Tax Planning 2017/18

Tax Planning 2017/18

Edited by

Mark McLaughlin CTA (Fellow), ATT (Fellow), TEP

With contributions by

Jackie Anderson LLB, ACA, CTA, LHA Consulting Ltd

Kye Burchmore LLB, RIFT Legal Services

Rebecca Cave CTA, FCA, MBA, FAIA (Hon)

George Duncan Solicitor, CTA, TEP, Partner, Charles Russell Speechlys LLP

Chris Erwood CTA, ATT, TEP, Director, Erwood & Associates Ltd

Anne Fairpo Barrister, CTA (Fellow), ATT

Robert Maas FCA, FTII, FIIT, TEP, Consultant, CBW Tax Ltd

Pete Miller CTA (Fellow), Partner, The Miller Partnership

Donald Pearce-Crump BA (Hons), LLB, CTA (Fellow), ATT

Partha Ray Cameron & Associates Ltd

Peter Rayney FCA, CTA (Fellow), TEP, Peter Rayney Tax Consulting Ltd

Douglas Sleziak Associate, Alec Ure & Associates

Alec Ure Associate, Alec Ure & Associates

David Whiscombe Barrister (Non-practising), CTA (Fellow), Director, BKL Tax

Chris Williams LLB

Bloomsbury Professional

Bloomsbury Professional
An imprint of Bloomsbury Publishing Plc

Bloomsbury Professional Ltd
41–43 Boltro Road
Haywards Heath
RH16 1BJ
UK

Bloomsbury Publishing Plc
50 Bedford Square
London
WC1B 3DP
UK

www.bloomsbury.com

British Library Cataloguing-in-Publication Data

A catalogue record for this book is available from the British Library.

ISBN: 978 1 52650 166 0

Typeset by Compuscript Ltd, Shannon
Printed and bound by CPI Group (UK) Ltd, Croydon, CR0 4YY

Preface

Welcome to Bloomsbury Professional's *Tax Planning 2017/18*. This book is now in its eleventh year of publication.

The calendar year 2017 has so far been a challenging one for taxpayers and tax advisers. The Finance Bill published in March 2017 was an eye-watering 776 pages long, not to mention 448 pages of explanatory notes. However, the general election on 8 June 2017 prevented the normal passage of the Finance Bill through Parliament, and resulted in a much shortened (156-page) Finance Bill and subsequent Finance Act 2017, mainly because of a lack of Parliamentary time to debate the original Finance Bill provisions.

This caused considerable uncertainty for a time, such as whether the 'missing' legislation from the original Finance Bill would appear in a subsequent Finance Act, and whether the commencement times for the various provisions would remain unchanged. Eventually, the government announced on 13 July 2017 that the legislation (subject to amendment in some cases) would be published in a Finance Bill after the end of Parliament's summer recess on 5 September 2017. The resulting Finance (No 2) Bill 2017 was published on 8 September 2017, comprising 674 pages.

Of course, this sequence of events has been most unsatisfactory for potentially affected taxpayers and tax professionals. It has not been much fun for tax authors and publishers either! At the time of writing, Finance (No 2) Bill 2017 containing the provisions omitted from Finance Act 2017 has not received Royal Assent. The law in this book is therefore stated as at 31 August 2017. However, the commentary in *Tax Planning 2017/18* aims to refer to those provisions where appropriate, including important tax changes relating to domicile, and helpful changes to the substantial shareholding exemption for group companies and institutional investors.

'Tax planning' continues to be a fairly emotive and controversial term. The government and HMRC continue to clamp down on what they regard as tax avoidance and unacceptable tax planning. This can have unfortunate and unexpected consequences for taxpayers, and is soon likely to have unpleasant implications for 'enablers' of defeated tax avoidance.

However, there is still much that can legitimately be done to save or reduce tax. *Tax Planning 2017/18* is therefore aimed at pointing out some of the areas where such planning opportunities still exist. Tax planning has an important role to play in managing one's financial affairs. Indeed, many clients of professional firms expect prompt, appropriate and up-to-date advice from their advisers on minimising tax liabilities. *Tax Planning 2017/18* is aimed at assisting professional advisers, among others, in delivering such advice.

Tax Planning 2017/18 takes into account new developments since the previous edition, including legislation introduced in the Finance Act 2017, and a number of noteworthy tax case decisions. This edition also includes new chapters on investors' relief and extracting funds from the company respectively.

The emphasis in *Tax Planning 2017/18* continues to be on providing topical content of practical use to the majority of small to medium-sized professional practices dealing with day-to-day tax planning issues. However, the practical importance of tax subjects can vary in accordance with changes to the law and other developments. The publishers would therefore warmly welcome constructive suggestions from readers on subjects they would like to see covered in 2018/19 and subsequent editions.

As always, I wish to express my sincere gratitude to all the authors who have contributed material to this book with such skill, professionalism and commitment. Their extensive tax knowledge and experience will hopefully make this book a useful and practical reference work for the reader.

Finally, my thanks to everyone at Bloomsbury Professional. In particular, many thanks to Claire McDermott for her considerable efforts and help during the preparation and editing of the book.

All commentary is based on the law in England and Wales. That applying in Scotland and Northern Ireland may occasionally be different.

Mark McLaughlin
General Editor
Manchester, 18 September 2017

Contents

Table of statutes

[All references are to paragraph numbers]

V

W

Table of statutory instruments and other guidance

[*All references are to paragraph number*]

Table of cases

A

B

I

X

Y

Z

List of examples

Chapter 17

Chapter 18

Chapter 19

Chapter 20

List of abbreviations

A&M	accumulation and maintenance
AA	annual allowance
ABA	agricultural building allowance
AC	amount crystallised
ACT	advance corporation tax
AFT	accounting for tax return
AIA	annual investment allowance
AIM	alternative investment market
APR	agricultural property relief
ASP	alternatively secured pension
ATED	annual tax on enveloped dwellings
AVC	additional voluntary contributions
BCE	benefit crystallisation event
BEIS	Department for Business, Energy and Industrial Strategy
BEPS	Base Erosion and Profit Shifting
BES	Business Expansion Scheme
BMT	bereaved minor's trust
BPR	business property relief
BSP	basic state pension
CA	Companies Act
CAA 2001	Capital Allowances Act 2001
CBI	Confederation of British Industry
CDC	collective defined contribution
CGT	capital gains tax
CIC	community interest company
CIHC	close investment holding company
CIOT	Chartered Institute of Taxation
CPI	consumer price index
CTA	Corporation Tax Act
CTAP	corporation tax accounting period
CTO	Capital Taxes Office
CTSA	corporation tax self-assessment
CVS	Corporate Venturing Scheme
CYB	current year basis
DA	defined ambition
DC	defined contribution
DOTAS	Disclosure of Tax Avoidance Schemes
DWP	Department for Work and Pensions
EBT	employee benefit trust
EEA	European Economic Area
EEIG	European economic interest grouping

EFPOS	employer-financed pension only scheme
EFRBS	employer-financed retirement benefit scheme
EGLP	expected group life policy
EIS	Enterprise Investment Scheme
EMI	Enterprise Management Incentives
EP	enhanced protection
ER	entrepreneurs' relief
ERA 1996	Employment Rights Act 1996
ESC	Extra-Statutory Concession
FA	Finance Act
FAS	Financial Assistance Scheme
FCA	Financial Conduct Authority
FHL	furnished holiday letting
FIFO	first in, first out
FPS	Full Payment Submission
FSA	Financial Services Authority
FURBS	funded unapproved retirement benefit scheme
FYA	first year allowance
GAAP	generally accepted accounting practice
GAAR	general anti-avoidance rule
GAD	Government's Actuary Department
GIA 2013	Growth and Infrastructure Act 2013
GPA	group payment arrangement
GWR	gifts with reservation
HMRC	Her Majesty's Revenue and Customs
IAS	International Accounting Standard
IBA	industrial building allowance
ICTA 1988	Income and Corporation Tax Act 1988
IHT	inheritance tax
IHTA 1984	Inheritance Tax Act 1984
IIP	interest in possession
IORP	institutions for occupational retirement provision
IOV	instrument of variation
IP	intellectual property
IPDI	immediate post-death interest
IRPS	investment-regulated pension scheme
ISA	Individual Savings Account
IT	income tax
ITA 2007	Income Tax Act 2007
ITEPA 2003	Income Tax (Earnings and Pensions) Act 2003
ITTOIA 2005	Income Tax (Trading and Other Income) Act 2005
LA	lifetime allowance
LBTT	Land and Buildings Transaction Tax
LBTT(S)A	Land and Buildings Transaction Tax (Scotland) Act
LEL	lower earnings limit
LIFO	last in, first out

LISA	lifetime Individual Savings Account
LLP	limited liability partnership
LS	lump sum
LSDB	lump sum death benefits
M&A	mergers and acquisitions
MPA	minimum pension age
MPP	maximum permitted pension
MSC	managed service company
NAO	National Audit Office
NAPF	National Association of Pension Funds
NEST	National Employment Savings Trust
NIC	National Insurance Contributions
NICA	National Insurance Contributions Act
NIRP	National Insurance Retirement Pension
NISA	New ISA
NMW	national minimum wage
NNP	non-natural person
NRB	nil rate band
OECD	Organisation for Economic Co-operation and Development
ONS	Office for National Statistics
OPS	overseas pension schemes
OTS	Office of Tax Simplification
PA 1890	Partnership Act 1890
PA 2007	Pensions Act 2007
PA 2008	Pensions Act 2008
PAYE	Pay as You Earn
PEP	Personal Equity Plan
PET	potentially exempt transfer
PIA	pension input amount
PILON	payment in lieu of notice
PIP	pension input period
PLSA	Pensions and Lifetime Savings Association
POAT	pre-owned assets tax
PP	primary protection
PPF	pension protection fund
PPR	principal private residence
PPS	personal pension schemes
PSA 2015	Pensions Schemes Act 2015
PSC	personal service company
PSN	Pensions Schemes Newsletter
PT	primary threshold
PTM	Pensions Tax Manual
QCB	qualifying corporate bond
QROPS	qualifying recognised overseas pension scheme
QRP	qualifying residual profit
R&D	research and development

RAC	retirement annuity contracts
RAS	relief at source
RBA	relevant benefit accrual
REIT	real estate investment trust
RICS	Royal Institution of Chartered Surveyors
RIPP	relevant intellectual property profits
RPI	Retail Price Index
RPSM	Registered Pension Schemes Manual
RTI	real time information
S2P	state second pension
SAAC	special annual allowance charge
SAYE	Save as You Earn
SDLT	stamp duty land tax
SEIS	Seed Enterprise Investment Scheme
SIP	share incentive plan
SLA	standard lifetime allowance
SP	Statement of Practice
SRN	scheme reference number
SSAS	small self-administered scheme
SSCBA 1992	Social Security Contributions and Benefits Act 1992
SSE	substantial shareholdings exemption
STSP	single-tier state pension
TAAR	Targeted Anti-Avoidance Rules
TCGA 1992	Taxation of Chargeable Gains Act 1992
TEE	taxed-exempt-exempt
TIOPA 2010	Taxation (International and Other Provisions) Act 2010
TiS	Transactions in Securities
TMA 1970	Taxes Management Act 1970
TOGC	transfer of a going concern
TOPA 2014	Taxation of Pensions Act 2014
TNRB	transferable nil rate band
TPAS	The Pensions Advisory Service
TUPE	Transfer of Undertakings (Protection of Employment) Regulations
UAP	upper accrual point
UEL	upper earnings limit
UITF	Urgent Issues Task Force
UTR	unique taxpayer reference
UURBS	unfunded unapproved retirement benefit scheme
VAT	value added tax
VATA 1994	Value Added Tax Act 1994
VCT	venture capital trust
VOA	Valuation Office Agency
VUR	value of uncrystallised rights
WDA	writing down allowance

Chapter 1

Starting a business – choosing an appropriate trading vehicle

Rebecca Cave CTA, FCA, MBA, FAIA (Hon)

SIGNPOSTS

- **Issues underlying the choice** – Number of people involved, flexibility, administration and tax costs, interest restrictions, commercial considerations, control and exit strategy (see **1.3–1.30**).
- **Sole traders** – Structure, regulation, business records, accounting date, cash-basis, fixed rate deductions and timing of tax payments (see **1.31–1.37**).
- **Partnerships** – Why use a partnership? Ordinary and limited partnerships, LLPs, benefits of all partnerships (see **1.38–1.72**).
- **Companies** – Types of company, tax treatment, tax benefits of a company, loans to participators (see **1.73–1.122**).
- **Company versus other vehicles** – Start as unincorporated, timing of tax payments, NIC burden, profit-extraction strategies, disadvantages of dividends, retention of profits (see **1.123–1.142**).
- **Long-term intentions** – Continuing or dissolving the business, double taxation charges (**1.143–1.147**).

INTRODUCTION

1.1 When an individual decides to form a business, he must decide on the most appropriate medium through which to conduct that business. The choice of the business vehicle can contribute to the ultimate success of the business, as it will affect the level and timing of tax payments, the availability of tax reliefs and the legal obligations of the business owners.

The basic choice for a new UK-based business is between a sole trader, ordinary partnership, limited liability partnership (LLP), or private limited company. Other alternatives for trading structures are the limited partnership, the trading trust, unlimited company, public company, co-operative, or a joint venture arrangement.

WHY THE CHOICE OF TRADING VEHICLE IS IMPORTANT

1.2 Unincorporated businesses (sole traders, trustees, partnerships and LLPs) pay income tax on their profits at 20%, 40% or 45%. In addition, Class 4 national insurance must be paid on profits above £8,164, at 9% with 2% due on profits above £45,000 (for 2017/18). Each owner of the business must also pay the Class 2 national insurance at a flat rate of £2.85 per week (£148.20 pa), if their annual profits exceed £6,025. Class 2 and Class 4 national insurance will be merged from 6 April 2018, and the revised rates should be announced in the 2017 Autumn Budget.

The combined tax and national insurance liability is generally payable in two equal instalments by 31 January and 31 July, irrespective of the date the business has chosen to draw up accounts to each year.

Incorporated businesses (companies of all types), pay corporation tax on their profits at the rate of 19% for the year commencing 1 April 2017, but this rate is due to drop to 17% on 1 April 2020. There are different rates of corporation tax for companies in the oil and gas industry.

An extra cost of using a company is the requirement to operate PAYE on the salaried remuneration of the owner. As such the company must also pay national insurance at 13.8% on salary, bonuses and benefits paid to employees or directors, which exceed £8,164 per year. The corporation tax is payable nine months and one day after the end of the accounting year, although large companies and those in groups must generally pay their corporation tax liabilities by quarterly instalments.

A company may pay less tax on its profits than an unincorporated business of a similar size, but its liability to national insurance may be greater, depending on the level of salaries and benefits paid out. A straight comparison of tax costs between different business vehicles is complicated by the fact that some tax reliefs apply only to companies or only to unincorporated businesses (see **Table 1.4** at **1.146**). Certain benefits can be provided to employees and directors tax free through the medium of a company, but are taxable if provided to the owners of an unincorporated business.

> **Focus**
>
> The choice of trading vehicle has a big effect on the quantum and timing of the tax liabilities generated by the business venture, but the choice should also be influenced by non-tax factors such as the need to protect the assets of the owner should the business fail.

ISSUES UNDERLYING THE CHOICE

1.3 A business may be expected to trade in a certain form by its customers or for traditional reasons (see **1.19**). In the absence of such external pressures the initial choice of business vehicle will turn on these issues:

- the number of people involved;
- current or future flexibility required;
- administrative costs;
- need to protect personal assets; and
- tax costs.

There are also a number of commercial considerations that should be raised with the client when discussing the trading vehicle to be used to start the business. One form of trading vehicle is rarely suitable for the entire lifetime of the business, and the type of business operated (eg property investment or trading) may influence the structure to use.

Number of people involved

1.4 The choice of business structure is partly determined by the number of people who will be involved in running and owning the business. A sole trader is restricted to single-person ownership and management. An ordinary partnership is effectively a group of individuals who have come together to run a business. The partners are taxed like individual sole traders on their share of the profits made by the partnership. The partners may appoint managers to run the business on their behalf, but they remain fully jointly and severally liable for the debts of the business.

An LLP or a limited partnership can offer the partners some protection from the debts of the business (see **1.61**). It is possible to form a partnership between a one-man company (see **1.6**) and the individual who controls that company. See **Chapter 3** for discussion of partnerships that include a company as a member.

A company may have any number of shareholders, and some or all of those shareholders may also be the company directors with responsibility for day-to-day management of the business. However, the company directors and managers can be a completely separate group of people from the owners (shareholders) of the business.

Flexibility

1.5 An ability to move smoothly from one form of business vehicle to another is important. Different levels of profits attract varying tax rates depending on the business structure, so a change from say sole trader to limited company may be made to reduce the overall tax liability. A dynamic business will benefit from a regular review of its structure.

A change in structure can be used to manage a new business risk. Where the business involves several separate projects or products that have different chances of succeeding or failing, a separate business vehicle may be set up to contain each project. This will isolate these different commercial risks and ensure that a successful project is not brought down by one that fails. This approach may lead to forming a joint venture company, creating a number of associated companies or a combination of partnerships and companies. A group of related businesses will also allow one project or product line to be extracted and sold on without disturbing the rest of the business. Where a series of similar ventures (eg property development) are carried on in successive companies, the taxation of the distributions on liquidation of those companies may be subject to income tax rather than CGT under *ITTOIA 2005, ss 396B* and *404A*, effective from 6 April 2016, for further discussion of this point, see **Chapter 8**.

1.6 A private limited company is a particularly flexible vehicle as it may be owned and run by just one individual, who will normally be the sole director. The only limitation laid down by the *Companies Act 2006* is that a private company is obliged to have at least one director, who must be a natural person, not a company.

A private limited company is not required to appoint or retain a company secretary unless the company's articles specify that it should. The role of a company secretary would include taking responsibility for filing returns with Companies House, maintaining records of director's meetings and share registers, and distributing accounts to all the shareholders. In the absence of a company secretary the directors need to undertake these tasks. A public company must appoint a qualified company secretary. The company secretary need not hold any shares in the company, and thus need not be a part owner of the business, and need not be involved in the day-to-day running of the business.

> **Focus**
>
> Where an individual holds the position of company secretary or director, that person may qualify for entrepreneurs' relief on disposal of the company shares, if he or she also holds at least 5% of the ordinary share capital and 5% of the voting rights (see **Chapter 8**).

Administrative costs

1.7 The administrative costs will tend to be higher where the business vehicle has greater reporting requirements, or it is required to run a PAYE scheme and thus make electronic returns under real time information (RTI). The costs of running a limited company tend to be greater than those for an ordinary partnership or sole-trader business, although the scale of the organisation and the complexity of the business will have a bearing on the total costs. The more official forms a business is required to file, the greater the risk of lateness or inaccuracy of a submission, which after the first default, normally generates an automatic penalty.

1.8 A company can be registered at Companies House for as little as £10 if the process is undertaken online, but an ordinary partnership or sole-trader business has no such registration costs. An LLP must also be registered at Companies House for a basic fee of £12. Limited partnerships are required to be registered with Companies House, which costs £20, and online registration is not offered.

1.9 Companies and LLPs must both file confirmation statements at Companies House at a cost of £40, or £13 for electronic submission. The filing fee must be paid whether or not the business has traded during the year. Partnerships that are not LLPs, and sole trader businesses, are not required to file a confirmation statement or annual return, submit to an audit, or file annual accounts at Companies House. This provides a high level of privacy for the business owners, and a cost saving.

Companies and partnerships, including LLPs, must submit an annual tax return to HMRC, in addition to the personal tax returns required for the business owners. Sole-traders submit details of their business profits or losses on their personal tax return, there is no separate tax return for the business.

1.10 The annual accounts of companies and LLPs must be filed annually at Companies House and certain of those accounts must be subject to an audit. Most LLPs and companies qualify as 'small', so they may take advantage of the audit exemption, under the *Accounts of Small and Medium-Sized*

Enterprises and Audit Exemption (Amendment) Regulations (SI 2004/16). However, some accounts will require an audit for other regulatory reasons, such as for businesses operating in the regulated financial services sector.

To qualify as 'small' the company or LLP must meet two of the three conditions set out in **Table 1.1** in its first financial year, or for later periods, in that year and the preceding year. Different limits apply to trading charities.

Table 1.1: Company size thresholds

For periods from 1 January 2016	*Micro-entity*	*Small Company*	*Medium Company*
Annual turnover not more than	£632,000	£10.2m	£36m
Balance sheet total not exceeding	£316,000	£5.1m	£18m
Average number of employees in financial year not exceeding	10	50	250

1.11 Companies and LLPs that qualify as 'small' or 'medium' (see **Table 1.1**) are also permitted to submit abbreviated accounts to Companies House, which only include a balance sheet and no profit and loss account. This prevents competitors from discovering the business turnover, profit, or whether a dividend has been paid. Medium-sized companies are required to include details of the business turnover within the abbreviated accounts.

Micro-entities, which can include LLPs, may prepare simplified financial statements which consist of an abridged profit and loss account, balance sheet with no notes and no director's report. The micro-entity is only required to file its balance sheet at Companies House. Charities and investment undertakings cannot qualify as micro-entities.

1.12 A full set of financial statements for a company including a profit and loss account and director's report must be submitted to HMRC to support the corporation tax return. Every figure in those documents must be 'tagged' using the extensible business reporting language (iXBRL) before it can be submitted with the corporate tax return.

Sole traders, partnerships and LLPs can still submit tax returns and accounts to HMRC in paper form, if the filing is completed by midnight on 31 October following the end of the tax year. A later filing of a partnership tax or individual tax return must be made electronically. Penalties for late filing of the partnership tax return apply per partner in addition to the penalty for late filing of the partnership return itself.

1.13 All businesses should consider registering the trading name and any trademarks to be used with the UK Intellectual Property Office. A domain name such as taxwriter.co.uk, in a recognisable form of the trading name, is also essential for most businesses to help establish a recognisable presence on the internet. A domain name should be reserved with a reputable registration agent. However, having a registered trademark does not give the holder an automatic right to the domain name containing that trademark.

Tax costs

1.14 The tax burden borne by the business is influenced by the differing tax rates applicable to profits made within the structure (see **1.2**), but also by how those profits are calculated. A number of tax reliefs for costs or losses are only available to businesses who operate as a company, or conversely as a sole-trader or partnership (see **Table 1.4** at **1.146**).

From 6 April 2017 a residential property letting business which is run as a sole trade or partnership suffers a restriction on the amount of finance and interest charges that can be deducted for tax purposes. This gives the corporate structure a distinct advantage for property letting (see **1.17**).

Where the business makes a loss, the ability to relieve that loss quickly can make an unincorporated structure more attractive, particularly in the early years of trading (see **1.15**).

If the business is expected to be consistently profitable, the choice of business vehicle may well be weighted towards a company. However, the expected profit level and the need to extract funds for personal use must be considered (see **1.91** onwards).

1.15 Many new businesses expect to make losses in the first few periods of trading before moving into profit. If those trading losses are generated within a corporate structure, the losses are essentially trapped within that company with only three possible avenues of relief:

- set against the other income of the company (*CTA 2010, s 37*);
- carried back against the profits of the company for up to 12 months (*CTA 2010, s 37(3)*); or
- carried forward to set against future profits of the same trade (*CTA 2010, s 45*).

The Government has proposed that corporate losses generated after 1 April 2017 would be available to set against the company's total taxable profits in future periods or surrendered in the form of group relief to other group members. However, where the company or group has profits of more than £5 million, the relief for all brought-forward losses (generated at any time) would be restricted to 50% of total profits. The relevant provisions to enact these changes are included in *Finance (No 2) Bill 2017*.

The losses made by an unincorporated business are not trapped within that business but can be relieved as follows:

(a) Losses made within the first four years of the life of the business can be carried back up to three years and set against the trader's other income of that tax year (*ITA 2007, s 72*).

(b) Trading losses made in any year can be set against the proprietor's other income of that year or the previous tax year (*ITA 2007, ss 64, 65*). This form of loss relief is known as sideways loss relief.

(c) If the claims to set the loss against net income have not exhausted all of the loss, the taxpayer can opt to relieve the remaining trading losses against any capital gains of the same year and the preceding year (*ITA 2007, s 71*).

(d) Where the trading loss remains unrelieved the loss is automatically carried forward to be relieved against profits of the same trade, profession or vocation arising in future years (*ITA 2007, s 83*). The loss is set against the next available profit without restriction.

(e) On incorporation of the business any unused losses from the unincorporated trade can be set against income received from that company by the former owner, including dividends, salary, interest or rents, if certain conditions are met (*ITA 2007, s 86*).

There is an HMRC toolkit available to help taxpayers assess whether income tax losses have been correctly claimed, but it does not deal with loss relief restrictions (http://tinyurl.com/psmxprv).

No loss relief can be claimed if the trade is not carried on commercially with a view to the realisation of profits (*ITA 2007, s 66*). The trades of market gardening or farming have sideways loss relief restricted where losses have been made in each of the previous five years.

Loss restrictions

1.16 The use of sideways, opening years or capital loss relief may be limited by five separate restrictions summarised in **Table 1.2**. Any loss not relieved sideways, or carried back, is carried forward to be set against the future profits of the same trade without restriction.

Table 1.2: Loss restrictions

Type of restriction:	*LLP partner (active)*	*Limited partner*	*Non-active partner or sole-trader*	*Active partner or sole-trader*
1. Capital contribution cap (*ITA 2007, ss 104–114*)	Yes	Yes	Yes	No
2. £25,000 cap (*ITA 2007, ss 74A & 103C*)	No	Yes	Yes	No
3. Greater of £50,000 or 25% of income cap (*ITA 2007, s 24A*)	Yes	Yes	Yes	Yes
4. Denied entirely due to tax avoidance scheme (*ITA 2007, s 74ZA*)	Yes	Yes	Yes	Yes
5. Cash basis used (see **1.34**)	N/A	Yes	Yes	Yes

Non-active partners or sole traders can be any individuals, limited partners, or sleeping partners (see **1.45**) who are personally engaged with the trade for, on average, less than ten hours per week.

Where the business is a partnership, HMRC are clear that they will apply the first two loss restrictions in **Table 1.2** in the order shown in that table, ie capital contribution first. Those restrictions only apply to trades, not to professions or vocations (HMRC Business income manual BIM82640).

From 6 April 2013 the relief for losses, interest and a number of other tax reliefs is restricted where the total relief given in the tax year exceeds:

- £50,000; or
- 25% of the taxpayer's adjusted total income for the tax year.

The use of sideways, opening years or capital loss relief is completely denied where tax avoidance arrangements have been entered into (*ITA 2007, s 74ZA*). Although HMRC say this anti-avoidance rule is targeted at persons who enter into tax-avoidance arrangements, the legislation is not restricted to such circumstances (BIM85762).

There are special rules for losses derived from qualifying film expenditure and film partnerships (*ITA 2007, ss 74D* and *103D*), which exclude the above loss restrictions, but impose their own restrictions to counter tax avoidance schemes.

Interest restrictions

1.17 Where a residential property letting business is carried on by individuals alone or in partnership, by trustees, or by personal representatives of deceased estates, the ability to deduct finance and interest charges from rental income is restricted as follows:

Tax year	Finance costs deductible:
2017/18	75%
2018/19	50%
2019/20	25%
2020/21	nil

The landlord receives a tax credit equivalent to 20% of the lower of:

- finance costs not deducted from rental income in the tax year;
- property business profits before deducting interest after deducting losses brought forward; and
- adjusted total income that exceeds personal allowances.

This tax credit is set against the taxpayer's income tax liability for the year (see **Example 1.1**). Any unused tax credit is carried forward to be relieved against the tax payable on the property income in a later tax year. This restriction on finance charges does not apply to corporate landlords.

Example 1.1 – Property letting run by sole trader or company

Peter lets residential property held in his own name and receives net rents of £140,000 per year after agents' fees and repairs. He pays interest and finance charges of £112,000 per year. He does not pay national insurance on his letting income as it is not regarded as a trade.

Paul holds his let property in a company he controls, which also receives net rental income of £140,000 per year and pays £112,000 in interest. Paul extracts the net income from his company as a dividend.

The tax payable by the two property businesses is calculated as follows:

2017/18 tax year	*Company*	*Individual*	
	£	*Paul £*	*Peter £*
Letting income	140,000		140,000
Interest deductible (75% deductible for individual)	(112,000)		(84,000)
Net income	28,000		56,000
Less personal allowance	–		(11,500)
Net taxable profits	28,000		44,500
Income tax due at 20% on first £33,500			6,700
Income tax due at 40% over £33,500			4,400
Tax credit: 20% × 25% × 112,000			(5,600)
Corporation tax at 19%	(5,320)		–
Income after CT – paid as dividend to Paul	22,680	22,680	
Less personal allowance		(11,500)	
Less dividend allowance		(5,000)	
Subject to dividend tax at 7.5%		6180	
Income tax paid	(463.50)		
Cash in hand for individual:	22,216.50		22,500
Total effective tax rate on net income:	20.65%		19.64%

Other tax-related decisions

1.18 There are a number of tax-sensitive decisions for a new business (listed below), which need to be addressed, irrespective of the structure adopted:

- choice of accounting date;
- ownership of real property;
- ownership of vehicles;

- ownership of intellectual property;
- how to attract investors;
- how and when to extract profits;
- how to provide for the proprietor's pension;
- how to pass the business on;
- how to extract capital.

Different business vehicles will produce different tax results for these issues. For example, the choice of accounting date for an unincorporated business can have a big influence on the timing and quantum of tax payable in the early years of the business (see **1.36**), but it is not so relevant for a corporate structure.

Commercial considerations

Credibility

1.19 A corporate structure can appear more credible to suppliers and customers, who may perceive unincorporated businesses as being small and risky. There may be considerable pressure from customers who receive a personal service from the proprietor of the business for that supplier business to be incorporated, to shift the risk of tax compliance on to the personal service company (PSC).

1.20 A corporate structure is thought to protect the customer from having to treat an individual contractor as an employee, subject to PAYE and NICs. Where an intermediary, such as a company or partnership, or even another individual such as an agent, is placed between the customer and the contractor who provides the personal service, the burdens of PAYE and employment rights for the individual should fall on the intermediary.

For contracts performed in the private sector, the intermediary is responsible for complying with the anti-avoidance rules known as IR35 (see **1.83**). From 6 April 2017, for contracts performed in the public sector, the public body that engages the PSC is responsible for deciding whether the IR35 rules apply, and the fee-payer who pays the PSC must deduct tax and NIC (employers' and employees') from the fee paid. This puts the contractor in a worse position than if he were an employee of his customer, so the advantages gained by working through a company are undermined.

The intermediary may also be subject to the additional constraints imposed by the Managed Service Companies (MSC) legislation (see **1.89**). There are particular rules for agency and temporary workers under which the worker may be treated as being an employee of the agency for tax and NIC purposes (see **Chapter 10**).

1.21 An LLP can also offer customers and suppliers a sense of security, as the reporting requirements mean the LLP's accounts are published for public view at Companies House. The LLP must also draw up accounts that comply with the same accounting standards as a company, and is not permitted to use the cash basis of accounting (see **1.34**).

Privacy

1.22 Those who prefer to keep the financial affairs of their business as a private matter between themselves and HMRC will see the disclosure requirements of a limited company or LLP as a disadvantage. However, micro-entities are permitted to file only a balance sheet at Companies House (see **1.11**).

Retention of control

1.23 The majority shareholders in a company, who hold more than 50% or 75% of the shares, can take the major decisions for the business, as those thresholds of share ownership provide rights under company law. The unanimous agreement of partners in a partnership is usually required for all major decisions, unless the partnership agreement states otherwise.

1.24 Shares in a private company can be created with diverse rights as to voting, dividends, entitlement to capital on winding-up, and so on. This offers not only great flexibility, but also the opportunity for the original proprietor to retain voting control in the company although he may not, at that stage, be entitled to the largest equity interest in the company. On the death of a shareholder, the legal continuity of the business is guaranteed. There is no automatic continuity of a partnership business on the death of a partner, but this may be provided for in the partnership agreement. The business of a sole trader will cease with the individual's death.

Raising finance

1.25 Companies may be able to raise additional finance from other shareholders, and minority and non-voting shareholders can provide finance that does not impinge on the majority's control over the running of the company. However, a private company cannot raise funds directly from the general public; only a public company can do this.

1.26 Companies may find it easier than unincorporated businesses to raise finance from other sources due to their equity structure. Although companies may become partners in most partnerships, a venture capitalist is unlikely to wish to become involved as a partner in an ordinary partnership, even as a limited partner. For further discussion of corporate partners see **Chapter 3**.

An LLP can offer a very flexible structure for companies and individuals to work together in a joint venture arrangement. However, the rules for taxing loans to participators (*CTA 2010, s 455*) can restrict the flow of funds within a group that consists of a close company and an LLP whose members are participators in the company (see **1.109**).

> **Focus**
>
> Anti-avoidance rules to prevent the manipulation of profits and losses, or the disposal of income streams or assets within mixed partnerships (ie partnerships with both individuals and non-individuals as members) apply from 6 April 2014. For further details see **Chapter 3**.

1.27 The personal liability of the business owners is often thought to influence the choice of business structure. However, in practice the limited liability achieved by the business owner by operating as a private limited company or an LLP is frequently undermined by the requirement to give personal guarantees to providers of business finance, or to provide a charge over their own personal assets in return for a business loan.

Unincorporated businesses are not able to offer a floating charge over their assets as security for borrowings, whereas companies and LLPs can do this.

National minimum wage

1.28 The national minimum wage (NMW) or national living wage (NLW) must be paid to all 'workers' (as defined for the NMW regulations). A director who does not have an explicit contract of employment with his company is unlikely to be a 'worker' for these purposes, so does not have to be paid the NMW (HMRC National Minimum Wage Manual NMWM05140). Family members who work in unincorporated businesses and live at home are also exempt from the NMW.

Sole traders and partners in ordinary partnerships, LLPs or limited partnerships are under no obligation to pay themselves any prescribed level of wages, as they are not treated as 'workers' for the purposes of the NMW. Although salaried partners in LLPs may be taxed as employees if they meet certain conditions, they are not actually employees and hence not treated as workers for the NMW legislation.

Share options

1.29 A company can incentivise employees by offering tax-advantaged share options or employee share schemes, which are not available to employees of a sole trader, partnership or LLP. For further details of the range of share-related incentives which can be provided, see *Employee Share Schemes* (6th edn, 2015, Bloomsbury Professional).

Exit strategy

1.30 A shareholder in a company can transfer small quantities of the company's shares to the next generation or to the management group, in order to gradually pass on control in the business. However, if shares are given to the company's employees, or to individuals who become employees when they acquire the shares, an income tax charge may arise under the employment-related securities legislation, on the basis that the shares are acquired due to the donee's employment (see **1.132**).

To transfer the interest of a sole trader or partner, the proprietor has to accept another person as a partner in the business, as an active or sleeping partner. This transaction will normally require a partnership agreement to be drawn up or amended.

It is easier to sell shares in a private company than to sell a partnership share in a similar-sized business. If the intention is to develop the business to the point where it can be sold as a trading unit, a corporate structure will normally be more appropriate.

Having said that, the assets and trade of a business can be sold out of any form of trading vehicle. An asset sale is often favoured by the purchaser of a business, as any liabilities attached to the business can be excluded from the transaction. For further discussion of the tax issues concerning owner-managed company sales, see **Chapter 8**.

SOLE TRADER

Structure

1.31 A business operated by one person as a sole trader is the simplest possible business structure. The owner is personally liable for all the debts of the business and is taxed on all of the profits. Essentially there is no legal distinction between the individual and the business.

Regulation

1.32 The regulation of a sole-trader business is minimal, although HMRC require the individual to register for national insurance and tax purposes as soon as possible after the business commences. A failure to notify penalty may be imposed if the individual has not registered with HMRC by 31 January following the end of the tax year in which he commenced his business. However, if the individual is not already within the self-assessment system, he must notify HMRC by 5 October after the end of the tax year in which the new source of income arose, as a failure to notify penalty can arise after that earlier date.

Business records

1.33 All taxpayers have an obligation to keep sufficient records to support entries made on their tax returns (*TMA 1970, s 12B*), but the form and extent of those 'statutory records' is not specified in law, except for VAT purposes. HMRC have a right to inspect all statutory records, and the taxpayer cannot appeal against a notice to produce his statutory records (*FA 2008, Sch 36, para 29*).

> **Focus**
>
> A private bank account that is used to pay off a credit card debt comprising partly of business expenses, was found to form part of the business's statutory records (*J Beckwith v HMRC* [2012] UKFTT 181 (TC)). An appointment diary for a private doctor was found not to form part of her statutory records (*Dr K Long v HMRC* [2014] UKFTT 199 (TC)).

Cash basis of accounting

1.34 Unincorporated trading businesses can elect to calculate profits/losses for tax purposes on the basis of the cash received and expenses paid out, known as the cash basis, as opposed to the accruals basis of accounting required by GAAP. The cash basis is supposed to make accounting easier for small businesses, who can start to used that method of accounting where their annual turnover is no more than £150,000.

Once a trading business has started to use the cash basis, it can carry on doing so until its annual turnover is twice the entry threshold (£300,000 from 6 April 2017). Alternatively, the business may leave the cash basis when its commercial circumstances change such that the cash basis is no longer appropriate.

It is proposed that a form of cash basis will be the default accounting regime for unincorporated landlords from 6 April 2017, where the landlord's annual gross property income does not exceed £150,000. However, the landlord will be permitted to opt out of the cash basis and use GAAP accounting instead. The provisions to introduce this form of cash basis for property businesses were not included in *FA 2017*. The relevant provisions to enact these changes are included in *Finance (No 2) Bill 2017*, to come into effect from 6 April 2017.

The following businesses cannot use the cash basis:

- companies;
- LLPs;
- farmers using the herd basis;
- persons using profit averaging under *ITTOIA 2005, s 221*;
- persons carrying on a mineral extraction trade;
- persons who have claimed business premises renovation allowance or R&D allowance; and
- Lloyd's underwriters.

When using the cash basis for a trade, the individual cannot claim a deduction for loan interest of more than £500 per year, although a full deduction for hire purchase (HP) costs is permitted. Landlords will be subject to different restrictions for interest and finance charges when they use the property cash basis for periods from 6 April 2017. These interest restrictions for property businesses will apply in addition to the restrictions for residential property businesses described in **1.17**.

When using either form of cash basis, losses cannot be offset against other income (sideways relief), or carried back as set out in **1.15**, but those losses may be carried forward.

Fixed-rate deductions

1.35 Any unincorporated trading business or profession, which does not have a corporate partner, can use fixed-rate expenses to replace the calculation of actual costs incurred in three areas:

- car and motorcycle expenses;
- use of home for business purposes; and
- private use of a business premises which is also used as the proprietor's home.

For details of the relevant fixed rates see Bloomsbury's *Tax Rates and Tables 2017/18*. These fixed rate deductions can be used whether or not the business opts to use the cash basis described in **1.34**, and are not restricted by the turnover of the business.

Accounting date

1.36 The date to which the sole trader's accounts are made up each year can have a significant effect on the timing of tax payments, particularly in the early years of the business. This is because an unincorporated business reports the profits or losses, for the accounting period which ends within the tax year, on the tax return for that year.

For example, profits from the accounting period ending on 30 April 2017 will be reported on the tax return for 2017/18, but equally the results for the accounting period ending on 31 March 2018 will be reported on 2017/18 tax return. Although those accounting periods have only one month in common, the tax will be payable on the same dates:

- 31 January 2018: on-account payment equivalent to half of the 2016/17 liability;
- 31 July 2018: on-account payment equivalent to half of the 2016/17 liability; and
- 31 January 2019: any balancing payment due for 2017/18.

In the first tax year of a new business, the profits arising in that tax year are assessed to tax from the date of commencement of the business to the end of the tax year. This can lead to double taxation of profits made in the first 24 months of the new business – see **Example 1.2**. The accounting date chosen (early or late in the tax year) will affect the degree to which the early profits are doubly taxed.

Example 1.2 – Doubly taxed profits

Alistair started trading on 1 July 2016 and drew up his accounts for the ten months to 30 April 2017. He then draws up accounts to 30 April each year. The profits to be taxed in the first three tax years are calculated as follows:

Tax year	*Profits taxed*	*Calculated from profits of:*
2016/17	Actual profits from 1 July 2016 to 5 April 2017	9/10 × accounting period to 30 April 2017
2017/18	First 12 months	10/10 × accounting period to 30 April 2017 plus
		2/10 × accounting period to 30 April 2018
2018/19	Year ending 30 April 2018	12/12 × accounting period to 30 April 2018

The proportions of the accounting periods have been calculated in months, when strictly a proportion of days in each period should be used. However, it can be seen that the 9/10ths of the profits for the period to 30 April 2017 and 2/10ths of the profits for the period to 30 April 2018 have been taxed twice, and will make up the amount of overlap relief to be used when Alistair ceases to trade.

Overlap relief

1.37 Any doubly taxed profits are relieved as overlap relief, which reduces the final amount of profits taxed when the business ceases, or when the business changes the date to which its accounts are made up. Either of these events may occur many years after the original double taxation arose, but the amount of overlap relief deducted at that time is not adjusted for the effect of inflation. The overlap relief thus loses its value over time.

PARTNERSHIPS

Why use a partnership?

1.38 The decision to trade as either a sole trader or an ordinary partnership (see **1.39**) is likely to be influenced largely by family, professional, or other commercial considerations. For example, in a sector where there is a strong tradition of family continuity, such as farming, there may be powerful domestic reasons that induce the proprietor into taking his children into partnership.

The liability of a sole trader is unlimited in respect of his business debts. A partner will have joint, or joint and several liability for partnership debts. This means that any one partner could be called upon to satisfy the whole of the debts of the business, albeit with the right to claim a contribution from his fellow partners. However, each partner can only be required to pay the tax due on his individual profit share from the partnership. In spite of this, many large partnerships retain funds within the business to pay the income tax and NIC due on behalf of the partners.

Ordinary partnership

1.39 A partnership may be referred to as an ordinary or general partnership to distinguish it from the forms of limited partnership (see **1.54**) and limited liability partnership: LLP (see **1.58**).

Is there a partnership?

1.40 It is sometimes difficult to prove whether two or more people are operating a business as a partnership, or if only one person is in business, or there are a number of connected sole-trader businesses. This point will be important as reporting under Making Tax Digital comes into effect, as the reporting rules for partnerships will be different from those which will apply for sole traders.

Where there is no written partnership agreement in existence, the *Partnership Act 1890* governs the operation of ordinary partnerships, and defines a partnership as the relationship which subsists between persons carrying on business in common with a view to a profit. The *Partnership Act 1890, s 2* sets out certain transactions, which do not by themselves create a partnership, such as the co-ownership of property, or an employee receiving part of his salary by way of a share in the profits of the business.

A partnership is not required by law to have a partnership agreement, but the existence of such an agreement is very good, but not conclusive, evidence that a partnership exists. Sharing profits raises a presumption that a partnership exists, but, again, is not conclusive evidence of a partnership. A thorough analysis of whether a partnership existed is contained in the report of *Phillips (Raymond John) v HMRC* [2009] UKFTT 335 (TC), see also HMRC Business Income Manual para BIM82005.

Focus

HMRC will try to assert that a partnership existed, to collect tax and penalties owing from a person connected with the business, even if that person has not been named as a partner (see *Valantine (Pauline) v HMRC* [2011] UKFTT 808 (TC)).

Types of partners

1.41 Normally, a partner in an ordinary partnership will take an active role in the partnership business, and take a proportion of the trading profits in recognition of their contribution to the business. However, some partners take no active role, and are referred to as 'sleeping partners'. A partnership may contain 'salaried partners', who may be employees described as partners for prestige reasons only, or they may be full equity partners who take a fixed profit share of the partnership profits.

Both sleeping and active partners will normally contribute capital to the partnership when they join the partnership. The trading profits of the partnership need not be distributed in proportion to the amount of capital each partner has contributed to the business, and equally capital profits and losses may be shared in different ratios to income profits and losses.

Tax treatment

Income tax

1.42 The taxation of partnerships is relatively simple where there are only a few partners. For tax and national insurance purposes each partner is treated as an individual sole trader. The amount of profit or loss taxed on each partner is determined by the profit-sharing ratio the partnership operates. Guidance on the taxation of partnerships is found in HMRC's Partnership Manual.

1.43 The partnership must file a partnership tax return to report the total partnership profits and any deductions from those profits such as capital allowances which are made before the net profits (or losses), are shared between the partners (*ITTOIA 2005, Pt 9*). It is the responsibility of the representative partner to file the partnership tax return either on paper by 31 October following the end of the tax year, or electronically by the following 31 January (see **1.12**).

> **Focus**
>
> If the partnership tax return is filed late, a penalty is issued to every person who was member of the partnership for the relevant tax year. However, only the representative partner can appeal against this penalty (see *Gorman (Andrew) v HMRC* [2011] UKFTT 818 (TC)).

Each partner is liable to pay income tax on their share of the taxable partnership profits, as reported on the partnership tax return. The individual partners are required to report this profit share on their personal tax returns, but problems can arise where some partners dispute the amount of profits allocated to them. The decision in the joined cases *Morgan & Self (Graham & Heather) v HMRC* [2009] UKFTT 78 (TC) found the partner can include additional information in their own tax return to indicate the correct amount of tax due from him. In *Phillips (Raymond John) v HMRC* [2009] UKFTT 335 (TC) the tribunal found that the partner does have the right to appeal against a consequential amendment to their own tax return because the taxable profit reported on the partnership tax return has been amended.

HMRC will generally only deal with the representative or nominated partner when enquiring into the partnership return, see the guidance in HMRC's Enquiry Manual (EM7020–EM7035).

1.44 When a partner joins a partnership, or the partnership starts trading there can be some double taxation of profits made from the date of commencement or from the date the new partner joins the partnership to the end of the tax year. This also applies when a sole trader starts to trade (see **1.36**). Overlap relief for the doubly taxed profits is given when the individual partner leaves the partnership, the partnership ceases to trade, or there is a change in the accounting date for the partnership.

Losses

1.45 A partner has the same choices as to how to relieve their portion of any trading loss as apply to a sole trader (see **1.15**). Each partner can make an independent choice as to how to obtain tax relief for their share of a trading loss, but see the restrictions for loss relief discussed in **1.16**.

1.46 The calculation of the tax charge for each individual partner can become complex if there are a large number of partners in the partnership and frequent changes in the profit-sharing ratios in any one tax year. A partner cannot have a taxable loss if another partner has a taxable profit in the same tax year. If a loss arises after allocating amounts paid out of the partnership profits as 'salaries', the loss must be reallocated to the partners with profits.

National insurance

1.47 Partners are generally self-employed earners for national insurance purposes (but see **1.62** for LLPs), so they must register as self-employed with HMRC and for self-assessment (on form SA401). Class 2 and Class 4 NIC are assessed and collected with the income tax self-assessment, and will be merged into one charge with effect from 6 April 2018.

> **Focus**
>
> HMRC and the DWP take the view that sleeping and inactive partners are subject to class 2 national insurance on their rewards from the partnership, as they are 'gainfully employed' as self-employed earners for the purposes of *SSCBA 1992, s 2(1)(b)*.

Capital gains

1.48 When a partnership buys an asset, each partner is treated as acquiring a fractional share in it; similarly on a disposal of an asset. In the absence of any agreements or evidence relating to the ownership of assets and the sharing of capital profits, the partnership assets are treated as being held equally by all the partners.

When a partner joins or leaves the partnership, or the agreement concerning the sharing of capital profits is altered there may be a disposal of a fractional share in a partnership asset. Each partner should compute his own gain or loss by reference to his interest in the partnership assets, and pay any capital gains tax due calculated according to their other gains and losses for the tax year (*TCGA 1992, s 59, Statement of Practice D12*). Whether or not capital gains tax is actually payable will depend upon the circumstances, and reference should be made to Chapter 6 of *Capital Gains Tax 2017/18* (Bloomsbury Professional).

Inheritance tax

1.49 An interest in a trading business, whether operated as a partnership or sole trader, potentially qualifies for 100% business property relief (BPR). However, BPR is denied if a binding contract for sale of the business or partnership interest exists at the date of death. To avoid this trap, the partnership agreement should contain an option for the existing partners to acquire the business interest following the death of a partner, but not a requirement that the business interest should be acquired. Alternatively, a tax liability may be avoided by claiming that the arrangements are part of a bona fide commercial bargain and were made without gratuitous intent.

Property held by a partner outside of the partnership and used by the partnership for its trade will qualify for 50% BPR, see further discussion in **Chapter 12.**

VAT

1.50 Although an ordinary partnership is not a separate taxable person in its own right in England and Wales, it is for VAT purposes. The partnership (not the individual partners) must register for VAT if its turnover exceeds the VAT registration threshold (£85,000 from 1 April 2017). However, the partners will be jointly and severally liable for the VAT debts of the partnership unless they have limited liability.

Partnerships formed in Scotland are treated as a separate legal person (*Partnership Act 1890, s 4(2)*).

1.51 No change in VAT registration is needed if there are changes in the composition of the partnership (ie partners leaving or joining). However, such changes should be notified to HMRC on form VAT2 as the departing partner will be regarded as a continuing partner and liable for the VAT debts of the business until the change is notified (see *Customs and Excise Comrs v Jamieson* [2002] STC 1418).

1.52 Where a sole proprietor takes another person into the business to form a partnership, or where a business carried on by two or more people in partnership is dissolved and continued by one person alone, HMRC must be informed. The change from sole proprietor to partnership or vice versa is a change of legal entity and will require registration of the new business for VAT purposes, although an election can be made to transfer the VAT registration number to the new entity (*VATA 1994, s 49(2)*).

1.53 If a sole trader carries on two or more distinct trades or businesses, the turnover of all those trades must be aggregated to determine if the individual is liable to be VAT registered. If he is VAT registered, all his trades must be subject to VAT. However, if the trades are conducted through separate legal entities such as a partnership, a limited company or sole trader, the trades will not be combined for VAT purposes, unless HMRC issue a direction for the businesses to be aggregated under *VATA 1994, Sch 1, para 2*.

Limited partnership

1.54 Limited partnerships are registered under the *Limited Partnerships Act 1907*. These are rarely used and should not be confused with LLPs incorporated under the *Limited Liability Partnerships Act 2000* (see **1.58**).

A limited partnership must include at least one general partner, whose liability is unlimited but it can be a limited company. Only the general partners can be involved in the management of the limited partnership. The liability of the limited partners for the debts and obligations of the partnership is limited to the amounts of their respective capital contributions. Limited partners lose their limited liability status if they become involved in the day-to-day running of the partnership.

Like an ordinary partnership, a limited partnership is not a separate legal entity when formed in England or Wales. Scottish partnerships do have a separate legal entity (*PA 1890, s 4(2)*).

Why use a limited partnership?

1.55 Limited partnerships are often used to undertake property developments or investments that are too big for a single person or organisation to take on. An investment manager will set up a subsidiary company to act as a general partner and invite third-party investors to become limited partners. Often the investment manager will then provide the general partner with the services of managing the limited partnership investment business.

Tax treatment

1.56 The tax treatment of a limited partnership is much the same as an ordinary partnership, as the partners are subject to tax on their share of the profits or losses as individuals (see **1.43**). However, the partners' freedom to utilise trading losses from a limited partnership has been restricted by the various provisions described in **1.16**.

VAT

1.57 The VAT regulations relating to partnerships detailed at **1.50** do not apply to limited partnerships. A limited partnership does not have to have one VAT registration. The limited partners can be separately registered for VAT as decided in *H Saunders and TG Sorrell v Customs & Excise Commissioners* (1980) VATTR 51.

Limited liability partnership

1.58 A limited liability partnership (LLP) is a corporate body with its own legal personality, and is formed by incorporating under the *Limited Liability Partnerships Act 2000*. The LLP must be registered at Companies House, and must submit annual accounts and a confirmation statement, which are open to public view. The LLP must have a minimum of two members, but there is no maximum. Limited companies or other LLPs can also be members, but ordinary partnerships and limited partnerships cannot.

1.59 An advantage of an LLP is that it is a legal body separate from its members. An ordinary partnership only has a separate legal personality from the partners if it is formed under Scottish law. The members of an LLP have their liability limited to the amount of capital the member has contributed to the LLP.

1.60 An existing ordinary partnership can convert into an LLP without tax charges arising on the conversion. For income tax or corporation tax each partner's notional trade is treated as continuing. However, a new self-assessment reference number (UTR) will be set up by HMRC for the new LLP, and the nominated partner should tell HMRC whether it wishes to continue to use the old UTR or the new one.

The PAYE scheme can be transferred from the old partnership to the new LLP, but the partners must ask HMRC to do this. The VAT number of the old partnership can be reallocated to the LLP using the election under *VATA 1994, s 49(2)*.

Why use an LLP?

1.61 An LLP offers protection for all of the partners from the acts of the other partners as the members do not have joint and several liability for the debts of the LLP, as is the case with an ordinary partnership. Limited partnerships, as opposed to LLPs, only offer limited liability to partners who do not participate in the management of the business.

Tax treatment

1.62 The individual members of the LLP are not regarded as employed by the LLP for any purpose, unless the conditions in **1.63** apply. Thus the members of the LLP pay income tax and national insurance on a self-employed basis on their share of the profits. A corporate member pays corporation tax on its share of the profits.

1.63 A salaried member of an LLP (not of an ordinary partnership) is treated as an employee of the LLP for income tax and NIC purposes, if the individual meets all of the following conditions (*ITTOIA 2005, ss 863A–863C*):

A. it is reasonable to expect that the member's remuneration for the work he performs for the LLP is substantially fixed, and does not vary in line with the overall profits or losses of the entire LLP (known as 'disguised salary');

B. the member has no significant influence over the affairs of the entire LLP; and

C. the member has contributed less than 25% of his disguised salary for the tax year as capital to the LLP.

Conditions A and B are considered only at the point when the individual becomes member of the LLP (or at 6 April 2014 if later); condition C must be examined annually.

> **Focus**
>
> Even if all the conditions A to C above are met, the individual continues to be treated as self-employed for employment law purposes until and unless his contract with the LLP is changed to an employment contract.

VAT treatment

1.64 As an LLP is a corporate body it is a recognised legal entity for VAT purposes and is separately liable for VAT registration, subject to the normal registration rules. As with ordinary partnerships this does not mean that the members will be seen as supplying their services to the LLP and therefore they will not normally have to register for VAT as individual partners.

1.65 As a corporate body the LLP can join a VAT group that has a company or other corporate bodies, such as universities, as members, as long as the conditions in *VATA 1994, ss 43* and *43A* are met. However, there are restrictions as to when an LLP can join a VAT group when it functions as the vehicle for a joint venture arrangement. For more information on VAT grouping see *HMRC VAT Notice 700/2: Group and divisional registration*. There are also anti-avoidance rules to consider in *VATA 1994, ss 43AA–44D* and *Sch 9A*.

Tax benefits of all partnerships

Income spreading

1.66 Tax issues may influence the decision to form a partnership. It is relatively common for a proprietor to take his spouse into partnership with a view to achieving an income tax saving. By spreading the profits of the business over two sets of basic rate income tax bands, and against two personal allowances, considerable tax savings may be achieved – see **Example 1.3**.

Example 1.3 – Comparing tax paid by sole trader or partnership

Frankie runs a sole trader business in England and makes taxable profits of £130,000 in the year to 31 March 2018, on which she pays £50,463 in tax and NIC, leaving £79,537 net income. If Frankie traded in partnership with Johnny, sharing the profits equally, the total tax and NIC payable would be £37,126, leaving a total net income of £92,874, thus increasing their net income by £13,337. Figures are rounded to nearest £.

2017/18 Tax Year	*As sole trader*	*As partnership*	
	Frankie	*Frankie*	*Johnny*
	£	*£*	*£*
Profits	130,000	65,000	65,000
Personal allowance*	Nil	11,500	11,500
Net taxable profits	130,000	53,500	53,500
Tax due at 20% on first £33,500	6,700	6,700	6,700
Tax due at 40% over £33,500	38,600	8,000	8,000
Class 2 NIC: £2.85 per week	148	148	148
Class 4 NIC: 9% between £8,164 and £45,000	3,315	3,315	3,315

Class 4 NIC: 2% above £45,000	1,700	400	400
Total tax and NICs payable	50,463	18,563	18,563
Net income after tax	79,537	46,437	46,437
Total effective tax and NI rate on gross profits:	38.82%	28.56%	28.56%

* Reduced to Nil where income is £123,000 or more.

1.67 HMRC should not challenge the apportionment of profits within a partnership but they may question the payment of a salary to a family member (see **1.97**). There is no legal requirement for the partners to contribute capital, participate in the management of the business, take an active part in running the business, or even be capable of performing the full range of activities of the business partnership (see HMRC Business Income Manual at BIM82020). Where there is a genuine partnership, the profits of that partnership may be split in any way which the partners desire, and that profit split may be changed at will.

1.68 Where the total business profits are split between two or more taxpayers, this can save considerable amounts of tax, as illustrated in **Example 1.3**. These tax savings are most effective where the income of an individual partner is reduced below a key tax threshold, such as £100,000 for loss of personal allowance, or £150,000 for the 45% tax rate. Tax at the higher and additional rates may also be saved by making pension contributions, or gift aid donations on behalf of both partners to expand their basic and higher rate bands.

Focus

Families who claim child benefit also need to observe two further thresholds for the imposition of the high income child benefit charge (HICBC) that claws back child benefit received by the family. This tax charge applies where the highest earner in the family has net adjusted income of over £50,000. The full amount of child benefit is clawed back where the income of the highest earner is £60,000 or more.

Limits to tax saving

Settlements legislation

1.69 The main weapon HMRC can use to attack tax savings achieved through profit-sharing arrangements is the settlements legislation primarily contained in *ITTOIA 2005, Pt 5, Ch 5*. Following the House of Lords decision in *Jones v Garnett* [2007] STC 1536, it is unlikely that HMRC would use this legislation to attack husband and wife businesses as any profits diverted to a spouse or civil partner would be covered by the spouse exemption, see **1.118–1.121**.

Where the partners in the business are not married it is unlikely that the settlements legislation could be used to challenge the split of profits. However, where the partnership was not effective for some other purpose, for example where professional or trade rules barred the involvement in the business of certain individuals held out as partners, HMRC may be able to prove a partnership did not exist.

1.70 To provide a robust argument against the settlements legislation being invoked it is important that all the partners have the attributes and trappings of full equity partners. Good evidence of a genuine partnership should be available, such as a partnership agreement that provides for the sharing of income and capital losses as well as profits or gains. The trade should be conducted through a partnership bank account, for which all partners are signatories.

IR35 provisions

1.71 If the partnership provides the personal services of the partners or employees in circumstances where the worker would be an employee of the customer if the partnership did not exist, the IR35 rules for personal services provided through intermediaries may apply (see **1.83–1.88**).

Estate spreading

1.72 The prospect of saving inheritance tax can influence a business proprietor to form a partnership. In the case of a partnership between husband and wife, the tax saving can come from the equalisation of their estates. Where the partnership is between a parent and child or grandchild, the partnership arrangement can form the basis for a long-term transfer of the business down the generations.

COMPANIES

Type of company

1.73 The following types of company may be used by a new business:

- private company limited by shares;
- private company limited by guarantee and not having share capital;

- private unlimited company, with or without share capital; and
- community interest company (CIC).

There are also various forms of co-operative and common share-ownership arrangements, which are not dealt with in this chapter.

Private limited company

1.74 This is the most commonly used corporate form. Its defining criterion is that the liability of its members is limited to the amount, if any, unpaid on the shares held by each of them. A private company may convert to a public limited company (Plc), but discussion of that topic is outside the scope of this chapter.

Company limited by guarantee

1.75 A company limited by guarantee is commonly used by not-for-profit organisations that do not have a requirement for working capital, such as trade associations, clubs, charities and trade protection societies. Membership of a company limited by guarantee is not transferable and ceases on death or earlier retirement.

It is also possible to form a charitable incorporated organisation, under the *Charities Act 2006,* which is not considered further in this chapter.

Unlimited company

1.76 An unlimited company cannot have 'Limited' in its title, as it does not confer limited liability on its members. This means the members' liability is similar to that of partners in a general partnership (see **1.43**). However, the unlimited company does have a separate legal existence and its members, unlike partners, have no direct obligation to contribute to the assets of the company while it is a going concern, save to be called upon to contribute to the company any capital unpaid on their shares.

Community interest company (CIC)

1.77 The CIC is designed to be used for community-based social businesses that are run as not-for-profit. A CIC may be a private or public limited company, limited by shares or guarantee. However, its articles of association must restrict the use of its assets for the benefit of the community. The CIC can attract investment under the social investment tax relief scheme.

Limited liability

1.78 Limited liability is perceived as being an important commercial advantage of carrying on a business through the medium of a limited company. The liability of the shareholders of a limited company is limited to the amount (if any) unpaid on their shares. Thus, if the company fails, they are not normally liable to make good any deficit. In the case of an unlimited company (see **1.76**), the shareholders' liability is not limited and they will be responsible for meeting all of the company's debts.

1.79 The actual degree of protection given by limited liability to the shareholders of private companies may be negated insofar as they have given any personal guarantees for the company's borrowings. A bank lending to a small company will almost invariably require personal guarantees from the directors or shareholders, and security over the personal assets of the major shareholders to support the loan provided. Shareholders will normally still be protected against claims by any creditors who have not taken such a security for their debts. The incorporation of a business will not absolve the proprietors from liability for pre-incorporation debts.

1.80 Individuals considering setting up a new business within a company, or incorporating an existing business, with a view to leaving creditors high and dry in the event of its being unsuccessful, should beware the provisions of the *Insolvency Act 1986, s 214* and the *Company Directors (Disqualification) Act 1986*. Under this legislation, directors can incur personal liability, notably in circumstances of wrongful trading or fraudulent trading, or when acting as a director when disqualified. For further discussion of the tax issues related to incorporation and disincorporation see **Chapter 2**.

Tax treatment

Corporate taxes

1.81 Corporation tax is levied at one rate for all sizes of company: 19% (from 1 April 2017), although different rates apply to companies in the oil and gas industry.

The tax savings to be made by operating through a limited company rather than as an unincorporated business have been diminished by the introduction of dividend tax from 6 April 2016. However, some tax savings can be realised by extracting profits from the company in a tax-efficient manner (see **1.91–1.112**).

1.82 In **Table 1.3** it is assumed the company owner is resident in England, takes a salary equal to the primary threshold for national insurance (£8,164) and extracts the balance of the profits as a dividend, of which the first £5,000 is taxed at 0%. This salary attracts no employees' or employer's NIC but the individual receives a full NI credit for the year. Note, these calculations would be different for an individual resident in Scotland, where the 40% threshold for earned income starts at £43,000.

Table 1.3: Comparison of net income in 2017/18

Gross profits by sole trader	*Net taxable profits*	*IT @ 20%*	*IT @ 40%*	*Classes 2 and 4 NIC*	*Total tax and NI*	*Owner's net income*
£	£	£	£	£	£	£
20,000	8,500	1,700	–	1,213.44	2,913.44	17,086.56
50,000	38,500	6,700	2,000	3,563.44	12,263.44	37,736.56
100,000	88,500	6,700	22,000	4,563.44	33,263.44	66,736.56
150,000	150,000*	6,700	46,600	5,563.44	58,863.44	91,136.56
Gross profits in company	*Net profits after salary*	*CT @ 19%*	*Dividend tax @ 7.5% & @ 32.5%*	*IT @ 20% on salary*	*Total tax and NI*	*Owner's net income*
£	£	£	£	£	£	£
20,000	11,836	2,248.84	93.84	–	2,342.68	17,657.32
50,000	41,836	7,948.84	1,916.34	–	9,865.18	40,134.82
100,000	91,836	17,448.84	14,341.63	–	31,790.47	68,209.53
150,000*	141,836	26,948.84	27,504.13	1,632.00	56,085.77	93,914.23

* No tax-free personal allowance given when income exceeds £123,000.

The cash savings for incorporation range from £570 at the £20,000 profit level to £2,777 at the £150,000 profit level. However, that is not a linear progression as the savings from incorporation dip at various thresholds.

Personal service companies

1.83 Where an individual personally performs a contract through a third party, such as his own personal service company (PSC), that contract can fall foul of the wide-ranging anti-avoidance legislation for provision of personal services through intermediaries, known as IR35 (*ITEPA 2003, Pt 2, Ch 8*). These provisions do not prohibit the payment of dividends, but can mean that any dividends or payments to other employees must be paid out of income that has been subject to tax under PAYE and NICs.

1.84 The IR35 rules can apply where the intermediary is a company, partnership, or even an individual, but different qualifying conditions exist in each case:

- Intermediary is a PSC: the worker who performs the services must either hold a material interest in the company, broadly defined as 5% or more of the ordinary share capital, or receive payments from the company that can be taken to represent remuneration for the services performed for the final client.
- Intermediary is a partnership: the individuals who perform the personal services must share 60% or more of the profits of the partnership.

Sole traders who do not themselves act as intermediaries cannot fall under the IR35 legislation.

1.85 The IR35 legislation is designed to increase the tax burden of businesses that fall within it, and thus reduce the tax advantage from working through a PSC rather than as a direct employee for the final client. The tax advantages are principally the ability to receive income free of NICs, paid as dividends, and to achieve tax relief for business expenses on the wholly and exclusively basis (*ITTOIA 2005, s 34*) rather than the wholly, exclusively and necessarily basis required for tax relief of expenses incurred by an employee (*ITEPA 2003, s 336*).

The IR35 rules seek to apply PAYE and NIC to the proceeds of contracts that would be treated as employment contracts if they had been performed by the individual working directly for the client and not through the intermediary. Where the contract is performed in the private sector, the PSC must decide whether a particular contract is within IR35. If the contract is performed for a public sector body, from 6 April 2017 that public body, and not the PSC, must decide whether the contract falls within IR35. In both cases, it is the PSC which bears the cost of the employer's NIC rather than the engager/client, so the client makes a significant tax saving by not employing the worker directly.

1.86 Whether income received by a personal service company falls within the IR35 rules will depend on the performance of the hypothetical contract represented by the actions of the worker, the final client, and any agent in between. Contractors and engagers are encouraged to use the HMRC online employment status tool to determine if a contract is caught by IR35.

1.87 Although the IR35 rules may remove many of the benefits of operating through a personal service company, some are retained:

- If the company has some intrinsic value this may attract CGT relief through the application of entrepreneurs' relief and the capital gains exemption when the company is sold or formally liquidated, although those reliefs will not apply if the shareholder starts a similar business within two years (see **Chapter 8**).

- The company may make contributions into a registered pension scheme set up for the director and other employees, saving both corporation tax and NIC.

1.88 All business proprietors who are potentially affected by IR35 need to make the following judgments:

- What proportion of income is caught by the IR35 rules?
- What additional costs will the business incur by keeping records to comply with the rules?
- Do the benefits of operating through a company outweigh the immediate costs?
- Will the business make losses under the IR35 rules that cannot be relieved?
- What is the risk of the proprietor's view of which income falls under IR35 being successfully challenged by HMRC?

Managed service companies

1.89 A company whose business consists wholly or mainly of providing the personal services of a worker to others can be defined as a managed service company (MSC) under *ITEPA 2003, Pt 2, Ch 9*, if the following conditions also exist:

- more than half of the income of the MSC is paid on to the worker in some form;
- the manner of payment of this income to the worker increases the worker's net receipt above the amount he would have received if all those payments were treated as employment income; and
- a person who carries on a business of promoting or facilitating the use of companies to provide the services of individuals (an MSC provider) is involved with the company.

1.90 The consequences of being an MSC are serious for the MSC provider and the company. All non-employment income extracted from the MSC (such as dividends) is deemed to be earnings of the worker for both PAYE and national insurance purposes. The tax and NICs are payable when the payment to the worker is made, not at the end of the tax year as under the IR35 provisions. The MSC provider, as well as the office holders of the MSC, and their associates, may also become liable to pay any PAYE and NICs debts which have been accrued by the MSC under the transfer of debt regulations (*SI 2007/1077* and *SI 2007/2068*). Where the MSC provisions apply to a company the IR35 provisions cannot also apply.

Profit extraction

Extract as dividends

1.91 Although tax is charged at only 19% on corporate profits, as compared to 20%, 40% or 45% on profits made within unincorporated businesses (see **1.2**), the net income cannot easily be placed in the hands of shareholders without suffering a further charge to tax. The obvious way of distributing such profits is by the payment of dividends, which don't create a liability to NIC.

A company can only pay a dividend if it has sufficient realised profits at the time that the dividend is paid. It may be necessary to prepare interim accounts to demonstrate the profits are available for distribution. If there are insufficient profits available, the dividend payment may be challenged by HMRC as a loan to the shareholder, or as remuneration of the director/shareholder.

1.92 Individuals who receive company dividends in excess of £5,000 per year must pay dividend tax on the excess at 7.5% within the basic rate band (£33,500 for 2017/18), at 32.5% within the higher rate band, and at 38.1% on dividends in the additional rate band. Dividends form the highest slice of a taxpayer's income.

Disadvantages of dividends

1.93 Taking profits out of the company as dividends rather than as salary or bonus can have a detrimental effect on the shareholder's financial affairs, as explained in **1.94–1.96**. Also paying dividends can increase the values of shareholdings for the purposes of IHT and CGT. However, the impact of IHT is usually limited because business property relief at the rate of 100% is given on transfers of shares in qualifying unlisted companies that do not hold significant non-business investments.

1.94 Dividends do not count as pensionable earnings. Thus taking a large proportion of income in the form of dividends could restrict the individual's ability to make tax-relieved personal contributions to a pension. However, employer's pension contributions could be paid instead, see **1.109**.

Extract as bonus or salary

1.95 Profits extracted in the form of remuneration give rise to NIC charges for both the employee and the employer, which makes this method of profit extraction relatively expensive, once the NIC threshold of £8,164 is exceeded (for 2017/18). However, where the business is eligible to claim the employment allowance, that can be set against up to £3,000 of employer's NICs.

In **Example 1.4** we have assumed the employment allowance is not available to set against NICs on the bonus, which will attract employer's NICs at 13.8%. The bonus is fully deductible for tax purposes, so there is no corporation tax charge where all the surplus profits are paid as a bonus. The dividend must be paid out of post-tax profits, so corporation tax must first be deducted from the gross profits. The employee is assumed to have already received a salary of exactly £11,500 which is covered by his personal allowance for the year. Figures are rounded to nearest £.

Example 1.4 – Choice between bonus or dividend

Company pays corporation tax at 19%	*Bonus*	*Dividend*
2017/18: calculation to nearest £	*£*	*£*
Gross profits before tax (after salary of £11,500)	100,000	100,000
Less bonus	87,874	Nil
Less employer's NIC at 13.8%	12,126	Nil
Corporation tax charged at 19%	Nil	(19,000)
Payable to employee/shareholder before deductions	87,874	81,000
Employees NIC at 12% on first £33,500 (£45,000 – salary: £11,500)	(4,020)	Nil
Employees NIC at 2% above £33,500 of bonus	(1,087)	–
Gross receipt for employee before income tax	87,874	81,000
Income tax at 7.5% on dividends in band to £33,500 – £5,000	–	(2,137)
Income tax at 20% on first £33,500	(6,700)	–
Income/dividend tax at 40%/32.5% above £33,500	(21,750)	(15,437)
Net receipts	54,317	63,426
Effective total tax rate on gross profits of company	45.68%	36.57%

1.96 **Example 1.4** demonstrates that paying a dividend is more tax efficient than a bonus or salary payment when the company pays corporate tax at 19%, taking into account NIC payable. When considering whether to incorporate the business, the total effective tax and NIC paid on the gross profits should be compared to the total effective tax and NIC paid by the sole trader or partner on the same profits; see **Example 1.3** above.

1.97 If remuneration is paid to a director or employee in circumstances where little is done in return, or little responsibility for the business is taken on, HMRC will seek to disallow the deduction of excessive remuneration (see **1.113**).

Extract value by rent

1.98 Where a property is held by the proprietor or their family personally, but used for the company for its trade, the company may pay rent for the use of that property. The rent received must be declared on the individual's personal tax return, and be subject to income tax on the net amount after deduction of expenses such as loan interest, repairs and insurance.

1.99 The payment of rent to an individual can be a useful way to extract funds from the company, and it has the following advantages:

- rent payments do not carry national insurance charges;
- the rent can be paid whether or not the company has made a profit in the period, unlike a dividend;
- the rent payments are tax deductible for the company;
- the property can be placed in the hands of a member of the family who does not work directly for the business, and hence direct some income from the company to that individual where it may be taxed at a lower rate;
- the rent paid does not affect the business property relief (BPR) available on the value of the property, which will be 50% whether or not a market rent is paid.

A lease should be drawn up between the company and the property owner, and if the property owner is a director of the company the rents should be set at a reasonable market value. The grant of a lease may incur SDLT (LBTT in Scotland) charges.

1.100 The proprietor of the business needs to balance the potential advantage of holding the property outside the company, in terms of profit extracted from the company, 50% BPR available on death compared to the 100% BPR available on the value of the property if it is held within the company. For further discussion of planning techniques available with BPR see **Chapter 12**.

A potential disadvantage of charging rent to the company for a building held privately is the loss of entrepreneurs' relief when the building is disposed of in association with the disposal of shares in the company and a withdrawal from the business. Where rent is received for the use of the building for periods after 5 April 2008, the entrepreneurs' relief will be restricted. Where the rent paid is less than the commercial market rent for the property the entrepreneurs' relief is restricted on a just and reasonable basis (*TCGA 1992, s 169P(2)*). For further discussion of entrepreneurs' relief on the disposal of a business see **Chapter 8**.

Extract value by interest

1.101 Where a shareholder or director has loaned money to the company, perhaps by not withdrawing amounts voted as dividends or remuneration, the company can pay interest on the outstanding balance. Where the interest is paid on a short-term loan from the individual to the company, the company can pay the interest due without deduction of tax.

If the period of the loan can exceed one year, the company should deduct income tax at 20% at the time the interest is paid, and report that tax deduction on a quarterly form CT61. Where the interest paid falls within the individual recipient's annual savings allowance (£1,000: basic rate taxpayer, £500: higher rate taxpayer), it is taxable at 0%, and the tax deducted at 20% can be reclaimed.

1.102 The interest paid by the company should be set at a commercial rate, which could be several points above the bank base rate. However, where HMRC perceive that the interest charge materially exceeds a commercial rate, they may seek to treat the excess interest as remuneration or a dividend distribution. There are also accounting issues to consider under FRS 102 or FRS 105 if the loan is not repayable on demand.

1.103 The payment of interest has the following advantages as a profit-extraction method:

- the interest can be paid whether or not the company has distributable profits, unlike a dividend;
- the interest payments do not carry national insurance;
- the interest payments are tax deductible for the company (but see **1.104**);
- payments are only made to those individuals who have outstanding credit balances with the company, rather than all of the shareholders, as with a dividend.

1.104 Where the company is a close company and the individual is a shareholder of that company, the company can only get a tax deduction for the interest due when it is actually paid, if the interest is paid more than 12 months after the end of the accounting period in which it was due (*CTA 2009, ss 373, 375*).

Extract value by benefits in kind

1.105 Value may be extracted from the company in the form of benefits in kind made available to directors, employees, and to shareholders who do not actually work for the company. Where the benefit is provided to a non-working shareholder, or an associate of that shareholder, the value of the benefit is not taxed as employment income, but is treated as a distribution under *CTA 2010, s 1064*.

1.106 Certain benefits in kind are tax free when provided to the company's employees or directors, but the private use of the asset or service would be taxable if paid for by the business and provided to a sole-trader or partner. Examples of tax-free benefits include:

- childcare vouchers – within limits;
- mobile phone;
- loan of up to £10,000 (see **1.108**);
- employer-provided training;
- relocation costs up to £8,000.

On the other hand, a car paid for by a partnership or unincorporated business may incur far lower tax charges than one provided for business and private use by the company.

Focus

A definite view on the potential tax savings which can be achieved by incorporating a business cannot be made without considering the levels of pension contributions, drawings or remuneration required by the individual, and the benefits in kind to be provided through the business, such as a company car.

Extract value by way of a pension

1.107 Pension contributions can be a tax-efficient way of extracting value from a company. An employer's pension contribution paid by the company into a scheme for a director or employee will be tax deductible if the individual's total remuneration package, including the pension contribution, is reasonable for the work done for the company.

Where the total pension contributions paid by or on behalf of the individual exceed the individual's annual allowance for the year, that individual will be subject to an annual allowance charge at their marginal tax rate. For further discussion of the tax treatment of pension contributions see **Chapter 11**.

Extract as a loan

1.108 Funds held within a private company may be loaned to directors, shareholders or employees, although tax charges may apply (see **1.109**). The following restrictions should also be noted:

- The *Companies Act 2006* prohibits loans to directors of more than £10,000 (*CA 2006, s 207*).
- A loan made available to an employee or associate of that employee through a third party may fall under the disguised remuneration provisions and thus be subject to PAYE (*ITEPA 2003, Pt 7A*).
- A loan to any director or to an employee which exceeds £10,000 at any point in the tax year, will generate a benefit in kind charge under *ITEPA 2003, s 175* equivalent to the interest due on the loan calculated at the official rate (2.5% since 6 April 2017), less any interest actually paid. The company will also be due to pay Class 1A NIC at 13.8% on the value of the benefit declared on the form P11D.

Loan to participators

1.109 Loans of any amount to participators in close companies can give rise to a charge under *CTA 2010, s 455* or *s 464A*, set at 32.5% of the loan advanced on or after 6 April 2016. This charge does not generally apply if the loan is repaid, written off or forgiven, within nine months of the end of the company's accounting period. However, the *CTA 2010, s 455* charge is extended in respect of loans or repayments made on and after 20 March 2013 where:

- A loan of £5,000 or more is repaid to the company, but within 30 days amounts totalling £5,000 or more are advanced to the same borrower or to one of his associates. In this case the first loan is treated as not having been repaid, and continues for the purposes of calculating the corporation tax charge. However, if the repayment is made by a dividend declared by the company and chargeable to income tax on the participator, it is not brought within this rule (*CTA 2010, s 464C*).
- The loan is £15,000 or more, the 30-day rule is ignored if at the time of the repayment of the first loan, if the borrower intends to borrow again from the company or has arrangements in place to do so. If those later loans are made they are treated as a continuation of the first loan. As above if the repayment is made by a dividend declared by the company it is not brought within this rule (*CTA 2010, s 464C*).

- Loans channelled from the company through LLPs or partnerships in which the participator is a member are treated as if the loan was made directly to the participator. This also applies if the loan is advanced to a trust of which a participator in the company is a beneficiary, or potential beneficiary.
- An arrangement, perhaps a partnership structure between the company and a participator, is used to transfer value from the company to the participator (*CTA 2010, s 464A*).
- The charge under *CTA 2010, s 455(2)* does not apply if:
  - the amount of the loan does not exceed £15,000; and
  - the borrower works full-time for the close company or any of its associated companies; and
  - the borrower *does not* have a material interest in the company (being 5% or more of the ordinary shares); or
  - the debt is incurred for the supply of goods or services in the ordinary course of the trade or business of the company.

Where the loan from a close company to a participator is written off or forgiven, the borrower is liable to income tax on the amount written off, as if that sum was a net dividend (*ITTOIA 2005, s 415*). This tax charge takes precedence over a charge as employment income under *ITEPA 2003, s 118*. Where a loan which has given rise to a *CTA 2010, s 455* charge is written off, the company cannot claim a tax deduction for the loan write-off under the loan relationship rules.

When the loan is repaid the company must make a claim for repayment of the *s 455* charge within six years from the end of the financial year in which repayment is made.

HMRC will demand NICs on amounts paid to directors that cause their loan accounts to become overdrawn. HMRC claim the payment to the director is an advanced remuneration and thus generates a Class 1 NI liability at the date it is paid or the director becomes entitled to those funds (*SSCBA 1992, s 2(1)*). If it was always the intention to clear the loan with a dividend payment or some other private funds introduced to the company, the overdrawn amount cannot be an advance of remuneration. For further details, see para 31 of leaflet CA44: *National Insurance for Company Directors*.

Extract by way of purchase of own shares

1.110 Limited companies may issue redeemable shares and purchase their own shares under certain conditions. The amount by which the purchase price for the shares exceeds the amount paid on subscription must normally be treated as a distribution (*CTA 2010, s 1000*). The shareholder who receives value for the shares will have to pay income tax on the net proceeds as if they were a dividend.

The proceeds of a share buy-back are treated as a capital payment subject to capital gains tax, if the conditions of *CTA 2010, s 1033* can be met for the transaction. For a full discussion of the tax implications of the company purchasing its own shares see **Chapter 4**.

Extract value on death

1.111 Gifts of shares in an unquoted trading business or company qualify for 100% BPR for inheritance tax (*IHTA 1984, s 105(1)*). If the gift is made during the lifetime of the donor, the share must also qualify for BPR at the later date of death of the donor, or the tax relief will not apply. So the company must still be unquoted and trading within the definitions of those terms as they apply under the *Inheritance Tax Act 1984*.

1.112 Where an asset, such as land, buildings, plant or machinery, is held by an individual and used for the purpose of a business, the value of that asset will qualify for 50% BPR if:

- the business is the individual's own sole-trading business; or
- the business is a partnership in which the individual is a partner; or
- the business is an unquoted trading company in which the individual is a controlling shareholder.

Control for IHT purposes is measured by the voting power on all questions affecting the company as a whole, which if exercised would yield a majority of the votes capable of being exercised on them. For further discussion of BPR on gifts or transfers of business assets see **Chapter 12**.

Tax benefits of a company

Income spreading using salaries

1.113 To obtain a tax deduction for business expenses those expenses must be incurred wholly and exclusively for the purposes of the trade or profession (*CTA 2009, s 54* for corporation tax; *ITTOIA 2005, s 34* for income tax). This applies to salaries, bonuses, wages, pension contributions and other employee benefits just as it does to any other business expenses.

A wage paid to a spouse or child is often seen by business owners as a legitimate way to redistribute some of the profits of the business into hands of those who will pay tax at a lower rate on that income. A spouse who otherwise has no other income can be paid up to the earnings threshold for NIC (£157 per week for 2017/18), and pay no tax or NIC on that income. If the wages exceed the lower earnings limit (£113 per week for 2017/18), the individual will also receive a national insurance credit that counts as Class 1 NIC for qualification for state benefits.

1.114 Wages paid to relatives of the principal owner of the business are particularly vulnerable to attack by HMRC as being a disguised distribution of profits, and not a business expense wholly and exclusively incurred for the business. HMRC will want to know not only that the wage was actually paid to the individual (*Abbott v IRC* (1995) Sp C 58), but also that it fairly represents the value of the work done by that individual (*Copeman v William Flood & Sons Ltd* (1940) 24 TC 53).

1.115 Employees who are close relatives of the main proprietor should have service contracts in place that set out their duties and remuneration in commercial terms to deflect challenges from HMRC. Any family members employed by the family company should also be paid at least the national minimum wage, unless that individual acts purely as a director or company secretary and has no employment contract with the company (see **1.28**).

In **Example 1.3**, Frankie could have reduced the total tax paid by the business by employing Johnny rather than taking him into partnership. If his salary was set at £58,108, this would amount to a gross liability for the business of £65,000 including employer's NICs of £6,892. The total employers' and employees' NICs paid by the business on Johnny's salary would be £11,574 which would significantly reduce the tax saving of £13,337, achieved by forming a partnership.

An alternative position is shown in **Example 1.5** where Johnny's wage was set at the level such that the employer's NICs due would just be covered by the employment allowance of £3,000. Although Johnny is the only employee, the employment allowance can be claimed as the business is not incorporated.

Example 1.5 – Tax saved by sole trader employing one person

Frankie makes annual taxable profits of £130,000 in the year to 31 March 2018, on which she pays £50,463 in tax and NIC, leaving £79,537 net income. If Frankie employs Johnny, on a wage of £29,903, the total tax and NIC payable by them both would be £39,611, leaving a total net income of £90,389, thus increasing their net income by £10,852. Figures are rounded to nearest £.

2017/18 Tax Year	*Sole trader*	*Sole trader*	*Employee*
	Frankie	*Frankie*	*Johnny*
	£	£	£
Profits/ pay	130,000	100,097	29,903
Personal allowance*	Nil	11,451	11,500
Employers' NIC covered by employment allowance			(3,000)
Net taxable profits/pay	130,000	88,646	18,403
Tax due at 20% on up to £33,500	6,700	6,700	3,680
Tax due at 40% over £33,500	38,600	22,058	–
Class 2 NIC at £2.85 per week	148	148	–
Class 4 NIC at 9% on profits between £8,164 and £45,000	3,315	3,315	–
Class 4 NIC at 2% above £45,000	1,700	1102	–
Employee's class 1 NIC @ 12% above £8,164	–	–	2,608
Total tax and NICs payable	50,463	33,323	6,288
Net income after tax	79,537	66,774	23,615
Total effective tax and NI rate on gross profits/pay:	38.82%	33.29%	21.03%

* Reduced by £1 for every £2 of income over £100,000.

Income spreading using dividends

1.116 Any problem over obtaining a tax deduction for the relative's wages may be circumvented by paying a dividend instead of a salary, if the family member holds shares in the company. However, HMRC may challenge the use of the following structures to divert income from the main shareholders/ workers to other less active shareholders:

- dividend waivers;
- paying separate dividends on different classes of shares;
- the gift of shares with restricted rights; or
- dividends paid to the minor children of the main shareholder.

Settlements legislation

1.117 In any of these cases HMRC may argue that a settlement has been created by the main worker in favour of the person who received the dividends, on the basis that the main worker has made a gift of income to another individual. The anti-avoidance rules in the settlements legislation (*ITTOIA 2005, ss 619–648*) would then apply so the diverted income is taxed as if it was that of the donor.

1.118 The gift of ordinary shares between spouses, and the receipt of dividend income that arose from those shares was examined in: *Jones v Garnett (Inspector of Taxes)* [2007] STC 1536. The House of Lords decided in favour of the taxpayer, agreeing with HMRC that there was gift of income between the spouses, but that income was not caught by the settlement rules in *ITTOIA 2005, Ch 5,* as the spousal exemption applied. Mr Jones could not be taxed on the dividend income correctly received by Mrs Jones.

1.119 The decision in *Jones v Garnett* does not mean the settlement provisions can be ignored as the provisions could be applied where the shareholders are not married, or some of the shareholders are children, as the spousal exemption would not apply.

The guidance in the HMRC Trusts, Settlements and Estates Manual suggests a settlement is created where shares in the company are gifted to the child by someone other than the parents who are responsible for generating the profits of the company (see Example 16 at TSEM4300). This was shown in the case of *PA & FJ Bird v HMRC* [2008] SpC 720.

Mr and Mrs Bird initially owned all the shares in their company, but suggested that their daughters, then aged 15 and 10, should subscribe for some shares. The Special Commissioner accepted that the issuing of shares to the daughters comprised a settlement, and the income from that settlement should be taxed on the parents in equal parts. Although it was not clear in this case whether the funds used to subscribe for the shares came from the parents or an inheritance the girls received from their grandfather, the parents were deemed to be the settlors as they were the directors of the company and they arranged for new shares to be issued to the children.

1.120 Another example of the use of the settlements legislation to challenge the use of dividend waivers was the case *SP Buck v Revenue & Customs* [2008] SpC 716.

Mr Buck owned 9,999 of the shares in his company and his wife owned one share. Mr Buck waived his entitlement to his company's dividend, so the whole of the dividend was paid to his wife. The Special Commissioner found that

Mr Buck had formed a settlement in favour of his wife by waiving his dividend entitlement, and this settlement consisted purely of a right to income. As a result the income from that settlement should be taxed on Mr Buck.

1.121 When setting up a company in which family members are to hold shares, the following actions may reduce the risk of attack under the settlements legislation:

- The shares issued should be ordinary shares with full voting rights and rights to capital on a winding-up.
- Where the shareholders are a married couple or registered civil partners the ordinary shares should be gifted from one spouse/civil partner to the other.
- Both spouses/civil partners should be made directors of the company so they are equally responsible for the decisions the board of directors takes for the business, including suggesting the level of dividends to be paid.
- The duties undertaken by each family member for the company should be recorded to show that each shareholder plays a key role in the operation of the business.

IR35 rules

1.122 If the company is subject to the IR35 rules (see **1.83**), the payment of dividends may not be effective in reducing the effective total tax paid by the shareholder and the company on the income received. However, operating through a company has other commercial advantages and disadvantages, as discussed in **1.19–1.30**.

Company versus another medium

Starting as unincorporated

1.123 If the business is starting from scratch and expects to make losses for the first few years, trading within the medium of a partnership or sole-trader business for the first year or so will allow those losses to be relieved against the trader's other income (see **1.15**). An incorporation of the business when it is profitable may mean a capital gain arises on the transfer of assets including goodwill to the company (if the goodwill is transferrable). The gain arising on the transfer of the goodwill is unlikely to qualify for entrepreneurs' relief, but incorporation relief or hold-over relief may be used to hold-over the gain. For a further discussion of the tax reliefs and problems encountered on the incorporation of a business, see **Chapter 2**.

Timing of tax payments

1.124 Any comparison of the tax savings available by operating through a company, rather than as a sole trader or partnership needs to take into account the timing of tax payments. The timing of tax payments for a sole trader or partner starting in business is discussed in **1.36**.

Salary payments have the shortest time-lag for collection of the tax due, as they must be subject to PAYE and NIC deductions at the point of payment. Benefits in kind may also be taxed immediately through inclusion in the PAYE code, and the employer will have to pay Class 1A NICs on most benefits within three months of the end of the tax year.

> **Focus**
>
> The RTI system for reporting PAYE deductions provides HMRC with details of the PAYE due within three days of the payment date for salaries and wages, the HMRC banking and debt management section will issue demands for any apparent underpayment of PAYE without delay.

Companies

1.125 Most companies must pay their corporation tax nine months and one day after the end of the accounting period in which that tax liability arises. Large companies which have taxable profits in excess of £1.5 million a year, or which are part of a group, generally pay their corporate tax liability in four instalments commencing six months and 14 days from the start of the accounting period which gives rise to the tax liability.

National insurance

1.126 The national insurance burden can be a significant influence on the decision whether or not to take income in the form of earnings from a company, and if it is not possible to take NIC-free income, whether to incorporate at all. National insurance is payable on remuneration at levels over £8,164 per year (for 2017/18), and there is no upper limit on the remuneration that bears Class 1 NIC, although the rate payable by the employee drops to 2% once the upper earnings threshold is reached (£45,000 for 2017/18). Class 4 NIC payable by the self-employed are also unlimited in a similar fashion, but the Class 2 flat rate is set at the relatively low rate of £2.85 per week to reflect the minimum entitlement to social security benefits it carries.

1.127 The difference in the burden of NICs between the employed and self-employed is difficult to justify, as the only difference in terms of social security benefits is the entitlement to Jobseeker's Allowance, which is not available to those who have been self-employed. Nevertheless, NICs represent a very considerable fiscal impost in their own right, and their impact needs to be carefully considered by any individuals thinking of incorporating their business. The employer must also pay Class 1A NICs on almost all benefits in kind provided for employees where those benefits are also taxable.

Combination of personal and corporate taxes

1.128 The sole trader or partner is taxed on all the profits he makes whether or not he extracts those profits from the business, but the proprietor of a corporate business has the flexibility to control the level of personal tax he pays by extracting just enough income to keep his net adjusted income below the significant thresholds of £45,000, £50,000, £100,000 or £150,000. This factor alone can influence the choice of business structure, particularly for businesses that expect to have widely fluctuating profits year on year.

Any profits extracted from the company, whether by way of remuneration, benefits in kind, dividends or other methods, will generally be chargeable to income tax, and in most cases national insurance.

Profit-extraction strategy

1.129 The level of tax savings which can be made by operating a business through a company will depend on the method by which the proprietor extracts profits from the business. Where profits are extracted from the company as remuneration, which is subject to NIC, the impact of the combined employers' and employees' NIC are capable of resulting in the overall fiscal cost being in excess of that which would be suffered without incorporation.

1.130 The payment of dividends does not carry national insurance, and the first £5,000 received by the taxpayer in the year is taxed at 0%, so that can be a tax-efficient method of profit extraction for a basic-rate taxpayer.

> **Focus**
>
> Where the IR35 or the MSC provisions apply, dividend income may be reclassified as earnings and taxed as such (see **1.84** and **1.89**). This may tip the balance back in favour of an unincorporated business.

Small salary, high dividends

1.131 Where a director takes a small salary and extracts the balance of his income requirements from his company in a form that does not attract NIC, such as dividends, interest or rent – see **1.91–1.103**), significant savings may be made. However, this strategy is only tax efficient for certain companies, as the dividend is not tax deductible and so does not reduce the corporation tax payable, as a salary payment does. The tax savings also depend on the marginal tax rate of the shareholder.

Example 1.6 compares the standard profit-extraction strategy for a small company of paying a low salary with the balance of profits taken out of the company as a dividend, with the taxation of the same business as a partnership. It assumes both partners have a basic rate band of £33,500 available, which has not been extended by Gift Aid donations or by paying pension contributions. Figures are rounded to nearest £.

Example 1.6 – Tax paid by partnership compared to company

2017/18 Tax Year	*As a company*	*As a partnership*	
	F&J Ltd	*Frankie*	*Johnny*
	£	*£*	*£*
Profits	130,000	65,000	65,000
Wages from company up to personal allowance *	23,000	11,500	11,500
Net taxable profits	107,000	53,500	53,500
Corporation tax at 19%	20,330		
Net income extracted as dividend	86,670		
Tax due on 2 × divs: £28,500 @ 7.5% £5,000 @ 0%	4,275	–	–
Income tax due at 20% on next £33,500 profits	–	6,700	6,700
Tax due at 32.5% or 40% over £33,500 of dividend/profits/ person	6,393	8,000	8,000
Class 2 NIC at £2.85 per week	–	148	148
Class 4 NIC at 9% on profits of £36,836 + 2% on £20,000	–	3,715	3,715
Class 1 NIC @ 12% on wages	800	–	–
Net wages received (£11,100 each)	22,200	–	–
Total tax, including CT and NICs payable	31,798	18,563	18,563
Net income, including wages, after tax	98,202	46,437	46,437

*employers' NIC covered by employment allowance

When operating as a partnership, Frankie and Johnnie have a net income after tax of £92,874. If they run their business through a company and take a small salary covered by their personal allowance, they will have a net dividend income of £76,002 plus a net earned income of £22,200, giving a total net income of £98,202. Using the structure of a company could thus increase their net income by £5,238, but the exact savings will depend on the method used to extract profits from the company.

Employment-related securities

1.132 To take profits out of the company as dividends the individual must first hold an appropriate proportion of the company's shares. Where the individual already works for the company, holds a directorship, is related to someone who is employed by the company, or is about to be employed by the company, any shares acquired in that company will almost certainly be 'employment-related securities' as defined in *ITEPA 2003, Pt 7*. Where this is the case, tax charges can arise at the point when those shares are acquired, or when benefits connected with those shares, such as dividends, are received.

1.133 Where employees are awarded shares, it is clear that those shares are employment-related, but shares acquired in many other situations are also caught by deeming provisions in *ITEPA 2003, Pt 7*. Even gifts of shares between family members or others are caught unless the gift is made in the course of the normal domestic, family or personal relationships of the donor. Where such a gift of shares is made there should be some contemporaneous recording of the motive for the gift, and preferably a suitably worded deed of gift.

1.134 The tax charges on acquisition of employment-related securities normally only apply where:

- the shares have unusual terms (restricted securities, conditional securities or convertible securities); or
- the value of the shares is abnormal (high or low) as against a market value.

1.135 An income tax charge on dividends paid on shares classified as employment-related securities arises under *ITEPA 2003, s 447*, as the dividends paid on those shares are a benefit received in connection with those shares. However, the provisions in *ITEPA 2003, s 447* only apply where something has been done that affects the shares as part of a scheme or arrangement, the main purpose of which (or one of the main purposes) is the avoidance of tax or national insurance (*ITEPA 2003, s 447(4)*). If this is proven, the market value of the benefit from the share (the net dividend received) becomes chargeable as employment income instead of as dividend income (see *PA Holdings Ltd v HMRC* [2008] SSCD 1185).

As employment income, the amount of the 'dividend' must be subject to NIC and taxed under PAYE at the individual's marginal rate rather than at the rate that applies to dividends: 7.5%, 32.5% or 38.1% (for 2017/18).

1.136 The burden of proof would be on the taxpayer to demonstrate that whatever was done to the share (such as issuing the share or an alteration of terms), these actions were not intended to avoid tax and NICs. It is thought that paying a dividend on a share is not something that is '... done which affects the employment-related securities as part of a scheme or arrangement the main purpose (or one of the main purposes) of which is the avoidance of tax or national insurance contributions' (*ITEPA 2003, s 447(4)*). The ability of the provisions in *ITEPA 2003, s 447* to apply to dividends issued by owner-managed companies has not yet been tested in the courts. However, it is possible that a decision to pay dividends in the place of salary in a small company could be caught as a scheme or arrangement to avoid tax or NIC.

Disadvantages of dividends

Pension contributions

1.137 Dividends do not count as earnings for pension contribution purposes. The maximum pension contribution an individual may make per tax year and receive tax relief for is £3,600 (gross) or 100% of their UK earnings, if higher (see **Chapter 11**), although the employer may make higher contributions.

1.138 A tax-efficient strategy for most owner-managed companies is to have the company pay the pension contribution as the employer. The employer's and employee's contributions into the pension scheme should not exceed the employee's annual allowance for the year (nominally £40,000 for 2016/17), or an annual allowance charge at the taxpayer's marginal rate will be due. The employer's pension contributions do not have to be linked to the employee's salary, and should qualify in full for a corporation tax deduction if the company can show the total remuneration package was made wholly and exclusively for the business. For further discussion of this point see **Chapter 11**.

Flexibility

1.139 Where the directors and shareholders are different individuals it is difficult to use dividends to replace salaries to reward the directors separately from the non-working shareholders. Dividend waivers are commonly used to remedy this problem, although great care should be taken where these involve the shareholder's spouse, civil partner or minor children to avoid the possibility of the settlements legislation applying to the arrangement (see **1.120**). It is essential that any dividend waiver is made before the dividend is paid.

Different classes of shares (known as alphabet shares) may be issued to working and non-working shareholders, although this strategy can create problems, as the shares issued to the employees are likely to be employment-related securities (see **1.132**).

> **Focus**
>
> The use of alphabet shares to pay differential dividends to selected directors or employees or the blatant use of dividend waivers by controlling shareholders to divert what could effectively be seen as bonuses to colleagues working in the business, could be attacked by HMRC using the ruling in *PA Holdings Ltd v HMRC* [2008] SSCD 1185. In each case, the payments made as dividends would be charged to income tax and NIC as remuneration.

Administration

1.140 When paying a dividend certain administrative formalities have to be observed; dividend certificates, directors' minutes and resolutions should be prepared. If dividends have not been properly declared in accordance with company law formalities, HMRC may challenge the payment and seek to treat the dividend as remuneration subject to Class 1 NICs, and require PAYE to be applied.

Retention of profits

1.141 Normally some profits will be retained within the business for future investment or to use as working capital. A company will generally have paid less tax on such retained profits (at 19%) than a sole trader or partnership where the marginal tax rates will be 29% (including NI) on profits per person up to £45,000 (£43,000 for Scottish residents), and 42%, 47% or 62% (including NI) beyond that threshold.

1.142 The proprietor needs to predict how long the business may remain in his hands and weigh up the difficulties of extracting capital value from the business in the long term. There is a potential double capital gains tax charge where appreciating assets are held within the company, and a potential double charge on retained earnings, both of which will crystallise when the company is liquidated (see **1.145**). If the company is sold rather than liquidated, this will not actually crystallise the double capital gains tax charge. However, the share price may reflect the gains held in the company and a charge on retained earnings will in effect arise at that time.

Long-term intentions

Continuing the business

1.143 The relative importance of the long-term disadvantage of the double charge on capital gains will depend upon the timescale that the proprietor has in mind for retaining the business. If he plans to run the company for many years, the cash-flow advantage from the lower tax rates on profits may outweigh the capital tax disadvantage at the time of liquidation or sale. Alternatively, there may in fact be no liquidation or sale because the business will be passed down to the next generation and continued within the family.

The decision in each case will depend very much on the precise circumstances of the business and the objectives of the proprietor. He will need to take a long view of the trends for both corporation tax and income tax rates, and weigh up the pros and cons of each course of action with considerable care.

Dissolving the company

1.144 Having once incorporated a business, it is not so easy to dissolve the company without incurring tax charges. Incorporation reliefs can apply to shelter gains when assets are transferred into a corporate body in return for shares, and disincorporation relief can protect the company from gains realised on the transfer of goodwill or property from a small company to the shareholders on its dissolution (see **Chapter 2**). However, the shareholders are not protected from the income tax or CGT charges that arise on the distribution of the company's assets.

Double tax charge

1.145 The received wisdom for capital gains tax planning has been to keep valuable assets used for the business outside the company if possible, to avoid the double tax charge when the company sells the asset and the shareholder extracts the proceeds. The potential double charge springs from:

- the charge to corporation tax in respect of a capital gain realised on disposal of the asset by the company; and
- the further charge to capital gains tax arising in the event of the shareholder wishing to liquidate the company and extract the net proceeds of the disposal of the asset; or

- a further charge to income tax when the shareholder extracts the proceeds of the sale from the company as a dividend.

The individual only obtains the benefit of the gain on the disposal of the asset by the company by suffering, at least to some extent, a duplicate tax charge.

Where the company pays corporation tax at 19% and the individual takes the net proceeds of the sale as a dividend, the total tax paid will be greater than the CGT rates of 10% and 20% that the individual would pay on the disposal of the asset (which is not a residential property) held outside the company, as shown in **Example 1.7**.

Example 1.7 – Gains made by company then distributed to shareholders

Assume the individuals have already received dividends of £5,000 each in that tax year. The gain is calculated per person.

Company	£
Chargeable gain	10,000
Less corporation tax at 19%	(1,900)
Available for distribution	8,100

Distributed to taxpayers paying tax at:	*Basic rate*	*Higher rate*	*Additional rate*
	£	£	£
Gross dividend	8,100.00	8,100.00	8,100.00
Tax due at 7.5% / 32.5% / 38.1%	607.50	2,632.50	3,086.10
Corporation tax paid on the gain	1,900.00	1,900.00	1,900.00
Total tax paid on gain	2,507.50	4,532.50	4986.10
Effective tax rate on gain	25.075%	45.325%	49.861%

Reliefs available for different structures

1.146 Comparing the corporate and personal tax rates as in **Example 1.7** does not tell the full story, as in practice the maximum tax rate is likely to be reduced by the various tax reliefs available to both the individual and the company, as summarised in **Table 1.4** below.

Table 1.4

Tax relief	*Unincorporated businesses*	*Companies*
Indexation allowance	Not available	Reduces effect of inflation on asset values held since the later of acquisition or 31 March 1982
Annual exemption	£11,300 for 2017/18	Not available
Entrepreneurs' relief on disposals (see **Chapter 8**)	CGT at 10% for gains on certain assets subject to a lifetime cap of £10m.	Not available
Substantial shareholding exemption (see **Chapter 6**)	Not available	Exempts gain or loss on shares if at least 10% stake is held for one year within two years of sale
Roll-over of gains on replacement of business assets in the following categories:	Land and buildings Fixed plant and machinery Ships, aircraft and hovercraft Satellites and space stations Goodwill Ewe and suckler cow premium quotas Basic payment rights for farmers Fish quota Lloyd's syndicate rights	Land and buildings Fixed plant and machinery Ships, aircraft and hovercraft Satellites and space stations Lloyd's syndicate rights
Roll-over relief on replacement intangible business assets	Included in the above categories of assets	For intangible assets acquired on and after 1 April 2002
Hold-over relief	Gifts of business assets and gifts of assets on which IHT is chargeable	Not available

EIS and SEIS to raise capital	Not available to raise business capital	Restricted to SMEs where investor is not connected to company
Transactions within a marriage/group (see **Chapters 16 and 6**)	Transfers between a married couple or civil partners who are living together are treated as no gain/no loss	Transfers within a group of companies where there is a 75% relationship are generally treated as no gain/no loss
R&D tax credits (see **Chapter 17**)	Not available	Enhanced deduction for revenue costs incurred in R&D projects. Losses made by small companies may be converted into tax credits
First-year tax credits	Not available	Surrender loss for payable tax credit where enhanced capital allowances claimed for the same period
Land remediation relief	Not available	Enhanced deduction for the cost of removing pollution from land or buildings
Patent Box regime (see **Chapter 18**)	Not available	Reduced rate of tax on profits derived from patented inventions or patent rights
Film, TV or video games tax relief	Not available	Cash rebates of 20% or 25% of film production expenditure
Cash basis accounting	Optional for most businesses where turnover is less than the VAT-registration threshold for the year	Not available
Interest relief for residential property lettings	Restricted from 2017/18, removed from 2020/21	No restriction

1.147 Where real capital gains are likely to arise, the potential double tax charge must be considered when incorporating a business that holds appreciating assets which are used for the trade. In such cases it may be sensible to leave the asset in the private hands of the proprietor and rent or lease the asset to the company. On the subsequent sale of the asset the individual will pay CGT on the gain at 10% or 20%, or at 18% or 28% if the asset is a residential property.

For further discussion of the current tax issues concerned with the sale of an owner-managed company, see **Chapter 8**.

Chapter 2

Incorporation and disincorporation

Mark McLaughlin CTA (Fellow), ATT (Fellow), TEP, Tax Consultant, Mark McLaughlin Associates Ltd
Jackie Anderson LLB, ACA, CTA, LHA Consulting Ltd

SIGNPOSTS

- **Scope** – The choice of trading medium is an important commercial decision, which should not generally be tax driven. However, a company can be a tax-efficient vehicle in which to shelter retained business profits at lower rates than personal tax rates for sole traders and individual partners in appropriate circumstances. Unfortunately, a number of tax measures have been devised to reduce the tax-efficiency of what has been termed 'tax motivated incorporations', but which potentially affect incorporations irrespective of their motive. A number of non-tax issues must be addressed when incorporating a business. Consideration should also be given to the implications if it is later decided to disincorporate the business (see **2.1–2.4**).
- **Income tax and NIC** – Incorporation gives rise to a number of income tax and national insurance contributions (NIC) issues, including cessation and overlap relief, the timing of tax payments, the treatment of stock and work in progress, capital allowances, income tax and NIC rates and planning, etc (see **2.5–2.32**).
- **Capital gains tax** – Incorporation often involves the disposal of chargeable assets to the company, such as business premises and goodwill. The sale of a business as a going concern may be subject to a claim for entrepreneurs' relief if the relevant conditions are satisfied. The scope for claiming entrepreneurs' relief on goodwill upon incorporation was restricted following legislation introduced in *Finance Act 2015*, subject to certain exceptions (following changes introduced in *Finance Act 2016*). Other forms of capital gains tax relief may be available on a disposal of assets to the company (see **2.33–2.57**).
- **Goodwill** – Care should be taken in identifying and valuing goodwill. For example, personal goodwill cannot be transferred, and valuation

difficulties can arise for certain businesses in respect of 'trade related property'. Overvaluations of goodwill can result in inadvertent tax charges (**2.58–2.70**).

- **Other tax issues** – Various tax considerations resulting from incorporation can include whether the company may claim a deduction in respect of intangible fixed assets (although the ability to do so was adversely affected following changes introduced in *Finance Act 2015* and subsequently), stamp taxes, inheritance tax, VAT and employment-related securities (see **2.71–2.102**).
- **Disincorporation** – While a company may have been chosen as the optimum operating vehicle for a business, there will be circumstances in which some businesses might benefit from 'disincorporating' and operating through a sole trader or partnership structure instead. Disincorporation can be implemented through a distribution or sale of the business to the shareholders (see **2.103–2.106**).
- **Key tax consequences of disincorporation** – These can include:
  - (a) For the shareholder – the legislation (which replaced ESC C16) only permits distributions made under an informal winding-up to be treated as capital as long as these do not exceed £25,000 (see **2.107** and **2.118**).
  - (b) For the company – the potential tax charges and events which arise on a disincorporation are similar to those which would occur on any sale of a company's business and assets to a 'third party' (see **2.108–2.117**).
- **Disincorporation relief** – A limited form of relief (introduced by *Finance Act 2013*) is available, so that small business owners may be able to avoid a double charge to tax upon disincorporation (see **2.121**). However, as there is likely to be a tax charge on the shareholder, the relief may not be attractive to some business owners.

INCORPORATION

Introduction

2.1 The choice of the most tax-efficient trading medium (ie sole trader, partnership or limited company) is a complicated subject, involving many different factors. With a top rate of income tax of 45% (for 2017/18), the incorporation of sole trader and partnership businesses is an important tax planning consideration. Incorporation might seem attractive to some business owners, particularly in view of a single corporation tax rate of 19% (for the financial year to 31 March 2018) for companies that do not have ring fence profits. Furthermore, the corporation tax rate was set at 19% for financial years beginning 1 April 2018 and 1 April 2019 in *Finance (No 2) Act 2015*. The corporation tax rate for the financial year beginning 1 April 2020 was reduced to 17% in *Finance Act 2016*.

A company may therefore be seen as a useful vehicle in terms of sheltering retained profits at lower tax rates than the personal tax rates applicable to many sole traders and business partners. However, the future extraction of profits as dividends was adversely affected in many cases by the reform of the dividend tax system in *Finance Act 2016* (see **2.32**).

A separate chapter of this book has been dedicated to choosing an appropriate trading vehicle when a new business commences (see **Chapter 1**).

2.2 This chapter covers tax issues in connection with the process of incorporation. The subject has been a popular one for many years. Historically, the 'heyday' for business incorporations probably followed *Finance Act 2002*, with the introduction of a 0% starting rate of corporation tax. Much has changed since then, including the withdrawal of the starting rate and fluctuating corporation tax rates generally. In some cases, it may be attractive for owner-managers to disincorporate an existing company's business, and to operate as a sole trader or partnership instead.

However, disincorporation has its own set of tax problems associated with it. Prior to legislation introduced in *Finance Act 2013,* there was no statutory relief when a business disincorporated and reverted back to the medium of a sole trader or partnership. However, a measure of relief is temporarily available by allowing qualifying business assets to be transferred from the company to one or more of its shareholders with no immediate tax charge (see **2.121**).

The tax issues surrounding disincorporation are later considered in a separate section of this chapter.

2.3

Focus

Whilst this chapter does not deal with non-tax issues arising from incorporation, it should be borne in mind that there are a number of legal and commercial issues. Those issues broadly include:

- company formation (eg appointment of directors, allotment of shares etc);
- shareholders' agreement (if there is one);

- company law obligations, such as statutory forms and accounts filing at Companies House;
- formalities of transferring the unincorporated business (eg documenting the transfer, accounting for the incorporation, notifications to HMRC, the transfer of employees between businesses, etc);
- professional fees (ie in connection with the incorporation process, and the costs of preparing company accounts, which are often higher than for unincorporated businesses);
- other practicalities (eg company accounts and their filing in XBRL format to HMRC, financing, notifying customers, suppliers, insurance companies, employees, amending trade and telephone directories, etc).

2.4 In some cases, it will also be necessary to address any potential implications of incorporation in terms of the business owner's entitlement to state benefits. For example, the impact of being a company director and shareholder may need to be considered in the context of tax credits and universal credit, including the level of remuneration from the company and (for universal credit purposes) the level of company profits.

A subject as wide as incorporation (and disincorporation) cannot be covered in detail in a single chapter. Readers are directed to the latest edition of *Incorporating and Disincorporating a Business* (Bloomsbury Professional) for more comprehensive coverage.

Income tax

2.5 There are specific provisions aimed at simplifying the calculation of income tax for small unincorporated business.

First, eligible small businesses can elect for a 'cash basis' to apply for the purposes of accounting for trading profits, instead of using generally accepted accounting practice. The *Finance Bill 2017* published on 20 March 2017 also provided for a mandatory cash basis in respect of property businesses with receipts for the tax year not exceeding £150,000, subject to an optional election facility for the cash basis not to apply. Those provisions were not subsequently included in *Finance Act 2017*, but were published in *Finance (No 2) Bill 2017* (which has not received Royal Assent at the time of writing).

Secondly, unincorporated businesses (ie self-employed individuals, or partnerships of individuals) can deduct certain expenses (ie motor expenses, use of home for business, and premises used for both home and business purposes) on a flat rate basis, if they choose.

However, companies are excluded from applying these 'simplification' measures. This presents a potential disadvantage in terms of incorporating a business, or at least an additional consideration.

The incorporation of a business involves the cessation of a former sole trade or partnership. It must be remembered that the company is a totally separate entity, chargeable to corporation tax and not income tax. It is therefore necessary to apply appropriate cessation adjustments to the unincorporated business. The cessation will, of itself, cause certain adjustments to the tax computation, especially as regards stock and capital allowances (see **2.13**, **2.17**).

Cessation computation

2.6 The general position under the current year basis (CYB) is that the income tax assessment for a given year is based on the profits of the accounting period ended in that year. Adjustments may be needed in the opening years to get to this position. Compensating adjustments may also be necessary when a business ceases.

There is no gap between the basis periods at cessation. The profits forming the basis of the assessment for the final tax year will be those earned in the period beginning immediately after the end of the basis period for the preceding year and ending on the date of cessation (*ITTOIA 2005, s 202*).

Depending on the accounting date and date of cessation, this could be a period of more or less than 12 months.

2.7 Unless the incorporation takes place on the usual accounting date, the accounts to cessation of the sole trade (or partnership) will be for a period other than 12 months. Use of a different date for the final accounting period will not normally trigger the change of basis period rules.

The cessation rules of *ITTOIA 2005, s 202* automatically take priority over the rules governing a change of accounting date (*ITTOIA 2005, ss 214–220*) for the year of cessation.

Overlap relief

2.8 Where 5 April has been used as the annual accounting date of a business, the total profits assessed will automatically equal the total profits earned. There will be no overlap between any income tax basis periods.

Accounts drawn up to 31 March (or 1, 2, 3 or 4 April) may be treated as coterminous with the tax year end (*ITTOIA 2005, s 209*).

Drawing up accounts to 5 April (or 31 March) has the advantage of simplicity. The profit earned during a tax year suffers income tax in that same year. No basis period adjustments are necessary. For that reason alone, many small sole traders and partnerships will choose this accounting date.

2.9 In using an accounting date other than one coterminous with the tax year end, there will be one or more years in which the basis periods for two adjacent tax years overlap. The logic to creation and use of overlap relief is that the profits earned throughout the life of a business are all subject to tax once, and once only. An adjustment may be made on a change of accounting date during the life of the business. Any remaining overlap relief can be useful in the tax year in which the business ceases.

Overlap relief is given as if it were an additional trading deduction incurred in that period (*ITTOIA 2005, s 205(1)*). In most instances, the use of overlap relief simply reduces the assessable profit in the final year. However, depending on the relative size of the profit and the overlap relief, a loss may be created. Equally, if a loss already arose in the period of cessation, the overlap relief will augment that loss.

A loss created or enhanced by overlap relief is generally treated in the same manner as any other trading loss; the usual loss relief claims may be made. The ability of sole traders and partners to obtain 'sideways loss relief' for trading losses against general income is subject to a limit (in *ITA 2007, s 24A*) on the amount of tax relief that can be deducted in their income tax calculation for the tax year (ie the greater of £50,000 and 25% of the individual's adjusted total income for the tax year). However, trading losses attributable to overlap relief may be deducted without restriction (*ITA 2007, s 24A(7)(c)*).

2.10

> **Focus**
>
> In any case other than a 31 March accounting date, there is no substitute for looking at the realised profits, projected future profits, amount of overlap relief and dates in each case. A wrong decision can result in a substantial income tax liability on cessation or, at least, a cash-flow disadvantage. The proprietor is not going to welcome that as a penalty for incorporation.
>
> There is also the issue of adjustments which vary the profits. Particular issues here include stock valuation and capital allowances (see below).

Payment of tax

2.11 Very few sole traders (and partnerships) seem to make any provision for tax in their business accounts. For the most part, tax liabilities falling due now are paid out of profits earned now.

Example 2.1 – Timing of tax payments

Chris drew up accounts to 30 June each year. Ignoring incorporation, the tax due for 2017/18 (ie based on the accounts for the year ended 30 June 2017) would be payable by two payments on account on 31 January 2018 and 31 July 2018, with a balancing payment on 31 January 2019.

He will quite probably meet the 31 January 2019 bill out of incoming funds at the end of 2018, despite the fact that he began earning the relevant profits as long ago as 1 July 2016.

2.12 The proprietor needs to be warned in advance of the change in timing of tax payments which is occasioned by incorporation:

- Chris's sole-trader self-assessment for 2017/18 was based on profits earned in the period 1 July 2016 to 30 June 2017. Tax is payable in instalments falling due between 31 January 2018 and 31 January 2019. Payment of the tax therefore falls much later than the inflow of the corresponding funds.
- If the incorporated business draws up accounts to 30 June 2018, tax is payable on 1 April 2019, a delay of only nine months.
- If Chris draws a taxable salary from the company, income tax and NIC is normally payable only 17 days after the tax month of payment if paid electronically (or 14 days in any other case (*SI 2003/2682, reg 69(1)*)).

The cash-flow considerations of funding the income tax (and NIC) liabilities of the unincorporated business up to the date of cessation should not be overlooked or underestimated. Forward planning (eg projecting tax liabilities and payment dates) based on the anticipated date of incorporation should be implemented as far as possible in advance.

However, it is proposed that 'making tax digital', when introduced, will provide unincorporated business owners with the opportunity to make regular payments towards their tax liabilities. This should help to mitigate cashflow difficulties resulting from incorporation in many cases.

Treatment of stock and work in progress

Stock

2.13 The basic position regarding the transfer of stock upon incorporation is that it is deemed to pass between connected persons at an arm's-length price (*ITTOIA 2005, s 177*).

The meaning of 'connected persons' is defined in *ITTOIA 2005, s 179*, and is rather wider than the usual definitions (in *CTA 2010, ss 1122–1123* or *ITA 2007, ss 993–994*). In particular, two persons are connected if one is a company and the other has control over it.

In most cases, the effect of the deeming provision in *ITTOIA 2005, s 177* is that the incorporation will result in additional taxable profits (ie if the arm's length value of stock exceeds its original cost) and a corresponding increase in the sole trader's or partner's income tax and Class 4 NIC liability.

2.14 However, the transferor and transferee (ie sole trader or partners and new company) may jointly elect that the stock is instead to be treated as transferred at the higher of cost or the amount actually paid (see *ITTOIA 2005, s 178*).

As the sale price or market value should be taken into account to determine the final profit of the unincorporated business, but is also deductible in arriving at the profits of the company, there is scope for planning. If the unincorporated business owner pays tax at (say) 40% but the company at only 19%, the stock should be transferred at a low value to reduce the income tax profits at the expense of corporate tax profits increasing but taxed at a lower rate. The choice of transfer value for these purposes is not infinitely variable though, as it must be lower than an arm's-length value (*ITTOIA 2005, s 178(2)*).

A flowchart illustrating the valuation of stock on cessation is included in HMRC's Business Income Manual at BIM33475. In addition, the practical application of the election is illustrated at BIM33480.

Where an election is appropriate, it must be made by the first anniversary of the normal self-assessment return filing date for the tax year of cessation (*ITTOIA 2005, s 178(4)*). However, it will often be practical to submit the election with the tax return covering the cessation period of the unincorporated business.

Note that such an election is only permissible where stock is sold or transferred for valuable consideration. It appears that if the stock is gifted to the company (which is not an impossible position in certain types of incorporation) then market value must prevail with no option available.

If a person who has made an election for the cash basis ceases carrying on a trade in that tax year, the value of any trading stock at the time of cessation is brought into account as a receipt on a basis that is just and reasonable in all the circumstances, for example, cost or net realisable value *(ITTOIA 2005, s 97A)*. In the case of a person carrying on a profession or vocation, the value of any work in progress at the time of cessation is brought into account in the same way as trading stock for a trader (*ITTOIA 2005, s 97B*).

Work in progress

2.15 For the vast majority of businesses, everything so far mentioned about stock applies equally to work in progress. There are, though, distinct rules concerning the valuation of work in progress on discontinuance of a profession or vocation. These are to be found in *ITTOIA 2005, ss 182–185*.

The basic position is that where there is valuable consideration (eg on a business transfer in exchange for shares) the work in progress is taken to have that value (*ITTOIA 2005, s 184(1)*). On a gift, market value must prevail (*ITTOIA 2005, s 184(2)*).

HMRC are normally prepared to accept whatever value is attributed to work in progress, unless it is blatantly unreasonable. They will not seek to make any adjustment so long as the value attributed to work in progress follows the basis consistently used for accounting purposes.

HMRC guidance in their Business Income Manual on valuing professional work in progress states that the proper valuation depends on the correct application of generally accepted accounting practice to the facts. The guidance points out that uncompleted contracts for services should be valued in accordance with section 23 of FRS 102, and adds (at BIM33020):

> 'In most cases revenue for service contracts should be accounted for under what is known as the "percentage of completion" method. In very simple terms, this means that if a contract is in progress at the year end, then the supplier of services would include the proportion undertaken to that date in its accounts. So if the contract is 50% complete, 50% of the contract value will be recorded in the accounts as revenue.'

In the case of construction contracts, HMRC guidance (at BIM33025) states that where the outcome of the contract can be estimated reliably, contract revenue and contract costs should be recognised as income and expenses by reference to the stage of completion of the contract at the end of the reporting period.

2.16 There is a further provision relating to the cessation of a profession or vocation in that the taxpayer may elect for the closing work in progress on cessation to be taken as having its cost value (*ITTOIA 2005, s 185*).

Any amounts received on the transfer of work in progress which exceed the actual cost of the work is then treated as a post-cessation receipt (under *ITTOIA 2005, s 243*). As a general rule, on the cessation of trading a sum received for the transfer of work-in-progress (or trading stock) is not a post-cessation receipt if a valuation has been brought into account under *ITTOIA 2005, Pt 2, Ch 12* (valuation of stock and work in progress). However, this does not prevent a post-cessation receipt arising as the result of the above election under *ITTOIA 2005, s 185* (see *ITTOIA 2005, s 252(2)*).

The deadline for making the election is the first anniversary of the filing date for the self-assessment return in respect of the tax year of cessation (*ITTOIA 2005, 185(2)*).

Capital allowances

Plant and machinery

2.17 Writing down allowances (WDA), annual investment allowances (AIA) and first-year allowances (FYA) are not available in the final chargeable period (nb since the introduction of the AIA (from 6 April 2008) the types of expenditure attracting FYA have been limited; see **2.22**).

Thus if a business incurs qualifying expenditure and incorporates very shortly afterwards, the opportunity to claim AIA and FYA may be lost (see, for example, *Keyl v Revenue & Customs* [2015] UKUT 383 (TCC)). The timing of incorporation may therefore be an important consideration.

The final chargeable period is (for the main pool or a 'special rate' pool) the chargeable period in which the qualifying activity is permanently discontinued (*CAA 2001, s 65(1)*). WDA in the final chargeable period is prohibited by *CAA 2001, s 55(4)*, AIA is prohibited by *CAA 2001, s 38B*, General Exclusion 1, and FYA is prohibited by *CAA 2001, s 46(2)*, General Exclusion 1.

2.18 In virtually every case, the new company will be connected with the proprietors of the unincorporated business. In most cases, the company's shareholders and directors will be identical to the sole trader or business partners. Connection follows under *CAA 2001, s 575*.

The disposal value of plant and machinery is to be interpreted in accordance with the table in *CAA 2001, s 61* ('Disposal events and disposal values'). Incorporation will involve either a sale of the plant and machinery, or a transfer for nil proceeds.

If the plant and machinery is sold, the disposal value for capital allowances purposes will generally be the net proceeds of sale (*CAA 2001, s 61(2), Table item 1*). If there are no proceeds at all, so there is a pure gift, then market value prevails (*CAA 2001, s 61(2), Table Item 7*).

This bears careful consideration because there may be important planning advantages. The result is that there will be a balancing allowance or balancing charge. A balancing allowance occurs when the disposal value is less than the written-down value of the pool (*CAA 2001, s 55(2)*) and is given as a deduction in the income tax computation in a similar fashion to a WDA, AIA or FYA. A balancing charge occurs when the disposal value is more than the written-down value of the pool (*CAA 2001, s 55(3)*) and is treated as an addition to profit.

There are anti-avoidance provisions for capital allowances purposes (*CAA 2001, Pt 2, Ch 17*), which apply to 'relevant transactions' such as the sale of plant and machinery (*CAA 2001, s 213*), including transactions between connected persons (*CAA 2001, s 214*). The effect is that no AIA or FYA is generally available for the buyer's expenditure (*CAA 2001, s 217*), and the buyer's qualifying expenditure is potentially restricted (*CAA 2001, s 218*).

In addition, the buyer's capital allowances are subject to adjustment (or other tax advantages such as in the timing of allowances may be cancelled out) where the transaction has an 'avoidance purpose' (as defined in *CAA 2001, s 215*), or relates to a scheme or arrangement with such a purpose. However, particularly in the latter case it is difficult to envisage an ordinary incorporation having a main purpose of obtaining a tax advantage in respect of plant and machinery, as capital allowances are not normally a primary consideration.

There is also a specific anti-avoidance rule to prevent the sale of a car allocated to a 'single asset pool' (ie within *CAA 2001, s 206*) at undervalue in order to generate a balancing allowance (*CAA 2001, s 208A*).

2.19 The parties do not necessarily have to suffer the balancing allowance or charge. Instead the transferor and transferee (the previous sole trader and the company) may make a joint election under *CAA 2001, s 266* that the plant and machinery are transferred at a price which gives rise to neither a balancing allowance nor a balancing charge. So what does that really mean? There is nothing in *CAA 2001, s 267* to override the rules in *CAA 2001, ss 46, 38B* and *55* that prohibit a WDA, AIA or FYA in the final chargeable period. The trade of the former sole trader *is* discontinued at the point of incorporation. So, the plant and machinery is actually transferred at the tax written-down value at the *start* of the final period of account of the sole trade.

The above election generally fixes the value of plant and machinery at its tax written-down value, notwithstanding that the plant and machinery may be sold to the company, and for a different value (eg original cost). HMRC guidance confirms: 'When an election is made any sale or transfer price is ignored' (CA29040). An election may be made within two years from the date of incorporation (*CAA 2001, s 266(4)*). However, there is a special provision preventing the election in successions involving businesses of leasing plant or machinery (see *CAA 2001, s 267A*).

If an election is made under *CAA 2001, s 266* and any of the assets are fixtures (eg on a sale of the business premises), a joint election is also required under *CAA 2001, s 198* ('Election to apportion sale price on sale of qualifying interest') in order that the company is able to claim capital allowances on the fixtures. This is due to the 'fixed value requirement' (see *CAA 2001, ss 187A–187B*), which was introduced (in *Finance Act 2012*) from April 2012.

An election under *CAA 2001, s 266* prevents a balancing adjustment in respect of the unincorporated business, whereas a *CAA 2001, s 198* election allows the company to claim capital allowances on any fixtures that are transferred. In many cases, an election under *CAA 2001, s 266* will include both fixtures and other plant and machinery; hence the amount specified in the *CAA 2001, s 198* election should not exceed the amount in the *CAA 2001, s 266* election.

In some cases, consideration should be given to not making a *CAA 2001, s 266* election, and entering into a joint election under *CAA 2001, s 198* for a low value, as this may generate a balancing allowance.

A 'pooling' requirement also applies in relation to fixtures (from April 2014), whereby the availability of capital allowances to a purchaser of fixtures is generally conditional on the pooling of relevant expenditure prior to transfer.

For guidance in this potentially difficult area, readers are referred to the latest edition of *Capital Allowances: Transactions and Planning* by Martin Wilson and Steven Bone (Bloomsbury Professional).

An election for transfers between connected persons is also available in respect of 'short life assets' (SLAs), if made within two years following the chargeable period of disposal (*CAA 2001, s 89*). The transfer of SLAs between connected persons otherwise takes place at market value (unless there is a tax charge under *ITEPA 2003*) (*CAA 2001, s 88*). The effect of a connected person election is broadly to treat the disposal as taking place at the capital allowances pool value, so that the original SLA election continues with the purchaser. If no such connected person election is made, the purchaser is still treated as having made the original SLA election with its original terminal date (see *CAA 2001, s 89(4)*), but a balancing allowance or charge will normally arise on the disposal.

This election has assumed greater significance since the period over which qualifying expenditure can be given short life asset treatment was increased (in *Finance Act 2011*) from four years to eight years.

2.20

Focus

The absence of any capital allowances at all in the final period of account means that great care should be taken in selecting the date on which to incorporate.

A tidy-minded adviser may favour incorporation at the traditional accounting date and make a *CAA 2001, s 266* election 'because it's easier'. This may result in the trader getting no capital allowances in the last period when, perhaps, there are substantial profits taxed at 40%, or possibly 45% (for 2017/18). The pay-off, of course, is that the company gets a higher writing down allowance in its first period of trade, but as companies generally pay corporation tax at 19% (for financial year 2017, commencing 1 April 2017) is this good planning, especially if the client bought a large piece of equipment just before incorporation in anticipation of capital allowances to mitigate tax on the profits?

Pre-incorporation planning must encompass the effect on capital allowances.

Remember that capital allowances are given for a period of account (not a year of assessment). Where accounts have traditionally been drawn up to 31 March, incorporation on that date will mean the loss of AIA, FYA or WDA for a full accounting period. What about incorporating at 30 April instead? The final period of account in which no capital allowances can be given is therefore only one month – a far more acceptable proposition.

How short might the final period actually be? In theory, perhaps as little as a day (though this might be unduly provocative to HMRC); a month is probably realistic.

2.21 The above analysis (subject to the point about a sale and election in respect of plant and machinery at **2.19** above) applies to incorporation by the *TCGA 1992, s 162* route.

There is an alternative. This is to ignore the incorporation relief in that section and go for the alternative afforded by *TCGA 1992, s 165*. This relates to a gift of business assets, though payment of some proceeds is possible. The company could actually pay the sole trader for the plant and machinery. Where there are actual proceeds, they are taken as the disposal value under *CAA 2001, s 61(2)*, Table Item 1. Market value is not substituted even where the vendor and purchaser are connected.

The sale proceeds could be left outstanding on loan account with the company. The proprietor can then draw down on the loan account at a later date without further tax charge.

Capital allowances rates

2.22 Historically, the regime for plant and machinery allowances changed significantly from April 2008 (ie 1 April for businesses within the charge to corporation tax, or 6 April for businesses liable to income tax). Those changes resulted in a reduction in the main rate of WDA to 20% (from 25%). In addition, most FYAs disappeared (although 100% allowances continue to be available for qualifying 'green' expenditure).

Further significant capital allowances changes were introduced in *Finance Act 2011*, reducing the WDA rate to 18% (from 20%) for expenditure allocated to the main rate pool, and to 8% (from 10%) for expenditure allocated to the special rate pool. These reductions apply to chargeable periods from 1 April 2012 (corporation tax) and from 6 April 2012 (income tax).

Furthermore, the maximum amount of the AIA has fluctuated widely since its introduction. It was originally set at £50,000 from April 2008, but increased to £100,000 from April 2010. The maximum subsequently reduced from £100,000 to £25,000 from April 2012 (subject to transitional rules in respect of expenditure incurred during an accounting period that spans 1 April or 6 April 2012).

However, the maximum amount of AIA was later increased (in *Finance Act 2013*) from £25,000 to £250,000 for a temporary period of two years from 1 January 2013, for both incorporated and unincorporated businesses. The maximum amount of AIA was further increased (in *Finance Act 2014*) to £500,000 in relation to expenditure incurred from 1 or 6 April 2014 to 31 December 2015. Thereafter, the limit was set to fall back to £25,000. However, the maximum amount of AIA was subsequently set at £200,000 (following a change introduced in *Finance (No 2) Act 2015*) in relation to qualifying expenditure incurred from 1 January 2016 (*CAA 2001, s 51A(5)*).

The above increases to £250,000 and £500,000 are subject to transitional rules (in *Finance Act 2014, Sch 2*) broadly where the business has a chargeable period straddling 1 January 2013 or 1 (or 6) April 2014 (ie the operative date of the AIA increases) or 1 January 2015 or 1 January 2016 (ie after the period for the increases has elapsed). The transitional rules for straddling accounting periods are generally complex. Care should therefore be taken when calculating the maximum capital allowance during such accounting periods.

Examples of AIA calculations for straddling accounting periods are included on the GOV.UK website (www.gov.uk/annual-investment-allowance-limit-changes-during-accounting-periods).

The AIA of 100% applies to qualifying expenditure for businesses of any size, with WDAs being available on any excess expenditure over that limit.

The rate of allowances on fixtures integral to a building is only 8% and is expenditure subject to separate 'special rate' pooling, and the rate of WDA for long-life assets is also 8% (*CAA 2001, ss 104A, 104D*). If expenditure is eligible for allowances at differing rates, the AIA should be allocated to expenditure otherwise attracting the lowest rate of allowances where possible.

Perhaps unsurprisingly, AIA restrictions (in *CAA 2001, ss 51A–51N*) include 'anti-fragmentation' provisions to restrict the availability of AIA for one or more companies or businesses under common control if 'related' by reason of a 'shared premises' and/or a 'similar activities' condition being met. The effect is that a single AIA is shared between them. However, if business owners control a combination of an unincorporated business and a company, entitlement to AIA for each business remains unaffected, as AIA is considered separately for different business entities. This may be helpful if only a particular element of an unincorporated business is being incorporated (eg the audit or payroll functions of an accountancy practice).

The AIA is not available for expenditure incurred in the period in which the business is permanently discontinued (*CAA 2001, s 38B,* General Exclusion 1), or where an asset is acquired from a connected person (see **2.18**). 'Connected persons' is defined (in *CAA 2001, ss 575–575A*) in terms of control over the company. This may prevent AIA being available in many cases, such as immediately following the incorporation of a family business. The AIA is also unavailable for certain transactions if a main purpose is to enable a person to obtain AIA to which they would not otherwise be entitled (*CAA 2001, s 38B,* General Exclusion 4). However, in practice capital allowances are unlikely to be a major consideration in the decision to incorporate in most cases.

Industrial and agricultural buildings

2.23 Following changes introduced in *Finance Act 2008*, industrial buildings allowances (IBAs) were gradually phased out, and ceased to be available altogether from April 2011 onwards (ie from 1 April for corporation tax purposes, or 6 April for income tax purposes) (*Finance Act 2008, ss 84, 85*).

2.24 In addition, *Finance Act 2007* withdrew balancing adjustments and the recalculation of WDAs on the sale of an industrial building with effect from 21 March 2007, subject to certain transitional and anti-avoidance rules.

2.25 Enterprise Zone Allowances were also withdrawn from April 2011, but are not subject to the phasing out rules for IBAs (*Finance Act 2007, s 36(1)*), and balancing charges therefore remain possible for a limited period of time thereafter (ie under *CAA 2001, ss 314, 328*); see CA35050.

However, first-year allowances of 100% were introduced in *Finance Act 2012* in respect of enterprise zones, which apply to companies investing in plant or machinery primarily for use in designated assisted areas within them, where qualifying expenditure is incurred in a specified eight-year period (*CAA 2001, s 45K*).

2.26 The phasing out provisions mentioned above also apply in the context of agricultural buildings allowances.

National insurance contributions

2.27 The impact on National Insurance contributions (NICs) must be taken into account in any consideration of incorporation. In some ways, it may seem paradoxical that one should want to move from self-employment where the 'mainstream' rate (of Class 4 NICs) is 9% to employment where the mainstream rate (Class 1 primary and secondary) is 25.8% (for 2017/18), with employees paying 12% and employers paying 13.8%; this combined rate falls to 15.8% on earnings in excess of the upper earnings limit (£866 per week for 2017/18), with employees paying 2% and employers continuing to pay 13.8%.

Of course, self-employed earners over the age of 16 and under pensionable age are also liable to pay Class 2 contributions at a flat rate (*SSCBA 1992, s 11*), which (for 2017/18) is £2.85 per week. Class 2 NICs is to be abolished from April 2018 and Class 4 contributions are to be reformed from the same date to provide the mechanism by which the self-employed build up entitlement to the state pension and contributory benefits.

In an owner-managed company, where earnings fall between the Class 1 NIC 'Primary Threshold' and the 'Upper Earnings Limit' (UEL), as mentioned the total NIC payable by employers and employees is at a rate of 25.8%, a not inconsiderable sum. This is well in excess of the 9% NIC payable by a self-employed person.

It was announced in the Budget on 8 March 2017 that, as part of the reforms to National Insurance for the self-employed, the main rate of Class 4 NICs would increase from 9% to 10% in April 2018, and to 11% in April 2019, to reduce the gap in rates paid by the self-employed and employees, and to reflect the introduction of the new state pension to which the self-employed have the same access. However, the government subsequently announced that the planned increases in Class 4 NIC rates would not be proceeding. Nevertheless, it is possible that the self-employed will face increases in the future.

NIC rates in respect of both employees and the self-employed for 2017/18 are as follows:

- the main rate of Class 1 NICs for employees and employers is 12% and 13.8% respectively;
- the additional rate of Class 1 NICs for employees is 2%;
- the main rate of Class 4 NICs for the self-employed is 9%, and the additional Class 4 NIC rate is 2%.

However, the rate of employers' NIC is 0% (for 2017/18) for those under the age of 21, with the exception of those earning more than the upper secondary threshold for under 21-year-olds (that matches the UEL). Employers' NIC is liable as normal beyond this limit (*SSCBA 1992, s 9A*). Furthermore, zero-rate employers' NIC applies to apprentices under the age of 25 on earnings not in excess of the apprentice upper secondary threshold (*SSCBA 1992, s 9B*). The upper secondary threshold for under 21-year-olds and the apprentice upper secondary threshold are aligned with the upper earnings limit for primary Class 1 purposes of £866 per week (for 2017/18).

To avoid the above Class 1 NIC rates, one must be prepared to withdraw funds from the incorporated business other than by way of salary. The payment of dividends is often the preferred method of profit extraction where possible, although difficulties can arise in certain circumstances if dividend payments take the place of a commercial salary (see **2.103** below). Further, the reform of the dividend tax regime from 6 April 2016 generally reduced the tax advantage of extracting profits in the form of dividends, although dividends remain NIC-free.

Employment allowance

2.28 The employment allowance was introduced (in the *National Insurance Contributions Act 2014* (*NICA 2014*) from April 2014. Businesses and charities (including community amateur sports clubs) are generally entitled to an allowance of up to £3,000 (for 2017/18) against their employers' NIC liability. Whilst the allowance appears to be aimed at benefiting small businesses in particular, it broadly applies to most businesses, regardless of size, and irrespective of whether the business is incorporated or unincorporated.

However, regulations introduced from 6 April 2016 prevent certain companies from claiming the allowance (*Employment Allowance (Excluded Companies) Regulations 2016 (SI 2016/344)*). The legislation prevents companies where the sole employee is at the time that the earnings were paid also a director. HMRC's subsequent guidance states that affected companies are those where the director is the only employee paid earnings above the secondary threshold for Class 1 NIC purposes. HMRC's guidance can be found at: tinyurl.com/HMRC-EA-SDC. However, a company which has only one employee is also entitled to claim the allowance if at the time of the payment that employee is not a director. Personal companies where the sole employee is also the director may wish to consider resigning as a director and appointing another family member as the director.

Not all businesses can claim the employment allowance (*NICA 2014, s 2*). Excluded employers include those carrying functions wholly or mainly of a public nature (eg NHS or general practitioner services). In addition, personal and managed service companies can only claim the allowance in respect of actual (not deemed) payments of employment income. If companies or charities are connected, only one nominated PAYE scheme with employers' NIC liabilities can claim the allowance.

There is also a restriction from claiming the allowance on 'transfers of businesses', which would appear to affect the transfer of employees upon incorporation. In broad terms, if one business takes over another business during the tax year there will be no entitlement to any remaining balance of the employment allowance in respect of the employees who worked for the business taken over, or for employees who are carrying on the work of the business taken over.

An anti-avoidance rule also prevents an employer from qualifying for the allowance by reason of 'avoidance arrangements' (ie arrangements with a main purpose of which is to secure that a person benefits (or benefits further) from the application of the employment allowance provisions.

Detailed guidance on the employment allowance is available on the GOV.UK website (tinyurl.com/HMRC-EA-Guidance).

Maximum contributions

2.29 Unless the incorporation of the business takes place on 6 April, there will be a tax year in which the proprietor is both self-employed (as a sole trader or partner of the existing business) and an employed earner (as director/

employee of the new company). There may be a liability for Class 1, Class 2 and Class 4 contributions. Fortunately, there are rules to limit the amount of contributions payable where an individual has more than one employment or both employment and self-employment.

Where both Class 1 and Class 2 contributions are payable, the liability for primary Class 1 contributions and Class 2 contributions is not to exceed an amount equal to 53 primary Class 1 contributions payable on earnings at the UEL for the year (*Social Security (Contributions) Regulations 2001, SI 2001/1004, reg 21*). An annual maximum also applies for Class 4 contribution purposes (*SI 2001/1004, reg 100*).

However, the position is complicated because there is required to be made a further adjustment in respect of the additional rate of 2% (for 2017/18), which has no upper earnings limit.

2.30 The possibility of total contributions exceeding the relevant maxima may not be identified during the course of the tax year. Thus, contributions actually paid may be excessive. Overpaid contributions may be recovered from HMRC (see www.gov.uk/claim-national-insurance-refund).

Where the situation of overpayment is foreseen, it is possible to make application to defer payment of Class 1 contributions (although Class 4 contributions can no longer be deferred). In theory, such applications should be made before the beginning of the tax year to which they relate. This may make it an impractical option in the case of incorporation unless this occurs early in the tax year. If an application is successfully made and the contributions actually paid prove insufficient, the shortfall must be satisfied by direct payment to HMRC. For applications to defer Class 1 NICs, see tinyurl.com/HMRC-NIC-CA72A.

None of the foregoing has any effect on the new company as secondary contributor. There are no provisions to limit the secondary contributions in respect of an employed earner. This is also true for Class 1A (and Class 1B) contributions which are payable only by employers.

State pension

2.31 A working individual (whether self-employed or an employee) pays NIC during his working life and generates a contribution record which determines the state pension which is paid after retirement age.

Focus

Employee Class 1 contributions start at the primary threshold (PT). However, contributions are treated as paid for state pension purposes where earnings are equal to or exceed the LEL, albeit that no contributions are actually paid (*SSCBA 1992, s 6A(2)*). On earnings between the LEL and PT notional contributions are paid at a zero rate in order to establish a contribution record for state pension purposes, even though no contributions are actually due.

This has traditionally been a very useful planning tool in remunerating small company directors. Note that the company must still submit a full payment submission under the real time information (RTI) regime in order to record the earnings for this purpose, even if no income tax or NIC is actually payable.

The state pension regime changed following the introduction of legislation in the *Pensions Act 2014* (and secondary legislation in the *State Pension Regulations 2015 (SI 2015/173)*), for those individuals reaching state pension age from 6 April 2016 (NB: those who reached state pension age before that date remain subject to the previous pension rules).

Individuals reaching state pension age on or after 6 April 2016 receive a flat rate (or 'single-tier') state pension. Consequently, it is no longer possible to build up entitlement to the second state pension (S2P) in addition to the basic state pension. However, S2P will continue to be paid to those who reached state pension age before 6 April 2016 and who have built up entitlement to it. Consequently, the ability for members of a defined benefit occupational pension scheme to contract out of S2P ended on 5 April 2016.

Entitlement to the single-tier state pension is subject to the individual's NIC payment record, and requires at least 35 qualifying years of National Insurance contributions in order to receive a full single-tier state pension. Those with fewer than 35 qualifying years, but with at least ten qualifying years will receive a proportionately smaller state pension. By contrast, a person needed 30 qualifying years for a full basic state pension if they reached state pension age before 6 April 2016. As indicated above, directors and employees can qualify for the state pension without actually paying any Class 1 contributions. Qualifying years under the new state pension are generated in the same way as qualifying years for the basic state pension. A qualifying year is broadly a tax year during an individual's working life in which they paid (or were treated as having paid, or were credited with) National Insurance contributions on earnings of 52 times the LEL.

The scope and calculation of state pension entitlement is beyond the scope of this chapter. General guidance is available from the GOV.UK website (www.gov.uk/new-state-pension/eligibility). Specialist advice from a pension expert should be sought if required.

Income tax rates

2.32 The basic personal allowance for income tax purposes gradually reduces (by £1 for every £2 of income) for individuals with adjusted net incomes over £100,000 a year (*ITA 2007, s 35(2)–(4)*). Based on current personal allowances levels (£11,500 for 2017/18) this means that the allowances would be extinguished for those with incomes of £123,000 a year or more.

Furthermore, an additional, higher rate of income tax of 45% (for 2017/18) applies to taxable incomes above £150,000.

The above restriction in personal allowances and a higher income tax rate of 45% could make incorporation seem a more attractive proposition for self-employed individuals who are potentially subject to higher income tax liabilities, in terms of sheltering profits at a lower rate of corporation tax. This assumes that the business owner would not need to extract all the profits, and may be prepared to restrict personal income levels to £100,000 (or £150,000) per annum or less.

Following the reform of dividend taxation (in *Finance Act 2016*) from April 2016, the 10% dividend tax credit was removed (ie such that dividends are received gross) and replaced with a dividend nil rate of up to £5,000 per tax year. It was announced in the Budget on 8 March 2017 that this dividend 'allowance' would be reduced from £5,000 to £2,000 for 2018/19 and subsequent tax years. That reduction was not enacted in *Finance Act 2017*, but was included in *Finance (No 2) Bill 2017* published on 8 September 2017 (which has not received Royal Assent at the time of writing).

Furthermore, dividend tax rates (for 2017/18) are 7.5% for basic rate taxpayers, 32.5% for higher rate taxpayers and 38.1% for additional rate taxpayers.

It should be noted that dividends within the £5,000 'nil rate' still count towards an individual shareholder's basic or higher rate bands, and therefore affect the rate of tax paid on dividends received in excess of the allowance.

Those individuals who receive dividend income of £5,000 or less following incorporation, and/or who extract income from the company at relatively low levels (eg preferring to retain profits within the company, perhaps with a view to a company purchase of own shares on retirement (see **Chapter 4**) or a later sale or winding up of the company) will perhaps not be unduly concerned about the dividend tax regime.

Conversely, business owners who receive all or most of their income from dividends at substantial levels will need to consider their remuneration strategy carefully, particularly in relation to the traditional 'salary v dividend' comparison.

Planning in this area may therefore include considering the transfer of shares to a spouse (or civil partner) to make use of an extra £5,000 dividend nil rate, and to take advantage of the spouse's personal allowances and basic rate tax band, if appropriate. However, care must be taken in view of the settlements anti-avoidance provisions (in *ITTOIA 2005, Pt 5, Ch 5*).

For detailed commentary on extracting funds from the company and remuneration strategies, see *Tax Planning for Family and Owner-Managed Companies 2017/18* (Bloomsbury Professional).

In terms of the decision whether to incorporate, despite the government's desire to remove the tax advantages arising from incorporating the business, tax savings are still achievable in some cases, although, as mentioned, any such savings will in general be significantly lower than before the reform of the dividend tax regime. In some instances, the tax saving may be extinguished by the additional cost of operating through a company. In all cases, it is recommended to 'do the sums' before making the decision whether or not to incorporate in the context of tax.

Of course, incorporation has commercial implications for the business, which should (and generally does) take precedence over any tax considerations in practice.

Capital gains tax

2.33 Historically, fundamental changes to the CGT regime were introduced from 6 April 2008, including a standard CGT rate of 18%. However, an additional CGT rate of 28% was introduced from 23 June 2010 to the extent that the individual is chargeable to income tax at higher rates (and also for trustees and personal representatives).

Subsequently, the above 18% and 28% rates of CGT for individuals were reduced (in *Finance Act 2016*) to 10% and 20% (from 2016/17). However, gains on the disposal of residential property interests that do not qualify for private residence relief, and gains arising in respect of carried interest, remain subject to the 18% and 28% rates.

The most important changes to business owners who were considering incorporation at the time of the above CGT reforms from 6 April 2008 were the withdrawal of taper relief and indexation allowance. The government responded to protests by the private equity sector about the withdrawal of business asset taper relief (giving an effective CGT rate of around 10% for higher rate taxpayers) by announcing the introduction of entrepreneurs' relief from 6 April 2008.

For entrepreneurs' relief purposes, a CGT rate of 10% applies to qualifying gains of up to £10m, in relation to business disposals from 6 April 2011. This upper limit was increased from £5m, which applied in relation to business disposals between 23 June 2010 and 5 April 2011. For business disposals between 6 April 2010 and 22 June 2010, entrepreneurs' relief applied to the first £2m of qualifying gains. The relief limit was increased from an original ceiling of £1m, which applied to qualifying disposals in 2008/09 and 2009/10.

The entrepreneurs' relief maximum is a cumulative lifetime limit. However, disposals before 6 April 2008 do not affect this lifetime limit, subject to transitional rules regarding company reorganisations and qualifying enterprise investment scheme and venture capital trust investments.

Many sole traders and partnerships sought to incorporate their businesses prior to 6 April 2008 in order to 'bank' business asset taper relief (and possibly indexation allowance, in the case of established businesses), typically by selling their business to a newly formed company at an effective CGT rate of 10% (or possibly lower), with a view to extracting the proceeds in due course without further tax implications. Incorporating the business before 6 April 2008 would generally preserve entrepreneurs' relief entitlement on a later disposal of shares in the company, subject to the relevant relief conditions being satisfied.

2.34

Focus

The sale of the business to a newly formed company as a going concern in the manner described above may be seen as a potentially tax-efficient way to dispose of the business (or its chargeable assets, to be more precise) at the 10% CGT rate, if entrepreneurs' relief is available.

However, the scope for claiming entrepreneurs' relief on a disposal of goodwill upon incorporation was restricted by changes first introduced in *FA 2015* for business disposals from 3 December 2014, subject to exceptions from this general rule in certain circumstances (see **2.36**).

This strategy of selling the business requires careful thought. For example:

- A business sale will trigger potential CGT liabilities. Whilst the tax charge could be financed via the company in part repayment of the debt owed following the sale, this assumes that the company is sufficiently in funds to do so.
- A sale of land and buildings (eg business premises) has stamp duty land tax (or land and buildings transaction tax) implications (see

2.73). In addition, an increase in value could result in a double layer of taxation (ie corporation tax on chargeable gains for the company, and potential tax and NIC liabilities when the net proceeds are extracted by the company owners) on a subsequent disposal of the property.

- A sale of intangible assets such as goodwill can give rise to valuation difficulties, resulting in disposal proceeds being overstated (see **2.60**).

It should also be noted that entrepreneurs' relief applies to a 'material disposal of business assets' such as the whole or part of a business (*TCGA 1992, s 169I(2)(a)*). The disposal of an identifiable part of the taxpayer's business as a going concern was held to be eligible for entrepreneurs' relief in *Gilbert (t/a United Foods) v Revenue & Customs* [2011] UKFTT 705 (TC). By contrast, the disposal of business assets does not necessarily satisfy this requirement (*Russell v HMRC* [2012] UKFTT 623 (TC)). HMRC's views on the distinction can be found in the Capital Gains Manual (at CG64015 and following).

In some cases, it may be difficult to determine whether there has been a cessation of the unincorporated business (eg if the business owner carries on another, similar business thereafter), and if so, when that cessation took place for entrepreneurs' relief purposes (see *Rice v Revenue & Customs* [2014] UKFTT 133 (TC)). The importance of clear evidence regarding cessation in such cases cannot be overstated.

Of course, businesses will continue to incorporate for commercial reasons, if not for tax savings.

2.35 What assets might the business own? There could be stock, tools and equipment, land and buildings, goodwill and investments. In all but the smallest businesses, there will be CGT considerations on the transfer of a business to a company. Many items of plant, tools and equipment, motor vehicles, fixtures and fittings in buildings, etc will have attracted capital allowances as plant and machinery. Income tax adjustments will be necessary. That does not stop assets of this type being chargeable to CGT (though chattels having a value of £6,000 or less and motor cars are exempt (*TCGA 1992, ss 262, 263*)).

However, *TCGA 1992, s 37* excludes from the CGT computation any consideration taken into account as a receipt in computing income. An actual gain in respect of this type of asset will therefore only arise where it is transferred for a value greater than original cost (which will be rare).

There are provisions to restrict allowable CGT losses by the amount of capital allowances on an asset (*TCGA 1992, s 41*). The rationale is to prevent the person making the disposal receiving a 'double allowance', ie relief for capital allowances and an allowable capital loss. However, see 'Harvesting capital losses' by Arthur Conway (*Taxation*, 6 June 2013) for possible limitations on the ability of *TCGA 1992, s 41* to restrict capital losses on sales of plant and machinery.

Prior to the abolition of industrial and agricultural buildings allowances, income tax consequences often needed to be considered in respect of buildings used in the business. However, following the withdrawal of those allowances, it is now generally necessary to concentrate on the CGT aspects on a transfer of land and buildings.

2.36 Goodwill, and whether it can be transferred, is a subject in itself. In many instances, goodwill will not appear on the balance sheet of an unincorporated business. Business owners should ensure that it is of a type which is transferable.

As indicated at **2.34**, a sale of the business to a newly formed company as a going concern upon incorporation may be seen as a tax-efficient disposal, particularly if it qualifies for entrepreneurs' relief. However, the availability of entrepreneurs' relief on disposals of goodwill upon incorporation was restricted by changes introduced in *Finance Act 2015*, in response to concerns by the government that some business incorporations were motivated by the potential tax advantages of doing so, and that business proprietors had been gaining an 'unfair advantage' in selling the business to a related close company in order to effectively extract funds from the business at the entrepreneurs' CGT rate of 10%, rather than the normal rates of income tax and National Insurance contributions.

The restriction (in *TCGA 1992, s 169LA*) as originally introduced in *FA 2015* applied broadly if the business owner transferred goodwill (directly or indirectly) to a 'related party' from 3 December 2014 as part of a qualifying business disposal for entrepreneurs' relief purposes, where the person was not a 'retiring partner'. However, the related party and retiring partner conditions were replaced (in *Finance Act 2016*) by different conditions in respect of close companies, ie broadly that immediately after the disposal the person (and any relevant connected person) together hold 5% or more of either the ordinary share capital or the voting rights in the company (or a group member). A 'relevant connected person' means a connected company or connected trustees, but not individuals in general. This restriction is subject to an exception in certain circumstances (see **2.37**). The changes in the entrepreneurs' relief restriction for transfers of goodwill were backdated, so that they apply to disposals from 3 December 2014.

The effect of the restriction, if it applies, is to exclude goodwill from the definition of 'relevant business assets' comprised in a 'qualifying business disposal' for entrepreneurs' relief purposes (in *TCGA 1992, s 169L*), so that a gain on an affected disposal of goodwill to a close company (or a company that would be close if it were resident in the UK) is charged at normal CGT rates (subject to other reliefs being claimed).

The entrepreneurs' relief restriction also applies where the goodwill disposal would otherwise be eligible for relief, but the business owner is party to 'relevant avoidance arrangements', ie broadly arrangements with a main purpose of ensuring that the above restriction does not apply.

2.37 If the entrepreneurs' relief restriction in **2.36** would otherwise apply by virtue of ownership of the company's share capital (ie by the disponer or any relevant connected person), it is nevertheless disapplied (by *TCGA 1992, s 169LA(1A)*) if certain conditions are satisfied. Firstly, there must be a disposal of all those shares to another company ('A') before the end of the 'relevant period' (ie 28 days beginning with the qualifying business disposal, or possibly longer if HMRC allow). Secondly, if company A is a close company, the disponer (and any relevant connected person) must hold less than 5% of the ordinary share capital and voting rights (of company A or any group member) immediately before the end of the relevant period (*TCGA 1992, s 169LA(1B)*).

Notwithstanding the entrepreneurs' relief restriction for transfers of goodwill in *TCGA 1992, s 169LA* (as amended by *Finance Act 2016*), an entrepreneurs' relief claim remains possible where, for example, the unincorporated business proprietor (and any relevant connected person) holds less than 5% of both the share capital and voting rights of the acquiring company; or where the business is incorporated prior to its disposal (within 28 days) to an unconnected company; or (say) on a disposal of the unincorporated business to a company wholly-owned by a family member. However, such exceptions from the restriction will probably not be relevant to most business incorporations.

2.38 It should be noted that the above entrepreneurs' relief restriction in respect of goodwill does not prevent the relief being claimed on other chargeable assets (eg business premises) that are relevant business assets comprised in the qualifying business disposal.

Other forms of CGT relief are considered in later sections of this chapter.

2.39 Capital gains are generally realised on the disposal of assets. There are various instances in *TCGA 1992* where tax on realised gains may be deferred until the happening of some later event. One such instance is where rollover relief is in point (*TCGA 1992, ss 152–160*). However, what if the gain does not relate to the (current) disposal of an asset? There is a potential trap for the unwary, as explained below.

A gain realised on the disposal of one asset, which has been used in a trade, may be deferred (or 'held over') against the acquisition of a second asset where the new asset is a wasting (or 'depreciating') asset, also used in the trade (*TCGA 1992, s 154*).

In that case, no adjustment is made to the base cost of the second asset. The gain on the first asset is calculated according to normal rules and simply deferred until the earliest of:

- the disposal of asset number two;
- the cessation of use of asset number two in a trade; or
- the expiry of ten years from the acquisition of asset number two.

If an asset carrying a deferred gain is transferred to a company on incorporation, there is a disposal. The original deferred gain comes back into charge; there is nothing you can do about it. None of the reliefs examined below cope with this. The deferred gain now chargeable arose on an earlier disposal and cannot be expunged by the incorporation reliefs. The tax will be due and payable.

> **Focus**
>
> In preparing to incorporate a business, always check whether there have been previous claims to rollover chargeable gains on business assets. Furthermore, note whether any such gains were merely deferred and not 'properly' rolled over.

2.40 The transfer of assets from an unincorporated business to a company is a disposal for CGT purposes. Further, it is invariably a disposal between connected persons. For this purpose, a company is connected with another person, if that person has control of it or if that person and persons connected with him together have control of it (*TCGA 1992, s 286(6)*).

Where the transactions are between connected persons, the rules of *TCGA 1992, s 18* prevail, in particular that the transaction is to be treated as a bargain not made at arm's length. This in turn brings *TCGA 1992, s 17* into play, to the extent that the consideration for the business proprietor(s) disposal of the assets is to be treated as their market value, and the company's corresponding acquisition value is also to be treated as market value. So, for the purposes of the CGT computation, the chargeable assets of a business are treated as passing at market value.

However, the actual consideration may be:

- shares in the company, which may be of more than one class;
- loan stock in the form of a debenture or similar (although this is rare in the case of small private companies);

- cash – often left outstanding on a director's loan account;
- nothing – it being quite common to gift the assets of a business to the company.

2.41 If there were to be a large chargeable gain, with tax payable, this would amount to a significant disincentive to incorporation. Certain reliefs exist to alleviate this problem and the rest of this chapter explores them:

- *TCGA 1992, s 162* ('Rollover relief on transfer of business');
- *TCGA 1992, s 165* ('Relief for gifts of business assets').

The latter is the more flexible of the two reliefs.

However, in addition EIS CGT deferral relief (*TCGA 1992, Sch 5B*) has sometimes been referred to as 'the third way'.

As indicated earlier, the sale of a business upon incorporation, whilst triggering a CGT charge, may nevertheless be an attractive alternative to the above reliefs, if a claim for entrepreneurs' relief is available at the reduced rate of 10% (although note the potential restriction in the relief at **2.36**).

TCGA 1992, s 162 relief

2.42 The relief under *TCGA 1992, s 162* (commonly referred to as 'incorporation relief') is mandatory if specified conditions are met, and therefore does not require a claim. The cost of the new assets (ie the company shares) is deducted from the chargeable gain. Correspondingly, the base cost of the new assets is reduced by the amount left out of the CGT computation on incorporation. There are provisions for apportionment where the consideration is not wholly in shares.

The relief applies where three conditions are satisfied (*TCGA 1992, s 162(1)*):

- a person who is not a company (ie sole trader or partner) transfers to a company a business as a going concern;
- together with the whole assets of the business, possibly excluding cash; and
- the business is so transferred wholly or partly in exchange for shares issued by the company to the person transferring the business.

With regard to the first bullet point above, it is important to ensure that what is transferred amounts to a 'business' as a going concern. There is no definition of 'business' for these purposes, although some assistance on its meaning may be derived from *Ramsay v HMRC* [2013] UKUT 226 (TCC). In that case, the Upper Tribunal allowed Mrs Ramsay's appeal against the decision of the First-tier Tribunal that she was not entitled to incorporation relief under *TCGA 1992, s 162*. Mrs Ramsay had inherited a one-third share of a large single building, which was divided into ten flats (five of which were occupied at the relevant time). She subsequently made a gift to her husband of one-half of her own one-third share, and later purchased the remaining two-thirds share of the property from her brothers. Mr and Mrs Ramsay transferred the property to a company, in exchange for shares in it.

Taking the activities of Mrs Ramsay as a whole, the Upper Tribunal concluded that Mrs Ramsay's activities fell within the business tests outlined in *Customs and Excise Commissioners v Lord Fisher* [1981] STC 238. The tribunal was also satisfied that the degree of activity undertaken in respect of the property overall was sufficient in nature and extent to amount to a business for the purpose of *TCGA 1992, s 162*.

It is also important to be able to demonstrate that the business is capable of being transferred, and that it was transferred as a going concern.

In *Roelich v Revenue & Customs* [2014] UKFTT 579 (TC), the taxpayer originally held 49 shares in a company (G). The other 51 of the 100 issued shares in G was held by another individual (B). In May 2006, the taxpayer made a transfer to G (valued at £523,363) in exchange for a further 49 shares (and at the same time B transferred a business into G in exchange for a further 51 shares). HMRC subsequently sought to charge CGT on the taxpayer's transfer to G. The taxpayer appealed, contending that incorporation relief under *TCGA 1992, s 162* was available in respect of the transfer.

HMRC considered that there was no business transferred to G that qualified for incorporation relief. The taxpayer had operated a property development consultancy business since 2003. In 2005, he reached an agreement with a contractor (PV), that if PV was successful in obtaining a landfill contract and if planning consent was obtained, PV would pay him a fee of £5 per load of infill. The infill contract was later awarded to PV. The taxpayer transferred the PV contract (which was valued on the basis of likely loads) to G in exchange for the 49 shares. The transfer was undertaken informally; there was no evidence of a disposal (or acquisition) of goodwill.

The First-tier Tribunal found that there was a business, and concluded that the business was a going concern from the outset. The tribunal did not accept HMRC's contention that the business was not capable of being transferred, as the taxpayer's knowledge was not incapable of being passed on to others. The tribunal also held that the business was transferred as a going concern, and was not merely the transfer of an income stream, as HMRC contended. Finally, the tribunal accepted that the issue of shares was primarily for the PV contract but was also in return for the transfer of the entire business. Incorporation relief was therefore available, and the taxpayer's appeal was allowed.

The taxpayer in *Roelich* was perhaps fortunate in the sense that the incorporation of his business was conducted informally, and there was very little documentary evidence of the transfer, whereas incorporation under *TCGA 1992, s 162* commonly involves some form of business transfer agreement.

Incorporation relief under *TCGA 1992, s 162* is very specific. All of the assets of the business (apart from cash which is, of course, not a chargeable asset) must be transferred to the company and this must be done wholly or partly in exchange for shares.

In fact, cash is not the only item which may be left out. HMRC Concession D32 states that relief under *TCGA 1992, s 162* is not precluded by the fact that some or all of the liabilities of the business are not taken over by the company. However, care is needed to ensure that liabilities remain within the terms of Concession D32. For example, if the company raises finance and uses the funds to pay the proprietors for the business to enable existing borrowings to be repaid, this will constitute (non-share) consideration for the business, resulting in any *TCGA 1992, s 162* relief being restricted.

'Cash' in the above context is considered by HMRC to include amounts left owing to the transferor as sums credited to a loan or current account with the company (CG65720).

Example 2.2 – TCGA 1992, s 162 relief in action

Janine decides to incorporate her business of producing personalised greetings cards from 1 June 2017. A very simplified closing balance sheet shows the assets to be stock £30,000, business premises £100,000 (cost £80,000) and goodwill £20,000 (cost nil). The entire business is transferred to a newly formed company, Super Cards Ltd, and 1,000 ordinary £1 shares are issued to her.

(a) The market value of the 1,000 shares is £150,000 being the total value of the assets transferred in (market value applies as this is a connected persons transaction).

(b) The consideration (shares issued) is apportioned in a just and reasonable manner, thus:

	£
Stock	30,000
Shop premises	100,000
Goodwill	20,000

(c) The chargeable gains are:

	£	£
Shop – consideration	100,000	
Less: Cost	(80,000)	20,000
Goodwill, consideration	20,000	
Less: Cost	nil	20,000
Total gain		40,000
The whole of this gain will be rolled over under *TCGA 1992, s 162.*		

(d) The CGT base cost of the shares, for a future computation on disposal is:

	£
Market value	150,000
Less: Gain rolled over *TCGA 1992, s 162*	(40,000)
Base cost	110,000

2.43 However, in some cases the gain may not be fully relieved. The business must be transferred as a going concern and must therefore reflect liabilities to be satisfied by the company. An undertaking to satisfy these liabilities amounts to further consideration. As indicated at **2.42**, Concession D32 prevents the assumption of liabilities from being treated as consideration for the purposes of the *TCGA 1992, s 162* computation. However, this does not mean that the liabilities can be ignored in determining the market value of the assets transferred.

Focus

Where the liabilities are relatively high, the net asset value of the business (which equals the value of the shares issued) may be low. If the chargeable assets have large inherent capital gains (watch for goodwill off the balance sheet), it may be impossible to roll over all of the gain – the base cost of the shares cannot go below zero.

Example 2.3 – TCGA 1992, s 162 relief limitation

Colin is a sole trader manufacturer of widgets. The balance sheet is as follows:

	£
Freehold property	300,000
Fixtures and fittings	25,000
Stock	25,000
	350,000
Less: Bank loan	(225,000)
Creditors	(50,000)
	£75,000
Represented by:	
Capital account	£75,000

The property originally cost £200,000, and there is goodwill off balance sheet of £75,000 for which Colin paid nothing.

He formed ABC Widgets Ltd on 1 May 2017 and 1,000 ordinary £1 shares were issued to him.

(a) The market value of the shares issued is £150,000, being the total net value of the assets transferred in (ie £75,000 balance sheet net assets, plus £75,000 goodwill).

(b) The chargeable gains are:

		£	£
Property:	Consideration (market value)	300,000	
	Less: Cost	(200,000)	100,000
Goodwill:	Consideration (market value)	75,000	
	Less: Cost	nil	75,000
			175,000
	Less: Rolled over under *TCGA 1992, s 162*		(150,000)
Chargeable gain			25,000

Subject to the annual CGT exemption, this gain is immediately taxable. However, on the disposal of an unincorporated business a claim for entrepreneurs' relief is potentially available, if the relevant conditions are satisfied and subject to the amount of relief claimed in respect of any earlier qualifying disposals.

However, the restriction on claims for entrepreneurs' relief in respect of the disposal of goodwill upon incorporation (from 3 December 2014) should be noted (see **2.36**). In the above example, gains were made on the disposal of property and goodwill, but only part of the total gains could be rolled over. How is the chargeable gain to be allocated between those assets, for the purpose of determining any entitlement to entrepreneurs' relief on the residual aggregate gain in respect of the property? There has been no formal HMRC guidance or any precedent at the time of writing, but it is understood that HMRC would accept a 'just and reasonable' apportionment of the residual aggregate gain, by reference to the component chargeable gains (but not any losses) which were taken into consideration for *TCGA 1992, s 162* purposes.

HMRC's view on the general interaction between incorporation relief and entrepreneurs' relief is understood to be that incorporation relief takes precedence over a claim to entrepreneurs' relief. At the time of writing, HMRC's approach on the interaction of the reliefs is not explicitly stated in the Capital Gains manual. However, the guidance indicates that a claim made under a provision which rolls over that gain against the acquisition cost of a replacement asset (of which incorporation relief would presumably be one) takes precedence over a claim for entrepreneurs' relief (CG64136).

It should also be borne in mind that entrepreneurs' relief requires a claim, and that an election is available for *TCGA 1992, s 162* not to apply (*TCGA 1992, s 162A*). It would therefore seem possible for taxpayers effectively to choose between the reliefs (or perhaps to take advantage of a combination of the two in some cases).

Care should be exercised when considering goodwill valuations in property-related businesses, such as pubs or nursing homes (see **2.62** and following below).

(c) The CGT base cost of the shares is:

Market value	150,000
Less: Gain rolled over *TCGA 1992, s 162*	(150,000)
	£nil

2.44 In the above situation where all the assets are transferred, only shares are issued and yet a chargeable gain still arises. Occasionally, though, other consideration might be taken. This could be in the form of loan stock issued by the company, or more simply the creation of a director's loan account with a credit balance.

In these circumstances, the gain which may be rolled over is limited to the fraction A/B of the amount of the gain on the old assets, where:

- A is the cost of the new assets (shares); and
- B is the value of the whole consideration received by the transferor in exchange for the business (*TCGA 1992, s 162(4)*).

Example 2.4 – Shares and other consideration (I)

Linda, a higher rate taxpayer, runs a fruit and vegetable wholesale business as a sole trader and decides to incorporate, with effect from 1 July 2017. The net asset value of her business is as follows:

Freehold property	200,000	(cost £100,000)
Fixtures and fittings	4,000	(cost £10,000)
Stock	6,000	(cost £6,000)
Goodwill	30,000	(cost nil)
Debtors	5,000	
	245,000	
Less: Trade creditors	(20,000)	
	£225,000	

Linda transfers the business to Fruit and Veg Ltd, which issues 1,000 ordinary £1 shares to her, and a director's loan account of £40,000 is created.

(a) The market value of the shares issued is £185,000 being the net asset value of the business transferred in (£225,000), less the loan account (£40,000).

(b) The chargeable gains are:

Property: Consideration	200,000	
Less: Cost	(100,000)	100,000
Goodwill: Consideration	30,000	

Less: Cost	nil	30,000
		130,000
Amount rolled over under *TCGA 1992, s 162*:		
A/B × 130,000 =		
$\frac{185{,}000}{225{,}000} \times 130{,}000 =$		(106,889)
		23,111
Annual exemption (2017/18)		(11,300)
Amount chargeable to CGT		£11,811
CGT liability (see Note):		
Property: £11,811 (× £100,000/£130,000) × 10%		908
Goodwill: £11,811 (× £30,000/£130,000) × 20%		545
		£1,453
The CGT base cost of the shares is:		
Market value		185,000
Less: Gain rolled over *TCGA 1992, s 162*		(106,889)
		£78,111

Note: As indicated at **2.43**, for the purpose of determining any entitlement to entrepreneurs' relief on the residual aggregate gain in respect of the property, it is assumed that HMRC would accept the above calculation of CGT based on a 'just and reasonable' apportionment, although there has been no formal HMRC guidance or any precedent at the time of writing.

2.45 The application of *TCGA 1992, s 162* is relatively inflexible, for two main reasons. First, it requires the transfer of all the business assets (with very limited exceptions) to the company. Secondly, most of the inherent value of the business is locked into the share capital of the company and cannot readily be extracted.

Some commentators recommend that if there is a substantial capital account in the unincorporated business then the proprietors should be advised to draw down on it before incorporation. Presumably such a capital account exists in the first place in order to fund continuing trading operations. If this is the case, then there is every likelihood that the funds withdrawn will be reintroduced into the company shortly afterwards by means of a credit to a director's loan account.

Perceived challenges to this process have sometimes been said to stem from *Furniss (Inspector of Taxes) v Dawson* [1984] STC 153, in that the transactions are preordained and the intermediate one has no real purpose. The net effect is to re-characterise the transaction as if the business had been transferred for a consideration partly in the issue of shares and partly in cash. A counter-argument might be demonstrated by the incorporation agreement (assuming that there is one) showing the intention to transfer the entire assets of the business in return for shares. Could a similar challenge stem from the principle in *Ramsay (WT) Ltd v IRC* [1981] STC 174, notably that there is a circular series of transactions leaving the business in the same position as before it started? The significance of *Ramsay* was effectively relegated to a rule of statutory construction following *Barclays Mercantile Business Finance Ltd v Mawson* [2004] UKHL 51.

However, a general anti-abuse rule (GAAR) was subsequently introduced in *Finance Act 2013*, and the government can also introduce targeted anti-avoidance rules where it is considered necessary to do so. Nevertheless, it is difficult (for the authors at least) to envisage business incorporations being affected by such measures.

It may be necessary to remove and retain part of the pre-incorporation capital account, for example to meet the tax liabilities of the unincorporated business. Provided that the final accounts of the unincorporated business have made full provision for outstanding tax liabilities, this should not be a problem.

2.46 It may be worthwhile thinking carefully about the consideration to be given by the company. If it is entirely the issue of shares, then the whole gain on the transfer of the business assets is (usually) deferred but then their full value is locked into the company. If some other consideration is given, there will be a chargeable gain, but does it need to be a taxable gain?

Example 2.5 – Shares and other consideration (II)

The facts are as in the previous example. The net asset value of Linda's business upon incorporation on 1 July 2017 is £225,000. The gross chargeable gains are £130,000.

Would Linda be better advised to create a loan account of (say) £19,500 as well as taking 1,000 ordinary shares?

(a) The market value of the shares is £205,500, being the net asset value of the business transferred in, less the loan account (£225,000 – £19,500).

(b)	Chargeable gains (gross), as before	130,000
	Amount rolled over under *TCGA 1992, s 162*:	
	A/B × 130,000 =	
	$\frac{205{,}500}{225{,}000} \times 130{,}000 =$	(118,733)
		11,267
	Annual exemption (to cover)	(11,267)
	Taxable gain	£nil

Linda has therefore created a director's loan account of £19,500 on which she is later free to draw with no additional tax liability, compared with a director's loan account of £40,000 in the previous example at a CGT cost of only £1,453.

(c)	The CGT base cost of the shares is:	
	Market value	205,500
	Less: Gain rolled over *TCGA 1992, s 162*	(118,733)
		£86,767

This is £8,656 higher than the previous example, in which Linda incurred a CGT liability of £1,453 but also had an additional credit of £20,500 to her loan account.

The availability of entrepreneurs' relief (in whole or part) may make a transfer in return for shares and a loan account with the company at a relatively low CGT cost seem like an attractive proposition, with the loan being repaid by the company as funds allow. The reduction in the base cost of the shares on a future disposal in those circumstances may be considered to be a price worth paying. However, the potential implications of a future increase in CGT rates should be borne in mind.

2.47 As mentioned, the CGT incorporation relief in *TCGA 1992, s 162* is mandatory. No claim is required. If the individual making the disposal of chargeable assets to the company meets the conditions laid down, then the relief is given.

However, *TCGA 1992, s 162A* permits a specific claim to disapply *TCGA 1992, s 162*. When this provision was introduced (in *Finance Act 2002*), it helped to overcome a potential problem involving the interaction of incorporation relief and taper relief, namely that the shares in the company issued on incorporation are a new asset and the qualifying holding period for taper relief must begin again. If the shares were sold shortly after incorporation, any previously earned entitlement to business asset taper relief on the assets transferred would be lost. This particular problem obviously disappeared with the withdrawal of taper relief from 6 April 2008.

However, the availability of entrepreneurs' relief for share disposals from that date is generally subject to a minimum ownership period of one year, and therefore the claim is still of some potential relevance.

2.48 If *TCGA 1992, s 162* relief is to be overridden, the business proprietor making the disposal to the company must make a claim, usually by the second anniversary of 31 January following the year of assessment in which the disposal took place (*TCGA 1992, s 162A(3)*). This is shortened to the first anniversary if the shares are sold before the end of the year following incorporation (*TCGA 1992, s 162A(4)*). Special rules apply where there has been a transfer between spouses (see *TCGA 1992, s 162A(5)*).

If the business was transferred from a partnership to a company, each individual partner may separately choose whether or not to make a *TCGA 1992, s 162A* claim (*TCGA 1992, s 162A(7)*).

The effect of the election is that the gain on disposal of business assets to the company is calculated in the usual way, taking the benefit of entrepreneurs' relief, if it is available and claimed. There is no deferral and tax is payable on the net gain. The base cost of the shares issued on incorporation is therefore market value.

TCGA 1992, s 165 relief

2.49 Many incorporations use the relief in *TCGA 1992, s 165* instead. Although the relief is headed 'Relief for gifts of business assets' it does not simply apply to gifts. It would be better termed a relief for transfers of business assets at undervalue.

A business asset for this purpose is defined as including an asset, or interest in an asset, used for the purposes of a trade, profession or vocation carried on by the transferor (*TCGA 1992, s 165(2)(a)(i)*). Any chargeable asset used in a sole trade or partnership by the asset owner is therefore encompassed.

2.50 The relief applies where the asset owner disposes of the asset by way of a bargain not at arm's length (*TCGA 1992, s 165(1)(a)*). As mentioned, the transfer of assets from an unincorporated business proprietor to the company will normally be such because it is a connected party transaction.

The effect of the relief is that a chargeable gain otherwise arising is reduced by the 'held over gain' and the amount of the company's CGT base cost is also reduced by the held over gain (*TCGA 1992, s 165(4)*).

2.51 Unlike *TCGA 1992, s 162* (application of which is mandatory in the relevant circumstances), a specific claim is required for gift relief to apply (*TCGA 1992, s 165(1)(b)*).

The claim must be made jointly by both the individual making the transfer and the company. HMRC require the claim to be made on the form contained in HMRC Helpsheet HS295 ('Relief for gifts and similar transactions') (tinyurl.com/HMRC-HS295).

No shorter time limit is specified, so the general time limit of four years from the end of the tax year in which the transfer takes place normally applies (*TMA 1970, s 43(1)*).

In practice, claims will nearly always be made long before the end of this time limit (normally on the business owner's tax return for the year of incorporation), because otherwise CGT on the gain would become payable.

Note that *TCGA 1992, s 165* contains no requirement that the transfer shall be the whole of the business or even all of the assets used in the business. It must simply be 'an asset' used in a trade, profession or vocation. Thus there is a flexibility which is absent from the *TCGA 1992, s 162* process.

Relief under *TCGA 1992, s 165* is available broadly if the asset is used for the purposes of the trade. The asset must be in 'trade' use immediately before it is gifted. Note that previous periods of non-trade use will generally restrict the relief (*TCGA 1992, Sch 7, para 5*).

Furthermore, if part of a property was used for the purposes of the trade and part of it was not, gift relief is generally subject to a restriction on a 'just and reasonable' basis (*TCGA 1992, Sch 7, para 6*).

2.52 The amount of the gain which can be held over is as follows:

- in the case of a pure gift (ie no proceeds at all), the gain which would otherwise arise in deeming the proceeds to be market value (*TCGA 1992, s 165(6)*), or
- in the case of a transfer at undervalue, the amount by which the deemed gain exceeds the excess of the actual consideration over the costs deductible in the CGT computation (*TCGA 1992, s 165(7)*).

The costs deductible are those given by *TCGA 1992, s 38* ('Acquisition and disposal costs etc').

Example 2.6 – TCGA 1992, s 165 relief: gift or sale at undervalue

Grant runs a musical supplies business. He decides to incorporate it, and transfers to the company the business premises now valued at £180,000. The CGT base cost is £75,000.		£
(a)	Capital gain arising:	
	Consideration (market value)	180,000
	Less: Cost	(75,000)
		£105,000
(b)	If Grant gifts the property to the company the whole of the gain is held over. The base cost of the property for the company is:	
	Market value	180,000
	Less: Held over gain	(105,000)
	Base cost for future disposal	£75,000
(c)	If Grant sells the property to the company for £50,000:	
	Actual proceeds	50,000
	Less: Allowable cost	(75,000)
	Excess	£nil

The result is as in (b) above. This is probably not a realistic scenario as Grant is missing the opportunity to take a further £25,000 tax free; the proceeds might as well be £75,000 – the result is similar.

(d)	If Grant sells the property to the company for £125,000:	
	Actual proceeds	125,000
	Less: Allowable cost	(75,000)
	Excess	£50,000
	Gross gain	105,000
	Less: Excess	(50,000)
	Gain held over	£55,000

The excess is also the chargeable gain subject to the annual exemption, if available. Entrepreneurs' relief may also be available for qualifying business disposals. *TCGA 1992, s 165* relief and entrepreneurs' relief both require claims, and some scope for planning may therefore exist in terms of choosing which relief to claim.

With regard to the interaction of gifts hold over relief and entrepreneurs' relief, HMRC's view is that *TCGA 1992, s 165* relief takes priority over entrepreneurs' relief (CG64137).

In the case of a disposal at undervalue, a claim to entrepreneurs' relief may be possible in respect of the amount of any gain remaining chargeable.

However, the restriction on entrepreneurs' relief claims in relation to disposals of goodwill to close companies (*TCGA 1992, s 169LA*) from 3 December 2014 should be taken into account, if appropriate.

The base cost of the property for the company is:

Market value	180,000
Less: Held over gain	(55,000)
Base cost for future disposal	£125,000

2.53

Focus

Unlike *TCGA 1992, s 162*, there is no fixed process to follow. An incorporation using *TCGA 1992, s 165* relief may therefore typically proceed on the following basis:

- Form the company (or acquire an 'off the shelf' company) and issue shares by cash subscription. Typically, the number of shares will be small.
- Some time later, on incorporation, transfer the required assets to the company either by pure gift or by sale for proceeds of a personally determined amount. Note that the company's undertaking to satisfy any liabilities of the unincorporated business will amount to proceeds for this purpose.
- At the outset, the company is unlikely to have substantial cash, so the proceeds are often left outstanding on the loan account.
- Sometime later, when the company is trading profitably, the proprietor may draw down from the loan account effectively taking the proceeds without further tax cost.

Prior to the entrepreneurs' relief restriction in respect of goodwill disposals (see **2.36**), it was relatively common for goodwill to be sold at market value, as opposed to being gifted. However, following the entrepreneurs' relief restriction, some business owners may prefer to gift the goodwill (or sell it at an undervalue) and claim relief under *TCGA 1992, s 165* instead.

There is perhaps less need in these circumstances for a formal incorporation agreement (which is essential for the *TCGA 1992, s 162* process). Any property transfer will be evidenced by a conveyance. However, because of its intangible nature, there ought to be a document evidencing any transfer of goodwill. Do not forget also that other items, such as stock and plant and machinery attracting capital allowances, may need to be sold to the company at particular prices. All in all, some sort of document is still a sensible step.

Summary – TCGA 1992, ss 162 and 165 compared

2.54

		TCGA 1992, s 162	*TCGA 1992, s 165*
1	How the relief is given	Mandatory. If certain conditions are satisfied, the relief is given automatically.	Optional. Claim required.
2	Method of incorporation	Fixed method:	Method more flexible:
		– form company, issue a few shares;	– form company, issue required number of shares;
		– transfer entire business and assets to company;	– transfer only assets required to company;
		– company issues more shares (and loan/cash) to the transferor of the business as consideration.	– company may pay for assets; price flexible.
3	CGT base cost of shares	Market value less gain rolled over.	Subscription price, minimal.
4	Base cost of assets in company	Market value. Incorporation was a connected party transaction; *s 162* depresses the share base cost, not that of the assets.	Market value less gain held over.
5	Flexibility	Can be overridden by a claim under *TCGA 1992, s 162A*. Partners in a partnership can separately choose to make this claim or not.	Claim may cover all assets or selected ones. Partners in partnership may make different claims to suit personal circumstances.

6	Funds potentially available	Value of assets locked into share capital of company unless cash/loan note issued. Amount which can be withdrawn relatively low.	Shareholder/director free to draw on loan account created as consideration for asset transfer, funds permitting. The amount may be quite high.
7	Debtors/other assets	Other assets, such as debtors, must go into the company.	Debtors may be left out of company. Care needed though if creditors exceed debtors and both are excluded from the transfer. The company's satisfaction of the creditors amounts to consideration for other assets transferred.
8	Losses	Permits the carry forward of losses under *ITA 2007, s 86*.	Cannot carry forward losses under *ITA 2007, s 86*.

For the most part, there is a straight choice between incorporation by the *TCGA 1992, s 162* route or the *TCGA 1992, s 165* route. There is no right or wrong answer. All the circumstances of the business, its asset values etc must be considered along with the future intentions of the proprietors. An appropriate decision must be made.

What you cannot do is to pick the best bits of *TCGA 1992, ss 162* and *165* and use them both. We have seen that there may be circumstances in which *TCGA 1992, s 162* can leave a residual chargeable gain. This is not eligible for a claim under *TCGA 1992, s 165* because there are actual market value proceeds (ie the shares).

Enterprise Investment Scheme (EIS)

2.55 A further opportunity in the CGT legislation to defer realised gains is afforded by EIS reinvestment relief under *TCGA 1992, Sch 5B*. This relief is related to investments in EIS companies and is perhaps better referred to as deferral relief. As mentioned at **2.41**, some refer to it as 'the third way'.

Following changes to the interaction of EIS deferral relief and entrepreneurs' relief from 23 June 2010, this potential route to incorporation may have been unattractive in many cases where entrepreneurs' relief would otherwise be available. However, the disincentive to claiming EIS deferral relief in respect of qualifying business disposals was relieved by further changes from 3 December 2014, as mentioned at **2.56**.

It has to be said that the EIS legislation (both for the income tax relief in *ITA 2007, Pt 5* and the CGT reliefs in *TCGA 1992, ss 150A–150C* and *Sch 5B*) is extraordinarily complicated. There are pitfalls aplenty and anyone seeking to use these reliefs should exercise great care. Even if a qualifying investment is successfully made, there is plenty of scope for things to go wrong after the event, due to a plethora of anti-avoidance rules. A detailed analysis of the EIS reliefs is beyond the scope of this chapter.

2.56 In broad terms, CGT deferral relief is potentially available where, *inter alia*, a 'qualifying investor' subscribes in cash for new ordinary shares which are fully paid up; in a 'qualifying company' which carries on a 'qualifying trade'; and the company uses the money received in a trade within specified time limits (*TCGA 1992, Sch 5B, para 1(2)*). If those and other relief conditions are satisfied, then a capital gain realised by the investor may be reduced by the amount of the investment (or a smaller amount specified in a claim) (*TCGA 1992, Sch 5B, para 2(1)*).

In theory, the route to EIS deferral relief upon incorporation appears to be as follows:

- Form the company and issue a small number of shares for cash. It is preferable that the initial shareholder is not (one of) the proprietor(s) of the business to be incorporated. This is for complex technical reasons which might lead the share issue to be regarded as a bonus or rights issue and not a new subscription (see *Dunstan v Young, Austen and Young Ltd* [1989] STC 69).
- The business proprietor then enters into an agreement to sell the assets of the business to the company for cash. The deal must be at market value, realising a chargeable gain. It is preferable that the company borrows money to do this, rather than have the proceeds left outstanding on loan account.
- The business proprietor then uses all or part of the cash consideration to subscribe for new ordinary shares in the company and claims deferral relief under the provisions of *TCGA 1992, Sch 5B*. It is important that cash must change hands to avoid falling foul of the anti-avoidance provisions in *Sch 5B, para 13* ('Value received by investor'). Further, the second and third steps above must not be combined. The shares must be subscribed for in cash – linking the steps would mean an asset/share exchange and the relief would not be due.
- The amount subscribed must be sufficient to cover the gain on disposal of the original business assets.

However, this approach must come with a huge health warning! The above is not necessarily a tried and tested route and HMRC could argue that the rather circular series of transactions is part of a scheme for the avoidance of tax.

There is an advance clearance procedure for establishing the qualifying nature of the shares to be issued and the company (form EIS(AA) 'Advance assurance application: Enterprise Investment Scheme/Seed Enterprise Investment Scheme'; see tinyurl.com/HMRC-EIS-SEIS-AA). Full explanation of the advance clearance procedure is included in HMRC's Venture Capital Schemes manual (at VCM14030-VCM14070), although individuals considering investing could contact the Small Company Enterprise Centre for comment on whether or not they would be eligible for EIS relief on their subscriptions.

Entrepreneurs' relief potentially applies to material disposals of business assets. If a gain on the disposal of the business qualifies for entrepreneurs' relief, a claim for relief can be made in respect of the gains arising. In terms of the interaction between entrepreneurs' relief and EIS deferral relief, it is possible (following changes introduced in *FA 2015*) for entrepreneurs' relief to be claimed on deferred gains when they are charged to tax, subject to the relief conditions that applied when they were first deferred, where the gains would originally have accrued on or after 3 December 2014 (see *TCGA 1992, ss 169U–169V*). Thus the individual can potentially benefit from both the deferral of gains and entrepreneurs' relief on the same gains.

For gains accrued before 3 December 2014, for qualifying business disposals from 23 June 2010 (following changes introduced in *Finance (No 2) Act 2010*), the individual may effectively choose between claiming entrepreneurs' relief and paying CGT on the gain at 10%, or claiming EIS deferral relief and paying CGT at the prevailing rate when the gain later comes into charge (*TCGA 1992, Sch 5B, para 1(5A)*). However, in (perhaps rare) cases where a gain has exceeded the £10m lifetime limit for entrepreneurs' relief purposes, entrepreneurs' relief can be claimed up to the lifetime limit, and EIS deferral relief claimed on gains above that limit.

For business disposals before 23 June 2010, the gain is first reduced by entrepreneurs' relief (of 4/9ths), before EIS deferral relief is applied. The deferred gain (net of entrepreneurs' relief) comes back into charge when a 'chargeable event' occurs in respect of the EIS shares (eg upon a disposal of the shares).

Entrepreneurs' relief can be claimed even if the business disposal was before 6 April 2008 (ie when the relief was introduced) and the chargeable event in respect of the qualifying EIS investment occurs on or after that date, provided that the original business disposal would have qualified for entrepreneurs' relief had it been available at that time (*Finance Act 2008, Sch 3, para 8*). Where all or part of a pre-6 April 2008 gain comes into charge following a chargeable event on or after 23 June 2010, entrepreneurs' relief (at the 10% rate) can be claimed under the *Finance Act 2008* transitional rules, if the relief conditions were satisfied when the gain arose. This revised form of relief applies if the first chargeable event since 6 April 2008 takes place from 23 June 2010.

For pre-6 April 2008 deferred gains coming into charge before 23 June 2010, chargeable gains on the subsequent disposal of the EIS shares (or other chargeable event) is net of entrepreneurs' relief (of 4/9ths). Any gain still remaining can be further reduced by losses and the CGT annual exemption, if available.

Various changes to the EIS legislation were introduced in *Finance (No 2) Act 2015*. One such change concerned how money raised by a share issue must be used. For shares issued from Royal Assent (18 November 2015), money used to acquire (directly or indirectly) a trade, goodwill or other intangible assets used for trade purposes does not amount to using that money for the purposes of a qualifying business activity (*ITA 2007, s 175(1ZA)*). This would appear to prevent existing trades being acquired upon incorporation, in the manner outlined above. However, it is understood that, whilst this restriction applies to EIS income tax relief, it was not intended to apply for CGT deferral relief purposes.

Seed EIS

2.57 The seed enterprise investment scheme (SEIS) was introduced (in *Finance Act 2012*) to encourage support in small, early stage companies (*ITA 2007, Pt 5A; TCGA 1992, s 150E, Sch 5BB*). The relief is available for shares issued on or after 6 April 2012 (*ITA 2007, s 257A*).

The SEIS offers qualifying investors the opportunity to claim income tax relief (worth 50% of the amount invested up to an annual maximum of £100,000) on subscriptions for shares in a qualifying company where certain conditions are satisfied.

For CGT purposes, there is an exemption for gains on shares within the scope of the SEIS. Reinvestment relief at 50% is also available on gains realised from disposals of assets (in 2013/14 and subsequent tax years) which are reinvested in the SEIS (*TCGA 1992, s 150G, Sch 5BB, para 1*). Reinvestment relief at 100% was available on gains realised in 2012/13 only (where the gains were reinvested through the SEIS in that or the following tax year).

However, it should be noted that SEIS involves a 'new qualifying trade' of an issuing company, which broadly means a genuine new venture, which has not been carried on within a defined two-year pre-investment period (*ITA 2007, s 257HF*).

In addition, HMRC can withdraw SEIS relief broadly if (*inter alia*) the company or a qualifying subsidiary carries on all or part of a trade previously carried on by another person during a specified period, or takes over assets during that period which were previously used by the investor (either alone or with other persons) in their trade where the person(s) had or has more than a half share in the trade (*ITA 2007, s 257FP(1)*).

Thus it seems that SEIS is aimed at encouraging genuinely new investment in companies by outside investors, and to ensuring that relief is not available to anyone who directly or indirectly owned the trade before it came to be owned by the company (VCM36100). The relief was not intended to apply for the purposes of incorporations.

Goodwill

2.58 Prior to changes restricting the availability of entrepreneurs' relief on the disposal of goodwill to a close company from 3 December 2014 (see **2.36**), the planning opportunity afforded by the business owner selling goodwill upon incorporation was relatively popular. The basic process of incorporation under *TCGA 1992, s 165* would be as follows:

- Sell some or all of the assets of the business, including goodwill, to the company either for full value or undervalue, leaving the proceeds outstanding on loan account.
- The first step is perceived to have created a capital gain, which may be reduced by entrepreneurs' relief and the annual exemption, if available. A sale at less than full market value could be considered in conjunction with a claim for holdover relief under *TCGA 1992, s 165*.
- Once the company starts to make profits, the proprietor can draw down on the loan account (representing the proceeds of sale of goodwill) without incurring further tax liabilities.

However, as indicated at **2.36**, claims for entrepreneurs' relief on disposals of goodwill to a close company (within *TCGA 1992, s 169LA*) are no longer possible, except in certain limited circumstances. The relevant restriction was aimed at countering perceived 'unfair' tax disadvantages on incorporation.

It should be noted that goodwill may still be the subject of a holdover claim under *TCGA 1992, s 165*, and that entrepreneurs' relief remains available on other relevant business assets comprised in the qualifying business disposal, such as trading premises. Goodwill may alternatively be sold upon incorporation at market value, albeit that any chargeable gain will be subject to normal CGT rates (10% and/or 20% for 2017/18).

2.59

> **Focus**
>
> Best practice for advisers who use the business sale route would be to follow the CG34 procedure and, shortly after the transaction takes place, seek agreement from HMRC on the valuations of the capital assets transferred to ensure that the CGT computations submitted are accurate so that the correct tax (if any) may be paid on the due date.
>
> Form CG34 ('Post-transaction valuation checks for capital gains') can be downloaded from HMRC's website: tinyurl.com/HMRC-CG34.

2.60 Some advisers may have experienced an unpleasant surprise following a goodwill sale, in the form of a letter from HMRC Shares and Assets Valuation. Typically, this will say that HMRC have sought guidance on the valuation of the goodwill transferred to the company, and in their view, this is little or nothing. What has been missed?

Nature of goodwill

2.61 What is goodwill? HMRC's Capital Gains Manual devotes a section to goodwill and intellectual property rights (see CG68000 and following). Readers who wish to steer clear (or at least be more aware) of potential conflicts with HMRC are advised to refer to that commentary.

The courts have tried to define goodwill, with varying success. Perhaps the leading commentary is that of Lord MacNaghten (in *IRC v Muller & Co's Margarine Ltd* [1901] AC 217, HL):

> 'What is goodwill? It is a thing very easy to describe, very difficult to define. It is the benefit and advantage of the good name, reputation and connection of a business. It is the attractive force which brings in custom. It is the one thing which distinguishes an old established business from a new business at its first start.'

HMRC's guidance on goodwill changed in September 2008. Previously, HMRC favoured a kind of zoological classification of goodwill, likening the behaviour of business customers to certain types of animal. Developing the theme there existed, in HMRC's view, three components to goodwill (ie personal, inherent and free) though they were not separable and, where the different types were present in one business, they became parts of an inseparable whole.

However, a Practice Note was issued by HMRC in January 2009 ('Apportioning the Price Paid for a Business Transferred as a Going Concern'), explaining that

HMRC and the Valuation Office Agency (VOA) consider that the price paid for a business as a going concern should be apportioned between goodwill and other assets included in the sale, and describing how this should be done. Referring to the various goodwill components (ie 'personal', 'inherent' and 'free' goodwill), HMRC state: 'These subdivisions are no longer considered helpful as they tend to cause confusion'.

In the context of business incorporations, HMRC state the following (CG68050):

> 'The incorporation of a business of a sole trader or a partnership is a common occurrence.
>
> If on the incorporation of a business the transferor has control of the company, the disposal of goodwill will be a transfer between connected persons within TCGA 92/S286(6).
>
> Where the transfer is between connected persons, any goodwill transferred to the company will be deemed to have been disposed of for a consideration equal to its market value in accordance with TCGA 92/S17 and TCGA 92/S18.
>
> If you are dealing with a transfer of goodwill between connected persons it is essential that you should establish by reference to the facts whether the transferee has, in fact, succeeded to the business as a going concern (as opposed to having acquired one or more of the business assets) before sending a request to SAV for a valuation of goodwill. You should not accept that there has been a disposal of goodwill unless there is factual evidence of a transfer of the business as a going concern.'

HMRC consider that, because goodwill is inseparable from the business from which it is derived, the disposal of a business as a going concern must involve the transfer of goodwill.

Goodwill and trade related property

2.62 In the case of businesses carried on from 'trade related property' (eg public houses, hotels, petrol stations, cinemas, restaurants, care homes etc), in their Practice Note (see **2.61**) HMRC appear to accept that there will be an element of goodwill in such businesses when sold as a going concern.

However, HMRC consider that the sale price will reflect the value of tangible assets and other assets such as goodwill, and that it is necessary to consider the contribution that each asset makes to the combined value. HMRC's approach appears to be to treat the difference between the purchase price of the business and values of the property, fixtures and fittings etc as being the value of the goodwill (and any other intangible business assets). Any goodwill etc will reflect the capitalised value of the excess of the estimated recurring profits of the actual business owner over those of what HMRC refer to as a hypothetical 'reasonably efficient operator'.

The broad implication of the Practice Note seems to be that goodwill valuations of businesses carried on from trade-related premises will generally be lower than for other types of businesses.

The Practice Note was expanded upon in September 2013, and includes a number of worked examples showing the approach of HMRC and the VOA in apportioning the proceeds on the sale of a business as a going concern, where the business was carried on from trade-related property (ie pubs and care homes). In each example, the HMRC/VOA approach results in a much lower goodwill valuation than had been claimed. The examples also outline the approach in calculating goodwill for the purposes of relief under the intangible fixed asset provisions. The current version of the Practice Note is available from the GOV.UK website (tinyurl.com/HMRC-PN-Price-TOGC).

Of course, the Practice Note is only a statement of HMRC's views regarding goodwill, and does not carry the force of law. The Royal Institution of Chartered Surveyors (RICS) rejected the approach described in the Practice Note. Discussions between HMRC, VOA and the Chartered Institute of Taxation (CIOT) subsequently took place with input from RICS and other professional bodies, but at the time of writing a consensus has still not been reached on a common approach.

In the meantime, the valuation of goodwill in trade-related properties should be treated with caution, and specialist valuation advice should be considered.

Personal goodwill

2.63

Focus

If any goodwill is attributable to the personal skills of the proprietor (eg a chef or hairdresser), in HMRC's view such personal goodwill is not transferable on a sale of the business (CG68010). This view has not changed, but unfortunately it presents a trap for the unwary.

Some commentators have indicated that HMRC have previously challenged the valuation of goodwill in professional practices in some cases, including whether there is any 'free' goodwill that is capable of being transferred.

However, in *Wildin v Revenue & Customs* [2014] UKFTT 459 (TC), the tribunal commented: 'the success of the firm was dependent on [the taxpayer's] own local contacts and work ethic.' There was no suggestion that this gave rise to personal goodwill (which cannot be transferred).

Advisers who have had goodwill valuations challenged by HMRC Shares and Assets Valuation possibly valued the goodwill by reference to the 'super profit' of the business.

Example 2.7 – Personal goodwill 'trap'

Mike is the chef and proprietor of a successful restaurant business, which incorporated on 1 May 2017. Last year, the gross profit was £200,000. The super profit might be established thus:

Gross profit	200,000
Less: Drawings (say)	(50,000)
Less: Interest on capital (say)	(20,000)
Super profit	£130,000

Goodwill valued at 1–2 times super profit (say £125,000–£250,000)

The problem? Most of the goodwill is personal (attaching to Mike and his reputed skills as a chef), or attaches to the location of his premises. Mike's adviser forgot this and merely included £200,000 (on a multiplier of 1½) as the goodwill proceeds upon the incorporation of the business.

The adviser is faced with explaining to Mike why HMRC will not agree the valuation.

Following the introduction of the restriction in the availability of entrepreneurs' relief on the disposal of goodwill to a close company (within *TCGA 1992, s 169LA*) from 3 December 2014 (see **2.58**), the above scenario involving a goodwill sale will probably be much less prevalent than before the restriction was introduced. However, it will still be a relevant issue in some cases, including for many business incorporations that took place before 3 December 2014 and which are subject to HMRC enquiry.

2.64 In the above example, could Mike's adviser have done anything better? As regards the personal goodwill, the answer is probably not. Mike does not want a service contract with the company. The advantage of taking dividends as opposed to salary has been explained to him and he wants to exploit this. In any case, it is questionable whether a service contract would make any difference. It merely gives the company an opportunity to exploit Mike's goodwill: it does not effect a transfer. HMRC guidance states (at CG68010):

> 'Any goodwill attributable to the personal skills of the proprietor, for example the personal skills of a chef or a hairdresser, will not be transferred to the new proprietor. Advice should be obtained from the CG Technical Group if it is claimed that the goodwill attributable to the personal skills of the proprietor have been transferred with the business because his/her services have been retained for the foreseeable future by means of an employment contract.'

As regards the goodwill attributable to the restaurant premises, the answer is 'perhaps'. Mike had various personal reasons for not placing this in the company. In the Practice Note to the 'Goodwill in Trade Related Properties Background Note' (tinyurl.com/HMRC-Goodwill-TRP-Note; see **2.62** above), HMRC express the view that, if a business such as a restaurant was transferred without 'some form of property interest', its value would be 'substantially diminished or removed'. It therefore seems likely that some measure of goodwill would be attributable to a lease, so Mike could have leased the premises to the company. This does not, however, transfer all of it.

2.65 HMRC seem to take the view that much of the goodwill attaching to any small business derives from the skills, abilities and other personal attributes of the proprietor. In other words, the transfer of goodwill might be a nice idea, but in many instances the scope to do it may be severely limited. You may have to face the fact that the personal goodwill must be left outside the company.

There is anecdotal evidence of HMRC challenging goodwill valuations for professional practices, particularly medical practitioners, on the basis that the goodwill of a professional is personal and therefore non-transferable. Care is therefore needed, and specialist advice in this area should be sought, if necessary.

2.66 In the above example, Mike's new company is paying him £200,000 and HMRC Shares and Assets Valuation maintain that the value of the free goodwill truly transferable is well below this. The majority of the goodwill remains outside the company. What then is the nature of the payment?

The capital gain will be calculated by reference to the market value of the goodwill as the parties are connected. How should the excess be handled? At this stage the company has not traded and, in the absence of any borrowings, has no funds. Its payment is therefore, to all intents and purposes, an IOU represented by a credit balance on a loan account.

HMRC's view, as stated in *Tax Bulletin,* Issue 76 (April 2005), is that the excess could fall to be treated in alternative ways, as follows:

- **Employment earnings** – HMRC have indicated that if goodwill was '... deliberately overvalued when it was sold to the company' the excess payment made by the company will be taxable as employment income (ie as earnings or, exceptionally, a benefit). The same applies to payments by the company for future services to be provided by the former business owner. Earnings will be subject to PAYE, and any benefit is reportable on form P11D. In either case, HMRC consider that the excess payment is liable to Class 1 National Insurance contributions.
- **Distribution** – It will normally be the case that goodwill is transferred before the company has commenced trading. HMRC consider that, in the majority of cases in which goodwill is transferred, any excess value will be received in the capacity of a shareholder, rather than an employee or director. A payment of excess value would therefore be treated by HMRC as a distribution (by reason of *CTA 2010, ss 1000(1)* or *1020(1)–(3)*).

HMRC's analysis of the tax treatment of payments for goodwill in *Tax Bulletin,* Issue 76 is based on the premise that the goodwill has been deliberately overvalued. HMRC appear to accept in the *Tax Bulletin* that goodwill valuations are not an exact science, and consider that distributions (within *CTA 2010, s 1020(1)–(3)*) can be 'inadvertent'. HMRC may therefore allow the transaction to be 'unwound' in those circumstances.

Focus

However, there are caveats to this let-out:

(1) 'Reasonable efforts' must be made to carry out the transaction at market value using a professional valuation (ie an 'independent and suitably qualified valuer on an appropriate basis').

(2) There can be no unwinding of intentional overvaluations.

(3) There must be no tax avoidance motive.

If a distribution is unwound, the shareholder must repay the excess value to the company. If the individual has already drawn down on the loan account then this repayment may give rise to an overdrawn loan account and a 'loan to a participator' under *CTA 2010, s 455*, leading to a tax charge on the company. There might also be an income tax charge on the individual under *ITEPA 2003, s 175*.

2.67 One could endeavour to ensure that the document of transfer includes an 'adjuster clause', which expresses the proceeds as being £x 'or such lesser amount as may be agreed with HMRC'. However, on enquiry this would seem likely to provoke a challenge, particularly if no serious attempt has been made to value the goodwill properly in the first instance.

Valuation of goodwill

2.68 The valuation of goodwill in businesses with non-trade related property is presently less controversial than for those businesses with trade-related property (see **2.62**). However, in both cases goodwill valuation is a specialist area. HMRC deal with such valuation issues through their Shares and Assets Valuation specialist office.

As mentioned, on incorporation it will be necessary to identify the value of non-personal goodwill which is readily transferable to the company. The usual method of valuation is by reference to the maintainable profits of the business. Allowance should be made for proprietor's remuneration, measured as the likely salary which an arm's length manager of the business might expect to be paid. Differential weighting might be applied over a period of time giving more significance to recent profits than the older ones.

In *Spring Capital Ltd v Revenue & Customs and Others* [2015] UKFTT 66 (TC), the First-tier Tribunal commented (albeit *obiter*) on whether, in valuing goodwill on its purported transfer by the proprietors of an unincorporated business to a company, a prudent purchaser would heavily discount the value of the business because there were no service contracts or non-competition clauses binding those individuals to the business, or whether it should be assumed (in the absence of such contracts or covenants) that the proprietors would remain with the company. The tribunal considered it reasonable to assume that the business should be valued on the latter basis. Whilst not creating any binding precedent, the tribunal's comments may be persuasive in appropriate cases, or at least act as a useful reminder of the complexities that can arise when valuing goodwill.

2.69 There is also the vexed question of an appropriate multiplier to use. Comparisons of quoted companies in similar fields of business are generally of little relevance. The business being transferred is non-corporate and probably quite small. The well-advised purchaser will assess the risk and, on an arm's-length basis, may make an offer well below what the business proprietor considers reasonable. However, this is the principle to be adopted and in many small trades a multiplier of only 1 or 2 is probably realistic.

In the context of businesses carried on from trade-related properties, as mentioned at **2.62** above, the Practice Note originally issued by HMRC in January 2009, and an expanded version of the Practice Note published in September 2013, set out how HMRC and the VOA consider the price paid for such a business as a going concern should be apportioned between goodwill and other assets. A particularly careful and prudent approach is required when valuing goodwill in those businesses.

2.70 Where the amounts involved are material, an independent expert valuation will be worth considering, particularly in view of HMRC's comments in *Tax Bulletin,* Issue 76. At a minimum, a record of the considerations taken in establishing the figure adopted should be maintained as a defence should there be an enquiry, which is likely to involve HMRC Shares and Assets Valuation.

HMRC guidance on the valuation of assets (tinyurl.com/HMRC-SAV-Goodwill) lists the types of information that should be provided to HMRC in support of goodwill valuations.

Intangible fixed assets

2.71 Historically, a major reform of the tax treatment of intangible fixed assets was introduced in *Finance Act 2002, Sch 29* (subsequently rewritten in *CTA 2009, Pt 8*). To take advantage, it is essential to operate through a corporate medium. Previously, intangible assets fell within the chargeable gains regime. The effect of the current provisions is to take specified intangible assets of companies out of that regime and into the normal trading rules.

In the context of business incorporations, the most common form of intangible asset is goodwill, although the rules also apply to 'intellectual property' as defined (in *CTA 2009, s 712(3)*). If the intangible fixed asset rules apply, the company may normally obtain a deduction for expenditure over a period of time, based on either generally accepted accounting principles, or by election on a fixed rate basis (*CTA 2009, s 726*), and receipts from disposal are treated as taxable.

However, HMRC may challenge tax relief claims for purchased intangible fixed assets if their value appears to be excessive, and there are anti-avoidance rules to prevent the perceived abuse of the intangibles rules.

Furthermore, changes introduced in *FA 2015* restrict corporation tax relief where a company acquires internally-generated goodwill and customer related intangible assets from a related party on the incorporation of the business generally in relation to transfers from 3 December 2014. However, those restrictions were largely superseded by further changes announced in *F(No 2) A 2015*, which (among other things) disallow corporation tax deductions for amortisation under the intangibles regime in respect of goodwill and certain other intangible assets linked to customers and customer relationships, with effect from 8 July 2015 (see **2.74** below).

2.72 As a general rule, the intangible fixed assets provisions broadly apply to assets of a company created on or after 1 April 2002, or where the company acquires such assets on or after that date from an unrelated party. The rules prohibit relief for expenditure on intangible fixed assets in respect of transactions between related parties, subject to certain exceptions (see **2.73**) (*CTA 2009, ss 835, 882*).

A 'related party' includes a participator in a close company (*CTA 2009, s 835(5)(a)*). Thus former sole traders or (say) partners in small partnerships will be related if they were already shareholders when the asset (eg goodwill) was acquired by the company (*Blenheims Estate and Asset Management Ltd v Revenue & Customs* [2013] UKFTT 290 (TC)), or became shareholders upon the goodwill transfer (*HSP Financial Planning v Revenue & Customs* [2011] UKFTT 106 (TC)).

For unincorporated businesses established before the intangible fixed assets rules were introduced (1 April 2002), it is therefore not possible to incorporate the business, have the company make a payment for intangible fixed assets acquired from the former sole trader or partnership and then write off the expenditure for tax purposes in the new company over time.

2.73 However, as indicated above, there are certain exceptions to the general rule prohibiting transfers between related parties from the intangible fixed assets regime, such as upon incorporation.

One such exception is where the related sole trader or partnership acquired the intangible fixed asset after 31 March 2002 from an unrelated third party (*CTA 2009, s 882(4)*).

A further, important exception from the related party prohibition of the intangibles provisions is where the unincorporated business (or any other person) created the asset after 31 March 2002 (*CTA 2009, s 882(5)*).

This exception has become increasingly significant with the passage of time. For example, more sole traders and partnerships which commenced trading from 1 April 2002 will have grown their businesses and enhanced the value of its intangible fixed assets.

Where intangible fixed assets are sold to the company upon incorporation on or after 1 April 2002 and one of the exceptions to the related party rules applies as outlined above, the company's acquisition will therefore normally be subject to the intangible fixed assets regime, rather than under the capital gains rules.

2.74 The availability of corporation tax relief for a company that acquires goodwill (and/or certain other types of 'relevant asset', such as unregistered trademarks) from related party individuals, including partnerships (eg upon incorporation) was restricted by measures introduced in *Finance Act 2015*.

The effect of those measures (in *CTA 2009, ss 849B-849D*) is broadly to restrict debits under the intangible fixed assets regime for internally-generated goodwill and other relevant assets acquired by a company from an individual who is a related party, or from a firm with an individual member who is a related party in relation to the company.

Where the goodwill includes previous third party acquisitions, a measure of deduction is available if certain conditions are met, ie the transferor must have acquired the relevant business (or part of it) in one or more 'third party acquisitions' (ie broadly from an unrelated party, where the acquisition did not have a main purpose of obtaining a tax advantage), and the company must have acquired that business or part from the transferor. The debit that would otherwise be taken into account under *CTA 2009, Pt 8, Ch 3* ('debits in respect of intangible fixed assets') is restricted by an 'appropriate multiplier' (nb the multiplier ensures that the company cannot claim relief for debits in an amount higher than the notional accounting value of the relevant asset acquired from the transferor).

Furthermore, on the subsequent realisation of the goodwill by the company, a debit (ie loss) that would otherwise be taken into account under *CTA 2009, Pt 8, Ch 4* ('realisation of intangible fixed assets') falls to be apportioned, ie between trading debits in respect of third party acquisitions, and non-trading debits in respect of other goodwill.

If no goodwill was acquired by third party acquisitions, the company is not allowed any debit under *CTA 2009, Pt 8, Ch 3* in respect of the acquisition of the goodwill (or other relevant asset). Any debit brought into account by the company on a subsequent realisation of the goodwill (under *Pt 8, Ch 4*), falls to be treated as a non-trading debit.

The above relief restrictions generally apply to transfers of goodwill etc from 3 December 2014 (unless made pursuant to an unconditional obligation entered into before that date). For company accounting periods straddling 3 December 2014, the accounting period is split and the restrictions apply to debits arising from that date.

However, as indicated at **2.71** above, the restrictions introduced in *Finance Act 2015* were largely superseded by further changes announced in *Finance (No 2) Act 2015*, with effect from 8 July 2015.

The effect of those changes is that no amortisation can be claimed by the company under the intangibles regime (under *CTA 2009, Pt 8, Ch 3*) in respect of a relevant asset. A 'relevant asset' includes goodwill, customer information and unregistered trademarks used in the business. In addition, any debit brought into account on the realisation of such assets (under *CTA 2009, Pt 8, Ch 4*) is treated as a non-trading debit (*CTA 2009, s 816A*).

The above changes introduced by *Finance (No 2) Act 2015* generally take effect for accounting periods beginning from 8 July 2015. Accounting periods straddling that date are treated as separate accounting periods for the purposes of apportioning debits. However, the changes do not apply to goodwill or other relevant assets acquired by a company before 8 July 2015, or under a contractual obligation that was unconditional before that date. Assets acquired between 3 December 2014 and 8 July 2015 where *CTA 2009, s 849B* applies therefore continue to be subject to the rules in *CTA 2009, ss 849C* and *849D* as outlined above.

The government's explanatory note to the changes states: 'This clause removes this relief with regard to the purchase of goodwill and other intangible assets closely related to goodwill. It will restrict the ability of companies to reduce their corporation tax profits following a merger or acquisition and removes this artificial incentive to buy assets rather than shares.' Whilst not specifically mentioned in the explanatory note, the above measures are also likely to make incorporation a less attractive proposition for some business owners from a tax perspective.

It should be noted that whilst the above restriction applies to goodwill and other relevant assets, corporation tax relief continues to be available for expenditure incurred on other types of intangibles falling within the intangible fixed assets regime in *CTA 2009, Pt 8*.

For further commentary on the intangible fixed assets regime generally, see *Corporation Tax 2017/18* (Bloomsbury Professional).

Stamp taxes

2.75 Stamp duty is not a tax levied on profits, income or gains. It is not even a tax on transactions. Stamp duty is charged on 'instruments', broadly defined as documents, transferring title to stock or marketable securities (principally shares and securities).

Goodwill ceased to be an asset liable to stamp duty in respect of instruments executed on or after 23 April 2002, and the transfer of debtors ceased to be liable to stamp duty from 1 December 2003.

Assets such as stock or plant and machinery are no longer chargeable to stamp duty. However, the transfer of 'fixtures', ie plant and machinery, which, in law, have become part of the land, is potentially chargeable to stamp duty land tax (or land and buildings transaction tax, if the land is situated in Scotland).

Stamp duty now only applies to instruments transferring stock and marketable securities, the issue of bearer instruments and transfers of interests in partnerships which hold stock and marketable securities. As regards bearer instruments, it should be noted that with effect from 26 May 2015 a UK incorporated company has been prohibited from issuing new bearer shares, and from 26 February 2016 all existing bearer shares issued by a UK incorporated company had to be converted into registered shares or cancelled (*Small Business, Employment and Enterprise Act 2015*). These changes are part of the UK government's promotion of corporate transparency as the ownership of unregistered shares can be hard to determine.

Stamp duty reserve tax is effectively an alternative to stamp duty. It relates to agreements to transfer chargeable securities (eg shares or loan capital), and is generally charged when no document of transfer is presented for stamping.

In the context of incorporation and small owner-managed or family companies, a stamp duty charge may be encountered in some cases, such as when relief is sought under *TCGA 1992, s 162*. However, there is no stamp duty on the issue of shares as such; only in the event that the business assets transferred include shares or securities will there be a stamp duty liability (at 0.5%) on the amount or value of the actual consideration given for the acquisition of the shares or securities. There is no market value rule for the purposes of stamp duty. It should be noted that there is an exemption (*FA 1986, s 79(4)*) for documents transferring certain categories of loan capital.

2.76 Stamp duty land tax (SDLT) applies to land transactions, ie broadly to the acquisition or enhancement of interests in UK land and buildings (*FA 2003, s 42*). It has no application to land outside the UK. From 1 April 2015, SDLT ceased to apply to land in Scotland, where it was replaced by land and buildings transaction tax (LBTT), administered by Revenue Scotland, the tax authority with responsibility for the taxes devolved to the Scottish Parliament, including LBTT.

The LBTT legislation borrows heavily from the SDLT regime and therefore in many situations the LBTT implications of a transaction may be the same, or similar, to the SDLT implications which would have arisen had the transaction been subject to SDLT. However, care must be taken as there are some fundamental differences between LBTT and SDLT. It is also possible that Revenue Scotland will take a different view of similar legislation compared to that taken by HMRC. There have been anecdotal instances where Revenue Scotland have, in fact, interpreted similar legislation differently to that of HMRC. Consequently, specific LBTT advice should normally be sought when dealing with a transaction over land in Scotland. For a detailed consideration of LBTT, see *Land and Buildings Transaction Tax 2017/18* (Bloomsbury Professional).

Note, in the commentary below, in relation to SDLT, the LBTT statutory references have been provided for the equivalent legislation.

SDLT and LBTT are in point regardless of whether or not the transactions are effected inside or outside the UK.

The chargeable consideration for a land transaction is defined in *FA 2003, Sch 4* (*LBTT(S)A 2013, Sch 2*). In most instances, it will be the consideration given in money or money's worth for the transaction.

However, if land and buildings are transferred to the company upon incorporation, invariably the parties will be connected with each other. If so, the land and buildings are deemed to pass at a chargeable consideration of not less than market value for SDLT purposes (*FA 2003, s 53*). The equivalent LBTT provision is *LBTT(S)A 2013, s 22*.

The rule for connection is found in *CTA 2010, s 1122*. Thus, for example, a controlling shareholder will be connected with the company. Whilst there may be some incorporation cases where the company has diverse shareholdings which will be outside the connection test in *CTA 2010, s 1122*, these are likely to be the exception rather than the rule.

Focus

However, upon the straightforward incorporation of a partnership of individuals, HMRC accept that the SDLT provisions for partnerships (*FA 2003, Sch 15, para 18*) effectively override the market value rule in *FA 2003, s 53* (SDLTM34160). In the Stamp Duty Land Tax manual, HMRC state (at SDLTM34170):

> 'Where the provisions of both *Finance Act 2003, s 53* and *para 18* apply to a transfer of a chargeable interest to a company, the provisions of *para 18* will take precedence to determine the chargeable consideration.'

The HMRC guidance at SDLTM34170 features an example, which indicates that the above SDLT provisions for partnerships will generally be more favorable than the market value rule in *FA 2003, s 53*, such as in circumstances involving the incorporation of a partnership.

As to the application of the SDLT provisions in relation to partnerships, see *Stamp Taxes 2017/18* (Bloomsbury Professional).

At the time of writing, it is not known whether Revenue Scotland take a similar view regarding the interaction of *LBTT(S)A 2013, Sch 17, paras 20, 21* (transfer of land from a partnership) and the market value rule in *LBTT(S)A 2013, s 22*. It is suggested that until this point is clarified in Revenue Scotland's technical guidance, the views of Revenue Scotland should be sought in relation to any transaction where this is an issue.

2.77 When a partnership acquires or disposes of a property from/to a partner or someone connected with a partner, special rules in *FA 2003, Sch 15* (or *LBTT(S)A 2013, Sch 17*) come into play to determine the amount of tax payable. When a property – possibly forming part of the assets of a business – is transferred from a partnership to a company or vice versa, if the company is owned by one or more of the partners or persons connected with them, actual consideration is irrelevant. The consideration for SDLT purposes (and also for LBTT purposes) is calculated using a formula which takes account of the market value of the property and the effective change in ultimate ownership. Where there is no change in ultimate ownership, and providing all of the partners are individuals, this can mean that the chargeable consideration for a transfer is zero.

However, the actual calculation can be complex, taking account of proportional partnership shares, other connections between the partners and whether the persons involved are individuals or companies. In relation to disposals of a property from a partnership to a partner or someone connected with a partner, it will also be important to consider relevant historic changes in partnership shares and whether SDLT (or stamp duty) or LBTT was paid on the acquisition of the property from a third party.

Detailed consideration of the various permutations is beyond the scope of this section. Specialist advice will generally be the best course of action.

If property is, for any reason, retained outside the company then rent may be paid. In many cases, this will be in respect of an informal licence without the need for a lease. A licence to use or occupy land is an exempt interest (*FA 2003, s 48(2)(b)*). For LBTT purposes, the grant, assignation or renunciation of a licence to occupy property (which is not a prescribed non-residential licence) is an exempt transaction (*LBTT(S)A 2013, Sch 1, para 3(1)(b)*).

However, care must be taken to distinguish a licence from a lease, as the distinction is important for SDLT purposes. The Stamp Duty Land Tax Manual states (at SDLTM00320):

> '[N]ote that a document which describes itself as a licence may in fact be a lease, especially if the practical consequence is that the grantee has exclusive occupation.'

This distinction is also important for LBTT purposes.

2.78 In the case of leasehold property, where an existing lease is transferred SDLT (and LBTT) is normally chargeable only on any actual consideration given by the transferee for the transfer. This is subject to the substitution of market value for consideration in the case of a transfer to a connected company (see **2.76**). No further SDLT or LBTT is normally chargeable in respect of rent payable under the lease, nor in respect of any premium previously paid on the original grant of the lease.

However, if the SDLT on original grant has not been finally determined when the lease is transferred (eg because the rent is variable and the transfer occurs during the first five years of the lease), the transferee inherits the ongoing obligations to finally determine the SDLT liability and pay any further tax due (*FA 2003, Sch 17A, para 12*).

If a new lease of commercial property is granted, SDLT is chargeable on both the premium payable, if any, and also on the rent payable (*FA 2003, Sch 5*).

In some circumstances the transfer of an existing lease is treated as the grant of a new lease and SDLT is charged accordingly. This happens when one of a range of reliefs (in *FA 2003, Sch 17A, para 11*) was claimed on the original grant of the lease, and the transfer is the first one since grant which does not qualify for one of the reliefs. The equivalent LBTT provision is *LBTT(S)A 2013,Sch 19, para 27.*

In relation to LBTT, the special rules for leases can be found in *LBTT(S)A 2013, Sch 19.* In principle, the manner of charging LBTT on the grant of a new lease will be similar to that under SDLT. Tax will be calculated separately on the rent and on any premium, and the two amounts added to give the initial tax charge for the grant of the lease. However, unlike SDLT, in calculating the LBTT liability on rent any known increase throughout the life of the lease will have to be taken into account in the initial assessment of the tax payable, apart from increases in line with the retail price index, consumer price index or similar index of inflation. But even then the position will not be finally determined.

In addition, assuming the grant of the lease was notifiable to Revenue Scotland, or became notifiable, the tenant (and any assignee) will be required to review the position every three years during the term of the lease, and again when the lease is assigned or terminates, to determine whether any further LBTT is payable. The aim of the legislation is to charge LBTT on the actual rent paid over the term of the lease. However, the requirement to file multiple returns may prove onerous for some tenants, particularly if they have a number of leased premises.

As to the application of the LBTT provisions in relation to commercial leases, see *Land and Buildings Transaction Tax 2017/18* (Bloomsbury Professional).

2.79 The rate at which SDLT is charged on consideration depends on the amount of the chargeable consideration, and whether the transaction is a residential property transaction or a non-residential property transaction. Historically, until 4 December 2014 the amount of the tax payable for both a residential property transaction and a non-residential property transaction was calculated using the so-called 'slab system'. Under that system, the rates were not progressive; rather, the whole consideration was chargeable at a single rate determined by the highest tax band into which the total chargeable consideration fell.

However, the tax payable in relation to a residential property transaction, with an 'effective date' on or after 4 December 2014, and in relation to a non-residential or mixed-use property transaction, with an 'effective date' on or after 17 March 2016, is now calculated using a 'progressive system' (like personal income tax). This means that it is only that part of the chargeable consideration falling within each tax band that is taxed at the rate for that tax band.

The rate at which LBTT is charged on chargeable consideration also depends upon the amount of the chargeable consideration, and whether the transaction is a residential property transaction or a non-residential property transaction. Like SDLT, the tax rates are applied on a progressive basis similar to income tax.

A 15% slab rate of SDLT (meaning that the whole of the consideration given for the dwelling is charged at a single rate of 15%) may apply to acquisitions of residential properties, for a consideration of over £500,000, purchased by companies and other 'non-natural persons' (see **2.99**).

With effect from 1 April 2016, higher rates of both SDLT and LBTT were introduced for purchases of additional dwellings by individuals and dwellings acquired by companies (whether it is the first such purchase or not). See **2.99** for further commentary.

The rates and bands applicable for both SDLT and LBTT are available on the GOV.UK (www.gov.uk/stamp-duty-land-tax) and Revenue Scotland (www.revenue.scot/land-buildings-transaction-tax/guidance/calculating-tax-rates-and-bands) websites respectively.

Inheritance tax

2.80 Incorporation is a commercial transaction. There should be no gratuitous intent to it. In theory, therefore, there is no charge to IHT, or it should be excluded by *IHTA 1984, s 10* ('Dispositions not intended to confer gratuitous benefit').

Where there is a gratuitous reduction in an individual's estate, most lifetime transfers are potentially exempt transfers (PETs). However, a transfer of value to a company does not constitute a PET (within *IHTA 1984, s 3A(1)(c), (1A)(c)(i)*), and is therefore an immediately chargeable transfer.

In addition, note that if a close company makes a transfer of value and this is apportioned to the participators, this is not a PET and IHT is immediately chargeable (*IHTA 1984, s 94*).

Whilst the interests of the shareholders in the newly formed company will, in most instances, be identical to the interests of the proprietors in the unincorporated business, this is not exclusively the case. To the extent that anyone other than the original business proprietor or spouse takes shares (eg adult children), a potential problem as indicated above is that the transfer of value made in such circumstances is not a PET. It is a chargeable transfer. The recipient of the gift is a company, not an individual, even though the effect of it is to increase the estates of the children. HRMC considers that this is the correct interpretation of *IHTA 1984, s 3A(2)* (see HMRC's Inheritance Tax Manual at IHTM04060, Example 2).

In most instances, the transfer of value in such circumstances will be relatively small. However, the proprietor needs to be aware of the erosion of his IHT nil rate band.

Business property relief

2.81 A separate chapter of this book deals with business property relief (BPR) (see **Chapter 12**). Every business proprietor must be aware of this relief and the impact that incorporation might have on it. For example, the rate could be halved in some cases, and the assets encompassed by it restricted.

2.82 Provided that the business of the sole trader is not excluded by the investment activity test in *IHTA 1984, s 105(3)*, the whole of the value should qualify for BPR in the event of death or a chargeable transfer for IHT purposes, unless there are any 'excepted assets' as defined in *IHTA 1984, s 112*.

As regards the business itself, a partner is in broadly the same position as a sole trader. 100% BPR should be available to a sole trader or partner in respect of a chargeable transfer of the business interest. As *IHTA 1984, s 105(1)(a)* refers only to an interest in a business, the extent of participation is irrelevant. Thus, a partner with (say) a 5% share in a business can obtain exactly the same relief pro-rata to value as a partner with a 90% share.

There is no relief for an asset held outside the partnership, unless the partnership interest itself is relevant business property (*IHTA 1984, s 105(6)*). Again, there is no minimum participation limit in the partnership. So a partner can get BPR in respect of property let to a partnership of which he is only a small minority partner. The rate of relief is 50% (*IHTA 1984, s 104(1)(b)*).

However, note that the loan account of a retired partner does not qualify for BPR (*Beckman v IRC* [2000] STC (SCD) 59).

2.83 Shares in unquoted trading companies generally qualify for BPR when there is a chargeable transfer for IHT purposes. BPR is available both to working and passive shareholders. It is not necessary for the shareholder to be a director of the company. There is no minimum size of holding, nor any specification as to the type of share, although there is a minimum ownership period for BPR purposes (see **2.86**). The rate of relief is 100% (*IHTA 1984, s 104(1)(a)*).

However, if business property is subject to a binding contract for sale at the time of a chargeable transfer, then BPR is not available (*IHTA 1984, s 113*). Beware company articles or shareholder agreements that impose 'buy and sell' arrangements on the members of the company. This pitfall is covered in greater detail in **Chapter 12**.

BPR is not denied by *IHTA 1984, s 113* if the reason for the binding contract is the incorporation of a sole trader or partnership in which the sale proceeds are wholly or mainly shares or securities in the company (*IHTA 1984, s 113(a)*). Note that there is no exception from *IHTA 1984, s 113* in the case of a cash sale of the business upon incorporation.

2.84 As with a partnership, a business proprietor who becomes a shareholder may decide to retain property outside the company. The property may qualify for BPR if it is used for the purposes of a business carried on by the company, the shares held are themselves relevant business property, and the transferor controlled the company (*IHTA 1984, s 105(1)(d), (6)*). However, the rate of relief is only 50% (*IHTA 1984, s 104(1)(b)*).

Thus for assets used but not retained within the business vehicle, the situation may worsen. A sole trader would get 100% BPR if the asset comprised part of the business, but a shareholder gets 50% relief, and only if he controls the company.

2.85

> **Focus**
>
> A simple loan to a company does not qualify for BPR. Whilst the incorporation transactions may lead to a positive balance on a director's loan account, this should not be left in place indefinitely. It gives a means of

drawing cash from the company without further tax charge but, if it is still in place when the shareholder dies or wishes to make a chargeable transfer of shares, the value is excluded from BPR.

The solution may be, if the funds are required in the company and IHT is a concern, to capitalise the loan for more shares. The freedom to draw down is then, of course, lost. A loan will sometimes be capitalised for more shares if the shareholder's life expectancy is possibly less than the normal two-year ownership requirement for BPR purposes, on the basis that the new shares may be identified with other shares in the company which have been held for at least two years.

For holdings of unquoted shares which would (under the capital gains tax rules in *TCGA 1992, ss 126–136*) be identified with other qualifying shares previously owned, for BPR purposes their period of ownership may be treated as including the ownership period of the original shares (*IHTA 1984, s 107(4)*).

However, as illustrated in *Executors of Dugan-Chapman (deceased) v Revenue and Customs Comrs* [2008] SpC 666, it is important that the documentation and implementation is complete and correct, and that the circumstances are suitable (see **12.10**).

2.86 The availability of BPR normally depends on the holding of a certain type of business asset for a minimum period of two years (*IHTA 1984, s 106*). This does not necessarily mean that the same relevant business property must be held throughout. The two-year minimum holding period need not be satisfied by the same relevant business property. It is possible to carry forward the qualifying conditions into replacement property. So, where one item of qualifying business property is replaced by another, the conditions for BPR can remain satisfied. There may even be a gap in ownership. The two-year minimum holding period is satisfied if both assets are held for a total of two years within five years before the transfer of value (*IHTA 1984, s 107(1)*).

The BPR available in respect of replacement property is generally restricted to what it would have been had the replacement(s) not been made. However, this general rule is subject to certain exceptions, one of which is the incorporation of a business, whereby the company is controlled by the former business owner(s) (*IHTA 1984, s 107(3)*).

Incorporation will generally involve a switch from a business held personally (qualifying under *IHTA 1984, s 105(1)(a)*) to shares in a trading company (qualifying under *IHTA 1984, s 105(1)(bb)*). All other conditions being satisfied, one replaces the other and the availability of BPR continues throughout. There is no need to establish a new minimum holding period for the shares.

However, as mentioned, an incorporation involving a business sale (as opposed to an exchange of the business for shares) would not attract BPR to the extent of the sale proceeds. There is also a possibility that HMRC could argue that a company set up in advance of the incorporation has not 'replaced' the unincorporated business in a strict sense, and that the shares are therefore not 'relevant business property'. Such an interpretation would appear harsh, but cannot be completely ruled out.

Agricultural property relief

2.87 A separate chapter of this book includes commentary on agricultural property relief (APR) (see **Chapter 12**). However, in broad terms APR is available in respect of the agricultural value of agricultural property, being the value which it would have if it were to be used perpetually for agriculture.

Much agricultural property will also satisfy the conditions for BPR. Where, on the face of it, both reliefs are available, APR takes precedence (*IHTA 1984, s 114(1)*). However, this does not necessarily prevent a claim for BPR on the excess over the agricultural value.

2.88 If, on incorporation, the land is placed within the company then the business proprietor ceases to own it. Rather, he has shares in the new company, the value of which reflects the value of the land held therein. These shares are clearly not agricultural property in themselves, but their value will reflect the underlying agricultural property. If that is the case, APR may be available on the share value to the extent that that value is attributable to the underlying agricultural land, providing that the shares give the transferor control of the company (*IHTA 1984, s 122(1)*).

The company must also satisfy certain conditions as to the occupation and ownership of the land. In addition, the shareholder must have owned the shares for whichever of the (two-year or seven-year) minimum periods is appropriate to the company, subject to provisions which preserve the relief where the shares replaced other eligible property during the relevant period (*IHTA 1984, s 123*).

Assuming that this will be a trading company, it is more than likely that BPR will be available in respect of the shares as well. This will relieve the excess value of the shares over the agricultural value of the land holding. If the control test is not satisfied, then BPR should be available on the whole value. Loss of APR should therefore be no real disaster.

If the agricultural land is held outside the company, on a new incorporation it is perhaps best to ensure that a formal tenancy is put in place. This would satisfy the conditions of *IHTA 1984, s 116(2)(c)* and, all other things being equal, 100% APR is maintained.

Value added tax

2.89 Most businesses will be registered for VAT. The disposal of the assets of a business is to be treated as a supply made in the course or furtherance of that business. Accordingly, VAT will be chargeable on the sale of such items as stock, plant and machinery, fixtures and fittings (*VATA 1994, Sch 4, para 5*). HMRC also regard a sale of goodwill as a taxable supply (C&E Press Notice No790, 10 December 1982).

However, the general rule is that no taxable supply is made and no VAT should be charged where the assets of a business are transferred to another person (eg a successor company) in connection with the transfer of all or part of the business as a going concern.

Therefore, the transfer of a business as a going concern is neither a supply of goods nor a supply of services for VAT purposes (*VAT (Special Provisions) Order 1995, SI 1995/1268, art 5*). This applies where the assets are to be used by the transferee in carrying on the same kind of business as that carried on by the transferor; and where the transferee is a taxable person, or immediately becomes one as a result of the transfer. If only part of the business is transferred as a going concern, the same rule applies where that part is capable of separate operation. The transfer of a going concern (TOGC) rule is mandatory provided all the statutory conditions are satisfied.

In the case of property rental businesses, HMRC accept (following *Robinson Family Ltd v Revenue & Customs* [2012] UKFTT 360 (TC)) that if the transferor of the business retains a small reversionary interest in the property transferred, this does not prevent the transaction from being treated as a TOGC for VAT purposes. Provided the interest retained is small enough not to disturb the substance of the transaction (no more than 1% of the pre-transfer value), the transaction will be a TOGC if the usual conditions are satisfied (Revenue & Customs Brief 30/12).

2.90 There is an exception to the TOGC rules. This is where the assets being transferred include land and buildings which are potentially taxable, ie on which the transferor has exercised the option to tax, or there is a sale of the freehold of a new or incomplete building liable to VAT at the standard rate, and the successor company has not notified HMRC of an election to waive exemption in respect of the property concerned and/or has not notified the vendor that its option to tax of the land and property concerned will not be disapplied (*SI 1995/1268, arts 5(2), (2A)*). The transferor must then charge standard rate VAT in respect of the supply of the property.

2.91 When the ownership of a business is transferred to a different legal entity it is possible for the transferee to take over the transferor's original VAT registration number. This treatment is broadly available if registration of the original business is cancelled from the date of the transfer, and the new business is not already registered, but is liable or entitled to be registered (*VAT Regulations 1995, SI 1995/2518, reg 6(1)*). The process is effected by completion of form VAT 68, which is available via the GOV.UK website (www.gov.uk/government/publications/vat-request-for-transfer-of-a-registration-number-vat68).

However, it should be noted that transferring a VAT registration number from one business to another transfers the responsibility for any debits and credits both before and after the transfer to the new owner. The decision to transfer a VAT number must be taken in the light of any adverse history or potential liability which may be assumed by the company.

2.92 Alternatively, if it is decided to break the link with the old business, the company may apply for fresh VAT registration. The former business proprietor must deregister immediately after the transfer (unless only part of the business has been transferred and thus the former business owner will continue to trade in some capacity). It is not necessary for the transfer of all the assets of a business to take place for it to be a TOGC. However, what is transferred should be sufficient to enable continued operation of the same business as was carried on by the transferor.

2.93

Focus

It is crucial for all businesses to establish whether or not there is a TOGC. There is no safe option – if VAT is charged on a transaction which turns out to be a TOGC, both parties will have misstated their VAT liabilities, where potentially HMRC can both require the vendor to account for the amount he has incorrectly treated as output tax and deny input tax recovery to the purchaser.

Conversely, if VAT is not charged, but HMRC decide there is no TOGC, the transferor will have a VAT liability which may be impossible to recover from the transferee.

For HMRC's internal guidance, see 'VAT Transfer of a going concern' manual (www.gov.uk/hmrc-internal-manuals/vat-transfer-of-a-going-concern).

For further commentary on the VAT issues surrounding the transfer of a business as a going concern, see *Value Added Tax 2017/18* (Bloomsbury Professional).

Investment businesses

2.94 Very often, the nature of an investment business will be the letting of property. Whilst for income tax purposes the receipt of rents from property is treated as a 'property business' (*ITTOIA 2005, ss 264, 265*), the real problem with the tax legislation is that there is no satisfactory definition of a 'business'.

There is abundant case law on activities in the nature of a trade, but very little on activities in the nature of a business. It is clear that a business is rather wider than (but includes) a trade, as well as a profession or vocation. Active management is a characteristic of a business, as is profit motive.

2.95 In any case, would one want to incorporate such an activity? For example, for IHT purposes no BPR would be available in respect of shares in the company. In addition, whilst the commercial letting of holiday accommodation may constitute a business, the business carried on may be mainly that of holding an investment, on which no BPR is due (eg *HMRC v Personal representatives of N Pawson, deceased* [2013] UKUT 050 (TCC)). The same may apply in respect of serviced office accommodation (*The Trustees of David Zetland Settlement v Revenue & Customs* [2013] UKFTT 284 (TC)), or a managed business centre (*Best v Revenue & Customs* [2014] UKFTT 77 (TC)).

Business owners may also perceive that there is a potential double tax charge by operating in corporate form. The company pays tax on its gain; the shareholder pays tax on extraction of the profit.

An unincorporated property letting business will derive gross rents against which may be set various expenses to arrive at a net property business profit. An individual receiving this will be chargeable to income tax at his highest marginal rate as it arises. Getting the profits into a company has the obvious attraction of the ability to withdraw profits by way of dividend rather than salary, just as with a trading company.

2.96 As indicated earlier in this chapter, there are two traditional routes of relieving the capital gains arising on incorporation of a business. These use either the general relief for gifts of business assets in *TCGA 1992, s 165*, or the specific incorporation relief in *TCGA 1992, s 162*.

A claim under *TCGA 1992, s 165* is generally a non-starter. This permits the holdover of a capital gain where an asset is transferred at undervalue and the asset is used for the purposes of a trade, profession or vocation. Whatever property letting may be, it is not a trade (although hotels are generally treated as such), or a profession or vocation. However, see **2.98** below as to the special treatment afforded to furnished holiday lettings.

2.97 By contrast, *TCGA 1992, s 162* provides a mandatory rollover of the gain where a person who is not a company transfers to a company a business as a going concern, together with the whole assets of the business. This must take us back to the question 'what is a business?' As already noted, there is no definition in *TCGA 1992*.

In *Ramsay v HMRC* [2013] UKUT 226 (TCC) (see **2.42**), the taxpayer was the landlord of a large Victorian property which had been converted into ten flats, of which five were occupied by tenants at the relevant time. The taxpayer (and her husband) transferred the property to a company, in exchange for shares in the company. Her tax return for the year of transfer included a claim for incorporation relief under *TCGA 1992, s 162*. Following an enquiry, HMRC issued a closure notice on the basis that *TCGA 1992, s 162* relief did not apply. The taxpayer appealed.

The First-tier Tribunal held that the taxpayer's activities were 'normal and incidental to the owning of an investment property', and dismissed her appeal. However, the Upper Tribunal allowed Mrs Ramsay's subsequent appeal, concluding that the activity undertaken in respect of the property overall was sufficient in nature and extent to amount to a business for *TCGA 1992, s 162* purposes. Whilst the activities could equally have been undertaken by a property investor, where the degree of activity outweighs what might normally be expected to be carried out by a mere passive investor, the tribunal held that this would amount to a business.

HMRC's Capital Gains Manual (at CG65715) tries to extract a meaning from case law. The guidance (rather unhelpfully) states that it is a question of fact whether a particular activity constitutes a business, and that it is not easy to draw the line. Following the *Ramsay* case (in which Mrs Ramsay was found to have worked in the property business for about 20 hours per week), HMRC's guidance instructs their officers as follows: 'You should accept that incorporation relief will be available where an individual spends 20 hours or more a week personally undertaking the sort of activities that are indicative of a business. Other cases should be considered carefully'.

Interestingly, it has been held for VAT purposes that the letting of property can amount to a business activity (see *D A Walker v Customs and Excise Commissioners* [1976] VATTR 10, and *G W and J A Green v Customs and Excise Commissioners* (1992, Decision 9016)). In the former case, the letting of three semi-detached houses on assured tenancies was considered to be a business in VAT terms.

In addition, the Upper Tribunal in the *Ramsay* case (see above) referred to various factors identified in another VAT case, *Customs and Excise Commissioners v Lord Fisher* [1981] STC 238, and considered that those factors are of general application to the question whether the circumstances describe a business:

1. whether the activity is a 'serious undertaking earnestly pursued';
2. whether the activity is an 'occupation or function actively pursued with a reasonable or recognisable continuity';
3. whether the activity has 'a certain measure of substance as measured by the quarterly or annual value of taxable supplies made';

4 whether the activity was 'conducted in a regular manner and on sound and recognised business principles';

5 whether the activity is 'predominantly concerned with the making of taxable supplies to consumers for a consideration'; and

6 whether the taxable supplies are 'of a kind which … are commonly made by those who seek to profit by them'.

2.98 Incorporation relief in *TCGA 1992, s 162* not only requires a transfer of the business, but of the business 'as a going concern'. The term 'going concern' predicates something more than transfer of a mere collection of assets. There must be an active infrastructure to go with it. On that basis, it seems unlikely in many cases that a property letting business could be transferred to a company with the benefit of *TCGA 1992, s 162* relief. However, some commentators have adopted a more optimistic view that active property letting is arguably a business activity (see, for example, Malcolm Gunn's article 'It's my business' in *Taxation*, 8 November 2007).

A cautious approach is advocated. If incorporation was successfully challenged by HMRC on enquiry, a very large unrelieved gain could ensue with no cash to meet the liability. This uncertainty will clearly be unsatisfactory for those taxpayers seeking to rely on incorporation relief under *TCGA 1992, s 162*. This has resulted in some taxpayers (or their advisers) seeking advance assurance from HMRC under the non-statutory business clearance service that their undertaking amounts to a business for these purposes (and is therefore capable of being transferred as a going concern).

There is no statutory clearance on the availability of *TCGA 1992, s 162* relief. A non-statutory business clearance application to HMRC could be considered (see www.gov.uk/guidance/non-statutory-clearance-service-guidance) in advance of the incorporation taking place. HMRC provide a checklist of information ('Annex A') to be included in the clearance application. However, there is anecdotal evidence that HMRC have been unwilling to provide such clearances in some instances where they consider that the incorporation is being undertaken for tax planning reasons.

Where properties meet the conditions to be treated as furnished holiday lettings, they are automatically deemed to be a trade for certain tax purposes. In particular, in the current context, *TCGA 1992, ss 241(3A)* and *241A(5)* treat the furnished holiday letting business as a trade for the purposes of *TCGA 1992, s 165*. Therefore, it is possible to transfer a property used for furnished holiday letting at undervalue (to a company) and hold over any capital gain arising by making a claim under *TCGA 1992, s 165*. In other words, it is possible to incorporate a property-letting business which consists entirely of furnished holiday lettings without triggering a taxable capital gain.

However, it should be borne in mind that a furnished holiday letting is unlikely to qualify for BPR for IHT purposes (see **2.95**), unless the level of services offered is exceptionally high.

2.99 One should also bear in mind the impact of SDLT. Where land and buildings are transferred to a company which is connected (*Corporation Tax Act 2010, s 1122*) with the transferor, SDLT (or LBTT)is normally charged by reference to market value (*Finance Act 2003, s 53* or *LBTT(S)A 2013, s 22*) (see **2.76**).

A higher rate of SDLT was introduced in *Finance Act 2016* for additional dwellings and dwellings purchased by companies, generally with effect from 1 April 2016 (*FA 2003, Sch 4ZA*). Consequently, the SDLT rates applying to higher rate transactions are 3% higher than the equivalent normal residential rates, subject to certain exceptions including purchases for consideration less than £40,000.

When several properties are transferred in a single transaction (or a series of linked transactions), it is normally necessary to aggregate the consideration for all to determine the SDLT rate, which then applies to all of the transfers (*FA 2003, s 55(4)*). However, where more than one dwelling is transferred in this way, the purchaser(s) may claim for the rate to be determined on the basis of the average consideration per property (ie a claim for 'multiple dwellings relief' – *FA 2003, Sch 6B*). It is not possible for the rate to drop below 1% if the claim is made (*FA 2003, Sch 6B, para 5(2)*). Note that, where a claim to multiple dwellings relief is made, the higher rates of SDLT apply in calculating the SDLT payable if the relevant transaction is a 'higher rates transaction' (*FA 2003, Sch 6B, para 5(6A)*). Any dwellings for which the 15% SDLT 'slab' rate applies (see below) are excluded (*FA 2003, Sch 6B, para 2(4)(aa)*). It should also be noted that, in the absence of a claim for multiple dwellings relief, where six or more dwellings are the subject of a single transaction, they are treated as wholly non-residential property (*FA 2003, s 116(7)*), so that the SDLT rates for non-residential property apply to the transaction.

The 15% 'slab' rate (ie meaning that the whole of the consideration given for the dwelling is charged at a single rate of 15%) of SDLT initially applied to residential properties over £2m purchased by companies and other 'non-natural persons' (NNPs) with effect from 21 March 2012 (*FA 2003, Sch 4A*). However, the threshold for the 15% SDLT rate was subsequently reduced in *FA 2014* to £500,000 for land transactions with an effective date on or after 20 March 2014, subject to transitional rules. There are, however, certain exemptions from the 15% slab rate, including acquisitions by property developers or dwellings acquired for the purposes of a property rental business (*FA 2003, Sch 4A, para 5(1)(a)* and *(b)*) or for a business using the dwelling in the course of a trading activity (*FA 2003, Sch 4A, para 5(1)(ab)*), and so on.

In Scotland, a higher rate of LBTT applies for purchases of additional residential properties, similar to its SDLT equivalent. The 'additional dwelling supplement' applies to individuals acquiring dwellings as second homes etc or as part of a business of investing or dealing in land (either conducting the business as a sole trader or as a partner in a partnership), and first purchases of residential properties (for £40,000 or more) by companies and certain trusts. The additional LBTT is 3% of the relevant consideration. The legislation can be found at *LBTT(S)A 2013, Sch 2A* ('Additional amount: transactions relating to second homes etc'). There are some important differences between the SDLT and LBTT higher rate regimes, which are beyond the scope of this chapter. For detailed commentary on this subject, readers are referred to *Stamp Taxes 2017/18* and *Land and Business Transaction Tax 2017/18* (both Bloomsbury Professional). Under LBTT, there is no equivalent of the SDLT 15% slab rate which applies to residential properties acquired for consideration of over £500,000 purchased by companies and other NNPs.

In addition, legislation in *FA 2013* introduced an 'annual tax on enveloped dwellings' (ATED) worth more than £2m, which are owned by NNPs (ie companies, partnerships with company members and collective investment schemes), subject to a limited range of reliefs (eg for property rental businesses, property developers, etc) (*FA 2013, Pt 3*). The ATED applies in relation to properties under the ownership of the NNP on or after 1 April 2013. The threshold of £2m was progressively reduced to £500,000 in *FA 2014*. From 1 April 2015, an annual charge of £7,000 applied for properties within a band with a value greater than £1m but not more than £2m. From 1 April 2016, an annual charge of £3,500 applied to properties within an additional band with a value greater than £500,000 but not more than £1m. Further changes introduced in *FA 2015* increased the annual ATED charges for properties valued at more than £2m, over and above the normal consumer prices index increase (eg an ATED charge of £23,350 applied for properties valued at more than £2m but not more than £5m). These increased charges applied with effect from the chargeable period beginning on 1 April 2015. It is specifically provided that the ATED charge will be increased each year in line with increases in the Consumer Price Index to the previous September, rounded down to the next £50 (*FA 2013, s 101*). The rates for the year commencing on 1 April 2017 are as follows:

Value	Tax
More than £500,000 but not more than £1 million	£3,500
More than £1 million but not more than £2 million	£7,050
More than £2 million but not more than £5 million	£23,550
More than £5 million but not more than £10 million	£54,950
More than £10 million but not more than £20 million	£110,100
More than £20 million	£220,350

Furthermore, *FA 2013* extended the capital gains tax (CGT) regime to gains on disposals by NNPs of UK residential property or interests in such property from 6 April 2013, where the consideration exceeds £2m (reduced proportionately if the NNP owns or disposes of only part of the property). The charge applies to both resident and non-resident NNPs, and affects those companies or collective schemes within the scope of the ATED (see above). A CGT charge of 28% is imposed. However, gains accruing before 6 April 2013 remain outside the scope of the CGT charge. The ATED-related CGT charge was extended from 6 April 2015 for properties worth more than £1m but not more than £2m, and further extended from 6 April 2016 for properties worth more than £500,000 and not more than £1m.

Further provisions introduced in *Finance Act 2015* extended the scope of CGT to include gains on the disposal of UK residential property interests by non-UK resident persons (or by individuals in the overseas part of a split year) from 6 April 2015. A restriction in private residence relief was also introduced in *Finance Act 2015* for properties located in a territory in which the individual is not tax resident, broadly where the person does not meet a 90-day test for time spent in the property over the year (*TCGA 1992, s 222C*).

2.100 Historically, care was needed to ensure that a company wholly or mainly in receipt of property rental income was not a close investment holding company (CIHC), which was subject to corporation tax at the main rate (although this would not be the case if, for example, all the properties were let to unconnected third parties).

However, the introduction of a single corporation tax rate and abolition of the small profits rate for companies that do not have ring fence profits (from 1 April 2015) have meant that there is no longer a disadvantage to a company being a CIHC in terms of corporation tax rates.

It should be noted that a disadvantage arising from CIHC status applies to an investor who borrows to buy shares in, or lend money to, a close company. While relief on the loan interest would normally be due for the shareholder (under *ITA 2007, s 392*), relief is denied where the close company in question is a CIHC. Whilst the CIHC rules were repealed from financial year 2015, *ITA 2007, s 393A* (which applies to interest paid from 2014/15) restricts the availability of income tax relief for payments of interest on loans to invest in, or lend to, close companies which are CIHCs.

Entrepreneurs' relief and property

2.101 Entrepreneurs' relief is generally not available on disposals of residential property. However, as indicated at **2.98** above, an exception to this general rule applies in respect of commercial furnished holiday lettings in the UK (*TCGA 1992, s 241(3A)*) or elsewhere in the EEA (*TCGA 1992, s 241A(5)*).

The disposal of a commercial property does not of itself qualify for entrepreneurs' relief. However, relief may be available if there is a disposal of the whole or part of a trading business including the premises.

In addition, a measure of relief may apply if the property disposal is 'associated' (within *TCGA 1992, s 169K*) with a disposal of the partnership interest, or a disposal of shares in the company, if certain conditions are satisfied (eg the disposal is associated with a material disposal of the whole or part of the partnership interest or all or some of the company's ordinary shares or securities, it is part of the individual's withdrawal from participation in the business, the property disposed of was used for business purposes throughout a one-year period ending with the material disposal (or cessation of the business, if earlier), and the disposal is of a property owned by the individual throughout the three-year period ending with the date of disposal).

However, it should be noted that entrepreneurs' relief is denied if a market rent is charged for the property, and is subject to restriction (on a 'just and reasonable' basis) if the rent charged is below market value (*TCGA 1992, s 169P*). The entrepreneurs' relief legislation as originally drafted also provided for the restriction or denial of relief if rent had been charged for periods before the relief was introduced. However, this provision was considered by many to be unduly harsh, and a transitional rule was therefore included so that periods prior to 6 April 2008 can be ignored for these purposes (*FA 2008, Sch 3, para 6*).

Employment-related securities

2.102 There is a requirement (in *ITEPA 2003, ss 421J* and *421K(3)(a)*) to notify HMRC when shares in a company are issued to employees (including past or future employees). The relevant return (ie HMRC's 'other' template, previously form 42) must be made to HMRC by 6 July following the relevant tax year.

HMRC guidance states that no report is required where a company is incorporated and all founder shares are acquired at nominal value (NB the other requirements are that no form of security is required; the shares are not acquired by reason of, or in connection with, another employment; and the shares are acquired by a director or prospective director of the company or someone who has a personal family relationship with the director, and the right or opportunity is made available in the normal course of the domestic, family or personal relationship of that person).

Furthermore, no report is required if further shares are allotted after a new company is incorporated, but before the commencement of business or transfer of assets to the company (ie broadly, where those shares are acquired by a founder shareholder or the person is a director or prospective director of the company, and the shares are acquired at nominal value and are not acquired by reason of, or in connection with, another employment).

However, if further shares are allotted after the company has commenced business, HMRC's view is that a return is required, albeit only in respect of those additional shares (see Example 3 at ERSM140040).

HMRC's requirement that the company's shares are acquired at nominal value effectively means that incorporations under *TCGA 1992, s 162* (ie under which the assets of the unincorporated business are transferred to the company wholly or partly in exchange for shares) will require a return to be made to HMRC.

An end of year return template, technical note and guidance notes can be accessed via the GOV.UK website (tinyurl.com/ERS-Template).

DISINCORPORATION

Background

2.103 While there can be clear benefits from operating through a company, and a company may at some stage have been chosen as the optimum operating vehicle for a business, there will be circumstances in which some businesses might benefit from 'disincorporating' and operating through a sole trader or partnership structure instead.

This decision might be prompted by some of the drawbacks of trading through a company, including substantial company car tax liabilities for the business owner (as a director or employee), operating PAYE on their 'drawings' (in the form of salaries and bonuses), additional accountancy fees, *Companies Act* compliance and reporting, etc.

And many businesses which incorporated to take account of the 0%/10% corporation tax rates in effect between the 2000 and 2005 financial years may have subsequently lost much of those tax savings as the corporation tax rate currently stands at 19% (from 1 April 2017).

The incorporation/disincorporation debate has certainly become more relevant as company profit extraction costs increase as a result of changes to the taxation of dividends from 5 April 2016 (in *Finance Act 2016*).

And while, as discussed above at **2.40** *et seq*, the legislation provides CGT relief on incorporation – the transfer of an existing sole trader or partnership business into a company – through the holdover of gains under *TCGA 1992, s 162* (see **2.42**), there were no equivalent CGT relieving provisions for disincorporation until *FA 2013*.

Finance Act 2013 partially addressed this by introducing a temporary disincorporation relief for small companies. The effect of this relief is that when a qualifying business disincorporates and its assets are transferred to individuals, there will be no immediate corporation tax on chargeable gains that arise (on qualifying assets) within the company. This relief is explained in more detail in **2.121**. Note that the relief does not prevent potential charges arising on the shareholders/owners of the company.

As the 'disincorporation' legislation applies only to the smallest companies, the next few sections (**2.104–2.120**) deal with the consequences of disincorporation for the majority of companies which are not eligible for disincorporation relief.

Planning a disincorporation

2.104 Disincorporation generally involves the transfer of the assets and liabilities of a business – including its goodwill, property, plant and machinery, stock and creditors – as a going concern to the shareholder(s) who then continue the business in an unincorporated form.

The potential tax charges and events which arise on a disincorporation are similar to those which would occur on any sale of a company's business and assets to a 'third party'. Disincorporation may, therefore, potentially be implemented with minimal tax costs where there are no significant property interests or business goodwill in the incorporated business.

Legal mechanics

2.105 Disincorporation can be implemented through a distribution or sale of the business to the shareholders.

From a company law perspective, the disincorporation of a business is likely to take place by means of a formal winding-up (a members' voluntary liquidation) or an informal winding-up (a simple dissolution or 'striking off').

A distribution may arise through a formal or informal winding up, or it can be made by way of a 'normal' distribution to the shareholders.

Members' voluntary liquidation

2.106 This type of liquidation is largely controlled by the company's shareholders and can be used only where the company being liquidated is solvent (*Insolvency Act 1986, Ch III, Pt IV*). Generally, a special resolution of the shareholders is required to place the company into voluntary liquidation, and the directors must make a statutory 'declaration of solvency' (so that, after having made a full inquiry, they declare that the company will be able to pay its debts within the following 12 months).

The liquidator can then wind up the company which, under a disincorporation, would entail the transfer of the business and assets to the shareholder(s). The liquidator will pay off the creditors and distribute the surplus to the shareholder(s).

The distribution to the shareholder(s) under a formal winding-up should be a capital one (under *TCGA 1992, s 122*).

However, the 'transaction in securities' anti-avoidance provisions contained in *ITA 2007, Pt 13, Ch 1* may also need to be considered (see **2.119**).

The main issue to consider before going down this route is the costs of a 'formal' voluntary liquidation in relation to the assets within the company.

'Dissolution' or 'striking off'

2.107 Due to the relatively high costs of a formal liquidation, many owner-managers prefer the informal winding-up route – where a company is 'dissolved' by being 'struck off' the Companies House register (*CA 2006, s 1000*).

However, where a company disincorporates by distributing its assets to its shareholders as part of an informal winding up, the shareholders will generally be subject to tax on an income (rather than capital) distribution basis (*CTA 2010, s 1020*). An income distribution will generally be less tax-efficient than a capital distribution in the hands of the shareholders – with entrepreneurs' relief only potentially being available in relation to capital distributions.

The distribution of the assets under an informal winding up may, however, be treated as a capital distribution in the hands of the shareholders where certain conditions are met.

Under a 'dissolution', the company will first transfer its trade and assets to an unincorporated business. (The transfer can be challenged by any minority shareholder or creditor who feels that this is prejudicial to their interests.) Liabilities can either be settled by the company or assigned to the successor business – provided that agreement is obtained from the relevant creditors. The company will then be dissolved under *CA 2006, s 1003*. A dissolution therefore involves fewer legal formalities and minimises costs. However, unlike a liquidation, it is not legally possible for a company to distribute its share capital (or any other non-distributable reserves).

Under Extra-Statutory Concession C16, HMRC were normally prepared to treat a distribution made to the shareholders prior to dissolution as having been made under a formal winding up. The company was required to give certain assurances to the Inspector beforehand. Such a distribution would therefore be treated as a capital distribution (*CTA 2010, s 1030*) for the shareholder, subject again to the 'transaction in securities' anti-avoidance provisions (see **2.119**). The benefit of ESC C16 was that the shareholders could take advantage of the lower tax rates applying to capital distributions.

Until October 2011, any 'unauthorised distributions' (of share capital, for example) could theoretically have been collected by the Office of the Treasury Solicitor. From October 2011, the Treasury Solicitor's Department withdrew its 'Guidelines about the Distribution of a Company's Share Capital', which had stated that the Treasury Solicitor would waive the Crown's right to any funds which a company distributes to its members prior to an informal striking off using ESC C16, where the amount of the 'unauthorised' distribution was less than £4,000.

The Office of the Treasury Solicitor then confirmed that in relation to distributions made from 14 October 2011, it would not seek to recover unauthorised distributions made prior to dissolution (http://www.bonavacantia.gov.uk/output/BVC17-FAQS.aspx).

However, from a tax perspective, the House of Lords decision in *R (on the application of Wilkinson) v Inland Revenue Commissioners* [2005] UKHL 30 made it clear that the scope of HMRC administrative discretion to make concessions which depart from the strict statutory position is not as wide as previously thought.

Accordingly, HMRC put ESC C16 on the statute books (*CTA 2010, ss 1030A* and *1030B*), but also took the opportunity to restrict the (favourable) capital treatment to distributions not exceeding £25,000. The legislation took effect from 1 March 2012 and the introduction of this limit has resulted in smaller companies, with relatively few assets, being able to take advantage of the informal winding-up route. Companies wishing to take advantage of this route could consider reducing their reserves below the new £25,000 limit prior to dissolution. Otherwise, it is likely that many owner-managers will now opt for a formal liquidation to take advantage of the beneficial capital gains tax treatment, even if the professional costs of doing so are likely to be significant.

Details of which companies are eligible for disincorporation relief are set out at **2.121** below.

The rest of this chapter assumes that the company is wound up rather than being dissolved.

Case study – B&B Ltd and Richard

2.108 Richard has run his bed and breakfast business for many years through his 100% owned company, B&B Ltd. He would now like to run the business as a sole trader, since this is more appropriate to its future scale of activities. The disincorporation date is 28 February 2017 (when the trade will be transferred to Richard and the company will be wound up).

The likely balance sheet at 28 February 2017 (reflecting the estimated trading profits to date) is shown in **Table 2.1**.

Table 2.1:

	Note		*Book value*	*Market value*
Freehold property	1		120,000	220,000
Goodwill	2		-	20,000
Fittings, plant and equipment	3			
Cost		20,000		
Less: depreciation	4	(8,000)	12,000	15,000
Stock	4		10,000	12,000
Debtors			7,000	
Bank overdraft			(4,000)	
Creditors	5		(9,000)	
Represented by share capital (£100) and reserves			£136,000	

Notes:

1 The freehold property has not been subject to depreciation – and represents the cost of the premises when it was acquired in March 2000.

2 The goodwill value is considered to represent 'free' (pre-1 April 2002) goodwill – and is not attributable to the premises or Richard personally!

3 The tax written-down value of the plant etc at 31 August 2016 was £9,000.

4 Stock and plant, etc will be transferred at their book values.

5 No tax provision has been made in the above figures.

In the six months to 28 February 2017, the tax-adjusted trading profit (before making any cessation adjustments) is expected to be £40,000.

Assume the trade and assets are transferred to Richard on 28 February 2017, so he can continue to operate the business as a sole trader. Provided the appropriate tax elections are made in relation to trading stock (*CTA 2009, s 167*) and plant (*CAA 2001, s 266*) the corporation tax computation for the six months to 28 February 2017 would be as follows:

Table 2.2:

	£
Tax-adjusted trading profit (no cessation adjustments)	40,000
Chargeable gain on sale of freehold property (£220,000 – £120,000) (ignore indexation allowance)	100,000
Chargeable gain on sale of goodwill (£20,000 – £nil base cost)	20,000
Taxable profits for the six months to 28 February 2017	160,000
Corporation tax liability @ 20%	32,000

Hence, B&B Ltd would incur a £32,000 corporation tax charge in its final trading period – of which £24,000 arises as a result of the chargeable gains realised on the transfer of its property and goodwill to the shareholder on disincorporation.

Main corporation tax consequences

Deemed cessation of trade

2.109 There is a deemed cessation of trade for corporation tax purposes on its transfer to Richard, in the case study above, even though the actual trade is continuing (albeit under different ownership) (*CTA 2009, s 41*).

Termination of corporation tax accounting period

2.110 The cessation of trade automatically brings to an end the current corporation tax accounting period (CTAP) of B&B Ltd. The company will therefore have a six-month CTAP to 28 February 2017 (*CTA 2009, s 10*).

Trading losses

2.111 If B&B Ltd incurred a trading loss in its final CTAP, this could be offset against any other corporation tax profits, including chargeable gains, of the current and preceding year (*CTA 2010, s 37(3)*). However, the current trading loss cannot be matched against gains arising from chargeable assets transferred / distributed to the shareholders during the course of the winding-up / dissolution, since these would arise in the subsequent CTAP (see below). In such cases, a sale of the chargeable assets to the shareholders at open market value before 'cessation' should be considered to achieve the appropriate loss offset.

The possibility of making a terminal loss relief claim should only be considered after all other forms of loss relief have been exhausted (*CTA 2010, s 39*).

If B&B Ltd had any unused trading losses, these would effectively be lost on the disincorporation since they cannot be carried forward beyond the deemed cessation of trade (*CTA 2010, s 45*). There is no provision for the transfer of trading losses to the unincorporated successor business.

Transfer of closing trading stock

2.112 In the Case Study above, as B&B Ltd (the transferor company) is 'connected' with Richard (see *CTA 2009, s 168*), who will continue to carry on the trade, the deemed 'market value' rule in *CTA 2009, s 166* will apply to the transfer of closing stock.

However, in most cases, it should be possible for the parties to make a joint election under *CTA 2009, s 167* to transfer the stock at its actual transfer value (or, if higher, the book value). In the unlikely event of the company being subject to UK-to-UK transfer pricing, the stock must be transferred at an arm's-length market value (*CTA 2009, s 162)*.

Capital allowances: plant and machinery

2.113 The normal 'capital allowance' cessation rules apply. No writing down allowances are given in the final basis period and a balancing adjustment is calculated (*CAA 2001, s 61* and Table Item 6). The balancing adjustment will generally be computed by reference to the actual transfer value, but market value would be applied where the parties are 'connected', as in the Case Study above (*CAA 2001, s 575)*.

However, if both parties make an election under *CAA 2001, s 266* the cessation rules will not apply and the plant can be transferred at its tax written-down value (*CAA 2001, s 267*). In this context, an election to transfer the plant at its tax written-down value may not be advantageous if the disincorporating company is going to have unrelieved trading losses. In such cases, the balancing charge could be used to absorb the loss, thus increasing the tax value of the plant for the successor business.

VAT

2.114 Assuming the business is VAT registered, the general rule is that where a trade ceases, the 'registered person' is deemed to make a taxable supply of all the goods then held by the business. However, since the business will be transferred to the shareholder(s) who will continue to carry it on as a sole trader/partnership, there should be no VAT levied on the transfer (by virtue of the 'transfer of going concern' provisions in the *VAT (Special Provisions) Order 1995, SI 1995/1268, art 5*).

To avoid any delays obtaining a new VAT registration it may be considered appropriate to elect to continue to use the business's existing VAT registration number (on form VAT 68), particularly as the history of the business will be well known to the shareholder(s).

Capital gains on transfer of assets

2.115 Chargeable gains will arise when the assets are transferred to the shareholders. The chargeable assets of the company (including goodwill) are deemed to be disposed of at market value for tax purposes (*TCGA 1992, s 17*).

The property held by B&B Ltd in the Case Study above might be distributed *in specie* during the winding-up to avoid SDLT (see **2.116**). This would still trigger a chargeable gain, but in the subsequent CTAP by reference to the property's market value.

Stamp duty land tax

2.116 A stamp duty land tax (SDLT) charge may arise on the shareholders where land or property is transferred to them on disincorporation. SDLT is generally charged on the consideration provided for the transfer so if, in the course of the disincorporation, the shareholders bought the property from the company, SDLT would be chargeable on the purchase price paid.

Where the property is owned by the company, the CGT cost of 'disincorporating' may prove to be prohibitive, particularly if a substantial capital gain is likely to arise. If the decision to disincorporate has been made and the tax cost of transferring the property is manageable, then it may often be preferable to 'distribute' it to the shareholders in specie during the winding-up. This will normally avoid any SDLT charge (see *Finance Act 2003, Sch 3, para 1*) and ranks as a capital distribution in the shareholder's hands. However, any assumption of a property loan/mortgage by the shareholders would represent 'consideration' for the transfer with a consequent SDLT charge.

If the property is sold to the shareholders as, or just before, the trade ceases (this may be done, for example, to access trading losses that might otherwise remain unused), then SDLT will potentially be payable.

Goodwill

2.117 Clearly, business goodwill will follow the transfer of the trade and may trigger a significant capital gain, depending on the market value agreed with HMRC. However, where a business was established after 31 March 2002, the gain will be treated as a taxable (trading) credit under the intangible fixed assets regime in *CTA 2009, Pt 8*.

Given HMRC's recent stance with regard to goodwill valuations on business incorporations (see **2.61** and following), for example where the trader has opted to sell goodwill to the newly incorporated company at its full market value, it will be interesting to see whether the same approach is adopted on a disincorporation. For many small businesses, HMRC have typically contended that the value of transferable goodwill is low or insignificant. This is because, HMRC argue, most if not all of the goodwill attaches to the proprietor personally and so is not capable of being transferred. (The over-analytical approach adopted by HMRC in relation to goodwill was questioned by the Special Commissioner in *Balloon Promotions v Wilson (Inspector of Taxes)* [2006] STC (SCD) 167.)

Whilst many small 'one-man-band' type businesses might have minimal goodwill, there will be a number of businesses which have built up significant 'free' goodwill attributable to the reputation built up by the business, its name and trade connections, and so on. Any potential uncertainty surrounding the value of goodwill in these cases must be carefully factored into the tax cost likely to arise on the disincorporation. Agreeing the value of goodwill with HMRC Shares & Assets Valuation could well turn out to be a protracted process. In some cases the CGT involved may well make the disincorporation too expensive.

Tax liabilities arising on shareholders

2.118 The company may be wound up as part of the disincorporation and any amounts/assets distributed will normally represent a capital distribution in the hands of the shareholder(s). The amount will therefore be subject to CGT (provided HMRC do not successfully invoke the transactions in securities anti-avoidance legislation).

Inevitably, a disincorporation will normally involve a classic 'double tax' charge, since the tax suffered by the shareholder on the capital distribution creates a further tax liability on the appreciation in the value of the company's chargeable assets, which has already been taxed in the company.

Entrepreneurs' relief may be available on any capital distributions. Otherwise, the capital distributions will currently attract CGT at either 10% or 20% from 6 April 2016 (in *Finance Act 2016*, compared to 18% or 28% rates from 2010/11). The rate applicable will be determined by each shareholder's income and other gains made in tax year of the distribution.

Where a shareholder receives a capital distribution in respect of any shares, he shall be treated as if he had received the consideration for the disposal of his shares (*TCGA 1992, s 122(1)*). This includes any distribution made in the dissolution or winding-up of the company. Therefore, if the conditions for entrepreneurs' relief are met the capital distribution received will suffer a 10% charge on the first £10m of gains (less any entrepreneurs' relief previously claimed). Based on the case study, the estimated CGT payable by Richard on the liquidator's distribution is shown below in **Table 2.3**:

Table 2.3:

	£	£
Net reserves at 28 February 2017 (before disincorporation)		136,000
Realisations:		
Goodwill – surplus on transfer		20,000
Freehold property – surplus on transfer/ distribution *in specie* – £220,000 less £120,000		100,000
		256,000
Less: Corporation tax liabilities – (see **Table 2.2**)	(32,000)	
Liquidator's fees and other costs (say)	(8,000)	(40,000)
Surplus available to distribute		£216,000

Based on the above, Richard's estimated CGT liability (ignoring his negligible base cost) would be approximately £20,490 calculated as follows:

	£
Distribution	216,000
Less: Annual exemption	(11,100)
Gain qualifying for entrepreneurs' relief	204,900
CGT liability @ 10%	20,490

Potential impact of transactions in securities rules

2.119 The 'transaction in securities' provisions now contained (for income tax purposes) in *ITA 2007, Pt 13, Ch 1* must always be considered in relation to transactions involving the company's shareholders.

Following the House of Lords decision in *IRC v Laird Group Plc* [2002] STC 722, the better view was that (by itself) the winding-up and distribution of the company's assets by a liquidator would not fall within the ambit of this legislation. On the other hand, *CIR v Joiner* [1975] STC 657 considered that these provisions would apply where a company's shareholders continue to carry on the trade in a new company *after liquidation*, having extracted the old company's distributable reserves as capital (rather than income). This view is also supported in HMRC's Company Taxation Manual (CTM36850).

Finance Act 2016 widens the 'transaction in securities' provisions in *ITA 2007, Pt 13* to include a distribution on liquidation. However, HMRC confirmed (in their meeting with the ICAEW Tax Faculty on 26 January 2016) that 'there would be no counteraction under the TIS as long as it was a simple liquidation with no successor company or other ancillary issues' (www.icaew.com/-/media/corporate/archive/files/technical/tax/tax-news/taxguides/taxguide-0216-tech-0616tax-company-distributions.ashx).

Even where the disincorporating trade is being transferred into personal ownership (rather than a commonly-owned company), there may in some cases be a risk that HMRC would seek to counteract the 'tax advantage' from the liquidation/dissolution (ie extracting the reserves in an income tax-free form as a capital receipt) under *ITA 2007, s 684*. However, provided it can be demonstrated that the disincorporation was motivated by sound commercial reasons, the normal 'let-out' in *ITA 2007, s 685* should still be available.

2.120 The practical application of *ITA 2007, Pt 13, Ch 1* clearly depends on HMRC's interpretation of the facts in each case. For example, HMRC are likely to challenge those cases where they suspect the shareholders have only disincorporated to extract the company's reserves at a beneficial CGT rate (assisted by entrepreneurs' relief). On the other hand, where all (or substantially all) of the company's funds need to be re-invested in the successor sole trade/partnership business, a more benign approach is likely to be taken. The overall tax costs of the disincorporation may also be an important factor in HMRC's deliberations.

The shareholders may require certainty on the tax treatment of the capital distribution and then could consider applying for advance clearance under *ITA 2007, s 701* to confirm HMRC's agreement that the bona fide test is satisfied.

Taxpayers also need to consider the new Targeted Anti Avoidance Rule (TAAR) introduced by *Finance Act 2016*. Where a number of conditions are satisfied, the TAAR will apply to tax a distribution in respect of share capital on a winding-up as if it was an income distribution. One of those conditions is that the main purposes, or one of the main purposes, of the arrangements is to gain a tax advantage. Hence, tax-motivated disincorporations will potentially be subject to the new TAAR.

There is no formal clearance procedure for the new TAAR, although HMRC have published examples of what transactions they consider to be caught by the new provisions, ahead of more detailed guidance to be published in due course.

Disincorporation relief

2.121 Following the recommendations of the Office of Tax Simplification, the *Finance Act 2013* introduced the disincorporation relief. The disappointing aspect of the relief is that it has been heavily watered down from the recommendation made by the OTS and the risk is that the uptake of this relief will be small. The relief was introduced so that a double tax charge does not arise (on both the company and the shareholders) where the company's business assets are transferred to the shareholder(s) who carry on the business either as a sole trader or within a partnership.

The effect of making a disincorporation relief claim is that the capital gains arising on the transfer of goodwill and land and buildings used in the business will be deferred when these assets are transferred to the shareholders who carry on the business. However, the disincorporation relief will only apply where the value of the qualifying assets does not exceed £100,000. This suggests that only the very smallest of businesses can benefit from this relief.

To enable a claim for disincorporation relief to be made five conditions need to be met:

1 The business is transferred as a going concern.

2 The business is transferred together with all the assets of the business (other than cash).

3 The total market value of the qualifying assets does not exceed £100,000 (as mentioned above, qualifying assets are restricted to goodwill and land and buildings).

4 All the shareholders to whom the business is transferred must be individuals.

5 All shareholders must have held their shares for at least 12 months prior to the date of disincorporation.

The relief claim must be made jointly by the company and all the shareholders to whom the business is transferred within two years from the business transfer date, and is irrevocable.

The measure is a temporary one and for businesses to qualify the transfer must take place between 1 April 2013 and 31 March 2018 inclusive. The reasoning behind this is that many businesses incorporated in 2002 when the 0% rate of corporation tax was introduced, and now that the 0% rate has been abolished the smaller businesses no longer wish to remain incorporated.

Even if a company meets all the conditions above there is still likely to be a charge on the shareholders when the assets are transferred to them. If the assets transferred (including non-qualifying assets) are below the £25,000 limit then the company can be dissolved and the shareholders will be subject to a capital gains tax charge. However, if the assets transferred exceed £25,000 then to obtain the capital gains tax treatment, the business would need to follow the winding-up route and the increased expenses likely to be incurred may persuade businesses to remain incorporated.

Chapter 3

Partnerships

David Whiscombe, BKL Tax

SIGNPOSTS

- **Scope** – Partnerships and LLPs are two of the possible structures available when a number of persons come together to carry on a business. Although different legally, partnerships and LLPs are treated in broadly the same way for tax purposes (see **3.1–3.4**).
- **Computational rules** – The same rules generally apply in computing partnership profits as to other traders but their application in particular areas can raise problems or opportunities (see **3.5–3.19**).
- **Profit-sharing** – The basis on which taxable profits are shared between partners may not always be straightforward (see **3.20–3.21**) and disputes may arise (**3.22–3.23**).
- **Capital gains tax** – Gains may arise not only on actual disposals but also on a change in profit-sharing ratios including on mergers and demergers (**3.24–3.29**).
- **Entrepreneurs' relief** – Entrepreneurs' relief may be available to partners, former partners and certain trustees (**3.30–3.34**).
- **Family partnerships** – Care must be taken with the settlements legislation but by no means all family or non-commercial arrangements are vulnerable (**3.35–3.38**).
- **Salaried partners** – May be treated differently as between ordinary partnership and LLPs, to which a special 'disguised remuneration' regime applies (see **3.39–3.41**).
- **Company partners** – Can be attractive in some circumstances but need to be used with care, especially when alongside connected individuals in the same partnership (**3.42–3.67**).
- **Stamp Duty Land Tax** – the SDLT regime applying to partnerships is complex but transfers between a partnership and its members can sometimes have a lower tax charge than expected (**3.68–3.80**).

CHOICE OF MEDIUM FOR CO-OWNED BUSINESSES

3.1 When a number of individuals decide to come together to carry on a business the choice of medium through which to operate raises a number of issues, including commercial, legal and taxation ones, which may be quite different from those which confront a sole trader. The position may be made more complicated by the fact that a structure which suits the personal needs of one of the individuals may not be attractive to the other co-owners and as a result the structure may be a compromise both between the legal commercial and taxation advantages and disadvantages of different structures and the requirements of different members.

Traditionally, the main structures considered by co-owners have been ordinary partnerships governed by the *Partnership Act 1890*, limited liability partnerships and limited companies (ie companies limited by share capital). The various consequences of each of these structures are summarised in **Chapter 1**. In this chapter we look in a little more detail at some specific issues arising with partnerships in the context of tax planning, including partnerships involving companies.

PARTNERSHIPS AND LLPs

3.2 An LLP is not, as a matter of law, a partnership. It is a legal entity which has an existence independent of its members. For certain tax purposes an LLP is treated as if it were a partnership and the members taxed as if they were partners in a partnership: but it is important to bear the limitations and restrictions in mind. More specifically, where an LLP carries on a trade or business with a view to profit, it is treated for income tax and corporation tax purposes as if its activities were carried on in partnership by its members and as if anything done by, to or in relation to the LLP for the purposes of, or in connection with, any of its activities were done by, to or in relation to the members as partners (*Income Tax Act 2007, s 863*; *Corporation Tax Act 2009, s 1273*). For CGT purposes, assets held by such an LLP are treated as held by its members as partners and as if any dealings by the LLP were dealings by its members in partnership (*Taxation of Chargeable Gains Act 1992, s 59A*). Interestingly, by the strict wording of the statute, transparency also extends for income tax purposes (but not for CT or CGT purposes) to an LLP which is carrying on a 'profession'. Since, however, such an LLP will also almost certainly be carrying on a 'business', the difference in wording is probably, in practice, of no significance.

In what follows, when we use the term 'partnership' we mean 'partnership or LLP', except where the context makes it clear that that is not the case.

> **Focus**
>
> In certain circumstances LLPs cease to be tax-transparent – advisers need to be alert to the possibility that CGT charges may arise both at that time and subsequently.

3.3 It is worth bearing in mind both that the tax-transparency of an LLP will come to an end in certain circumstances (the most common being the appointment of a liquidator) and the consequences should that happen. In particular, for CGT purposes the LLP will thereafter be treated as if it were a company rather than as a partnership. This does not retrospectively affect the treatment of gains made before the liquidation, but any chargeable gains arising on disposals of assets after the commencement of the liquidation etc, are computed as if the LLP had never been treated as a partnership. Where business assets roll-over relief has been claimed by rolling over a gain into a share of an asset owned by an LLP, a tax liability (based on an amount equal to the postponed gain which has not come into charge) will arise on the relevant member(s) when the LLP ceases to be tax-transparent. Similarly gains deferred on the gift of business assets under *TCGA 1992, s 165*, or under *TCGA 1992, s 260*, crystallise.

On and from liquidation etc, the interest which each of the members has in the LLP as a member is treated in the same way as a shareholding in a company, the acquisition cost of which is the amount of capital subscribed. Hence the realisation of assets by an LLP which is in liquidation can give rise both to gains subject to Corporation Tax at the LLP level and gains subject to CGT in the hands of members when distributed by the LLP (to the extent that the share of proceeds exceeds the capital contributed by the members).

3.4 In addition to the potential loss of tax transparency, special tax rules apply to LLPs including in regard to:

- treatment of 'salaried members';
- availability of relief for trading losses.

COMPUTATION OF PARTNERSHIP PROFITS

3.5 Where all partners in a partnership are individuals, the taxable income of the partnership (whether from trading or from any other source) is computed using the same rules as apply to individuals. Where a partnership includes individuals who are not resident in the UK, income is computed (in relation to those individuals) using the rules applicable to non-UK-residents.

Where a partnership includes one or more companies, the profit share of corporate partners is computed using, broadly speaking, the computational rules applying to companies (which may be different according to whether the company is resident in the UK or not). Often the computational rules for a particular source will be the same for UK resident and non-resident individuals and for UK resident and non-resident companies: but in theory where a partnership includes both resident and non-resident individuals and companies it may be necessary to produce four separate computations of each source of income using four different sets of computational rules.

The position of a partnership which is itself a partner in a partnership has historically been unclear. For accounting periods commencing after 6 April 2018, legislation is to be introduced to clarify the position, following responses to HMRC's August 2016 Consultation Document *Partnership Taxation: proposals to clarify tax treatment*. It is proposed that, where a partnership includes among its partners a partner which is itself a partnership, it will be required to report to HMRC the details of that partner and provide to both HMRC and the partner computations of taxable profit on all four possible bases (ie UK-resident individual, UK-resident company, non-UK-resident individual and non-UK-resident company). Alternatively, where the details of all ultimate recipients (ie identity and amount of profit share allocated) have been provided to HMRC (and to the ultimate recipients), the partnership will have to prepare computations only on the basis appropriate to each ultimate recipient.

Focus

Where a partnership has non-resident members and/or corporate members up to four separate computations of tax-adjusted profit may need to be produced and filed with the partnership tax return.

Some specific areas of doubt or difficulty in relation to the computation of profit are considered below.

Drawings and profit share

3.6 Partners' drawings and salaries are an appropriation of profit, not a deduction in calculating it (*PDC Copyright (South) v George* [1997] STC (SCD) 326, SpC 141). However, this does not mean that no payment made by the partnership to a partner is deductible: the true character of the payment must be identified.

For example, it may be that the partnership agreement allocates a slice of profit between partners by reference to the amount of capital each has invested in the partnership. That allocation of profit remains an allocation of profit and not a payment of interest, however it may be described. But it is equally possible for a partner to loan money to the partnership under a separate documented loan agreement providing for the payment of interest. This might be the case if, for example, the arrangements required that the interest was paid by the partnership even if there were no profits out of which to pay it. If that is the case, what has been paid by the partnership and received by the partner will be interest and not profit-share, which will be tax-deductible for the partnership to the same extent and subject to the same rules as any interest paid to any other lender: and taxable on the hands of the partner-lender in the same way as interest received from any other source.

Similarly, the partnership agreement may allocate an enhanced share of profit to a partner who personally owns the property from which the partnership trades. Such an enhanced profit share remains profit share and not rent. But it is equally possible that a partner may enter into a formal lease or licence agreement which requires the partnership to pay rent for occupation of the property. In that case the partner is taxed on the rent like any other landlord, with the partnership having a deduction in calculating its profits in the same way as if the rent had been paid to any other landlord (so long as the rent in relation to the property is not so excessive as to fall foul of the 'wholly and exclusively' rule).

The leading case establishing the principle is *Heastie v Veitch & Co* [1934] 1 KB 535. In this case, a partnership of chartered accountants carried on its business from premises which were owned by the senior partner and for which the partnership paid a rent which was found by the General Commissioners to be a fair and proper rent. It was held by the Court of Appeal that the rent was deductible by the partnership in computing the partnership profit. But it is clear from the judgment in the Court of Appeal that the principle is not limited to rent but extends to any goods or services provided by a partner independently of his position as partner:

> 'suppose two people are carrying on business in partnership as hotel proprietors and it is necessary for the purpose of carrying on that hotel, that business, that they should be supplied from time to time with wine, and suppose one of the partners is carrying on a wholly independent business on his own account in the wine business and supplies wine to the partnership, it would be idle to suggest, would it not, that for the purpose of ascertaining the profits of the hotel you could not deduct the sums paid to the partner who was the wine merchant?' (Romer LJ at p319)

Salaries, fees, etc

3.7 It is not unusual for partners in a professional partnership to hold offices or employments in the course of the partnership business on terms that the income from them is regarded as partnership income and divided between partners in accordance with the partnership profit-sharing arrangements. Subject to ESC A37 (see below), the income remains taxable as employment income and the normal rules of taxing employment apply to it. It remains taxable as employment income in the hands of the partner earning it and the same limited expenses are deductible for tax purposes as for any other employment income. In particular, costs of travelling to the place of employment are not deductible for tax purposes in computing the amount of employment income, nor are any other incidental expenses such as secretarial or support costs. Where these costs are borne for convenience by the partnership they will not be incurred 'wholly and exclusively' for the purposes of the partnership business and will not be deductible in computing partnership profits. Even if it is clearly demonstrable that the employment itself was undertaken at the instigation of the other partners for reasons closely connected with, and beneficial to, the partnership business, the illogical and unsatisfactory decision by the House of Lords in the case of *Mitchell and Edon v Ross HL* (1961) 40 TC 11 presents an insuperable hurdle to any claim to deduct expenses of the employment in computing the taxable income of that business.

Focus

It is only in certain closely-defined circumstances that salaries and fees received in respect of offices (but not employments) held by partners in connection with the partnership can be treated as partnership income. But VAT may be due even where the income does not pass the test for inclusion in the partnership accounts but remains chargeable as employment income.

3.8 In certain circumstances Extra-Statutory Concession A37 provides that earnings of a partner as director of a company (but, it should be noted, not earnings as an employee) may be treated as part of the professional income of the partnership and brought into the calculation of the profits of the partnership, with expenses incurred being allowed in the normal way. ESC A37 will apply if:

- the fees are only a small part of the profits;
- the directorship is a normal incident of the profession and of the particular practice concerned;
- there is an agreement between the partners that the fees from the appointment are to be treated as partnership income and divided between the partners, and that arrangement actually happens in practice; and
- all the partners agree that the income is to be treated as part of the partnership profits for tax purposes, and written confirmation of this is given to HMRC.

ESC A37 is paralleled by a similar treatment in respect of national insurance contributions (NICs) under *SI 2001/1004, reg 27.*

3.9 Where a person, in the course or furtherance of a trade profession or vocation, accepts any office, services supplied by him as the holder of that office are treated as supplied in the course or furtherance of the trade, profession or vocation (*Value Added Tax Act 1994, s 94(4)*) so will bear VAT. Note that *VATA 1994, s 94(4)* applies only to offices, not employments; but it applies even if the conditions for ESC A37 are not fulfilled (or the benefit of ESC A37 is not taken) such that the income from the office in question is charged to tax as employment income of the individual concerned. In other words, in cases where *VATA 1994, s 94(4)* applies it is not possible to avoid the imposition of VAT by accepting or procuring that the income is treated as employment income rather than as business income of the partnership.

Costs relating to partnership changes

3.10 The costs of drawing up or amending a partnership agreement will usually be disallowable as capital expenditure. This would extend to costs of transferring a partnership's business to a limited company or to an LLP. Similarly, the costs of dissolving a partnership will be capital in nature. However, it is likely that (at least in some circumstances) the legal and professional costs which an ongoing partnership business incurs in getting rid of (or otherwise settling a dispute with) a recalcitrant partner will be revenue in nature and tax-deductible. This is to be contrasted with the position where a partnership dispute is resolved by a splitting of the business, with two or more groups of partners each taking part of the business and going their separate ways: the costs in such a case are likely to be capital in nature.

Focus

Although most costs of dealing with or altering internal partnership arrangements are disallowable, costs of hiring and firing partners (even equity partners) will often prove to be deductible.

3.11 In the past, HMRC have resisted claims to tax relief on the costs of recruiting partners on the basis that they, like the costs of drawing up a partnership agreement, are in the nature of capital costs. HMRC now accept that recruitment costs are normally allowable as revenue expenditure save where there is some additional factor involved. They give as examples of relevant factors (at PM30800) cases where:

- The admission of the partner has a fundamental impact on the structure of the firm's business involving more than a mere expansion of the business.

- The partner is recruited as part of the acquisition of a business.
- The new partner's capital contribution is a material factor in the recruitment.

It is likely that the legal and professional costs which an ongoing partnership business incurs in getting rid of (or otherwise settling a dispute with) a recalcitrant partner will be viewed in the same light as those of recruiting a partner, with similar factors determining the tax-deductibility of the expense.

3.12 The treatment of any payment made to a partner on leaving a partnership depends on its true character. In some circumstances a payment may simply be an additional share of profit which will be taxable on the partner and non-deductible for the partnership in the same way as any other profit share. In others the payment may be in settlement of some alleged grievance which the leaving partner has against the firm which will usually be tax free. Two cases in particular have come before the First-tier Tribunal. In *Self and Morgan v Commissioners of HMRC* [2009] UKFTT 78 (TC) the payments represented allocations of profits to the leaving partners as they were made to them in their capacity as partners and not as an entirely collateral payment made to them otherwise than in their capacity as partners.

However, there are occasions when a payment will not be an allocation of profits, as in *AB v HMRC* [2011] UKFTT 685 (TC). The taxpayer had received termination payments from two unconnected partnerships on two successive occasions. On each occasion the relationship between AB and the partnership had broken down and on each occasion a payment had been made by the partnership on AB's leaving. On the first occasion the payment was described as and held to be a share of profit: in the other it was held to be in the nature of compensation for the adverse treatment AB had suffered at the hands of the partnership. The discussion in the case of the factors to be considered and the reasons why different conclusions were reached in respect of the two payments is well worth reviewing.

Although in the cases cited the tribunal was required only to determine the treatment of the receipts in the hands of the ex-partner concerned (rather than the treatment of the payment in the hands of the partnership), it would seem that the payment would be deductible in computing partnership profits (if, and only if) it had the character of compensation.

Interest paid by a partnership

3.13 Normally interest paid by a partnership is deductible in computing business profits or losses of a business subject to the usual requirements including that it be incurred wholly and exclusively for the purposes of the business. The position may, however, be more complex.

3.14 If a partner's capital account becomes overdrawn, HMRC may argue that part of the partnership's borrowing has been used to fund the overdrawn account such that tax relief for interest on partnership borrowings should be restricted. In the simple case of a sole trader preparing accounts on a cash basis with a bank overdraft, an overdrawn capital account and few business assets, it may be reasonable to say that the overdraft has funded the excess drawings. But things will rarely be that simple, even for a sole trader. If there are both liabilities and assets in the balance sheet, who is to say that the business assets have not been financed by the overdraft and the overdrawn loan account by the business creditors? Or if the capital account has become overdrawn because of losses, how much of the loss is attributable to non-cash items such as depreciation or amortisation?

> **Focus**
>
> Tax relief for interest on third-party borrowings may need to be examined very carefully where one or more partners have overdrawn capital accounts but there are a number of arguments which can be deployed to support a claim for full tax relief.

3.15 The potential complexity of the analysis is apparent from HMRC's somewhat superficial analysis at BIM45690. The Special Commissioners case of *Silk v Fletcher* [1999] STC (SCD) 220 gives some guidance, but not much. In that case the taxpayer was originally in partnership but he then worked as a sole practitioner. His capital account was substantially overdrawn and for many years his drawings exceeded his profits. The taxpayer sought, in calculating profits, to deduct the interest incurred on several loans. The Special Commissioner held that, even if the capital account was not overdrawn, it would not necessarily follow that the interest would be tax deductible. It had to be ascertained how much of the borrowed money was actually used for business purposes. As drawings exceeded profits, the implication was that at least part of the interest was used to fund private expenditure. The taxpayer also argued that his capital account was not overdrawn because the accounts did not reflect goodwill. The former Special Commissioner disagreed with this contention, although the appeal was allowed in part after making adjustments for depreciation, debtors and creditors.

3.16 If the matter is complicated even for a sole trader, it is that much more complicated for a partnership. If one partner's capital account is overdrawn, but others are in credit, it may well be possible to argue that the overdrawn account is being funded not by any partnership bank borrowings but by the positive capital accounts of the remaining partners, such that no restriction to tax relief on interest paid by the partnership should be made. However, each situation will depend on its own facts: at the end of the day the question to be asked is – what was the purpose for which any interest was paid?

3.17 A partner may borrow money to acquire an asset personally but permit the partnership to use the asset on the understanding that the partnership will pay the interest on the loan and charge it in the partnership accounts. The interest payable by the partnership will normally be allowable in this situation as a substitute for payment of rent to the partner. It is a moot point whether strictly speaking the partner should treat himself both as receiving rent equal to the interest paid on his behalf and as paying out the interest which has been paid on his behalf. In practice, HMRC do not seem to take the point. Difficulties will arise if the amount of the interest paid by the partnership exceeds the market value of occupancy of the property or part of the property occupied by the partnership – the excess is in effect a distribution of profit to the partner and is not deductible for the partnership.

Personal expenses of partners

3.18 There is no rule restricting tax-deductible expenses to those incurred by the partnership as a whole. On the contrary, where a partner defrays out of his personal resources some expense which is incurred wholly and exclusively for the purposes of the partnership trade, tax relief for such an expense is available. In the past, one of the most common circumstances in which this arose was in the case of doctors' partnerships. Before the days of self-assessment it was quite common to see a partnership assessment allocating shares of profits to individual doctors and for the statement of partnership share to show further deductions for such personally-incurred expenses as 'use of home as surgery', 'wife's wages', 'conference expenses' and the ubiquitous 'motoring expenses'. Similarly, one would encounter individual capital allowance claims covering assets provided by the doctors individually but used in the partnership business. Such claims were not, of course, restricted to medical practitioners but, in practice, seemed to be most commonly encountered in that context.

Focus

Partnership expenses borne directly by partners are deductible subject to the normal rules for trading deductions but must be deducted in the partnership tax computation and not as a separate adjustment in the partners' personal; self-assessment returns.

Although self-assessment swept away the machinery of such stand-alone expense and capital allowance claims for partners, it changed nothing as regards the tax-deductibility. However, the process now is that any claim for relief for expenditure incurred by partners (as distinct from by the partnership) is nonetheless claimed at the level of the partnership taxation computation. There is no longer any 'second stage' at which individual claims may be made.

Preparing the partnership return correctly therefore involves adding together the partnership expenditure and the expenditure incurred by the individual partners in order to arrive at the total expenditure figure for the partnership. This is then included in the Standard Accounts Information.

HMRC state (at BIM82075) that it is necessary that 'the adjustments are made before apportionment of the net profit between the partners', and they instruct that officers 'should not accept any deductions for expenses from the net profits allocated to a partner'. In practice, HMRC generally accept that tax relief should be effectively given to the partner incurring the relevant expense, by appropriate allocation of the tax-adjusted partnership profit between partners.

Overseas aspects

3.19 Care is needed where a partnership either has non-UK-resident members or has trading profits arising outside the UK (or both).

A UK-resident member of a partnership is liable to UK tax on his share of the worldwide income of the partnership. He may also be liable to foreign taxes on any profits of the partnership which arise outside the UK: the UK will give double tax relief for any such taxes either under a treaty or unilaterally.

A partnership is not of itself taxable. The concept of residence status is therefore meaningless in the context of partnerships themselves. It follows that a partnership cannot itself claim any benefits as a 'dual resident' under any Double Taxation Convention ('DTC'), nor will HMRC normally issue a 'certificate of residence' for the purposes of any DTC. A few DTCs do state that a partnership may be regarded as having a residence status and, in those cases, a 'certificate of residence' may be issued. In other cases, partners may be able to claim treaty benefits and HMRC will assist by providing a 'letter of confirmation' confirming UK-residence status where appropriate.

A non-UK-resident member of a partnership is liable to UK tax only on his share of partnership profits arising in the UK. He has no UK tax liability in respect of profits arising outside the UK. For this purpose, where the partnership carries on a single trade in the UK and overseas, HMRC will regard each member's share of profit as arising partly in the UK and partly overseas.

For example, suppose that a UK LLP has members resident in the UK and members resident in Country Y, and branches in both the UK (which makes a profit of £9m) and Country Y (which makes a profit of £1m). Suppose that under the LLP agreement profits are 'streamed' so that the members resident in Country Y share between them the £1m profits arising from the Country Y branch and the members resident in the UK share the £9m profits of the UK branch. Common sense would suggest that UK tax would be payable only by

UK members, and on a total of £9m (since the non-resident members take as a matter of fact no share of UK-sourced profits). In fact, HMRC will take the view that profits cannot be 'streamed' in this way for tax purposes (even if they are 'streamed' commercially). They will regard UK members as being entitled to and taxable on 90% of global profits (so £9m) of which £8.1m arises in the UK and £0.9m arises overseas: and the overseas members as being entitled to 10% of global profits (so £1m) of which £0.9m arises in the UK and is taxable in the UK and £0.1m arises overseas and is tax free.

> **Focus**
>
> A non-resident partner is liable to UK tax only on his share of UK income of the partnership which arises in the UK. However, if he fails to pay his tax, the UK-resident partners may be liable to make payment to HMRC as his deemed UK tax agents.

One solution to this difficulty may be to create separate LLPs (or local equivalents) in the UK and overseas, or perhaps to employ the overseas-resident members in Country Y (or even deliberately to arrange matters so as to procure that they are caught by the 'salaried members' legislation described at **3.40** below).

Although a partner resident outside the UK is liable to UK tax on trading profits arising in the UK, there may be obvious practical difficulties in the way of HMRC actually collecting tax from him. For this reason, the *Taxes Acts* make provision (at *ITA 2007, Pt 14, Ch 2C*) for income tax liabilities of a non-resident to be collected from any 'UK representative' of the non-resident. *CTA 2009, Pt 22, Ch 6* makes similar provision in respect of non-resident companies. In relation to partnerships, the partnership itself is treated as the UK representative of the non-resident partners. It may thus be assessed to tax in the name of the non-resident partners. In such circumstances, each of the partners is jointly liable for the non-resident partners' tax – this is the only circumstance in which one partner can be liable for another's tax liability. In the case of an LLP, it is the LLP itself which is liable, but since, in general law, members of an LLP are not personally liable for the LLP's liabilities, no personal liability attaches to members.

In either case, a partnership with UK income and non-resident partners may be wise to take a very close interest in the UK tax compliance arrangements of non-resident partners, including withholding distributions until evidence that all tax liabilities have been met is available.

This is to be distinguished from the case where a UK-resident member of a partnership or LLP leaves the UK, leaving tax debts unpaid. There is, in that case, no UK representative and no liability on the partnership, partners or LLP.

SHARING OF PROFITS AND LOSSES

3.20 Taxable profit is allocated between partners 'in accordance with the firm's profit-sharing arrangements during that period' (*ITTOIA 2005, s 850(1)*). The phrase is simple enough but in some circumstances it may not be clear what it means. Examples in HMRC's guidance notes suggest that the preferred method may be to allocate tax-adjusted profits by applying to them the same formula as has been used commercially. But this can give capricious results – as in **Example 3.1** below where Brown, despite having 50% of the commercial profit, has a smaller tax charge than Smith, who has 31.25% of the commercial profit.

Example 3.1 – Complex profit-sharing ratios

Smith, Jones and Brown share profits as follows:

	Smith	*Jones*	*Brown*
First £30,000 (salary)	20,000	10,000	0
Next £50,000 (return on capital)	5,000	5,000	40,000
Balance	45%	45%	10%
Allocation of commercial profit £80,000	25,000	15,000	40,000
Allocation of tax adjusted profit £130,000	47,500	37,500	45,000

3.21 An alternative, which would also arguably meet the statutory requirement of allocation 'in accordance with the firm's profit-sharing arrangements', and which would seem fairer, would be to allocate taxable profits in the same proportion as commercial profits. Probably either method would be acceptable to HMRC if agreed between the partners and applied consistently.

What is clear is that partners cannot agree to allocate profits between them for tax purposes in a way which is different from that in which commercial profits are in fact allocated. Further, 'the allocation of profits or losses for an accounting period cannot be varied retrospectively after the end of that accounting period' (HMRC guidance at BIM82055). While this may be true as far it goes – once profits and their allocation between partners are agreed and the accounts signed off, that is final – it must not be taken too far. In many cases a final decision on dividing up profits is not taken until after the end of the period and the amount of the profit (as well as the relative contributions of the partners) is known. To suppose that this is in any way problematic would be absurd. What is, however, crucial is that the allocation for tax purposes follows the commercial allocation.

The August 2016 Consultation Document *Partnership taxation: proposals to clarify tax treatment* (referred to at **3.5** above) included proposals dealing with profit-sharing arrangements and allocation of tax-adjusted profit to partners.

Proposal 5 in the Consultation Document addressed government concerns arising from the 'potential for uncertainty where partners dispute the allocation of profits made to them for tax purposes on the basis that the actual profit-sharing arrangements are different from the written agreement or as stated by the nominated partner'. The original proposal was that legislation should be introduced to confirm that the arrangements set out in the partnership or LLP agreement should be conclusive, unless overridden by notification to HMRC from the nominated partner. Following consultation, it is now proposed that the profit allocation stated in the partnership return will be 'the first point of reference for HMRC in determining the taxable profits of each partner' but that, where that allocation is disputed by a partner, 'the Government intends to legislate to protect the partners from being taxed on incorrect profit shares'.

Proposal 6 in the Consultation Document identified government concerns that flexibility in allocating profits 'is seen by some partnerships as an opportunity to manipulate profit, loss and capital gains allocations for tax purposes. For example, by allocating specific items of income and expenditure to particular partners or classes of partner or by determining profit shares after the end of the accounting period'. Following consultation, it is proposed that, 'to reduce the scope for allocating profits for purely tax-motivated purposes', the following changes will be made:

- Clarifying (presumably by legislation) how to apply a firm's profit-sharing arrangements consistently in allocating taxable profits among the partners, including in cases where different partners' taxable profits are computed on different bases.
- Legislation will provide that any retrospective variation to a partnership's profit-sharing arrangements made after the period-end will not apply. How this will work where there is no agreed allocation of profit at all until after the end of the period is not yet clear.

Where a partner joins or leaves a partnership during an accounting period, legislation will provide that such partners will be treated as taxable on their share in profits or losses that arose during the period in which they were partners or members. The profit arising during the part of the accounting period when a person is a partner should be used as a basis, and the allocation agreement in force at that time (the time of their joining the partnership) will be applied to that proportion to determine the partner's share of taxable profit.

One further practical point should be considered. Sometimes one or more partners has his profit share underpinned at a guaranteed minimum figure. This kind of arrangement, which has historically been fairly common in businesses in the financial dealing sector, can give some anomalous results.

Example 3.2 – Guaranteed profit shares

A is sole trader. He takes B and C into partnership with him. He guarantees that their share of profit in the first year will be not less than their previous salary of £55,000 each.

The partnership loses a large customer and the first year's results show a profit (also the tax-adjusted profit) of only £50,000 in total. Commercially, A suffers a loss of £60,000 (ie the 'guaranteed minima' of £110,000 less the actual profit of £50,000).

B and C will each pay tax on £25,000 of profit. A gets no tax relief for his commercial loss of £60,000 (for there is in fact no partnership loss to be relieved). The planning point here is that any guarantee given by A should be stated in the partnership agreement in terms of after-tax not pre-tax income, or should provide for suitable tax indemnities.

Tax disputes between partners

3.22 A return of partnership profits is required to be made by the nominated partner. The return must show, inter alia, the amount of partnership profit and the allocation between partners. There is no problem if the return is made, it is made on time, and all partners agree with the figures on it. If the return is late, is not made, or is not agreed by all the partners then complexities can arise.

The question of what happens if a partner does not agree with the amount of profit allocated to him in the partnership return was the subject of the First-tier Tribunal decision in *Morgan and Self v CIR* [2009] UKFTT 78 (TC). Although the case was decided on other grounds so that the comments of the tribunal chairman are strictly *obiter dicta*, the judge concluded that the obligation of the member to make his own self-assessment return 'to the best of his knowledge and belief' trumps the requirement to include on the personal return the share of profit allocated on the partnership return. The solution, the judge concluded, was that in cases of dispute the member should include on his personal return the figure which he believes to be the correct share of taxable profit, together with a note explaining that this differs from the figure shown on the partnership return.

Focus

Where a partner disagrees with the taxable profit or share of disposal proceeds allocated to him on the partnership return he should notify HMRC on his own tax return both of the figures used on the partnership return and the figures which he believes to be correct.

3.23 A similar difficulty may arise if the partner who has been required to make the partnership return fails to do so. The legislation (*FA 2009, Sch 55, para 55*) then imposes penalties not only on the defaulting partner but on all the partners. Thus the law can have the effect of imposing a penalty on a sleeping partner with no practical means of access to the books and records necessary to make the return and no real power either to make the return himself or force the nominated partner to do so. Furthermore, as confirmed in *Dyson v CIR* [2015] UKFTT 131 (TC), it is only the defaulting partner who has the right of appeal against the penalties imposed on himself and on the other partners: if he chooses not to exercise that appeal right the other partners have no recourse. This is, as the judge in the case observed, clearly a breach of Article 6 of the Human Rights Act: but the tribunal was nonetheless bound.

CAPITAL GAINS TAX

3.24 Capital gains tax (CGT) may be relevant to a partnership either in relation to acquisitions or disposals of partnership assets from or to third parties, or in relation to transactions between the partners in those partnership assets which are chargeable assets for CGT purposes. Detailed guidance for partnership capital gains is to be found in HMRC Statement of Practice SP D12

External disposals

3.25 Partnerships (and, in most circumstances, LLPs) are effectively transparent for the purposes of CGT such that any charge to CGT on the disposal of partnership assets arises in the hands of each individual partner. In so far as the disposal of partnership assets is concerned, the entitlement to the disposal proceeds depends on the agreement between the partners. There is nothing to prevent the partners having a different capital-sharing ratio from that in which trading, professional, or indeed any other income profits are shared. Each partner will have an independent base cost, and each will have the separate ability to roll over or hold over gains through the purchase of qualifying assets within the stipulated time limits.

Focus

Partnerships may share capital profits in whatever way they choose. CGT will follow the commercial allocation. Any change in profit-sharing ratios may give rise to chargeable gains, even where there has been no external disposal. This may apply in particular on mergers and demergers but the possible availability of business asset roll-over relief should not be overlooked.

Transactions between partners

3.26 A change in capital profit-sharing ratios between partners is treated as a disposal for CGT purposes. A partner reducing his share is deemed to make a disposal and a partner increasing his share to make an acquisition. The consideration in each case is deemed to be the relevant proportion of the value at which the asset in question appears in the partnership balance sheet plus any off-balance-sheet payment. Market value is substituted only where the partners are connected other than by being in partnership: even then, market value will be substituted only if it is considered that the transaction would have been undertaken at market value but for the connection.

It follows that if assets are carried in the balance sheet at a figure which equates to original cost, any change of capital profit-sharing ratios will (although a disposal) not give rise to any gain or loss for CGT purposes.

It also follows that a revaluation of partnership assets does not of itself amount to a disposal for CGT purposes. This is logical: by simply changing the value at which they choose to recognise an asset in the partnership balance sheet, partners have not changed their financial assets. This remains the case even if the revaluation is used to support further borrowings in the partnership which are then drawn down as additional drawings.

3.27 Thus, there will not be a CGT charge by reason *only* of:

(i) cash being withdrawn in excess of the capital introduced and retained profits; or

(ii) assets being revalued and the capital accounts credited with any revaluation surplus in the capital profit-sharing ratio,

or because of a combination of both.

If assets are revalued, however, and a change in capital profit-sharing ratio then takes place, a disposal is deemed to arise in the case of those partners whose shares reduce, whether or not accompanied by a withdrawal of cash. To that extent, the gain on revaluation is regarded as having been realised.

Where partnerships merge, there will normally be a change in the profit-sharing ratios of all chargeable assets held by either of the merging firms. If gains arise (due to an earlier revaluation of assets or payment outside the accounts) each partner may be able to claim rollover relief in respect of shares acquired in the other firm's assets. Similarly, a demerger is likely to involve changes in the profit-sharing ratios. If gains arise on the relinquishment of an interest in some assets (or payment outside the accounts) the partner may be able to claim rollover relief in respect of any enhanced share in other assets; ESC D25 provides that the acquisition of a further interest in an asset already in use for the purposes of a trade is for roll-over relief purposes treated as the acquisition of a new asset.

Writing off goodwill

3.28 Some special care is needed in regard to 'negligible value' claims under *TCGA 1992, s 24* in respect of partnership goodwill. It is not uncommon for partnership agreements to be 'modernised' by providing that all goodwill shall be written out of the balance sheet, and that going forward there shall be neither payment demanded of incoming partners in respect of goodwill nor any payment made to outgoing partners. In these circumstances, partners owning goodwill who have an acquisition cost (or a 1982 value) might consider that since it will be impossible for them to realise any value for goodwill, a 'negligible value' claim should be made so as to crystallise a loss for CGT purposes.

Unfortunately, it is the view of HMRC (see CG28000) that an agreement of this kind does not of itself mean that the goodwill is of negligible value within the meaning of the Act. A claim under *TCGA 1992, s 24* may be made only if the entire goodwill of the partnership as a whole has become of negligible value. This is a question of fact, and is quite different from an agreement between the partners that they will not, as between themselves, attach any value to goodwill. Of course, it may be that the agreement to treat the goodwill as valueless simply reflects the fact that the goodwill has in the real world actually become valueless: but if a negligible value claim is to be sustained it will be necessary to produce evidence to that effect.

As with any revaluation upwards or downwards, the writing off of the goodwill in the balance sheet will affect the consideration deemed to pass on a future change in capital profit-sharing ratios, including on retirement. Thus a partner who, after goodwill has been written off, disposes of his interest in goodwill on reducing his share of capital profits will realise a loss equal to his acquisition cost.

Partners as connected persons and associates

3.29 For the purposes of CGT, partners are 'connected' with each other (and with each other's spouses, civil partners or relatives) except in relation to bona fide acquisitions or disposals of partnership assets (*TCGA 1992, s 286*). Similarly, partners are 'associates' of each other (*CTA 2010, s 448*). These definitions are widely relevant throughout the tax code. Given that for certain tax purposes LLPs are in certain circumstances treated as in the same way as partnerships, the question arises whether the treatment of partners as 'connected' and 'associated' persons also means that fellow members of an LLP are also to be treated in the same way. The answer is probably no.

Focus

The general rule that partners are 'connected persons' for tax purposes probably does not apply to individuals who are fellow members of an LLP and not otherwise connected.

In commercial and legal terms an LLP is, as a body corporate with separate legal identity, quite different from a partnership. Legally the relationship which subsists between fellow members of an LLP is much closer to that which subsists between fellow members of a limited company than to a partnership. HMRC have published no general guidance but it is worth noting that in the specific case of 'association' for the purposes of EIS relief (*ITA 2007, s 253*), which defines 'associate' to include 'partner', HMRC regard 'partner' as meaning 'anyone with whom the individual carries on a business as described in the *Partnership Act, 1890*' – which would, of course, exclude fellow members of an LLP. It seems probable therefore that HMRC would agree that the general rule is that fellow members of LLPs are neither connected persons nor associates.

Entrepreneurs' relief for partnerships

3.30 For the purposes of applying entrepreneurs' relief to the circumstances of a partnership, *TCGA 1992, s 169I(8)* provides that:

- an individual who disposes of (or of interests in) assets used for the purposes of a business carried on by the individual on entering into a partnership which is to carry on the business is to be treated as disposing of a part of the business,
- the disposal by an individual of the whole or part of the individual's interest in the assets of a partnership is to be treated as a disposal by

the individual of the whole or part of the business carried on by the partnership, and

- at any time when a business is carried on by a partnership, the business is to be treated as owned by each individual who is at that time a member of the partnership.

Thus, in the context of partnerships, entrepreneurs' relief may potentially be relevant to gains made:

- by a partner on the disposal by the partnership of the whole or part of the partnership business;
- by a partner on the disposal of the whole or part of an interest in a partnership (including on a change of capital profit-sharing ratios);
- by an individual, on actual or deemed disposals when he admits partners into the business for the first time;
- by a partner on a disposal, following the cessation of the partnership business, of assets used by the business at the time of cessation;
- by certain trustees, in relation to 'trust business assets';
- by a partner making an 'associated disposal'; or
- by shareholders of a company which is a member of a partnership in circumstances where the relevant conditions are fulfilled (see **3.47** below).

The first three of these are reasonably straightforward, and substantially similar issues arise as arise on the disposal of a business by a sole trader. Note, however, that the requirement that a business must have been carried on for at least one year if relief is to be available is applied separately to each partner. This means that some partners may qualify and others may fail to qualify on the same disposal event.

Example 3.3 – One year of trading required for business to qualify

Rachel and Martyn established a nursery business as a partnership on 1 October 2013. Helen joins the partnership on 1 May 2014, paying £30,000 for her share of the goodwill of the business. Entrepreneurs' relief is not available on the gains realised by Rachel and Martyn, as the business has not been established for at least one year. If Rachel had run the nursery business as a sole trader for some years before Martyn joined as a partner on 1 October 2013, the gains realised by Rachel on 1 May 2014 would qualify for entrepreneurs' relief, but the gain made by Martyn on that date would not qualify.

Cessation of business

3.31 Relief may be claimed by a partner in respect of gains arising on a disposal of assets which were in use for the purposes of the partnership business at the time at which business ceased, provided the partner had been a partner in the business for at least one year before cessation and provided the asset is disposed of within three years of the cessation of the business. The relief applies equally to assets owned by the partnership and to assets owned personally. Although the circumstances in which this relief may be claimed has a superficial similarity to relief under the 'associated disposal' rules, the disposal described here remains a 'material disposal' and, in particular, is not subject to the restrictions on relief which apply to 'associated disposals' (see **3.34** below).

Example 3.4 – Cessation

Mr and Mrs Last have been trading in partnership as shoe repairers for many years from two shops. One of the shops is a partnership asset shown in the balance sheet, and the other is owned personally by Mrs Last. On receiving an offer from a property developer for one of the shops, Mr and Mrs Last decide to close down the business and retire. Assuming both shops are sold within three years of the date the business closes, gains on both the shops will qualify for entrepreneurs' relief.

Trust disposals

3.32 Trustees may, in certain circumstances, claim entrepreneurs' relief.

It is very important to appreciate that, although trustees may be partners in a partnership, the relief is not available in respect of gains made by trustees on the disposal of their interest in a partnership in which the trustees are themselves partners. Nor is it available in respect of gains arising when a partnership in which the trustees are partners makes a disposal of a business or part of a business.

Relief is available only in respect of gains on assets owned by the trustees but used by a partnership in which a 'qualifying beneficiary' is a partner. If there is no 'qualifying beneficiary', there can be no relief. Whether the trustees themselves are partners in the partnership is irrelevant.

The relief is given in respect of gains on disposals of 'settlement business assets'. In the context of a partnership, a trust asset is a 'settlement business asset' if:

- it is used, throughout a period of at least one year ending not more than three years before the date of disposal, for the purposes of a business carried on by a partnership of which a 'qualifying beneficiary' is or was a member; and

- the 'qualifying beneficiary' ceases to carry on the business (either because the partnership ceases to do so or because he ceases to be a partner) on the date of disposal or has done so within three years before that date.

A 'qualifying beneficiary' is one who has an interest in possession (other than for a fixed term) in the 'settlement business asset'. If more than one beneficiary has such an interest, the gain is apportioned and only that part apportioned to the qualifying beneficiary who carries on the business qualifies for relief.

Where the relief is claimed, it counts towards the lifetime limit of the qualifying beneficiary; consequently, any claim must be made jointly by the trustees and the qualifying beneficiary.

Example 3.5 – Trust disposal

Adolphus and his sister Cyrene each have a 50% life interest in a family trust which owns farmland. Adolphus (but not Cyrene) is a partner in the partnership which farms the land. Part of the land is re-zoned for residential development and is sold to a developer for £15m. The partnership continues to farm the remainder of the land.

Provided Adolphus has ceased to be a partner before the land is disposed of, entrepreneurs' relief can be claimed in respect of 50% of the gain (the claim to be made jointly by Adolphus and the trustees).

Note that, if Adolphus is still a partner at the date of disposal, the conditions for relief are not met.

Associated disposals

3.33 Where a partner disposes of the whole or part of his interest in a partnership in circumstances qualifying for entrepreneurs' relief (a 'material disposal'), a disposal of an asset held personally may qualify for entrepreneurs' relief as an 'associated disposal'. There is no requirement that the 'material disposal' actually gives rise to a gain – merely that the circumstances are such that, if there were a gain, it would qualify for entrepreneurs' relief. The conditions for 'associated disposal' relief were significantly restricted by *Finance Act 2015* and again by *Finance Act 2016*, the effect of which is to make rules which were already complex even more so.

The following sets out the position for disposals after 17 March 2015:

- If the material disposal in question is a complete disposal of the partner's interest in the partnership (such as where the partnership business is sold or the partner completely retires), the requirement is that either:
  - the interest disposed of is at least a 5% interest in the partnership; or
  - the partner's interest in the partnership must have been at least 5% throughout a continuous period of at least three years in the eight years ending with the date of the material disposal.
- If the material disposal is a disposal of something less than the partner's complete interest in the business, the material disposal itself must be of at least a 5% interest in the partnership assets.

In each case, there must be no 'partnership purchase arrangements' in existence – that is, arrangements whereby the partner making the disposal (or someone connected with him) can re-acquire an interest in (or increase an interest in) the partnership.

Subject to the above restrictions on which material disposals may be taken into account, entrepreneurs' relief is available on the disposal of an asset which:

- is disposed of as part of the partner's withdrawal from participation in the business carried on by the partnership (*TCGA 1992, s 169K(3),(5)*);
- was used for the purpose of the partnership business for at least one year to the date of disposal of the partnership interest, or the date or cessation of the partnership business if earlier (*TCGA 1992, s 169K(4)*); and
- had (if acquired on or after 13 June 2016) been owned by the partner throughout the period of three years ending with the date of disposal (*TCGA 1992, s 169K(4A)*). Where the asset is or has been jointly owned and the extent of the partner's interest in the asset has changed within the three years ending with the date of disposal, an appropriate apportionment of the gain is made and entrepreneurs' relief is available on the proportion of the gain which corresponds to the smallest share owned in the period.

HMRC manuals give some guidance on the interpretation of the phrase 'part of the partner's withdrawal from participation in the business' – see CG63995. It is explicitly stated that it is not necessary (in the case of a partial disposal) that the individual should actually reduce the amount of work done in the business, but the associated disposal and the material disposal should be 'part and parcel' of one single withdrawal from participation in the business. This means that there should normally be no significant interval between the two disposals. However, where the partnership ceases to trade, HMRC will accept that a disposal is capable of being 'associated' with the material disposal arising on cessation if it takes place within a year after cessation (it may not, by definition, take place before cessation, because of the requirement that it is still in use for the purposes of the partnership business on cessation). It will also qualify if it is disposed of:

- within three years after cessation, provided it has not been leased or used for any other purpose after the cessation of the business; or
- in cases where the partnership business has not ceased, within three years of the material disposal, provided it has not within that period been used for any purpose other than that of the business.

Example 3.6 – Disposal of partnership interest

Graham is in partnership with his son Tristan, sharing all profits: 7/8ths to Graham, 1/8th to Tristan. Graham owns the office from which the partnership has traded for a number of years. On his 60th birthday, Graham gifts the office to his son, and the profit-sharing ratios are changed to 1/4 to Graham and 3/4 to Tristan, but Graham continues to work full-time for the partnership. The disposal of the office to Tristan qualifies as an associated disposal, as Graham has at the same time made a disposal of at least 5% of his interest in the assets of the partnership.

Restrictions

3.34 There are four circumstances in which entrepreneurs' relief on an associated disposal is reduced to such amount as is 'just and reasonable':

(a) The asset has only been used by the business for only part of the period of ownership by the individual, in which case the gain taken into account will reflect the period of business use.

(b) Only part of the asset has been used for the purposes of the business, so the gain taken into account will reflect the proportion of the asset used for business purposes.

(c) The individual has been concerned in the carrying on of the business (whether as sole trader or as a partner of the partnership) for part only of the time during which the asset was used by the business. This is less likely than situations (a) or (b), but is possible where an individual was a salaried partner before becoming a full partner or perhaps where property is owned by a spouse who is subsequently taken into partnership.

(d) Any payment of rent was made for the use of the asset by the personal company or partnership for a period after 5 April 2008.

The payment of 'rent' in the final restriction means any form of consideration paid for the use of the asset, including licence fees for the use of intellectual property. Where the rent paid is less than a full market rent for the use of the asset, the gain is restricted proportionately.

Note that these restrictions apply only in the context of a claim to 'associated disposal' relief. They are of no relevance where relief is claimed on a 'material disposal' or to a claim by trustees on a disposal of 'settlement business assets'.

FAMILY PARTNERSHIPS

3.35 Family partnerships are often created with a view to spreading income between husband and wife (or more widely within a family) with a view to minimising tax. The first concern in such cases may be whether HMRC are able to challenge the validity of the partnership. Usually, if proper care has been taken with the planning, the answer is no. In HMRC's words:

> 'Where the spouse or civil partner has signed a deed declaring an intention to carry on the business and the deed gives a right to share in the profits, and subsequently accounts of the business show that that person has been allocated a share of the profits, there will not usually be much chance of mounting a successful challenge.' [BIM82065]

There is no reason in law why a child may not be a partner in a business, provided the child has the intellectual capacity to understand the nature of the business and the obligations of partnership. Thus a three-year-old could not be a partner: quite possibly a twelve-year-old could. The law is different in Scotland: there it is very unlikely that a child under the age of 16 could be a partner.

Focus

Partnerships between spouses or civil partners can be an easy and effective way of splitting income for tax purposes though the commercial and legal consequences of entering into partnership (including the exposure to unlimited liability in the case of an ordinary partnership) should be considered very carefully before taking such a step. Partnerships involving minor children (even where the children's capital contribution to the partnership has been funded by, for example, grandparents) are usually best avoided except in very special circumstances.

3.36 Quite separate from the question whether a spouse or other family member can be a partner is that of whether a partnership is capable of amounting to an arrangement conferring bounty and therefore a 'settlement' within the meaning of *ITTOIA 2005, Part 5, Chapter 5*. There are at least three circumstances in which this may be the case.

First, if a parent introduces a minor child into partnership, any share of income awarded to the child will almost always constitute income arising under a 'settlement' made on the child by the parent such that the income remains taxable on the parent. The only exception would be where, despite the minority, the child had genuinely 'earned' the income by his or her efforts: for example where the partnership exists to exploit the talents of a child performer.

Second, a partnership between husband and wife is potentially within the settlements legislation if the 'passive spouse' both (a) has no right to capital but only a right to income and (b) receives a greater share of income than is commensurate with the work done in the partnership. But this will not normally be the case: normally the spouse will share in capital as well as income of the partnership.

Third, a partnership may in some circumstances amount to a 'revocable settlement' and as such caught by the legislation even if the settlement is made on an adult.

Example 3.7 – Revocable settlement

Mr T is in partnership with his wife Mrs T. Their daughter is a university student. The deed is altered to admit the daughter as a partner. All the partners agree that on finishing her course the daughter's interest in the partnership will come to an end. The amendment of the partnership agreement under which the daughter is included without any additional capital or value being added by her is an arrangement with the requisite element of bounty. The gift from the parents is subject to conditions under which the property given will revert to them. The daughter's income is therefore treated as the income of the parents under *ITTOIA 2005, s 624*.

(Based on HMRC guidance at TSEM4215.)

3.37 Although entering into a partnership on favourable terms is likely to amount to the making of a settlement within the definition of the legislation, there are normally no tax consequences where the person benefitted is an adult other than the settlor's spouse or civil partner. In particular, it will not normally be possible for HMRC to challenge arrangements whereby the person benefitted is the settlor's adult child, parent or unmarried cohabitee.

Example 3.8 – Settlement on unconnected adult

Mr S is a tax adviser. He lives with Mr T but they are not in a civil partnership. Mr S and Mr T form a partnership to exploit Mr S's talents as tax adviser, sharing assets, profits and losses of the business equally. Mr T has no knowledge of tax, contributes no capital and does no work in the business. Nonetheless the partnership is not vulnerable to attack under the settlements legislation.

CGT implications of family partnerships

3.38 The introduction of a person into a partnership normally results in a change in the asset profit-sharing ratios and therefore a deemed disposal of chargeable assets held by the partnership. Where the parties are not connected the deemed disposal value will be the value at which the assets are recognised in the partnership balance sheet plus any off-balance-sheet payment. Where the parties are connected other than by being in partnership (as when family members join the partnership) and a different value would have been used had they not been connected, the disposal will be deemed to take effect at the open market value of the interest transferred. Thus, if in a family partnership an adult daughter is admitted to partnership without payment for her share of goodwill and business premises, and it is established that, were it not for the family relationship, values of £20,000 and £50,000 would have been attributed to the interests in the assets transferred to her by the other family members, those values will be used and the CGT consequences will follow.

If the partnership is a trading partnership and the asset is used wholly for the purpose of the trade it will normally be the case that the transferor(s) and transferee may jointly elect for the otherwise chargeable gain to be deducted from the deemed acquisition cost of the transferee (ie the said market value) under the business assets gifts relief provisions of *TCGA 1992, s 165*.

SALARIED PARTNERS

General partnerships

3.39 A person described as a 'salaried partner' may be a true partner; or he may be an employee given the title as matter of prestige. Which he is, is a question of fact.

The question is – is the 'salaried partner' a party to the partnership agreement and entitled under it to participate as principal in the general management and conduct of the business? It is, as HMRC put it at BIM82025, 'inherent in the contract of partnership that a true partner (as opposed to an employee) is permitted, indeed has the right, to participate in the general management and administration of the firm'.

The question of status may arise not only in relation to HMRC but also where a salaried partner, on leaving the firm, seeks to establish that he or she was an 'employee' with full employment rights. This has happened in a number of cases, including *Tiffin v Lester Aldridge LLP* [2012] EWCA Civ 35. The position is now possibly further muddied by the so-called 'gig economy' cases, such as *Aslam, Farrar & others v Uber BV and others*, *Pimlico Plumbers v Gary Smith*, *Boxer v Excel Group Services* and *Dewhurst v City Sprint*. The *Employment Rights Act 1996*, the *Working Time Regulations 1998* and the *National Minimum Wage Act 1998* all apply not only to employees but also to 'workers'. This term is defined to mean an individual working under a contract whereby the individual:

> 'Undertakes to do or perform personally any work or services for another party to the contract whose status is not by virtue of the contract that of a client or customer of any profession or business undertaking carried on by the individual.'

Thus, an individual working under a contract may be, depending on the facts:

- employed; or
- self-employed, but a 'worker' entitled to the protections of the *Employment Rights Act* etc; or
- self-employed and not a 'worker'.

Whether this now means that a 'salaried partner' may fall into the third category has not yet been established by the courts.

Limited liability partnerships

3.40 Until *FA 2014* changed the law, it was regarded as impossible for HMRC to challenge the 'employment' status of a member of an LLP: a member of an LLP could not in practice be re-categorised as an employee of it. The obvious scope which this gave for NIC avoidance led to legislation (now *ITTOIA 2005, s 863A et seq*) which treats any member of an LLP as an employee for tax purposes unless at least one of three possible 'escape routes' is satisfied. The legislation in this area is detailed and complex: what follows is a summary highlighting key planning areas. What is important to understand is that these three 'escape routes' are largely mechanistic and are different from the normal tests of employment. It is possible to envisage situations where a person who would not be treated as an employee of an ordinary partnership may be treated as an employee of an LLP and vice versa.

> **Focus**
>
> 'Salaried members' of an LLP are subject to a special rule designed to counter 'disguised employment' which does not apply to ordinary partnerships. The special rule differs significantly from the ordinary tests of employment with the result that 'salaried members' who would not be regarded as employees under the ordinary case law tests may nonetheless be caught by the special rule: but some 'salaried members' who have all the normal characteristics of employees may nonetheless be able to take steps to ensure that they are not caught by the special rule.

3.41 The first 'escape route' is that it is reasonable to expect that more than 20% of the member's share of profit from the LLP will be something other than 'disguised salary'. An amount is 'disguised salary' if either: (a) it is fixed; or (b) it varies by reference to something other than the overall profits of the LLP as a whole; or (c) it is not in practice affected by the overall profits of the LLP as a whole. Thus, counter-intuitively, a share of departmental profits, however variable and inconstant, remains 'disguised salary'. A share of profit which is nominally dependent on overall LLP profit but which is subject to underpinning or capping arrangements which mean that the amount actually payable is all but certain will also rank as 'disguised salary'.

3.42 The second 'escape route' is that the member has 'significant influence' over the affairs of the LLP. In small LLPs it is probable that every member has 'significant influence': in larger ones, where management is delegated to a management or executive committee, it is likely that only members of such a committee will have it.

The third 'escape route' is that the member's 'contribution' to the LLP is at least 25% of the amount of the 'disguised salary' which it is reasonable to expect that the member will receive. 'Contribution' means broadly the amount of the member's capital account with the LLP. Artificial arrangements whereby the capital account does not truly represent the amount which the member has at risk are countered by the legislation. Thus a contribution does not count if and to the extent that the 'real' equity members guarantee the LLPs obligations to a 'salaried member' or the contribution is financed by limited-recourse loans or loans guaranteed by the LLP itself.

COMPANIES IN PARTNERSHIP

> **Focus**
>
> There is no reason why a company may not be a member of a partnership, and in some circumstances this may be attractive for tax and other reasons. However, care must be taken with regard to the possible application of anti-avoidance legislation introduced by the *Finance Act 2014*.

Trading status of corporate partners

3.43 Certain tax advantages are afforded to trading companies. The definition may vary according to the relief concerned but one might need to consider, for example, the scope of IHT business property relief (BPR), CGT entrepreneurs' relief or CGT hold-over relief for gifts.

> **Focus**
>
> Is a company whose purpose and activity is to be a partner in a partnership a trading company for tax purposes? On first principles the answer is yes: a corporate partner will as a matter of fact be carrying on in common with the other members of the partnership the business of the partnership; so if the business is a trade, the company is carrying on that trade. It should however be noted that, just like any other trading company which accumulates and invests profits, its status as a trading company may be compromised by its use of the accumulated profits. And, from 18 March 2015, the status of shares in a corporate partner for CGT entrepreneurs' relief requires very careful consideration, having regard to amendments to the definition of 'trading company' made both by *Finance Act 2015* and *Finance Act 2016*.

3.44 Thus, a corporate partner which uses its surplus profits from the partnership business to build, say, an investment portfolio outside the partnership business, may find that, on the facts, the relative sizes of its partnership trading activity and its non-partnership non-trading activity may have the result that IHT BPR or CGT entrepreneurs' relief may be restricted or denied. Overlaid upon that is a special rule applying only to entrepreneurs' relief on which we give further detail at **3.47** below.

Inheritance tax: BPR

3.45 *IHTA 1984, s 105(3)* denies BPR altogether in respect of shares in a company if the company's business is mainly making or holding investments. But even if the company's business is mainly trading so that relief is in principle due, relief may be restricted by virtue of *IHTA 1984, s 112*. This requires relief to be restricted by reference to the value of any assets which are neither used nor required for use in the business ('excepted assets'). HMRC do, however, accept that 'the business' means here the entirety of the company's activities and not just the trading activity (see SVM111220). Hence in the case of a company whose business is mainly trading but which also carries on an investment activity, assets will be 'excepted' only if used for neither the trading nor the investment part of the 'hybrid' business.

> **Focus**
>
> IHT Business Property Relief is denied if the partnership agreement contains obligations and provisions which together amount to a binding contract for sale of a partner's interest in the partnership on death. This can be avoided by careful drafting involving the use of cross-options.

3.46 In HMRC's view, cash which is surplus to the present and future needs of a trading business can almost never be regarded as an asset of a separate investment business (because holding it 'requires no effort and involves no activity') so will almost always constitute an 'excepted asset'. IHT considerations would therefore tend towards recommending investment of surplus cash into other investments so as to demonstrate the existence of an 'investment activity' element to the company's business rather than simply retaining it in cash.

The relief is incidentally denied if, on the death of the shareholder, there are provisions that amount to a binding contract for sale (*IHTA 1984, s 113*). Accordingly, when drafting the partnership agreement, care should be taken regarding the relevant provisions.

Entrepreneurs' relief

3.47 The entrepreneurs' relief position is very different. Shares in a company will qualify for the relief only if the company is a 'trading company' at all relevant times. The basic definition of 'trading company' is at *TCGA 1992, s 165A* – a company which (a) carries on trading activities; and (b) whose activities do not include to a substantial extent activities other than trading activities. 'Substantial' is undefined, but HMRC apply a rule of thumb which treats 'substantial' as meaning more than 20% (see CG64090 for more detail on the application of the 20% test). Thus a company which satisfies the 'wholly or mainly' requirement of IHT BPR may nonetheless fail to meet the stricter test for entrepreneurs' relief. On the other hand, the entrepreneurs' relief test at *TCGA 1992, s 165A* is by reference to 'activities'. It is at least arguable (especially in view of what HMRC say about 'lack of activity' in the IHT context – see SVM111220 above) that the mere passive holding of surplus cash (of whatever amount) can never amount to a non-trading 'activity' so that, while a holding of surplus cash may restrict IHT BPR it can never of itself disqualify a company from entrepreneurs' relief. Thus the best advice if entrepreneurs' relief is to be secured may be diametrically opposed to that which best secures IHT BPR, namely to retain surplus assets in cash and to avoid the further 'activity' implicit in making other investments. Even in this case, the entrepreneurs' relief position is not completely clear: for further guidance on HMRC's current views on the impact on entrepreneurs' relief of the investment of surplus cash, see CG64060.

In summary, a corporate partner which accumulates profits from its partnership trading and either retains those profits in cash or diversifies into other (non-trading) activities may need to take great care lest it be at risk of losing its trading status for the purposes of BPR, entrepreneurs' relief or both.

3.48 It is also necessary to take into account the changes effected first by the *Finance Act 2015* and subsequently by *Finance Act 2016* (with retrospective effect to 18 March 2015). These specify (via *TCGA 1992, Sch 7ZA*) the circumstances in which activities carried on by a company as a member of a partnership are to be treated as trading activities.

Specifically, such activities count as trading activities only if the person disposing of the shares ('P') passes both the 'profits and assets test' and the 'voting rights test' in relation to the partnership. At their simplest, these tests require that P should indirectly possess (via his interest in the corporate member) a right to at least 5% of the profits, assets and votes of the partnership throughout a period of at least one year ending with the disposal. Thus, if the members of a trading partnership comprise four companies all with equal rights, any shareholder who holds at least 20% of one of the companies could potentially qualify for Entrepreneurs Relief on a disposal of his interest in the company (since 20% × 25% = 5%).

> **Focus**
>
> The *Finance Act 2015* and *Finance Act 2016* amended the entrepreneurs' relief rules to apply an indirect 5% test to the holding of shares in a company which is a member of a partnership.

There is a sting in the tail of the *Finance Act 2015* change. Normally, when a company ceases for any reason to qualify as a 'trading company', a disposal of shares (including by way of liquidation) can continue to qualify for entrepreneurs' relief if it is made up to three years after the trading status is lost. But where a company loses its trading status as a result of the coming into force of the *Finance Act 2015* change, this 'three-year' rule does not apply.

Capital allowances: annual investment allowance (AIA)

3.49 A partnership consisting of, or including, companies is debarred from claiming AIA.

By *CAA 2001, s 38A* the relief is available only to companies, individuals and partnerships of individuals.

MIXING PERSONAL AND CORPORATE PARTNERS

3.50 It has historically been possible to seek to get the 'best of both worlds' by use of a 'mixed' partnership whereby the members of a trading partnership include both the individual members and one or more companies controlled by the members, either individually or jointly.

With effect from 6 April 2014, *ITTOIA 2005, s 850C* removes virtually all the tax advantages that might otherwise have been expected to flow from mixed member partnerships. From that date mixed member partnerships will seldom be attractive. Nor, unfortunately, is there any 'grandfathering' provision to protect mixed member partnerships already in existence as at the date the law changed.

> **Focus**
>
> Since the enactment of the *Finance Act 2014* the involvement of companies in a partnership should be approached with great care. Existing fully corporate arrangements should normally be safe, but new arrangements may be vulnerable.

Mixed member partnerships: Finance Act 2014 provisions

3.51 Very broadly, *ITTOIA 2005, s 850C* bites where a share of partnership income which would otherwise have arisen to an individual partner in a partnership is in some sense diverted to a company partner in which the individual has some kind of economic interest with a consequent reduction in tax. It operates by re-attributing the income back to the partner from whom it was diverted.

More specifically, the rules apply where one of two conditions ('Condition X and Condition Y') is fulfilled, though there is considerable overlap between the conditions and there are many situations where both conditions will be fulfilled. In each case, the rules apply only if the 'diversion' of profit share from the individual to the company results in a reduction in the overall tax bill. There is no motive test: it is not necessary that the 'diversion' should have been undertaken with the purpose or intention of reducing the tax charge: merely that it does in fact do so.

Condition X

3.52 Condition X is that it is 'reasonable to suppose' that the corporate partner's profit share includes amounts representing the individual's 'deferred profit' – that is, a share of partnership profit which will, or even might, be allocated to the individual in the future. So much of the company's profit share as it is reasonable to suppose is attributable to an individual's 'deferred profit' as determined on a 'just and reasonable' basis is then re-allocated for tax purposes to the individual. The most obvious case will be where profits required for retention as working capital in the business are allocated to a corporate partner but in some way earmarked for individual partners, as in **Example 3.9**.

Example 3.9 – Re-allocation of company profit share: Condition X

Smith, Jones, Green and Brown are in partnership together with SJGB Ltd, a company which they own in equal shares. £100,000 of profit is allocated to SJGB Ltd. In this case the 'deferred profit' is re-allocated equally. More complicated arrangements might involve the use of different share classes with separately designated reserves or simply through a memorandum note; in that case the 'deferred profit' would be reallocated in whatever way is just and reasonable.

3.53 There is no scope for any re-allocation of profit to be retrospectively changed if an individual never receives the 'deferred profit' allocated to him.

Example 3.10 – Non-receipt of re-allocated profit

Following from **Example 3.9**, Brown leaves the partnership some years later and, under the terms of the partnership agreement, his shares in SJGB Ltd are bought back at par value. The law provides no remedy to Brown as against HMRC for the fact that he will have paid Income Tax on £25,000 of profit which he never in fact receives. Any adjustment to be made as between the partners is a matter for private agreement between them, and it would be prudent to cover this in the partnership agreement.

Condition Y

3.54 It is also necessary to consider the alternative condition which may apply to mixed member partnerships, 'Condition Y'. This operates where:

- a corporate member's profit share exceeds the 'appropriate notional profit';
- an individual member of the partnership has 'power to enjoy' any part of the company's profit share; and

- it is reasonable to suppose that the whole or part of the company's profit shares is attributable to the individual's power to enjoy it.

Where these conditions are fulfilled, so much of the company's profit share as exceeds the 'appropriate notional profit' and as, it is reasonable to suppose, is attributable to the individual's power to enjoy (determined on a just and reasonable basis) is re-allocated for tax purposes to the individual. **Example 3.11** illustrates a very straightforward example of the operation of Condition Y.

Example 3.11 – Re-allocation of company profit share: Condition Y

Smith and Jones are in partnership along with Smith Ltd and Jones Ltd (100% owned by Smith and Jones respectively). Profits are allocated 50% to Smith/Smith Ltd and 50% to Jones/Jones Ltd with each individual able to determine how 'his' share of profit is allocated between himself and his company. The effect of *ITTOIA 2005, s 850C* is that (subject to what is said later in this chapter) Smith and Jones will each be assessed to income tax on 50% of the partnership profit.

Appropriate notional profit

3.55 'Appropriate notional profit' is defined as the sum of the appropriate notional return on capital and the appropriate notional consideration for services. The first is, essentially, interest at a commercial rate on any capital which the company has contributed to the partnership. 'Contribution' for this purpose has the same meaning as in *ITA 2007, s 108* – broadly the permanent capital of the partnership as distinct from short-term loans. All relevant circumstances are to be taken into account; these would presumably include the risk profile of the firm's business, what other assets and liabilities the firm had and the rates of interest being paid by the firm on commercial loans from unconnected lenders. HMRC guidance underlines that the rate must be a reasonable rate of interest; it is not relevant that an equity return on the same investment might have been much greater. Thus if, in **Example 3.11**, the partnership was borrowing from commercial lenders at say 6%, and Smith Ltd and Jones Ltd each had capital accounts with the partnership of £100,000, an 'appropriate notional return on capital' might (at least in HMRC's view) be £6,000 per annum for each corporate partner and it would be only the excess of each company's profit share over that amount which would be re-allocated.

3.56 An appropriate notional consideration for services is the arm's length value of services provided to the partnership by the corporate member, but disregarding any services involving other members of the partnership. Thus, in **Example 3.11**, if the only services provided to the partnership by Smith Ltd are the services of Smith himself, the 'appropriate notional consideration for services' would be nil. But if (for example) Jones Ltd owns property which is made available to the partnership rent-free, the 'appropriate notional return for services' would be the market rent of the property.

Power to enjoy

3.57 It is important to appreciate that although the legislation refers to 'mixed membership' it does not attack the mixing of corporate and individual members per se. It is only where an individual partner has 'power to enjoy' all or part of a corporate partner's profit share – very broadly speaking, where he has some sort of connection with the corporate partner – that the legislation comes into play. Thus if, in **Example 3.11**, Mr Smith had been in partnership only with Jones Ltd (a company with which he has no economic interest or connection other than being in partnership), the legislation would not have been relevant. 'Power to enjoy' is, however, very widely defined, with three main branches.

3.58 First, an individual has 'power to enjoy' a company's profit share if he is connected with the company within the meaning of *ITA 2007, s 993* (otherwise, of course, than simply by being in partnership with it). This is itself a very wide-ranging definition and would include the case where the company is controlled (within the meaning of *CTA 2010, s 450*) by the individual or his associates, and can lead to some counter-intuitive results. For example, if Smith is in partnership with a company owned by the trustees of a charitable trust of which his grandfather was the settlor, he has 'power to enjoy' the company's profit share and it will be vulnerable to re-allocation to him.

3.59 Second, there is 'power to enjoy' if any of five specified 'enjoyment conditions' is met. These are, in fact, substantially the same as the notoriously wide enjoyment conditions which apply for the purposes of *ITA 2007, s 723* (the 'transfer of assets abroad' legislation). Thus profits will be vulnerable to re-allocation if:

- the company's profit share is in fact so dealt with as to be calculated at some time to enure to the benefit of the individual; or
- the receipt of the company's profit share operates to increase the value of assets held by or for the benefit of the individual; or
- the individual is entitled to receive any benefit provided out of the company's profit share; or
- the individual may become entitled to the beneficial enjoyment of the company's profit share if one or more powers are exercised by any person; or

- the individual is able to control the application of the company's profit share.

3.60 Third, even if none of these enjoyment conditions is met and the individual is not connected with the company, the legislation provides that the individual will nonetheless be deemed to have 'power to enjoy' if he is a party to any arrangements one of the main purposes of which is to secure that an amount included in the company's profit share is charged to Corporation Tax and not Income Tax. Read strictly, this would seem to put at risk any individual who merely acquiesced in the introduction to the partnership of a corporate partner even though the individual himself derived no direct or indirect benefit from the arrangement, though it is to be hoped that the courts would draw back from such a draconian interpretation of the law.

Attribution

3.61 Having established that the corporate partner's profit share exceeds the appropriate notional profit and that an individual partner has the 'power to enjoy' it in some degree, it remains to determine whether it is reasonable to suppose that any part of the company's profit share is attributable to the power to enjoy. In other words, would the company have received the profit share but for the individual's power to enjoy it? Sometimes the answer to the question will be obvious: in **Example 3.11**, it would defy credibility to suppose that Smith Ltd would have received its profit share had not Smith owned it. In other circumstances there may be a point to be taken. As a rule, it is probably fair to say that the more remote and indirect the individual's 'power to enjoy' interest in the company, the less reasonable it may be to suppose that the company's profit share is attributable to it. It is, however, worth pointing out that one of the odder features of the new law is that it may reallocate to an individual income which would not have been caught by the settlements legislation. For example, if an individual sole trader were to take into partnership his adult children and his spouse, or were to transfer the sole trade to a company in which they were shareholders, neither the profit share nor the dividend income of the family members would normally be within the scope of the settlements legislation and would remain taxable on the recipients. Yet if he were to take into partnership a company in which his family were shareholders, *ITTOIA 2005, s 850C* would be likely to re-allocate the company's entire profit share to him.

Double taxation

3.62 As one would expect, where income of a corporate partner is re-allocated under the new rules to an individual member, a 'just and reasonable' adjustment is made to the corporate partner's taxable profit. Usually this will simply be to reduce the company's taxable profit by the amount taxed on the individual, but in some cases the differing computational rules applying to companies and to individuals will mean that the 'just and reasonable' adjustment is less straightforward.

The other area in which double taxation needs to be considered is in relation to the extraction from the company of amounts representing the re-allocated income. Where income of a company has been taxed on an individual it would plainly be absurd for a second charge to be imposed on the subsequent distribution of that income to the individual. The new rules do indeed provide that any such payment is ignored for tax purposes, but only:

- if there is an agreement in place in relation to the amount re-allocated;
- the payment is made as a result of the agreement; and
- the payment is not made under arrangement one of the main purposes of which is the avoidance of tax.

The legislation is silent as to the form of the agreement or when it must be in place: but best practice may be for the agreement to take the form of a deed and for it to be entered into as soon as it becomes apparent that re-allocation is a possibility.

One possible difficulty may arise where the application of the legislation is not recognised (or not conceded) until some years after the income has arisen in the company and after distributions have been made (whether as salary or as dividend) to the individual in question and after they have been included on that individual's tax return and tax paid on them. Can it really be said either that 'there is an agreement in place in relation to the amount re-allocated' or that the payment is made 'as a result of' that agreement when the payments were in fact made some years before the possibility of re-allocation was recognised? And in such a case can the rule operate to allow a refund to be claimed of the tax previously paid on the relevant remuneration or dividends? One would hope that HMRC would take the same broad and teleological approach to the interpretation of relieving legislation of this kind as to assessing legislation; but there must be a doubt.

And one case in which there would certainly be a difficulty would be if income of a company were to re-allocated after the company had applied the income in, for example, making pension contributions for the benefit of the individual, as shown in the example below.

Example 3.12 – Inability to distribute re-allocated income

Adam Ltd, controlled by Adam, is a member of a partnership. In the year to 31 March 2015 its share of profit is £100,000. It uses its entire profit share to make a pension contribution to Adam's pension fund. Following enquiry and appeal to the First-tier Tribunal it is held in 2018 that £75,000 of the income of Adam Ltd should be re-allocated to Adam for tax purposes.

The consequence would appear to be that Adam is liable to tax for 2014–15 on the £75,000 even though (a) he has never received it and (b) the company is not able to pay it to him. Logically, the legislation should give him relief against the £75,000 deemed income for the contribution made by the company to the pension fund; but there is no machinery by which this can be done. Adam is therefore significantly worse off than he would have been had he been a member of the partnership personally.

Anti-avoidance, grandfathering and the scope of the new rules

3.63 It might reasonably be supposed that if what is perceived to be objectionable is a 'mixed member' partnership, HMRC would raise no objection to pure corporate partnerships or to the restructuring of existing 'mixed member' partnerships so as to become pure corporate partnerships. That this is not so must be one of the most puzzling features of the legislation. Yet this is the intention and effect of the anti-avoidance rule introduced as *ITTOIA 2005, s 850D*. This rule applies where a partnership is not in fact a mixed member partnership but:

- an individual personally performs services for the firm;
- a non-individual partner has a share of the firm's profit; and
- it is reasonable to suppose that the individual would have been a partner in the firm but for the new rules introduced by *ITTOIA 2005, s 850C*.

Where *ITTOIA 2005, s 850D* applies, the individual is treated as if he had been a partner in the firm with the result that the main provisions at *ITTOIA 2005, s 850C* potentially apply.

Example 3.13 – Restructuring ineffective in avoiding re-allocation of profit

Smith and Jones are in partnership together with their respective companies Smith Ltd and Jones Ltd. As a result of the new legislation all or part of any profit share allocated to the companies is at risk of being re-allocated by *ITTOIA 2005, s 850C* to the individuals. This remains the case even if Smith and Jones now resign from the partnership leaving only their companies as members, since the anti-avoidance rule will bite: plainly is it 'reasonable to suppose' that Smith and Jones would have continued to be partners alongside their companies but for *ITTOIA 2005, s 850C*.

3.64 In theory, *ITTOIA 2005, s 850D* (and thus *ITTOIA 2005, s 850C*) would not be in point if it could be shown that the motivation of Smith and Jones in resigning from the partnership owed nothing to a desire to avoid the impact of *ITTOIA 2005, s 850C*. In practice, it is difficult to envisage any circumstances in which that could credibly be argued to be the case.

Although in general it is a question of fact whether it is 'reasonable to suppose' that a given individual would have been a member of a given partnership but for *ITTOIA 2005, s 850C*, the legislation at *ITTOIA 2005, s 850D* gives one specific example where it is conclusively deemed to be the case. That is, where the individual is a member not of the partnership itself but of a partnership (or, more likely, an LLP) which is in turn a member of the partnership. Hence structures such as **Example 3.14** will be caught by the new rules.

Example 3.14 – Deemed membership of LLP by individuals

XYZ LLP has as its members X LLP, Y LLP and Z LLP whose members are respectively Mr X and his company X Ltd, Mr Y and his company Y Ltd, and Mr Z and his company Z Ltd. Although XYZ LLP is not a 'mixed member' partnership, it is deemed to be reasonable to suppose that X Y and Z would have been members but for *ITTOIA 2005, s 850C* with the result that the profits of their respective companies are vulnerable to re-allocation.

Grandfathering

3.65 There is no 'grandfathering' for mixed member partnerships which were in existence before the introduction of the new rules: thus, from 6 April 2014, any mixed member partnership must have regard to *ITTOIA 2005, s 850C*.

However, because the anti-avoidance rule at *ITTOIA 2005, s 850D* applies only if it is reasonable to suppose that an individual would have been a member 'but for' *ITTOIA 2005, s 850C*, it logically follows that a pure corporate partnership which antedates *ITTOIA 2005, s 850D* cannot be within its scope. HMRC have confirmed their agreement with that interpretation and accept that it cannot be inferred that an individual would have been a member of a partnership but for the new rules if the individual withdrew from the partnership before the new rules were announced on 5 December 2013. Thus if, in **Example 3.11**, Smith and Jones had by good fortune or by virtue of a reliable crystal ball resigned as individuals before 5 December 2013, leaving a pure corporate partnership as at that date, the profits of their companies would not be at risk of re-allocation to them. HMRC have further confirmed that a change taking place on or after

5 December will be treated in the same way provided the decision to make the change was made before 5 December. One example of this might be where a member who is required to give notice of resignation gave such notice before 5 December 2013 but did not cease to be a member until the expiry of the notice period after that date.

3.66 The position of corporate members joining existing pure corporate partnerships after 5 December 2013 is not completely clear. The key question is whether it is reasonable to suppose that the new member would have joined in an individual capacity if *ITTOIA 2005, s 850C* had not been enacted. In the case of a partnership which has historically been a pure corporate partnership with a track record of new members joining as companies, it may be unreasonable to make such a supposition; on the other hand, if a company joins what has historically been a mixed member partnership it may be more likely that *ITTOIA 2005, s 850D* may be in point.

New pure corporate partnerships

3.67 The position of new pure corporate partnerships is even less clear. Where a new pure corporate partnership is created to acquire the business of an existing 'tainted' mixed member partnership it seems likely that *ITTOIA 2005, s 850D* would be in point. But what of a pure corporate partnership created to undertake an entirely new project or trade? It seems to be HMRC's view that it depends on whether the decision to use corporate rather than individual members is driven by tax or by wider commercial considerations, though it must be said that this seems to be a very broad interpretation of *ITTOIA 2005, s 850C* which may not be supported by the courts. Thus if two established companies come together to form a partnership to carry out a particular project – something which is common in, for example, the property development sector – the likelihood that HMRC would seek to invoke *ITTOIA 2005, s 850D* is small. But if a number of individuals wishing to establish a new business form new companies to become members of a new partnership through which the trade is to be conducted, HMRC may feel more confident in seeking to apply *ITTOIA 2005, s 850D*.

STAMP DUTY LAND TAX

3.68 Chargeable interests held by or on behalf of a partnership are treated for SDLT purposes as held by, or on behalf of, the partners, and land transactions entered into for the purposes of a partnership are treated as entered into by, or on behalf of, the partners (and not by the partnership as such). This is the case irrespective of whether the partnership has a legal personality or is a body corporate under the law of the country in which it is formed (*FA 2003, s 104* and *Sch 15, Pt 1*).

The partnership is treated as continuing, regardless of changes in composition, as long as one partner continues.

> **Focus**
>
> Although third-party sales and purchases by partnership are relatively straightforward in SDLT terms, the rules applying to transfers between partnerships and their partners and on sales of interests in a partnership are not only complex but have changed regularly since the introduction of SDLT in 2003. The general rule is now, in essence, to look through to the underlying ownership of the property (but in terms of entitlement to income, not capital). This can create unwelcome charges but is also capable of resulting in a much reduced or zero charge to SDLT on some transfers.

3.69 Purchases and sales of land by the partnership are therefore reasonably straightforward in SDLT terms. The main complexities arise with *Part 3* of *FA 2003, Sch 15* – 'Transactions to which special provisions apply'.

Transactions to which special provisions apply: FA 2003, Sch 15, Pt 3

3.70 Special provisions apply to

- the transfer of a chargeable interest to a partnership by a partner or a person connected with a partner;
- the transfer of an interest in a partnership;
- the transfer of a chargeable interest from a partnership to a partner or a person connected with a partner.

Transfer of a chargeable interest to a partnership

3.71 The transfer of a chargeable interest to a partnership by a partner or a person connected with a partner (or a person who become a partner as a result of the transfer) will in principle give rise to a charge to SDLT (*FA 2003, Sch 15, para 10*). The broad aim of the legislation here is to 'look through' the partnership to the partners so as to identify the value that is actually changing hands and to charge SDLT on that amount.

The simplest example is where an individual transfers a chargeable interest to a partnership with whose members he is otherwise unconnected. The amount on which SDLT is charged is in that case the percentage of the market value of the asset which is equal to the percentage which he gives up – that is, the difference between the 100% of the asset which he owns at the outset and the share of the asset which he owns (via his membership of the partnership) after the transfer.

Example 3.15 – Transfer from a partner to a partnership

Smith owns a property. He joins a partnership in which he takes a 25% share and on joining it transfers to the partnership as partner's capital a property worth £400,000.

Smith has effectively given up 75% of the value in the property. SDLT is due on 75% × £400,000 = £300,000. Note that the value which the partners attribute to the property is irrelevant: SDLT will be due by reference to a percentage of the market value.

The same SDLT would be payable if Smith were already a 25% member of the partnership and was selling the property to the LLP for value. Again, he would be giving up a 75% interest and SDLT would be due on 75% of the value (regardless of the selling price).

For this purpose (as for *FA 2003, Sch 15* generally) the shares in which partners are treated as owning partnership assets are determined by reference to the shares in which income profits of the partnership are allocated (*FA 2003, Sch 15, para 34*). This may, of course, be different from the shares in which capital profits are allocated (which is what is relevant for CGT purposes) and may be a trap for the unwary.

Taking a slightly more complex case, where the individual who is making the transfer is connected with other members of the partnership, regard is had not only to share of the asset which he himself owns (via his membership of the partnership) after the transfer but also to that owned by partners connected with him.

Example 3.16 – Effect of connected parties in partnership

If, in **Example 3.15**, Smith's civil partner Jones was also a member of the partnership, with a 15% share of profits, Smith would be regarded as having effectively given up 60% (that is, 100% – 25% – 15%) of the property so that SDLT would be due on 60% × £400,000 = £240,000.

3.72 A charge to SDLT can arise where land has been transferred into a partnership by a partner and within three years of the date of transfer a 'qualifying event' occurs. This is defined as the transferor:

(a) withdrawing from the partnership any money or money's worth other than income profit; or

(b) obtaining repayment of any loan he has made to the partnership.

In such circumstances the 'qualifying event' is treated as a chargeable transaction and the chargeable consideration is taken to be the amount of the withdrawal or repayment up to the market value of the chargeable interest transferred (less any amount previously chargeable).

3.73 If the partnership to which the chargeable interest is transferred is a property-investment partnership (PIP) an election can be made to disapply the treatment described at **3.71** above and instead to pay SDLT by reference to the full market value of the chargeable interest transferred (*FA 2003, Sch 15, para 12A*). Although such an election would initially seem counter-intuitive, the advantage of making the election is that it will avoid any subsequent charge as described under **3.72** above and will also reduce the amount of SDLT payable on a subsequent transfer of an interest in the PIP.

For this purpose, a PIP is not, as might reasonably be supposed, simply a partnership which invests in property. Instead, it is defined (by *FA 2003, Sch 15, para 14(8)*) as a partnership whose sole or main activity is investing or dealing in chargeable interests (whether or not that activity also involves the carrying out of construction operations on the land in question). A property development partnership and a land dealing partnership will therefore both be PIPs.

Transfer of an interest in a partnership

3.74 SDLT is in principle payable on the transfer of an interest in a PIP where the partnership property includes a chargeable interest. This includes not only the case where a person becomes a partner but also the case where one partner's share reduces (including a reduction to zero on leaving the partnership) and the share of another partner or partners increases. Any person whose partnership share increases (including any new partner) is treated as the 'purchaser' for SDLT purposes and is answerable for the relevant SDLT.

A transfer of an interest in a partnership other than a PIP is not subject to SDLT (regardless of the amount of chargeable property held within the partnership).

3.75 On a transfer of an interest in a PIP, SDLT is chargeable on the proportion changing hands of the market value of 'relevant partnership property'. Thus, if a partner in a PIP having a 10% share in the partnership retires from the partnership, the remaining partners will suffer a charge to SDLT on 10% of the 'relevant partnership property'.

3.76 What is included in (or excluded from) 'relevant partnership property' depends on the type of transfer, styled either a 'Type A' transfer or a 'Type B' transfer.

3.77 A Type A transfer is one where:

- a partner's share is acquired (in whole or part) by another person (either an existing or a new partner) for consideration in money or money's worth; or
- a person becomes a partner; the interest of an existing partner reduces (or ceases) and money or money's worth is withdrawn from the partnership by the existing partner (other than out of resources available to the partnership prior to the transfer).

For a Type A transfer, the 'relevant partnership property' taken into account is every chargeable interest held by the partnership immediately after the transfer of the partnership interest except for:

- any chargeable interest transferred to the partnership in connection with the transfer;
- leases at a market rent; and
- any chargeable interest that is not attributable economically to the partnership interest transferred.

3.78 Any other transfer is styled a Type B transfer. In the case of a Type B transfer, the 'relevant partnership property' excludes (in addition to the exclusions for a Type A transfer):

- any chargeable interest transferred to the partnership on or before 22 July 2004;
- any chargeable interest for which the *FA 2003, Sch 15, para 12A* election has been made; and
- any other chargeable interest which was transferred to the partnership other than by a partner or a person connected with a partner.

Transfer of a chargeable interest from a partnership

3.79 As with a transfer to a partnership, the transfer of a chargeable interest from a partnership to a partner or a person connected with a partner (or to a person who ceases to be a partner as a result of the transfer) will in principle give rise to a charge to SDLT (*FA 2003, Sch 15, para 18*). As with transfers the other way, the broad aim of the legislation is to 'look through' the partnership to the partners so as to identify the value that is actually changing hands and to charge SDLT on that amount.

3.80 Thus on a transfer of land from a partnership consisting of husband and wife (or other connected parties) to a company controlled by those persons (or by any one of them), no SDLT is payable (including in the particular case where a business is incorporated). This may be thought anomalous given that there is no corresponding SDLT relief on the incorporation of a sole trade. Those contemplating taking advantage of the anomaly by converting a sole trade to a partnership shortly before incorporation would, however, be well advised to contemplate the anti-avoidance rules at *Finance Act 2003, s 75A et seq.*

Chapter 4

Company purchase of own shares

Mark McLaughlin CTA (Fellow), ATT (Fellow), TEP, Tax Consultant, Mark McLaughlin Associates Ltd

SIGNPOSTS

- **Scope** – A purchase of own shares (eg by an owner-managed company) generally falls to be treated as an income distribution. However, there is an exception in respect of unquoted trading companies if certain conditions are satisfied, such that the vendor is normally treated as receiving a capital payment instead. The distinction between income and capital treatment for the transaction can be significant, particularly due to the difference in the rates of income tax and capital gains tax (see **4.1–4.4**).
- **Conditions** – A number of statutory conditions must be satisfied for a company purchase of own shares to be excluded from income distribution treatment and to be treated as a capital payment for tax purposes instead (see **4.5–4.34**).
- **Practical issues** – The transaction may need to be structured and implemented carefully, according to whether capital or income distribution treatment is sought. A clearance application can be made in advance to obtain certainty about HMRC's view of the tax treatment on the company's purchase of its own shares (see **4.35–4.62**).
- **Company law** – A company purchase of its own shares must comply with certain *Companies Act* requirements. Otherwise, the transaction may be void and legally unenforceable, and unforeseen tax implications may result (see **4.63–4.66**).
- **Other points** – Separate tax considerations apply to corporate and trustee vendors. In addition, sundry issues on a company purchase of own shares include returns of share purchases, stamp duty costs and returns, share valuations and the loan relationships 'unallowable purposes' anti-avoidance provisions (see **4.67–4.78**).

INTRODUCTION

4.1 This chapter is mainly concerned with the purchase by an unquoted trading or holding company of its own shares from an individual shareholder, particularly in respect of family and owner-managed companies.

As a general rule, when a company buys back its own shares from a shareholder, any 'premium' (ie payment in excess of the capital originally subscribed for the shares) constitutes a distribution. For tax purposes, the transaction generally falls to be treated as an income distribution (*CTA 2010, s 1000(1)*), such as on a purchase of own shares by a quoted company.

However, there is an exception in the case of unquoted trading companies (*CTA 2010, s 1033*). If certain conditions are satisfied, the transaction is automatically excepted from income distribution treatment. The effect is that the vendor is treated as receiving a capital payment instead (unless the vendor is a share dealer, in which case the receipt is treated as trading income). This treatment provides shareholders with a potentially tax-efficient exit route from the company.

A 20% rate of capital gains tax (CGT) (for 2017/18) makes capital payments less attractive in some cases, where the proceeds are relatively small. The normal lower CGT rate of 10% (for 2017/18) does not apply to the extent that an individual is liable to higher rates of income tax, However, if the conditions for entrepreneurs' relief are satisfied, the first £10m of an individual's qualifying gains are taxable at a rate of 10% (*TCGA 1992, s 169N*). Entrepreneurs' relief has become increasingly valuable over time. The relief limit was increased to £10m from £5m in *Finance Act 2011*, which in turn was increased to £5m from £2m (in *Finance (No 2) Act 2010*), and to £2m from the original ceiling of £1m (in *Finance Act 2010*) with effect from 6 April 2010 (the £1m limit applying in relation to disposals in 2008/09 or 2009/10). For disposals before 6 April 2008 (ie prior to the abolition of taper relief), the position was potentially better, as full business asset taper relief could result in an effective 10% CGT rate with no upper gains limit.

Furthermore, a claim for investors' relief (which was introduced in *Finance Act 2016*) separately provides for a CGT rate of 10% on chargeable gains from the disposal by a qualifying person of shares where certain conditions are satisfied, subject to an overall limit of £10m (*TCGA 1992, ss 169VC, 169VK*). Some shareholders may be eligible to claim investors' relief in due course.

By contrast to the potential CGT rates, the reform of the system of dividend taxation from April 2016 (introduced in *Finance Act 2016*) resulted in the removal of the dividend tax credit of 10% and replacement with a dividend nil rate (£5,000 a year per individual for 2017/18; note that the government announced that the nil rate would be reduced to £2,000 a year for 2018/19 and, although this reduction was not enacted in *Finance Act 2017*, it was included in *Finance Bill (No 2) 2017* published on 8 September 2017, which has not received Royal Assent at the time of writing). The rate of income tax on dividends (for 2017/18) is 7.5% for basic rate taxpayers, 32.5% for higher rate taxpayers and 38.1% for additional rate taxpayers.

The differential between CGT and income tax rates may vary depending on individual circumstances, but in general terms it is sufficiently wide (in 2017/18) to make capital treatment an important consideration for many individual shareholders.

Conversely, subscriber shareholders in unquoted trading companies may be able to claim a capital loss arising from a purchase of own shares where CGT treatment applies, upon which income tax relief may be available, if certain conditions are satisfied (*TCGA 1992, s 24(2)*; *ITA 2007, s 131*).

A company purchase of own shares can be useful in a variety of situations, particularly in the context of family or owner-managed businesses. For example, a controlling director shareholder may wish to retire and make way for younger management, some or all of whom may be family members. Alternatively, shareholder disputes over the running of the company's trade may be resolved by using a company purchase of own shares to provide dissenting parties with an opportunity to depart from the company and realise the value of their shares. In both cases, this route may seem particularly attractive if a direct purchase of the shares (eg by other shareholders, family members or managers) is not possible due to an insufficiency of funds.

A company purchase of own shares also provides personal representatives or legatees with an opportunity to realise the value of shares following the death of a shareholder. It should be noted that (for 2017/18) the standard rate of CGT for gains accruing to settlement trustees and personal representatives (eg for share disposals) is 20%.

A number of conditions must generally be satisfied in order to qualify for capital gains treatment on a company purchase of own shares, including a 'trade benefit' test, as well as requirements as to residence, length of ownership of the shares and the degree (if any) to which the vendor remains connected with the company. In some cases, it may not be possible to satisfy all the requirements. The business owners may therefore wish to consider alternative exit strategies for the vendor shareholder (eg a management buyout). Such considerations are outside the scope of this chapter.

Employee shareholder shares

4.2 An 'employee shareholder' employment status was introduced from 1 September 2013 (*Employment Rights Act 1996, s 205A*). This status initially offered various tax incentives to encourage employee share ownership, in return for the individual agreeing to forego certain employment rights. Those tax incentives originally included a CGT exemption in respect of qualifying shares issued or allotted to an employee under an employee shareholder agreement with a total 'unrestricted market value' not exceeding £50,000 on receipt (*TCGA 1992, s 236C*). However, this exemption was restricted (in *Finance Act 2016*) to a lifetime limit of £100,000 on the disposal of shares acquired under employee shareholder agreements entered into after 16 March 2016. The CGT exemption was removed completely in *Finance Act 2017*, in relation to shares acquired in consideration of an employee shareholder agreement entered into on or after the 'relevant day' as defined (ie normally 1 December 2016).

There was also specific provision in respect of a company purchase of own shares. No income tax charge originally arose as a distribution (under *ITTOIA 2005, Pt 4, Ch 3*) if shares were sold back to the company (ie the payment was made in respect of shares in the company), those shares were exempt employee shareholder shares (within the meaning of *TCGA 1992, ss 236B–236D*), and the individual was not an employee (or office holder) of the employer company or associated company at the time of disposal (*ITTOIA 2005, s 385A*). However, this income tax relief was removed in *Finance Act 2017*, once again in relation to shares acquired in consideration of an employee shareholder agreement entered into on or after the 'relevant day' (see above).

The remainder of this chapter deals with the company purchase of shares in an unquoted trading company, which are not employee shareholder shares eligible for the above tax reliefs.

Tax and company law

4.3 The tax legislation on company distributions is contained in *CTA 2010, Pt 23, Ch 3*. This legislation contains provisions specifically dealing with the purchase of own shares by an unquoted trading company (*CTA 2010, ss 1033–1048*). The purchase of own shares rules exclude from distribution treatment payments made by a company on the redemption, repayment or purchase of its own shares, if certain conditions are satisfied.

This chapter outlines those rules, and considers planning points and potential pitfalls in relation to them.

4.4 It is important to note that a purchase of own shares must comply with company law requirements to be valid. In practice, the *Companies Act 2006* requirements are often an after-thought, and have the potential to be overlooked completely by the uninitiated. As this book is mainly concerned with tax law rather than company law, priority is given to tax considerations. However, whilst company law is discussed later in this chapter, strictly speaking it should be the primary consideration. The implications of 'getting it wrong' can be unfortunate to say the least.

A company purchase of own shares should not be confused with a reduction of share capital, for which separate company law provisions apply (*CA 2006, Pt 17, Ch 10*). As to the circumstances in which a reduction of share capital may be appropriate, as well as the company law requirements and tax implications, see **Chapter 5**.

Guidance on the tax treatment of a company purchase of own shares is contained in HMRC's Company Taxation Manual (at CTM17505 onwards), mainly in respect of income distribution treatment, and in the Capital Gains Manual (at CG58600 onwards) relating to capital gains treatment.

Additional commentary on the subject can also be found in *Tax Planning for Family and Owner-Managed Companies 2017/18* by Peter Rayney (Bloomsbury Professional).

CHECKLIST

4.5

> **Focus**
>
> Aside from the company law requirements mentioned above, the following checklist is intended as a brief summary of the conditions to be satisfied for a company purchase of its own shares to be excluded from income distribution treatment, and to be treated as a capital payment instead (within *CTA 2010, ss 1033–1048*). These conditions are considered further in this chapter.

Table 4.1: Conditions for company purchase of own shares within CTA 2010, s 1033(1)

- **Company status** – the purchasing company must be an unquoted trading company, or the unquoted holding company of a trading group (*CTA 2010, s 1033(1)(a)*).
- **Purpose of the payment** – either the 'trade benefit' (see **4.12**) and 'no scheme or arrangements' (see **4.19**) tests are met, *or* the payment is applied by the recipient in discharging an inheritance tax liability within two years after a death (Note – in the latter case, the further conditions below do not need to be satisfied) (*CTA 2010, s 1033(1)(b)*).
- **Residence** – the vendor shareholder must be UK resident (and for individuals in respect of purchases before 6 April 2013, ordinarily resident) for the tax year in which the purchase takes place (*CTA 2010, s 1034*).

- **Period of ownership** – the shares must have been owned for a minimum of five years ending with the date of purchase. However, if the shares were acquired by will or intestacy, the minimum ownership period is reduced to three years (*CTA 2010, ss 1035–1036*).
- **'Substantial reduction'** – the vendor shareholder's interest in the company must normally be substantially reduced (eg if the vendor retains some shares after the purchase) (*CTA 2010, ss 1037–1041*).
- **No 'continuing connection'** – the vendor must not be connected with the company (or group company) immediately after the purchase (*CTA 2010, ss 1042, 1043, 1062–1063*).

If these conditions are satisfied, capital treatment is automatic. This assumes, of course, that the transaction is valid under company law.

An application can be made to HMRC under *CTA 2010, s 1044* for advance clearance that capital treatment will be available to the vendor shareholder (see **4.57**). This is normally accompanied by an application for clearance under *ITA 2007, s 701* that the anti-avoidance rules regarding 'transactions in securities' in *ITA 2007, Pt 13, Ch 1* do not apply to counteract any income tax advantage (*ITA 2007, s 684*).

4.6 Alternatively, a 'negative' clearance application can be made that the transaction should be treated as an income distribution.

It can be possible to break the conditions for capital treatment, if income distribution treatment is preferable. For example, this could be achieved by the vendor leaving the sale proceeds outstanding as a loan, such that the 'no continuing connection test' is broken. Alternatively, the shares could be bought in stages, so that the 'substantial reduction' test is not met.

Breaching the capital treatment conditions is further considered later in the chapter (see **4.61**).

IHT and 'undue hardship'

4.7 The purpose of the company purchase of its own shares (or redemption or repayment) for which this chapter is mainly concerned is broadly that the payment is wholly or mainly to benefit a trade carried on by the company or group, and is not part of a scheme or arrangement a main purpose of which is to allow the owner to participate in company profits without receiving a dividend, or for tax avoidance.

However, it should be noted that there is a second, alternative allowable purpose. This is that substantially the whole proceeds from the share transaction relating to an unquoted trading company or holding company of a trading group (apart from any payment towards a CGT liability arising in respect of it) are applied in discharging an IHT liability of the recipient on a death, within two years of that event (*CTA 2010, s 1033(3)*).

4.8 If this purpose is relevant, it is not necessary for the vendor to demonstrate that the transaction was for the benefit of the company's trade, and the other conditions which apply to the first purpose need not be satisfied by the vendor of the shares. However, there is a further specific requirement for the second purpose to apply, which is broadly that the relevant IHT liability could not otherwise have been paid without 'undue hardship' (*CTA 2010, s 1033(4)*).

The remainder of this chapter considers the conditions to be satisfied for a purchase of own shares by an unquoted trading company (or unquoted holding company of a trading group) to fall within *CTA 2010, s 1033(2)*.

COMPANY STATUS

4.9 The purchasing company must be an unquoted trading company or the holding company of a trading group (*CTA 2010, s 1033(1)(a)*). The terms 'unquoted company', 'trading company' and 'trading group' (among others) are specifically defined for the purposes of the purchase of own shares rules, and broadly have the following meaning (*CTA 2010, s 1048*):

- An 'unquoted company' is a company which is neither quoted nor a 51% subsidiary of a quoted company. A 'quoted company' is a company whose shares (or any class of them) are listed on the official list of a stock exchange. However, shares listed on the Alternative Investment Market, or dealt in on the Unlisted Securities Market, are regarded as unquoted for these purposes (CTM17507).
- A 'trading company' is a company whose business consists 'wholly or mainly' (ie more than 50%) of carrying on one or more trades (*CTA 2010, s 1048(1)*). This differs from the definition of trading company for entrepreneurs' relief (or investors' relief) purposes, which requires that the company's activities do not include to a substantial extent activities other than trading activities (*TCGA 1992, s 165A(3)*). 'Substantial' in an entrepreneurs' relief context is taken by HMRC to mean more than 20% of certain categories of measure, such as non-trading income (see CG64090).

  Hence, it is possible that a company may satisfy the 'wholly or mainly' test of trading status on a purchase of its own shares, and yet a gain on the disposal of those shares may be denied entrepreneurs' relief in the hands of an individual shareholder because the company's non-trading activities are substantial.

- A 'trading group' is one in which the business of its members taken together consists wholly or mainly of carrying on one or more trades (*CTA 2010, s 1048(1)*). In this context 'group' means the company itself and its 75% subsidiaries.

4.10 There is a distinction between 'trade' and 'business' which must be recognised. For example, property investment activities may amount to a business, but on general principles do not constitute a trade. In addition, a 'trade' for the above purposes specifically excludes dealing in shares, securities, land or futures (*CTA 2010, s 1048(1)*).

Finally, in HMRC's view it is not sufficient that the company was formerly trading, or intends trading in the future. It must be a trading company when the transaction takes place (*Tax Bulletin,* Issue 21 (February 1996)).

PURPOSE OF THE PAYMENT

4.11

> **Focus**
>
> The condition for a company purchase of its own shares to be excepted from distribution treatment includes a purpose test containing two separate limbs, both of which must be satisfied (*CTA 2010, s 1033(2)(a), (b)*).
>
> These limbs are considered separately below.

Limb 1: The 'trade benefit' test

4.12 The first limb of the 'purpose' condition mentioned above is that the company's purchase (or redemption or repayment) of shares must be wholly or mainly for the purpose of benefiting a trade carried on by the company, or by any of its 75% subsidiaries. The requirement is referred to in this chapter as the 'trade benefit' test.

As indicated in the Checklist at **4.5**, in addition to the 'trade benefit' condition in *CTA 2010, s 1033(2)(a)*, there are various other conditions for a company purchase of own shares to be excluded from income distribution treatment. Those further conditions are contained in *CTA 2010, ss 1034–1043* (see below), and are relatively unambiguous.

By contrast, a particular difficulty with the 'trade benefit' test is that it is not defined anywhere in the legislation. However, this test was considered in *Allum v Marsh* [2005] STC (SCD) 191, which is discussed below.

STATEMENT OF PRACTICE 2/82

4.13 The 'trade benefit' test is also the subject of guidance by HMRC in Statement of Practice 2/82 ('Company's purchase of own shares: *ICTA 1988*'), which includes examples of situations in which the trade benefit test would normally be regarded as satisfied:

- Disagreements between shareholders over the company's management, which has or could have an adverse effect on the company's trade.

  As a general rule, the company must buy back all the dissenting shareholder's shares and remove him entirely. However, there are possible exceptions to this rule, such as if the company cannot afford them all, but buys back as many as it can afford and intends buying the rest as soon as possible, or if the retiring director shareholder wishes to retain up to 5% for sentimental reasons.

- An 'unwilling shareholder' wants to end their association with the company.

  The trade benefit test may be satisfied if the purpose of the share buyback is to ensure that the shares are not sold to someone who could be unacceptable to the other shareholders. Statement of Practice 2/82 provides examples of 'unwilling shareholders':

  - 'business angels' (ie outside shareholders who wish to withdraw equity finance);
  - retiring controlling director shareholders wanting to make way for new management;
  - personal representatives of deceased shareholders wishing to realise the shares; and
  - legatees of a deceased shareholder not wishing to hold shares in the company.

RETAINING AN INTEREST IN THE COMPANY

4.14 Statement of Practice 2/82 indicates that if the vendor shareholder retains an interest in the company (eg if the company is not buying all the vendor's shares, or if the vendor is retained as a director or consultant) the trade benefit test will probably not be satisfied. However, the possibility of a retained interest is not ruled out as mainly benefiting the company's trade in certain circumstances. For example:

- the company does not currently have the resources to purchase all the shares of a retiring controlling shareholder immediately; or

- a retiring director wishes to retain no more than 5% of the company's shares for sentimental reasons.

It should be remembered that statements of practice only represent the views of HMRC, and are not legally binding. Nevertheless, taxpayers and their advisers should be aware of Statement of Practice 2/82 and its contents.

An Annex to Statement of Practice 2/82 helpfully contains the suggested format of advance clearance applications on a purchase of own shares, including a statement of the expected 'purpose and benefits' of the purchase, trading and otherwise.

HMRC's Help Sheet 'Company Purchase of Own Shares' also contains checklists of information to be provided in clearance applications for a purchase benefiting a company's trade, and a purchase in connection with an IHT liability (tinyurl.com/HMRC-CPOS).

4.15 Despite the non-statutory nature of the trade benefit test, prior to *Allum v Marsh* (see below) case law had not offered much guidance on its meaning. In *Moody v Tyler (Inspector of Taxes)* [2000] STC 296, the taxpayer resigned as the director of a family company in 1989. The company lent him £50,000. In 1995 the company purchased 2,247 shares from his holding for £50,000. Those monies were offset against the loan. The taxpayer appealed against an assessment to tax as an income distribution, on the grounds that the purchase had been made wholly or mainly to benefit the trade carried on by the company within what is now *CTA 2010, s 1033(2)(a)*.

The General Commissioners dismissed the appeal and the Court of Appeal upheld their decision. Whether the trade benefit test had been satisfied was a pure question of fact, and there was no basis upon which the court could interfere with the Commissioners' decision. In any event, it is interesting to note that the purchase of own shares in this case was in breach of company law, as the proceeds were used to cancel the vendor's outstanding loan account with the company. As noted elsewhere in this chapter, consideration for the transaction must be paid in full, in cash, on completion.

ALLUM v MARSH

4.16 The subsequent case of *Allum v Marsh* [2005] STC (SCD) 191 offers some assistance on the application of the 'trade benefit' test. In that case, the company's purchase of the taxpayer's shares was held not to be for the benefit of the company's trade. The taxpayers, Mr and Mrs A, were the directors of an unquoted trading company. They held all the shares except one held by R, their son. When the taxpayers were approaching age 70, a property developer expressed an interest in purchasing the company's premises. Mr and Mrs A wished to retire from the business and dispose of their shares without selling them outside the company, so that R could run the company and continue trading. The property sale was completed. The company voted to purchase Mr and Mrs A's shares, and to repay an outstanding directors' loan. In the following year, the company's trading operations reduced considerably. Suitable trading premises were not found, and the company's business was carried out from a limited facility shared with another company.

HMRC assessed the taxpayers on the sale proceeds for their shares as an income distribution, on the grounds that the conditions for capital gains tax treatment (in what is now *CTA 2010, s 1033(2)(a)*) were not satisfied. HMRC considered that the company's purchase of its own shares had not benefited the company's trade. The taxpayers appealed.

The Special Commissioner, Dr Brice, dismissed the taxpayers' appeal. In determining whether a company purchase of its own shares had been made 'for the purpose of benefiting a trade', it was necessary to take account of consequences closely linked to the payment, so that unless those consequences were merely incidental, they had to be regarded as a purpose for which the payment had been made. The offer to purchase the property had been made when Mr and Mrs A were approaching age 70, and wished to retire. The company's decision to purchase the taxpayer's shares had been inextricably linked to its need for the sale proceeds from the property to enable it to do so. The company had been left without permanent premises from which to trade, without the benefit of the directors' loan, and without Mr and Mrs A's services. Those consequences were so closely linked to the company's purchase of the shares that they had to be regarded as a purpose for which the payment was made. The purchase of the shares had therefore not been made wholly or mainly for the purpose of benefiting the trade, but to enable the directors to retire.

FACTORS TO CONSIDER

4.17 The Special Commissioner considered a number of principles established in the case *Vodafone Cellular Ltd v Shaw* [1997] 69 TC 376, to decide whether the company's payment for the shares was made wholly and exclusively for the purposes of the trade, or whether there was some element of personal advantage:

- 'For the purposes of the trade' was taken to mean to serve the purposes of the trade, and not for the purposes of the company or for the benefit of the company.
- Was the payment made for the purposes of the taxpayer's trade? To answer this question, it was necessary to discover his object or subjective intentions in making the payment.
- The taxpayer's object in making the payment must be distinguished from the effect of the payment.

- The taxpayer's subjective intentions are not limited to his conscious motives. Consequences which are so inevitably and inextricably linked to the payment must be taken to be a purpose of the payment, unless they are merely incidental.
- The primary question to ask of the taxpayer is 'what was the particular object of the taxpayer in making the payment?'

The Special Commissioner concluded that the purchase of shares was not made 'wholly or mainly' to benefit the company's trade, but to facilitate the retirement of Mr and Mrs A. The purchase allowed the trade to continue, but Dr Brice said that surplus funds could have been paid to Mr and Mrs A, and the trade could still have continued.

4.18 Whilst advance clearance from HMRC on the tax treatment of a purchase of own shares is not mandatory, it will be beneficial to do so in the vast majority of cases, not least in terms of obtaining certainty in cases where the trade benefit requirement is in any doubt.

Limb 2: 'Scheme or arrangement' test

4.19 The second limb of the 'purpose' condition mentioned above is that the company purchase (or redemption or repayment) of its own shares must not form part of a scheme or arrangement, a main purpose of which is either to enable the share owner to participate in the company's profits without receiving a dividend, or the avoidance of tax (*CTA 2010, s 1033(2)(b)*).

'Scheme' or 'arrangement' is not defined for these purposes in the legislation. Both terms require consideration of the motive for the transaction. This is largely a question of fact. However, it may be more difficult to discern whether the 'main purpose' test is breached. It is therefore important that any clearance application made by the company to HMRC in respect of the transaction contains complete and correct details. Otherwise, any clearance given by HMRC cannot subsequently be relied upon.

RESIDENCE OF VENDOR

4.20 A further condition for exception from income distribution treatment on a company purchase of its own shares is that the vendor (and any nominee, if appropriate) must be resident in the UK in the tax year of purchase (*CTA 2010, s 1034(1)*). Prior to changes introduced in *FA 2013*, there was also a requirement to be ordinarily resident in the UK, but this requirement ceased to apply in relation to a purchase of own shares by an unquoted trading company on or after 6 April 2013 (*FA 2013, Sch 46, para 145*).

The statutory residence test (SRT) (in *FA 2013, Sch 45*) generally applies to determine an individual's residence for tax purposes, with effect from 2013/14. For tax years prior to 2013/14, the individual's residence status is determined according to the prevailing legislation and case law at that time.

If it is necessary for SRT purposes (in relation to tax years 2013/14 to 2017/18 inclusive) to determine the individual's residence status for an earlier tax year than 2013/14, an election is available to apply the SRT provisions to determine residence status for the earlier tax year (although the election does not change the individual's actual tax residence status for that year) (*FA 2013, Sch 45, para 154*).

For commentary on residence and the SRT, see **Chapter 9**.

4.21 If the vendors are trustees, the CGT rules for determining their residence status (and ordinary residence status, for tax years before 2013/14) apply (*TCGA 1992, s 69*). A detailed consideration of those rules is outside the scope of this chapter. However, it should be noted that (following changes to the rules for determining the residence status of trustees from 6 April 2007) trustees are resident in the UK if all of the trustees are UK resident, or if the following conditions are satisfied (*TCGA 1992, s 69(2)*):

- at least one trustee is UK resident; and
- a settlor was resident, ordinarily resident (for tax years before 2013/14) *or* domiciled in the UK at the 'relevant time' (ie broadly when the settlement was made, or immediately before the settlor's death if the settlement was made by will, intestacy or otherwise). It should be noted that the government originally intended introducing tax changes relating to domicile in *Finance Act 2017*, including that domicile in the UK for these purposes would include deemed domicile in the UK. The domicile changes were not subsequently included in *Finance Act 2017*, but they were included in *Finance (No 2) Bill 2017* published on 8 September 2017, which has not received Royal Assent at the time of writing.

4.22 Thus a UK-resident trust may inadvertently become an offshore trust (eg by one of the trustees becoming non-UK resident, and the settlor not meeting the above UK residence or domicile requirements when the settlement was made).

The trustees need only be resident in the UK for the purposes of this chapter for the tax year in which the share purchase takes place.

4.23 The residence status (and ordinary residence status, in relation to a purchase of own shares by an unquoted trading company before 6 April

2013) of personal representatives is somewhat more straightforward, as their status follows that of the deceased immediately before death (*CTA 2010, s 1034(3)*).

PERIOD OF OWNERSHIP

4.24 The general rule is that the vendor must have owned the shares throughout the five-year period ending with the share purchase (*CTA 2010, s 1035(1)*). However, this basic requirement is modified in certain respects, depending on the circumstances:

- In the case of transfers to the vendor from a spouse or civil partner, periods of ownership may be combined for the purposes of the five-year test, unless the parties are no longer living together (other than by reason of death) (*CTA 2010, s 1036(1), (2)*).
- If the vendor acquired the shares by will or intestacy, or is the deceased's personal representative, periods of ownership by the deceased (or his personal representatives) may be combined, and the required period of ownership is reduced from five years to three years) (*CTA 2010, s 1036(3)*).
- If the shares were acquired as part of a company reorganisation of share capital (eg the 'stand in shoes' provisions on a share-for-share exchange) within the capital gains tax legislation (*TCGA 1992, Pt 4, Ch 2*), the same treatment applies in terms of the ownership test. There are certain exceptions from this relaxation, in respect of allotments for payment and stock dividends within *CTA 2010, s 1049* (*CTA 2010, s 1035(3)*).

If the vendor's shares of the same class were acquired at different times, care may need to be taken in matching the disposal with those acquisitions. For the purposes of the ownership test a FIFO ('first in, first out') basis applies, so that earlier share acquisitions are taken into account before later ones. This rule is helpful, as it gives the longest possible period of ownership for the purpose of this test.

In addition, any previous share disposals by the vendor are matched with earlier acquisitions on a LIFO ('last in, first out') basis, so that later acquisitions are taken into account first (*CTA 2010, s 1035(2)*).

4.25 Aside from the above exceptions, if the company has been incorporated for less than five years, the shareholder cannot satisfy the five-year ownership test. This includes on the incorporation of a sole trader or partnership business.

THE 'SUBSTANTIAL REDUCTION' TEST

4.26

> **Focus**
>
> Two separate arithmetic tests (referred to below as the 'substantial reduction' test and the 'no continuing connection' test) must be satisfied for the exception from income treatment in *CTA 2010, s 1033(2)* to apply, which are relevant if the vendor retains an interest in the company following the share sale. The interests of 'associates' (see below) are taken into account for these purposes.

The first test is that the vendor's interest as a shareholder in the company must be substantially reduced. The combined interests of the vendor (and any associates) are taken into account for the purpose of this test (*CTA 2010, s 1037(1), (2)*).

The term 'substantially reduced' broadly means that the nominal value of shares owned by the vendor (and any associates) immediately after the purchase, expressed as a fraction of the company's share capital at that time, does not exceed 75% of the corresponding fraction immediately before the purchase (*CTA 2010, s 1037(3)–(5)*). This test is illustrated below.

Example 4.1 – 'Substantial reduction' test

Lee owns 4,000 shares in Express Retail Ltd, an unquoted trading company. The company's issued share capital is 10,000 ordinary £1 shares. Express Retail Ltd agrees to purchase 2,000 of Lee's shares. The relevant fractions are as follows:

Before the purchase: 4,000/10,000 (40%)

After the purchase: 2,000/8,000 (25%)

Therefore 75% (the substantial reduction threshold) × 40% = 30%. Lee holds 25% of the company's shares following the purchase.

Lee's remaining holding of 2,000 shares therefore represents a substantial reduction based on his original holding. Note that his interest in the company has actually been reduced by 37.5% (ie (40% – 25%)/40%), but Lee's shareholding in the company has reduced by 50%.

The calculation of the minimum number of shares required for the substantial reduction test to be satisfied can be expressed by formula, as follows:

$$\text{Minimum number} = \frac{nx}{4x - 3n}$$

Where:

n = the number of shares in the vendor's holding (including associates); and

x = the company's issued share capital

Thus in **Example 4.1**, the minimum company purchase of shares required for the above purposes is:

$$\frac{(4{,}000 \times 10{,}000)}{40{,}000 - 12{,}000} = \underline{1{,}429 \text{ shares}}$$

In *Preston Meats Ltd v Hammond; Sharples v Hammond* SpC 2004, [2005] SSCD 90 (SpC 435), the company shareholdings of the taxpayer and his wife amounted to 49.6% of the whole. The taxpayer wished to retire. It was agreed that the company would purchase his shares, with a view to falling within what is now *CTA 2010, s 1033(1)* so that the proceeds would be treated as a capital receipt. However, the company did not have the funds to pay for the shares immediately. The company therefore issued 130,000 £1 redeemable interest-bearing preference shares at par, carrying no voting rights, which were acquired by the taxpayer and his wife. HMRC issued assessments on the taxpayer and the company, on the basis that the taxpayer's shareholding had not been 'substantially reduced', as required by what is now *CTA 2010, s 1037(3)–(5)*. The taxpayer appealed, contending that 100,000 of the preference shares had been acquired for the benefit of his daughter.

The taxpayer's appeal was dismissed. The evidence indicated that the taxpayer had retained ownership of the 100,000 shares. It therefore followed that the condition in *CTA 2010, s 1037(3)–(5)* had not been satisfied. It was held that the taxpayer intended no more than that his daughter should benefit from the money received on redemption of the shares. The taxpayer's holding was also considered to breach the connection test in *CTA 2010, s 1042(1)* (see **4.31**).

4.27 A second 'substantial reduction' test must also be satisfied, broadly in terms of the vendor's interest in the company's profits. Even if the substantial reduction test is met in terms of share capital, it is not regarded as satisfied if the vendor shareholder's interest (expressed as a fractional share) in the company's profits available for distribution exceeds 75% of the corresponding fraction immediately before the purchase.

'Profits available for distribution' has the meaning given in *Companies Act 2006, s 830(2)*, except that the amount is increased by £100 per company plus any fixed distributions to which the shareholder may be entitled. Added to that figure is the excess of all sums payable on share purchases (or redemptions or repayments) over distributable profits available immediately before the purchase (*CTA 2010, s 1038*).

HMRC's Help Sheet 'Company Purchase of Own Shares' (see **4.14**) states in the context of this test: 'Where there are complex profit sharing arrangements, the Clearance Team will be able to advise.'

Groups of companies

4.28 If the purchasing company is a group member, the vendor's interest as a shareholder in the group (together with any associates) must be substantially reduced.

A 'group' is defined as a company (which is not itself a 51% subsidiary) plus its 51% subsidiaries (*CTA 2010, s 1047(1)*). There are two tests to be satisfied.

The first test is a calculation, which involves aggregating the nominal value of shares (expressed as a fraction of the issued share capital) of each company in the group in which the vendor owned shares immediately before or after the purchase, and dividing that aggregate by the number of group companies in which the vendor owned shares immediately before, or immediately after, the purchase. The vendor shareholder's interest in the group is substantially reduced if it does not exceed 75% of the vendor's interest before the purchase (*CTA 2010, s 1040(2)*).

4.29 The second test to be satisfied is expressed in terms of the vendor's entitlement to a share of the group's 'profits available for distribution' (see above). This test involves aggregating the vendor's share of such profits from each group member to which there was a notional entitlement immediately after the share purchase, and dividing that aggregate by each company's profits available for distribution in which the vendor owns shares immediately before, or immediately after, the purchase (including 51% subsidiaries of such companies). The vendor's entitlement to distributable group profits is substantially reduced if it does not exceed 75% of his interest before the purchase (*CTA 2010, ss 1040(1), 1041*).

4.30 There are anti-avoidance provisions to extend the group for these purposes in two specific circumstances.

First, if an unquoted company acquired all or a significant part of the business of the purchasing company (or group member) less than three years before the purchase (or redemption or repayment) of the shares, that outside company (and any 51% subsidiaries) is treated as a member of the same group as the purchasing company (*CTA 2010, s 1047(2), (3)*).

Secondly, a company that has ceased to be a group member continues as such if there are any arrangements under which it could rejoin the group (*CTA 2010, s 1047(4)*).

THE 'NO CONTINUING CONNECTION' TEST

4.31 In addition to the 'substantial reduction' test, there is a further arithmetic test to be satisfied in order to qualify for exception from income distribution treatment on a purchase of own shares. This test requires that the vendor must not be connected with the company (or a group company) immediately after the purchase (*CTA 2010, s 1042*).

4.32 'Connection' is broadly defined in terms of direct or indirect ownership or entitlement to acquire (now and in the future) more than 30% of the company's issued ordinary share capital, loan capital (except in limited circumstances involving money lending companies; see below) and issued share capital, voting power or the entitlement of equity holders to assets available for distribution on a winding-up of the company (*CTA 2010, s 1062(2), (4)*).

However, if the company's loan capital was acquired in the ordinary course of a business carried on by the shareholder that includes the lending of money, and the vendor takes no part in the management or conduct of the company, his interest in the loan capital is disregarded in applying the above 30% test (*CTA 2010, s 1062(3)*).

The rights of associates are also taken into account for these purposes (*CTA 2010, s 1063(4)*). 'Associates' in this context includes spouses or civil partners who are living together, but does not include (for example) adult offspring, or siblings (*CTA 2010, s 1059*).

The vendor is also connected with the company if he controls it (*CTA 2010, s 1062(7)*). 'Control' in this context has the meaning given in *ITA 2007, s 995* for individuals or *CTA 2010, s 1124* for companies (*CTA 2010, Sch 4*), ie broadly a person's power to secure that the company's affairs are conducted in accordance with his wishes, through shareholdings, voting or other powers in respect of the company.

Anti-avoidance

4.33 There are anti-avoidance provisions to prevent the 'substantial reduction' and 'no continuing connection' arithmetic tests being circumvented:

- The purchase must not at any time be part of a scheme or arrangement with a view to the vendor (or an associate) having an interest immediately after the share purchase that would breach the arithmetic tests (*CTA 2010, s 1042(2), (3)*). This condition is subject to the exception at **4.34** below.
- A transaction within one year after the purchase is deemed to be part of a 'scheme or arrangement' for the above purposes (*CTA 2010, s 1042(4)*).

Disposals by associates

4.34 There is a relaxation in the arithmetic tests. An associate may dispose of shares to the company, to enable the vendor shareholder to satisfy the substantial reduction tests (in *CTA 2010, s 1037(2)* or *1039(4)*).

In those circumstances, the arithmetic tests do not apply to the company's purchase of the associate's shares, to the extent that the number of shares purchased enables the vendor shareholder to comply with the test (*CTA 2010, s 1043*).

MEETING THE CONDITIONS

4.35 In many cases, in order to satisfy the 'trade benefit' test it may be necessary for the vendor shareholder to dispose of virtually their entire shareholding. However, the purchasing company may have insufficient funds to acquire the vendor's shares without causing cash-flow difficulties. It may therefore be argued that it would be of greater benefit to the company's trade to purchase the shares in tranches.

> **Focus**
>
> However, to avoid income distribution treatment the two arithmetic tests mentioned above (ie the 'substantial reduction' and 'no continuing connection' tests) must be satisfied. In addition, if the shares are being purchased in stages, HMRC clearance should strictly be sought for each transaction.
>
> As well as the 'arithmetic' conditions being met, HMRC would also need to be satisfied that the 'trade benefit' test was passed in each clearance application.

'Loan back' by vendor

4.36 If the company wants to purchase all the vendor's shares but cannot afford to do so, HMRC accept that there is no reason why the vendor should not lend part of the consideration back to the vendor immediately after the purchase. Clearly, the 'substantial reduction' requirement can be satisfied.

However, the 'no continuing connection' test must also be considered, ie the vendor (and any associates) must not have interests in the company of more than 30% of the combined issued share and loan capital (or voting power; see *CTA 2010, s 1062(2)*). A loan back to the company may breach this requirement, particularly if the market value of the shares is relatively high and the remaining issued share capital is relatively small.

4.37 In *Tax Bulletin,* Issue 21, HMRC helpfully point out that it is acceptable for the company to satisfy the connection test by making a bonus issue before the purchase of own shares takes place, in order to increase its issued share capital, as illustrated below.

Example 4.2 – Purchase and loan back to the company

Martin owns 2,500 shares in Express Widgets Ltd, an unquoted trading company. His shareholding represents 25% of the company's issued share capital of 10,000 shares.

Martin wishes to retire, and Express Widgets Ltd therefore agrees to buy Martin's 2,500 shares on 30 September 2017 for their market value of £100,000. Martin has owned his shares for six years, and satisfies the entrepreneurs' relief conditions for CGT purposes. The parties agree that they would like the transaction to fall within *CTA 2010, s 1033*, with the transaction giving rise to a capital gain for Martin, on which full entrepreneurs' relief can be claimed.

However, the company is experiencing temporary cash-flow difficulties. Martin therefore agrees to loan £50,000 of his proceeds back to the company. However, this would mean that Martin held loan capital of £50,000. The company's combined share and loan capital would be £57,500 (ie £7,500 plus £50,000). Martin would therefore be connected with the company (*CTA 2010, s 1062(2)(b)*).

The company's accountants therefore suggest that before the purchase of own shares takes place, the company should make a bonus issue of 20 shares for each share held, out of its distributable reserves. Martin now holds 52,500 shares out of 210,000 in issue. The company then purchases

Martin's 52,500 shares for £100,000, and Martin loans £50,000 back to the company.

Martin therefore holds loan capital of £50,000. The company's combined share and loan capital is £207,500 (ie £7,500 original share capital, plus £150,000 bonus share capital, plus Martin's loan of £50,000). Martin's interest in the company is less than 30%.

However, in certain circumstances a bonus issue of shares followed by a repayment of share capital may result in the application of the distribution provisions (see **4.50**).

'Phased' purchases

4.38 For a purchase of own shares to be valid under company law, the company must make full cash payment on purchase. It is questionable whether the transfer of a company asset, or alternatively leaving the proceeds outstanding on loan account, strictly represents 'payment' for these purposes. HMRC's view is that it does not, and that in such circumstances the shares are not treated as cancelled and the vendor retains legal ownership of the shares (CTM17505). The tax implications of any payments already made to the shareholder would then need to be considered, such as whether the proceeds fall to be treated as a loan to a close company participator, within *CTA 2010, s 455*.

However, it should be noted that *Companies Act 2006, s 691* merely requires that 'the shares must be paid for on purchase'.

Note there is a limited relaxation to this rule for private company share purchases in relation to an employee share schemes (see **4.66**).

In the company law case *BDG Roof-Bond Ltd v Douglas* [2000] 1 BCLC 401, the court held (*obiter*) that payment can be made by a transfer of assets *in specie*. The alternative position is that the House of Lords' decision in *CIR v Littlewoods Mail Order Stores* [1965] AC 135 is authority for the proposition that the words 'sale' and 'purchase' require an exchange of property for cash and not for any other form of property (*Taxation* Readers' Forum, 17 December 2009).

4.39 An alternative to the 'loan back' following the purchase of the vendor's entire shareholding is a 'phased' purchase (ie the purchase of shares in tranches). Statutory clearance (if required) should be sought from HMRC in respect of each purchase. HMRC have indicated (subject to the 'trade benefit' test being satisfied) that it is possible for the vendor to make a series of disposals phased over a period (ICAEW Technical Release 745).

However, for the transactions to be eligible for capital gains treatment, the 'substantial reduction' and 'no continuing connection' tests must be satisfied on each occasion. In addition, HMRC may argue that the 'trade benefit' test is not passed on the first disposal, unless there is a clear intention for the company to purchase the remainder of the vendor's shares.

For entrepreneurs' relief purposes, the relevant relief conditions will need to be satisfied if a claim is to be made in respect of each disposal.

Contracts with multiple completion

4.40 As indicated above, a company purchase of its own shares by instalments is prohibited under company law, except in relation to employee share schemes (see **4.66**).

However, a company may enter into a single, unconditional share sale contract with the vendor, with completion taking place on different dates in respect of separate tranches of shares within the agreement. The effect is that the 'substantial reduction' test mentioned above need only be considered once (ie at the contract date), and not at the date of each completion.

The vendor must also satisfy the 'no continuing connection' test. However, if the vendor loses beneficial ownership of the shares at the contract date (see below), he will only remain connected with the company if there is ongoing ownership of, or entitlement to, more than 30% of its issued ordinary shares, loan capital, voting rights and/or assets on a winding-up. The rights and powers of any associates must also be taken into account (see below).

Completion of the contract in stages should not create a debt for connection purposes. In the event that the company defaults on a stage of the purchase, the vendor could sue under breach of contract for the right to enforce specific performance.

4.41 HMRC may be prepared to accept that a multiple completion contract is possible, provided that beneficial ownership passes at the contract date (ICAEW Technical Release 745). This is more a point of non-tax law, but nevertheless HMRC will insist that the contract satisfies this requirement.

In particular, HMRC may argue that until the full purchase price is paid for the shares, the company law position is that the vendor remains on the register and is entitled to vote in respect of the shares without reference to the wishes of the purchaser. Furthermore, HMRC may argue that the seller cannot lawfully give up his voting rights under a contract with multiple completion. Alternatively, if the shares are claimed to be held as nominee for the company, HMRC may contend that this gives rise to a trust, which could make the vendor connected to the company (*CTA 2010, s 1048(3)*).

It may be possible to prevent such arguments by amending the company's articles, to provide that on the company entering into a contract for the purchase of its own shares, the shareholder's rights (including voting rights in relation to the shares) cease with immediate effect. However, such a change to the articles would need to be made before the multiple completion share purchase contract takes effect (*Tax Insight*, March 2011).

Alternatively, after the share purchase agreement has been entered into, consideration could be given to simply re-designating the uncancelled shares as a separate class of non-voting share (see 'Multiple attraction' *Taxation*, 13 October 2011).

The retention of a 'special share' of a separate class following the share repurchase (possibly by re-designating the special share from the vendor's existing holding prior to the proposed repurchase) may be considered if there are 'anti-embarrassment' terms in the contract (eg such that upon a subsequent sale of the company's shares at an enhanced price, the exiting shareholder will become entitled to part of the enhanced share price received by the remaining shareholders). The company's articles would need to reflect that the special share carries no voting or dividend rights, but has capital rights on a subsequent share sale to reflect the anti-embarrassment terms in the contract. The various conditions for capital gains treatment would need to be considered (eg the 30% connection test in *CTA 2010, s 1062(4)*), and the arrangements should be fully disclosed in a clearance application to HMRC under *CTA 2010, s 1044* (see *Taxation* Readers' Forum response by Peter Rayney, 23 January 2014).

The above argument about beneficial ownership may be avoided if it is possible to structure the share tranches in such a way that the arithmetic tests mentioned in the preceding paragraph are satisfied after completion in respect of the first tranche.

It should be noted that until the shares are (or are treated as) cancelled, they remain part of the company's issued share capital, and (for example) may need to be taken into account for entrepreneurs' relief purposes in determining whether the company's other shareholders satisfy the 'personal company' requirement in *TCGA 1992, s 169S(3)*. It may therefore be relevant to consider the time when the shares are (or are treated as) cancelled in this context (see below).

It has commonly (but not universally) been assumed that the date of disposal for CGT purposes under a company purchase of own shares is determined in accordance with *TCGA 1992, s 28* ('Time of disposal and acquisition where asset disposed of under contract'). The date of disposal under an unconditional contract according to those provisions is when the contract is made (*TCGA 1992, s 28(1)*), notwithstanding that payments are made at later dates. This means that the tax liability arising from the disposal could fall due before the consideration for all the shares is received. However, this may not be a significant problem where, for example, entrepreneurs' relief applies to the entire gain on the disposal. In addition, if the consideration is payable over a period exceeding 18 months, the capital gains legislation allows tax on a chargeable gain to be paid by instalments over a period of up to eight years, if appropriate (*TCGA 1992, s 280*).

In the event that the company fails to complete on one or more outstanding tranches of shares, it may be necessary to consider whether relief can be claimed in respect of the unpaid consideration for the shares (under *TCGA 1992, s 48*).

As indicated above, the time of disposal under a company purchase of own shares is not necessarily straightforward. The above provision setting the time of disposal in relation to contracts (in *TCGA 1992, s 28*) generally applies where an asset is disposed of and acquired under the contract. However, upon a company acquiring its own shares, any shares that are not cancelled on acquisition are treated as cancelled (*FA 2003, s 195(4)(b)*). Thus, shares (including those held in treasury; see **4.64**) that are not cancelled are generally treated as such for tax purposes. Furthermore, the acquisition by a company of its own shares is not treated as the acquisition of an asset (*FA 2003, s 195(2)*). In the case of contracts with multiple completion, there is anecdotal evidence of HMRC sometimes contending that the time of disposal is determined under *TCGA 1992, s 22(2)* (instead of *TCGA 1992, s 28*), being the dates when each capital sum is received. This is understood to be on the basis that there is a disposal under the contract, but no corresponding acquisition as required by *TCGA 1992, s 28(1)*. Where an entrepreneurs' relief claim is potentially in point, it would therefore be prudent to consider ensuring that the relevant relief conditions are satisfied when each capital sum is received (see **4.44**).

It should be noted that loss of beneficial ownership of the shares effectively means that the vendor shareholder is unable to participate in dividends paid after the contract date, or exercise voting rights in relation to the shares during the completion period. The vendor shareholder would need to consent to the loss of rights to any dividends or other shareholder rights as a result of entering into the agreement and will therefore probably wish to take legal advice in advance, to ensure that the contract offers appropriate safeguards to protect his position. A contract with multiple completion normally only requires a single clearance application to HMRC under *CTA 2010, s 1044*.

There is also anecdotal evidence of HMRC previously having accepted that although the date of disposal for CGT purposes is the date of the unconditional contract, the other conditions for a purchase of own shares not to be a distribution must be satisfied at the date of acquisition, ie the completion date. Thus the five-year ownership condition and the residence requirement etc would need to be met at the date of completion (*Monthly Tax Review* by Matthew Hutton, January 2010).

INCOME OR CAPITAL?

4.42 This chapter has so far mainly been concerned with the conditions to be satisfied by the individual shareholders of unquoted trading companies for a purchase of own shares to be excluded from income distribution treatment, and to be treated as a capital payment instead. This emphasis on capital treatment is understandable. For example, entrepreneurs' relief, if available, can result in a CGT rate of 10% on gains of up to £10m for qualifying business disposals (see **4.1**). Entrepreneurs' relief can apply after a qualifying period of only one year subject to the other relief conditions being satisfied, although in the context of a purchase of own shares the qualifying period of ownership for capital treatment should be noted (see **4.24**).

However, even if the CGT rate of 10% is not available, it may still be preferable for the transaction to be treated as a capital distribution. Income treatment was generally more desirable for disposals during earlier tax years in which the CGT rate exceeded the effective income tax rate on company distributions.

A CGT rate of 10% (for 2017/18) applies where an individual is not liable to income tax at the higher rate; there is also a CGT rate of 20% to the extent that the individual is a higher rate taxpayer, or chargeable gains exceed the unused part of the individual's basic rate band (although these rates are subject to certain exceptions, such as in relation to chargeable gains accruing on disposals of residential property (that do not qualify for private residence relief) and carried interest); the corresponding CGT rates in those cases are 18% and 28% instead.

Following the reform of dividend taxation in *Finance Act 2016* including the abolition of the 10% tax credit, for 2017/18 the rate of income tax on distributions (subject to a £5,000 nil rate) is 7.5% for basic rate taxpayers, 32.5% for higher rate taxpayers and 38.1% for additional rate taxpayers. The government intended to introduce legislation in *Finance Act 2017* to reduce the dividend nil rate (from 2018/19) to £2,000 and, although the amendment did not appear as originally planned, it was included in *Finance (No 2) Bill 2017* published on 8 September 2017 (which has not received Royal Assent at the time of writing).

> **Focus**
>
> Thus, if (for example) the shareholder was ineligible for entrepreneurs' relief, a CGT rate of 20% (for 2017/18) will often be more attractive than income treatment, particularly where the individual is a high earner, and/or substantial sums are involved.

However, there may occasionally be cases where income treatment is preferable, such as if the disposal proceeds are relatively small and/or the shareholder's income and gains remain within the basic rate income tax threshold.

It will generally be prudent to compare the relative tax costs of income and capital distributions respectively as a preliminary measure.

4.43 In the case of an income distribution, a purchase of own shares by a company with surplus advance corporation tax (ACT) at 5 April 1999 will give rise to notional (or 'shadow') ACT, which must be taken into account before any offset of actual ACT, in accordance with the shadow ACT provisions (*SI 1999/358*).

STATUS OF THE SHARES

4.44 Under the entrepreneurs' relief provisions, a 'material disposal' of shares in the company can be subject to relief. The rules broadly require that, for a qualifying period of at least one year ending with the date of disposal, the company is the shareholder's personal company and is either a trading company or the holding company of a trading group, and that the individual is an officer or employee of the company or a trading group member (*TCGA 1992, s 169I*).

'Personal company' in this context requires ownership of at least 5% of the company's ordinary share capital and voting rights (*TCGA 1992, s 169S(3)*). However, the 'personal company' requirement does not apply in relation to disposals of relevant EMI shares, and the above one year requirement runs from the date on which the EMI option was granted, rather than exercised (*TCGA 1992, s 169I(7A)*).

Care should be taken to avoid the inadvertent loss of entrepreneurs' relief, such as by the vendor's resignation as a director prior to the date on which the share purchase contract becomes unconditional (under *TCGA 1992, s 28(2)*), which may be determined by the date on which company law requirements were met (*Moore v Revenue and Customs* [2016] UKFTT 115 (TC); see **4.66**), although if there is an employment relationship with the company following the vendor's resignation, entrepreneurs' relief is not necessarily lost (see *Corbett v Revenue & Customs* [2014] UKFTT 298 (TC); *Hirst v Revenue & Customs* [2014] UKFTT 924 (TC)). The availability (or otherwise) of entrepreneurs' relief is likely to have a significant impact on the effective CGT rate on a share disposal to which capital treatment applies, and the relief conditions therefore need to be followed closely.

Furthermore, as indicated at **4.41** above in the context of contracts with multiple completion, for entrepreneurs' relief purposes it would be prudent to ensure that the individual vendor continues to be an officer or employee of the company when each capital sum is received under the contract for the purpose of own shares.

Following the introduction of investors' relief (in *Finance Act 2016*), a CGT rate of 10% also applies (subject to a lifetime cap of £10m) if the relevant conditions (in *TCGA 1992, Pt 5, Ch 5*) are satisfied and a claim is made. Those conditions include that the shares have been held for a period of at least three years starting from 6 April 2016 (that were acquired on or after 17 March 2016). This minimum ownership period is in contrast to the normal five-year minimum ownership period for CGT treatment on a company purchase of own shares (see **4.24**).

As noted elsewhere in this chapter, capital gains treatment in *CTA 2010, s 1033* applies automatically if the relevant conditions are satisfied. However, a claim is required for entrepreneurs' relief (and investors' relief) purposes (*TCGA 1992, ss 169M, 169VM*).

COMPANY STATUS

4.45 The definition of 'trading company' for the purposes of a company purchase of own shares requires that the company is 'wholly or mainly' trading (*CTA 2010, s 1048(1)*).

This is a less stringent test than for CGT purposes in respect of entrepreneurs' relief, which generally requires that the company's activities must not include non-trading activities to a substantial extent (*TCGA 1992, s 165A(3), Sch 7ZA, para 1(2)*). For investors' relief purposes, the definitions of 'trading company' and 'holding company of a trading group' in *TCGA 1992, s 165A* are applied (*TCGA 1992, s 169VV*).

HMRC consider 'substantial' in the context of entrepreneurs' relief to mean more than 20% (see CG64090).

4.46 The circumstances in which HMRC will provide a ruling on the status of a company for entrepreneurs' relief purposes is set out in the Capital Gains Manual. If the company has genuine doubt or difficulty over its trading status, it can seek an opinion under HMRC's Non-Statutory Business Clearance Service to assist the individual taxpayer. A firm opinion should normally be provided on the status of a company for periods that have ended, where all the relevant facts have been provided (CG64100). The company's request for an opinion should be in the format, and contain the material, prescribed in HMRC's Non-Statutory Business Clearance Guidance manual.

Guidance is also available on the GOV.UK website (www.gov.uk/guidance/non-statutory-clearance-service-guidance).

It is possible to apply for a 'negative clearance' from HMRC that the conditions for capital treatment on a purchase of own shares are not satisfied (see **4.60**).

Even if the disposing shareholder's genuine concerns over the trading status of the company for entrepreneurs' relief purposes prove to be well founded, capital treatment is still likely to be more beneficial in most circumstances.

Example 4.3 – Company status

Edward has owned 20% of the shares in Dotcom Ltd, an unquoted company, for nearly six years. The company traded very successfully and quickly grew during that time, accumulating a significant amount of surplus cash at bank, most of which was invested. In May 2017, Edward wished to retire, and it was agreed that Dotcom Ltd would purchase his shares, realising proceeds of £500,000. Edward's taxable income for 2017/18 was £125,000 (NB: his dividend nil rate has been used elsewhere).

Edward is concerned that Dotcom Ltd is not a 'trading company' for entrepreneurs' relief purposes, and asks the company to apply to HMRC for an opinion on its trading status. Unfortunately, HMRC's opinion is that the company is not a trading company for entrepreneurs' relief purposes, on the grounds that its non-trading activities are 'substantial'.

Nevertheless, the company is a trading company in terms of a company purchase of own shares, as it is 'wholly or mainly' trading (*CTA 2010, s 1048(1)*). The CGT rate of 20% is still preferable to the tax liability on an income distribution (ignoring the original cost of the shares, and any reliefs and exemptions available):

Capital payment: CGT liability	
£500,000 × 20%	£100,000
Income distribution: income tax liability	
	£
£25,000 × 32.5%	8,125
£475,000 × 38.1%	180,975
	189,100

However, where the vendor's income will be modest following the purchase of own shares (eg following retirement), income distribution treatment may be preferable. Consideration could be given in such cases to disposing of the shares over a number of years instead, and possibly seeking 'negative clearance' from HMRC, if appropriate, that income distribution treatment applies. Alternatively, it may be relevant to consider whether the transactions in securities anti-avoidance provisions (*ITA 2007, s 684*) apply for income tax purposes.

Comparing tax rates

4.47 As indicated above, for higher rate or additional rate taxpayers who do not qualify for entrepreneurs' relief (and ignoring the annual CGT exemption), a CGT rate of 20% (for 2017/18) compares favourably with the 32.5% rate on an income distribution for a higher rate (40%) taxpayer, and/or the 38.1% rate faced by an additional rate (45%) taxpayer on an income distribution (see **4.48** below).

Income tax rates may apply if the company does not qualify for capital treatment on a purchase of own shares, as illustrated in the example below.

Example 4.4 – Income distribution treatment

Sarah is a 45% taxpayer. She owns 20% of the shares in Alpha Ltd. She wished to retire, and the company bought back her shares on 30 September 2017 for £250,000. Sarah originally subscribed for the shares at par in 1990, at a cost of £100. The conditions for capital treatment are not satisfied.

Her income tax liability on the sale is calculated as follows (NB: Sarah's dividend nil rate is assumed to have been used elsewhere):

	£
Proceeds	250,000
Less: Subscription cost	(100)
Amount of distribution	249,900
Income tax liability:	
£249,900 × 38.1%	95,212
Effective income tax rate (rounded): (£95,212/£250,000)	38.08%

Note – the effective rate is slightly lower than the rate of 38.1% mentioned above, due to the subscription cost of the shares.

4.48 For individual shareholders who are 40% taxpayers, the income tax position (for 2017/18) is potentially more complicated. Personal allowances are gradually reduced (by £1 for every £2) to nil to the extent that the individual's adjusted net income exceeds £100,000.

In addition, as illustrated in **Example 4.3**, an additional income tax rate of 45% applies to taxable income over £150,000, with an additional tax rate of 38.1% applying to distributions otherwise taxable at the 45% rate. An income distribution to a shareholder on a purchase of own shares may result in a higher rate taxpayer falling partly within the 32.5% dividend rate in respect of the distribution, and partly within the 38.1% dividend additional rate.

If the consideration for the shares is relatively low and/or their base cost is relatively high, the individual vendor shareholder may not be liable to higher rate tax. In such circumstances, income distribution treatment may be more beneficial. However, in practice, such cases are likely to be relatively few.

Income distribution treatment

4.49 As indicated in the above example, the amount of the income distribution is broadly the consideration for the shares, less the original subscription price (*ITA 2007, s 989*; *CTA 2010, s 1000(1)*, category B).

It should be noted that, if the vendor shareholder did not originally subscribe for the shares, but instead bought them for a premium from another shareholder, the original subscription price is taken into account in calculating the amount of the distribution, as opposed to the higher sum actually paid for the shares. Thus a tax charge could arise on a deemed distribution even though the shareholder may have disposed of the shares for no actual profit.

In some cases, share capital may be issued at a premium, representing new consideration (eg following a share exchange on a previous company takeover). The amount of such a premium is generally treated as part of the share capital when considering the amount of any repayment of share capital (*CTA 2010, s 1025*; see CTM17510–CTM17520).

4.50 There are potential traps to avoid in the distributions legislation:

- A previous bonus issue of shares followed by a repayment of share capital may result in the application of the distribution rules in certain circumstances (see *CTA 2010, s 1026(1), (2)*). This applies to the purchase of own shares by a 'relevant company' (broadly a closely controlled or unquoted company) at any time after an earlier issue of bonus shares, but for other companies it only applies to repayments of share capital within ten years of the bonus issue (*CTA 2010, s 1026(3)*).

The effect is that on a subsequent purchase of own shares, share capital is only treated as repaid to the extent that the repayment exceeds the earlier bonus issue. Thus if (for example) the amount of earlier bonus issues exceeds the amount that would otherwise be treated as a repayment of share capital on the purchase of own shares, HMRC guidance points out that the whole payment for the purchase of own shares will be treated as an income distribution (see CTM17530).

- If a purchase of own shares satisfies the conditions for capital gains treatment (in *CTA 2010, s 1033*), it will not give rise to an income distribution. HMRC accept that exemption from income distribution treatment includes the amount that would otherwise be a distribution because of the earlier bonus issue.

  However, different treatment applies in the case of repeat bonus issues. HMRC guidance indicates that if a company makes a bonus issue followed by a purchase of own shares, and then another bonus issue, the provisions of *CTA 2010, s 1026* dealing with distributions following a bonus issue are considered to apply before *CTA 2010, s 1033* (see CTM17550).

- A purchase of own shares followed or accompanied by a bonus issue of shares can result in the latter being treated as an income distribution in certain cases, including close companies, irrespective of capital treatment having applied to the share repurchase, or clearance having been given under *CTA 2010, s 1044* (*CTA 2010, s 1022*). This applies to bonus issues by 'relevant' companies (see above) at any time after the purchase of own shares, but for other companies it only applies to bonus issues within ten years of a repayment of share capital (*CTA 2010, s 1023(1), (2)*).

  The effect is that a distribution can arise up to the amount of share capital repaid from the purchase of own shares. HMRC guidance states that this will be the case even if the recipient of the bonus issue is not the same as the vendor on the company purchase of own shares (see CTM17540).

4.51 As a result of income distribution treatment, the proceeds received by an individual vendor shareholder may partly represent a return of share capital for capital gains tax (CGT) purposes, and partly an income distribution. The fact that the transaction is an income distribution does not prevent it from being a disposal for CGT purposes as well. The amount charged to income tax is excluded from the taxable consideration when calculating the CGT position (*TCGA 1992, s 37(1)*).

The net proceeds in the CGT computation would be matched with the original amount paid for the shares. This will often mean that no capital gain or loss arises, as illustrated below.

Example 4.5 – CGT position where income treatment applies

In January 2013, Jason subscribed for 10,000 ordinary £1 shares in Delta Ltd, an unquoted trading company, representing 50% of the company's share capital. The company is successful.

On 30 September 2017, Delta Ltd agrees to purchase Jason's shares for £500,000. Unfortunately for Jason, the company's purchase of his shares does not qualify for capital gains treatment, as the five-year ownership condition has not been satisfied. The transaction is therefore treated as an income distribution.

His CGT computation for 2017/18 is as follows:

	£
Proceeds	500,000
Less: Treated as a distribution (£500,000 – £10,000)	(490,000)
Net proceeds	10,000
Less: Cost	(10,000)
Chargeable gain/(allowable loss)	Nil

4.52 However, in some situations (eg if the vendor shareholder held the shares at 31 March 1982, and the shares had a high value at that time) an allowable capital loss may be generated.

Example 4.6 – Income treatment and capital loss

Gerald subscribed for 100 ordinary £1 shares in Beta Ltd in 1980, representing 75% of the company's share capital. The company's trade is successful, and Gerald's shares are worth £200,000 at 31 March 1982.

On 31 August 2017, Beta Ltd agrees to purchase Gerald's shares for £1.4m. The conditions for CGT treatment in *CTA 2010, s 1033* are not satisfied in respect of the transaction.

Gerald's tax position (for 2017/18) is as follows:

	£
Income distribution	
Proceeds	1,400,000
Less: Subscription cost	(100)
Amount of distribution	1,399,900
CGT computation	
Proceeds	1,400,000
Less: Charged to income tax	(1,399,900)
	100
Less: Value at 31 March 1982	(200,000)
Allowable loss	(199,900)

4.53 The rule regarding disposals between connected persons (ie which restricts loss relief to transactions with the same connected person) in *TCGA 1992, s 18(3)* does not apply in the above example. This is because the 'connected persons' rule is engaged when a person 'acquires' an asset, whereas in the above example for company law purposes Beta Ltd cancelled the shares, so in that sense would not 'acquire' anything (*FA 2003, s 195(2)*).

As indicated at **4.41**, there is anecdotal evidence that HMRC sometimes use similar reasoning to contend that the date of disposal on a purchase of own shares under a multiple completion contract is when each capital sum is received (within *TCGA 1992, s 22(2)*), and not the date of the contract (within *TCGA 1992, s 28(1)*), as the latter provisions require that an asset is 'acquired' under the contract. On that basis, the conditions for entrepreneurs' relief would need to be considered when the proceeds are received, as opposed to the date of the contract.

The tax treatment for company or trustee vendor shareholders is considered later in this chapter.

4.54 If an individual vendor subscribes for ordinary shares in an unquoted trading company and a capital loss arises such as in the circumstances outlined above, it may be possible to offset the loss against the taxpayer's total income for the same and/or the preceding year, subject to any restriction in the amount of such 'sideways' loss relief, if the capping of such losses to the greater of £50,000 and 25% of adjusted total income applies for the tax year (*ITA 2007, ss 24A, 131*).

This income tax loss relief is subject to a number of conditions (in *ITA 2007, Pt 4, Ch 6*), a detailed consideration of which is outside the scope of this chapter. However, there appears to be no reason why an eligible loss cannot relieve total income, including the distribution arising from the company purchase of its own shares.

Capital gains treatment

4.55 The conditions for automatic capital gains treatment were described earlier in this chapter. If those conditions are satisfied, the income distribution rules are disapplied, and the entire proceeds are treated as a capital receipt instead. For individual vendor shareholders, this presents an opportunity to claim CGT reliefs, allowances and exemptions, if applicable.

For example, the CGT liability of an individual shareholder may be reduced or extinguished by a high base cost (or March 1982 value, if the shares have been held for a sufficient time), capital losses, entrepreneurs' relief and the annual CGT exemption.

Even if the CGT liability is not completely extinguished, capital treatment can result in a relatively low effective tax rate, as illustrated below.

Example 4.7 – Effective rate of CGT

The facts are as in **Example 4.6** above, except that the conditions for capital gains treatment in *CTA 2010, s 1033* are satisfied in relation to Gerald's disposal of 100 ordinary £1 shares to Beta Ltd for £1.4m on 31 August 2017. In addition, the conditions for entrepreneurs' relief have been satisfied throughout Gerald's relevant ownership period.

His CGT position for 2017/18 is as follows:

	£
Proceeds	1,400,000
Less: Section 104 holding (value at 31 March 1982)	(200,000)
	1,200,000
Less: Annual exemption	(11,300)
Chargeable gain	1,188,700
CGT at 10% (entrepreneurs' relief rate)	118,870
Effective CGT rate (rounded)	8.5%

4.56 If entrepreneurs' relief applies to reduce the gain without restriction, the effective CGT rate (ie the CGT rate as a percentage of disposal proceeds) can be considerably lower than the special 10% rate. This is because the effective CGT rate is subject to additional factors including allowable costs, capital losses and the annual exemption (if available). Capital gains treatment will therefore be the preferred path for many vendor shareholders of unquoted trading companies.

It should be remembered that capital treatment under *CTA 2010, s 1033* is mandatory if the relevant conditions are satisfied. Otherwise, income tax distribution treatment will automatically apply instead.

CLEARANCE APPLICATIONS TO HMRC

4.57

> **Focus**
>
> As noted above, the legislation on the purchase (or redemption or repayment) by an unquoted trading company of its own shares in *CTA 2010, ss 1033–1048* contains various conditions which must be satisfied before the tax treatment allowed by *CTA 2010, s 1033* can apply. Provision is made (in *CTA 2010, s 1044*) for the company (or its agent) to make a written clearance application in advance to HMRC.

It is worth noting the following general points in relation to clearance applications:

- A clearance application is not necessarily required in order for *CTA 2010, s 1033* to apply (ie the application of *CTA 2010, s 1033* is mandatory; either the conditions for capital treatment are satisfied, or they are not). However, if a complete and accurate clearance application is submitted to HMRC, this does provide certainty of tax treatment.
- Clearances applications can either be 'positive' under *CTA 2010, s 1044(2)* (ie that *CTA 2010, s 1033* does apply), or 'negative' under *CTA 2010, s 1044(3)* (ie that it does not). 'Negative' clearance applications are discussed further below.
- Clearance by HMRC under *CTA 2010, s 1044* differs from certain other statutory clearances, such as under *ITA 2007, s 701* in respect of transactions in securities. Clearance under the latter provisions merely confirms that the proposed transactions are not considered to be undertaken for a main purpose of obtaining an income tax advantage (see **4.59** below). Clearance under *CTA 2010, s 1044* confirms that

CTA 2010, s 1033 will (or will not) apply to the purchase of own shares. Thus, provided that the clearance application correctly and fully discloses all material facts, it should be possible to rely on the clearance given by HMRC, even if it transpires that capital treatment was not technically in point for some reason.

4.58 To assist companies and agents in preparing clearance applications under what is now *CTA 2010, s 1044*, HMRC included as an Annex to Statement of Practice 2/82 pro forma applications for clearance for the purchase of own shares under what is now *CTA 2010, s 1033(2)* (ie relating to the benefit of a trade), and *CTA 2010, s 1033(3)* (ie relating to the payment of inheritance tax).

In more recent guidance, as indicated at **4.14**, HMRC's Help Sheet 'Company Purchase of Own Shares' also contains separate checklists of information to be provided in clearance applications for a purchase benefiting a company's trade, and a purchase in connection with an IHT liability (tinyurl.com/HMRC-CPOS). The pro forma clearance application relating to a purchase benefiting a company's trade is included below.

The application must give particulars of all 'relevant transactions' (*CTA 2010, s 1045(1)(b)*), and must fully and accurately disclose all material facts and circumstances. Otherwise, any resulting clearance given by HMRC is void (*CTA 2010, s 1045(6)*).

4.59 An application to HMRC under *CTA 2010, s 1044* for advance clearance that capital treatment will be available to the vendor shareholder is normally accompanied by an application for clearance under *ITA 2007, s 701* that the 'transactions in securities' anti-avoidance rules do not apply.

Those provisions (in *ITA 2007, Pt 13, Ch 1*) are of relevance to most owner-managed businesses, as they relate to close companies (ie under the control of five or fewer persons, or participators who are directors). They broadly apply to company distributions not otherwise taxable as income (*ITA 2007, s 685*, referred to in the legislation as condition 'A' or 'B') unless HMRC are satisfied that obtaining an income tax advantage was not a main object of the purchase of own shares and no counteraction adjustment (under *ITA 2007, s 698*) ought to be made in respect of the transaction.

Where a joint clearance application is made under *CTA 2010, s 1044*, and also *ITA 2007, s 701* concerning the transactions in securities provisions, a single letter can be used for both clearances, which should be sent to HMRC's Clearance & Counteraction Team, Anti-Avoidance Group. Contact details can be obtained from the GOV.UK website (www.gov.uk/guidance/seeking-clearance-or-approval-for-a-transaction#3). No extra copy is required as the same person will deal with each of the clearances asked for. A single response will be given covering all of them.

'Negative' clearance applications

4.60 As mentioned elsewhere in this chapter, capital gains treatment in *CTA 2010, s 1033* applies automatically if the relevant conditions are satisfied. This will normally be the preferred tax treatment for vendor shareholders if entrepreneurs' relief is due, or otherwise if the CGT rate (20% in most cases) is lower than the effective rate of income tax on an income distribution (eg 38.1% for a 45% taxpayer in 2017/18).

Historically, in the case of family or owner-managed companies before 6 April 2008, it was often desirable to structure the company purchase of own shares so that the relevant conditions for capital gains treatment were breached (eg if little or no taper relief was available for CGT purposes). Income tax treatment also became potentially more attractive in some cases following the introduction of a 28% CGT rate for higher rate taxpayers in respect of gains accruing from 23 June 2010. However, following the general reduction in CGT rates and increase in tax rates for income distributions (from 2016/17), breaching the conditions for capital gains treatment will be even less of a consideration than before in most cases.

Of course, it is also important to be aware of circumstances in which capital treatment can be lost, to ensure that an inadvertent breach of the rules does not occur.

BREACHING THE CONDITIONS FOR CAPITAL TREATMENT

4.61 A breach of the rules for capital gains treatment can be caused in various ways. For example:

- The vendor selling the shares in stages under separate contracts, or immediately lending the sale proceeds back to the company for a time, such that the 'substantial reduction' and/or the 'no continuing connection' tests are not satisfied.
- The vendor breaching the residence condition, such as by transferring the shares to a nominee who is not resident or ordinarily resident in the UK in the tax year of purchase. The acquisition of shares by the nominee does not trigger a disposal by the vendor for CGT purposes, as transactions between them are specifically disregarded (*TCGA 1992, s 60(1)*). However, the rules for capital treatment on a purchase of own shares require that both the vendor and nominee must be resident in the UK (and ordinarily resident in the UK, for share purchases before 6 April 2013) (*CTA 2010, s 1034(1), (2)*). The transfer of shares to a nominee prior to a company purchase of own shares could also be challenged by HMRC, based on *Furniss v Dawson* [1984] AC 474 principles.

- It may be the case that the purchase of own shares was not wholly or mainly for the benefit of the company's trade. For example, the vendor may be retained as a full-time director. Alternatively, it may be that the transaction wholly or mainly benefited the vendor shareholder as opposed to the company, eg that the transaction was undertaken wholly or mainly to provide funds to facilitate the retirement of a director shareholder (as was held by the Special Commissioner in *Allum v Marsh*; see **4.16**), rather than to benefit the company's trade.

There is a 'negative' advance clearance application procedure available to the company by virtue of *CTA 2010, s 1044(3)*, ie to the effect HMRC are satisfied that the transaction is *not* one for which capital gains treatment in *CTA 2010, s 1033* applies.

HMRC are required to give their decision within 30 days of receiving the application, or to request further particulars.

APPLICATION FOR CLEARANCE UNDER *CTA 2010, S 1044* – PURCHASES WITHIN *CTA 2010, S 1033(1), (2)*

4.62

Focus

It should be clearly stated at the top of the letter what clearances are requested (eg *CTA 2010, s 1044* and *ITA 2007, s 701*). It should also be confirmed whether the purchase of shares is regarded as falling within *CTA 2010, s 1033(1)* by virtue of *CTA 2010, s 1033(2)* or *(3)*.

If the purchasing company has previously made an application under *CTA 2010, s 1044* (or its predecessor, *ICTA 1988, s 225*) it will be helpful if HMRC's reference can be quoted.

1. **Information about the company**

   1.1 The name of the company making the purchase

   1.2 The company UTR

   1.3 Confirmation that the company is unquoted

   1.4 Confirmation that the company is a trading company or the holding company of a trading group

   1.5 Where the company is a member of a group, the names of the group companies together with their UTRs

2. Information about the payment

2.1 Details of the shares to be purchased, the name of the present owner, the purchase price and the number of shares to be bought

2.2 Details of any other transactions taking place between the company and the seller at or about the same time

2.3 Confirmation that the company's Articles of Association allow it to purchase its own shares

2.4 Details of how the payment will be made

3. Information about the shareholders

3.1 A list of the current shareholders in the purchasing company, showing for each person their current holdings including amount, class and dividend rights. Where appropriate include details for each company in the group (as per 1.5)

3.2 Details of any relationships between the shareholders

3.3 Where the shareholder is the son or daughter of another shareholder, confirmation that he or she is over 18 or else details of their age

3.4 Where the shareholder is a trust please provide details of the names of the trustees, the settlors, and the beneficiaries of the trust

4. Information about the purpose

4.1 A statement of the reasons for the purchase, including the trading and any other benefits expected to accrue from it, whether or not to the purchasing company

4.2 Confirmation that the purchase does not form part of a scheme or arrangement where the main purpose or one of the main purposes is to enable the owner of the shares to participate in the profits of the company without receiving a dividend, or for the avoidance of tax

4.3 Confirmation that the seller will receive no other payment from the company, or details of any such payment to be made

4.4 Particulars of any prior transactions or arrangements to be carried out in preparation for the purchase

5. Information about the seller

5.1 The present residence status of the seller and any intended change

5.2 The UTR or NI number of the seller, or if not known, his or her private address

5.3 The period of beneficial ownership by the seller of the shares to be purchased and any other relevant holdings

5.4(a) Confirmation that the combined interests of the seller and any associates in the company will be substantially reduced, or,

5.4(b) If the company is a member of a group, confirmation that the combined interests of the seller and any associates in the group will be substantially reduced

5.5 Confirmation that the seller (after including any interests held by his associates) will not, immediately after the purchase, be connected with the company making the purchase or with any company which is a member of the same group as that company

6. Accounts and other financial information

The application should be accompanied by:

6.1 Copies of the latest available financial statements for the purchasing company

6.2 If appropriate, copies of the latest financial statements for the group and for any group companies

6.3 A note of any material relevant changes since the balance sheet date or confirmation that there are no changes

6.4 Details of any loan or current account which the seller maintains with the company or with any group company

COMPANY LAW

4.63 A company purchase of its own shares must comply with certain *Companies Act 2006* requirements. HMRC can only consider a request for clearance on a transaction which appears to be a valid purchase of own shares (*Tax Bulletin,* Issue 21 (February 1996)).

Focus

A detailed consideration of company law issues is outside the scope of this chapter. However, compliance with the law is fundamental to the transaction, and the tax treatment is dependent on the legal analysis. The main company law considerations (ie for an unquoted or 'off market' purchase) are therefore outlined below.

Professional advisers who are unfamiliar with company law should obtain the necessary legal advice. Failure to comply with the legal requirements could make the transaction void and legally unenforceable, and render the company and its officers liable to sanctions (*CA 2006, s 658(2), (3)*).

In *Baker v Revenue & Customs* [2013] UKFTT 394 (TC), a company purchase of own shares was held to be void by reason of the failure to comply with Companies Act requirements, which included an insufficiency of distributable profits. The appellant was therefore under an obligation to return funds to the company. This meant that those proceeds did not (as HMRC contended) amount to an income distribution for tax purposes. Thus the appeal was allowed.

The facts in *Baker* were distinguished from an earlier (non-tax) case, *Kinlan & Anor v Crimmin & Anor* [2006] EWHC 779 (Ch). In that case, the company (in liquidation) was seeking the repayment of proceeds paid to a departing shareholder on a purchase of own shares. The court held that the transaction was void as it breached company law (ie by reason that part of the consideration for the shares was deferred). However, it was also held that the shareholder was entitled to keep the money received from the company, based on certain 'important and unusual features of the case'. The tax implications of the decision were not addressed.

The rationale applied in the *Baker* case suggests that HMRC's approach in similar situations would be to treat such funds retained by departing shareholders as liable to income tax as a distribution.

4.64 Shares purchased by an unquoted company are normally treated as cancelled. However, as indicated at **4.66** below, the company may, if authorised to do so by its articles, make a company purchase of own shares out of distributable profits (or the proceeds of a fresh share issue for the purpose of financing the purchase), or alternatively out of capital up to an aggregate purchase price in a financial year of the lower of £15,000 and the nominal value of 5% of the company's fully paid share capital as at the beginning of the financial year (*CA 2006, s 692(1)*).

If the company purchases its own shares in accordance with *CA 2006, Pt 18, Ch 4* (*ss 690–708*), such shares may be held as treasury shares if the purchase is made out of distributable profits (*CA 2006, s 724(1)*). Shares held in treasury are not actually cancelled, and are retained by the company. However, the rights attaching to the shares are effectively suspended whilst they are held in treasury (ie the company may not vote in respect of the shares or receive distributions in respect of them) (*CA 2006, s 726(2), (3)*).

The purchase by a company of its own shares is not treated as the acquisition of an asset (*FA 2003, s 195(2)*). See **4.41**.

Requirements

4.65 The Companies Acts give a company power to purchase its own shares, if certain conditions are satisfied. Otherwise, the shares are not treated as cancelled and legal ownership remains with the vendor (CTM17505). The tax implications of the company's payment to the shareholder would then need to be considered. For most owner-managed companies, this would include a potential liability for the company under the 'loans to participators' provisions (*CTA 2010, s 455*), and for the vendor as a taxable benefit under the beneficial loan rules (*ITEPA 2003, s 175*).

Companies Act 2006 specifies a procedure for share buy-backs, which restates some provisions of its predecessor (*Companies Act 1985*), and changed others.

4.66 The following is a brief outline of the main company law requirements.

- **Power to purchase own shares**

  A company is not required to have the power in its Articles of Association to purchase its own shares, although the members may restrict or prohibit a purchase of own shares through the company's Articles if they wish. This provision is helpful, because the Articles of some older companies do not contain an authority.

  The share purchase must not leave the company with only redeemable and/or treasury shares (*CA 2006, s 690*).

- **Authority for purchase**

  A contract for an 'off-market' company purchase of own shares is generally required to be approved in advance (*CA 2006, s 693*). (Note: separate conditions apply (since 30 April 2013) if the purchase is for the purposes of or pursuant to an employee share scheme (*CA 2006, 693A*)).

  However, the Act allows a company to enter into a contract to purchase its own shares, on condition that the shareholders approve the contract terms by an ordinary resolution, which requires a majority of over 50% (*CA 2006, ss 282, 694(2)*). (Note: prior to changes introduced by the *Companies Act 2006 (Amendment of Part 18) Regulations 2013, SI 2013/999* with effect from 30 April 2013 a special resolution was necessary, which required a majority of over 75% (*CA 2006, s 283*.)

  If the contract (or its terms) is not approved, the company may not purchase the relevant shares and the contract lapses.

  The purchase authority requirements in *CA 2006, ss 693, 694* were considered in the context of an entrepreneurs' relief claim on a company purchase of own shares in *Moore v Revenue and Customs* [2016] UKFTT 115 (TC). In that case, a director shareholder who was employed under a contract of employment agreed that the company would purchase his shares following a dispute with the other director shareholders, and would leave the business. At a general meeting of the company on 29 May 2009, it was resolved that the company would purchase 2,700 out of the taxpayer's 3,000 shares. On the same day, the taxpayer signed a compromise agreement for the termination of his employment, and the company purchase of shares agreement. All Companies House papers concerning the taxpayer's resignation as a director were also signed on that day. However, those documents stated that the effective date of his resignation as a director was 28 February 2009.

Following an enquiry into the taxpayer's return, HMRC concluded that the taxpayer was not entitled to entrepreneurs' relief, because he was not an officer or employee of the company throughout the period of one year ending with the disposal of his shares (as required by *TCGA 1992, s 169I(6)(b)*). The taxpayer appealed. He accepted that he had ceased employment with the company and was no longer an office holder from 28 February 2009. However, it was contended that the completion of the negotiations resulted in a binding contract for sale in February 2009, and it followed that this was the date of disposal for CGT purposes (*TCGA 1992, s 28*). However, the First-tier Tribunal noted that company law (*CA 2006, ss 693, 694*) required a contract for a company's own purchase of shares to be approved in advance by a special resolution. That resolution was not passed until 29 May 2009. Accordingly, the company was incapable of entering into a valid contract to purchase the shares until the resolution had been passed. Even if there had been a contract, it had to be conditional on approval by special resolution. The date of disposal under a conditional contract would (by virtue of *TCGA 1992, s 28(2)*) be the date on which the condition was satisfied, ie 29 May 2009. The appellant's appeal was dismissed.

- **Disclosure of contract details**

  A copy of any written contract (or a memorandum of its terms) must be made available to the members. For resolutions at meetings, it must be available for inspection at the company's registered office for at least 15 days prior to the meeting, and also at the meeting itself (*CA 2006, s 696(2)*).

- **Payment for the shares**

  The shares purchased must be fully paid. In addition, the company is generally required to pay for the shares on completion (*CA 2006, s 691*). However, the latter condition is subject to an exception (since 30 April 2013) allowing private companies to purchase shares for the purposes of or pursuant to employee share schemes by instalments (*CA 2006, s 691(3)*, as inserted by *SI 2013/999, reg 3*).

- **Distributable profits**

  Subject to certain exceptions (see below), a company must purchase its own shares out of distributable profits, or out of the proceeds of a fresh share issue to finance the purchase (*CA 2006, s 692(2)*). An amount equal to the par value of the shares bought back must be transferred to a capital redemption reserve account.

  However, a private company may purchase its own shares out of capital subject to conditions in *CA 2006, s 692(1)* (see 4.64), or under *CA 2006, Pt 18, Ch 5* (*ss 709–723*) ('Redemption or purchase by private company out of capital'), consideration of which is outside the scope of this chapter.

- **Cancellation of shares**

  Following the company share repurchase, the relevant shares are treated as cancelled. The company's share capital is reduced by the nominal value of the cancelled shares (*CA 2006, s 706*). This rule does not apply to treasury shares (see above).

- **Return to Companies House**

  A return must be made to Companies House within 28 days of the transaction, stating the number of shares purchased, their nominal value and the date of purchase (*CA 2006, s 707*).

  Except in the case of treasury shares which are not cancelled, the company must also give notification of the cancellation of the shares within 28 days, normally with a statement of the company's share capital (except where it would be the same as a statement required under *CA 2006, s 720B* in relation to an employees' pension scheme) (*CA 2006, s 708*).

- **Inspection of contract**

  The company must keep a copy of the contract (or a memorandum of its terms) available for inspection at its registered office for a period of at least ten years from conclusion of the contract (*CA 2006, s 702*). Alternatively, a copy of the contract (or any variation) may be kept for inspection at a specified place (in regulations made under *CA 2006, s 1136*).

  The company must notify the registrar of the place where the contract is available for inspection, unless it has always been kept at the company's registered office. A contract (or memorandum of terms) relating to a private company must be made available for inspection by any of its members.

CORPORATE VENDORS

4.67 Whilst this chapter is mainly concerned with individual owner-managers of unquoted trading companies, it should be noted that a company purchase of own shares by a UK company from another UK company has potentially different tax implications.

In those cases, if the purchase gives rise to a distribution, the disposal proceeds are not reduced by the amount of the distribution for the purposes of calculating corporation tax on chargeable gains. HMRC originally adopted this approach on the basis that the distribution does not suffer a tax charge as income within *TCGA 1992, s 37(1)* (Statement of Practice 4/89). The distribution is included in the computation of corporation tax on chargeable gains. HMRC guidance states that this treatment only applies to a purchase of own shares, not to a redemption or reduction in share capital (CG58623).

The above approach by HMRC is based on previous distributions legislation (*ICTA 1988, s 208*), which stated: 'except as otherwise provided by the *Corporation Tax Acts*, Corporation Tax shall not be chargeable on dividends and other distributions of a company resident in the United Kingdom, nor shall any such dividends or distributions be taken into account in computing income for corporation tax'. This legislation was subsequently replaced by *CTA 2009, s 1285*, which was itself subsequently repealed (see below).

4.68 HMRC's view on the treatment of a purchase of own shares from a corporate shareholder in Statement of Practice 4/89 was upheld by the Court of Appeal in *Strand Options and Futures Ltd v Vojak* [2003] EWCA Civ 1457. In that case, HMRC had previously confirmed that chargeable gains treatment under what is now *CTA 2010, s 1033* (previously *ICTA 1988, s 219*) did not apply to the taxpayer company, but considered that Statement of Practice 4/89 applied with the effect that not only would the proceeds from the purchase of part of its shareholding in another company be treated as a distribution for tax purposes, but the distribution must also be included in the chargeable gain computation in respect of the shares. The Court of Appeal considered that a true interpretation of the effect of *ICTA 1988, s 208* (except where otherwise expressly provided by the Tax Acts) was that it related directly to dividends and other distributions, rather than indirectly as part of the computation of a taxable amount. If it had been intended to exclude the distribution from the capital gains computation, a specific reference could have been made in *ICTA 1988, s 208.* Accordingly, it was held that the distribution element should be brought into account in computing the taxpayer's chargeable gains.

The above legislation on UK company distributions in *ICTA 1988, s 208* was subsequently replaced by *CTA 2009, s 1285*, which expressly provided that UK dividends and other distributions were not prevented from being taken into account in the calculation of chargeable gains. This provision therefore made the decision in the *Strand Options* case explicit in statute.

However, *CTA 2009, s 1285* was also replaced by legislation (introduced by *Finance Act 2009*) for distributions paid on or after 1 July 2009, which removes the general exemption for UK company distributions. The current provisions (*CTA 2009, Pt 9A*) determine the scope of the corporation tax charge on both UK and foreign company distributions. A detailed consideration of these rules is outside the scope of this chapter. However, it is perhaps worth noting that although, in the majority of cases, company distributions will be exempt from corporation tax, this is not automatically the case.

Unlike the previous legislation in *CTA 2009, s 1285*, the rules in *CTA 2009, Pt 9A* as originally enacted did not expressly state the treatment of distributions in the company's calculation of chargeable gains. However, legislation introduced in *F(No 3)A 2010* explicitly preserves the corporation tax charge on chargeable gains resulting from share capital. It broadly provides that whilst a distribution may be exempt from tax as income, this does not prevent the amount of the distribution from being taken into account in computing a company's chargeable gains (*CTA 2009, s 931RA*). This amendment to *CTA 2009, Pt 9A* applies to distributions from 1 July 2009, and hence the treatment of repurchases of share capital effectively remains unchanged from HMRC's previous position and the decision in the *Strand Options* case, as outlined above.

Whilst a chargeable gain may therefore arise for a corporate vendor on a purchase of own shares, the substantial shareholding exemption (SSE) may apply to the disposal if certain conditions are satisfied (*TCGA 1992, Sch 7AC*). Commentary on the SSE is included at **6.58** and following.

TRUSTEE VENDORS

4.69 As explained in this chapter, a company purchase of own shares is generally treated as a distribution for tax purposes. Under trust law, such a transaction usually gives rise to a capital receipt. Certain types of capital receipts by trustees are treated as income receipts in their hands, and are liable at 'special trust rates', ie the rate applicable to trusts of 45% or the dividend trust rate of 38.1% (for 2017/18). This includes the receipt from a company which is buying back its own shares from the trustees.

The tax treatment of such a disposal by trustees was called into question following changes to what has now become *ITA 2007, s 482* (previously *ICTA 1988, s 686A*) in *FA 2006*. The original legislation in *ICTA 1988, s 686A* provided that what was taxable was only the distribution element, excluding the original subscription price for the shares. However, the effect of an omission in the wording of the *FA 2006* amendments was to treat the whole payment to the trustees (ie including the original subscription price) as being taxable, rather than just the distribution element. The circumstances in which capital gains treatment applied were not distinguished either. This omission was corrected in *FA 2007* (see below), which ensures that distributions are liable to income tax (ie the 'profit' element, excluding the original subscription price), with the amendment having effect from 6 April 2006.

The correct position is stated in *ITA 2007, s 482* ('Types of amount to be charged at special rates for trustees') as amended. A distribution for the purposes of that legislation broadly includes a payment made on the redemption, repayment or purchase of shares in the company. However, a company purchase of own shares which satisfies the conditions for capital treatment is specifically excluded from the meaning of 'distribution' for the purposes of the *Corporation Tax Acts* (*CTA 2010, s 1033(1)*), and the same treatment is applied for income tax purposes by virtue of the definition of 'distribution' in *ITA 2007, s 989*. Hence a capital payment under trust law, and for tax purposes by virtue of *CTA 2010, s 1033*, on a company purchase of own shares should not be subject to income tax as a distribution.

HMRC's Trusts Manual confirms (at TSEM3205):

> 'Where CTA 2010, s 1033 applies a sale of shares is not treated as a distribution. So if the conditions in s 1033 are satisfied, ITA Sections 481 and 482 will not apply to a company purchase of own shares. You should not apply ITA Sections 481 and 482 if the company in question has received 'clearance' that s 1033 does apply.'

4.70 There was some concern that where the vendors of shares are trustees, a 'double' charge to income tax and CGT could arise effectively on the same transaction, for reasons other than those outlined above. For CGT purposes, *TCGA 1992, s 37(1)* provides that disposal proceeds are excluded from the chargeable gains calculation if '... charged to income tax as income of, or taken into account as a receipt in computing income of, *the person making the disposal* ...' (emphasis added).

In the case of a settlor-interested trust, the person making the disposal will be the trustees, but the income tax liability will arise on the settlor. In strictness, relief under *TCGA 1992, s 37* would therefore be unavailable in the CGT computation, as the person making the disposal would be different than the person incurring the income tax charge. However, it is understood that HMRC accept that a relief claim is available to vacate the CGT assessment (under *TMA 1970, s 32(1)*).

A similar problem potentially arises in respect of life interest trusts which are not settlor-interested, whereby the trustees are liable to CGT on the gain, but the income tax liability otherwise belongs to the life tenant. HMRC are reported to consider that because a purchase of own shares is generally capital under trust law, the income tax liability will not usually belong to the life tenant. The trustees would therefore be liable to income tax instead, and the protection of *TCGA 1992* would then be available. However, as a precaution, the trust deed should not define the life tenant's entitlement to income by reference to 'taxable income' (see 'A problem of trust' by John Barnett, *Taxation*, 9 June 2005).

OTHER POINTS

Associated persons

4.71 For the purposes of the company purchase of own shares rules providing for capital treatment if the conditions in *CTA 2010, ss 1033–1047* are satisfied (eg in respect of the 'substantial reduction' and 'no continuing connection' tests), the interests of associated persons need to be considered. Such interests are added to those of the vendor for these purposes.

'Associated persons' include the following (*CTA 2010, ss 1059–1061*):

- spouses or civil partners living together;
- parents and minors under the age of 18;
- a person connected with a company is associated with that company, and with any other companies which it controls;
- if a person connected with one company controls the other, the two companies are associated;
- if a person is accustomed to acting on the directions of another person in respect of the company's affairs, the two persons are associated;
- settlement trustee shareholders are broadly associated with any settlor(s), their associates and with any person who has an actual or potential beneficial entitlement to a significant interest in the shares (subject to certain exceptions relating to pension schemes and employee trusts); and
- the personal representatives of a deceased shareholder are associated with any person who has an actual or potential beneficial entitlement to a 'significant interest in the shares.

An interest is 'significant' in the context of trustees and personal representatives if its value exceeds 5% of the beneficial interest in the settlement or estate concerned (*CTA 2010, ss 1060(4), 1061(2)*).

Returns of own share purchases

4.72

> **Focus**
>
> The company must submit a return to HMRC within 60 days of making a payment for the purchase of own shares to which capital treatment is considered to apply (*CTA 2010, s 1046*).

> This requirement applies whether or not clearance was requested and obtained from HMRC that capital gains treatment applies to the payment (CTM17580).

In practice, if a clearance application was made this requirement can often be satisfied in a short letter to HMRC drawing the officer's attention to the clearance letter and outlining any changes between the proposed transactions in the letter and the actual transactions that took place.

If a clearance application was not made, HMRC will need to know the date of the purchase, the name of the vendor, the number of shares, the amount of consideration, and the grounds on which the 'trade benefit' test are considered to be satisfied.

A person connected with the company must give notice to HMRC if the company treats a purchase of own shares as satisfying 'Condition A' in *CTA 2010, s 1033*, within 60 days of becoming aware of any scheme or arrangement within *CTA 2010, s 1042* that affects the payment. *CTA 2010, s 1042(2)* broadly states that the purchase must not be part of a scheme or arrangement which may result in the seller or associate having a disqualifying interest in the company (*CTA 2010, s 1046(3), (4)*).

4.73 HMRC can apply their information and inspection powers if necessary.

Historically, an HMRC officer who (prior to 13 August 2009) had reason to believe that a company payment subject to capital gains treatment formed part of a 'scheme or arrangement' could issue a notice requiring the company (or any connected person) to provide certain information relating to the transaction within a period of not less than 60 days (*ICTA 1988, s 226(3)*, prior to repeal), with the threat of possible penalties for failing to comply.

However, this provision was rendered otiose following the introduction of HMRC's information and inspection powers in *FA 2008, Sch 36* (as amended), and was therefore repealed with effect from the above date.

In addition, from 1 April 2012, HMRC's data-gathering powers (in *FA 2011, s 86(1), Sch 23*) broadly provide that HMRC can by written notice require relevant data to be provided by a relevant data holder (as widely defined), subject to penalties for non-compliance. A 'relevant data holder' for these purposes includes a person who receives a payment from the company within *CTA 2010, s 1033* (*FA 2011, Sch 23, para 14(1)(c)*).

For notices given or requests made prior to 1 April 2012, if a payment for a purchase of own shares within *CTA 2010, s 1033* is received on behalf of another person, HMRC can require the recipient to disclose the name and address of that other person. HMRC can also require the other person to state the name and address of any other person on whose behalf the payment was received (*CTA 2010, s 1046(5)–(7)*).

4.74 Vendor shareholders will need to ensure compliance with statutory requirements in connection with a company purchase of their shares. For example, they should ensure that the disposal is properly notified and returned to HMRC, and that any tax liabilities are duly paid, within the appropriate time limits. Consideration should also be given to the level of tax return disclosure required to minimise the possibility of an HMRC enquiry, and reduce the risk of a discovery assessment by HMRC outside the normal enquiry window (*Brown & Anor v Revenue & Customs* [2012] UKFTT 425 (TC)).

If an advance clearance application was made and HMRC gave clearance that capital treatment applied, consideration should be given to submitting a copy of the application and HMRC's clearance letter with the tax return, or at least making reference to them in the white space on the return (of course, this assumes that the clearance application fully and accurately discloses all material facts and circumstances).

If a clearance application was not submitted to HMRC but capital gains treatment is still sought, the tax return should disclose all the information that a full and accurate clearance application would have contained, and highlight any areas of uncertainty or potential disagreement on the tax treatment (eg the grounds on which the 'trade benefit' test are considered to be satisfied).

Stamp duty

4.75 The purchasing company is generally liable to a stamp duty charge of 0.5% on a return to Companies House under *CA 2006, s 707*, as if it were an instrument transferring the relevant shares on sale to the company pursuant to a purchase agreement *(FA 1986, s 66)*. This stamp duty liability is rounded up to the nearest multiple of £5.

However, for documents executed from 13 March 2008, if the consideration is £1,000 or less, the return does not need to be stamped by HMRC before being sent to Companies House, although the company must certify that the transaction does not form part of a larger transaction the consideration for which is more than £1,000 (*FA 1999, Sch 13, para 1(3A)*).

The return (Form SH03) provides details of the share buyback. This form can be downloaded from the GOV.UK website: www.gov.uk/government/publications/notify-a-purchase-of-own-shares.

As indicated above, Form SH03 is a stampable return, and the duty is charged on the consideration for the shares. Note that the return itself is stampable, rather than the share transfer form. If no stamp duty is payable, due to the above consideration threshold of £1,000, it must be certified on the form that this is the case, and it should be sent directly to Companies House.

The company must deliver the return to Companies House within 28 days from the first date on which the shares were delivered to the company.

Professional fees

4.76 Professional costs incurred by the company on the purchase (or redemption or repayment) of its shares are generally not an allowable deduction from trading profits for corporation tax purposes. This is on the basis that such fees are capital expenditure in respect of the company's share capital, and/or that they are excluded from relief under the 'wholly and exclusively' rule (*CTA 2009, ss 53, 54*).

It may seem somewhat anomalous that HMRC can give clearance that a purchase of own shares is wholly or mainly for the benefit of the company's trade, and yet deny a deduction for the professional costs of securing that benefit. However, it does not automatically follow (at least in HMRC's view) that the related professional costs of a purchase of own shares are considered to be 'wholly and exclusively' for the purposes of the trade (see CTM17600).

Professional advisers may therefore wish to word their fee notes carefully, to distinguish between allowable and non-allowable services, with a view to minimising any disallowance for the latter.

For the vendor, if capital gains treatment applies, a deduction for professional fees is available if directly related to the cost of acquiring or disposing of the shares (*TCGA 1992, s 38(2)*). HMRC regard the reasonable professional fees of valuing the shares for the purpose of making a capital gains computation as allowable (CG15260). However, fees incurred in computing the tax liability are not considered by HMRC to be allowable (CG15280).

Valuation of shares

4.77 For valuation purposes, the market value rule for transactions between connected persons for CGT purposes in *TCGA 1992, s 18* does not generally apply to a company purchase of own shares, such as in the case of a family company, as there is no acquisition by the company corresponding to the disposal by the shareholder.

However, market value may still be substituted if the purchase is not considered to be at arm's length (*TCGA 1992, s 17*; see CG58645).

A purchase at what HMRC consider to be overvalue may be referred to HMRC Shares and Assets Valuation. The end result may be that HMRC seek to tax the excess over an arm's-length value, perhaps as an income distribution (within *CTA 2010, s 1020*), or possibly as employment income within *ITEPA 2003, s 446X* ('Securities disposed of for more than market value').

However, reports by HMRC officers to Shares and Assets Valuation on this basis are understood to be rare.

Loan relationships

4.78 The loan relationships regime for companies (*CTA 2009, Pt 5*) includes anti-avoidance provisions that can restrict debits (eg loan interest payments) to the extent that the loan relationship has an 'unallowable purpose' as defined (*CTA 2009, ss 441–442*).

HMRC guidance in their Corporate Finance Manual (at CFM38180) lists transactions that they consider will not normally fall within the unallowable purposes anti-avoidance provisions. In the context of a company purchase of own shares, HMRC state that *CTA 2009, ss 441–442* will not normally apply to loan relationship debits 'that relate to a straightforward borrowing by a UK plc in order to fund a repurchase of its shares provided that there are no attempts to structure the arrangement in such a way as to provide a tax advantage for any other person and/or the amount borrowed (the level of gearing up) is dictated by market forces and hence is at arm's length'.

However, it should be noted that HMRC's guidance refers to a purchase of own shares by a public limited company, as opposed to companies in general.

Chapter 5

Reduction of capital

Pete Miller CTA (Fellow), Partner, The Miller Partnership

SIGNPOSTS

- **Reduction of capital simplified** – The new rules in *Companies Act 2006* make reducing a company's capital simpler and cheaper (see **5.1–5.3**).
- **Reduction of capital cannot be used for takeover schemes under** ***CA 2006, s 899*** – Changes were made by secondary legislation in March 2015 to prevent perceived avoidance of stamp duty (see **5.4**).
- **Enhancing distributable reserves** – A reduction of capital can eliminate negative reserves and allow a company to pay dividends (see **5.5–5.7**).
- **Repayment of cash** – The cash subscribed for shares can be returned to shareholders using a reduction of capital (see **5.8–5.13**).
- **Transactions in securities** – Reductions of capital were added to the list of transactions in securities potentially subject to counteraction of an income tax advantage, with effect from 6 April 2016 (see **5.14–5.19**).
- **Forming a group** – Reductions of capital are another useful way to group companies together, and can save stamp duty in contrast with a share exchange (see **5.20–5.23**).
- **Demergers** – Reductions of capital are a helpful mechanism for demergers and other schemes of reconstruction, and should be added to every adviser's toolkit (see **5.24–5.27**).

REDUCTIONS OF CAPITAL – COMPANY LAW

5.1 The reduction of capital of a company is a potentially useful mechanism for a number of transactions, including both merging companies into groups and for demergers. Furthermore, a reduction of capital can potentially be a useful way of returning cash to shareholders.

5.2 *Reduction of capital*

Although the facility for reducing capital has existed for some time, until recently this was a complex, time-consuming and expensive process, in particular because it required a Court Order (under *CA 1985, s 135*). However, for private companies the process is substantially simplified by the new rules in *CA 2006, Pt 17, Ch 10*.

5.2 The main provision is *CA 2006, s 641(1)(a)*, which states that a limited company with share capital may reduce that capital by a special resolution supported by a solvency statement, where the company is a private company. It may reduce its capital in any way it wishes, subject only to the restriction that there must be at least one member holding at least one non-redeemable share (*CA 2006, s 641(2), (3)*).

The rules for the statement of solvency are at *CA 2006, s 642*. The statement must be signed by all of the directors of the company, no more than 15 days before the date of the special resolution reducing the company's capital. Both the resolution and the solvency statement must then be registered with Companies House. The solvency statement itself must state that each director considers the company able to pay, or otherwise discharge, all its debts on the date of the statement, along with any debts as they fall due in the year immediately following.

Alternatively, if it is intended to wind the company up within 12 months, the company must be able to pay, or otherwise discharge, all of its debts in full within 12 months of the commencement of the winding up (*CA 2006, s 643*).

5.3 Once the special resolution has been passed, a copy of that resolution, of the solvency statement and also a statement of capital must be delivered to Companies House (*CA 2006, s 644*). The statement of capital must state the total number of shares of the company, the aggregate nominal value and details of each class of share, along with the amounts paid up or unpaid on each share. The special resolution only takes effect when the registrar has registered the relevant documents.

The statement of solvency must then be sent to each member of the company before, or at the same time, as the proposed special resolution is sent. If a solvency statement is delivered to the registrar but has not been provided to the members, this is an offence by the officers of the company who are in default and they are potentially liable to a fine.

5.4 A reduction of capital cannot be used to facilitate a takeover of one company by another, if the takeover is the subject of a court order under *CA 2006, s 899* (*SI 2015/472*, with effect from 3 March 2015). The stated purpose of the new regulation is that using a reduction of capital for a takeover constitutes avoidance of stamp duty, as there is no stamp duty on either the cancellation or the issue of shares, only on the transfer of shares.

Takeovers that do not rely on *CA 2006, s 899* are not affected, so it is unlikely that the new regulations will have any effect on transactions involving owner-managed businesses.

COMPARISON WITH PURCHASES OF OWN SHARES

5.5 A reduction of capital is a different transaction from a company purchase of own shares, for which the relevant provisions are at *CA 2006, Pt 18, Ch 4* (see **Chapter 4**). Essentially, a reduction of capital involves reducing the company's capital base, and the maximum amount that can be involved is the nominal share capital plus any premium originally paid on the shares.

Usually, a purchase of own shares is made out of distributable profits or the proceeds of a fresh issue of shares made specifically to finance the purchase (*CA 2006, s 692*). It is possible for a purchase of own shares to be made out of capital, but only after exhausting the available profits and proceeds of any fresh issues of shares. The limitations and process are described at *CA 2006, Pt 18, Ch 5* and are materially more onerous than for a reduction of capital, requiring an auditor's report as well as a statement from the directors.

A capital redemption reserve (which is non-distributable) must be set up to the extent that shares are purchased from distributable reserves (*CA 2006, s 733*). The amount transferred is equal to the nominal value of the shares purchased. This facilitates the maintenance of the company's capital base. The capital redemption reserve can be used to pay up new share capital (*CA 2006, s 733(5)*) or it can be reduced using the same mechanism as for a reduction of capital (*CA 2006, ss 733(6), 641*).

ENHANCING DISTRIBUTABLE RESERVES

Reduction of capital is usually distributable

5.6 When a company reduces its capital under *CA 2006, Ch 10*, whether using the simplified process for private companies or a court order, available to both public and private companies, the reserve so arising is stated by *CA 2006, s 654(1)* not to be a distributable reserve. This reserve is usually referred to as a capital redemption reserve.

However, *CA 2006, s 654(2)* gives the Secretary of State the power to suspend the application of *CA 2006, s 654(1)*, which was done by the *Companies (Reduction of Share Capital) Order 2008, SI 2008/1915*. This states that, where a private company limited by shares reduces its capital, the reserve is to be treated as a realised profit and, hence, as a distributable reserve. Indeed, the statutory instrument gives the same result for reductions of capital by unlimited companies and also where companies with share capital have used the court order route, unless the court orders otherwise. In effect, this appears to render *CA 2006, s 654(1)* somewhat otiose.

As a result of the above analysis, the most common use of a reduction of capital, in the author's experience, is for a company to enhance its distributable reserves. That is, if a company has negative reserves, or insufficient reserves to pay out the dividends that it would like to pay, a reduction of capital might be an appropriate way to enhance the reserves to allow the payment of the required dividends.

Example 5.1 – Eliminating a profit and loss deficit

Acer Limited has been trading at a loss for some time, and the profit and loss account deficit is £63,000. The company has recently had an injection of capital from new investors and is starting to make profits. However, the new investors are keen to have a return on their investment as soon as possible, and do not wish to wait for the profit and loss deficit to be eliminated before they can start to receive dividends. The company has £100,000 of share capital.

Using the provisions of *CA 2006, s 641* onwards, the company resolves to reduce its capital by £65,000, leaving a profit and loss account in credit by £2,000. Future profits from the trading activities can then be paid out to the shareholders by way of dividends.

5.7 In many cases, the company does not have sufficient share capital to allow this approach to creating distributable reserves. However, it is possible that the company has other, non-distributable reserves that might be capitalised, to create share capital that can then be reduced to create distributable reserves. For example, it is common for a company to have a valuable property and, therefore, possibly a revaluation reserve.

Example 5.2 – Property revaluation and share capital reduction

Beech Limited has a profit and loss deficit of £173,000 but only £100 of share capital. However, Beech Limited has a property which stands on the balance sheet at £30,000 historical cost, which is estimated to currently be worth £400,000. The profit and loss deficit can be resolved by taking the following steps:

1. Carry out a formal revaluation of the property and create a revaluation reserve of £370,000. This is not a distributable reserve.
2. Use the revaluation reserve to pay up, say, £370,000 of new share capital.
3. Reduce the company's capital by, say, £200,000, so that the profit and loss account is in credit by £27,000.

Tax analysis

5.8 The use of the profit and loss account for this purpose should not be a taxable event. No cash is actually returned to the shareholders, so there should be no capital gains or distribution charge on them. In many cases, a straightforward reduction of capital constitutes a reorganisation (under *TCGA 1992, s 126(3)*), which is specifically removed from the charge to capital gains tax for the shareholders by *TCGA 1992, s 127*.

Nor is there any provision to charge any corporation tax on the company in respect of such transactions.

There is a theoretical possibility that the shares issued in a capitalisation of a revaluation reserve might be employment related securities. However, where it is intended that the shares be cancelled almost immediately afterwards, it seems unlikely that the shareholders could be seen as having any benefit from holding those shares ephemerally, and the author is not aware of HMRC even taking this point.

RETURNING CAPITAL TO SHAREHOLDERS

5.9 A reduction of capital can also be used to actually return cash to shareholders. Essentially, instead of the reduction of share capital having a contra-entry enhancing the profit and loss reserve, the reduction of share capital is balanced by a payment of cash to the shareholders.

Similarly, the reduction of capital could be used to reduce an outstanding balance on a shareholder's loan account.

Tax analysis

5.10 As far as the company is concerned, there are no tax consequences. No deduction is allowed for the payments to reduce the share capital.

5.11 As far as the shareholders are concerned, there would, *prima facie*, be a disposal of some or all of their share capital. Therefore, one would expect a capital gains computation to be necessary.

In simple cases, however, what is being returned to the shareholders is no more or less than what they originally subscribed for the shares, so there should be no gain and no loss. This arises generally out of the share pooling rules.

Example 5.3 – Capital reduction resulting in no gain

Barbie and Ken each subscribe £50,000 for shares in their new company JK Enterprises Limited. Some years later, they decide the company does not need a £100,000 capital base and that £75,000 should be returned to them as shareholders, £37,500 each.

In capital gains terms, we would expect the computation to match the £37,500 share capital originally subscribed with £37,500 share capital returned, leaving a zero gain.

The computation would be different if they had bought the shares from a third party, rather than having subscribed the share capital themselves, as the base cost of the shares and the amounts originally subscribed would not be the same in such cases, so a capital gain or allowable loss might accrue.

5.12 There is a theoretical argument that the actual market value for the shares should be substituted in the capital gains computation. This arises from *TCGA 1992, s 17*, which states that a bargain otherwise than on arm's-length terms should be adjusted to arm's-length terms, so the question revolves around whether a reduction of capital is a disposal of the shares for an arm's-length price.

Taking the previous example, suppose at the time of the reduction of capital the company was actually worth £1m. If 75% of the share capital were sold to a third party, clearly the shareholders would expect to realise something closer to £750,000 for that disposal. The counter-argument, of course, is that on a reduction of capital, they have not, in fact, made an arm's-length disposal, and they have only diminished the value of the company by the £75,000 cash extracted. There is no obvious conclusion to this discussion, except to note that HMRC must be aware of the point, as it has been raised several times in the tax press, but to date HMRC have not been seen to argue the point.

In this author's view, however, the better argument is that the arm's-length price for a reduction of capital is, in fact, the original capital subscribed, so that there is no adjustment to be made under *TCGA 1992, s 17*.

5.13 It is also worth noting that a reduction of capital can be, and often is, a reorganisation, under *TCGA 1992, s 126(3)*. Technically, this means that the amounts received are taxed under the provisions of *TCGA 1992, s 128*, not the normal disposal provisions. However, it is suggested that this is not of any practical significance.

5.14 So far, this looks like a relatively tax-efficient way of returning cash to shareholders, as they do not pay any tax on the amounts returned to them. If there is a chargeable gain, for example because the shares were acquired by purchase, rather than subscription, it may well be that entrepreneurs' relief is available and that capital gains tax is only due at 10%.

Indeed, it may well be that an allowable loss arises, where there is a reduction of capital in respect of purchased shares, if the amounts returned are less than the purchase price per share.

Transactions in securities

5.15 The 'fly in the ointment' of repaying capital to shareholders is the transactions in securities legislation in *ITA 2007, Pt 13, Ch 1* (*ss 682–713*). Very broadly, this legislation is designed to prevent shareholders accessing the company's distributable reserves in a capital form, so that they pay less in capital gains tax than they would otherwise have paid in income tax on a dividend. This legislation only applies where the transaction or transactions in securities are carried out with the intention of avoiding income tax. It is unfortunate that HMRC have taken the view that a reduction of capital in return for cash is likely to be income tax avoidance and therefore susceptible to challenge under this legislation.

HMRC legitimised their position by adding the repayment of share capital or share premium to the list of transactions in *ITA 2007, s 684(2)* that are specifically deemed to be transactions in securities for the purposes of this legislation, with effect from 6 April 2016.

The sanctions that HMRC possess effectively involve 'counteracting' the tax advantage. So, to extend **Example 5.3** further, the reader will recall that Barbie and Kenneth have each received £37,500 tax free, being the return of the capital they originally subscribed into JK Enterprises Limited. If HMRC decided that this transaction was carried out for tax avoidance purposes, then an assessment can be raised to charge tax as if the £37,500 each of them had received had been a distribution from the company and was therefore chargeable to income tax at the relevant rate for distributions.

The transactions in securities rules can only apply if, and to the extent that, the company concerned has distributable reserves (*ITA 2007, s 684*) or, from 6 April 2016, if there are distributable reserves in any companies it controls (see **5.19**). So, if JK Enterprises Limited in **Example 5.3** does not have any reserves, HMRC are powerless.

5.16 There are a number of reasons why the author, and many other observers, considers HMRC's approach to be completely wrong-headed here. Firstly, one thing that many tax avoidance arrangements have in common is a degree of complexity or artificiality. While this is not a universal rule, it is suggested that in situations like this the shareholders have a simple choice between taking a distribution from the company or reducing its capital. They both require a certain degree of process and pre-transaction scrutiny (for distributions, it is important to ensure that the company has sufficient distributable reserves, for example), they are both relatively straightforward transactions, and neither of them involves any degree of artificiality or contrivance. The main difference, of course, is that a reduction of capital actually has a permanent effect on the company's capital base, for which there might, in any case, be commercial reasons. In this context, a straightforward choice between two relatively straightforward transactions does not seem to the author to constitute the avoidance of income tax.

There is also support for this approach in decided tax cases. In *Duke of Westminster v CIR* 19 TC 490, Lord Tomlin said in the House of Lords that:

> 'Every man is entitled if he can to order his affairs so that the tax attaching under the appropriate Acts is less than it otherwise would be. If he succeeds in ordering them so as to secure this result, then, however unappreciative the Commissioners of Inland Revenue or his fellow taxpayers may be of his ingenuity, he cannot be compelled to pay an increased tax.'

Similarly, in *Ayrshire Pullman Motor Services and Ritchie v CIR* 14 TC 754, Lord Clyde said that:

> 'No man in this country is under the smallest obligation, moral or other, so to arrange his legal relations to his business or to his property as to enable the Inland Revenue to put the largest possible shovel into his stores.'

Of course, these cases date from 1936 and 1929, respectively, and things have moved on since then. However, the comments remain good law in most people's views, and certainly apply where there is no contrivance or artificiality. So we have judicial assurance that we are entitled to make decisions about how we order our financial and commercial affairs, taking the likely tax bill into account. In the author's view, none of this constitutes tax avoidance (unlike the planning in *Duke of Westminster* which was clearly quite egregious).

5.17 In the context of the transactions in securities legislation itself, there was a similar comment in the case of *Brebner v CIR* 43 TC 705. In this case, a group of trawlermen had arranged their financial affairs in order to finance the acquisition of a coal supplier, which was accepted to have been a wholly commercial reason, despite the fact that a tax advantage was obtained. In terms of the tax avoidance test, Lord Upjohn, in the House of Lords, said this:

> '... When the question of carrying out a genuine commercial transaction, as this was, is considered, the fact that there are two ways of carrying it out – one by paying the maximum amount of tax, the other by paying no, or much less, tax – it would be quite wrong as a necessary consequence to draw the inference that in adopting the latter course one of the main objects is, for the purposes of the section [ie the transactions in securities legislation, then in *FA 1960, s 28*], avoidance of tax.'

In summary, therefore, not only does general case law support the proposition that straightforward tax planning is acceptable, but so does a decided case relating specifically to the transactions in securities rules themselves.

5.18 Finally, for transactions completed before 6 April 2016, the reduction of capital transaction may be outside the scope of the transactions in securities rules, as *ITA 2007, s 685(6)* states that the legislation does not apply to the return of sums paid by subscribers on the issue of securities. This seems to be a relatively straightforward technical point, and it is hard to see why HMRC do not accept, therefore, that the transactions in securities legislation cannot apply to a reduction of capital. This provision was repealed for all transactions taking place on or after 6 April 2016. Also, a reduction of share capital or share premium was added to the list of specific transactions in securities to which these rules apply, in *ITA 2007, s 684(2)*, also for all transactions taking place on or after 6 April 2016.

Even under the old rules, HMRC stated in a number of cases that they would consider counteraction on the basis that there were distributable reserves and, therefore, paying out the share capital, and only paying capital gains tax, if that, must be the avoidance of income tax. In discussion of the *FA 2016* proposals, HMRC's view was that there was scope for tax avoidance by reducing capital and returning cash to shareholders, even where the cash represented the amounts originally subscribed by those shareholders out of their own taxed income.

As a result, it is recommended that, if a client wishes to reduce their capital in this way, they should not apply for clearance under *ITA 2007, s 701*. Instead, if they are prepared to take the risk that there may be counteraction and that the sums concerned might be taxed as a dividend, they should merely complete the relevant self-assessment returns in the proper way, noting, if appropriate, any capital gains consequences on the disposals of the shares. However, they are not required to state the possible application of the transactions in securities rules on their tax returns, as these rules are outside self-assessment, a view which has been specifically published by HMRC (in *Tax Bulletin 42*). Although this was some years ago, the administrative status of the transactions in securities rules has not changed in the interim and, so it seems, nor has HMRC's view on this point.

In these cases, if HMRC subsequently form the view that the transactions in securities rules may be in point, having inspected the relevant returns and accounts, as noted above the author believes there is substantial ammunition to argue against any counteraction proceedings or to win a case in front of the tribunals or courts. In the final analysis, if the company was potentially going to pay out the amounts, anyway, as a distribution, then the clients are no worse off (apart from relevant professional fees).

5.19 There are, also, circumstances where HMRC will not be able to challenge the reduction of capital under these rules. Firstly, if there are no distributable reserves, no lawful distribution could have been paid, so the transactions in securities legislation cannot apply. Strictly, therefore, HMRC should grant clearance in advance in these cases, although personal experience is that they refuse to grant clearance, they merely confirm that, in the absence of distributable reserves, no counteraction is possible.

There will also be cases where the recipient of the cash would not, in any case, have paid UK income tax, for example where the shareholder is either a non-UK resident individual or company, or indeed a UK company. While there is a corporate equivalent of the transactions in securities rules (*CTA 2010, Pt 15*), they very rarely apply, largely because UK companies are effectively exempt from corporation tax on distributions received, anyway (see *CTA 2009, Pt 9A*). So it is hard to see how a reduction of capital to a corporate shareholder could constitute the avoidance of corporate tax on income.

There may also be rare cases where the commercial drivers for reducing capital are sufficiently strong that HMRC would accept that these commercial reasons demonstrate that the avoidance of income tax was not one of the main reasons for entering into the transactions. For example, in a recent case where a reduction of capital was used to facilitate a shareholder exit, HMRC accepted that no counteraction was required.

5.20 In summary, therefore, it is entirely acceptable for a company to reduce its capital and return that capital subscribed to the shareholders. HMRC may, if they spot the point, attempt counteraction under the transactions in securities rules, although it is hoped that they would fail for the reasons detailed above.

While this is not a strategy for the faint-hearted, a reduction of capital remains an option, particularly where there are no distributable reserves or the shareholders cannot be avoiding income tax.

FORMING A GROUP

5.21 The previous section might lead to the impression that reductions of capital, while having been simplified, are relatively useless. This is, however, not the case and the rest of this chapter looks at two areas in which they can lead to substantial tax savings, stamp duty and demergers.

When a new company is inserted over an existing company, this is usually done by way of a share exchange. That is, a person will exchange their holdings of shares in company A by transferring those shares to company B which, in turn, will issue shares to that original shareholder. These forms of share exchange are generally free of capital gains tax, by virtue of the share exchange rule at *TCGA 1992, s 135* (see **7.12** *et seq*).

Stamp duty savings

5.22 The other tax charge that might arise on such transactions is the stamp duty charge, at 0.5% of the value of the consideration, for the transfer of the shares in company A. In general, of course, the market value of the shares issued by company B in consideration will be the same as the market value of company A, so essentially the stamp duty charge is at 0.5% on the market value of the shares of company A. This sounds like a low rate but can, of course, be a large amount when the companies are very valuable.

There is a relief from stamp duty at *FA 1986, s 77*. The relief is available so long as the transaction is for *bona fide* commercial reasons and not part of a scheme or arrangement for the avoidance of tax. But for the relief to apply, the shareholdings of company B must be of the same class and in the same proportions as the shareholdings of company A immediately prior to the exchange.

The availability of relief under *FA 1986, s 77* is complicated by *FA 1986, s 77A*, introduced for instruments executed on or after 29 June 2016. *FA 1986, s 77A* denies stamp duty relief under *FA 1986, s 77* where it is reasonable to assume that one of the purposes of the transaction is to secure a change of control of the original company. However, there is an exemption for mergers, which would normally apply to mergers such as we are discussing here (*FA 1986, s 77A(3), (4)*). This provision will be more relevant for certain demergers (see also **5.25**, and **Example 5.5** at Step 1).

Example 5.4 – New holding company: stamp duty implications

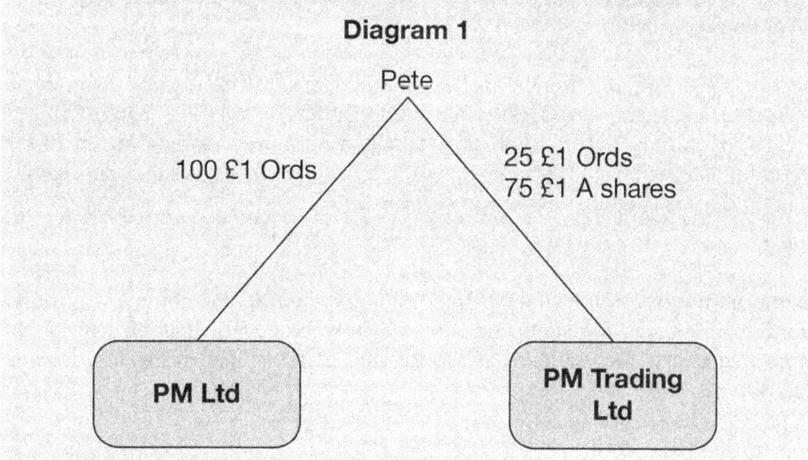

Diagram 2

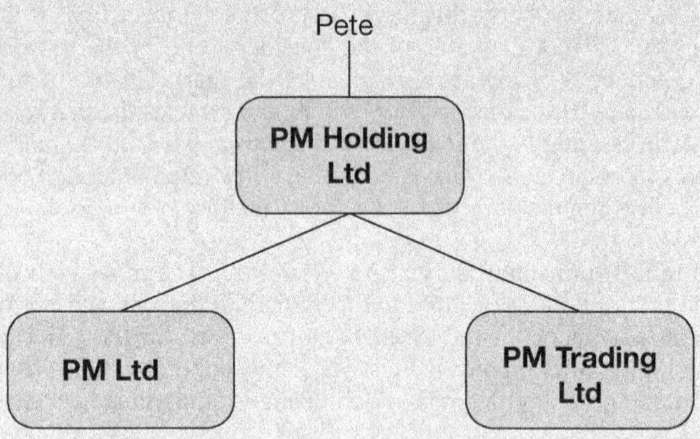

Pete holds the 100 £1 ordinary shares of PM Limited. For commercial reasons he decides a new holding company is required and exchanges all his shares in return for 10,000 £1 shares in PM Holdings Limited. Stamp duty relief under *FA 1986, s 77* should be available, as Pete holds 100% of the ordinary shares prior to the transaction and 100% of the ordinary shares of PM Holdings Limited immediately afterwards.

Pete also holds all of the share capital of PM Trading Limited and wishes to exchange that company too, so that it is also a subsidiary of PM Holdings Limited. Pete's holding of shares in PM Trading Limited is 25 £1 ordinary shares and 75 £1 A shares. He proposes to transfer these to PM Holdings Limited in return for the issue of 5,000 more £1 ordinary shares by PM Holdings Limited.

While Pete will remain the 100% shareholder of PM Trading Limited, directly before the transaction and indirectly afterwards, his shareholding in PM Holdings Limited will not exactly mirror his shareholding in PM Trading Limited, as all the shares will be ordinary shares, so no relief from stamp duty is available for this transfer.

In the above example, while this does not matter if the company is only worth £50,000 (as the stamp duty would only be £250), it is clearly much more material if the company is worth, say, £5m, so that the stamp duty is £25,000

5.23 One way around this problem is to use a reduction of capital and issue of new shares, rather than a share exchange.

To effect the second exchange in **Example 5.4**, PM Trading Limited could reduce its capital under *CA 2006, s 641* and issue new shares to PM Holdings Limited. PM Holdings Limited will then issue shares to Pete. There is no transfer of shares from Pete to PM Holdings Limited, so no transaction on which stamp duty can be charged.

The shares will have to be cancelled in two tranches. *CA 2006, s 641*, as already noted, requires the company always to have at least one participating ordinary share issued. So we cannot reduce the share capital to nothing, even for an instant of time. Instead, in a case like this, it is generally advised that a reduction of the A share capital and the issue of new shares (which can be ordinary shares) to PM Holdings Limited. Then we reduce the ordinary share capital and issue new shares to PM Holdings Limited; finally, PM Holdings Limited will issue the relevant number of shares to Pete.

Clearly this transaction is not a share exchange within *TCGA 1992, s 135*. It is, however, a scheme of reconstruction (see **7.22** *et seq*), so that clearance under *TCGA 1992, s 138* should be available, just as it would have been for the share exchange. The restriction at *TCGA 1992, s 137(1)* requires that the transactions be carried out for *bona fide* commercial reasons, which will almost always be the case, and it also requires that the transaction not be part of a scheme or arrangements with a major purpose of avoiding corporation tax or capital gains tax. Therefore, if you take the view that the structuring of the proposed transaction this way is to avoid stamp duty, HMRC are not allowed to refuse the capital gains relief, as *TCGA 1992, s 137(1)* does not refer to stamp duty.

5.24 This is perfectly acceptable structuring of a transaction in a way that carries a lower tax bill than it might have had it been structured another way. This is squarely within the parameters of the *Duke of Westminster* and *Ayrshire Pullman* cases referred to above, and not, it is ventured, tax avoidance at all.

In any case, the practical experience is that HMRC have never refused clearance for any of the author's clients on these cases. When first using this technology, HMRC tended to ask why the transaction was not carried out by way of share exchange, but they seemed perfectly comfortable with the response that we did not wish to incur a stamp duty charge on the transactions.

That said, however, do not forget the restriction for schemes under *CA 2006, s 899* (see **5.4** above).

DEMERGER MECHANISM

Demergers

5.25 A demerger is a method of splitting up a company or group into more than one company or group, sometimes owned by the same shareholders and sometimes segregated between the shareholders. There are several ways that the split can be achieved but most of them required the transfer of assets from the original single company to one or more successor companies, as part of a scheme of reconstruction.

For this to be a tax-free transfer, it has to be for no consideration (see **7.29**), so the question that arises is what mechanisms are available to a company to transfer their assets in this way, without any consideration being given.

5.26 There are three mechanisms available in most cases:

- **Distribution**: the original company distributes assets *in specie* to one or more successor companies.
- **Liquidation**: the original company distributes assets *in specie* to one or more successor companies, under the provisions in *Insolvency Act 1986, s 110*.
- **Reduction of capital**: the original company distributes assets *in specie* to one or more successor companies, as consideration for a reduction of capital.

All of these are used in schemes of reconstruction, particularly demergers. The distribution *in specie* route, however, is only available for trading companies, as there is a specific relief from the income tax charge on a distribution *in specie* where trading activities or groups are being split up (*CTA 2010, Pt 23, Ch 5*). This relief does not apply where trades are being separated from non-trading activities or where non-trading activities are being split.

The liquidation route has been the most common alternative to the distribution *in specie*, simply because of the complexities of a reduction of capital prior to the enactment of *Companies Act 2006*. Reductions of capital were usually only used as a mechanism for demergers of large or public companies, for which the extra fees were not a major issue. However, liquidation demergers are not always desirable, as it can be commercially difficult to put a company into liquidation, the liquidator's fees can be quite high and, in some cases, there can be a substantial charge to SDLT in some cases.

5.27 Consider, for example, what would have happened if, instead of separating two parts of a trade, as illustrated above, the business comprised a portfolio of investment properties. Let us work through the differences between a liquidation demerger and a reduction of capital.

Example 5.5 – Demerger of property investment company

Bill and Ted own PropCo, a property investment company with investment properties. They wish to separate the business between themselves.

The first steps are common to both transactions:

Diagram 3

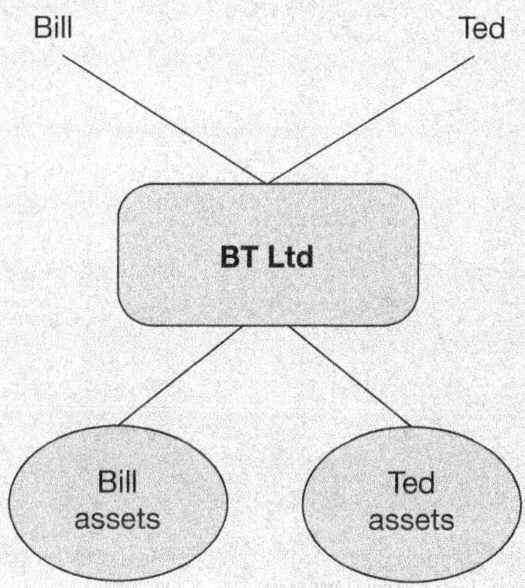

Step 1

Insert a new holding company, HoldCo by way of a tax free share-for-share exchange. *Prima facie*, we would expect the relief from stamp duty at *FA 1986, s 77* to apply. However, one problem with demergers is that the insertion of a new holding company at Step 1 can fall foul of the stamp duty rule in *FA 1986, s 77A*, because a demerger separating a company between two equal shareholders will perforce mean that one company changes control when it ceases to be controlled by two people and becomes controlled by just one of them. As a result, we can replace Step 1 with a transaction whereby the shares of PropCo are cancelled under

CA 2006, s 641 and new shares are issued to HoldCo, which in turn issues shares to Bill and Ted. Since neither the cancellation nor the issue of new shares carry stamp duty, no stamp duty arises in the first place, so the relief at *FA 1986, s 77* is simply not in point.

See **5.23** for a more detailed technical analysis.

Diagram 4

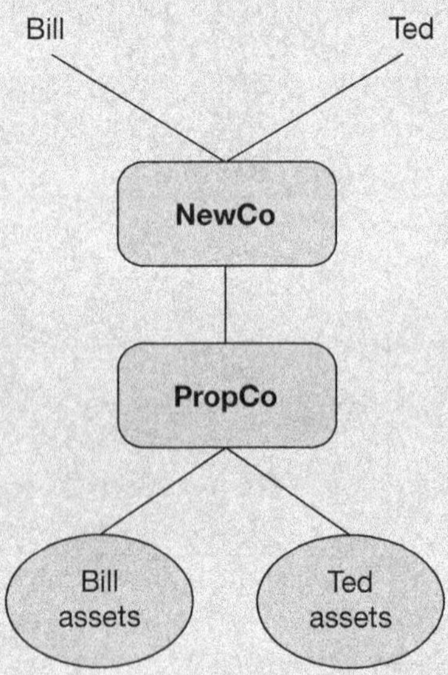

Step 2

Transfer, say, Bill's property portfolio from PropCo to HoldCo.

Generally speaking, it is preferable to do this by way of distribution in specie, which should then be free of SDLT by virtue of *FA 2003, s 54* ('Exceptions from deemed market value rule').

Where this is not possible, or not possible with the whole of the portfolio, usually due to an insufficiency of distributable reserves, the transfer can be done for book value consideration, in which case it will be necessary to rely on the SDLT group relief in *FA 2003, Sch 7*. This does introduce a few more complexities, which is why it is preferable to use a distribution in specie for this step.

Diagram 5

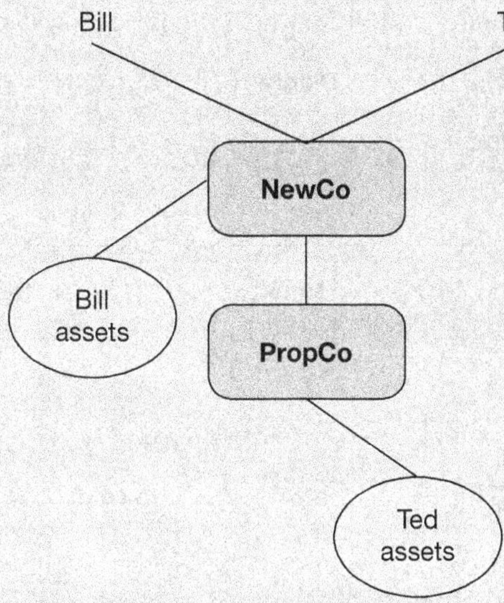

Liquidation demerger

In a liquidation demerger, HoldCo will then be liquidated.

Diagram 6

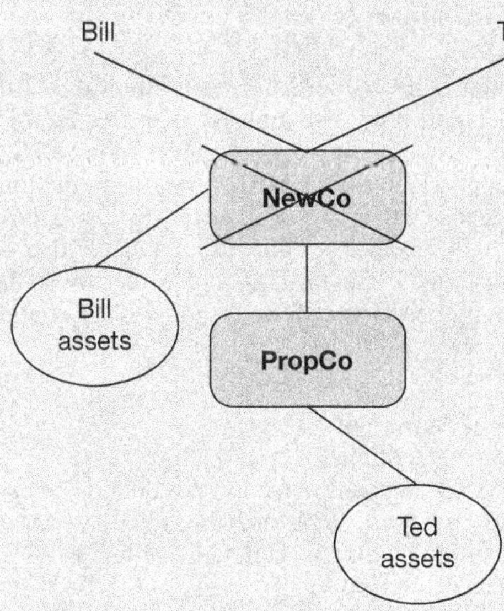

The shares of PropCo, containing Ted's portfolio, will be transferred to TedCo, which will issue shares only to Ted. Bill's portfolio will be transferred from HoldCo to BillCo, which will issue shares only to Bill.

Diagram 7

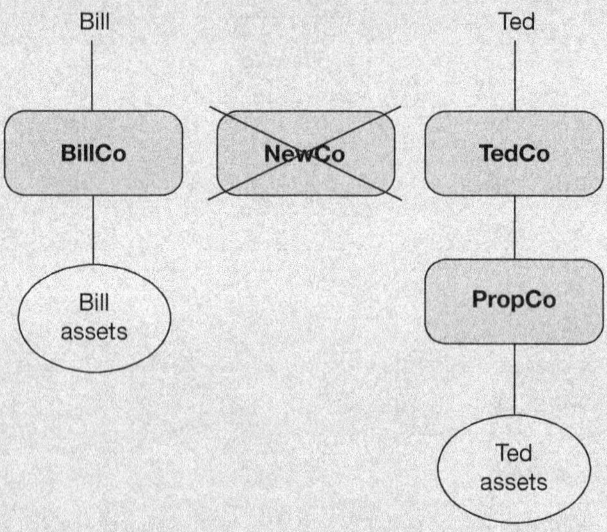

As a result, Bill and Ted will each hold their own separate portfolio of properties and both sets of transactions should be free of capital gains tax, as a scheme of reconstruction.

However, the transfer of Bill's portfolio from HoldCo to BillCo gives us a problem for SDLT purposes. This transfer is, prima facie, a distribution in the winding up of HoldCo, so we would expect the SDLT exemption at *FA 2003, s 54* to apply. However, HMRC's view, and that of a number of other commentators, is that the issue of shares by BillCo is the consideration for the transfer of the portfolio, so that SDLT will be due on the market value of those shares issued. This will, of course, usually be the same as the market value of the properties transferred, so the SDLT charge can be very substantial in such cases.

Reduction of capital demerger

Let us now look at what happens if we use a reduction of capital to effect the demerger. The first two steps are the same as for a liquidation demerger, so our starting point is HoldCo owning Bill's portfolio and PropCo (as above).

Diagram 8

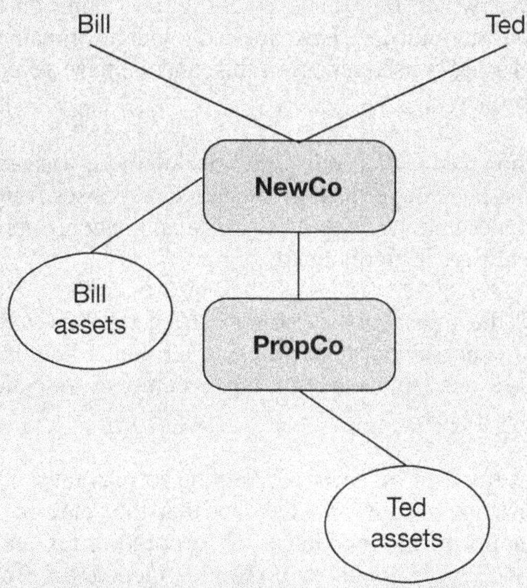

Instead of putting HoldCo into liquidation, we reduce the capital of HoldCo by cancelling all of Ted's shares (we will probably have reorganised the shares into Bill and Ted classes immediately prior to that step).

In consideration of the reduction of Ted's share capital, PropCo is moved to TedCo which issues shares to Ted only.

Diagram 9

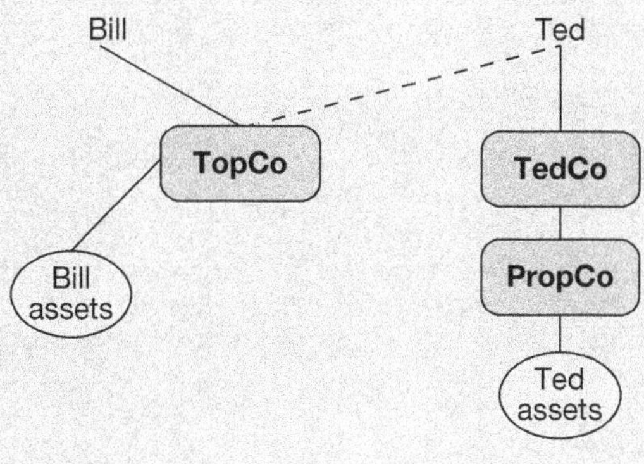

Thus we have effected the demerger, with Bill owning HoldCo with his portfolio and Ted owning TedCo which owns PropCo and his portfolio.

By avoiding a liquidation of HoldCo we have avoided the necessity to transfer Bill's portfolios out of one company and into another, so there is no SDLT as there is no transfer, which represents a substantial saving on the liquidation demerger route. Furthermore, we have not had to put a company in liquidation, with all the commercial consequences of this, and we have saved the fees of an insolvency practitioner.

5.28 The author has carried out a number of these transactions over the last three years and has not yet had any negative responses from HMRC. Pre-transaction clearances under *TCGA 1992, s 138* and, where appropriate, *TCGA 1992, s 139* have always been obtained.

When asked why the transaction is being carried out this way, the fact was highlighted that it is actually structurally simpler than a liquidation demerger, commercially more desirable than putting a company into liquidation, and saves the liquidator's fees.

To the extent that this can be seen as planning to prevent a charge to SDLT arising, it is important to highlight the fact that the relevant anti-avoidance provisions only apply to the avoidance of corporation tax and capital gains tax (for *TCGA 1992, s 138*) or those taxes plus income tax (for *TCGA 1992, s 139(5)*).

Chapter 6

Groups

Pete Miller CTA (Fellow), Partner, The Miller Partnership
Based on chapter originally written by John Baldry LLB, LLM (London)

SIGNPOSTS

- **Different definitions of 'group'** – The definition of a 'group' of companies is different for different parts of the *Corporation Tax Acts*.
- **Definition of group relief group** – A group for group relief purposes requires one company to be a 75% subsidiary of the other, or both to be 75% subsidiaries of a third company (**6.9** *et seq*).
- **Definition of capital gains group** – A group for capital gains purposes comprises a 'principal company' and its 75% subsidiaries, together with their 75% subsidiaries, and so on, so long as all the companies are 'effective 51% subsidiaries' of the principal company (**6.25** *et seq*).
- **SSE groups** – For the purposes of the substantial shareholdings exemption, a group comprises a 'principal company' and its 51% subsidiaries, together with their 51% subsidiaries, and so on, so long as all the companies are 'effective 51% subsidiaries' of the principal company (**6.58** *et seq*).
- **Anti-avoidance** – *CTA 2010, Pt 5, Ch 6* contains anti-avoidance rules common to most of the definitions of a 'group' (**6.4** *et seq*).
- **EEA group relief** – Group relief can be given for losses on non-UK subsidiaries resident in the EEA in restricted circumstances (**6.20** *et seq*).
- **Degrouping** – A degrouping charge arises where a company leaves a group holding assets transferred to it from another group company within the previous six years. This charge is treated as part of the disposal proceeds for most disposals where the transferred asset is a chargeable asset, so that it arises on the vendor company (**6.33** *et seq*). The degrouping charge for intangible assets arises on the company leaving the group (**6.74**).

- **Transfers of trades** – There are special rules for transfers of trades between companies under 75% common ownership, preserving losses and capital allowances on the trade transfer (**6.40** *et seq*).
- **Loss-buying, etc** – There are targeted anti-avoidance rules which prevent buying in capital losses and gain washing transactions, and to prevent the artificial reduction of gains or creation of losses (**6.47** *et seq*).
- **Group payment arrangements** – There are administrative arrangements whereby all payments of corporation tax by a group can be carried out through a single group company (**6.75**).

INTRODUCTION

6.1 This chapter deals with the principal considerations which arise for companies which fall to be treated (under tests which differ according to the tax in question) as members of a group for one or more corporation tax purposes. This brings with it both benefits and opportunities for the careful and less desirable consequences for the unwary.

Unlike some other taxing jurisdictions, such as the US, the UK does not operate a consolidated system of group taxation, at least for corporation tax. Rather, the UK tax system respects each company within the group as distinct legal entities, each subject to the general tax regime, but then overlays various additional substantive and administrative rules in order to take into account the fact that the companies are in reality part of one economic unit.

The principal day-to-day issue for a group of companies will be how to deal with situations where certain members of the group are making profits and others losses. This is dealt with through the group relief rules. Companies may also be concerned about the transfer of assets, businesses or assignment of debts between members of the group. The tax code attempts to provide for all these scenarios, but in doing so also provides certain anti-avoidance rules which must be carefully negotiated in order not to cause immediate or future tax concerns.

That is not to say, however, that the rules achieve, or even attempt to achieve, neutrality between the position where an economic entity operates through one company (or 'divisions'), and where it operates through more than one company. Inefficiencies may arise because the group has many companies (eg losses may become stranded by being carried forward in a non-profit making member of the group when other members are profitable), or fortuitous planning using subsidiaries may lead to tax advantages not available if the enterprise had been carried on through a different corporate structure (eg a business to be sold is carried on in a separate subsidiary so that substantial shareholdings relief is available on the sale).

The tax consequences of a particular group structure are myriad and infiltrate through every area of tax. The main focus of this chapter is on the basic rules which a practitioner or in-house tax adviser to a group is likely to come across, both in the operation of the group and in transactions undertaken by it. It therefore deals principally with group relief, capital gains tax groups, transfers of trades, pre-entry loss provisions, depreciatory transactions and the substantial shareholdings exemption. On the administrative side, group payment arrangements are also dealt with.

There are also numerous anti-avoidance rules which are applicable to groups in a number of areas of corporate tax legislation, including the various specialist regimes, for example those relating to intellectual property and derivatives. Detailed consideration of those rules is outside the scope of this work, and is best dealt with in those works which consider the areas concerned. Some of the rules in those regimes which apply specifically to groups are, however, noted in this chapter.

DEFINITIONS

6.2 Certain of the provisions which apply for the various definitions of a 'group' of companies have common elements. They are therefore considered together in this section. In the process of the re-write in *CTA 2010*, the provisions in *TCGA 1992* which referred to *ICTA 1988* have been amended to refer to the re-written Act, although the *TCGA 1992* provisions themselves have not, and will not be, rewritten, as the re-write project has been discontinued.

75% subsidiary

6.3 For the purposes of most group tests, *CTA 2010, s 1154(3)* provides the definition for one body corporate being a 75% subsidiary of another. A body corporate will be a 75% subsidiary of another body corporate if and so long as 75% of its ordinary share capital is owned directly or indirectly by that other body corporate. There are two points to note here. First, ordinary share capital is itself defined in *CTA 2010, s 1119* and means all share capital of the company, whatever it is called, other than capital the holders of which have the rights to a dividend at a fixed rate but have no other rights to share in the profits of the company. Essentially, therefore, this removes fixed-rate preference shares from the test. Other preference shares, however, count as ordinary share capital.

Secondly, the test is an indirect one. Therefore if A owns 100% of B and C, each of which owns 50% of D, D will be a 75% subsidiary of A, even though it is not a 75% subsidiary of B or of C.

The basic tests of capital ownership for grouping purposes are often referred to as the 'nominal' ownership requirements, referring to the 'nominal' amount of share capital which is required to establish the group, as contrasted with the economic tests discussed below.

CTA 2010, Pt 5, Ch 6

6.4 *CTA 2010, Pt 5, Ch 6* provides what are often referred to as the 'economic' tests for ownership. Without these, it would obviously be easy to manipulate the ownership of companies so that they fell within a particular group, but where the real economic interest in the company lay elsewhere.

6.5 The basic premise of *CTA 2010, Pt 5, Ch 6* is to establish what a shareholder (still referred to as an 'equity holder') would receive by way of share of profits or assets if all the profits or assets were distributed by the company. For these purposes, equity holder means any person who holds ordinary shares in the company or is a loan creditor of the company in respect of a loan which is not a 'normal commercial loan' (*CTA 2010, s 158*).

6.6 For *CTA 2010, Pt 5, Ch 6* purposes there is a self-contained definition of ordinary shares, which is not the same as that in *CTA 2010, s 1119* referred to above. The effect is similar, but more prescriptive. Here the definition of ordinary shares is 'all shares other than restricted preference shares' (in the new re-write terminology).

The definition of restricted preference shares is that they must satisfy conditions A to E in *CTA 2010, s 160*. In summary:

A the shares must be issued for 'new consideration';

B they must not carry conversion rights, except into (broadly) other restricted preference shares or quoted shares in the company's parent;

C they must not carry any right to the acquisition of shares or securities;

D they must carry no right to dividends or a restricted right to dividends;

E they must not carry rights to repayment of an amount exceeding the new consideration given, except in so far as those rights are comparable with those for fixed dividend shares listed on a recognised stock exchange.

CTA 2010, s 161 then provides the meaning of 'restricted right to dividends' which includes fixed amount or fixed rate shares and 'fluctuating percentage rate' shares, the latter being shares linked to a published rate of interest, the retail prices index, or a similar prices index of the country or territory in whose currency the shares are denominated. The requirement that the dividends must represent no more than a reasonable commercial return on the consideration received by the company for the issue of the shares is also now included in *CTA 2010, s 161*.

6.7 The definition of 'normal commercial loan', is contained in *CTA 2010, s 162*. In summary, the loan must have been for 'new consideration' and satisfy the following conditions:

A it must not carry conversion rights except (broadly) those which could be carried by a restricted preference share within *CTA 2010, s 160*;

B it must not carry any right to the acquisition of shares or securities;

C it must not carry interest which depends on the results of the company's business, or the value of its assets, or which exceeds a reasonable commercial return on the consideration lent;

D it must not carry a right to repayment in excess of the amount of new consideration lent, except in so far as that right is comparable with those for debt listed on a recognised stock exchange.

For loans made on or after 21 March 2012 condition A is not breached if the loan is convertible into shares of an unconnected company that is listed on a recognised stock exchange.

Condition C is not breached if the interest rates decrease as the company's results or asset values increase, or *vice versa* (*CTA 2010, s 163(1), (2)*). Nor is condition C breached if a loan is used to buy land by the company and is secured on that land, so that the creditor can enforce payment by exercising rights over the land (*CTA 2010, s 163(3)–(6)*).

6.8 In order to deal with situations where shares carry rights to dividends which are limited or which may change by reason of arrangements which exist, or which may change because of the existence of options which may be exercised, *CTA 2010, Pt 5, Ch 6* contains a number of provisions which provide for the recalculation of the distribution of profits. Not all of these apply to all group tests; in particular the group relief test is more stringent than the capital gains tax test. Further reference is made to the differences in these tests in the relevant sections below (see, in particular, **6.28**).

> **Focus**
>
> These anti-avoidance rules apply with modifications across many of the definitions of a group for the purposes of the *Corporation Tax Acts*.

GROUP RELIEF

6.9 The group relief rules allow the transfer ('surrender' in the statutory terminology) of various types of losses, including but not limited to trading losses, from one member of a group (the 'surrendering company') to another (the 'claimant company'). The rules are concerned with income-type losses rather than capital losses (which are dealt with in a different way, see further below). One consequence of the introduction of the various specific regimes over the last decade or so (loan relationships, intangibles, etc) has been that the non-trading losses under such regimes also fall to be dealt with under the group relief regime.

6.10 It is important to remember that group relief operates on an annual basis. It is this fact that causes many inefficiencies to arise in groups of companies. A company can only claim losses in any year to the extent that it has profits to absorb them. If, therefore, a company in a group has surplus losses in a year which cannot be surrendered to other members of the group, then its only option will be to carry those losses forward to use against its own profits. This may result in the losses being stranded and becoming more or less worthless, particularly, for example, in the case of a holding company which ends up with a brought forward non-trading deficit on its loan relationships.

Qualifications for membership of a group

6.11 The group relief provisions occupy the seven chapters of *CTA 2010, Pt 6*. For the purposes of the group relief provisions (which apply to all types of losses available for group relief), two companies are members of a group of companies if one is the 75% subsidiary of another, or both are 75% subsidiaries of a third company (*CTA 2010, s 152*). *CTA 2010, s 151(4)* introduces the economic tests of ownership referred to in the discussion on *CTA 2010, Pt 5, Ch 6* above, so that a company will not be treated as a subsidiary of another company at any time where the parent company would not be entitled to 75% of the profits available for distribution to equity holders or 75% of the assets of the company available for distribution to equity holders on a winding-up. For these purposes, the full provisions of *CTA 2010, Pt 5, Ch 6* apply, so the effect of options will need to be taken into account.

6.12 In addition, *CTA 2010, Pt 5, Ch 5* has its own anti-avoidance provision in *CTA 2010, s 154* where there are arrangements under which the relationships between two group members (the 'first company' and the 'second company' may change. In particular the section applies where there are arrangements in existence whereby they may have any of the following effects (referred to as Effects 1 to 3):

- the first company (or any successor company under *CTA 2010, Pt 22, Ch 1*; see further the discussion at **6.40** below) could cease to be a member of the same group of companies as the second company and could become a member of the same group of companies as a third company; or
- any person or persons together have or could obtain control of the first company but not of the second; or

- a third company could begin to carry on the whole or part of a trade which is carried on by the first company either as successor to the first company or as successor to another company which has begun to carry on part of that trade.

6.13 The most obvious application of *CTA 2010, s 154* is when a group member is being sold to a third party. In such a case, there will come a point where the transaction between the seller and purchaser is at a stage where arrangements will be considered to have come into place, and group relief will no longer be possible. It is not always easy to determine at exactly what time that will be. Although the terminology of *CTA 2010, s 154* is very broad, there is a necessity for 'arrangements', and it is accepted generally that this means arrangements with another party or parties. There is some guidance to be found in HMRC manuals, in particular at CTM80165 (and the other paragraphs referred to therein) and SP 3/93 as to HMRC's view, which is that such arrangements may or may not be legally binding and may or may not be in writing. It is often the case that it is unclear where a sale of a group member will take place until very shortly before signing, the parties' negotiations being continuous until that point with the prospect of no transaction taking place at all. In that case, it would usually be relatively safe to conclude that there were no arrangements in place until agreement had been reached. Obviously once a written agreement is reached, even though it may be conditional, there will be arrangements in place, and group relief will not be possible during a period between sale and completion. In joint venture arrangements, ESC C10 provides HMRC's practice in relation to arrangements between joint venture parties which might otherwise fall foul of *CTA 2010, s 154* and also deals with share mortgages.

Residence qualifications for group relief

6.14 Since the *Finance Act 2000*, it is possible for members of a group to be resident outside the UK and to 'trace' groups through ownership of foreign bodies corporate. However, it is obviously not the intention of the legislation to give worldwide relief for losses, and therefore *CTA 2010, s 131* provides that the surrendering company (the group member with the loss) and the claimant company (the group member with the profit against which the loss is to be offset) must either be resident in the UK, or carry on a trade in the UK through a permanent establishment (this is referred to in the re-write as 'UK related', which is defined in *CTA 2010, s 134*).

From 1 April 2006 this was extended for certain cases involving companies in the European Economic Area following the *Marks & Spencer* group relief case. The conditions for relief in cases involving companies resident in EEA member states are dealt with separately in *CTA 2010, Pt 5, Ch 3* (see further **6.20** below).

Types of loss available for group relief

6.15 The types of loss which may be surrendered by way of group relief are set out in *CTA 2010, s 99(1)* and are trading losses, excess capital allowances, non-trading deficits on loan relationships, qualifying charitable donations, UK property business losses (formerly Schedule A losses), management expenses and non-trading losses on intangible fixed assets.

6.16 It should be noted that trading losses, excess capital allowances and non-trading deficits on loan relationships may be surrendered even where the surrendering company has other profits against which they could be set (*CTA 2010, s 99(3)*). However, charges on income, UK property business losses, management expenses and non-trading losses on intangibles may only be group relieved to the extent they exceed the surrendering company's gross profits for the period (see *CTA 2010, s 105*), and are subject to further restrictions (see *CTA 2010, s 99(5)*).

Limits on group relief

6.17 *CTA 2010, s 137* provides for the amount of group relief to be given and deals with the limits on group relief. The basic limitation is the lower of the amount of the loss (the 'surrenderable amount' as defined in *CTA 2010, s 99(7)*) and the claimant company's total profits. The limitations are applied by reference to the 'overlapping period', which is the part of the accounting period which is common to both the surrendering company and the claimant company in relation to the claim in question (*CTA 2010, s 142*).

6.18 If all members of the group have the same accounting period, then such complications do not arise, but otherwise it is necessary to apportion amounts of profits and losses between accounting periods of the claimant and surrendering companies. The basic rule is that this is to be done on a time basis (*CTA 2010, ss 139(2)* and *140(2)*). However, where that would give rise to a result which is 'unjust or unreasonable', then the apportionments may be made on such other basis as may be just and reasonable (*CTA 2010, s 141(3)*). It is worth bearing this provision in mind where a business is very seasonal or where unusual events during an accounting period have given rise to particular losses, and it would be more advantageous to the taxpayer to attribute those losses to a particular part of an accounting period. Further guidance may be found in the HMRC manuals at CTM80260. It should be noted however, that HMRC interpret this provision as including the position where a time apportionment would be unjust to HMRC.

6.19 If, in any period, a company is a 'dual-resident investing company' then that company may not surrender any amounts by way of group relief (*CTA 2010, s 109*). This is an anti-avoidance provision which is intended to prevent the double usage of losses by companies which are resident in more than one country; see HMRC manuals at CTM34500 and following paras for history and HMRC's view. The legislation contains restrictive provisions on the types of trading company which fall outside the provision. Trading companies which have as their main function or one of their main functions the activities set out in *CTA 2010, s 109(4)* will still be considered to be investment companies (mainly holding company, finance company and analogous activities).

They may, however, have unexpected application to certain companies which are incorporated in tax-haven jurisdictions, but which may technically be considered within the charge to tax of that territory, and which are also tax resident in the UK by reason of their management and control being exercised in the UK. This is particularly the case in jurisdictions which apply tax to certain types of companies but exempt others. In such cases it may be wise to seek guidance from HMRC if group relief is to be of particular significance in the group in question. There is nothing to prevent such companies being claimant companies for group relief purposes.

Relief for overseas losses of non-resident companies

6.20

> **Focus**
>
> In *Marks & Spencer plc v Halsey (Inspector of Taxes)* Case C-446/03 [2006] STC 237, Marks & Spencer successfully claimed before the ECJ that as a matter of principle the UK group relief laws breached EU law as, whilst they would allow losses of a UK company arising from a branch in France (for example) to be relieved against another UK group member's profits, it would not allow relief if, as in the case of Marks & Spencer, those losses arose in a French company.

6.21 In response to the *Marks & Spencer* decision, provisions were introduced to permit losses from companies resident in the European Economic Area (or EEA permanent establishments of non-EEA resident companies) to be surrendered to other members of a UK group. Those provisions are in *CTA 2010, Pt 5, Ch 3*. Apart from the conditions therein, it is also subject to its own anti-avoidance provision in *CTA 2010, s 127* where arrangements are entered into to ensure that losses would be available for group relief (eg by taking certain corporate actions to ensure that the conditions discussed below were satisfied). If that is the case, the amount of loss is excluded from relief.

The availability of overseas losses of EEA subsidiaries was highly restricted and was reviewed by the ECJ as potentially being too restrictive for EU purposes. As a result, changes were made in *Finance Act 2013* to make the losses less restrictive and, therefore, possibly more compliant with EU legislation.

6.22 The four conditions for group relief to be permitted in this situation are:

- the equivalence condition: *CTA 2010, s 114*;
- the EEA tax loss condition: *CTA 2010, ss 115* and *116*;
- the qualifying loss condition: *CTA 2010, ss 117–120*; and
- the precedence condition: *CTA 2010, s 121*.

All four conditions must be satisfied in order for a loss to be relieved. In broad terms the principles of the conditions are as follows.

The loss must be equivalent (ie it must correspond in all material respects) with a type of loss which would be surrendered under the domestic rules (the equivalence condition).

It must be calculated in accordance with the relevant rules under the relevant territory for the calculation of losses or other amounts eligible for relief (the EEA tax loss condition).

From 1 April 2013, EEA-resident companies can surrender losses from their UK permanent establishments as group relief in the UK, even if that loss can also be used against the profits of the surrendering company or of any other person (the qualifying loss condition). Where a loss that has been surrendered is later used against non-UK profits, then the benefit of the UK group relief will be withdrawn to the extent that the loss has been used elsewhere. This ensures that the losses are not relieved twice, once as group relief in the UK and then again in another country. This change will not apply to non-UK resident companies which are resident outside the EEA.

Until *FA 2013*, the legislation required that the loss must not have been relieved or be able to be relieved in previous, current or future periods whether against profits of the surrendering company or of any other person (the qualifying loss condition). It was this condition which effectively reduced the use of the overseas loss to cases where the loss has become legally (and not just practically) impossible to use. This rule was challenged by the European Commission in Case C-172/13 *European Commission v UK* (3 February 2015). The challenge was unsuccessful, however, finding that the Commission's examples did not demonstrate that the legislation was unnecessarily restrictive.

This test, whether the losses can be used in the non-UK jurisdiction, must be considered at the end of the accounting period in which the losses arose (*CTA 2010, s 119(4)*). However, in May 2013 the Supreme Court decided (in *R & C Commrs v Marks and Spencer plc* [2013] BTC 162) that this was incompatible with EU law and that the test should be considered at the time that the claim is made, instead. So far, however, no legislative changes have been proposed. So the Supreme Court decision will only apply to what we might call Marks & Spencer claims, ie those pre-dating the UK legislation.

The final qualification is that there is no other territory (not limited to EEA countries) in which effective relief could be given for the relevant loss.

Once those conditions have been satisfied, *CTA 2010, ss 123–126* provide for rules for the recalculation of the amount of the loss in accordance with UK tax rules and the assumptions to be made in making the surrender as regards accounting periods etc.

Administrative requirements for group relief

6.23 Claims for group relief are part of the corporation tax self-assessment regime (CTSA) and are dealt with by *FA 1998, Sch 18, para 66*ff. A claim must be made in the CTSA return or in an amendment to that return. The surrendering company must give its consent to the claim, and consent must be given at or before the time of the claim and the claim must contain a copy of that consent, otherwise the claim for group relief will be ineffective (*FA 1998, Sch 18, para 70*) Revised claims may only be dealt with by amendment of the CTSA return, and strictly this is by withdrawal of one claim and resubmission of another rather than by amendment of the claim (*FA 1998, Sch 18, para 73*).

There are separate time limits for the claiming or withdrawal of a claim for group relief from the general CTSA return amendment rules, which are set out in *FA 1998, Sch 18, para 74*. The basic rule is that the claim must be made by the first anniversary of the CTSA filing date for the company, but this is extended if there is an enquiry into the return or an appeal in relation to the return up to 30 days after the completion of the enquiry or the final determination of the appeal. This obviously gives time for consequential amendments to the group relief claims which may be affected by other matters which are the subject of the enquiry or appeal.

Payment for group relief

6.24 Payments for group relief are ignored for corporation tax purposes provided they do not exceed the amount of the loss (*CTA 2010, s 183*). Obviously, the benefit to the claimant company is that amount multiplied by the effective corporation tax rate for the period in question, and so it will usually be that, lesser, amount which is paid, if any payment is made. The company law relating to corporate benefit and maintenance of capital should be taken into account when deciding whether or not and how much to pay for group relief.

CHARGEABLE GAINS GROUPS

6.25 The provisions relating to corporation tax on chargeable gains in groups principally deal with the transfer of assets from one company in a group to another, and provide for the transfer to be on a 'no-gain-no-loss' basis. The corollary of this is that a potential 'exit charge' is created if the transferee company leaves the group within six years of the transfer, subject to certain exceptions which are discussed further below.

Qualifications for membership of a group

6.26 The primary qualification for being a member of a group is to be a 'company', as defined by *TCGA 1992, s 170(9)*. For these purposes, 'a company' is:

(a) a company as defined in *CA 2006, s 1(1)*;

(b) a company which is constituted under any other Act or a Royal Charter or letters patent or is formed under the law of a country or territory outside the United Kingdom, but not an LLP;

(c) a registered industrial and provident society;

(d) an incorporated friendly society within the meaning of the *Friendly Societies Act 1992*;

(e) a building society.

6.27 Grouping for capital gains tax purposes is dealt with in a conceptually different way to groups for group relief purposes. The legislation works in terms of first determining a particular capital gains tax group with one parent company. This is principally so that it can then be determined whether a company has left a particular group for the purposes of applying the exit charge. However, this way of viewing the group does create complications in trying to determine whether a group is the same group or not, for example if a new parent company is formed and the existing parent company transferred to it.

6.28 A group for chargeable gains purposes is therefore defined as a company (the 'principal company of the group') and all its 75% subsidiaries (*TCGA 1992, s 170(3)*). No company which is itself a 75% subsidiary of another company can be a principal company of a group. In economic ownership terms, a group does not include any company which is not an 'effective 51% subsidiary' of the principal company. *TCGA 1992, s 170(7)* provides the definition of 'effective 51% subsidiary' with the usual tests of profits available for distribution and beneficial entitlement to assets on a winding-up, and *TCGA 1992, s 170(8)* brings in the tests in *CTA 2010, Pt 5, Ch 6* discussed above in relation to group relief. For these purposes, *CTA 2010, Pt 5, Ch 6* is modified so that loans from banks in the normal course of their business are excluded from the meaning of 'loan creditor' for the definition of equity holders, and the 'arrangements' and options provisions are also ignored for the purposes of the chargeable gains group tests.

These rules were tested in the case of *Gemsupa and Another v RCC* [2015] UKFTT 97 (TC), where the existence of options was specifically held not to be relevant in determining whether the companies were members of a group. As a result, transfers of properties were accepted as being tax free, under *TCGA 1992, s 171(1)* (see **6.31**), even though the vendor companies' shares were the subject of call options allowing the previous owners to reacquire the companies immediately after the property transfers.

6.29 Because the definition of a group revolves around identifying a particular group rather than simply the relationship between two companies, it is necessary to identify when the group has remained the same group. *TCGA 1992, s 170(10)* provides that a group will remain the same group for as long as the principal company of the group is the same. If the principal company becomes a member of another group, then the two groups are also regarded as the same group.

Residence qualifications

6.30 As with the group relief provisions discussed above, *FA 2000* introduced changes to the definitions of chargeable gains groups so that it is possible for the principal company of a group to be a company resident outside the UK, and for members of the group to be non-UK resident companies. This can give rise to issues where the constitution of groups changes by reason of a transaction taking place entirely outside the UK, and the parties involved overlook a charge to capital gains tax because no-one envisages that such a transaction would cause a UK tax effect. At the same time as the *FA 2000* amendments to the constitution of groups, residence qualifications were inserted into the transfer provisions in *TCGA 1992, s 171* to ensure that the provisions did not permit transfers outside the UK tax net on a tax-free basis.

Transfer provisions

6.31 The principal provision on transfers is *TCGA 1992, s 171*, which provides that where a transfer is made between two members of a chargeable gains group, and they are either resident in the UK, or the asset is (or will be) a chargeable asset in relation to them, then the transfer is deemed for corporation tax to be one at a consideration which will give rise to neither a gain nor a loss.

The use of the phrase 'disposes of an asset to another company', as well as the general framework of the provisions, means that there must be both a disposal and an acquisition of an asset for the provisions to apply, and a disposal without an acquisition (such as the redemption of shares), or an acquisition without a disposal (such as the subscription for shares) will not be within *TCGA 1992, s 171*. There are also some specific exclusions in *TCGA 1992, s 171(2)* and *(3A)*. Of note is the exclusion for transfers to dual-resident investing companies. The point made at **6.19** above in relation to unexpectedly dual-resident companies is worth remembering.

6.32 It may be the case that the assets which are the subject of the transfer are trading assets for one of the companies but capital assets for the other. If the transferee is acquiring the asset as part of its trading stock, then *TCGA 1992, s 173(1)* deems it to have acquired it as a capital asset and then immediately appropriated it to trading stock. This will give rise to a charge under *TCGA 1992, s 161* either as a capital gain, or, by election, by an adjustment to the trading profits of the acquirer.

If the transferor is the trader, then *TCGA 1992, s 173(2)* deems the transferor to have appropriated the stock from trading stock immediately before the transfer. *TCGA 1992, s 161* treats the transferor as having acquired it for the value which is taken into the accounts in respect of it, and *TCGA 1992, s 171* then applies to the transfer. There is no specific statutory provision which provides the figure to be placed in the trading accounts on the deemed appropriation from trading stock in such a case, although in practice market value has been used, on the basis of the principle in *Sharkey v Wernher* (1955) 36 TC 276. There are relatively new provisions introduced by *FA 2008, Sch 15, Pt 2* and now in *CTA 2009, Pt 3, Ch 10* which apply market value to appropriations in general, although their interaction with *TCGA 1992, s 173(2)* is still not entirely clear because *TCGA 1992, s 173(2)* only deems there to have been an appropriation for the purposes of *TCGA 1992, s 161*. However, use of any other figure is likely to lead to an argument with HMRC.

Although the provisions of *TCGA 1992, s 173* open up the possibility of planning by, for example, the triggering of losses, it should be borne in mind that attempts to rely on trading or non-trading status have not received much sympathy before the courts when taxpayers have sought to rely on different group members having a different status. See, in particular, *Reed v Nova Securities Ltd* [1985] STC 124 and *New Angel Court Ltd v Adam* [2004] STC 779.

Company ceasing to be a member of a group

6.33

Focus

These rules were substantially amended for capital gains purposes by *Finance Act 2011*. The old rules apply for degrouping events prior to Royal

Assent to *FA 2011*, and can be found in *Tax Planning 2016–17* (Bloomsbury Professional). The new rules apply after that date. An election could be made for the effective date to be 1 April 2011, but it had to have been made (or rescinded) by 31 March 2012.

Of particular practical importance is the new facility to require a degrouping charge to be reduced or eliminated where it is just and reasonable to do so.

These new rules do not apply to degrouping charges applicable to chargeable intangible assets, under *CTA 2010, Pt 8*.

Without anti-avoidance measures, the intra-group transfer provisions would obviously be open to abuse as assets could effectively be transferred to third parties by the mechanism of a company. However, rather than adopt any mechanism which depends on there being arrangements in place at the time of the transfer, or any reliance on any motive test, the chargeable gains legislation imposes a charge when a transferee company leaves the group within six years of the transfer under *TCGA 1992, s 179*. These rules were changed substantially by *FA 2011*.

6.34 The basic rule is that if a company, Company A, leaves the group and either it, or an associated company also leaving the group, owns the asset (or an asset into which a gain on the asset has been rolled under the replacement of business assets rules) otherwise than as trading stock, then company A is deemed to have sold and immediately reacquired the asset on its acquisition from Company B. How this gain is then taxed depends on when and how Company A leaves the group, and is covered below.

There are several points worth making in relation to the basic application of *TCGA 1992, s 179*. First, as mentioned above, it is a blanket charge and does not depend on the circumstances of the original transfer being tax motivated or carried out at otherwise than market value. Secondly, the asset may no longer be owned by Company A but may have been transferred on to another company leaving the group at the same time (leading to the mistaken conclusion that *TCGA 1992, s 179(2)* applies (see further below)). Finally, the asset which was the subject of the original transfer to Company A may no longer be owned by the group at all, but *TCGA 1992, s 179* will still impose a charge if a gain on the disposal of the asset has been rolled into another asset under *TCGA 1992, s 151*.

The conditions for the charge (commonly referred to as an 'exit charge') are:

- there has been a transfer from Company B to Company A when both were members of a group;
- at the time of the transfer Company A and Company B were either resident in the UK or the asset was a chargeable asset in relation to them;

- within six years of the time of the acquisition, Company A ceases to be a member of the group.

If company A ceases to be a member of the group by virtue of a disposal of shares (a 'group disposal'), the chargeable gain computed in respect of the asset is not charged on Company A. Instead, the gain is treated as further consideration accruing to the vendor company. This means, first, that the charge falls on the vendor company and not in Company A, which simplifies due diligence and warranty issues in transactions. And secondly, it means that any reliefs or exemptions that apply to the group disposal, such as the substantial shareholdings exemption (*TCGA 1992, Sch 7AC*) or the reorganisations provisions (*TCGA 1992, s 135*), will also apply to the degrouping element.

This rule also applies where there is no taxable group disposal but an exit charge still arises, to which the substantial shareholdings exemption would apply. For example, if Company A, a member of a trading group, holds shares in a trading company that were transferred to it within the previous six years, and Company A is sold by a non-UK vendor, the gain is added to the consideration received by the vendor and, since the vendor is outside the scope of UK corporation tax, no charge arises. In many cases, the gain on the deemed disposal by Company A would have been exempt under the substantial shareholdings exemption, but the degrouping provisions apply anyway, even if the substantial shareholdings exemption does not.

6.35 If the exit charge arises other than through a disposal (eg where a new investor subscribes for more than 25% of the enlarged share capital), the charge arises as a chargeable gain in Company A, instead, as there is no vendor company to which it can be applied. Where this happens, the company may be able to transfer the charge to another company in the vendor group by an election under *TCGA 1992, s 171A* (see **6.39**).

Companies leaving a group at the same time

6.36 The primary exemption from the charge under *TCGA 1992, s 179* is contained in *TCGA 1992, s 179(2)* which prevents a charge arising on a transfer between two companies when those companies leave the group together. No exit charge arises in respect of a transfer from one company to another if either:

- both are 75% subsidiaries and effective 51% subsidiaries of another company on the date of the acquisition, and they remain both 75% subsidiaries and effective 51% subsidiaries of that other company until immediately after the degrouping event, or
- one is a 75% subsidiary and an effective 51% subsidiary of the other on the date of the acquisition, and remains both a 75% subsidiary and an effective 51% subsidiary of the other until immediately after the degrouping event.

These are very restrictive rules, as they permit very little intra-group movement in respect of the transferee and transferor companies.

Claim for 'just and reasonable' adjustments

6.37 One problem with the exit charge rules was always the potential for double taxation, inherent in there being a charge in respect of the disposal of the shares and another in respect of the deemed disposal of an underlying asset owned by a company whose shares were being sold. In such cases, the company making the disposal may claim to have the degrouping charge reduced or eliminated (the reduction must be specified in the claim), and HMRC are required to reduce the gain 'by such amount (if any) as is just and reasonable', taking into account the transaction whereby the asset-holding company acquired the asset.

Where a reduction is made, the base cost of the asset concerned is also reduced by the same amount. This prevents the double relief that might accrue if the asset were to be rebased without the commensurate exit charge.

Merger exemption: TCGA 1992, s 181

6.38 The merger exemption in *TCGA 1992, s 181* is sometimes overlooked, but it can be useful. The exemption applies where Company A (the transferee) leaves the group as part of a merger carried out for bona fide commercial reasons and the avoidance of tax is not the main or one of the main purposes of the merger. This principally assists in cases where two groups exchange interests in each other's businesses, either via the transfer of business to a new company, or to one of the group companies involved in the transaction. The value of the interests acquired by each group must be substantially the same as the value of the business interest given up (ie this relief is not restricted to 50:50 joint ventures), and the consideration must be substantially in the form of the acquisition of the interest in the business, or applied in acquiring such an interest (ignoring any small amounts) (*TCGA 1992, s 181(4)*).

Notional transfers prior to a sale: TCGA 1992, s 171A

6.39 Prior to the introduction of *TCGA 1992, s 171A*, it was common for groups to marshal their gains and losses by the transfer of assets intra-group prior to their disposal to third parties. This type of planning was generally accepted by HMRC, and effectively allowed group relief for allowable (capital) losses. *TCGA 1992, s 171A* is restated by *FA 2009* to dispense with the need actually to deem an intra-group transfer of the relevant asset, which had given rise to issues in some circumstances. Under the new drafting, there is simply an election to transfer the gain or loss between group companies. It should, however, be noted that the gain or loss must be made in respect of an asset to which a transfer under *TCGA 1992, s 171* could have applied.

TCGA 1992, s 171A also permits an exit charge gain to be transferred within a group, so that, if an exit charge arises on a company leaving a group (see **6.35**), that charge can be transferred to another company in the vendor group.

TRANSFERS OF TRADES UNDER *CTA 2010, PT 22, CH 1*

6.40 The transfer of a business between members of the group will of course have more tax implications than just tax on chargeable gains. There may be brought forward trading losses in the transferring trading company which may be lost, or there may be capital assets on which capital allowances have been claimed where a disposal would lead to a balancing charge or a balancing allowance. *CTA 2010, Pt 22, Ch 1* aims to avoid those events where a trade is transferred between parties under common ownership, and avoids the effects of the statutory discontinuance of the trade under *CTA 2009, s 41*. It is subject to its own anti-avoidance provisions.

Common ownership requirements

6.41 The common ownership requirement in *CTA 2010, s 941* is stated in a different way to the grouping tests. *CTA 2010, Pt 22, Ch 1* is intended to be broad in application, and can itself be viewed as an anti-avoidance provision. The terminology of the common ownership test has been somewhat re-written, but the principle is the same, and requires a 75% common interest. The test compares the ownership of the company at the time of the transfer or at any time within the subsequent two years with the owners at any time within the year prior to the transfer. If there is a 75% commonality of ownership between the two dates, the common ownership requirements are met.

Although *CTA 2010, Pt 22, Ch 1* itself only applies to transfers between companies (as it applies for corporation tax), the 'common ownership' requirement can be traced through persons other than companies. *CTA 2010, s 942* sets out the options by which the ownership condition may be satisfied Basically, ownership is traced through the ordinary share capital of the company carrying on the trade. 'Ordinary share capital' for this purpose bears its *CTA 2010, s 1119* meaning discussed above in relation to group relief. A trade is therefore regarded as belonging to the persons owning the ordinary share capital of the company carrying on the trade, or if it is carried on in a subsidiary, by the persons owning the ordinary share capital of the parent.

There is also a particular rule, in *CTA 2010, s 941(7)*, which treats for this purpose persons who are related (being husbands, wives, civil partners, ancestors or lineal descendants, and brothers and sisters) as the same person.

Shares owned by non-charitable trusts are treated as owned by the persons entitled to the income under the trust (*CTA 2010, s 941(5)*), and for these purposes if there is more than one such person, they are treated as the same person (*CTA 2010, s 941(7)*).

Effect of application

6.42 *CTA 2010, Pt 22, Ch 1* applies for two specific purposes only. First, it prevents a disposal event under the capital allowances legislation, and effectively gives future allowances to the purchaser in the same amounts as would have been given to the seller (*CTA 2010, s 948*). Secondly, it allows the carry forward of losses in the trade under *CTA 2010, Pt 4, Ch 2* to continue to be carried forward by the purchaser (*CTA 2010, s 944*).

Anti-avoidance

6.43 *CTA 2010, s 948* (the capital allowances provision) does not apply if the transferee company is a dual-resident investing company (see the discussion at **6.19** above).

Where liabilities of the transferor company are not assumed by the transferee, and these exceed the value any assets of the transferor not transferred, the loss carry-over under *CTA 2010, s 944* is restricted to the amount of losses over and above that excess (*CTA 2010, s 945*). This provision is designed to prevent the hiving down of trades and associated losses where the liabilities of the trade remain with the transferor (eg in an insolvency proceeding), and the subsequent sale of a company with those losses.

Finance Act 2013 also introduced a further restriction on the transfer of trading losses under this legislation, relating to the interaction with the rules for a change of ownership of a company (*CTA 2010, Pt 14, Ch 2*). The new anti-avoidance rule is designed to stop any device whereby the trade is transferred to another group company. Before this amendment, the effect of *CTA 2010, s 676* was to restrict the carry forward of losses by a successor company where the loss had been sustained by a predecessor if the transfer of the trade occurred before the change in ownership (of the successor). The effect of the new legislation is to extend the restriction of carried forward losses by a company even if the transfer of the trade occurs after the change in ownership (ie where the successor company has not itself undergone a change in ownership). The new rules apply to all changes of ownership on or after 20 March 2013.

Other issues on a transfer of trade

6.44 It should be noted that *CTA 2010, Pt 22, Ch 1* makes no provision about trading stock. The basic provisions in *CTA 2009, Pt 3, Ch 11* will therefore apply by reason of *CTA 2009, s 41* and an amount will have to be brought into account in respect of the disposal of it, which is either the value obtained on transfer, or the market value if the parties are connected (subject to the ability to elect otherwise).

6.45 If only part of a trade is transferred under *CTA 2010, s 951*, a question arises as to whether the transferor continues to carry on the remaining trade as part of the previous trade, or whether there has been a discontinuance of that part (which will not be assisted by *CTA 2010, Pt 22, Ch 1* unless that part is also transferred); see *Rolls-Royce Motors Ltd v Bamford* [1976] STC 162.

This point was further considered in *Leekes Ltd v RCC* TC04298, where a trading company, Coles, was acquired by Leekes and the trade hived up to Leekes, which was agreed to be a succession. Leekes therefore claimed the losses of the acquired trade under what is now *CTA 2010, s 944* (previously *ICTA 1988, s 343(1)* and *(3)*) and HMRC contended that they could only be used against the future profits of the acquired trade, not against the full profits of the combined trade. The First-tier Tribunal found for the company but there was (and remains) some confusion as to whether *CTA 2010, s 944* applies, as accepted by both parties, or whether *CTA 2010, s 951* should apply, in which case HMRC would be correct in their analysis. The Upper Tribunal overturned the First-tier Tribunal decision, on the basis that *ICTA 1988, s 343(3)* implicitly required streaming of losses, because it referred to loss relief for 'for any amount for which the predecessor would have been entitled', which necessarily restricted the loss relief to the amount that Coles would have been entitled to. The current legislation, at *CTA 2010, s 944(3)*, is probably clearer in allowing this interpretation, as it refers to 'relief that would have been given … to the predecessor had it continued to carry on that trade'. As the Coles trade continued to be loss making, no relief could be given for past losses, as that trade had no profits to shelter.

6.46 If the transferee already carries on a trade, the transfer of the new trade may be an expansion of the existing trade, it may result in two separate trades being carried on by the transferee, or it may represent a discontinuance of the previous trade (which, again, will not be assisted by *CTA 2010, Pt 22, Ch 1*).

PRE-ENTRY GAINS AND LOSSES

6.47

> **Focus**
>
> These rules are very effective at preventing the buying in of allowable losses from another company. It is therefore highly unlikely that the losses in a recently acquired company will be available to use in the wider group.

These rules were substantially amended by *Finance Act 2011*. The old rules apply for degrouping events prior to Royal Assent to *FA 2011* and can be found in *Tax Planning 2016–17* (Bloomsbury Professional).

It will be obvious from the discussion above in relation to chargeable gains groups that there is room for manipulation of the rules by reason of companies joining groups having either made a gain or loss in the accounting period in which they join (which is then offset by a later disposal of an asset in the acquiring group or used to offset a gain on an asset about to be disposed of in the acquiring group), or by the acquisition of companies with assets which have inherent unrealised gains or losses. These are referred to as pre-entry (ie into the new group) gains and losses.

The provisions which have been enacted to counter various sorts of these activities have changed over time. The main provision in *TCGA 1992, Sch 7A* (given effect by *s 177A*) (loss buying) was enacted by *FA 1993*, and remains in force. It was joined in 1998 by *TCGA 1992, Sch 7AA* (gain buying). *FA 2006* inserted two new provisions, *TCGA 1992, s 184A* (loss buying avoidance schemes) and *TCGA 1992, s 184B* (gain buying avoidance schemes) (these are referred to as 'targeted anti-avoidance rules'). *FA 2006* also repealed *TCGA 1992, Sch 7AA*, as it was felt to have been superseded by *TCGA 1992, s 184B*. The same was not felt to be true of *TCGA 1992, Sch 7A*, and therefore that provision now exists in tandem with *TCGA 1992, s 184A* (which takes precedence over *TCGA 1992, Sch 7A*). *TCGA 1992, Sch 7A* was amended by *FA 2011*.

Pre-entry losses: TCGA 1992, Sch 7A

6.48 *TCGA 1992, Sch 7A* restricts the use of allowable losses which accrued to a company before it became a member of a chargeable gains group (a 'pre-entry loss'). There is no motive or commerciality test in *TCGA 1992, Sch 7A*. The provisions are therefore commonly applicable to groups of companies, and can therefore result in a significant compliance burden in relation to the second leg of the restriction.

6.49 Pre-entry losses which have accrued prior to the time the company joined the group may be deducted from chargeable gains which have arisen on:

- a disposal by the company before the date on which it became a member of the relevant (new) group;
- the disposal of an asset which was held by the company before it became a member of that group; or

- the disposal of an asset which was acquired after the date the company became a member of the group from a person who was not a member of that group at the time of the acquisition, and which was used in a business carried on by that company before it joined the group and continued to be carried on by that company or by another member of the group until the time of the disposal of the asset.

The order in which losses are to be offset against gains is set out in *TCGA 1992, Sch 7A, para 6*.

6.50 The rules which apply when companies join capital gains tax groups, including where *TCGA 1992, s 170(10)* deems there to be a continuity of groups, would undermine the efficacy of these anti-avoidance rules, so *TCGA 1992, Sch 7A, para 1(6)* disapplies *TCGA 1992, s 170(10)* generally. *TCGA 1992, Sch 7A, para 1(6)* works by treating all the members of the first group as becoming members of the second group at the time they actually joined the second group, and not, by reason of *TCGA 1992, s 170(10)*, when they joined the first group.

There is an exception in *TCGA 1992, Sch 7A, para 1(7)*, whereby *TCGA 1992, s 170(10)* may not be disapplied where the transaction is simply the insertion of a new holding company with the same shareholders.

Pre-entry losses: TCGA 1992, s 184A

6.51 *TCGA 1992, s 184A* is a broader provision than *TCGA 1992, Sch 7A*, in that it is drafted to apply in wider circumstances. It does, however, contain a motive test, and so to that extent is likely to apply in a much more restricted range of circumstances than *TCGA 1992, Sch 7A*. *TCGA 1992, Sch 7A* remains in force. Note, however, that the tax advantage in question does not have to be secured for the company making the loss.

TCGA 1992, s 184A applies wherever there has been a 'qualifying change of ownership' and a 'qualifying loss' arises in relation to a 'pre-change asset'. A qualifying change of ownership includes where a company has joined or left a group of companies and also where a company becomes subject to different control (*TCGA 1992, s 184C(6)* – control for this purpose bearing its wider meaning in *CTA 2010, s 450* (formerly *ICTA 1988, s 416*); *TCGA 1992, s 288(1)*). If the provisions apply, a qualifying loss may not be deducted from gains accruing to the company other than those on pre-change assets.

Pre-entry gains

6.52 As mentioned above, *TCGA 1992, Sch 7AA* was repealed by *FA 2006*, and replaced by *TCGA 1992, s 184B*. *TCGA 1992, Sch 7AA* is not dealt with further in this chapter.

TCGA 1992, s 184B applies in the same circumstances to *TCGA 1992, s 184A*, save that there must have been a 'qualifying gain' made on a pre-change asset rather than a qualifying loss. Again, the motive test should mean that this will not apply otherwise than in avoidance cases, subject to the usual questions of interpretation as to what is meant by tests encompassing 'one of the main purposes' language, as is the case in both *TCGA 1992, ss 184A* and *184B*.

DEPRECIATORY TRANSACTIONS

6.53 The fortunate aspect of these parts of the tax legislation is that it is now irrelevant for disposals to which the substantial shareholdings exemption in *TCGA 1992, Sch 7AC* applies. Its existence should not, however, be forgotten. The two sets of provisions are *TCGA 1992, ss 176* and *177* on the one hand, and *TCGA 1992, s 30* onwards on the other.

TCGA 1992, ss 176 and 177

6.54 *TCGA 1992, s 176* is an anti-avoidance provision which aims to restrict the creation of losses by the reduction in the value of shares or securities prior to their disposal by means of a 'depreciatory transaction'. It only restricts the creation of losses, and does not result in a gain being imposed.

For the purposes of *TCGA 1992, s 176*, a depreciatory transaction is either a disposal of assets between two group members at an undervalue, or any other transaction which involved the company to be disposed of, or one or more of its 75% subsidiaries, where that transaction involved two or more group members. The classic application of *TCGA 1992, s 176* is squarely within the main heading and occurs where assets are transferred intra-group at an undervalue, and the transferor company is then sold at a loss.

Where the section applies, any allowable loss is reduced to the extent 'just and reasonable'.

6.55 *TCGA 1992, s 177* is aimed at the reduction in the value of a target by basic dividend stripping in the form of a payment of a dividend by the target company. It applies where the recipient has a holding of 10% or more of any one class of shares. The consequences are the same as the application of *TCGA 1992, s 176*.

These rules only apply to depreciatory transactions in the six years immediately preceding the disposal.

TCGA 1992, s 30 onwards

6.56

> **Focus**
>
> This rule is of wide application as there is no description of the types of transaction that might be caught. Instead, the rules concentrate on their effect.
>
> These rules were substantially amended by *Finance Act 2011*. The old rules apply for degrouping events prior to Royal Assent to *FA 2011* and can be found in *Tax Planning 2016–17* (Bloomsbury Professional).

Unlike *TCGA 1992, s 176*, *TCGA 1992, s 30* can result in the imposition of an actual charge to tax, and has historically therefore given more concern to tax advisers than *TCGA 1992, s 176*. This is partly because the provisions are drafted generally, and then further refined in the context of groups. Approached in this way, they are slightly easier to understand.

The basic criteria for *TCGA 1992, s 30* to apply are that in the context of a disposal of an asset:

- the value of the asset (or of a 'relevant asset') has been materially reduced; and
- a tax-free benefit has been or will be conferred on the person making the disposal, a connected person, or, where there is an avoidance motive, any other person.

For this purpose 'relevant asset' means an asset owned by a company associated with the disposing company. This only applies in limited circumstances, and if there is a charge under *TCGA 1992, s 179*, this element of the provision is excluded.

6.57 Where arrangements have been made materially to reduce the value of those shares or securities, or of a relevant asset, and the arrangements are intended to create a tax advantage, the consideration for the gain or loss on the disposal is adjusted by an amount which is 'just and reasonable', taking into account the arrangements themselves and any tax otherwise payable. This rule does not apply if the arrangements are simply the making of an exempt distribution, being broadly a distribution that would not be taxed under *CTA 2009, Pt 9A*.

For these purposes, a relevant asset is an asset owned by a member of the same group as the disposing company.

SUBSTANTIAL SHAREHOLDINGS EXEMPTION

6.58 The scope of the capital gains tax charge was radically changed for companies by *FA 2002* by the introduction of the substantial shareholdings exemption. As mentioned above, this made many of the loss buying and depreciatory transactions effectively redundant, certainly as far as M&A practitioners were concerned. The regime does, however, have some uncertainties. These are usually largely factual, as the regime only applies to disposals of trading companies or groups by trading companies or groups. The 'trading' issue is therefore of paramount importance, and is often the subject of a clearance application under Code of Practice 10 other than in very obvious cases. It should be noted that the exemption is not limited to actual disposals to third parties; disposals for chargeable gains purposes in general are exempted (the losses are of course correspondingly unallowable).

Following consultation during 2016 (see 'Reform of the Substantial Shareholdings Exemption' published by HM Treasury in May 2016), changes were proposed for the *Finance Act 2017*. Due to a surprise general election that year, the changes were deferred but, at the time of writing, HMRC have announced that the changes will be brought into a second Finance Act of 2017 and will be effective from 1 April 2017 (ie the originally proposed start date). At the time of writing, the *Finance (No 2) Bill 2017* was being debated by Parliament.

Basic application

6.59 Despite the drafting of *TCGA 1992, Sch 7AC, Pt 1*, the basic exemption is very simple. There are requirements to be met as regards the shareholding, the disposing company (referred to unhelpfully as the 'investing company' in the legislation), and the company whose shares are being disposed of (the 'company invested in').

6.60 A 'substantial shareholding' is where a company has a holding of not less than 10% of the company's ordinary share capital, is beneficially entitled to at least 10% of the profits available for distribution to equity holders, and is beneficially entitled to 10% of the assets available for distribution on a winding-up. *CTA 2010, Pt 5, Ch 6* (as modified for capital gains) applies for the purposes of the latter two tests (*TCGA 1992, Sch 7AC, para 8*). The holdings of groups are generally aggregated for this purpose (*TCGA 1992, Sch 7AC, para 9*).

The shareholding must have been held throughout a 12-month period beginning not more than two years before the day on which the disposal takes place, for disposals up to 31 March 2017. For disposals on or after 1 April 2017, the shareholding must have been held throughout a 12-month period beginning not more than six years before the day on which the disposal takes place, assuming that the *Finance (No 2) Bill 2017* receives Royal Assent.

Investing company requirements

6.61 For disposals up to 31 March 2017, the disposing company must be a sole trading company or a holding company of a trading group in order for the exemption to apply. This criterion must be satisfied for the 12-month period ended at the time of disposal, and it must also be satisfied immediately after the disposal. Therefore a disposal of its sole trading subsidiary by a non-trading holding company will not satisfy the exemption, but the disposal of such a subsidiary by a trading holding company would satisfy the exemption. The lessons for group structuring could hardly be clearer.

The provisions imposing requirements on the investing company will be repealed for disposals on or after 1 April 2017, assuming that the *Finance (No 2) Bill 2017* receives Royal Assent.

Investee company requirements

6.62 The requirements for the company invested in are that it must be a sole trading company or a holding company of a trading group or subgroup in order for the exemption to apply. (This is really due to the fact that the concept of group in *TCGA 1992, Sch 7AC* is by reference to chargeable gains tax groups, so there can be only one group, hence the adoption of the subgroup.)

This criterion must be satisfied for the 12-month period ended at the time of disposal, and it must also be satisfied immediately after the disposal. For disposals on or after 1 April 2017, the investee company does not have to satisfy the condition immediately after the transaction, unless the disposal is to a connected party or it is a disposal that relies on *TCGA 1992, Sch 7AC, para 15A* (see **6.66**). This assumes that the *Finance (No 2) Bill 2017* receives Royal Assent.

Meaning of trading

6.63 'Trading company', 'trading group' and 'trading subgroup' are defined in *TCGA 1992, Sch 7AC, paras 20, 21* and *22* respectively, but the essence of the primary definition in each is the same – the company (or group or subgroup as a whole) means 'a company carrying on trading activities whose activities do not include to a substantial extent activities other than trading activities'. There is an extended meaning of 'trading activities' which is expressed to include preparatory activities and activities in preparing for acquiring a trade or a company which carries on a trade, as well as activities in the course of or in furtherance of a trade.

In practice, it is usually obvious which activities of a company, group or subgroup are or are not trading, the most frequently seen non-trading activities being property leasing (including intra-group of course), financing (by companies other than those which can qualify as financial traders), and the holding of large amounts of cash (perhaps arising from a disposal) on a temporary basis. What is often less obvious is whether those activities will be 'substantial' to the extent that they taint the rest of the activities of the company, group or subgroup. In the case of the wider group, intra-group activities can usually be ignored (on the basis that the provisions refer to the activities of the members of a group 'taken together'), and the problem usually arises where there is intra-group activity between a company or subgroup which has to be examined, and other members of a wider group.

In relation to non-trading activities, and whether they are substantial, HMRC take a similar approach to that taken for taper relief. For these purposes 'substantial' means more than 20%. HMRC have published guidance on their approach at CG53116 and the following paragraphs. The 20% test is applied to turnover, the value of assets, management time spent and the company's history. The latter test is intended to avoid a 'snapshot' approach to the tests, by looking at them over a period of time.

Because of the difficulties in applying the trading tests, it had become fairly standard practice to seek a ruling from HMRC under Code of Practice 10. Code of Practice 10 rulings are usually available for up to four Finance Acts, and thereafter the legislation is no longer considered new enough to warrant the system being available. However, HMRC relaxed this approach in relation to substantial shareholdings and introduced a new facility in June 2007. This system has now been replaced in effect by the non-statutory clearance procedure; see HMRC's Non-Statutory Business Clearance Guidance Manual for details on how to make an application.

The subsidiary exemptions

6.64 *TCGA 1992, Sch 7AC, paras 2* and *3* contain subsidiary exemptions. *TCGA 1992, Sch 7AC, para 2* deals with disposals of 'assets related to shares' (see *TCGA 1992, Sch 7AC, para 30*), which is intended to cover disposals of options and convertible securities where the main exemption would be met. As the HMRC manuals state, this is effectively to ensure that companies do not have a choice as to whether to dispose of assets which are within the capital gains tax charge or those which are not (and indeed, the same applies generally to the legislation, as otherwise companies would have the choice of creating capital losses).

6.65 *TCGA 1992, Sch 7AC, para 3* contains a further subsidiary exemption. It is rather impenetrably drafted, but its effect can be very useful and it should not be overlooked. The substantial shareholding condition must still be met. *TCGA 1992, Sch 7AC, para 3(2)(d)* then applies a 'look back' provision to the previous two years as regards the exemption to find a time when it would have been satisfied (ie applying all the tests of the exemption at that time). *TCGA 1992, Sch 7AC, para 3(2)(e)* then looks to the two years before disposal and tests the 'company invested in' requirement, and deems that requirement satisfied if that company was controlled by the disposing company or companies connected with the disposing company.

TCGA 1992, Sch 7AC, para 3(3) then limits the application of the *TCGA 1992, Sch 7AC, para 3* exemption in cases where the investing company requirement immediately after disposal is not met, where the failure to meet that requirement is due to the disposing company being wound up or dissolved or the fact it is about to be wound up or dissolved. This provision is repealed for disposals on or after 1 April 2017, assuming that the *Finance (No 2) Bill 2017* receives Royal Assent.

In practice, therefore, *TCGA 1992, Sch 7AC, para 3* applies particularly where the status of the company invested in (or indeed the group, but this may be less likely) has changed prior to the disposal, or where the disposing company is in the process of being wound up.

Packaging trades for disposal

6.66 The substantial shareholdings exemption also applies to situations where a company is disposing of a trade or part of a trade and wishes to do so by transferring that trading activity into a new company which can be sold as a clean vehicle to the purchaser. This is intended to ensure that the disposal of the new company by the vendor will, itself, be exempt, subject to certain conditions being satisfied (*TCGA 1992, Sch 7AC, para 15A*).

The conditions are that:

- immediately before the disposal the vendor company holds a substantial shareholding in the new company;
- an asset which, at the time of the disposal is being used for the purposes of a trade carried on by the new company has been transferred to it by the vendor or another company in the group at a time when all the relevant companies were members of the same group; and
- the asset was previously used by a member of the group, other than the new company, for the purposes of a trade carried on by that company.

If these conditions are satisfied the vendor company is treated as having held the substantial shareholding in the new company for the period of 12 months ending with the time of the disposal, so long as, during the whole of that period, the relevant asset had been in use for the purposes of a trade carried on by a company in the group. Furthermore, if the conditions are met, then *TCGA 1992, Sch 7AC, para 19* treats the new company as having been a trading company throughout that 12-month period.

As a result, the substantial shareholdings exemption is available for the 'packaging' of trading activities by a vendor company without the vendor suffering an exit charge.

It is also to be noted that the change in the exit charge rules is not mirrored in the degrouping rules for chargeable intangible assets under *CTA 2009, Pt 8*. This means that the exemption will be of no use to trades with material amounts of intellectual property created or acquired since 31 March 2002 or where the trade started after that date and a major asset is goodwill.

Furthermore, HMRC's stated view is that this extension to the exemption only applies where the vendor company is a member of a group (see HMRC's Capital Gains Manual at CG53080C), which means that the exemption is not available to single companies with several trades. This is an odd interpretation of the legislation, as these new rules were specifically designed with single companies in mind, and not everyone agrees with HMRC's interpretation.

Interaction with other provisions

6.67 The application of *TCGA 1992, Sch 7AC* is more complicated in group situations where there has been a reorganisation prior to sale. The overall aim of the legislation is to ensure that ownership which is split between different members of a group, whether in amount or in time, is taken together for the purposes of the Schedule (*Sch 7AC, paras 9* and *10*).

The first point to make is that *TCGA 1992, Sch 7AC* does not displace *TCGA 1992, s 171*, and that provision operates in its usual way as a disposal for a consideration which results in neither a gain nor a loss accruing (*TCGA 1992, Sch 7AC, para 6*).

The second point, where the difficulty arises, is its application of *TCGA 1992, s 135* to intra-group share exchanges. *TCGA 1992, Sch 7AC, para 4(1)* effectively gives priority to the substantial shareholdings rules over *TCGA 1992, s 127*. However, removing *TCGA 1992, s 127* leaves one with a transaction under *TCGA 1992, s 171*, over which the exemption does not have priority. That is not, it would seem, what was intended by the legislation.

The answer to this was given by HMRC at the time the provisions were passing through the legislative process, and is, in summary, that there is a disposal for substantial shareholdings purposes, with the result that on a disposal by company A to company B of company C in return for an issue of shares by company B to company A, company A has a substantial shareholdings exempt disposal, company B acquires company C at market value, and company A acquires the shares in company B at the value it held the shares in company C (ie *TCGA 1992, s 127* does apply for that purpose). That is perhaps a sensible result, but it is very difficult to reach that conclusion on the wording of the legislation, and HMRC's circular explanation has to be read to be believed.

This does, however, mean the position remains the same as if *TCGA 1992, Sch 7AC, para 4(1)* had not prevented *TCGA 1992, s 127* applied to the transaction as a whole, and means that companies which carry out such internal share-for-share reorganisations should ensure that clearance is obtained so that they know what their base costs in the various subsidiaries are. The previous position, where companies can, to at least a limited extent, indulge in base cost planning in the context of reorganisations (subject to the commercial purpose test) remains the same.

Anti-avoidance

6.68 *TCGA 1992, Sch 7AC* has its own anti-avoidance provision, contained in *TCGA 1992, Sch 7AC, para 5*, which is perhaps considered less than it should be in practice. It is necessary for it to apply that the sole or main benefit that could be expected to arise be that a gain which would otherwise have accrued be exempt, but note that this is not a motive test, rather it is an objective test based on the facts of the case.

The other conditions in *TCGA 1992, Sch 7AC, para 5* are that the disposing company 'acquired' control of the target and there was a significant change in trading activities of the target company when the disposing company controlled the target. The main target of this provision can therefore be seen as artificial manipulation of the trading requirement for the company invested in.

OTHER RELEVANT PROVISIONS FOR GROUPS

6.69 The aim of this section of the chapter is to provide an overview of other provisions which are relevant to groups, although detailed consideration of the regimes is outside the scope of this chapter.

Transfer pricing

6.70 The amendment of the transfer pricing legislation in *TIOPA 2010, Pt 4*, to include transactions between UK companies rather than just between

UK and overseas companies has undoubtedly increased the burden on many groups. The pricing of each transaction between group members needs, strictly, to be justified on the basis of arm's-length principles. It should be remembered that this applies in relation to all sorts of transactions, including loans.

There is an exemption for small and medium-sized companies in *TIOPA 2010, s 166*, which applies to transactions between companies resident in the UK and between companies resident in the UK and companies resident in a territory which is party to a double tax treaty with an anti-discrimination provision and subject to certain designation powers of HM Treasury.

Should an adjustment under the transfer pricing provisions apply, then there is the possibility of a compensating adjustment under the provisions. Obviously, all of these provisions need to be considered in the context of the wider tax attributes of the companies concerned and the group as a whole.

Loan relationships

6.71 The loan relationships legislation contains a number of provisions which apply between connected parties and/or members of groups of companies.

The provisions in *FA 2006* were substantially amended by *FA 2004* to cope in particular with the introduction of International Accounting Standards (IAS) accounting, and have now been re-written into *CTA 2009, Pt 6. Finance Act 2009* has amended the provisions relating to late-paid interest and accrued discounts between connected parties in an attempt to bring them into line with EU law. *FA 2010, Sch 19* has inserted provisions into both the loan relationships and derivative provisions in *CTA 2009* enabling the provisions to be amended by statutory instrument to deal with changes in accounting rules.

6.72 The rules in *CTA 2009, Pt 5* require careful examination where groups and connected companies are concerned. The main provisions are as follows:

CTA 2009, ss 373–379 may apply to delay an interest deduction where the payee does not accrue the interest under the loan relationships regime and it is not paid within 12 months of the accounting period in which it would have otherwise accrued. The impact of this is much reduced by the amendments made by *FA 2009*, the effect of which is to allow deductions on an accruals basis where the counterparty to the debt is (broadly speaking) in a territory with which the UK has an appropriate double taxation treaty.

CTA 2009, s 361 may cause there to be a deemed release by a creditor company of an amount where it acquires a loan relationship for less than its face value and the debtor is a connected party. The debtor company may therefore suffer a tax charge on that deemed release. Note that these rules have been substantially amended by *FA 2010, Sch 16.*

CTA 2009, s 358 may prevent a charge arising between connected companies on the release of a debt.

CTA 2009, Pt 5, Ch 6 contains the rules for impairment losses between parties having a connection or becoming connected. *CTA 2009, Pt 5, Ch 4* provides for the continuity of treatment where a loan relationship is transferred between members of a group of companies (within the capital gains tax meaning). It is broadly intended to provide for a tax-neutral transfer, whatever the actual value paid on the transfer.

CTA 2009, ss 373–379 has a provision which is very similar to *TCGA 1992, s 179*. It provides for a deemed assignment and reacquisition at market value where a company has acquired a loan relationship within a group and leaves the group within six years. This will obviously only give rise to a charge in practice where the value of the loan relationship was not equal to the carrying value at the time of the transfer.

CTA 2009, s 407 applies to deeply discounted securities, and provides for a deferral of the discount accrual where the parties are connected until the time of redemption of the security. There are equivalent amendments to the late-paid interest rules made by *FA 2009* in this provision.

Derivative contracts

6.73 The derivative contracts regime formerly in *FA 2002, Sch 26* and now re-written to *CTA 2009, Pt 7,* also contains provisions which apply between connected parties and groups. In particular, *CTA 2009, Pt 7, Ch 5* contains provisions on continuity within groups and transferees leaving groups which are modelled on the equivalent loan relationships provisions.

Intangibles

6.74 *CTA 2009, Pt 8* contains its own particular group regime in relation to intangible assets, which is similar to the chargeable gains tax system. The provisions provide for tax-neutral transfers within a group and for a degrouping charge, and there is an exemption for companies leaving the group together in the same way as for chargeable gains (see *CTA 2009, Pt 8, Chs 8* and 9).

Note that there is an important difference between the degrouping charge for chargeable assets, under the capital gains regime, and for chargeable intangible assets, under *CTA 2009, Pt 8*. The new rules for the degrouping charge for chargeable assets do not apply to chargeable intangible assets, so that the degrouping gain for chargeable intangible asset still arises in the company leaving the group, not in the disposing company, as for chargeable assets.

CTA 2009, Pt 8, Ch 13 provides for general rules in transactions between related parties, and *CTA 2009, s 851* provides for deferral of accrual of debits if they are not paid within 12 months of the accounting period in which the debit would otherwise accrue (whether or not the recipient accrues the receipt within the charge to corporation tax).

GROUP PAYMENT ARRANGEMENTS

6.75 *FA 1998, s 36* permits HMRC to enter into 'arrangements' for the payment of tax for a group to be made by one designated member. This is done by way of contract with HMRC, and the standard form contract is published on HMRC's website, together with guidance notes.

The arrangements are purely administrative, and *FA 1998, s 36(3)* specifically provides that it shall not affect the liability of any company for corporation tax. The group payment arrangements (GPA) contract provides that HMRC will not pursue individual companies for tax until after the final filing date for corporation tax for all the companies in the group.

The contract only provides for arrangements between the companies and HMRC, and does not deal with arrangements between the companies themselves. It is obviously necessary for there to be some arrangements between the group members and the representative member for the payment of tax. Tax advisers need to take account of these arrangements in the context of company sales and purchases and ensure that agreement is reached, and/or an indemnity obtained in respect of the apportionment of payments under the GPA.

Chapter 7

Reorganisations and reconstructions

Pete Miller CTA (Fellow), Partner, The Miller Partnership

SIGNPOSTS

- **Reorganisations** – A reorganisation of a company's share capital is effectively tax free. It is not treated as a disposal or an acquisition and the new shares/securities effectively stand in the shoes of the original shares (**7.3** *et seq*).
- **Conversions of securities** – The treatment of conversions of securities is similarly tax free (**7.8** *et seq.*).
- **Share-for-share exchanges** – Share-for-share exchanges, schemes of reconstruction and conversions of securities are treated in the same way, so far as possible (**7.12**).
- **Cash consideration given** – Any cash given is taken into account for capital gains tax purposes as further consideration enhancing the base cost of the new shares or securities (**7.6**).
- **Cash received** – Any cash received in such transactions is treated as a part disposal of the holdings (**7.6**).
- **QCB exchanges** – In share-for-debenture exchanges, where the debenture is a qualifying corporate bond, the gain is computed at the time of the exchange and comes into charge when the bonds are redeemed or otherwise disposed of (**7.17** *et seq*).
- **Different rules for stamp taxes** – The rules for stamp taxes do not follow those for capital gains, although there are acquisition reliefs and reconstructions reliefs available (**7.34**).

INTRODUCTION

7.1 This chapter covers a number of transactions, collectively referred to as 'reorganisations' or 'reconstructions', which are largely tax free. These include actual reorganisations of a company's share capital, certain transactions that are treated as if they were reorganisations of share capital and more complex schemes of reconstruction, such as mergers and demergers.

This chapter perforce is only an overview of complex legislation. For a more detailed discussion of most of the issues, consult *Taxation of Company Reorganisations* by Pete Miller and others (Bloomsbury Professional).

REORGANISATIONS OF SHARE CAPITAL

Effect of the legislation

7.2 The effect of the legislation is best summed up by quoting the provision directly: 'a reorganisation shall not be treated as involving any disposal of the original shares or any acquisition of the new holding or any part of it, but the original shares (taken as a single asset) and the new holding (taken as a single asset) shall be treated as the same asset acquired as the original shares were acquired' (*TCGA 1992, s 127*).

In other words, the 'original shares' and the 'new holding' (see below) are treated as being the same asset for capital gains tax purposes and there is no disposal or acquisition. So the new holding is treated as having been acquired at the same time and for the same price as the original shares. This is often referred to as the 'no disposal fiction'.

Meaning of 'reorganisation'

7.3 The relevant provisions apply to a reorganisation or reduction of share capital. The shares held before the reorganisation are referred to as the 'original shares' and the shares or debentures held afterwards are called the 'new holding'. In *Unilever (UK) Holdings Ltd v Smith* 76 TC 300 a class of preference shares was cancelled and the shareholders were paid off. The company argued that this was a reorganisation but the court held that there was no identifiable new holding when an entire class of shares is cancelled, so the transaction was not a reorganisation.

It is clear, however, that a reorganisation can also include converting share capital into other securities (*TCGA 1992, s 126(1)*). The conversion of other securities into share capital is also treated as a reorganisation by virtue of *TCGA 1992, s 132* (see below).

'Reorganisation' is not specifically defined in either tax law or company law. On the plain English approach, it is taken to refer to a company organising its share capital differently.

Example 7.1 – Reorganisation of share capital

Albert subscribed for the issued share capital of Company A, 100 £1 shares, in June 2008. Company A reorganises the £1 shares into 10p shares, so that the issued share capital now comprises 1,000 10p shares.

Since this is a reorganisation, Albert's shareholding still has a capital gains base cost of £100 and the shares are treated as having been acquired in June 2008. The reorganisation of the share capital is not treated as a disposal.

Increases in share capital

7.4 In *Dunstan v Young, Austen & Young Ltd* 61 TC 448, the company successfully argued that an issue of shares to its parent was a reorganisation within the general meaning of the word and it is now accepted that the general meaning of a reorganisation can include share increases. However, a reorganisation requires the continued identity of the shareholders (of each class) holding their shares in the same proportions.

Focus

Not all changes to a company's share capital will be a reorganisation. The transaction must fall within the general meaning of 'reorganisation' or one of the specific inclusions.

Increases in share capital by, for example, bonus issue or rights issue are specifically deemed to be reorganisations for these purposes, as long as the allotments of shares or debentures are in proportion to the original holdings (*TCGA 1992, s 126(2)(a)*).

The alteration of rights of any class of shares, where there are more than one class, are also deemed to be reorganisations (*TCGA 1992, s 126(2)(b)*).

Example 7.2 – Bonus issue of shares

Basil and Claude bought the shares of Company B for £1,500 each in August 2001. They each own 50 £1 shares. In order to increase its capital, it issues 450 £1 bonus shares to each shareholder, so that they each have 500 £1 shares.

Since this is a reorganisation, Basil and Claude are not treated as having disposed of their original shares (which they clearly have not, anyway), nor as having acquired the new shares. Their capital gains base cost is still £1,500 each, treated as having been incurred in August 2001.

It is not immediately obvious from the legislation whether changing the rights on shares to increase the number of classes of share capital necessarily constitutes a reorganisation, such as a company converting its single class of ordinary shares into A and B shares prior to a demerger. An example might be a company that has two shareholders, each with 50 £1 ordinary shares, which reorganises its capital so that one shareholder now had 50 £1 A shares and the other has 50 £1 B shares, which is a common change as part of many demergers.

Following the principle established in *Dunstan v Young, Austen & Young Ltd*, we would say that the same shareholders hold the capital of the company in the same proportions, which indicates that the transaction is a reorganisation on first principles. This is an important step in many demergers and we are not aware that HMRC have ever questioned this analysis.

Reductions of share capital

7.5 Not every reduction is a reorganisation. Specifically, the paying off of redeemable share capital is not a reduction of share capital that is treated as a reorganisation. Instead, it is treated as a disposal for tax purposes and reorganisation treatment is not available.

The exception to this rule is where the consideration for the redemption of the redeemable shares is newly issued shares or debentures, so the 'redemption' of redeemable shares by issuing new share capital or debentures will be a reorganisation. Similarly, this rule does not apply where the shares are redeemed in a liquidation (*TCGA 1992, s 126(3)*).

It is not clear whether all other reductions of capital are reorganisations, or whether they are required to satisfy the principle established in *Dunstan v Young, Austen & Young Ltd* (above). The uncertainty is because *Dunstan v Young, Austen & Young Ltd* applied to the definition of a reorganisation on first principles, as in *TCGA 1992, s 126(1)*, which refers to 'a reorganisation or reduction of a company's share capital'. So the principles may only apply to a reorganisation and not to a reduction of share capital.

Consideration given or received

7.6 The basic tax treatment of a reorganisation is based on the policy that the shareholder has not actually given or received any value in respect of the reorganisation. If value is given or received, the policy requires adjustment.

Where additional consideration, such as payment for a rights issue, is given for a new holding on a reorganisation, that extra consideration is to be treated as having been given for the original shares (as part of the composite asset fiction). This includes incurring the liability to give additional consideration. However, the surrender, cancellation or other alteration of the original shares or the rights attached to them is not consideration, and nor is the application of value which is, in effect, derived from the assets of the company itself, such as profits or revaluation reserves used to pay up new share capital (*TCGA 1992, s 128(1), (2)*).

The consideration given cannot increase the base cost of a new holding by more than the actual increase in value achieved by an injection of capital on an arm's-length transaction. This amendment was following the *Young, Austen & Young* case, as the consideration given for the new shares was greatly in excess of the market value of the shares issued, which was nil (*TCGA 1992, s 128(2)*).

Where new consideration is given, any indexation allowance will run from the time at which the consideration is given or becomes liable to be given (*TCGA 1992, s 131*).

Where a shareholder receives consideration on a reorganisation, apart from the new holding itself, the shareholder is treated as having made a part disposal of the original shares in return for that consideration. This means that the base cost of the original holding is reduced, as for any part-disposal computation, although for all other purposes the no-disposal and composite asset fiction is maintained.

The receipt of consideration includes consideration from other shareholders for surrendering rights derived from the original shares, as well as any consideration deemed to have accrued on a capital distribution under *TCGA 1992, s 122* (*TCGA 1992, s 128(3)*).

Example 7.3 – Rights issue

Company C has 100,000 issued £1 shares. In order to increase its capital, it offers shareholders a 1 for 1 rights issue (ie each current shareholder can subscribe for 1 new share for each share they already hold). The price is £2.50 a share.

A corporate shareholder, Desmond Ltd, holds 1,000 shares, for which it was an original subscriber at £1 per share. Desmond Ltd takes up its rights, paying £2,500 for the 1,000 extra shares in January 2011. Desmond now has 2,000 shares with a total base cost of £3,500. However, indexation allowance for the recently paid £2,500 only runs from January 2011.

Apportionment of base cost

7.7 Where any part of a new holding is disposed of or deemed to be disposed of by this provision, the base cost of the shares or securities comprising the new holding must be apportioned by reference to the market value of the shares or securities at the date of disposal. HMRC's view is that this means that the base cost is apportioned by reference to the market value of the part disposed of divided by the market value of the entire holding (*TCGA 1992, s 129*; see also CG51892).

There are special computational rules for the apportionment of base costs where the new holding consists of more than one class of shares or debentures, or more than one class of rights in a unit trust, and one or more of those classes or shares or units are quoted on a recognised stock exchange (in the case of shares or debentures) or have published prices (in the case of units) and the listings occurred within three months of the date of the reorganisation. In these cases, the base cost of the different classes of share, debenture or unit is by reference to the market value on the first day on which market values or prices were quoted, whether or not the reorganisation has taken place at that time (*TCGA 1992, s 130*).

HMRC say that this 'gives the taxpayer the advantage of knowing the base cost of his shares in advance of any disposal' and that it also avoids 'difficulties with the interaction between the reorganisation provisions and the pooling rules of section 104 TCGA'.

Conversions of securities

7.8 Broadly, a conversion of securities should be treated as a reorganisation for tax purposes, with 'necessary adaptations' to the rules in *TCGA 1992, ss 127–131*. This deemed equivalence to a reorganisation of share capital tells us that the securities held before the conversion should be treated as if they were the 'original shares' and the securities held after the conversion should be treated as the 'new holding'. Therefore, the converted securities are treated for capital gains purposes as having been acquired at the same time and at the same cost as the original securities (*TCGA 1992, s 132(1)*).

The legislation gives a non-exhaustive list of the transactions to which this rule will apply (*TCGA 1992, s 132(3)*):

- a conversion of securities of a company into shares in the company;
- a conversion of a security which is not a qualifying corporate bond into a security of the same company which is such a bond;
- a conversion of a qualifying corporate bond (QCB) into a security which is a security of the same company but is not such a bond;

- a conversion at the option of the holder of the securities converted as an alternative to the redemption of those securities for cash;
- any exchange of securities effected in pursuance of any enactment (including an enactment passed after this Act) which provides for the compulsory acquisition of any shares or securities and the issue of securities or other securities instead (this is rare these days but this occurred when an industry or business was taken into public ownership (such as nationalisation of an industry) and the shareholders were given government bonds in exchange).

The conversions of a non-QCB into a QCB or vice versa are dealt with by *TCGA 1992, s 116*, but a transaction only gets into that provision by being a transaction to which *TCGA 1992, s 135* would otherwise apply. So conversions to or from a QCB are deemed to be within *TCGA 1992, s 135* so that *TCGA 1992, s 116* can then apply. In the case of *Hancock* [2016] UKUT 81 (TCC), it was decided that *TCGA 1992, s 132* applies to each conversion of a type of security separately. Thus, if *TCGA 1992, s 116* is in point, that provision also applies to each separate type of security, not to a mixed portfolio of securities (as was argued by Mr and Mrs Hancock) (see **7.21**).

The rules apply regardless of whether the conversion is effected by a transaction or occurs in consequence of the operation of the terms of any security or debenture. This change followed the case of *Harding v HMRC* 79 TC 885. Mr Harding purported to have a security that changed its status without a transaction, by the use of a clause that expired after a set period of time, and claimed that the redemption of the bond escaped taxation altogether. HMRC won the case, but the legislation was amended to avoid further doubt.

For the purposes of this legislation, 'security' includes any loan stock or similar security whether of the government of the UK or of any other government, or of any public or local authority in the UK or elsewhere, or of any company, and whether secured or unsecured (*TCGA 1992, s 132(3)*).

Certain debentures, issued on or after 16 March 1993, are deemed to be securities (*TCGA 1992, s 251(6)*). The rules for conversions of securities apply to these, too, so that a conversion of such debentures into QCBs, or a conversion of a QCB into a debenture that is deemed to be a security, are also treated as reorganisations (*TCGA 1992, s 132(4), (5)*).

Premiums received on conversions of securities

7.9 The normal case is to tax the premium as a part disposal of the securities under *TCGA 1992, s 128* (with any 'necessary adaptations').

When the premium received is small compared to the value of the securities, there is a mandatory alternative approach, whereby the premium is deducted from the base cost of the converted securities. In effect, this defers any gain until the securities are disposed of (*TCGA 1992, s 133(2)*).

The meaning of 'small' in this context is not defined but HMRC will usually accept that 'small' means less than 5% of the value or less than £3,000, even if that exceeds 5% of the value of the securities. There may be cases where a premium in excess of 5% of the value of the securities should be treated as being small or where a premium of less than 5% should not be treated as small. These cases will be decided on their merits (see CG57836 and RI 164 (February 1997)).

Where the premium exceeds the allowable expenditure (ie the base cost), this provision does not apply so the premium would be charged to tax in the normal way. However, the recipient can elect that only the excess of the premium over base cost is to be charged, instead. If this election is made, then no base cost of the securities is available to set against the proceeds of any subsequent disposal (*TCGA 1992, s 133(4)*).

There are similar provisions for any cash received on the redenomination of a security into euros from the original currency in which it was denominated on issue (*TCGA 1992, s 133A*).

Compensation stock

7.10 There are special rules for the compulsory acquisition of shares in return for gilt-edged stock, which was most likely to occur on a nationalisation. This legislation requires a gain or loss to be computed as if the shares had been sold at the exchange value deemed by the enabling (nationalising) legislation. The gain (or loss) will then come into effect when the gilt-edged securities are eventually disposed of by sale, redemption, etc. A disposal of only part of the holding of gilt-edged securities will bring into charge an appropriate part of the gain (*TCGA 1992, s 134*).

Stamp duty and reorganisations of share capital

7.11 In general, a reorganisation of share capital does not carry a charge to stamp duty, as there is no transfer of a security. However, a company purchasing its own shares under *Companies Act 2006, s 690* is chargeable to stamp duty under *FA 1986, s 67*.

SHARE-FOR-SHARE EXCHANGES

Introduction

7.12 The issue of shares or debentures in one company in exchange for the shares or debentures in another is not a reorganisation of share capital. However, it is treated as one for capital gains tax purposes, with the necessary adaptations, so long as the appropriate conditions are satisfied. The treatment of such transactions as reorganisations is mandatory and there is no option for a shareholder to choose to have the transaction treated as a disposal (*TCGA 1992, s 135(1), (3)*).

Generally, the treatment of share-for-share exchanges as if they were reorganisations of share capital will only apply if the transactions are carried out for bona fide commercial reasons and not for the avoidance of capital gains tax or corporation tax (unless the members concerned, along with persons connected with them, do not hold more than 5% of the relevant class of shares or debentures of the original company). Pre-transaction clearance to that effect can be obtained from HMRC (*TCGA 1992, ss 135(6), 137(1), (2), 138*). A sample letter applying to HMRC for pre-transaction clearance is attached at the end of this chapter.

Transactions affected

7.13 The fundamental requirement is that there be a disposal by a person of shares or debentures to a company, which then issues shares or debentures as consideration (or as part of the consideration) for the acquisition. It does not matter whether this is an intra-group transaction or an acquisition (*TCGA 1992, s 135(1)*).

There are three circumstances to which the reorganisations treatment applies (*TCGA 1992, s 135(2)*):

Case 1 – Where the acquiring company holds, or in consequence of the exchange will hold more than 25% of the ordinary share capital of the target company. If the acquiring company already holds at least 25% of the ordinary share capital of the target, any further transfer of shares or debentures in the target company to the acquiring company in exchange for the issue of shares or debentures will satisfy Case 1.

The ordinary share capital of a company is defined in *CTA 2010, s 1119* ('all the company's issued share capital (however described), other than capital the holders of which have a right to a dividend at a fixed rate but have no other right to share in the company's profits'). For the purposes of this rule, however, it also includes units in unit trusts and, for companies without share capital, it includes any interests in the company possessed by members of the company (*TCGA 1992, s 135(4), (5)*).

Case 2 – Where the acquiring company issues the shares or debentures in exchange for shares as a result of a general offer made to members of the target company or any class of them (with or without exceptions for persons connected with the acquiring company). The offer must be made in the first instance on a condition such that if it were satisfied the acquiring company would have control of the target company. This Case is more relevant to takeovers of public companies or other companies with many shareholders. Usually, the offer is conditional upon the acquiring company receiving sufficient acceptances to give it control of the target company. The initial terms of the offer are the critical factor here and CG52525 clarifies HMRC's view that Case 2 is satisfied even if the condition is dropped whilst the offer is still open. If the condition were to be dropped and the acquiring company did not receive sufficient acceptances to give it control, Case 2 would nevertheless have been satisfied in respect of any shares exchanged as a result of the offer.

Case 3 – Where the acquiring company holds or in consequence of the exchange will hold the greater part of the voting power in the target company. This Case was introduced to comply with EU law following the introduction of the EU Mergers Directive (Council Directive 90/434/EEC of 23 July 1990 on the common system of taxation applicable to mergers, divisions, transfers of assets and exchanges of shares concerning companies of different Member States (as amended)).

There is no requirement that either party involved in the transaction be UK resident. So, subject to the anti-avoidance provisions, neither the acquirer nor the target company need be UK resident. Obviously, the vendor must be UK resident for there to be a charge to tax in the UK to which the provision can apply.

> **Focus**
>
> Not all share-for-share exchanges will satisfy these conditions and it is important to ensure that the vendor does not have an unexpected tax charge.

Effect of share exchanges

7.14 If there is an exchange that satisfies one of the Cases, the shares issued by the acquiring company are to be taken as being the same as the shares that it acquires in the target on the exchange. So the original shareholders of the target company are treated as having acquired their shares in the acquiring company at the same time and for the same cost as their original shareholdings in the target company. The effect of the legislation is to roll over any gain arising on the disposal of the target company shares until there is a disposal of the shares issued by the acquiring company (*TCGA 1992, s 135(3)*).

In essence, the legislation applies the two fictions of the reorganisation provisions: the no-disposal fiction and the single composite asset fiction.

All the other consequences of *TCGA 1992, ss 127–131*, such as consideration received or given as part of the exchange transaction, will also apply as appropriately adapted.

The legislation is silent as to what 'necessary adaptations' are required to enable a share-for-share exchange to be treated as a reorganisation.

Example 7.4 – Share-for-share exchange

Fred owns Company D and Company E and had paid £100,000 for each company. He decides that he wants to form a group with them, so he sells Company D to Company E and, as consideration, Company E issues more shares to Fred. This is a share-for-share exchange and Company E now owns all the shares of Company D, satisfying Case 1 and Case 3.

Fred is therefore treated as not having disposed of Company D. The capital gains base cost of his shares in Company E is £200,000, being the combined original base cost of the companies.

Incidentally, Company E is treated as having the market value base cost in Company D, by virtue of *TCGA 1992, s 171(3)*. (See also *Westcott v Woolcombers Ltd*, 60 TC 575 and *NAP Holdings (UK) Ltd v Whittles*, 67 TC 166.)

Where the consideration is an issue of debentures, we have two possibilities, depending on whether the debentures are qualifying corporate bonds or not (QCBs or non-QCBs) (see **7.19** below).

In general, therefore, a disposal of shares by a company in return for debentures will be dealt with under *TCGA 1992, s 116* (see below), as will a disposal of shares by an individual in return for debentures that are QCBs. For the corporate shareholder, any future gain or loss on the QCB will be dealt with under the loan relationships legislation (**6.71** *et seq*).

A disposal of shares by an individual in return for non-QCBs will be treated as a reorganisation of share capital, so that the shareholder (now a bondholder) is treated as not having made a disposal. The QCBs will have a capital gains base cost the same as the original shares.

Interaction with capital gains degrouping charge

7.15 Where a target company leaves a group as a result of a share-for-share exchange, it may be holding assets transferred to it within the last six years, and so be potentially subject to the capital gains degrouping charge (**6.33** *et seq*). Under the rules introduced by *FA 2011, Sch 10*, the gain on the deemed disposal and reacquisition of those assets is to be held over until there is a chargeable disposal of the new holding, ie the shares issued by the acquiring company on the exchange (*TCGA 1992, s 179(3E)*).

Stamp duty and share exchanges

7.16 In general, an exchange of shares will carry a charge to stamp duty at 0.5%. However, there is a relief for acquisition of the whole of the share capital of a company, at *FA 1986, s 77*, subject to the conditions for relief being satisfied. Broadly, those conditions are:

- the acquisition is effected for bona fide commercial reasons and does not form part of a scheme or arrangement of which the main purpose, or one of the main purposes, is avoidance of liability to stamp duty, stamp duty reserve tax, income tax, corporation tax or capital gains tax;
- the consideration for the acquisition consists only of the issue of shares in the acquiring company to the shareholders of the target company, so that after the acquisition each person who immediately before it was made was a shareholder of the target company is a shareholder of the acquiring company;
- after the acquisition has been made, the shareholdings in the acquiring company are proportionately identical to the shareholdings in the target company.

This relief clearly does not apply to exchanges in return for debentures, as it fails the initial test of involving an issue of shares.

There is no formal clearance for the availability of this relief. In practice, HMRC will usually accept that it applies in cases where they also accept the bona fide commercial reasons for the transaction for capital gains tax purposes. But this cannot be relied upon. For example, the transaction may have a component involving avoidance of stamp duty reserve tax, which would mean that the stamp duty relief would not be available but would have no bearing on the availability of the capital gains relief (which is only restricted where there is an intention to avoid capital gains tax or corporation tax).

The position is complicated further by *FA 1986, s 77A*, introduced by *FA 2016, s 136* for documents executed on or after 29 June 2016. *FA 1986, s 77A* denies stamp duty relief under *FA 1986, s 77* where it is reasonable to assume that one of the purposes of the transaction is to secure a change of control of the original company. There is an exemption for mergers but this provision will be important for share exchanges that precede certain demergers (see **5.22** and **5.25**, and **Example 5.5** at Step 1).

Where the relief from stamp duty is not available, the transaction may be carried out by a reduction of capital, instead (see **5.21**).

EXCHANGES INVOLVING QUALIFYING CORPORATE BONDS (QCBs)

Introduction

7.17 QCBs are exempt from capital gains tax under *TCGA 1992, s 115* (the same provision that takes gilt-edged securities out of the scope of capital gains tax). Where there is a conversion to which *TCGA 1992, s 132* applies, or an exchange to which *TCGA 1992, s 135* applies, the normal reorganisation rules will not work without special provision. For example, in the absence of specific rules, shares standing at a large gain could be converted (actually or by exchange) into QCBs, which would then be exempt from tax, offering a major avoidance opportunity.

The rules apply to any transaction that would otherwise be or be treated as if it were a reorganisation of share capital, where either the original shares or the new holding, but not both, would be or contain a QCB. A transaction in this context includes a conversion of securities as defined by *TCGA 1992, s 132*, even if this is effected without a transaction (*TCGA 1992, s 116(1), (2)*).

Where these rules apply, the reorganisation provisions are disapplied from any transaction which involves a QCB and the new asset is treated as having been acquired when it actually was acquired, rather than when the original asset was acquired (*TCGA 1992, s 116(5), (6)*).

What is a QCB?

7.18 For the purposes of corporation tax (ie for a corporate bond-holder), a QCB is any asset representing a loan relationship of a company (*TCGA 1992, s 117(A1)*).

Broadly speaking, for any other tax purposes (ie a non-corporate bond-holder) a corporate bond is a security that has at all times represented a normal commercial loan (as defined by *CTA 2010, Ch 6, Pt 5*) and which is expressed in sterling with no provision made for conversion or redemption into any other currency.

Generally, a non-convertible debenture denominated in sterling and issued on normal commercial terms will be a QCB (*TCGA 1992, s 117(A1), (1)*).

The important issue here is that the status of an instrument as a QCB depends on the holder. Since 'any asset representing a loan relationship of a company' is a QCB, any security issued in a reorganisation or deemed reorganisation will be a QCB if it is issued to a company.

If it is issued to an individual, as is common, particularly in the private equity field, then the status of an instrument as a QCB or not will depend on its terms. This was important as individuals were often concerned to ensure that they had an adequate holding period for the purposes of business asset taper relief, in which case they would want to receive non-QCBs in a share-for-debenture exchange, so that the instrument would continue to qualify for the relief. However, since business asset taper relief was abolished in 2008, and entrepreneurs' relief operates rather differently, these considerations are likely to be less relevant in future transactions.

There are two common methods of ensuring that the loan notes do not constitute QCBs. One is to incorporate a provision into the loan note instruments enabling them to be converted into a currency other than sterling at a date prior to the redemption date, which would mean that the loan note fails the condition of *TCGA 1992, s 117(1)(b)* that it be expressed and redeemable in sterling. This was challenged in the case of *Nicholas Trigg*, where the First-tier Tribunal decided ([2014] UKFTT 967 (TC)) that clauses allowing conversion into Euro-denominated bonds did not mean that certain bonds were non-QCBs. However, this decision was overturned by the Upper Tribunal ([2016] UKUT 165 (TCC)).

The other method is to incorporate a provision into the loan note instruments enabling the holder to subscribe for additional shares or securities, which would mean that the QCBs do not represent a 'normal commercial loan' as defined in *CTA 2010, Ch 6, Pt 5*.

> **Focus**
>
> HMRC scrutinise the terms of corporate bonds and may challenge whether the terms are sufficiently robust to ensure that a corporate bond is not a qualifying bond. Proper legal advice on the terms of the bond is essential.

Exchanges of QCBs for non-QCBs

7.19 If the original holding consists of QCBs, the exchange, conversion or reorganisation is treated as a disposal of the QCBs, exempt from tax on gains, and the shares or debentures issued in the transaction are treated as being acquired at market value, ie the reorganisation provisions are disapplied and there is a market value acquisition of the new holding. So the no-disposal fiction and the single composite asset fiction do not apply in these circumstances (*TCGA 1992, s 116(9)*).

If, on the exchange, some cash consideration is also given by the vendor, the total cost of the non-QCB for capital gains tax purposes, ie its base cost on a future disposal, is the market value of the QCB plus the cash consideration given (*TCGA 1992, s 116(8)*).

If cash consideration is received on the exchange, this is deducted from the base cost of the non-QCB. This is completely logical: the vendor has disposed of an asset worth £X for consideration with a total value of £X. If he receives £Y in cash, the deemed cost of the new asset must be £(X–Y) (*TCGA 1992, s 116(7)*).

Exchanges of shares or of non-QCBs for QCBs

7.20 If, on the other hand, shares or non-QCB debentures are exchanged for or converted into QCBs, the original securities are treated as not having been disposed of, but the gain that would otherwise have accrued at the time of the exchange is held over. That gain (or loss) then comes into charge when there is an actual disposal of the QCB. If only part of the QCB holding is disposed of, then an appropriate part of the gain or loss is deemed to accrue.

If cash consideration is also given in a non-QCB for QCB transaction, this is taken into account to reduce the held-over gain under *TCGA 1992, s 116(10)* (*TCGA 1992, s 116(6), (8)*).

If cash consideration is received by the vendor in such an exchange, this is charged to tax on the basis of the proportion of the market value of the old asset represented by the cash consideration. So, for example, if the cash represents half the value of the old asset, half the chargeable gain is chargeable immediately and the other half is rolled over to come into charge on disposal of the QCBs.

If there is such a charge on cash received, this gain is then deducted from the gains coming into charge when there is a disposal of the whole or part of the QCB, to prevent double taxation.

However, if the cash receipt is small in comparison to the market value of the old asset, this provision is not applied, 'to avoid the delay and expense of a full computation where this would be disproportionate, and to avoid the need for assessments in trivial cases' (RI 164). In such a case, therefore, the entire gain is rolled over into the new QCBs, and the sum received appears to escape taxation. In most cases, HMRC will accept that 'small', for these purposes, means less than 5% of the value or less than £3,000, even if that exceeds 5% of the value of the securities (see above) (*TCGA 1992, s 116(7), (12), (13), (14)*).

In this context, 'disposal' of the QCB is wider in meaning than just a sale. In particular, redemption or waiving of the security will also constitute a disposal in this context.

These provisions only apply to gains held over in the relevant transaction. So if the QCB increases or decreases in value before eventual disposal, that increase or decrease is outside the scope of capital gains tax, although it may be chargeable on a company under the loan relationships legislation (*TCGA 1992, s 116(10)*). One impact of this is that the charge comes into force even if the QCB is subsequently worthless. There is no capital loss relief for any reduction in value of a QCB (unless the QCB was issued before 17 March 1998 and the now repealed provisions of *TCGA 1992, s 254* apply (*TCGA 1992, s 116(15)*).

Focus

Where a gain is held over into a QCB, but the borrower becomes insolvent, it is very difficult to avoid the gain coming into charge. It might be worth considering insurance or a bank guarantee of the bonds so the vendor does not end up with a 'dry' tax charge.

A held-over gain does not come into charge if the disposal is within one of the following categories:

- husband and wife transfers (*TCGA 1992, s 58(1)*);
- transfers to a legatee on death (*TCGA 1992, s 62(4)*);
- intra-group transfers between UK-resident companies (*TCGA 1992, s 171(1)*);
- incorporation of a UK permanent establishment of a company resident in another Member State (*TCGA 1992, s 140A*);
- merger to form a company which is UK resident or has a UK permanent establishment (*TCGA 1992, s 140E*).

In each of these cases, however, the recipient under any of these provisions will suffer the held-over tax charge on the eventual disposal of the securities (*TCGA 1992, s 116(11)*).

Example 7.5 – Conversion of QCBs

Gregory holds loan notes (a form of debenture) of F Plc, a listed company. The loan notes are QCBs and are currently worth £10,000. The company decides to capitalise its debt by conversion into shares and issues Gregory with 173 shares, which have a market value of £10,200 at the date of issue.

For the purposes of capital gains tax, the 173 shares of F Plc have a base cost of £10,200, ie market value. The disposal of the loan notes is outside the scope of capital gains tax.

Example 7.6 – Redemption of QCBs

Harvey Ltd, an investment company, has a wholly-owned subsidiary, Impasse Ltd, which it sells for £15m. All of the consideration is in the form of loan notes, which are therefore QCBs for Harvey Ltd. The loan notes will be redeemed at £1m a year starting on the 5th anniversary of the sale.

There is no actual gain on the disposal but the putative gain is computed (and the substantial shareholdings exemption does not apply). As each tranche of loan notes is redeemed, one-fifteenth of the gain comes into charge on Harvey Ltd.

Note that the charge arises on disposals of the loan notes. So an appropriate proportion of the charge would arise if Harvey Ltd were to sell any of them or if any of the loan notes were to be extinguished, eg on a liquidation of the issuer.

7.21 *TCGA 1992, s 116(1)(b)* applies, *inter alia*, where '… the original shares would consist of or include a qualifying corporate bond and the new holding would not …'. This implies that *TCGA 1992, s 116* cannot be applied to a situation where the starting point is a mixture of QCBs and non-QCBs and the portfolio is wholly converted into QCBs. This analysis was successfully relied upon by the taxpayers (or non-payers) in *Anthony and Tracy Lee Hancock*, where the First-tier Tribunal decided ([2014] UKFTT 695 (TC)) that a mixed holding was converted into all QCBs, then redeemed free of capital gains tax by virtue of the exemption in *TCGA 1992, s 115*. This decision was overturned by the Upper Tribunal ([2016] UKUT 81 (TCC)), and the Court of Appeal upheld the Upper Tribunal's decision ([2017] EWCA Civ 198) (see **7.8**).

SCHEMES OF RECONSTRUCTION

Introduction

7.22 Schemes of reconstruction can also be treated as if they were reorganisations of share capital. Broadly, the principles are the same as for exchanges, with the new holding being treated as if it were the same as the original shares, acquired at the same time and at the same price.

Definition of a scheme of reconstruction

7.23 Broadly, a scheme of reconstruction requires the business carried on by one or more original companies to be carried on by one or more successor companies and it requires the shareholders of the original company or companies, taken together, to be the same as the shareholders of the successor company or companies, taken together.

The definition refers to any 'scheme of merger, division or other restructuring', and so attempts to cover every possible restructuring of corporate-owned businesses. So it covers the situations where:

- one company splits into more than one company, each carrying on part of the business carried on by the original (a demerger);
- two or more companies merge all their businesses into one company (a merger or amalgamation);
- two or more companies mix and merge their businesses into more than one company.

At the same time, the definition of 'reconstruction' requires the shareholder base to be essentially maintained, even if it is split between more than one company.

There is no requirement that a scheme of reconstruction involves only UK companies. Although the tax consequences of a scheme of reconstruction will only be relevant to a company or shareholder that is UK resident for tax purposes, the other companies involved in the scheme need not be UK resident. Indeed, for there to be any such restriction might offend against some of the fundamental freedoms required by the EU, such as freedom of establishment and free movement of capital. So it is entirely possible to have, say, a scheme that involves all non-UK companies where the only person to whom the tax consequences matter is a UK-resident individual shareholder, but so long as the appropriate conditions are satisfied for the scheme to constitute a scheme of reconstruction, the shareholder should be able to claim the benefits of the relevant exemptions.

Essentially, the definition has four conditions, of which the first two, along with one other must be satisfied. However, preliminary reorganisations of share capital and subsequent issue of shares or debentures are disregarded, so in deciding whether the conditions are satisfied, we look at the position after any preliminary reorganisation and before any subsequent issues of shares or debentures (*TCGA 1992, Sch 5AA, paras 1, 6, 7*).

First and second conditions: pro rata issue of ordinary share capital

7.24 The scheme must involve the issue of ordinary share capital of one or more 'successor companies' to the shareholders of one or more 'original companies'. Alternatively, the scheme can involve the issue of shares to the shareholders of one or more classes of share of the original company or companies, so a scheme of reconstruction can be carried out without involving all the shareholders of the original company. The issue of shares must also be pro rata to the shareholders' rights as shareholders of the original company.

The ordinary share capital of a successor company or companies can only be issued to the holders of ordinary share capital of one or more original companies and to no one else, so a reconstruction is not a way of bringing new shareholders into a company or companies. It may well be possible to introduce new shareholders to a company either before or after carrying out a scheme of reconstruction, but the scheme of reconstruction itself requires that shares of the successor company or companies are only issued to shareholders of the original company or companies (*TCGA 1992, Sch 5AA, paras 2, 3*).

Issues of fixed rate capital or of debentures, which are less concerned with proprietary rights over the issuing companies, are excluded from the definition of reconstructions. This does not mean that fixed rate shares or debentures cannot be issued in a scheme of reconstruction, however, merely that there must be an issue of ordinary share capital for the scheme to qualify as a scheme of reconstruction in the first place.

Ordinary share capital means issued share capital other than fixed rate shares with no other rights of participation, as well as units in unit trust schemes and the interests of members in companies that do not have share capital (*TCGA 1992, Sch 5AA, para 8*).

Both the first (issue of ordinary share capital) and second (pro rata) conditions must be satisfied.

Third condition: continuity of business

7.25 The third condition has several alternative components:

- A single original company can be reconstructed into one or more successor companies. The condition is that the business or substantially the whole of the business carried on by the original company must, after the reconstruction, be carried on by a new company or by two or more successor companies, which may include the original company.
- There may be more than one original company, being reconstructed into a single company (a merger). Here the condition is that the businesses or substantially the whole of the businesses carried on by the original companies must, after the reconstruction, be carried on by the successor company, which can also be one of the original companies.
- Less commonly, there may be more than one original company being reconstructed into several successor companies. Here the condition is that the businesses or substantially the whole of the businesses carried on by the original companies must, after the reconstruction, be carried on by different successor companies, some or all of which can also be one of the original companies. That is, the businesses must have moved companies to be a scheme of reconstruction.

The activities of the successor companies are to be considered altogether in considering whether those activities constitute the whole or substantially the whole of the activities carried on by the original company or companies prior to the reconstruction. CG57027c gives a very simple example: imagine an original company with a retail and a manufacturing trade. This company is subject to a scheme of reconstruction whereby one successor company carries on the retail trade and another carries on the manufacturing trade. Taking the overall activities of the successor companies together, they constitute the whole of the activities of the original company.

Where groups of companies are involved, the group structure is largely ignored and the activities of a controlled company are treated as being the activities of the controlling company.

If any original companies retain assets to distribute as share capital on being wound up, this is ignored in considering whether the third condition is satisfied (*TCGA 1992, Sch 5AA, para 4*).

If the third condition is not satisfied, a transaction can still qualify as a scheme of reconstruction if the fourth condition is satisfied, instead.

Fourth condition: compromise or arrangement with members

7.26 This condition requires that the scheme be carried out pursuant to a compromise or arrangements under the 'arrangements and reconstruction rules' of *Companies Act 2006, Pt 26* in the UK or similar provisions applicable in other jurisdictions. No one, apart from the company or companies subject to the compromise or arrangements, can acquire any part of the business or businesses of the original company or companies (*TCGA 1992, Sch 5AA, para 5*).

> **Focus**
>
> HMRC will challenge transactions that they do not think qualify as schemes of reconstruction. It is imperative to take advice and to ensure that the appropriate conditions are satisfied.

THE RECONSTRUCTION RELIEFS

Introduction

7.27 Where there is a scheme of reconstruction, certain reliefs are available to both the shareholders of the companies concerned and, where appropriate, to the companies themselves. To see why these reliefs are necessary, let us look at a simple reconstruction.

> **Example 7.7 – Simple reconstruction**
>
> Company A is liquidated and transfers all its assets to a new company, company B, in consideration for which company B issues shares to the shareholders of company A.
>
> So far as the shareholders of company A are concerned, they still own a company carrying on the same business as before, they have not taken any money out of the corporate structure and nothing material has changed, but the capital gains legislation says that the shareholders have disposed of their shares in company A and received in consideration the shares in company B. Therefore, absent the exemption, the shareholders of company A would suffer a chargeable gain.
>
> Furthermore, company A has disposed of all its assets to company B, which should give rise to a chargeable gain, too.
>
> The reconstruction reliefs at *TCGA 1992, ss 136* and *139* prevent either charge applying (see **7.28** and **7.29**).

Shareholder and creditor reconstruction relief

7.28 The relief for shareholders treats the scheme of reconstruction as if it were a share-for-share exchange to which the reorganisation provisions can apply with 'necessary adaptations' (*TCGA 1992, ss 136(2), 135(3)*).

The relief requires an arrangement between a company and its shareholders or debenture holders, in connection with a scheme of reconstruction, whereby another company issues new shares or debentures to those shareholders or debenture holders pro rata to their holdings. There is also provision for the arrangements only to affect specific classes of share or debenture. This is similar in approach to *TCGA 1992, Sch 5AA*, with the added ability to involve debentures as well as shares (but not instead of shares or the transaction would fail Condition 1 in *TCGA 1992, Sch 5AA*).

This provision applies regardless of whether the originally held shares or debentures are retained or cancelled – in a simple reconstruction. In the example in the Introduction, where company A is liquidated, the shares would obviously be cancelled, whereas on a merger or a demerger it is likely that the original shares will be retained (*TCGA 1992, s 136(1)*).

Remember, however, that an issue of loan notes that are qualifying corporate bonds will invoke the hold-over provisions of *TCGA 1992, s 116.*

Note, also, that there is no requirement for the companies involved to be UK resident for tax purposes. The exemption relates to the tax charge on the shareholders and is not concerned with the residence status of the companies.

Preliminary reorganisations of the shareholdings of the original company are permitted and the relief applies *mutatis mutandis* to companies without share capital (but not to units of unit trusts, for some reason) (*TCGA 1992, s 136(3), (5)*).

The relief only applies if the scheme of reconstruction is carried out for bona fide commercial reasons and not part of a scheme or arrangement to avoid capital gains tax or corporation tax (unless the members concerned, along with persons connected with them, do not hold more than 5% of the relevant class of shares or debentures of the original company). Pre-transaction clearance to that effect can be obtained from HMRC (*TCGA 1992, ss 136(6), 137(1), (2), 138*). A sample letter applying to HMRC for pre-transaction clearance is attached at the end of this chapter.

Company reconstruction relief

7.29 Referring back to the example in the Introduction to this section, we see company A passing assets to company B. The reconstruction relief treats this transfer as being at no gain and no loss, so the successor company effectively inherits the original base cost, plus indexation, of the original company (*TCGA 1992, s 139(1)*).

The relief only applies if the scheme of reconstruction is carried out for bona fide commercial reasons and not part of a scheme or arrangement to avoid capital gains tax or corporation tax. Pre-transaction clearance to that effect can be obtained from HMRC (*TCGA 1992, ss 139(5), 138*). A sample letter applying to HMRC for pre-transaction clearance is attached at the end of this chapter.

For the exemption to apply there must be a transfer of a business or part of a business for no consideration from the perspective of the transferring company, except for taking on any of the debts of that business. The word 'business' is much wider than a trade and a transfer of a business is apt to include a wide range of activities. HMRC accept that the holding of subsidiaries is a 'business' for the purposes of this legislation, too, so the relief is available for the transfer of subsidiaries in a reconstruction, as well as for the transfer of businesses per se.

HMRC have always taken the view that 'a company's business' means a business (or subsidiary) that is at least 75% owned by the transferor company, although there is nothing in the statute to support this interpretation.

Both companies involved must be UK resident or carrying on a trade in the UK through a permanent establishment. That said, this provision is clearly contrary to EU legislation (The Treaty for the Functioning of the European Union prescribes the fundamental freedom to establish in any Member State and to move capital freely between Member States) and may be invalid, at least for transactions between EU Member States (*TCGA 1992, s 139(1A)*).

The relief does not apply to assets held as trading stock or to the transfer of a business into an authorised unit trust, a venture capital trust or an investment trust (*TCGA 1992, s 139(2), (4)*).

Interaction with capital gains degrouping charge

7.30 Where a company leaves a group as a result of a transfer under a scheme of reconstruction, it may be holding assets transferred to it within the last six years, and so be potentially subject to the capital gains degrouping charge (see **6.33**). Under the rules introduced by *FA 2011, Sch 10*, this charge would prima facie be treated as consideration received by the transferor company, which would breach the no consideration rule for this relief to apply. However, such deemed consideration is ignored for the purposes of that rule (*TCGA 1992, s 139(1B)*).

HMRC have also stated in correspondence that, in these circumstances, the degrouping charge just disappears. It does not fall on the transferor company and it is not held over until some later event. While this might appear to be a potentially useful tax-planning opportunity, it is important to remember that this relief only applies if the reconstruction is not part of a scheme for the avoidance of corporation tax, so clearance might be refused if a scheme of reconstruction were seen by HMRC as being intended to achieve a tax-free degrouping using this mechanism.

Interaction with the substantial shareholdings exemption

7.31 Where the business transferred is the holding of trading subsidiaries, the substantial shareholdings exemption might prima facie apply. However, that exemption specifically does not apply where there is a no gain, no loss transfer, such as under this reconstruction relief (*TCGA 1992, Sch 7AC, para 6(1)(a)*).

Tax liabilities

7.32 If a business transfer was not for bona fide commercial reasons or was for the avoidance of tax, and the transferor company has been wound up, the tax can be collected from the transferee company. If the tax is not paid within six months of the assessment, HMRC can claim a corresponding part of the unpaid tax from any other person who holds any of the assets in respect of the disposal of which the tax is charged, in so far as that person has acquired those assets through another scheme of reconstruction or by an intra-group transfer. Any person so charged to tax is entitled to try and recover both the tax and any interest charged from the original transferee company (*TCGA 1992, s 139(6), (7), (8)*).

Reconstructions and intangible fixed assets

7.33 The regime for intangible fixed assets (*CTA 2009, Pt 8*) effectively takes intangible fixed assets, created or acquired by a company since 31 March 2002, outside the capital gains regime (*CTA 2009, s 906(1)*).

Such assets, where a disposal would give rise to a credit or debit under *CTA 2009, Pt 8*, are referred to as 'chargeable intangible assets' (*CTA 2009, s 741(1)*).

A transfer of a business in a scheme of reconstruction can include the transfer of chargeable intangible assets, so *CTA 2009, Pt 8* contains a relief designed largely to mirror the provisions of *TCGA 1992, s 139*, with appropriate modifications for the different type of asset (*CTA 2009, s 818*).

The relief applies where there is a transfer of a business as part of a scheme of reconstruction and there is no consideration, apart from the assumption of debt (*CTA 2009, s 818(1)*).

The relief does not apply to intra-group transfers, or if either company is a qualifying friendly society entitled to exemption from tax or a dual-resident investing company (there is no obvious policy reason for the fact that these exclusions are very different from those for chargeable assets) (*CTA 2009, s 818(3), (4)*).

The relief also does not apply unless the transactions have been carried out for genuine commercial reasons and not as part of a scheme or arrangements for the avoidance of corporation tax, capital gains tax or income tax. Pre-transaction clearance that this is so can be obtained from HMRC (*CTA 2009, ss 818(5), 831, 832, 833*).

The transfer must include intangible fixed assets that are chargeable intangible assets to both the transferor and transferee companies, which mirrors the potentially unlawful residence requirements of *TCGA 1992, s 139(1A)*, as assets can only be chargeable intangible assets of UK-resident companies and UK trading permanent establishments (*CTA 2009, s 818(2)*).

Where the relief applies, the transfer is deemed to be tax neutral, meaning that the transfer is deemed not to be a realisation (ie disposal) or acquisition and anything done by the transferor while owning the asset is deemed to have been done by the transferee (*CTA 2009, ss 776, 818(2)*).

Stamp duty and schemes of reconstruction

7.34 The definition of a scheme of reconstruction for capital gains purposes does not apply to either stamp duty or stamp duty land tax. There is no statutory definition of a scheme of reconstruction for stamp taxes, so these taxes use the definition developed by company law, requiring substantially the same business to be carried on after a reconstruction as before, with substantially the same shareholders (see, for example, *Re South African Supply and Cold Storage Co* [1904] 2 Ch 268 and *Brooklands Selangor Holdings Ltd v IRC* [1970] 2 All ER 76).

The practical effect of this is that transactions that are exempt from capital gains tax as schemes of reconstruction might still carry charges to stamp duty or SDLT.

A transfer of shares under a scheme of reconstruction may qualify for the relief at *FA 1986, s 77* (see **7.17** above) if the conditions are satisfied and if *FA 1986, s 77A* does not apply.

A transfer of assets under a scheme of reconstruction may qualify for the relief at *FA 2003, Sch 7, Pt 2*, subject to satisfying the conditions for that relief. These are:

- The consideration for the acquisition consists wholly or partly of the issue of non-redeemable shares in the acquiring company to all the shareholders of the target company.
- After the acquisition has been made each shareholder of each of the companies is a shareholder of the other and the proportion of shares of one of the companies held by any shareholder is the same, or as nearly as may be the same, as the proportion of shares of the other company held by that shareholder.
- The acquisition is effected for bona fide commercial reasons and does not form part of a scheme or arrangement of which the main purpose, or one of the main purposes, is the avoidance of liability to stamp duty, income tax, corporation tax, capital gains tax or stamp duty land tax.

There is no statutory right to a pre-transaction clearance as to the availability of this relief. As noted previously, however, HMRC will, in many cases, accept that the relief applies if they are also satisfied for the purposes of the capital gains reliefs that the transaction is for bona fide commercial reasons and not part of a scheme or arrangement to avoid tax.

APPENDIX – SAMPLE CLEARANCE LETTER

7.35 Dear Sirs

We are writing on behalf of the shareholders of [*name the company or companies involved*] to seek formal clearances under [*statutory provisions*] in respect of the proposed transaction(s) below.

Parties involved

List all the relevant shareholders and companies (this can be in an appendix to the main letter). For individuals, always provide:

- national insurance numbers
- unique taxpayer references
- home addresses
- shareholding(s) in relevant companies
- residence status.

For companies or LLPs, always provide:

- company registration numbers
- unique taxpayer references
- registered office addresses
- residence status.

This will help HMRC identify the parties and ensure that the relevant tax offices are sent details of the application and whether clearance was granted or refused.

History and background

Brief history of the company or companies involved, their business(es), etc. This helps put the whole transaction into context for HMRC.

Bring it up to date with an explanation of the current position and what the transactions are meant to achieve.

Prior transactions

It is sensible to mention any previous transactions that may be relevant within, say, the last five years.

Proposed transactions

Describe these in detail, together with the reasons behind each element of the transactions. Either here, or in the History and background section, you need to explain why the transactions are being carried out and why in this particular way, to demonstrate the commercial drivers and the lack of any tax-avoidance motives.

For more technically based clearances, such as for demergers, it is also important to demonstrate that all the relevant technical conditions are satisfied.

Commercial reasons for the transaction

Some applicants like to spell out the commercial drivers as a separate section of the letter.

Future transactions

For completeness, you should cover any other transactions in contemplation for the near to medium term. This should cover both definite transactions and transactions that have been thought about, albeit they are not definitely going to happen.

Examples might be:

- After a demerger, one of the new companies will be offering shares or share options to key employees. The ability to do this may, indeed, have been one of the reasons behind the demerger.
- Following a reconstruction, it is possible that one of the businesses or companies in a group would be sold, were an appropriate offer to be made. This will probably not affect whether HMRC grant a clearance.
- Following a reorganisation, one of the businesses or companies in a group will definitely be sold. This may affect whether HMRC grant a clearance, depending on the circumstances, such as whether HMRC see the reorganisation as reducing the tax liability on the subsequent disposal, which might be seen as tax avoidance.

Clearance sought

Specifically request the clearances sought and the statutory references.

Enclosures

Always enclose the latest statutory accounts of all the companies involved.

Contact details

If you require any further details concerning the transactions please contact Mr J Smith by email (email address) or by telephone (telephone number). It is relatively uncommon for HMRC to do this but it can help to ensure that minor queries can be dealt with quickly and efficiently.

Chapter 8

Selling or winding-up an owner-managed company

Partha Ray, Cameron & Associates Ltd

SIGNPOSTS

- **Scope** – there are two possible methods of selling a business, either by selling the shares of a company or by a company disposing of its assets. Selling a trading business might entitle a vendor to entrepreneurs' relief resulting in a favourable CGT rate.
- **Entrepreneurs' relief (ER)** – to be eligible for ER, certain conditions need to be met and the main qualifying conditions are set out in **8.5**.
- **Consideration satisfied by shares or loan notes** – purchasers may not wish to pay for the business by all the cash upfront, and part of the arrangement may be to settle this deferred consideration. We look at the rules for QCBs and non-QCBs although these are now similar (see **8.11–8.25**).
- **Practical issues** – there are corporation tax consequences on a winding-up, including the sale of trading stock and how best to use trading losses (see **8.28–8.38**).
- **Anti-avoidance provisions** – there are restrictions on the surplus available for distribution to shareholders on an informal winding-up (see **8.47–8.49**), and for businesses which are wound up and then continue to trade under a new company (phoenix companies – see **8.59–8.62**).
- **Other points** – there is tax relief for shareholders of insolvent companies who can either make a negligible value claim or it may be possible to obtain income tax relief for capital losses on certain shares (see **8.65–8.77**).

SALES UNDER THE CGT REGIME

8.1 Most owner-managers selling their businesses are likely to qualify for entrepreneurs' relief (ER), which provides the benefit of a 10% CGT rate. However, ER is restricted to the first £10m of eligible share sale gains. Any gains in excess of the £10m limit (which is a cumulative lifetime allowance) are, from 6 April 2016, chargeable at a CGT rate of either 10% or 20%. The rate which will apply is determined by an individual's income and other gains which arise during the tax year in which the disposal is made.

If ER has already been fully utilised then any capital gains, in 2017/18, are taxable at either 10% or 20% depending on the vendor's other income. Where an individual's total taxable income and gains are below the upper limit of the basic rate income tax (currently £33,500) then the gains will be taxable at 10% (the same rate as ER). Any gains (or part of the gains) which are above the threshold will be taxable at 20%. In this chapter, it is assumed that all gains, for which ER is not available, are taxable at 20%. Under the CGT rules, an important planning consideration will be to ensure that maximum possible use is made of ER, and some owner-managers may wish to fragment their shareholdings to other family members to achieve this.

Table 8.1 shows how an owner-manager's CGT liability rises on larger gains.

Table 8.1

Gains on shares	*CGT payable 2017/18 (with ER)*
£000	*£000*
100	10
1,000	100
5,000	500
10,000	1,000
15,000	2,400

Focus

ER continues to be a very valuable relief for entrepreneurs as the disposal of their business should, in most cases, be subject to capital gains tax at 10% rather than the standard 20% capital gains tax rate for higher and additional rate taxpayers (the gains arising from the disposal of residential property are taxed at 28%). Therefore, advisers should ensure that, where possible, all qualifying conditions are met.

When calculating the gain on a disposal there are a couple of points that individuals and trustee shareholders need to consider:

- Indexation relief is no longer available. For those shareholders who acquired their shares (well) before April 1998 the loss of indexation may prove to be costly in terms of additional CGT.
- March 1982 rebasing is now compulsory for shares held at 31 March 1982. In many cases, this should not affect the shareholder's capital gain (since the March 1982 rebasing value will be used in any case). However, it will no longer be possible to use the original cost of the shareholding, even if that produces a *lower* gain.

All shares in a particular company (of the same class) are generally treated as a single 'pooled' asset, regardless of when they were actually acquired.

Until 2010, HMRC applied the 'Transaction in Securities' anti-avoidance rules in *ITA 2007, s 684* more vigorously. It was therefore very important for the vendor shareholders to make use of the statutory clearance procedure under *ITA 2007, s 701*. Provided the main aspects of a transaction have been fully disclosed, the vendor can obtain some certainty before the sale that HMRC are satisfied that the transaction is being made for genuine reasons and will not subsequently be challenged under this legislation.

However, the application of *ITA 2007, s684* should not apply for sales to unconnected third parties (*ITA 2007, s 686*). The new exemption provides greater clarity and certainty and, targets the application of the rules to transactions which are *mainly* motivated towards obtaining a tax advantage.

BASIC DEAL-STRUCTURING ISSUES

8.2 Generally, vendors can either sell their shares in the company or arrange to sell the trade and assets out of the company. In the majority of cases, the vendor shareholders will seek to structure the deal as a sale of their shares (which is the main focus of this chapter). This is attractive for a number of reasons. The sale proceeds are received directly in the hands of the vendor and would normally be subject to a lower CGT rate (with the benefit of ER). For any disposals in 2017/18, the marginal income tax rate of 45% will mean that, for vendors, obtaining the capital gains tax treatment becomes even more imperative.

A share sale also limits the vendor's commercial exposure, subject to the protection obtained by the purchaser through warranties and indemnities under the sale agreement.

In contrast, an asset deal frequently gives rise to an element of double taxation. This is because capital gains and 'clawbacks' of previously claimed capital allowances typically arise within the company on the sale of the assets (such as goodwill and plant). A further tax charge then arises when the company's post-tax sale proceeds are extracted by the shareholders from the company. Vendors generally tend to be 'forced' to sell the trade and assets out of their company in 'distress' sale situations. Companies that are very small can now take advantage of the disincorporation relief. This is covered in detail in **Chapter 2**.

Purchasers have tended to prefer to acquire the trade and assets since this involves less commercial risk and, for acquisitions until 7 July 2015, the prospect of obtaining tax relief (against trading profits) on the assets purchased, such as on goodwill and other intangible assets. However, in recent years, asset deals are likely to be more expensive in terms of stamp duty land tax (SDLT), where the acquisition contains a substantial element of UK land and property. For example, if the amount paid for (say) trading premises is £1m, the SDLT cost (from 17 March 2016) would be £2,000 on the first £250,000 and £37,500 on the remaining £750,000 (£750,000 × 5%). Goodwill and all transfers of intellectual property or debts no longer attract any stamp taxes.

On the other hand, share purchases only attract stamp duty at 0.5% but this is levied on the *total* value of the company (reflecting the value of non-dutiable assets but reduced by the company's debt and liabilities).

The rest of this chapter concentrates on the CGT consequences and planning opportunities of selling shares in an owner-managed company.

BASIC CAPITAL GAINS TAX (CGT) RULES ON SHARE SALES

Date of disposal

8.3 The vendor will normally generate a capital gain when they sell their shares. The nature of the contract will determine the date of disposal:

(a) A disposal of an asset will be recognised for CGT purposes when an unconditional contract is executed for its sale (*TCGA 1992, s 28(1)*).

(b) In the case of a conditional contract, the date of disposal is deferred until the relevant condition precedent is satisfied (or waived) (*TCGA 1992, s 28(2)*). A condition precedent refers to an event which is outside the control of the contracting parties – for example, obtaining satisfactory tax clearances or relevant regulatory approval etc. (On the other hand, a 'condition subsequent' is merely a term of the contract required to be fulfilled by one of the parties and does not create a conditional contract for CGT.)

Cash consideration is immediately chargeable to CGT in the tax year of disposal (*TCGA 1992, s 28*). Tax must be paid on any *fixed* (ie ascertainable) deferred consideration, even it if is conditional, although HMRC will refund the tax when they are satisfied that the conditional amount will not be paid. Instalment relief may be available for the tax payments; given the difficulty of paying the tax before the full cash proceeds are received (*TCGA 1992, ss 48* and *280*). However, fixed deferred consideration is usually best structured through the use of loan notes, as this enables the relevant tax to be held over (see **8.15**).

Calculation of capital gain

8.4 In broad terms, an individual or trustee vendor's capital gain is calculated as the amount by which the sale proceeds (net of allowable incidental costs of disposal) exceeds the amount they originally paid for the shares – often referred to as the 'base cost'.

Where a vendor held his shares at 31 March 1982, he must deduct the market value of the shareholding at 31 March 1982 as his base cost (instead of his pre-March 1982 acquisition cost).

Example 8.1 – Comparative CGT computation for sale of shares (under taper relief and entrepreneurs' relief regimes)

For some months, James has been in serious negotiations for the sale of 'his' company, Anderson Ltd. He expects to sell his company for a cash consideration of £12m (net of legal and professional costs). James acquired his 100% shareholding in June 1995 for £100,000. Anderson Ltd has always been a trading company.

The CGT liabilities for a sale made during 2017/18 is set out below:

	2017/18
	£
Net sale proceeds	12,000,000
Less: Acquisition cost (June 1995)	(100,000)
Chargeable gain	11,900,000
Less: Annual exemption	(11,300)
Taxable gain	11,888,700
CGT @ 10% (first £10m & @ 20% on balance)	1,377,780

ENTREPRENEURS' RELIEF

Main qualifying conditions

8.5 For normal share sales the following conditions must be met throughout the one year before the disposal (*TCGA 1992, s 169I(1), (2)(c), (5), (6)*). The vendor shareholder must:

- hold shares in a trading company or holding company of a trading group (see **8.8**); and
- be a director or employee of that company (or fellow group company) and it must be their 'personal company' – ie they must own at least 5% of the ordinary share capital (carrying at least 5% of the voting rights).

Most owner-managers should have little difficulty in satisfying the relevant tests. However, the 'director/employee' requirement should not be that onerous, since there is no requirement to work on a 'full-time' basis – part-time working would therefore suffice. The 5% 'shareholding/votes' test must be satisfied by the individual vendor alone (eg there is no attribution of a spouse's or any relatives' share).

From 17 March 2016, the favourable 10% rate is potentially also available to shareholders who are not connected with the company (investor relief) but this chapter only focuses on the tax aspects of owner-managed companies.

Relaxation of conditions for EMI share options

8.6 The tax advantages of the EMI scheme were enhanced by allowing gains made on shares acquired through exercising EMI qualifying options after 5 April 2012 to be eligible for the beneficial 10% entrepreneurs' relief.

The effect of the rules is that an individual will be entitled to entrepreneurs' relief (for disposals after 5 April 2013) in respect of EMI shares as long as the qualifying option was granted a year before the date of disposal of the shares. There will not be a requirement for the company to be their personal company (ie holding at least 5% of the ordinary share capital), so that entrepreneurs' relief is now more easily available to those who exercise their EMI share options.

The main reason for the change is that the government recognised that EMI options are typically exercised just before the employing company is taken over. This means that the shares would not be owned by the employee for one year and would, therefore, be ineligible for entrepreneurs' relief.

ER must be claimed (broadly) within 22 months after the end of the relevant tax year in which the share sale is made. Thus, for example, an ER claim on a qualifying gain in 2017/18 must be made by 31 January 2020. Once claimed, ER is applied to the complete eligible gain (up to the maximum £10m cumulative threshold) – it cannot be restricted in any way. However, some flexibility could be provided by selling shares in separate tranches, with an ER election being made against specific disposals.

The ER conditions are more restrictive than those which applied to the business taper regime. For example, a large number of minority and employee shareholders will be unable to meet the conditions necessary to secure ER. They will therefore suffer CGT rate of either 10% or 20% under the new regime (compared with their typical rate of 10% under the taper regime).

Trustees can also claim ER in certain special cases where their trust has one or more beneficiaries holding an 'interest in possession' (see **8.8**).

Basic mechanics of ER

8.7 To obtain ER, the shares only need to be held on a qualifying basis for at least one year to obtain ER.

ER provides that the first £10m of 'qualifying business gains' are taxed at a lower rate of 10%. This £10m ER allowance is available, separately, to both husband and wife which may be an important consideration when structuring shareholdings.

In 2017/18, gains qualifying for ER are taxed at 10%. The following example shows the computation of ER for different levels of qualifying business gains:

Example 8.2 – ER available on varying levels of eligible gains

	£000	*£000*	*£000*
Eligible gain	1,000	10,000	15,000
CGT @ 10% (first £10m) & 20% (on balance)	100	1,000	2,400

Trading company/group test

8.8 The ER 'trading company/group' test is relatively stringent (*TCGA 1992, s 165A*). Broadly, the relevant company/group must be wholly engaged in carrying on trading activities, subject to the *de minimis* rule for 'substantial' non-trading activities.

HMRC's practice is to interpret this rule as permitting non-trading activities, provided they do not exceed 20% of the company's/group's total activities (although this is not a statutory test). Vulnerable *non-trading* activities would include property letting to third parties, investment in shares etc, loans to shareholders/connected companies, and surplus cash not required for future trading activities which is actively managed as an investment activity.

HMRC generally test whether non-trading activities are within the 20% benchmark by looking at a range of measures, such as:

- turnover;
- the asset base of the company;
- expenses;
- time spent by management and employees.

Thus, for example, the turnover/sales income from a company's non-trading activities would be compared with the total turnover generated by the company and so on. It may be necessary to build up the correct picture over time and this may involve striking a balance between all these factors (*see IR Tax Bulletin,* Issue 62).

Although many considered that substantial surplus cash could invalidate a company's trading status, HMRC now seem to take a more relaxed approach in this area. It would appear that provided the cash had been generated from a company's trading operations and it has not been applied for an investment purpose, then it should be treated as a trading asset.

When determining whether a company/group satisfies the 'trading' status test for ER, qualifying equity investments in joint venture trading companies (which would otherwise be regarded as investment activities) are deemed to represent an appropriate part of the trading activities of a trading company/group. A shareholding in a 'joint-venture' company qualifies for 'trading' treatment provided the participating company (or group) holds at least 10% of its ordinary shares and:

(a) the joint-venture company is a trading company or holding company of a trading group; and

(b) at least 75% of the joint-venture company's equity share capital is held by five or fewer participating shareholders (irrespective of their tax residence status).

It should be possible to obtain an advance (non-statutory) clearance from HMRC as to whether the company satisfies the relevant 'trading' company/group criteria for ER.

Disposals by trustees

8.9 Trustees can also claim ER in certain special cases where their trust has one or more 'qualifying' beneficiaries holding an 'interest in possession' (over the entire trust fund or the relevant part (such as a 'sub-fund') containing the shares) (*TCGA 1992, s 169J*).

The main trust conditions are directed at the 'qualifying beneficiary' rather than the trustees. Thus, the trustees can make a claim for ER provided the *qualifying beneficiary*:

- is a director or employee of the company (or any fellow-group company); and
- holds at least 5% of the ordinary shares in the company (carrying at least 5% of the voting rights) in their own right.

There is no minimum shareholding condition for the trustees. These 'trust' conditions must be satisfied throughout a period of *one year* ending within the *three years* before the sale. The company must also be a trading company or a holding company of a trading group (see **8.8**) throughout this period.

The conditions mean that to facilitate a potential ER claim by a trust, the (qualifying) beneficiary must have a personal holding of at least 5% of the shares (carrying at least 5% of the votes). However, the trustees do *not* have their own separate £10m ER allowance. The qualifying beneficiary effectively assigns to the trustees all or part of their unused ER allowance (by entering into a joint election). Therefore, if the beneficiary has used all of their £10m allowance, this will preclude any ER claim by the trustees.

Entrepreneurs' relief on associated disposals of personally held property

8.10 Where an individual qualifies for the relief on the disposal of shares, they can also obtain relief on an associated disposal of an asset that has been used by the company (*TCGA 1992, s 169K*). This would typically be a property that is personally owned by a shareholder/director which has been used by the company for its business, but it might also cover the sale of intellectual property that is personally held (outside the company) by the vendor shareholder.

The relief is only allowed for 'associated' disposals so they must therefore take place at the same time as (or shortly after) the share sale – an isolated disposal of personally held property will not qualify for any relief.

TCGA 1992, s 169K requires the following conditions to be satisfied for a qualifying 'associated disposal' (in the context of an ER-related share sale):

- The vendor shareholder must make the 'associated disposal' as part of their 'withdrawal from participation' in the business carried on by the company. (This appears to imply a 'hands-on' working test, so if the vendor continues to work in the target company post-sale, they may not satisfy this condition.)
- Throughout the *one-year* period (normally) prior to the sale of the shares, the relevant property is used for the purposes of the company's trade.

The conditions for associated disposal relief are therefore quite restrictive in terms of timing. For example, the sale of the property some time before the share sale would not qualify (since it would then not have been used for the purposes of the company's trade up to the date of the share sale).

The ER on an associated disposal can also be scaled down on a 'just and reasonable' basis (under *TCGA 1992, s 169P*) to reflect cases where (among other things):

- the property has only been *partly* used for the purposes of the company's trade throughout the vendor's period of ownership;
- a rent has been charged by the 'vendor' to the company for its use of the property.

This means that the gain eligible for 'associated disposal-ER' would now have to be reduced to the extent that a rent had been charged for the property over its entire period of ownership. Thus, if (say) only 40% of the market rent had been charged throughout this period, then 60% of the property gain would be eligible for 'associated disposal' relief. However, there is a provision whereby the restriction, to an individual who has charged rent for the use of an asset by the company, will only apply for rents charged after 5 April 2008.

Focus

Many businesses keep the property, from which the business trades, outside the company as it may belong to one of the directors. In these situations rent is paid for use of the property but the downside is that it may affect eligibility to ER when the property is subsequently disposed of.

TREATMENT OF SALE CONSIDERATION SATISFIED BY SHARES/LOAN NOTES IN THE ACQUIRER

Different types of consideration

8.11 Vendors may sell their shares for a consideration satisfied in cash, loan notes or shares issued by the acquiring company. Very often the vendor is likely to be offered a combination of cash and loan notes/shares. In some cases, vendors may also be given additional deferred consideration in the form of an 'earn-out'.

Consideration shares in the acquirer

8.12 Many private company takeovers, particularly by quoted companies, will entail the purchaser issuing new shares to the vendor shareholders as part of the sale consideration.

Many company takeovers, particularly by listed companies, will entail the purchaser issuing new shares to the vendor shareholders as part of the sale consideration. This enables the vendor to defer their capital gain until the shares are sold. The CGT reorganisation rule in *TCGA 1992, s 127* is applied here so that the vendor is treated as not having made any disposal of his old shares. Instead, he is treated as receiving the new 'consideration' shares at the same time and at the same cost as his old shares.

The share-for-share exchange 'reorganisation' rules are circumscribed by the 'commercial purpose' test in *TCGA 1992, s 137*. Consequently, the beneficial CGT treatment will only apply where the transaction is being undertaken for bona fide reasons *and* where one of the main purposes is not to obtain a tax advantage. Advance clearance should generally be applied for under *TCGA 1992, s 138* to obtain certainty that HMRC agree that these requirements are satisfied in relation to the proposed deal.

The 'commercial purpose' test in *TCGA 1992, s 137* does *not* apply to very small minority shareholders (ie those holding no more than 5% of the target company), presumably because they are not in a position to influence the structure of the transaction (*TCGA 1992, s 137(2)*).

Special election to obtain entrepreneurs' relief on share exchange

8.13 As the 'reorganisation' rule provides that there is no CGT disposal, the vendor would normally be unable to claim ER on the value of the acquirer's shares received as part of their sale consideration. This would be unfortunate if the vendor was unable to claim ER on a later sale of their 'consideration' shares – for example, because they did not possess the requisite 5% shareholding in the acquiring company.

The ER legislation recognises this problem and provides that the vendor can make a special election (under *TCGA 1992, s 169Q*) to opt out of the normal share-for-share exchange treatment. By making a *TCGA 1992, s 169Q* election the vendor is treated as having made a normal CGT disposal with the value of the acquirer's shares being reflected as all/part of their overall sale consideration. In such cases, the benefit of the ER would be reflected in the (higher) market value base cost of the shares in the acquiring company.

Example 8.3 – Effect of special ER election on share exchanges

Sue has been a 'management' shareholder since June 2002 and holds 10% of the equity share capital of Cook Ltd (a successful music publishing and recording company). She acquired her 10,000 £1 shares at their full market value of £20,000.

In August 2017, Cook Ltd was taken over by Stokes Plc. As part of this transaction, Sue received sale consideration of £600,000, which was satisfied as follows:

	£
Cash	200,000
Shares in Stokes Plc, valued at	400,000

Sue's shares in Stokes Plc represented a 3% shareholding (with commensurate voting rights). She is therefore unlikely to qualify for ER on their subsequent sale. However, by making a *TCGA 1992, s 169Q* election, she could benefit from ER on the *total* consideration received on the August 2017 sale, as shown below:

		£
Sale consideration	Cash	200,000
	Stokes Plc shares	400,000
		600,000
Less: Base cost		(20,000)
		580,000

	£
Less: Annual exemption	(11,300)
Taxable gain (qualifying for ER)	568,700
CGT @ 10%	56,870

Sue's base cost of her Stokes Plc shares would be their full market value of £400,000 (as opposed to £13,333 (4/6 × £20,000), being the pro-rata original cost of her Cook Ltd shares if the reorganisation rules had applied).

Making a TCGA 1992, s 169Q election

8.14 The *TCGA 1992, s 169Q* election is made on an 'all or nothing' basis. Therefore, it is not possible to restrict its application to gains of £10m. Such elections must be made within 22 months after the end of the tax year in which the sale occurs.

The potential consequences of making a *TCGA 1992, s 169Q* election should always be considered when structuring any deal. Because the reorganisation rule is disapplied, the vendor would generally incur a CGT liability on the 'ER-relieved' gain. The vendor would, therefore, need to ensure they had sufficient cash consideration to fund the tax liability. Furthermore, the timing of any future tax liability (when the higher base cost comes into play) must also be considered.

Clearly, such an election would not be appropriate where the 'cash' element of a company share sale produced chargeable gains exceeding the ER limit of £10m.

Focus

Before making a *TCGA 1992, s 169Q* election, make sure there is sufficient cash to pay the upfront CGT liability.

Consideration satisfied in loan notes (up to 22 June 2010)

8.15 In many deals, the vendor may agree to accept deferred payment for part of the sale consideration by taking loan notes in the acquiring company. As a general rule, where the purchaser satisfies part of the consideration by issuing loan notes, an appropriate part of the vendor's gain is deferred until the loan note is redeemed for payment. The precise mechanics of the deferral depended on the tax status of the loan note, as until 22 June 2010, this varied between Qualifying Corporate Bonds (QCBs) (see **8.16**) and non-QCBs (see **8.20**).

This CGT deferral rules are subject to HMRC being satisfied that the loan note has been issued for genuine commercial reasons and not mainly to avoid tax (*TCGA 1992, s 137*) (see **8.11**). The vendor would normally apply for a *TCGA 1992, s 138* clearance to seek advance confirmation of this point from HMRC.

Dealing with QCBs

8.16 Broadly, most 'non-convertible' loan notes will represent QCBs. The capital gains deferral mechanism for a QCB is governed by the rules in *TCGA 1992, s 116(10)*. These provide that the *chargeable gain* on the loan note consideration is computed at the date of sale. This gain is then postponed and becomes taxed only when the loan note is encashed (or disposed of *outside* the cases specified in *TCGA 1992, s 116(11)*).

Where QCBs were received on a post-6 April 2008 (but before 23 June 2010) share sale, any available ER was deducted in arriving at the gain held over under *TCGA 1992, s 116(10)*. Until 23 June 2010 this meant that the 'carried-forward' gain reflected any ER that was available and claimed at the original sale date.

From 23 June 2010, if there is an exchange of shares for QCBs and no *TCGA 1992, s 169R* election is made to bring the gain immediately into charge, it is likely that when the gain subsequently comes into charge, it will not qualify for ER.

Example 8.4 – Claiming ER on QCBs (up to 22 June 2010)

In May 2010, John sold his 40% shareholding in Arthur Ltd to Lehmann Plc for £2.5m, of which:

- £500,000 was paid in cash on completion; and
- £2m was satisfied by the issue of a QCB loan note (bearing interest at 5%, bank guaranteed and redeemable after 12 months).

John subscribed for his 40,000 £1 shares in Arthur Ltd at par in May 2002.

John would incur a CGT liability on the cash consideration and would be able to defer the capital gain on the part satisfied in QCBs.

2010/11 – CGT on cash consideration

Cash

		£
Sale consideration – Cash		500,000
Less: Base cost	$£40{,}000 \times \dfrac{£500{,}000}{£500{,}000 + £2{,}000{,}000}$	(8,000)
Capital gain		492,000
Less: ER – £492,000 × 4/9		(218,667)
Gain after ER		273,333
Less: Annual exemption		(10,100)
Taxable gain		263,233
CGT @ 18%		47,382

Postponed QCB gain (with ER)

		£
QCB consideration		2,000,000
Less: Base cost	$£40{,}000 \times \dfrac{£2{,}000{,}000}{£500{,}000 + £2{,}000{,}000}$	(32,000)
Capital gain		1,968,000
Less: ER – £1,508,000 (£2,000,000 *less* £492,000) × 4/9		(670,222)
Postponed gain		1,297,778

QCB gains and TCGA 1992, s 169R elections to gain the benefit of ER (disposals after 22 June 2010)

8.17 The *Finance (No 2) Act 2010* changed the way ER is dealt with on QCB gains held over from 23 June 2010. This follows the change in ER to a straight 10% CGT charge. In such cases, any available ER is no longer factored into the held-over gain, so that now it is the 'gross' gain which is postponed.

If the seller wishes to claim ER on their QCB gain, they must make a special election under *TCGA 1992, s 169R*. This treats the QCB gain as being a chargeable disposal at the time of the share sale (ie the original shares are treated as sold for the QCB consideration), against which the ER CGT 10% rate can be claimed. By making an election, the normal QCB hold-over rules in *TCGA 1992, s 116(10)* do not apply. The *TCGA 1992, s 169R* election must be made by the 31 January following the tax year of the share sale.

This change therefore gives rise to a dilemma for sellers – should they elect under *TCGA 1992, s 169R* and pay 10% ER CGT 'upfront' on the share gain or defer their share gain under *TCGA 1992, s 116(10)* and (probably) pay CGT at 20% on the full held-over gain on redemption (with no ER)?

If a seller wishes to tax the QCB gain upfront to obtain a low ER CGT 10% rate, they would need to ensure that the deal structure provides sufficient cash funds to pay the CGT liability on the 31 January following the tax year of the sale. Where the *TCGA 1992, s 169R* election is made, there is no QCB hold-over and thus the redemption does not trigger any taxable gain.

Example 8.5 – Treatment of QCB gains and ER (post-22 June 2010 share sale)

In May 2017, Mark sold his 40% shareholding in Green Ltd to Blues Plc for £2.5m of which:

- £500,000 was paid in cash on completion; and
- £2m was satisfied by the issue of a QCB loan note (bearing interest at 9%, bank guaranteed and redeemable after 12 months).

Mark subscribed for his 40,000 £1 shares in Green Ltd at par in May 2003.

Mark's CGT position is as follows:

2017/18 – CGT on cash consideration

Cash		£
Sale consideration – Cash		500,000
Less: Base cost	$£40{,}000 \times \dfrac{£500{,}000}{(£500{,}000 + £2{,}000{,}000)}$	(8,000)
Capital gain		492,000
Less: Annual exemption		(11,300)
Taxable gain		480,700
ER CGT @ 10%		£48,070

If Mark does *not* make an election under *TCGA 1992, s 169R*, all the QCB gain is held over (without the benefit of ER).

Postponed QCB gain

		£
QCB consideration		2,000,000
Less: Base cost	£40,000 *less* £8,000	(32,000)
Postponed gain		1,968,000

The postponed gain is likely to become taxable on redemption at 20%, being £393,600 (ignoring the annual exemption).

2017/18 – Taxable QCB gain at ER CGT rate

If Mark makes an election under *TCGA 1992, s 169R* for the QCB consideration to be taxable in 2017/18, he can obtain a 10% ER CGT rate on the QCB gain.

	£
QCB consideration	2,000,000
Less: Base cost	(32,000)
Capital gain	1,968,000
ER CGT @ 10%	196,800

An election to benefit from ER would give Mark a substantial tax saving provided he can manage the acceleration of his tax liability.

Transitional ER for pre-6 April 2008 QCBs

8.18 Special rules apply to QCB loan notes that were acquired as consideration for a pre-5 April 2008 share sale. Taper relief ceases to be relevant where QCB gains are crystallised under the new CGT regime. However, the benefit of any indexation allowance that was built into the held-over gain is retained on a post-5 April 2008 redemption.

Special rules enable ER to be claimed against the QCB gain becoming chargeable on a post-5 April 2008 redemption (*FA 2008, Sch 3, para 7*). Clearly, the QCB holder must have unused ER available to offset against the crystallised gain. However, relief is only given provided the vendor would have been entitled to ER on the original pre-6 April 2008 share sale (on the assumption that the ER legislation had been in force at that time). ER relief will not always be available – for example, the vendor may have sold a very small (less than 5%) holding on the original sale.

For these purposes, the transitional ER claim must be made within 22 months following the tax year in which the held-over gain crystallises.

QCB loss problem

8.19 No capital loss relief is available as a QCB is not a chargeable asset for CGT (*TCGA 1992, s 115*). Furthermore, any capital gain deferred under *TCGA 1992, s 116(10)* can also be triggered if the purchasing company defaults on a QCB loan note which is cancelled or settled via a 'compromise arrangement'. In these dire circumstances, HMRC generally permit the worthless loan note to be 'gifted' to a charity without triggering the held-over gain. Having said that, vendors should always seek to obtain 'commercial bank' guarantees for their loan notes to avoid these types of nightmare scenarios!

Non-qualifying corporate bonds (non-QCBs)

8.20 Where the purchaser issues non-QCB loan notes, the terms of such loan notes will be designed so as to fall outside the criteria for a QCB. Thus, for example, a non-QCB loan note would be one which is convertible into the acquirer's shares or contains the right to subscribe for additional shares or securities. Where such notes are issued in exchange for shares they are deemed to be a security (and therefore do not necessarily have to be 'marketable', readily transferable and so on) (*TCGA 1992, s 251(6)*).

Non-QCB loan notes represent a security for CGT purposes and their receipt falls to be treated as a share reorganisation under *TCGA 1992, s 127* (by virtue of the share exchange rules in *TCGA 1992, s 135*) (see **8.11**). The appropriate part of the vendor's original base cost in the target company's shares is therefore treated as given for the non-QCB security at the original acquisition date(s). (Non-QCBs were often used under the taper relief regime to extend the vendor's taper relief period, but these taper relief issues ceased to be relevant after 5 April 2008.)

Since the CGT deferral in relation to the sale consideration satisfied by non-QCBs is governed by the CGT reorganisation rules in *TCGA 1992, s 127*, it is possible for ER to be claimed on the non-QCB consideration (assuming the relevant ER conditions are satisfied) by making a *TCGA 1992, s 169Q* election). By making this election, the value of the non-QCB consideration is brought into the vendor's CGT computation at the date of the sale (as explained in **8.12**). Before structuring any deal or deciding whether an election would be beneficial, the relevant factors in **8.13** should be considered.

Where the vendor is unable to obtain a commercial bank guarantee for the loan note, many feel that a non-QCB would be a more prudent alternative – this avoids the QCB-type risk of triggering a CGT charge on the cancellation of the loan note (eg where the acquiring company becomes insolvent) (see **8.19**).

EARN-OUT DEALS

Basic tax treatment of 'cash-based' earn-outs

8.21 Owner-managed companies are sometimes sold on an 'earn-out' basis with deferred consideration being provided, calculated on a formula basis relating to the post-sale profits, over (normally) the next two or three years. This will generally enable the vendor to enjoy extra consideration, calculated by reference to a formula based on the level of profits achieved by the target company in the two or three years following the sale. An earn-out also limits the purchaser's 'downside' risk as the vendor will receive little or nothing if the anticipated profits are not met.

Under the principles established in the case of *Marren v Ingles* [1980] STC 500, the expected net present value of the earn-out right falls to be included as part of the vendor's taxable consideration for the disposal of the shares. Thus, where the vendor's share sale gain qualifies for ER, the value of the earn-out right will effectively attract the relief (subject to the £10m threshold).

As and when the earn-out payments are received, further CGT charges will arise in respect of the earn-out *right* itself (representing capital sums derived from the right to receive the earn-out (under *TCGA 1992, s 22*) and *not* the disposal of shares). Thus, assuming the vendor had unused ER relief, this would not be available against the disposals of the earn-out right (since these do *not* constitute a disposal of shares). Capital gains on the earn-out payments (taxed under *TCGA 1992, s 22*), which are based on the earn-out payments received less the appropriate deductible base value of the right, will therefore attract CGT at either 10% or 20%.

One of the main potential problems arising from the '*Marren v Ingles*' treatment is the risk of being taxed on an unrealised gain, ie the vendor would suffer tax on the *value of the right* (when their shares are sold). Where the earn-out falls (well) below expectation, this could result in a capital loss arising on the disposal of the right in a subsequent tax year. In such cases, it is now possible to make an election under *TCGA 1992, s 279A* to carry the subsequent loss back to reduce the vendor's original capital gain.

Earn-outs satisfied in shares/loan notes under TCGA 1992, s 138A

8.22 An earn-out may also be structured so that it must be satisfied in the form of shares and/or loan notes in the acquiring company (when the relevant earn-out consideration is determined). This enables the 'deferral' mechanism in *TCGA 1992, s 138A* to apply (automatically without the need for an election) and thus avoids the 'upfront' tax charge based on the value of the right. Broadly speaking, provided the original share sale could meet the conditions for a *TCGA 1992, s 135* share exchange (but there does not necessarily have to be one), the vendor is *automatically* treated as (partly) exchanging their original shares for the deemed *TCGA 1992, s 138A* security.

This treatment was particularly beneficial under the (pre-6 April 2008) taper relief regime. Since the vendor was in effect 'rolling-over' into a non-QCB, their taper relief would continue to accrue (normally) at the business rate. This treatment generally enabled vendors to obtain full business taper on their earn-out payments (when they redeemed their actual loan notes). Thus, even where an earn-out was originally proposed to be settled in cash, vendors were advised to amend its terms so as to require the purchaser to satisfy the agreed earn-out amounts in the form of short-dated loan notes. Typically, the sale agreement would require the purchaser to issue these loan notes once the earn-out profits had been computed and the vendor's entitlement had been agreed. After a minimum six-month redemption period, the vendors would encash their loan notes and pay the relevant CGT on their earn-out 'gains' at an effective CGT rate of around 10%.

Treatment of TCGA 1992, s 138A earn-outs after 6 April 2008

8.23 When the earn-out is quantified, the acquiring company will issue the relevant loan note or shares for the agreed amount.

QCB loan notes

8.24 Where the earn-out consideration is satisfied in the form of a QCB loan note, this will be dealt with under the company security conversion/exchange rules in *TCGA 1992, s 132*. This treats the event as a CGT reorganisation and therefore brings the QCB rules in *TCGA 1992, s 116(10)* into play.

Broadly, the gain held over against the QCB would be the amount of the relevant earn-out consideration less the pro-rata base cost. (The pro-rata base cost is derived from the original cost of the shares that was carried into the deemed security when the vendor sold their original shares: see **8.2**.) The postponed gain would generally be taxed at the 18%/28% CGT rate when the QCB is finally encashed (HMRC require a minimum redemption period of six months from issue).

From 23 June 2010, if there is an exchange of shares for QCBs and no election is made to bring the gain immediately into charge, it is likely that when the gain subsequently comes into charge, it will not qualify for ER.

Shares/non-QCB loan notes

8.25 In some cases, the acquiring company satisfies the earn-out in the form of a fresh issue of its shares (or a non-QCB). The number of shares issued would generally depend on the earn-out consideration and the (agreed) prevailing market price/value of the acquirer's shares. In such cases, a combination of the *TCGA 1992, s 132* exchange and *TCGA 1992, s 127* CGT reorganisation rules will apply to treat the new shares/security as having been acquired at the same time (and pro-rata) base cost as the vendor's original shares. Any subsequent gain on sale/encashment would generally attract CGT at 10%/20%.

Exceptionally, there may be cases (assuming the vendor has unused ER relief available) where the subsequent disposal of the shares/non-QCB securities could attract ER. However, the vendor would generally need to have satisfied the relevant ER conditions from the time the shares/securities were issued as part of the earn-out. This is because (assuming they remain employed in the target company) it is only from this date that they would generally be able to satisfy the 5% ordinary shares/voting rights test: see **8.5**.

APPLICATION OF ITA 2007, s 684 ANTI-AVOIDANCE RULES

8.26 As there is a significant difference between the rates of income and capital gains tax, HMRC may invoke the anti-avoidance provisions found in *ITA 2007*. The 'Transactions in Securities' (TiS) anti-avoidance rules (as they apply for income tax purposes) in *ITA 2007, s 684* can potentially apply to counter the tax advantage obtained by selling family or owner-managed (ie 'close') companies in such a way so as not to suffer income tax.

Whilst all owner-managed company sales can, potentially, be caught by the provisions of the TiS legislation, most should be exempted under the 'fundamental change of ownership' rules (see **8.27**). The intention of the revised TiS provisions is mainly aimed at cases where the seller benefits from receiving the (net of tax) ER proceeds, but maintains a significant interest in the business after the sale (eg by selling to a 'connected' company).

The Transactions in Securities legislation will now apply only where all the following conditions are met:

- the shareholder is a party to a Transaction in Securities;
- broadly, they must receive relevant (non-income taxable) consideration in connection with the distribution, transfer or realisation of assets of a close company;

- the shareholder does not fall under the 'fundamental change of ownership' exemption;
- the shareholder's main purpose of the Transaction in Securities is to obtain an income tax advantage and an income tax advantage is obtained.

Fundamental change of ownership

8.27 *FA 2010* substantially relaxed the application of *ITA 2007, s 684* by introducing a 'carve-out' exemption for sales to unconnected third parties, which applies from 24 March 2010. This represents a fundamental and significant shift in HMRC's approach. The new exemption provides greater clarity and certainty and carefully targets the application of the TiS rules to transactions which are *mainly* motivated towards obtaining a tax advantage.

The refocused TiS legislation should only catch those who enter into a relevant transaction with a tax-avoidance objective.

A key component of the revised TiS regime is 'the fundamental change in ownership' exclusion rule, since sales which meet the relevant conditions are completely exempt from the TiS legislation. The conditions are (*ITA 2007, s 686*):

- Before the transaction a person holds shares in a close company and Conditions A, B and C are met for at least two years after the change in ownership.
- Condition A – after the sale at least 75% of the ordinary shares are held by persons who are not connected with the vendor.
- Condition B – the shares above must carry at least a 75% entitlement to any distributions.
- Condition C – the shares must carry at least 75% of the voting rights.

Focus

The introduction of the fundamental change of ownership criteria is a welcome piece of legislation as it should provide greater certainty for genuine business sales as the legislation is intended to catch transactions with a tax-avoidance motive.

WINDING-UP THE FAMILY OR OWNER-MANAGED COMPANY

Background

8.28 If the asset sale route is taken, the shareholders of a family or owner-managed company may decide to wind it up voluntarily. In such cases, there will often be a surplus available for distribution to the shareholders after the interests of the creditors have been satisfied. It will be essential to ensure that the surplus funds are distributed in a tax-efficient manner (see **8.47–8.56**). Where a company is wound up voluntarily, there may be time to implement appropriate corporate tax planning measures to increase the amount ultimately available to the company's shareholders.

In some cases, the existing shareholder(s) may simply wish to 'disincorporate'. This would normally entail winding the company up and transferring its trade and assets to the shareholder(s). The shareholders would then continue to carry on the trade through a sole trader or partnership structure (see **Chapter 2**).

8.29 If the company is wound up by a receiver or creditor, then the shareholders are likely to lose most if not all of their capital stake. It will then be necessary to consider what tax relief can be claimed in respect of their shares and any irrecoverable shareholder loans (see **8.68–8.79**). If the company is insolvent, the actions of the receiver/liquidator will be dictated by commercial requirements but, where possible, these should be conducted in the most tax-efficient basis to enhance the amount available for both creditors and shareholders. However, there is no point in planning to reduce tax liabilities that are never going to be paid due to insufficiency of funds.

CONSEQUENCES FOR THE COMPANY

Pension provision

8.30 Before the company ceases trading the proprietors'/directors' pension provision should be considered. Unless full provision has been made, there will be a tax advantage in making 'top-up' payments to an approved scheme. Provided the pension contributions are *paid* in the final corporation tax accounting period (CTAP) (ie up to cessation of trade), a trading deduction can normally be claimed with no spreading of contributions. This will have the effect of reducing the funds remaining for distribution and hence the shareholder's exposure to tax. However, care needs to be taken where pension contributions exceed the annual allowance of £40,000 (in 2017/18 subject to any unused allowance from earlier years) as the director/proprietor is likely to be subject to an additional tax liability.

Where a company has not made any pension provision for its proprietors/directors, it may be possible for it to enter into a Hancock annuity arrangement. The company would purchase an annuity from an insurance company before the trade ceases. Following the case of *Hancock v General Reversionary & Investment Co Ltd* (1918) 7 TC 358, the purchase of an annuity to fund a future pension was held to be deductible against profits – it was not a capital payment. The insurance company would then be responsible for paying the pension.

8.31 HMRC have confirmed that Hancock annuities can still be purchased post-A Day as long as they comply with the new pension rules. A specially purchased Hancock annuity for a retiring employee would normally be set up through a registered scheme in the same way as any other pension scheme, especially if a tax-free lump sum is to be provided. Tax relief for the employer contribution is subject to the 'wholly and exclusively' rule. (It is also possible for the company to purchase a Hancock annuity through a registered scheme.)

Under a Hancock-type arrangement, all benefits will have vested, so it does not have to satisfy the annual allowance rules. The lifetime allowance does apply.

Termination of CTAP and closure costs

8.32 The company's trade will usually have ceased before it is wound up and this will have a number of important tax consequences.

The cessation of the company's trade will bring about a termination of the company's current CTAP (*CTA 2009, s 10*). Generally, this will accelerate the date on which the company pays its tax liability. Companies which do not pay their tax in instalments must pay the corporation tax for the final CTAP within nine months following the end of that period. For other companies, the final instalment date is effectively brought forward, being due three months and 14 days after the end of the CTAP. Any unprovided expenses incurred after the cessation of trade (known as 'post-cessation' expenses) can only be offset against post-cessation receipts (see **8.38**), which reduces the prospect of obtaining relief (*CTA 2009, s 197*).

In drawing up the tax computation to cessation, particular care must therefore be taken to ensure that specific provisions are made for all known trade expenses that have been incurred up to the date of cessation. This will include provisions for warranty claims and bad and 'impaired' trading and loan relationship debts.

8.33 HMRC will disallow any expenses incurred in connection with the cessation of trade. However, following the Privy Council's decision in *IRC v Cosmotron Manufacturing Co Ltd* [1997] STC 1134, HMRC will normally allow relief for contractual redundancy or severance payments made on the cessation of trade. The rationale for allowing relief is that the payment is made under a pre-existing contractual or statutory obligation incurred as a consequence of the employees being employed for the purposes of the trade (*Tax Bulletin,* Issue 39).

Termination payments that do not qualify under the above principle, such as *ex gratia* payments, can be specifically relieved under the statutory trading deduction rules. Specific statutory relief is given for statutory redundancy payments and any additional redundancy payments (up to three times the amount of the statutory redundancy payments). Such payments are treated as paid on the date of cessation *if* they are paid after the trade ceases (*CTA 2009, ss 77(4), 79(2)*).

Sale of plant and industrial buildings

8.34 The cessation of trade will give rise to a deemed disposal of plant and machinery for capital allowance purposes, resulting in a balancing adjustment (*CAA 2001, s 61(2),* Table, item 6). If the plant is sold either before or shortly after the trade ceases, the disposal value will generally be the net disposal proceeds (*CAA 2001, s 61(2),* Table, item 1).

The sale of an industrial building no longer gives rise to any balancing adjustment. For a post-20 March 2007 disposal, the vendor avoids any recapture of industrial buildings allowances (IBAs) where the building is sold for an amount exceeding its tax residue. However, as part of the phasing out of IBAs, the purchaser could have claimed IBAs on the building (on the transitional basis) until the abolition of IBAs on 31 March 2011.

Capital gains on property sale

8.35 The sale of the company's chargeable assets may also produce capital gains, giving rise to a significant tax liability. Broadly, the disposal of a property etc is recognised for capital gains purposes when an unconditional contract for the sale is made (*TCGA 1992, s 28*). If the company has significant trading losses in the final CTAP, the company should enter into the sale contract for the property on or before it closes down the trade (although completion can take place afterwards). This would enable any gain on the property sale to be sheltered by the current trading losses (that might otherwise be forfeited on cessation).

Inevitably, there will be situations where it is not possible to sell the property until some time after the trade has ceased so that any gain cannot be offset by the trading losses generated in the final CTAP to cessation. Furthermore, the gain might be taxed at the full 20% corporation tax rate (for the year ended 31 March 2017) if the company becomes a close investment holding company.

In these cases, it may be beneficial to crystallise the gain before the trade ceases by arranging for the property to be sold to the owner-manager and then possibly licensed back to the company. The sale of the property would attract SDLT. Where appropriate, it might be possible for the property to be distributed *in specie* to the owner-manager. This would be treated as a distribution (taxable at an effective rate of 32.5%/38.1% in the owner-manager's hands), but would be exempted from any SDLT charge. The company's disposal would be deemed to take place at market value.

Sale of trading stock

8.36 Where the company's trading stock and work in progress is sold to an *unconnected* UK trader, the actual sale proceeds will be credited in the trading account for tax purposes. In such cases, HMRC cannot impute a market value for tax purposes (*CTA 2009, s 165*).

Trading losses

8.37 The liquidator must consider how to make best use of any remaining tax-adjusted trading losses. Trading losses can only be carried forward for offset against profits of the same trade (*CTA 2010, s 45(4)*). Consequently, any unrelieved tax losses cannot normally be carried forward beyond the date of cessation except where they can be offset against post-cessation receipts.

The main reliefs which are likely to be relevant for (tax-adjusted) trading losses are as follows:

- The offset of trading losses for the final CTAP to cessation against the company's other profits (before charges on income) of that period (*CTA 2010, s 37(3)(a)*).
- The offset of any remaining trading losses by carrying it back against the total profits (after deducting trading charges on income) for the previous year (*CTA 2010, s 37(3)(b)*)).
- Tax-adjusted trading losses arising in the final 12 months before cessation of trade can be carried back against the company's total profits (*after* deducting trading charges on income) against the CTAPs falling within the *three* previous years on a LIFO basis (*CTA 2010, s 39(2)*). A company's CTAP terminates on cessation of trade – if an earlier CTAP straddles and ends in the final 12-month period, any trading loss for that CTAP is time apportioned and added to the terminal trading loss claim.
- Trade charges for the final 12-month period can be used to augment the terminal loss claim.

Trade charges for CTAPs partly straddling the final 12 months are apportioned. However, trade charges are now likely to arise only in rare cases. Patent royalties recognised for accounting purposes are now normally included within the trading loss calculation (under the *CTA 2009* intangible fixed assets regime).

Setting off trading losses against post-trading receipts

8.38 Income receipts arising after a company has ceased to trade are assessable as 'non-trading' post-cessation receipts (*CTA 2009, ss 188–190*). This would include the write-back of excessive provisions (upon which tax relief was originally claimed), the unanticipated recovery of a bad debt that had been provided against or written-off and the release of trading liabilities after the trade has ceased.

Post-cessation expenses can be deducted against post-cessation receipts. However, if the company had unused trading losses at the date of cessation, HMRC accept that they can (exceptionally) be carried forward and offset against post-cessation receipts (see HMRC Business Income Manual (at BIM80535) which indicates that 'any unrelieved losses and unused capital allowances of the discontinued business' can be deducted for the purposes of *CTA 2009, s 196*).

A company may make an election (*CTA 2009, s 198*) which enables post-cessation receipts, received within six years of cessation, to be carried back and treated as received *immediately prior* to the cessation. This enables such receipts to be offset, for example, by trading losses brought forward under *CTA 2010, s 45*. The election must be made within two years of the end of the accounting period in which the receipt is received.

Close investment holding company status

8.39 Where a close company ceases to carry on a trade or property investment business, it will usually be treated as a close investment holding company (CIHC) (*CTA 2010, s 34*). A CIHC cannot benefit from the lower small profits rate of corporation tax, nor can it claim small companies' marginal relief, whatever the level of its profits. In such cases, the company's post-cessation income and gains would be taxed at the main corporation tax rate of 20% (for the year ended 31 March 2017).

If the company is not a CIHC throughout the CTAP which ends on the commencement of its winding-up, it will not be treated as a CIHC for the next CTAP (*CTA 2010, s 34(5)*). However, where the company has ceased trading before it is wound up, this exemption is unlikely to apply. However, there is an HMRC concession whereby they might still allow the exemption.

Pre-liquidation tax liabilities

8.40 The liquidator will need to take account of pre-liquidation tax liabilities as either preferential or ordinary claims (*Insolvency Act 1986, ss 175, 386*). Broadly, preferential creditors have the right to repayment of their debts ahead of the *unsecured* creditors. Since 15 September 2003, preferential creditors have been confined to liabilities broadly representing unpaid employee remuneration, etc for the four months before the winding-up. Previously, certain 'government' debts were also counted as preferential debts which included unpaid PAYE and national insurance contributions, etc for the 12 months prior to the receiver's/liquidator's appointment and unpaid VAT arising within the previous six months. However, unpaid PAYE and NIC ceased to be a preferred creditor from 15 September 2003 onwards.

8.41 Assessed taxes are not preferred debts, so any unpaid pre-liquidation corporation tax would rank as an unsecured creditor. Corporation tax arising during the liquidation is, however, normally treated as a liquidation expense (*Re Toshoku Finance UK Plc, Kahn (liquidators of Toshoku Finance UK Plc) v IRC* [2002] STC 368).

A practical approach will normally be required by the liquidator of the insolvent company when dealing with the company's tax affairs. He must inform HMRC of his appointment and determine the outstanding corporation tax position. Where the company is insolvent or has substantial brought-forward tax losses, HMRC may be prepared to agree a 'nil liability' position without the need to submit detailed tax computations (but a CT 600 must be submitted). However, if the liquidator wishes to agree an amount of trading losses for the purposes of a loss relief claim, HMRC will require detailed computations and accounts.

Post-liquidation tax liabilities

8.42 The commencement of a winding-up terminates the company's current CTAP and a new accounting period will begin. Each successive accounting period will last for 12 months, with the final accounting period ending on the date the winding-up is completed (*CTA 2009, s 12*). Similar rules now apply where a company goes into administration.

Corporation tax liabilities which arise during the course of the winding-up would be treated as an expense or disbursement of the liquidation (see *Re Beni-Felkai Mining Co Ltd* (1933) 18 TC 632). In most cases, the only taxable income received during the winding-up period is interest receivable on realised funds. However, interest received from HMRC, by companies in liquidation, on overpaid corporation tax is exempt from tax where the amount is less than £2,000 (*CTA 2010, s 633*).

As a necessary disbursement of the liquidation, the tax liabilities must (together with any overdue tax) be met in priority to the claims of all creditors and the liquidator's remuneration. However, where appropriate, the liquidator can apply to the court for an Order of Priority to be made to ensure that his remuneration and expenses can be dealt with equitably.

Legal formalities

Members' voluntary liquidation

8.43 The shareholders of a solvent company can proceed to wind up the company voluntarily. Generally, a special resolution of the shareholders is required to place the company in voluntary liquidation. Before this is done, the directors must make a statutory declaration of solvency. After having made a full inquiry, the directors must declare that the company will be able to pay its debts within 12 months following the commencement of the winding-up.

A member's voluntary liquidation must be dealt with by a licensed insolvency practitioner. Under a liquidation, a company can only be restored to the Register within a period of two years after the winding-up has been completed (although claims for death or serious injury can be made at any time). Such an order can be brought by a member or creditor or any other interested person. It therefore provides greater protection as regards dealing with creditors. The creditor who surfaces after the company has been liquidated has only two years to put the company back on the register and even then can only overturn distributions made if the liquidator did not take proper steps to contact creditors. Quite often, the costs of a formal voluntary liquidation may seem relatively high compared to the value of the company's assets.

Dissolution under CA 2006, s 1000

8.44 A solvent company may also be dissolved as a result of the company's name being struck off the register by the Registrar of Companies under *Companies Act 2006, s 1000*. This route is sometimes preferred to a liquidation. HMRC are prepared to treat a dissolution under *CA 2006, s 1000* as a 'winding-up' for tax purposes (see **8.47**).

8.45 Where the dissolution route is used, there is now less reason for concern where the share capital exceeds £4,000. This follows the Treasury Solicitor's withdrawal of its 'Guidelines about the Distribution of a Company's Share Capital', which stated that the Crown would be entitled to any funds which a company distributes to its members prior to an informal striking-off (unless the share capital was below £4,000). The main reason for the withdrawal of the Guidelines is that Companies Act 2006 makes it relatively easy to reduce capital below the £4,000 limit (see below).

8.46 A (private) limited company can reduce its share capital by a special resolution which is supported by a solvency statement. The amount by which the share capital is reduced is treated as a distributable reserve. Therefore, from 1 October 2008 if the share capital exceeds £4,000, a company can reduce its share capital (below this amount) and distribute all assets before applying for dissolution.

In contrast to the 'two-year' period allowed for liquidations, a dissolved company can be restored by a court order within six years from the publication of the striking-off notice in the Gazette (*CA 2006, s 1024*). Any member or creditor who 'feels aggrieved' can apply to the court for such an order. It would therefore be possible for a creditor to come forward at any time during the six-year period to overturn a transfer of assets to the members.

DEALING WITH SURPLUS AVAILABLE TO SHAREHOLDERS

Capital distributions

8.47 Where a company has surplus funds (ie after its creditors have been paid), it is necessary to decide how these can be extracted for the shareholders' benefit in the most tax-efficient manner.

Distributions made in the course of dissolving or winding up the company are treated as 'capital distributions' (subject to distributions not exceeding £25,000) and are therefore chargeable to CGT (*TCGA 1992, s 122*). A distribution made to shareholders during the course of the winding-up does not count as an 'income' distribution for tax purposes and therefore no tax credit is available to the recipient shareholder (*CTA 2010, s 1030*).

For CGT purposes, a shareholder is treated as making a disposal of an interest in the relevant shares when he becomes entitled to receive the capital distribution from the company (*TCGA 1992, s 122(1)*). The commencement of the liquidation does not trigger any deemed disposal for the shareholder.

Capital distributions under an informal winding-up

8.48 Previously it was preferable for a solvent company to be struck off the Register of Companies under, what is now *CA 2006, s 1000*, as the costs of winding-up are much lower. However, since 1 March 2012 when ESC C16 was put on a statutory footing within *CTA 2010, ss 1030A* and *1030B*, most owner-managers prefer the route of a formal liquidation in order to obtain the benefit of the capital gains tax treatment.

The informal winding-up route still works for businesses where the amount available for distribution does not exceed £25,000. Where it still applies, HMRC will treat a distribution made prior to a dissolution as having been made under a formal winding-up, and therefore as a capital payment. Certain assurances must be given to the Inspector beforehand. Normally, the Inspector will require that any remaining tax liabilities are paid and also confirm that, once the assets have been distributed, the company will request the Registrar of Companies to strike the company off the register.

Focus

This route no longer provides the favourable capital treatment where the reserves of a company exceed £25,000. In such cases, especially where the company is a husband and wife company, it is possible to formally liquidate the company for relatively little cost.

CGT on capital distributions

8.49 In many cases, capital distributions may be entitled to entrepreneurs' relief (ER) (see **8.50**). Such capital distributions do not carry any indexation allowance or taper relief entitlement as the legislation for both reliefs has been repealed. ER enables the gain arising on the capital distribution to be taxed at a rate of 10%, up to the maximum 'lifetime' limit of £10m or, if lower, the shareholder's unused ER.

From 23 June 2010, any gain qualifying for ER is taxed at 10%. Other gains are taxable, from 6 April 2016, at either 10% or 20%. This is dependent on whether an individual's income and gains exceed the upper limit of the basic rate income tax band. Any gain (not qualifying for ER) is taxable at 10% if it falls within the basic rate band (£31,500 for 2017/18). If the gain, or part of a gain, falls above that limit it will be taxable at 20%.

Entrepreneurs' relief on post-5 April 2008 capital distributions

Qualifying conditions for entrepreneurs' relief

8.50 Capital distributions made during a winding-up (or distributions treated as capital under *CTA 2010, ss 1030A and 1030B*) are eligible for ER, since they are treated as a disposal of an interest in shares under *TCGA 1992,* *s 122 (TCGA 1992, s 169I(2)(c))*. ER is given in such cases provided the conditions in *TCGA 1992, s 169I(7)* are satisfied:

1 The company must be a trading company (or holding company of a trading group) in the *one year* before it *ceases* to trade (or ceases its 'holding company of a trading group' status).

2 Throughout the *one year* before the company ceases to trade (or be a qualifying holding company), the recipient shareholder is required to have:

 - held at least 5% of the ordinary share capital (carrying at least 5% of the voting rights) in the one year;

 - served as a director or employee of the company (or fellow group company).

3 The relevant capital distribution must be made within *three years* after the date the trade ceases (or the company ceases to be a qualifying holding company). HMRC have no discretion to extend this 'three-year' period.

Planning considerations

8.51 These special ER rules are based around the date the company ceases to trade (or loses its qualifying 'holding company' status without becoming a trading company).

Particular care must be taken to ensure that the company is in a position to pay a capital distribution within the three years after it has ceased to trade. The liquidator must therefore endeavour to realise the company's assets within this time frame.

Example 8.6 – Calculation of taxable gain on capital distribution

White Ltd ceased trading on 30 May 2017 after selling its trade and assets. The company was then immediately wound up with a capital distribution of £25,000 being paid on completion of the winding-up on 6 December 2017.

Mr Jones incorporated White Ltd with 1,000 £1 ordinary shares and his shareholding was worth £2,000 at 31 March 1982.

Mr Jones's capital gain on the capital distribution would be calculated as follows:

	£
Capital distribution	25,000
Less: March 1982 value	(2,000)
Chargeable gain	23,000
Less: Annual exemption	(11,300)
Taxable gain	11,700
CGT at 10%	1,170

* Mr Jones has been a director of White Ltd since its incorporation holding 100% of the shares and voting rights in the company. He therefore qualifies and claims ER on the capital distribution (which is made within three years of the company's ceasing to trade).

Taper relief on pre-6 April 2008 capital distributions

8.52 Under the pre-6 April 2008 taper relief rules, the shares in a company were deemed to have become 'non business assets' from the date it ceased to trade. The gains on such distributions would therefore usually have been subject to time apportionment for business/non business taper relief periods. With ER there are no such restrictions.

Multiple capital distributions

8.53 If a shareholder receives more than one capital distribution, all but the last one will be treated as a part disposal in respect of the shares. The normal

$$\frac{A}{A + B}$$

part disposal formula in *TCGA 1992, s 42* will be used to apportion the base cost of the shares where:

A = the amount of the interim capital distribution

B = the residual share value at the date of the interim distribution.

In practice, a relatively relaxed approach is taken with regard to agreeing interim valuations of shares (for the purpose of calculating 'B') where the liquidation is expected to be completed within two years of the first distribution (SP/D3). For example, if all the distributions are made before the CGT is calculated, HMRC will normally agree that the residual share value at the date of any interim distribution equals the total amount of subsequent distributions, without any discount for the delay in the receipt of the subsequent payments.

8.54 Depending on the amounts involved it may be beneficial to phase the timing of the capital distributions over as many tax years as possible. This will enable the shareholders to benefit from more than one annual exemption. Although all parties may be anxious to conclude the liquidation as quickly as possible, by timing the liquidation shortly before the start of the tax year, it may be possible to pay capital distributions over three separate tax years (but paid over a period of only (say) 18 months). Where there are a number of shareholders, the benefits from using multiple annual exemptions may be considerable.

Example 8.7 – Tax treatment of multiple capital distributions

Black Ltd went into (a Members' Voluntary) liquidation on 10 March 2017, having ceased trading on 6 February 2017. After the trade ceased, the company leased out its trading premises on a short lease until the property was sold during the liquidation. Entrepreneurs' relief is available on the capital distributions.

Mr Root formed the company in September 1990, subscribing for all the 2,000 ordinary £1 shares at par.

The liquidator made the following distributions to Mr Root from the residual profits and initial capital:

	£	
6 July 2017	15,000	
31 March 2018 (final)	4,000	
CGT at 10%		£570 (see below)

ER is available and claimed by Mr Root on the capital distributions which are made within three years of the company ceasing to trade.

Mr Root's CGT computations would be as follows:

	£	£
2017/18:		
6 July 2017		
Capital distribution	15,000	
Less: Part disposal cost		

2017/18:	£	£
£2,000 × £15,000/(£15,000 + £4,000)	(1,579)	
Chargeable gain		13,421
31 March 2018	£	
Final capital distribution	4,000	
Less: Cost: £2,000 *less* £1,579 used in July 2017	(421)	
Chargeable gain		3,579
Total chargeable gains		17,000
Less: Annual exemption		(11,300)
Taxable gain		5,700

Small capital distributions

8.55 'Small' interim distributions are deducted against the shareholder's base cost, effectively postponing any gain (*TCGA 1992, s 122(2)*). For these purposes, a distribution not exceeding £3,000 is always taken as small. In all other cases, the distribution is accepted as 'small' provided it does not exceed 5% of the value of the relevant shareholding at the relevant date. However, HMRC do not insist on deducting the small proceeds against the cost where it is beneficial for the shareholder to crystallise a capital gain, for example, if it can be covered by an otherwise unused annual CGT exemption (*Tax Bulletin*, Issue 27).

Where the capital distribution exceeds the allowable CGT base cost, the 'small proceeds' rule does not apply. Instead, the shareholder can elect to offset the capital distribution against his base cost (*TCGA 1992, s 122(4)*). Once the base cost has been fully used, the balance of proceeds and any subsequent distributions will be fully chargeable to CGT.

Distributions in specie

8.56 If a liquidator distributes assets to the shareholders in lieu of their entitlement to a cash distribution, this will still constitute a capital distribution for tax purposes (*TCGA 1992, s 122(5)*). *In specie* capital distributions can rank for ER in the usual way.

Capital distributions of assets are always treated as a transaction at market value because the shareholders are connected with the company (*TCGA 1992, s 17(1)(a)*).

In contrast to a capital distribution for cash, a distribution *in specie* involves two disposals – one by the company in respect of the asset disposed of (which should be exempt from stamp duty or stamp duty land tax (as appropriate)) and one by the shareholder in respect of his shares. As there is no tax credit available on a capital distribution, this gives rise to an acute form of the 'double charge' effect.

PRE-LIQUIDATION/DISSOLUTION DIVIDEND VERSUS CAPITAL DISTRIBUTION

Benefits of CGT treatment

8.57 Most capital distributions made by owner-managed companies should be eligible for ER although care is needed to ensure that the relevant conditions are satisfied in the 12 months before the trade ceases (see **8.49**). There is an added advantage in that payments paid out up to three years after the cessation of trade will still qualify for ER. Provided the individuals have not used any of their ER, they will pay a CGT rate of 10% on gains (of up to £10m on disposals after 5 April 2011). On substantial gains (over £10m), their averaged CGT rate will exceed 10% (due to gains over £10m attracting tax at 20%).

Certain groups of shareholders will *not* benefit from ER (such as small minority shareholders holding less than 5% of the voting equity, and 'non-working' passive shareholders) and will therefore pay CGT at either 10% or 20% on their capital distributions (subject to any annual exemption).

In contrast, pre-liquidation dividends received by a higher rate taxpayer would be subject to income tax at the rate of 32.5%/38.1% on the amount received. In such cases, it will always be preferable to wait until the company is wound up before extracting its retained profits as a capital distribution (which is taxed at a lower rate). Similarly, where a company with assets in excess of £25,000 is being liquidated (see **8.43**), the liquidation should be carried out under a members' voluntary liquidation to obtain 'capital' treatment.

Dividends taxed at basic rate

8.58 There may be some cases where it would be advantageous to extract the company's reserves as a (pre-liquidation) income distribution. For example, if the amounts to be distributed (perhaps over several years) could be paid within the shareholders' 'basic rate' income tax bands no further tax would arise on their dividends (due to the availability of the 10% tax credit). Such planning must be considered and implemented before the company is wound up, since *income* dividends can only be paid before the company is placed into liquidation.

LIQUIDATION AND ITA 2007, s 684 ISSUES

Phoenix company arrangements

8.59 The availability of an effective 10% CGT rate under ER may tempt some owner managers to retain profits in their companies with a view to subsequently liquidating them and extracting the reserves as a capital payment. It would be feasible to extract fairly significant sums in this way.

8.60 The business could subsequently be carried on under identical or similar ownership via a new company – often called a 'phoenix company'. There may of course be tax charges and stamp duty land tax arising on the transfer of the assets to the new company.

HMRC felt they needed more legal teeth to catch this kind of arrangement so the *Finance Act 2016* intends to amend the Transactions in Securities legislation so that distributions on a winding-up which would otherwise be treated as capital will be caught by the TiS provisions.

A new Targeted Anti Avoidance Rule (TAAR) will apply to distributions in respect of share capital in a winding up where the following conditions are met:

- an individual holds at least 5% of the company;
- upon receiving a distribution he continues to be involved, directly or indirectly, with the carrying on of a similar trade; and
- the main purpose of the winding up is to obtain a tax advantage,

ITA 2007, s 684 and the Joiner *case*

8.61 Previously, it was firmly established that *ITA 2007, s 684* could apply where a company (with retained profits) is liquidated with its business being sold to another company under the same or substantially similar ownership. This is broadly what happened in *IRC v Joiner* [1975] STC 601. However, in that case, the House of Lords held that the arrangement was only caught by the 'transactions in securities' legislation because an agreement which varied the shareholders' rights to a capital distribution on a winding-up constituted a 'transaction in securities'.

8.62 The *Joiner* case also concluded that simply putting a company into liquidation was not sufficient (by itself) to be a transaction in securities. HMRC subsequently issued a statement that *ITA 2007, s 684* would *not* be applied to an 'ordinary liquidation'. This effectively means a genuine winding-up of a company, whether it comes to an end or its business is taken over by another entity that is under substantially different control, is unlikely to be vulnerable to a challenge.

On the other hand, HMRC are likely to challenge the transfer of a business to another 'commonly controlled' company in the course of a winding-up. A similar stance may be taken where the shareholder(s) seek(s) to 'disincorporate' their company to enable them to continue to carry on the trade as a sole trade or partnership.

In contrast, HMRC are likely to accept cases where the businesses are being transferred as part of a genuine reconstruction operation within *TCGA 1992, ss 136* and *139* using *Insolvency Act 1986, s 110*.

ENTREPRENEURS' RELIEF ON ASSOCIATED DISPOSALS OF PERSONALLY HELD PROPERTY

Conditions for associated disposal relief

8.63 Some owner managers prefer to hold the company's trading premises personally (away from the clutches of the company's creditors). In such cases, it is likely that the owner manager may wish to sell the property to a third party at the same time or shortly after the company has ceased trading.

There are special rules which extend the availability of ER to mitigate the gain arising on such disposals (known as 'associated disposals') where the shareholder makes a qualifying disposal for ER (*TCGA 1992, s 169K(1), (2)*). In the context of a disposal arising on a capital distribution, the vendor shareholder must meet the conditions summarised in **8.50**.

Furthermore, to obtain ER under the 'associated disposal' rules, two additional conditions must be satisfied:

- The associated disposal must be made as part of the 'withdrawal from participation' in the company. In HMRC's view, this is taken to mean the individual reducing their shareholding in the company (rather than scaling down the amount of work they do for the company). Since a capital distribution creates a disposal of an interest in the relevant company's shares, this test should normally be met (*TCGA 1992, s 169K(3)*). Broadly, HMRC would expect the associated disposal to be triggered by the liquidation/dissolution of the company (giving rise to the shareholder's exit).
- The property (or other personally owned asset) disposed of must have been used in the company's trade throughout the one year before it ceased trading (*TCGA 1992, s 169K(4)*). It is therefore important to ensure that the property etc is used in the trade right up to the cessation of that trade.

Restrictions on gain qualifying for associated disposal entrepreneurs' relief

8.64 As a general rule, associated disposal relief only comes into play if the shareholder has unused ER remaining after calculating their taxable gains on the capital distributions. Associated disposal relief is relatively restrictive and the gain on the associated disposal qualifying for relief may be restricted under *TCGA 1992, s 169P*. The main areas in which relief may be restricted and the basis on which this is done (on a *'just and reasonable'* basis) is summarised below:

Circumstances	*TCGA 1992 reference*	*Restriction to relief*
Property only used for the purposes of the company's business for only part of the period of ownership.	*s 169P(4)(a)*	Relief restricted to period of business use only.
Only part of the property is used for the purposes of the company's business.	*s 169P(4)(b)*	Relief is given on a pro rata basis for the time that it was used for business purposes.
Company pays rent to shareholder for using the asset.	*s 169P(4)(d)*	No relief is available if a full market rent was received. Partial relief is available where the rent received was less than the full market rent. For these purposes, no account is taken of rent received relating to a pre-6 April 2008 period (*FA 2008, Sch 3, para 6*)

Any restriction of the gain qualifying for associated disposal relief is made on a 'just and reasonable basis' by reference to the full ownership period of the relevant asset (subject to the special 'transitional' rule noted above which prevents any pre-6 April rent receipts restricting relief). However, where the shareholder continues to charge a full commercial rent to the company for its use of 'their' asset after 5 April 2008, HMRC will deny relief for the period the asset is held after 5 April 2008 (since it will be regarded as an investment asset as opposed to a trading one).

The restriction in respect of rental income is likely to cause particular difficulties to individuals who borrowed to acquire a commercial property and let it to their company. They will generally wish to charge a rent to the company to fund their personal loan interest payments.

RELIEF FOR SHAREHOLDERS OF INSOLVENT COMPANIES

Negligible value claim

8.65 Where the shares are worthless, a shareholder can make a 'negligible value' claim. There is no specified form for making the claim, but it should clearly identify the shareholding which is claimed as becoming of negligible value, the date on which the capital loss is deemed to arise (see below), and the claim is being made under *TCGA 1992, s 24(2)*.

HMRC should accept a 'negligible value' claim where the shares are 'worth next to nothing' (see Capital Gains Manual at CG13124). This will enable the shareholder to be treated as disposing of their holding for no or virtually no consideration. Where a capital loss is deemed to arise before 6 April 2008, any available indexation cannot be used to increase or create a capital loss.

The deemed disposal does not take place until the claim is made (*TCGA 1992, s 24(2)(a)*). However, *TCGA 1992, s 24(2)(b)* permits a negligible value 'capital loss' claim to be backdated to an earlier date specified in the claim, which must be within two years before the start of the tax year in which the claim is made. Importantly, a 'backdated' claim can only be made if the shares were (held by the claimant and) also worthless at that earlier date.

8.66 Sometimes, negligible value claims are negated because HMRC successfully show that the shareholder's base cost is substantially less than the amount paid for the shares. This is often the case where the shares have been subscribed for shortly before the date of the negligible value claim and are deemed to have been acquired at a (low) market value either by way of the 'non arm's length bargain rule' in *TCGA 1992, s 17(2)*, or on a share reorganisation within *TCGA 1992, s 128(2)*.

It is perhaps worth noting that the Inspector has the discretion to accept certain types of negligible value where the claim is free from any doubt or difficulty (such as the need to agree share valuations). These are for capital losses of under £100,000 on shares in UK unquoted companies which, at the date of the claim or any earlier specified date:

- were in an insolvent liquidation; or
- had ceased trading with no assets.

8.67 If a shareholder does not make a negligible value claim, their capital loss will then be deemed to arise when the company is finally dissolved. In practice, this would be when the liquidation is completed or when the company is finally dissolved – a disposal arises for CGT purposes when the shares are finally extinguished (*TCGA 1992, s 24(1)*).

Example 8.8 – Backdated negligible value claim

Mr Khan's company, Craven Cottage Ltd, went into liquidation in July 2016. The liquidation was completed in July 2017 without Mr Khan receiving any distributions from the liquidator.

Mr Khan formed the company in June 1987 subscribing for 10,000 £1 ordinary shares.

A negligible value claim is made in January 2018, which backdated the deemed disposal of his shares to March 2017 (ie 2016/17).

The calculation of the allowable loss arising in 2015/16 is as follows:

	£
Capital distribution	–
Less: Cost	(10,000)
Allowable loss	(10,000)

Income tax relief for capital losses on shares

Application of *ITA 2007, s 131* relief to companies in liquidation

8.68 In certain circumstances, shareholders may be able to make a claim to offset the capital loss arising on their shares against their other *taxable* income (under the share loss relief provisions in *ITA 2007, s 131*.

For shares issued after 5 April 1998, *ITA 2007, s 131* relief is only available if the company is a qualifying company for EIS purposes. Income tax relief is particularly valuable, as capital losses cannot be relieved unless and until the shareholder makes a capital gain.

In relation to liquidations, income tax relief can be claimed in respect of a capital loss arising on:

- a capital distribution during a winding-up;

- the cancellation (extinction) of the shares under *TCGA 1992, s 24(1)*; or
- a negligible value claim under *TCGA 1992, s 24(2)* (*ITA 2007, s 131(3)*).

8.69 In many cases, it may be beneficial to establish that a deemed capital loss has arisen by making a negligible value claim. This treats the shares as having been disposed and immediately reacquired at their negligible value. As far as timing is concerned, the deemed capital loss can be specified to arise at the date of the claim or at any time within the two years before the start of the tax year in which the claim was made (provided the shares were also 'negligible' at that time). Where *ITA 2007, s 131* is claimed for a deemed 'negligible value' loss, a clear claim must also be made under *TCGA 1992, s 24(2)*. This was confirmed by the Special Commissioner's decision in *Marks v McNally* (2004) SSCD 503, where a share loss relief claim was denied because of the failure to show unambiguously that the capital loss was being claimed under *TCGA 1992, s 24(2)*.

8.70 Strictly, *ITA 2007, s 131* relief cannot be claimed for a capital loss arising on the dissolution of the company. However, by concession, the relief can be claimed where:

(a) the company has no assets and is dissolved; *and*

(b) the shareholder has not received a capital distribution in the course of the dissolution or winding-up of the company *or* where an anticipated final distribution has not been made; *and*

(c) a negligible value claim has not been made under *TCGA 1992, s 24(2)*.

If reliance cannot be placed on the concession to obtain relief on a dissolution, then a negligible value claim must be made while the shares still exist.

'Subscriber share' requirement

8.71 Shareholders can only obtain share loss relief (against their taxable income) if they originally *subscribed* for the shares. Therefore, relief cannot be claimed for shares acquired 'second-hand'.

Special identification rules deal with cases where the claimant shareholder has a 'mixed' shareholding (ie has 'subscriber' shares qualifying for *ITA 2007, s 131* relief and other shares acquired by purchase, gift, etc). However, these are unlikely to be necessary on a liquidation since all the shares would generally be treated as disposed of at the same time.

Where the shareholding is made up of BES shares, EIS 'income tax' relief shares and EIS 'CGT deferral' shares, these 'subscription' shares are broadly identified on a FIFO basis.

Operation of *ITA 2007, s 131* relief

8.72 *ITA 2007, s 131* relief for disposals (or deemed 'negligible value' disposals) is claimed against the shareholder's income for the tax year of the disposal *and/or* the previous tax year. Where a claim is made for both years, the claim must specify the year against which the *ITA 2007, s 131* deduction is to be claimed first. Otherwise, the claim must specify the relevant year being claimed (*ITA 2007, s 132*). Under self-assessment, any carry-back claim is treated as a claim for the later year. The relief is calculated as the reduction in the previous year's tax liability as a result of the claim. The consequent reduction in the previous year's tax liability is treated as an additional 'payment on account' of the later year (*TMA 1970, Sch 1B, para 2*).

The claim must be made within 12 months after the 31 January following the tax year in which the loss is incurred (*ITA 2007, s 132(4)*).

RELIEF FOR SHAREHOLDER LOANS

Capital loss relief for irrecoverable loans

Outline of *TCGA 1992, s 253* relief

8.73 Generally, a simple debt is outside the scope of CGT and therefore if it becomes irrecoverable, relief would not be available for the creditor's loss. However, an individual shareholder (or indeed any other individual lender) can make a claim under *TCGA 1992, s 253* to obtain a capital loss equal to the *principal* element of their irrecoverable loan (which can include credit balances on current accounts). Corporate lenders generally obtain relief under the loan relationship regime unless they are 'connected' with the borrowing company.

The claimant will receive a capital loss equal to the amount that the Inspector has agreed is irrecoverable. The capital loss *cannot* be offset against income under *ITA 2007, s 131* (as it does not relate to shares).

The capital loss on an irrecoverable loan arises when the claim is made. However, it is also possible to establish the loss at an earlier time, being within the two previous tax years before the start of the tax year in which the claim is made, provided the loan was also irrecoverable at that earlier date (*TCGA 1992, s 253(3), (3A)*).

Conditions for *TCGA 1992, s 253* relief

8.74 To make a competent claim under *TCGA 1992, s 253*, a number of conditions must be satisfied, the most important of which are:

(a) The loan must be irrecoverable and the claimant must not have assigned their right of recovery.

(b) The amount lent must have been used wholly for the purposes of a trade (which can include capital expenditure and trade setting-up costs) carried on by a UK-resident company. This trade application test is also satisfied where the borrowing company has lent the monies to another 'fellow' group company for use in its trade. The fellow group company must be in a 75% group relationship – the wider 'group' definition (which includes non-resident companies) applies for loans made after 31 March 2000. Since 6 April 2003, that group company must be a 'trading company'. (Relief is also available where the borrowed amount is used to repay a loan that would have qualified.)

 The relief is not therefore available for loans to investment companies or to purchase 'investment' assets.

(c) The loan must not constitute a 'debt on security' (broadly, a debt on security represents a loan held as an investment which is both marketable and produces a return or profit to the holder) (*TCGA 1992, s 253(1), (3)*).

8.75 In judging whether a loan has become 'irrecoverable' at the date of the claim (or earlier date), HMRC are likely to examine the prospects of its recovery based on relevant balance sheets and other information. The Inspector would seek to determine whether there is a reasonable likelihood of the loan (or part of it) being repaid, having regard to the borrowing company's current and probable future financial position. In practice, where the borrower is insolvent and has ceased trading and it is clear that the loan (or part of it) would not be repaid, a *TCGA 1992, s 253* claim would usually be accepted for the relevant amount. On the other hand, relief may be denied where the borrowing company is still trading (albeit making losses). Similarly, if the borrower was in a parlous state when the loan was made, the Inspector may refuse the claim on the grounds that the loan had not *become irrecoverable* as required by *TCGA 1992, s 253(3)(a)*.

8.76 In *Crosby (Trustees) v Broadhurst* [2004] STC SSCD 348, the Special Commissioners agreed that relief was available on an irrecoverable loan that had (as part of the terms of the borrowing company's sale) been waived before the formal claim was submitted to the Inspector. They did not accept the Inspector's view that the loan had to be in existence at the time the claim was made.

Any subsequent recovery of part or all of the debt will be treated as a chargeable gain arising at the date of repayment. Capital loss relief cannot normally be claimed on intra-group loans under *TCGA 1992, s 253*.

Guarantee payments

8.77 Where an *individual* shareholder has provided a personal guarantee which is called in by the lender, they will be able to claim capital loss relief on any payment made under the guarantee. Claims for guarantee payments made by an individual must be made within four years of the end of the year of assessment in which the payment is made.

Capital loss relief may also be available where a group company makes a payment under a guarantee in relation to a borrowing by a fellow group company. The claim must be made within four years of the accounting period end in which the payment is made. The group guarantor company would become entitled to the rights of the original lender and can therefore claim capital loss relief if it is prevented from claiming a deduction under the loan relationship legislation (*TCGA 1992, s 253(3), (4)(c)*).

Example 8.9 – Capital loss relief for irrecoverable loan

Wright Ltd has traded profitably for a number of years. However, the company has experienced a downturn in trading during the last three years. In May 2006, Mr Billy, the controlling shareholder, had to make a cash injection of £80,000 to the company to ease its ailing finances. However, in December 2017, the company's bankers called in the receiver and the company was subsequently wound up. No part of Mr Billy's loan account was repaid.

Mr Billy can therefore claim under *TCGA 1992, s 253* for the £80,000 to be treated as an allowable loss for CGT purposes.

If Mr Billy realises a capital gain of, say, £50,000 in 2017/18, he should be able to relieve it with his capital loss on the loan, provided he makes the claim by 5 April 2022. To do this, Mr Billy must be able to satisfy the Inspector that the full amount of the loan (or substantially all of it) was irrecoverable by 5 April 2018.

CONVERTING LOANS INTO NEW SHARES

8.78 Given the potential advantages of income tax relief by making a claim under *ITA 2007, s 131* shareholders may be tempted to 'capitalise' their loans by subscribing for further shares. However, if the company is *insolvent*, the amount subscribed for the new shares is unlikely to be reflected as part of the shareholder's CGT base cost. This is because *TCGA 1992, s 17(1)* deems the shares to be acquired at their (negligible) market value (where the amount subscribed is greater than market value).

Alternatively, the capitalisation of the loan for new shares may constitute a 'reorganisation' for CGT purposes. This would be the case where, for example, all shareholders subscribe for additional shares in proportion to their existing holdings. On a 'reorganisation', *TCGA 1992, s 128(2)* effectively provides that the amount subscribed will only be reflected in base cost to the extent that the relevant shareholding increases in value, which in such cases is unlikely.

Given the above difficulties in securing a CGT base cost, it will normally be disadvantageous to substitute share capital for shareholder loans (where the company has a deficiency of net assets). The shareholder should be able to claim capital loss relief for his irrecoverable loan under *TCGA 1992, s 253*, whereas if it is 'converted' into shares there is unlikely to be any relief.

Losses incurred on qualifying corporate bonds (QCBs)

8.79 In some cases, the shareholder may hold a loan note evidencing the debt. This will invariably constitute a qualifying corporate bond (QCB) and represent a 'debt on security'. However, provided the loan was made *before 17 March 1998*, an allowable capital loss can still be claimed for the irrecoverable part of the debt under the provisions of *TCGA 1992, s 254* for CGT loss relief.

However, to qualify the QCB must comply with the 'qualifying loan' rules and the funds concerned must have been lent wholly for the purposes of a trade carried on by the borrower. It follows that if the holder received the QCB as consideration for the acquisition of shares relief will not be available (*TCGA 1992, ss 253, 254*).

No CGT loss relief is available for QCB loans made after 16 March 1998.

Loans made by companies

8.80 Capital loss relief under *TCGA 1992, s 253* is not available where the lender is able to claim a deduction under the loan relationship rules (*TCGA*

1992, s 253(3)). In many cases, a corporate lender should be able to claim a 'non-trading' loan relationship deduction for an impairment loss on a 'non-trading' loan (ie where the loan is effectively written off or provided against as an irrecoverable bad debt). A trading deduction would only be available where the loan was made in the course of a trade.

However, if the borrower is a *connected person*, such as a fellow group member or a 'parallel' company under common control, then it is not generally possible to claim a tax allowable impairment loss (*CTA 2009, s 354*). In this context, *CTA 2009, s 355* provides a mechanism for a lender to obtain relief *only* on amounts which become subject to an impairment 'write-off' after it ceases to be 'connected' with the borrowing company. This means that amounts remaining outstanding when the borrower goes into liquidation cannot be relieved. It should be noted that GAAP usually requires impairment of debts that are not expected to be recovered. Hence the lender is likely already to have impaired most, if not all, of the loan balance prior to the commencement of liquidation, etc. Relief will only be available on such amounts that remain 'unimpaired'.

8.81 The legislation in *CTA 2009, s 355* works by preventing any tax deduction being taken for impairment losses that were denied relief whilst the companies were 'connected'. It is helpful to understand why the 'connection' test in *CTA 2009, s 466* would be broken where the 'connected party' debtor goes into insolvent liquidation or administration. In broad terms, *CTA 2009, s 472* provides that a person has control of a company for this purpose if they are able to conduct the company's affairs in accordance with their wishes through holding the requisite shares, voting power or powers conferred by the Articles of Association or any other documents (such as a shareholders' agreement). Where the borrowing company goes into liquidation or administration, this 'control' nexus would be broken since the liquidator/administrator would take over the management of the company's affairs. A parent company would therefore lose its ability to control the affairs of its subsidiary (eg by appointing and removing directors) and hence would no longer 'control' the company within *CTA 2009, s 472*.

Exceptionally, where the lending company is able to deduct an impairment loss for amounts becoming impaired post-liquidation, it will be allowed as a non-trading (or trading) deduction by virtue of *CTA 2009, s 355*.

Chapter 9

Tax planning for the non-resident and non-domiciled

Robert Maas FCA, FTII, FIIT, TEP, Consultant, CBW Tax Ltd

SIGNPOSTS

- **Concepts** – From 2013/14 onwards there is a statutory definition of residence. For earlier years the concept was not defined.
- **Planning to emigrate** – There are various ways that a person can cease to be UK resident. However the absence of a statutory definition of residence prior to 2013/14 made it uncertain whether a person had achieved this (see **9.7–9.29**).
- **The concept of domicile** – A person's tax position can be affected by his domicile. This again is not defined. However, it is a concept of general law, not a tax concept, so there is a lot of judicial guidance on its meaning (see **9.30–9.32**).
- **The tax significance of the two concepts** – Why do these concepts matter? What taxes depend on each concept? (see **9.33–9.35**).
- **The remittance basis** – A person who is resident but not domiciled in the UK can claim to be taxed on overseas income and gains only to the extent that they have been brought into the UK. Where a person has been resident in the UK for over seven years a fee of £30,000 to £90,000 has to be paid to HMRC if it is wished to use the remittance basis. This fee is in addition to the tax on remittances. The legislation contains some detailed rules to treat money as being remitted if it is economically used here (see **9.36–9.55**). The rules altered significantly from 6 April 2017.
- **Employment income** – Special rules apply to employment income (see **9.46–9.54**).
- **Taxation of non-UK residents** – Non-residents are not normally taxed in the UK on investment income other than property income. They are however taxed on employment income, trading income

and property income where the employment or trade is exercised in the UK (including partly in the UK) or the property is here. Non-residents are not normally taxed on UK capital gains. From 2014/15 (in some cases from 2013/14) this exclusion does not apply to UK residential property. Inheritance tax depends primarily on domicile. A non-resident who is domiciled in the UK or has assets in the UK is within the scope of inheritance tax (see **9.57–9.89**). From 6 April 2017, shares in, and certain loans to, overseas companies that own UK residential property are also brought into inheritance tax.

- **Company residence** – A company is normally resident where its central control and management takes place. The courts have laid down principles to determine how to identify this place. A UK-incorporated company is normally UK resident, even if it is controlled and managed from elsewhere. A non-UK resident company does not wholly escape UK tax; it is taxable here if it carries on a trade in the UK or has property income here (see **9.90–9.103**).

INTRODUCTION

9.1 Chargeability to UK tax depends on two concepts:

- residence; and
- domicile.

Up to 5 April 2013, there was a third, ordinary residence, but this concept was abolished by the *Finance Act 2013* (*FA 2013*) as part of the introduction of a statutory residence test. Prior to 2013/14 residence and ordinary residence were concepts of general law that were left to be formulated for tax purposes by the courts. In practice most people relied on the HMRC guidance as set out in the booklet IR20 and its more recent replacement HMRC6. HMRC claimed to base this guidance on the decided cases, but it was often difficult to reconcile the two. HMRC6 seemed to be largely concessionary in parts and more rigid than the court decisions in others. The statutory residence test fundamentally altered the concept of residence. The previous tests are however still of relevance in two circumstances. The first is that they apply for all years up to 5 April 2013 and HMRC have until 5 April 2017 (5 April 2019 if they can show a failure to take reasonable care and 5 April 2033 if they can show fraud) to challenge a person's residence status for 2012/13. Secondly, the statutory residence test is actually a series of tests. One of these takes account of whether the taxpayer was UK resident in either of the two previous tax years. This looks at residence under the rules that applied at the time (subject to a right to elect to use the new rules instead), so if one of those years was 2011/12 or 2012/13 it may still be necessary to look at the old rules to determine residence up to 2015/16. Accordingly, the previous residence tests are reproduced below as a separate self-contained section following the review of the current residence test.

A person who is resident and domiciled in the UK is liable to UK tax on worldwide income and assets. If a person does not meet both of these tests then some of his income or assets may well escape UK tax.

The starting point is accordingly these two concepts.

RESIDENCE FROM 6 APRIL 2013

9.2

Focus

From 5 April 2013 a person is UK resident for a tax year if either:

1 He is present in the UK for more than 183 days in the tax year (*FA 2013, Sch 43, para 7*).

2 He has a home in the UK during the tax year, he spends some time there (however short) on at least ten days in the tax year, and for a period of at least 91 days (30 of which fall in the tax year) either he has no home outside the UK or, if he does, he spends time there on fewer than 30 days in the tax year (*FA 2013, Sch 43, para 8*).

3 He works 'sufficient hours in the UK' over a 365-day period (all or part of which falls into the tax year), during that period there are no significant breaks from UK work, and more than 75% of the total number of days in the 365-day period on which he does more than three hours' work are days of work in the UK (*FA 2013, Sch 45, para 9*). Whether a person works sufficient hours in the UK is calculated by reference to a formula. Start from 365. Deduct disregarded days, ie days on which the person works at least three hours overseas (even if he does three hours here as well). Deduct annual leave, parenting leave, sickness, and non-working days embedded in a block of such days. Divide the resulting figure by seven and round down to the nearest whole number (or round up to 1). Ascertain the total hours that the person works in the UK (other than on disregarded days) during the 365-day period. Divide that by the number previously calculated. If this gives 35 or more, the person worked sufficient hours in the UK for the tax year.

Example 9.1 – Working in the UK

Johann comes to the UK from Belgium to work on an installation project in 1 January 2015. He works seven hours a day, five days a week for six months. He then takes four weeks' holiday. He works four hours a day for the next six weeks. He is off sick for the next eight days, after which he resumes work for another 32 days (of which 24 are work days). Johann then returns to Belgium where he works seven hours a day for six weeks. He comes back to the UK for a day to sort out a problem. On that day he works four hours in Belgium and 3.5 in the UK. He then returns to Belgium. Of the first 30 days in Belgium, ie the number required to bring the total days up to 365) Johann works on 20.

From 365 deduct the disregarded days, ie days working in Belgium = 30 + 1 + 20 = 51. From the resultant 314 deduct holidays, etc (28 + 8 = 36) giving 278. Divide by 7 = 39. Ascertain Johann's total hours worked in the UK (26 weeks × 5 days × 7 hours (910) + 6 × 5 × 4 hours (120) + 24 × 4 (96) = 1,126. Divide by 39 = 28.8. As that is less than 35 Johann has not worked sufficient hours in the UK, so is not UK resident under this test.

4 The person dies during the tax year, was UK resident for each of the previous three years under one of the above tests, had a home in the UK during the tax year and, if he were not resident in the tax year, the previous year would not have been a split year (*FA 2013, Sch 45, para 10*).

5 He was resident here in any one of the previous three tax years, spends at least 15 days in the UK in the tax year and satisfies one or more of five connecting factors (see below). The number of factors that count vary with the time spent in the UK, namely:

Days spent in UK	*Impact of connection factors on residence status*
Fewer than 16 days	Always non-resident
16–45 days	Resident if individual has 4 factors or more (otherwise not resident)
46–90 days	Resident if individual has 3 factors or more (otherwise not resident)
91–120 days	Resident if individual has 2 factors or more (otherwise not resident)
121–182 days	Resident if individual has 1 factor or more (otherwise not resident)
183 days or more	Always resident

The five connecting factors are:

- **Family** – the individual's spouse or civil partner (or common law equivalent) or minor children are resident in the UK.
- **Accommodation** – the individual has accessible accommodation in the UK and makes use of it during the tax year (subject to an exclusion for a short stay with a relative).
- **Substantive work in the UK** – The individual does substantive work in the UK (but does not work here full time).
- **UK presence in the previous year** – The individual spent more than 90 days in the UK in either of the previous two tax years.
- **More time in the UK than in other countries** – The individual spent more days in the UK in the tax year than in any other single country.

(*FA 2013, Sch 45, paras 17, 18*).

6 If the individual was not resident in the UK in any of the previous three tax years, he is present here for more than 45 days in the tax year and meets one or more of the first four of the above five factors. Again the number of factors that count vary with the time spent in the UK but the table differs from that at above. The rules are as follows (*FA 2013, Sch 45, para 19*):

Days spent in UK	*Impact of connection factors on residence status*
Fewer than 46days	Always non-resident
46–90 days	Resident if individual has 4 factors or more (otherwise not resident)
91–120 days	Resident if individual has 3 factors or more (otherwise not resident)
121–182 days	Resident if individual has 2 factors or more (otherwise not resident)
183 days or more	Always resident

The connecting factors appear to apply throughout the year if they apply on a single day in the year, although split-year treatment (see **9.5**) will often apply in the year that a person comes to, or leaves, the UK. Split-year treatment will not apply where a person ceases to be, or becomes, UK resident because of a change in the number of factors taken into account under (5) or (6) above.

9.3 Even if he would be UK resident under one of the above tests, a person is not UK resident for a tax year if either:

1 He was UK resident in at least one of the previous three tax years, spends less than 16 days here in the tax year concerned and does not die in that year (*FA 2013, Sch 45, para 12*).

2 He was not UK resident in any of the previous three tax years and spends less than 46 days here in the tax year concerned (*FA 2013, Sch 45, para 13*).

3 He works sufficient hours overseas in the tax year, there are no significant breaks from overseas work in that year, he does more than three hours' work in the UK on no more than 30 days and he spends no more than 90 days here in the tax year (ignoring days on which he is deemed to be in the UK) (*FA 2013, Sch 45, para 14*). Sufficient hours overseas is calculated in the same way as sufficient hours in the UK (see above) but by reference to the tax year, not by reference to any 365-day period.

4 He dies during the tax year, he was not UK resident for either of the previous two years (or was not UK resident for the previous year and the year before that was a split year) and he spent less than 46 days in the UK in the tax year (*FA 2013, Sch 45, para 15*).

5 He dies during the tax year, was not UK resident in either of the previous two years by virtue of head 3 above (or was not UK resident in the previous year by virtue of that head and the year before that was a split year) and he would have been non-UK resident under head three if it applied only by reference to the part of the tax year up to the date of his death (*FA 2013, Sch 45, para 16*).

9.4 For the above purposes a person is normally present in the UK on a day if he is here at midnight on that day. However a day on which he is in transit as a passenger is ignored provided that he does not engage in activities that are to a substantial extent unconnected with his passage through the UK. HMRC seem to interpret this last condition as meaning that any activities entered into must not be pre-planned. This looks at social activities as well as business ones. The intention seems to be to exclude the day only if the sole reason for being in the UK overnight was because travel connections made it impossible or difficult to travel onwards on the day of arrival (HMRC6, para 2.3).

Up to 60 days on which he would not have been present here but for exceptional circumstances beyond his control that prevent him leaving the UK can also be ignored provided that he intends to leave the UK as soon as circumstances permit. If (ignoring this special rule) a person has at least three UK connecting factors (see **9.2**), was UK resident in one of the previous three tax years and is present in the UK at some point in the day (but not at midnight) on more than 30 days, those excess days are deemed to be days of presence in the UK

(*FA 2013, Sch 45, paras 22, 23*). This prevents a person who lives overseas but works in the UK from avoiding UK residence by coming here on a Monday morning and leaving on Thursday and counting only one day of presence, when the reality is that he is here for virtually three. This restriction does not apply for the purpose of determining whether the automatic UK resident tests (items 1–4 in **9.2** above) and the automatic overseas resident tests (**9.3** above) are met (*FA 2013, Sch 45, para 23(5)*). HMRC indicate in RDR3 that this means that it does not affect the 91-day test (see **9.3**(3)).

If the only reason for a family connection is that the taxpayer's infant child is resident in the UK, that tie can be ignored if the taxpayer sees the child in the UK for less than 61 days in the tax year (*FA 2013, Sch 45, para 32*). If the child is UK resident only because he is in full-time education here, the child can be treated as non-UK resident if he spends less than 21 days here outside term time (*FA 2013, Sch 45, para 33*). Term time for this purpose includes half-term breaks and other breaks during a term when education is not provided.

Accommodation is accessible only if it is available to the taxpayer to live in when in the UK for a continuous period of at least 91 days and he spends at least one night there in the tax year (*FA 2013, Sch 45, para 34*). If the accommodation is the home of a parent or grandparent, a sibling or an adult child or adult grandchild of the taxpayer (or of the spouse or civil partner of such a person) it is only accessible accommodation if the taxpayer spends at least 16 nights there during the tax year.

A person does substantive work in the UK only if he works here for at least three hours a day for at least 40 days (*FA 2013, Sch 45, para 35*).

Where residence for any year up to 2017/18 depends on whether the individual was resident in the UK in 2012/13 or earlier, residence for those earlier years is determined on the basis of the rules that applied at the time (*FA 2013, Sch 45, para 154(2)*). However the individual can elect for residence for all or any of those earlier years to instead be determined on the basis of the new statutory residence rules (*FA 2013, Sch 45, para 154(3)*). Such an election must be made within 12 months of the end of the tax year concerned and is irrevocable.

Split-year treatment

9.5 There are eight circumstances (or 'cases') in which the tax year can be split, ie the taxpayer is regarded as UK resident only for the part of the year in which he is living in the UK. These are:

1 The taxpayer was UK resident in the previous tax year, is non-resident during the following year by virtue of **9.3**(3), and in the current year there is a period that begins within the tax year on a day on which the

taxpayer does more than three hours' work overseas, ends at the end of the tax year, and during which the taxpayer works sufficient hours overseas, has no significant breaks from overseas work, works in the UK for no more than the permitted limit and does not spend more than the permitted number of days in the UK (*FA 2013, Sch 45, para 44*). Sufficient hours overseas is calculated in a similar way to that at **9.2**(3). The permitted limit is 30 days reduced proportionately for the number of whole months in the tax year prior to the start of the non-resident period. The permitted number of days in the UK is 90 reduced for the number of whole months in the tax year prior to the start of the non-resident period.

2 The taxpayer was UK resident for the previous tax year, is not UK resident in the following year, has a spouse or partner who meets the above condition, moves overseas during the current tax year so that they can continue to live together, and for the remainder of the year has no home in the UK (or if he does, spends more time in an overseas home than in the UK one) and spends no more than the permitted number of days in the UK (calculated as above) (*FA 2013, Sch 45, para 45*).

3 The taxpayer was UK resident for the previous tax year, is non-UK resident for the following year, had a home in the UK at the start of the current tax year but ceases to do so during the year (and has no home here thereafter in the tax year) and following that cessation spends no more than 15 days in the UK and establishes a sufficient link with an overseas country within six months of ceasing to have a UK home (*FA 2013, Sch 45, para 46*). For this purpose a person establishes a sufficient link with an overseas country if either he is treated as a resident there, he has been present there at midnight on every day in the six-month period, or his only home (or homes) is in that country.

4 The taxpayer was non-UK resident for the previous tax year, did not have his home (or all of his homes) in the UK at the start of the current year but comes to do so during the year and, for the part of the year prior to that time did not have sufficient UK ties (ie the four connecting factors but with the figures pro rated by reference to the number of months in the part of the year following the acquisition of the UK home) (*FA 2013, Sch 45, para 47*).

5 The taxpayer was non-UK resident in the previous tax year, there is a period of 365 days beginning in the current year (on a day on which the taxpayer does more than three hours' work in the UK) before the start of which the taxpayer did not have sufficient UK ties, the taxpayer works sufficient hours in the UK (calculated as above), has no significant breaks from UK work and in that 365-day period at least 75% of the days on which the taxpayer did more than three hours' work were days working in the UK (*FA 2013, Sch 45, para 48*).

6 The taxpayer was non-UK resident in the previous year by virtue of the test at **9.3**(3), is UK resident for the following tax year, and there is a period beginning at the start of the current year and ending during the current year on a day on which the taxpayer does more than three hours work overseas, and the taxpayer satisfies the overseas work criteria (*FA 2013, Sch 45, para 49*). A period satisfies the overseas work criteria if the taxpayer works sufficient hours overseas (see earlier), there are no significant breaks from overseas work, the number of days on which the taxpayer does more than three hours' work in the UK does not exceed the permitted limit (see earlier) and the total number of days spent in the UK does not exceed the permitted number of days (see above).

7 The taxpayer was non-UK resident for the previous year, is UK resident during the following year, in the current year he moves to the UK so that he can continue to live with his spouse or partner (who satisfies head 6 above), and in the part of the year before coming to the UK the taxpayer had no home in the UK (or if he did, spent more of his time in a non-UK home) and the number of days he spent in the UK does not exceed the permitted number of days (as defined earlier) (*FA 2013, Sch 45, para 50*).

8 The taxpayer was non-UK resident for the previous tax year, is UK resident for the following year (and that is not itself a split year) and in the current year had no home in the UK but acquired one during the year and continues to have a home in the UK for the remainder of that year and the whole of the following year, and in the period before acquiring the UK home the taxpayer did not have sufficient UK ties (as defined earlier) (*FA 2013, Sch 45, para 51*).

It will be seen that split-year treatment is more limited than under the old rules. Split-year treatment on coming to the UK can apply only if the taxpayer (or spouse) is coming to the UK to work or had no home in the UK and acquires one here during the tax year. Split-year treatment on leaving the UK can apply only if the taxpayer (or spouse) goes abroad to work or he disposes of his UK house (or does not do so but acquires an overseas property and spends more time in that than in the UK one).

Temporary non-residence

9.6 In the same way as for capital gains tax (see **9.62**) a person who ceases to be non-UK resident and becomes UK resident again within five years can be taxed on certain types of income that arise during his period of non-residence. A person is a temporary non-resident if he is solely UK resident for a complete tax year (or the UK part of a split tax year), following that period one or more tax years (or parts of a split tax year) occur for which he does not have sole UK residence, the temporary period of non-residence is five tax years or less, and at least four out of the seven tax years immediately preceding the tax year in which he ceased to be solely UK resident were tax years for which he had sole UK residence (or a split year for part of which he had sole UK residence) (*FA 2013, Sch 45, para 110*). An individual has sole UK residence for this purpose if he is resident here under UK domestic law and is not treated as non-resident under a double tax treaty (*FA 2013, Sch 43, para 112*). The temporary period of non-residence is of course the period between ceasing to be UK resident and again becoming UK resident.

Where a person is temporary non-UK resident:

1 Withdrawals from a registered pension scheme or a non-UK pension scheme under a flexible drawdown arrangement paid in the period of temporary non-residence are treated as paid in the period of return, ie the first tax year (or taxable part of a split year) following the individual's return to the UK (*ITEPA 2003, ss 576A, 579CA* inserted by *FA 2013, Sch 45, paras 116, 117*).

2 Relevant foreign income (ie foreign investment income) taxed on a remittance basis received prior to the individual's departure from the UK and remitted during the period of temporary non-residence is treated as remitted in the period of return (*ITTOIA 2005, s 832A* inserted by *FA 2013, Sch 45, para 118*).

3 Employment income which is not earnings or share-related (and as such is taxable in the year of receipt under *ITEPA 2003, s 394*) which is in the form of a lump sum and is received during the period of temporary non-residence is treated as received in the period of return (*ITEPA 2003, s 394A* inserted by *FA 2013, Sch 45, para 125*).

4 A relevant step under the rules in relation to employment income provided by third parties which consists of the payment of a lump sum in the period of temporary non-residence is treated as having been received in the period of return (*ITEPA 2003, s 554Z4A* inserted by *FA 2013, Sch 45, para 126*).

5 A relevant benefit provided under an EFURBS in the form of a lump sum and remitted to the UK in the period of non-residence is treated as having been remitted to the UK in the period of return (*ITEPA 2003, s 554Z11* inserted by *FA 2013, Sch 45, para 127*).

6 A UK pension paid in the form of a lump sum which accrued in the period of temporary non-residence is a treated as having accrued in the period of return (*ITEPA 2003, s 572A* inserted by *FA 2013, Sch 45 para 129*).

7 A dividend or other distribution by a close company to a material participator in the company (or an associate of his) in the period of temporary non-residence must be treated as received in the period of

return (unless it is a cash dividend paid out of trading profits arising after the start of the period of temporary non-residence) (*ITTOIA 2005, s 401C* inserted by *FA 2013, Sch 45, para 133*). A material participator is one who has a material interest in the company (ie over 5%). The dividend attracts a tax credit for the year of return in the normal way.

8 Such a dividend from a non-UK company which would be a close company if it were UK resident is similarly treated as received in the period of return (*ITTOIA 2005, s 408A* inserted by *FA 2013, Sch 45, para 134*).

9 A stock dividend paid by a UK company to a material participator during the period of temporary non-residence is similarly treated as received in the period of return (*ITTOIA 2005, s 413A* inserted by *FA 2013, Sch 45, para 135*).

10 If a loan or advance by a close company to an individual is written off by the company during the period of temporary non-residence it is treated as having been written off in the period of return (*ITTOIA 2005, s 420A* inserted by *FA 2013, Sch 45, para 136*).

11 Any other distribution by a close company (or an overseas company that would be close if it were UK resident) to a material participator (or associate) in the period of non-residence is treated as made in the period of return if it would be taxable in the UK if it were made in that period (*ITTOIA 2005, s 689A* inserted by *FA 2013, Sch 45, para 137*).

12 if an individual's UK tax liability in a period of temporary non-residence is limited under *ITA 2007, s 811* and his income includes dividends or other distributions made by a close company to a material participator, the individual's total income for the period of return must be increased by the amount of such income (unless the distribution is out of trading profits arising in the period of temporary non-residence) (*ITA 2007, s 812A* inserted by *FA 2013, Sch 45, para 138*).

13 If in the period of temporary non-residence an individual receives a chargeable event gain from an insurance policy issued before the start of that period and no one is liable to UK income tax on that gain, the chargeable event is treated as having occurred in the period of return (*ITTOIA 2005, s 465B* inserted by *FA 2013, Sch 45, para 140*).

CEASING TO BE UK RESIDENT

9.7 Under the statutory residence test it is relatively easy for a person to become non-UK resident for a tax year. He can:

1 Limit his visits to the UK in that tax year to 15 days (45 days if he was UK resident for only one tax year).

2 Take up full time work overseas throughout that tax year and not work in the UK at all (or work here for less than 31 days) and limit his visits to the UK in the tax year to 90 days. Full-time work for this purpose aggregates all employments and self employments and any day on which more than three hours' work is done counts as a working day.

3 Arrange his life to seek to minimise the number of connections that he has with the UK and keep his visits to the UK within the appropriate trigger point for his remaining connections. A point to watch is that one of the connecting factors is that the person spent over 90 days in the UK in one of the previous two tax years. Accordingly it might in some cases be necessary to keep visits to 90 days even though the test may allow a longer period in the UK. This is because if the 90 days is exceeded that might not make the individual resident for the year concerned, but will create an extra connecting factor for the following two years.

An individual can also be treated as non-UK resident under a double tax agreement. Most such agreements provide that where a person is UK resident under UK tax rules and also resident in the other country under its tax rules, a series of tests must be applied to determine which country is to treat him as a resident. If those tests result in his being treated as a resident of the other country, he cannot be taxed (to income tax and capital gains tax) as a UK resident.

A point to watch is that a double tax treaty does not prevent a person being UK resident; it simply taxes him as if he were non-UK resident. Accordingly using a double tax agreement will not break the 17-year period of residence under the deemed domicile test for inheritance tax or the seven or more years of residence for the remittance basis rules.

Deemed non-residence

9.8

Focus

Remember that a client might be dual-resident as a result of being also resident in another country at the same time as he is resident in the UK. If the UK has a double taxation agreement with the other country that agreement will contain a tie-breaker clause to determine which country is entitled to treat the client as a resident, rather than both doing so. Claiming the benefit of the agreement may make the client non-UK resident even though he is UK resident under the UK domestic rules.

However this deemed non-residence applies only to taxes covered by the agreement. In particular it will not necessarily apply to income arising in third countries.

As indicated above, most, but not all, of the UK's full double tax agreements contain a 'tie-breaker' clause to treat an individual as resident in only one of the countries concerned where he would otherwise be treated by each as resident there under its domestic laws. A fairly standard example is that with the US which provides that where an individual is both resident in the UK under UK law and resident in the US under US law then:

- He is deemed to be resident only in the country in which he has a permanent home available to him.
- If he has a permanent home available in both countries he is deemed to be resident only in the country with which his personal and economic relations are closer (often called his 'centre of vital interests').
- If either his centre of vital interests cannot be determined or he does not have a permanent home available to him in either country he is deemed to be resident only in the country in which he has a habitual abode.
- If he has a habitual abode in both countries (or neither) he is deemed to be resident only in the country of which he is a national.
- If he is a national of both (or neither) the tax authorities of the two countries must endeavour to settle the question by mutual agreement.

(Article 4(4), US/UK Double Tax Agreement)

9.9 The notes to the OECD model double tax convention expand on the second point above:

> 'It is necessary to look at the facts in order to ascertain with which of the two States his personal and economic relations are closer. Thus, regard will be had to his family and social relations, his occupations, his political, cultural or other activities, his place of business, the place from which he administers his property, etc. The circumstances must be examined as a whole, but it is nevertheless obvious that considerations based on the personal acts of the individual must receive special attention. If a person who has a home in one State sets up a second in the other State while retaining the first, the fact that he retains the first in the environment where he has always lived, where he has worked, and where he has his family and possessions, can, together with other elements, go to demonstrate that he has retained his centre of vital interests in the first State.'

Some double tax agreements include a provision that relief from UK tax is due to a resident of the other country only to the extent that the person is liable to tax on the income in that other country. This particularly applies where the other country taxes the income on a remittance basis. Such countries include Australia, Canada, Ireland and Jamaica. Conversely, the US agreement does not grant exemption from US tax where the income is taxed in the UK on a remittance basis and has not been remitted.

RESIDENCE UP TO 5 APRIL 2013

9.10 As indicated earlier, for 2012/13 and earlier years the concept of residence relied on a large number of court decisions but it was difficult to draw much firm guidance from them. HMRC sought to do so in their booklet HMRC6, 'Residents and non-residents – Liability to tax in the UK' (which replaced IR20). This was an extremely useful booklet. It is unwise to seek to decide a person's residence under the pre-5 April 2013 rules without first becoming familiar with this booklet, not only because it highlights areas to which HMRC attach particular importance but also because the HMRC interpretation is to an extent concessionary.

Broadly speaking, a person was resident in the UK if he normally lived here; whether or not he did so was a question of fact.

The HMRC view seemed to be that in order for a UK resident to cease to be resident here he needed to go abroad permanently or for a settled purpose. Once he was accepted as having left the UK he would become UK resident again only if he returned to the UK for more than 90 days a year on average.

In deciding whether or not a person had left the UK, HMRC consider all the relevant evidence, including the pattern of presence in the UK and elsewhere (Revenue & Customs Brief 01/07). It is not wholly clear what this means. Prior to the issue of this statement in January 2007, most people thought that HMRC's approach to residence was an arithmetical one, ie that a person was UK resident if he was physically present in the UK for 183 days or more in a tax year or if he was physically present here for more than 90 days a year on average.

HMRC6 gave the following guidance:

- There are many different factors which will determine whether a person is resident in the UK during a tax year. It is not simply a question of the number of days the person is physically present in the UK during a tax year although this is an important consideration (para 2.2).
- Different considerations apply depending on whether the person is arriving in the UK for the first time from another country or whether he has been resident in the UK in earlier years (this is not in the latest version of HMRC6 but is implicit in the text of para 2.2).
- Residence in the UK will depend on how often and for how long a person is here, the purpose and pattern of his presence and his connections with

the UK. These might include the location of his family, his property, his work life and social connections (para 2.2).

- From 6 April 2008 when considering days of presence in the UK, all of the days in which the person is present at the end of the day (ie at midnight) must be included (para 2.2.1).
- A person will always be resident in the UK in any tax year in which he is physically present in the UK for more than 183 days. There are no exceptions to this (para 2.2).
- It is possible to be resident in the UK and some other country (or countries) at the same time (introduction to Chapter 2). However, if the other country is one with which the UK has a double taxation treaty the agreement is likely to contain a 'tie-breaker clause' which might prevent the UK from treating the individual as UK resident for the purpose of the agreement. Double tax agreements do not usually deal with income from third countries.
- Strictly speaking, a person is UK resident for the whole of a tax year if he is resident here for any part of it (para 2.4). However, Extra-statutory Concession A11 provides that if an individual ceases to reside in the UK and he has left for permanent residence abroad (or comes to the UK to take up permanent residence or to stay for at least two years) he will be taxed only for the part of the year up to the date of his departure (or from the date of his arrival). This is known as the split-year concession. It will not apply if the individual remains ordinarily resident in the UK (see below) after his departure or was ordinarily resident in the UK prior to becoming resident here. HMRC6 states that ESC A11 applies if a person has been resident in the UK and 'leaves to live abroad permanently or for a period of at least three years'. There is a further concession (ESC A78) which allows split-year treatment for a person accompanying a spouse or civil partner when they leave the UK to work full-time abroad, or in the year of return to the UK (para 2.4). There is a corresponding CGT concession (ESC D2) but this is much more limited. It does not apply where a person leaves the UK (unless he was not resident and not ordinarily resident here for the whole of at least four out of the last seven tax years preceding that in which he leaves the UK). It applies to a person coming to the UK only if he has not been either resident or ordinarily resident in the UK at any time during the five tax years preceding that in which he becomes resident here.
- If a person comes to the UK to live here permanently or to remain here for three years or more, he will be resident and ordinarily resident from the date of arrival (para 7.2).
- If a person whose home has been abroad comes to the UK as a student for less than four years for a period of education or study he will be resident here, but not ordinarily resident as long as he does not own or

buy (or rent for three years) accommodation here and when he leaves the UK he is not planning to return here regularly for visits that average over 90 days in a tax year (para 7.3).

- If a person whose home has been abroad comes to the UK intending to remain for less than three years, he may simply be visiting (para 7.4). Such a person will be resident and ordinarily resident in the UK from the fifth year he visits if his visits average over 90 days or from such earlier year as he realises that his visits will exceed a 90-day average (para 7.5).
- A person is not regarded as simply visiting if he comes to the UK for a purpose which means that he will be remaining here for at least two years (eg an employment). Such a person may well be resident (but not necessarily ordinarily resident) from the day of his arrival (para 7.4).
- If a person comes to the UK voluntarily and for a settled purpose, he will be ordinarily resident from the time he comes to the UK. If he owns or buys (or rents for over three years) accommodation in the year of arrival, that *may be* an indication that his presence in the UK forms part of the regular and habitual mode of his life for the time being and so he is ordinarily resident from when he arrives (but if he already owned accommodation here and sells it within three years of his arrival he will not be ordinarily resident here) (para 7.7.3). He will also not normally be regarded as ordinarily resident if he actually leaves the UK within three years of arrival (para 7.7.3).
- If a person does not become ordinarily resident when he first comes to the UK he will do so from the beginning of the tax year in which the third anniversary of his arrival falls (eg a person who comes to the UK on 4 April 2010 will become ordinarily resident from 6 April 2012 as 4 April 2013 falls in 2012/13) (para 7.7.3). He can become ordinarily resident here earlier (from the beginning of the tax year in which the trigger event falls) if he makes a decision to stay for three or more years or buys a property here (para 7.7.4).
- If a person leaves the UK permanently (ie to live abroad and not return) or indefinitely (ie to live abroad for at least three years but acknowledging that he might eventually return to live here) the act of going abroad does not mean that he will automatically become non-resident or non-ordinary resident. This depends on a number of factors including:
  - the reason he has left the UK (eg to work or live abroad permanently);
  - what visits he makes to the UK after he has left; and
  - what connections he keeps in the UK such as family, property, business and social connections (para 8.1).
- If a person leaves the UK permanently or indefinitely he will become non-resident and non-ordinarily resident from the time of his departure

only if he has physically left the UK for the purposes stated. If he goes abroad on holiday until he moves into his new home or begins his overseas employment, he is regarded as remaining resident here during his holiday period (para 8.2).

- Even if a person has left the UK permanently or indefinitely he will remain resident and ordinarily resident in the UK if his visits back are not such as to show that he has made a definite break with the UK (para 8.2). Prior to the issue of the 2010 version of HMRC6, HMRC accepted that a person would not again become UK resident if his visits back did not exceed an average of 90 days but while this test is still included in the 2010 version its significance has been reduced.
- A person will be ordinarily resident in the UK if:
  (a) he has come to the UK voluntarily (which would include at the request of his employer); and
  (b) his presence here has enough continuity to be properly described as settled (business, employment and family all provide a settled purpose); and
  (c) his presence in the UK forms part of the regular and habitual mode of his life for the time being (para 3.2).
- A person who leaves the UK to work full-time abroad under a contract of employment is treated as not resident and not ordinarily resident in the UK if his absence from the UK and the employment abroad both last for at least a whole tax year (and visits back do not breach the 183- or 91-day rule) (para 8.5). This is considered further below.
- In applying the 90-day and 183-day tests a day must be counted as a day of presence in the UK if the individual is physically present here at midnight on that day. There is an exception if the individual is in transit (ie he arrives in the UK as a passenger and departs from the UK on the next day) and while in the UK he does not engage in activities that are to a substantial extent unrelated to his passage through the UK. HMRC appear to consider that any activity that the individual plans to carry out while he is in transit will prevent the exception applying.

The tests formulated by the courts

9.11

Focus

HMRC claimed to base their approach on court decisions. It should be borne in mind that was simply HMRC's view. In the event of a dispute there is no reason to assume HMRC's interpretation of the court decisions is superior to yours. Consider how the facts of your client's case conform with the principles laid down by the courts.

The above guidance represents HMRC's views only – although of course where possible it is sensible to plan on the basis of HMRC's views as to ignore them invites challenge. HMRC do stress that HMRC6 'only offers general guidance … and does not have legal effect. Whether this guidance is appropriate in a particular case will depend on all of the facts of that case'.

The tests that the courts have laid down to determine residence were summarised by Lewison J in *HMRC v Grace* ([2009] STC 213) as follows:

'(i) The word "reside" is a familiar English word which means "to dwell permanently or for a considerable time, to have one's settled or usual abode, to live in or at a particular place": *Levene v Commissioners of Inland Revenue* (1928) 13 TC 486, 505. This is the definition taken from the Oxford English Dictionary in 1928, and is still the definition in the current on-line edition;

(ii) Physical presence in a particular place does not necessarily amount to residence in that place where, for example, a person's physical presence there is no more than a stop gap measure: *Goodwin v Curtis* (1998) 70 TC 478, 510;

(iii) In considering whether a person's presence in a particular place amounts to residence there, one must consider the amount of time that he spends in that place, the nature of his presence there and his connection with that place: *Commissioners of Inland Revenue v Zorab* (1926) 11 TC 289, 291;

(iv) Residence in a place connotes some degree of permanence, some degree of continuity or some expectation of continuity: *Fox v Stirk* [1970] 2 QB 463, 477; *Goodwin v Curtis* (1998) 70 TC 478, 510;

(v) However, short but regular periods of physical presence may amount to residence, especially if they stem from performance of a continuous obligation (such as business obligations) and the sequence of visits excludes the elements of chance and of occasion: *Lysaght v Commissioners of Inland Revenue* (1928) 13 TC 511, 529;

(vi) Although a person can have only one domicile at a time, he may simultaneously reside in more than one place, or in more than one country: *Levene v Commissioners of Inland Revenue* (1928) 13 TC 486, 505.'

It may be helpful also to set out the tests adopted by the Special Commissioner in *Shepherd v HMRC* ([2006] STC 1821), which Lewison J in *Grace* commended as 'impeccable conclusions that represent the correct approach to be adopted':

> 'From these authorities I derive the following principles: (i) that the concept of residence and ordinary residence are not defined in the legislation; the words therefore should be given their natural and ordinary meanings (*Levene*); (ii) that the word "residence" and "to reside" mean "to dwell permanently or for a considerable time, to have one's settled or usual abode, to live in or at a particular place" (*Levene*); (iii) that the concept of "ordinary residence" requires more than mere residence; it connotes residence in a place with some degree of continuity (*Levene*); "ordinary" means normal and part of everyday life (*Lysaght*) or a regular, habitual mode of life in a particular place which has persisted despite temporary absences and which is voluntary and has a degree of settled purpose (*Shah*); (iv) that the question whether a person is or is not resident in the United Kingdom is a question of fact for the Special Commissioners (*Zorab*); (v) that no duration is prescribed by statute and it is necessary to take into account all the facts of the case; the duration of an individual's presence in the United Kingdom and the regularity and frequency of visits are facts to be taken into account; also, birth, family and business ties, the nature of visits and the connections with this country, may all be relevant (*Zorab*; *Brown*); (vi) that a reduced presence in the United Kingdom of a person whose absences are caused by his employment and so are temporary absences does not necessarily mean that the person is not residing in the United Kingdom (*Young*); (vii) that the availability of living accommodation in the United Kingdom is a factor to be borne in mind in deciding if a person is resident here (*Cooper*) (although that is subject to *s 336*); (viii) that the fact that an individual has a home elsewhere is of no consequence; a person may reside in two places but if one of those places is the United Kingdom he is chargeable to tax here (*Cooper* and *Levene*); (ix) that there is a difference between the case where a British subject has established a residence in the United Kingdom and then has absences from it (*Levene*) and the case where a person has never had a residence in the United Kingdom at all (*Zorab*; *Brown*); (x) that if there is evidence that a move abroad is a distinct break that could be a relevant factor in treating an individual as non-resident (*Combe*); and (xi) that a person could become non-resident even if his intention was to mitigate tax (*Reed v Clark*).'

9.12 *Tax Bulletin,* Issue 52 dealt with the position of mobile workers, namely people such as lorry or coach drivers who drive their vehicles to and from the Continent, those who work on cross-channel transport and salesmen who make frequent short business trips abroad.

HMRC did not accept that such people had gone abroad for full-time work, even where they did little work in the UK. They considered that even though such a person may have been here for less than 91 days on average he was resident and ordinarily resident here if he usually lived in the UK and made frequent and regular trips abroad in the course of his employment or business. They regarded a person as usually living in the UK if his home and settled domestic life remained here. It is probable that this was the test that they also applied to decide whether a person who went abroad for a longer period had left the UK. It should be particularly noted that HMRC regarded someone 'travelling to France most Sundays or Mondays in connection with their employment but returning to the UK by or at the following weekend' as a mobile worker (*Tax Bulletin,* Issue 52).

Leaving the UK

9.13 There were four ways that a person who was UK resident could cease such residence:

- leaving to go abroad for one tax year under a contract of employment (or a self-employed assignment);
- leaving the UK permanently or indefinitely for at least three tax years;
- not being physically present in the UK at all during a tax year;
- as now, becoming resident in a country with which the UK has a double tax agreement and being deemed to be non-tax resident for the purpose of that agreement.

Contract of employment

9.14 The individual needed to work full-time abroad under a contract of employment spanning at least one complete tax year (HMRC6 para 8.5). If this condition was met he was regarded as ceasing to be both resident and ordinarily resident in the UK from the date of his departure (or such later date as his employment actually began).

HMRC gave guidance on what they meant by 'full-time' for this purpose in *Tax Bulletin,* Issue 6 (February 1993). In general where a job involves a standard pattern of hours they expected the individual to put in what a layman would clearly recognise as a full working week.

They said that 'there is no fixed minimum number of hours for this purpose but 35–40 hours is obviously a typical UK working week'. However, it is probable that it was sufficient to look at a normal working week in the country where the person was working if this was less than the norm in the UK.

9.15 Where a job did not have a straightforward structure they looked at the nature of the job and, where appropriate, took account of local conditions and practices in that particular occupation. This probably meant that they would expect the individual to put in the number of hours that a person doing a similar job would normally be expected to work.

HMRC also said that where a person had several part-time jobs overseas concurrently, particularly if they were with the same employer or group of companies, it might be reasonable to aggregate the time spent on them. This might also be done where the person simultaneously worked abroad both as an employee and as a self-employed person.

They also warned that where a person had a main employment abroad but also worked in the UK in some unconnected occupation (eg he had a directorship of a UK company), they would want to consider whether the extent of the UK activities might cast doubt on the full-time nature of the overseas employment.

9.16 If the employment was terminated prematurely and a new employment contract entered into with someone else, HMRC reviewed the position but were normally prepared to aggregate the two employments. It is conceivable that they might aggregate them even if the individual returned temporarily to the UK between the employments, planning to go abroad again.

A person was also regarded as having ceased to be UK resident and ordinarily resident if he left the UK to work full-time in a trade, profession or vocation and he met conditions similar to those in HMRC6, paragraph 8.5 (para 8.8). It is not clear what this meant. Did it merely mean that the self-employment overseas must span a complete tax year or might it mean that there needs to be a contract requiring the person to be abroad for such a period?

9.17 If a person was treated as non-resident under either para 8.5 (employed) or 8.8 (self-employed) of HMRC6 his spouse was also treated as non-resident if she accompanied him (or later joined him) even though the spouse was not in full-time employment – provided that the spouse was abroad for at least a complete tax year (para 8.9 and ESC A78).

Where a person was regarded as non-UK resident under this test he could still visit the UK for up to an average of 90 days. However, it is hard to envisage a genuine full-time employment that allowed three months holiday every year.

Leaving the UK permanently or indefinitely

9.18 HMRC said in the original version of HMRC6:

> 'If you say that you are no longer resident and ordinarily resident in the UK, we might ask you to give some evidence that you have left the UK

> permanently or indefinitely. For example, we would expect you to show that when you left the UK you had acquired accommodation to live in as a permanent home. The act of leaving the country is not likely to be sufficient evidence that you have left the UK permanently and have become non-resident and not ordinarily resident. If you still have property in the UK which you can use after you leave, we might want you to explain why you are retaining that property when you say you have left the UK' (para 8.2).

9.19 HMRC's Inspector's Manual (IM) (which has been withdrawn) stated:

> 'If an individual goes to live outside the UK, acquires a permanent home abroad, has a reason for having accommodation for use in the UK which is consistent with the aim of permanent residence abroad, [and] returns to the UK only on visits which do not average 91 days or more a tax year, he will be regarded as having ceased to be resident and ordinarily resident. For tax years before 1993–94 an individual also had to cease to retain accommodation in the UK.
>
> Where an individual claims that he had ceased to be resident and ordinarily resident in this country, his claim may be admitted on a provisional basis at the outset … if the grounds on which it is based are adequately proved, but in no circumstances can a final decision be made until the individual's absence from the UK has extended over a period which includes a full tax year. If adequate proof is not immediately available a decision on the claim is postponed for up to three years from the date of departure and the position is determined by reference to what has actually happened since the date of departure.' (IM41)

These quotations suggest that HMRC were likely to regard a person as ceasing to be UK resident from the time of his departure if he went abroad with an intention to live outside the UK for three years or more (and in fact fulfilled that intention) and did not retain significant ties with the UK. However, he had to go abroad 'for a settled purpose'. This probably required an identifiable change in the person's lifestyle and possibly a specific reason for going abroad. There was no statutory basis for adopting a three-year period. That was simply HMRC's longstanding practice. Indeed the one-year full time work route was undoubtedly based on a presumption that where a person is working full time overseas that is of itself normally sufficient evidence that the person has left the UK for a settled purpose if that purpose lasts for at least one complete tax year. It is easy to overlook that a person is taxed by reference to the law and is entitled to challenge an HMRC practice that he feels does not reflect the application of the law to his particular circumstances.

No presence in UK during tax year

9.20 If a person did not set foot in the UK at all during a tax year it is unlikely that he would have been resident here for that year. He could well have been ordinarily resident though – but see *Reed v Clark* below.

There are two early cases, *Re Young* (1875) 1 TC 57 and *Rogers v CIR* (1879) 1 TC 255, in which the taxpayer was held to be resident in the UK even though they did not set foot here at all during the tax year. These cases involved master mariners, whose voyages lasted for over a year and whose home and family were in the UK. As the taxpayers lived in the UK when not on a voyage these decisions are understandable. In the former case the Lord President commented that 'every sailor has a residence on land'.

9.21 In *Reed v Clark* (1985) 58 TC 528, Nicholls J said that:

> 'The word "reside" is a familiar English word and is defined in the Oxford English Dictionary as meaning "to dwell permanently or for a considerable time, to have one's settled or usual abode, to live in or at a particular place" and that "the task of the fact finding tribunal … was to consider and weigh all the evidence and then, giving the word 'residing' its natural and ordinary meaning, reach a conclusion on the factual question of whether or not the taxpayer was residing in the UK in the year of assessment".'

In that case he felt that:

> 'I am in no doubt that the true and only reasonable conclusion from the primary facts found by the Commissioners was that Mr Clark was not residing in the UK in the tax year 1978/79. For the whole of that year his home and place of business was in Los Angeles.'

This suggests that it was possible for a person to be UK resident in a tax year in which he did not set foot in the UK if he is normally resident here and does not have a settled abode somewhere else during that year.

HMRC6 gave no indication that this escape route existed. That is probably because HMRC did not like it. Clearly, though, HMRC guidance cannot override court decisions.

The 91-day test

9.22 Where a person had left the UK (or had never been UK resident) HMRC practice was to treat him as UK resident in any year in which he was physically present here for 183 days or more, or for any year in which his visits to the UK exceeded on average 90 days (the 91-day test).

This average was calculated over the period from a day of departure using the formula:

$$\frac{\text{Days in the UK}}{\text{Total days since leaving the UK}} \times 365$$

If the period since the person left the UK exceeded four years (or the person had never been UK resident) the calculation was done by reference to the last four years only.

9.23 For the purpose of the 91-day test (but not the 183-day one) HMRC were prepared to ignore days spent in the UK because of exceptional circumstances beyond the individual's control such as the illness of himself or a member of his immediate family (Statement of Practice 2/91 and HMRC6 para 2.2). Statement of Practice 2/91 states that 'each case where this relaxation of the normal rules may be appropriate will be considered in the light of its own facts'. In the self-assessment era the notes to the non-residence page of the tax return indicated that it was for the taxpayer to make this judgement himself. It would probably be sensible to flag up in the 'white space' on the return what days have been ignored and why.

IR20 added a caveat that: 'If during your absence the pattern of your visits varied substantially year by year, it might be appropriate to look at the absence as being made up of separate periods for the purpose of calculating average visits. This might be necessary if, for example, a shift in the pattern of your visits suggested a change of circumstances, which altered how we viewed your residence status.' This appears to have been dropped in HMRC6.

9.24 In calculating the days in the UK a day was normally counted only if the taxpayer was in the UK at midnight (HMRC6 para 2.2). This was probably concessional. In *Wilkie v IRC* (1952) 32 TC 495, Donovan J concluded: 'there is nothing in the language … to prevent hours being taken into the computation, but that … since what has to be determined is the period of actual residence it is legitimate to do so'. In that case Mr Wilkie arrived in the UK around 2pm on 2 June 1947. He intended to leave on 30 November 1947 but owing to the cancellation of his plane was compelled to remain until he was able to fly out around 10am on 2 December. HMRC claimed that he had been in the UK for more than 182 days as both 2 June and 2 December were days in the UK. Mr Wilkie was held to be non-resident for 1947/48 as he was in the UK for only 182 days and 20 hours, which is less than 183 days.

Although there was no statutory definition of residence, the test of presence at midnight reflected the amendment to *ITA 2007, s 831* (foreign income of individuals in UK for temporary purpose) made by *FA 2008, s 24*. It is likely that HMRC will in practice apply the whole of this amendment in determining residence; it also provides that a day can be ignored if the individual arrives in the UK as a passenger on that day, leaves the UK on the following day and during the time between arrival and departure does not engage in activities that are to a substantial extent unrelated to the individual's passage through the UK. HMRC seem to interpret this last condition as meaning that any activities entered into must not be pre-planned. This looks at social activities as well as business ones. The intention seems to be to exclude the day only if the sole reason for being in the UK overnight was because travel connections made it impossible or difficult to travel onwards on the day of arrival (HMRC6, para 2.3).

HMRC say that they derived the 91-day test from decided cases. However, it seems to give a generous interpretation to such decisions. In *Cooper v Cadwalader* (1904) 5 TC 101 the taxpayer was held to be resident even though he was here for only about two months a year. In *Lowenstein v De Salis* (1926) 10 TC 424 he was here on average for between two and three months a year. In *Lysaght v IRC* (1927) 13 TC 511 the taxpayer was here for 101 days in one year and 94 in the next.

Available accommodation

9.25 Up to 1992/93, a person was regarded as resident in the UK in any year in which he visited the UK, however short the period, if he had accommodation available for his use in the UK. This 'available accommodation' rule was excluded for the purpose of *ICTA 1988, s 336* (now *ITA 2007, s 831*) by *F(No 2)A 1993*. At that time the Minister indicated that the available accommodation rule had been abolished completely as: 'it has been held in the courts in the case of *Lysaght v IRC* (1927) 13 TC 511 … that the language of *s 336* has "illustrative value" in relation to the definition of residence elsewhere in the *Taxes Act 1988*'.

However, the view of HMRC was that this did not mean that the existence in the UK of accommodation available for the person's use was no longer relevant. They still regarded both the existence of available accommodation in the UK and whether or not the taxpayer had accommodation overseas as relevant in relation to the question of whether or not he has left the UK for a settled purpose. It was not, however, decisive; it was simply one of the factors to be taken into account. Accommodation did not have to be owned by the taxpayer for it to be available for his use. It was a question of fact whether it was so available.

Ordinary residence

9.26 HMRC said that the word 'ordinary' indicates that a person's residence in the UK is typical for him and not casual. A person would be ordinarily resident here if his residence had all of the following attributes:

- he had come to the UK voluntarily;
- his presence here had a settled purpose;
- his presence in the UK formed part of the regular and habitual mode of his life for the time being. This pattern could include temporary absences from the UK. They considered that if a person came to live and work in the UK for three years or more he would have established a regular and habitual mode of life here.

HMRC also considered that the pattern of a person's presence, both in the UK and overseas, was an important factor. So were the person's reasons for being in the UK, his intentions when coming to or leaving the UK and his lifestyle and habits.

HMRC practice was to treat a person who came to the UK intending to live here permanently or to remain here for at least three years (four if he came to study) as being ordinarily resident from the date that he arrived in the UK. They treated someone who came here without such an intention as ordinarily resident from the beginning of the tax year after the third anniversary of his arrival or, if earlier, the beginning of the tax year in which the person decided to stay in the UK for three years or more.

If a person already owned accommodation in the UK or acquired accommodation (bought or took a lease of three years or more) in the year of arrival he was again treated as ordinarily resident from the date of his arrival (assuming that he became resident here). If he disposed of the accommodation and left the UK within three years he could however be treated as not ordinarily resident. A person who acquired accommodation after his arrival (and not in the same tax year) was treated as ordinarily resident from the beginning of the year in which he acquired such accommodation. However paragraph 3.2 of HMRC6, after using a three-year period in an example, stated: 'This example looks at a period of three tax years as the appropriate period. This in no way indicates that you can be in the UK for three years before you have to consider whether you are ordinary resident.'

9.27 In *Reed (Inspector of Taxes) v Clark* (1985) 58 TC 528, Nicholls J said:

> 'The approach which I have found most helpful is to start from the contrast, which has been commented upon more than once, drawn in *s 49* itself (now

ITA 2007, s 829) between ordinary residence and departure abroad for occasional residence. In the section occasional residence is the converse of ordinary residence. This seems to me to conform to the common usage of the phrase "occasional residence" – a person's occasional residence is contrasted with his usual (or ordinary) residence.

For the meaning of ordinary residence one need look no further than the recent decision of the House of Lords in (*Shah v Barnet London Borough Council* [1983] 2 AC 309). In that case the issue was the meaning of the phrase "ordinary resident" in the context of a student's entitlement to receive an educational grant under an Act and regulations excluding a local authority from being under a duty to bestow an award upon a person who had not been ordinarily resident in the United Kingdom throughout a specified period of three years. In delivering the leading speech, with which Lord Fraser, Lord Lowry, Lord Roskill and Lord Brandon concurred, Lord Scarman observed that "ordinary residence" was not a term of art in English law and that in *Levene v IRC* (1928) 13 TC 486 and *Lysaght v IRC* (1927) 13 TC 511 the House of Lords construed those words in their tax context as bearing their natural and ordinary meaning as words of common usage in the English language. Lord Scarman said (at pages 343–344) "Unless, therefore, it can be shown that the statutory framework or the legal context in which the words are used requires a different meaning, I unhesitatingly subscribe to the view that 'ordinary resident' refers to a man's abode in a particular place or country which he has adopted voluntarily and for settled purposes as part of the regular order of his life for the time being, whether of short or of long duration". He added that a settled purpose did not require an intention to stay indefinitely, but that the purpose, while settled, might be for a limited period only: "all that is necessary is that the purpose of living where one does have a sufficient degree of continuity to be properly described as settled."

On that basis it seems to me plain that a British resident's departure abroad for a period of a few weeks or months with the firm intention of returning at the end of the period to live here as before would be likely always to be for the purpose only of occasional residence. At the opposite end of the scale, it seems to me equally plain that the departure of such a resident abroad for a limited period of (say) three years would not necessarily be for the purpose only of occasional residence just because from the outset he had a firm intention of returning at the end of the period to live here as before … For my part I think this latter conclusion is also true of residence abroad for just over one year in duration. The difference between these examples is one of degree, and there is an area in which different minds may reach different conclusions. In my view a year is a long enough period for a person's purpose of living where he does to be capable of having a sufficient degree of continuity for it to be properly described as settled. Hence, depending on all the circumstances, the foreign country could be the place where for that period he would be ordinarily and not just occasionally resident.'

Accordingly, the HMRC three-year rule was not necessarily correct.

The tests formulated by the courts

9.28 The tests of ordinary residence adopted by the courts were summarised by Lewison J in *HMRC v Grace* ([2009] STC 213) as follows:

'(i) "Ordinarily resident" refers to a person's abode in a particular place or country which he has adopted voluntarily and for settled purposes as part of the regular order of his life, whether of short or long duration: *R v Barnet LBC ex p Shah* [1983] 2 AC 309, 343;

(ii) Just as a person may be resident in two countries at the same time, he may be ordinarily resident in two countries at the same time: *Re Norris* (1888) 4 TLR 452; *R v Barnet LBC ex p Shah* [1983] 2 AC 309, 342;

(iii) It is wrong to conduct a search for the place where a person has his permanent base or centre adopted for general purposes; or, in other words to look for his "real home": *R v Barnet LBC ex p Shah* [1983] 2 AC 309, 345 and 348;

(iv) There are only two respects in which a person's state of mind is relevant in determining ordinary residence. First, the residence must be voluntarily adopted; and second, there must be a degree of settled purpose: *R v Barnet LBC ex p Shah* [1983] 2 AC 309, 344;

(v) Although residence must be voluntarily adopted, a residence dictated by the exigencies of business will count as voluntary residence: *Lysaght v Commissioners of Inland Revenue* (1928) 13 TC 511, 535;

(vi) The purpose, while settled, may be for a limited period; and the relevant purposes may include education, business or profession as well as a love of a place: *R v Barnet LBC ex p Shah* [1983] 2 AC 309, 344;

(vii) Where a person has had his sole residence in the United Kingdom he is unlikely to be held to have ceased to reside in the United Kingdom (or to have "left" the United Kingdom) unless there has been a definite break in his pattern of life: *Re Combe* (1932) 17 TC 405, 411.'

HMRC seemed to have clearly changed their approach to both residence and ordinary residence in recent years, albeit that they denied having done so. Their new approach was to require a person who claimed to have ceased to be UK resident to demonstrate that he had left the UK before he could be regarded as non-resident. It is only after they had accepted that he had become non-resident that the 91-day test applied.

The Gaines-Cooper case

9.29 In *R Gaines-Cooper v CIR* [2008] STC 1665, HMRC claimed that, in applying the 91-day test, the Commissioners should look at nights in the UK, whereas their previous approach had been to count a day only if the person was in the UK throughout that day. Furthermore, Mr Gaines-Cooper was held to be resident in the UK in some years even though he spent well under 90 days in the UK. This is what prompted HMRC to state in Revenue & Customs Brief 01/07 that they had not adopted a new approach and to seek to justify their approach in that case.

The facts of that case are complex and it is not intended to consider them here. The case emphasises that much of IR20 (the predecessor to HMRC6) was concessional. The courts and the Commissioners must apply the law. They cannot take any account of HMRC concessions (other than in the context of judicial review). In such circumstances it is not surprising that HMRC should argue the case on the basis of the law where this conflicts with their normal practice. An unfortunate side effect of relying on HMRC concessions is that if agreement cannot be reached with HMRC, an appeal to the Commissioners inevitably carries with it a need to forfeit the benefit of such concessions.

It should also be noted that both parties asked the Commissioners to look at the overall position over a period of 11 years, so it is not surprising that they did not hold him to be non-resident in years when his visits to the UK were minimal. Indeed HMRC view this as a case where the taxpayer, although living part of his time abroad and part of his time in the UK for over 20 years, had never left the UK, so the length of his visits were irrelevant. The High Court agreed with the Commissioners and the Court of Appeal refused leave to appeal. Mr Gaines-Cooper also sought judicial review of HMRC's approach on the basis that IR20 gave him a legitimate expectation that if he limited his time in the UK to under 91 days on average he would not be resident here. High Court, Court of Appeal and Supreme Court all held that he did not meet the precise wording of IR20 and thus could not rely on it ([2009] EWHC 2617 (Ch)).

Domicile

9.30

> **Focus**
>
> It is not easy to change one's domicile. Unlike with most tax issues it is for a person alleging a change of domicile to prove it. This means that if someone starts with a non-UK domicile, it is for HMRC to show that this has changed. Unless the person has stated on an HMRC form that he intends to live in the UK indefinitely, it is virtually impossible for HMRC to do this while the individual is still alive and able to go to the Tribunal and tell it what his intention is.
>
> Where a client comes to the UK, take care with the completion of form P86 as completing it carelessly can seriously damage his domicile position.

There is no statutory definition of domicile. It is not a tax concept. It is a general legal concept. It ties a person to a system of law. It is accordingly an important concept in matrimonial and family law.

Domicile is largely a question of intention. It is the country (or state in the case of a country with a federal system where each state has its own legal system) that a person regards as his homeland.

A person starts life with a 'domicile of origin'. This is not the place where he was born. It is his father's domicile at the time of his (ie the son or daughter's) birth. If the father is not known it will be the mother's domicile.

A person's domicile can change during their lifetime. However, it is a fairly enduring concept. It is not easy to change one's domicile. If a person does acquire a new domicile and subsequently abandons his new country, his domicile of origin will revive.

9.31 There is an inference that a person retains his original domicile. It is for the person who alleges a change of domicile to prove it. This differs from the normal tax approach where it is for the taxpayer to disprove HMRC's contention.

To change one's domicile one must go to a new country with the intention of living there permanently or indefinitely. It is obviously difficult to prove intention. Indeed there are no published tax cases where HMRC have sought to show that a person who started life with a non-UK domicile of origin has become UK domiciled and that person is still alive. This is because if the individual can go before the First-tier Tribunal and give evidence of his intention, HMRC know that it is virtually impossible for them to show a change of domicile.

This does not mean that HMRC do not challenge domicile; it means that they defer doing so strongly until after a person's death as at that stage he is no longer able to say what his intention was, so the Tribunal has to discern that from the surrounding facts.

9.32 A person who starts life with a non-UK domicile of origin does not become UK domiciled merely by living in this country for many years. This is a common misconception. Many people who have lived in the UK even for 40 or 50 years are not domiciled here because they have retained an intention to return to their home country. Indeed, the probability is that a person who started life with a foreign domicile and came to the UK for a specific purpose, such as to study, to work or to marry, has retained his domicile of origin as it is unlikely that such a person has formed a decision never to return to his home country. Indeed such a person does not even need to show an intention to return to his home country; an intention to go somewhere else is sufficient as the test is whether or not he has ever had an intention to remain permanently in the UK.

Conversely, of course, a person who started life with a UK domicile of origin will have difficulty in convincing HMRC that he has obtained – and retained – a foreign 'domicile of choice', particularly if the claim to be non-UK domiciled is made at a time when he is living in the UK. That is not to say that it is not possible to do so. It depends on the facts. A UK-domiciled person who goes to, say, the US to study and while there marries and decides to stay there may well acquire a US domicile of choice. If his employer were later to send him to the UK to work, or he takes a job in the UK, he will retain his US domicile whilst he is in the UK provided that his intention is always to return to the US at some stage.

Whilst the UK and the US are referred to above, this is a form of shorthand. They are in fact both federal countries. A person cannot actually be domiciled in the UK. He must be domiciled in one of England and Wales, Scotland or Northern Ireland. It is important to realise that. If the hypothetical taxpayer envisaged above had gone to New York to study and now feels that when he retires he will not return to New York as it is too cold but will retire to Florida, his English domicile of origin will have revived when he made the decision not to return to New York as he would have abandoned his intention to live permanently in New York and could not have acquired a Florida domicile of choice as he would have to actually live there for a period before he could do so.

Although a person may retain his non-UK domicile, that does not necessarily mean that he retains the tax benefits of being non-domiciled. From

6 April 2017, a non-domiciled person who has been resident in the UK for all or part of 15 of the previous 20 tax years will be fully taxable here for all of income tax, capital gains tax and inheritance tax in the same way as a UK domiciled individual. Currently such 'deemed domicile' applies only for inheritance tax and only where the person has been UK resident for 17 of the previous 20 years. In addition, an individual, who both was born in the UK and has a UK domicile of origin, will be taxable on worldwide income and gains (and within the scope of inheritance tax on UK assets) for any tax year in which he is resident in the UK.

The UK has a small number of double tax agreements in relation to inheritance tax. In some of those agreements the reference to UK domicile includes deemed domicile but the older agreements refer only to domicile. Those agreements can protect from inheritance tax a person who is domiciled in the other country and deemed domiciled in the UK.

The tax significance of the two concepts

9.33 The most important concept for income tax is residence. A person is taxable on world-wide income if he is resident in the UK. He is taxable only on UK income – and even then there are some exemptions – if he is not resident here. This is subject to a major caveat. A person who is resident in the UK but not domiciled here (or, up to 5 April 2013, was not ordinarily resident here) is often taxable on non-UK source income only to the extent that it is brought into the UK.

From 6 April 2017, this remittance basis can apply only if:

(1) the individual has been resident in the UK for less than 15 of the previous 20 tax years, and

(2) he was not born in the UK with a UK domicile of origin.

If these two tests are met, the individual can use the remittance basis if either:

(a) the individual has been UK resident for less than seven of the previous nine tax years;

(b) the individual is under 18;

(c) the individual pays a fee (albeit called a tax charge) to be able to use the remittance basis. The amount of the fee depends on the number of years that the taxpayer has been UK resident. It is £30,000 if he has been resident for at least seven of the previous nine tax years, and £60,000 if he has been resident for at least 12 of the previous 14 tax years; or

(d) the individual's unremitted overseas income for the year is under £2,000.

Heads (a), (b) and (d) above also applied prior to 6 April 2017. In addition, the individual had to have been UK resident in at least 17 of the previous 20 years and paid a £90,000 fee for the year to purchase the privilege of using the remittance basis (nil if he has been resident less than seven of the previous nine years, £30,000 if he had been resident for less than 12 years but for at least seven of the previous nine tax years, and £60,000 (£50,000 for 2012/13 and 2014/15) if he has been resident for less than 17 years but for at least 12 of the previous 14 years). The £90,000 figure applied only for 2015/16 and 2016/17, the £50,000 figure applying to earlier years.

A person who is entitled to use the remittance basis under (a) to (c) above must complete a tax return and claim that basis in the return, unless (a) or (b) applies and he has both no UK income or gains and no remittances of overseas income or gains. Where (c) above applies the individual can choose year by year at the time he completes his tax return whether to claim the remittance basis and pay the fee. This is nominally tax on specified unremitted overseas income. The taxpayer must nominate at least £1 of such income and can nominate sufficient income and gains to cover the £30,000, £60,000 or £90,000. However, HMRC recommend that people should nominate only £1 unless they intend to claim double tax relief in an overseas country. This is because the nominated income is deemed to be the last amounts remitted and if such income is accidentally remitted the identification of remittances in subsequent years becomes a nightmare!

It is not at all clear that nominating overseas income will enable the £90,000 (or £60,000 or £30,000) to be treated as a 'tax' qualifying for double tax relief. That is up to the overseas country. It cannot be expected to take kindly to the UK introducing a device to seek to shift such money from the overseas treasury to the UK one. However, the nomination requirement was introduced primarily to seek to achieve relief against US tax, and the US tax authority has accepted that it does so. Indeed it is understood that they accept that it does so irrespective of the amount of income that is nominated, although that seems counter-intuitive so it would be safer to nominate sufficient to cover the whole of the taxable US income.

Up to 5 April 2013, one of the main income tax anti-avoidance provisions, *ITA 2007, ss 714–730* (transfer of assets abroad), only applies if a person was ordinarily resident in the UK.

9.34 Capital gains tax is also triggered by residence. Again, capital gains on overseas assets realised by a person who is not domiciled in the UK are taxable here only to the extent that they are remitted to the UK. Prior to 6 April 2013, capital gains tax was also triggered by ordinary residence here.

The restrictions on the use of the remittance basis rules from 2017/18 does not, of course, make unremitted income or gains of years up to 2016/17 freely remittable. Such income and gains will continue to be taxed on the remittance basis and will trigger tax here for the year in which they are remitted if the funds are brought into the UK.

9.35 Inheritance tax depends almost wholly on domicile. A person who is domiciled in the UK is taxable here on world-wide assets. A person who is not domiciled here is taxable only on UK assets. Residence is irrelevant with one exception. If, at the time of death or an *inter vivos* gift, the decedent or donor has been resident here during more than 15 of the previous 20 tax years (17 out of 20 prior to 6 April 2017) or, from 6 April 2017, is deemed domiciled because he was born here, he is chargeable to inheritance tax as if he were domiciled here.

A point to watch is that a person who is resident here at any time in the tax year is treated as resident throughout that year for this purpose. Accordingly, a person who comes to the UK on 5 April and makes a gift on 7 April 15 years later is deemed domiciled in the UK even though he has only been resident here for 15 years and three days.

The remittance basis

9.36

> **Focus**
>
> The key to the remittance basis is to ensure that the client has sufficient overseas bank accounts that he does not need to mix income with capital – and, of course training him (and his overseas bank) to operate those accounts properly.

Where income and gains are taxable on a remittance basis it is up to the taxpayer to demonstrate that he has not remitted income or gains. If he cannot do so statutory rules apply to determine what has been remitted in relation to receipts into the account after 5 April 2008 (see **9.40**). The legislation is silent as to what happens after all such receipts have been identified. HMRC are likely to regard remittances as representing overseas income on a first-in, first-out basis up to the amount of such income that has arisen since the individual came to the UK. They will probably then treat further remittances as a mixture of capital gains and capital in proportion to the amount of gains and capital in the bank or other account from which the funds were remitted. That was their approach before 6 April 2008.

To avoid these presumptions a non-UK domiciled individual should maintain a number of overseas bank accounts and should take care to ensure that the money in the separate accounts is not mixed. In this context it is important to realise that income does not lose its nature by being invested.

For example, suppose a person has £100,000 of income overseas which he invests in overseas shares and that five years later he sells the shares for £150,000. The £150,000 is £100,000 of income and £50,000 of capital gain, not £100,000 of capital and £50,000 of capital gain. Accordingly, an individual who wants to avoid remitting capital needs to monitor very carefully what is paid into his overseas bank accounts.

9.37 At a minimum a non-domiciled individual needs to maintain two overseas bank accounts, one for income and the other for capital. He then needs to ensure that all income arising overseas is paid into the income account. It can be difficult to convince some overseas banks of the importance of keeping a rigid separation between the two. In particular it is unwise to credit the interest on a capital deposit account to that account and then immediately transfer it to the income account. This is not necessarily fatal, as it may well be possible to convince the First-tier Tribunal that what has been transferred out is the same funds as were paid in. However, it becomes more difficult to do this if other transactions take place in the account between the time of the credit and the time of the transfer out, particularly if the account is overdrawn. It also of course needlessly presents HMRC with the opportunity to argue the point.

9.38 If a person generates capital gains overseas, he also ideally ought to have one or more capital gains accounts. It needs to be appreciated though that the sale proceeds of an asset is itself a mixed fund. It is not possible to demonstrate which part is the original capital and segregate it from the gain. The whole of the sale proceeds need to be paid into the capital gains account. There are two caveats to this. The first is that if a share is sold at a loss no part of the proceeds can be gain; the whole amount must be original capital (unless of course the initial purchase price represented income or earlier capital gains). Accordingly, where a share or other asset is sold at a loss the whole of the proceeds ought to be paid into the capital account (which represents freely remittable funds). The second is that it probably does not matter if small gains are paid into the capital account. This is because if capital gains are remitted the amount remitted is deemed to be gains of the year they are remitted.

A person is not taxable on (and does not need to declare) capital gains which total in aggregate less than £11,100 pa. Accordingly, if the total capital gains paid into the capital account are below this figure it is irrelevant whether or not they are remitted (unless the taxpayer has already utilised his annual allowance against UK gains). If they exceed that figure there is a problem particularly if the gains form a large proportion of the capital in the account.

9.39 If a person makes a large number of disposals of overseas assets it may be sensible to pay the disposal proceeds into one capital gains account where the taxable gain element of a disposal is high in proportion to cost, into a different bank account where the proportion is relatively low and perhaps into the capital account where it is small. Remittances would be made from the capital account until it is exhausted; then from the second capital gains account (as the taxable proportion is lower); then from the first capital gains account; and finally from income.

HMRC take the view that it is impossible to remit a loss. Accordingly, a person who is taxed on the remittance basis obtained no relief for losses prior to 5 April 2008. From that date it is possible to make an irrevocable election to qualify such losses for relief. Such an election normally needed to be made by 5 April 2012. It is not necessarily beneficial. This is because the taxpayer's UK losses are then set against unremitted overseas gains in preference to UK gains. That makes the election unattractive if the taxpayer has significant UK assets and is unlikely to remit overseas gains.

Remittances from mixed funds

9.40 The legislation spells out in detail how remittances from mixed funds are to be identified. A mixed fund for this purpose covers two things. Anything which contains both income and capital, or capital gains and capital, or all three, is a mixed fund. As indicated above, the sale proceeds of an asset will automatically constitute a mixed fund under this test. In addition a single fund, such as an income bank account, which contains items arising in more than one year, is also a mixed fund.

The order of remittances is:

(a) employment income that is taxable in the UK whether remitted or not and that is not liable to foreign tax;

(b) employment income for non-UK duties (if not ordinarily resident) or from a separate overseas employment and which is not liable to foreign tax;

(c) income from employment-related securities that is not liable to foreign tax;

(d) overseas investment income that is not liable to foreign tax;

(e) overseas chargeable gains that are not liable to foreign tax;

(f) employment income liable to a foreign tax;

(g) overseas investment income liable to a foreign tax;

(h) overseas chargeable gains liable to a foreign tax; and

(i) income or capital not falling within any other head.

The tests are applied first to the amounts of income, capital gains or other items for the tax year in which the payment out occurs that have been paid into the mixed fund in the same tax year prior to the date of the remittance. They are then applied to the income or gains of the previous year, and so on until the whole of the amount remitted has been identified. Curiously, if overseas income of year 1 is invested overseas and the investment is realised in a later year the capital gain element is identified against remittances in priority to the income element, which is the reverse of the rule that applied before 6 April 2008.

The above identification rules apply to all remittances in 2008/09 or later. However if remittances exceed the post 5 April 2008 income and gains, so that earlier income or gains are deemed to be remitted, the previous 'rules' apply to determine what income or gains have been remitted. That is a bit of a misnomer. Prior to 6 April 2008, the legislation was silent on the order of remittances. HMRC practice was to identify remittances against income as far as possible and then against a mixture of income and capital, in both cases on a first in, first out basis. As it is for the taxpayer to demonstrate that the HMRC identification is incorrect it is difficult to challenge this.

Up to 5 April 2019, a person to whom the remittance basis applied for any year up to 2016/17 (whether or not it still applies) and who was not born in the UK with a UK domicile of origin can rearrange money held in a mixed fund by segregating each element into separate overseas bank accounts (*Finance (No 2) Bill 2017*). However, he can only do this once in relation to a particular bank account. This is a potential problem because it is only money that can be recategorised; if an investment derived from a mixed fund is held, this cannot be recategorised, albeit that the proceeds can be if the investment is sold during 2017/18 or 2018/19. Accordingly, the timing of the reallocation can be important in individual cases. The taxpayer must, of course, also have maintained records to be able to demonstrate the source of the balance on the bank account. If he cannot do so, back to the opening of the account, he can at least segregate the funds for the part of the period for which he has records. For pre-6 April 2008 balances, the legislation allows for a rough and ready split in certain circumstances, but that does not apply to post-5 April 2008 deposits.

Example 9.2

Carl is Canadian domiciled. He was born in Canada but has lived in the UK for 25 years. He has a bank account in Jersey on which the balance at 31 December 2018 is £80,000. He analyses the make-up of the account (applying the above rules to payments out of the account since 5 April 2008) and discovers that the balance is made up as follows:

Income	£20,000
Capital gains element of sales of assets	£25,000
Original capital	£35,000
	£80,000

Carl moves £35,000 to a new capital account in Jersey and £25,000 to a new capital gains account. Following the transfers (and probably the notification to HMRC of the segregation), Carl can remit the £35,000 to the UK without tax and, if he remits the £25,000, it will be taxed wholly as a capital gain. Carl can, of course, split the existing balance into nine separate overseas accounts if he has amounts in the account falling into each of the categories (a) to (i) above.

What is a remittance?

9.41

Focus

In looking at whether funds have been remitted it is not sufficient to look only at what the client has done. You need to identify all of his relevant persons and ensure that the client's overseas income has not been indirectly remitted by a relevant person. In particular it is usually unsafe to allow an overseas company to invest in the UK if it has been funded by the client.

Money or property is remitted to the UK if it is brought to, or received or used in, the UK by or for the benefit of a 'relevant person' and the property is or derives from overseas income or gains of the taxpayer. There is also a remittance if a service is provided in the UK to, or for the benefit of, a 'relevant person' and the property is, or derives from, overseas income or gains. There can also be a remittance if property gifted to a third party is brought to, or received or used in, the UK and enjoyed by a relevant person. It is important to realise that bringing assets into the UK that have been purchased overseas out of foreign income or gains can trigger a remittance. There are some limited exceptions including a £1,000 *de minimis* exemption. It should particularly be stressed that the quantum of the remittance where goods are brought to the UK is their cost, not their value at the time they come into the UK.

There is also a remittance if the funds are used (directly or indirectly) outside the UK in respect of a 'relevant debt'. A relevant debt is of course one that relates to property or services that would have triggered a remittance had it been financed otherwise than by the borrowing. Unlike under the previous legislation, the payment of interest on a relevant debt outside the UK constitutes a remittance. There is an exception for interest on a mortgage made before 12 March 2008 for the purpose of enabling the individual to acquire an interest in residential property in the UK (and for no other purpose). This exception will cease if terms of the loan (or any supporting guarantee) are varied, the loan ceases to be secured on the property, any other debt is secured on the property or the property ceases to be owned by the individual.

Relevant persons

9.42 A relevant person is:

(a) the individual;

(b) the individual's spouse or civil partner;

(c) a person living with the individual as if they were their spouse or civil partner;

(d) a child or grandchild of a person within (a) to (c) who is under 18;

(e) a close company (or one that would be close if it were UK resident, or a 51% subsidiary of a close company) in which a relevant person is a participator (however small the shareholding may be), or a 51% subsidiary of such a company;

(f) the trustees of a settlement of which a relevant person is a beneficiary, or a body connected with such a settlement.

This can create extreme difficulties in determining what is a remittance. For example, suppose that the individual makes a gift out of a capital gain to his adult son in France. The son later visits the UK with his young children and uses his credit card to pay for a family meal in the UK. The credit card is settled from the French bank account into which the gift was deposited. The cost of the meal for the son and his wife is not a deemed remittance of the capital gain but the cost of his children's meal is as they are relevant persons in relation to the donor under (d). It is unclear how the donor is expected to obtain the information that he needs to complete his tax return.

The government view is that:

> 'individuals giving unremitted money or assets offshore to a relevant person would need to make arrangements with that person, to enable them to keep track of any remittances to the UK. I acknowledge that there is a complexity for the taxpayer' (Jane Kennedy PBC, 19 June 2008 Col 830).

Unfortunately, she did not mention the added complexity of a gift to a non-relevant person who might use some of it to benefit a relevant person.

Exemptions

9.43 The following do not constitute a remittance:

(a) the payment of the £30,000, £60,000 or £90,000 fee, but only if it is made direct to HMRC from an overseas bank account;

(b) clothing, footwear, jewellery and watches that are acquired out of foreign income or gains and are both the property of a relevant person and for the personal use of a relevant person;

(c) any other property that derives from foreign income or gains where its cost is under £1,000;

(d) any other property that derives from foreign income or gains that is temporarily imported into the UK, ie that is here in aggregate for not more than 275 days (counting from 6 April 2008 onwards indefinitely, so that track will need to be kept of each such item, perhaps over a 20- or 30-year period until the 275-day figure is breached, making the cost taxable);

(e) property that derives from foreign income or gains that is brought into the UK solely for repair or restoration and taken out again once it has been repaired;

(f) items that are brought to the UK for public display at an approved museum, gallery or other establishment approved by HMRC (this used to be restricted to works of art and collectors pieces and antiques but this limitation no longer applies from 6 April 2013);

(g) payments outside the UK (ie to a non-UK bank account) in consideration of services provided in the UK which relate wholly or mainly to property situated outside the UK (unless they fall within anti-avoidance rules).

None of these exemptions (other than (g)) can apply to money. Furthermore, if the property ceases to qualify for the exemption there is a deemed remittance at that time. Again, it should be stressed that if the property is sold in the UK the deemed remittance is of the cost not of the sale proceeds. A deemed remittance can arise in some unexpected circumstances. For example if an expensive dress is gifted to a UK charity shop it will cease to meet the exemption (but if it is gifted to a foreign charity shop no tax charge should arise). If an expensive dress is brought into the UK for use by a mother and while in the UK is gifted to her 17-year-old daughter that will not trigger a tax charge as the daughter is a relevant person. However, it will trigger a tax charge on the daughter's 18th birthday, as she will then cease to be a relevant person (but if on that day the dress is outside the UK, no tax charge will arise).

From 6 April 2013, the exemption will not be lost if the property is lost, stolen or destroyed unless compensation, such as insurance proceeds, is received in respect of it. From 6 April 2012, the tax charge on a sale of exempt property can be avoided by taking the sale proceeds overseas. The proceeds are then not treated as having been remitted provided that the sale is not to a relevant person, it is by way of a bargain at arm's length, once the property is sold no relevant person has an interest in it or can benefit from it, the whole of the sale proceeds are received by the seller within 95 days of the sale date, the sale is not made as part of (or as a result of) a scheme or arrangement one of the main purposes of which is the avoidance of tax, and the whole of the sale proceeds are taken out of the UK (or used to make qualifying investments) within 45 days of the receipt of the proceeds (or of the receipt of the last instalment of them). It should particularly be noted that the whole amount must be taken overseas – except to the extent of fees deducted before the consideration is paid to the seller. If the asset is sold at a gain, that will, of course, be a UK chargeable gain. Similarly from 6 April 2013 compensation received for the loss, theft or destruction of the property will not trigger a tax charge if the compensation is taken overseas within 45 days of its receipt.

CGT rebasing

9.44 A person who paid the remittance basis fee for any tax year from 2008/09 to 2016/17, was not born in the UK with a UK domicile of origin, meets Condition B in *ITA 2007, s 835BA*, remains non-UK domiciled (albeit excluded from use of the remittance basis) and was not born in the UK with a UK domicile of origin, can rebase CGT assets that he personally held at 5 April 2017 (and did not transfer overseas after 16 March 2016) (*Finance (No 2) Bill 2017*). This is an attractive concession because it will enable the entire gain on the asset to be remitted, with no UK tax being payable on the pre-6 April 2017 element of the gain.

Example 9.3

Jay is domiciled in India. He was born in India but has lived in the UK for the last 20 years. He owns a house in New York which cost £400,000, but was worth £2 million at 5 April 2017. Jay sells the house for £2.2 million in 2018/19. Although he will realise a capital gain of £1.6 million, Jay is taxed as if it were £200,000 (£2.2 million less £2 million). Assuming that the initial £400,000 was capital, Jay can remit the whole of the £2.2 million and pay tax of only £40,000 (20% of £200,000).

No election is required. The rebasing is automatic. However, if an asset is disposed of for which the taxpayer would prefer not to use the 5 April 2017 value, he can elect to calculate the tax by reference to the figure that would otherwise have applied. He might want to do this if the asset fell in value between the acquisition and 5 April 2017. Such an election is irrevocable.

It should particularly be noted that this rebasing applies only to assets held personally. It will not apply to assets held within an overseas company or trust. Also the asset must remain outside the UK until it is sold (subject to the same exemptions as are set out above).

Relief for remittances for investment purposes

9.45 From 6 April 2012, a taxpayer can make a claim to treat income or chargeable gains as not having been remitted if they are either used by a relevant person to make a qualifying investment, or brought to the UK in order to be used to make such an investment. An individual makes a qualifying investment if either shares in a company (or securities of a company) are issued to the individual, or the individual makes a loan (secured or unsecured) to the company and Conditions A and B are met when the investment is made.

Condition A is that the company is either an eligible trading company or an eligible stakeholder company. An eligible trading company is a private limited company which carries on one or more commercial trades (or is preparing to do so within the next two years), and carrying on commercial trades is all or substantially all of what it does (or what it is reasonably expected to do once it begins trading). An eligible stakeholder company is a private limited company which exists wholly for the purpose of making investments in eligible trading companies (ignoring any minor or incidental purposes), and holds one or more such investments or is preparing to do so within the next two years. For this purpose, a private limited company is a body corporate whose liability is limited, which is not an LLP, and none of whose shares is listed on a recognised stock exchange. A trade includes anything that is treated for corporation tax purposes as if it were a trade, and also a business carried on for generating income from land. Carrying on research and development activities from which it is intended that a commercial trade will be derived, or will benefit, is treated as the carrying on of a commercial trade but preparing to carry on such R & D activities is not.

Condition B is that no relevant person has (directly or indirectly) obtained (or become entitled to obtain) any related benefit, and none expect to obtain any such benefit. For this purpose a benefit includes the provision of anything that would not be provided to the relevant person in the ordinary course of business or would only be so provided on less favourable terms. A benefit excludes anything provided to the relevant person in the ordinary course of business and on arm's length terms. A benefit is a related benefit if it is directly or indirectly attributable to the making of the investment (whether it is obtained before or after the investment is made), or it is reasonable to assume that the benefit would not be available in the absence of the investment. The provision of a benefit includes any arrangements that allow a person to enjoy any benefit from the thing in question (either temporarily or permanently) and covers things provided in money or money's worth including property, capital, goods or services of any kind.

The investment must be made within 45 days of the money being brought into the UK. This could cause a problem if a loan is to be drawn down over a period. The election cannot be made where exempt property is brought into the UK and is subsequently used to make the investment, even though *ITA 2007, s 809Y* treats the property as triggering a remittance charge when the investment is made.

There is a tight time limit for the claim; the first anniversary of 31 January following the tax year in which the income or gains are remitted to the UK. It does not appear that the company needs to be a UK company or that its trade needs to be in the UK. The relief does not apply if there is a scheme or arrangement the main purpose of which, or one of the main purposes of which, is the avoidance of tax. From 6 April 2013, compensation received in the UK for the loss, theft or destruction of property brought into the UK from overseas can also be invested in such qualifying investments rather than having to be taken overseas to avoid a tax charge. It must be invested within 45 days of receipt.

The amount will be treated as remitted at a later date if:

(a) the target company ceases to be an eligible trading company or an eligible stakeholder company and the entire shareholding is not sold and the money taken out of the UK within 45 days of the relevant person becoming (or ought to become) aware of that fact;

(b) the relevant person who made the investment ceases to be a relevant person and the entire shareholding is not sold and the money taken out of the UK within 45 days of the relevant person becoming (or ought to become) aware of that fact (remember that a child ceases to be a relevant person on his 18th birthday);

(c) the relevant person disposes of all or part of the holding and does not take the money out of the UK within 45 days of receiving the disposal proceeds;

(d) relief is received by (or for the benefit of) a relevant person from an involved company/the target company, an investee company or a connected company (other than by a disposal of all or part of the holding) and the money is not taken out of the UK within 45 days of the value being received; or

(e) the two-year start-up rule is breached and the entire shareholding is not sold and the money taken out of the UK within 45 days of the relevant person becoming aware of the fact.

There is no deemed tax charge if the company takes an insolvency step for genuine commercial reasons (except to the extent of money received from that step). As an alternative to taking the money overseas, it can be reinvested in another qualifying investment. It is only necessary to take the income or gains amount out of the UK. If part of the investment was capital that does not need to be taken overseas again – but the entire holding still needs to be sold. The sale proceeds must be taken out of the UK 'in the form in which they are received'. That is a potential problem as it is not always possible to take an IOU out of the UK as its *situs* is normally treated as being in the UK. Curiously, although the legislation requires a disposal of the entire holding, it seems to allow the proceeds to be reinvested in the same company. If a disposal is not by way of a bargain at arm's length, it is deemed to be made at market value – and it is that market value amount that needs to be taken outside the UK. It is not clear how this can be done if it exceeds the actual proceeds. Where investments are made at different times in the same company, disposals are deemed to take place on a first in, first out basis. There are special rules for mixed funds.

Employment income

9.46

Focus

Where a client will work partly in the UK and partly overseas consider whether a dual-contract structure is appropriate. However to do this the work must be capable of being compartmentalised. It is not sufficient for one contract to cover UK work and the other non-UK as HMRC contend that any UK work that is integral to the overseas work prevents that work being carried out wholly outside the UK. If a job involves some pure overseas tasks and some where the work will be partly done in the UK and partly overseas, consider putting the pure overseas tasks into an overseas employer and leaving the mixed ones to be performed under the UK employment contract.

Employment income is taxable on a remittance basis only if the employee is resident but not domiciled in the UK, the employment is with a foreign employer and the duties of the employment are performed wholly outside the UK (*ITEPA 2003, ss 21–23*). (Prior to 6 April 2013 he also had to be not ordinarily resident here.) For this purpose, duties performed in the UK can be treated as performed outside the UK if they are 'merely incidental' to the performance of overseas duties (*ITEPA 2003, s 39*). In practice, HMRC tend to ignore less than ten days of UK duties as *de minimis*.

9.47 In *Robson v Dixon (Inspector of Taxes)* (1972) 48 TC 527, Pennycuick V-C observed that the words 'merely incidental' are upon that ordinary usage apt to denote an activity (here the performance of duties) which does not serve any independent purpose but is carried out in order to further some other purpose'. In that case an airline pilot who was based in the Netherlands made 38 take-offs and landings in the UK out of 811 in the year. The UK landings were held not to be merely incidental to the Netherlands ones. HMRC interpret this as meaning that duties performed in the UK that are of the same type as those performed overseas are not merely incidental even if performed for only a very short time (*Tax Bulletin*, Issue 76). Visits to the UK to report to a group's head office are likely to be merely incidental to the overseas performance of the subject of the report.

9.48 A non-UK domiciled employee should consider whether he can use a dual-contract arrangement under which he is employed by an overseas company for non-UK duties and a UK company for UK ones. However, *ITEPA 2003, s 24A*, which was inserted by *FA 2014, Sch 3, para 3*, makes this very difficult although not wholly impossible. HMRC do not like such arrangements and are likely to look at them closely. HMRC have said that:

> 'Given the way in which modern business operates and the ease and speed of communication, some employees may find it increasingly difficult to avoid performing substantive UK duties under their overseas contracts. For example, an employee who is responsible under their overseas contract for servicing the business of overseas clients may have to respond to a telephone call or e-mail from a worried overseas client with an urgent problem when the employee is in the UK. Formulating and communicating a response to such a problem would be regarded as a fundamental duty under the overseas contract. It follows that the performance of such duties in the UK will not be merely incidental to the performance of duties outside the UK as they will be of equal importance to the overseas duties. It is the quality of the UK duties and not the time devoted to their performance that determines whether they are merely incidental' (*Tax Bulletin*, Issue 76).

9.49 It is questionable whether that is wholly correct. For example, if a person carries out overseas duties and sends a report to his UK office and next time he is in the office he responds to a telephone call from the client and the response could have been equally made by someone else in the office who had read the report, answering the telephone is unlikely to be a duty of the overseas employment. In other words, the duties are normally segregable if the employee can deal with the UK and overseas aspects wearing two different hats, but would not be segregable if the only person who can perform the UK activity is the person who performed the overseas one, eg because it requires information that is in his head or they are both part of an ongoing negotiation.

9.50 It is generally sensible to list the duties of the overseas employment in detail in the employment contracts. This not only makes clear what those duties are but it highlights when the contract is drawn up the extent to which segregation is practical. Where some duties can be segregated and some cannot, it is advisable to limit the overseas employment to the segregable ones and leave the remaining duties in the UK employment. It does not matter that that includes overseas duties; the key thing is that the overseas employment should not include any UK duties.

9.51 Where a dual-contract arrangement is used it also needs to be borne in mind that the remuneration for the overseas employment needs to be paid outside the UK (as payment in the UK is equivalent to a remittance).

Care also needs to be taken with expenses. If the UK company reimburses expenses incurred on the overseas contracts, HMRC are likely to contend that the arrangements are a sham. If a group has a policy of channelling all expenses through the UK and recharging them to the appropriate company there should be no problem though.

9.52 Where an employee has two or more employments with the same employer or with associated employers (ie under common control), and any of the duties are performed in the UK the emoluments must be aggregated and re-apportioned between the UK and overseas duties in such manner as is reasonable having regard to the nature of, and time devoted to, the UK and overseas duties respectively, and all other relevant circumstances (*ITEPA 2003, s 24*).

Accordingly, if a dual-contract arrangement is used, the split of the salary between the two needs to be done on a basis that can be justified. HMRC's starting point is likely to be to expect the split to reflect the time involved in the respective duties. They are unlikely to accept that overseas work deserves a higher daily rate because it is inconvenient, but should accept that it does so because the employee works longer hours when he is overseas.

9.53 In addition to the rules on UK-linked debts referred to earlier, earnings are treated as remitted to the UK if they are paid, used or enjoyed in the UK or transmitted or brought to the UK in any manner or form (*ITEPA 2003, s 33*). Accordingly, if the employee uses overseas earnings to purchase assets such as a car or a painting and brings them into the UK the earnings used to purchase the assets are regarded as remitted to the UK (Employment Income Manual at EIM40302). HMRC indicate that in general the purchase of investments abroad should not be regarded as a remittance even if the share certificate is brought into the UK, as they will not be enjoyed here, but the sale of such investments in the UK will constitute a remittance.

Travelling expenses

9.54 An employee who is non-UK domiciled is not taxed on travelling expenses (including accommodation) from and to his home country in the five years from the date he comes to the UK (not any later date on which he starts the employment) provided that the cost of the travel is either borne by his employer or is paid by the employee and reimbursed to him by his employer (*ITEPA 2003, s 379*). This relief applies only if the employee did not visit the UK in the two years prior to coming to the UK to work and was not resident in the UK in the two years preceding that in which he came to the UK. There is no limit on the number of journeys qualifying for relief in the five-year period.

Where this relief applies it also extends to the costs of two return journeys per year made by each of the employee's spouse and his infant children either accompanying him when he came to the UK or to visit him in the UK (*ITEPA 2003, s 374*). Again, the cost must either be borne by the employer or paid by the employee and reimbursed to him by his employer.

Self-employment income

9.55 It is virtually impossible for a person who is resident in the UK to carry on a trade outside the UK as a sole trader. This is because a trade is carried on where its control and management takes place. If the proprietor is UK resident the trade will inevitably be controlled and managed from the UK. In such circumstances overseas income will simply be a receipt of the UK trade.

It is possible for a trade carried on in partnership to be controlled and managed outside the UK if one of the partners is non-UK resident. In such circumstances the UK-resident partners' share of profits will be taxed on a remittance basis.

Overseas workday relief

9.56 Where a person comes to the UK and works both in the UK and overseas a special relief applies for the first three tax years of UK residence (provided that he has not been UK resident for any of the three tax years prior to coming here). Provided that such a person is non-UK domiciled (as will normally be the case), he can use the remittance basis for those three years in respect of overseas earnings from an employment with a non-UK resident employer even if that employment is not carried on wholly outside the UK.

The earnings are apportioned between UK and overseas work on a just and reasonable basis (*ITEPA 2003, ss 15, 23, 26A, 41ZA* as amended or inserted by *FA 2013, Schs 6* and *44*).

In practice HMRC are likely to contend that this requires the apportionment to be made on a time basis. The proportion attributed to UK work is taxed irrespective of whether or not it is remitted but the part attributed to overseas work is taxed here only if and when it is brought into the UK. The operation of this rule creates an identification problem with remittances to ensure that the part attributable to UK work is not taxed twice.

Accordingly, a taxpayer who wants to use this relief can nominate a separate overseas bank account into which his earnings will be paid and to which simplified identification rules can apply. Such a nomination must be made by 31 January following the end of the first tax year to which it applies. The account must be an ordinary bank account. It cannot be the nominated account of more than one person (so spouses cannot use a joint account).

Nothing must be paid into the nominated account other than earnings from the employment, disposal proceeds of employment-related securities and interest on the account. If something else is accidentally paid into the account it must be transferred out within 30 days of its being discovered (together with any later prohibited receipts). However this applies only to the first two mistakes. A third mistake cannot be remedied; the account will cease to be a nominated account. Where an individual has such a nominated account special identification rules apply. The total amount remitted to the UK in the year is first identified and treated as a single transfer made at the end of the tax year. All other transfers out of the account are treated as a second single transfer made immediately after the first. The normal mixed account rules are then applied to those two deemed single transfers. These treat employment income (ie UK earnings) for a tax year as being remitted in priority to foreign employment income for that year. Having determined the deemed make up of the two deemed single payments, each individual transfer is treated as containing the same proportions of the different types of income (*ITA 2007, ss 809RA–809RD* inserted by *FA 2013, Sch 6, para 6*).

TAXATION OF NON-UK RESIDENTS

Investment income

9.57 As indicated above, the UK charges non-UK residents to income tax only on income arising in the UK. Even then not all UK income is taxable. The tax chargeable on a non-UK resident is limited to the tax that would be payable on the individual's UK employment income, trading income and property income (plus, where applicable, deemed income from the release of a loan to a participant of a close company, gains from certain UK insurance policies, disposals of futures and options involving guaranteed returns, non-trading income from intellectual property and film and sound recordings) if he were not entitled to personal allowances, plus any tax deducted at source from other types of income (*ITA 2007, ss 811–814*).

This means that the following types of UK income are not taxable except to the extent of any withholding tax (*ITA 2007, s 813*):

- interest (there is a 20% withholding tax unless the interest is bank interest;
- purchased life annuity payment;
- profits from deeply discounted securities;
- distributions from unauthorised unit trusts;
- transactions in deposits;
- royalties and other income from intellectual property (there is a 20% withholding tax);
- certain telecommunication rights;
- annual payments not otherwise chargeable to tax (there is a 20% withholding tax);
- dividends from UK companies;
- UK social security pensions;
- certain other UK pensions and employment-related annuities;
- social security income (other than income support or jobseekers allowance, although these are unlikely to be paid to non-residents);
- some trading transactions carried out by an independent broker in the normal course of his business;
- any other types of income tax that the Treasury may exclude by regulation.

The above types of income are however taxable if they are received through a UK representative of the non-resident who is carrying on a trade in the UK on behalf of the non-resident through a branch or agency (*ITA 2007, s 814*).

Employment income

9.58 A person who is not UK resident is taxable on employment income only to the extent that it relates to duties performed in the UK. The applicable earnings are obviously calculated by apportioning the person's salary between that attributable to UK and non-UK work. Up to 5 April 2008, this limitation also applied to an individual who was resident in the UK but not ordinarily resident here in the tax year in which it was earned (*ITEPA 2003, s 25*). This relief has been preserved as overseas workday relief (see **9.56**).

Most of the UK's double tax agreements prevent the UK from taxing the UK earnings of a resident of the other country if that person is present in the UK for 183 days or less in any 12-month period commencing or ending in the year of assessment concerned, the employer is not UK resident and the remuneration is not borne by a UK permanent establishment. This exclusion does not normally apply to entertainers and sportsmen.

If a person is resident but not ordinarily resident in the UK he is also taxable here on earnings for duties performed outside the UK to the extent that they are remitted to the UK (*ITEPA 2003, s 26*).

Trading income

9.59 A non-resident who carries on a trade in the UK through a branch or agency is taxable on the profits of that branch or agency. It is unclear whether it is possible for a non-resident to carry on a trade here as a sole trader other than through a branch or agency. This is because a trade is normally carried on at the place from which it is controlled and managed, and it would be fairly unusual for that not to take place where the proprietor is resident.

It used to be thought that a trade could not be carried on in the UK if all of its sales contracts were made outside the UK. However, the courts now tend to look at the overall substance of the trade. Where the substance of the trade is primarily in the UK – such as a trade of dealing in UK property – it is sensible for a non-resident to seek to ensure that all contracts are entered into outside the UK and also to evidence that he makes decisions in relation to the trade in his home country.

Property income

9.60 The basic rule is that the rental agent (or the last agent in the chain if there is more than one) must deduct tax at 20% from the rent and account for it quarterly to HMRC (*ITA 2007, ss 971, 972* and the *Taxation of Income from Land (Non-Residents) Regulations 1995, SI 1995/2902*). He can calculate this deduction on the rents that he receives less any expenses he pays on the landlord's behalf during the quarter that he reasonably believes are deductible in calculating the taxable income of the UK property business. He cannot deduct expenses paid direct by the landlord. In most cases the largest expense is likely to be loan interest and this is normally either paid by the landlord or the rents are paid into a bank account with the lender. It is rare for it to be paid by the agent.

Accordingly, where there are borrowings the tax deduction is likely to exceed the tax actually due on the profits of the UK property business. Where there is no agent the tenant is obliged to deduct tax at 20% from the rent and to account for it to HMRC.

9.61 Alternatively, the non-resident can elect to be taxed directly under the Non-Resident Landlord's Scheme. This requires the approval of HMRC. When approved, HMRC will authorise the agent or tenant not to deduct tax from the rents. Until he receives such authorisation the agent must deduct tax. Most non-resident landlords opt to use this scheme. It ensures that only the right amount of tax is paid. The non-resident has to file an annual tax return and must pay tax in accordance with the normal self-assessment rules, which of course require interim tax payments to be made based on the previous year's income.

A non-resident individual should normally consider holding UK property through a non-UK company. There are two reasons for this. The individual will pay tax on rental income at rates of up to 45% if the income exceeds the basic rate tax band, whereas an overseas company pays income tax at the 20% basic rate. The second is that as the property is situated in the UK it is within the scope of UK inheritance tax if it is held by the individual but will be outside the scope of IHT if held through an overseas company. This exception will cease to apply from 6 April 2017 to the extent that the property is residential property.

Capital gains tax

9.62 An individual is normally chargeable to CGT only if he is resident in the UK at some time during the tax year in which the gain is realised. Prior to 6 April 2013 the tax also applied if he was ordinarily resident here. Split-year treatment can apply in the circumstances set out in the statutory residence test (see **9.2**).

9.63 There are three important exceptions to this basic rule. The first is that if a non-UK resident is carrying on a trade, profession or vocation in the UK through a branch or agency he is liable to tax on gains on the disposal of UK assets which are used in (or held for the purpose of) the branch or agency at the time the gain accrues, or were used (or held for) such a purpose at an earlier time or have been acquired for use for such a purpose. For the charge to apply the trade must be carried on at the date of the disposal (*TCGA 1992, s 10*). The provision can be overridden by double tax agreements. The same rule applies for corporation tax (*TCGA 1992, s 10B*).

9.64 The second is that a taxpayer who is a temporary non-resident (see **9.6**) is chargeable to CGT in the period of return on some gains realised during his period of non-residence (*TCGA 1992, s 10A* as amended by *FA 2013, Sch 43, para 117*).

9.65 Where *TCGA 1992, s 10A* applies, the individual is treated as realising in the year of return capital gains equal to the aggregate of the gains that arose to him during his period of temporary non-residence and gains that would have been deemed to arise to him during that period under *TCGA 1992, s 13* (gains of overseas company with a UK shareholder) or *TCGA 1992, s 86* (gains of overseas settlement with a UK settlor). He is similarly treated as realising any losses that accrued to him during the period of non-residence (or would have been deemed to so accrue under *TCGA 1992, s 13*) (*TCGA 1992, s 10AA(3)* inserted by *FA 2013, Sch 43, para 117*). It should be noted that if losses actually realised by the taxpayer exceed the taxable gains, the excess loss is an allowable loss deemed to accrue in the year of return.

There is an exception for assets that were acquired during the period of temporary non-residence and disposed of during that period. This exception does not apply if the asset was acquired under a no gain, no loss acquisition, it was an interest created by (or arising under) a settlement, or a gain on another asset was rolled over into that asset (*TCGA 1992, s 10A(3)*).

The third is residential property in the UK. From 6 April 2015, non-residents are liable to capital gains tax on the disposal of (or of an interest in) UK residential property (see **9.73** below).

9.66 Where an individual would have been resident in the UK but was excluded from doing so by a double tax treaty, deemed gains taxable on the individual under *TCGA 1992, s 13* or *TCGA 1992, s 87* or *89(2)* (gains of overseas settlement) are not taxable on him. However, the double tax treaty is to be interpreted so as to permit actual gains arising to the individual in the period of non-residence to be taxed on his return (*TCGA 1992, s 10(9B), (9C)*).

This prevents an individual seeking to establish residence in a treaty country which did not itself tax capital gains for a year, realising a large gain, and then returning to the UK in the following year. Belgium was a popular country. It is questionable whether that device was in any event effective. It is hard to see why another country should want to argue that a person was resident there in circumstances where it would collect no tax by doing so and could see that the reason for claiming residence there was to seek to avoid UK tax. Furthermore, it is by no means clear that taxing an amount equal to a gain is the same thing as taxing the gain.

9.67 To prevent a non-resident being able to escape a CGT charge under *TCGA 1992, s 10* where he carries on a trade in the UK, there is a deemed disposal if he takes the asset outside the UK or ceases the UK trade prior to selling the asset. Where an asset held by a non-resident for the purpose of a UK trade is removed from the UK, and so ceases to be a chargeable asset, it must be treated as being disposed of and re-acquired at its market value immediately before it left the UK (*TCGA 1992, s 25(1)*). This does not apply if the asset is taken outside the UK contemporaneously with the person ceasing to carry on his UK trade (or if it is an oil exploration asset) (*TCGA 1992, s 25(2)*).

9.68 If an asset ceases to be a chargeable asset by virtue of the owner ceasing to carry on a trade, profession or vocation in the UK through a branch or agency he is deemed to have disposed of the asset and re-acquired it at its market value immediately before the trade ceased (*TCGA 1992, s 25(3)*). This does not apply if the asset again becomes a chargeable asset in the same tax year or accounting period (*TCGA 1992, s 25(5)*). For example, it would not apply if the non-resident set up a new UK trade before the end of the tax year. In the case of a company the charge also does not apply if the trade is transferred to another company by way of an intra-group transfer within *TCGA 1992, s 139* or *171* (*TCGA 1992, s 25(5)*).

This provision will of course also prevent a UK resident who carries on a trade in the UK from emigrating and avoiding tax on the trading assets by ceasing the trade and selling the asset after he becomes non-UK resident. However, this is a question of timing. Neither *TCGA 1992, s 10* nor *s 25* will apply if a person ceases to carry on the trade while UK resident but defers selling the assets previously used for the trade until he becomes non-resident. *TCGA 1992, s 25(3)* will not apply in such circumstances as, if the owner is UK resident when the trade ceases, the asset will not cease to be a chargeable asset as it is still within the scope of CGT by virtue of the owner being resident and ordinarily resident in the UK.

9.69 Provided that a person intends to remain non-resident for more than five tax years, it is still possible to emigrate while owning UK assets which are not trading assets of a UK branch or agency by deferring a sale until after the owner has become non-resident. Where a person carries on a business in the UK as a sole trader or in partnership and he intends to become non-resident, consideration should be given to incorporating the business for shares under *TCGA 1992, s 162*. *TCGA 1992, ss 10* and *25* will not apply to a subsequent sale of the shares.

Alternatively, such a person could cease to use the asset in the trade while he is UK resident. For example, at a time when he is UK resident he could transfer the trade to a company but keep the asset personally. After emigration he could then sell both the shares and the asset.

9.70 An individual who is domiciled outside the UK but resident here and has claimed the remittance basis for income tax is also liable to CGT on that basis in relation to gains on overseas assets (*TCGA 1992, s 12(1)*). As with income, the charge can be avoided by spending the sale proceeds outside the UK. The rules considered above in relation to deemed remittances of investment income also apply to capital gains (*TCGA 1992, s 12(2)*).

The gain is deemed to arise when it is remitted. HMRC consider that if a person becomes domiciled in the UK and subsequently remits gains arising at a time when he was non-domiciled they can still tax the remittance under *TCGA 1992, s 12*. It is not wholly clear that this view is correct but anyone who wished to challenge it would need to litigate the point. The wording of the legislation is ambiguous.

9.71 Where an individual intends to become non-resident and sell an asset after he has ceased to be UK resident it needs to be borne in mind that the date of disposal for CGT is the date of contract, not that of completion. A contract does not need to be a formal written document. An offer to sell and the acceptance of that offer creates a contract. HMRC may well want to review all of the correspondence in relation to the sale to look for evidence that a contract came into existence at a time when the individual was still UK resident (or before the end of the tax year in which he ceased to be resident here).

9.72 A conditional contract does not create a disposal until the condition is satisfied. However, it is often difficult to be sure whether the contract is conditional. Lawyers draw a distinction between a condition precedent (ie one the non-fulfilment of which will mean that the contract never became enforceable) and a condition subsequent (ie one which does not destroy the contract but the non-fulfilment of which will give rise to a claim for damages). It is only the former that can qualify as a conditional contract for CGT purposes.

It is accordingly safest to use options if it is wished to make a contract conditional. An option does not create a contract until the option is satisfied. There is a risk with cross-options (ie where the prospective vendor has an option to require the other person to acquire the asset and the proposed purchaser has an option to require the other person to sell it to him). HMRC have been known to contend that cross-options are equivalent to a contract as both parties are able to enforce the bargain. Accordingly, if cross-options are used it is safest for both not to be exercisable at the same time. For example, the vendor could have an option to require the purchaser to buy the asset from him exercisable only during the following May and the prospective purchaser could have an option to require the vendor to sell the company to him exercisable only during the following July. There would then be no time at which both parties could bring the bargain into existence.

Capital gains tax – UK residential property

9.73 As indicated at **9.65**, from 6 April 2015, non-residents have to pay capital gains tax (NRCGT) on the disposal of (or of an interest in) UK residential property (*FA 2015, s 37* and *Sch 7*). They are taxable only on the part of the gain that arises after 6 April 2015. This is normally achieved by revaluing the property at 6 April 2015 and treating that value as the cost of the property. Alternatively the taxpayer can elect to time apportion the gain, ie to calculate the gain over the entire period of ownership and exclude the proportion of that gain that the part of that period ending with 5 April 2015 bears to the entire period of ownership.

A residential property for this purpose includes a property which is only partly a dwelling (such as a shop with a flat above) and a property which has been a dwelling at any time during the owner's period of ownership, but the calculation of the gain limits the charge to tax on only the residential element. The definition also includes an off-plan purchase of a yet-to-be constructed residence.

An NRCGT loss is ring-fenced. It can be used against NRCGT gains but nothing else. If a non-resident who incurs an NRCGT loss subsequently becomes UK resident, the loss becomes a normal CGT loss available to be utilised against any capital gains.

A non-resident who realises an NRCGT gain must submit a tax return for the disposal and pay the tax due within 30 days of the disposal.

9.74 There are few exclusions. It applies to disposals by individual trusts and companies. It applies to let properties and other investment properties. It does not apply to properties included in the stock of a property dealing trade though. The tax does not apply to disposals by widely-held companies (one not under the control of five or fewer people, but shares held by certain connected persons are treated as owned by one of the five or fewer for this purpose) or widely marketed unit trust schemes or OEICs.

There is an exemption for an individual's principal private residence, but this will rarely apply to non-residents. Where a non-resident individual has residences in several countries, his UK property can be regarded as his principal residence only if he occupies it for at least 90 days during the tax year, and anyone who does so risks becoming UK resident for the year under the statutory residence test.

9.75 The normal tax rates apply. This means that an individual is entitled to his £11,100 annual allowance and to his 18% tax band (the amount of which, if any, depends on the size of his UK taxable amount) with the balance being taxed at 28%. A trust pays a flat rate of 28%. A company is taxable at 20% and is entitled to deduct the indexation allowance (to reflect inflation) in calculating the gain.

9.76 A non-resident company can also be liable to CGT on ATED-related gains. ATED (annual tax on enveloped dwellings) is a special tax on high-value residential property held by a company or by a partnership which includes a corporate partner. Where ATED applies to a property, ATED-related CGT applies on its disposal. This is at the rate of 28% on the entire gain, with no deduction for the annual allowance or the 18% lower rate.

There are a great number of exemptions from ATED. The intention is that it should apply only to UK residences available for occupation by shareholders of the owning company or connected persons of theirs.

ATED was introduced from 1 April 2013 for residential properties worth over £2m. It was extended from 1 April 2015 to include those worth over £1m and from 1 April 2016 to residential properties worth over £500,000. These limits are based on the value of the property at 1 April 2012 or, if later, the date of acquisition. Only the part of the gain applicable to the period after 1 April 2013 (or 1 April 2015 or 1 April 2016 as appropriate) is taxable. As with NRCGT, the taxpayer can achieve this by either revaluing the property at the time it comes within the NRCGT net or using time apportionment.

9.77 If the disposal of a property by a company attracts both ATED-related CGT and NRCGT, the two gains must be calculated separately and the tax due aggregated. The part of the ATED-related gain attributable to the period after 6 April 2015 can be deducted in calculating the NRCGT gain. This avoids double taxation, but ensures that the ATED-related gain is taxed at 28% (and without indexation) rather than at the lower rate that applies to disposals by a company.

When ATED and ATED-related CGT was introduced, the government anticipated that properties within the tax would be taken out of the company, so that little tax would actually be collected. This has been proved wrong. Many non-residents are prepared to accept ATED rather than own the property direct. One of the reasons for this is that ownership of the property by a non-UK company can take the property out of the scope of CGT, whereas ownership direct by an individual subjects it to CGT. However, this will cease to apply to residential property from 6 April 2017.

9.78 Curiously, although ATED was introduced to discourage ownership of residences through a company (and has to an extent done so as there are other ways of avoiding or minimising IHT if a property is held by an individual or a trust), the NRCGT rules encourage ownership through a company because the 20% corporate rate is significantly lower than the 28% rate potentially payable by individuals and trusts. This anomaly is a by-product of the UK being a member of the EU. ATED applies to ownership by both UK and non-UK companies and both are taxed at 28%. NRCGT does not apply to UK companies and the European rules do not permit the UK to impose a higher tax on EU companies than on a UK company, so the rate of NRCGT for companies has to match the corporation tax rate that a UK company pays on its capital gains.

Inheritance tax

9.79 Inheritance tax is based partly on domicile and partly on the location of the assets. Residence and ordinary residence are irrelevant – except to the extent that continuous residence can create a deemed UK domicile (see below). A person is liable to inheritance tax on UK assets irrespective of where he is domiciled or resident. A person who is domiciled in the UK (or to be precise in one of the countries that constitute the UK) is chargeable to IHT in relation to worldwide assets.

From 6 April 2017, some overseas assets are within the scope of IHT to the extent that their value derives (directly or indirectly) from UK residential property. The assets concerned are:

(a) an interest in a close company, or one that would be a close company if it were UK resident,

(b) an interest in a partnership,

(c) a loan that was made to finance (directly or indirectly):

  (i) the acquisition by an individual, a partnership or a settlement of an interest in a UK residential property or of an interest in a company or partnership within (a) or (b),

  (ii) the acquisition of an interest in a UK residential property by a close company (or foreign equivalent) or partnership,

  (iii) the maintenance or enhancement of a UK residential property interest, and

  (iv) any money or other asset held as security, collateral or guarantee for such a loan.

(*Finance (No 2) Bill 2017*)

Heads (a) and (b) do not apply if the interest in the company or partnership is less than 5%. A loan ceases to be a UK asset when the UK residential property is sold. However, if a UK property (or any other asset) is sold and the proceeds are used to buy another UK property, a loan to acquire the first asset is treated as being to indirectly acquire the second.

It should be noted that what falls to be treated as UK property is the value of the shares or partnership interest, and not the value of the UK property.

Example 9.4

Jack and Jill and their daughter Jenny are all non-UK domiciled. They each own one-third of a Jersey company that owns their UK house. The house is worth £900,000.

On Jack's death, his one-third interest in the Jersey company is treated as a UK asset. Its value will be significantly less than a third of £900,000, because it is a minority interest in an unquoted company. If Jill has been UK resident for less than 15 years and pays the remittance basis charge, she might consider gifting her shares in the Jersey company to grandchildren or others, so as to create smaller minority interests, which will have a lower value per share.

Example 9.5

Ali, a non-domiciled individual, owns 100% of a Guernsey company that hold six UK residential investment properties. The company owes Ali £100,000, which was used towards the purchase of the first property. The other properties all have bank mortgages to finance 80% of their cost, the other 20% having been financed out of the company's rental income.

On Ali's death, his shares in the Guernsey company are a UK asset. Their value is probably the net asset value of the company. As the company has been largely financed by borrowings, this is probably 20–30% of the value of the properties. In addition, Ali's £100,000 loan is treated as a UK asset; in theory, so are the bank loans but, as the bank is not within the scope of IHT, that is irrelevant. Curiously, if during his lifetime the company had re-mortgaged its first property and repaid Ali, the only taxable item would have been the shares.

Example 9.6

John, a non-domiciled individual, owns 100% of a Guernsey company that owns six residential investment properties, one in the UK and the other five in Germany. There are bank mortgages on the German properties, but not on the UK one.

A proportion of the value of the shares will be regarded as a UK asset on John's death. This has to be arrived at on a just and reasonable basis. Bearing in mind that the mortgages have to be allocated rateably to all of the properties, this is probably the proportion of the net asset value that the value of the UK property bears to the total value of all of the properties. Curiously, re-mortgaging the German properties will reduce the value of the deemed UK proportion of the value of the shares.

It is not wholly clear what the position would be if John had lent the company funds to finance the acquisition of the German properties. The attribution of part of the loan to the UK property in valuing the shares probably does not mean that the loan has indirectly financed the acquisition of the UK property.

9.80 Where a person is non-UK domiciled, a holding in an authorised unit trust, a share in an open-ended investment company and a number of UK government securities are excluded from inheritance tax even though they are UK assets (*IHTA 1984, s 6(1A), (2)*). If the individual is domiciled in the Channel Islands or the Isle of Man, Ulster savings certificates, national savings certificate, premium bonds and certified SAYE saving arrangements are also excluded from IHT (*IHTA 1984, s 6(3)*). So are emoluments from the foreign government and tangible moveable property of members of visiting forces if the presence of the property in the UK is due to the individual being in the UK as a serving member of such an overseas military force (*IHTA 1984, s 155*). There is also an exclusion from IHT on death for a foreign currency account with a UK bank where at the time of his death the holder is domiciled outside the UK and neither resident nor ordinarily resident here (*IHTA 1984, s 157*).

9.81 A person who is not domiciled in the UK is treated, for IHT purposes only, or if he were domiciled here (and not elsewhere) at any time if either:

- he was domiciled here at some time within the previous three years; or
- he was resident in the UK for income tax purposes in at least 15 of the 20 tax years ending with the year in which that time falls (17 out of 20 prior to 6 April 2017).

(*IHTA 1984, s 267(1)*)

This deeming does not apply for the purpose of *IHTA 1984, s 6(2)* and *(3)* (which deems certain securities etc to be outside the scope of IHT if they are held by a person who is not UK domiciled), *s 48(4)* (which applies *IHTA 1984, s 6(2)* to settlements) or *s 158(6)* (double tax relief) (*IHTA 1984, s 267(2)*). The change in the deemed domicile rules from 6 April 2017 will, in practice, extend the first of these periods to up to five years where the individual was deemed domiciled at the time of his emigration.

9.82 The IHT exemption for transfers between spouses or civil partners is limited to £325,000 (£55,000 for disposals before 6 April 2013).where the transferor is domiciled in the UK but the transferee is not (*IHTA 1984, s 18(2)*). This provision might well be overridden by the non-discrimination clause of a double tax agreement. It also needs to be borne in mind that any lifetime transfer of value to an individual is a potentially exempt transfer which will be taxable only if the transferor dies within seven years of making the gift (*IHTA 1984, s 3A*). Accordingly, a lifetime gift to a non-domiciled spouse – or indeed any other non-UK domiciled individual – is exempt, whatever the amount, if the donor survives for the seven-year period.

9.83 Where one spouse or civil partner only is UK domiciled, consideration accordingly ought to be given to putting the majority of the family assets into the ownership of the non-UK domiciled spouse (or into a trust for the benefit of the non-UK domiciled spouse if this can be done without a significant entry charge) during the lifetime of the UK-domiciled spouse.

Where one spouse is UK-domiciled and the other is not, the non-domiciled spouse can elect to be treated as domiciled for IHT purposes. That will avoid the limitation on spousal gifts, but will also bring the spouse's worldwide assets into the scope of IHT, so is not necessarily desirable. The election can be made at any time and can be backdated by up to seven years. The election can be made by the personal representatives of a deceased spouse but such an election must be made within two years of the death. Accordingly, there is no need to elect until the domiciled spouse dies and it can be seen that the election will avoid tax on a failed PET by the deceased to the spouse (made after 6 April 2013) or on a transfer to the spouse on death.

The election is irrevocable but if the individual ceases to be UK resident it ceases to have effect once the individual has been non-resident for four tax years (*IHTA 1984, ss 267ZA, 267ZB*).

9.84 Non-UK property included in a settlement is outside the scope of IHT if the settlor was non-UK domiciled (and not deemed to be UK domiciled) at the time of the creation of the settlement (*IHTA 1984, s 48(3)*). So are units in a UK-authorised unit trust and shares in a UK open-ended investment company which are held by such a settlement (*IHTA 1984, s 48(3A)*). This does not apply if an interest in possession in the property is held by a UK-domiciled person and that interest was acquired for a consideration in money or money's worth (*IHTA 1984, s 48(3B)*).

UK government securities within *IHTA 1984, s 6(2)* are also exempt if they are held by such a settlement and either a non-domiciled person has an interest in possession in them or all possible beneficiaries of the settlement are non-UK domiciled (*IHTA 1984, s 48(4)*).

9.85 If an interest in possession in a pre-22 March 2006 settlement comes to an end there is a deemed disposal of the settled property for IHT purposes. However, no tax is chargeable if, when that interest in possession comes to an end, the settlor's spouse or civil partner becomes entitled to the property, provided that he is domiciled in the UK (*IHTA 1984, ss 53(4), 54(2)*).

Again, this is not necessarily a problem if the interest in possession terminates during the beneficiary's lifetime as the deemed disposal is deemed to be a potentially exempt transfer by the person with the interest in possession so it does not matter that the spouse is not UK domiciled provided that the beneficiary survives for seven years.

A transfer of value made by a close company is apportioned amongst its participators and treated as a transfer of value by the participators (*IHTA 1984, s 94*). However, if a participator is non-UK domiciled this does not apply to the extent that the value apportioned to him relates to non-UK property held by the company (*IHTA 1984, s 94(2)*).

Double tax treaties

9.86 The UK has only ten tax treaties in relation to inheritance tax. Those that it does have fall into two categories, namely those that were entered into pre-1975 and originally related to estate duty (which was payable only on death) and those entered into after 1975 which originally related to capital transfer tax (the original name of inheritance tax) and thus also cover lifetime gifts.

The first category comprises the agreements with France, Italy, India and Pakistan. These treaties now apply to IHT on death only (*IHTA 1984, s 158(6)*).

The second category comprises the agreements with Ireland, Netherlands, South Africa, Sweden, Switzerland and the US.

9.87 Clearly, the individual agreement needs to be looked at in a particular case. However, they normally apply where a person is domiciled in both countries under their domestic law. The category two agreements refer to a person being domiciled in the UK in accordance with its law or treated as domiciled for the purposes of IHT. This raises an interesting question as to the application of the category one agreements where a person is not domiciled in the UK under UK law but is deemed domiciled here for IHT purposes.

The probability is that such a person is automatically regarded as French (or Italian, Indian or Pakistani) domiciled for the purposes of the treaty. Where a person is domiciled in a category two country, such as the US, and deemed domiciled in the UK, then the tie-breaker clause of the agreement will apply in the same way as if he was domiciled in both countries.

9.88 The category one agreements (other than that with Italy which is more limited) prevent the UK charging IHT on property situated outside the UK where the decedent was domiciled in the other country and not in the UK for the purpose of the agreement. They also contain rules to determine the *situs* of specific assets. However, these agreements also allow the UK to charge IHT on property which 'passes under a disposition or devolution regulated by the law of some part of Great Britain'. This will allow the UK to tax non-UK property if it passes under a UK will or is held in a UK settlement. Where the other country imposes tax on assets situated in that country, the UK has to give credit for such tax in determining the UK tax payable. This is subject to an important proviso from 6 April 2017: a UK residential property interest held by the non-domiciled individual is brought within the scope of IHT, unless a similar tax to IHT is chargeable on its value under the law of the other country (*Finance (No 2) Bill 2017*).

The category two agreements normally lay down more detailed rules as to what can be taxed by each country. They determine the *situs* of property and normally allow the UK to tax land and business property situated in the UK.

Where the UK does not have a double tax agreement with the other country it allows a credit for foreign tax paid both on death and on lifetime gifts (*IHTA 1984, s 159*).

Use of overseas trusts

9.89 An overseas trust can be an attractive vehicle in which to hold assets where the taxpayer is resident but not domiciled in the UK. Such a trust does not have income tax advantages but can be attractive from both a CGT and IHT point of view.

It enables CGT to be deferred whilst the funds remain within the trust. The tax charge on the settlor under *TCGA 1992, s 86* does not apply where the settlor is non-UK domiciled. Accordingly, capital gains are taxed only under *TCGA 1992, s 87* when they are distributed from the settlement. This applies to gains on both UK and non-UK assets. On distribution a surcharge is however payable. This is 10% pa up to a maximum of 60% (giving an effective CGT rate of 32% where the 20% rate of CGT applies). However, if the gain will be retained within the settlement for significantly more than six years the cash-flow benefit is likely to outweigh this disadvantage. The charge under *TCGA 1992, s 87* is considered in **Chapter 14**.

Non-UK assets held in a trust are normally outside the scope of IHT if the settlor was non-UK domiciled (and not deemed domiciled) at the time he created the trust. This exemption continues to apply even if the settlor subsequently becomes deemed domiciled in the UK (except where the settlor was born in the UK with a UK domicile of origin). The general IHT benefits that can be obtained from the use of trusts in relation to UK assets are considered in **Chapter 14**.

The residence of trusts and settlements is dealt with in **Chapter 14**.

COMPANY RESIDENCE

9.90 A company is domiciled where it is incorporated, but domicile is rarely important in a corporation tax context.

A company is resident in the country in which its central control and management takes place. This was established by the House of Lords in a commendably brief judgment in *De Beers Consolidated Mines Ltd v Howe (Surveyor of Taxes)* (1906) 5 TC 198. De Beers was incorporated in South Africa where it operated diamond mines. Its head office was in South Africa. The company held weekly board meetings in both London and South Africa. The majority of the directors lived in the UK. Attendance at the London meetings was far greater than at the South African ones and in practice the major decisions were taken at the London meetings. The Lord Chancellor, Lord Loreburn, opined:

> 'In applying the conception of residence to a company, we ought, I think, to proceed as nearly as we can upon the analogy of an individual. A company cannot eat or sleep, but it can keep house and do business. We ought, therefore, to see whether it really keeps house and does business. An individual may be of foreign nationality, and yet reside in the United Kingdom. So may a company. Otherwise, it might have its chief seat of management and its centre of trading in England, under the protection of English law, and yet escape the appropriate taxation by the simple expedient of being registered abroad and distributing its dividends abroad. The decision of Chief Baron Kelly and Baron Huddleston, now thirty years ago, involved the principal that a company resides, for purposes of income tax, where its real business is carried on. Those decisions have been acted upon ever since. I regard that as the true rule; and the real business is carried on where the central management and control actually abides. It remains to be considered whether the present case falls within that rule. This is a pure question of fact, to be determined, not according to the construction of this or that regulation or bylaw, but upon a scrutiny of the course of business and trading.'

As the Commissioners had found as a fact that 'the head and seat and directing power of the affairs of the Appellant Company were at the office in London from whence the chief operations of the Company, both in the UK and elsewhere, were, in fact, controlled, managed and directed', the company was held to be resident in the UK.

9.91 HMRC say that 'Although central management and control depends ultimately on the facts, a review of residence normally starts with the question of law. A company is governed first by the law of the country in which it is incorporated and second by its constitution … In the UK, management is normally entrusted to the directors, although it can be given to a single individual such as a managing director who has exclusive authority under the terms of the Articles. Where the company is incorporated abroad, it will be necessary to take into account the system of company management under the law of the country of incorporation' (International Tax Manual, ITM120180). The company law cases have held that normally this is the Board of Directors.

However, as residence is a question of fact it is possible that the people legally charged with the management and control of the company did not in fact exercise it. In *Bullock (Inspector of Taxes) v Unit Construction Co Ltd* (1959) 38 TC 712, the issue in dispute was the residence of a number of Kenyan subsidiary companies of Unit Construction. These were incorporated in Kenya and their Boards of Directors met only in Kenya. In 1950, the parent company directors decided that they would in future make all the major decisions in relation to the operation of the subsidiaries, and the Boards of the subsidiaries acquiesced in this. The East African companies were held to be resident in the UK. In the House of Lords, Lord Radcliffe said:

> 'Ought we, then, to adopt this principle that evidence of what has happened in fact must be excluded by a rule of law if what has been done is inconsistent with the regulations of a company? In my opinion it would be wrong to do so. I cannot see how the corollary of such a principle could fail to be that, if you cannot look beyond what the regulations of the company provide for, it is only those regulations which need to be or indeed can be referred to when a question of residence arises. Companies could be equipped with the most comprehensive sets of constitutions providing for management to be located in this or that selected taxing jurisdiction, and, however much the written requirements were in fact departed from for reasons of convenience or otherwise, all efforts to establish the true facts relating to the actual seat of management would founder on the ground that what had been done was merely "unconstitutional" … I cannot think that such considerations are sufficient to introduce an important qualification upon this accepted test by which you try to ascertain what are the real facts about the seat of management and control and to put in its place what seems to be the merely formal device of studying a set of

written regulations. I do not believe that this would conduce to the health of revenue administration. I think it much better to adhere to the approach laid down by Lord Loreburn, LC, in the De Beers case. "This is a pure question of fact, to be determined, not according to the construction of this or that regulation or by-law, but upon a scrutiny of the course of business and trading".'

9.92 HMRC are very alert to the risk that the decisions might in reality not be made by the Board of Directors. They tell their staff, under a heading 'what is the reality', that:

> 'it has been said that the management and control test is bad because it leads to the nonsense of directors flying to Jersey for board meetings ... It is quite easy for a company operating here to incorporate in Jersey and claim to be managed and controlled there with only a minimal tax cost in Jersey provided the shareholders are not resident there.
>
> On the face of it the point is a valid one. But criticism of that kind is concerned as much with questions of fact as of concept and the two things must be kept separate in our minds. There is, in principle at any rate, no reason why a business which is visibly in this country should not be managed and controlled from, let us say, Jersey. But if the directors of that company are working in this country on a regular basis and probably living here as well, it may be highly unlikely that they will be doing anything more in Jersey than reaffirming decisions already taken here. If that is so the mere fact of having board meetings in the Channel Islands is irrelevant. The question is, where do the people concerned exercise management and control. If they really do it in this country and go through a meaningless form of words in Jersey, that will achieve nothing for them' (International Manual ITH334).

9.93 HMRC have given guidance on residence in Statement of Practice 1/90 where they emphasise:

> 'In general the place of directors' meetings is significant only insofar as those meetings constitute the medium through which central management and control is exercised. If, for example, the directors of a company were engaged together actively in the UK in the complete running of a business which was wholly in the UK, the company would not be regarded as resident outside the UK merely because the directors held formal meetings outside the UK. While it is possible to identify extreme situations in which central management and control plainly is, or is not, exercised by directors in formal meetings, the conclusion in any case is wholly one of fact depending on the relative weight to be given to various factors. Any attempt to lay down rigid guidelines would only be misleading.

Generally, however, where doubts arise about a particular company's residence status, the Revenue adopt the following approach –

(i) they first try to ascertain whether the directors of the company in fact exercise central management and control;

(ii) if so, they seek to determine where the directors exercise this central management and control (which is not necessarily where they meet);

in cases where the directors apparently do not exercise central management and control of the company, the Revenue then look to establish where and by whom it is exercised.'

They also warn:

'In outlining factors relevant to the application of the case law test, this statement assumes that they exist for genuine commercial reasons. Where, however, as may happen, it appears that a major objective underlying the existence of certain factors is the obtaining of tax benefits from residence or non-residence, the Revenue examine the facts particularly closely in order to see whether there has been an attempt to create the appearance of central management and control in a particular place without the reality.'

9.94 An important case before the courts is *Wood v Holden* [2006] STC 443 which was heard by the Court of Appeal in January 2006. This is a significant case partly because it relates to a tax-avoidance scheme, so the courts might be expected to seek to interpret the law so as to thwart the scheme, and partly because it draws a clear distinction between simply implementing decisions of someone else and considering what that other person proposes and deciding that it is in the best interest of the company to adopt that proposal.

9.95 A CGT avoidance scheme was formulated by Price Waterhouse Corporate Finance Ltd in the UK which involved one non-UK company, CIL, being gifted shares in a UK company, Holdings, CIL selling those shares to its wholly owned Dutch subsidiary, Eulalia, at market value and Eulalia subsequently selling the shares in Holdings to an arm's-length purchaser. The Special Commissioners decided that CIL was non-UK resident but that Eulalia was UK resident. They felt that the taxpayer had failed to satisfy them that Eulalia was not UK resident (and both HMRC and the Woods had claimed that CIL was non-resident). This received short shrift from Park J in the High Court:

'There plainly comes a point where the taxpayer has produced evidence which, as matters stand then, appears to show that the assessment is wrong. At that point the evidential basis must pass to the Revenue. … In this case … Mr and Mrs Wood had to show to the civil standard of proof that the adjustment was wrong. I accept that the onus was on them to show that Eulalia was not resident in the United Kingdom, but rather was resident in the Netherlands. They showed that Eulalia was incorporated in the Netherlands. They showed incontrovertibly that it had been resident only in the Netherlands until it was acquired by CIL. They showed that CIL was not itself a United Kingdom company, and indeed was a company which the Revenue asserted to have been resident outside the United Kingdom. They showed that, from the time when Eulalia was acquired by CIL, its managing director was [ABN AMRO] Trust, a large Dutch company with offices in Amsterdam. They showed resolutions and consequential actions being taken in the offices in Amsterdam. They accepted that what Eulalia was doing was part of a tax scheme which was being superintended by Price Waterhouse in their Manchester offices. They called evidence from the Price Waterhouse partners who at the time were heads of the firm's departments for corporate finance and for tax in Manchester. They produced a witness statement from the head of the legal department at [ABN AMRO] Trust. They were willing for the appeal to be adjourned in order that the witness could attend in person to be available for cross-examination. They produced all the documents which existed (so I assume, and no one has suggested that any documents were suppressed). The documents showed guidance and influence coming from Price Waterhouse, but no more than that. Mr and Mrs Wood were able to point out that the Netherlands Revenue had stated to the United Kingdom Revenue that the actual management of Eulalia was carried out by [ABN AMRO] Trust, "meaning that the taxable domicile of Eulalia Holding BV is located in the Netherlands". Surely at that point they can say: "We have done enough to raise a case that Eulalia was not resident in the United Kingdom. What more can the Special Commissioners expect from us? The burden must now pass to the Revenue to produce some material to show that, despite what appears from everything which we have produced, Eulalia was actually resident in the United Kingdom."'

He also thought it was not enough for HMRC to demonstrate that the steps taken were part of a single tax scheme, that there were overall architects of the scheme in Price Waterhouse Corporate Finance Ltd and that those involved all shared the common expectation that the various stages of the scheme would in fact take place. These matters were not denied. However, he felt that, taken together they did not, of themselves, lead to the conclusion that Eulalia was resident in the UK.

9.96 The Court of Appeal agreed with the judge. Furthermore, Lord Justice Chadwick added that:

> 'A further flaw in the Special Commissioners' approach was to treat the decisions which were made by ABN AMRO as not "effective decisions" because they were reached without proper information or consideration. But a management decision does not cease to be a management decision because it might have been taken on fuller information; or even, as it seems

to me, because it was taken in circumstances which might put the director at risk of an allegation of breach of duty. Ill-informed or ill-advised decisions taken in the management of a company remain management decisions.'

Companies incorporated in the UK

9.97 From 15 March 1988, a company that is incorporated in the UK must be regarded as UK resident for tax purposes (*CTA 2009, s 14*).

This can, of course, be overridden by double tax treaties (*CTA 2009, s 18(4)*). As with individuals, double tax treaties normally contain a tie-breaker clause to treat a company as resident in one only of the two countries which are party to the treaty. This normally provides that the company is deemed to be a resident only of the country in which its place of effective management is situated. This is probably the same test as central management and control.

Non-resident company trading in the UK

9.98 A non-UK resident company will of course be taxable in the UK to the extent that it has taxable income arising here. A non-UK resident company is within the charge to corporation tax if, and only if, it carries on a trade in the UK through a permanent establishment in the UK. It is so taxable on all profits, wherever arising, that are attributable to its permanent establishment in the UK, including income from property or rights used by, or held by or for, the establishment, and on chargeable gains falling within *TCGA 1992, s 10B* (see above) by virtue of assets being used in or for the purposes of the trade carried on through the establishment or being used or held (or acquired for use) for the purposes of the establishment (*CTA 2009, s 19*). From 5 July 2016, it is also taxable on profits from dealing in or developing UK land, even where these do not arise through a UK permanent establishment.

9.99 A company has a permanent establishment in the UK if, and only if, it has a fixed place of business here through which its business is wholly or partly carried on, or an agent acting on behalf of the company has, and habitually exercises in the UK, authority to do business on behalf of the company (*CTA 2010, ss 1141–1145*).

For this purpose, a fixed place of business includes a place of management, a branch, an office, a factory, a workshop, an installation or structure for the exploration of natural resources, a mine, an oil or gas well, a quarry or any other place of extraction of natural resources, a building site and a construction or installation project (*CTA 2010, s 1141(2)*). A company cannot have a permanent establishment in the UK by reason only of the fact that it carries on business here through an agent of independent status acting in the ordinary course of his business (*CTA 2010, s 1142(1)*). A company is not regarded as having a permanent establishment if the activities carried on in the UK are only of a preparatory or auxiliary character, such as the use of facilities for the purpose of storage, display or delivery of goods or merchandise belonging to the company, the maintenance of a stock of goods or merchandise belonging to the company for the purpose of storage, display or delivery or of processing by another person, or purchasing goods or merchandise for the company, or collecting information (*CTA 2010, s 1143*).

The legislation lays down rules for attributing profits to a permanent establishment (*CTA 2009, ss 20–24*).

Where a company is not within the charge to corporation tax it will be chargeable to income tax at the basic rate on UK source income. It is not clear if it can be chargeable to income tax on trading income which does not arise through a permanent establishment. It can of course also be chargeable to CGT in relation to UK residential property both under the ATED-related CGT and the NRCGT regimes. These are considered at **9.73–9.78**.

Change of residence

9.100 There is no bar on a UK company changing its residence, although if the company is incorporated in the UK it can do only by becoming dual resident or being deemed to be non-resident under a double tax agreement, as a UK-incorporated company is treated as resident here (with some exceptions where a company ceased to be UK resident before 1988).

9.101 There are a number of provisions that can impose a tax charge where a UK-resident company ceases to be resident here or which relate to non-resident companies. The main ones are *CTA 2009, ss 41(2)* and *289* (company beginning or ceasing to be within the charge to corporation tax), *TMA 1970, s 109B* (provisions for securing payment by company of outstanding tax), *TMA 1970, s 109E* (liability of other persons for unpaid tax), *TCGA 1992, s 14* (non-resident groups of companies), *TCGA 1992, s 185* (deemed disposal of assets on company ceasing to be resident in the UK), *ITA 2007, ss 835C–835S* (UK representatives of non-residents), *CTA 2010, ss 973–980* (recovery of tax payable by non-resident company), *CTA 2010, ss 969–972* (non-resident companies: assessment, collection and recovery of corporation tax (non-resident companies: extent of charge to income tax), *CTA 2010, s 1142* (non-resident companies: transactions carried out through broker, investment manager or Lloyd's agent), *CTA 2010, ss 107–110* (group relief where surrendering company not resident in UK) and *ITA 2007, s 5(1)* (companies within the charge to income tax).

Dual-resident companies

9.102 As with an individual, it is possible for a company to be resident in two or more countries simultaneously, because the test for residence is different in each country. Where this occurs the legislation can restrict the deductibility of specified expenditure and capital allowances to prevent double relief being obtained. Accordingly, it is normally best to seek to avoid such a status.

Companies treated as non-resident

9.103 Where a UK-resident company is treated as non-resident under a double tax treaty, it is treated as non-resident for all the purposes of the *Taxes Acts* (*CTA 2009, s 18*). For this purpose a company is regarded as treaty non-resident if it meets the appropriate conditions, even if it has not claimed the benefit of the treaty (*CTA 2009, s 18(4)*).

Chapter 10

Agency workers and intermediaries

Originally written by David Heaton, FCA, CTA, David Heaton Tax Ltd and updated by Kye Burchmore LLB, RIFT Legal Services

SIGNPOSTS

- **Background** – Agency workers have been a feature of the economy for many years and most have been deemed to receive employment income. However structures had developed enabling them to be paid gross by intermediaries, without PAYE or NIC, on an increasingly widespread basis because they were technically self-employed and outside the scope of the agency provisions in *ITEPA 2003* and the NIC *Categorisation Regulations 1978.* The government reacted by changing the deeming rules in 2014 and the reporting arrangements in 2015 (see **10.1–10.3**).
- **Status** – Workers supplied by third parties to work for a client are technically self-employed unless they are deliberately given a contract of employment (see **10.4**).
- **Liabilities** – The government attempted in April 2014 to counteract avoidance via intermediary self-employment, and evasion via offshore intermediaries, by changing the deeming rules and imposing new liabilities on businesses within the UK, by removing the requirement for a personal service obligation from the agency provisions and adding new targeted anti-avoidance rules and transfer of debt provisions (see **10.5–10.23**). In addition to this, from April 2017, liabilities for IR35 for public sector work moved from the PSC to the public sector body or agency engaging the PSC (see **10.12**).
- **Reporting obligations** – From April 2015, intermediaries paying gross for the services of workers who are self-employed or supplied by another business must submit quarterly reports of their payments so that HMRC may identify and penalised abuse of the 2014 provisions at an early stage (see **10.24–10.37**).
- **Restrictions on travel and subsistence expenses** – From April 2016, umbrella companies and personal service companies supplying

agency workers lost the right to pay tax- and NIC-free travel and subsistence expenses for home-to-work travel to any employee subject to supervision, direction or control as to the manner of carrying out the work, which undermined the business model of most umbrella employers (see **10.38–10.42**).

INTRODUCTION

10.1 This chapter examines the changes made between 2014 and 2017 to the tax and national insurance contribution (NIC) rules for agency and 'temporary' workers and their 'intermediary' suppliers.

Agency workers have been a feature of the economy for many years and according to the Office for National Statistics (ONS) around 1.5 million people were classed as 'temporary workers' in the first quarter of 2017. Only around a third of 'temps' were 'temping' because they were unable to find a permanent job.

Agencies have been supplying workers for many years, to cover for permanent staff who are absent and to deal with peaks and troughs in demand, but it is not the classic 'temp' who was the target of the changes made in 2014. The mischief at which those changes were aimed has been developing since before the introduction of IR35 in 2000. The problem, as perceived by HMRC, was that the agency worker provisions for PAYE and NIC were being abused so as to save tax and NICs for employers, and payroll deductions were in danger of becoming optional as the problem grew.

The nub of that problem lies in the categorisation of workers as employed or self-employed. Agency workers have for many years been treated as receiving employment income, despite the fact that they are not employees, but certain providers had established alternative employment models that enabled agencies, acting fully within the law, to supply nominally temporary workers as if they were self-employed contractors, thereby saving the employer NICs that would ordinarily be paid in respect of the earnings of agency workers, and deferring the tax for the individual workers by moving the income from the PAYE regime to the self-assessment regime.

An associated but fundamentally different problem was also addressed by changes in 2014. UK NIC law does not levy secondary contributions on employers who have no presence in the jurisdiction (although the jurisdiction now – at least until formal 'Brexit' – extends technically to the whole of the European Economic Area (EEA) when dealing with migrant workers). The jurisdiction normally extends only as far as the 12-mile limit (and beyond the limit is not classed as EEA territory), so employers of workers operating on the UK Continental Shelf have for many years avoided having an onshore presence that would attract a secondary contribution liability. The government identified this as an unacceptable anomaly and created a new system of levying contributions in respect of Continental Shelf workers.

The third problem, addressed by the *Finance Act 2016* changes, centres on intermediary workers employed under 'umbrella' contracts who have been receiving part of their pay as tax- and NIC-free commuting and subsistence expenses. Typical agency workers have been deemed for many years to have a new permanent workplace for each assignment, so they have never been able to receive tax-free commuting expenses. This led to the growth of an 'umbrella' employment industry, in which workers were deliberately given a single, overarching or 'umbrella' employment contract covering all their assignments, rather than an agency contract for services. The same principle applied to workers who set up their own personal service company (PSC) to cover all their assignments. This arrangement meant that they were being sent to a series of temporary workplaces in a single employment, with relief due under *ITEPA 2003, s 338*. Umbrella employers reduced taxable pay and substituted tax-free expenses under 'payday-by-payday' relief models. *ITEPA 2003, s 339A* blocks this approach by deeming each engagement to be a separate employment, putting umbrella employees on the same footing as agency workers and the clients' employees alongside whom they work.

The relevant law

10.2 The tax rules relevant to agency workers and the changes made to them are found in *ITEPA 2003, Pt 2, Ch 7 (ss 44–47)*, with a new record-keeping requirement in *ITEPA 2003, s 716B* and the addition of *ITEPA 2003, ss 61K–61X* to address the perceived non-compliance with IR35 in the public sector. The record-keeping requirement provides power to extend the PAYE record-keeping requirement to cases of self-employed workers supplied by intermediaries.

The NIC rules and changes made to them are found in the *Social Security (Categorisation of Earners) Regulations 1978, SI 1978/1689* (the '*Categorisation Regulations*') and the *Social Security (Contributions) Regulations 2001, SI 2001/1004* (the '*Contributions Regulations*').

The 2014 changes were aimed at ensuring that agency workers who work in a similar way to ordinary employees of the client businesses are subjected to the same PAYE and NIC obligations as those ordinary employees, irrespective of their contractual terms. Why this was necessary is explained below (see **10.4**).

For cases where this was (for perfectly valid reasons) not achieved, HMRC also introduced, with effect from 6 April 2015, a new reporting regime so that it at least has visibility over the businesses continuing to use workers supplied by intermediaries, and over which of them are paid gross. The *Income Tax (Pay As You Earn) (Amendment No 2) Regulations 2015, SI 2015/171* added *Regulations 84E–84H* into the *Income Tax (Pay As You Earn) Regulations 2003, SI 2003/2682* to create a new quarterly reporting regime for those intermediaries who contract with end users, referred to as 'clients' in the regulations. The reporting requirements and mechanics are discussed below (see **10.24**).

For oil and gas workers, any employment on the UK Continental Shelf has for many years been treated as employment within the UK and therefore subject to primary NIC liability (*SSCBA 1992, s 120* and *Contributions Regulations, Reg 114*), but this deeming rule does not extend to employers of such workers. To impose a secondary contribution liability on such employers or intermediaries (or their clients, if the employers do not pay) for the first time, *NIC Act 2014, s 12* and *Social Security (Contributions) (Amendment No 2) Regulations 2014, SI 2015/572* added new *Regs 114A–114D* to the *Contributions Regulations* from 6 April 2014. There is now a licensing and certification regime to provide rig operators with a safe way to hire workers through intermediaries, without exposing themselves to potential NIC obligations.

The reliefs for expenses for necessary travel to a temporary workplace are found in *ITEPA 2003, ss 338–339*. They were created to allow a measure of relief for journeys other than ordinary commuting but were being exploited by the umbrella employment sector in a way that Parliament never envisaged. From 6 April 2016, *FA 2016, s 14* introduced two sections to counter the use of 'salary sacrifice' in connection with this relief:

- *ITEPA 2003, s 339A* restricts *ITEPA 2003, ss 338* and *339* relief by treating as a separate employment each engagement of a worker personally providing services through an intermediary (umbrella or PSC) while under some right of supervision, direction or control. This has the effect of turning more journeys into ordinary commuting, for which no relief is due.
- *ITEPA 2003, s 688B* creates new powers to recover unpaid PAYE in certain circumstances from directors and officers of companies where:
  - (i) fraudulent documents have been provided that purport to evidence an absence of supervision, direction and control, or
  - (ii) the intermediary has no evidence to support a claim that there is no supervision, direction or control, or
  - (iii) the intermediary is an 'IR35' personal service company without being a managed service company (MSC).

The four mischiefs

10.3 The main target of the changes in 2014 and 2015 was avoidance by means of ensuring that agency workers were legally classed as self-employed. The change in statutes and regulations now deem many of these workers to be employed by the agency or intermediary supplying them to the client.

The second target in 2014 was employers of offshore workers in the oil and gas industry who previously had had no liability to pay secondary contributions if they had no place of business within the UK. The regulations now deem the secondary contributor to be:

- the employer, if it has a presence or place of business in the UK, or in the absence of such an employer;
- an associated company of the employer that is present in the UK, or in the absence of either of these:
- the oilfield licensee.

The third target in 2014 and 2015 was evasion rather than avoidance. Some intermediaries had deliberately set themselves up outside the jurisdiction so that they were under no obligation to comply with UK law. The law has for many years included 'host employer' provisions for both income tax (*ITEPA 2003, ss 687, 689*) and NIC (*Categorisation Regulations, Sch 3, para 9*), imposing a liability, broadly on somebody within the jurisdiction against whom HMRC could take enforcement action. However, that UK person was unable to comply if the overseas intermediary refused to supply the relevant information, and HMRC was powerless to penalise the UK client who had an obvious 'reasonable excuse' for non-compliance. The new regulations attempt to ensure that the liability for PAYE and NIC in respect of workers supplied by such intermediaries is transferred to the agency in the UK that has the contract with the client.

The fourth target is the exploitation of the temporary workplace provisions to pay what are effectively agency workers a tax-free travel payment in substitution for part of their true pay. *FA 2015* made changes that would catch all expenses paid under salary sacrifice arrangements from 6 April 2016, making them subject to PAYE but leaving open the possibility of a claim by the employee for retrospective relief under *ITEPA 2003, s 338*. *FA 2016, s 14* turns most temporary workplaces for intermediary workers into permanent workplaces, thereby preventing relief under *ITEPA 2003, s 338*.

AGENCY WORKERS' EMPLOYMENT STATUS

10.4 A full analysis of the employment status of agency workers is beyond the scope of this brief chapter, but the principles may be stated succinctly.

It has been established for many years (see *Ready Mixed Concrete (South East) Ltd v Minister of Pensions and National Insurance* [1968] 2 QB 497, page 515) that, for there to be a contract of service, three conditions must be fulfilled:

- the servant agrees to provide his own work in exchange for a wage;
- he agrees to accept the master's control; and
- the other provisions of the contract are consistent with its being a contract of service.

MacKenna J noted that 'Freedom to do a job either by one's own hands or by another's is inconsistent with a contract of service, though a limited or occasional power of delegation may not be …'.

In the context of a typical agency worker, these conditions may never be fulfilled, even if the worker is supplied by the agency to the same client for many years. The worker contracts with the agency or intermediary and is paid by him, but control is exercised by the client, who is not a party to that agreement, having entered into a separate bilateral agreement with the agency. The tripartite arrangement therefore automatically falls outside the scope of a contract of service (see **Figure 10.1**). The typical agency worker therefore works in law under a 'contract for services', ie, as a self-employed contractor.

> **Focus**
>
> Employment contracts have only two parties, so agency workers are self-employed on common law principles. Tax law applies different rules.

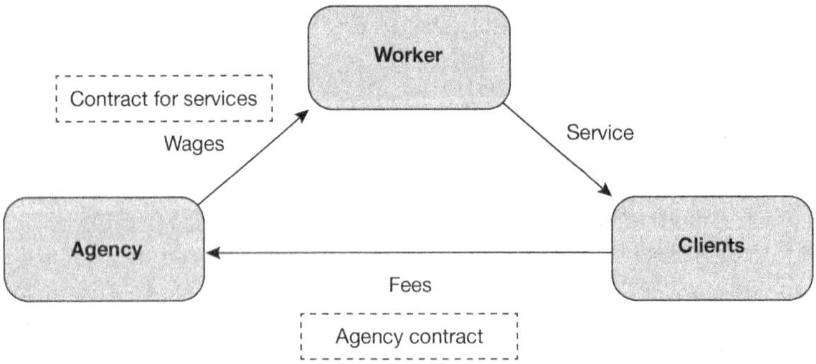

Figure 10.1: The tripartite relationship for agency work

It has been recognised for a long time that agency workers who work alongside permanent staff, doing the same work, broadly in the same circumstances, should be taxed and subjected to NIC deductions just like those permanent staff. This was originally achieved by *ITEPA 2003, s 44* and the *Categorisation Regulations* deeming them to receive employment income if three conditions were fulfilled:

- their income was not already employment income (some agency workers do in fact have a contract of employment, as do almost all 'umbrella' company workers);
- they were obliged to provide personal service; and
- they were subject to supervision, direction or control as to the manner of carrying out the work.

In other words, they were de facto employees, even if they could never be employees in law because they were working via an agency.

A number of activities were specifically excluded for historical reasons. Services as an actor, singer, musician or other entertainer or as a fashion, photographic or artist's model have traditionally been provided via agencies but it has been accepted that the workers concerned ought to be genuinely self-employed. Also excluded were services provided wholly in the worker's own home or at other premises which were neither controlled nor managed by the client nor prescribed by the nature of the services (see *ITEPA 2003, s 47*).

> **Focus**
>
> Not every agency worker is deemed to fall within PAYE and Class 1 NIC: there are a number of exceptions.

There have been occasional examples of agency workers being able to establish that they were employed under a contract of service by the agency (see, eg *McMeechan v Secretary of State for Employment* [1996] EWCA Civ 1166), but the normal position has been and remains that the typical agency worker is self-employed on basic principles (see, eg *Dacas v Brook Street Bureau (UK) Ltd* [2004] EWCA Civ 217). Most agencies therefore pay their temporary workers through payroll, subject to deduction of PAYE and Class 1 NIC.

There were two major exceptions to this: 'umbrella' company workers and those workers who did not meet the three conditions stated.

Firstly, umbrella companies emerged after 1998 as a way of exploiting the tax-free and NIC-free status of expenses for employees travelling between home and a temporary workplace (see **Figure 10.2**). Workers were deliberately given employment contracts for what was, in essence, agency work (with all jobs carried out under the 'umbrella' of a single 'over-arching' contract) and were paid at a lower rate than normal. This was topped up by expenses payments for home-to-work travel that would not be paid to a normal employee of the business. Since only part of the remuneration package was taxable, the actual gross pay required to keep the workers' net pay at the same level as that enjoyed by agency workers was lower than otherwise would have been the case. This enabled the employer, or often a related employment agency, to reduce the rate charged to its clients for supplying the workers' services, giving it a competitive edge. Clearly, no deeming rules were required to bring their income within PAYE and Class 1 NIC. Umbrella workers were therefore very attractive to employment agencies, as costs were lower and payroll administration was undertaken by the umbrella business.

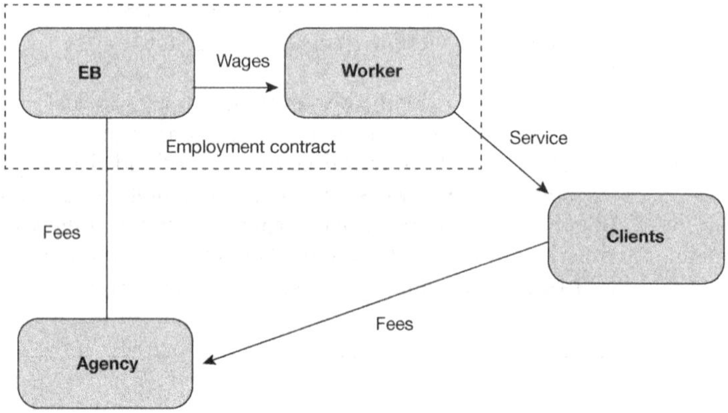

Figure 10.2: The classic umbrella-agency structure

Secondly, some intermediaries began, with those temporary workers who went on to their books, to enter into contracts for services that explicitly permitted the worker to send a substitute rather than commit to carrying out the work personally. Agencies often ensured that actual substitution took place from time to time so that it could be demonstrated that the right was genuine. This had the effect of ensuring that the second condition set out above could not be met, and that the workers would therefore be outside the PAYE and NIC deeming provisions. Here again, a cost saving arose (ie, due to the absence of employer contributions) that could be passed on to clients in the form of lower hourly rates.

These structures first became widespread in the construction industry, but the imposition of a 20% deduction under the Construction Industry Scheme meant that HMRC had few concerns about delayed or reduced remittances. However, when the use of self-employed agency contracts began to spread to other industries where there was no similar requirement for deduction at source, and to businesses that moved their entire workforce onto an intermediary's books, HMRC's concerns grew. In *Commissioners for HMRC v Talentcore Limited (t/a) Team Spirits* [2011] UKUT 423 (TCC) the tribunals found against HMRC in a challenge to the arrangements for the company's self-employed sales 'consultants', supplied like ordinary agency staff to work in airport duty-free shops over an eight-year period but not subjected to payroll deductions for tax and NIC.

The intermediary businesses using these arrangements had developed a way of working that threatened the Exchequer, as more employers began to transfer their workforce to an intermediary, sometimes known as a 'payroll company', who was not obliged to make deductions, or to pay employer NICs. The adoption of this type of arrangement was entirely legitimate, provided the freedom to send a substitute was genuine, but the government dubbed it 'false self-employment'. It was of course not false: it was inconvenient that the law made these workers self-employed, so the law had to be changed.

THE 2014 RULES: LIABILITY

10.5 The government announced in its Autumn Statement 2013 that it would tackle the use of employment intermediaries facilitating false self-employment to avoid employment taxes. The results of its consultations, with the amendments to legislation, are noted in the introduction above. New rules deeming most workers supplied by intermediaries to be employees of those intermediaries were in place by 6 April 2014, although the reporting requirements could not be introduced at the same time because of the lead time for software development, so the reporting elements of the legislation were delayed until 2015–16.

FA 2014, ss 16–21 and the matching NIC regulations (*Social Security (Categorisation of Earners) (Amendment) Regulations 2014, SI 2014/635*) changed the basis of deeming workers engaged through intermediaries to be employees for tax and NIC purposes. The NIC equivalent of the anti-avoidance rule in the new *ITEPA 2003, s 46A* required primary legislation, which appeared in *NIC Act 2015, s 6*, adding a new *Reg 5A* into the *Categorisation Regulations*.

What is now caught?

10.6 Whereas the old agency rules had set a personal service obligation as one of the conditions for their application, the new version in *ITEPA 2003, s 44(1)* looks simply for:

- actual personal service (other than the traditionally excluded services such as acting, entertaining, modelling and home working) by a worker; together with

- a contract involving the end client (or a person connected to that client) and a third party (ie, the 'agency', which need not necessarily be a recognised employment agency, and certainly is not a person connected with the client).

The 2014 rules apply where, under or in consequence of this contract between client and agency:

- the worker's services are provided; or (NB: the draughtsman deliberately did not choose the word 'and' at this point, as the net is to be cast widely)
- the client or a connected person pays or provides consideration for those services.

This defeats the device of creating a contractual structure that avoids the direct provision by the agency of the worker's services, or direct payment by the client for those services, which will not suffice to sidestep the new rules: both conditions must be met if the parties are to escape *ITEPA 2003, s 44*.

10.7 Having noted that the net has been cast widely, it must also be said that HMRC's ambitions are not unlimited: it would make no sense for the rules to encompass every working relationship involving a third party because most of them do not involve any kind of avoidance and many of the workers involved are indeed genuinely self-employed or already on somebody's payroll. *ITEPA 2003, s 44(2)* therefore disapplies the deeming rule so that neither PAYE nor Class 1 NICs are due if:

- it is shown that the manner in which the worker provides the services is not subject to (or to the right of) supervision, direction or control by any person (see further below); or
- remuneration receivable by the worker in consequence of providing the services constitutes employment income of the worker apart from under the agency provisions (which means that umbrella companies supplying their own payrolled employees as temporary workers are out of scope).

Disregarding the personal service obligation and instead relying on seeking actual personal service prevents the simple use of a substitution clause as an escape route from PAYE and Class 1 NIC liability. Many temporary workers who previously worked under a contract with a substitution clause will meet these revised conditions, because the new focus is on the work they do personally, rather than whether they are obliged to do it personally, so they will be deemed to be employees of the agency for PAYE and NIC purposes.

> **Focus**
>
> Anyone working through a one-man personal service (PSC) and finding work through an agency is automatically outside the scope of the PAYE and NIC deeming (but not necessarily the reporting regime).

The impact of *ITEPA 2003, s 44(2)(b)* is that anyone working through a one-man personal service (PSC) and finding work through an agency is automatically outside the scope of the PAYE and NIC deeming (but not necessarily the reporting regime – see **10.29** below). Salary drawn from the PSC is employment income, but dividends paid to the director-shareholder will not be 'remuneration receivable by the worker', as it is classed as investment income. Any salary drawn by the director-shareholder will therefore fall within *ITEPA 2003, s 44(2)(b)* and the arrangement will not require the agency to operate payroll deductions. This exclusion merely reflects reality: an agency paying a company cannot operate PAYE, because the PAYE regulations only apply to payments made to an individual or his nominee, not to the company that employs that individual and contracts to provide his services. The position is a little different, however, for PSCs in the public sector, where the client or agency may now have an obligation to operate PAYE (see **10.12** below).

Those working for an umbrella company under an overarching contract, whose wages are subject to PAYE and Class 1 NICs, are also excluded from the scope of *ITEPA 2003, s 44* by this rule, although the agency that places the worker (if it is not the umbrella company itself) will still have a reporting obligation (see further below).

10.8 Where the conditions are indeed met, *ITEPA 2003, s 44(3)* provides that the work for the client is treated as an employment of the worker with the agency, and all remuneration received by the worker, from anybody, in respect of the work is treated as earnings from that deemed employment with that intermediary. Where intermediaries work in a chain, so that the final agency in the chain with the contractual relationship with the client does not pay the worker directly, this rule means that this final agency is responsible for the PAYE and NIC obligations if other intermediaries or employers in the chain default. The same intermediary is also obliged to make reports under the 2015 changes (see further below).

Chains are not uncommon, and sometimes it is not easy to identify the end of a chain. While the typical agency temp (an office worker, a fruit picker, an event steward, etc) works under a simple contract for services with an agency (as in **Figure 10.1** above), many thousands of temporary workers are now employed by umbrella companies who supply their services to agencies for onward supply to the agencies' clients (as in **Figure 10.2** above).

In some cases, there is even a chain of businesses recognisable as employment agencies: a UK agency may, for example, have a contract to supply workers to a UK construction business that is a subcontractor to a large building company that is in turn working for a utility that is building a power station, and the UK agency may source its workers from an agency in, eg, Poland that takes on the job of finding enough workers to staff the contract. Less obviously perhaps, in the context of major projects, a main contractor will usually let contracts for elements of the project to a number of subcontractors, who may deliver the services with their own staff, supplemented by expertise bought in from elsewhere, such as specialists working through their own PSCs. An example might be a quantity surveyor (QS) with his own PSC who works on a project basis for a QS practice, which is not obviously an employment agency but may fall within the definition of *ITEPA 2003, s 44* in appropriate circumstances. The QS practice might supply his services to one of the subcontractor businesses on a major construction site, and in reality he may be working for the main contractor on that site, whose client will pay for and use the facility that is eventually constructed. In these circumstances, it is often difficult to identify exactly who is the client and who is the last intermediary in the chain with a contract to supply the individual's personal services.

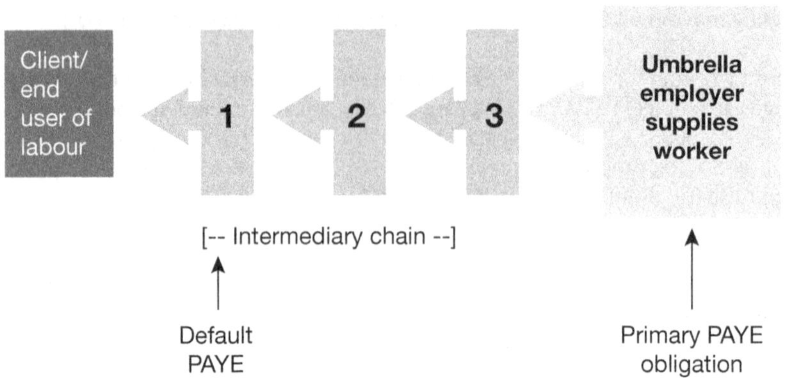

Figure 10.3: The agency supply chain and default responsibilities

Supervision, direction or control

10.9 Note the retention of the second condition from the old rules, the existence of a right of supervision, direction or control as to the manner of doing the work, in *ITEPA 2003, s 44(2)(a)*. This ensures that genuinely self-employed tradesmen and professionals will not be dragged into the deductions net even if they find work through agencies – the rules are intended to collect PAYE and Class 1 NICs from those who are working like employees without meeting all the conditions for a contract of employment. One of the examples issued in HMRC's early guidance on the new rules (now incorporated into the Employment Status Manual at ESM2060) illustrates the point.

Example 10.1 – Agency construction worker

Joiner John, who is supplied by an agency to work on a building project, is asked to build an oak-panelled door from a drawing, and then hang it. He is free to work as he sees fit, using his own workshop at home. He is not supervised as to how he carries out the contracted task, and is not caught by Class 1 NIC or PAYE.

In an alternative scenario, joiner John turns up on site and is allocated to the existing joinery team, working under the contractor's supervisor/foreman, who will direct, oversee and provide guidance over his work. He is also shown how to complete the work where necessary. The *Categorisation Regulations* and *ITEPA 2003, s 44* are clearly in point.

In real life, of course, there are multiple shades of grey between these black and white examples. There are only a couple of notable court cases to date on the point of supervision, direction and control. In *Staples v Secretary of State for Social Services* (CO/1073/84, 1985, unreported), a relief head chef was found to have worked without supervision, direction or control over how he worked, and was accordingly outside the deeming rules of the *Categorisation Regulations*. In contrast, one of his colleagues, supplied as a relief sous chef – whose very job title pointed to his being under the head chef's supervision – was held to fall within the deeming rules. This case is picked up in one of the case studies included as ESM2058 in official guidance.

In the more recent case of *Gabriel Oziegbe v Revenue & Customs* [2014] UKFTT 608 (TC), the First-tier Tax Tribunal considered whether security guards on a construction site were subject to supervision, direction and control, and Nowlan J commented as follows at paragraph 14:

> 'The most obvious situation in which the "control" requirement will not be satisfied is where the particular service being rendered is one that is extraneous to the basic activity of the client, such that it is entirely natural that the client will have no control or right of control over the way in which the services are provided.'

This approach is entirely logical: there would not usually be any control over how an independent contractor works if they are engaged specifically for their expertise in a field where the client lacks the knowledge or specialism. Another noteworthy point highlighted in this case is that the question to be asked is whether there is supervision, direction or control over how the work is done, not what job is to be done. This is only a First-tier Tribunal case but it does at least start the process of shaping the boundaries of when an individual is subject to supervision, direction or control.

In view of the absence of reported cases, HMRC issued 19 pages of guidance and examples to elaborate on their view of how supervision, direction or control might look in a range of industries, such as IT consulting, restaurants, haulage, security, pharmacy, care work, market research, etc (see http://bit.ly/1jnTcah and now ESM2037 and ESM2057–ESM2068). The fact that HMRC's example of a site security operative reaches the opposite conclusion, as was seen in Gabriel Oziegbe, illustrates how complicated this area can be and just how many shades of grey there are.

> **Focus**
>
> HMRC has added guidance to the Employment Status Manual to explain 'supervision, direction or control'.

Some of the agencies targeted by the change in the *Categorisation Regulations* have responded by arguing that most of their temporary workers are too experienced and too qualified to need supervision, and those who are not have been moved onto a subcontractor payroll subject to PAYE, so it remains to be seen how effective the change will be in imposing Class 1 NIC and PAYE on workers who are technically self-employed on basic principles. It is easy to foresee HMRC experiencing the same difficulties with this supervision rule as they have faced for many years with IR35: every individual case is different, and every single one needs a full investigation, for which resources do not exist in HMRC. HMRC are known to have created a number of dedicated compliance teams in late 2015 and an employment status and intermediaries team in 2016 to focus on intermediary workers, using the intelligence gathered via the quarterly returns described below (and on the absence of such returns from some businesses from which they were expected) to identify targets for compliance interventions.

Use of personal service companies

10.10 Other suppliers of self-employed temporary workers responded to the changes by ensuring that the *ITEPA 2003, s 44(2)(b)* escape route is followed: the deeming rules do not apply if the workers are already employees. As noted above, those who wish to avoid liability are free to work through their own PSC and pay themselves principally by dividend, provided that, in the process, they do not fall within the IR35 or managed service company rules. It is not entirely clear why the *FA 2014* rules did not forestall this entirely predictable turn of events, since HMRC knew in advance of the likely response by the temporary employment industry.

The Budget report in July 2015 promised measures to prevent or discourage this type of 'avoidance', if the structures adopted may legitimately be so described, given the limited savings to be made after the introduction of the new dividend tax in April 2016. In particular, small companies have been disqualified for 2016–17 onwards from claiming the employment allowance (£3,000 pa from April 2016) if there is only one recipient of NICable earnings and that person is a director. That said, the one-man company need only employ and pay a single casual worker for a few hours to protect its entitlement to the allowance, but most will have simply appointed and paid a second director, so the value of the restriction is doubtful and seems unlikely to raise the £70m–£80m pa scheduled in the Budget Red Book. In addition, the new dividend tax is clearly aimed at narrowing the gap between taking remuneration and dividends from close companies, but the rates may have to be increased if it is to be effective. From April 2018 the dividend allowance will reduce from £5,000 to £2,000, as seen in *Finance (No 2) Bill 2017*. Its omission from the *Finance Act 2017* led many to believe that the government had scrapped the idea of lowering the allowance, but this is evidently not going to be the case. It is not impossible that *ITEPA 2003, s 44* will be redrafted again to carve out PSC structures.

10.11 HMRC consulted in July 2015 on potential new rules that would make the engager or client responsible for making the decision about whether a PSC worker is engaged like an employee, and transfer any overlooked IR35 liability for PAYE and NICs to the engager or client if the worker is found to have been in disguised employment but to have failed to comply with the IR35 rules. HMRC estimate (albeit on the basis of unpublished evidence and assumptions) that only 10% of PSCs who are within IR35 rules comply with those rules. The aim of the change was to collect money from engagers, who are more likely to be in existence and traceable several years down the line than are PSCs, although the problem of policing their decisions as to whether an individual could be deemed an employee is likely to be no less acute than the present HMRC problem with IR35 non-compliance. The idea was considered and rejected as impractical when IR35 was conceived, and little has changed apart from the government's need for more taxes.

Many informed parties told HMRC that the proposals were impractical. The ICAEW's published comments included this:

> 'how would "earnings" be calculated so as to exclude agents' profit margins, which PAYE code would apply, how would engagers know that they were dealing with a PSC, and which earnings periods and limits would apply for NIC? The plan is impracticable, even if the engager has enough knowledge of the contractor's circumstances to be certain that

> the worker is employed by a PSC, which may not always be the case, especially where workers are supplied up a chain of intermediaries.'

The government response in May 2016 was another consultation entitled 'Off-payroll working in the public sector: reform of the intermediaries legislation', which set out proposals, that were ultimately introduced in April 2017, to make public sector bodies and agencies responsible for operating the tax rules that apply to off-payroll working in the public sector. The rules are to remain unchanged in the private sector.

'Responsible' means going further than the existing Whitehall procurement rules, under which many public sector bodies are already required to check that some of their off-payroll workers are paying the correct taxes. The new rules:

> 'move the liability to make the determination about whether the intermediaries rules apply, and the associated tax liability if so, from the PSC to the public sector end-client or agency or other third party closest in the chain to the PSC if there is one.'

The scope of the term 'public sector' is to be based on the definition in the *Freedom of Information Act 2000* and its Scottish equivalent. This includes 'educational establishments' without differentiating between state and private sector institutions, but the latter logically cannot be in scope.

10.12 Agencies (and other businesses that are not registered employment businesses but act as intermediaries) supplying PSC contractors to any public sector organisation, and paying them, will be expected to put in place systems to determine in conjunction with the public sector client if an engagement is in scope, collect the necessary standing data (eg name, address, NINO) and to operate PAYE and NIC deductions and make RTI reports as if they are the employer. The normal 5% reduction when calculating the deemed payment for IR35 will not be available to those working within the public sector and within the scope of IR35.

The detail over how payments would be made to a PSC through RTI were half-baked at best and seem not to have been thought through (or, more accurately perhaps, not set out in the proposals), and HMRC have all but said that software developers will have to find solutions as to how this will work. To ensure there is no double taxation, the intermediary will get relief for tax and national insurance but only insofar as it has distributed the net deemed payment to the worker.

There is no explanation from HMRC of how the RTI system will issue a correct PAYE code to the agency when the system will still show the PSC as the employer. To date, HMRC have been unable to ensure that duplicate employments are not created when a person with one job moves to another and is paid (with the timeous submission of a Full Payment Submission (FPS)) before the old employer submits its final FPS (eg because payday is at the end of the month after the month of leaving, once commissions have been calculated). The deliberate creation of a double employment record in a public sector PSC case is yet another complexity that the RTI system may struggle with but is something that software developers have had to deal with. It is highly likely that many companies will simply ignore the PSC and employ the individual directly under PAYE.

The change in legislation assumed that public sector engagers and agencies would simply be able to operate the proposed new system from 6 April 2017, despite the fact that HMRC did not even know what that system would look like. It seems more than likely that HMRC will have to accept, as they have with the legislation on payrolling benefits in kind, that the official implementation date bears no relation to reality, because they have been tardy with the specification of the changes for the software industry. One would hope that, given the above, HMRC would adopt a 'light touch' with regard to compliance monitoring (little to none) for the first 12 months, even though the legislation was enacted in April 2017.

10.13 Where agencies and other intermediaries are in a contractual chain, the new IR35 legislation is to apply to the agency that contracts directly with the PSC, which the government believes to be best placed to collect the personal details and deduct the tax and NICs. The public sector body will, however, be required, if asked, to provide its opinion within 31 days as to whether the work is caught by the IR35 legislation or not, as they will be the entity that will have a working knowledge of how the individual works and whether it is akin to an employment relationship. If the public sector body confirms that the individual is outside IR35 and the agency or intermediary relies on that information in good faith, or if the public sector body fails to provide an opinion, the public sector body will be the party that is liable to HMRC. This approach has unfortunately led to the unsurprising result of many public sector bodies opting for a cautious approach and simply saying that all individuals are within IR35, without any actual assessment of how the individuals work.

Anti-avoidance and anti-evasion

10.14 The *FA 2014* changes attempted to forestall both of these approaches (ie, non-supervision and working via a PSC) by introducing both transfer of debt provisions and a Targeted Anti-Avoidance Rule (TAAR).

Transfer of debt

10.15 The obligation to deduct PAYE in a simple agency situation under *ITEPA 2003, s 44* falls on the agency (*ITEPA 2003, s 44(3)*), which is deemed to be the employer. *Categorisation Regulations, Sch 3, para 2* places the NIC obligation in the same hands.

Logically, an agency seeking to avoid having to operate PAYE would seek evidence from the client that the worker was under no right of supervision, direction or control. The temptation for the client is clear: a worker who is free to work without supervision is outside Class 1 NIC liability, so the hourly rates charged by the agency can be lower. An unscrupulous client under pressure to meet a contractual budget might be tempted to simply tell the agency that there is no right of supervision. However, if an agency is provided with a fraudulent document by the client that dishonestly purports to evidence the fact that there is no supervision, direction or control as to the manner of working, or by any other party to the contractual relationship purporting to show that the worker is already an employee and therefore outside the scope, the provider of the fraudulent document (if he is resident or has a place of business in the UK) becomes the deemed employer (*Categorisation Regulations Sch 3, para 2*, and *ITEPA 2003, s 44(5)*).

It remains to be seen how this rule might be applied in practice, and whether an employee of a client issuing such a document without authority to do so, and without full knowledge of the facts, can validly be accused of 'fraud' as opposed to carelessness or recklessness. Fraud generally requires mens rea (*Fraud Act 2006, s 2* refers to dishonestly making a false representation) so the provision may prove difficult to enforce and time-consuming even to argue (which has long been HMRC's major problem with IR35). An agency open to being pursued for PAYE, that intends to rely on a document purporting to evidence freedom from supervision, would arguably be well advised to ensure that the letter has been signed by someone with clear authority to do so, such as a director of the client. Unconfirmed reports suggest that the special intermediary compliance teams set up in late 2015 are focussing on false claims of a lack of supervision as their first foray into countering the perceived avoidance and evasion.

TAAR

10.16 The TAAR in *ITEPA 2003, s 46A* was added in an attempt to catch any third person entering into 'arrangements' (a term defined widely in *ITEPA 2003, s 46A(2)*), the main purpose, or one of the main purposes, of which is to sidestep *ITEPA 2003, s 44*. That third person is to be treated as the agency under the new *ITEPA 2003, s 44*.

HMRC originally saw this rule being used where, for example, an agency insists that all workers are supplied via their own PSCs so as to avoid the agency rules. Their guidance currently states clearly that the TAAR will not apply to people who set up a PSC for a reason other than reducing tax, such as the limited liability protections provided by incorporation (para 3.69, Onshore Employment Intermediaries: False Self-Employment, summary of responses, 13 March 2014, and ESM2041).

NIC law changed in the same way as the tax rules for agencies, albeit somewhat belatedly, because it (rather inexplicably) required primary legislation: *NIC Act 2015, s 6* added a new *Reg 5A* to the *Categorisation Regulations* to do the same job, with its effect backdated to 6 April 2014, except for the elements related to foreign employers and agencies within paras 9(a)–(d), which took effect from 12 February 2015 when *NIC Act 2015* was passed.

PAYE personal liability notices

10.17 To prevent evasion of responsibility by corporate deemed employers being liquidated with unpaid PAYE debts, the government added *Ch 3A* into the *Income Tax (PAYE) Regulations 2003, Pt 4*. This will allow HMRC to issue personal liability notices to the directors of the deemed employer when 'relevant' PAYE debts (ie, those transferred under the fraudulent documents or TAAR provisions) remain unpaid at the due date, although the actual timing will of course be some years later when HMRC has (a) identified the default and (b) exhausted other avenues to collect from the entity that is primarily liable.

Directors of employment businesses are ordinarily open to personal liability notices only for unpaid NICs (*SSAA 1992, s 121C*), but not for PAYE. The new *Ch 3A* is aimed directly at countering PAYE avoidance and evasion in the context of the new rules, but *SSAA 1992, s 121C* may conceivably be used against those to whom liability for NICs is transferred under the new *Sch 3, para 2* rules in the *Categorisation Regulations* if the companies concerned fail to pay their NIC debts and cannot do so.

10.18 The *Finance Act 2016* also added *ITEPA 2003, s 688B* and introduced additional PAYE regulations (*Pt 4, Ch 3B, regs 97ZG–97ZM*) to extend the transfer of PAYE debt provisions to arrears arising from any failure to deduct PAYE from non-allowable home-to-work travel expenses of intermediary workers who are subject to supervision, direction or control or work through IR35 companies. The liability may be transferred to the directors of the company that provides fraudulent documents purporting to evidence a lack of supervision, direction or control, or to the directors of the intermediary where it holds no reasonable evidence of an absence of a right of supervision.

Offshore intermediaries

10.19 UK intermediaries exploiting the gaps in the agency rules outlined above were not the only focus of HMRC's efforts to increase NIC revenues.

There were also two perceived major problems with offshore intermediaries: failure to comply with existing 'host employer' rules for workers supplied by overseas employers, and an absence of secondary Class 1 NIC liability for non-EEA employers of workers active on the UK Continental Shelf in the oil and gas sector. Both were addressed by the 2014 and 2015 changes.

When a UK worker is employed by an EEA-based employer, normal UK and EEA NIC rules apply, with the employer liable (since 1 May 2010, when EU social security rules were updated by the introduction of Regulations (EC) No 883/2004 and 987/2009, and until the UK leaves the EU) to register in the UK and pay both primary and secondary Class 1 NICs under Real Time Information (RTI) rules.

It is debatable whether HMRC is correct in asserting that the provisions of the EC regulations are of relevance where a worker is a UK resident working on the UK Continental Shelf, since he will have done nothing to bring himself within the scope of the European migrant worker rules, but that is an argument beyond the scope of this chapter.

When a worker is supplied by a non-EEA employer, with no UK place of business, the foreign employer is not generally so liable, but the 'host employer' rules in *Categorisation Regulations, Sch 3, para 9* place the employer's obligations (payment and reporting) on the UK host employer to which the services of the individual are supplied. However, this latter approach requires cooperation between the supplying employer and the host employer, and if the offshore agency or intermediary refuses to supply the relevant information, the UK host cannot comply and has a reasonable excuse for not doing so (assuming no collusion or fraud).

10.20 A small number of offshore employment businesses outside EEA territory were abusing this position to supply tens of thousands of temporary workers to public sector employers (eg supply teachers and nurses) with no secondary NICs being paid, despite the host employer rules. The 2014 offshore intermediary rules collect the NICs from any onshore agency that facilitates the supply of the worker or, in the absence of any such agency, the end client. The target is plainly to put non-compliant offshore suppliers out of business, but this type of evasion is not easy to stop.

Example 10.2 – Host employers

Chrissie, a qualified nurse, signed up with Warezatkair, an online agency based in Niue, a Pacific territory that has no tax or social security treaties with the UK but good internet services. W maintains a database of nursing personnel and has contracts with a number of nursing agencies and nursing banks in the UK for the supply of agency nursing services. It agrees fees with the UK agencies who source their staff via Niue but does not disclose financial details, so the UK agencies do not know how much the agency nurses are paid per shift. The UK users and agencies could not comply with the host employer rules without information from Niue, which was never forthcoming.

UK agencies are now explicitly liable for the PAYE and NIC obligations, but still have the same problem of lacking the necessary information.

To counter both evasion and avoidance, changes were also made to *Categorisation Regulations, Sch 3, para 9* from 6 April 2014 (under the *Social Security (Categorisation of Earners) (Amendment) Regulations 2014, SI 2014/635*) to create a secondary Class 1 NIC liability, where none existed or was enforceable before, in respect of workers provided by foreign employers.

Under the new provisions, the end client may be liable where there is a foreign, but no UK, agency. Where there is a foreign employer or agency, but also a UK agency, the UK agency that has the contractual relationship with the end client may be liable. This is represented in **Figure 10.4** below.

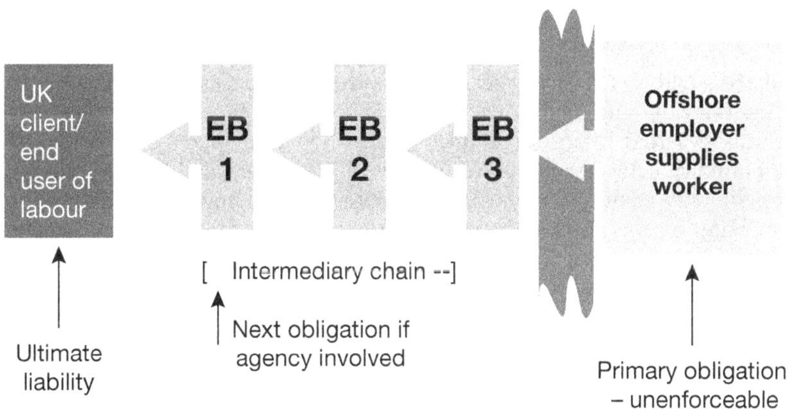

Figure 10.4: Liabilities of Employment Businesses (EB) for workers employed from outside the UK

The liabilities for NICs (other than for pure oil & gas workers offshore) after the introduction of the 2014 offshore intermediary changes may be summarised in the following table:

Table 10.1: Liable employers where workers employed via intermediaries from outside the UK

Mr X working for	Deductions due by
UK host employer via foreign employer	UK host employer
UK client of foreign agency	UK client
UK client of UK agency but via overseas employer or agency	UK agency ('EB1' in **Figure 10.4**)
UK employer, but X works outside UK for UK agency, selling to foreign client, X 'eligible' for UK NIC	UK employer or UK agency with contract with foreign purchaser of services
Foreign employer, but X works outside UK for UK agency, selling to foreign client, X 'eligible' for UK NIC	UK agency with contract with foreign purchaser of services

Oil and gas

10.21 The offshore intermediary rules apply if the worker is engaged to work on an offshore oil and gas installation on the UK Continental Shelf. Many employments carried out on oil and gas rigs are under contracts with intermediary companies other than those that operate the rigs. However, the 2015 reporting rules (see **10.24** below) do not apply.

In the oil and gas business, it has always been the case that most of the operators in the UK North Sea have been foreign companies, bringing their overseas expertise to bear on extracting the offshore oil and gas reserves. UK law normally extends only as far as the 12-mile limit, and Class 1 liability normally only applies to workers within UK jurisdiction, but workers earning their living on rigs (or 'offshore installations') in the UK sector are deemed to be employed earners for NIC purposes, so they are within primary Class 1 NIC liability.

Until 6 April 2014, though, no similar rule applied to their foreign employers to impose a secondary liability if they were not UK resident and had no UK place of business. The UK Continental Shelf is also outside the territory of the EEA, so the foreign employers could not be treated as having a UK place of business even under Regulation (EC) No 883/2004 unless they were established onshore in an EEA state. Many workers were therefore supplied to rig operators by non-EEA operators or agencies (typically in Jersey, Guernsey, Panama, the United Arab Emirates (UAE) or Singapore) so as to avoid the secondary Class 1 NIC liability.

> **Focus**
>
> The wages of oil and gas workers on the UK Continental Shelf now attract a secondary NIC liability even if their employer is outside the UK.

Changes were therefore made to the *Contributions Regulations, Reg 114* from 6 April 2014 (empowered by *NICA 2014, s 12*) to create a secondary Class 1 NIC liability where none existed or was enforceable before in respect of workers on 'offshore installations'. The liability may be paid by the legal employer offshore, but if it is not, it falls on an associated company present in the UK, and if there is more than one, on the group company with the largest corporation tax profits in the UK for the accounting period which precedes the tax year in which the contributions are due. If there is no such onshore company, the liability moves to the licensee of the field.

The potential for transfers of secondary NIC liability means that oilfield operators will be justifiably concerned about hiring workers supplied by an overseas business that may or may not have paid the requisite secondary NICs, so in addition to the *Categorisation Regulations*, we now also have, in *Contributions Regulations, Regs 114A–114D*, a new certification process. It gives hirers certainty over the credentials of their labour suppliers in Continental Shelf operations. The new provisions provide for the issue of certificates to offshore labour suppliers and licensees who use their labour, excluding the licensees from any NICs liability in respect of the supplied workers. Certification is handled by an HMRC office in Edinburgh – see NIM33800.

Mariners

10.22 The new offshore intermediary rules do not extend to mariners working on ships (as opposed to vessels qualifying as offshore installations, now defined in *Contributions Regulations, Reg 114D*), to whom the normal mariner provisions of *Contributions Regulations, Reg 115* continue to apply and who may still be employed in appropriate circumstances without a UK secondary NIC liability. The new oil and gas rules are excluded in respect of certain mariners on board vessels that qualify as offshore installations if they fall within certain grade descriptions that relate to marine rather than oil and gas activities (see below).

Meaning of 'at sea' and 'offshore installation'

10.23 *Contributions Regulations, Reg 114* deems employment 'at sea' in any designated area of the UK Continental Shelf in connection with oil and gas operations to be work carried out in the UK, even if the contributor does not satisfy the conditions of residence and presence in the UK prescribed in the *Contributions Regulations, Reg 145.*

The term 'at sea' could present a conflict with *Contributions Regulations, Reg 115* – a worker on a ship in the UK North Sea could potentially fall under either regulation – but the scope of the Continental Shelf rule is limited by *Contributions Regulations, Reg 114(4)* so that it applies only to work on or in connection with an 'offshore installation', with the exception of certain grades of mariner set out in a table at the foot of *Contributions Regulations, Reg 114,* who will still be treated as mariners within *Contributions Regulations, Reg 115* even when working on such structures. The table essentially identifies certain types of worker on board ships or vessels that may be classed as offshore installations (eg, jack-ups or semi-submersibles) whose job is essentially that of a mariner rather than a rig worker and whose duties are covered by the *Merchant Shipping (Safe Manning, Hours of Work and Watch Keeping) Regulations 1997, SI 1997/1320.*

As ever, there are grey areas. For example, *Contributions Regulations, Reg 114D* includes a definition of 'offshore installation' specific to these provisions. The term means 'a structure which is, is to be, or has been, put to a relevant use while in water'. The regulation includes a list of relevant uses, all related to exploitation of oil and gas reserves, and defines 'put to use while in water' to mean while standing in any waters, stationed (by whatever means) in any waters, or standing on the foreshore or other land intermittently covered with water. Fixed rigs, and jack-ups that are working, clearly 'stand' on the seabed, while semi-submersibles, flotels (accommodation vessels) and FPSOs (floating production, storage and offloading units) are 'stationed'. The regulation specifically excludes ships or vessels used for the transport of supplies, or as safety/standby vessels, or for the laying of cables, but ships that work while stationary but move around could fall either side of the line (eg, dive support vessels, inspection/construction support vessels and subsea pipe-laying vessels that remains stationary using dynamic positioning while working). As a rule of thumb, HMRC will regard any such ship that remains stationary for no longer than five days as falling outside the definition of offshore installation, which is the same basis it uses for claims to seafarers' earnings deduction (EIM33108–EIM33109).

Note that the *Contributions Regulations, Reg 114* rules do not apply to offshore wind and wave farms and vessels that install and maintain them, as exploiting the wind and waves is not a 'relevant use'. These workers, if they are within UK jurisdiction, may therefore fall within the scope of *ITEPA 2003, ss 44–47* and the *Categorisation Regulations.*

THE 2015 RULES: REPORTING

10.24 The problem of allegedly false self-employment will clearly not have disappeared with the introduction of the anti-avoidance changes in 2014. There will still be a significant number of workers who are outside the scope of PAYE and Class 1 NIC because they do not fall within *ITEPA 2003, s 44* and the *Categorisation Regulations*. Some of the escapees will be legitimate (ie, there is genuinely no right of supervision, direction or control, or they are already employed by an umbrella company or a PSC), but HMRC needed a way of checking that payments made gross by agencies (and anyone else falling within the scope of the intermediary rules) are indeed legitimate. There is therefore a quarterly online reporting obligation from 6 July 2015 for any payments made by 'agencies' outside the RTI system, intended to alert HMRC to any possible disregard shown for the rules by intermediaries. Where workers are still being paid gross despite the new rules, HMRC wants to know why, from the intermediary with the contract for the supply of the worker to the client.

Example 10.3 – Who has control?

Bean & Co offers bookkeeping services to numerous clients. At times of high demand, it subcontracts work to Jackie, a freelancer who is highly experienced, has her own self-employed business and does not normally take on supervised engagements.

A client, Stalker, has a problem when its financial controller goes off on long-term sick leave and asks Bean if it can supply a temporary replacement for a month. Bean subcontracts the work to Jackie. No PAYE or NICs are due because Jackie is not subject to supervision, direction or control, so Bean pays her gross. A quarterly report is required from Bean, though, because Jackie is supplying her personal services to Stalker via an intermediary.

Any new returns designed by HMRC will now always be digital by default, but there was insufficient time between the conception of the 2014 changes and their introduction for the relevant software to be developed. Design and implementation of the reporting regime required a delay until 6 April 2015.

Where a worker meets the revised conditions in *ITEPA 2003, s 44*, the 'agency' must operate PAYE and Class 1 NICs and make online reports under the RTI rules. HMRC will therefore have information about payments made to these workers and be able to check that the deductions have been paid over.

However, many temporary workers will be outside the scope of PAYE, so intermediaries may not pay wages under deduction, perhaps because they do not pay workers directly (eg, they are sourced from an umbrella company), or they pay workers gross because they are not subject to supervision, direction or control as to the manner in which they work.

HMRC can see both the financial accounts and the RTI returns but has no further information, so it may look as if significant sums are being paid to agency workers without deduction of PAYE and NICs, which would call for compliance action. There would be little point in investigating compliant umbrella company structures, but those agencies paying workers gross are seen as a real compliance risk.

10.25 The quarterly reporting rules from 6 April 2015 are found in the *Income Tax (Pay As You Earn) (Amendment No 2) Regulations 2015, SI 2015/171* which inserted new *Regs 84E–84H* into the *PAYE Regulations*. These require specified information from 'specified employment intermediaries' and impose record-keeping requirements on those intermediaries.

Details must be reported even if the workers are paid (by someone else) under deduction of PAYE and NICs. Oddly, their 'employers' may not be the ones doing the reporting.

The reporting requirements depend on the type of worker and the structure in which the engagement is made.

Focus

RTI deductions for umbrella workers are reported by their employers, but agencies must still make quarterly reports of payments to the umbrella companies.

The major exception from the new reporting regime is the classic 'temping' structure: the intermediary must deduct and account for PAYE and Class 1 NICs using the RTI system. This type of engagement is of little interest to HMRC's compliance teams, as there is less likelihood of avoidance of deductions, so nothing is required beyond the normal RTI reporting.

This exception applies equally to businesses that would ordinarily not be classed as agencies: for example, an accountant sending an employee on secondment to a client continues to process the earnings through payroll. The client pays the accountant's fee without deducting PAYE or NICs, but the new quarterly reporting requirements are irrelevant.

10.26 In contrast, where temps are actually employees of an umbrella company under an overarching contract of employment, and PAYE and NICs are deducted, with a full payment summary (FPS) for every payment, a report may nevertheless be required by the agency if the umbrella company is not the person who has the contract with the client.

If the umbrella company contracts directly with the client, it accounts for PAYE and NIC and need not file quarterly reports. However, if the umbrella company merely acts as a provider of labour to an agency, and it is the agency that has the contract with the client, the agency will be paying gross fees for the workers' services. Without the full picture, this looks to HMRC as if the agency is paying the workers gross, so the agency must make quarterly reports.

The new rules began to apply from 6 April 2015, with the first reports due between 6 July and 5 August for the quarter to 5 July 2015. HMRC received many more reports in the first quarter than in later quarters, which gave an instant target list for its compliance teams. HMRC believes that the drop in the number of returns signifies a problem with non-compliance, but it seems much more likely that the initial absence of comprehensive guidance about the new rules, especially about what did not have to be reported, led to intermediaries reporting for the first quarter payments that were not in fact in scope. The correct analysis followed in the second quarter, with the help of better guidance, which was issued only on 30 July 2015. It seems inevitable that compliance with the proposed public sector IR35 rules will follow a similar pattern due to the tardiness of HMRC in finalising and specifying the design and guidance.

Who reports?

10.27 An 'employment intermediary' is within the new reporting rules if specified in *PAYE Regulations, Reg 84E*. The definition of 'employment intermediary', for the purposes of the agency rules only, is now found in *ITEPA 2003, s 716B(2)*:

> 'a person who makes arrangements under or in consequence of which –
>
> (a) an individual works, or is to work, for a third person, or
>
> (b) an individual is, or is to be, remunerated for work done for a third person.'

ITEPA 2003, s 716B(3) states that:

> 'an individual works for a person if –
>
> (a) the individual performs any duties of an employment for that person (whether or not the individual is employed by that person), or

(b) the individual provides, or is involved in the provision of, a service to that person.'

10.28 The latter definition appears to be very wide in scope, which is unsurprising in view of the fact that the 2014 changes were intended as an anti-avoidance measure. However, it is doubtful that HMRC intended the reporting obligation to encompass every subcontract arrangement involving an individual worker. The obligation will clearly apply to any organisation, large or small, in any sector, supplying workers to an end client to work *for that client*, but it will be of no relevance where the worker works for the contracting business itself.

HMRC has still, despite this being a real problem, issued no guidance on where the dividing line is between working for a client and working for a supplier to the client, so each case will depend on its facts, which is not very helpful to employers and agencies trying to understand their obligations. The guidance on GOV.UK simply assumes that a supplier will know it is an intermediary and will know when it is in scope.

If an accountant subcontracts work to a self-employed freelancer (see **Example 10.3** above), it should be reasonable to assume that the accountant charging a flat fee for the provision of, eg, a quarterly VAT return would involve the freelancer working for the accountant rather than for the client, so the accountant would not be an employment intermediary. In contrast, if the accountant arranged for the freelance bookkeeper to cover for somebody in-house who was absent, paying the bookkeeper and charging the client a fee for the services, it would perhaps be difficult to avoid characterising the accountant as an employment intermediary.

The specific conditions

10.29 The intermediary will be 'specified', and therefore required to fulfil the reporting obligations, if it meets four conditions set out in *PAYE Regulations, Reg 84E*:

(i) it is an agency (as defined in *ITEPA 2003, s 44*, ie, not just a registered employment agency);

(ii) more than one individual provides services to a client under or in consequence of a contract between the intermediary and one or more clients (this excludes PSCs from scope if they simply sell their director's services direct to a client without involving an agency);

(iii) the services are not provided exclusively on the UK Continental Shelf (so oil and gas workers are out of scope because they are certified under the *Contributions Regulations, Regs 114A–114D* arrangements instead); and

(iv) the intermediary makes one or more payments in respect of, or connected with, the services provided by one or more individuals that is subject to RTI reporting (ie, PAYE under *PAYE Regulations, Reg 67B*) but has been omitted from the intermediary's FPS, or is not subject to PAYE under RTI because the worker is neither an employee nor treated as an employee under *PAYE Regulations, Reg 10* (ie PAYE for agency workers).

Note that a PSC that subcontracts its work to another PSC will be an 'agency' for these purposes. If the first PSC holds a direct contract with the client, it will have a reporting obligation, because it will be paying gross for what is, in effect, agency work. In contrast, if the first PSC has found its work through an agency, it will not hold the contract with the client and will have no reporting obligation: that will fall on the agency.

Example 10.4 – PSC obligations

Daisy is a marketing consultant operating through her own personal service company, Chain Ltd. When she finds work directly, without agency involvement, Chain is not an intermediary: it is her employer. She can draw salary under PAYE and NIC deduction, or dividends out of distributable profits.

When her work comes via Buttercup, an agency, Buttercup must pay Chain gross – it cannot deduct PAYE from payments to a company – but report the payments quarterly.

Occasionally, Daisy wins several contracts in quick succession, and rather than disappoint clients, she subcontracts some of the work to a former colleague, Rose, who also operates via a PSC, Garland Ltd. When Chain pays Garland for Rose's services, Chain can pay gross but it is an intermediary in the context of the transaction and must include the payment on the next quarterly return.

From April 2017, if Daisy is seen to be working under an IR35-type contract for a public sector organisation, Buttercup will have to put Daisy on its payroll and deduct tax and NICs from the fees paid. If her contract with the public sector organisation explicitly and genuinely allows her to subcontract any of her work to someone like Rose, via Garland or otherwise, Buttercup should not have to worry about the new IR35 rules, as the absence of a personal service obligation should preclude the application of *Chapter 8*, but Buttercup would still have to report quarterly the gross payments made to Chain.

It is, as yet, unclear (if HMRC have even considered the point) how the quarterly reporting of gross payments to PSC employers will interact with the inclusion of the PSC's employee on the agency's payroll.

Making returns

10.30 *PAYE Regulations, Reg 84F* provides that the specified intermediary must, for each quarter, provide specified information by the 5th of the month following the end of each quarter. Errors in returns may be corrected before the reporting deadline for the next quarter. Agencies need not make just one submission for each quarter if it is more convenient to report weekly or monthly.

The return must be made online (using the reporting intermediary's Government Gateway account – see http://bit.ly/1FEYFmR), in accordance with a specified HMRC template (http://bit.ly/1B5ZKnT), and it must include a declaration of correctness and completeness by the person submitting it. An agent may make reports on behalf of a client by whom it is authorised to file PAYE returns (http://bit.ly/1ItWO2w). Any self-employed person acting as an employment agency without himself being an employer will have to register as an employer so as to obtain a PAYE reference for this purpose, and then make clear to HMRC that it is not in fact an employer and will not be submitting FPS, EPS or P11D returns. HMRC has recognised this problem and advises such agents to send an email to mailbox.employmentintermediariesunit@hmrc.gsi.gov.uk, which suggests that an internal protocol has been agreed for these unusual cases.

The submission (quarterly or more frequent) must be in the form of an open document spreadsheet (.ODS) file or a comma-separated values (.CSV) file in the exact format set out in the template. Data validation rules are set out in a document for software developers at http://bit.ly/1g4eUBm.

Reporting must continue every quarter until the agency has not fallen within the definition of specified intermediary for four consecutive quarters, or has notified HMRC that it is no longer in business as such.

Overseas aspects

10.31 The reporting requirement applies to agencies in the UK who are specified employment intermediaries. However, many UK agencies also have contracts to find workers for overseas projects, and since many applications will now be processed wholly online, not requiring the presence in the UK of the worker, it may be that non-residents, be they British or foreign, are engaged to work on those overseas projects.

The reporting requirements apply only to workers subject to UK tax (if the workers are non-resident and not working in the UK, HMRC has no interest), so agencies in the UK taking on self-employed workers overseas to work for clients solely overseas should not include them in their reports, provided the workers are not UK resident for tax purposes (see ESM2180).

It is unclear how an intermediary is to know or assess the residence status for tax purposes of any such worker, since the statutory residence test requires much information that is not available to an employer (and the NIC rules are different in any case, so an intermediary would need to assess under two sets of criteria, if aware of the distinction and capable of making such a judgment). Sometimes a worker's residence status will be immediately clear: if a UK business wins a contract to build a desalination plant in the Persian Gulf and the UK staffing agency contracted to find the workers recruits them from, eg, India, they are non-UK residents working overseas. The position will be less clear-cut when the new recruits are expatriate British citizens or other nationalities who have lived and worked in the UK in the past and may or may not be UK resident for tax purposes at the time of recruitment or at some point during the contract period.

10.32 When proposals were mooted in 2014 to withdraw personal allowances from non-residents, they were dropped because there was no practical way for an employer reliably to identify a new worker's residence status when first applying PAYE to their remuneration, or for HMRC to assess the worker's residence status without imposing a requirement for a new return of personal information outside the requirements of a tax return. Where an employer takes on a worker, it at least has the advantage that the employer has a direct relationship with the worker, but where an agency is recruiting over the internet for overseas jobs, and the worker is supplied by an offshore employer, the question of residence is much harder to establish reliably. HMRC has not yet indicated how it expects intermediaries to approach the question of a worker's residence status when recruiting for work outside the UK.

Required information

10.33 *PAYE Regulations, Reg 84G* sets out the information requirements, which are straightforward provided the agency has a direct relationship with the worker. The intermediary must:

- identify itself by giving specified details:
  - name;
  - address;
  - postcode; and

- employer PAYE reference (if it has one);
- identify each worker:
  - full name;
  - address;
  - postcode;
  - NI number *or* gender and date of birth if the worker has no NI number; and
  - unique taxpayer reference (UTR) *if* the worker is self-employed or a member of a partnership;
- state the start date of the relevant services for *each worker* in the period;
- state the end date of the relevant services for *each worker* in the period.

It remains to be seen how the system will cope with foreign workers who work temporarily in the UK and have no permanent UK address or postcode, no NI number and no UTR. A NI number is of course required by anyone liable to NICs, and a UTR is required by anybody within self-assessment, but many new arrivals looking for work through agencies will have neither, and it is unlikely that a temporary UK address will be of use to HMRC. As soon as a new hire moves home while still on the payroll, HMRC's database will be instantly out of date. The address on the NI and PAYE System (NPS) database is updated from FPS data only when a new worker's record is added to the payroll for the first time, not when a subsequent FPS reports a changed address.

10.34 Where a payment is made to an individual outside the RTI regime (or someone who should have been paid under PAYE but was not), further details are required by *PAYE Regulations, Reg 84G(c)*:

- the full name and address of the recipient if paid to someone other than the individual worker whose details are included above, and if the recipient is a partnership, the name under which it trades;
- the total of the payments to that person in the quarter (in either £ or €, indicating which currency has been used, although that is not explicit in the regulations);
- a reason code for why no tax was deducted;
- if the reason is that the recipient is a limited company, the full name of the company and its registration number; and
- an indication of whether the payment included any VAT.

PAYE Regulations, Reg 84G(c) is arguably incoherent, as it could be read as not requiring these further details where a payment is made to a company, partnership or LLP in respect of the services to clients. However, it must clearly be read as a payment made by *anybody* to an individual in respect of that individual's services to a client, otherwise bullet point four would be nonsensical: paying outside the RTI regime is clearly not limited to paying a self-employed individual without PAYE; it applies equally to paying an umbrella company or PSC for the individual's services.

Gross payment reason codes

10.35 There are six possible circumstances and reason codes listed in the guidance why PAYE might not have been deducted:

A the payee is self-employed

B the worker is a member of a partnership

C the worker is a member of an LLP

D the worker is supplied by a limited company (including personal service companies)

E the worker is on a non-UK engagement and is supplied from a company, partnership or person outside the UK

F PAYE has already been applied by someone else

One of the reasons for falling into the intermediary reporting regime, namely omitting to apply RTI to the earnings of an agency worker who is subject to PAYE, does not appear in the above list. The obvious corrective action would be to file an FPS (or earlier year update (EYU) if there is significant delay) and account for the PAYE.

The specified intermediary is instructed in the guidance to use the reason that comes first in the above list, even if more than one reason applies. This demonstrates further incoherence, because many workers are supplied to the agency by an umbrella company, which will typically be employing the worker. It will apply PAYE, but reason D will have to be used when reason F is more logical.

Information and record-keeping obligations

10.36 *PAYE Regulations, Reg 84H* requires the specified employment intermediary to keep and preserve information, records and documents which evidence the specified information when the details are not already required to be sent to HMRC under any other provision of the regulations.

Agencies putting workers on their own payroll will keep RTI records, but where they have no PAYE obligation, the normal PAYE and NIC record-keeping requirements would not apply.

Under *PAYE Regulations, Reg 84H*, relevant information, records and documents must be retained for not less than three years after the end of the tax year to which they relate, although it is specifically provided that they may be kept in any form or by any means, so a digital archive should be acceptable.

It should be noted that the record-keeping requirement is imposed only on the 'specified employment intermediary'. Where workers are supplied along a chain of contracts, via a number of intermediaries, only the last intermediary in the chain must make the reports and keep the records. It is not clear how that specified intermediary is to enforce the requirement for items of personal data that it may not hold and that it may not be able to access if the employer or intermediary higher up the chain is outside UK jurisdiction and subject to foreign data protection laws.

Penalties

10.37 Unsurprisingly, late returns, non-submission and inaccuracies will be subject to penalties, although there is nothing specific in the regulations, so the PAYE penalty regime in *TMA 1970, s 98* (as amended by *FA 2015, s 18*) applies.

HMRC guidance (http://bit.ly/1SHnsQo) states that the first offence in a 12-month period will attract an automatic penalty of £250, the second offence £500, and further offences £1,000, all of which are below the statutory maximum in *TMA 1970, s 98* and the guidance at ESM2190. It also threatens daily penalties for continued failure to submit a report. *TMA 1970, s 98* does not impose automatic penalties, so the guidance must be taken merely as a statement of HMRC's intentions.

HMRC's guidance (ESM2190) states that penalties will be imposed proportionately, and will be used where:

- the payments declared for workers contained in the return are significantly incorrect and understated;
- workers have been omitted from the return;
- identity details have been omitted on a significant number of occasions; or
- the return uses reason F (PAYE under RTI already applied by somebody else) to justify gross payment when in fact no PAYE has been accounted for.

TRAVEL AND SUBSISTENCE RESTRICTIONS – APRIL 2016

10.38 As noted above, workers supplied to agencies through 'umbrella' companies have typically been given permanent employment contracts so that they can legitimately claim to have a series of temporary workplaces and legitimately claim a tax- and NIC-free amount of commuting costs between home and those temporary locations.

Generally, umbrella employers have obtained dispensations for paying the expenses of travel and subsistence for their workers, and they have exploited this by reducing taxable pay and exchanging it for tax-free expenses. Sometimes part of the tax saving has been passed to the workers by increasing their net take-home pay including expenses, but some umbrella employers have simply protected net pay and used the tax and NIC savings to reduce their rates to clients, arguing that the workers are no worse off because they would in any event have been incurring the relevant commuting costs out of their own pocket.

Contracts often allowed for variable gross pay but protected net pay, at a known hourly rate. HMRC warned that this type of 'payday-by-payday' relief structure was ineffective, but in the only case so far to have been considered by the courts (*Reed Employment plc and Others v HMRC* [2015] EWCA Civ 805) the (losing) employer's problem was a failure to implement permanent contracts (and thereby create a series of temporary workplaces for the 'temps' in question) rather than any salary sacrifice or exchange, so HMRC's opinion is still open to question.

Example 10.5 – Workplace type: 2015/16 rules

Roy needed to assemble a team of workers in 2015/16 for a temporary project in Wembley. He sourced the workers from elsewhere, as he had few resources of his own and needed workers who knew what they were doing.

If the workers had been hired via an agency, the Wembley site would have become their permanent workplace for the duration of the contract and their commuting costs would not have been deductible, so Roy sourced them from a range of umbrella employers, with whom they already had permanent employment contracts and who sent them to various sites around the UK every week. The Wembley site was therefore just another temporary workplace for them, and their expenses of travelling between home and the site were therefore generally deductible where the journey to the site was not substantially the same as ordinary commuting for them.

Raheem, one of the workers who is an additional rate taxpayer, travelled to Wembley from his home in Cheshire every week, and chose to stay in an hotel, at a total cost of £1,000 per week. Raheem's employer, Sky Blue plc, in order to minimise its employment costs, agreed with him that it would reduce his pay and reimburse his travel and subsistence expenses instead, for which it held a P11D dispensation, but it would ensure his net pay was protected.

Switching £1,000 from pay to expenses would have increased net pay by the income tax and primary NIC liability saved (£470 per week), so Raheem's revised taxable pay was agreed to be £1,886 lower (ie £1,000 for the expenses and £470 ÷ (100% – 47%) for the grossed-up tax saving). This saved tax and NIC of £886, so Raheem was only £1,000 out of pocket, which was covered by the tax-free expense reimbursement. Sky Blue also saved £260 in employer NICs, so its employment costs were reduced by £1,146 (£1,886 + £260 – £1,000), some of which it chose to pass on to Roy to make the contract price more attractive, some of which it retained to cover administration costs and make a contribution to profit.

Raheem's friend Harry, who lives near Wembley, and his umbrella employer were also spurred on by Roy's agency to use the same salary exchange arrangement, but they couldn't, as Harry's travel to Wembley was very similar to his normal commute to a permanent site in North London, only a few miles from Wembley.

Tackling the tax loss

10.39 Whether or not HMRC could have blocked this structure by litigating its view that 'payday-by-payday' salary sacrifice was ineffective, the government chose instead to tackle the perceived loss of tax and NICs at the root by yet more legislation, blocking the temporary workplace rule for intermediary workers who are, in effect, working in exactly the same way as an ordinary employee of the client, alongside whom they work, and who cannot claim tax relief for their ordinary commuting costs.

With retrospective effect from 6 April 2016, *Finance Act 2016, s 14* introduced *ITEPA 2003, s 339A* to achieve this, together with a new *ITEPA 2003, s 688B* and new PAYE personal liability notices for the directors of companies who disregard the new rules or who provide fraudulent documents in an effort to sidestep the block.

In summary, *ITEPA 2003, s 339A* blocks any claim under *ITEPA 2003, ss 338* and *339* by a worker who is supplied by an intermediary or PSC (other than a managed service company, which is taxed under existing rules) by deeming each engagement to be a separate employment. This has the effect of applying the normal travel and subsistence rules to such workers: they cannot claim relief for travelling to the base for that assignment, but they can still claim if the client sends them to a temporary location in the course of carrying out the duties of the assignment.

Example 10.6 – Workplace type: 2016/17 rules

Roy's successor, Sam, needs to assemble a new team of workers in 2016/17 for a different temporary project based in Wembley. He again sources the workers from a series of umbrella employers.

Raheem again commutes from his home in Cheshire every week, and again stays in a hotel, at a total cost of £1,000 per week. Raheem's employer, Sky Blue plc, can no longer pay Raheem's expenses of travel and subsistence tax-free for the Wembley contract, because the Wembley engagement is treated as a new, separate employment, which means that Wembley becomes his permanent workplace for the duration of the engagement. Its price to Sam increases accordingly to cover the costs of Raheem's extra salary, the associated employer NICs and pension costs, and its profit margin.

In the middle of this contract, Sam decides that the team all need a few days at specialist training facilities at Lilleshall in Shropshire, so Raheem incurs the expense of travelling to a temporary workplace, just like the permanent members of Sam's staff at Wembley. These expenses may be reimbursed tax-free. The same applies to Harry and his employer, as he incurs expenses in travelling from London to Shropshire for a temporary, wholly business purpose.

Scope

10.40 Not every worker finding work through an intermediary is caught by the 2016 changes. The government's aim was to raise more taxes by curbing relief to umbrella and PSC employees who work just like the client's own staff, since it is unfair that an employer can outsource its workforce to an agency and an umbrella employer and pay less because some of the pay is called travel and subsistence expenses and is paid tax-free.

For the purposes of *ITEPA 2003, ss 338* and *339* ('travel for necessary attendance') only, *ITEPA 2003, s 339A* therefore deems each engagement to be a separate employment if the worker provides personal service (other than solely in the home of the client, which means that domestic cleaners, in-home carers, etc are not caught) under an intermediary contract rather than under a direct contract with the client or a connected person of the client. Note that the restriction to *ITEPA 2003, ss 338* and *339* means that the normal rules in

ITEPA 2003, ss 336 (expenses incurred wholly, exclusively and necessarily in the performance of the duties) and *337* (travel in performance of duties, which generally applies to travelling appointments such as meter readers, district nurses and salesmen) are unaffected.

To ensure that only quasi-employees are in scope, and that genuine freelance contractors hired in for their expertise rather than as a cheaper employee-substitute are not, the block on claiming relief for travel and subsistence expenses does not apply 'if it is shown that the manner in which the worker provides the services is not subject to (or to the right of) supervision, direction or control by any person' (*ITEPA 2003, s 339A(3)*).

However, this exclusion cannot apply where the engagement is through a PSC within the *Chapter 8* IR35 rules (*ITEPA 2003, s 339A(4)*). Managed service companies are excluded from the exclusion (Tax Law Rewrite principles appear to have been forgotten by the draughtsman), but for this purpose the definition of MSC is extended beyond that in the *Chapter 9* MSC rules to include not only those companies within the meaning given by *ITEPA 2003, s 61B*, but also companies that would be classed as such if they were not avoiding classification as an MSC by virtue of paying the whole of the worker's income out as employment income (*ITEPA 2003, s 339(11)*).

10.41 There is a further exclusion from *ITEPA 2003, s 339A* for engagements where the *Chapter 8* IR35 rules do not apply because there is no disguised employment (ie the circumstances in *ITEPA 2003, s 49(1)(c)* are not met), but the intermediary otherwise meets the conditions for IR35 in *ITEPA 2003, s 51*, *52* or *53*, and the intermediary is not an MSC (applying the extended MSC definition above) (*ITEPA 2003, s 339(5)*). In determining whether a corporate intermediary meets the *ITEPA 2003, s 51* conditions, it is only necessary to consider whether the worker has a material interest in the intermediary company, and any link between payments from client to PSC and from PSC to worker is regarded as irrelevant (*ITEPA 2003, s 339(6)*).

There are special provisions to guard against abuse and attempts to evade liabilities by somebody providing fraudulent evidence purporting to show that the exclusion for absence of supervision in *ITEPA 2003, s 339(3)* applies: where the client or some other person (other than the worker or a person connected with the PSC) who is resident or has a place of business in the UK and is involved in the relevant services contract provides the intermediary with a fraudulent document intended to constitute such evidence, and as a result the intermediary fails to account for PAYE that should have been due, the worker is then treated as having an employment with the client or other person who provided the document and the PAYE liability is transferred to that client or other person, who is then treated as the employer and payer of the earnings (*ITEPA 2003, s 339A(7), (8)*).

There is also a catch-all targeted anti-avoidance rule intended to forestall attempts at circumventing *ITEPA 2003, s 339A*: no regard is to be had to any arrangements the main purpose, or one of the main purposes, of which is to secure that the denial of a deduction for the expenses is not to apply (*ITEPA 2003, s 339A(10)*).

Deterrence: transfer of liability

10.42 As is the case with the reformed 2014 agency provisions, the directors and officers (ie any manager, secretary or other similar officer, or any person acting or purporting to act as such) of companies involved in the provision of services through intermediaries are also threatened with personal liability notices in respect of amounts of PAYE, interest and penalties that their company is to account for under the *ITEPA 2003, s 339A* provisions.

ITEPA 2003, s 688B provides power for PAYE regulations to specify rules for the issue of personal liability notices. These may be issued in a number of cases to:

- persons providing fraudulent documents (ie the directors of the companies that issue such documents);
- the directors of the intermediary companies or LLPs who have failed to deduct PAYE from non-deductible travel expenses on the basis that the worker was not subject to supervision, direction or control without holding evidence on the basis of which it would be reasonable in all the circumstances to conclude that *ITEPA 2003, s 339A(3)* applies; and
- the directors of PSCs (other than MSCs) within IR35.

Chapter 3B (*Regs 97ZG–97ZM*) was also added to *Part 4* of the *Income Tax (Pay As You Earn) Regulations 2003, SI 2003/2682* setting out the details of the recovery mechanisms for such 'relevant PAYE debts'. They are broadly similar to the personal liability notice rules for NICs and a group of directors is jointly and severally liable for any amounts due, but there are also key differences. The accelerated payment notice provisions have clearly affected the draughtsman's approach: the only grounds of appeal are that the specified amount does not represent the amount of relevant PAYE debt or that the person served with a notice was not a director of the company on the relevant date. The possibility that a director or officer might not be culpable, which is recognised in the NIC legislation, does not appear to have been contemplated.

Chapter 11

Pensions

Written by Alec Ure, Associate of Alec Ure & Associates, and updated by Douglas Sleziak, Associate of Alec Ure & Associates

SIGNPOSTS

- **Latest developments** – There have been major restrictions on pensions tax reliefs in recent years. They have impacted on private and state pension provision. The tax relievable allowances for the annual allowance (AA) and lifetime allowance (LA) were severely restricted by *Finance Act 2011* (*FA 2011*), and were further cut back by *Finance Act 2013* (*FA 2013*). The latest cuts in *Finance (No 2) Act 2015* (*F(No 2)A 2015*) include a tapered AA for high earners from 6 April 2016 (see **11.26**). Additionally, a reduction of the LA to £1m is confirmed in the *Finance Act 2016* (*FA 2016*) from 6 April 2016 (see **11.35**). This will encourage high earners to seek alternative products for providing income in their old age, including the new-style individual savings accounts described below. Of significance are the current income tax (IT) rates for the tax year 2016/17. These are:

  - basic rate 20%;
  - higher rate 40%; and
  - additional rate 45%.

  The above rates of income tax (IT) are retained for the tax year 2017/18.

  The IT basic rate limit for 2017/18 is £33,500 and the personal allowance for 2017/18 is £11,500.

  The above changes have resulted in an astonishingly complex system of protections and transitional arrangements. Also, HMRC have become increasingly vigilant in tackling UK and overseas tax avoidance, including pensions liberation. Its extended powers to collect information for pension schemes, the introduction of the UK's first general anti-avoidance rule (GAAR) and the revised disclosure of tax avoidance schemes legislation (DOTAS) – see **11.119** – mean that it is essential to understand the new rules if effective tax-planning is to be achieved.

Nevertheless, *Finance Act 2014* (*FA 2014*) contained significant relaxations to the capped drawdown pension limit and pension death benefit limit and the amount of minimum income requirement for flexible drawdown for defined contribution/money purchase (DC) schemes (see **11.63–11.65**). Additionally, there was an increase in the trivial commutation lump sum limit and transitional provision in relation to a new standard LA for the tax year 2014/15. The Tax Avoidance Disclosure regimes were strengthened and *FA 2016* introduces protection from the latest reduction in the LA.

The *Taxation of Pensions Act 2014* (*TOPA 2014*) confirmed major changes to permitted access of DC pension pots; lifetime annuity rules; death benefits and short-term annuities (see **11.64–11.65** and **11.83–11.87**). It also allowed all of the funds in a DC scheme to be taken as an authorised taxed lump sum, removed the higher unauthorised payment tax charges, increased the flexibility of the income drawdown rules and increased the maximum value and scope of trivial commutation lump sum death benefits (see **11.76** and **11.77**). New information requirements were brought in to ensure individuals who have flexibly accessed their pension savings (this is termed 'flexi-access') are made aware of the tax consequences of doing so. The special lump sum death benefits charge and the serious ill-health lump sum charge were reduced from 55% to 45%, which rate has since been reduced to the individual's marginal rate (see **11.85**). A pension death benefit may now be paid to a nominee or successor as well as to a dependant as can drawdown pensions. New types of short-term annuities that are similar to dependants' short-term annuities may be paid to individuals who are not dependants of the pension scheme member.

FA 2015 included the extension of relaxation to the annuities rules on death, and strengthened the DOTAS regime. The DOTAS rules are further extended by *FA 2016* (see **11.119**).

Following the last general election, the new Pensions Minister promised to safeguard pensions and to keep the recent pension 'freedoms'. Her stated primary objectives were to:

> 'take forward work to bring in the new state pension (the single-tier pension), help millions more to be enrolled into good quality workplace pension schemes, and safeguard new freedom and choice as to how people access their savings.'

The Chancellor's second budget on 8 July 2015 included £12 billion of welfare cuts and additional anti-tax avoidance laws. On the same day, a Green Paper entitled 'Strengthening the incentive to save: a consultation on pensions' tax relief' was published for consultation. In a sweeping move, the Chancellor stated that he was proposing to put pensions on a footing similar to individual savings accounts (ISAs). This would be a most radical change, meaning that pension schemes would operate on a 'taxed-exempt-exempt' (TEE) basis, and then topped up by the government. The windfall for HM Treasury would be far more substantial than the amount raised by flexi-access. There was also a suggested alternative, to retain the current system and to further change the AA and the LA, with various options in between. The long-standing National Association of Pension Funds (NAPF) rebranded itself as the Pensions and Lifetime Savings Association (PLSA) in acknowledgement of the government's announcement of proposed radical change to future retirement savings.

There was strong feeling in the pensions industry that the government had already made up its mind on the matter. 20–20 Trustees published its response to consultation on its website, stating:

> '[W]e believe a switch to an ISA savings regime would primarily be about bringing forward tax revenue and cutting relief further: bringing forward tax under the guise of simplification. We don't believe that having a pension system which is essentially an ISA with employers topping up your contribution is going to work'.

It also expressed its concern that the reforms target the young, who experience huge barriers to long-term saving. Additionally, the Pensions Minister has called the proposal a '*big mistake*'. In a later, significant, development, a Confederation of British Industry (CBI) survey showed almost 80% of employers wanted a period of pensions stability. Around 96% of respondents said there was a good business case for providing a pension to staff. Employers said having a decent scheme helped them attract and keep workers, and enhanced their reputation. Additionally, two-thirds of large firm respondents, and four-fifths of small companies, said there was a paternalistic obligation on employers to contribute to schemes.

In the face of such ongoing pressure, HM Treasury confirmed in October 2015 that the Chancellor would not be making any major announcements concerning pension tax relief in the Autumn Statement in November 2015, and that he had been persuaded to take more time to consider further radical reforms. However, it became clear in the budget on 16 March 2016 that the Chancellor was determined to push through alternatives to the existing EET pension provision. He raised the ISA limit from £15,000 pa to £20,000 pa from 6 April 2017 and introduced the launch of a 'lifetime ISA' (LISA) for those aged from 18 to under 40.

Under the new LISA, for every £4 saved, the government will put in £1. There will be a limit of £4,000 pa, with a £1,000 government contribution. Individuals can continue saving until they reach the age of 50. They can use the cash to buy a home any time from 12 months of opening, or access it from age 60 for use in retirement. All withdrawals will be tax free. Savers who have already taken out a 'Help to Buy ISA' will be able to roll their savings into a LISA. The government will set a limit on any property purchased at £450,000, with this limit applying nationally, and consult on plans to allow borrowing against the funds without incurring a charge if the borrowed funds are fully repaid. In addition, regulations will provide that ISAs can retain their tax-advantaged status following the death of the account holder. The government is also exploring the possibility of introducing a USA 401k-type model.

Unimpressed, on 22 February 2016, the former Pensions Minister accused the Chancellor of 'daylight robbery', and on 10 June 2016 he said that the almost total takeover of pension policy by the Treasury is profoundly concerning.

The second budget on 8 July 2015 had confirmed the proposed cut to the LA to £1m from April 2016 and unexpectedly cut the AA from the same date to £10,000 for high earners. The growth of salary sacrifice schemes is being closely monitored and the government is consulting over the use of unfunded employer-financed retirement benefit schemes (EFRBS) which are used to gain a tax advantage that was not intended to apply.

- **Types of pension scheme, and their provisions** – There are various types of pension scheme which are described in *FA 2004*. They are open to virtually anyone. There are no limits on contributions to UK-registered pension schemes, only on the tax reliefs which are available, and carry-forward provisions for unused reliefs are available.

  The increased longevity of citizens has long resulted in a challenge to UK governments to find a pensions product for those who have no private pension provision. As a result, we have seen the birth, and gradual demise, of stakeholder schemes, and the introduction of auto-enrolment and the National Employment Savings Trust (NEST). However, as a result of significant policy changes, flexi-access, and new-style ISAs (as described above) are encouraging individuals to crash down their pension pots in their entirety.

A major concern for the high earner (in particular) was contained in *FA 2011, Sch 2* (Employment income provided through third parties), which introduced a charge on 'disguised remuneration', largely affecting EFRBS. The legislation is aimed at preventing the avoidance of IT and national insurance contributions (NICs) by trusts (see **11.10–11.41**).

- **Wide investment choice** – There are few restrictions on investments for UK-registered pension schemes, apart from those which apply to investment-regulated pension schemes (IRPS). However, special rules apply to loans (see **11.42** and **11.44**).
- **Drawing lifetime benefits** – There is a minimum pension age (MPA) for drawing benefits. There are exceptions for certain categories of individual and in circumstances of ill-health (see **11.51–11.53**).
- **Flexi-access** – The drawdown rules for DC schemes were highly flexible, and are constantly being re-written. The new freedoms described above have brought in significant changes (see **11.63–11.65**). Complex protections exist from the LA charge in specified circumstances (see **11.35** and **11.80–11.82**).
- **Death benefits** – General death benefit rules apply on the death of a member for children's and dependant's pensions. The tax situation depends on whether the member dies before or after age 75 and the nature of the payment made. The new drawdown rules apply in most cases, and there have been significant repeals from the inheritance tax (IHT) charge (see **11.93** for IHT exemptions and charges and **Chapter 14** for IHT tax planning with trusts). Again, the new relaxations described above have brought in significant changes (see **11.63–11.65**).
- **Special rules apply on divorce** – The rules mainly concern pension-sharing (see **11.95–11.99**).
- **The reporting to HMRC regime is constantly changing** – The forms and requirements both for UK schemes (whether or not they are UK-registered pension schemes) and for overseas pension schemes (OPS) are described in **11.100–11.102**, **11.121** and **11.150**.
- **Severe tax charges can be incurred on unauthorised payments** – The forms and requirements (referred to in the last edition) have been further extended, both for UK pension schemes and OPS, whether or not they are UK-registered pension schemes (see **11.103–11.120**).
- **Reviews of current pension scheme provisions can be beneficial** – Many pension schemes continued to operate under out-of-date documentation (see **11.122** and **11.123**). This could have

unintended side effects on cost and benefit provision. Reviews of documentation should be undertaken regularly in view of the ongoing changes to pensions legislation.

- **Alternative retirement and savings provisions** – Many employers and savers are exploring alternative tax-efficient methods of saving due to the severe restriction of tax reliefs on pension saving. These methods can include (see **11.126–11.141**):
  - cash payments by employers;
  - benefits in kind and share schemes etc;
  - excepted group life policies;
  - incentive exercises;
  - ISAs/NISAs/LISAs;
  - venture capital trusts;
  - Hancock annuities and employer-financed pension only schemes (EFPOS);
  - salary sacrifices;
  - business loans;
  - unfunded schemes.
- **Overseas pension schemes, and DOTAS** – OPS can be an important tool in tax planning for many. The main HMRC guidance on taxation was HMRC6. This was replaced by new guides for residents and non-residents on the residence, domicile and remittance basis rules for tax years 2012/13 onwards. They are:
  - Information Note: Remittance Basis (RDRI);
  - Guidance Note: Statutory Residence Test (SRT); and
  - Guidance Note: Overseas Workday Relief (OWR).

  (See **Chapter 9** for further details concerning the above).

  Cross-border provision is becoming popular within the European Union and European Economic Area (EU and EEA). Additionally, migrant member relief is available to certain individuals.

  Qualifying recognised overseas pension schemes (QROPS) enable transfers to be made from UK-registered pension schemes, and other forms of overseas pension provision are available. The rules which apply to QROPS are subject to ongoing change and regulation. It is important to follow the guidance on DOTAS and GAAR if penalties are to be avoided (see **11.119**).

- HMRC's Pensions Schemes Newsletters (PSN) regularly include guidance on pension scheme transfers.
- There had been a proposal by government to introduce automatic transfers for small pension pots which have been built up over an individual's lifetime (known as '*pot follows member*'), together with defined ambition (DA) and collective defined contribution (CDC) schemes. However, in October 2015 the Department for Work and Pensions (DWP) stated that the proposal had been put on the back-burner. On 29 October 2015, a statement tabled by the Pensions Minister confirmed that the government will not pursue DA, CDC or automatic transfers. In a later statement the minister indicated that the ideas for change may not have been completely abandoned as future policy.
- A glossary of terms used in this chapter can be found at **11.154** below.

INTRODUCTION

11.1 From A-Day the '*simplified*' tax regime provided wider opportunities for efficient tax planning by extending the thresholds which had previously applied to tax-relievable savings. However, before long the true concept of simplification began to be eroded. The most recent developments have been far-reaching and are complex in the extreme. They impose new charges on savers, whether for members of registered pension schemes or for members of EFRBS and severely restrict tax reliefs on contributions. These charges not only affect high earners, they now encompass a far wider category of people than ever before. They also encourage members of DC schemes to melt down their pensions from age 55.

Until a few years ago, government thinking was becoming directed at protecting pensions at a low level, but discouraging people from saving at a level which is commensurate with their needs and income levels through pension schemes. This former principle seems to have been largely abandoned, whilst the latter remains in place. There had been some procedural easements and repeals of some existing charges, in particular in the area of IHT, and there are new and greater freedoms in accessibility to pension funds, but these mainly affect DC schemes only. However, DC schemes are now being subjected to new regulations and standards by HMRC, the Pensions Regulator and other regulatory bodies. These important developments are described in some detail later in this chapter. 'The latest developments' as summarised above are leading the pensions industry into an even more uncertain future.

11.2 HMRC's Registered Pension Schemes Manual (RPSM) has been replaced by the HMRC Pensions Tax Manual (PTM). Whereas it is an essential source of reference for pension practitioners, trustees, scheme managers, tax advisers and members, the welter of changes to the pension and tax rules in the past few years has resulted in the content of HMRC's manuals falling behind changes to legislation and practice.

The PTM has just one level, focusing on providing technical guidance.

THE LATEST DEVELOPMENTS

11.3 The government has been seeking to raise revenue steadily from pension schemes and from a greatly extended category of persons. A list of the major changes which were brought in by *FA 2011* and subsequent legislation is provided below. The changes from 6 April 2015 were a move by government to gain a sudden windfall of tax receipts from members of DC pension schemes. As described above, the government later had ideas to raise a far greater sum under new proposals and it is actively encouraging individuals to seek alternative provision for their old age.

A detailed description of the changing rules which govern access rights to pension pots for members of DC schemes can be found in **11.61–11.69**. A brief guide to the statutory sources which introduced these changes and other changes in recent years to pensions law and practice is given below.

FA 2011 brought in the following changes:

- a severe cut in the level of the AA under *FA 2011, Sch 18* to £50,000 from the tax year 2011/12;
- a cut in the level of the standard LA to £1.5m from the tax year 2012/13 onward under *FA 2011, Sch 17*, subject to a protection now known as 'fixed protection 2012' (FP 2012) – see **11.35**, with attaching changes to trivial commutations;
- a greatly increased lump sum death benefit charge (an increase from 35% to 55%), except for benefits which became payable on death before age 75 in respect of an individual who had not taken a pension (which are tax free);
- limiting the tax relief for employers when they make asset-backed contributions to their defined benefit (DB) pension schemes;

- exemption from income tax for certain lump sums and lump sum death benefits (LSDB);
- repeal of alternatively secured pension (ASP – see **11.60**), and the attaching IHT charges which applied;
- replacement drawdown pension rules, with a special option for the high earner;
- charging '*employment income provided through third parties*' ('disguised remuneration'), primarily under EFRBS and employee benefit trusts (EBTs);
- abolition of life assurance premium relief in relation to payments by employers to EFRBS from 2012;
- extensions to the DOTAS legislation;
- an announcement that individuals cannot hide behind double taxation agreements to avoid UK tax if they are UK resident and the action concerns UK transferred assets and a tax-avoidance scheme from 6 April 2011; and
- major restrictions on QROPS, mainly from 6 April 2012.

FA 2012 brought in the following changes:

- a small pension rule to permit individuals who are aged over 60 to commute pension funds of £2,000 or less into lump sums – for personal pensions or similar vehicles – without the need to take into account other pension savings, with a maximum of two commutations in a lifetime;
- government monitoring of the use of unfunded pension arrangements to ensure that that they are not used to circumvent the restriction of pensions tax relief and the disguised remuneration requirements under *FA 2011, Sch 2*;
- a limit on the tax reliefs which apply to asset-backed pension contributions with effect from 29 November 2011 (*FA 2012, Sch 13* concerned a scheme acquiring an asset from an employer with an employer contribution and receiving an income stream for, say, 15 years from which time the property reverts to the employer). This further limited the circumstances in which upfront relief is given to asset-backed arrangements;
- an annual tax on enveloped dwellings (ATED), to deter 'non-natural persons' (ie companies) from being used as corporate envelopes to avoid stamp duty land tax (SDLT). SDLT is payable when a property is purchased in the UK, at a level dependent on the property's value. The rate of SDLT for enveloped properties was increased to 15% and the capital gains tax (CGT) regime was extended to include the disposal of

UK residential property by non-resident, non-natural persons for more than £2m.

- a review of QROPS, to facilitate legislation to exclude such schemes in any jurisdiction that makes legislation or otherwise creates or uses a pension scheme to provide tax advantages which UK tax and pensions legislation does not intend (see **11.150**);
- confirmation of the reduction in the top rate of tax from 50% to 45% from 2013;
- an increase for age-related allowances;
- an increase in basic state pension (BSP);
- confirmation of the proposed introduction of a single tier flat-rate pension at a future date to replace BSP and the state second pension (S2P);
- the intention to integrate IT and NICs at a future date.

FA 2013 contained the following changes:

- a reduction in the AA to £40,000 for the year 2014/15 onwards – see **11.26**;
- a cut in the standard LA to £1.25m from the tax year 2014/15 onward, subject to a protection known as 'fixed protection 2014' (FP 2014) – see **11.35**;
- further changes to the tax rules which apply to asset-backed pension contributions (see *FA 2012* under **11.3** for the relevant legislation) – under *FA 2012, s 48* and *Sch 13* there were protection provisions for all asset-backed arrangements that fall into the categories of new arrangements, November–February arrangements and pre-November 2011 arrangements (*FA 2013, Sch 13*);
- an additional form of individual protection (IP 2014') – see **11.35**;
- the introduction of a flat-rate state single-tier pension, targeted to have effect from April 2016 – see **11.4**;
- confirmation of the 'triple lock guarantee' on state pension (SP) – see **11.5**;
- the introduction for employers of an employment allowance – see **11.6**;
- an increase to the limit on the amount of pension an individual may take each year under capped drawdown – see **11.62**;
- a change to the testing of LSDBs – see **11.84–11.88**;
- accommodating the removal of contracting out of S2P through a DC pension scheme from 6 April 2012;

- QROPS to re-notify HMRC every five years that they continue to meet the requirements to be QROPS – see **11.150**;
- the introduction of UK's first GAAR – see **11.119**;
- changes to the rules for bridging pensions for individuals receiving, or with a right to receive, a bridging pension on or after 6 April 2013. *FA 2013, s 51*, aligned the tax rules with the social security changes to state pension age (SPA) from that date to enable a scheme to continue to pay a bridging pension until a member's SPA.

Additionally:

- consultation on the impact of the future withdrawal of relief for interest on loans to purchase life annuities taken out by pensioners before 1999;
- introducing 'family pensions' – see **11.117**;
- keeping the use of the index of retail prices (RPI) for indexation purposes under evaluation until after the UK Statistics Authority has concluded reviewing the governance arrangements and structures supporting the production of price indices and how best to ensure that these statistics best meet the needs of users in future;
- a limit on the premiums that can be paid into life insurance qualifying policies to £3,600 a year from 6 April 2013, with transitional arrangements for policies issued before that date.

FA 2014 brought in the following changes:

- under *FA 2014, s 41* (with effect from 27 March 2014):
  - an increase in the capped drawdown pension limit and pension death benefit limit from 120% to 150%;
  - a reduction in the amount of minimum income requirement for flexible drawdown from £20,000 to £12,000;
- under *FA 2014, s 42* (with effect from 27 March 2014):
  - an increase in the aggregate amount of commutation limit for purposes of trivial commutation lump sum from £18,000 to £30,000;
  - an increase in the trivial commutation lump sum limit of £2,000 to £10,000;
- *FA 2014, Sch 5* provided the necessary further provision in connection with the increased pension flexibility;
- under *FA 2014, Sch 46* there is transitional provision in relation to the new standard LA for the tax year 2014/15 etc;

- under *FA 2014, s 45* the application of certain charges to non-UK pension schemes is amended by a new formula for the pension input amount (PIA) for cash balance and DB arrangements;
- under *FA 2014, Sch 7* there are further provisions concerning HMRC's extended powers;
- additionally:
  - with effect from 5 December 2013, stamp duty for shares purchased in exchange traded funds was abolished in order to encourage those funds to locate in the UK;
  - there were some improvements to film tax relief;
  - from April 2014, there was a new tax relief for investment in social enterprises and new social impact bonds;
  - the rate relief scheme was extended for another year;
  - the rules that discourage firms from expanding and opening extra premises were relaxed;
  - the inflation increase in business rates for all premises was capped at 2% from April 2014;
  - businesses could pay their rates in 12-monthly instalments;
  - for 2014–2016 every retail premise in England with a rateable value of up to £50,000 was entitled to a discount on their business rates. The discount was worth £1,000 off their bills;
- following government consultation on the impact of withdrawing the relief for interest on loans to purchase life annuities, it was decided to retain the relief.

Pensions Act 2014 (*PA 2014*) brought in the following changes:

- provisions to roll out the single-tier state pension;
- voluntary NICs (Class 3A), to allow pensioners who reach SPA before 6 April 2016 to top-up their additional state pension;
- an increase in SPA to 67;
- a framework for future changes to SPA with a regular review based around the principle that people should spend a given proportion of their lives receiving a SP;
- provisions to introduce bereavement support payment to replace the existing bereavement benefits for new customers. The reforms will significantly simplify the system by moving to a more uniform payment

structure with support focused on the period immediately following bereavement and a single contribution condition;

- automatic transfers of small pension pots so that a person's pension will follow them to their new pension scheme when they change jobs (now put on hold, or possibly abandoned);
- some clarifications relating to automatic enrolment;
- powers to allow the government to introduce minimum governance and administration standards and restrict charges in workplace pensions.

TOPA 2014 brought in the following changes:

- *TOPA 2014, s1* and *TOPA 2014, Sch 1*:
  - all funds in a DC scheme may be taken as an authorised taxed lump sum – the higher unauthorised payment tax charges were removed;
  - maximum caps on withdrawal and minimum income requirements for all new drawdown funds were removed from 6 April 2015;
  - individuals in capped drawdown may convert to a new drawdown fund once arranged with their scheme;
  - pension schemes may make payments directly from pension savings – 25% will be tax-free;
  - there is a limited right for scheme trustees and managers to override their scheme's rules to pay flexible pensions from money purchase pension savings, if they so wish;
  - some restrictions on lifetime annuity payments were removed;
  - in order to ensure that individuals do not exploit the new system to gain unintended tax advantages, a money purchase annual allowance (MPAA) of £10,000 will apply for any future savings in DC schemes where the individual has flexibly accessed their savings;
  - the maximum value and scope of trivial commutation lump sum death benefits are increased;
  - new information requirements ensure that individuals who have flexibly accessed their pension savings are aware of the tax consequences of doing so;
  - there is a restriction on, or reduction to, certain tax charges that apply to death benefits; and

   - there are changes to the rules for individuals who receive UK tax relief in respect of pension savings in non-UK pension schemes so that the flexibilities and restrictions to relief will apply equally to them.

- *TOPA 2014, s 2* amends *FA 2004, Pt 4, Ch 5*, to make the special lump sum death benefits charge apply in respect of a member who had reached the age of 75 at their date of death. Further amendments reduce both the special LSDB charge and the serious ill-health lump sum charge from 55% to 45% from 6 April 2015;
- *TOPA 2014, s 3* and *Sch 2* permit a pension death benefit to be paid to a nominee or successor as well as to a dependant, and drawdown pensions may be paid to a nominee or successor from 6 April 2015.
- *TOPA 2014, s 4* provides definitions and the power to make regulations appropriate to *TOPA 2014, ss 1–3*.
- nominees' and successors' short-term annuities are introduced, being short-term annuities that are similar to dependants' short-term annuities but may be paid to individuals who are not dependants of the pension scheme member.

An HMRC policy paper was issued, accompanied by a draft Explanatory Note entitled 'Pension Flexibility: Draft Explanatory Note – Taxation of Pensions Bill' and a document entitled 'Pension Flexibility: Draft Guidance' (5 August 2014).

FA 2015 brought in the following changes:

- an extension of the death relaxation to annuities from April 2015 – beneficiaries of individuals who die under the age of 75 with a joint life or guaranteed term annuity, are able to receive any future payments from such policies tax-free where no payments had been made from the policy to the beneficiary before 6 April 2015. Joint life annuities may *to be passed to any beneficiary*;
- *FA 2015, s 34* introduced *Sch 4* which contains the relevant provision about pension annuities, and other pension, paid in respect of deceased members of pension schemes to nominees or successors;
- the DOTAS regime was *further* strengthened.

The *Pension Schemes Act 2015* (*PSA 2015*) brought in the following changes with effect from 6 April 2015:

- *PSA 2015, Pt 4* is concerned with pensions liabilities:
   - *Ch 1* contains pension guidance;

  - *Ch 2* concerns independent advice;
  - *Ch 3* concerns drawdown, conversion of benefits and lump sums;
  - *Ch 4* concerns transfers;
  - *Ch 5* concerns the interpretation of some of the terms used in *Pt 4*; and
  - *Sch 3* contains general pensions guidance and the regulators who are concerned with pensions;
- *PSA 2015, ss 4* and *5* define what is meant by a money purchase (DC) scheme.

The main purpose of *PSA 2015* is to:

- introduce a requirement for trustees to check that a member has taken independent advice from an appropriate person before converting any DB into flexible benefits or transferring them to a different scheme in order to acquire flexible benefits;
- give power by regulation to specify the circumstances in which an employer must arrange or pay for such independent advice from an appropriate person;
- introduce a ban on transfers out of unfunded DB public service schemes to schemes in which the member can obtain flexible benefits; and
- remove a restriction so that members have the right to take a cash equivalent transfer value up to their scheme's normal pension age (NPA), rather than up to one year before they are due to reach their scheme's NPA.

The Chancellor announced in the budget on 18 March 2015 that the LA will reduce from £1.25m to £1m from 6 April 2016. Transitional protection for pension rights already over £1m will be introduced alongside this reduction to ensure the change is not retrospective. The LA will be indexed annually in line with consumer prices index (CPI) from 6 April 2018.

F(No 2)A 2015 received Royal Assent on 18 November 2015. There are transitional regulations from 9 July 2015. Pension savings will now always be measured over a tax year, and include those to the taxation of LSDBs and there are changes to the carry-forward rules (see **11.34**). Additionally, tax will be payable on lump sum death benefits at the recipient's marginal rate of IT as from 6 April 2016 (see **11.85**).

The *Finance Act 2016* received Royal Assent on 15 September 2016. It is of considerable length. Its progress through the House was tracked on the

Parliament website under the title of the *Finance (No 2) Bill 2015–16 to 2016–17.*

For pensions and related planning matters it brings in the following changes:

- *FA 2016, ss 1–3* state the IT rates.
- *FA 2016, s 18* makes several changes to disguised remuneration rules under *Part 7A* of the *Income Tax (Earnings and Pensions) Act 2003* and to the *Finance Act 2011*. There is a withdrawal of transitional relief on certain investment returns for those who have not settled their liabilities before 1 April 2017 (previously 1 December 2016). The change is intended to encourage those who used certain types of disguised remuneration schemes to settle their liabilities.
- *FA 2016, s 19* contains the reduction of the LA and amends *FA 2004* accordingly:
  - the LA is £1m from 6 April 2016;
  - it will be increased in line with increases in the CPI for the year to the previous September where it is higher than it was 12 months earlier, rounded up to the nearest £100. If the index is not higher in that 12-month period, then the standard LA for the tax year will be same as the standard LA for the previous tax year;
  - where an individual has a LA enhancement factor and the event giving rise to the enhancement factor occurs between 6 April 2014 and 5 April 2016, enhancement factor is multiplied by £1.25m if this is greater than the standard LA at the time the benefit crystallisation event (BCE) occurs;
  - *FA 2016, s 19(4)* provides for the reference to the standard LA to be replaced by a figure of £1.25m where certain LSDBs are paid (BCE 7 refers) on or after 6 April 2016 in respect of the death of the individual in either tax year 2014/15 or 2015/16. When uncrystallised funds are designated for dependants' or nominees' flexi-access drawdown, following the death of a member before 6 April 2016, the BCE is tested against the standard LA in force at the time of the member's death. This has effect from 6 April 2015. When the entitlement to a beneficiary's or dependent's annuity arises following the death of a member before 6 April 2016, the BCE is tested against the standard LA in force at the time of the member's death. This has effect from 6 April 2016, and has effect in relation to BCEs occurring on or after that date.
- *FA 2016, Sch 4* contains the main provisions for transitional protection from the reduction of the LTA.

- *FA 2016, Sch 4, Pt 1* introduces fixed protection 2016 (FP 2016):
  - *FA 2016, Sch 4, paras 1* and *2* state that individuals will have a protected LA of £1.25m. The protection is available to individuals who, on 6 April 2016, had one or more arrangements under a registered pension scheme, or a relieved non-UK pension scheme of which the individual is a relieved member. Individuals with fixed protection 2012 (FP 2012); fixed protection 2014 (FP 2014); primary protection (PP) or enhanced protection (EP) at any date on or after 6 April 2016 will not be able to hold FP 2016 at that date;
  - *FA 2016, Sch 4, para 3* sets out certain events known as 'protection-cessation events'. These are events which occur on or after 6 April 2016. They are:
    - where there is benefit accrual;
    - where there is an impermissible transfer;
    - where there is a transfer of sums or assets that is not a permitted transfer;
    - where a new pension arrangement relating to the individual is made otherwise than in permitted circumstances;
  - *FA 2016, Sch 4, para 4(1)* provides definitions of benefit accrual for each type of arrangement;
  - *FA 2016, Sch 4, para 4(2)* and *(3)* provides how to determine the increase in the value of the individual's rights;
  - *FA 2016, Sch 4, para 4(4)* provides a definition of when a relevant contribution is paid;
  - *FA 2016, Sch 4, para 4(5)* provides that increases in an individual's rights under an arrangement are to be ignored for the purposes of determining whether benefit accrual has occurred if they do not exceed the relevant percentage in a tax year;
  - *FA 2016, Sch 4, para 4(6)* describes the relevant percentage as an annual rate of increase specified in the scheme rules as at 9 December 2015, plus any relevant statutory increase percentage as defined in *FA 2016, Sch 4, para 4(8)*. Where there is not a rate of increase specified in the scheme rules, the relevant percentage is either the annual percentage increase in the CPI or, if it is higher, the relevant statutory increase percentage;
  - *FA 2016, Sch 4, para 4(7)* provides for a 'predecessor arrangement' or 'predecessor registered pension scheme' to apply where appropriate for the purposes of *FA 2016, Sch 4, para 4(6)*;

- *FA 2016, Sch 4, para 4(8)* defines 'relevant statutory increase percentage';
- *FA 2016, Sch 4, para 4(9)* provides that *FA 2016, Sch 4, para 4(10)* applies when the individual's rights are under a deferred annuity contract and that contract limits increases in rights to annual increases in the RPI;
- *FA 2016, Sch 4, para 4(10)* provides that, where *FA 2016, Sch 4, para 4(9)* applies, the relevant percentage in *FA 2016, Sch 4, para (6),* which allows for CPI increases, is replaced by the annual rate of increase in the value of the individual's rights during the tax year;
- *FA 2016, Sch 4, para 4(11)* provides detail on the calculation of the annual increase in the RPI;
- *FA 2016, Sch 4, para 5* defines impermissible transfers;
- *FA 2016, Sch 4, para 6* defines permitted transfers;
- *FA 2016, Sch 4, para 7* defines permitted circumstances;
- *FA 2016, Sch 4, para 8* concerns the rules for individuals who receive UK tax relief on pension savings in relieved non-UK schemes;

- *FA 2016, Sch 4, Pt 2* introduces a further type of transitional protection for those who think they may be affected by the reduction in the LA from 6 April 2016. This is known as individual protection 2016 (IP 2016):
  - *FA 2016, Sch 4, para 9* sets out who can rely on IP 2016, how their pension rights are valued and the level of protected LA that they will be entitled to;
  - *FA 2016, Sch 4, para 9(1)* provides that individuals can rely on IP 2016 if they have pension rights (their 'relevant amount') of greater than £1m on 5 April 2016, if they do not have PP and if they have a reference number issued by HMRC;
  - *FA 2016, Sch 4, para 9(2)* provides that where an individual has IP 2014 their standard LA is the greater of their relevant amount (subject to an overall limit of £1.25m) and the standard LA at that time;
  - *FA 2016, Sch 4, para 9(3)* provides a definition of 'relevant arrangement';
  - *FA 2016, Sch 4, para 9(4)* defines the 'relevant amount' as the sum of amounts A to D which are *FA 2016, Sch 4, paras 10–13*. This is

the value on 5 April 2016 of the individual's pensions in payment plus their pension savings, not yet taken, that have benefited from UK tax relief;

- *FA 2016, Sch 4, para 9(5)* provides that, where an individual who has notified HMRC that they intend to rely on IP 2016, has one of five specified existing protections, ie:

  (i) EP;

  (ii) FP 2012;

  (iii) FP 2014;

  (iv) IP 2014;

  (v) FP 2016.

  IP 2016 does not apply for so long as the existing protection continues to apply;

- *FA 2016, Sch 4, para 9(6)–(9)* deals with the position where the pension rights of an individual with IP 2016 are subject to a pension debit, as a result of the sharing of the individual's pension rights following a divorce on or after 6 April 2016. In such a case, the individual's relevant amount is reduced by the amount of the debit. However, for IP 2016 purposes the amount of debit is reduced by 5% for each complete tax year between 5 April 2016 and the date of the pension debit. Where the individual's relevant amount is reduced below £1m as a result of the pension debit, they will no longer be entitled to rely on IP 2016;

- *FA 2016, Sch 4, para 10* sets out how to calculate amount A, which is the value of the pensions that the individual was receiving on 6 April 2006 (A-day);

- *FA 2016, Sch 4, para 10(2)–(5)* applies where a BCE has occurred, in respect of the individual on or before 5 April 2016. The factor is applied to take account of any change in the standard LA since the event, so that that percentage of the standard LA used up by the pre A-day pension is the same on 5 April 2016 as it was on the date of the BCE;

- *FA 2016, Sch 4, para 10(6)* and *(7)* applies where no BCE has occurred in respect of the individual since A-day, in which case amount A is 25 times the annual rate at which the pre A-day pension is payable on 5 April 2016;

- *FA 2016, Sch 4, para 10(8)* and *(9)* defines 'relevant existing pension';
- *FA 2016, Sch 4, para 11* sets out how to calculate amount B, which is the value of any BCEs in respect of the individual occurring on or before 5 April 2016. Amount B is the aggregate of the value of each BCE, multiplied by a factor of £1.25m over the standard LA at the date of the event;
- *FA 2016, Sch 4, para 12* sets out how to calculate amount C, which is the value of any uncrystallised pension rights that the individual has in a registered pension scheme on 5 April 2016. Amount C is calculated In accordance with the method set out in *FA 2004, s 212*;
- *FA 2016, Sch 4, para 13* sets out how to calculate amount D, which is the value of any uncrystallised pension rights that the individual has under relieved non-UK pension schemes on 5 April 2016. It is assumed that there is a BCE in respect of those rights at that date and the amount that would have been crystallised in accordance with *FA 2004, Sch 36, para 14.*

- *FA 2016, Sch 4, Pt 3* sets out when a valid application for FP 2016 or IP 2016 is made, and the issue by HMRC of a reference number that the individual can use to prove that they are entitled to that protection when they take any benefits on or after 6 April 2016:
  - *FA 2016, Sch 4, para 14* makes provision for individuals to apply for a reference number, and the form of that application, for FP 2016 and IP 2016, and for HMRC to issue a reference number;
  - *FA 2016, Sch 4, para 14(1)* defines that an individual has a reference number for the purposes of FP 2016 or IP 2016 if one has been issued by HMRC and it has not been withdrawn;
  - *FA 2016, Sch 4, para 14(2)* defines the form of the reference number and when it will be issued;
  - *FA 2016, Sch 4, para 14(3)* sets out what information is required in order for an application to be a valid application;
  - *FA 2016, Sch 4, para 14(4)* requires HMRC to notify the individual if their application for a reference number for FP 2016 or IP 2016 is unsuccessful or, in the case of IP 2016, the application was successful but a reference number is not being issued because the protection is dormant;

- *FA 2016, Sch 4, para 14(5)* defines the terms 'relevant arrangement', 'appropriate amount' and 'transfer day';
- *FA 2016, Sch 4, para 14(7)* defines what is meant by 'dormant basis' for the purposes of IP 2016, that is the application would have been successful but for the fact that the individual held another form of transitional protection at the time of the protection at the time of the application;
- *FA 2016, Sch 4, para 14(8)* sets out the prior provisions which would result in the dormant basis;
- *FA 2016, Sch 4, para 15* sets out the circumstances in which HMRC may withdraw a reference number and requires HMRC to tell the individual the reasons for doing so;
- *FA 2016, Sch 4, para 16* provides for an appeal against the non-issue or the withdrawal of a reference number;
- *FA 2016, Sch 4, para 17* sets out the requirement for individuals who have a reference number, or a pending application for a reference number, for the purposes of FP 2016 or IP 2016 to notify HMRC within 90 days if a protection-cessation event occurs;
- *FA 2016, Sch 4, para 18* sets out the requirement for individuals who have a reference number, or a pending application, for the purposes of IP 2016, to notify HMRC within 60 days if they receive a discharge notice related to a pension debit;
- *FA 2016, Sch 4, para 19* provides for personal representatives of deceased individuals to be able to apply for FP 2016 and IP 2016;
- *FA 2016, Sch 4, para 20* amends the table in *s 98* of the *Taxes Management Act 1970* (*TMA 1970*) to add *paras 17* and *18* of the *Schedule* to column 2 of the table. Where an individual fails to comply with the requirements in either *para 17* or *18*, the penalties apply. This includes a penalty of up to £300 where required information is not provided.

• *FA 2016, Sch 4, Pt 4* sets out the information requirements in connection with FP 2016 and IP 2016:

- *FA 2016, Sch 4, para 21* sets out that individuals who have a reference number for the purposes of IP 2016 are required to preserve the documents that have been used in the calculation of their relevant amount, for six years from the date of application for the reference number;

- *FA 2016, Sch 4, paras 22–25* make various amendments to the *Registered Pension Schemes (Provision of Information) Regulations 2006 (SI 2006/567)*, so that, where an individual relies on FP 2016 or IP 2016, similar information is required to be provided by the member to the scheme administrator and from the scheme administrator to HMRC as for the similar existing LA regimes;
- *FA 2016, Sch 4, para 26* inserts new *para 14C* into *SI 2006/567*. If the member requests it, and as long as the request is received by the scheme administrator before 6 April 2020, scheme administrators are required to provide information, to enable a member to calculate their relevant amount. Scheme administrators may, if they so choose, provide this information for requests received after this date but there is no requirement to do so.

- *FA 2016, Sch 4, Pt 5* sets out changes to *FA 2004* in respect of PP and EP to ensure that certain individuals with one of these protections are able to receive the right amount of tax free lump sums intended by legislation:
  - *FA 2016, Sch 4, para 28(1)* applies where an individual has PP or EP but no lump sum protection. If the member becomes entitled to a pension commencement lump sum (PCLS) after 6 April 2014, when making the adjustment to the relevant amount for a previous BCE that also occurred after 6 April 2014, where £1.5m is greater than the standard LA at the time of the previous BCE, the standard LA at the time of the earlier event is treated as being £1.5m;
  - *FA 2016, Sch 4, para 28(2)* applies where an individual has PP with lump sum protection. Where more than one BCE occurs after 6 April 2012, and a further BCE occurs on or after 6 April 2014, the definition of standard LA for the purposes of revaluing the earlier BCEs is the greater of £1.8m and the standard LA at the time the individual became entitled to the lump sum.
- *FA 2016, Sch 4, Pt 6* sets out the interpretation of expressions used in the *Schedule* and provides a power to make regulations amending *Parts 1, 2* and *3* of the *Schedule*. Such regulations may be retrospective providing they do not increase any person's liability to tax and do not have effect before 6 April 2016.
- *FA 2016, s 20* removes existing legislation in the *FA 2004, Sch 28*, to align pensions tax legislation with *PA 2014* and allow the payment of bridging pensions to continue, without adverse tax consequences, as set out in current legislation. HMRC will consult with industry representatives on the drafting of new regulations and to clarify the exact implications of the single-tier state pension on the legislation relating to bridging pensions.

- *FA 2016, s 21* introduces exceptions from the anti-avoidance calculations that must otherwise be carried out in respect of annual increases in dependants' scheme pensions where an individual who was entitled to a scheme pension, dies having reached age 75. The change has effect on or after 6 April 2016:
  - *FA 2016, s 21(2)* provides that application of the limits operates subject to the new provisions;
  - *FA 2016, s 21(3)* provides when the anti-avoidance calculations do not apply in connection with dependants' scheme pensions. The general limit for 2016/17 is £25,000. The personal limit is the total of the annual rate of the member's scheme pensions, both in payment and to which they were entitled but not yet in payment, in the year that they died. There are formulae for both to be increased for future years. The amount by which an individual's pension under a public service pension scheme had been reduced in their lifetime is ignored
- *FA 2016, Sch 5*, as introduced by *s 22*, makes various changes to *FA 2004* to ensure that the pension flexibility changes introduced from 6 April 2015 operate as intended. They make changes to the tax rules for serious ill-health lump sums, charity lump-sum death benefits, dependants' with drawdown pension funds and flexi-access drawdown funds where the dependant reaches age 23, trivial commutation lump sums and dependants' death benefits under cash balance arrangements. The changes have effect on the day after Royal Assent to *FA 2016:*
  - *FA 2016, Sch 5, paras 1(1)–(4)* amend the taxation of serious ill-health lump sums to remove the 45% charge and replace it with a charge at the recipient's marginal rate, where the individual is over 75. The definition of 'serious ill-health lump sum' is amended to allow a lump sum to be paid out of unused funds in a drawdown fund and the *Income Tax (Earnings and Pensions) Act 2003* (*ITEPA 2003*) is amended accordingly;
  - *FA 2016, Sch 5, para 5* allows payment of a charity lump-sum death benefit from uncrystallised funds in respect of a member who had not reached age 75 at the time of their death;
  - *FA 2016, Sch 5, para 6* amends the conditions that must be met for a drawdown fund to be a dependants' flexi-access drawdown fund or a dependants' drawdown fund to enable dependants with these type of funds who would currently have to use all of this fund before age 23, to be able to continue to access these funds as they wish after their 23rd birthday.

- *FA 2016, Sch 5, para 6(2)* extends the meaning of dependant in certain circumstances to include a child who has reached age 23;
- *FA 2016, Sch 5, para 6(3)* extends the meaning of dependant for dependants' short-term annuities and dependants' income withdrawal respectively;
- *FA 2016, Sch 5, para 6(5)* provides that a recipient may be a dependant under the extended meaning;
- *FA 2016, Sch 5, para 7(1)–(3)* allows a scheme pension to be paid as an authorised payment where it is commuted to be a trivial commutation lump sum;
- *FA 2016, Sch 5, para 8* amends *ITEPA 2003* in respect of a lump sum paid out of uncrystallised rights;
- *FA 2016, Sch 5, para 8(2)* ensures that only 75% of rights that have not been accessed (uncrystallised rights) are taxed, even when they are paid together with crystallised rights. This aligns the tax treatment with lump sums that are paid entirely out of uncrystallised rights;
- *FA 2016, Sch 5, para 9* states that the amendments made by *FA 2016, Sch 5, paras 7* and *8* have effect in relation to lump sums paid after the day on which the *FA 2016* was passed;
- *FA 2016, Sch 5, para 10* allows employers to top up the amount of any shortfall in funds in a promised uncrystallised funds LSDB in a cash balance arrangement at the time of the member's death. The top up can only be made in respect of a shortfall at the time of the death;
- *FA 2016, Sch 5, para 11* provides that where an annuity is payable on death to a nominee, and some or all of the cost of the annuity could instead have been paid to a personal representative, those funds shall not form part of that person's chargeable estate for IHT purposes.

- *FA 2016, s 23* inserts new *ITEPA 2003, s 642A*, to provide that any payments received by individuals under the Netherlands 'Wuv' scheme will be exempt from IT from 6 April 2016. The 'Wuv' scheme makes payments to individuals who were victims of persecution in Europe or Asia during the Second World War. To benefit from the scheme, recipients must either have had Dutch nationality, been a Dutch subject or persecuted on Dutch territory and later acquired Dutch nationality. Payments from the Netherlands' government via the scheme had been included in the calculation of an individual's income tax liability.

In April 2014 an appeal on a Housing Benefit claim contended that the failure to treat the payments in the same way as pensions and annuities from Germany or Austria was unlawful discrimination. The relevant changes to the inheritance tax rules are contained in *FA 2016, s 84.*

- *FA 2016, s 94* introduces an exemption so that an IHT charge will not arise where a person has failed to exercise their rights to draw designated funds from a drawdown pension fund or a flexi-access drawdown fund during their lifetime and so has left unused funds when they die.
- *FA 2016, ss 156–158* concern the general anti-abuse rule (GAAR) provisional counteractions; binding of tax arrangements to lead arrangements and penalties.
- *FA 2016, ss159–161* and *Schs 18–23* concern serial tax avoidance; promoters of tax avoidance schemes and large businesses: tax strategies and sanctions for persistently unco-operative behaviour respectively.
- *FA 2016, ss 162–166* concern penalties in connection with offshore matters and offshore transfers; offshore tax errors etc; publishing details of deliberate tax defaulters; asset-based penalties for offshore inaccuracies and failures; and offences relating to offshore income, assets and activities respectively.
- *FA 2016, Sch 6* concerns the deduction of IT at source; the abolition of duty to deduct tax from interest on certain investments, the deduction of tax from yearly interest: exception for deposit takers and the deduction of tax from UK public revenue dividends.

The *Finance Act 2017* (*FA 2017*) received Royal Assent on 27 April 2017. It has been considerably truncated from the final draft of the *Finance (No 2) Bill 2017*, due to the calling of the general election on 8 June 2017. In the circumstances, significant parts of the *Finance (No 2) Bill 2017* have been shelved for the time being.

For pensions and related planning matters, *FA 2017* brings in the following changes for the tax year 2017/18:

(a) *FA 2017, ss 1–3* state the IT and savings rates for the tax years 2017/18.

(b) *FA 2017, Sch 3, Pt 1* as introduced by *s 9* makes provisions relating to registered pension schemes established outside the United Kingdom and payments made in respect of overseas pension entitlement. *FA 2017, Sch 3, para 1(1)* inserts new *FA 2004, Pt 4, ss 242C, 242D* and *242E.* New *FA 2004, s 242C* applies the tax provisions in *FA 2004, Pt 4* in relation to non-UK-based registered pension schemes as follows:

  - in relation to UK-relieved funds held under a non-UK-registered pension scheme, the rules apply as they would to the sums or assets held under a UK-based registered pension scheme;

- in relation to non-UK-based registered pension schemes, the rules apply as they would to a UK-based registered pension scheme to the extent of the scheme's UK-relieved funds;
- in relation to members of non-UK-based registered pension schemes, the rules apply to their rights under the scheme to the extent that they are represented by UK-relieved funds, in the same way as funds held under a UK-based registered pension scheme; and
- in relation to contributions to a non-UK-based registered pension scheme the rules apply as they do to contributions to a UK-based registered pension scheme.
- The new *FA 2004, s 242C* gives HMRC the power to make regulations to clarify how UK provisions of *FA 2004, Pt 4* and tax relief applies in relation to non-UK-based registered pension schemes. Amendments may also be made to *ITEPA 2003, Pt 9*.
- The new *FA 2004, s 242D* sets out how the annual allowance charge applies to non-UK-registered pension schemes and confirms that an individual's input into a non-UK-registered pension scheme is to be included in the calculation of the amount to be tested against the annual allowance only if HMRC have set out in regulations that they are taken to have been made in respect of that individual under the scheme in the year.
- The new *FA 2004, s 242E* refers to investment-regulated non-UK-registered schemes and sets out that the taxable property provisions apply in relation to non-UK-registered pension schemes as if the scheme were established in the UK.

(c) *FA 2017, Sch 3, Pt 2, para 2* brings 100% instead of 90% of the foreign pension income of UK residents into charge for UK tax purposes.

(d) *FA 2017, Sch 3, Pt 2, para 3* removes the facility for tax relief in respect of new savings in the specialist pension schemes ('Section 615 Schemes') for those working outside the UK.

(e) *FA 2017, Sch 3, Pt 3, para 4* amends *ITEPA 2003* in relation to lump sums for UK residents from foreign pension schemes.

(f) *FA 2017, Sch 3, Pt 3, para 5* amends *ITEPA 2003, s 395B* to remove foreign service relief for UK resident members of an employer-financed retirement benefits scheme ('EFRBS') who receives a lump sum in the tax year 2017/18 and subsequent tax years.

(g) *FA 2017, Sch 3, Pt 3, para 6* inserts a new *ITEPA 2003, s 395C* which sets out the meaning of foreign service.

(h) *FA 2017, Sch 3, Pt 3, para 7* inserts new *ITEPA 2003, s 554Z4(7)* and *(8)* which sets out that the value of a relevant step is not reduced for foreign service when the relevant step is a lump sum relevant benefit under an EFRBS paid to a UK resident.

(i) *FA 2017, Sch 3, Pt 3, para 8* inserts a new *ITEPA 2003, s 573(4)* which provides for a UK tax charge on the payment of a relevant lump sum under a pension scheme established outside the UK where the member is UK resident (or, if the member has died, was UK resident immediately before their death), including where the beneficiary is not UK resident.

(j) *FA 2017, Sch 3, Pt 3, para10* inserts a new *ITEPA 2003, s 574A* as follows:

- it defines a relevant lump sum as a lump sum paid from a pension scheme that is not a registered pension scheme, relevant non-UK scheme or EFRBS established in the UK and the lump sum is not a relevant step to which disguised remuneration rules in *ITEPA 2003, Pt 7A, Ch 2* apply;
- it provides that a lump sum paid under a relevant non-UK scheme is a relevant lump sum if the member payment provisions in *FA 2004, Sch 34* do not apply to the lump sum;
- it sets out the steps to calculate the amount of pension that is treated as arising in relation to a relevant lump sum paid under a relevant foreign pension scheme;
- it sets out that the amount arrived at by following the steps referred to above is treated as the amount of taxable pension income arising in the tax year;
- it provides a power for HMRC to make relevant regulations; and
- it provides for the changes to take effect in relation to lump sums paid on or after 6 April 2017.

(k) *FA 2017, Sch 4, Pt 1* amends *FA 2004, Sch 34* with effect from 6 April 2017 to extend from five to ten years the period of an individual's non-UK residence during which UK tax charges can apply to payments out of pension savings in overseas pension schemes that have had UK tax relief. This refers to transfers from UK-registered pension schemes to qualifying recognised overseas pension schemes and subsequent transfers during the relevant period. It also provides for HMRC to make regulations to reduce a member's UK tax-relieved fund in certain circumstances.

(l) *FA 2017, Sch 4, Pt 2, para 11* amends *FA 2004, Pt 4* by inserting new *FA 2004, ss 244A–244N*. These set out how the overseas transfer charge will operate with the exclusions from the charge, liability to the charge, the amount of the charge and how those liable will account for the charge:

- New *FA 2004, s 244A(1)* provides that the overseas transfer charge arises when a recognised transfer is made to a Qualifying Recognised Overseas Pension Scheme ('QROPS') or an onward transfer from a QROPS or former QROPS except where the transfer is excluded from the charge.
- New *FA 2004, s 244A(2)* sets out how the exclusions are limited.
- New *FA 2004, s 244A(3)* defines an onward transfer as a transfer from a QROPS or former QROPS to another QROPS. The sums or assets transferred that represent the individual's accrued rights must be held under the new scheme to represent that individual's rights in that new scheme.
- New *FA 2004, s 244A(4)* defines relevant period as any period from the transfer to the next 5 April plus five years.
- New *FA 2004, s 244A(5)* defines the original transfer in relation to an onward transfer as the most recent transfer from a registered pension scheme or where the transfer was from a currently-relieved scheme rather than a registered pension scheme, the most recent transfer from that scheme.
- New *FA 2004, s 244A(6)* and *(7)* provides that, if a transfer is made that is made up of the different types of onward transfer, they are counted as separate onward transfers for *FA 2004, ss 244A* to *244N*.
- New *FA 2004, s 244B(1)* provides that a transfer is excluded from the overseas transfer charge if in the five tax years beginning with the date of the transfer, the individual who made the transfer is resident in the same country as the QROPS to which the transfer was made and no onward transfer is made that is subject to the overseas transfer charge.
- New *FA 2004, s 244B(2)* provides that the position at the point of transfer is assumed to remain for five tax years but if, within the five-tax year period from the date of transfer, the individual is no longer resident in the same country, as their transferred pension savings, then the overseas transfer charge will apply to those transferred funds in the QROPS at that point.
- New *FA 2004, s 244B(3)* provides that an onward transfer to a QROPS is excluded from the overseas transfer charge if, in the remainder of the five tax years from the date of the original transfer, the individual who made the transfer is resident in the

same country as the QROPS to which the onward transfer was made, and no subsequent onward transfer is made that is subject to the overseas transfer charge.

- New *FA 2004, s 244B(4)* provides that the position at the point of the onward transfer is assumed to be the case for the remainder of the five-tax year period from the date of the original transfer but if, within that time, the individual is no longer resident in the same country as their transferred pension savings, then the overseas transfer charge will apply to those same funds at that point.
- New *FA 2004, s 244C(1)* and *(2)* provides for a transfer to a QROPS in an European Economic Area (EEA) state to be excluded from the overseas transfer charge if, in the five tax years beginning with the date of the transfer, the individual who made the transfer is resident in a country within the EEA and no onward transfer is made that is subject to the overseas transfer charge.
- New *FA 2004, s 244C(3)* provides that the position at the point of transfer is assumed to remain for five tax years but if, within the five-tax-year period from the date of transfer, the individual ceases to be resident in an EEA state then the overseas transfer charge will apply to the transferred funds in the QROPS at that point.
- New *FA 2004, s 244C(4)* provides for an onward transfer to a QROPS in an EEA state to be excluded from the overseas transfer charge if, in the five tax years beginning with the date of the transfer, the individual who made the transfer is resident in a country within the EEA and no subsequent onward transfer is made that is subject to the overseas transfer charge.
- New *FA 2004, s 244C(5)* provides that the position at the point of the onward transfer is assumed to be the case for the remainder of the five-tax-year period from the date of original transfer but if, within that period, the individual ceases to be resident in an EEA state then the overseas transfer charge will apply to the transferred funds in the QROPS at that point.
- New *FA 2004, s 244D* provides that a transfer is excluded from the overseas transfer charge if the transfer is made to the occupational pension scheme and the individual is an employee of a sponsoring employer of the QROPS.
- New *FA 2004, s 244E(1)* provides that a transfer is excluded from the overseas transfer charge if the transfer is made to a QROPS established by an international organisation and the individual making the transfer is an employee of that international organisation at that time.

- New *FA 2004, s 244E(2)* defines international organisation as an organisation to which *International Organisations Act 1968, s 1* applies, so it is clear that it is not simply a company or group of companies that operate internationally.
- New *FA 2004, s 244F(1)* provides that a transfer is excluded from the overseas transfer charge if the transfer is made to a QROPS that is an overseas public service pension scheme and the individual making the transfer is an employee of one of the public service employers that participates in the pension scheme at that time.
- New *FA 2004, s 244F(2)* defines an overseas public service pension scheme as a pension scheme that is established by the law or government of the country in which it is established to provide benefits for or in respect of public service carried out by employees of the participating public service employer.
- New *FA 2004, s 244F(3)* provides that an employer will be considered to participate in an overseas public service pension scheme that is a QROPS if it is established to provide benefits [solely] to or in respect of its employees.
- New *FA 2004, s 244G(1)* excludes a transfer from the overseas transfer charge if it is made in respect of a transfer requested before 9 March 2017.
- New *FA 2004, s 244G(2)* provides that an onward transfer is excluded from the overseas transfer charge if; the charge was paid on an original transfer and it has been repaid; the charge was paid on a transfer from another QROPS to the QROPS making the onward transfer, certain conditions set out in subsection (4) are met and it has not been repaid and is not capable of being repaid; the original transfer from a registered pension scheme to a QROPS was made before 9 March 2017; or the original transfer from a registered pension scheme to a QROPS was made on or after 9 March 2017 but was requested before that date.
- New *FA 2004, s 244G(3)* excludes an onward transfer from the overseas transfer charge if the transfer is made out of funds other than an individual's ring-fenced transfer fund.
- New *FA 2004, s 244H* provides a power for HMRC to exclude further transfers from the overseas transfer charge if the transfer is specified in the regulations.
- New *FA 2004, s 244I* sets out that a transfer that would be excluded from the overseas transfer charge will be subject to the charge if the individual doesn't provide all the necessary information to the scheme administrator of the registered pension scheme or QROPS scheme manager of the scheme concerned.

- New *FA 2004, s 244J(1)* sets out that the scheme administrator of the registered pension scheme making a recognised transfer to a QROPS and the individual making the transfer are jointly and severally liable for the overseas transfer charge.
- New *FA 2004, s 244J(2)* sets out that where the transfer to a QROPS is an onward transfer, the scheme manager of the QROPS or former QROPS making the transfer and the individual making the transfer are jointly and severally liable to the overseas transfer charge.
- New *FA 2004, s 244J(3)* to *(5)* provides that the scheme manager of the QROPS or former QROPS that holds the transferred funds and the individual who made the transfer will be jointly and severally liable to the overseas transfer charge where a transfer is initially excluded from the charge because the individual and the QROPS to which they had transferred were both in the same country or both in different EEA states, but the charge arises within five tax years of the transfer because one of the conditions of the exclusion is no longer met.
- New *FA 2004, s 244J(5)* sets out that the scheme manager of a former QROPS is liable to the overseas transfer charge only if the scheme was a QROPS on or after 9 March 2017, it received a recognised transfer from a registered pension scheme or an onward transfer from another QROPS on or after that date.
- New *FA 2004, s 244J(6)* provides that individuals, scheme administrators and scheme managers will be liable to the overseas transfer charge whether or not they are resident or domiciled in the UK.
- New *FA 2004, s 244K(1)* provides that the rate of charge for the overseas transfer charge is 25% of the transferred value.
- New *FA 2004, s 244K(2)* and *(3)* provides that the transferred value of the transfer from a registered pension scheme established in the UK is the amount of the sums and the value of the assets transferred. If the registered pension scheme is established outside the UK then the transferred value subject to the overseas transfer charge is limited to the amount of UK-relieved funds in the scheme.
- New *FA 2004, s 244K(4)* provides that the transferred value subject to the overseas transfer charge on a transfer from a QROPS or former QROPS is the amount of the sums and the value of the assets that can be attributed to the individual's ring-fenced transfer fund subject to subsections (5) to (9).
- New *FA 2004, s 244K(5)* and *(10)* provides that, if a lifetime allowance charge arises on a transfer, the transferred value subject

to the overseas transfer charge is the amount after the deduction of the lifetime allowance charge and that the lifetime allowance charge is to be calculated without reference to the overseas transfer charge.

- New *FA 2004, s 244K(6)* provides that, where the transfer was initially excluded from the overseas transfer charge because the individual and the QROPS to which they had transferred were both in the same country or both in different EEA states, but the charge later arises because the exclusion is no longer met within five tax years beginning with the date of transfer, the overseas transfer charge applies to the funds representing the individual's ring-fenced transfer fund held in the QROPS or former QROPS.
- New *FA 2004, s 244K(7)* provides that, if the scheme administrator or scheme manager pays the overseas transfer charge but does not deduct the amount of the charge from the value of the funds to be transferred, the amount of the charge is grossed up as defined in *Income Tax Act 2007, s 998*, in effect added to the value to be transferred and itself subject to the overseas transfer charge.
- New *FA 2004, s 244K(8)* sets out that, if the scheme administrator or scheme manager deducts the amount of the overseas transfer charge from the value to be transferred, the transferred value is the amount given by subsection (2) to (6) before any deduction of the overseas transfer charge.
- New *FA 2004, s 244K(9)* sets out that, if the individual pays the overseas transfer charge, the transferred value is the amount given by subsections (2) to (6) without any deduction for the charge.
- New *FA 2004, s 244L(1)* confirms that the charge referred to in this section is the overseas transfer charge for which the scheme manager of a QROPS or former QROPS is liable.
- New *FA 2004, s 244L(2)* provides a power for HMRC to set out how scheme managers of QROPS and former QROPS account for the overseas transfer charge. HMRC can make provision for or in connection with the payment date when the charge is due, when interest arises on the charge paid after the due date, how the scheme manager notifies HMRC of errors in the information provided, and the making of assessments, repayments and adjustments.
- New *FA 2004, s 244M* sets out the circumstances in which a repayment of the overseas transfer charge will arise.
- New *FA 2004, s 244M(1)* provides that there can be a repayment of the overseas transfer charge only if the overseas transfer charge arose on a transfer when it was made and, in the relevant period

beginning with the original transfer, circumstances arise that would have led to the transfer being excluded from the overseas transfer charge.

- New *FA 2004, s 244M(2)* and *(3)* provides that the overseas transfer charge can be repaid only to the extent that it has not been repaid already, but any penalties or interest that were payable in relation to the overseas transfer charge are not repayable.
- New *FA 2004, s 244M(4)* provides that a repayment of the overseas transfer charge depends on the scheme administrator or scheme manager claiming the repayment and meeting all of the requirements to provide information to HMRC about the repayment.
- New *FA 2004, s 244M(5)* provides that a repayment of the overseas transfer charge is not a relievable pension contribution, so the scheme administrator (or the scheme manager) cannot claim UK tax relief on it.
- New *FA 2004, s 244M(6)* provides that, if the amount repaid is then transferred to a QROPS, that amount should not be tested against the lifetime allowance on the basis of a transfer to a QROPS.
- New *FA 2004, s 244M(7)* provides that, in the circumstances where an individual can make a claim (on the basis that they paid the tax out of funds that did not come directly from the pension scheme), they must do so within a year of the end of the relevant period.
- New *FA 2004, s 244N* sets out the circumstances in which a scheme administrator or a scheme manager that is liable to the overseas transfer charge may seek to be discharged from that liability.
- New *FA 2004, s 244N(1)* and *(2)* provides that the scheme administrator of a registered pension scheme or the scheme manager of a QROPS liable to the overseas transfer charge may apply to HMRC for the discharge of their liability to the charge.
- New *FA 2004, s 244N(3)* sets out the ground as the scheme administrator or scheme manager reasonably believed that there was no liability to the overseas transfer charge on a transfer and it would not be just and reasonable for that scheme administrator or scheme manager to be liable to the charge on the transfer.
- New *FA 2004, s 244N(4)* and *(5)* provides that HMRC must decide whether to discharge the liability and tell the scheme administrator or scheme manager the decision.

- New *FA 2004, s 244N(6)* provides that a discharge under this section does not affect the liability of anyone else who is liable to the overseas transfer charge on the transfer concerned.
- New *FA 2004, s 244N(7)* provides a power for HMRC to provide further details on the discharge of the liability of the scheme administrator or scheme manager.

(m) *FA 2017, Sch 4, Pt 2, para 12* provides for the recognised transfer provisions in Pt 4 of FA 2004 to be amended.

(n) *FA 2017, Sch 4, Pt 2, para 13* amends *FA 2004, s 169* by adding various subsections. These include: (1) a new *FA 2004, s 169(2)(ba)* which provides for a new declaration and undertaking that scheme managers must make for their scheme to be a QROPS. It requires scheme managers of recognised overseas pension schemes to confirm that they understand their potential liability to the overseas transfer charge and is willing to operate the charge, including paying the tax; (2) a new *FA 2004, s 169(2A)* which provides a power for HMRC to make regulations to require information or evidence in a particular form in relation to the notification of recognised overseas pension schemes; and (3) a new *FA 2004, s 169(4ZA)* which provides a power for HMRC to make regulations to require members or former members of QROPS or former QROPS to provide information to the scheme manager of a QROPS or former QROPS;

(o) *FA 2017, Sch 4, Pt 2, para 14* adds a new *FA 2004, Ch 5A*. This adds new *FA 2004, ss 242A* and *242B* as follows:

- *FA 2004, s 242A* defines non-UK-registered pension scheme established in a country or territory outside the UK.
- *FA 2004, s 242B* defines UK-relieved funds as funds that have had UK tax relief that are held in a non-UK-registered scheme.
- *FA 2004, s 242B(1)* sets out that UK-relieved funds are sums or assets that represent accrued rights that at any time were held under a registered pension scheme established in the UK, at any time formed the UK tax-relieved fund under a relevant non-UK scheme or represent accrued rights when the individual member accrued rights under the scheme and is taken to have benefited from UK tax relief.

(p) *FA 2017, Sch 4, Pt 2, para 15* adds a new *FA 2004, s 254(6)(ba)* which includes repayments to scheme administrators in the list of regulations that HMRC may make in relation to scheme administrators accounting for tax to HMRC.

(q) *FA 2017, Sch 4, Pt 2, para 16* adds a new *FA 2004, s 255(1)(da)* which provides the power for HMRC to make regulations in connection with the liability of scheme administrators of registered pension schemes and scheme managers of QROPS or former QROPS to assessments to the overseas transfer charge.

(r) *FA 2017, Sch 4, Pt 2, para 19* adds a new *Taxes Management Act 1970, s 9(1A)(aa)* which removes a scheme manager of a QROPS or former QROPS from the scope of self-assessment [which they would otherwise be within as a result of their liability to the overseas transfer charge].

(s) *FA 2017, Sch 4, Pt 2, para 20* adds a new paragraph 3A to the Table in *FA 2009, Sch 56* in relation to the payment of penalties for failure to make payments on time.

(t) *FA 2017, Sch 4, Pt 2, para 21* amends the *Registered Pension Schemes (Accounting and Assessment) Regulations 2005 (SI 2005/3454)* in relation to overseas transfer charges and claims for repayments of overseas transfer charges.

(u) *FA 2017, Sch 4, Pt 2, para 22* amends the *Pension Schemes (Information Requirements for Qualifying Overseas Pension Schemes, Qualifying Recognised Overseas Pension Schemes and Corresponding Relief) Regulations 2006 (SI 2006/208)* (‘*Information Regulations*’) as follows:

- Includes a definition of ‘onward transfer’ in relation to QROPS.
- Includes a reference to ring-fenced transfer funds in addition to a relevant transfer fund.
- Adds a new *Information Regulations, reg 3(2)(da)* which sets out that a scheme manager of a QROPS or former QROPS, when making a transfer to another QROPS, must provide to HMRC information on whether the transfer is subject to the overseas transfer charge and, if so, the details of the transferred value and the amount of the charge deducted from the payment by the scheme manager and if not the reasons why not. The scheme manager must also provide information to HMRC on the remaining value of the individual’s relevant transfer funds and ring-fenced transfer funds immediately after the payment.
- Adds new *Information Regulations, reg 3(2A)–(2C)*.
- New *Information Regulations, reg 3(2A)* provides that *Information Regulations, reg 3(2B)* and *(2C)* applies if a recognised transfer is made to a QROPS or an onward transfer is made by a QROPS or former QROPS.
- New *Information Regulations, reg 3(2B)* provides that if, within five tax years beginning with the date of the original transfer of the funds from a registered pension to a QROPS, the scheme manager of the QROPS or former QROPS is notified that there is a change

in circumstances such that the exclusion no longer applies, that scheme manager must tell HMRC within 90 days of being notified of the change; details of the change, the transferred value of the transfer, the amount of overseas transfer charge that now arises and confirmation of whether the scheme manager intends to account for the charge and details of the funds remaining in the individual's ring-fenced transfer fund or relevant transfer fund immediately after the change.

- New *Information Regulations, reg 3(2C)* provides that the scheme manager of a QROPS or former QROPS must notify HMRC where, within five tax years beginning with the date of the original transfer of the funds from a registered pension scheme to a QROPS, they become aware that an individual's principal residential address has changed such that the exclusion which applied to the transfer charge on the individual and the QROPS to which they had transferred were both in the same country or both in different EEA states no longer applies.
- Adds a new *Information Regulations, reg 3(3A)* to include a reference to the expiry after ten years of the obligation by a scheme manager to provide information to HMRC in relation to ring-fenced funds.
- Includes various references in the *Information Regulations* to ring-fenced transfer funds and the provision of information to HMRC.
- Adds new *Information Regulations, regs 3AE–3AL.*
- New *Information Regulations, reg 3AE* sets out the information and details the time scales which applies to the provision of such information that an individual must provide to a QROPS scheme manager when they want to transfer their funds to another QROPS. This is similar information to that which the individual is required to provide to the scheme administrator of a registered pension scheme when they want to transfer from that scheme to a QROPS.
- New *Information Regulations, reg 3AF* sets out the information and details the time scales which apply where the scheme manager of the QROPS or former QROPS must provide to the individual member where an onward transfer gives rise to the overseas transfer charge.
- New *Information Regulations, reg 3AG* sets out how the scheme manager of the QROPS or former QROPS, who is liable to an overseas transfer charge, accounts for the tax to HMRC.
- New *Information Regulations, reg 3AH* provides that HMRC will raise a tax assessment on the scheme manager for any overseas

transfer charge that is not paid by the due date. The charge is payable within 30 days of the issue of the notice of assessment.

- New *Information Regulations, reg 3AI* sets out the action that HMRC may take if the correct overseas transfer charge has not been paid on or before it becomes due.
- New *Information Regulations, reg 3AJ* sets out that interest applies to overdue overseas transfer charges.
- New *Information Regulations, reg 3AK* sets out how adjustments, repayments and interest on overpaid charges are calculated.
- New *Information Regulations, reg 3AL* sets out how claims for repayments of charges on subsequent excluding events are calculated.

(v) *FA 2017, Sch 4, Pt 2, para 23* amends the *Registered Pension Schemes (Transfers of Sums and Assets) Regulations 2006 (SI 2006/499)* in order to provide that the circumstances in which the scheme pension may be reduced includes, in particular, payment of the overseas transfer charge.

(w) *FA 2017, Sch 4, Pt 2, para 24* amends the *Information Regulations* as follows:

- to set out the additional information in relation to the overseas transfer charge that the scheme administrator of a registered pension scheme must provide to HMRC after making a transfer to a QROPS;
- to insert under reportable event 9 (transfers to QROPS) that the scheme administrator must provide details of whether or not the transfer gave rise to the overseas transfer charge and, if so, details of the charge and, if not, the reason for exclusion from the charge;
- to bring forward the deadline for the scheme administrator to provide information to HMRC in relation to a transfer to a QROPS where the scheme administrator applies for a repayment of the overseas transfer charge before the deadline would have occurred otherwise; and
- to set out the additional information in relation to the overseas transfer charge that the scheme administrator must obtain from the individual who requests a transfer to a QROPS.
- New *Information Regulations, reg 11BB* is added and provides that, following a recognised transfer that is excluded from the overseas transfer charge because the individual and the QROPS to which they transferred are in the same country or in different EEA states, the individual member must, within 60 days of the change,

tell the scheme administrator that made the transfer if, within five tax years of that transfer, their country of residence changes.

- New *Information Regulations, reg 12A* is added and provides that, if an overseas transfer charge arises on a transfer from a registered pension scheme to a QROPS, the scheme administrator must, within 90 days, provide the individual with details of the transfer and the overseas transfer charge, the extent to which the scheme administrator has paid the tax or intends to do so and, if paid, the date the charge was paid.
- New *Information Regulations, reg 14ZCA* is added and sets out the information that a scheme administrator must provide to a scheme manager of a QROPS when making a recognised transfer to that QROPS, together with the specified time scale.

(x) *FA 2017, Sch 6* as introduced by *FA 2017, s 15* makes amendments to *ITEPA 2003, Pt 7A* (employment income provided through third parties) as follows:

- It amends *ITEPA 2003, s 554A(2)* to make it clear that a relevant step still occurs where the underlying transaction is void or in breach of trust.
- It inserts new *ITEPA 2003, s 554C(1)(aa)* and *(ab)* which make it clear that *ITEPA 2003,* s 554C applies where a third party receives a right to a payment, or an asset, and a related payment, or asset transfer, has been made to the relevant person. It also provides that a *Pt 7A* charge will now arise where a loan, or right to payment, is written off, or released by a third party.
- It inserts new *ITEPA 2003, s 554C(3A)–(3C)* which defines 'loan' and makes it clear that a *Pt 7A* charge arises where a borrower acquires the right to the sum or asset they have borrowed.
- *FA 2017, Sch 6, para 4* amends *ITEPA 2003, s 554A(4)* so that the release or write-off of a loan by a third party does not give rise to a *Pt 7A* charge where it occurs, on or after the death of the employee.
- *FA 2017, Sch 6, para 5* inserts a new *ITEPA 2003, s 554OA* which provides that a charge does not apply where an employment related loan of £10,000 or less is transferred to a new employer, unless the transfer is connected to a tax avoidance arrangement.
- *FA 2017, Sch 6, para 8* inserts a new *ITEPA 2003, s 554RA* which ensures repayments of loans are not relevant steps.
- *FA 2017, Sch 6, para 9* inserts a new *ITEPA 2003, s 554XA* which refers to exclusions in relation to payments to HMRC in respect of a tax liability.

- *FA 2017, Sch 6, para 10* replaces the existing *ITEPA 2003, s 554Z5* with a new *ITEPA 2003, s 554Z5*. This ensures that where there are two income tax charges that relate to the same underlying money, or asset, the later charge is reduced to nil where the earlier charge has been paid in full.
- *FA 2017, Sch 6, para 11* inserts new *ITEPA 2003, ss 554Z11B–554Z11G*. New *ITEPA 2003, ss 554Z11B–554Z11D* provide relief from double taxation where there is more than one unpaid liability relating to the same underlying money or asset. New *ITEPA 2003, ss 554Z11E* and *554Z11F* relate to provisional payments of tax. New *ITEPA 2003, ss 554Z11G* contains additional provisions relating to the introduction of new *ITEPA 2003, s 554Z11C*.
- *FA 2017, Sch 6, paras 13–16* provide for the changes to *ITEPA 2003, Pt 7A* to apply from 6 April 2017, or such other date as specified.

The following clauses of the *Finance (No 2) Bill 2017* relate to pensions (previously omitted from the *Finance Act 2017* in view of the general election being called on 8 June 2017):

(1) *Clause 3: Pensions Advice*. This clause adds a new *ITEPA 2003, s 308C*. This clause introduces a new income tax exemption to cover the first £500 worth of pensions advice provided to an employee (including former and prospective employees) in a tax year. It will allow advice not only on pensions, but also on the general financial and tax issues relating to pensions, allowing individuals to make more informed decisions about saving for their retirement. The changes replace existing provisions which limited the exemption solely to pensions advice and was capped at £150 per employee per year.

(2) *Clause 7: Money purchase annual allowance*. This clause amends *FA 2004, Pt 4*. It will reduce the money purchase annual allowance from £10,000 to £4,000 with effect from 6 April 2017. This refers to individuals who flexibly access or have already flexibly accessed registered pension scheme savings.

The *Pension Schemes Act 2017* (*PSA 2017*) received Royal Assent with effect from 27 April 2017. The *PSA 2017* provides for the following:

(a) It provides that an authorisation and supervision regime for Master Trusts will be introduced, so that Master Trusts will have to demonstrate to the Pensions Regulator that they meet certain key criteria on establishment and continue to do so; existing Master Trusts will be brought into the regime and required to meet the new criteria, and trustees will be required to protect members in the event of a winding-up or closure of a Master Trust.

(b) *PSA 2017, s 1* defines what is a 'Master Trust'.

(c) *PSA 2017, s 2* refers to relevant public service pension scheme.

(d) *PSA 2017, s 3* refers to a prohibition on operating a Master Trust without being authorised.

(e) *PSA 2017, s 4* refers to how trustee may apply to the Pensions Regulator to have the Master Trust authorised.

(f) *PSA 2017, s 5* refers to the Pensions Regulator's power to make a decision on whether such a Master Trust meets the authorisation criteria.

(g) *PSA 2017, s 6* gives the trustee the power to appeal to a Tribunal against any decision made by the Pensions Regulator to refuse authorisation of a Master Trust.

(h) *PSA 2017, s 7* refers to the authorisation criteria. This includes the Pensions Regulator determining if the persons who wish to operate the Master Trusts are fit and proper persons.

(i) *PSA 2017, ss 8, 9, 10, 11* and *12* refer to the Pensions Regulator's power to determine if the Master Trust meets the financial sustainability requirements., the systems and processes requirements and continuity strategy requirements.

(j) *PSA 2017, s 13* requires the Pensions Regulator to maintain and publish a list of authorised Master Trusts schemes and provide ongoing supervision of such Master Trusts.

(k) *PSA 2017, s 14* requires trustees of Master Trusts to submit annual accounts of the scheme to the Pensions Regulator.

(l) *PSA 2017, s 15* gives the Pensions Regulator the power to require the trustees to submit supervisory returns.

(m) *PSA 2017, s 16* requires the trustee to notify the Pensions Regulator of any significant events which affect the Master Trust.

(n) *PSA 2017, ss 17* and *18* give the Pensions Regulator the power to issue a fixed penalty notice and escalating notices for failure to comply with a request for information.

(o) *PSA 2017, s 19* gives the power for the Pensions Regulator to withdraw authorisation of a Master Trust.

(p) *PSA 2017, ss 20* and *21* refer to triggering events and duties of trustees.

(q) *PSA 2017, s 21* refers to notification requirements of specified events.

(r) *PSA 2017, s 23* refers to continuity options where an event is triggered.

(s) *PSA 2017, s 24* refers to continuity option 1 being transfer out and winding-up.

(t) *PSA 2017, s 25* refers to continuity option 2 resolving triggering event.

(u) *PSA 2017, ss 26* and *27* refer to the approval of an implementation strategy and the content of an implementation strategy.

(v) *PSA 2017, s 28* refers to the duty to pursue a continuity option.

(w) *PSA 2017, s 29* refers to a prohibition on winding-up except with continuity option 1.

(x) *PSA 2017, s 30* refers to periodic reporting requirements.

(y) *PSA 2017, s 31* gives the Pensions Regulator the power to make a pause order.

(z) *PSA 2017, s 32* refers to a prohibition on new employers during a triggering event period.

(aa) *PSA 2017, s 33* refers to a prohibition on increasing charges during a triggering event period.

(bb) *PSA 2017, ss 34* and *35* refer to the circumstances when it becomes clear that authorisation should or should not be withdrawn.

(cc) *PSA 2017, s 36* refers to fraud compensation.

(dd) *PSA 2017, ss 37* and *38* refer to transitional provisions and minor amendments.

(ee) *PSA 2017, ss 39* and *40* refer to 'interpretation' and the making of regulations under the Act.

(ff) *PSA 2017, Pt 2* refers to administration charges.

Regulations. A considerable number of regulations were made in order to accommodate the changes to practice. The main ones are listed below, together with brief descriptions of their effect:

- The *Pension Protection Fund and Occupational Pension Schemes (Levy Ceiling) Order 2015 (SI 2015/66)* came into force on 14 March 2015 in relation to *Article 2*, on 31 March 2015 in relation to *Article 3* and on 1 April 2015 in relation to *Article 4*. The Order specifies the levy ceiling for use in relation to the PPF in the year commencing 1 April 2015 and revokes *SI 2014/10, Articles 2* and *3*. It also amends the calculation of the PIA, the rules which apply to block transfers and a refund of excess contributions lump sum and prevents an individual giving a '*scheme pays notice*' after that individual has taken all their pension benefits.

- The *Social Security (Miscellaneous Amendments) Regulations 2015 (SI 2015/67)* came into force on 23 February 2015 and amended the *State Pension Credit Regulations 2002 (SI 2002/1792)* regarding the State Pension Credit.

- The *Finance Act 2004 (Registered Pension Schemes and Annual Allowance Charge) (Amendment) Order 2015 (SI 2015/80)* came into force on 28 January 2015 and made amendments to provisions about the AA charge in *FA 2004, Pt 4*. *Article 11* amended *FA 2004, s 228A*, where a first pension input period (PIP) ends in the tax years 2011/12, 2012/13 or 2013/14. Any unused AA is to be available to be carried forward for those tax years. There are revisions to the calculation of the pension input amount, block transfers, refunds of an excess contributions lump sum and prevention of an individual giving a '*scheme pays notice*' after that individual has taken all their pension benefits.

- The *Occupational Pension Schemes (Levies) (Amendment) Regulations 2015 (SI 2015/84)* came into force on 1 April 2015 in relation to *Regulations 1–3*, on 1 April 2016 in relation to *Regulation 4*, and on 1 April 2017 in relation to *Regulation 5*. The Regulations amend the *Occupational Pension Schemes (Levies) Regulations 2005 (SI 2005/842)* regarding the amount of the administration levy for the years ending 31 March 2016, 31 March 2017, 31 March 2018 and for subsequent years.

- The *Occupational Pension Schemes (Power to Amend Schemes to Reflect Abolition of Contracting-out) Regulations 2015 (SI 2015/118)* came into force on 5 April 2015. They set out checks on employers' powers to amend their salary-related pension scheme rules in order to offset the loss of the employer's NIC rebate once contracting-out ends in April 2016. They also provide for certification of any rule changes by an actuary, and impose restrictions to ensure that amendments involving reductions in scheme benefits or increases in members' pension contributions do not go beyond specified limits.

- The *Pensions Act 2014 (Commencement No 4) Order 2015 (SI 2015/134)* brought into force on 5 February 2015 the provisions of *PA 2014*. It includes provisions relating to the new SP for people reaching pensionable age on or after 6 April 2016 and to occupational pension schemes on short service benefits and on the abolition of contracting-out for salary-related schemes.

- The *State Pension Regulations 2015 (SI 2015/173)* came into force on 6 April 2015. They set out some of the detailed rules relating to the new single-tier state pension, and state that the minimum number of qualifying years for the purposes of entitlement to the single tier state pension at the reduced and transitional rates is 10. *Regulation 15* and the *Sch* contain provisions regarding pension sharing on divorce or dissolution of a civil partnership and amend the *Sharing of State Scheme Rights (Provision of Information and Valuation) (No 2) Regulations 2000 (SI 2000/2914)* and the *Pensions on Divorce (Pension Sharing) (Scotland) Regulations 2000 (SI 2000/1051)*.

11.3 *Pensions*

- The *Social Security Pensions (Flat Rate Accrual Amount) Order 2015 (SI 2015/185)* came into force on 6 April 2015 following a review under the *Social Security Administration Act 1992 (SSAA 1992), s 148AA(1)* of the general level of earnings to determine whether that level has increased in the year to 30 September 2014. The review shows the general level of earnings has increased by 1.5% during that period and so the Order directs that the flat rate accrual amount for the tax year 2015/16 shall be £93.60.

- The *Social Security Pensions (Low Threshold) Order 2015 (SI 2015/186)* came into force on 6 April 2015, following a review under the *SSAA 1992, s 148A,* of the general level of earnings to determine whether the amount of the low earnings threshold should be increased for future tax years. The review shows the general level of earnings during the year to 30 September 2014 has increased by 1.5% and so the Order directs that the low earnings threshold for the tax years following 2014/15 shall be £15,300.

- The *Social Security Revaluation of Earnings Factors Order 2015 (SI 2015/187)* came into force on 6 April 2015 following a review under the *SSAA 1992, s 148, of* the earnings factors relevant to the calculation of the additional pension in the rate of any long-term benefit, or of any graduated minimum pension, or to any other calculation required under *Pt 3* of the *Pension Schemes Act 1993*. The review shows the relevant earnings factors have increased by 1.5% and so the Order directs earnings factors for 2014/15 shall be increased by 1.5%.

- The *Pensions Act 2004 (Code of Practice) (Governance and Administration of Public Service Pension Schemes) Appointed Day Order 2015 (SI 2015/456)* came into force on 1 April 2015 and brought into force the Pension Regulator's *Code of Practice No 14: Governance and administration of public service pension schemes.*

- The *Automatic Enrolment (Earnings Trigger and Qualifying Earnings Band) Order 2015 (SI 2015/468)* came into force on 6 April 2015 and maintains alignment of the automatic enrolment earnings trigger for 2015/16 with the PAYE income tax personal allowance threshold and continues to align the qualifying earnings band for contributions in 2015/16 with the NICs lower earnings limit (LEL) and the upper earnings limit (UEL). The Order revokes the *Automatic Enrolment (Earnings Trigger and Qualifying Earnings Band) Order 2014 (SI 2014/623), Article 3.*

- The *Guaranteed Minimum Pensions Increase Order 2015 (SI 2015/470)* came into force on 6 April 2015 following the review of the general level of prices laid down in the *Pension Schemes Act 1993* (*PSA 1993*), *s 109(1)*. The percentage by which that part of any guaranteed minimum pension (GMP) attributable to earnings factors for the tax years 1988/89 to 1996/97 and payable by contracted-out DB occupational pension schemes is to be increased by 1.2% from 6 April 2015.

- The *Social Security (Miscellaneous Amendments No 2) Regulations 2015 (SI 2015/478)* came into force on 6 April 2015. They amend the *Social Security (Contributions) Regulations 2001 (SI 2001/1004)* and take account of a number of changes introduced in *FA 2014* and *NICA 2015* concerning inclusion of class 2 NIC in self-assessment; replacement of the term 'general earnings' with 'earnings' for class 1 NIC purposes; disregard NIC for payments made under the armed forces early departure payment scheme; align NIC rules with the tax rules on apportionment of employment-related securities income received by internationally-mobile employees; and simplify reporting of NIC agreements and elections in relation to employer's NIC on employment-related securities.

- The *Occupational and Personal Pension Schemes (Disclosure of Information) (Amendment) Regulations 2015* (*SI 2015/482)* came into force on 6 April 2015 and amend the *Occupational and Personal Pension Schemes (Disclosure of Information) Regulations 2013 (SI 2013/2734)*. They are consequential to the provisions of *TOPA 2014* and to *PSA 2015*. They make provision concerning the information that certain pension schemes must give a person with flexible benefits and when that information must be given.

- The *Financial Services and Markets Act 2000 (Regulated Activities) (Amendment) (Pension Guidance Exclusions) Order 2015* (*SI 2015/489*) came into force on 26 March 2015 and provide for exclusions from regulated activities to ensure that those persons providing pensions guidance pursuant to arrangements with HM Treasury are not carrying on a regulated activity.

- The *Occupational Pension Schemes (Consequential and Miscellaneous Amendments) Regulations 2015* (*SI 2015/493*) came into force on 6 April 2015. *Regulation 2* amends the *Occupational Pension Schemes (Preservation of Benefit) Regulations 1991 (SI 1991/167)* to ensure an occupational pension scheme can provide a short service benefit using one of the new types of authorised payment – an uncrystallised funds pension lump sum (UFPLS). *Regulation 3* amends the *Occupational Pension Schemes (Contracting-out) Regulations 1996 (SI 1996/1172)* to ensure that the prohibition on commutation of a pension under an occupational pension scheme does not apply to payment of an uncrystallised pension lump sum. *Regulation 5* amends the *Occupational Pension Schemes (Modification of Schemes) Regulations 2006 (SI 2006/759)* providing a power for trustees to modify their scheme for the purpose of offering the new types of authorised payments and also providing a power for trustees to ensure they are not required to make a transfer payment under the scheme rules if they are unable to carry out a check required by *PSA*

2015, s 48, or the check does not confirm that the person seeking the transfer has received appropriate independent advice.

- The *Occupational and Personal Pension Schemes (Transfer Values) (Amendment and Revocation) Regulations 2015* (*SI 2015/498*) came into force on 6 April 2015 save for *Regulation 14* which comes into force on 1 April 2017. The Regulations amend the *Occupational Pension Schemes (Transfer Values) Regulations 1996 (SI 1996/1847)* and revoke the *Transfer Values (Disapplication) Regulations 2010 (SI 2010/6)* and are consequential to the provisions of *PSA 2015* and *FA 2015, Sch 4*, which provides greater flexibility to pension scheme members when accessing and transferring pension rights.
- The *Occupational and Personal Pension Schemes (Automatic Enrolment) (Amendment) Regulations 2015* (*SI 2015/501*) came into force on 1 April 2015 and amend the *Occupational and Personal Pension Schemes (Automatic Enrolment) Regulations 2010 (SI 2010/772)* by reducing the information requirements on employers, introducing certain circumstances where the employer duty is turned into a discretion and prescribing alternative quality requirements for DB schemes.
- The *Social Security (Contributions) (Amendment) Regulations 2015 (SI 2015/543)* came into force on 6 April 2015 and amend the *Social Security (Contributions) Regulations 2001 (SI 2001/1004)* so that an employer will not be liable to pay earnings-related NICs in respect of payments for, or re-imbursements of, the cost of advice about the conversion or transfer of a pension scheme which they are required to provide under *PSA 2015*.
- The *Financial Services and Markets Act 2000 (Banking Reform) (Pensions) Regulations 2015 (SI 2015/547)* came into force on 5 March 2015 and introduce requirements in relation to the pension liabilities of ring-fenced bodies such as banks to ensure that they do not participate in multi-employer pension schemes or where they do participate for the trustees or managers to modify the scheme so that the ring-fenced body may meet the requirements.
- The *Social Security (Contributions) (Limits and Thresholds) (Amendment) Regulations 2015* (*SI 2015/577*) came into force on 6 April 2015 and amend the *Social Security (Contributions) Regulations 2001 (SI 2001/1004)* to specify the levels of the LEL and UEL for class 1 contributions and the primary and secondary thresholds for primary and secondary class 1 contributions for the tax year commencing 6 April 2015. They also introduce an upper secondary threshold for the age-related secondary percentage for secondary class 1 contributions which applies in relation to primary contributors who are under the age of 21. The amendments also provide for equivalents of the UEL, primary and secondary thresholds, where the earnings period is a month or a year.

- The *Social Security (Contributions) (Re-rating and National Insurance Fund Payments) Order 2015 (SI 2015/588)* came into force on 6 April 2015 and amends the *Social Security Contributions and Benefits Act 1992* (*SSCBA 1992*), *ss 13, 15* and *18* by specifying the rates and relevant earnings limits for class 3 and 4 NICs for 2015/16 tax year.

- The *Registered Pension Schemes (Provision of Information) (Amendment) Regulations 2015* (*SI 2015/606*) came into force on 6 April 2015. They amend the *Registered Pension Schemes (Provision of Information) Regulations 2006 (SI 2006/567)* by specifying the information that scheme administrators must provide to the receiving scheme administrator when transferring pension funds which can be paid tax-free; and to HMRC when schemes change their structure, range or number of members, in the interests of preventing scheme liberation. Individuals do not have to provide information to schemes before they become subject to the MPAA.

- The *Registered Pension Schemes (Transfer of Sums and Assets) (Amendment No 2) Regulations 2015 (SI 2015/633)* amended the *Registered Pension Schemes (Transfer of Sums and Assets) Regulations 2006 (SI 2006/499)* so that they also apply to new types of pension annuities.

- The *Registered Pension Schemes (Splitting of Schemes) (Amendment) Regulations 2015 (SI 2015/667). Regulation 3* amends the list in *Pt 1* of *Sch 3* to *FA 2004* to add three new public service pension schemes, *Regulations 4* and *5* amend the responsibilities and liabilities that are assumed by sub-scheme administrators. The Regulations came into force on 6 April 2015.

- The *Pension Increase (Review) Order 2015* (*SI 2015/671*) came into force on 6 April 2015. The review carried out by HM Treasury under the *Social Security Pensions Act 1975* (*SSPA 1975*), *s 59* resulted in an increase of 1.2% for pensions which began before 7 April 2014 and an increase as set out in Table 1 for pensions which began on or after 7 April 2014.

- The *Overseas Pension Schemes (Miscellaneous Amendments) Regulations 2015 (SI 2015/673)* came into force on 6 April 2015 and amend the *Pension Schemes (Categories of Country and Requirements for Overseas Pension Schemes and Recognised Overseas Pension Schemes) Regulations 2006 (SI 2006/206)* to align the reporting requirements for OPS more closely with those for UK-registered pension schemes. They make amendments to the *Pension Schemes (Categories of Country and Requirements for Overseas Pension Schemes and Recognised Overseas Pension Schemes) Regulations 2006 (SI 2006/206)* and the *Pension Schemes (Information Requirements – Qualifying Overseas Pension Schemes, Qualifying Recognised Overseas Pension Schemes and*

Corresponding Relief) Regulations 2006 (SI 2006/208) Regulations 2 and *3* amend the overseas pension scheme regulations by adding a condition that must be met by a scheme before it becomes a recognised overseas pension scheme (ROPS). Benefits must be payable to the member no earlier than if *pension rule 1* in *FA 2004, s 165*, applied (ie no earlier than the age of 55). *Regulations 4* and *5* amend the information regulations so that QROPS, former QROPS or their members must provide information where a member obtains access to their pension rights by means of the provision for flexible access introduced by *TOPA 2014*.

A QROPS or former QROPS must also provide specified information to the member and to a QROPS in relation to specified payments to or in respect of the member from the scheme. This is required for the purposes of determining the AA charge and any member payment charges in relation to the individual where the individual flexibly accesses their pension or where there are payments of funds in connection with the member. Information must be provided within 91 days of the trigger events mentioned in the new provisions. The new information requirements are contained in new *Regulations 3AA* to *3AD*.

- The *Pensions Act 2011 (Commencement No 6) Order 2015* (*SI 2015/676*) came into force on 6 April 2015 and it brings into force *Pension Schemes Act 2011* (*PSA 2011*), *s 7*, to ensure that automatic re-enrolment will not happen more frequently than once in every period of two years and nine months.
- The *Financial Services and Markets Act 2000 (Regulated Activities) (Amendment) (No 2) Order 2015* (*SI 2015/731*) came into force on 6 April 2015 and amends the *Financial Services and Markets Act 2000 (Regulated Activities) Order 2001 (SI 2001/544)* to provide that advising on the conversion or transfer of pension benefits which are safeguarded benefits is a regulated activity for the purposes of *FSMA 2000*.
- The *Financial Services and Markets Act 2000 (Regulated Activities) (Transitional Provision) Order 2015* (*SI 2015/732*) came into force on 6 April 2015 and makes transitional arrangements for the new activity of advising on conversion or transfer of pension benefits provided for in the *Financial Services and Markets Act 2000 (Regulated Activities) (Amendment) (No 2) Order 2015 (SI 2015/731)*.
- The *Pension Schemes Act 2015 (Transitional Provisions and Appropriate Independent Advice) Regulations 2015 (SI 2015/742)* came into force on 6 April 2015 and make provision in relation to the requirement in *PSA 2015, s 48*, that trustees or managers of a pension scheme check that appropriate independent advice has been received by a member or survivor before the trustees or managers can carry out the transactions specified. They also make provision under *PSA 2015, s 49* specifying

circumstances in which an employer must pay for the provision of appropriate independent advice to a member or survivor when this is required under *PSA 2015, s 48*.

- The *Occupational Pension Schemes (Charges and Governance) Regulations 2015 (SI 2015/879)* came into force on 6 April 2015, save for *Regulations 11* and *23* which come into force on 6 April 2016. The Regulations amend the *Occupational Pension Schemes (Scheme Administration) Regulations 1996 (SI 1996/1715)*, the *Stakeholder Pension Schemes Regulations 2000 (SI 2000/1403)*, the *Register of Occupational and Personal Pension Schemes Regulations 2005 (SI 2005/597)*, the *Occupational Pension Schemes (Investment) Regulations 2005 (SI 2005/3378)*, the *Occupational and Personal Pension Schemes (Consultation by Employers and Miscellaneous Amendment) Regulations 2006 (SI 2006/349)* and the *Occupational Pension Schemes (Modification of Schemes) Regulations 2006 (SI 2006/759)*. They impose obligations on trustees and managers of certain occupational pension schemes in relation to charges imposed by and governance of those schemes.

- The *Occupational Pension Schemes (Charges and Governance) (Amendment) Regulations 2015 (SI 2015/889)* came into force on 6 April 2015. They amend the *Occupational Pension Schemes (Charges and Governance) Regulations 2015 (SI 2015/879)* to correct an error so that an arrangement which only provides benefits attributable to additional voluntary contributions (AVCs) will not be a default arrangement under the definition in the *Occupational Pension Schemes (Charges and Governance) Regulations 2015 (SI 2015/879)*.

- The *Superannuation (Admission to Schedule 1 to the Superannuation Act 1972) Order 2015 (SI 2015/919)* came into force on 16 April 2015 and adds further employments to, and removes from, the list of employments and offices in *Superannuation Act 1972 (SA 1972), Sch 1*. It also corrects an error made by the *Superannuation (Admission to Schedule 1 to the Superannuation Act 1972) Order 2003 (SI 2003/1073)*.

- The *Registered Pension Schemes (Provision of Information) (Amendment No 2) Regulations 2015 (SI 2015/1455)* amend the *Registered Pension Schemes (Provision of Information) Regulations 2006 (SI 2006/567)* and require scheme administrators to tell beneficiaries where the payment of an annuity is subject to the LA charge. They will also require that when beneficiaries annuities are transferred between insurance companies then the transferring insurance company must provide certain information to the receiving insurance company so that the correct tax treatment can be applied following the transfer. The Regulations have effect from 6 April 2015.

11.3 *Pensions*

- The *Registered Pension Schemes (Audited Accounts) (Specified Persons) (Amendment) Regulations 2015 (SI 2015/1518)* concern the requirements around who can audit accounts under the *Registered Pension Schemes (Audited Accounts) (Specified Persons) Regulations 2005 (SI 2005/3456)*. The changes to the 2005 Regulations are intended to mirror those to various Regulations which were amended from April 2014 by *Reg 2* of the *Occupational Pension Schemes (Miscellaneous Amendments) Regulations 2014 (SI 2014/540)*.

- The *Pensions Act 2014 (Abolition of Contracting-out for Salary Related Pension Schemes) (Consequential Amendments and Savings) Order 2016 (SI 2016/200), Parts 1* and *2* came into force on 6 April 2016, *Part 3* comes into force on 6 April 2017, *Part 4* comes into force on 6 April 2019 and *Part 5* comes into force on 6 April 2021. As a result of the introduction of the new flat-rate SP and the ending of contracting-out from 6 April 2016, this Order makes consequential amendments to the *Occupational Pension Schemes (Contracting-out) Regulations 1996 (SI 1996/1172)*, the *Occupational Pension Schemes (Preservation of Benefit) Regulations 1991 (SI 1991/167)*, the *Contracting-out (Transfer and Transfer Payment) Regulations 1996 (SI 1996/1462)*, the *Occupational Pension Schemes (Modification of the Pension Schemes Act 1993) Regulations 1998 (SI 1998/1466)*, the *Occupational Pension Schemes (Cross-border Activities) Regulations 2005 (SI 2005/3381)*, the *Employers' Duties (Registration and Compliance) Regulations 2010 (SI 2010/5)*, the *Occupational Pension Schemes (Transfer Values) Regulations 1996 (SI 1996/1847)*, the *Pension Sharing (Implementation and Disclosure of Liability) Regulations 2000 (SI 2000/1053)* and the *Pension Sharing (Pension Credit Benefit) Regulations 2000 (SI 2000/1054)*.

- The *Occupational and Personal Pension Schemes (Modification of Schemes – Miscellaneous Amendments) Regulations 2016 (SI 2016/231)* came into force on 6 April 2016. As a result of the ending of contracting-out from 6 April 2016, the Regulations make consequential amendments to the *Occupational Pension Schemes (Modification of Schemes) Regulations 2006 (SI 2006/759)*, the *Occupational and Personal Pension Schemes (Consultation by Employers and Miscellaneous Amendment) Regulations 2006 (SI 2006/349)* and the *Occupational Pension Schemes (Schemes that were Contracted-out) (No 2) Regulations 2015 (SI 2015/1677)*.

- The *State Pension (Amendment) (No 2) Regulations 2016 (SI 2016/240)* came into force on 6 April 2016. As a result of the introduction of the new flat-rate SP from 6 April 2016, the *Regulations* make consequential amendments to the *State Pension Regulations 2015 (SI 2015/173)* regarding the crediting of NICs.

- The *Pensions Act 2014 (Contributions Equivalent Premium) (Consequential Provision) and (Savings) (Amendment) Order 2016*

(SI 2016/252) came into force on 6 April 2016. As a result of the ending of contracting-out from 6 April 2016, this Order makes provision for the payment of contributions equivalent premiums and makes consequential amendments to the *Pensions Act 2014 (Savings) Order 2015 (SI 2015/1502)*.

- The *Pension Sharing (Miscellaneous Amendments) Regulations 2016 (SI 2016/289)* came into force on 6 April 2016. The Regulations make amendments to various statutory instruments concerning pension sharing orders in consequence of *TOPA 2014* and *PSA 2015*. The amended statutory instruments are the *Pensions on Divorce etc (Provision of Information) Regulations 2000 (SI 2000/1048)*, the *Occupational and Personal Pension Schemes (Disclosure of Information) Regulations 2013 (SI 2013/2734)*, the *Pensions on Divorce etc (Charging) Regulations 2000 (SI 2000/1049)*, the *Pension Sharing (Valuation) Regulations 2000 (SI 2000/1052)*, the *Pension Sharing (Pension Credit Benefits) Regulations 2000 (SI 2000/1054)*, the *Divorce etc (Pensions) Regulations 2000 (SI 2000/1123)*, the *Dissolution (Pensions) Regulations 2005 (SI 2005/2920)*, the *Pension Schemes Act 2015 (Transitional Provisions and Appropriate Independent Advice) Regulations 2015 (SI 2015/742)* and the *Divorce etc (Pensions) (Scotland) Regulations 2000 (SI 2000/112)*.

- The *Pension Protection Fund and Occupational and Personal Pension Schemes (Miscellaneous Amendments) Regulations 2016 (SI 2016/294)* came into force on 6 April 2016. The Regulations make amendments regarding the payment of pension lump sums by occupational pension schemes, the Pension Protection Fund (PPF), and the provision of information by occupational and personal pension schemes (PPS), some of which are consequential on changes introduced by *TOPA 2014* and *PSA 2015*. The Regulations amend the *Occupational Pension Schemes (Winding-up) Regulations 1996 (SI 1996/3126)*, the *Occupational Pension Schemes (Assignment, Forfeiture, Bankruptcy etc) Regulations 1997 (SI 1997/785)*, the *Pension Protection Fund (Compensation) Regulations 2005 (SI 2005/670)*, the *Pension Protection Fund (Entry Rules) Regulations 2005 (SI 2005/590)*, the *Pension Protection Fund (General and Miscellaneous Amendments) Regulations 2006 (SI 2006/580)* and the *Occupational and Personal Pension Schemes (Discharge of Information) Regulations 2013 (SI 2013/2734)*.

- The *Occupational Pension Schemes (Charges and Governance) (Amendment) Regulations 2016 (SI 2016/304)* came into force on 6 April 2016. The Regulations make amendments to the *Occupational Pension Schemes (Charges and Governance) Regulations 2015 (SI 2015/879)*.

- The *Registered Pension Schemes (Provision of Information) (Amendment) Regulations 2016 (SI 2016/308)* came into force on 6 April 2016. The Regulations make amendments to the *Registered Pension Schemes (Provision of Information) Regulations 2006 (SI 2006/567)* to specify the information that scheme administrators must provide to members for the transitional year 2015/16 in relation to the tapered reduction in the AA which affects individuals with income over £150,000 from 6 April 2016.

- The *Occupational and Personal Pension Schemes (Automatic Enrolment) (Miscellaneous Amendments) Regulations 2016 (SI 2016/311)* came into force on 6 April 2016. The Regulations make various amendments to the *Employers' Duties (Implementation) Regulations 2010 (SI 2010/4)*, the *Employers' Duties (Registration and Compliance) Regulations 2010 (SI 2010/5)* and the *Occupational and Personal Pension Schemes (Automatic Enrolment) Regulations 2010 (SI 2010/772)* relating to automatic enrolment.

- The *Income Tax (Pay As You Earn) (Amendment) Regulations 2016 (SI 2016/329)* came into force on 6 April 2016. *Regulation 5* amends The *Income Tax (Pay as you Earn) Regulations 2003 (SI 2003/2682), Sch A1* to specify the lump sum payments made to individuals under the pension flexibility rules which pension providers are required to report to HMRC and which may be paid as a consequence of *TOPA 2014* and *F(No 2)A 2015.*

- The *Social Security (Contributions) (Limits and Thresholds Amendments and National Insurance Funds Payments) Regulations 2016 (SI 2016/343)* came into force on 6 April 2016. The Regulations make amendments to the *(Social Security Contributions and Benefits Act 1992* and the *Social Security (Contributions) Regulations 2001 (SI 2001/1004)* giving effect to the annual uprating of class 1 and class 4 NICs to apply from 6 April 2016. They also specify the new class 4 NICs upper profits limit; class 1 NICs upper earnings limit; class 1 NICs upper secondary threshold for employees under 21; and apprentice upper secondary threshold for apprentices under 25.

- The *Occupational Pension Schemes (Scheme Administration) (Amendment) Regulations 2016 (SI 2016/427)* came into force on 6 April 2016. The Regulations make various amendments to the *Occupational Pension Schemes (Scheme Administration) Regulations 1996 (SI 1996/1715)* regarding scheme administration and to the *Occupational Pension Schemes (Investment) Regulations 2005 (SI 2005/3378)* regarding an error in the definition of default arrangement.

- The *Registered Pension Schemes (Provision of Information) (Amendment) Regulations 2017 (SI 2017/11)*. The Regulations make various amendments to the *Information Regulations* in relation to payments of lump sum death benefits made by registered pension schemes to trustees on or after 6 April 2016. They also impose information requirements on pension scheme administrators when a lump sum death benefit payment is made to a trustee in specified circumstances.

- The *Pension Protection Fund and Occupational Pension Schemes (Levy Ceiling and Compensation Cap) Order 2017 (SI 2017/50)*. *Article 2* specifies that the increase in the general level of earnings for the period from 1 August 2015 to 31 July 2016 is 2.6%. Accordingly, *article 3* specifies the levy ceiling for the financial year beginning on 1 April 2017. *Article 4* increases the amount of the compensation cap from 1 April 2017.

- The *Occupational and Personal Pension Schemes (Automatic Enrolment) (Amendment) Regulations 2017 (SI 2017/79)*. The Regulations amend the *Occupational and Personal Pension Schemes (Automatic Enrolment) Regulations 2010 (SI 2010/772)* with effect from 6 March 2017 by adding two new circumstances where the employer duties are turned into a discretion.

- The *Occupational and Personal Pension Schemes (General Levy) (Amendment) Regulations 2017 (SI 2017/203)*. The Regulations amend the *Occupational and Personal Pension Schemes (General Levy) Regulations 2005 (SI 2005/626)* by specifying the new figures with effect from 1 April 2017.

- The *Pension Protection Fund (Modification) (Amendment) Regulations 2017 (SI 2017/324)*. The Regulations make amendments to the *Pension Protection Fund (Compensation) Regulations 2005 (SI 2005/670)* for the purposes of the compensation cap. In addition, they amend the *Pension Protection Fund (General and Miscellaneous Amendments) Regulations 2006 (SI 2006/580)* in relation to the discharge by the board of liabilities in respect of money purchase benefits by payment of a lump sum, where the value of a person's money purchase benefits does not exceed a specified maximum.

- The *Registered Pension Schemes (Authorised Payments) (Amendment) Regulations 2017 (SI 2017/397)*. The Regulations make various amendments to the *Registered Pension Schemes (Authorised Payments) Regulations 2009 (SI 2009/1171)*. This would include the provision of a pensions advice allowance being an authorised payment for the purposes of *FA 2004*.

- The *Pension Schemes (Categories of Country and Requirements for Overseas Pension Schemes and Recognised Overseas Pension Schemes) (Amendment) Regulations 2017 (SI 2017/398)*. The Regulations make various amendments to the *Pension Schemes (Categories of Country and Requirements for Overseas Pension Schemes and Recognised Overseas Pension Schemes) Regulations 2006 (SI 2006/206)* (the '*Overseas Pension Schemes Regulations*'). This includes removing what is known as the 70% rule from the *Overseas Pension Schemes Regulations*, which required the rules of a scheme to designate a minimum of 70% of the funds that have had UK tax relief to be used to provide the member with an income for life.

- The *Social Security (Contributions) (Rates, Limits and Thresholds Amendments and National Insurance Funds Payments) Regulations 2017 (SI 2017/415)*. The Regulations amend the *Social Security and Benefits Act 1992* and the *Social Security (Contributions) Regulations 2001 (SI 2001/1004)* with effect from 6 April 2017 in relation to current liabilities to pay any Class 1 to Class 4 National Insurance contributions.

State benefits, contracting-out and indexations

11.4 SPA for men is 65 and for women born before 6 April 1950 is 60. It is intended that SPA for women should reach 65 by November 2018 and rise to 66 for both men and women by April 2020. Five-yearly reviews of SPA will remain. The first review must be completed by May 2017.

The Chancellor announced in the Budget 2014 that SPA will further increase to 67 between 2016 and 2028. He said that it was the government's intention that the proposed increase to 68 will occur by the mid-2030s and to 69 by the late 2040s. Future statutory reviews based on life expectancy figures will emanate from the Office for National Statistics (ONS).

There was a 2.5% increase in BSP from April 2015. This took the weekly payment up to £115.95. The rate for the current year is £122.30. The cash rise in BSP in April 2015 was passed through to the standard minimum guarantee in Pension Credit, which pushed the guarantee up to £151.20 for single people from April 2015. The cost of the measure to raise the standard minimum guarantee for Pension Credit was offset by an increase in the Savings Credit threshold of 5.1%. However, BSP and S2P were replaced by a single-tier pension from 6 April 2016. The full amount for those who have made full qualifying contributions is £159.55, but those who reached SPA before 6 April 2016 will receive their SP in line with existing rules. It is proposed that the single-tier pension will be increased each year by at least the percentage that average national earnings have grown in the previous year.

Individuals should be made aware that the single-tier is based on 35 qualifying years of NICs, for those with fewer than 35 years a pro-rata amount will be paid subject to a minimum number of ten qualifying years at SPA. Individuals may get less than the new full single-tier pension if they were contracted out before 6 April 2016, but may get more than the full single-tier pension if they would have had over a certain amount of Additional State Pension under the old rules.

It is noteworthy that existing pensioners who reached SPA before the introduction of the single-tier pension may make voluntary NICs to boost their income in retirement. The government is campaigning in order to get more individuals to make such contributions.

Contracting-out was abolished with effect from 6 April 2012 for DC schemes. *FA 2013, s 51*, addressed the abolition of contracting out of S2P and made consequential amendments to existing legislation.

An overseas scheme can only receive transfers of contracted-out rights if its documentation makes it eligible to hold such rights. The transferring scheme administrator will need to provide transfer forms together with the details which apply to any transferring member, in order to comply with the regulatory requirements. Benefits in contracted-out salary-related schemes may be transferred to any UK-registered pension scheme (contracted-in or out), or to a QROPS subject to certain conditions (see *PSA 1993, s 159* and *Pts III* and *IV*, as amended, and *FA 2013, s 51*). The *Registered Pension Schemes (Authorised Payments) (Amendment) Regulations 2013 (SI 2013/1818)* had effect from 6 April 2013 and brought the tax legislation into line with DWP legislation.

HMRC will gross-up of the minimum contributions paid in respect of an individual who is contracted-out of S2P through a PPS. A specified amount will then be paid into the NI Fund. HMRC ceased to pay minimum contributions to pension schemes from 6 April 2015.

11.5 The earnings link for SP was restored with a triple guarantee that pensions will be increased by the higher of earnings, prices or 2.5%. The increases commenced in 2012 and apply to England, Scotland and Wales. However, the uprating method for most state benefits and tax credits from April 2011 moved from RPI to the traditionally lower CPI. A statutory minimum requirement continues to apply to the revaluation and indexation of pension rights. The changes apply to DB rights in occupational pension schemes, and certain DC rights in occupational pension schemes. The sustainability of the triple guarantee appears to be in doubt at the time of writing.

The revaluation order uses data on price inflation to the previous year ending 30 September based on CPI. The same index is used in determining increases for all occupational pensions and payments made by the PPF and FAS.

National insurance contributions

11.6 For non- contracted-out employees. the 2017/18 employee contribution is 12% of all earnings between £157 and £866 pw, plus 2% of all earnings above £866 pw. The employer contribution is 13.8% of all earnings in excess of the first £157 pw. It is reduced to 0% of all earnings between

£157 and £866 pw where the employee is under 21, and for certain apprentices under 25. Employers can normally claim up to £3,000 a year against their liability for employer contributions.

The non-contracted-out rates for employees were reduced for salary related schemes in 2015/16 on the band earnings between £122 to £770 pw by 1.4%. For the employer they were reduced by 3.4%. Contracting-out was abolished for 2016/17 and there are no reductions.

Independent commission for public sector

11.7 An Independent Public Service Pensions Commission (IPSPC) investigating the viability of public sector pensions was established and reported back to government on its findings. There had been much opposition and legal challenge to the introduction of CPI which did not meet with success. The *Public Service Pensions Act 2013* (*PSPA 2013*) was the government response to the 2011 report of the IPSPC recommending scheme redesign, reform and regulation that was sustainable, affordable and fair. In a further blow to occupational pension provision, the Chancellor announced that employer contributions to unfunded public sector schemes will increase from 2019/20.

Default retirement age

11.8 The default retirement age was phased out between 6 April and 1 October 2011. Nevertheless, human resources departments and scheme trustees and managers will still need to plan accordingly as employers are able to operate a compulsory retirement age 'provided that they can objectively justify it'.

FSA replaced by FCA and PRA

11.9 The Financial Services Authority (FSA) was replaced in 2013 with a subsidiary prudential regulator under the Bank of England. The Bank of England has been given wide-ranging powers. The regulator is represented by two bodies, known as the Financial Conduct Authority (FCA) and Prudential Regulation Authority (PRA).

MEMBERSHIP AND TYPES OF SCHEME

Methods of retirement saving

11.10 For most earners, the post A-Day rules provided valuable benefits and savings for employers and members of registered pension schemes, including members of QROPS and EFRBS. Subsequent Acts and secondary legislation swept away many of these benefits and continue to do so. Nevertheless, DC schemes have increased greatly in popularity and benefits are becoming more accessible to members. DB schemes have high running costs and place the risk on the employer. They also have stringent funding requirements impose on them, largely in compliance with UK law which generally tracks *Directive 2003/41/EC of the European Parliament and the Council on the activities and supervision of institutions for occupational retirement provision* ('the *IORPS Directive*') and EU investment laws. In consequence, closures and conversions of such schemes continue to rise steadily.

Employers and trustees need to take into consideration the Pensions Regulator's website statements and Code of Practice 13 entitled 'Governance and administration of occupational defined contribution trust-based schemes' which calls for higher standards for DC schemes. There is a draft replacement DC Code of Practice dated November 2015 under consideration. The key point is to keep employees accurately and fairly informed about the employer's pension arrangements.

Wide choice

11.11 Tax relief is available on scheme investments held by UK-registered pension schemes in a similar manner as applied before A-Day, and on contributions for the employed or self-employed whatever their residence, subject to the AA and LA limits. Individuals can be members of more than one type of registered pension scheme, whether or not they are employees of participating companies. They can choose from occupational pension schemes, personal pension schemes, etc. Any persons regulated by the PRA (previously the FSA – see **11.9**) are able to establish a UK-registered pension scheme other than an occupational pension scheme (*FA 2004, s 154*, as amended by the *Finance Act 2007* (*FA 2007*), *Sch 20, para* 2).

The role of the Pensions Regulator is a relevant consideration when designing a pension scheme, as penalties and fines can be imposed on schemes and trustees where they are in conflict with statutory requirements of compliance or acceptable standards of governance.

For DB schemes, COP 3 had effect from July 2014. It is entitled 'Funding Defined Benefits' and is designed to help support trustees and employers to make use of the full flexibility of the scheme specific funding regime in their negotiations. It had effect for Northern Ireland from July 2015.

COP 14 had effect from April 2015 and is entitled 'Governance and administration of public service pension schemes'.

For DC schemes, the Regulator's 'DC Code' requires trustees to complete the trustee toolkit or demonstrate that they otherwise meet the requirement for appropriate knowledge and understanding. DC COP 13 is entitled 'Governance and administration of occupational defined contribution trust-based schemes'. It came into effect on 21 November 2013, and was brought in by the *Pensions Act 2004 (Code of Practice) (Governance and Administration of Occupational Defined Contribution Trust-Based Pension Schemes) Appointed Day Order 2013 (SI 2013/2869)*. The Regulator also published regulatory guidance to be read in conjunction with the DC Code in November 2013.

Consultation on the Regulator's new DC Code of Practice on the governance and administration of occupational DC schemes closed on 29 January 2016. The revised Code came into effect in July 2016, entitled 'Governance and administration of occupational trust-based schemes providing money purchase benefits'. Certain themes remain constant, but the Code sets them out differently. The Code addresses three principles:

- to have all of the standards expected of trustees in one place – the Code sets out all of the standards of conduct and practice that apply to occupational trust-based schemes providing DC benefits, rather than having them spread across a number of separate documents;
- to be clear and unambiguous; and
- to be short and simple – practical guidance and 'how to' guides are not part of the Code.

Consideration may be given to *hybrid pension schemes*. They can be an attractive means for employers to share risk with their employees, but they are complex to administer. It is necessary to manage DB entitlements as if they were a DB scheme and manage DC entitlements as if they were a DC scheme. The Pensions Regulator publishes guidance entitled 'Hybrid scheme management' on its website.

Master Trust DC schemes are very much in the news and have proven to be very popular for the purpose of auto-enrolment. The Institute of Chartered accountants in England and Wales and the Pensions Regulator published a Master Trust voluntary framework document on 1 May 2014. The document was intended to reassure members of such schemes and arrangements, and other larger DC schemes, that their schemes are being properly run, based on a set of control objectives. Master Trusts should obtain annual independent assurance.

However, investors and tax-planners should be aware that, in more recent years, the government and the Regulator have been less than comfortable with the way such products are developing.

On 28 January 2016 the Regulator warned there are real risks from new Master Trusts being subject to far less regulatory scrutiny than new contract-based providers. It is concerned about the sustainability of some of the schemes entering the market, and has lobbied for tighter regulation. In February 2016, HM Treasury said that new rules would be published 'as soon as practically possible'. On 10 March 2016, the Pensions Minister said that legislation must be introduced to stop the cost of Master Trust wind-ups falling on member, and on 24 March 2016 it was announced that the government will introduce legislation to boost the governance and monitoring of Master Trusts (see **11.3**).

CDCs and *DA schemes* have also been proposed, and have been subjected to scrutiny to the extent that the Pensions Minister has stated that they have been put on the back burner for the time being. The background to these products and a brief description of their nature is given below:

- Initially, DWP rejected a call from the Association of Consulting Actuaries for CDC schemes. The Association had felt that CDCs would spread risk and costs by pooling individual pension contributions to form a single 'mega-fund' for investment purposes. It believed that such schemes would potentially offer greater economies of scale and smoothing. However, the DWP expressed concerns about managing risk effectively. Despite the DWP's pronouncement, the government announced in the Queen's Speech on 4 June 2014 that it would provide for the introduction of such schemes in 2016 (when contracting-out for DB schemes was to cease).
- Subsequently a UK parliamentary committee recommended a review of the impact of the changes to the DC market and auto-enrolment. It said the DWP should not divert resources towards developing CDC or shared-risk schemes (now known as DA schemes). DA schemes are a kind of company retirement scheme where employers and employees share the burden of pension saving.
- Unfortunately, the experience in those European countries which have introduced such schemes has been such that there has been a reduction in the level of pensions in payment. Indeed, in CDCs in the Netherlands employers have felt obliged to pump in more contributions to make up the loss rather than face worker unrest.
- Representatives of the UK pensions industry, unsurprisingly, expressed concern about the lack of consistency in bringing in CDC and DA schemes with other government proposals, in particular the right to melt down DC schemes in their entirety (see **11.64**).

Contract-based schemes have become increasingly prevalent. The Regulator publishes guidance on *contract-based schemes*, entitled 'Voluntary Employer Engagement in Work Place Contract-based Pension Schemes', on its website, together with case studies.

An important new definition of 'money purchase benefits' was introduced in response to the Supreme Court case of *Houldsworth and another v Bridge Trustees Ltd* [2011] UKSC 42. *PSA 2015, ss 4* and *5* define what is meant by a money purchase scheme. The case meant that DC benefits could include benefits where there is a risk that the pension scheme could incur a funding deficit. The government had not intended such an interpretation, so the DWP took action to negate the effect of the decision. Under the new definition, benefits will only be money purchase where assets are equal to liabilities and a funding deficit cannot arise. Pension schemes with a guarantee or internal annuitisation option will no longer be treated as money purchase. It is important, therefore, that trustees, administrators and employers of such schemes should consider how the changes will affect their schemes.

Non-associated employers

11.12 The tight restrictions which had been imposed on membership and member benefits for *centralised schemes for non-associated employers* before A-Day were removed by *FA 2004*. Therefore, employers are able to minimise administrative costs and overhead costs by acting in a group (eg in their geographical area or within their own industry). This form of pension provision can also be most attractive for international employers. Different types of overseas and offshore trusts, including QROPS are also becoming increasingly popular (see **11.150** below), but are under increasing scrutiny by HMRC.

Focus

There are statutory definitions for pension schemes in *FA 2004*. Essentially, a pension scheme is a scheme which has or is capable of having effect so as to provide benefits to or in respect of persons:

1 on retirement;

2 on death;

3 on having reached a particular age;

4 on the onset of serious ill health or incapacity; or

5 in similar circumstances.

Statutory definitions of pension schemes

11.13 *FA 2004, s 150(1)* describes the criteria which apply to types of schemes; benefit provision and membership categories.

A *pension scheme* is described as follows:

> 'a scheme or other arrangements, comprised in one or more instruments or agreements, having or capable of having effect so as to provide benefits to or in respect of persons –
>
> (a) on retirement;
>
> (b) on death;
>
> (c) on having reached a particular age;
>
> (d) on the onset of serious ill health or incapacity; or
>
> (e) in similar circumstances.'

Therefore, it is important that any new or restructured schemes or arrangements meet the above conditions.

11.14 An *occupational pension scheme* is a pension scheme set up by an employer (known as a sponsoring employer) to provide benefits for, or in respect of:

- any or all of its own employees;
- any or all of the employees of any other employer,

and any other person who is not an employee of any sponsoring employer who is invited to join.

Tax relief on contributions is available for members who:

- have earnings which are subject to UK tax for a tax year;
- are resident in the UK some time during a tax year;
- are resident in the UK some time during the five tax years before the tax year when they became a member of the scheme; or
- for the tax year concerned have, or their spouse has, earnings from overseas Crown employment which are subject to UK tax.

Permitted members

11.15 UK-registered pension schemes may be open (depending on their own rules) to anyone without restriction. Employers are free to design their schemes and arrangements as they see fit, and to include broad eligibility rights. For example, they will wish to consider whether to include waiting periods for scheme membership, and whether to permit an employee or other member to be re-admitted to membership (and, if so, on what terms).

Some examples of the wide class of permitted members for whom contribution relief is available are:

- a non-working spouse or minor for whom contributions are paid by a third party, eg a working spouse, parent or grandparent;
- a self-employed individual in membership of an occupational scheme of which they are the sponsoring employer in the role of a sole trader or partnership in relation to their self-employed earnings.

UK earnings are widely drawn. They can include patent income, share options treated as employment income, the taxable element of a golden handshake over £30,000, and earnings of directors and members of their families who are employees of private investment or property companies.

Ex-gratia payments or golden handshakes can be an efficient tax saving means of rewarding employees, as payments of £30,000 or less are tax free. The threshold has not increased since its introduction in 1989, and for no tax or NICs liability to arise, any ex-gratia payment or golden handshake must not be 'earnings' (see HMRC's National Insurance Manual at NIM02010) and there must be no legal or contractual obligation on the employer to pay it. Even if the employee has no legal or contractual right to the payment it will still be earnings for NICs purposes if the payment can be held to derive from the employment.

Auto-enrolment

11.16 Employers were required to review their employment policy for any employees who are not already offered membership of a scheme or arrangement which met at least the minimum requirements of the requirement under *Pensions Act 2007 (PA 2007)* and *Pensions Act 2008 (PA 2008)*, as amended, for NEST. Employers may put alternative arrangements into place before their auto-enrolment. These require employer contributions of 1% rising to 3% from October 2018. Cost will be a major consideration for employers, and some may wish to regularly review their employment policy as the rules change and the use, or potential use, of self-employed services.

The DWP published proposals to improve the automatic enrolment process in a consultation on 25 March 2013. The key proposals included:

- streamlining the process for assessing who is eligible for automatic enrolment;
- lifting the requirement for people to be automatically enrolled if they have recently been put in their company pension scheme and have left it;
- asking wider questions about whether the process can be made easier for some employers.

The *Automatic Enrolment (Earnings Trigger and Qualifying Earnings Band) Order 2014 (SI 2014/263)* amended *PA 2008* regarding the amount a jobholder must receive before an employer is subject to certain duties in relation to that jobholder. The Order also specified rounded figures in respect of the pay reference periods other than 12 months. The latest Order is the *Automatic Enrolment (Earnings Trigger and Qualifying Earnings Band) Order 2017 (SI 2017/394)*.

Employers need to be alert to the fact that the Pensions Regulator has issued notices to employers which failed to meet their auto-enrolment duties, and has conducted fact-finding and compliance visits. Guidelines for employers were published on 15 January 2014, to counter them mistakenly referring to contractual enrolment as auto-enrolment. A second phase of amendments to secondary legislation came into force on 1 April 2014 which extended the deadlines for employers to comply with their employer duties from one month to six weeks. From 6 April 2014, the annual updates to the earnings figures used for thresholds and limits came into effect.

Schemes which are used for automatic enrolment must offer a default strategy. New joiners must not be asked to make a choice or provide information in order to become an active member of a qualifying scheme.

However, since the auto-enrolment regime was introduced, concerns were raised that the 6% minimum employer contribution to a DC arrangement could lead to a two-tier workforce, with employees who have been transferred-in following a TUPE transfer receiving more generous contributions from their employer (adding to the employers' costs) than the rest of the workforce (see the *Transfer of Undertakings (Protection of Employment) Regulations 2006 (SI 2006/246)*).

The DWP consulted on the above issue in February 2013. The upshot is that amending regulations came into effect on 6 April 2014 (applicable to TUPE transfers on and after this date) which adds a further option. Basically, where a transferor employer was required to make contributions solely for the purpose of providing DC benefits, the transferee employer may provide, as a minimum, the same level of contributions as the transferor employer for the employees immediately before the transfer took place. The Regulator issues regular guidance for small employers.

There is a cap on member charges of 0.75% from April 2015 on the defaults available under all DC schemes under automatic enrolment. This cap includes all member-borne deductions. Consultancy charges are banned from April 2015, and there is a ban on all arrangements which are incompatible with auto-enrolment rules from April 2016. As from April 2015, trustees and independent governance committees have had new duties to consider and must report on costs and charges. The government will introduce new mandatory requirements for standardised disclosure of all pension costs and charges.

NEST

11.17 Multiple contracts apply under NEST, including ones for consultancy services and software development support. The charges for all members, whether a member is contributing or not, whatever fund they're contributing to, and no matter how much is in their retirement pot are made up of two parts:

- an annual management charge (AMC) of 0.3% on the total value of a member's fund each year;
- a contribution charge of 1.8% on each new contribution into a member's retirement pot.

FA 2011 removed unintended potential charges on members, and prevented other unintended tax consequences which may result from the interaction of current tax rules. It confirmed that:

- NEST is exempt from taxation in respect of any borrowing; and
- NEST members are exempt from taxation on interest in relation to late payment of contributions by the employer.

With effect from October 2012, employers could enroll workers into a workplace pension, provided that they are not already in a pension at work; and

- are aged 22 or over;
- are under SPA;
- earn more than £10,000 a year; and
- work in the UK.

There are staging processes to comply with auto-enrolment for employers. These are:

- with more than 250 employees (October 2012–February 2014);
- with between 50 and 249 employees (1 April 2014–1 April 2015);
- for new employers setting up business from 1 April 2012–30 September 2017 (1 May 2017 and 1 February 2018).

Employers with fewer than 50 persons in their largest PAYE scheme are staged between 1 June 2015 and 1 April 2017. Some employers with fewer than 50 workers may have earlier staging dates, perhaps because their PAYE scheme also includes non-workers (eg pensioners being paid pension benefits). In this case, if they meet certain conditions, they can choose to move their staging date back to a prescribed date between 1 August 2015 and 1 April 2017.

Employers will also need to enrol non-eligible jobholders and workers without qualifying earnings, up to £5,824 a year, also known as entitled workers, if they apply to join.

NEST is able to register with HMRC and to operate as an occupational pension scheme for tax purposes by way of amendment to *PA 2008, s 67*.

For 2015/16 the entry level for NEST was for employees earnings between £10,600 and £42,385 pa. The maximum level of contribution was set at £4,600 pa until 31 March 2017. The *National Employment Savings Trust (Amendment) Order 2015 (SI 2015/178)* removed the annual contribution limit for contributions made in each tax year by, or on behalf or in respect of, a member of the scheme with effect from 1 April 2017, and removed the restriction on trustees to accept transfers in which were cash transfer sums. It also lifted the restrictions on transfers of a member's pension account to another pension scheme. For the 2016/17 tax year there is a lower limit for qualifying earnings of £5,824; and an upper limit for qualifying earnings of £43,000 a year.

On 27 June 2015, it was announced that a default system will blend income drawdown, a cash fund and saving towards an annuity, to run simultaneously. On retirement, 90% of the member's fund will transfer to the income drawdown fund and be invested in an income-generating portfolio. The monthly returns will provide a retirement income while 2% of the fund, annually, will move into another fund to purchase a deferred annuity. The remaining 10% will be moved into a cash fund for members to access as and when required, and be topped up should the income-drawdown fund provide excess returns.

Employers and employees will need to pay minimum contribution rates, as a percentage of a worker's pensionable earnings, as follows:

Date	*Minimum contributions*
October 2012 – September 2017	2% – the employer must pay at least 1% of this.
October 2017 – September 2018	5% – the employer must pay at least 2% of this.
October 2018 onwards	8% – the employer must pay at least 3% of this.

The dates for the increases to 5% and 8% are due to change to April 2018 and April 2019, subject to parliamentary approval.

The *National Employment Savings Trust Order 2010 (SI 2010/917)* was amended by a consolidated *National Employment Savings Trust (Amendment) Order 2013 (SI 2013/597)* applicable from 1 April 2013 to align itself with the changes to auto-enrolment described above. In addition, it removed the requirement to admit as a member a person whose place of work is sufficiently located in an EEA state other than the UK so as to make that person subject to the social and labour law of that EEA state. NEST may refuse to accept contributions made in respect of a member's employment that is subject to the social and labour law of another EEA state.

With effect from 1 April 2017, the *National Employment Savings Trust (Amendment) Order 2015 (SI 2015/178)* removes the £4,600 pa limit on contributions that can be paid to NEST in relation to each member; allows NEST to receive bulk transfers without member consent if the separate bulk transfer without consent conditions are satisfied (which require the trustees of the transferring scheme to obtain an actuarial certificate) and the employer concerned is making contributions to NEST and lifts the restrictions on NEST receiving and making transfers in respect of individuals.

FUNDING FLEXIBILITY AND RULES

Funding and actuarial input

11.18 There are no statutory HMRC funding rules, only thresholds on tax-relievable levels of contributions (see **11.19–11.34**). Practitioners and advisers will need to inform their clients of the thresholds which apply to the tax reliefs which are available. The need to obtain actuarial advice arises mainly for the purpose of compliance with DWP legislation and the Pensions Regulator's requirements, which apply chiefly to DB schemes. This enables DC schemes to cut their overheads, although the advice of an actuary may be required by trustees or administrators as a matter of prudence in appropriate circumstances.

It should, however, be noted that the Pensions Regulator has stated on its website that it will implement sanctions against trustees and managers against '*unacceptable behaviour*'. In its statement, the Regulator said that trustees and scheme managers should contact it if they were worried. It also reminded trustees and advisers of the important role of whistleblowers, and the risk of incurring sanctions (see **11.10** above).

It is important to submit scheme returns on time in order to avoid penalties. On 15 March 2016 the Regulator stated that it had warned a number of trustees that it could crack the whip and fine them for not completing their scheme returns. It had also reminded trustees on 1 March 2016 that they will be fined if they fail to prepare the new annual governance statements within the statutory deadline. The statements must be produced within seven months of a scheme year's ending on or after 6 July 2015. The first DC statements were already due on 6 February 2016 and failure to comply could result in a fine of between £500 and £2,000. The Regulator issued a further warning of fines in April 2016 if trustees fail to make the necessary changes to their returns from July 2016, and said that 'any schemes which fail to prepare their statement within the statutory timescale will be in breach of the law and should report the breach to us.'

Contributions tax relief

Members

11.19 There is no limit on the level of contributions which may be paid by a member. Members receive tax relief on personal contributions up to 100% of their annual earnings, or £3,600 if higher – subject to the AA threshold described at **11.26** below. Any person other than the employer or a former employer who contributes in respect of a member, where relief at source (RAS) is in point for personal pensions, must gross up the contribution at the basic tax rate (and higher relief will be available, where appropriate, through self-assessment or pay-as-you earn (PAYE) coding). Even where a member of a personal pension has taxable income below the basic rate tax threshold, or no taxable income at all, basic rate tax relief is still available assuming the residency requirement is met. A person who contributes under a net pay arrangement (only available for occupational pension schemes) will have contributions deducted from earned pay before tax is calculated, thereby obtaining immediate relief at the marginal rate.

Individuals who joined a UK scheme and who were resident in the UK at some time in the last five tax years still qualify for tax relief on contributions through RAS even though they are no longer UK resident and have no UK chargeable earnings (*FA 2004, s 189).* However, the maximum relievable contribution is limited to £3,600. This may have an impact on overseas members of pension schemes.

Employers

11.20 Employers' contributions are allowable as deductions against their corporation tax/profits, subject to the AA threshold described in **11.26**. The circumstances are that in the case of:

- a trade or profession, they must be incurred wholly and exclusively for the purposes of the employer's trade or profession (*Income and Corporation*

Taxes Act 1988 (*ICTA 1988*), *s 74(1)(a)* – CT; and *Income Tax (Trading and Other Income) Act 2005* (*ITTOIA 2005*), *s 34* – IT).

- a company with investment business, they are an expense of management (*ICTA 1988, s 75*).

However, relief will only be given on cash contributions made, not the amount shown in the company accounts. If contributions exceed 210% of the amount paid in the preceding year, unless the excess does not exceed £500,000 or there is a cessation of business, spreading will normally apply. The spread will be for up to four years – the maximum period applying where the excess contributions are £2m or more. *FA 2004, Sch 36, Pt 4, para 42*, contained transitional protection for existing arrangements as at A-Day.

Of potentially significant interest for tax-planning by employers is that HMRC have indicated that high levels of contributions may be treated as made wholly and exclusively for the purpose of the business if the aggregate salary and contributions are comparable to that paid to unconnected employees performing similar tasks. If there is no comparable task, the decision will be a commercial decision. HMRC's Business Income Manual, BIM46030, BIM46035 and BIM47105–BIM47106 refer.

Repayment claims

11.21 Reclaiming overpaid tax is an important aspect of tax planning. The procedures which apply to the following claims are:

- **Flexi-access pension, and small pension lump sum repayment, claims**

  Use the online service for a flexibly accessed pension payment repayment claim and for a repayment claim where small pension taken as a lump sum. The forms are P55 and P53 respectively.

- **In-year repayment, where funds have been fully extinguished.**

  The process for members to claim an in-year repayment in circumstances where funds have been fully extinguished mirrors the current in-year trivial commutation repayment process.

- **Lump sum death benefits**

  Where a scheme administrator pays one of the following lump sum death benefits (LSDBs) to an individual and it is taxable, instead of deducting the special LSDB charge they should deduct IT using an emergency code:

  - defined benefit LSDB;
  - uncrystallised funds LSDB;

- drawdown pension fund LSDB;
- flexi-access drawdown pension fund LSDB;
- pension protection LSDB;
- annuity protection LSDB.

The forms are:

- P50Z(DB) – individuals should only use the P50Z(DB) form if:
  - they have taken a pension fund LSDB that uses up their pension pot; and
  - they have no other income
- P53Z(DB) – individuals should only use the P53Z(DB) form if:
  - they have taken a pension fund LSDB that uses up their pension pot; and
  - they have other taxable income in this tax year.
- P55(DB) – individuals should only use the P55(DB) form if:
  - they have taken a pension flexibility death benefit payment that does not use up all of that fund;
  - they will not be taking regular payments; and
  - the pension body is unable to make any tax refund

If one of the LSDB listed above is taxable and the scheme administrator pays it to a non-qualifying person such as a company, a trust or the member's estate when they die, the scheme administrator must continue to deduct tax and report it to HMRC on the AFT return. This tax is the liability of the scheme administrator.

- **Reclaiming tax deducted from investment income**

  An APSS146 is only required from administrators or trustees if:

  - they have not previously submitted an APSS146 for that pension scheme;
  - the scheme's assets owner has changed, for example, if there has been a change in the scheme's trustees;
  - they wish to change the scheme's bank account details; or
  - the person sending in the repayment claims is changing.

EFRBS

11.22 EFRBS have potentially been a tax-efficient method of saving for high earners. However, HMRC published some early guidance on contributions to such schemes where they perceive that tax avoidance may be involved:

1 There is a restriction of tax relief where an employer routes the funding of an EFRBS through a registered pension scheme. (The *Registered Pension Schemes (Restriction of Employer's Relief) Regulations 2005, SI 2005/3458* apply.) In addition to this restriction, HMRC sought to prevent the spreading rules from being circumvented by routing them through a new company. *FA 2004, s 199A* was inserted by *FA 2008, s 90.* The measure had effect for payments made on or after 10 October 2007 under binding obligations entered into on or after 9 October 2007, with effect from 10 October 2007.

2 HMRC Spotlight 6: (EFRBS) states:

> 'We are aware of schemes where companies claim a corporation tax deduction for employer contributions to an EFRBS on the basis that either (a) the contribution to the EFRBS or (b) a subsequent transfer to a second EFRBS is a "*qualifying benefit*". This would allow the company to secure a corporation tax deduction before any benefits are actually paid by the scheme to the employee. Our view is that neither transaction involves the provision of a "*qualifying benefit*". Whilst it has been argued that there may be some ambiguity in the law around the meaning of the phrase "*transfer of assets*" since it does not state to whom the transfer is to be made, in our view the context resolves any ambiguity. The law defines "*qualifying benefits*" and such benefits are plainly, from the context, benefits that if paid under the terms of an EFRBS might fall within the employment income charge. So in that context, a "*transfer of assets*" should be interpreted as a transfer that could give rise to such a charge. This will primarily mean a transfer of assets to the employee but also includes a transfer to a member of the employee's family. Neither an employer contribution to an EFRBS nor a transfer between EFRBS gives rise to a possible employment IT charge on the employee. So there is no "*qualifying benefit*" entitling the employer to a deduction.
>
> We will actively challenge examples of such arrangements as and when they arise.'

A major development was contained in *FA 2011, Sch 2 'Employment income provided through third parties'* which introduced a charge on '*disguised remuneration'* despite strong representations by industry. The legislation is aimed at preventing the avoidance of income tax and national insurance contributions (IT and NICs) by trusts and other intermediaries, including employee benefit trusts (EBTs) and EFRBS. Legislation was amended to extend PAYE and NICs to such payments or deemed payments, and to arrangements for employees to receive a loan and the earmarking of assets by a third party. *Part 7A* was introduced into *ITEPA 2003*. HMRC published a frequently asked questions document on the subject in March 2011 which was revised following consultation with industry in July 2011. The main current guidance is in EIM45000 onwards.

The tax charge is imposed on the sum of money involved or on the higher of the cost or market value where an asset is used to deliver the reward or recognition. The legislation also included anti-forestalling provisions applying to payments made after 9 December 2010. There is some mitigation of the tax charge on emerging assets where IT and NICs have been levied on such events at the time they occurred.

This was a punitive measure and it seemed to be an extreme reaction to a limited incidence of blatant tax avoidance by the very few. IT could be charged on employment income or benefits whether or not they have been received or will ever be received. In the event, there have been very few reported cases of a *Part 7A* charge being incurred.

It should be noted that life assurance premium relief in relation to payments by employers to EFRBS was abolished from 2012 (see **11.3** in relation to changes to EFRBS).

PPF levy

11.23 DB schemes remain an expensive form of pension provision compared to other types of scheme. The pension protection fund (PPF) levy is important in considering pensions cost. The levy system can be a drain on a company's business at a time when it is least able to pay.

The PPF 7800 Index and Compensation Cap Factors are published by the PPF on a regular basis. The index reflects the use of CPI rather than RPI to revalue relevant payments made by the PPF and the PPF takes into account the level of pricing in the bulk annuity market and the assumptions used for valuations under *Pensions Act 2004, s 179* in order better to reflect the current level of pricing.

Under the *Pensions Act 2011 (Transitional, Consequential and Supplementary Provisions) Regulations 2014 (SI 2014/1711)* certain benefits that were formerly treated as money purchase cease to be treated as such and thus fall under PPF protection for the first time.

The PPF website for 2016/17 contains the following (abbreviated) information:

The *scheme-based levy* (SBL) is based on a scheme's liabilities to members on a *Pensions Act 2004, s 179* basis. It is calculated using the formula:

SBL = 0.000021 × UL

UL is the scheme's liabilities on a *Pensions Act 2004, s 179* basis rolled forward to 31 March 2016 and smoothed but not stressed.

All schemes pay the scheme-based levy, irrespective of their funding position.

The *risk-based levy* (RBL) is based on the likelihood of a scheme making a claim on the PPF and the potential size of that claim. It is calculated using the formula:

RBL = underfunding risk (U) × insolvency risk (IR) × levy scaling factor (LSF)

Underfunding risk represents the size of a scheme's potential claim on the PPF.

U is the underfunding amount of the scheme determined using the scheme's rolled-forward assets and liabilities, taking account of any valid Type B or C contingent asset arrangements, deficit reduction contributions and certified asset backed contribution value and coupon payments. In the great majority of cases, U is calculated using stressed assets and liabilities (it is calculated using unstressed assets and liabilities if this results in a higher underfunding amount).

Insolvency risk reflects the likelihood of a scheme's employer(s) becoming insolvent. It reflects the risk of insolvency of the sponsoring employer(s), taking into account the scheme structure. From levy year 2015/16 probabilities of insolvency were provided to the PPF by Experian. IR may be modified where there is a Type A contingent asset.

The *levy scaling factor* **(LSF)** scales the amount we collect from all schemes down to ensure that the total levy collected matches the levy estimate. The levy scaling factor is 0.65.

The *risk-based levy* is capped to protect the most vulnerable schemes. The cap for 2016/17 is 0.75 per cent (represented by K in the formula) of unstressed liabilities. Where the risk-based levy calculated using the above formula exceeds 0.75 per cent of unstressed liabilities, the cap is applied and the risk-based levy is calculated using the following formula:

Risk-based levy cap = Unstressed liabilities (UL) × K

When carrying out this calculation, we use 0.007500 for K.

FAS

11.24 As well as equalisation, the financial assistance scheme (FAS) regulations enable the FAS to absorb a scheme's remaining assets so payments can be made to people whose benefits would have been met in full by the scheme, as well as to people qualifying for FAS payments. The FAS is now under the wing of the PPF. It will close to Notification and Qualification of new schemes from 1 September 2016.

TAX-RELIEVABLE ALLOWANCES

Introduction

11.25 There are tax relievable ceilings on aggregate annual input and aggregate pension fund entitlement. These are a tax-efficient means of saving for employers and members. New constraints were placed on the thresholds and tax reliefs for high earners by the *Finance Act 2010* (*FA 2010*). However, some were repealed and replaced by a very severe reduction in the level of the AA. There have since been further reductions in the AA (see below). It is therefore important to review arrangements for contributions in respect of all such persons, and to take advantage of the opportunities to mitigate tax levels within the permitted boundaries. The LA has also been severely cut back on more than one occasion (see **11.35** below).

Annual allowance

11.26 The AA is the maximum aggregate amount of annual tax-free input that can be put into a registered scheme. It was set at £215,000 in 2006/07 and it increased steadily to £255,000 by the year 2010 as shown below:

- tax year 2007/08 – £225,000;
- tax year 2008/09 – £235,000;
- tax year 2009/10 – £245,000;
- tax year 2010/11 – £255,000.

The level in the first review period had been frozen at the 2010/11 level up to and including the tax year 2015/16. After some further, mainly abortive, tinkering, however, *FA 2011, Sch 17*, brought in a reduced AA of £50,000 from tax year 2011/12, and *FA 2013, s 49*, further reduced AA to £40,000 from 2014/15.

There is also a cut back to £10,000 for those who enter flexi-access and a cut back for high earners (see **11.64**). Furthermore, in the budget on

8 July 2015, the Chancellor unexpectedly announced that there will be a reduction in the AA from 2016/17 for high earners with incomes including pension contributions of over £150,000. It will be tapered down to £10,000 with a reduction of £1 for every £2 by which an individual's earnings exceed £150,000. The tapering will not apply if the individual's earnings excluding pension contributions are below £110,000. Any salary sacrifice set up on or after 9 July 2015 will be included in the threshold definition. *Section 23* and *Sch 4* to *F(No 2)A 2015* contain the relevant changes. Additionally, the period over which pension savings are measured will now always be measured over a tax year. PSN 57 covered the changes to the AA and 'Scheme Pays'. Members whose pensionable earnings exceeded £110,000 in the tax year will be able to request a pension savings statement from their scheme if they want one. Schemes must provide a statement if either the member's PIAs for 2015 to 2016 as a whole exceed £80,000, or the member's PIA for the post-alignment tax year exceed £40,000.

HM Treasury is endeavouring to prevent 'payments of benefits in lieu of salary' *i*n order to prevent reimbursed business expenses being commingled with salary sacrifice. In the budget on 8 July 2015, the Chancellor stated that the government will actively monitor salary sacrifices and their effect on tax receipts.

On 6 April 2016, HMRC published guidance for administrators if a member pays in more than their AA. The guidance is entitled 'Pension administrators: check your member's annual allowance'. The administrator will need to send the member a pension savings statement if the member's pension savings are more than the AA or MPAA.

Annual allowance charge

AA charge

11.27 An AA charge of 40% arose on any excess input under *FA 2004, s 227*. Under *FA 2011, Sch 17*, the excess charge of 40% was replaced by a charge at the '*appropriate rate*', which is for the current year the marginal rate which applies to the taxpayer concerned.

The main details are:

- the excess AA charge is levied at the individual's marginal tax rate, and it applies in the year of taking benefits;
- unused AA may be carried forward for three years;
- inflation-linked increases in expected pensions for deferred members of schemes do not count when determining the excess AA charge;

- the valuation factor used to calculate the value of DB pension savings has increased from 10 to 16;
- the opening value of rights under DB schemes is subject to a revaluation rate.

The AA charge is not treated as income for any of the purposes of the Taxes Acts. It applies whether or not the administrator or member are resident, ordinarily resident or domiciled in the UK. Excess monies may remain in the scheme subject to the ultimate LA at retirement, and any excessive tax withheld by the scheme may be refunded to the member. Where tax relief has been given on an excess in the scheme, it will be clawed back from the fund. The allowance cannot be set off against the AA from one year to another if the value of a defined benefit falls during the year. Importantly, there are some exemptions which do not count towards the allowance:

- contributions in excess of a member's earnings that do not qualify for tax relief;
- AVCs which are paid for the purpose of securing added years (as the increase in benefits will be counted);
- before the end of the year, the individual has become entitled – meaning an actual right to draw all of the benefits;
- before the end of the tax year, the individual has died.

From 6 April 2011 the AA charge has applied in the year pension benefits are drawn except where the benefits are in the form of a serious or severe ill health lump sum. It also applies to those who have enhanced protection (EP). Inflation-linked increases in expected pensions for deferred members of schemes do not count when determining the excess charge, and transitional rules applied from 14 October 2010.

Schemes must report the AA charges that are met by *Scheme Pays* (see below) using the quarterly Accounting for Tax (AFT) Return. (For example, AA charges that arose in the 2011/12 tax year needed to be reported by the quarter ending 31 March 2014, with the AFT return filed and the tax charge paid by 15 May 2014.)

Pension input amounts, and pension input periods

11.28 The AA applies to the pension input amount (PIP), which depends on the type of scheme or arrangement concerned. *FA 2004, s 152* identifies four types of scheme, and a summary of the method of calculation of the increase in the value of an individual's rights in the pension input period (PIP) for each type is given below, subject to the later summary of the proposals which are contained in *FA 2011, Sch 17*, and are described in **11.33** below. PTM054300 concerns PIA and carry forward from 2008/09, 2009/10, 2010/11 (see **11.34**). From the tax year 2011/12 onwards it is possible to carry forward to a current tax year any available unused AA from the preceding three tax years. The AA each of the tax years 2008/09, 2009/10 and 2010/11 is deemed to be £50,000. The method of calculating how much of the deemed AA of £50,000 has been used up for each of those tax years by reference to the total PIAs for those tax years is based on the current methods of valuing PIAs generally, and in the case of certain DB and cash balance arrangements that existed before the start of the first PIP for the arrangement there are deemed PIPs before the start of the first PIP.

F(No 2)A 2015, Pt 1, Sch 4, aligns PIPs with tax years from 8 July 2015. A technical note of the same date explains how the PIA for the 2015/16 tax year is modified for cash balance and DB arrangements. The taper has effect on and after 6 April 2016.

From tax year 2015/16 onwards, certain individuals might be subject to the MPAA instead of the AA. It is still possible to carry forward from a previous tax year when the MPAA applied but the amount that can be carried forward is calculated by reference to the alternative AA that applied for that previous tax year (see **11.34**).

Amidst strong opposition, the government replaced the RPI with the CPI for pensions legislation (see **11.34** below). This has an adverse effect on the level of members' benefits whilst reducing the funding level for their employers.

The following are the PTM sources which describe how the increase in savings is calculated in each type of arrangement:

- PTM053200 for pension savings under an other DC arrangement;
- PTM053300 for pension savings under a DB arrangement;
- PTM053400 for pension savings under a cash balance arrangement;
- PTM053500 for pension savings under a hybrid arrangement;
- PTM023100 for further details about the meaning of an arrangement;
- PTM056500 for further details about the application of the AA or MPAA.

Cash balance arrangement

11.29 The PIA is the difference between the pension value at the beginning of the opening period and the pension value at the end of the closing PIP in the tax year concerned. The opening value is the amount which would be available for the provision of benefits to or in respect of the individual on the assumption that the individual became entitled to the benefits at the beginning of the PIP. This is uprated by CPI or 5%, whichever is higher. The closing value is the amount which would be available for the provision of benefits to or in respect of the individual on the assumption that the individual became entitled to the benefits at the end of the PIP.

Any pension debit in the period is added back; pension credit is deducted. If there has been a transfer to a registered or recognised overseas scheme during the period, the amount of the sums transferred plus the market value of the assets is to be added (or deducted if there has been a transfer in). Any benefit that has crystallised in the period is to be added, unless the member has become entitled to the whole benefit or died. Any minimum payments under *PSA 1993* are to be subtracted.

Transitional rules for calculating total PIAs for tax year 2015/16 can be found in PTM058070. The rules for deferred members are contained in PTM058080.

Other money purchase arrangement

11.30 The PIA is the total of any relievable pension contributions paid by or on behalf of the individual under the arrangement, and contributions paid in respect of the individual under the arrangement by an employer of the individual, at the end of the closing PIP in the tax year concerned. When at any time contributions paid under a pension scheme by an employer otherwise than in respect of any individual become held for the purposes of the provision under an arrangement under the pension scheme of benefits to or in respect of an individual, they are to be treated as being contributions paid at that time in respect of the individual under the arrangement.

Transitional rules for calculating total PIAs for tax year 2015/16 can be found in PTM058060.

Defined benefits (final salary) scheme

11.31 The PIA is the difference between the pension value at the beginning of the opening period and the pension value at the end of the closing PIP in the tax year concerned. The opening value is ten times the pension value at the opening value (had it been taken then), plus the lump sum entitlement other than by commutation. This is uprated if no rights accrue during the PIP. The alternative percentage by reference to which the opening value of DB arrangements is calculated as the greatest of:

- 5%;
- the percentage by which CPI for the month in which the PIP ends is higher than it was for the month in which it began; and
- the percentage to which regulations made by HMRC refer.

The closing value is 16 (previously 10 – see below) × the pension value at the closing value (had it been taken then), plus the lump sum entitlement (other than by commutation). Any pension debit in the period is added back; pension credit is deducted. If there has been a transfer to a registered, or recognised overseas, scheme during the period, the amount of the sums transferred plus the market value of the assets is to be added (or deducted if there has been a transfer in). Any benefit that has crystallised in the period is to be added, unless the member has become entitled to the whole benefit or died. Any minimum payments under the *PSA 1993* are to be subtracted.

Under *FA 2011, Sch 17*, the valuation factor used to calculate the value of DB pension savings increased from a factor of 10 to a factor of 16.

Adjustments were made for the change to CPI.

Transitional rules for calculating total PIAs for tax year 2015/16 can be found in PTM058070. The rules for deferred members are contained in PTM058080.

Hybrid arrangement

11.32 The PIA is the greater or greatest of such of input amounts A, B and C as are relevant input amounts.

- *A* is what would be the PIA if the benefits provided to or in respect of the individual under the arrangement were cash balance benefits.
- *B* is what would be the PIA if the benefits provided to or in respect of the individual under the arrangement were other money purchase benefits.
- *C* is what would be the PIA if the benefits provided to or in respect of the individual under the arrangement were DB.

Transitional rules for calculating total PIAs for tax year 2015/16 can be found in PTM058070. The rules for deferred members are contained in PTM058080.

Input period, and transitional rules

11.33 The PIP applies in each tax year. It commences on the day that the member begins to accrue pension rights under the scheme, but it should be noted that there was wide flexibility in the choice of an end date (*FA 2004, s 238*). There was accordingly scope to make large contributions at the most tax-efficient time for the contributor concerned – but see the changes under **11.34** below. The end period may be the end of the scheme accounting period, the end of the tax year, or any other chosen date.

Note that start and end dates in the past may be nominated for a PIP. Note also that just because large contributions can be made, for example by sacrificing bonuses and manipulating the AA, it does not always mean it is a sound course of action. If an employee uses up too much LA early on, he may not benefit fully from contributions an employer may make on his behalf later. Careful consideration will be required when dealing with large contributions.

Under *FA 2011, Sch 17*, transitional rules applied from 14 October 2010. They applied to individuals who had pension savings relating to a pension input period that started before 14 October 2010 and which would end in the 2011/12 tax year – and was therefore subject to the new AA limit. There are options for enabling individuals to meet high tax charges out of their pension benefits, rather than current income.

FA 2011, Sch 2, inserted a new *FA 2004, s 227A*, describing how to carry forward unused AA. There is provision for the carry forward of unused AA for a period of up to three years to 2011/12 and following years. The unused allowance for the three years preceding the current year may be added to the allowance for the current year for determining whether a charge is applicable for the current year. Unused AA is only available for carry forward where it arises during a tax year in which the individual is a member of a UK-registered pension scheme but applies to a tax year even if the pension input amount for that year is nil. The earlier year's unused allowance is to be set off against the current year before that of the later year.

The revisions, and carry-forward

11.34

> **Focus**
>
> The PIP is an important consideration in tax planning. HMRC have published detailed guidance. There are also carry forward provisions which enable unused AA to be carried forward to future years.

HMRC's first published guidance on PIPs remains of importance in tax planning and it is reproduced below. (The reductions to the AA (see **11.26**) need to be taken into consideration from 6 April 2014.). HMRC have stated that, for the purpose of carrying forward unused AA to the 2014/15 tax year, the AA for each of the previous three tax years (2013/14, 2012/13 and 2011/12) remains at £50,000.

HMRC's first guidance on PIPs is reproduced below. However, it should be noted that PIPs are changed to bring them in line with the fiscal year from

8 July 2015 (*F(No 2)A 2015, s 23* and *Sch 4, Pt 1*). So, the first PIP starts from the date that the first contribution is paid and ends on the following 5 April except for pre 8 July 2015 where another end date was nominated.

The first guidance:

> 'A scheme can only have one PIP in each income tax year and each PIP must not exceed 12 months. Therefore, following the introduction of the AA charge on 6 April 2006, any scheme that did not nominate to change their PIP to an alternative date in their first year will have a first PIP ending on 6 April 2007 and will have PIPs ending on 6 April going forward.
>
> It would seem that some scheme administrators did not realise that this was the case and thought that if they had not nominated for an alternative end date for their first PIP, the default was to the tax year, so that their PIP runs to the 5 April each year. Having realised that this is not so, they are now looking to change their PIP so that it does align with the income tax year. The nomination rules mean that a scheme can bring forward the end date of PIP to a date earlier in the tax year.
>
> Under the current legislation a scheme can, where no previous nomination has been made, make a retrospective nomination to unwind their PIP back to the first PIP. By retrospectively nominating for their first pension period to end on 5 April 2007, the scheme can align their PIP to the income tax year for all subsequent periods. Once you have made a nomination to change the PIP then you can't make a second nomination for the same tax year.
>
> Changing the scheme's PIP in this way may have an impact on a member's tax liability, as it may result in a member's contributions or benefit accrual falling within a different tax year for the purposes of the AA charge. If the scheme has always worked on the basis that their PIP ended on the 5 April this is likely to have little if any effect and is only likely to affect members who have made large contributions close to the end or beginning of the income tax year. However, it is worth noting that members will be liable to any AA charge that arises as a result of the change in the PIP and will be able to claim any repayment of any overpayment that may arise as a result of the change. A repayment claim can be made up to four years after the end of the tax year in which the overpayment arises.
>
> The scheme must advise their members if they nominate for their first PIP to end other than on the scheme anniversary. If a scheme does not do so, that member's PIP automatically defaults to the anniversary of the date they joined the scheme or 6 April if the member joined the scheme before 6 April 2006.
>
> If a scheme wishes to retrospectively nominate for their first pension input period to end on 5 April 2007, they need to do so before the draft

legislation receives Royal Assent. Under the draft legislation, from 6 April 2011 it will not be possible for a nominated date to be a date before the date on which the nomination is made.'

The details of who can change the end date of a PIP vary depending on the type of arrangement.

F(No 2)A 2015, s 23 and *Sch 4* contain the following changes to the carry-forward provisions for earlier years which are described later (PTM054300 concerns PIAs and carry-forward from 2008/09, 2009/10, 2010/11):

- From tax year 2015/16 onwards, certain individuals might be subject to the MPAA instead of the AA. It is still possible to carry forward from a previous tax year when the MPAA applied, but the amount that can be carried forward is calculated by reference to the alternative AA that applied for that previous tax year (PTM055200 and, for tax year 2015/16, PTM058030).
- Every member of a registered pension scheme has an AA of £80,000 for the 2015/16 tax year, but this is subject to an allowance of £40,000 for the period from 9 July 2015 to 5 April 2016. This is in addition to any existing unused AA carried forward from the three previous tax years.
- *F(No 2)A 2015, Sch 4, para 6* inserts a new *FA 2004, s 228C* as follows:
  - new *FA 2004, s 228C* amends the amount of the AA for 2015/16 to prevent any retrospective taxation arising as a consequence of aligning PIPs with the tax year during 2015/16;
  - new *FA 2004, s 228C(2)* splits the 2015/16 tax year into two parts for the purposes of the AA: the pre-alignment tax year which ends on 8 July 2015; and the post-alignment tax year which starts on 9 July 2015 (PTM058010);
  - new *FA 2004, s 228C(3)* ensures that only one AA charge can arise in 2015/16 which is the sum of any charge arising under the pre-alignment and post-alignment tax years. It also ensures that the rate of any charge arising is, as intended, at the individual's marginal rate for 2015/16, but where their taxable income includes any excess pension savings over the AA;
  - new *FA 2004, s 228C(4)* doubles the normal AA for the pre-alignment tax year to £80,000. For those who have flexibly accessed their pension savings, their MPAA for this period is £20,000;
  - new *FA 2004, s 228C(5)* sets out that, for members of registered pension schemes in the pre-alignment tax year, the AA and the alternative AA for the post-alignment tax year will be nil.

The MPAA for this period will be £10,000 less any amount that their DC savings for the pre-alignment tax year exceeded £10,000. As carry forward is not available for the MPAA, this means that up to £10,000 will be available for the DC savings in the post-alignment tax year. If an individual is not a member of a registered pension scheme in the pre-alignment tax year, this subsection does not apply, and their AA will be £40,000 for the post-alignment tax year;

- new *FA 2004, s 228C(6)* allows up to £40,000 of unused AA from the pre-alignment tax year to be carried forward and therefore added to the nil AA for the post-alignment tax year. However, where an individual exceeded the MPAA in the pre-alignment tax year, this carry-forward is limited to £30,000;
- new *FA 2004, s 228C(7)* amends the carry-forward rules for tax years 2016/17 to 2018/19. It ensures that, although tax year 2015/16 has been split into two for the purposes of the AA, the period over which unused AA can be carried forward is not reduced as a result, and remains at three full tax years;
- new *FA 2004, s 228C(8)* sets out the amount of unused AA that can be carried forward to future years from 2015/16. For those not subject to the MPAA, the maximum that can be carried forward is the amount of unused AA in the pre-alignment tax year, subject to a maximum of £40,000, less any amount of this used up in the post-alignment tax year. For those subject to the MPAA, the maximum that can be carried forward is the amount of unused AA in the pre-alignment tax year, subject to a maximum of £30,000, less any amount of this used up in the post-alignment tax year. *FA 2004, s 228C(7)* also preserves the order in which unused AA is used up, initially using the AA for the current year and then any unused AA carried forward from the earliest available year first; and
- new *FA 2004, s 228C(9)* ensures that, where an individual dies or becomes severely ill in the post-alignment tax year, they will not have a PIA for any savings for the pre-alignment tax year as well as the post-alignment tax year.

- The following contain the PTM references to the guidance for each type of arrangement:
  - see PTM053200 for pension savings under another DC arrangement;
  - see PTM053300 for pension savings under a DB arrangement;

- see PTM053400 for pension savings under a cash balance arrangement;
- see PTM053500 for pension savings under a hybrid arrangement;
- see PTM023100 for more details about the meaning of an arrangement; and
- see PTM056500 for more details about the application of the annual allowance or MPAA.

The carry-forward years for the future are:

- For tax year 2016/17 – from the post-alignment tax year, the pre-alignment tax year, 2014/15, 2013/14.
- For tax year 2017/18 – from 2016/17, the post-alignment tax year, the pre-alignment tax year, 2014/15.
- For tax year 2018/19 – from 2017/18, 2016/17, the post-alignment tax year, the pre-alignment tax year.

The following HMRC website extracts describe how the carry-forward changes worked for earlier years:

> 'From April 2011, the annual allowance for tax-relieved pension savings reduces from £255,000 to £50,000. You will not be affected by this change, regardless of level of income, if you are:
>
> > self-employed and contribute less than £50,000 a year into your personal pension scheme(s)
> >
> > a member of a "*money purchase*" workplace pension scheme and the total contributions made by you and your employer together with any contributions you may make to other pension arrangements (such as Additional Voluntary Contributions (AVCs) or private pensions) is less than £50,000
> >
> > a member of DB (for example, a final salary or career average) scheme and your pension savings are less than £50,000 a year
> >
> > not an active member of any registered pension scheme.'
>
> *'How does carry forward work?*
>
> If you have not used all your AA in one or more of the last three tax years, the unused amount is added to the AA available for the current tax year. This would enable you to make pension savings above the normal AA in one year and not have to pay an AA charge if you had sufficient unused AA from the previous three tax years. For example, carry forward might be helpful if you receive a promotion or are made redundant and wish to

make a large contribution to your pension arrangement as part of your redundancy agreement.'

'Do I use the £255,000 AA for 2010/11 to work out how much I can carry forward to 2011/12?

No, the amount you can carry forward from 2010/11 to offset 2011/12 pension savings is worked out as though the AA for 2010/11 was £50,000, and (for those in DB/final salary schemes) the new rules for valuing savings are used. The amounts available to carry forward from 2008/09 and 2009/10 are worked out using the same assumptions.

The new rules for valuing contributions to DB schemes use a flat factor of 16 (not the current factor of 10), and up-rate the opening value of your expected pension in line with inflation, using the CPI for September before the start of the tax year.'

HMRC have received a number of queries particularly around who can take advantage of the facility and how the amount of unused AA available for carry forward from the years 2008/09, 2009/10 and 2010/11 should be calculated. Again, HMRC's guidance on this matter is summarised below:

'An individual can carry forward unused AA from any year during which they were a scheme member, regardless of whether they made any contributions during that year or had a nil PIA during that year.

The amount of any unused AA for the years 2008/09, 2009/10 and 2010/11 should be calculated by applying the rules that would apply if the PIP for each of those years were a PIP ending in the tax year 2011/12 and using an assumed AA of £50,000 for each of those years.

The CPI up-rating factors to use for each of the above years is:

September 2007 (for use for 2008/09) 1.8

September 2008 (for use for 2009/10) 5.2

September 2009 (for use for 2010/11) 1.1

September 2010 (for use for 2011/12) 3.1.

For years 2008/09 and 2009/10, a member can only carry forward unused AA to 2011/12 if it has not been used up in a subsequent year.'

PSN 56 was published on 29 January 2013 and covered the changes to the carry forward rules as they applied at that date.

Lifetime allowance and protections from charge

11.35 LA is the maximum aggregate amount of pension savings that can benefit from tax reliefs in a fund during an individual's lifetime. It was set at

£1.5m in 2006/07 and it increased steadily to £1.8m by the year 2010. Again, this was a tax-efficient means of saving for employers and members as shown below:

- tax year 2007/08 – £1.6m;
- tax year 2008/09 – £1.65m;
- tax year 2009/10 – £1.75m;
- tax year 2010/11 – £1.8m.

The LA was frozen at the 2010/11 level up to and including the tax year 2015/16. However, the government decided to cut back the LA:

- *FA 2011, Sch 18*, brought in a reduced LA of £1.5m from 6 April 2012 for those with savings above £1.5m or with a pension pot expected to rise above this level through investment growth without any further contributions or pension savings. Application could be made before 6 April 2012 for a new personalised LA ('FP 2012') of £1.8m, providing that the member ceased accruing benefits in all registered pension schemes before 6 April 2012.

  Under FP 2012 the standard LA was replaced by a figure of £1.8m when calculating the enhancement factor where the individual is relying on protection under *FA 2004, ss 220, 222, 223* or *224*, (which apply a lifetime enhancement factor in respect of pension credits, relevant overseas individuals and transfers from QROPS). The substitution related only to events taking place before 6 April 2012.

  Savings in DB schemes cannot increase above a specified rate and no contributions may be made in the future to registered pension schemes without losing such protection. Protection can also be lost in circumstances where there is an impermissible transfer or a transfer of sums or assets that is not a permitted transfer, or a transfer into a DB scheme under a pension sharing order.

- Further changes were announced in the budget on 20 March 2013. *FA 2013, s 48* and *Sch 22* restricted tax relief for pension savings by reducing the level of the LA from £1.5m to £1.25m from 6 April 2014. Members could apply for FP 2014 of £1.5m. An individual could apply regardless of the current level of their pension savings. Members of RNUKS were also able to apply, subject to their not having a PIA of greater than nil in the non-UK pension scheme in any tax year from 2014/15. Application had to be made before 6 April 2014.

  The rules of FP 2014 are similar to those which apply to FP 2012, meaning that protection could be lost by future events in the circumstances described above.

- IP 2014 is described in *FA 2014, Sch 6*. It entitles individuals to an LA of the greater of the value of their pension rights on 5 April 2014, up to an overall maximum of £1.5m, or the level of the standard LA. It is available to individuals with UK tax-relieved pension rights of more than £1.25m or who think they may have rights in excess of that amount by the time they take their pension benefits. There is no restriction on the individual making future contributions or accruing further benefits. If, however, they exceed the limit, they will be subject to the LA charge when they take their benefits. Individuals with IP 2014 may retain FP 2012 or FP 2014, as appropriate. However, IP 2014 will apply if they subsequently lose their fixed protection.

- IP 2014 will remain at the above level unless the standard LA rises above this figure, in which case the individual's LA would revert to the standard LA. Applications may be made to HMRC until 5 April 2017, and those who may be affected will wish to obtain a valuation of their pension rights by reference to that date. A form is available on HMRC's website. Any pension commencement lump sum under IP 2014 shall be limited to 25% of the individual's pension rights, subject to an overall cap of 25% of the personalised LA. IP 2014 will cease if the monetary value of savings falls below £1.25m following a pension sharing order on divorce. However, if the pension debit reduces the value to a figure above £1.25m, IP 2014 will remain and the reduced level will apply from the date of the pension debit. The pension debit will be treated as reduced by 5% for each full tax year between 5 April 2014 and the date of the pension debit. PSNs 58, 61 and 63 cover IP 2014.

- The LA was further reduced to £1m from 6 April 2016. Transitional protection for pension rights already over £1m ensure the change is not retrospective. The LA will be indexed annually in line with CPI from 6 April 2018. These changes are included in *Finance Act 2016, s 19* and *Sch 4* (see **11.3**). They are referred to as fixed protection 2016 (FP 2016) and individual protection 2016 (IP 2016). They provide individuals with pension savings of up to £1.25m protection from retrospective taxation, subject to certain conditions. On 6 April 2016, HMRC announced what administrators need to do to check their members' protection status. The Business Guidance is entitled 'Pension administrators: check your member's protection status'.

- PSN 76 addresses members planning on taking benefits between 6 April 2016 and July 2016. They can apply to HMRC for FP 2016 or IP 2016 using the interim application process. To help members with this, HMRC have produced pro forma letter text for members to apply for both. They are appended to the PSN. For FP 2016 this will be AJ followed by four digits – for example, AJ1234. For IP 2016 this will be four digits followed by AJ – for example, 1234AJ. The reference numbers provided by the online application process will be very different from the temporary reference numbers provided through the interim process. This makes it easy for HMRC, scheme administrators and members to identify whether protection is temporary and needs to be followed up with an online application.

- The scheme member must provide HMRC with amounts A to D and their total relevant amount. The total relevant amount is the sum of amounts A to D (A + B + C + D) shown in the PSN. The member must confirm that as at 5 April 2016 they did not hold PP; EP; FP 2012 or FP 2014. PSN 77 provides appendices, which describe the interim application processes:

  - Appendix 3 – FP2016; and
  - Appendix 4 – IP2016.

PSN from 58 onward cover all the changes to the fixed protection and the individual protection regimes. They can be found at www.hmrc.gov.uk/pensionschemes/newsletterXX.pdf.

PTM is being rebuilt and does not yet reflect the new FP2016 and IP2016.

The above forms of protection are important considerations for the high earner, and scheme administrators should ensure that they are not be inadvertently lost.

11.36 Any amount over the LA threshold will be subject to a tax charge. Where excess monies are paid out in lump sum form, a charge of 55% arises on the amount paid out ('the chargeable amount'). The administrator shall withhold the charge, and remit it to HMRC. Any remaining part of the chargeable amount is referred to as the '*retained amount*'. This is the amount that will be retained by the scheme, or an overseas pension scheme (OPS) or an insurance company to fund pension benefits etc. The retained amount is subject to a lower charge than the lump-sum amount to reflect the fact that those funds will be taxed at a later point when paid from the scheme, ie when paid as a pension. The LA charge on the retained amount is therefore 25%.

Accordingly practitioners may wish to compare the value of a tax-relievable contribution combined with investment yield in a registered scheme (and an ultimate 55% charge on any excess over the allowance) with a cash payment by the employer.

A member may have a higher certified allowance than that prescribed by *FA 2004* from A-Day under primary protection (PP) but this may only increase in line with the main allowance. It was of little appeal to high earners as any future payments into the fund will be highly tax-inefficient; any growth in the fund above the increase in the standard LA would ultimately be subject to the LA charge. An alternative form of protection from A-Day was EP. Both forms of protection are described later. The later forms of fixed protection are described at **11.35**.

Test for the LA charge

11.37 Payment of a pension commencement lump sum (PCLS) and payment of a pension, whether scheme pension, lifetime annuity, or drawdown pension will occasion a test against the LA to determine whether a LA charge is due. Each benefit has slightly different characteristics when it comes to valuing it for this purpose.

11.38 Prior to the changes under *FA 2011*, scheme pension was valued at £20 per £1 pa of pension. A different factor can be agreed with HMRC if greater contingent benefits are payable. The value of a lifetime annuity is the purchase price of the annuity. It is also possible to value the annuity paid under a DC arrangement not as a lifetime annuity but as scheme pension. This means that some investment-linked annuities may be unsuitable for this purpose if they permit the level of annuity to fall below the original annuity level and therefore breach one of the scheme pension conditions. Although pension may be taken to be scheme pension under this method, the lump sum from a DC arrangement is still calculated as one-third of the annuity purchase price.

11.39 The value of unsecured pension is the actual amount that is designated for income withdrawal/drawdown (or short-term annuity). Unfortunately, the LA problem does not end with the test at that point. If unsecured pension is later used to buy scheme pension or lifetime annuity there will be a second LA test. The amount crystallised at the second test will be 20 times the scheme pension or the purchase price of the annuity less the original funds designated as available for income withdrawal. Note that the original amount of funds designated is not indexed in any way. Therefore, if the LA has been exhausted and no income is drawn from the fund, and assuming that investment returns are not negative, there would be an LA charge upon buying scheme pension/lifetime annuity. If investment growth in an unsecured pension fund is strong, it may even outstrip the maximum GAD rate (**11.62** below) that applies each year. As before, the charge may be mitigated or even avoided by treating the annuity purchased as a scheme pension, but as a member gets older the more likely it is that the cost of an annuity will drop below £20 per £1 pa.

As stated above in **11.64**, there have been significant relaxations to the pension access and annuity rules under recent legislation.

Contributions in specie

11.40 It is possible to transfer an asset into a registered pension scheme, if the rules so permit. However, this will effectively be a gift and so will not enjoy tax relief. On the other hand, an asset transferred in satisfaction of a contribution to be made may be acceptable, with tax relief being available on the amount of contribution due. *In specie* contributions will potentially be chargeable to CGT as a disposal but will not be subject to stamp duty or stamp duty land tax. It will be necessary to seek specialist guidance on the IHT position (eg with regard to pre-owned assets).

Shares granted in an employer's share incentive plan or under an SAYE share option scheme may nonetheless be transferred to a UK-registered pension scheme within 90 days of entitlement and will be treated for tax relief as if they were a contribution made by the member. Tax relief is available on the market value of the shares. Corporate advisers may want to consider possibilities for using a share incentive plan or save-as-you earn (SAYE) scheme in conjunction with a company's pension scheme.

Recycling tax-free cash lump sums

11.41 *FA 2004, Sch 29, para 3A* restricts the recycling of tax-free cash lump sums from A-Day. Examples that illustrate situations where the recycling rule applies are given at PTM133850. HMRC expressed concern that some practitioners had identified that a member may take a tax-free cash lump sum and immediately re-invest it in a registered scheme. The payment would obtain tax relief, and the member could then take another tax-free cash lump sum to enable the cycle to be repeated. Such arrangements are blocked by the (revised) legislation, which removed the tax advantages relating to any cash lump sums artificially recycled. However, HMRC state that it is not intended to affect cases where an individual takes a tax-free cash lump sum as part of the normal course of taking pension benefits.

The legislation applies to contributions which are greater than 30% of the relevant cash lump sum made at the time a tax-free cash lump sum is paid. All or part of the pension commencement lump sum is treated as an unauthorised member payment for tax purposes. Recipients of unauthorised member payments are liable for special stand-alone tax charges of either 40% or 55% of the payment depending on whether the amount of the lump sum in question that is deemed to be an unauthorised payment exceeds a set surcharge threshold of 25%.

Members must notify their scheme administrator when such an unauthorised payment is made and its amount, and practitioners/advisers will wish to apprise them of this requirement.

INVESTMENT OPPORTUNITIES

Introduction

11.42 Pension investment funds may build up tax free. The relief provisions are described in *FA 2004, ss 186* and *187*. Many of the investment restrictions which had been imposed on tax-approved schemes before A-Day were relaxed. In particular, the removal of the restriction on investment in residential property was a major relaxation. Therefore, a review of the investments of existing schemes is to be recommended if best advantage is to be taken of the new opportunities which have arisen. However, contrary to the true principles of simplification, restrictions were imposed on schemes which contain an element of member-direction on their investment activity. These restrictions were inserted into the Act by *FA 2006*. The rules which apply to the category of schemes which contain member-direction powers (IRPS see **11.46–11.50** below).

The rules which apply

11.43 In addition to the relaxations in the area of property acquisition, most of the restrictions on transactions between connected persons were removed by *FA 2004*. The pensions tax regime depends largely on the prudence of trustees and administrators, and compliance with their wider statutory duties. The main rules are as follows.

For large schemes, shareholdings in the sponsoring company and associated/ connected companies remain limited to 5% of the fund value, a restriction imposed not by tax law but by the *Occupational Pension Schemes (Investment) Regulations 2005 (SI 2005/3378)*, issued under *Pensions Act 1995* (*PA 1995*). The Regulations were amended to provide an exception for investments by the operator of a collective investment scheme, and a transitional provision which allows certain schemes to retain employer-related investments in excess of the 5% limit required by *Directive 2003/41/EC of the European Parliament and the Council on the activities and supervision of institutions for occupational retirement provision* ('the *IORPS Directive*').

Although *FA 2004, s 179* permits loans of up to 50% of fund value to participating employers and to companies associated with them, *SI 2005/3378* contains a general prohibition on making loans to a sponsoring employer. However, the pre A-Day exemptions which applied to small self-administered schemes (SSASs) have remained, and there are certain limited exemptions for existing loans from schemes with fewer than 100 members:

- Underwriting commissions applied for the purposes of a scheme are not liable to income tax and other forms of income, such as stock-lending fees, and income derived from futures and options contracts are similarly exempt from tax, as previously.
- Borrowing must not exceed 50% of fund value (*FA 2004, ss 182–185* and *FA 2004, s 163*).
- Debts between the scheme, the employer or the member must be on commercial terms, and unpaid debts are taxed as unauthorised payments.

- All investments, including loans to third parties, must be on commercial terms, not remove value from the fund and annuities must not provide for a return of the balance of insurance funds on death except in specific authorised circumstances.
- Trading income is taxable under the self-assessment procedure.
- Income derived from investments or deposits held as a member of a property investment limited liability partnership are liable to tax, as previously.
- Non-commercial use of assets by a member or associate attracts a benefit-in-kind charge on the member.
- Member loans are prohibited (this means that personal pension schemes and retirement annuities that have no sponsoring employer are unable to make loans to their members' businesses or partnerships where a partner is the scheme member – loans to third parties are, however, permitted, but they must be on fully commercial terms).

Further information on loans

11.44 The other requirements of the *FA 2004* for loans are:

- the meaning of a 'loan' is given in *FA 2004, s 162*;
- employer loans are permitted up to five years' duration – if it is not possible for an employer to repay a loan within the agreed period, it may be rolled over once for a maximum period of five years;
- loans must be secured against assets of at least equal value;
- any amounts which exceed 50% of total fund value (or are otherwise unauthorised employer payments) will be taxed at 40%;
- under the *Pension Schemes (Prescribed Interest Rates for Authorised Employer Loans) Regulations 2005, SI 2005/3449* a loan reference rate must be charged, being an average of the base rates of a specified group of banks (the rate is 1% more than the reference rate found on the reference date preceding the start of the period (ie on 6 April));
- *FA 2004, Sch 30* contains various loan definitions and explains the treatment of unauthorised payments;
- *FA 2004, Sch 36, Pt 4, para 38* describes the transitional arrangements for loans.

Surcharges and sanctions may be imposed if the provisions are abused and, where high levels of unauthorised payments are made, the registration of the scheme may be withdrawn.

It is important that investments are held securely and under a 'prudent person' principal. Satisfactory arrangements must be in place for holding the scheme's assets, which must be separate from the employer's account. Trustees/scheme administrators have a statutory duty to consult with the employer about the scheme's statement of investment principles,

The DC Code contains guidance in areas such as lifestyling and the investment of contributions, reviewing performance, changing funds and monitoring and reviewing the scheme's default strategy. A default strategy of investment should be selected automatically for a member joining the scheme, unless the member chooses to set their own strategy and chooses funds themselves from those made available by the trustees.

Pre A-Day transitional provisions

11.45 In general, investments which were held as at A-Day in accordance with the relevant HMRC requirements at the time may be retained if they are left undisturbed. Changes to loans, borrowings, leases, etc will normally mean that the new investment rules will apply.

Investment-regulated pension schemes

11.46 Following the enactment of the *FA 2004*, the government declared its intent to impose new restrictions on small schemes, and to extend those restrictions to schemes in which investments may be self-directed or controlled by members and connected persons. The outcome was that the term IRPS appeared in *FA 2006* and prohibitive charges can be incurred by such schemes. If a scheme holds, say, 10% of the company shares, it will be taxed on 10% of the taxable property of the company. The area is a most complex one, which requires specialist advice. A description of the main criteria which apply is accordingly given below.

Definition of IRPS

11.47 An IRPS is a scheme or arrangement which fits one of the following descriptions:

- *An occupational scheme*: where there are 50 or fewer members and at least one meets the following condition, or 10% or more of the members of a scheme meet that condition. The condition is that one or more of those members or a person related to one of those members is or was able (directly or indirectly) to direct influence or advise on investments held by the scheme.

- *A scheme which is not an occupational scheme*: where one or more members, or a person related to the member is or was able (directly or indirectly) to direct, influence or advise on investments for the purpose of the scheme under an arrangement for that member.
- *An arrangement, within an occupational scheme which is not an IRPS:* which has one or more members or a person related to one of the members who is or was able (directly or indirectly) to direct, influence or advise on investments which are linked to an arrangement relating to that member ('linked' means the sums or assets are held for the purpose of an arrangement under the scheme relating to that member, but not merely by virtue of apportionment of scheme assets).

The definition of an IRPS was relaxed retrospectively to 6 April 2006. It excludes schemes in which the individual members could not realistically be expected to influence scheme decisions to invest in taxable property. This will primarily affect large occupational pension schemes, although the precise meaning of the relaxation is at present unclear.

The tax charges

11.48 It is important to note that the use of funds to acquire, improve, convert or adapt taxable property is deemed to be an unauthorised member payment by the scheme, so triggering an unauthorised payment charge at 40% on the member, and a 40% scheme sanction charge on the scheme administrator, which may be reduced to 15% when the member has paid his liability. Income from such property is liable to income tax. Additionally, the administrator will be liable to capital gains on the disposal of assets. If the net income from the property is less than 10% of the value of the property then in place of the actual income the administrator will be taxed on a deemed income. The amount of the deemed income will be 10% of the value of the property.

The member may also face a further 15% unauthorised payment surcharge if the taxable property is a wasting asset (eg a leasehold interest in property for less than 50 years or plant and machinery). In a worst-case scenario, HMRC may de-register the scheme, resulting in a further charge on the administrator of 40% of the scheme value.

The meaning of taxable property

11.49 Taxable property is residential property and most tangible moveable property. Residential property (wherever based) is a building or structure, including associated land, that is used or suitable for use as a dwelling. Tangible moveable property is things that you can touch and move (eg assets such as art, antiques, jewellery, fine wine, classic cars, yachts, stamps, autographs, gems and certain machinery).

The provisions apply to taxable property held directly or indirectly, except through genuinely diverse commercial vehicles. The benefit in kind charge on personal use of registered scheme assets will not apply to assets taxed under these measures.

There are some specific exceptions from the meaning of tangible moveable property under the *Investment-regulated Pension Schemes (Exception of Tangible Moveable Property) Order 2006 (SI 2006/1959).* These are gold bullion, and items with a market value of £6,000 or less which no member of the scheme or connected person has a right to use or occupy, and in which the scheme does not hold an interest directly, and which is held by a 'vehicle' (*FA 2004, Sch 29A, para 20*) for the purpose of management or administration of that vehicle. There are also some exemptions from a charge for investments in various types of investment vehicle, including certain types of property investment vehicles unless one of the purposes for which the scheme holds an interest in the vehicle is to enable a member or person connected to a member to occupy or use taxable property of the vehicle. However, the exemption from the charge on indirect holdings for UK real estate investment trusts (unless such investment is made to enable a scheme member or a connected person to occupy or use residential property) does not apply if the holding by any relevant person is 10% or more.

The transitional exemptions

11.50 The taxable property provisions do not apply if:

- the scheme held an interest in such property on A-Day which it had acquired before that date, and which it was not prohibited from holding up to 5 April 2006; or
- before A-Day the property was held by a person other than the scheme and the scheme was not prohibited from holding the interest it held in that person at that time; or
- the scheme or a person in whom the scheme directly or indirectly held an interest entered into a contract to acquire an interest in such property before A-Day and was not at that time prohibited from acquiring such an interest, but acquires the property on or after that date.

It should be noted that the exemption is lost on a change in occupation or use, or where there is a change in the scheme's interest in any person who holds a direct interest in the property or in anyone who has entered into a contract to acquire the property (if the change would not have met pre A-Day conditions).

DRAWING BENEFITS

Minimum payment age

11.51

> **Focus**
>
> It is important to follow the rules which apply to the minimum pension age for drawing benefits if prohibitive tax charges are to be avoided. However, there are exceptions for certain categories of member as shown below.

Unless a pension is being brought into payment on grounds of ill health it must not commence before age 55 (50 pre-6 April 2010). However, anyone entitled to a low retirement age before A-Day may continue to benefit from that low retirement age if certain conditions are met. This is known as the member's protected pension age. This will mainly affect sportsmen or those in hazardous occupations (see the *Registered Pension Schemes (Prescribed Schemes and Occupations) Regulations 2005 (SI 2005/3451)*, but can also affect employees who may be entitled to early payment of pension as of right in certain conditions (eg redundancy).

Where a member has a protected pension age, the tax rules provide that the protected pension age replaces the normal prevailing pension age for all purposes of the pensions tax legislation other than the reduction in the member's LA that may apply where the protected pension age is less than 50 and benefits are taken before normal minimum pension age (MPA).

Members of personal pension schemes (PPS) and retirement annuity contracts (RAC) may retain their low normal retirement age if:

- there was an unqualified right to take a pension before age 50;
- they draw all uncrystallised pension and/or lump sum rights under the scheme on the same day; and
- they hold one of the following occupations:
  - athlete
  - badminton player
  - boxer
  - cricketer
  - cyclist

- dancer
- diver (saturation, deep sea and free swimming)
- footballer
- golfer
- ice hockey player
- jockey – flat racing
- jockey – national hunt
- member of the reserve forces
- model
- motor cycle rider (motocross or road racing)
- motor racing driver
- rugby league player
- rugby union player
- skier (downhill)
- snooker or billiards player
- speedway rider
- squash player
- table tennis player
- tennis player (including real tennis)
- trapeze artiste
- wrestler.

Benefits may only become payable on cessation of any related employment. The right will be lost upon a transfer of benefit, but not if it is part of a block transfer.

11.52 Members of occupational pension schemes or deferred annuity contracts with a low normal retirement age are able to retain that right if:

- they had an unqualified right on 5 April 2006 to take a pension and/or lump sum before the age of 55;
- the provision was set out in the governing documentation of the retirement benefit scheme or deferred annuity contract on 10 December 2003;

- they draw all of their uncrystallised pension and/or lump sum rights under the scheme on the same day;
- they have left the employment to which the scheme relates; and
- they either:
  - had the right under the scheme or contract on 10 December 2003; or
  - acquired the right in accordance with the scheme provisions as they were on 10 December 2003 upon joining the scheme after that date.

Although those with a low normal retirement age may continue to enjoy this right under transitional protection, their LA will be reduced by 2.5% for each complete year between the date they draw benefits and the date on which they would have reached MPA (50 or 55, depending on occupation). The 2.5% reduction will not apply, however, in the case of benefits from certain public sector schemes.

Ill health retirement

11.53 Dependent on a scheme's rules, benefits may be paid before age 55 in circumstances of ill health. A member must have left the employment to which the pension relates (either now or at a previous date) and the administrator must obtain proper medical evidence that the member is incapable of continuing in his current occupation. If scheme rules permit, ill health pension may be temporarily suspended if the member recovers sufficiently to return to his original job.

Ill-health insurance contracts, which were approved for PPSs before 6 April 2001, or for RACs, are not to be regarded as unauthorised payments.

Pensions

11.54 There is no overall limit on the amount of pension which can be paid under *FA 2004*, and, except in cases referred to above, there is no requirement that a member must have left employment for a benefit to be paid. Pension could only be paid in one of the following forms:

- scheme pension (this *must* be paid under a defined benefit arrangement);
- lifetime annuity;
- unsecured pension before age 75 (income withdrawal or short-term annuity);
- ASP after age 75 (income withdrawal).

The last two bullet points were replaced by drawdown pensions under *FA 2011, Sch 16,* rules from 6 April 2011 and flexi-access for DC schemes from 6 April 2015. The rules which apply to drawdown pensions were ever-changing. They are described at **11.61–11.65** below.

Scheme pension

11.55 Scheme pensions maybe paid under a DB arrangement or a DC arrangement. Scheme pensions are described in PTM062310–PTM062340. They must meet the following conditions:

- It must be payable by the scheme administrator or by an insurance company selected by the scheme administrator.
- It must be payable in at least annual instalments until the member's death or until the later of the member's death and a guaranteed period of up to ten years.
- The level of scheme pension must not decrease from one year to the next except in permitted circumstances.

If it is paid under a DC arrangement, the member must first have had the choice to select a lifetime annuity.

Scheme pensions do not have to be provided by age 75 – they can come into payment at any time from the member's 55th birthday onwards. But any undrawn entitlements are tested for LA purposes at age 75.

Members lose the right to have benefits payable in any form other than a scheme pension when they take scheme pension. They also lose their right to the funds available – that right was exchanged for a guaranteed pension. A scheme pension may be guaranteed for a term certain of no more than ten years. So if the member dies before that term has ended, the scheme pension will continue to be paid until the end of the guarantee period, but to another person. These guarantee payments cannot be commuted and paid as a lump sum.

11.56 The circumstances in which a scheme pension would decrease were:

- reduction of an ill health pension upon full or partial recovery;
- a reduction applying to all pensions in payment;
- reduction between the ages of 60 and 65 (or later SPA depending on age) to take account of integration with the state pension (bridging pension);
- pension sharing order or provision;

- forfeiture of pension under provisions allowed by *PA 1995* and regulations made by HMRC;
- court order;
- abatement under a public service pension scheme;
- the rate of scheme pension payable is being reduced in consequence of a court order;
- the rate of scheme pension payable to a member is being reduced on or after 6 April 2013 in consequence of the scheme administrator paying an amount of AA charge in relation to the member;
- certain other circumstances relating to the PPF, contracted-out rights affected by the *Gender Recognition Act 2004* and admission to the Royal Hospital at Chelsea.

There is a further relaxation from 6 April 2015 as described in **11.64**.

11.57 If the level of pension decreased other than in permitted circumstances, future instalments would be subject to unauthorised payment charges. Furthermore if the level of scheme pension was reduced to below 80% of its original level, any tax-free lump sum paid in connection with the pension will become an unauthorised payment. There is a relaxation from 6 April 2015 as described in **11.63**.

Lifetime annuity

11.58 A lifetime annuity may be paid under a DC arrangement. It may be purchased from either uncrystallised funds, a drawdown pension fund or a flexi-access drawdown fund. From 6 April 2015 onwards, the following conditions must be met:

- the member must become entitled to the annuity on or after 6 April 2015, ie if the member became entitled to the annuity before 6 April 2015 that annuity must satisfy the previous lifetime annuity conditions set out below;
- the annuity must be purchased from an insurance company (the previous condition which required the member to have the opportunity to select the insurance company providing the annuity does not apply from 6 April 2015;
- the annuity must be payable for the member's life or until, if later, the expiry of a specified period (a 'term certain') of any duration for which payment of the annuity is guaranteed (the previous condition which limited the period of a term certain to a maximum of 10 years' duration no longer applies);

- the member must have had an opportunity to select the insurance company (open market option);
- it must be payable until the member's death or until the later of the member's death and a guaranteed period of up to ten years;
- it must not decrease in payment except where the variation relies on investment performance, tracks an investment index or the retail prices index. A lifetime annuity may also be reduced in consequence of a pension sharing order.

There are flexible rules for annuities from 6 April 2015 as described in **11.64**.

Unsecured pension and ASP before 6 April 2011

Unsecured pension

11.59 Under *FA 2004*, unsecured pension could take the form of a short-term annuity, purchased with pension scheme funds and payable for no more than five years (and not beyond age 75). However, unsecured pension was more likely to take the form of income withdrawal/ASP.

The maximum amount of income that could be drawn annually was 120% of a notional annuity rate calculated using tables drawn up by the Government Actuary's Department (GAD). The GAD rates were based on a single-life, non-escalating annuity for a person of the same age and gender as the member.

However, there are new rules for annuities from 6 April 2015 as described in **11.64**.

ASP

11.60 ASP was permitted for DC and cash balance arrangements. It was the same as for income withdrawal under age 75 with two important differences:

- the GAD rate to be applied was the rate for a 75-year-old whatever age the member was;
- a minimum amount of 55% of the GAD rate had to be drawn each year, and the maximum amount that could be drawn was 90% of the GAD rate.

ASP could therefore be unattractive to anyone unless there existed a genuine objection to the mortality pooling that comes with purchasing an annuity, or even just an objection to leaving money to an insurance company.

The age 75 rule was raised to 77 by *F(No 2)A 2010, Sch 3*. The provisions concerning the pension and pension death benefit rules for unsecured pensions, secured pensions, lump sums, ASPs and pension and lump sum death benefit (LSDB) rules had effect as if any reference to an age of 75 were a reference to a person's 75th birthday were a reference to a person's 77th birthday. The rules applied to an annuity that was purchased on or after 22 June 2010. Anyone who had not annuitised before 22 June 2010, but had reached age 75 by that date, would have had to enter into ASP.

Under the provisions of *FA 2011, Sch 16*, from 6 April 2011, IHT was not charged on drawdown funds which remain in a UK-registered pension scheme, whatever age the individual was at the date of death. However, IHT charges remain in circumstances where the scheme trustees have no discretion over the payment of lump sum death benefits, and to lump sums from non-registered pension schemes or non-qualifying non-UK pension schemes.

The drawdown rules from 6 April 2011

11.61 There has been much meddling with the post-6 April 2011 drawdown rules for DC schemes. The latest development was flexi-access, which is described in **11.63**. A chronological list of changes prior to 6 April 2015 is given in **11.62** and **11.63**.

Capped drawdown

11.62 *FA 2004, s 167, pension rule 4*, was amended so that an increase in the drawdown level to 120% applied to pension years starting on or after 26 March 2013. *FA 2014, s 14*. subsequently brought in an increase in the capped drawdown limit from 120% to 150% of the basis amount from 27 March 2014.

The 120%/150% maximum income levels also applied to dependants' drawdown pension.

The general rules for capped drawdown are:

- there was a maximum income level which could be purchased whilst the member retains the fund (see above);
- the above amount must be determined at least every three years until the end of the year in which the member reaches the age of 75 (thereafter, annual reviews must be carried out);
- there was a maximum income level of 100% of the equivalent annuity which could be purchased whilst the member retains the fund for capped drawdown;
- the budget on 20 March 2013 stated that the limit on the amount of pension an individual may take each year under capped drawdown would increase from 100% to 120%;

- *FA 2013, s 50,* increased the capped drawdown limit from 26 March 2013 to 120%, and made a similar revision to legislation in order to increase the maximum dependants' drawdown pension amount;
- *FA 2014, s 14*, increased the capped drawdown limit from 150%, and made a similar revision to legislation in order to increase the maximum dependants' drawdown pension amount;
- the age 75 ceiling was removed from most lump sums (eg pension commencement lump sums, serious ill health lump sums, winding-up lump sums and trivial commutation lump sums);
- withdrawals which are made whilst a member is resident overseas for a period of less than five full tax years will be taxed in the tax year in which they become UK resident again;
- any tax-free cash sum must be taken when income drawdown commences;
- the age 75 limit for taking cash was removed;
- an individual may take no income at all in a year;
- the drawdown rules only apply where an individual has ceased to be an active member of any registered pension schemes, and any future pension savings by that individual anywhere will attract the excess AA charge.
- any future pension savings attract the AA charge;
- IHT is not chargeable on drawdown funds which remain in a UK-registered pension scheme, whatever the member's age at death. It is also not chargeable on QROPS or qualifying non-recognised overseas pension schemes (QNUPS). However, IHT remains chargeable where the scheme trustees have no discretion over the payment of lump sum death benefits, and to lump sums from non-registered pension schemes or RNUKS.

The *EU Gender Directive*, from 21 December 2012, means that the scheme administrator should use the GAD table for men to obtain the relevant annuity rate for women if the woman is aged:

- over 23 with a reference period starting on or after 21 December 2012 (including when the nominated period is before that date);
- 75 or over with a drawdown pension year starting on or after that date (including when the nominated period is before that date).

Where an individual became entitled before 6 April 2006 to a capped drawdown pension and no benefit crystallisation event (BCE) has yet occurred, the amount of LA treated as used up by that pension when the first benefit crystallisation event occurs will be reduced to 80% of the maximum drawdown pension payable under that arrangement.

Flexible drawdown

11.63 For flexible drawdown, individuals with a lifetime pension income of at least £20,000 a year (excluding any temporary pension or drawdown pension, but including state benefits) could, subject to the rules of their scheme, access their drawdown funds without any cap on the amount of the withdrawals made. Any subsequent pension savings for an individual who applied to access the whole of their drawdown pension fund would be liable to the AA charge on all PIAs.

FA 2014, s 14, subsequently brought in a cut in the minimum income requirement for flexible drawdown from £20,000 to £12,000 from 27 March 2014.

FA 2014 removed the revaluation factor for determining how much of the commutation limit is used up by crystallisation of previous pension rights. Additionally, the 55% tax charge on lump sums taken in excess of 25% was reduced to the individual's normal marginal tax rates.

Subsequent changes and flexi-access

11.64 In his budget speech on 19 March 2014, the Chancellor said that major changes to DC scheme access would have effect from 6 April 2015. The changes were:

- complete freedom for individuals to draw down as much or as little of their pension pot as they want, anytime they want;
- a removal of all caps and drawdown limits;
- no one will have to buy an annuity;
- a new right to advice on decision-making.

FA 2014, Sch 5, provided a temporary relaxation to allow a transfer of pension rights after a lump sum is paid and a temporary relaxation to allow lump sum to be repaid to pension scheme that paid it. The provisions widened the six-month lump sum window to 18 months in order to give DC members who have already taken their PCLS flexibility to delay drawing their pension until after April 2015.

This was all very well but, sadly, the UK has a very low level of state retirement provision compared with its European neighbours. It has traditionally relied on private pension provision for the employed, and provided tax-incentives to employees and their employers to save for retirement. It is quite clear that this approach is now considered by the government to be unnecessary, as the previous Pensions Minister asserted after the budget that members can make extravagant purchases (*'If people do get a Lamborghini, and end up on the state pension, the state is much less concerned about that, and that is their choice*').

Clearly, for those members of DC schemes in need of ready cash, this offers a clear incentive to melt down their pension entitlements. It also makes it attractive for members of DB schemes to transfer to DC schemes and to crash out their future pension entitlements. However, in the latter case, HM Treasury stated that it will only allow private DB scheme members to transfer to DC schemes 'if the risks and issues around doing so can be shown to be manageable'. In a seemingly discriminatory statement, it added that it will ban or restrict such transfers for public sector workers, and would impose special restrictions on private sector members. HM Treasury later bowed a little to pressure from the pension industry and, on 21 July 2014, it stated that most members will have freedom to effect such transfers but not members currently drawing down their DB pensions or still those who wish to make transfers from unfunded public sector pensions.

The windfall tax receipts at taxpayer's marginal rates were obviously a one-off gain for the Chancellor. Naturally, the changes have a marked effect on the insurance market, and new-style annuity provision are being developed.

The government backed down on the Chancellor's pledge during consultation on DC access '*to introduce a new guarantee, enforced by law, that everyone who retires on the defined contribution pensions will be offered free, impartial, face-to-face advice on how to get the most from the choices they will now have*'. The government replaced the word '*advice*' with the word '*guidance*'. This meant that individuals will not receive regulated financial advice unless they pay for it.

It was announced later in the budget on 18 March 2015 that there will be an exemption from an IT charge and NICs when the employer bears the cost of providing the advice and does not pass this on to employees through the use of salary sacrifice arrangements.

On 4 March 2015, the FCA stated that it requires all pension transfer advice to be verified by a qualified specialist.

Representatives of the pensions industry began to respond to the changes, unsurprisingly focusing largely on their own business streams. The comments from various parties were contained in the previous edition of this chapter.

The previous Pensions Minister admitted that the new 'freedoms' are a calculated risk. He said:

> 'We wouldn't be doing it if we thought it was a disaster, but you do take a risk when you trust people with their own money'. He added that where an

individual has spent all their pension pot 'You enjoyed it and then intend to live on your state pension and, perhaps, other savings. Is that the wrong outcome?'

Additionally, on 24 October 2014, he stated that men who withdraw large sums from their pension pots should be forced to sign a waiver admitting they know their widows could be left destitute.

The Green Paper entitled 'Strengthening the incentive to save: A consultation on pensions' tax relief' was intended to produce an even greater windfall, by means of considerable tax savings. This was later abandoned (see under 'Signposts' at the beginning of this chapter).

The latest position is given in **11.65**.

11.65 *PSA 2015* contains the following provisions:

- a requirement for trustees to check that a member has taken independent advice from an appropriate person before converting any DB into flexible benefits or transferring them to a different scheme in order to acquire flexible benefits;
- power by regulation to specify the circumstances in which an employer must arrange or pay for such independent advice from an appropriate person;
- a ban on transfers out of unfunded DB public service schemes to schemes in which the member can obtain flexible benefits; and
- the removal of a restriction so that members have the right to take a cash equivalent transfer value up to their scheme's normal pension age, rather than up to one year before they are due to reach their scheme's NPA.

TOPA 2014 describes the drawdown facility as '*Flexi-access drawdown funds*'. Individuals will be treated as flexibly accessing their pension if they receive any of the following on or after 6 April 2015:

- a payment from a flexi-access drawdown fund, including a payment from a capped drawdown fund that would breach the cap;
- an uncrystallised fund pension lump sum (UFPLS);
- a payment under a flexible annuity contract;
- a payment of a DC scheme pension where the scheme has fewer than 11 other pensioner members and they became entitled to the scheme pension on or after 6 April 2015;
- a stand-alone lump sum from a DC arrangement where the individual was entitled to PP but not EP, that is where *Circumstance A* in *Article 25B(2),*

Taxation of Pension Schemes (Transitional Provisions) Order 2006 (SI 2006/572), as amended, applies.

Additionally, any person who had a valid notification for flexible drawdown before 6 April 2015 will be deemed to have flexibly accessed their rights at the start of 6 April 2015.

The latest rules are very detailed and complex. They are listed in the summary below.

- It is confirmed that members of DC schemes aged over 55 may draw down as much or as little of their pension pot as they want, at any time they want.
- There are no transitional arrangements for payments that are requested before 6 April 2015 but paid after. Therefore if (for example) an application for trivial commutation under a DC arrangement was received prior to 6 April 2015 but the individual's payroll system was unable to process it in time for the year end and the payment is made after 6 April 2015 and can't be paid as a small pot commutation, the payment must be treated as an UFPLS and reported (see **11.102**).
- It is proposed to raise the age at which an individual can take their private pension savings under the tax rules from 55 to 57 by 2028 (see **11.4**), at the point that the SPA increases to 67.
- All caps and drawdown limits are removed.
- No one will have to buy an annuity.
- Any individual who accesses their pension fund under the flexi-access rules will be subject to the MPAA of £10,000 or 100% of their salary, whichever is lower, and unused allowance cannot be carried forward. The object is to prevent individuals who have drawn cash from benefiting if they subsequently reinvest the cash taken into a new pension and receive tax relief again.
- Scheme administrators must provide individuals who are subject to the MPAA with a pensions savings statement if their DC savings, which will include savings in certain hybrid arrangements, exceed £10,000 in that particular scheme.
- The MPAA restriction does not apply to individuals who are already in capped drawdown. They may retain the £40,000 annual limit.
- Individuals who access their pension savings flexibly from a flexi-access drawdown fund will retain an AA for DB pension savings of up to £40,000, depending on the value of new DC pension savings.

- All existing funds used for pre-6 April 2015 flexible drawdown will automatically become flexi-access drawdown funds.
- Up to 25% of the fund payment will be tax free as an UFPLS. The balance will be taxed at the member's marginal rate (currently 20%; 40%; or 45%).
- Normal PAYE rules should apply to flexi-access payments which are not tax-free lump sums. All payments should be reported on the real time information basis (RTI) Full Payment Submission (FPS) in a similar way to annuity payments currently, but with data item 168 populated. There are two new value fields for reporting flexibility payments: 'taxable amount' (data item 173) and 'non-taxable amount' (data item 174). Where data item 168 is set, details of the taxable and non-taxable elements of the payment should be entered in these fields.
- The lump sum tax-free payments should not be reported at all under RTI. The *Income Tax (Pay As You Earn) (Amendment) Regulations 2016 (SI 2016/329)* amend the *Income Tax (Pay As You Earn) Regulations 2003 (SI 2003/2682)* regarding information which employers and scheme administrators must report to HMRC on making a payment to an employee or pensioner. The obligation for employers to complete 'end of year questions' when submitting the final return of the year is removed.

  Where payment is made for the first time, and there is no existing PAYE scheme, one must be set up. Where the fund is exhausted in one payment, an end date must appear on the RTI FPS and a P45 issued, to enable the member to claim any tax refund that might be due in-year.
- Where a member decides to receive their money over more than one payment, for example, in five annual payments, the end date should only be entered on the FPS and a P45 issued once the final payment is made.
- Withdrawals may be made in stages. In most cases, HMRC will apply an emergency month 1 tax code 1060L M1. It was announced on 7 April 2015 that providers will need to apply the emergency code (circa 36%) to payments unless a P45 is produced. HMRC have given a 'promise' that they will repay any overcharge 'within one month'. To reclaim the excess tax, the individual will need to complete a repayment form, ie:
  - a P50 if their sole income is a state pension, or
  - a P53 if they have other income.

  Alternatively, pensioners will receive a refund at the end of the tax year.
- PSN 75 states:

  > 'Due to the forthcoming changes to the taxing of certain death benefits from 6 April 2016 and following feedback from the industry about

the reporting of pension flexibility payments from April 2015, HMRC have introduced 3 new RTI data items to enable the reporting and quantifying of flexibly accessed pension rights (including UFPLSs) and death benefits. You can find details of these in *Pension Schemes Newsletter 74*'.

- HMRC have agreed a process for members to claim an in-year repayment in circumstances where funds have been fully extinguished. This process mirrors the in-year trivial commutation repayment process.
- The tax surcharge of 55% for DC members who withdraw their full savings will be charged at the individual's marginal income tax rate.
- The scheme administrator must provide the member with a statement confirming the date the first payment occurred and setting out what they must do when a member first flexibly accesses their pension savings,. The statement must be provided within 31 days of the flexible access occurring. If the member (or another scheme administrator) has already informed the scheme administrator that they have flexibly accessed another scheme then the scheme administrator does not need to provide the member with a statement. Members then need to tell any other pension scheme that they are an active member of, that they have flexibly accessed their pension savings, but excluding any DB only schemes. This notification must be provided within 91 days of receiving the statement or within 91 days of becoming an active member, whichever is the later.
- Where a member uses funds from a flexi-access drawdown fund to buy an annuity or scheme pension from an insurance company, the scheme administrator must inform the insurance company providing that scheme pension or lifetime annuity. This is an extension to the information that must be provided to insurance companies where payments are made from drawdown funds, to include flexibly accessed funds.
- When an individual under age 55 with a protected pension age transfers benefits in payment as part of a recognised transfer, the transfer won't cause any pension payment made before the member's 55th birthday to be unauthorised.
- When making a transfer, if a transferring scheme has been notified by a member that they also have flexibly accessed rights elsewhere or the member has flexibly accessed their rights in that scheme, the scheme administrator will be required to notify the receiving scheme of the date they believe the first flexible access occurred. This notification must be made within 31 days of the transfer, or if later, within 31 days from the date the scheme administrator became aware that the member had flexibly accessed their pension rights.
- There is no requirement for the receiving scheme administrator to provide the member with a statement on receipt of a transfer for a member who

has already flexibly accessed their rights, and there is no requirement for the scheme administrator to notify HMRC.

- As from 6 April 2015, annuities can be provided that can decrease and increase in value, as the annuitant chooses. Lump sums may be taken from annuities. Lifetime annuities may reduce as well as increase in value. However, where an individual is paid an annuity that can reduce, other than in prescribed circumstances, this can trigger the MPAA.
- Where an individual becomes entitled to a lifetime annuity before the normal minimum pension age and without the ill-health condition applying, the amount treated as crystallised by that annuity at age 55 will be the higher of the annual rate of the annuity multiplied by 20 and the original value of the sums and assets used to buy the lifetime annuity.
- The government is proposing to permit existing pensioners to sell their annuities for cash. Tax will be applied at individual's marginal rate. Annuity holders that assign to a third party the right to their annuity payments will get the £10,000 MPAA that applied to DC schemes from April 2015. HM Treasury's view was that a second-hand annuity market may fail to emerge.
- In the budget on 8 July 2015, it was announced that it has been decided to put back the implementation from April 2016 to April 2017.
- On 15 December 2015, the government announced that, on the agreement of their annuity provider, individuals will be able to assign their annuity to a third party buyer in return for a capital lump sum or a drawdown pension which can be accessed flexibly. The annuity provider would continue to retain the underlying assets and would pay the annuity income to the third party for the lifetime of the annuity holder.
- The annuity must belong to an individual and be held in their own name. DC annuities held as general scheme assets (and not in the name of the individual) will be out of scope, as will be DB scheme annuities which are within an occupational scheme. However, scheme trustees will be able to permit assignment, if both they and the member wish to do so.
- PSN 77describes the secondary annuities market.
- It is now stated that the promised 'free, impartial, face-to-face' guidance will not have to be face-to-face, it could be by means of telephone calls or online. However, it will be funded by a levy on insurers that will be paid for through higher charges on pension schemes.
- Guidance under a new single entity to replace PAS, PW and MAS (see **11.3**) will be closely monitored by the FCA.
- Transferees from DB schemes to DC schemes must pay for financial advice. The government has abandoned the requirement for DB members to take regulated advice before transferring a small pot into a DC scheme.

- Transfer values can be well below the value of the pension pot – perhaps only 60% in value – and indexation for future years will be lost.
- Members of unfunded public sector schemes are banned from transferring to DC schemes.
- A drawdown pension fund existing on 5 April 2015 is not prevented from remaining a drawdown pension fund by the member designating additional funds to it on or after 6 April 2015 unless *FA 2004, s 165(3A),* applied in respect of the arrangement before 6 April 2015, where the scheme administrator accepted the member's flexible drawdown declaration in respect of that arrangement.
- The capped annual drawdown limit can be retained if the member or dependant wishes.
- Individuals should revisit their '*expression of wish*' forms and wills etc in view of the new freedoms.
- Certain benefits can be cut back or lost for those who take advantage of the new pension flexibilities. The cuts are described in great detail in a DWP Housing Benefit Circular. The main headings are '*Effects on claimants below Pension Credit qualifying age*' and '*Effects on claimants who are of Pension Credit qualifying age*'.

TOPA 2014 contains a permissive override that allows trustees and managers of UK-registered pension schemes to make certain designated payments regardless of any provisions in the scheme's rules that would otherwise prevent such payments. However, the scheme trustees or manager are able to choose to whether or not to make such payments as there is no compulsion to provide flexible access provisions. The override extends to:

- drawdown pensions;
- the purchase of a short-term annuity;
- dependants' drawdown pensions;
- the purchase of a dependants' short-term annuity; and
- an UFPLS.

Lump sums

11.66 A PCLS could only be paid in connection with a pension coming into payment. The pre A-Day possibilities for cash-only schemes no longer exist except where provided for under transitional protection. Under *FA 2007, Sch 20*, a PCLS can be paid up to six months and before 12 months after the date of entitlement, and up to 12 months after age 75 if the retirement date was before age 75. This provision extended the previous three-month period.

How the lump sum is calculated depends on whether the arrangement it comes from is a DB or DC arrangement.

The changes described in **11.65** offer greater access to lump sums for members of DC schemes.

11.67 In a DC arrangement the lump sum is expressed as one-third of the annuity purchase price, where a lifetime annuity is provided, or one-third of the sums designated for income withdrawal. This equates to 25% of funds being vested, but expressing it in such a manner ensures the lump sum calculation is tied to the amount of funds actually crystallised at the time.

Calculation of the PCLS is more complicated under a DB arrangement. The lump sum is calculated according to the formula ¼ × (LS + AC) where:

- LS is the amount of lump sum actually taken; and
- AC is the amount crystallised by the scheme pension coming into payment (normally 20 times the initial rate of scheme pension in a DB arrangement).

Under *FA 2004, paras 1–3, Sch 29*, from 6 April 2011:

- For pension benefits not taken until after the age of 75, a PCLS may be paid to a member aged 75 or over (previously the entitlement had to arise before age 75).
- An entitlement to a PCLS arises immediately before the entitlement to the pension in connection with which the lump sum is being paid arises. The PCLS must be tested against the LA as a BCE 6. If the entitlement to pension and the PCLS arises shortly before the member reaches age 75, it is possible that they may not be paid their PCLS until after they have reached that age. If the PCLS is in respect of a DC arrangement the funds which will be used to pay the lump sum will have been treated as remaining unused funds when the member reached age 75 and tested against the LA as a BCE 5B at that time. To prevent double testing, there is no BCE 6 – the only BCE that occurs is a BCE 5B. So, contrary to the usual position, the amount of the PCLS will be tested against the member's LA after, rather than before, the pension in connection with which it is paid is tested. This will affect the amount of the member's available LA at the time their PCLS is tested.
- When calculating the applicable amount, AC in the statutory formula is, where the member became entitled to the pension before reaching age 75, the amount crystallised by reason of the member becoming entitled to the pension or, where the member becomes entitled to the pension after reaching age 75, the amount that would have crystallised had there been a BCE in relation to the pension.

- The member must have available LA in order to qualify for a PCLS. If the lump sum is being paid after age 75 from uncrystallised funds or rights, those funds or rights will have already been tested against the member's LA under BCE 5B or BCE 5 respectively when the member reached age 75. This BCE will have used up some or all of the member's available LA at that time.

For the purposes of deciding whether the member satisfies the condition that they have available LA, when they take a PCLS after age 75:

- the fact that a BCE 5 or 5B has occurred is disregarded. This means that any LA used up by that BCE does not count in calculating whether the member has available LA; and
- if the member has already taken benefits from the same or another arrangement under a registered pension scheme after reaching age 75 or some other event has occurred that would have been a BCE but for the fact that the event occurred on or after the member reaching age 75, then, again solely for the purposes of calculating whether the member has available LA, those events are treated as though they were BCEs and so are treated as having used up LA.

11.68 In a DB arrangement where a lump sum is provided by the commutation of pension, the maximum amount of lump sum depends on the commutation rate used within the scheme. The lump sum formula may more usefully be expressed as:

(20 × full pension × commutation factor) / (20 + 3 × commutation factor)

Therefore a £10,000 pa pension in a DB scheme with a commutation rate of, say, £14 per £1 pa may be partially commuted for a lump sum of up to:

(20 × 10,000 × 14) / (20 + 3 × 14) = £45,161

The residual pension will be 10,000 – 45,161 / 14 = £6,774.21 pa.

Note that the lump sum will always be 6 2/3 times the residual pension in a DB arrangement unless transitional protection applies.

11.69 If a person has taken a lump sum prior to A-Day, this will be taken into consideration for the purpose of calculating the maximum lump sum that may be taken from the same arrangement after A-Day. Additionally, any person who has taken a lump sum prior to A-Day, but deferred his pension until after A-Day, will not be permitted to take a further tax-free lump sum in relation to that employment.

Any additional voluntary contributions (AVCs) that were not commutable before A-Day because they were started after 8 April 1987 may be commutable post A-Day subject to scheme rules permitting. Where DC AVCs have been paid under a DB scheme, the entire AVC fund may be used first to provide a PCLS before it is necessary to commute DB pension, subject again to scheme rules permitting.

Unless transitional protection applies, the maximum PCLS that may be taken tax free is limited to 25% of the available LA.

Protected lump sums

11.70 Where lump sum rights on 5 April 2006 are more than 25% of the value of pension rights under an occupational pension scheme on the same date, they may be protected and a different calculation will apply. If all pension rights are transferred out of the scheme post A-Day protection will be lost unless the transfer is part of a block transfer or rights are transferred to a buy-out policy upon scheme wind-up. If a partial transfer occurs, the protected lump sum in the ceding scheme is reduced by one quarter of the transfer value.

The protected lump sum is expressed as VULSR × CSLA/FSLA, where:

- VULSR is the value of lump sum rights on 5 April 2006;
- CSLA is the LA at the time of paying the lump sum; and
- FSLA is the LA for 2006/07 (£1.5m).

The protected lump sum may be calculated using the same formula as applies where relevant benefit accrual has occurred (*FA 2008, s 92, Sch 29, para 13).*

11.71 A further protection was provided for lump sum rights exceeding £375,000 with PP. Individuals can choose, subject to scheme rules, how much lump sum they wish to take from each scheme. So an individual may take all the benefits from a particular scheme as a stand-alone lump sum. This can happen where:

- the member is aged less than 75 (this condition does not apply after 5 April 2011);
- the member has reached the normal MPA (or any earlier protected pension age they may have under the scheme) or is taking benefits earlier due to ill-health; and
- all the member's uncrystallised rights under the scheme come into payment as a single BCE.

Payment of a stand-alone lump sum is a BCE 6, and so it is liable to the LA charge if there is insufficient LA to cover the payment. The amount of the stand-alone lump sum is limited by the formula:

VULSR – APCLS

where:

- VULSR is the value of the member's uncrystallised lump sum rights as at 5 April 2006 increased in line with the increase of the standard LA or, from 6 April 2012, by 20% until such time as the prevailing standard LA taken is more than £1.8m when the previous method of determining the increase re-applies; and
- APCLS is the value of any PCLS and/or stand-alone lump sum that has previously been paid to the member (increased in line with the increase of the standard LA). From 6 April 2012, the lump sum paid previously is increased by multiplying the amount of that lump sum by £1.8m (or the standard LA at the time the further lump sum is paid if this is greater), then dividing by the standard LA at the time of payment. For example, if the further lump sum had been paid in tax year 2012/13 when the standard LA was £1.5m, and the previous lump sum (£300,000) was paid in tax year 2007/08 when the standard LA was £1.6m, the previous lump sum was increased as follows – £300,000 × £1.8m/£1.6m giving an increased amount of £337,500.

11.72 Scheme administrators are not obliged to pay the maximum protected lump sum. If scheme rules permit they may pay a lump sum of up to the protected amount. The HMRC limit on 5 April 2006 is calculated as 3/80 of final remuneration times company service, uplifted 80ths where the member had continued rights under the scheme, or, where the member was a post-1989 member of a money purchase scheme, as 2.25 times the level of pension. The level of pension in this case can be calculated using the GAD drawdown rate applicable on 5 April 2006 or by simply dividing the DC fund by 20. Advisers therefore need to work out which method proves the most beneficial for their clients.

Existing lump sum certificates could be ignored once post A-Day valuations for transitional protection had taken place. However, for personal pension schemes that received a transfer from an occupational pension scheme, the lump sum must not exceed that shown on the certificate.

Refunds of contributions, and compensation payments

11.73 The rules which apply to refunds of contributions can be found in PTM045000. Where a member has less than two years' qualifying service, refunds of contributions made by the member will be permitted, and will be taxed on any excess (*FA 2004, Pt 4, Ch 5, s 205*). Such refunds will be permitted on leaving pensioned employment or on winding up the scheme. Where a member leaves pensionable service before acquiring rights to short service benefit (for example, before completing two years qualifying service) DWP legislation requires that the member be given certain benefit options, provided that they have by then completed at least 3 months of pensionable service under the scheme.

IT is payable by the scheme administrator whether the administrator and recipient are resident, ordinarily resident or domiciled in the UK. The banded tax rates are:

- 20% up to £10,800 and at 40% on the excess in the tax years 2006/07 to 2009/10; and
- 20% up to £20,000 and at 50% on the excess in tax years 2010/11 onwards.

The additional types of refunds of member contributions which are permitted are:

- a refund of excess contributions lump sum where a member has paid relievable pension contributions in a tax year of more than the maximum amount that can receive tax relief; and
- a contributions refund lump sum where a member would have been be liable to the SAAC on their contributions.

The tax rates are as follows:

- a refund of excess contributions lump sum is not subject to any income tax charge. It is paid tax-free. The payment must be made before the end of the period of six years beginning with the last day of the tax year in which the 'excess contributions condition' was met, ie the tax year in which the 'excess' contribution was paid;
- a tax charge of 50% will apply in respect of the payment of a contributions refund lump sum. The tax charge is the scheme administrator's liability. The individual is not liable to this tax charge.

The Pensions Minister stated on 24 October 2014 that, as from October 2015, employees who leave their employer after less than two years' service will no longer be pushed into withdrawing their pension contributions. Short service refunds were abolished other than within the first 30 days of membership. However, DB occupational pension schemes and PPSs are not affected.

Compensation payments may be made to authorised employers in respect of a criminal, fraudulent or negligent act or omission by a scheme member (*FA 2004, Ch 3, s 178*).

Retained benefits

11.74 It was no longer necessary to take retained benefits into account when testing HMRC limits if members' earnings (ie P60 plus P11D) were less than £50,000 in the tax year which preceded A-Day. This was important when calculating the HMRC maximum lump sum available on 5 April 2006 for protection purposes.

Serious ill health

11.75 Serious ill health commutation is permitted for registered schemes, out of uncrystallised benefits (*FA 2004, Sch 29, para 4*). The administrator must obtain written medical evidence that the member's life expectancy is less than one year and must notify HMRC. There is no charge to income tax on payment to a member who has not reached the age of 75, either on the individual or the scheme administrator (unless the LA charge is an issue).

Under the flexi-access rules (see **11.65**), the special LSDB charge on serious ill-health lump sums was reduced from 55% to 45% from 6 April 2015 (see PTM063400). The 45% rate for individuals who have reached age 75 has since been replaced with tax at the individual's marginal rate, and a requirement that a serious ill-health lump sum can only be paid from an arrangement that has never been accessed has been removed. The scheme administrator is the person liable for paying this charge so they will normally deduct the tax from the lump sum before payment.

If a member in circumstances of serious ill health with a life expectancy of less than a year fails to exercise an option to wholly commute their benefits, the value of the benefits foregone is liable to IHT.

The *Finance Act 2016* removes the requirement that a serious ill-health lump sum can only be paid from an arrangement that has never been accessed and replaces the 45% tax charge with tax at the individual's marginal rate.

Trivial commutations and small pension pots

11.76 *Trivial pensions*: The rules which apply to triviality lump sums are given in PTM063500 *et seq*. Under *FA 2014, s 42*, with effect from 27 March 2014, individuals aged over 60 who have not touched their pension pot, and whose total pension savings are no more than £30,000, can withdraw all of their savings. The first 25% will be tax free, and the remainder will be taxed as the top slice of their income in the tax year of withdrawal. The affected payments are payments that would be trivial commutation lump sums but for the continuing payment of an annuity, and which satisfy the other conditions set out in *reg 10* of the *Registered Pension Schemes (Authorised Payments) Regulations 2009 (SI 2009/1171)*.

The trivial commutation lump sum amount was previously set at £18,000 – which had replaced the earlier maximum of 1% of the LA. There must be no other trivial commutation paid. All benefits under the pension arrangement must be extinguished. *FA 2013, Sch 22, para 8(4)* revised the calculation of the maximum amount that can be paid where the individual has previously taken some pension benefits. From 6 April 2014 the calculation is by reference to any change in the trivial commutation limit.

Pension rights must be valued at no more than the commutation limit on what is called the '*nominated date*'. The member must have the opportunity to nominate the date when their pension rights are valued for triviality purposes, within certain limitations. It cannot be earlier than three months before the first trivial commutation lump sum paid to the member by any registered pension scheme.

Where the lump sum is being paid after age 75 from uncrystallised rights or funds, those rights or funds will have been tested against the member's LA under BCE 5 or BCE 5B respectively when the member reached age 75. This BCE will have used up some, or all, of the member's available LA at that time. So, solely for the purposes of deciding whether the member satisfies the condition that they have available LA, the fact that a BCE 5 or 5B has occurred is disregarded. This means that any LA used up by that BCE does not count in calculating whether the member has available LA. On the other hand, if the member has already taken benefits from the same or another arrangement under a registered pension scheme after reaching age 75 or some other event has occurred that would have been a BCE but for the fact that the event occurred on or after the member reaching age 75, then, again solely for the purposes of calculating whether the member has available LA those events are treated as though they were BCEs.

PSN 57, dated 14 May 2013, describes trivial commutation payments through RTI from 6 April 2013. Pension schemes must now report to HMRC through RTI any payments they make where tax is deducted under PAYE.

Under the flexi-access rules (see **11.65**), the definition of a trivial commutation lump sum is amended so that they will be payable from DB arrangements only. The lump sum must extinguish the member's entitlement to all DBs under the scheme. Pension providers will continue to deduct tax at the basic rate from these lump sums before paying them. Additionally, the age limit for taking trivial commutation lump sums is reduced from age 60 to MPA, or when the ill-health condition has been met.

DC pensions in payment may now be paid as a trivial commutation lump sum.

11.77 *Small pots:* Under *FA 2014, s 42*, with effect from 27 March 2014, there was an increase in the size of the lump-sum small pot that can be taken from *occupational pension schemes* to £10,000, an increase in the total pension savings that can be taken from age 60 as a taxed lump sum from other small pots to £30,000 and an increase in the number which can be taken to three. All benefits under the pension arrangement must be extinguished. The small pot limit had previously been set at £2,000. Small pots can be taken without taking into account other pension benefits (*FA 2004, s 164(1)(f)*). There must not have been a transfer-out of the scheme in the three years preceding the date of payment and the first 25% of the payment is tax free (unless the pension is in payment, when the whole amount is liable to IT) with the remaining 75% taxable under PAYE.

If a member has small benefits in a *non-occupational pension*, such as a PPS, *section 32* (buyout policy), stakeholder plan or *section 226* contract (RAC), it may be possible to cash them in even if the main rules above have not been met. The member must have reached the age of 60 and the payment must not exceed £10,000. It must extinguish all their pension rights under the arrangement, and they must not have previously received more than two payments under one of these types of scheme. This excludes any separate lump sum under the special rule for occupational schemes only. The first 25% of the payment is tax-free, with the remaining 75% taxable under PAYE. If the pension is in payment, the whole amount is liable to income tax.

Under the flexible access rules (see **11.65**), the age limit for taking small pot lump sums is reduced from age 60 to the MPA (currently 55), or when the ill-health condition has been met.

The rules which apply differ depending on whether the individual is a member of a company or public pension scheme, or a personal pension scheme, as shown in the following examples.

Example 11.1 – Company or public sector pension scheme

If the individual's pension pot is worth £10,000 they may take their pension pot as a lump sum subject to the conditions:

- *Condition 1:* They must take all their pension pots with the same pension scheme as a lump sum.
- *Condition 2:* They must not have transferred any funds out of the pension scheme in the last three years.
- *Condition 3:* They are not a controlling director – or someone connected with a controlling director (ie a director of a limited company who owns or controls 20% or more of the ordinary share capital of the company inclusive of that person's immediate family – whether or not the director owns or controls at least 20% of the company) of an employer that participates in the pension scheme.

- *Condition 4:* They belong to more than one company or public sector scheme for the same job and their total pension pots are worth £10,000 or less.

If they meet the first three conditions but not Condition 4 they may still be able to take their whole pension pot as a lump sum but they will need to check with their scheme administrator.

Example 11.2 – Personal pension scheme

If the individual's pension scheme is not a company or public sector scheme they may still be able to take all their pension pot as a lump sum if their pension pot is worth no more than £10,000. They must take all the money in that pension pot as a lump sum.

They may only take a lump sum three times (previously two) under this rule.

Only 75% of the lump sum is taxable. The scheme administrator will deduct any tax due at the basic rate of 20% using PAYE and issue the member a P45 showing how much tax has been paid. If the individual normally does not pay tax, they can claim back the overpaid tax from HMRC. If they are a higher or additional rate taxpayer they may need to pay more tax through self-assessment.

On 29 October 2015 the government confirmed that it will not pursue automatic transfers (more commonly referred to as 'pot follows member' by the industry), at least for the time being.

Buy-out policies

11.78 Buy-out policies must be provided through a UK-registered pension scheme, and not be free-standing. There need be no monetary limits, and a tax-free lump sum of up to 25% of value may be paid. DC contracts must use a factor of 20:1 for determining limits. Pre A-Day bought-out benefits remain subject to the limits that were written into those contracts.

Transfers

11.79 Benefits may be transferred freely between UK-registered pension schemes including pensions in payment as long as certain conditions are met. None of these transfers occasions a test against the LA, but where benefits are transferred to a QROPS the amount of the transfer value is tested against the

LA. Any excess over the LA is simply taxed at 25%; it is not possible to draw the excess as an LA excess lump sum in this situation.

Primary protection and enhanced protection from A-Day

11.80 The two methods of protecting accrued rights under *FA 2004* from A-Day are described below. Despite the amazingly complex system of transitional protections which have since developed against later diminutions of the LA (see **11.36** above), these protections are still of great benefit to those who applied for them before 5 April 2009. Whichever protection was sought, it was necessary to value the accrued rights as at A-Day. The valuation of rights which had not yet come into payment depended on the type of arrangement from which they derived. Details of calculation are contained in the PTM. Rights already in payment were valued as 25 times the annual rate of pension being paid (disregarding any lump sum already paid). Payments in the form of income drawdown were valued as 25 times the maximum annual rate of drawdown that could be received on 5 April 2006.

Enhanced protection

11.81 EP enabled members to avoid the LA and AA charges completely. No further relevant benefit may accrue to the individual from A-Day. The value of aggregate uncrystallised rights on 5 April 2006 must not have exceeded an amount calculated as 20 × MPP, where MPP is, broadly, the maximum permitted pension that would be allowed by reference to the appropriate tax regime in force before A-Day. Any excessive amount had to be surrendered if EP was to apply. Practitioners will wish to continue to be vigilant by ensuring that their clients are aware of the actions which may inadvertently trigger a loss of EP by way of relevant benefit accrual, such as further contributions, new death benefit provision, higher accrual rates, non-permitted transfers, etc. Note that a transfer from a DB scheme to a DC scheme, although being a permitted transfer for EP, will cause the loss of EP if the transfer value is greater than the appropriate limit allowed for relevant benefit accrual under EP. A similar loss of protection will occur to fixed protection members. Details are provided in the PTM.

The member's benefits can be recalculated at the first BCE, according to various assumptions. A member's earnings for the three-year period to the earliest of his death, leaving employment with the sponsoring employer and the first relevant event are taken into account.

'Relevant benefit accrual' means:

- *For a DC arrangement* (but not a cash balance arrangement): where a contribution is paid which is:

  (1) a tax relievable contribution paid by or on behalf of the individual;

(2) a contribution in respect of the individual by his employer;

(3) any other contribution which becomes held for the benefit of the individual.

- *For a cash balance or DB arrangement*: where, at the time when a benefit payment is made (or on making a permitted transfer to a money purchase arrangement), the crystallised value of the benefit exceeds the higher of the value of an individual's rights on 5 April 2006, increased to the date of payment by the highest of:

  (1) 5% compound;

  (2) the increase in the RPI (CPI from 2012/13); and

  (3) an increase specified in statutory order applicable to contracted-out rights.

Primary protection

11.82 PP allows further benefit to accrue post A-Day, and it provided a protection for accrued rights by way of an uplift to an individual's LA in the form of an LA enhancement factor which is the percentage by which the value of rights on 5 April 2006 exceeded £1.5m and was expressed in the following formula:

$$\frac{(RR - SLA)}{SLA}$$

where:

- RR was the value of pension rights on 5 April 2006;
- SLA was the standard LA for the 2006/07 tax year (£1.5m).

Any other further benefit will almost certainly attract an LA charge. Examples of how this works in practice are contained in the PTM.

DEATH BENEFITS

General rules

11.83 General death benefit rules apply on the death of a member for children's and dependants' pensions, which are subject to PAYE but are not subject to the LA. Children's pensions had to cease at age 23 unless dependency continued by reason of disability. The *Finance Act 2016* enables dependants with drawdown or flexi-access drawdown pension who would currently have to use all of this fund before age 23 or pay 45% (marginal rate tax from 6 April 2016) on any lump sum payment, to continue to access their funds as they wish after their 23rd birthday.

There were also transitional arrangements which protected pensions in payment at A-Day and pensions from arrangements for a person who had retired by A-Day.

Where an individual started taking their pension from 6 April 2016, and had reached age 75 at the time of their death, any dependants' scheme pensions must be tested annually against the amount of the member's scheme pension, no matter the size of the member's pension savings or the dependants' scheme pensions. If a part of the dependants' pension exceeds the permitted maximum for that year, the excess is taxed as an unauthorised payment.

In order to reduce the administrative burden on UK industry, the *Finance Act 2016* makes the administration of dependants' scheme pensions simpler by providing exceptions from the test of dependants' scheme pensions for low value pensions and where the risk of abuse is low. It removes the need for calculations to be carried out each year comparing the value of the dependants' scheme pension to the scheme pension of the member in certain circumstances.

If the total value under a pension scheme is not more than 25% of the standard LTA at the earlier of member's death (if the member did not have an actual right to a scheme pension at death) or the date the member became entitled to the pension (rounded up to the nearest £100), then the scheme administrator is authorised to pay the dependants' scheme pensions without the test being carried out.

The value of tax-free lump sums taken before death may be uprated when calculating the maximum dependants' scheme pension. Increases to the rate of dependants' scheme pensions are authorised if that rate is the same as that applicable to at least 20 other members of the pension scheme.

The *Finance Act 2016* also enables the full amount of dependants' benefits to be paid as authorised payments where there are insufficient funds in a cash balance arrangement when the member dies.

With the exception of:

- UFPLS lump sum death benefits paid on the death of member before age 75 and within 2 years of notification of death; and
- DBLSDB paid on the death of member before age 75 and within 2 years of notification of death,

all other death benefits should be reported through RTI, including payments that are now non-taxable.

Payments made to trusts continue to be liable to the special LSDB charge and should be reported on the AFT.

The other permitted death benefits are described below.

Permitted benefits

11.84 In general, death benefits may be paid to any person, with exceptions in cases of triviality commutation, small pension pots and winding up (in which circumstances payment must be made to dependants (*FA 2004, s 168* and *Sch 29, Pt 2*). The meaning of '*dependant*' is widely drawn, and may include an ex-wife or civil partner who had been married or a civil partner to the member when the pension commenced. The changes brought about by flexible access (see **11.65**) are described in **11.85.**

DC and other permitted death benefits

11.85 A DC arrangement can potentially provide a dependant's annuity, a dependant's scheme pension, or a dependant's drawdown pension. There is no limit on the amount of a dependant's pension. A dependant's pension does not count as a BCE. Accordingly, it is not subject to the LA, but it is subject to IT under PAYE.

The current rules which apply to death benefits, primarily as a result of flexi-access, are described below.

- Annuities are placed on a level playing field with drawdown as far as tax is concerned. In general, IHT is payable on the pension pot. Monies withdrawn on death whilst in flexible drawdown before age 75 shall be tax-free. Holders of flexible pensions may nominate an individual to inherit the remaining pension fund as a '*nominee's flexi-access drawdown account*'. This can be anyone at any age and is no longer restricted to 'dependants'. Any beneficiary (that is, a dependant or a nominee) with unused drawdown funds on their death can pass those funds to a successor to be designated to provide a drawdown pension for that individual (a successor's flexi-access drawdown fund) or to be paid as a LSDB.
- Pension death benefits from DC arrangements in the form of an annuity can be paid to anyone, not just a dependant, and payments from the annuity can be made tax-free where the member died before age 75.

- The maximum ten-year guarantee period for lifetime annuities, which enabled annuities to continue to be paid after the member's death is removed.

- The maximum ten-year guarantee period for lifetime annuities, which enabled annuities to continue to be paid after the member's death is removed.

- Under *FA 2015* beneficiaries of individuals who die under the age of 75 with a joint life or guaranteed term annuity, are able to receive any future payments from such policies tax-free where no payments had been made from the policy to the beneficiary before 6 April 2015. Joint life annuities may to be passed to any beneficiary. However, pensioners that have already selected a '*joint life*' annuity which is passed to spouse are not allowed to change their policy.

- With effect from 1 April 2015 survivors' pensions need no longer cease when a widow or widower of a deceased member of a public service pension scheme finds a new partner. The same right will be granted to former partners of police officers or firefighters killed on duty, and the government will consult on rolling out the reform to former partners of members of the security services who are killed on duty.

- Where the death occurred before age 75, LSDBs from DC arrangements can be paid tax-free, subject to the member having sufficient available LA. The 55% tax charge that applied to lump sums paid from drawdown funds (when death occurs both before and after age 75) and uncrystallised funds (when death occurs after age 75) has been abolished.

- From 6 April 2011, LSDBs had been taxed at 55% (previously 35%), except those payable on death before age 75 in respect of an individual who had not taken a pension. If the member died having reached age 75. For the year 2015/16, lump sums were taxed at 45%. Where an uncrystallised or crystallised LSDB is paid out after age 75, it will be taxed at the recipient's marginal rate from 6 April 2016 (*FA 2016*).

  The following payments made in respect of an individual who dies before reaching age 75 may, subject to meeting the required conditions, also be tax-free:

  - DBLSDB;
  - pension protection LSDB;
  - annuity protection LSDB;
  - uncrystallised funds LSDB;
  - drawdown pension fund LSDB;
  - flexi-access drawdown fund LSDB (from 6 April 2015).

However, if the entitlement to any of the above last three LSDBs above is paid more than two years after the scheme administrator became aware of the death, it is subject to the same tax treatment as if the member died having reached age 75, that is in 2015 to 2016, it would be taxed at 45%, thereafter at the individual's marginal rate of tax.

The previous tax treatment of lump sums, subject to the changes under flexi-access described above, is summarised below.

From 6 April 2011, LSDBs had been taxed at 55% (previously 35%), except those payable on death before age 75 in respect of an individual who had not taken a pension, which remained tax free (*FA 2011, Sch 16*). The scheme rules may provide for the tax to be recovered from the payment. However, no charge arises on a DBLSDB if:

- the benefit is payable on death before age 75 in respect of an individual who had not taken a pension;
- the benefit is paid in respect of a DB arrangement;
- the benefit is paid before the earlier of the day on which the scheme administrator first knew of the member's death and the day on which the scheme administrator could first have reasonably been expected to have known of it; and
- the benefit is paid before the end of two years from date of death; and
- the benefit is not a pension protection LSDB, a trivial commutation LSDB or a winding-up LSDB.

As from 6 April 2011, the following types of authorised LSDBs can be paid after age 75:

- a DBLSDB;
- UFLSDB;
- pension protection LSDB;
- annuity protection LSDB;
- drawdown pension fund LSDB (previously called an unsecured pension fund LSDB);
- trivial commutation LSDB;
- winding-up LSDB;
- charity LSDB;
- life cover lump sum.

The following types of lump sum were taxed at 55% from 6 April 2011 (*FA 2011, Sch 16*):

- pension protection LSDB if the member died after 5 April 2011;
- annuity protection LSDB if the member died after 5 April 2011;
- drawdown pension fund LSDB if the member dies after 5 April 2011;
- UFLSDB taxed at 55% if paid after age 75;
- DBLSDB if the member dies after 5 April 2011 whilst aged 75 or above.

All the IHT charges that arose before 6 April 2011 on pension funds left over on death no longer applied. Similarly, the IHT charges that were due when a person chose not to take any benefits from their scheme no longer applied.

An UFLSDB could be paid if the member died on or after 6 April 2011, whatever the age of the member when he died. If the member died before the age of 75, the UFLSDB must be paid within two years of the earlier of the following dates:

- the date the pension scheme administrator first knew of the member's death; and
- the date the scheme administrator could reasonably have been expected to know of the member's death.

If the member died age 75 or over, there is no two-year time limit on making the payment of an UFLSDB.

The amount of UFLSDB paid must be no more than the value of the uncrystallised funds, as were held in the arrangement when the member died, at the point of the LSDB payment. So any growth of those uncrystallised funds up to the point of payment may be covered in the payment.

If the member was aged under 75 when he died, the lump sum must be tested against the LA. If the member was aged 75 or over when he died, there is no LA test but the special LSDB charge applies. The scheme administrator, not the recipient, is responsible for paying this special tax charge, and the tax may be deducted from the payment due. IHT will not apply (*FA 2011*).

A scheme may also pay any guaranteed annuity pension protection LSDB*t* chosen by the member when they started to be paid a scheme pension. If the member died on or after 6 April 2011, the benefit can be paid whatever age the member was when he died. There is no time limit for the payment of this lump sum. It is not tested against the LA, but the 55% tax charge, since reduced on two occasions, as stated above, was due, payable by the scheme administrator or, if the benefit is paid by an insurance company, the company.

Any drawdown pension may continue to be paid to a dependant, or he or she may choose to purchase an annuity. If the member was in receipt of an annuity at date of death, the terms of the annuity could provide for payment of a dependant's annuity. If a member was in receipt of *drawdown* (that is, not classed as a short-term annuity), the remainder of the fund may be paid out on death as a lump sum (a drawdown pension fund LSDB). If the member died on or after 6 April 2011, the lump sum can be paid whatever the age of the member when he died. There is no time limit for the payment of this lump sum. A drawdown pension fund LSDB cannot be more than the value of the drawdown pension fund held in the arrangement when the member died, at the point of the lump sum payment. Any growth of that drawdown pension fund up to the point of payment may be covered in the payment. (Any sum used to purchase a short-term annuity cannot go towards the LSDB, which must simply be a return of existing funds.) The special tax charge applied in the circumstances described above.

Defined benefits

11.86 Subject to the changes listed in **11.85**, a DB arrangement can provide a dependant's scheme pension. PTM072110 and PTM072120 describe the rules which apply.

A ten-year guarantee may be provided from schemes and on lifetime annuities. Where a scheme provides for a dependant's pension, if the scheme rules permit, it may be possible to convert it into a LSDB before the dependant becomes entitled to it.

If the member died on or after 6 April 2011, a DBLSDB can be paid, whatever age the member was when he died.

If the member died before his 75th birthday, the DBLSDB must be paid within two years of the earlier of:

- the date the pension scheme administrator first knew of the member's death; and
- the date the scheme administrator could reasonably have been expected to know of the member's death.

IHT will not normally apply (*FA 2011*).

An annuity protection LSDB can be paid where the deceased member was in receipt of a lifetime annuity, as described above.

A charity LSDB may be paid, if the member or dependant dies before attaining age 75, to a charity nominated by the member before their date of death. If the member died after age 75, such a benefit may be paid from uncrystallised funds provided that there is no dependant.

Legal personal representative

11.87 Subject to the changes listed in **11.85**, where LSDBs are not paid directly to the legal personal representative, that person must be notified of the payment. The amount of the LA used up must be declared, and the special LSDB charge is chargeable on the beneficiary. However, there will be no additional charge on any pension payments made.

Tax charges

11.88 The special LSDB charge (see **11.85**) also applies to members of RNUKS who have received UK tax relief in respect of their contributions or transferred assets.

Where an individual died before 6 April 2014, and LSDBs were not paid until on or after that date, the lump sum is tested against the standard LA at the time of the individual's death, rather than at the point the lump sum is paid.

Transitional arrangement for five-year guaranteed lump sums

11.89 A five-year guarantee may continue for a DC scheme, but it may not necessarily be tax-free. For a DB scheme, it is tax-free if the sum is within the LA.

Transitional arrangement for lump sums arising before A-Day

11.90 Protection was given to lump sums paid by schemes in existence before A-Day in respect of members and dependants who died before that date, and the period within which a LSDB can be paid is extended to two years from the date on which the scheme administrator could reasonably have known of the death of the member or dependant instead of from the date of death.

Enhanced protection – lump sums

11.91 A DB scheme may pay a death-in-service lump sum calculated as a multiple of salary at date of death. This can continue under EP even though the salary may have increased. It must be tested against the appropriate limit to determine whether a relevant benefit accrual has occurred. If it has not the EP is unaffected. For a DC arrangement an UFLSDB may be paid equal to the accumulated value of the assets in a member's pension fund at the date of death, and EP would not be lost.

Funeral benefit

11.92 Existing one-off, tax-free payments to be made upon the death of a member to cover funeral expenses may continue in certain circumstances. If the registered pension scheme was, immediately before A-Day, an approved scheme and the member had a right under the pension scheme to such cover on 5 April 2006 *provided that* the rules of the scheme included the provision as at 10 December 2003 and the member was in receipt of benefits from the scheme on or before 5 April 2006. The payment is not included in the LA.

Inheritance tax

11.93 It is prudent to avoid the prospect of a charge to IHT on lump sum death-in-service benefits. For certainty, the benefit can be dispensed through a discretionary trust, meaning that the trustees have discretion to decide to whom the benefit shall be paid. Members should be asked to complete a statement of wishes form, indicating the person/s or body/ies that they would like to benefit. The trustees are not to be bound by this statement, but they will usually be guided by it.

FA 2016 concerns IHT pension drawdown funds. It introduces an important exemption so that an IHT charge will not arise where a person has failed to exercise their rights to draw designated funds from a drawdown pension fund or a flexi-access drawdown fund during their lifetime and so has left unused funds when they die. It also provides that where an annuity is payable on death to a nominee, and some or all of the cost of the annuity could instead have been paid to a personal representative, those funds shall not form part of that person's chargeable estate for IHT purposes.

11.94 The following special rules applied to IHT before the changes made by the provisions of *FA 2011, Sch 16*, from 6 April 2011, Thereafter, IHT has not been charged on drawdown funds which remain in a registered pension scheme, whether or not the individual dies after reaching the age of 75. However, IHT charges will remain in circumstances where the scheme trustees have no discretion over the payment of LSDBs, and to lump sums from non-registered pension schemes or RNUKS:

- *FA 2006* stated that monies held in an ASP by an investor aged 75 or over would be subject to IHT at 40% when the investor died, deducted directly from the fund by the administrator. Funds passed to charities escaped the tax, and funds paid to provide pension benefits for a spouse, civil partner or financial dependant were not be chargeable until the entitlement to the benefit ceased.

- *FA 2006* also stated that ASP funds which were passed on at death (eg to other family members) were prohibited. The minimum ASP withdrawal level was increased from nil to 55% of the notional annuity, and the maximum level was increased from 70% to 90%.
- In mitigation of the above, there could have been merit, where another family member was earning, in a member drawing maximum income and paying it directly into an arrangement for that person. The family member would obtain tax relief on the contribution and payments out of income, including income from ASP, would be free from IHT.
- The *FA 2008* stated that tax-relieved pension savings diverted into IHT using scheme pensions and lifetime annuities in other circumstances than ASP would be subject to unauthorised payment charges and IHT where appropriate. This was inserted by *FA 2008, s 90, Sch 28*. This applied to transfers and assignments after 10 October 2007 or increases in pension rights attributable to the death of a member when the member died on or after 6 April 2008. The charges would not apply where the pension scheme had at least 20 members whose rights were increased at the same rate because another member had died.
- *FA 2006* legislated an existing 1992 concessionary practice in relation to an IHT charge which could arise when a person aged under 75 exercised a choice which reduced his chargeable estate and increased that of another (unless on an arm's length basis, and so excepted as a transfer of value). The exemption could apply in a pension scheme where the member exercised his right not to take pension. For example, where the member was in good health when the decision was made, but subsequently his life expectancy was seriously impaired and an enhanced death benefit was paid. The *Act* also extended the concession to dispositions to charities.
- Accumulation and maintenance trusts and interest in possession trusts have been chargeable on establishment from 2006 if the value of the trust is higher than the nil IHT band, and a further tax charge will be levied on the tenth anniversary after they are set up. These measures have also applied to existing trusts from 2008. Transfers into new trusts are taxable at 20% above the nil rate band plus a further 6% charge every ten years. Existing trusts will only be charged at 6% – the ten-yearly charge. These rules also extend to certain divorce cases.
- IHT relief was back-dated by legislation to A-Day on savings in certain overseas pension schemes. Effectively this protects monies in QROPS,

s 615(3) schemes and schemes which provide a pension for life (see *FA 2008, s 91, Sch 29, para 18*).

PENSION SHARING

Pre A-Day pension debit and credit

11.95 Pension sharing on divorce operates so as to reduce a member's pension rights by a pension debit, and to award the ex-spouse with a pension credit. Before A-Day a pension debit counted against the HMRC maximum benefit that a member was allowed to accrue under the pre A-Day tax regime. The pension credit was ignored in assessing the HMRC maximum benefit of the ex-spouse.

Post A-Day pension credit

11.96 The position changed on A-Day. If a person acquires a pension credit post A-Day it will count towards that person's LA. However, in a case where the pension being shared is one that has been brought into payment on or after A-Day, the person receiving the pension credit can apply for an uplift to their LA. Since the pension being shared will already have been tested against the LA once before, when it was brought into payment, it would be unfair to test it against a LA a second time. The uplift is calculated according to the formula APC/SLA, where:

- APC is the appropriate amount of the pension credit rights at the date they were acquired (ie that part of the original member's cash-equivalent transfer value which was split in favour of the ex-spouse); and
- SLA is the standard LA at the time when the pension credit rights were acquired.

Example 11.3

An example is given below for an earlier year (2007/08). For years commencing from 6 April 2011 the reduced levels of LA should be employed, as appropriate.

If £1m worth of pension rights are shared in the 2007/08 tax year in the proportion 50:50, the pension credit recipient can claim an uplift of £500,000/£1,600,000 = 0.3125, which is rounded up to two decimal places, 0.32. If the person with pension credit draws benefits in the 2010/11 tax year when the LAI was £1.8m, their LA will be increased to £1.8m × 1.32 = £2,376,000.

11.97 To receive this uplift the recipient of pension credit must notify HMRC on form APSS201 by 31 January five years after the 31 January following the tax year in which the pension sharing order took effect.

A similar uplift is available for anyone who acquired pension credit before A-Day, given that pre A-Day pension credit did not count against HMRC limits. The uplift is available whether or not the pension credit relates to rights which were already in payment. The uplift is calculated according to the formula IAPC/SLA, where:

- IAPC is the appropriate amount of the pension credit rights at the date they were acquired (ie that part of the original member's cash-equivalent transfer value which was split in favour of the ex-spouse), and
- SLA is the standard LA for the 2006/07 tax year (ie £1.5m).

11.98 To determine the amount of IAPC it is increased in line with increases in the index from the month in which the pension credit was acquired.

Anyone seeking an uplift for pre A-Day pension credit had to notify HMRC on form APSS201 on or before 5 April 2009. Note, however, that this uplift was not available for pre A-Day pension credit if the person with pension credit was also relying on PP.

Post A-Day pension debit

11.99 For those subject to a pension debit before A-Day, the good news is that this does not count towards the post A-Day LA, despite the fact that it counted towards pre A-Day HMRC limits. This means that someone with a pension debit acquires scope to fund his benefits up to their original level. However, if any transitional protection is being relied on that requires the calculation of HMRC maximum benefits on 5 April 2006, the pension debit may have to be taken into account for those purposes.

For the seriously wealthy this means divorce may not necessarily be all bad news post A-Day. If 100% of pension rights are given away post A-Day as part of a divorce settlement, the person giving the rights away will be able to fund up to the LA once again essentially benefiting from contribution tax relief twice. Unfortunately for such individuals, the LA threshold is under constant attack. PTM describes the effect of a pension sharing order on the transitional protections from the ever-reducing LA.

REPORTING AND TAX RETURNS

11.100

> **Focus**
>
> It is important to comply with the reporting regime and not to miss deadlines. Penalties will be incurred if there is failure to do so. There are four main reporting requirements:
>
> - event reports (*FA 2004, s 251*);
> - quarterly accounting for tax return – AFT (*FA 2004, s 254*);
> - the registered scheme return (*FA 2004, s 250*); and
> - notices requiring documents or particulars (*FA 2004, s 252*).
>
> Fines of £300, plus £60 per day for continued non-compliance, can be imposed where there is a failure to comply. Fraudulent statements or negligence in making returns, transfers, statements and information, may see these fines increased up to £3,000.
>
> The reporting rules and forms have been amended and extended many times since their inception. The latest versions are described below.

UK-registered pension scheme events reports should be filed online by 31 January, although nil reports are not required. The main requirements are stated in the *Registered Pension Schemes (Provision of Information) Regulations 2006 (SI 2006/567),* amended as described below, and they include the administrator's general duty to report certain events to HMRC and other parties. All reporting, registration and returns must be made online (see the *Registered Pension Schemes and Overseas Pension Schemes (Electronic Communication of Returns and Information) Regulations 2006 (SI 2006/570)*, as amended). It is not mandatory to file the SA970 (self-assessment return for pension schemes) electronically. SA975 provides a guide to completing the tax return for trustees of an approved self-administered pension scheme.

The main reportable events are:

- unauthorised payments made to scheme members and employers, including benefits in kind;
- payments in excess of 50% of the standard LA – LSDBs (in aggregate) only;
- early provision of benefits – payments before age 50 (up to April 2010), 55 (from April 2010) – to persons who were directors in any of the six years prior to the reporting current reporting year, or any connected persons;

- payment of a serious ill health lump sum – to persons described in the third point above;
- suspension of an ill health pension – where the ill health condition is no longer met;
- BCEs, enhanced LA or EP – where the amount crystallised (in aggregate) exceeds the standard LA;
- payment of a pension commencement lump sum – where the sum crystallised exceeds 25% of the combined pension and lump sum, and is more than 7.5% but less than 25% of the standard LA;
- payment of a PCLS under PP or EP – where the amount exceeds 25% of the standard LA and is protected from charge by transitional protection;
- payment of a 'standalone' lump sum – transitional protection lump sums which are reportable under the terms of *SI 2006/572*;
- transfer payment to a QROPS, as defined in the *FA 2004* – the HMRC website lists such schemes;
- IRPS status – on acquiring or losing such status – some transitional protection exists for already qualified schemes;
- making changes to scheme rules which permit unauthorised payments or widen investment beyond insurance policies or contracts of insurance;
- making changes to the rules of pre A-Day 'split scheme' rules;
- making changes to the legal structure of a scheme – movement between the categories of single trust, annuity contract, body corporate and other types of vehicle;
- making a change to scheme membership numbers – meaning a head count as at 5 April each year;
- transfer of a LSDB;
- payment of a LASDB after the death of a member aged 75 or over; but see the changes described in **11.62–11.64** above);
- making a scheme chargeable payment from an IRPS;
- changing the country or territory of the scheme establishment;
- attaining or losing the status of an occupational pension scheme.

FA 2008, Sch 36, empowered HMRC to request information and documents from a taxpayer or third party for the purpose of checking a taxpayer's tax position, and to require information from a third party for the purpose of checking another person's tax position where that person's identity is not known.

The *Registered Pension Schemes (Provision of Information) (Amendment) Regulations 2011 (SI 2011/301)* amended the *Registered Pension Schemes (Provision of Information) Regulations 2006 (SI 2006/567)* and changed the information which the scheme administrator of a registered pension scheme is required to report to HMRC in respect of certain events. They have been amended regularly since they were made. The key changes appeared under the following regulations:

- the *Registered Pension Schemes (Provision of Information) (Amendment) Regulations 2006 (SI 2006/1961)*;
- the *Registered Pension Schemes (Provision of Information) (Amendment) Regulations 2008 (SI 2008/720)*;
- the *Registered Pension Schemes (Provision of Information) (Amendment) Regulations 2010 (SI 2010/581)*;
- the *Registered Pension Schemes (Provision of Information) (Amendment) Regulations 2011 (SI 2011/301)*; and
- the *Registered Pension Schemes (Provision of Information) (Amendment) (No 2) Regulations 2011 (SI 2011/1797)*.

These were followed by major changes in 2013 which were brought in by the following regulations:

- the *Registered Pension Schemes and Relieved Non-UK Pension Schemes (Lifetime Allowance Transitional Protection) (Notification) Regulations 2013 (SI 2013/1741)* – scheme administrators must provide HMRC with additional information where there is a recognised transfer to a QROPS;
- the *Registered Pension Schemes (Provision of Information) (Amendment) Regulations 2013 (SI 2013/1742)*, which amended the *Registered Pension Schemes (Provision of Information) Regulations 2006 (SI 2006/567)* to reflect changes made under *FA 2013*; and
- the *Registered Pension Schemes and Overseas Pension Schemes (Miscellaneous Amendments) Regulations 2013 (SI 2013/2259)* further amended UK-registered pension schemes and QROPS in respect of the information requirements. They made transitional provision in respect of the requirements for the scheme administrator and member of a UK-registered pension scheme to provide information in relation to transfers from UK-registered pension schemes to QROPS which were in existence immediately before 6 April 2012 and which would have ceased to meet the necessary conditions for QROPS status as at 6 April 2012 but for the coming into force of those Regulations. Where the transfer request made by the member to the scheme administrator in respect of the transfer or the transfer itself took place on or after 6 April 2102 but before 14 October 2013, the time limits for the delivery of information

from the scheme administrator to HMRC and from the member to the scheme administrator were extended.

The following is a summary of the main extended information requirements which have applied from 2013:

- Where the date of birth, address and NI number were previously required, subject to some exceptions, only the NI number was needed. The amendments applied to all reports delivered on or after 6 April 2011.
- Where, in respect of unauthorised payments, the person is neither an individual nor a company, the scheme administrator needs to obtain a number from HMRC and provide it in the event report.
- Where the scheme administrator is required to provide certain members with the information ('pension savings statement') they will need to work out whether or not the AA charge will be payable for a tax year and if so, the amount of the charge.
- A sponsoring employer must supply the scheme administrator with the information required to calculate the PIA relating to an employee or director for a tax year, by 6 July following the end of that tax year.

  The following matters were addressed:

  - the reduction of the LA from £1.5m to £1.25m from tax year 2014/15;
  - the FP 2014 application procedure and definition;
  - requirements concerning pension savings statements relating to pension input periods that end in tax year 2013/14 and subsequent years, including where the AA for the relevant tax year has been exceeded in that scheme – the pension savings statement must be provided by 6 October following the end of the tax year;
  - a requirement for the scheme administrator to provide HMRC with additional information where there is a recognised transfer to a QROPS;
  - a requirement for the scheme administrator to provide HMRC with additional information if a member of a UK-registered pension scheme intends to rely on FP 2014 (the member must give to the scheme administrator the reference number issued by HMRC under the *Registered Pension Schemes and Relieved Non-UK Pension Schemes (Lifetime Allowance Transitional Protection) (Notification) Regulations 2013 (SI 2013/1741)*); and
  - a requirement the member of a UK-registered pension scheme to give additional information to the scheme administrator when the member makes a request for a recognised transfer.

Further amendments and extensions continue to appear. The latest are:

- the *Registered Pension Schemes (Provision of Information) (Amendment) Regulations 2014 (SI 2014/1843)* which amend the *Registered Pension Schemes (Provision of Information) Regulations 2006 (SI 2006/567)* to reflect the reduction of the LA from £1,500,000 to £1,250,000 with effect from 6 April 2014. They also contain a definition of IP 2014 (see **11.35**) and make the necessary amendments to legislation; and
- the *Registered Pension Schemes (Provision of Information) (Amendment) Regulations 2015 (SI 2015/606)* which amend the *Registered Pension Schemes (Provision of Information) Regulations 2006 (SI 2006/567)* to support compliance work by HMRC to prevent pension liberation and to reflect the new pensions flexibilities. *Regulation 6* reflects the new pensions flexibilities (see **11.65**).
- the *Registered Pension Schemes (Provision of Information) (Amendment) Regulations 2016 (SI 2016/308)* which amend the *Registered Pension Schemes (Provision of Information) Regulations 2006 (SI 2006/567)* to reduce the pensions annual allowance for *high income* individuals with effect from 6 April 2016 and make related changes to PIP, PIAs and the carry-forward of unused AA. Also, the scheme administrator will only be required to provide a pension savings statement to a member for tax year 2015/16 if either PIAs for 2015/16 as a whole exceed £80,000, or the PIAs for the post-alignment tax year exceed £40,000.
- the *Income Tax (Pay As You Earn) (Amendment) Regulations2016 (SI 2016/329)* which amend the *Income Tax (Pay As You Earn) Regulations 2003 (SI 2003/2682), Sch A1* to specify the lump sum payments made to individuals under the pension flexibility rules which pension providers are required to report to HMRC and which may be paid as a consequence of *TOPA 2014* and *F(No 2)A 2015.*
- the *Registered Pension Schemes (Provision of Information) (Amendment) Regulations 2017 (SI 2017/11)* which make various amendments to the *Information Regulations* in relation to payments of lump sum death benefits made by registered pension schemes on or after 6 April 2016. They also impose information requirements on pension scheme administrators when a lump sum death benefit payment is made in specified circumstances.

11.101 *FA 2004* has been amended by later statutes with regard to information powers and requirements:

- *FA 2008, Sch 36,* gave HMRC extensive powers to request information and documents. The information can be requested from a taxpayer or third party for the purpose of checking a taxpayer's tax position. HMRC can also require information from a third party for the purpose of checking another person's tax position where that person's identity is not known.

- *FA 2013, Sch 7,* extended the powers of HMRC further. The new powers concerned:
  - applications for registration;
  - power to inspect documents in relation to applications for registration;
  - penalties for failure to comply with information notices etc;
  - penalties for inaccurate information in applications;
  - penalties for inaccurate information or documents provided under information notice;
  - penalties for false declarations;
  - the de-registration process;
  - HMRC power to require information or documents for purpose of considering if the scheme administrator is fit and proper;
  - HMRC power to inspect documents for purpose of considering if scheme administrator is fit and proper;
  - penalties for failure to comply with information notices etc; and
  - penalties for inaccurate information or documents provided under information notice.
- *FA 2014, Sch 7,* extended HMRC's powers to obtain information and impose penalties in respect of disclosure matters.

As many of the above tax charges are severe and most arduous, it is important that advisers, administrators and members are familiar with, and follow, these and later ongoing changes to legislation. The main area of greatest risk for high earners who are members of small schemes concerns the activities of IRPS, and transferees to QROPS (see **11.150** below). It is also important to avoid inadvertently losing transitional protection for affected members. Specialist advice should be sought as appropriate in order to avoid potential significant loss.

Advisers and scheme administrators will also need to be acquainted with the DWP's revised disclosure rules. The *Occupational and Personal Pension Schemes (Disclosure of Information) Regulations 2013 (SI 2013/2734)* consolidate the core personal and occupational pension schemes disclosure requirements and simplify some of the previous rules with effect from 6 April 2014. In brief, the main rules are as follows:

- *Basic information:* must be provided automatically. This includes lifestyling (where appropriate), statutory money purchase illustrations, retirement and death benefits, changes to benefits in payment, changes to scheme information, any scheme modifications made by the Pensions Regulator, a summary of the funding statement, automatic enrolment information and the winding-up rules.
- *Requested information:* must be made available on request, including scheme documentation, employer details, annual reports and accounts, defined benefit funding principles, winding-up procedures, transfer information and a statement of non-money purchase benefits.

11.102 In addition to the self-assessment returns:

- The AFT is the mechanism for paying tax charges incurred. There are no notice requirements on HMRC for this return, which must be made on a quarterly basis and must be provided within 45 days of the relevant quarter end. The main areas covered are: LA charges, repaid lump sums, taxable death benefits, taxable refunds of surpluses and de-registration charges.
- A UK Registered Pension Scheme Return (PSR) must be completed if a Notice to File is received from HMRC. There are two different versions, one for occupational schemes and the other for non-occupational schemes. It is separate from the scheme return that needs to be sent to the Pensions Regulator or form SA970.
- Pension Schemes Online can be used to submit forms by either a scheme administrator or a practitioner appointed by a scheme administrator. Some functions – such as registering a pension scheme or changing the scheme administrator – cannot be carried out by a practitioner. Pension Schemes Online cannot be used for:
  - RAS repayment claims;
  - submitting form SA970;
  - reclaiming tax paid on investment income.

A current list of reporting forms for schemes and their actions is provided below:

Form number	*Description*
APSS100	Pension Scheme Tax Registration
APSS100 (Insert 1)	Supplementary page to Q6

APSS101	Election to contract out
APSS102	Election for industry-wide money purchase schemes to contract out
APSS103	Relief at Source Details
APSS103A	Relief at Source Details – Specimen Signatures
APSS105	Relief at Source Interim Claim
APSS106	Relief at Source Annual Claim
APSS107	Relief at Source Annual Statistical Return
APSS108	Declaration as a Scheme Administrator of a deferred annuity contract scheme
APSS109	Notification of succession to a split scheme
APSS109 (Insert)	Supplementary page
APSS110	Notification of succession to a sub-scheme
APSS146	Registered Pension Scheme Registration for Income Tax Repayments
APSS146A	Registered Pension Scheme Repayments Third Party Authority
APSS146B	Registered Pension Scheme Repayments Specimen Signatures
APSS150	Authorising and De-authorising a practitioner
APSS151	Add Scheme Administrator for second and subsequent notifications of pre-A day Scheme Administrators or for any post-A day Scheme Administrators
APSS151	Add Scheme Administrator for first notifications of Pre-A day Scheme Administrators
APSS152	Amend Scheme Details
APSS153	Change of Scheme Administrator/Practitioner user details
APSS154	Associate Scheme Administrator to Scheme
APSS155	Election to vary a Contracting out or Appropriate Scheme Certificate
APSS155A	Election to surrender/Request to cancel a contracting-out or appropriate scheme certificate
APSS155B	Election to vary a contracting-out or appropriate scheme certificate
APSS160	Cessation of Scheme Administrator

APSS161	Pre-register as a Scheme Administrator/Practitioner
APSS200	Protection of Existing Rights
APSS201	Enhanced Lifetime Allowance (Pension Credit Rights)
APSS202	Enhanced Lifetime Allowance (International)
APSS203	To authorise HMRC to allow scheme administrators to view lifetime allowance certificates
APSS209	Request by Scheme Administrator for Lifetime Allowance Certificate Details
APSS227	Fixed protection
APSS241	Scheme member to both transferring and receiving scheme
APSS242	Overseas transfer charge scheme administrator repayment claim
APSS243	Overseas transfer charge scheme manager repayment claim
APSS244	Scheme manager notification of change of member's circumstances
APSS250	Qualifying Overseas Pension Schemes
APSS251	Qualifying Recognised Overseas Pension Schemes
APSS251	Qualifying Recognised Overseas Pension Schemes Notes
APSS251A	Qualifying Recognised Overseas Pension Schemes – Change of details
APSS251B	Qualifying Recognised Overseas Pension Schemes – Change in status and notification of fund value
APSS251B	Qualifying Recognised Overseas Pension Schemes – Notification of fund value – insert
APSS252 (Insert)	Supplementary page for relevant migrant members
APSS253	Qualifying Recognised Overseas Pension Schemes – Payments in respect of qualifying members
APSS253 (Insert)	Qualifying Recognised Overseas Pension Schemes – Payments in respect of qualifying members – Additional page
APSS254	Election for a deemed BCE
APSS254 (Notes)	Election for a deemed BCE Completion notes

APSS255	Member information for the overseas manager
APSS262	Transferring UK tax-relieved assets to a QROPS (amended due to *SI 2013/1742* – the new regulations for recognised transfers apply to transfer requests made by the member from 12 August 2013)
APSS263	Member information
APSS300A	Amendment to registered pension scheme event report for 2006/07 or 2007/08
APSS300B	Amendment to registered pension scheme event report for 2008/09 onwards
APSS301	Amendment to information declared on the original occupational pension scheme return
APSS301 (Notes)	Amendment to information declared on the original occupational pension scheme return – Guidance notes
APSS313	Amendment to registered pension scheme return for non-occupational pension schemes, supplementary page
APSS315	Form to complete to report the value of payments to an individual in tax year ending 5 April 2012 from a flexible drawdown pension. For later tax years, payments must be reported on the online Event Report
APSS413	To appeal against an assessment or penalty made by Audit and Pension Schemes Services
PS199	Scheme Wind-Up pre-A Day
R63N	Form to make a request for repayment of income tax deducted from the investment income of a registered pension scheme
SA970	Tax return for trustees of registered pension schemes

On 15 March 2016, the Pensions Regulator stated that it had warned a number of trustees that it could crack the whip and fine them for not completing their scheme returns. The Regulator also reminded trustees on 1 March 2016 that they will be fined if they fail to prepare the new annual governance statements within the statutory deadline. The statements must be produced within seven months of a scheme year's ending on or after 6 July 2015. The first DC statements were due on 6 February 2016 and failure to comply could result in a fine of between £500 and £2,000.

UNAUTHORISED TRANSACTIONS AND TAX CHARGES

11.103 *FA 2004* brought in the greatest change to UK pensions tax law since the Second World War. The current rules are heavily dependent on direct compliance with the law, and are constantly changing. Accordingly, it is essential for practitioners to be fully aware of the current statutory requirements, as tax charges can be inadvertently incurred by the unsuspecting. Many of these charges fall on the scheme administrator.

Unauthorised payments

11.104 Unauthorised payments are payments to or in respect of current or former members or employers (or those who are deemed to be so) which are not authorised payments. They include, subject to the relaxations for DC schemes in **11.65**:

- transfers of assets or of monies or monies' worth;
- taking value out of a pension scheme for unauthorised reasons;
- assignment or surrender of benefits, rights or debts;
- value shifting of assets;
- non-commercial transactions;
- increases in rights of a connected person on death;
- allocating an unallocated employer's contribution;
- member use of assets;
- taxable property held by an IRPS;
- acquisition of wasting assets (ie assets that have an anticipated life of less than 50 years, such as properties with less than 50-year leases, cars, racehorses, plant and machinery etc);
- pension liberation;
- tax free lump sums in excess of 25% of a member's pension pot;
- trivial lump sums in excess of £30,000;
- continued payment of pension after the member's death;
- death in service lump sum paid more than two years after the scheme administrator was told the member had died;
- a scheme realises it incorrectly calculated the amount of the member's pension pot following a transfer of funds or purchase of an annuity and the balancing payment is made directly to the member;

- lump sum payments to cash-in or access pension funds before age 55 in other than permitted circumstances;
- excessive benefits in general.

Any liberated funds are repatriated, and *FA 2004, s 266,* provides relief from the charge. The member has to claim the relief within a year of the repatriation of the funds.

Where a surrender of pension rights is made to fund an authorised surplus payment to a sponsoring employer, the surrender is to be treated as an unauthorised payment of the value of the rights surrendered. A surrender of rights in favour of dependants will be treated as an unauthorised payment unless the new rights are provided under the same scheme under which the surrendered rights were held.

The main charges, surcharges, penalties and sanctions

The unauthorised payments charge

11.105 *FA 2004, s 208:* The charge is at 40% on payments to a member or sponsoring employer that are not authorised by the scheme rules. It is payable by the member, the recipient or the sponsoring employer according to the circumstances.

The unauthorised payments surcharge

11.106 *FA 2004, s 209:* The member charge is 15% of the surchargeable unauthorised payment and it is payable by the same person who is subject to the unauthorised payments charge and arises when:

- a member gets unauthorised payments of 25% or more of their pension pot in a year;
- an employer gets unauthorised payments of 25% or more of the value of the pension scheme in a year.

For employers the 25% percentage is calculated based on the amount of the employer payment divided by the value of the total rights under the scheme.

Members must declare the surcharge on their tax returns. A discharge is available under *FA 2004, ss 267* and *268* if 'it would not be just and reasonable for the person to be liable'.

The scheme sanction charge

11.107 *FA 2004, s 239:* The charge is 40% of the chargeable payments. It is reduced where an unauthorised payment charge above has already been paid. This reduction is the lesser of 25% of the scheme chargeable payments on which tax was paid under the unauthorised payments charge; and the actual amount of tax paid on the unauthorised payment.

The charge applies to most unauthorised payments; unauthorised borrowing and investments in taxable property.

A scheme administrator can apply to be discharged from the tax charge under *FA 2004, ss 267* and *268* if 'it would not be just and reasonable for the person to be liable'.

The de-registration charge

11.108 HMRC can de-register a scheme where it has failed to meet certain statutory requirements. Although this is an unlikely course of action, the most vulnerable schemes will be those which have attracted the scheme sanction charge. De-registration can occur where there has been serious compliance failures (such as defaulting on large tax payments or providing false information) by the scheme, and where the total percentages of the fund used up by scheme chargeable payments exceeds 25% in any 12-month period. The rate of tax chargeable is 40% of the value of the whole fund, and it may be appealed (see **11.118**).

Payment methods

11.109 The payment methods for the above charges are as follows.

Unauthorised member payments: Members can pay the unauthorised payments tax charge and surcharge on either by getting the scheme to pay the tax using the mandating procedure or by completing a self-assessment tax return.

To use the mandating system, the scheme administrator will require the member to complete a mandate giving them authority to deduct the member's tax from the unauthorised payment and pay the tax to HMRC. The scheme administrator will thereafter pay any unauthorised payment less the tax to the member and remit the tax to HMRC giving details of the member's, name, date of birth and NIC number.

Unauthorised employer payments: The company must report all the following information to HMRC by 31 January following the end of the tax year in which the unauthorised payment was made. It must state:

- the details of the scheme making the payment;
- the nature of the payment;
- the amount; and
- the payment date.

An employer that is not a company should report and pay the tax due on the unauthorised payment on their tax return.

Scheme sanction charge: The scheme administrator must report an unauthorised payment on the Event Report. HMRC will work out the amount of tax due using information from the Event Report and any reports of tax paid using the mandating procedure. HMRC will then send the scheme administrator an assessment of the tax due.

The payment date for the tax is 30 days after the assessment notice is issued. Late payment penalties become payable if the tax still has not been paid 30 days after the due date.

Interest will be charged if the scheme sanction charge is not paid by 31 January following the tax year in which the charge arose.

Scheme administrators can make payments on account.

De-registration charge: The charge is payable by the person who was the scheme administrator immediately before HMRC de-registered the scheme. If more than one person is the scheme administrator at that time, each person is jointly and severally liable for the tax due. If there is no scheme administrator, liability passes to other persons (such as trustees) who have responsibility for the scheme. Only as a last resort will liability pass to members of the scheme.

The percentages used up are calculated as follows: (scheme chargeable payment / the value of the scheme at that time) × 100.

The value of the scheme funds is the market value of the assets held for the purposes of the scheme plus the amount of the sums held for the purposes of the scheme, both taken at the time of the payment.

Penalties

11.110 HMRC have power to seek penalties for failures to provide information and the provision of false information. The penalty regime is subject to continuing change and extensions. It is important to avoid incurring prohibitive charges on scheme administrators and members. The following table summarises the main penalties which apply:

Statutory reference	*Reason for penalty*	*Amount of penalty*
FA 2004, s 257(1)	Failure to comply with a notice issued under *FA 2004, s 250* (pension scheme return)	Initial penalty £100
FA 2004, s 257(2)	Continuing failure to comply with a notice issued under *FA 2004, s 250* (pension scheme return)	Daily penalties up to £60 per day
FA 2004, s 257(4)	Fraudulent or negligent return or delivery of incorrect documents etc	Up to £3,000
FA 2004, s 258 and *TMA 1970, s 98(1)(b)(i)*	Failure to supply event report required by regulations under *FA 2004, s 251(1)(a)* or *(4)*	Initial penalty up to £300
FA 2004, s 258 and *TMA 1970, s 98(1)(b)(ii)*	Continuing failure to supply event report required by regulations under *FA 2004, s 251(1)(a)* or *(4)*	Daily penalties up to £60 per day
FA 2004, s 258 and *TMA 1970, s 98(2)*	Fraudulent or negligent return or delivery of incorrect documents etc	Up to £3,000
FA 2004, s 258(2)	Failure to preserve documents as required by regulations made under *FA 2004, s 251(b)*	Up to £3,000
FA 2004, s 261(3)	Producing an incorrect document or certificate or providing false information in connection with any matter registered in accordance with the EP regulations	Up to 25% of the relevant excess
FA 2004, s 262	Failure to produce any document or certificate or to provide any information, when required to do so by the EP regulations	Up to £3,000
FA 2004, s 263(2)	Failure to notify HMRC within 90 days of a relevant benefit accrual where EP applies	Up to £3,000

Statutory reference	*Reason for penalty*	*Amount of penalty*
FA 2004, s 264(1)	Making a false statement or representation to obtain a tax relief or repayment or to make an unauthorised payment	Up to £3,000
FA 2004, s 264(2)	Preparation of an incorrect document that may cause a registered pension scheme to make an unauthorised payment	Up to £3,000
FA 2004, s 265(3)	Winding up a registered pension scheme wholly or mainly for the purpose of facilitating the payment of winding-up lump sums or winding-up lump sum death benefits (or both) under the pension scheme	Up to £3,000 in respect of: (a) each member to whom a winding-up lump sum is paid under the pension scheme; and (b) each member in respect of whom a winding-up lump sum death benefit is paid under the pension scheme
FA 2004, s 266(2)	Transfer to an insured scheme is not made [*sic*] the administrator or insurance company of the receiving scheme	Up to £3,000
FA 2004, s 95 and *TMA, s 95*	Fraudulent overclaims for relief at source	Tax geared penalty
FA 2008, Sch 36	Failure to comply with a notice issued under *FA 2008, Sch 36*	See PTM160800
FA 2008, Sch 36	Providing inaccurate information when complying with an information notice issued under *FA 2008, Sch 36*	See PTM160800
FA 2009, Sch 55	Late filing or failure to file an accounting for tax return	See PTM162300
FA 2009, Sch 56	Late payment or failure to pay tax due	See PTM162300
FA 2007, Sch 24	Providing inaccurate information on an accounting for tax return	See PTM160800

Authorised surplus payments charge

11.111 A tax charge applies where an authorised surplus payment is made by a scheme to a sponsoring employer. The charge is payable on the amount of any surplus payment authorised by HMRC, at a rate of tax of 35% on the amount of the surplus.

The tax charge on benefits in kind

11.112 This charge arises where members or their relatives occupy residential property or enjoy the use of a pride in possession asset owned by a scheme at less than a commercial rent. The rate of tax is 40% of the value of the benefit in kind so enjoyed. The charge is payable by the member or any other recipient of the benefit regardless of their effective rate of tax.

Registration for enhanced protection from the standard lifetime allowance

11.113 Any provision of incorrect or false documents, certificates or information when registering for EP from the standard LA can incur a penalty of up to 25% of the excess allowance claimed on the individual concerned.

Enhanced protection – relevant benefit accrual

11.114 Failure to notify HMRC within 90 days of relevant benefit accrual, where required, occurring for a person with EP can incur a penalty of up to 25% of the excess allowance claimed can render the individual concerned liable to a penalty of up to £3,000.

Winding-up

11.115 Subject to the relaxations for DC schemes in **11.65**, if a scheme is deliberately wound up to provide winding-up lump sums to the members or winding-up LSDBs to others, the administrator is liable to a penalty not exceeding £3,000 in respect of each person to whom a winding-up lump sum is paid.

Transfers to the appropriate person

11.116 A penalty of up to £3,000 may be imposed on an administrator who fails to ensure that transfers to another scheme that invests in insurance policies are made to the appropriate person.

Family pensions

11.117 *FA 2013, s 11*, reflects the budget 2012 statement that, with effect from 6 April 2013, any employer pension contribution to a UK-registered pension scheme of an employee's spouse or family member as part of the employee's flexible remuneration package will give rise to IT and NIC charges on the employee and the employer respectively. The government refers to such arrangements as 'family pensions' (see HMRC at 'Family Pension Plans'). The provisions were included in *FA 2013, s 11*.

Appeals

11.118 Until 31 March 2009, appeals against HMRC action could be made to the General or Special Commissioners, normally within 30 days of the relevant event:

- against a failure to register a scheme;
- against an action to de-register a scheme;
- against a decision to exclude a recognised overseas pension scheme;
- against notices requiring documents or particulars; and
- in respect of the discharge of the LA charge.

The General and Special Commissioners were both abolished with effect from 31 March 2009 and replaced with effect from 1 April 2009 by a single Tribunal. Tax appeals in the First-tier Tribunal are allocated to one of four procedural tracks according to their ascending order of complexity and value. The Upper Tribunal principally replaces the Chancery Division of the High Court for tax appeals. The Upper Tribunal can hear complex cases of sufficient value transferred from the First-tier. Appeals against a First-tier or Upper Tribunal decision go on to the Court of Appeal. So, on the pensions front all appeals made against HMRC's tax charges, adverse decisions, etc go to the Tribunal. Appeals pending before 31 March 2009 also go to the Tribunal.

On 31 March 2016, HMRC published a form to use to notify an appeal and postpone payment against an assessment or penalty determination made by Audit and Pension Schemes Services. The form is APSS413. HMRC stated 'if you appeal against an assessment, you may also use this form if you want to postpone payment of all or part of the tax charged by the assessment'.

Disclosure of tax avoidance schemes and the general anti-abuse rule

11.119 The DOTAS legislation does not affect bona fide pension schemes. However, it is important to be vigilant when checking the probity of pension arrangements, as severe penalties can be incurred in the event of a failure to disclose a non-compliant scheme.

Under the DOTAS rules and legislation, scheme promoters must disclose information about a tax-avoidance scheme that meets certain definitions within five days of it being made available to clients. The promoter is then issued with a scheme reference number (SRN) which must be passed on to clients. HMRC are empowered to investigate non-compliance and impose penalties for failing to disclose a scheme and for failing to pass on or report an SRN.

The daily penalty for failure to comply with a disclosure obligation is up to £5,000. HMRC have adopted a practice of '*naming and shaming*' proposals for tax-avoidance schemes alongside a range of targeted disclosure requirements and associated penalties, and has brought in enhanced information requirements.

FA 2013, s 223, increased HMRC's powers. The main changes concerned the duty of a client to provide information to a promoter. Where HMRC suspect that a person other than the client is, or is likely to be, a party to the arrangements, they may by written notice require the promoter to provide prescribed information in relation to any person other than the client whom the promoter might reasonably be expected to know is, or is likely to be, a party to the arrangements. Disclosure forms must be completed in circumstances where there is a UK promoter, an overseas promoter and where there is no external promoter.

There is a new threshold condition for promoters of tax-avoidance schemes (POTAS) who have marketed multiple tax avoidance schemes that are regularly defeated. Three such defeats over an eight-year period will trigger the threshold condition and bring the scheme promoter into consideration for a conduct notice. For this threshold condition, a defeat is defined as:

> '[L]itigation finally being in HMRC's favour; the user of the scheme reaches agreement with HMRC about their case or makes no appeal against an assessment; a GAAR counteraction has been issued; or the user of the scheme corrects their return on receipt of a follower notice.'

Where there are multiple users of a defeated scheme, a scheme will be defeated if litigation is finally found in HMRC's favour or 75% of the scheme users agree with HMRC that the scheme does not provide the asserted tax advantage.

In addition, corporate trustees must maintain a register of persons with significant control from 6 April 2016. The information must be filed at Companies House from 30 June 2016. Scheme administrators should note that non-compliance constitutes a criminal offence.

The changes to HMRC's definitions of 'hallmarks' (the descriptions of the types of tax-avoidance schemes that are disclosable) can be found in the following:

- *Finance Act 2010, Schedule 17 (Appointed Day) Order 2010 (SI 2010/3019).*
- *Tax Avoidance Schemes (Prescribed Descriptions of Arrangements) (Amendment) Regulations 2010 (SI 2010/2834).*
- Explanatory Memorandum to *Tax Avoidance Schemes (Prescribed Descriptions of Arrangements) (Amendment) Regulations 2010.*
- August 2011, forms to notify HMRC of tax avoidance – guidance with effect from 6 April 2011 covering income tax, CT, CGT, NICs, stamp duty land tax and IHT. The guidance contained a description of a promoter, an introducer and the tests associated with DOTAS.
- HMRC's guide on '*Disclosure of Tax Avoidance Schemes (DOTAS) Regime – the confidentiality and employment income hallmarks*', published on 17 July 2013 and covering the confidentiality hallmark for promoters and the employment income hallmark on disguised remuneration rules in *Pt 7A* of the *Income Tax (Employment and Pensions) Act 2003*.
- '*Disclosure of Tax Avoidance Schemes*' dated 4 November 2013 covering income tax, CT, CGT, NICs, stamp duty land tax and IHT.
- '*Disclosure of Tax Avoidance Schemes*' dated 14 May 2014. This was guidance on dealing with HMRC for tax agents and advisers:

  > 'what to do if you promote or use arrangements (including any scheme, transaction or series of transactions) that will or are intended to provide the user with a tax and/or National Insurance contribution advantage. Decide if arrangements need to be disclosed and how to notify HMRC.'

  It was updated on 13 January 2016.
- *FA 2014, Pt 5*, introduced greatly extended obligations on POTAS. *FA 2014, Pt 6* contains further anti-avoidance provisions, in particular with regard to DOTAS and new taxation codes of practice for banks.
- *FA 2015* further strengthened the DOTAS and POTAS rules, including the hallmarks, to ensure avoidance that is being marketed and used must be disclosed to HMRC. It also empowers HMRC to identify and pursue those who are required to disclose but do not and to obtain information about employees who are party to avoidance schemes, and allows it to publish information about promoters and schemes that are notified under the strengthened regime. HMRC are able to issue conduct notices to a broader range of connected persons under the common control of a

promoter of tax avoidance schemes. The new provisions provide that the three-year time limit for issuing notices to promoters who have failed to disclose avoidance schemes to HMRC applies from the date when the failure comes to the attention of HMRC. *FA 2015, Pt 3* introduced a new 'diverted profits tax', and *FA 2015, Pt 4* and *Sch 17* brought in further anti-avoidance provisions. The penalties under *TMA 1970, s 98C*, were increased.

- *Disclosure of tax avoidance schemes (DOTAS)*: '*Income Tax, Corporation Tax, Capital Gains Tax, National Insurance contributions (NICs), Stamp Duty Land Tax (SDLT), Annual Tax on Enveloped Dwellings (ATED) and Inheritance Tax (IHT)*' dated 2 September 2015.
- *Disclosure of Tax Avoidance Schemes: hallmark regulations – summary of Dealing with HMRC and Tax agent and adviser guidance*' dated 2 February 2016.
- The *Tax Avoidance Schemes (Prescribed Descriptions of Arrangements) Regulations 2016 (SI 2016/99)* amending the *Tax Avoidance Schemes (Prescribed Descriptions of Arrangements) Regulations 2006* (*SI 2006/1543*). They extend the scope of the confidentiality and premium fee hallmarks to include IHT; make changes to aspects of the standardised tax products and losses hallmarks; and introduce a new hallmark relating to financial products.
- There is a new threshold condition for the POTAS regime in *FA 2016, ss 159–161*. These ensure that avoidance that is being marketed and used must be disclosed to HMRC. HMRC may identify and pursue those who are required to disclose but do not, to obtain information about employees who are party to avoidance schemes and may publish information about promoters and schemes that are notified under the strengthened regime.
- *FA 2016, Schs 18–23* concern serial tax avoidance; POTAS and large businesses: tax strategies and sanctions for persistently unco-operative behaviour respectively.
- *FA 2016, ss 162–166* concern penalties in connection with offshore matters and offshore transfers; offshore tax errors, etc: publishing details of deliberate tax defaulters; asset-based penalties for offshore inaccuracies and failures and offences relating to offshore income, assets and activities respectively.

The disclosure forms are:

- AAG1. Disclosure of avoidance scheme.
- AAG2. Notification by scheme user where offshore promoter does not notify HMRC.

- AAG3. Notification by scheme user where there is no promoter, or the scheme is promoted by lawyer unable to make full notification.
- AAG4. Notification of scheme reference number by scheme user.
- AAG5. Continuation form.
- AAG6. Form for providing scheme reference numbers to users of notifiable stamp duty land tax arrangements.
- AAG7. From 13 January 2016 employers should use this form to provide a SRN to an employee where a tax advantage is expected to arise relating to their employment as a result of notified arrangements.

GAAR was brought in from 1 April 2013 by *FA 2013, Pt 5*. It is the UK's first general anti-abuse rule. The *National Insurance Contributions Act 2014* (*NICA 2014*) came into effect on 13 March 2014. *NICA 2014, ss 10* and *11* provide for the GAAR to apply to NICs. GAAR is primarily aimed at the individual taxpayer. It imposes a burden of proof on HMRC. A designated HMRC officer may notify a taxpayer in writing where the officer considers that the taxpayer has obtained a tax advantage which should be counteracted. The taxpayer has 45 days from the day on which the notice is given to provide written representations in response to the notice to the designated officer.

HMRC guidance was published on 18 December 2013 under the title 'Offshore employment intermediaries', together with a technical note and some frequently asked questions. Legislative changes are contained in *NICA 2014, ss 10* and *11*, to extend NICs to various circumstances under GAAR. A quarterly return must be completed and, from April 2014, UK tax is levied on the full employment income where the division of duties and remuneration between a UK and overseas contract is artificial and where tax is not payable on the overseas contract at a rate broadly comparable to UK tax rates.

There is an extended accelerated payment of tax to users of schemes disclosed under DOTAS, and to taxpayers involved in schemes subject to counteraction under GAAR. The amount in dispute will be held by HMRC while the dispute is resolved. In cases where taxpayers have used avoidance schemes which are defeated in another party's litigation, and where they do not settle the dispute, they must pay the disputed amount to HMRC on demand.

There are penalties for criminal offences in law and for deliberate offshore tax evasion. A GAAR Advisory Panel will enable counteraction of equivalent arrangements by other users. A new penalty of 60% of tax due to be charged in all cases successfully counteracted by GAAR is introduced from 6 April 2017.

FA 2016, ss 156–158 concern GAAR provisional counteractions; binding of tax arrangements to lead arrangements and penalties.

FA 2017, s 24 made further amendments to provisions relating to POTAS as follows:

(a) It replaces *FA 2014, Sch 34, para 13(6)–(8)* and inserts new *FA 2014, Sch 34, para 13A(9)–(12)*. These provisions refer to who controls a body corporate and/or a partnership and define promoter.

(b) It inserts new *FA 2014, Sch 34, paras 13B–13D* concerning 'relevant bodies controlled by other persons treated as meeting a threshold condition', 'persons who control a relevant body treated as meeting a threshold condition', and 'relevant bodies controlled by the same person treated as meeting a threshold condition'. These provisions refer to control or significant influence in relation to a POTAS.

(c) It replaces existing *FA 2014, Sch 34A, paras 20–22* with new paragraphs concerning 'relevant bodies controlled by other persons treated as meeting a *s 237A* condition', 'persons who control a relevant body treated as meeting a *s 237A* condition', and 'relevant bodies controlled by the same person treated as meeting a *s 237A* condition'. These provisions also refer to control or significant influence in relation to a POTAS.

Employer asset-backed pension contributions

11.120 Asset-backed contributions to DB pension schemes, which are not structured finance arrangements, were not permitted from April 2012 by virtue of *FA 2012, s 48* and *Sch 13*. These schemes concern acquiring an asset from an employer with an employer contribution and receiving an income stream for, say, 15 years from which time the property reverts to the employer.

On 19 November 2013, the Pensions Regulator called for trustees to examine such schemes carefully, and it recommended that trustees explore less risky alternatives. It issued guidance on its website on 18 December 2013.

Finance Acts, and extended compliance and reporting

11.121 Scheme administrators, members and promoters will need to take into consideration the provisions of recent *Finance Acts*, which extended the compliance rules for UK pension schemes and UK citizens as described in **11.119** and **11.120**.

FA 2014, Pts 5 and *6* targeted pension liberation fraud, in particular where members are encouraged to access their pension savings before reaching the age of 55. Additionally, *Sch 7* included changes supporting future regulatory action by the Pensions Regulator, which may require independent trustees or scheme administrators to be appointed at the instigation of the Regulator.

It also provides for HMRC to send information notices and inspect documents in connection with an application to register a pension scheme and associated penalties and appeals and contains various additional circumstances when HMRC may decide not to register a pension or may de-register a pension scheme.

The advent of flexi-access for DC schemes from 6 April 2015 (see **11.65**) effectively mean that the pensions liberation application to such schemes is confined to those aged under age 55.

There has been a strengthening of the powers of Whitehall to expand its efforts to recover money that is owed.

It is also necessary to familiarise oneself with the Pension Regulator's current approach to compliance matters. It announced on 13 June 2013 that it was expanding its compliance unit. It has been targeting its actions based on the risk and potential impact of non-compliance, and uses its power to audit companies' records going back six years. It can impose fines of up to £10,000 a day or pursue a criminal prosecution.

11.122 From A-Day all approved schemes were designated as UK-registered pension schemes, unless they opted out of the post A-Day regime. The *Registered Pension Schemes (Modification of Rules of Existing Schemes) Regulations 2006, SI 2006/364* provided a rule of construction and gave the trustees discretion over whether or not to make a payment which would fall to be treated as an unauthorised payment under the new regime. However, from a tax-planning perspective it was advisable to review existing documentation and make any desirable revisions, after having sought appropriate legal advice. Considerations included:

- any agreed changes in the level of pensionable pay and the method of calculation;
- whether or not to put in place the scheme's own earnings cap as a means of controlling maximum benefit accrual (the earnings cap must now be calculated by the scheme administrator or replaced by an alternative limit of pensionable earnings if one is desired);
- how the removal of HMRC limits has impacted on intended member benefits;
- whether to extend the scheme to overseas employers and employees;
- whether to widen the transfer powers and income withdrawal facilities to take advantage of the new freedoms;
- how the current tax rules affect benefit payments (eg transfers and income withdrawal);

- whether to change scheme indexation provisions, or remove them in the case of DC schemes, in accordance with the *Pensions Act 2004* relaxations.

A particular area of concern was what the trustees should do in the event of a surplus arising which, under the existing regime, should be returned to the employer but, under the post A-Day regime, could remain within the member's LA.

REVIEWING EXISTING UNAPPROVED ARRANGEMENTS

General

11.123 *FA 2004* removed the pre A-Day tax rules applicable to funded unapproved retirement benefit schemes (FURBS) and unfunded unapproved retirement benefit schemes (UURBS), with the result that FURBS became classified as EFRBS and lost virtually all attraction for investors. Transitional protection applies to funds accumulated up to A-Day, but it is not total. Members may wish to take advantage of the options available under the rules of their schemes, such as drawing or transferring benefits before fund growth attracts unwelcome tax charges. The long-established concept of a service agreement or unfunded promise by means of an UURBS may still have some attraction. However, from the employee viewpoint it does not offer security and government monitoring of the use of unfunded pension arrangements was announced in *FA 2012* (see **11.3**).

11.124 The main rules changed markedly for schemes where *'disguised remuneration'* is in point for the purpose of gaining a tax advantage, as described in **11.22** above. Otherwise, the rules are summarised below:

- Contributions may continue to be made to FURBS (now EFRBS) from A-Day. The lump sum will be adjusted to take account of the tax-free lump sum accumulated to A-Day. From the tax perspective there seems to be no attraction in taking up this option.
- The protection of the tax-free lump sum (where such payments qualified for relief either by virtue of the taxation of employer contributions on the member or the taxation of all income and gains under the fund), is only inclusive of indexation and not the fund yield on values from that date.
- The normal IHT exemptions apply only to pre A-Day assets under an existing discretionary trust (for unregistered schemes with no post-A-Day contributions, and those with post- A-Day contributions, the IHT treatment for the former is that in place as at 5 April 2006, limited relief shall be given for the latter for protected funds inclusive of indexation).

- No additional tax charge arises on the fund/lump sum for a FURBS which ceased contributions/input before A-Day.
- Investment gains are taxable at the 45% rate applicable to trusts. The first £1,000 is taxed at the standard rate. The current tax rates are below.

  Trust income up to £1,000:

Dividend-type income	7.5%
All other income	20%

  Trust income over £1,000:

Dividend-type income	38.1%
All other income	45%

  Trustees do not qualify for the new dividend allowance, introduced for individuals from 6 April 2016. This means trustees pay tax on all dividends depending on the tax band they fall within.

  Previous tax years:

  For 2015/16 there was a 10% tax credit on dividends from UK companies (and some non-UK companies).

  This means:

  - the first £1,000 of dividends were not taxed as the tax credit covered them;
  - dividends over £1,000 were taxed at 30.56%.
- Amounts held in the fund will not be included in the LA.
- NIC will be payable on benefits, although it is likely that there will be no charge on any benefits which are within the limits of benefits that could be paid out of a registered pension scheme.
- Tax relief on employer contributions is only allowable when the benefit is paid out.

The timing of benefit payments from existing FURBS

11.125 The rules of each scheme will require review. HMRC produced very little guidance on FURBS – the main pre A-Day publication was last updated in 1991. The guide states that benefits outside the approved scheme regime are '*unlimited*', and 'there are no tax rules which govern the structure of schemes, the type of benefits or their amount'. The guide also says that benefits may be given '*when a person retires or died, in anticipation of retirement, after a person has retired or died …*' Nevertheless, the rules themselves will take precedence over benefit payments, transfers and winding-up payments. The guide also states:

> 'there are no tax problems where a cash equivalent is paid between funded schemes. The funds held in the transferring scheme will have accrued from contributions, investment income and gains which have been taxed. For this reason there will not be any tax liability on the transfer payment.'

ALTERNATIVE PROVISION TO UK REGISTERED SCHEME BENEFITS

Introduction

11.126 In view of the impact of the LA charge on senior employees who had already accrued significant pension entitlements by A-Day, and the recent severe cuts to the LA (see **11.35** above), employers and their advisers may wish to consider providing alternative means of reward for such persons in the future. Additionally, although the registered pension scheme is an attractive and tax-efficient means of providing benefits for members who are unaffected by the LA charge (or the other charges which can be incurred under such schemes), it may best suit company policy to provide additional or alternative benefits across the workforce.

Some alternative means of saving by high earners and rewarding them for services are considered below.

Cash payments by employers

11.127 The company may consider making a direct cash payment to employees, subject to PAYE and NIC charges. This may be attractive to higher paid employees, providing ready access to monies and freedom of choice on expenditure. It is also likely to be more tax-attractive than the company paying an LA charge on behalf of an employee, as that action would in itself create a further tax charge. Additionally, any contributions to EFRBS are likely to be taxed under PAYE and subjected to NICs.

Cash payments are simple in concept, flexible and need not bind the employer to make future payments at the same level. They could also be used to invest in individual savings accounts (see **11.129**) where there is scope to do so.

Benefits-in-kind, share schemes, etc

11.128 Many companies have found that the provision of benefits to employees, such as cars, accommodation, membership fees, school fees, company cars, etc attracts new personnel. There will be tax charges on the recipients of such benefits, but these are mitigated by certain allowances and exemptions. In addition, any such expenditure which is deemed to be for the furtherance of the company's trade or undertaking will secure tax reliefs for the company. Other popular means of providing incentives to employees, and increased performance, include bonuses, share incentive schemes and share options.

Individual savings accounts, and savings allowance

11.129 ISAs have always been an attractive tax-free investment media. The government is constantly revising ISA rules and types, seemingly in an attempt to lure people away from pension savings. From 1 July 2014, ISAs became a simpler product known as NISA. From that date, savers were able to subscribe their full amount to a cash account, and investors have rights to transfer their investments from a stocks and shares account to a cash account. A wider range of securities (including certain retail bonds with less than five years before maturity) can be invested. In addition, core capital deferred shares issued by building societies are eligible to be held in a NISA, junior ISAs or child trust funds (CTFs). The amount that can be subscribed to a child's Junior ISA or CTF in 2015/16 is £4,080. The chancellor announced in the budget on 16 March 2016 that the ISA limit will be raised from £15,240 to £20,000 per annum from 6 April 2017. In addition, regulations will provide that ISAs can retain their tax-advantaged status following the death of the account holder following Royal Assent to the *Finance Act 2016*.

A consultation response document was published by the government in July 2015 containing the comments received on including peer-to-peer loans in ISAs. This included the decision to introduce a new type of ISA for peer-to-peer loans – the *innovative finance ISA* (IFISA) – alongside cash ISAs and stocks and shares ISAs. IFISA is available from 2016/17. Such lending can be risky but also can bring in higher returns. *FA 2016, s 32* amended the *Income Tax Act 2007*, backdated to 6 April 2015, to allow tax relief for losses on the irrecoverable principal of peer-to peer-loans. The government decided not to make peer-to-peer loans eligible for CTF accounts as holding peer-to-peer loans in these accounts could restrict the diversity of investments that can be held in these accounts for children.

The chancellor also announced in the budget on 16 March 2016 that a 'lifetime ISA' (LISA) will be introduced for those aged from 18 to under 40 to encourage saving for retirement and first-time home-buying. For every £4 saved, the government will put in £1. There will be a limit of £4,000 pa, with a £1,000 government contribution. Individuals can continue saving until they reach the age of 50. They can use the cash to buy a home any time from 12 months of opening, or access it from age 60 for use in retirement. All withdrawals will be tax-free. Savers who have already taken out a 'Help to Buy ISA' will be able to roll their savings into a lifetime ISA. The government will set a limit on any property purchased at £450,000, with this limit applying nationally, and consult on plans to allow borrowing against the funds without incurring a charge if the borrowed funds are fully repaid. The government will discuss the implementation of the LISA with the savings and investment industry ahead of April 2017. It is also exploring the possibility of introducing still greater flexibility and is looking at the USA 401k model.

The government is considering whether savers should be allowed to withdraw money for '*other life events*' than those envisaged by LISA. However, they will not qualify for the government bonus, plus any interest or growth on it will be lost and a 5% charge will be levied.

There is also a personal savings allowance (PSA) from 2016/17. This means that every basic rate taxpayer can earn £1,000 per year in interest without paying tax on it (£500 for higher rate taxpayers).

Excepted group life policies

11.130 Practitioners may wish to seek specialist advice on excepted group life policies (EGLPs). These products can be an attractive alternative to in-house pension scheme death benefit cover if properly drawn. There is no IT charge, LA does not apply, they can provide tax-free lump sum death benefits and be efficient on IHT where a discretionary trust is in place. Employer contributions are tax-relievable under the 'wholly and exclusively' test and there is no benefit-in-kind charge on the member.

There is no need to register an EGLP with HMRC and no need to comply with the new registered pension schemes reporting requirements. However, they must meet the conditions in *ITTOIA 2005, ss 480–482*. This means that an EGLP must be a group policy whose terms provide for the payment of benefits on the death of more than one individual and for those benefits to be paid on the death of each of those individuals. An EGLP must meet the four benefit conditions in *ITTOIA 2005, s 481* and the three beneficiary conditions in *ITTOIA 2005, s 482*.

11.131 EGLPs are not subject to the punitive taxation that applies to EFRBS. There is no need to register an EGLP with HMRC and no need to comply with

HMRC reporting requirements. Since EGLPs sit outside the registered pension scheme tax regime, they could therefore be used to provide lump sum life cover for:

- employees whose group life cover already exceeds their LA;
- employees whose group life cover, together with lump sum death benefits from other registered pension schemes, exceeds their LA;
- employees with EP where payment of the lump sum insured would jeopardise EP;
- employees with EP where payment of life assurance premiums would jeopardise EP;
- employees with PP where PP may not fully protected against an LA charge;
- new employees who have EP and would lose it if they became members of a registered pension scheme for life assurance benefits.

A similar policy may be put in place where it covers only one employee. This is known as a 'relevant life policy'.

Pension term assurance

11.132 *FA 2007* brought in a change to pension term assurance policies whereby tax relief on pension contributions which are paid as premiums to such policies is withdrawn. Existing policies had to be reviewed. Pre-6 December 2006 applications continue to benefit from tax relief, as do applications which had been sent to the insurance company on or before that date and receipt recorded by that insurance company by midnight on 13 December 2006.

HMRC's Helpsheet 347 states:

> 'You are not entitled to tax relief when you make personal term assurance contributions. Few payments are personal term assurance contributions. This helpsheet tells you whether or not any of your contributions are personal term assurance contributions.'

Although this legislative change has generally made pension term assurance unattractive, the restriction does not apply to member life assurance premiums under an occupational pension scheme if they are to a group policy and the other members covered by the policy are not connected with the individual paying the premiums (ie spouse, relative, civil partner). Additionally, life assurance which is paid by an employer for the benefit of his employees may continue.

Focus

The payment of incentive payments needs careful handling. HMRC and the Pensions Regulator have published a great deal on this matter. The Regulator replaced its guidance on incentive exercises with a '*Code of good practice on incentive exercises*', together with a statement which cross-refers to the Code. Importantly, trustees should be consulted and engaged when an incentive exercise is proposed. Additionally, trustees are expected to start from a presumption that incentive exercises are not in most members' interests and are required to take advice when an incentive exercise is proposed. The new rules came into effect on 1 July 2012.

Inducement/incentive offers

11.133 Inducement/incentive payments are payments by employers or UK-registered pension schemes to incentivise scheme members into giving up certain rights in place of alternative provision or benefit enhancement. This can give rise to long-term savings on funding assumptions. However, care and specialist advice is essential if an employer is to consider making such an offer.

HMRC's Employment Income Manual (EIM) at EIM15155 states:

> 'An employer/third party may offer to pay lump sums to employees and/or former employees who are members of the employer's registered pension scheme. In return the employee/former employee exchanges or surrenders their rights under the registered pension scheme, thereby reducing the employer's future liability for the scheme's funding. Such offers have been made in a number of circumstances.'

Back in January 2007, HMRC stated that the payment of cash sums 'in connection with the surrender or exchange of rights' are employment income, and are chargeable to IT, regardless of the age of the recipient or whether or not the recipient is retired, as they are deemed to fall within the meaning of relevant benefits payable from an EFRBS. They considered that the payment of a cash sum attracts NICs if it is deemed to be '*earnings*'. Earnings 'paid to or for the benefit of the individual' (payments made direct from employer to individual) attract Class 1 NICs. Where payment is made by the employer into the registered scheme, it attracts neither Class 1 nor Class 1A NICs. However, HMRC stated that the above does not apply to payments that 'enhance the transfer value of the pension fund and which are included in the funds transferred between schemes'.

11.134 The Pensions Regulator has now opted for the term 'incentive exercises', and its website guidance to trustees dated 19 July 2012 is summarised below:

- trustees should be consulted and engaged when an incentive exercise is proposed;
- trustees should start from a presumption that incentive exercises are not in most members' interests;
- trustees should take advice when an incentive exercise is proposed, to ensure they understand the extent of their legal obligations.

Despite the HMRC pronouncements above, the Regulator has since stated that trustees should presume that enhanced transfer exercises are not in members' interests. It stated: 'If a company is willing to encourage the transfer, the company's gain is likely to be the member's loss'. The *Pensions Act 2014, s 34* provides for regulations to be made which prohibit the practice of offering incentives to members to leave their DB schemes and transfer to alternative arrangements. The Regulator issued guidance on the matter, requiring members to be fully informed of the implications of transferring out and recommending that trustees should seek independent financial advice. It has stated that trustees should start from the presumption that such exercises and transfers are not in members' interests and should therefore approach any exercise cautiously and actively. The Regulator said trustees may decide to refuse to release data as a release would 'enable such an exercise to be run without their scrutiny'.

The Regulator's main guidance is summarised below:

- any offer must be clear, fair and not misleading;
- trustees should be actively involved and be sure that the selection, remuneration and broader commercial interests of advisers are aligned with members' interests;
- no pressure should be placed on members to make a decision to accept the offer;
- the Regulator points out that the Pensions Ombudsman can direct that compensation be made to the members.

The Regulator has updated its scheme returns to include questions on incentive exercises including enhanced transfer values and pension increase exchanges. It may give a Determination Notice under *PA 2004, s 96(2)(d)*.

Hancock annuities and EFPOS

11.135 A Hancock annuity is an immediate annuity for a retiring employee. These products remained available post A-Day as UK-registered pension schemes, and they are subject to the LA. Alternatively, an EFPOS (an acronym in an amendment to the *Social Security (Contributions) Regulations 2001, SI 2001/1004)*) could be considered. An EFPOS enjoys exemptions from NIC charges both on the employer contribution and the benefit paid from the scheme (as for an EFRBS), although it provides only a pension.

Salary sacrifices

11.136 Salary sacrifices were popular before A-Day primarily for those employees who wished to avoid the 15% restriction on employee contributions. Some arrangements have remained in place. The requirement that salary sacrifices of £5,000 a year or more must be notified to the employer's local Tax Inspector remains in place. Sacrifices must be in accordance with HMRC earnings guidelines (EIM42750). HMRC published guidance on what impacts salary sacrifice arrangements have on statutory maternity pay and what non-cash benefits employers should provide to their employees during statutory maternity leave.

Bonus waivers are similar to salary sacrifices and can appeal in particular to high earners. Following a long consultative process, HMRC confirmed that salary sacrifices and bonus waivers are not caught by the disguised remuneration rules if they are *bona fide* sacrifices and not tax-avoidance schemes.

Statutory clearance from HMRC of the effectiveness of existing waivers can be obtained by writing to: HMRC Clearances Team, Alexander House, 21 Victoria Avenue, Southend-on-Sea, Essex, SS99 1BD; email hmrc.southendteam@hmrc.gsi.gov.uk.

Scheme pensions

11.137 Scheme pensions can be more tax-efficient than drawdown or secured pensions, subject to meeting prescribed conditions. For DC schemes, the new freedoms in **11.65** can be considered.

Increases in benefits

11.138 Benefits which are increased under a discretionary power were not treated as a material change for the purpose of the SAAC, subject to meeting certain conditions.

Business loans

11.139 Loans of up to 50% of fund value may be made by SSASs in the employer's workplace. This can be a significant aid to cash flow – the maximum level of employer-related investments for most other schemes is 5% only. Self-instead personal pension schemes (SIPPS) may invest in commercial property. If such schemes cannot meet mortgage repayments due to a failure to pay rental income, the scheme may by HMRC concession re-mortgage, subject to certain rules.

Unfunded schemes

11.140 An unfunded promise could be given. Under such an arrangement tax is only payable when the benefit is paid, and employer NICs will be deferred. Of course, there is no certainty of payment and employer tax relief will be deferred until the benefit becomes payable.

Save as you earn/share incentive plans/ EIS/VCT etc

11.141 SAYE is a savings-related share scheme where an individual can buy shares with their savings for a fixed price. They can save up to £500 a month under the scheme. At the end of their savings contract (three or five years) they can use the savings to buy shares. The tax advantages are:

- the interest and any bonus at the end of the scheme is tax-free;
- savers don't pay IT or NIC on the difference between what they pay for the shares and what they are worth.

Savers might have to pay capital gains tax (CGT) if they sell the shares – but not if they put them into a NISA or pension as soon as they buy them.

Share incentive plans offer tax and NIC advantages to employees when they buy or are given shares in the company they work for. If an individual gets shares through a Share Incentive Plan and keeps them in the plan for five years they won't pay IT or NIC on their value. They won't pay CGT shares they sell if they keep them in the plan until they sell them. If they take them out of the plan, keep them and then sell them later on, they might have to pay CGT if their value has increased. There are four ways an individual can get shares:

Free shares – those given by their employer (who can give up to £3,600 of free shares in any tax year).

Partnership shares – an individual can buy shares out of their salary before tax deductions. There's a limit to how they can spend – either £1,800 or 10% of their income for the tax year, whichever is lower.

Matching shares – their employer can give up to two free matching shares for each partnership share they buy.

Dividend shares – they may be able to buy more shares with the dividends they get from free, partnership or matching shares (but only if their employer's scheme allows it). They won't pay IT if they keep the dividend shares for at least three years. They will have to pay IT and NIC on any shares they take out. The budget on 8 July 2015 made changes to existing enterprise investment schemes (EIS) and venture capital trust (VCT). The main changes are that:

- companies must raise their first investment under EIS, VCT or other risk finance investment within seven years of making their first commercial sale, or 10 years if the company is a 'knowledge intensive company';
- in addition to the cap on annual investments to £5m, there is a new cap on total investments of £12m, or £20m if the company is a 'knowledge intensive company'.

However, the government is making a number of changes to employee share schemes, and the option to acquire employment-related securities. It has published a list of events which would cause a tax-advantaged share incentive plan to cease to qualify as such as from Royal Assent to the *Finance Act 2016*.

Hybrids, Master Trusts and CDCs

11.142 A description of hybrid pensions schemes, Master Trusts and CDCs as differing styles of securing retirements savings is given in **11.11**.

Tax charges and exemptions for EFRBS

11.143 No special CGT provisions apply to EFRBSs. Whether a benefit is paid out of cash realised from the sale of scheme assets, or by a transfer *in specie* of those assets, both actions are a disposal of trust assets and trigger CGT charges.

The legislation is not specific on IHT charges for EFRBS. It is presumed that the normal provisions for discretionary settlements apply. In other words, the 6% ten-yearly charge may apply, and the exit charge up to 6% may well be triggered on death. The content of the documentation will again be paramount, and specialist advice should be sought. It was often recommended for FURBS that the employee's estate was excluded from the potential beneficiaries for reasons of certainty of IHT relief and to avoid dispute with HMRC.

OVERSEAS TAX PLANNING

Introduction

11.144 UK-registered pension scheme eligibility is available to virtually all – the employed or self-employed, the non-employed and qualifying non-residents – and the advent of ROPS, brought in far wider tax-planning opportunities than those which had been available before A-Day. In addition to these significant changes, many of the restrictions on transfers to and from UK-registered pension schemes to overseas schemes were removed. Of course, there are specific rules to follow if tax reliefs are to be obtained and/or unwelcome tax charges are to be avoided. These rules have been extended greatly in recent years. The rules are described below.

Background, and EU influence on investments

11.145 The relaxations of UK tax rules for overseas pension schemes, and the cross-border opportunities, were in no small part driven by EU law. The free movement of capital, labour and services around Member States has long been a central plank of the aims of the EC. The *IORPS Directive* (*2003/41/EC* on the activities and supervision of institutions for occupational retirement provision) represented the first step on the way to an internal market for occupational retirement provision on a European scale. The *Occupational Pension Schemes (Investment) Regulations 2005 (SI 2005/3378)* adopted a 'prudent person approach' as the underlying principle for capital investment, in accordance with the *IORPs Directive, Art 18*. Mainly, the IORPs guidance has been followed in a proportionate and flexible manner, namely:

- a triennial review of the statement of investment principles;
- trustees must consider 'proper advice' on the suitability of a proposed investment;
- there are specific requirements in relation to borrowing and a restriction on investment in the '*sponsors*' undertaking' to no more than 5% of the portfolio (where a group is concerned, the percentage is no greater than 20%).

Significantly, the 'small scheme exemption' which is contained in *Art 5* of the Directive means that schemes with fewer than 100 active and deferred members are exempted from many of the requirements of the regulations, but are still required to have regard to the need for diversification on investment rule.

The European Commission (EC) announced on 23 May 2013 that it had postponed the introduction Solvency II-style rules for DB pension schemes. This has been a bone of contention for Member States as it would make

DB schemes very costly to maintain. However, the debate on solvency continues. The EU holistic balance sheet closed on 13 January 2015. More than 100 questions had been put to the European pensions industry, following a proposal for six different models to harmonise DB funding across the European Union. Pension fund representative groups across Europe, as well as consultancies, heavily criticised the project and told the European Insurance and Occupational Pensions Authority (EIOPA) that its proposals undermined itself.

The Actuarial Association of Europe has stated that informing pension fund members about the true value of liabilities is the key to avoiding social unrest in future. The actuaries have compiled a discussion paper calling on regulator EIOPA to push for 'Clarity before Solvency'. One major demand is for EIOPA to rule out the application of a single discount rate for all IORPs.

Meantime, it was announced on 11 May 2015 that EIOPA had decided to press ahead with stress tests for IORPs, accompanied by another round of quantitative assessment.

The UK decision to opt out of the EU may well have an impact on how UK legislation on the above freedoms and funding rules will impact on pensions in the longer term. Meanwhile, on 3 June 2016, it became clear that European institutions have yet to agree a final stance on key measures proposed in the revised *IORP Directive*. IORP 11 came into force from January 2017 and must be implemented by EU States by January 2019. IORP 11 aims at providing better protection for members and other beneficiaries of pension schemes. It also aims to make cross-border provisions easier. However, the proposal to include provisions for a new harmonised solvency standard for IORPs has been dropped.

Cross-border provision, and the remittance basis

11.146 EU employers may join a UK-registered pension scheme, provided that there are clauses or rules in the scheme documentation to allow this, and compliance with the relevant Member State's requirements. Additionally, *PA 2004, ss 287* and *294*, permit *cross-border* activities within the EU. These activities include accepting contributions, ring-fencing of assets and preventing the disposal of assets which are held in the UK for an EU occupational pension institution. The principal regulations are the *Occupational Pension Schemes (Cross-border Activities) Regulations 2005, SI 2005/3381*. The purpose of the regulations is to enable occupational pension schemes for a qualifying person to be sponsored by a European employer in other Member States. Practitioners will wish to consider the advantages which are offered by the new rules, and to revise their clients' rules if necessary.

For UK residents who are either non-domiciled or not ordinarily resident in the UK, there is an opportunity to use the *remittance basis* on overseas funds (see **11.153** below). They must make a claim each year if all non-UK income and capital gains for that year is to be taxed on the remittance basis. They will not pay tax on overseas income, unless it is brought into the UK. HMRC require non-domiciled individuals to pay a charge of £50,000 (£30,000 before 2012/13) on top of the tax that would be due under the remittance basis, unless their unremitted foreign income and capital gains amount to less than £2,000.

The annual charge of £30,000 applied to individuals who had been UK resident for at least seven of the previous nine tax years. This rose to £50,000 once they had been UK resident for 12 of the previous 14 years). For reason of tax-efficiency the payment should be made from an overseas source. The government has stated that there will be a new £90,000 charge for people who are non-domiciled in the UK for tax purposes but have lived there for 17 of the past 20 years.

Migrant member relief

11.147 Migrant member relief is available where an individual:

- is resident in the UK but was not resident in the UK at the time he joined a qualifying overseas pension scheme (QOPS);
- comes to the UK as a member of that scheme, and remains a member of the overseas scheme;
- notifies the scheme manager that he intends to claim migrant member relief (UK tax relief against UK earnings on contributions paid to the overseas scheme);
- has earnings chargeable in the UK; and
- was eligible for tax relief on contributions to the overseas scheme in the country in which they were resident immediately before coming to the UK (alternatively, where a member had received tax relief on contributions paid to the pension scheme in the country of residence at any time in the ten years prior to coming to the UK).

11.148 The overseas scheme must either be EU or EEA registered, or one that generally corresponds with a UK scheme, and must:

- notify HMRC that it is an OPS, providing supporting evidence if required;
- undertake to notify HMRC if it stops being an OPS;

- undertake to provide HMRC with certain information in accordance with regulations; and
- notify any member claiming migrant member relief that it has undertaken to comply with the information requirements.

Employers may claim a deduction for contributions paid to a QROPS in respect of employees who are eligible for migrant member relief.

Special rules apply tax charges that arise in respect of RNUKS, where UK tax relief has been given on contributions under migrant member relief, or under the terms of a double taxation treaty, or where a transfer has been made from a UK-registered pension scheme to an overseas scheme. Member payment charges apply under *FA 2004, Sch 34,* where the individual is resident in the UK in the year in which the payments are made or was resident in the UK in any of the immediately preceding five years.

Pension portability in the EU

11.149 The *EU Portability Directive* was adopted by the EC on 21 June 2013. The EC urged the European Parliament to adopt the Directive as soon as possible. The Directive requires Member States to implement minimum requirements for the acquisition and preservation of pension rights for people who go to work in another EU country. The Commissioner for Employment, Social Affairs and Inclusion, László Andor, said the news was 'an important step' towards ensuring people could work in another Member State without losing their occupational pension benefits: 'People who exercise their right to free movement should not be penalised'.

Practitioners will need to be aware of the latest developments, as it is likely that Member States will have to ensure the fair treatment of dormant pension rights and gradually improve their transferability. The changes may require a review of existing pension scheme documentation. It is currently intended that the Directive will apply to all work-related pension schemes both funded and unfunded.

The agreement would see a vesting period for pension rights of three years for workers caught by the Directive. This is controversial as a number of Member States apply a longer period for domestic workers. Member States will have four years to apply the changes to national law.

It should be noted that unequal tax treatment of foreign pension funds in the EU is not permitted. The EC referred Germany to the European Court of Justice (ECJ) over its existing legislation. It has also reported several other EU states over their dividend tax legislation, which it says discriminates against overseas pension funds.

Qualifying recognised overseas pension scheme, and transfers

11.150 There is no doubt that there are considerable funds which are tied up in UK-registered pension schemes for internationally mobile employees, expatriates and employees of overseas companies. Before A-Day there was little that could be done to move these monies to an overseas scheme. *FA 2004* introduced sweeping changes and specialist practitioners have acquainted themselves with the new (and ever-changing) rules, leading to reviews of their own clients' status and contact with specialist overseas providers and scheme administrators where appropriate.

A key opportunity for members lies in joining a QROPS. The advantages are that pension monies may be transferred to and from UK-registered pension schemes to such schemes without tax charge, and tax reliefs are available on contributions to such schemes. Future accrual of benefits from monies which have received no UK tax reliefs will not attract the LA charge.

A transfer to a QROPS is a 'relevant transfer' under *FA 2004, s 169*, which includes pensions in drawdown, and a BCE is triggered. Additionally, there are wide potential tax savings for individual members on their benefits, dependent on their residence and/or domicile status.

There are no specific UK restrictions on borrowing by QROPS. However, if a member borrows money back from funds he has transferred, it will trigger an unauthorised payment charge.

FA 2008 contained a significant change in legislation concerning IHT charges. It provided IHT relief on savings, generally for QROPS, backdated to A-Day (*FA 2008, para 18, Sch 29*, which amended *IHTA 1984, s 58*, concerning 'relevant property').

Unfortunately, some practitioners/providers have been perceived by HMRC to have abused the transfer opportunities offered by QROPS. As a result, HMRC issued a consultation document entitled '*Overseas Transfers of Pension Savings – Draft Guidance*' on 20 December 2011. HMRC's main concern was that UK pension funds which have been transferred, or may be transferred in future, could be forced out of bona fide pension schemes into unregulated and insecure domains. A specific concern is those schemes which permit a full collapse of the fund after five years' absence from the UK. Accordingly, the reporting requirements have been tightened up.

FA 2012 heralded a review of QROPS to exclude such schemes in any jurisdiction that makes legislation or otherwise creates or uses a pension scheme to provide tax advantages which UK tax and pensions legislation does not intend. Scheme administrators/managers will need to be aware that the following additional requirements were introduced:

FA 2013 extended *FA 2008, Sch 36,* so that the same rules in relation to inspection and requiring information apply to all pension matters whether the pension scheme is registered in the UK or is a QROPS or former QROPS. *FA 2013, ss 52* and *53* contain the main changes, which apply to all transfers to QROPS made free of tax and empower HMRC to make regulations setting out additional information requirements from a new or existing QROPS and an ex-QROPS. There is a new provision that a notice requiring old documents in relation to a QROPS or former QROPS is extended to documents that originate up to ten years before the date of the notice. A copy of such a notice must be given by HMRC to the scheme manager. Reports may be made to HMRC (at www.hmrc.gov.uk/qropsonline).

Where there has been a change to the circumstances which were declared under an earlier report, the information must be provided to HMRC:

- within 30 days beginning on the day that the change occurred or the scheme manager became aware of the lack of completeness or inaccuracy; or
- by such other time as may be agreed between HMRC and the scheme manager.

There is a cut-off point from which scheme managers of former QROPS no longer need to report changes to information. Scheme managers of former QROPS will not need to report changes to information if:

- there are no relevant transfer funds under the scheme; or
- the transfer to which the relevant information correction/change relates was made more than ten years ago and the member is neither UK resident nor resident at any point earlier in the tax year or in any of the previous five tax years.

Where a scheme ceased to be a QROPS on or after 14 October 2013, HMRC can require the scheme manager of a former QROPS to provide information if that scheme received transfer whilst the scheme still had QROPS status and the transfer came from:

- a UK-registered pension scheme; or
- another QROPS where the transfer included rights that originated from a registered pension scheme.

The information must be provided:

- within 90 days beginning on the day the notice is given by HMRC; or
- by such other time as may be agreed between HMRC and the QROPS.

Legislation was intended to take effect from 1 April 2015, requiring scheme managers to re-notify HMRC of their recognised overseas pension scheme (ROPS) status every five years from the date that HMRC give the scheme manager their QROPS number. As part of this re-notification process the scheme manager must tell HMRC how the scheme continues to meet the conditions to be a ROPS. Scheme managers can re-notify at any time in the six-month period before the re-notification is due. However, the start of the QROPS re-notification process is being delayed until 6 April 2016. PTM112600 provides further information about the QROPS re-notification process.

The effective removal of the '70% rule', which was brought about by the flexible access changes (see **11.65**), was to have applied to overseas schemes which hold UK tax relieved assets, for example, QROPS. This was contained in draft regulations but has now been incorporated in *FA 2017* (see **11.3**). As a result of the changes, an overseas scheme cannot be a QROPS unless the scheme manager has given HMRC an undertaking that he will operate the new overseas transfer charge and pay this to HMRC. This means that any existing QROPS will only continue to be treated as a QROPS until 13 April 2017, if it does not comply with the new undertaking requirements.

Other types of overseas pension schemes

11.151 *QNUPS:* QNUPS are described in the *Inheritance Tax (Qualifying Non-UK Pension Schemes) Regulations 2010 (SI 2010/51)*. IHT exemptions are available for such schemes, with retrospective effect to 6 April 2006. Transfers from RPS to QNUPS are not recognised transfers unless the scheme is also a QROPS. A QNUPS is a 'pension scheme' within the meaning of *FA 2004, s 150(1)*. There are far fewer reporting requirements than apply to QROPS.

OPS: An OPS cannot be a registered pension scheme, and it must be established outside the UK. Normally, a scheme will be treated as established in the country where its registered office and main administration is, or, if there is no registered office, where its main administration is. The scheme's location of main administration is where the scheme's decisions are made. In the case of a trust-based scheme, that would normally be determined by reference to where the scheme trustees are resident. An OPS must be regulated as a pension scheme in the country in which it is established, or, if there is no body by which it could be regulated, then certain conditions must be met. Additionally, it must be 'recognised for tax purposes' by the country or territory in which it is established.

QOPS: A qualifying overseas pension scheme (QOPS) is a scheme which can accommodate migrant members. It must be an OPS and notify HMRC of its status on form APSS 250.

ROPS: A ROPS is an OPS which meets the criteria described in the *Pension Schemes (Categories of Country and Requirements for Overseas Pension Schemes and Recognised Overseas Pension Schemes) Regulations 2006 (SI 2006/206)* – see below.

The governing legislation

11.152 The main legislation which affects the above overseas schemes is weighty, but it is a critical source of information. The changes made by the *Registered Pension Schemes and Overseas Pension Schemes (Miscellaneous Amendments) Regulations 2012 (SI 2012/884)* are of particular interest, draconian and far-reaching. A list of the legislation, with brief commentaries, is provided below:

- *Pension Schemes (Categories of Country and Requirements for Overseas Pension Schemes and Recognised Overseas Pension Schemes) Regulations 2006 (SI 2006/206)* – the requirements to qualify as an OPS.
- *Pensions Schemes (Application of UK Provisions to Relevant Non-UK Schemes) Regulations 2006 (SI 2006/207)* – the method of calculation of tax on a payment made by a RNUK in respect of a payment which is referable to a member's UK tax-relieved funds.
- *Pension Schemes (Information Requirements – Qualifying Overseas Pension Schemes, Qualifying Recognised Overseas Pension Schemes and Corresponding Relief) Regulations 2006 (SI 2006/208)* – the information which must be sent to HMRC for a QOPS and a QROPS to be recognised.
- *Pension Schemes (Relevant Migrant Members) Regulations 2006 (SI 2006/212)* – the application of migrant member relief for a member of an OPS.
- *Registered Pension Schemes (Provision of Information) Regulations 2006 (SI 2006/567)* – the requirements for the provision of information, which have recently been largely extended to QROPS.
- *Registered Pension Schemes and Overseas Pension Schemes (Electronic Communication of Returns and Information) Regulations 2006 (SI 2006/570)* – electronic reporting and tax return rules for UK and overseas schemes.
- *Registered Pension Schemes (Extension of Migrant Member Relief) Regulations 2006 (SI 2006/1957)* – extending eligibility for relief where a person was not resident in the UK at the time they joined a scheme, other than where:
  - a member's rights have been subject to one or more block transfers;
  - a series of block transfers have occurred; and

  - the scheme to which the member originally belonged is closed to new accruals for existing members and a further scheme for members of that scheme is set up.

- *Pension Schemes (Categories of Country and Requirements for Overseas Pension Schemes and Recognised Overseas Pension Schemes) (Amendment) Regulations 2007 (SI 2007/1600)* – amending Primary Condition 2 of the principal *QROPS Regulations* and introducing a Schedule relating to Australian schemes.
- *Special Annual Allowance Charge (Application to Members of Currently-Relieved Non-UK Pension Schemes) Order 2009 (SI 2009/2031)* – introducing SAAC into legislation – SAAC was repealed in April 2011.
- *Inheritance Tax (Qualifying Non-UK Pension Schemes) Regulations 2010 (SI 2010/51)* – bringing in inheritance tax exemptions for QROPS and RNUKS retrospectively to 6 April 2006 for the purposes of the *IHTA 1984, s 271A.*
- *Registered Pension Schemes etc (Information) (Prescribed Descriptions of Persons) Regulations 2010 (SI 2010/650)* – circumstances in which HMRC will not require a copy of information to be sent to certain persons.
- *Registered Pension Schemes and Overseas Pension Schemes (Miscellaneous Amendments) Regulations 2012 (SI 2012/884)* – very significant changes with effect from 6 April 2012, in particular for an OPS to be recognised, the scheme must be established in a country or territory where there is a system of taxation of personal income under which tax relief is available in respect of pensions and:

  (a) tax relief is not available to the member on contributions made to the scheme by the individual or, if the individual is an employee, by their employer, in respect of earnings to which benefits under the scheme relate; or

  (b) all or most of the benefits paid by the scheme to members who are not in serious ill-health are subject to taxation,

  where tax relief in respect of benefits is available to a member of the scheme who is not resident in the country or territory in which the scheme is established, the same or substantially the same tax relief must also be available to members of the scheme who are resident in the country or territory; and apply regardless of whether the member was resident in the country or territory:

  (i) when the member joined the scheme; or

  (ii) for any period of time when they were a member of the scheme.

Transfers which were made to existing QROPS before 6 April 2012 may retain their status without penalty if the scheme loses its QROPS status from that date.

- *Pension Schemes (Categories of Country and Requirements for Overseas Pension Schemes and Recognised Overseas Pension Schemes) (Amendment) Regulations 2006 (SI 2012/1221)* – excluded new Guernsey exempt pension contracts and exempt pensions trusts under the *Income Tax (Guernsey) Law 1975, s 157E*, from being ROPS – and therefore QROPS – if they are open to non-residents of Guernsey. Additionally, certain conditions on New Zealand schemes, dependent on whether or not the scheme is a local Kiwisaver scheme.
- *Pensions Schemes (Application of UK Provisions to Relevant Non-UK Schemes) (Amendment) Regulations 2012 (SI 2012/1795)* – replacing 'unsecured pension' and 'ASP' with 'drawdown pensions' with retrospective effect from 6 April 2011.
- *Registered Pension Schemes (Provision of Information) (Amendment) Regulations 2013 (SI 2013/1742)* –amendments to the registered pension scheme information requirements.
- *FA 2013* – extending HMRC's information and inspection powers.
- *Registered Pension Schemes and Overseas Pension Schemes (Miscellaneous Amendments) Regulations 2013 (SI 2013/2259)* – further amended registered pension schemes and QROPS in respect of the information requirements.
- *Registered Pension Schemes and Relieved Non-UK Pension Schemes (Lifetime Allowance Transitional Protection) (Individual Protection 2014 Notification) Regulations 2014 (SI 2014/1842)*. The Regulations make provision for individual protection 2014 following the reduction in the lifetime allowance.
- *Registered Pension Schemes (Provision of Information) (Amendment) Regulations 2014 (SI 2014/1843)*. The Regulations amend the *Information Regulations* in relation to the reduced annual allowance.
- *Overseas Pension Schemes (Miscellaneous) Regulations 2015 (SI 2015/673)*.
- *Pension Schemes (Categories of Country and Requirements for Overseas Pension Schemes and Recognised Overseas Pension Schemes) (Amendments) Regulations 2017 (SI 2017/398)*. The Regulations make various amendments to the *Pension Schemes (Categories of Country and Requirements for Overseas Pension Schemes and Recognised Overseas Pension Schemes) Regulations 2006 (SI 2006/206)* (the '*Overseas Pension Schemes Regulations*'). This includes removing what is known as the 70% rule from the *Overseas Pension Schemes Regulations*, which

required the rules of a scheme to designate a minimum of 70% of the funds that have had UK tax relief to be used to provide the member with an income for life.

Foreign pensions of UK residents and anti-avoidance

11.153 *FA 2011, s 72*, prevented individuals from taking advantage of a tax loophole. Notwithstanding the terms of a double taxation arrangement with another territory, a payment of a pension or other similar remuneration may be taxed in the UK where:

- the payment arises in the other territory;
- it is received by an individual resident of the UK;
- the pension savings in respect of which the pension or other similar remuneration is paid have been transferred to a pension scheme in the other territory; and
- the main purpose or one of the main purposes of any person concerned with the transfer of pension savings in respect of which the payment is made was to take advantage of the double taxation arrangement in respect of that payment by means of that transfer.

In the event that tax is paid in the other jurisdiction, appropriate credit will be available against the UK tax chargeable.

The legislation had effect in relation to payments of pensions or other similar remuneration made on or after 6 April 2011.

British pensioners who live abroad will have to provide evidence that they are alive if they wish to keep their state pensions. At present, the DWP sends 'life certificates' to individuals who have retired abroad, which they have to get countersigned. It is increasing the frequency with which the certificates are issued, although these new 'push on life certificates' will only apply to countries such as France which do not automatically share the information with the UK.

In the future, non-UK residents will have to pay CGT on gains on UK residential properties that are not their primary residence. This will have impact on the investments of some pension schemes.

The main HMRC guidance on tax reliefs for residents and non-residents in the HMRC guide HMRC6 entitled 'Residence, Domicile and the Remittance Basis' was a useful guide for tax-planners. It has now been replaced by the following publications:

- *RDR1*: Guidance Note: Residence, Domicile and the Remittance Basis – published 8 June 2016;
- *RDR3*: Guidance Note: Statutory Residence Test – published August 2016;
- *RDR4*: Guidance Note: Overseas Workday Relief – published May 2013;
- HS264: Remittance Basis – published 2017;

  Guidance Note: Changes to the Remittance Basis – published May 2012;

  Information Note: Changes to the Remittance Basis – published May 2012.

See also **11.119–11.121**.

GLOSSARY OF TERMS

11.154

AA	=	annual allowance
ABI	=	Association of British Insurers
ACA	=	Association of Consulting Actuaries
A-Day	=	6 April 2006
AFT	=	accounting for tax return
AMC	=	annual management charge for NEST
APPS	=	appropriate personal pension scheme
ASP	=	alternatively secured pension
ATED	=	annual tax on enveloped dwellings
AVC	=	additional voluntary contribution
BCE	=	benefit crystallisation event
BIM	=	HMRC Business Income Manual
BSP	=	basic state pension
CBI	=	Confederation of British Industry
CDC	=	collective defined contribution schemes
CEIOPS	=	Committee of European Insurance and Occupational Pension Supervisors
CGT	=	capital gains tax
COP	=	code of practice
CPI	=	consumer prices index

CT = *Corporation Tax Act 2010*

CT = corporation tax

CTF = child trust fund

DA = defined ambition scheme

DB = defined benefit

DBLSDB = defined benefit lump sum death benefit

DC = defined contribution

DCA = Department of Constitutional Affairs

DC COP = Code of Practice 13 'Governance and administration of occupational defined contribution trust-based schemes'

DOTAS = disclosure of tax avoidance schemes

DRA = default retirement age

DTA = double taxation agreement

DWP = Department for Work and Pensions

EBT = employee benefit trust

EC = European Commission

ECJ = European Court of Justice

EEA = European Economic Area

EET = exempt-exempt-taxed

EFPOS = employer-financed pension only schemes (an acronym in an amendment to the *Social Security (Contributions) Regulations 2001 (SI 2001/1004)*)

EFRBS = employer-financed retirement benefits scheme

EGLP = excepted group life policy

EIM = HMRC Employment Income Manual

EIOPA = European Insurance and Occupational Pensions Authority

EIS = enterprise investment schemes

EP = Enhanced protection

ETV = enhanced transfer value

EU = European Union

FA = *Finance Act*

FAS = Financial Assistance Scheme

FCA	=	Financial Conduct Authority – which, with the PRA, replaced the FSA in 2013
FP 2012	=	fixed protection 2012
FP 2014	=	fixed protection 2014
FP 2016	=	fixed protection 2016
FPS	=	Full Payment Submission to tell HMRC about payments made to employees and what deductions the employer has made.
FSA	=	Financial Services Authority, replaced by the FCA and PRA in 2013, under the auspices of the Bank of England
FSCS	=	Financial Services Compensation Scheme
FSMA 2000	=	*Financial Services and Markets Act 2000*
FURBS	=	funded unapproved retirement benefit schemes
GAAR	=	general anti-abuse rule
GAD	=	Government Actuary's Department
GMP	=	guaranteed minimum pension
GPP	=	group personal pension
HIERC	=	high income excess relief charge
HMRC	=	Her Majesty's Revenue and Customs
HMRC PSS	=	HMRC Pension Scheme Services
ICTA 1988	=	*Income and Corporation Taxes Act 1988*
IFISA	=	innovative finance ISA
IHT	=	inheritance tax
IHTA 1984	=	*Inheritance Tax Act 1984*
IM	=	Inspector's Manual
IORP	=	institution for occupational retirement provision
IORPS Directive	=	*Directive 2003/41/EC of the European Parliament and the Council on the activities and supervision of institutions for occupational retirement provision*
IP 2014	=	individual protection 2014
IP 2016	=	individual protection 2016
IPTM	=	HMRC Insurance Policyholder Taxation Manual
IRPS	=	investment-regulated pension scheme
ISA	=	individual savings account

IT	=	income tax
ITA	=	*Income Tax Act*
ITEPA 2003	=	*Income Tax (Earnings and Pensions) Act 2003*
ITTOIA	=	*Income Tax (Trading and Other Income) Act 2005*
LA	=	lifetime allowance
LAM	=	HMRC Life Assurance Manual
LEL	=	lower earnings limit
LISA	=	lifetime individual savings account
LLP	=	limited liability partnership
LSDB	=	lump sum death benefit
MAS	=	Money Advice Service, to be replaced by a new single entity
MPA	=	minimum pension age
MPAA	=	money purchase annual allowance
NAO	=	National Audit Office
NAPF	=	National Association of Pension Funds
NEST	=	National Employment Savings Trust
NI	=	National Insurance
NIC	=	National Insurance Contribution
NICA 2015	=	*National Insurance Contributions Act 2015*
NICO	=	National Insurance Contributions Office
NIM	=	HMRC National Insurance Manual
NISA	=	new individual savings account
NPA	=	normal pension age
NRD	=	normal retirement date
OEIC	=	open-ended investment company
ONS	=	Office for National Statistics
OPS	=	oversea pension scheme
PA	=	*Pensions Act*
PAS	=	Pensions Advisory Service, to be replaced by a new single entity
PAYE	=	Pay As You Earn
PCLS	=	pension commencement lump sum
PFLSDB	=	pension fund lump sum death benefit

PIA	=	pension input amount
PIP	=	pension input period
PLSA	=	Pensions and Lifetime Savings Association, formerly the NAPF
PP	=	Primary Protection
PPS	=	personal pension scheme
PPF	=	Pension Protection Fund
PRA	=	Prudential Regulation Authority which, with the FCA, replaced the FSA in 2013
PSA	=	personal savings allowance
PSA 1993	=	*Pension Schemes Act 1993*
PSA 2015	=	*Pension Schemes Act 2015*
PSN	=	HMRC's Pension Schemes Newsletter
PSR	=	Pension Scheme Return
PSTR	=	Pension Scheme Tax Reference
PTM	=	HMRC Pensions Tax Manual
PW	=	Pension Wise, to be replaced by a new single entity
QNUPS	=	Qualifying Non-Recognised Overseas Pension Scheme
QOPS	=	Qualifying Overseas Pension Scheme
QROPS	=	Qualifying Recognised Overseas Pension Scheme
RAC	=	retirement annuity contract
RAS	=	relief at source
REIT	=	Real Estate Investment Trust
RNUKS	=	relevant non-UK scheme
ROPS	=	Recognised Overseas Pension Scheme
RPI	=	retail prices index
RPSM	=	HMRC Registered Pension Schemes Manual
RTI	=	real time information
SA 1972	=	*Superannuation Act 1972*
SAAC	=	special annual allowance charge
S2P	=	state second pension
SA 970	=	Tax return for trustees of registered pension schemes
SA 975	=	Guidance notes on the tax return for trustees of registered pension schemes

SAYE	=	Save As You Earn
SDLT	=	Stamp Duty Land Tax
SCO	=	HMRC Special Compliance Office
SERPS	=	state earnings-related pension scheme
SIPPS	=	self-invested personal pension scheme
SP	=	state pension
SPA	=	state pension age
SRN	=	scheme reference number
SSAS	=	small self-administered scheme
SSAA 1992	=	*Social Security Administration Act 1992*
SSCBA 1992	=	*Social Security Contributions and Benefits Act 1992*
SSPA 1975	=	*Social Security Pensions Act 1975*
TEE	=	Tax-exempt-exempt
TOPA 2014	=	*Taxation of Pensions Act 2014*
TSEM	=	HMRC Trusts, Settlements and Estates Manual
TUPE	=	*Transfer of Undertakings (Protection of Employment) Regulations 2006 (SI 2006/246)*
UAP	=	upper accrual point
UEL	=	upper earnings limit
UFPLS	=	uncrystallised fund pension lump sum
UURBS	=	unfunded unapproved retirement benefit scheme
VAT	=	value added tax
VCT	=	venture capital trust
WRPA 1999	=	*Welfare Reform and Pensions Act 1999*

Chapter 12

Business and agricultural property relief and woodlands relief

Mark McLaughlin CTA (Fellow), ATT (Fellow), TEP, Tax Consultant, Mark McLaughlin Associates Ltd

Chris Erwood CTA, ATT, TEP, Erwood & Associates Ltd

SIGNPOSTS

- **Business property relief (BPR)** – BPR reduces the value of transfers of relevant business property by a specified percentage. The rate of relief depends on the type of business property. BPR must be claimed, and is subject to certain conditions (see **12.1–12.3**).
- **Business carried on** – BPR does not generally apply in respect of businesses wholly or mainly carrying on certain types of activity, such as making or holding investments (see **12.4–12.8**).
- **Ownership** – No BPR is generally due unless the transferor has owned the relevant business property for a minimum period of two years before the transfer. However, this general rule is subject to certain exceptions, such as for replacement property (see **12.9–12.12**).
- **Practical issues** – Various issues may need to be addressed in respect of BPR. For example, BPR is subject to restriction for 'excepted assets'. In addition, groups of companies may need to structure their activities and assets carefully to ensure that BPR is not inadvertently lost or restricted. BPR is not normally available if the business property is subject to a binding contract for sale at the time of the transfer. Business property transferred within seven years before death may affect the availability of BPR unless certain conditions are satisfied (see **12.13–12.46**).
- **Other planning** – BPR planning opportunities and pitfalls exist in respect of the death estate. Other planning has sometimes included the use of multiple ('pilot') trusts and 'placing' debt to maximise the relief, although the former arrangement has been affected by provisions (introduced in *F(No 2)A 2015*) on 'same day additions', and

the latter is subject to anti-avoidance rules on liabilities (introduced in *FA 2013*). BPR clearance applications may be made to HMRC in some cases (see **12.47–12.61**).

- **Agricultural property relief (APR)** – APR operates to reduce the value of transfers of qualifying property by either 50% or 100%, dependent on the terms of occupation (see **12.62–12.64**).
- **Time qualification** – Unlike its BPR sibling, APR is subject to a two-tier time test which pivots on end use and ownership of the underlying farming activity (see **12.70–12.73**).
- **The 'piggy back' facility** – The landowner can gain access to APR by reference to the qualification of the underlying farmer tenant (see **12.73** and **12.81**).
- **Complexity** – The complex rules surrounding the scope and application of APR should not be understated and as a consequence it remains a risk area for the professional practitioner tempted to 'dabble' (see **12.70–12.71**, **12.85–12.86**, **12.102**).

BUSINESS PROPERTY RELIEF

INTRODUCTION

12.1 Business property relief (BPR) is an important and valuable relief from inheritance tax (IHT). It reduces the value transferred by a transfer of value of certain types of business or business property by a specified percentage. The current rates of BPR are 100% and 50% respectively. The actual rate of relief applied to a transfer depends on the type of business property.

The relief applies to actual or deemed transfers. It is available for lifetime transfers, or to relevant business property included in an individual's estate on death. There are no territorial limits to the relief, so it can apply to business property situated worldwide. BPR also applies to settled property included in the death estate, and is available to trustees in respect of the periodic and exit charges that apply to discretionary trusts, and to most other types of trust following changes introduced in *FA 2006*.

The law on BPR is contained in *IHTA 1984, ss 103–114*. The relief must be claimed. The claimant must therefore be aware of the categories of business property that qualify, and the correct rate of BPR applicable. A number of conditions must be satisfied before the relief is available, and a number of potential traps exist for the unwary.

The first part of this chapter outlines the conditions for BPR, and highlights some planning points and possible pitfalls in connection with the relief.

Conditions

12.2 BPR applies if the value transferred by a transfer of value relates to relevant business property. The categories of business property, and the rates of BPR attributable to them, are broadly as listed below (see *IHTA 1984, ss 104, 105(1)*):

- a business or an interest in a business – 100%;
- control holdings of unquoted securities in a company – 100%;
- unquoted shares in a company – 100%;
- control holdings of quoted shares in a company – 50%;
- land, buildings, plant and machinery used by a company controlled by the transferor, or by a partnership of which the transferor was a member – 50%;
- land, buildings, plant and machinery of a settlement in which the transferor had an interest in possession and was used in his business – 50%.

12.3 In the context of companies, the term 'unquoted' applies for BPR purposes to shares listed on the Alternative Investment Market (AIM). The same applies to shareholdings in OFEX companies (see HMRC's Inheritance Tax Manual at IHTM18336, IHTM18337).

Shares traded on NASDAQ Europe are similarly treated as unlisted at present. However, shares traded on NASDAQ are currently treated as listed for IHT purposes, and BPR does not apply except (rarely) for controlling shareholdings (IHTM18340, IHTM18341).

In general, if a company is not listed on the UK Stock Exchange, any foreign recognised Stock Exchange or alternative market, its shares and securities will be unquoted (*IHTA 1984, s 105(1ZA)*). However, in relation to those companies and in general, it is necessary to consider whether the business carried on makes the shares or securities (or a business interest) eligible for BPR. Furthermore, a company that is initially treated as unquoted for BPR purposes (eg by only being listed on the AIM) should be monitored regularly to ensure that it does not subsequently obtain a secondary listing on (for example) a foreign recognised stock exchange.

It is worth noting that securities forming part of a controlling holding in an unquoted trading company (ie securities that give control either by themselves or together with other securities owned by the transferor and any unquoted shares so owned) are eligible for BPR at the 100% rate (*IHTA 1984, s 105(1)(b)*), such as loan notes with rights in general meetings of the company forming part of a single holding giving the holder control.

In the case of land, buildings, plant and machinery used by a company, it is important to note the requirement that the company must be controlled by the transferor. 'Control' for these purposes is defined in *IHTA 1984, s 269*, broadly in terms of the exercise of a majority of voting power on all matters affecting the company as a whole. In *Walding and others (Walding's Executors) v CIR* [1996] STC 13, Mrs Walding held 45 out of 100 shares in a company on her death. Her executors claimed that the deceased had control of the company for BPR purposes, on the basis that 24 shares were in the name of her four-year-old grandson, but the court dismissed the executors' appeal against the Revenue's refusal of a BPR claim on factory units owned by the deceased and occupied by the company.

However, note that a company chairman with a 50% shareholding and a casting vote under the company's articles has been held to have control for these purposes (*Walker's Executors v IRC* [2001] STC (SCD) 86).

It should be noted that the 'related property' provisions (*IHTA 1984, s 161*) apply for the purposes of determining control (*IHTA 1984, s 269(2)*). This can be helpful if, for example, spouses or civil partners each hold shares in the company which are not controlling holdings in isolation, but are deemed to give control as related property. This situation will be encountered in unquoted companies in particular.

A group structure (see **12.23**) may be considered in appropriate cases, such as to hold the shares in a trading company and also the trading premises, with a view to securing BPR at 100% on the business premises (and shares), as opposed to only 50% if the premises is owned by a controlling shareholder (or no BPR at all, if the shareholder does not hold a controlling interest in the company).

A beneficiary with a qualifying life interest in trust property is treated for IHT purposes as owning the underlying assets. A qualifying life interest for these purposes means an interest in possession within *IHTA 1984, s 49(1)*. If those assets were used in the beneficiary's business on death, they will normally qualify for 100% BPR (*Fetherstonaugh and others v IRC* [1984] STC 261). As to HMRC's view in relation to lifetime transfers, see **12.12**.

The *Fetherstonaugh* (or '*Finch*' as HMRC refer to it at IHTM25154) case was successfully relied upon by the executor in *Revenue and Customs v Brander (personal representative of the Fourth Earl of Balfour)* [2010] UKUT 300 (TCC), in terms of satisfying the two-year ownership test for BPR purposes (in *IHTA 1984, s 106*; see **12.9** below).

What is a 'business'?

12.4 'Business' has a wider meaning than 'trade' for BPR purposes; it specifically includes a profession or vocation. However, it does not include a business carried on otherwise than for gain (*IHTA 1984, s 103(3)*; see, for example, *Grimwood-Taylor and another (executors of Mallender, deceased) v Inland Revenue Commissioners* [2000] STC (SCD) 39). A 'hobby business' may therefore be excluded (see IHTM25051), unless it can be demonstrated that it has been run in a proper, business-like manner.

Prior to the decision in the *Nelson Dance Family Settlement Trustees* case (see below), and it was commonly thought that the transfer of business *assets* (as opposed to a transfer of the business itself) did not qualify for BPR. The *Nelson Dance* case concerned the transfer of some farmland with development value to the trustees of a family settlement. The trustees claimed BPR on the basis that there had been a transfer of value which resulted in a reduction in the value of 'relevant business property' within *IHTA 1984, s 105*. HMRC sought to disallow the BPR claim, but the trustees' appeal was successful. The Special Commissioner ([2008] SpC 682) held that BPR was due on the basis that: 'all that is required is that the value transferred by the transfer of value is attributable to the net value of the business.'

HMRC's subsequent appeal (*Revenue and Customs Commissioners v Trustees of the Nelson Dance Family* [2009] EWHC 71 (Ch)) was dismissed. The High Court held that it was sufficient for BPR purposes that the diminution in value of the transferor's estate by reason of the transfer was attributable to the value of relevant business property. As the land had been used in the farming business, its transfer could be regarded as attributable to the value of the business, and BPR was therefore available on the transfer.

The *Nelson Dance* decision would therefore seem to offer an opportunity for sole traders and partners wishing to transfer business assets (ie not 'excepted assets' – see **12.14**) into trust with the benefit of BPR (and CGT holdover relief in most cases), whilst continuing to carry on the business. Particularly in the case of trading assets, the decision whether to transfer them into trust must be considered carefully if the business interest would qualify for 100% BPR in any event. The same might be said of the investment assets of a 'mixed' trading and investment business which is mainly trading, although a transfer may be attractive if, for example, the business owner wishes to secure CGT entrepreneurs' relief on all assets of the business, on the basis that 'substantial' investments would preclude any relief (*TCGA 1992, s 169L(4)(b)*).

It should be remembered that relevant property trusts are liable to periodic and exit charges for IHT purposes. There are traps for the unwary. For example, on an exit charge in the first ten years of the trust, BPR is ignored when determining the initial value of the asset. This can be problematic if BPR is not available on exit. In addition, a transfer to a relevant property trust of (for example) land with development value could (following *Nelson Dance*) attract BPR, but at the next ten-year anniversary the trustees might be found to hold a mere business asset or a mere investment, in respect of which no relief would be available.

The decision in *Nelson Dance* does not seem to accord with HMRC's interpretation of the BPR rules. A change in the law is therefore possible, and so any planning opportunities may be limited.

> **Focus**
>
> Business property is generally precluded from relief if the business consists wholly or mainly of dealing in securities, stocks or shares or land or buildings, or in making or holding investments (*IHTA 1984, s 105(3)*).
>
> There are some limited exceptions, in respect of market makers or discount house businesses carried on in the UK. This exception for market makers was extended with effect from 31 December 2012, to apply BPR if the business concerned is a market maker within the EEA (other than the UK) in a recognised regulated market (*The Inheritance Tax (Market Makers and Discount Houses) Regulations 2012, SI 2012/2903*).
>
> There is also an exception in group situations, if a company's business is wholly or mainly to be the holding company of one or more companies whose business is not an excluded one (*IHTA 1984, s 105(4), (4A)*).
>
> Groups of companies are discussed later in this chapter (see **12.23–12.29**).

Property consisting of farmland, which was let for grazing under seasonal grazing arrangements described as conacre (ie a temporary easement creating a licence to use land) but which, more precisely, were agistment agreements (ie the letting of land for grazing) in Northern Ireland was held to be enough to constitute a business within *IHTA 1984, s 105(1)* on the facts in *McCall and another (Personal Representatives of McClean, dec'd) v Revenue and Customs Commissioners* [2009] NICA 12.

However, the Court of Appeal upheld the conclusion of the Special Commissioner ([2008] SpC 678) that the arrangements could not be viewed as a business of providing grass, but rather as a business of holding an investment, such that BPR was not due. Girvan LJ stated:

> 'The agisting farmer had exclusive rights of grazing; he was entitled to exclude other graziers including the deceased; the deceased could not use the land for any purpose that interfered with the grazing and the letting for grazing was the way in which the deceased decided that the grasslands could be used and exploited as uncultivated grassland short of the creation of a lease. The deceased's business consisted of earning a return from grassland whose real and effective value lay in its grazing potential. The activities which were regarded as just sufficient to lead to the lettings of the land being regarded as a business were all related to enabling that potential value to be released.'

Thus although there was sufficient activity to constitute a business, that business was held to be excluded from BPR, on the grounds that it consisted wholly or mainly of making or holding investments, within *IHTA 1984, s 105(3)*. The Court of Appeal supported the view of the Special Commissioner that the activities of the business consisted in making available its major asset (ie the farm fields) to others for payment, without the separate provision of other goods or services to any substantial degree. The deceased had made the land available, not to make a living on it, but from it; the management activities related to letting the land; it was unlike 'hotel accommodation for cattle' as argued by the taxpayers (as to investment businesses, see **12.15** below). Thus although the letting of land does not necessarily constitute an investment business, the availability of BPR is likely to depend on the nature and extent of other services also provided.

Caravan parks

12.5 A number of cases have considered what constitutes a 'business' for BPR purposes. This is particularly so in relation to caravan park businesses, for the purposes of determining whether they were substantially investment in nature due to rental receipts, or whether the trading (eg sales and service) components of the businesses were sufficient to enable them to qualify for BPR.

In *IRC v George and another (executors of Stedman, dec'd)* [2004] STC 147, Lord Justice Carnwath accepted on the facts that a caravan site qualified, commenting that it was '… difficult to see why an active family business of this kind should be excluded from business property relief, merely because a necessary component of its profit-making activity is the use of land'.

HMRC's Inheritance Tax Manual (IHTM) provides a useful insight into its approach following the decision in *George*, and commentary is therefore repeated below. In practice, HMRC are likely to refer caravan park cases in which BPR is claimed to their Technical Group.

'Caravan sites and furnished lettings' (extracts from IHTM25279)

> 'The judgment in *George* is helpful in clarifying what is to be regarded as either investment or non-investment activity. It makes clear that the provision of services under the terms of a pitch agreement is a non-investment activity. This means that in cases where a large part of the business's activities (measured in both time and money) consists of providing services to residents, we would be more likely to consider that the business was neither wholly or mainly investment in nature. However, we need to be satisfied that the figures for pitch fees, for instance, are not artificially depressed in the accounts in favour of inflated figures for wages or other non-investment expenses.'
>
> 'The judgment in *George* also recognises that the time and money spent on maintaining amenity areas is in part designed to maintain the value of the owner's investment. It follows that the taxpayers are entitled to return a reduced level of investment income by offsetting against it part of the maintenance costs. As this could lead to the net investment income being, proportionally, a smaller part of the overall income of the business we might well conclude in a particular case that the business was neither wholly or mainly one of holding investments. On the other hand, we would also need to take into account the time spent by the owner and/or his employees in the maintenance work. When taken together with other work carried out in the business, the evidence might lead us to conclude that the majority of work done is involved in maintaining the value of the owner's investment. If so, then we would seek to deny the claim under *s 105(3)*.'
>
> 'The judgment in *George* also suggests that the holding of land as an investment is separate and distinct from the service element of the business. Finally, when looking at the facts "in the round", trading figures are only a part of the overall picture.'
>
> 'When dealing with a claim for business relief on a caravan park, you will need to obtain detailed business accounts, including breakdowns of both the income and expenditure between the investment and non-investment elements of the business. In addition, you should ask the taxpayers to state precisely what services were provided to the park residents and how long was spent by the deceased (as park owner) and his partners and/or employees providing those services.'

The 'right' business?

12.6 A detailed consideration of what constitutes an eligible business for BPR purposes is outside the scope of this chapter. However, the following points are worthy of note:

- *Property construction* – the restriction on dealing in land and buildings does not prevent a property construction business from qualifying for BPR, such as a building company holding houses or plots as stock in trade for development. However, if a house builder has not built any houses recently and is selling off its land, in HMRC's view the business will not qualify for BPR at the time of the business transfer, on the basis that it consists wholly or mainly of dealing in land and buildings, for which relief is precluded by *IHTA 1984, s 105(3)* (IHTM25266).

  However, in *Executors of Piercy (dec'd) v Revenue and Customs Commissioners* [2008] SpC 687, a property development company owned land on which it had built workshops for letting. The executors of a major shareholder claimed BPR, but HMRC denied it on the ground that the company received substantial investment income and its business was therefore mainly making or holding investments. The executors claimed that the company was still trading: it still held undeveloped land that it wished to develop for housing but had to wait for uncertainty to be resolved concerning proposals for a new railway line.

  The Commissioner found that the land was still held as trading stock, not as an investment, and allowed the appeal. A land-dealing company will not qualify for BPR if it is a speculative trader or dealer, but land-dealing companies that actively develop land or build on land are outside the exclusion. For a company to be wholly or mainly holding investments, the Commissioner held that it must actually have investments: thus holding the land as trading stock was highly relevant here.

- *Hotels, nursing homes, etc* – other property-backed businesses such as hotels and nursing homes will also usually qualify for relief, in view of the level of services provided. However, HMRC guidance (at IHTM25277) indicates that BPR in respect of certain types of hotel (ie the 'self-service/budget hotel industry') may be susceptible to challenge: '…you should also ascertain the nature of a "hotel" business to establish whether on the facts it actually falls at the investment end of the spectrum'.

- *Holiday lettings, etc* – HMRC have tended to examine BPR claims in respect of holiday lettings relatively closely, presumably to establish if the activity constitutes a 'business', and if so, whether it is wholly or mainly one of holding investments.

  In *HMRC v Personal Representatives of N Pawson, Deceased* [2013] UKUT 050 (TCC), Mrs Pawson owned an interest in a large bungalow

('Fairhaven') on the Suffolk coast at the time of her death. Her executors claimed BPR in respect of the property. Their claim was on the basis that Fairhaven had been used for a holiday letting business, and that it was not disqualified (by *IHTA 1984, s 105(3)*) from being relevant business property on the basis of being a business consisting wholly or mainly of making or holding investments. The First-tier Tribunal (FTT) allowed the executors' appeal ([2012] UKFTT 51 (TC)), finding that the exploitation of Fairhaven had constituted a business, which did not consist wholly or mainly of holding an investment. HMRC appealed.

The Upper Tribunal noted that some business activities carried on at Fairhaven naturally fell on the investment side of the line, but that certain additional services were provided to occupants as part of the holiday letting business. Those additional services comprised: a cleaner/caretaker to clean the property between each letting and carry out regular inspections of the property; space heating and hot water; a television and telephone at the property; being on call to deal with queries and emergencies; and minor matters such as the replenishment of cleaning materials as and when necessary, and the provision of an up-to-date welcome pack (laundry services were also provided, but only after Mrs Pawson's death).

The Upper Tribunal considered that the critical question was whether those additional services prevented the business from being mainly one of holding Fairhaven as an investment. The Upper Tribunal noted that the judgment in *IRC v George* (see **12.5**) made it clear that the provision of such services is 'unlikely to be material' in the case of a property letting business because they were not enough to prevent the business remaining 'mainly' one of property investment. The services provided were considered to be of a relatively standard nature. Looking at the business in the round, in the Upper Tribunal's view there was nothing to distinguish it from any other actively managed furnished holiday letting business, and there was certainly no basis for concluding that the services comprised in the total package were such that the business ceased to be one which was mainly of an investment nature. HMRC's appeal was allowed.

The decisions in *Pawson* (and *George*) were subsequently considered in *Green v Revenue and Customs* [2015] UKFTT 236 (TC), where it was held that lifetime transfers of interests in a furnished holiday lettings business to a settlement were not eligible for BPR, as the First-tier Tribunal decided that the business consisted mainly of making or holding investments.

Similarly, in *Ross v Revenue and Customs* [2017] UKFTT 507 (TC), it was held that a two-thirds share of a partnership that carried on a business of running and managing eight holiday cottages plus two staff flats in Cornwall and a property in Weymouth consisted mainly of making or holding investments, and hence BPR was precluded by *IHTA 1984, s 105(3)*. The First-tier Tribunal referred to the above decisions in *Pawson* and *Green*, and held that (despite the high level of services provided to holiday cottage guests in the present case) the business activity nevertheless consisted mainly of investing in property.

HMRC's guidance in the Inheritance Tax Manual previously indicated that BPR would normally be allowed if the lettings were short term (eg weekly or fortnightly) and there was substantial involvement with the holidaymakers, both on and off the premises. This applied even if the lettings were for only part of the year.

However, HMRC's guidance (IHTM25278) was amended in late 2008 and subsequently. At the time of writing, it states the following:

> 'HMRC's view is that furnished holiday lets will in general not qualify for business property relief. The income derived from such businesses will largely consist of rent in return for the occupation of property. *There may however be cases where the level of additional services provided is so high that the activity can be considered as non-investment, and each case needs to be treated on its own facts*' (emphasis added).

HMRC's revised approach suggests that the active involvement of the holiday lettings proprietor is of less importance than the degree of service and nature of services offered to guests. In the absence of more specific guidance from HMRC, it would seem logical to assume that the closer the comparison between the holiday accommodation and a traditional hotel in terms of services provided, the better would appear the prospect of securing BPR.

Other types of lettings involving land may fall foul of *IHTA 1984, s 105(3)* in HMRC's view. Their guidance states (at IHTM25280): 'You will need to consider whether the exploitation of land ownership in other ways, such as self-storage, car parks, business parks, DIY livery, moorings or beach huts, is an investment activity'. However, in *Vigne Deceased, Personal Representative of the Estate of v Revenue and Customs* [2017] UKFTT 632 (TC), a livery business was held to be a business which was not wholly or mainly one of holding investments (within *IHTA 1984, s 105(3)*), and was therefore eligible for BPR.

- *Property lettings* – difficulties can arise with property lettings. For example, in *Clark and another (executors of Clark, dec'd) v HMRC* [2005] STC (SCD) 823, a company's business comprised rents from properties it owned (ie investment income), plus trading income from management charges in respect of a number of dwellings owned by family members. Viewed 'in the round', the company's business was held to consist mainly of investments. The company's maintenance of the rented properties was held not to constitute the separate provision of services, but was inherent in the property ownership.

- *Loans* – In *Phillips and others (Executors of Rhoda Phillips, dec'd) v HMRC* [2006] SpC 555, shares in a company which made informal, unsecured loans to related family companies were held to be relevant business property, on the basis that the company's business was making loans, and therefore did not consist wholly or mainly of making or holding investments within *IHTA 1984, s 105(3)*.

'Wholly or mainly'

12.7 The 'wholly or mainly' business test (see also **12.4**) applies to a business, business interest or company shares or securities. For the purposes of determining whether a company satisfies this test, it is necessary to consider all the company's activities 'in the round'. HMRC state the following (at SVM111150):

> 'It is not possible to lay down any precise ground rules. Each company has to be looked at in the round. It may however be readily accepted that, where the majority of both the tangible asset value and profit of the company is attributable to trading activities, relief is available.'

HMRC's guidance adds that the 'wholly or mainly' test should be considered over a reasonable period prior to the transfer in case of temporary fluctuations in activity and performance.

The likely approach by HMRC in appropriate cases will therefore be to consider the company's activities, assets and income or gains, not only when business property is transferred, but also over what they regard as a 'reasonable period' leading up to it (IHTM25263).

In *Brown's Executors v IRC* [1997] STC (SCD) 277, HMRC refused a BPR claim on shares, on the grounds that the business consisted wholly or mainly of making investments at the date of death. The company had traded as a nightclub, but the business was sold before the shareholder's death and the proceeds held on a short-term bank deposit pending the acquisition of a new nightclub. However, the executors' appeal was upheld.

12.8

Focus

An important point to note is that BPR is only denied if the business activities mentioned in *IHTA 1984, s 105(3)* (ie dealing in securities, stocks and shares, dealing in land or making or holding investments) represent more than 50% of all business activities.

Thus, for example, the shareholder of an unquoted company undertaking 51% trading activities and 49% investment business activities can benefit from full BPR if the other relief conditions are satisfied. Conversely, if trading activities represent 49% and investment business activities 51%, no BPR is due at all.

In practice, it may be difficult to measure the respective activities accurately. The Special Commissioner's decision in *Farmer and another (executors of Farmer, dec'd) v IRC* [1999] STC (SCD) 321 offers some guidance on the possible approach to this problem.

In *Farmer*, the deceased carried on the business of farming and letting properties which were surplus to the requirements of the farm. The net rental profits were greater than the net farming profits, but the farming assets had a higher value at death than the properties used for letting. HMRC denied BPR on the basis that the business consisted mainly of making or holding investments.

However, the executors' appeal was upheld. The Special Commissioner held that it did not follow that the level of net profit was the only or principal test in *IHTA 1984, s 105(3)*. The business and its activities had to be looked at 'in the round'. The letting of properties was subsidiary to the main farming activity, and although they were more profitable in the overall context of the business, this was not conclusive. The overall context of the business, capital employed, the time spent by employees and consultants and the levels of turnover supported the conclusion that the business consisted mainly of farming.

Subsequently, in *Executors of Piercy (dec'd) v Revenue and Customs Commissioners* [2008] SpC 687 (see **12.6**), the Special Commissioner held that a property development company whose land was stock did not thereby hold investments, such that its business could not be excluded for BPR purposes by *IHTA 1984, s 105(3)* as consisting wholly or mainly of making or holding investments. This was notwithstanding that slow trading meant that some of the development sites could not be sold and had to be leased, thereby generating substantial investment income for the company.

The issue of mixed usage was considered in *Revenue and Customs v Brander (personal representative of the Fourth Earl of Balfour)* [2010] UKUT 300 (TCC), in the context of a landed estate. In that case, the Earl of Balfour inherited a life rent interest in the family estate in 1968, including land used for farming. The activities carried on included in-hand farming and management of commercial woodlands, but there was also substantial letting activity. He entered into a farming partnership with his nephew in November 2002. In June 2003, he died. HMRC considered that BPR was not due. However, the First-tier Tribunal held that the ownership requirements of *IHTA 1984, s 107* as to replacement property were satisfied, and that *IHTA 1984, s 105(3)* did not apply to deny BPR.

The Upper Tribunal dismissed HMRC's subsequent appeal. In deciding the meaning of 'the business of holding investments' the tribunal said the test to be applied is that of the intelligent businessman who would be concerned with the use to which the asset is being put and the way it was being turned to account. Furthermore, the question of whether a business consists wholly or mainly of making or holding investments is a decision of fact for the decision-maker, who should look at the business in the round to form an overall picture of the relative importance of the investment and non-investment activities in that business. This exercise involves looking at the business over a period of time.

Looking at the overall context of Lord Balfour's business in operating a unitary landed estate with in-hand farming, forestry/woodland, sporting activities and the letting of farms, the First-tier Tribunal was entitled to treat that context as a factor which pointed towards a business that was mainly a trading business. It was also entitled to conclude that the turnover and net profit figures supported the conclusion that management of the estate was mainly a trading activity. The Upper Tribunal agreed that *IHTA 1984, s 105(3)* did not apply. BPR was therefore available.

In *The Trustees of David Zetland Settlement v Revenue and Customs* [2013] UKFTT 284 (TC), HMRC refused a BPR claim in respect of an IHT charge arising on the ten-year anniversary of a settlement. The trustees appealed. The BPR claim had been made in respect of (among other things) a commercial building divided into units let to tenants. The trustees contended that the services provided to the tenants were such that its business activities were prevented from being 'mainly' one of making or holding investments within *IHTA 1984, s 105(3)*.

The tribunal noted from the Upper Tribunal decision in the *Pawson* case (see **12.6**) that the relevant test is the nature of the activities carried out, not the level or degree of activity, and commented: 'In the *Pawson* case the bar has been set quite high. The facts do not get the Appellants over the bar. The services provided were mainly of a standard nature aimed at maximising income through the use of short term tenancies.' The trustees had pointed towards various services and facilities as being additional over and above those normally provided to tenants (eg a café, communal events, internet services, cleaning services, a gym, hair salon). However, the tribunal concluded that the non-investment activities were primarily concerned with increasing the return on the building, and were not sufficient to tip the balance in favour of obtaining BPR. The trustees' appeal was dismissed.

In *Best v Revenue and Customs* [2014] UKFTT 77 (TC), a claim for BPR in respect of unquoted company shares was denied by HMRC, on the basis that the business of the company consisted wholly or mainly of holding investments. The deceased shareholder's executor appealed. The company owned a business centre, which provided industrial and warehouse space for small to medium-sized businesses. The tribunal noted the authorities (in *George* (see **12.5**), *McCall* (see **12.4**) and *Pawson* (see **12.6**)) in the context of land and whether a business consists wholly or mainly of holding investments. The tribunal held that the nature and extent of additional services provided by the company did not predominate when considering its activities as a whole, and that the company's business was mainly holding investments. The executor's appeal was dismissed.

PERIOD OF OWNERSHIP

12.9 The general rule is that no BPR is due unless the relevant business property has been owned by the transferor for a minimum period of two years (*IHTA 1984, s 106*).

In terms of IHT lifetime planning, this two-year minimum holding period compares favourably with the seven-year period required for potentially exempt transfers to become exempt. It makes investment in (for example) unquoted shares (see **12.3**) potentially more attractive to individuals whose life expectancy is likely to exceed two years but uncertain to exceed seven years due to age or ill health, particularly while BPR is available at the 100% rate. However, such investments are generally risky in nature, and their commercial implications must therefore be carefully considered.

HMRC appear to apply the ownership test to businesses as a whole, rather than individual assets of the business. It therefore follows that capital and assets introduced into a business less than two years before death or transfer will qualify for BPR as part of the net value of the business (within *IHTA 1984, s 110*), provided that they were used in the business at the relevant time (IHTM25342).

12.10

Focus

Changes in the business during the two-year period are not necessarily fatal for BPR purposes. The nature of the business need not be the same, but there must have been a business throughout that period (IHTM25303).

There are also certain exceptions to the basic two-year ownership requirement, in connection with replacement property, acquisitions on death and successive transfers respectively.

These exceptions broadly apply as outlined below.

- *Replacement property* – the ownership test is treated as satisfied if the property replaced other business property eligible for relief, provided that the combined period of ownership is at least two years out of the preceding five years (see, for example, *Revenue and Customs v Brander (personal representative of the Fourth Earl of Balfour)* [2010] UKUT 300 (TCC)).

  However, the BPR available is restricted to what it would have been had the replacement or any one or more of the replacements not been made (*IHTA 1984, s 107(2)*), subject to the exceptions below.

  The replacement property rule may be helpful in certain circumstances:

  - *incorporation of a business* – the acquisition of the business by a company controlled by the former business owner(s);
  - *partnerships* – changes resulting from the formation, alteration or dissolution of a partnership (eg retiring from one partnership to form another);
  - *company reorganisations, etc.* – holdings of unquoted shares which would (under the capital gains tax rules in *TCGA 1992, ss 126–136*) be identified with other qualifying shares previously owned may treat their period of ownership as including the ownership period of the original shares (*IHTA 1984, s 107(4)*).

    In *Executors of Dugan-Chapman (deceased) v Revenue and Customs Commissioners* [2008] SpC 666, a BPR claim relied on the company reorganisations exception to the two-year ownership rule. Mrs Dugan-Chapman was allotted one million ordinary shares in the company on 27 December 2002, two days before her death. The issue was broadly whether those shares could be identified for BPR purposes with other shares in the company which she had held for at least two years prior to her death. The Special Commissioner dismissed the executors' appeal against HMRC's determination that the value of those shares could not be reduced by BPR. HMRC had contended that the shares were issued as the result of a simple subscription for shares. There was insufficient evidence or documentation to support the executors' argument that a reorganisation had actually taken place.

    As a postscript, subsequently in *Vinton and others v Fladgate Fielder* [2010] EWHC 904 (Ch), the executors, trustees and residuary beneficiaries of Mrs Dugan-Chapman's estate sued the solicitors for damages to recover the IHT that became payable and the costs of the above unsuccessful tax appeal. The solicitors applied to have the claim struck out as 'fanciful', but the court refused to strike out the claim.

Although a BPR claim was unsuccessful in the above case (albeit that 300,000 shares allotted to Mrs Dugan-Chapman on 23 December 2002 pursuant to a valid rights issue did qualify for BPR), there is still a potential planning opportunity available in 'deathbed' situations (eg where a shareholder has a life expectancy of less than two years).

However, as the *Dugan-Chapman* case illustrates, it is important to get the facts and the paperwork right. For example:

- There should be a commercial need for cash, since otherwise the money used to acquire the new shares will be an excepted asset (within *IHTA 1984, s 112*).
- The directors should record the need for funds for the purposes of the business of the company.
- The rights issue should be executed correctly (eg so that all shareholders can participate (and several should actually do so), in addition to the 'target' shareholder).
- If possible, the balance of voting rights should be left as it was before the share arrangement.
- No attempt should be made to 'water down' the arrangement in any way. For example, the new money must not be a mere loan, nor be seen as such by attempting to distinguish between one class of share and another.

The above BPR limit for replacement property in *IHTA 1984, s 107(2)* does not apply to changes in value resulting from the formation, alteration or dissolution of a partnership, nor from the acquisition of a business by a company controlled by the former owner of the business. Thus, in the case of the first two instances listed above, the potential restriction in BPR mentioned earlier is disregarded (*IHTA 1984, s 107(3)*).

- *Successions* – for the purposes of the two-year ownership requirement and the replacement property rule, business property inherited on death is generally treated as owned from the date of death. However, if the deceased was a spouse or civil partner, the ownership periods of both individuals are combined (*IHTA 1984, s 108*). This applies irrespective of how long they have been married (IHTM25321). However, note that this provision applies to business property acquired on the death of another person, and not where that other person made a lifetime gift.
- *Successive transfers* – BPR is broadly available for relevant business property if that property was eligible for relief when it was originally transferred to its owner (or their spouse or civil partner), and that

(or replacement) property would be relevant business property on the later transfer (but for the two-year rule), provided that either the original or later transfer was made on death (*IHTA 1984, s 109(1)*). However, BPR can be subject to limitation in certain specific circumstances (in *IHTA 1984, s 109(2), (3)*), broadly relating to replacement property and to earlier partial acquisitions (see IHTM25333).

For the purposes of the ownership requirement in *IHTA 1984, s 106* (and *IHTA 1984, s 107*), it would seem that shares are owned when they are acquired, whether they are issued fully or partly paid up, as there are no specific BPR provisions regarding partly paid shares. Acquiring shares on that basis may therefore seem attractive in terms of starting the ownership 'clock'.

What if some of an individual's shares meet the two-year ownership requirement, but other shares do not? In terms of identifying the shares for BPR purposes, HMRC's approach is stated to be as follows (SVM111090):

> 'Where the transferor acquired additional shares during the 2 years prior to the transfer and it is claimed that the shares transferred derived from the holding acquired earlier, the agents should be asked to provide the necessary evidence – such as a copy of the relevant entries in the register of transfers or of the relevant share certificates. However if, exceptionally, firm evidence does not exist (for example because, following a reorganisation of the share capital, a fresh certificate was issued to cover the whole of the transferor's holding) relief may be given to the extent that it would be available **on the basis of a "first in-first out" assumption**' (emphasis added).

BPR and interests in possession

12.11 In the context of BPR, 'ownership' generally applies in terms of beneficial entitlement.

HMRC consider ownership in relation to settled property to mean legal ownership by the trustees of a settlement in which there is no interest in possession (IHTM25302).

Beneficial entitlement includes a beneficiary's beneficial entitlement to an interest in possession in the settled property (*IHTA 1984, s 49(1)*). The IHT regime for interests in possession was changed significantly by *FA 2006*, and only certain post-22 March 2006 interests in possession (eg immediate post-death interests) are subject to this treatment.

If an unadministered residuary estate includes business property, the residuary beneficiary is treated as owning the business property (or an appropriate share of it) (*IHTA 1984, s 91*; see IHTM25302).

12.12 As noted at **12.2** above, land, buildings, plant and machinery of a settlement in which the transferor had an interest in possession and was used in his business qualify for BPR at the 50% rate. However, if the transferor has a qualifying interest in possession in the assets used for his business, those assets will normally be treated as part of his business and will be entitled to 100% relief (*Fetherstonaugh v IRC* [1984] STC 261; see **12.3**).

HMRC consider that there is 'some doubt' whether the *Fetherstonaugh* decision can apply to lifetime as well as death transfers, and will refer claims for 100% BPR on lifetime transfers to their Technical Group (IHTM25154).

Value of the business

12.13 BPR is available in respect of the net value of the business. 'Net value' is the value of business assets (including goodwill) less business liabilities (*IHTA 1984, s 110(b)*). Any assets not used in the business cannot qualify for relief. In addition, BPR is not available for assets not used wholly or mainly for business purposes throughout the preceding two years, nor required for future business use (*IHTA 1984, s 112(2)*; see **12.14**).

In *Hardcastle and another (executors of Vernede, dec'd) v IRC* [2000] STC (SCD) 532, the Lloyd's assets of a non-working name was accepted to qualify as business property eligible for 100% relief. Uninsured underwriting losses were held to be liabilities deductible from the value of the deceased's other estate rather than the deceased's underwriting interests. The losses were not considered to be liabilities incurred for the purposes of the business under *IHTA 1984, s 110(b)*.

In *IRC v Mallender* [2001] STC 514, the deceased's Lloyd's underwriting business was also considered to be business property eligible for relief. However, a tenanted investment property used to support a security for a bank guarantee did not qualify as business property. The land was worth considerably more than the maximum sum guaranteed. The court held that the bank guarantee was the asset used in the business rather than the investment property itself.

Subsequently, in *Seymour (Ninth Marquess of Hertford) v IRC* [2005] STC (SCD) 177, a stately home (Ragley Hall) was operated as a business. 78% of Ragley Hall was open to the public, and 22% was occupied as a private residence. The deceased's executors claimed BPR on the value of the building as a whole, as being one of the assets of the business within *IHTA 1984, s 110(b)*. They appealed against HMRC's refusal to allow relief for 100% of the property value. The Special Commissioner held that the asset attracting business property relief was Ragley Hall in its entirety, not just 78% of it.

Unfortunately, HMRC appear to view this case as an 'unusual' one, on the basis that '... it was the nature of the business in this particular case and the part that the physical structure of the hall played in that business that most influenced the Commissioner's decision'. BPR claims on buildings based on the decision are therefore likely to attract the attention of HMRC's Technical Group (see IHTM25342).

Excepted assets

12.14 There is a potential restriction of BPR in respect of 'excepted assets', ie assets not used wholly or mainly for business purposes for at least the last two years, nor which are required for future business use (*IHTA 1984, s 112*). This provision therefore has the potential to restrict BPR such as, for example, in relation to surplus cash held by an unquoted trading company (see **12.17**).

The 'future use' requirement provides a useful let-out in cases where an asset has not been used wholly or mainly for business purposes throughout the last two years. If the asset is in actual business use at the relevant point in time, it will probably be required for future business use as well.

Different rules apply to land or buildings, plant or machinery used wholly or mainly for the business of a company controlled by the transferor, or by a partnership of which he was then a partner, for which 50% BPR is available. The description of relevant business property in *IHTA 1984, s 105(1)(d)* only requires that the asset is in business use immediately before the transfer. However, the excepted asset provisions broadly require business use throughout the preceding two years, subject to relaxations for replacement property and under the rules in *IHTA 1984, s 109* for successive transfers (*IHTA 1984, s 112(3)*).

A helpful relaxation in the excepted asset rules applies to land and buildings, where part is used exclusively for business purposes but the whole of the land or building is not used wholly or mainly for business purposes (eg it was used wholly or mainly for the benefit of a transferor or a connected person). In those circumstances, the part used exclusively for business purposes, and the rest of the property, are treated as separate assets and BPR is applied accordingly to the business part. The value of the entire land or building is apportioned between those parts for this purpose (*IHTA 1984, s 112(4)*).

Example 12.1 – Partial BPR

Stanley owned a three-storey building on his death. The ground floor was a shop from which he operated a confectionery business. He used the second and third floors for his living quarters. The value of the whole building is £600,000, of which the upper floors are valued at £350,000.

The ground floor shop is treated as a separate asset, which is not an excepted asset.

In the case of property subject to a mortgage (or other loan), prior to changes introduced in *FA 2013*, BPR could be maximised if the mortgage was secured on the non-business part of the property. However, this planning strategy has been blocked in relation to mortgages or loans taken out on or after 6 April 2013 (see **12.56**).

Investment 'business'?

12.15

Focus

Investment assets will not necessarily be excepted assets. A trading company that includes a 'business' of making or holding investments may qualify for BPR, provided that the investment business does not predominate. A 'wholly or mainly' test applies for these purposes (*IHTA 1984, s 105(3)*).

HMRC accept that a 'hybrid' company that is mainly trading will not be subject to the excepted assets rule in respect of assets used in the investment element of the business (see Shares and Assets Valuation Manual at SVM111220).

However, HMRC consider that a 'business' involves a degree of activity. In *American Leaf Blending Co v Director-General of Inland Revenue (Malaysia)* [1978] 3 All ER 1185 (a Malaysian tax case) (see **12.20**), Lord Diplock held: 'The carrying on of "business", no doubt, usually calls for some activity on the part of whoever carries it on, though, depending on the nature of the business, the activity may be intermittent with long intervals of quiescence in between.'

In the case of surplus cash, the company's holding of it generally requires no effort and involves no activity. In *Jowett v O'Neill and Brennan Construction Ltd* [1998] STC 482 (a corporation tax case), the holding of cash on interest-bearing deposit was held not to constitute a business. On the other hand, a holding of investment shares or securities may constitute a business, depending on the size of holdings, the degree of active management and the reason for acquiring them.

12.16 Another corporation tax case (*Revenue and Customs Commissioners v Salaried Persons Postal Loans Ltd* [2006] STC 1315) gives rise to the possibility that a company owning property and deriving a rental return from it may be considered not to be carrying on an investment business.

In that case, the company's only source of income was rental income from a former business premises. HMRC contended that the company was carrying on a business, but the Special Commissioner allowed the taxpayer's appeal. It was relevant to consider why the company received income and what it actually did to receive the income. The company had merely continued letting its old trading premises, which it had done for nearly 30 years. The circumstances in which a company letting property is found not to be carrying on a business are likely to be exceptional. However, the possible application of the decision in the *Postal Loans* case in a BPR context should be borne in mind.

In *McCall and another (Personal Representatives of McClean, dec'd) v Revenue and Customs Commissioners* (discussed at **12.4** above) the Special Commissioner ([2008] SpC 678) considered that the business in that case consisted wholly or mainly of the making of investments, on the basis that:

> 'the activities of the business consisted of the making available of its major asset to other persons for payment without the separate provision of any substantial other goods or services.'

He added:

> 'The activities surrounding the letting (except perhaps the provision of water) were not so substantial as to constitute themselves a part of the business distinct from holding the land: this was not like a car hire business where income derives from the letting of a car but where the cleaning, servicing, insuring and dealing in the cars may be such a large part of what is done to say that it is not just a business of holding cars; instead the major part of what was done was letting the land and the other activities a necessary part of that or small in comparison.'

The Special Commissioners' decision was upheld in the High Court ([2009] NICA 12). It would therefore seem that, whilst the letting of land does not necessarily constitute an investment business, the availability of BPR is likely to depend upon what other services are provided as well, and the extent of those services.

'Surplus' cash

12.17

> **Focus**
>
> It may be relevant to ask: is surplus cash 'surplus' at all? For example, what is the company's working capital requirement? Could the funds be applied towards repaying creditors? Or expanding the company's trade?

> In the context of the 'future use' test in *IHTA 1984, s 112(2)(b)*, HMRC have stated that, unless there is evidence that cash is held for an identifiable future purpose, it is likely that the surplus cash will be treated as an excepted asset. Thus the holding of funds as an 'excess buffer' to weather an adverse economic climate is not considered by HMRC to be a sufficient reason for it not to be classed as an excepted asset (*ICAEW Taxguide 1/14*).

HMRC's Shares and Assets Valuation Manual states (at SVM111220):

> '[Surplus cash] cannot be regarded as a separate investment business nor as part of the hybrid business, as it requires no effort and involves no activity. It is a factual test.'

The guidance then lists the following questions, which may provide a helpful checklist (or at least a useful insight into HMRC's approach) when considering if cash is indeed 'surplus':

- Was the cash used for the business?
- Was the cash used to finance the business carried on by the company?
- How much cash did the company use regularly?
- What were its short-term cash requirements?
- Does the amount of cash fluctuate?

The excepted assets restriction for BPR purposes (see **12.14**) can apply to assets which are not wholly or mainly required for future business use. This condition was considered in *Barclays Bank Trust Co Ltd v IRC* [1998] STC (SCD) 125.

In that case, the deceased had been a shareholder in a company operating the business of selling bathroom and kitchen fittings. At the date of the deceased's death, the company held £450,000 in cash. Turnover was around £600,000. HMRC accepted that £150,000 of that cash was required by the company at that time, but maintained that the remaining £300,000 was an excepted asset. The Special Commissioner accepted HMRC's view, and dismissed the appeal against the BPR restriction. The possibility of using the money at some future point if a suitable opportunity arose was not sufficient. To be required for future use, there must be some evidence that the money will be required for a specific project or business purpose.

The *Barclays* case perhaps provides a helpful 'rule of thumb', on the footing that a cash balance equivalent to 25% of turnover was accepted as being required for the day-to-day running of the business. However, it may be possible to justify a higher proportion in practice, subject to the working capital requirements of the particular business. For example, some trades may be subject to seasonal fluctuations, which could perhaps mean that a larger proportion of cash is required.

12.18 By contrast, in *Brown's Executors v IRC* [1996] STC (SCD) 277, the deceased owned shares in an unquoted trading company which operated a nightclub. The nightclub was sold to third parties. Proceeds from the sale of the nightclub were held in a short-term interest-bearing deposit account with a bank pending acquisition of a new nightclub business. The deceased investigated the possibility of acquiring other nightclubs, but then died suddenly. The executors appealed against HMRC's refusal of a BPR claim on the shares. HMRC claimed that the company's business consisted wholly or mainly of making or holding investments, within *IHTA 1984, s 105(3)*. However, the Special Commissioner accepted the executors' evidence that the company had been actively seeking alternative sites for another nightclub, and allowed the appeal.

The issue in the *Brown's Executors* case differs from the *Barclays Bank* case, but it does illustrate two points. First, the question of excepted asset status is only relevant if the shares are relevant business property. Secondly, in the context of excepted assets and generally, it is important that clear evidence of future trading requirements for apparently 'surplus' cash is available. HMRC guidance states (at SVM111230):

> '**[T]he future use should clearly be in contemplation at the valuation date**. In other words, as regards capital expenditure, there has to be some positive decision or firm intention existing at that time. The mere toying with an idea or some distant thought should circumstances change cannot suffice' (emphasis added).

Thus formal business plans and meeting minutes may be helpful in this context.

12.19 As mentioned (see **12.14**), in the case of land and buildings, the excepted assets rule also contains an apportionment provision (*IHTA 1984, s 112(4)*). This rule applies if part of the asset is used exclusively in the business, where the whole of the land and buildings would otherwise be an excepted asset because it was not used wholly or mainly for business (or would be excluded from relief under a separate provision relating to land and buildings, machinery and plant in *112(3)*). Its effect is that the part used exclusively for business purposes and the rest of the property are treated as separate assets, and the value of the land or building as a whole is apportioned between them.

This apportionment may apply where, for example, a dentist operates a practice from home. The house is mainly the dentist's residence, but rooms on the ground floor are used for a surgery, office and waiting room.

Investment 'business'

12.20 The BPR restriction for surplus cash as an excepted asset can be overcome by applying those funds towards an investment 'business'. However, care is needed to ensure that the company's trade remains the dominant business.

In addition, the question arises as to what constitutes a 'business' for these purposes. In the case of shares and securities, HMRC's Shares Valuation Manual suggests that some caution is required (SVM111220):

> '… much will turn on the size of the holdings, the time spent on their management (including buying and selling) and the reason for their acquisition. You should however, bear in mind the conclusion of the Privy Council in *American Leaf Co v Director General* [1979] AC 676 that "in the case of a company incorporated for the purpose of making profits for its shareholders any gainful use to which it puts any of its assets prima facie amounts to the carrying on of a business." If a company does carry on an investment business ancillary to its trading business, it cannot be said that the investments made have not been used for the purposes of the hybrid (mainly trading, partly investment) business. Thus those investments cannot be regarded as excepted assets.'

12.21 If the asset was used wholly or mainly for the personal benefit of the transferor or a person connected with him (eg a yacht), it is deemed not to have been used wholly or mainly for the purposes of the business concerned (*IHTA 1984, s 112(6)*).

However, what is the practical effect of excluding the excepted asset? HMRC accept that, in some cases (eg minority shareholdings), the exclusion of an asset would make little or no difference to the value transferred (SVM111220). This will particularly be the case if shares are valued on a capitalisation (or 'earnings' basis) as opposed to an 'assets' basis, as the existence of an excepted asset may only have a minor effect on value. However, HMRC guidance states:

> 'Where, however, shares are being valued by reference to the capitalisation value of a company, you should remember that the value of any substantial non-business asset ought to be added to the capitalisation value of the company. The added value of the non-business asset will clearly have to be excluded from relief.'

12.22 The BPR restriction for surplus cash as an excepted asset can also be mitigated by repaying trade and other creditors (eg hire purchase liabilities, long-term loans).

In addition, following *Phillips and others (Executors of Rhoda Phillips, dec'd) v HMRC* [2006] SpC 555 (see **12.6** above), BPR can seemingly be secured by engaging in the business of making loans (eg to related businesses).

Groups of companies

12.23 Without a special rule for holding companies in group situations, their shareholders would be denied BPR under the general rule in *IHTA 1984, s 105(3)*, which excludes shares (and also businesses or business interests) from relief if the company's business is wholly or mainly dealing in securities, stocks or shares, land or buildings or making or holding investments.

The exception for shares or securities in holding companies applies if the company's business is wholly or mainly as a holding company of at least one subsidiary whose business does not fall into any of the excluded categories mentioned above (*IHTA 1984, s 105(4)(b)*).

A group may be considered as an appropriate structure for BPR purposes in certain circumstances, such as to allow a group member to hold the premises of a trading group member (*IHTA 1984, s 111b*), if it is desired to keep the trading company and premises separate (eg for asset protection reasons).

By contrast, where an individual holds shares in an unquoted trading company and personally owns the business premises, the latter attracts BPR (at 50%) only if he has control of the company (*IHTA 1984, s 105(1)(d)*).

12.24 The value of a company's shares or securities is reduced for BPR purposes if it is a holding company and one or more group members is not within the definition of relevant business property.

A company is treated as not being a group member in a valuation context unless it either satisfies the conditions for being wholly or mainly a trading company (subject to exceptions for a market maker or discount house business carried on in the UK (or in an EEA state, with effect from 31 December 2012 (*IHTA 1984, s 105(4), (4A)*; *SI 2012/2903*)) or holding companies, as described above), or unless its business is wholly or mainly of holding land or buildings mainly occupied by group members whose business would not preclude its shares from being relevant business property (*IHTA 1984, s 111*).

Thus on a transfer of shares in the holding company, the value of any 'excluded' subsidiaries would not be taken into account when considering how much of the transfer of value is eligible for BPR.

There is also an exclusion from the excepted asset rules in the case of groups. An asset will not be an excepted asset in a group situation provided that the company using it was a member of the group at the time of use and immediately before the transfer, and that the use is in a company not excluded by virtue of *IHTA 1984, s 111* as outlined above (*IHTA 1984, s 112(2)*).

12.25

Focus

Where a group of companies carries on investment business activities, some care may be required to prevent the restriction or denial of BPR.

Example 12.2 – BPR planning: group investments (1)

Holdco Ltd has three wholly-owned subsidiaries, A Ltd, B Ltd and C Ltd. Each of the subsidiaries is trading. However, Holdco owns a valuable portfolio of investment properties. The value of those properties is such that Holdco is not 'mainly' a holding company within *IHTA 1984, s 105(4)(b)*. Consequently, the shareholders of Holdco would not be entitled to BPR on their shares under the existing structure.

If one of the subsidiaries (say, A Ltd) owned all the investment properties, Holdco may qualify as a holding company. However, for the purposes of calculating BPR on the Holdco shares, the value of A Ltd's shares would be excluded, as though it was not a group member.

By contrast, if the assets were not investments but properties from which A Ltd and the other group members traded, the value of the A Ltd shares could be taken into account for BPR purposes as a qualifying company (*IHTA 1984, s 111(b)*).

12.26 It might be possible to arrange for an alternative allocation of investments between group members, which could result in BPR being available to the Holdco Ltd shareholders.

Example 12.3 – BPR planning: group investments (2)

Following on from **Example 12.2**, the investment properties are divided so that Holdco Ltd, A Ltd, B Ltd and C Ltd each hold their own separate, smaller investment property portfolios, which are carefully structured so that each subsidiary is mainly trading.

Each property portfolio constitutes a business, so there is no BPR restriction in respect of their value. Similarly, Holdco is mainly carrying on the activities of a holding company. The investment property portfolios do not cause BPR to be denied, and there is no 'excepted asset' restriction because the property holdings represent a smaller business on which BPR also falls to be due.

If it is not possible to spread investments between group members in such a way, consideration could be given to extracting the investments from the group, although this may have other tax implications, such as corporation tax for the company in respect of chargeable gains.

12.27 Care is needed. The 'wholly or mainly' test in terms of qualifying activities should ideally be considered before the group asset structure is put in place. The test is particularly important in the case of the holding company, as the availability of BPR for the entire group may depend on it. The test should be measured on any appropriate basis (eg turnover, profitability or asset values), and also 'in the round' to take account of the overall nature of the group.

For further guidance on the potential approach and the categories of measure to consider (albeit in a different context), see **12.8** above and the Special Commissioner's decision in *Farmer and anor (executors of Farmer, dec'd) v IRC* [1999] STC (SCD) 321.

The position should be monitored on an ongoing basis, as trading activities may fluctuate and property values may increase, to the point where the 'wholly or mainly' test ceases to be met.

Intra-group loans

12.28 What is the position if intra-group loans are made by the holding company to one or more subsidiaries? If a loan falls to be treated as part of the holding company's business of being a holding company (within *IHTA 1984, s 105(4)(b)*), BPR status should not be adversely affected. However, it is necessary to consider not only whether the holding company's business consists mainly of being a holding company, but also whether providing loan finance to subsidiaries can properly be treated as forming part of that business.

HMRC confirmed (in a letter to the Chartered Institute of Taxation in January 2011) that, whilst all cases depend on their own facts, the provision of loan and other finance to subsidiaries is an activity which is indicative of the business of a holding company.

Thus, if the subsidiaries are themselves qualifying (ie non-investment) companies, and if the holding company's business as a holding company predominates, BPR would normally be available for the shares in the holding company. Intra-group loans are regarded as non-investment if the subsidiaries use them for the purposes of their non-investment business, and if the amounts are reasonable in the context of the group's business as a whole.

In correspondence with the Institute of Chartered Accountants in England and Wales (ICAEW), HMRC subsequently confirmed that the BPR implications depend on where the funds are held within the group, and the purpose for any loans. A loan made to support non-investment business activity would not of itself be regarded as an investment. However, each case will depend on its own facts. HMRC would look critically at any loans with an apparent non-commercial purpose, but these would still be viewed in the context of the group as a whole.

The correspondence between the above professional bodies and HMRC on intra-group loans can be found in ICAEW Taxguide 5/11 (tinyurl.com/ICAEW-Taxguide5-11), to which reference should be made for detailed guidance on BPR and groups of companies. Subsequent correspondence between Society of Trusts and Estates Practitioners member, Emma Chamberlain, and HMRC in 2015 (which was reconfirmed in 2017) clarified some points in relation to groups and intra-group activities (see www.step.org/sites/default/files/Policy/BPR_Correspondence.pdf).

'Deep' group structures

12.29 In some cases, the group may be deeper than a single holding company with one or more direct subsidiaries. More than one layer of holding company and subsidiary may exist. The legislation provides for the availability of BPR for a group parent company holding shares in a qualifying trading company (*IHTA 1984, s 105(1)(b)*). However, it may be necessary to carefully consider the availability of BPR for group structures involving a second layer of holding company.

It was initially thought that HMRC may be prepared to accept that a group structure with up to six levels of holding company potentially falls within the BPR regime, subject to meeting the general criteria regarding qualifying activities and not having excepted assets (see *Taxation*, 1 October 2008).

However, in subsequent correspondence with the ICAEW, HMRC indicated that there is no limit to the number of intermediate holding companies (provided that Companies Act requirements are met – see, in particular, the definition of 'holding company' in *CA 2006, s 1159*), but that such companies cannot be ignored or looked through. In practice, HMRC will look at the group as a whole to determine whether it is mainly investment or non-investment in nature, before considering each individual company separately within the group structure to determine whether any relief restriction is necessary in accordance with *IHTA 1984, s 111*.

See **12.28** above on the correspondence between professional bodies and HMRC and subsequent guidance regarding BPR issues in connection with group structures and financing, particularly in the context of a complex holding company structure (which is common in large privately owned groups) with a number of different ('intermediate') underlying holding companies, each effectively being its own separate group.

OTHER POINTS

Company liquidations, reorganisations, etc

12.30 When a company is no longer required, the business owners may decide to liquidate or informally wind up the company. The company's shares or securities generally cease to be eligible for BPR when the decision is made to end the company (eg when a winding-up order or resolution has been passed).

However, there is an exception from this general rule if the company's business is to continue after a reconstruction or amalgamation. This exception applies either if the reconstruction or amalgamation is the reason for the winding-up, or if the reconstruction or amalgamation takes place no more than a year after the transfer of value (*IHTA 1984, s 105(5)*).

With regard to company reorganisations, as indicated at **12.10** above for the purposes of the two-year ownership requirement in *IHTA 1984, s 106*, holdings of unquoted shares which would (under the capital gains tax rules in *TCGA 1992, ss 126–136*) be identified with other qualifying shares previously owned may treat their period of ownership as including the ownership period of the original shares (*IHTA 1984, s 107(4)*).

Partnerships

12.31 There is no general requirement for an asset to have been eligible for BPR throughout the period of ownership. However, it must be relevant business property immediately before the chargeable event. For example, a partner's interest in a partnership is property which is relevant business property (*IHTA 1984, s 105(1)(a)*). Upon retirement, the partner's capital account is converted into a debt, and the retiring individual becomes a creditor of the partnership. The debt is not relevant business property (*Beckman v IRC* [2000] STC (SCD) 59).

To preserve entitlement to BPR, the partner may wish to make a gift of the capital before retiring (ie an interest in the business, as opposed to a simple gift of cash; see IHTM25250), or possibly to delay retirement by taking a lesser role on the business in return for a reduced partnership share.

BPR may be available to a business partner under two separate headings:

- an interest in a business (*IHTA 1984, s 105(1)(a)*) – eligible for 100% BPR;
- land, buildings, plant and machinery used by a partnership of which the transferor was a member (*IHTA 1984, s 105(1)(d)*) – eligible for 50% BPR.

In the latter case, consideration could be given to restructuring the partnership agreement in appropriate circumstances, with the asset (eg land and buildings) becoming part of the partnership's assets (see 'Staying alive' by Kevin Slevin, *Taxation*, 21 November 2013).

If the partnership holds the land and buildings (or plant and machinery) and the partner retains an interest in the business until death, HMRC are understood to accept BPR claims on the partner's interest in the land and buildings at the 100% (not 50%) rate, on the basis that the interest is comprised in the notional transfer of his business interest within *IHTA 1984, s 105(1)(a)*. The position is thus distinguishable from the notional transfer on death of land owned outside the partnership, on which only 50% BPR is due within *IHTA 1984, s 105(1)(d)*.

12.32 However, what is the BPR rate on a lifetime transfer of the partner's interest in land and buildings held by the partnership? Unless the transfer is of the partner's interest in the partnership as a whole, it cannot fall within *IHTA 1984, s 105(1)(a)*, so would fall within *IHTA 1984, s 105(1)(d)* instead, giving BPR of 50%. On that basis, in terms of the BPR rate it makes no difference whether the partner's lifetime transfer is of land and buildings held within the partnership or outside it, as the BPR rate in both cases is 50% (IHTM25225).

However, in the case of a retiring partner, it would seem at least arguable that the transfer of an interest in land and buildings held by the partnership as part of the partner's overall withdrawal from the business and the transfer of his qualifying interest to another partner falls within *IHTA 1984, s 105(1)(a)* and is therefore eligible for 100% relief. Unfortunately, there is no indication that this view is accepted in HMRC's guidance on partnerships (at IHTM25250).

Limited liability partnerships

12.33 Limited liability partnerships (LLPs) are not normally treated as owned by the individual partners, in the same way that shareholders own shares in a company. Instead, a business carried on by the LLP is treated as carried on by the partners. The LLP's property is treated as that of the partners. Property occupied or used by the LLP is treated as occupied or used by the partners. The incorporation (ie. formation) of an LLP is treated as the formation of a partnership, and a transfer of value by or to an LLP is treated as made by or to its members (*IHTA 1984, s 267A*).

For BPR (and APR) purposes, there is no change in the treatment of assets held outside, but used in, the partnership. The incorporation of a partnership into an LLP is not treated as interrupting a partner's period of ownership in terms of BPR (see *Tax Bulletin,* Issue 50).

There is a difference between loans to, and interests in, an LLP. Thus, BPR will be available only on the capital, not on any loans, in line with the rule in *Beckman v IRC* (see **12.31**, and also below).

HMRC's view is that LLPs differ from other partnerships, on the basis that an LLP interest is deemed to be an interest in every asset of the partnership, whereas an interest in a 'traditional' partnership is a 'chose in action'. However, when considering if an LLP is an investment business, HMRC will look at the nature of the LLP's business, rather than the nature of the LLP's assets.

For example, HMRC guidance indicates that, in the case of an LLP investing in unquoted shares in a trading company, BPR is not available on an interest in the LLP. This appears to be on the basis that the LLP's business is investment in nature if its activities consist wholly or mainly of holding shares in the company, notwithstanding that the underlying assets constitute business property (IHTM25094).

HMRC subsequently affirmed the view set out in IHTM25094, stating that, if an LLP simply takes the place of a holding company, the effect of *IHTA 1984, s 267A* is that BPR (within *IHTA 1984, s 105(4)(b)*) is prevented from applying in respect of its holding of shares in the unquoted trading company (*ICAEW Taxguide 1/14*).

However, HMRC also state:

> 'in cases where the LLP also carries on a qualifying business, the business may be regarded as a hybrid, and if the shares in the subsidiary companies are used in the business (rather than being held as investments), then it is possible that the interest in the LLP may qualify for BPR if it does not fail the "wholly or mainly" test (IHTM25264). The question of whether an asset is used in the business or held as an investment will be highly fact specific.'

This view by HMRC is reflected in their responses to two hypothetical scenarios (ie examples 2 and 5) in the above ICAEW guidance, which indicate that BPR may be available in respect of interests in LLPs in certain specific circumstances.

It should be noted that HMRC's view is not universally accepted. For example, in 'A merry dance' (*Taxation,* 20 March 2014), James Kessler QC and Oliver Marre consider that HMRC's view is incorrect, on the basis that it is necessary to consider the relevant statutory provision for BPR (*IHTA 1984, s 104(1)*), and ask whether the value transferred by a transfer of value is attributable to the value of any relevant business property.

Where BPR is available (under HMRC's approach) on the basis that the LLP is itself trading, it may be necessary to consider whether the shares in subsidiaries are excepted assets within *IHTA 1984, s 112*.

Retirement of a partner

12.34 The timing of lifetime transfers of land or buildings, plant or machinery used by the partnership is important in terms of qualifying for any BPR at all. As noted above in relation to partnership interests, the asset must have been wholly or mainly used for business purposes immediately before the transfer, by a partnership of which the transferor was then a partner. A transfer after retirement therefore attracts no BPR.

This point was illustrated in *Beckman v IRC* [2000] STC (SCD) 59. The deceased (H) and her daughter (B) had been business partners until H's retirement. H's financial interest in the business immediately before her retirement, represented by her capital account, remained the same after her retirement.

However, the Special Commissioner held that her legal interest was radically changed on her retirement. Previously, she had all the rights of management conferred by the *Partnership Act 1890* and all the liabilities of a partner. Following retirement, in the absence of any agreement to the contrary, she became simply a creditor of B. Accordingly, on H's death four years later, business property relief on the sum due to her was denied. For the purposes of *IHTA 1984, s 105*, H's interest in the business ceased when she retired from the partnership that carried on that business.

In terms of BPR planning, as indicated at **12.31**, partners wishing to avoid a similar outcome could consider making a gift of the capital prior to retiring, or alternatively remaining a partner with a reduced profit share.

Contracts for sale

12.35 BPR is not normally available where the subject matter of the transfer is itself already subject to a binding contract for sale at the time of the transfer (*IHTA 1984, s 113*).

This may result in a loss of relief, in that the owner of the property can no longer claim the relief on a transfer made after a 'buy and sell' agreement has been entered into. However, arrangements between partners and shareholders can often be structured in such a way that BPR is not jeopardised.

Focus

It is important to recognise the types of agreement that constitute a 'binding contract for sale'. HMRC identify three key elements (see IHTM25292) (emphasis added):

- an *agreement* for the deceased partner's business interest or shareholder's shares to pass to his personal representatives;
- a *requirement* for the personal representatives to sell to the surviving partners or shareholders; and
- an *obligation* for the surviving partners or shareholders to buy the asset under the terms of the agreement (funds for the purchase often being provided by life assurance policies).

HMRC's stated view is that such terms (referred to as 'buy and sell' agreements) prevent BPR from being due on the business interest or shares (Statement of Practice 12/80).

However, BPR is not prevented by *IHTA 1984, s 113* from applying to company shares or securities, if the company's articles of association require the personal representatives to offer his shares for sale to the company, or to other shareholders or directors. However, there should be no obligation to buy; nor should there be a mutually binding obligation to buy and sell (SVM111120).

12.36 The types of agreement which are not 'caught' by *IHTA 1984, s 113* include:

- *'Accruer'* clauses – the deceased's interests pass ('accrue') to the surviving partners, who are required to pay the personal representatives a particular price (eg based on a valuation or formula). The agreement in these circumstances will generally be at arm's length.
- *Options* – the deceased's interest falls into the estate, but with an option for the surviving partners to purchase it. Agreements sometimes provide for a two-way (or 'cross') option. There is (in principle, at least) an argument that cross-options are not materially different in substance to a binding contract for sale. This argument seems unlikely in the case of genuine options, but in any event such concerns could be set aside by using a single option (ie put or call), or by providing for successive put and call options with their own separate and distinct exercise periods.

12.37 HMRC are alert to planning involving lifetime transfers of unquoted shares, shortly followed by a sale of the company (IHTM25291). They are likely to investigate such transfers (in the context of a possible binding contract for sale within *IHTA 1984, s 113*) if, for example, the company is sold within six months of the transfer, or possibly longer if the circumstances suggest that a sale was in prospect when the lifetime transfer was made (SVM111120).

However, it should be noted that BPR is not denied by *IHTA 1984, s 113* if the reason for the binding contract is the incorporation of a sole trader or partnership in which the sale proceeds are wholly or mainly shares or securities in the company, or in the case of company shares or securities if the purpose of the sale is a reconstruction or amalgamation (*IHTA 1984, s 113(a), (b)*).

Lifetime gifts and BPR

12.38 An important point to consider for IHT planning purposes is whether to make gifts during lifetime, or to leave assets in the estate until death. In the case of assets eligible for 100% BPR, there are potential benefits to delaying gifts until death. These include a possible CGT-free uplift in value on death, no concerns about the possible clawback of BPR on lifetime gifts, and the retention of control over the asset in question.

On the other hand, there is the constant danger that BPR rates may be reduced, or that the relief may be abolished altogether. These concerns may make transferring business property into a relevant property trust to 'bank' BPR seem an attractive proposition, with the donor retaining a degree of control over the asset as a trustee.

However, this type of planning needs to be considered 'in the round', taking account of factors including the loss of CGT-free uplift on death.

Avoiding a clawback of BPR

12.39 IHT charges can arise on a transferor's death if, for example, the transferee has disposed of the business property without replacement, or if the asset is no longer relevant business property. A gift of business property from one individual to another generally constitutes a potentially exempt transfer, in which case BPR is not an immediate issue. However, the availability of BPR will need to be considered in the event of the transferor's death within seven years.

Alternatively, if a chargeable lifetime transfer (eg a gift to a discretionary trust) was reduced by BPR and the transferor dies within seven years, the additional IHT on death is calculated as if the transfer had not been reduced by BPR unless certain conditions are satisfied, as outlined below (*IHTA 1984, s 113A(1), (2)*).

12.40 The BPR clawback provisions do not apply if the following conditions are satisfied (*IHTA 1984, s 113A(3), (4)*):

- the transferee continued to own the business property until the donor's death (or until the transferee's death, if earlier); and
- the original property is still relevant business property at that time (but see below). The two-year ownership test does not apply for the purposes of this rule.

The first condition above is relaxed if the transferee has replaced the original asset with other business property. BPR may still be available, subject to further conditions (*IHTA 1984, s 113B*; see below).

The second condition above does not have to be satisfied for lifetime transfers of shares or securities which were quoted at the time of the transfer, or of unquoted shares which remained as such until the transferor's death, or of unquoted securities which, either by themselves or together with other such securities owned by the transferor and any unquoted shares so owned, gave the transferor control (*IHTA 1984, s 113A(3A)*).

12.41 A potential trap exists in the meaning of transferee. A 'transferee' is defined as the person who became the owner of the property on the transfer, or where on the transfer the property became (or remained) settled on discretionary trusts, the trustees of the settlement (*IHTA 1984, s 113A(8)*).

For example, if the original transfer was to the trustees of a discretionary trust, the first condition above will not be satisfied if, before the transferor's death, a beneficiary becomes absolutely entitled to the trust property (eg following an appointment by the trustees, or the termination of the trust). HMRC guidance warns that the meaning of transferee is precise in this context (IHTM25367).

12.42 If the BPR clawback rules apply to an immediately chargeable lifetime transfer, only the additional IHT on that transfer is affected by the loss of BPR. The additional tax on the transferor's death is calculated on the basis of no BPR (ie the additional tax payable on death is the difference between the IHT at death rates (after taper relief, if appropriate) on the value excluding BPR and the tax paid at lifetime rates on the reduced value). However, for the purposes of cumulating the lifetime transfer with subsequent transfers within the seven-year period before death (including the death estate), the value transferred by the transfer remains as reduced by BPR.

Therefore, it can be advantageous to make chargeable lifetime transfers of business property subject to 100% BPR, compared with making potentially exempt transfers which become chargeable on death (ie where the transfer must be aggregated in full) (*IHTA 1984, s 113A(1), (2)*).

For example, if an individual dies within seven years of settling shares worth up to his available nil rate band on a discretionary trust (on which 100% BPR was claimed), the effect of a clawback of BPR is that the chargeable transfer is of an amount that falls within the individual's nil rate band. The individual's cumulative total is unchanged. Thus the clawback of BPR in this case does not result in an IHT liability.

It should be noted that if the BPR clawback provisions only apply to a part of the gifted property, BPR may still apply to the balance (*IHTA 1984, s 113A(5)*).

For example, if the original transfer was a potentially exempt transfer (PET) of 1,000 unquoted shares worth £100,000, and the transferee sells 500 shares for £25,000, BPR of £50,000 remains available on the other half of the shares.

Replacement property

12.43 As indicated above, the condition that the transferee must generally own the original property at the transferor's death is relaxed in the case of replacement property.

The 'replacement property' rules apply if the transferee has sold all or part of the original property before the transferor's death and invested the whole of the proceeds in the purchase of other qualifying property. The conditions are broadly as follows (*IHTA 1984, s 113B(1), (2)*):

- the whole of the consideration must be reinvested in the replacement property (HMRC consider 'whole of the consideration' to mean the proceeds net of any professional costs and CGT; see IHTM25369);
- the replacement property must be acquired (or a binding contract for its acquisition entered into) within the 'allowed period' of three years (or such longer period as HMRC may allow) after the disposal of the original property; and
- the disposal and acquisition must both be made in transactions at arm's length, or on arm's length terms (eg exchanges of business property).

12.44 If the above conditions are met, the basic conditions for BPR on lifetime gifts within seven years of the transferor's death in *IHTA 1984, s 113A(3)* (see above) are taken to be satisfied in relation to the original property, provided that the following conditions are also met in relation to the replacement property (*IHTA 1984, s 113B(3), (4)*):

- the replacement property is owned by the transferee immediately before the transferor's death (or until the transferee's death, if earlier);

- throughout the period from the date of the chargeable transfer until death (disregarding any period between the disposal and acquisition) either the original property or the replacement property was owned by the transferee; and
- the replacement property is relevant business property immediately before the death (or would be, apart from the minimum period of ownership requirement in *IHTA 1984, s 106*).

It should be noted that if the transferor has died (before the transferee) after disposal of all or part of the original property by the transferee, but before the replacement property is acquired, BPR remains available if the replacement property is acquired (or a binding contract for its acquisition entered into) within the 'allowed period' mentioned in **12.43** (see *IHTA 1984, s 113B(5)*).

12.45 A special rule applies where shares owned by the transferee immediately before the transferor's death (or before the transferee's earlier death) represent the original property received from the transferor. This rule may apply if, for example, the transferee holds shares following a company reorganisation (within *TCGA 1992, ss 126–136*), or if the shares were issued to the transferee in consideration of the transfer of business property consisting of the original property. The effect is that the shares are treated for replacement property purposes as the original property (*IHTA 1984, ss 113A(6), 113B(6)*).

Interestingly, where the replacement property treatment in *IHTA 1984, s 113A(6)* is claimed, HMRC guidance indicates that the claim will be referred to their Technical Group for adjudication (IHTM25370).

The order of gifts

12.46 The making of lifetime gifts of business assets should be considered carefully, as the availability of BPR may depend upon the order of such gifts.

For example, BPR (at the 50% rate) applies to land and buildings, machinery or plant used wholly or mainly in a business carried on by a company of which the transferor then had control (*IHTA 1984, s 105(1)(d)*).

The controlling shareholder of an unquoted trading company who owns its business premises may wish to make gifts of the shares and the premises at different times. It is important that he retains the controlling interest in the company when the property is given away. Otherwise, BPR at 50% may be lost on the subsequent gift of the premises. See **12.3** above on the meaning of 'control' in this context.

A loss of BPR in the above circumstances is not necessarily fatal for IHT purposes if the gifts are to another individual, as the gifts (including the property) are potentially exempt transfers which become exempt after seven years. It may be possible, and desirable, to insure against the risk of the donor's death within that time. However, if the gift is chargeable when made (ie as for most lifetime transfers into trust), the non-availability of BPR could result in an immediate, and perhaps unnecessary, IHT charge.

DEATH AND BPR

Maximising BPR

12.47 Planning involves not only taking advantage of possible tax savings, but also avoiding potential pitfalls which could, for example, result in the loss of an available relief or allowance.

For example, BPR is generally wasted if qualifying assets are left to the spouse or civil partner, because such legacies are normally exempt in any event. There is also a danger that BPR may not be available on the spouse's later death (eg due to a change in law).

Assets that may qualify for 100% BPR could therefore possibly be given to a future generation (eg the grandchildren), or to appropriate trusts. However, consideration should be given to whether the surviving spouse requires the business assets (eg shares in the family trading company, which could provide income through future dividends).

Avoiding the loss of BPR

12.48

> **Focus**
>
> If an estate includes assets eligible for BPR and other assets, and the deceased's will provides for both chargeable beneficiaries (eg adult children) and an exempt beneficiary (eg a UK-domiciled spouse, civil partner or a charity), it is important to ensure that specific business property (eg unquoted trading company shares) is left to chargeable beneficiaries, if possible.
>
> If an estate includes property attracting BPR (or APR), special provisions apply for the purposes of valuing specific and residuary gifts where part of the estate is exempt. The provisions can result in an apportionment of relief between the chargeable beneficiaries and exempt surviving spouse or civil partner (*IHTA 1984, s 39A*).

If any residuary gifts (after 17 March 1986) include business (or agricultural) assets, any specific gifts of non-business assets (eg cash gifts) will be entitled to a due proportion of BPR. The value of such specific gifts is the 'appropriate proportion' of their value (*IHTA 1984, s 39A(3), (4)*).

This apportionment of BPR can have unfortunate consequences.

Example 12.4 – BPR and a partly exempt estate

Scott died on 10 May 2017. His estate of £1,625,000 consists of shares in an unquoted trading company worth £800,000, and other assets (ie cash, shares and an investment property) worth £825,000. Scott's nil rate band (£325,000 for 2017/18) is available in full on his death.

Scott's will leaves cash and specific other (non-business) assets amounting to £500,000 to his spouse. The residue of Scott's estate, including the trading company shares (eligible for 100% BPR) is left to his adult children, together with the remaining other non-business assets worth £325,000.

The value of Scott's estate (net of BPR) is £825,000. As he left £500,000 to his spouse, his personal representatives assume (incorrectly) that the remaining £325,000 will be covered by Scott's nil rate band, and that no IHT will be payable. However, the result of applying the 'appropriate proportion' (see above) to the spouse's exempt legacy is:

$$\pounds 500{,}000 \times \frac{\pounds 825{,}000}{\pounds 1{,}625{,}000} = \pounds 253{,}846$$

The residue (ie the chargeable free estate) is (£825,000 – £253,846) = £571,154. The decrease in the amount subject to the spouse exemption has resulted in a significant (and unexpected) IHT liability.

12.49 As the above example illustrates, if an exempt legacy receives a proportion of BPR, the relief is effectively wasted because the legacy is subject to IHT exemption (ie the spouse exemption) in any event. On the death of an individual with business (or agricultural) property, a will which provides for a 'nil rate band' legacy in non-specific terms (eg words such as 'the maximum amount of funds without incurring a liability to IHT on my death') will probably not have the intended effect. However, if the business property is given by a chargeable, specific gift, its value is reduced by BPR (*IHTA 1984, s 39A(2)*).

BPR (or APR) can be optimised by ensuring that specific gifts of business (and agricultural) assets which attract 100% relief are made to chargeable parties in addition to the nil rate band, if appropriate. If the deceased's will does not provide for such specific legacies, it may be possible to vary the dispositions in the will using a deed of variation within two years of the deceased's death, and including a statement in the deed that it is to apply for IHT purposes (*IHTA 1984, s 142;* see **Chapter 14**).

12.50 The rates of BPR available may be 100%, 50%, or some other effective rate due to the operation of the excepted assets rule in *IHTA 1984, s 112*. A married (or civil partner) testator with business (or agricultural) property may therefore wish to consider a chargeable legacy comprising all business property qualifying for 100% relief, plus property qualifying for less than 100% relief (see below). The remainder may be left to the surviving spouse or civil partner absolutely, or possibly as an 'immediate post-death interest' (*IHTA 1984, s 49A*).

If the nil rate band legacy comprises (say) business property qualifying for 50% BPR, the maximum specific legacy to a chargeable party without giving rise to an IHT liability is equal to twice the available nil rate band.

Example 12.5 – BPR at the 50% rate

Mr A dies on 10 July 2017, owning a controlling interest in quoted trading company shares, and had made no gifts in the preceding seven years. The maximum 'nil rate band' legacy is £650,000, calculated as follows:

	£
Shares	650,000
Less: BPR (50%)	(325,000)
	325,000
Less: nil rate band (2017/18)	(325,000)
Chargeable	Nil

12.51 An alternative form of chargeable legacy has traditionally been to a discretionary trust. BPR is available to the trustees of such a settlement (*IHTA 1984, s 103(1)(b)*). In addition, following *FA 2006*, lifetime gifts to the trustees of most types of settlement are immediately chargeable transfers for IHT purposes (*IHTA 1984, s 3A(1), (2)*), and therefore the availability of BPR in connection with trusts has assumed added importance generally.

A trust to which the rules for 'relevant property' (as defined in *IHTA 1984, s 58*) apply, which consists entirely of business property eligible for BPR at the 100% rate, can avoid ten-yearly or exit IHT charges. BPR does not necessarily reduce the IHT rate for trusts, but it can apply to reduce the value transferred to nil.

'Doubling up' BPR

12.52 BPR can effectively be obtained twice on the same property in certain circumstances.

For example, the first spouse (or civil partner) to die leaves business property on discretionary trusts in favour of the survivor and issue. BPR (and a CGT-free uplift of the business property's base cost to market value) is obtained on the first death. The surviving spouse subsequently purchases the business property from the trustees at arm's length (under an option granted on the first death). Subject to surviving the required two-year period, BPR may be secured on that property for a second time, whether on death or on a lifetime transfer.

Example 12.6 – Two bites of the cherry

Mr Smith died on 31 August 2017, having made no lifetime gifts and owning the following assets:

	£
Family home	600,000
Shares in the family trading company	1,000,000
Investment properties	450,000
Building society and bank deposits	1,225,000
Portfolio of quoted shares	550,000
	3,825,000

In his will, Mr Smith leaves the family company shares to a discretionary trust in favour of Mrs Smith, his adult children, and grandchildren. He also leaves cash from his bank and building society accounts to the trust, up to the nil rate band (£325,000 for 2017/18), which is available in full. The residue of his estate is left to Mrs Smith absolutely, which is made up as follows:

	£
Family home	600,000
Investment properties	450,000
Building society and bank deposits (£1,225,000 – £325,000)	900,000
Portfolio of quoted shares	550,000
	2,500,000

The legacy into the discretionary trust amounts to £1,325,000. This comprises the family trading company shares worth £1,000,000, on which BPR of 100% is available, plus cash of £325,000, which utilises Mr Smith's nil rate band. Hence no IHT is payable on Mr Smith's death.

Mrs Smith buys the family company shares from the trustees for £1,000,000, which equates to market value in this example. The purchase is financed partly in cash of £300,000. The balance is financed by selling the investment properties for £450,000, plus part of the portfolio of quoted shares for £250,000 (no CGT liabilities arise on the properties or shares, the values of which were uplifted to market value on Mr Smith's death).

If Mrs Smith survives for at least two years following the share acquisition, and assuming that BPR at 100% is then available in respect of her family company shares, only her remaining estate would be liable to IHT, comprising (based on current values):

- the family home (£600,000);
- building society and cash deposits (£600,000); and
- the portfolio of quoted shares (£300,000).

After deducting the available nil rate band, the IHT liability on her death estate is significantly reduced (the residence nil rate band is ignored in this example). In addition, she may have benefited from the income generated by the funds held by the discretionary trust in her capacity as a beneficiary.

Protecting against future BPR changes

12.53 Given the undoubted generosity of BPR (particularly at the 100% rate), it is open to speculation how long the BPR rates will remain at their present levels. It may therefore be considered prudent to 'bank' the relief to protect against future changes in BPR.

This could be achieved by making a lifetime transfer of the business property to (say) a discretionary trust (or, following *FA 2006*, to most other types of trust).

Prior to anti-avoidance legislation introduced in *Finance (No 2) Act 2015* (see **12.54**), if the value of business property exceeded the nil rate band, the use of a number of trusts was a potentially attractive strategy.

Example 12.7 – Multiple trusts (I)

Mrs Jones had business property worth £975,000. She created three 'pilot' discretionary trusts early in 2014/15 with nominal amounts at staggered intervals, and subsequently added (on 30 November 2014) business property so that each settlement was worth £325,000. There was no IHT liability on the transfers into the trusts, as BPR applied at the 100% rate.

Following the transfers, each trust should be protected by a nil rate band, even if the BPR rates are changed in the future, and even if the assets cease to be relevant business property.

12.54 Even before the anti-avoidance rules (outlined below) were introduced, this strategy carried potential risks. First, the arrangements could be challenged on the grounds of artificiality. Second, HMRC could seek to invoke the 'associated operations' rule (*IHTA 1984, s 268*), although this risk was lessened somewhat following the decision in *Rysaffe Trustees (CI) Ltd v IRC* [2003] STC 536.

These risks were arguably reduced by ensuring that each trust was properly and separately administered. It may also have been preferred if there were genuine differences between the trusts (eg different trustees and beneficiaries), that the trusts were created as far apart as practicable in terms of time periods, and that they were not pre-ordained.

The implications for other tax purposes (eg capital gains tax – see below) must be considered as well.

Anti-avoidance legislation (*IHTA 1984, ss 62A–62C*) was introduced in *Finance (No 2) Act 2015* with effect from 18 November 2015 to counter the use of multiple pilot trusts, through a 'same day addition' rule. The legislation broadly provides that where a transfer of value is made to one settlement ('Settlement A') and on the same day the same settlor adds value to one or more other settlements ('Settlement B'), in calculating the rate of tax for the purposes of relevant property trust IHT charges in Settlement A (eg ten yearly and exit charges) the added value in Settlement B and (if Settlements A and B are not 'related settlements') the original value of Settlement B is taken into account under these provisions.

A 'same-day addition' (as defined in *IHTA 1984, s 62A*) can include a transfer of value on the creation of a settlement, but not if Settlement A and Settlement B are 'related settlements' (ie settlements created by the same settlor on the same day (*IHTA 1984, s 62A(4)*)).

Example 12.8 – Multiple trusts: same day additions (II)

The facts are in **Example 12.7**, except that Mrs Jones added the business property to the three pilot trusts after the anti-avoidance legislation in *IHTA 1984, s 62A* was introduced.

In calculating (for example) the rate of IHT on a distribution from one of the trusts before its first ten-year anniversary (under *IHTA 1984, s 68*), the value of the 'same-day additions' must be taken into account.

The trusts are not related settlements in this instance (ie they were created on different days), so the value of the relevant property in those settlements immediately after they were created is also taken into account in the *IHTA 1984, s 68* calculation (*IHTA 1984, s 68(5)(e)–(f)*).

The above anti-avoidance legislation is aimed at same day additions to other relevant property trusts (*IHTA 1984, s 62A*), subject to certain limited exceptions (see *IHTA 1984, s 62B*), such as a *de minimis* provision for lifetime transfers to exclude small same-day additions, and for transfers of value to charitable trusts.

Furthermore, the same day addition provisions do not apply if either or each of Settlement A and Settlement B is a protected settlement (*IHTA 1984, ss 62B(1)(c), 62C*). A settlement is a 'protected settlement' if it commenced before 10 December 2014 and either of two conditions (A or B) is satisfied.

Condition A is broadly that the settlor has not added value to the settlement since 10 December 2014. Thus, in **Example 12.7**, the settlements created by Mrs Jones will not be affected by the above anti-avoidance provisions, provided she makes no further transfers resulting in the value of the settled property being increased.

Condition B is that the settlor makes a transfer on or after 10 December 2014 resulting in the value of the property being increased, where the transfer arises (under *IHTA 1984, s 4*) on the settlor's death before 6 April 2017 by reason of a 'protected testamentary disposition' (ie under the settlor's will, where its provisions are substantially the same as they were immediately before 10 December 2014).

It should be noted that it remains possible for the settlor to create a new settlement every seven years, each with its own nil rate band (assuming that no other chargeable transfers or potentially exempt transfers have been made in the intervening periods). Consideration could also be given to adding business property to existing pilot settlements on different days. The additions would fall to be aggregated with earlier transfers, but the aggregation is of the values transferred by any chargeable transfers made by the settlor (*IHTA 1984, s 67(3)*), and BPR operates to reduce the value transferred by a transfer of value (*IHTA 1984, s 104*).

BPR and CGT

12.55 A disadvantage of making lifetime gifts of assets eligible for 100% BPR is often the CGT position. Whilst hold-over relief may be available in many cases under *TCGA 1992, s 165* (eg on a gift of unquoted trading company shares to a UK-resident individual), a tax-free uplift to market value on the death of the owner will often be preferable.

One possible solution in appropriate cases would be to gift the business asset to an elderly relative (eg a grandparent). The gift to the elderly relative would be free of IHT, and a CGT hold-over relief claim may be considered. On the elderly relative's death, 100% BPR should be available (the normal minimum period of ownership being relaxed because the conditions in *IHTA 1984, s 109* are satisfied). The property may then pass under the relative's will to the intended beneficiaries with the benefit of the CGT uplift to market value.

Example 12.9 – BPR and CGT uplift on death

Donald is a shareholder of Titanic Ltd, an unquoted trading company. The shares currently qualify for 100% BPR. He wishes to gift the shares to his son Michael during 2017/18. The shares are worth £1.4m, and there is an inherent capital gain on them, on which the potential CGT liability is approximately £250,000. Entrepreneurs' relief is not available.

Donald gives the shares (ie his desired gift to Michael) to his father Edward, who is in his late eighties. The gift is a PET, which would otherwise be subject to full BPR. The chargeable gain is held over under *TCGA 1992, s 165*. Donald hopes that Edward will leave the shares to his grandson Michael in his will (note there must be no prior agreement or arrangement).

On Edward's death, there is no IHT as 100% BPR is available. However, there is a CGT free uplift in the base cost of the shares to market value as at Edward's death. A CGT saving of £250,000 has therefore been achieved.

If Edward's will did not leave the shares to Michael, a deed of variation could achieve the same result, subject to the co-operation of the beneficiary under the will.

BPR, debt and charging business property

12.56 The value of relevant business property for BPR purposes is its net value (*IHTA 1984, s 110(a)*). 'Net value' is broadly the value of business assets, less any liabilities incurred for the purposes of the business (*IHTA 1984, s 110(b)*). For example, a sole trader's fixed and current business assets (eg plant and machinery and stock) are reduced by business liabilities (eg a bank overdraft) in determining the net value of the business.

However, the business property itself may be acquired with a mortgage or other loan. In such cases, the general rule for a debt (or 'incumbrance') charged on property is that it reduces the value of that property as far as possible (*IHTA 1984, s 162(4)*). This treatment applies to the extent that the liability is not already taken into account under *IHTA 1984, s 162B*, which is an anti-avoidance provision introduced in *FA 2013*. It broadly provides that if a liability was incurred (directly or indirectly) to acquire, maintain or enhance assets on which BPR (or agricultural property relief, or woodlands relief) is due, the liability reduces the value of those assets. BPR then applies to the resulting net value. However, if any excess liability remains, it may be allowable as a deduction against the estate in general, subject to another anti-avoidance rule (in *IHTA 1984, s 175A*) regarding unpaid liabilities after death.

For example, a sole trader may have had a loan secured on his house, the funds from which were applied in financing the business. Prior to the introduction of *IHTA 1984, s 162B*, as the borrowings were charged on the house, *IHTA 1984, s 162(4)* provided that the 'incumbrance' on the house should be taken to reduce its value for IHT purposes. However, for mortgages and loans incurred on or after 6 April 2013, such borrowings would be deducted from the value of the business, before BPR is applied (*IHTA 1984, s 162B(2)*).

If a liability financed a mixture of business property and investment asset, and the liability has been partially repaid before an IHT charge arises, supplementary provisions set out the order in which the liability is treated as having been discharged (see *IHTA 1984, s 162C*).

As stated earlier in this chapter, 'business' has a wider meaning than 'trade' and can include the making or holding of investments. However, in determining whether a business interest or company shares are relevant business property, the investment 'business' must generally not predominate (*IHTA 1984, s 105(3)*).

12.57

> **Focus**
>
> Investors can no longer use BPR and the mortgage or charging provisions to their advantage as before, such as by borrowing on non-business assets (eg the home) and investing the proceeds in assets giving entitlement to BPR (eg AIM listed shares in trading companies), or possibly subscribing for shares in an unquoted family trading company. The borrowing must first be applied to the business property as opposed to the home, resulting in a loss of BPR. This treatment applies to liabilities incurred on or after 6 April 2013 (*FA 2013, Sch 36, para 5(2), (3)*).
>
> In any event, the commercial risk generally inherent in such investments must be measured against any potential IHT benefit.

BPR and gifts with reservation

12.58 A lifetime transfer of business property may be treated as remaining comprised in the donor's estate, if the 'gifts with reservation' (GWR) rules apply (in *FA 1986, s 102* and *Sch 20*). An asset subject to the GWR rules can qualify for BPR, broadly if the following conditions are satisfied:

- the asset was relevant business property at the time of the gift; and
- the asset would qualify for BPR at the time of the GWR charge (ie on the donor's death or earlier release of the reservation) if the donee made a notional transfer of it.

For the purposes of the two-year ownership test, any period of ownership by the donor before the gift is treated as that of the donee (*FA 1986, Sch 20, para 8(2)*). If the donee dies before the GWR charge, the period of ownership of the personal representatives or beneficiaries is also treated as that of the donee (*FA 1986, Sch 20, para 8(5)*).

A GWR is not generally a problem for IHT purposes if BPR at 100% is available and maintained, but there are specific circumstances where reservation can be fatal. For example, where BPR is at 50% on an asset used by a company controlled by the transferor, and the asset passes to a minority shareholder such that clawback is in point, the donee cannot satisfy the requirements of the relief (*FA 1986, Sch 20, para 8(1A)(b)*). Such a lifetime disposal can also be disadvantageous for CGT purposes, as it sacrifices the market value uplift on death.

If BPR is claimed on the basis that the original property has been sold and the proceeds used to buy other property which would (on a notional transfer of value by the donee immediately before the donor's death, apart from the ownership tests) qualify for BPR, HMRC guidance indicates that the replacement property provisions are 'complicated' and cases will be referred to their Technical Group (IHTM25384).

BPR and APR

12.59 Agricultural property relief (APR) is considered in the second part of this chapter (see **12.62** *et seq*). APR also applies automatically, and for the purposes of this chapter it should be noted that if the same property qualifies for both BPR and APR in respect of a transfer, APR takes precedence (*IHTA 1984, s 114(1)*).

However, the agricultural value may be lower than its value for BPR purposes (eg farmland with planning permission or development value), in which case if both reliefs are in point it may be possible to claim APR on the agricultural value, and BPR on the excess.

BPR clearances

12.60 It can often be difficult to know whether property qualifies for BPR. However, HMRC provide a BPR clearance procedure. It was initially described in HMRC Brief 25/08, and is a non-statutory clearance as to the application of the tax law to a specific transaction or event.

HMRC's BPR clearance service was originally introduced for a six-month trial period only (1 May 2008 to 31 October 2008), but was subsequently extended (in January 2009) to apply indefinitely.

HMRC will give a view of the tax consequences of a transaction or event in the following circumstances (www.gov.uk/guidance/non-statutory-clearance-service-guidance):

- the relevant HMRC guidance has been fully considered, and/or the relevant helpline has been contacted; and
- the information needed could not be found; or
- there is remaining uncertainty about HMRC's interpretation of recent tax legislation.

Conversely, HMRC will not provide guidance or advice in some cases. On 13 June 2017, HMRC updated their general online guidance and also their BPR checklist (Annex C). The section 'When HMRC will not provide advice under this service' was amended to state that HMRC will confirm the reason why the advice requested has not been provided, if appropriate; listed examples include:

- Where all necessary information has not been provided.
- HMRC do not consider there are genuine points of uncertainty.
- The advice requested amounts to tax planning advice or approval of tax planning products or arrangements.
- The application is about the treatment of transactions that HMRC consider are for the purpose of avoiding tax.
- HMRC are already checking the tax position for the period in question.
- Any related return for the period in question has become final (except for clearance applications in connection with an offshore disclosure facility being made via HMRC's digital disclosure service).
- There is a statutory clearance procedure applicable to the transaction.
- The advice sought relates to the application of the settlements legislation (in *ITTOIA 2005, Pt 5, Ch 5*) or the tax consequences of executing non-charitable trust deeds or settlements.

Annex C (BPR checklist) was updated to make clear that it may not be used for gifts to individuals, ten-year anniversary charges, conditional dispositions of property under a will, deeds of variation, the tax consequences of executing a trust deed, the application of *ITTOIA 2005, Pt 5, Ch 5*, valuations, or general confirmations of the status of businesses for BPR purposes.

The clearance facility is available if the transfer involves an immediately chargeable transfer. This means that (for example) a share transfer to a discretionary trust is possibly eligible for a clearance application as to the availability of BPR in respect of the shares, but (as indicated above) a potentially exempt transfer, such as a gift from one individual to another, is not.

The clearance facility is potentially helpful. However, for BPR applications involving a change of ownership of a business (succession), any clearance given will only remain valid for six months.

A checklist and guidance on HMRC's BPR clearance service (Annex C) is available via the GOV.UK website (tinyurl.com/HMRC-BPR-Clearance-App).

Testing for BPR

12.61 In cases where the BPR clearance service is not appropriate, it may be possible to 'test' the availability of BPR. There is a specific problem where a will has created, or has been varied so as to create, a nil rate band discretionary trust and the executors wish to put into it property that qualifies for relief.

Consider the following, which has previously been suggested by Emma Chamberlain and Chris Whitehouse as a possible solution to the problem:

- set up the discretionary will trust;
- transfer from the estate of the deceased to the will trust substantial value in the form of specific 'target' property which (it is hoped) qualifies for BPR, but without making the transfer dependent on its availability; and
- transfer to the will trust such cash sum as would not attract a tax charge (eg the available nil rate band, ignoring the target property).

The thinking is that the transfer to such a trust will prompt HMRC to adjudicate the BPR issue, since unless the trustees within two years of death appoint property to an exempt beneficiary such as the spouse there has been a chargeable transfer. If BPR is allowed, fine: the trust can roll forward or can be the vehicle for further IHT saving, such as where the spouse buys the business property so as to recycle the relief.

If relief is denied, provided the decision is reached quickly enough, the trustees have the option of appointing the 'failed' assets to the spouse within two years under *IHTA 1984, s 144* to avoid paying the tax.

AGRICULTURAL PROPERTY RELIEF

AGRICULTURAL ASSETS: PROPERTY

12.62 Agricultural property relief (APR) is, as the name implies, a relief not an exemption. The distinction is important. APR operates by reducing the value transferred by a reduction set at 100% or 50% dependent on determinative tests. The code is set out in *IHTA 1984, ss 115–124C* and is very similar to that for business property relief (BPR), but there are important differences of detail.

HMRC have published their guidance on the entire APR section of the Inheritance Tax Manual and reading is strongly recommended – it is generally well expressed and carefully written (see IHTM24000 et seq).

The HMRC website also contains a short but readable 'Customer Guide' to APR (see www.hmrc.gov.uk/cto/customerguide/page17.htm), which contains useful and helpful information aimed at both the professional adviser and the client. Accordingly, as clients become better informed and seek, naturally, to keep the cost of advice to a minimum, it is not unreasonable for them to expect practitioners to know at least as much as, but preferably much more than, is available in that HMRC Customer Guide.

APR is available on 'agricultural property' (ie primarily agricultural land or pasture used for agricultural purpose), but it is also extended to include:

- woodland and buildings used for the intensive rearing of livestock or fish, *but* only if the occupation of that woodland or those buildings is ancillary to the occupation of the agricultural land or pasture: see *Williams v HMRC* [2005] STC (SCD) 782;
- cottages, farm buildings and farmhouses and the land occupied with them, but only if of a *character appropriate* to the property;
- stud farms. HMRC consistently argue that for APR purposes the stud farm must be 'viable', hence run for profit along established business lines and not a mere hobby enterprise, but there is scant authority for that former view. Running a stud can be a business but one difficulty is enthusiasm and an absence or lack of a business approach: a person who loves horses and spends all their time caring for them, showing them and talking to like-minded people who may occasionally buy horses, may have little time or interest in keeping detailed stock records or year-end valuations and the like so as to prove that their passion is actually also a trade. It is therefore necessary if not critical to demonstrate that the stud farm is run on business lines and has the attributes and makings of a business.

IHTA 1984, s 115(5) used to restrict APR to property located in the UK, the Channel Islands and the Isle of Man but this was amended by *FA 2009, s 122* with effect from 23 April 2009 – the relief is now extended to land within the European Economic Area (note that, for BPR purposes, relief was always operative on a worldwide basis).

12.63 Following the well-publicised Lands Tribunal decision in *Lloyds TSB Private Banking Plc (personal representative of Rosemary Antrobus, dec'd) v HMRC* DET/47/2005 (*Antrobus (No 2)*), the distinction between the purchasing power (and attributes) of a 'working' and 'lifestyle' farmer may be significant when considering the agricultural value of agricultural property. Another difficulty is the link, or nexus, between land and a farmhouse since often the main value of APR will be not be in the land but in the farmhouse. If that link between the land and the farmhouse is not strong enough, APR will be denied on the latter. HMRC are also leaning more actively toward denial of APR on the farmhouse where the supporting land is subject to grazing licences – the argument pivots on the notion that merely allowing others to use the land for grazing does not in itself amount to farming and as such it cannot be said that the farmhouse is the centre of farming operations.

12.64 In broad terms, APR at 100% applies to vacant property, or property subject to a lease created or succeeded to on or after 1 September 1995; else APR at the reduced rate of 50% applies otherwise unless vacant possession can be obtained within 12 months (or within 24 months under ESC F17) or the property is broadly valued at market value. Importantly, the value to which APR attaches is not market value but the value which the property would carry if subject to a perpetual covenant prohibiting its use otherwise than as agricultural property. As a consequence, this latter value will typically be less than the open market value, and this disparity will be greater to the extent there is development potential or where the land, for any reason, commands a premium. Accordingly, even APR at 100% will often fail to eliminate the entire transfer of value attributable to the agricultural property in question. Examples include:

- small areas of grassland that would attract indulgent parents of pony-riding offspring;
- agricultural land bought at a premium price as a 'safe haven' investment by non-farmers; and
- areas of land of particular beauty that command a 'leisure' or 'vanity' premium in excess of their agricultural value.

Some factors may now limit this trend – in recent years there has been some resurgence in the value of farmland, perhaps driven by better commercial yields; indulgent parents and others may now have less spare liquidity as a consequence of the far-reaching shadow of the past recession, the legacy of which still persists. In the light of this and where supported by relevant facts, HMRC's standard opening argument that not all of that value should qualify for agricultural relief should be strongly resisted.

However, such a resistant approach should be distinguished from the situation where it is clear there is a dominant development value, as demonstrated in the BPR case of *McCall and Keenan (personal representatives of McLean, dec'd) v Revenue and Customs* [2009] NICA 12 (see **12.4**), a decision of the Court of Appeal in Northern Ireland. In that case the land had an agricultural value of £165,000, but was zoned for redevelopment and was thus worth an impressive £5.8 million at the date of death. It was accepted that the owner, having lost her mental faculties, could not be said herself to be carrying on a business, but her son-in-law looked after the land on her behalf.

The Court of Appeal confirmed the view of the Special Commissioner that there was a business (just) but it was held to be an investment business; the test applied was that of an intelligent businessman; a landowner who derives income from land is an investor if he carries out only incidental maintenance work. The use of the land by graziers was sufficiently exclusive for the land to be an investment. The agisting farmer could exclude other graziers, including the landowner, which prevented the owner from using the land in a way that interfered with the grazing. The case is a useful and detailed reconsideration of the BPR issues considered earlier in this chapter.

CLAWBACK

12.65 If a donor has made a lifetime gift of business or agricultural property which is a PET but dies within seven years such that the PET fails, there is a risk that APR attaching to the original gift will be clawed back. However, clawback can be avoided if the donee retained the original property from the date of the transfer until the date of death and it continued to qualify at that latter point (by reference to the donee) or if he disposed of it during that period and reinvested the net proceeds of sale in qualifying replacement property. In the latter scenario, the reinvestment must take place within three years of the sale of the original property (*IHTA 1984, s 118(1)*). In contrast to the position for CGT rollover relief, 'reinvestment' during the 12 months before the disposal of the original property is not permitted.

It is generally accepted that professional costs and CGT may be deducted in computing the net proceeds of sale before reinvestment; importantly, reinvestment into business property is permitted even when the original property was agricultural property (see RI95).

Can the donee of a PET of a qualifying business or agricultural property safely dispose of it four years after the gift, thus before expiry of the donor's seven-year survival window? Yes, but only if it is the donor who dies within the next three years (the replacement window), because the donee can smartly reinvest the net proceeds in qualifying replacement assets – there is no requirement to retain the reinvested assets for a minimum period (*IHTA 1984, s 124B*). If, however, the *donee* dies within the seven-year period, the opportunity to reinvest and thereby prevent clawback is lost. Reinvestment by the donee's personal representatives will not prevent clawback.

Use of chargeable transfer to limit clawback

12.66 If the death of the donor (or donee) within seven years is likely, then the classification of the lifetime gift as a chargeable transfer may be preferable to PET status. This is so since in the case of a failed PET, there may be full clawback which would impact on the donor's cumulative clock whilst for the chargeable transfer there is only a clawback on the death rate uplift – it does not affect the seven-year cumulation principle of the donor's lifetime clock.

For a PET, once the seven years have elapsed the donee may sell the asset without risk of clawback. Likewise, APR is still available on death even though the inheritor may sell the very next day.

INVESTMENTS IN THE CONTEXT OF FARMING

12.67

> **Focus**
>
> The *Farmer* case (below) is critical in its demonstration of the overlap and interaction of APR and BPR in a business context. The established principles have been soundly reinforced by later case decisions, notably *Brander*, but *Farmer* remains the main reference point where there is any element of diversification away from the central farming activity.

In *Farmer and another (executors of Farmer dec'd) v IRC* [1999] STC (SCD) 321 (see **12.8**), the deceased was a shareholder in a company that carried on the business of letting properties as well as the business of farming. The profits of the letting business were greater than the farming profits, but the farming assets, which admittedly included the farmhouse itself, were (at death) more valuable than the properties used for letting. HMRC refused BPR arguing that since the profits of the letting business were greater than those derived from the farming activity, the business was wholly or mainly one of making investments.

The executors appealed to the Special Commissioners, who found in their favour. It was held that the nature of the business had to be considered in the round and that no single factor – such as profitability – should be determinative. On the facts, although the lettings were more profitable than the farm, the overall context of the business, the capital employed, the time spent by the employees and consultants and the levels of turnover supported the conclusion that the business consisted mainly of farming.

It should be noted that *Farmer* was a case on BPR rather than APR but, until the decision in *McCall* noted above, it was helpful and a point of reference for those borderline cases where BPR, as is nearly always the case, might be more valuable than APR, ie where agricultural land has development value but APR, even at 100%, is restricted to the lower agricultural value as noted at **12.64** above.

The 'fallout' from *McCall* has had a significant impact and local HMRC Inspectors are not shy of relying on it to deny relief on initial application, as noted at **12.64** above.

The principles drawn from the *Farmer* case were further underpinned in *Brander (personal representative of the fourth Earl of Balfour v Revenue and Customs* [2009] UKFTT 101. Here the First-tier Tribunal had to consider the replacement property provisions of *IHTA 1984, s 107*; but in doing so found it necessary to decide whether farming and related operations fell within the 'wholly or mainly' exclusion from business relief under *IHTA 1984, s 105(3)*. The tribunal followed the *Farmer* case in allowing that the running of a typical Scottish landed estate, consisting mainly of farming and of management of cottages (that were often let to people whose expertise could benefit the estate), was not an investment business. HMRC failed in their appeal to the Upper Tribunal heard in May 2010 (*Revenue and Customs v Brander (personal representative of the Fourth Earl of Balfour)* [2010] UKUT 300 (TCC)) (see **12.8**).

FARMING PARTNERSHIP

12.68 For a fuller discussion of partnerships, please refer to the first half of this chapter which considers the BPR perspective (see **12.31** and following).

In relation to a limited liability partnership (LLP), under the *Limited Liability Partnerships Act 2000* the LLP is not treated as owned by the individual partners. For APR there is no change in the treatment of assets held outside, but used in, the partnership, nor is incorporation into an LLP regarded as an interruption for APR and/or BPR.

Partnership farmland

12.69 The old rule that treated partnership property as personal or moveable property was repealed by the *Trusts of Land and Appointment of Trustees Act 1996*. Land held outside a partnership (or company controlled by the taxpayer) and used for an agricultural purpose attracts 100% APR (*IHTA 1984, s 116*). If held as another business asset, 50% BPR is available (*IHTA 1984, s 105(1)(d)*), but free of the restriction as to agricultural value imposed by *IHTA 1984, s 115(3)*.

PERIOD OF OWNERSHIP OR OCCUPATION

Minimum period of ownership

12.70

> **Focus**
>
> Access to APR pivots on satisfying the minimum ownership period of two or seven years but critically this rule is modified in two key circumstances where death is a common factor.

Unlike BPR where a single ownership period test applies, for APR there are two alternative time rules which must be considered, namely the owner occupier and the landlord tenant occupier. Under *IHTA 1984, s 117(a)*, APR is available where the transferor has occupied and farmed the land for the purposes of agriculture (farmed in hand) for *two years*, whilst under *IHTA 1984, s 117(b)* that period is extended to *seven years*, during which the transferor has owned the land and it has been occupied (by anyone) for the purposes of agriculture (the landowner).

Contrast these rules with those for BPR, where a period of ownership will count towards the qualifying period even though the asset may not have been used for business until just before the transfer (note that in Scotland the relevant date for ownership may be that of execution of the disposition, not later recording in the Register of Sasines: see *Marquess of Linlithgow v HMRC* [2010] CSIH 19).

Slightly amended rules apply to farming companies: see below. The quality of occupation is considered towards the end of **12.111**: it is always wise to document the basis on which land is being used, to support the claim when the time comes. As will be seen in the commentary below on the case of *Atkinson v HMRC* (see **12.111**), the precise basis of occupation can determine the tax analysis.

Spouses and civil partners: a special succession rule

12.71 The minimum period of ownership requirement is modified where the transferor who acquired the APR property did so on the death of his spouse or civil partner. *IHTA 1984, s 120(1)(b)* deems such a transferor to have owned the property for the combined period of his own and deceased spouse's ownership and where that aggregate is equal to or greater than two years then the ownership test is satisfied.

Importantly, this aggregation applies only to periods of ownership falling either side of a transfer on the death of the first spouse. It does not apply where the first spouse made a lifetime gift of the land to the second spouse who later dies, and the author is aware of many cases where flawed reliance has been placed on the misunderstanding of the rule. This point demonstrates the sheer complexity of APR, which underpins the need of the professional advisor to continually review and consider the applicable rules pertinent to the individual facts in each case.

Successions

12.72 Under *IHTA 1984, s 120(1)(a)*, a legatee is deemed to own an inherited asset from the date of death and where the legacy was from his spouse, the spouse's period of ownership is also deemed to be counted for the purpose of determining the qualifying ownership period – see **12.71** above.

However, a lesser-known provision will also assist the legatee who has inherited agricultural property from a person (whether his spouse or not) who satisfied the minimum period of ownership requirement, where the ownership requirement is effectively waived on a subsequent transfer by the legatee: see **12.73**.

Successive transfers

12.73 Where there are two successive transfers, of which at least one was on death, and the earlier transferor satisfied the ownership or occupation requirements, these time requirements (subject to certain conditions) are waived for the transferee (*IHTA 1984, s 121*).

Example 12.10 – Legacy of agricultural land

A owns agricultural land which qualifies for APR in all respects including minimum period of ownership and, on his death in September 2017, he leaves that agricultural land to B. The land can still qualify for APR on a later transfer by B, even if that transfer occurs less than two years after A's death – B can 'piggyback' on A's time qualification. Furthermore, as the transfer by A to B ('the earlier transfer') was on A's death, the transfer by B ('the subsequent transfer') can be either a lifetime or a death transfer.

Example 12.11 – Lifetime gift of farming company shares

On 30 September 2017, C, who also owns land which qualifies for APR in all respects including minimum period of ownership, makes a lifetime gift of his majority shareholding in a farming company to D. That land will qualify for APR on a transfer by D on his later death by 'piggybacking' on C's qualification even if D's death is within two years of the gift. Since the original transfer by C to D ('the earlier transfer') was a lifetime transfer, the transfer by D ('the subsequent transfer') will benefit from *IHTA 1984, s 121* only if it is on D's death. If D wishes to make a lifetime transfer which qualifies for APR, he will need to build up his own period of ownership.

In both of the examples above, it is irrelevant whether A and B or C and D are spouses/civil partners because in each case, A and C had owned the shares for the required period. The special treatment given to spouses/civil partners would only be relevant if:

- the earlier transferor had not satisfied the minimum period; and
- the earlier transfer was on death.

Revisiting the example of A and B above, consider that A and B were married/ civil partners and that A had owned the land for one year only – B could benefit from APR on a subsequent transfer by holding the land for a further year after A's death in order to achieve the minimum two-year combined ownership period (*IHTA 1984, s 120(1)(b)*). The rule would be disapplied if the transfer had been made during lifetime – see **12.71** above.

Replacements

12.74 Consider the case of a farmer, who having owned agricultural property and occupied it for qualifying agricultural purposes for the requisite period, is now minded to sell. If he reinvests no more than the (net) proceeds of sale of his original farm in the purchase of new agricultural assets, there is no need to re-qualify under the ownership and occupation tests as *IHTA 1984, s 118(1)* credits him with his past occupation period. However, if the farmer invests additional funds perhaps to buy a larger unit, *IHTA 1984, s 118* relief will extend only to the replacement proportion of the new farm and a fresh qualification period will apply to the excess (*IHTA 1984, s 118(3)*), but note that this restriction does not apply if the replacement was brought about by the formation, alteration or dissolution of a partnership (*IHTA 1984, s 118(4)*).

Residuary estates

12.75 A legatee or transferee whose minimum period of ownership has been waived or reduced by *IHTA 1984, s 120* or *IHTA 1984, s 121* (see **12.72** and **12.73** above) must nevertheless hold that property as qualifying agricultural property in order to access APR. Would there be a problem if the legatee died or made a gift before the administration of the estate has been completed? No.

IHTA 1984, s 91(1) treats the legatee as being *entitled as from the date of the death*, and therefore the administration period will count as time during which the legatee could occupy or own the land. However, as soon as the complexities of administration of this estate will allow, and liquidity is assured, the personal representatives should assent or appropriate the agricultural assets to the legatee.

AGRICULTURAL VALUE

Introduction

12.76

> **Focus**
>
> It is critical to be aware that APR, if in point, is restricted to the agricultural value of the asset alone – this may not be and, certainly in the case of realty, is unlikely to be the same as market value, which may be significantly higher.

As was noted at **12.62** above, APR is available on only so much of the value transferred as is attributable to the agricultural value of the property, which is the value that it would have if it were subject to a perpetual covenant prohibiting its use otherwise than as agricultural property (*IHTA 1984, s 115(3)*).

In the case of an attractive farmhouse or of land with development potential, this will normally be much less than its value in the open market without such a restriction; and (as noted in the leading case next mentioned) lower than property that is merely subject to a planning tie. A restriction in a planning permission can, and quite often is, varied after a number of years.

Often in the case of small parcels of land there will be a transfer of value equal to the excess of market value over agricultural value, but as noted this should not apply to larger parcels of bare land sold as farms in the present economic climate.

12.77 In the landmark case of *Lloyds TSB (personal representative of Antrobus, dec'd) v IRC* [2002] STC (SCD) 468 ('*Antrobus (No 1)*'), a farmhouse, Cookhill Priory, attracted APR, as being of a 'character appropriate' to the agricultural land and pasture forming part of the estate, within *IHTA 1984, s 115(2)*.

Subsequently, in *Lloyds TSB Private Banking Plc (personal representative of Rosemary Antrobus, dec'd) v HMRC* DET/47/2005 ('*Antrobus (No 2)*'), the Lands Tribunal was required to consider the 'agricultural value' of Cookhill Priory for the purposes of *IHTA 1984, s 115(3)*. The tribunal concluded that the agricultural value should be determined on the basis that the assumed perpetual covenant in *IHTA 1984, s 115(3)* would have prohibited use of the land in any other way and, after excluding 'lifestyle' farmers from the theoretical market, the open market value was eventually set at £608,475 and the agricultural value set at 70% thereof, at £425,932. This was a point that HMRC pursued vigorously, so the practitioner should allow for it in valuing a transfer of land as well as farmhouses, as noted at **12.62** above.

Availability of relief since Antrobus (No 2)

12.78 The question 'what is a farmhouse?' had been discussed in *Antrobus (No 2)* even though, strictly, it was of no concern of the Lands Tribunal, having already been determined in *Antrobus (No 1)*. It was noted, in *McKenna v HMRC* [2006] SpC 00565, that the test in *Antrobus (No 2)* should be approached with caution, though in *McKenna* that was not enough to secure APR for Rosteague House, a fine house by the sea (a house with land rather than the more accepted view of land with a house).

The test that has emerged with some strength is that a farmhouse is the dwelling, the hub, the centre from which the farmer manages the farm, so where the land is actually all subject to a contracting agreement and the landowner does virtually no farming himself it is more difficult to sustain that argument. This is an area of prime interest for HMRC and, in the author's experience, there is clear evidence that HMRC are sharpening their attack by probing closely into the depth and nature of the farming activities undertaken. The moral is clear in that relief for the farmhouse should never be assumed, but rather should be carefully reviewed in anticipation that any claim may need to be robustly defended.

Special valuation issues

12.79 Where a person has both freehold land and a share in a partnership to which the land is let on an agricultural tenancy, there is a natural question as to whether the two interests should be valued on the assumption that they are sold together, and if so, how that valuation should be calculated.

In *IRC v Gray (Executor of Lady Fox)* [1994] STC 360, the testatrix was the freeholder and had a 92.5% interest in the partnership which held the tenancy of that freehold estate. The Court of Appeal decided that, for valuation on death purposes, a freehold reversion in land *must* be aggregated with a partnership interest which holds a tenancy of that land (following the principle of realising the maximum realisable price without undue expenditure of time and effort: *Duke of Buccleuch v IRC* [1967] 1 506, HL). In other words, it is a single 'natural unit'. The existence of a tenancy can therefore bring about the worst of both worlds. The valuation will be initially on vacant possession principles notwithstanding the tenancy, but, by virtue of *IHTA 1984, s 116(2)(c)*, only a 50% agricultural property discount may be available (where tenanted prior to 1 September 1995) rather than 100%.

12.80 *Walton's Executors v IRC* [1996] STC 68, CA, concerned the valuation of an agricultural tenancy for capital transfer tax purposes, where the W family were the freeholders which had let the farm to a partnership of Mr W and son. On Mr W's death, HMRC claimed that the capital transfer tax value of the lease was the difference between the value of the freehold with vacant possession and its value subject to the lease. HMRC's reasoning was that, on Mr W's death, there was a hypothetical sale of the tenancy valued at £70,000.

The taxpayer's claim, accepted by the Land Tribunal and the Court of Appeal, was that there was no hypothetical sale, as the son did not wish to sell but to continue the farming. Therefore, the value of the tenancy was based on a potential profit rental basis (£6,300), ie a real-world situation. This was typically a small value in the absence of any special purchaser, who did not exist in this case.

THE LEVEL OF RELIEF

Assets qualifying for 100% relief

12.81

> **Focus**
>
> The landowner can secure APR on agricultural land and buildings used in the farming activity carried on by the underlying tenant by '*piggy backing*' on the qualification of that tenant. However, be aware of the denial of APR for the farmhouse where the latter and the land are not in common tenant occupation.

The circumstances in which 100% APR is available are set out in *IHTA 1984, s 116(2)(a)–(c)*, namely:

- *Transferor has vacant possession or the right to obtain it within 12 months (IHTA 1984, s 116(2)(a))*

  This provision covers owner-occupied farms and farms where the transferor's interest entitles him to vacant possession or will do within the next 12 months (by concession, extended to 24 months (ESC F17)). It is important to note that a partnership could, according to the terms of its agreement, have occupation rights but these must not prejudice the landowner's right to vacant possession.

- *Transferor has held his interest since before 10 March 1981 (IHTA 1984, s 116(2)(b))*

  'Working farmer' relief is still available under this heading and is still seen occasionally in practice. It applies where the transferor held his interest beneficially since before 10 March 1981 where had he given away that interest before then and made an appropriate claim, *FA 1975, Sch 8, para 2* would have applied in computing the value transferred without limitation by *FA 1975, Sch 8, para 5*. The main elements of these pre-1981 rules are:

  - a limit of £250,000 in value and 1,000 acres in area; and
  - the requirement that the transferor was wholly or mainly engaged in farming during five out of the previous seven years. The latter test is deemed to be satisfied if not less than 75% of his income was derived from agriculture.

Relief will be denied if at any time between 10 March 1981 and the transfer of value in question the transferor acquired the right to vacant possession, acquired the right to obtain vacant possession within 12 months, or failed to acquire either such right by reason of an act or deliberate omission.

Relief may be cut down in certain circumstances: see *IHTA 1984, s 116(4)*.

- *The property is let on a tenancy beginning on or after 1 September 1995 (IHTA 1984, s 116(2)(c))*

This relief, designed to encourage the granting of fresh agricultural tenancies, coincided with the introduction of the *Agricultural Tenancies Act 1995* which deregulated the market for let farmland.

Where a tenant dies on or after 1 September 1995 and his tenancy vests under his will or intestacy in another person, that other person's tenancy is deemed under *IHTA 1984, s 116(5A)* to commence at the date of the earlier death for the purposes of determining whether 100% APR is available. Similar provision is made (although this is not applicable to property in Scotland) where, on the death of the surviving tenant on or after 1 September 1995, another person obtains a tenancy under a legislative right.

Where the tenant has given notice to retire in favour of a new tenant, but before such retirement takes place the landlord dies, then the new tenant is deemed to have commenced his tenancy immediately before that latter death, so the estate of the landlord benefits from 100% APR under this head as if the new tenancy had already commenced. This extension of the relief is subject to the condition that the tenant does indeed retire in favour of the new tenant after the landlord's death and within 30 months of the giving of notice.

Landlords and tenants may work together to bring an old arrangement under the post 31 August 1995 rules (surrender and re-grant), ie the landlord might add land to the tenancy, making it a new one. There are two points to consider:

1 The surrender of an existing lease followed by a re-grant on a non-arm's length basis undertaken purely in order to obtain 100% APR in the future might amount to a PET by the tenant but this is thought unlikely through absence of gratuitous intent (*IHTA 1984, s 10*).

2 The surrender of the old lease could constitute a CGT disposition by the lessee under either the value-shifting provisions in *TCGA 1992, s 29* or by reason of valuable consideration (re-grant). There is a strong argument that this might be avoided if a new lease is granted in an arm's-length transaction on the same property at a

different rent but otherwise on the same terms, but only if that could be justified commercially. Further relief is also available under the lesser-known ESC D39 ('Extension of leases'). If the surrender is regarded as a chargeable disposal, it is HMRC's view that the gain on the extinguishment of the old lease cannot be the subject of holdover on grounds that the new lease is a separate asset.

Assets qualifying for 50% relief

12.82 50% APR is available on agricultural property which qualifies in all other respects but which does not fall within any of the three heads of 100% APR. This will mainly comprise property which has been let since before 1 September 1995 and there is no right to vacant possession within the next 12 (or 24) months.

Concessionary reliefs

12.83 Two Extra-statutory Concessions are relevant here:

1 ESC F17 treats the condition in *IHTA 1984, s 116(2)(a)* as satisfied where the transferor's interest in the property, immediately before the transfer, carried the right to vacant possession within 24 months (as opposed to 12 months) of the date of the transfer (see **12.81** above). It also treats the conditions as satisfied where, notwithstanding the terms of the tenancy, the transferor's interest is valued at an amount broadly equivalent to the vacant possession value. See *IRC v Gray (Executor of Lady Fox)* [1994] STC 360, CA – see **12.79**.

2 ESC F16 also gives 100% APR in respect of transfers of agricultural property which include a cottage occupied by a retired farm employee or spouse. This is subject to the occupier being a protected tenant or having a lease for life as part of his contract of employment. In practice, as fewer people actually work on the land and, of those who do, fewer are employed but rather are contractors, this relief will eventually become obsolete.

THE MAIN ESTATE-PLANNING LESSONS

12.84 APR in its current form is very generous if not to the farmer then to the non-farmer investment landowner and for that reason its continued existence will always be the subject of debate and concern. Since APR is available on lifetime gifts as well as transfers on death, those who currently qualify for relief might wish to consider making lifetime gifts to insulate themselves as far as possible against future changes in the law which would deny/restrict relief.

On the other hand, there are some advantages in delaying making gifts, which need to be considered too.

Shareholdings and partnerships (LLP)

12.85

> **Focus**
>
> BPR and APR work closely together where there is central farming business activity but there can be complications where that activity is incorporated.

The difficulty with a limited farming company is (see *IHTA 1984, s 122*) that only a majority shareholding qualifies for APR. If the company qualifies in all respects for BPR then that will not matter, but if it does not, then a minority shareholder may find that his asset is in a mere investment company carrying no access to relief. Subject to that, several issues must be considered:

- Selling the shares or retiring from the partnership could cause significant loss of relief. Not only will the possibility of 100% APR on the shares or partnership interest themselves be lost, but so will the 50% BPR on assets belonging to the individual and used in the business of the company or partnership.
- If it is likely that shares, which qualify for APR now, will in the future cease to do so, consider making a lifetime gift now. It may be possible to hold over CGT under *TCGA 1992, s 165*. The downsides to this are:
  - the possibility of clawback (see **12.65** above);
  - the lack of CGT uplift on death;
  - the gift with reservation provisions are still relevant even where a lifetime gift of business or agricultural property is made. *FA 1986, Sch 20, para 8* modifies the gifts with reservation provisions. In general terms, if the donor reserves a benefit, then the conditions for relief must continue to be met by reference to the donor until the donor's death in order to preserve the relief and reduce the charge on death. However, by *FA 1986, Sch 20, para 8(1A)(b)* the rate at which relief is given is calculated by reference to the donee; thus these provisions cause difficulty where a transferee, for some reason, does not have that control.

The rules as to gifts with reservation contain several complexities. One of them is illustrated with agricultural land.

Example 12.12 – Gift with reservation of agricultural land

On 31 October 2013, Boris made a gift of the land but continued to occupy and farm it until his death on 30 September 2017 such that the transfer fell within the gift with reservation rules. For APR purposes, the donor farmer was in occupation at death so APR should be available under *FA 1986, Sch 20, para 8*; but will BPR be available in respect of any 'premium' value not qualifying for APR?

FA 1986, Sch 20, para 8(1A)(b) provides a 'piggyback' quality by treating the deemed transfer as being made by the donee of the land, disregarding the shortness of period of ownership if less than two years. Thus, if the donee qualifies for BPR, there will be no clawback.

Use of 'relevant property' trusts

12.86

Focus

Be aware of the conflicting APR application to the value of non-qualifying assets leaving the confines of a relevant property trust before and after the first ten-year charge.

APR can reduce IHT otherwise chargeable under the IHT regime applicable to 'relevant property' trusts which, since *FA 2006*, now comprises nearly all lifetime settlements. In determining whether certain conditions, such as the minimum period of ownership, are met, references to the transferor are treated as references to the trustees (*IHTA 1984, ss 103(1)(b)* and *115(1)(b)*).

A trust in which the assets comprise only property that qualifies for 100% APR, with no market value premium, can neatly sidestep the impact of any ten-yearly or exit charges. Although APR does not reduce the effective rate at which tax is charged on an exit before the first ten-year anniversary, this is not a problem provided the value transferred is, post application of APR, reduced to nil – in other words, the asset subject to the exit charge, with identical agricultural and market value, qualifies for 100% APR in its own right (see **12.87** below).

12.87 The position is not so simple where:

- APR is at 50% (ie on let land pre-1 September 1995); or
- APR is given against part of the actual value (ie a farmhouse).

In these cases the impact of APR on both the ten-yearly charge and exit charges *after* the first ten-yearly charge can reduce both the rate of tax and the value transferred.

However, it is important to be aware that a different rule applies during the first ten years of the trust's life. In this period, APR operates to reduce only the initial value transferred into trust (thus from the settlor's perspective) or else to attach the exiting asset if it qualifies for APR in its own right. Its impact is ignored in arriving at the exit charge itself of which the principal component is the value of trust property on creation/added later ignoring APR. Accordingly, to obtain maximum benefit from APR, it is recommended that distributions during the first ten years are, where possible, avoided.

12.88 The transfer of farming assets into a trust, whether by lifetime gift or on death, is often one of the best estate-planning methods available due to the availability of APR of a maximum 100%. Subject to any premium over agricultural value, agricultural assets can be held in such a trust almost indefinitely without attracting any ten-yearly charges or exit charges (post first ten-year charge) after that first ten-year anniversary.

It is therefore critical that the trustees fully satisfy the relevant APR conditions at each ten-year anniversary. Assuming that the 100% rate applies and that any other assets in the trust fall within the nil rate band (to include any premium over agricultural value) – the effective ten-year anniversary charge rate will be nil%. A curious feature of the regime is that this nil rate will continue to apply until immediately prior to the next ten-year anniversary, even if the assets comprised within the trust are no longer business or agricultural assets (ie because the trust fund consists of the proceeds of sale). This provides ample scope for tax planning.

APR 'recycled'

12.89 In certain circumstances, APR can effectively be obtained twice on the same property. This is also considered in the context of business property (see **12.52**). Assume that, on the death of the first spouse/civil partner, agricultural property is left on discretionary trust in favour of the surviving spouse and issue. APR and a CGT uplift of the base cost to market value should be obtained on that first spouse's death.

The surviving spouse/civil partner has the option to purchase the agricultural property from the trustees at its market value. Subject to surviving the requisite two-year period (note that the benefit of the aggregation period under *IHTA 1984, s 120* is not available here, since the asset did not pass directly from spousal partner to partner but from spousal partner into trust), the spouse may then obtain APR a second time – either on their death or on a lifetime transfer. The CGT-free uplift should also be available a second time.

12.90 Life assurance is worth considering where, as in this example, the effectiveness of a plan to minimise IHT is dependent on a particular individual's survival for a specific period. One option would be to purchase term cover for the surviving spouse for at least two years, and this would be appropriate if the matter is being considered at or after the date of the first spouse's death.

Alternatively, even before the death of the first (business-owning) spouse, life assurance could be taken out to cover the risk of the second spouse dying first. Obviously, if that risk materialised, it would prevent the plan for double relief from working. In this case, the cover should be against:

- the risk of the second (non-business owning) spouse dying first; *and*
- the risk of that second spouse dying within two years of the first spouse. This would be a form of term assurance, but that term would be dependent on the date of death of the first spouse, ie the life of X + two years.

Example 12.13 – 'Doubling up' on APR/BPR

Celia Johnson was married with children and grandchildren. Her estate (after allowing for funeral and debts) comprised net liquid assets and savings, of £2,325,000; 30% of the family trading company, Johnson Knitwear Ltd, which makes socks, and is worth £500,000; and Hill Top Farm which Mrs Johnson farmed under an agreement with her neighbour. The farmhouse is worth £500,000 and the land and other buildings £780,000.

By her will made in August 2015, Mrs Johnson left, to a discretionary trust for close family members:

- the shares in the knitwear company; and
- the farmland (but not the house); and
- cash equal to the nil rate band at her death.

The drafting of the will made it clear exactly how much passed to the trust, avoiding the difficulties noted in *RSPCA v Sharp* [2010] EWHC 268 (Ch). The remaining assets were left to her widower. He was also given an option to buy the business and agricultural assets from the trust at market value.

April 2017: death of Mrs Johnson

There is no IHT due to the interaction of APR, BPR, spousal exemption and the nil rate band. There will also be a CGT-free uplift to market value of the base cost of all the assets. The nil rate band for 2017/18 is £325,000 so, on the basis that Mrs Johnson had made no chargeable lifetime gifts, the amount of cash that would go into the trust would be determined by any adjustments, as for example 30% of the value of the farmhouse not qualifying for APR. Of the cash, therefore, up to £325,000 would go into the trust but about £2m would go to Mr Johnson absolutely. He also, of course, acquired the option to buy the business and agricultural assets from the trust at market value.

Mr Johnson promptly (ie in May 2017) buys the business and agricultural assets from the trust using £1,280,000 from the cash that he inherited absolutely. Having little else to do, he takes a more active interest in running the farm than his late wife had done, using the farm kitchen as the place from which he works. The trustees made substantial distributions to the family. Mr Johnson survives a further two years from the exercise of the option.

May 2019: Death of Mr Johnson

The assets in his estate would be:

- the farmhouse (given to him in April 2017);
- the land, with 100% APR (owned since May 2017);
- the shares, with 100% BPR (also owned two years); and
- cash (about £720,000 less any living expenses and small gifts).

There was never any need for the trustees to pay income to Mr Johnson: he had sufficient in his own right.

The IHT taxation of the trust created under the will of Mrs Johnson is complex. There is a single transfer on death under *IHTA 1984, s 4*, of which the transfer of the nil rate band is only part, with the balance comprising property qualifying for APR/BPR. However, the general rule for relevant property trusts is that, even though they may be established within the nil rate band, that is ignored when calculating the exit charge in the first ten years. This is because what is measured is the transfer itself and not the value transferred as reduced by reliefs such as, in this case, APR/BPR. Thus, unless the exit is a distribution *in specie* of property qualifying for APR/BPR such that it is itself reduced to nil, an exit charge may still trigger.

The business and agricultural property will benefit from a second capital gains tax-free uplift of their base costs to market value on Mr Johnson's death. Although the introduction of the transferable nil rate band in *FA 2008* reduces the necessity for its use on the first death, this example demonstrates how it can still be helpful to utilise the nil rate band on that first death.

It should be noted that when dealing with relevant property trusts the capital gains tax position is different if they are created on death rather than in lifetime. There was some uncertainty about the availability of holdover relief under *TCGA 1992, s 260* on non-business assets, on the basis that, if 100% APR/BPR applied, there was no chargeable transfer. However, HMRC have confirmed that, in their view, a gift qualifying for 100% BPR/APR is nonetheless treated as a chargeable transfer for the purposes of *TCGA 1992, s 260* (see CG67041). That must be right: it is chargeable, but at 0%.

Creation of several lifetime trusts to achieve protection against future changes in the reliefs

12.91 A specific and popular arrangement involved the use of a number of small relevant property trusts (pilot trusts) to maximise the respective trust's nil rate band. It could be adapted where 100% BPR or APR applies see – *Trust and Estates 2017/18* (Bloomsbury Professional) for more detail.

Example 12.14 – Multiple trusts

Fred owns farmland with an agricultural value in excess of £2m. He created six relevant property trusts at staggered intervals over the course of 2016/17 each with a nominal amount of cash. He later transfers assets (all carried out on the same day) carved out of the landholding which, applying the 'loss to estate' principle, amounts to less than £325,000 each, thus leaving Fred with only nominal value at the end.

Provided (see below) that 100% APR applies, all of the transfers will escape exposure to IHT, and a CGT liability can be avoided by use of holdover relief under *TCGA 1992, s 260*: the terms of the changes introduced in *FA 2008* do not restrict the operation of *TCGA 1992, s 260*.

Under current law each trust should be protected by the nil rate band rule even if:

- the BPR/APR rules are altered in the future (unless in the extremely unlikely event that retrospective legislation is introduced); or
- the assets cease to be relevant business property or agricultural property (ie they are sold).

However, there are, as always, several risks associated with this type of scheme:

First and foremost there is its artificiality.

Second, HMRC could invoke the associated operations rule, although this risk has been severely curtailed following the decision in *Rysaffe Trustees (CI) Ltd v IRC* [2003] STC 536. The risk can be further reduced by ensuring that there are genuine differences between the trusts (ie different trustees and beneficiaries), whilst the staggered intervals are as far apart as practicable and are not preordained (it should be noted that HMRC were successful in invoking *IHTA 1984, s 268* to show that life policies, when taken out with annuities, constituted associated operations: see *Smith and others* [2008] STC 1649). This landmark case decision did provide good protection from HMRC attack and was further reinforced by inclusion of the same in an HMRC publication of illustrative situations not considered to be tax abusive and hence outside the reach of the general anti-abuse rule (GAAR).

However, this route (which was first thought to have been negated through HMRC's proposal to introduce a settlement nil rate band, which was itself later withdrawn) has nonetheless been overshadowed by targeted anti avoidance legislation contained in *Finance (No 2) Act 2015* aimed at the use of multiple trusts. The rules (*Finance (No 2) Act 2015, ss 62A–62C*), effective from 10 December 2014, provide that, where property is added to two or more relevant property settlements on the same day and after the commencement of those settlements, the value of the added property together with the value of property settled at the date of commencement (that is not already in a related relevant property settlement) will be brought into account in calculating the rate of tax for the purposes of trust IHT charges (eg ten years and exit charges).

Third, where land is carved up into smaller lots, valuation issues become complicated. The value of a lifetime transfer is the loss to the donor's estate measured on a pre/post transfer basis, thus if the third trust included part of two 'natural letting units' it might depress the value of retained land. If it did, the value transferred (subject to APR) might well be different from the value of the actual parcel of land. This issue is even more important where a share or interest in land is transferred, rather than merely the separation of an enclosure from neighbouring land.

Fourth, there is the possible loss of CGT rollover relief under *TCGA 1992, s 152*.

Fifth and finally, consideration should be given to the potential loss of entrepreneurs' relief, which might otherwise be available on a material disposal of business assets such as the whole or part of a farming business (*TCGA 1992, s 169H*). The disposal of an asset is not necessarily a disposal of the whole or part of a business (CG64015). In addition, HMRC's view appears to be that a claim for holdover relief takes precedence over a claim for entrepreneurs' relief (CG64137), although this has yet to be established at tribunal level.

OTHER WAYS OF USING APR

Gifts to elderly relatives

12.92 The main disadvantage to a lifetime gift of valuable assets eligible for 100% APR/BPR, is the CGT position, albeit of lesser importance given the current low 10/20% rate (18/28% rate for residential property/land). Whilst holdover relief may be available under *TCGA 1992, s 165*, the tax-free uplift to market value on the death of the owner is clearly a much better alternative.

Consider the position of an asset given to a trusted but elderly relative, ie grandparent. The gift, as a PET, would be potentially free of IHT and normally holdover relief would be available to avoid exposure to CGT. On the grandparent's death, 100% APR/BPR should be available and the normal minimum period of ownership may also be relaxed under the succession provisions of *IHTA 1984, s 109* (BPR) or *121* (APR), discussed at **12.72**, such that the IHT exposure is effectively reduced to nil. The property may then pass under the grandparent's will to the intended beneficiaries, but with the added benefit of the CGT uplift to market value.

Elderly relative transfers to offshore trust on death

12.93 A scheme to limit gains may be put into effect through a deed of variation.

WILL PLANNING

12.94

> **Focus**
>
> Be aware of the impact of the *IHTA 1984, s 39A* rule resulting in a dilution of APR (and BPR) on a gift of qualifying property where the spousal exemption is in point. This little-known but so damaging provision can lead to a wholly unexpected tax outcome.

Some aspects of planning through wills rely on detailed consideration of the special rules which apply to APR/BPR relieved property and thus are dealt with in this chapter. Leaving agricultural property to a spouse/civil partner may suit family purposes but will waste APR which is traded away against the spousal exemption. From a purely tax perspective, agricultural property that may qualify for 100% APR should be given to the lower generations (children and grandchildren) or to appropriate trusts.

Key to the choice is the running of the farming business: a careful balance must be struck between fairness, as between siblings, and the need for 'those who work the land to own it'. Will an agricultural asset retain its character in the hands of a family member who treats it as a mere investment? Will APR continue or remain at its present level? A gift to the next generation may 'lock into' the reliefs at present levels. Frequently, a surviving spouse does not need the business assets, such as shares in the family company, which may be illiquid, but would prefer (or need) the liquid or cash assets instead.

12.95 If the surviving spouse/civil partner does need the agricultural assets, those assets can be placed into a 'wait and see' mini discretionary trust and, if needed, distributed to the surviving spouse at a later point: previously if the distribution was absolute then this had to take place more than three months but not later than two years after the first spouse's death (*IHTA 1984, s 144*) – see *Frankland v IRC CA* [1997] STC 1450. However, *Finance Act (No 2) 2015* removed this three-month stipulation where such appointment is made to a surviving spouse and this mirrors the existing approach applied where the distribution is on IPDI terms (*IHTA 1984, s 144(3)(c)*).

A word of warning – if the testator wants to give agricultural assets to chargeable beneficiaries to supplement a nil rate band gift, and leave the residue to the surviving spouse, he must ensure that the specific property, ie the farm, is given to the non-exempt beneficiaries to avoid an apportionment (and hence dilution) of APR between them and the exempt surviving spouse under *IHTA 1984, s 39A*.

The burden of IHT can create unfairness between more than one chargeable beneficiary, ie a gift of shares qualifying for 100% BPR to the testator's daughter and a gift of an equivalent cash sum to the testator's son would result in an effectively exempt gift to the former while the son's gift would be subject to IHT.

OTHER ADVANTAGES OF DELAYING SUCH GIFTS UNTIL DEATH

12.96 If an estate owner is reasonably confident that 100% APR/BPR will be available on his death, there is little incentive to relinquish control or reduce a substantial minority holding by making lifetime gifts. Indeed, there can even be a disadvantage by reason of the clawback operation. The case of *Rosser v IRC* [2003] STC (SCD) 311 illustrates a situation where, for IHT purposes, it would have been preferable to defer gifting agricultural property until death.

The advantages of delaying gifts until death are as follows:

- There is no question of clawback of APR/BPR as this only applies to lifetime gifts (*IHTA 1984, ss 124A* and *124B*). It should be noted that there is a specific problem in relation to business property that falls within *IHTA 1984, s 105(1)(d)* where the donor had the necessary control but the donee does not but this has no exact parallel for APR.

- There will be full CGT exemption and tax-free uplift on death, which is more favourable than CGT holdover relief, itself more akin to a deferral. This matter has perhaps become more of an issue since the CGT overhaul in *FA 2008* when rebasing, indexation and taper relief ceased to apply, although entrepreneurs' relief may provide some shelter. In relation to business assets and farming assets qualifying as business assets, the change in tax burden could be dramatic.
- The estate owner can retain control of his shareholding and for many 'self-made' individuals, this advantage will be hard to resist: they may feel that their children should earn their own living, rather than rely on an inheritance.
- If the estate owner would really like to tie up the land for successive generations, this is best done by creating an immediate post-death interest (IPDI) by will which thus becomes effective on their death – the same form of trust if created in lifetime would enter the relevant property regime and hence the value of lifetime gifted assets therein would be treated as a chargeable transfer. However, the creation of an IPDI trust on death whilst carved out of the chargeable estate would not enter the relevant property regime but would continue to be treated as an old-style interest in possession (IIP).

12.97 In the past a common alternative saw the estate owner create a settlement in which he retained a lifetime interest with capital appointment at trustee discretion. If he wanted his children to have control of decisions in the meantime, this could be achieved by their appointment as trustees. The creation of such a trust in this post-21 March 2006 era would now be a chargeable transfer (rather than PET under the pre-22 March 2006 regime) and, whilst the value transferred would still benefit from APR, the CGT-free uplift on the life tenant's death would no longer apply as the trust would be within the relevant property regime. Notwithstanding, the IHT analysis would conclude that, by reason of the potential for the trustees to exercise discretion over capital in favour of the life tenant, a benefit in the gifted trust assets had been reserved under *FA 1986, s 102*, but that APR would be available to cushion its impact.

The obvious flaw in the plan is that holdover relief would not be available at the time of making the post-21 March 2006 lifetime settlement, as the trust would be settlor interested (*TCGA 1992, s 169B*). Until 6 April 2008, this restriction was not considered a real concern in practical terms as the gain could benefit from a substantial amount of taper relief accrued during the settlor's personal ownership, thus softening the CGT exposure. However, the *FA 2008* CGT rules (with its repeal of taper relief in favour of the more restrictive entrepreneurs' relief) did not replicate the favourable pre-6 April 2008 regime. During the lifetime of the settlor, the trust would be of 'relevant property'. Periodic charges to IHT would be mitigated by APR or BPR, but cash in the trust could suffer IHT charges.

DEEDS OF VARIATION (*IHTA 1984, S 142*)

12.98 In the context of APR where death occurred less than two years ago, consideration should be given to the redirection of gifts of agricultural property attracting 100% APR from the exempt spouse to non-exempt persons, such as children, grandchildren or discretionary trusts. This would make good use of nil rate band trusts that are no longer needed by virtue of the transferable nil rate band introduced with effect from 9 October 2007.

MORTGAGING OR CHARGING AGRICULTURAL OR BUSINESS ASSETS

12.99 The placing, moving or rearrangement of debt to achieve instant tax savings has been dealt a severe blow as a result of *IHTA 1984, s 162B* as introduced in *FA 2013*, and its impact should be studied in detail.

Avoid mortgaging or charging a farm?

12.100 In the past there were two situations to consider when securing debt:

- charge the farm;
- charge non-APR assets.

In the first, the pre-*IHTA 1984, s 162B* prevailing wisdom dictated that this should be avoided wherever possible since on a transfer of value, APR would be restricted to the net value of the farm namely the value of the farm less the mortgage. Thus the second option was the preferred route since it maximised the APR and reduced the chargeable value of the non APR asset against which secured, but this was subject to the approval of the mortgagor which gave rise to practical rather than tax difficulties.

However, the introduction of *IHTA 1984, s 162B* in *FA 2013* demands that irrespective of the actual asset against which the borrowing is secured such borrowing must first be attributed to relievable agricultural property to the extent that the borrowing (directly or indirectly) has been used to finance the acquisition, maintenance or enhancement of the agricultural property. This has the effect of reducing the value of the asset otherwise attracting the benefit of APR and instantly thwarts any attempt to maximise APR through repositioning of the charge. See **12.56** for a more detailed discussion of *IHTA 1984, s 162B*.

12.101 In the BPR case of *IRC v Mallender and others (executors of Drury-Lowe, dec'd)* [2001] STC 514 (see **12.13**), the deceased had given security to a bank over some land in return for a bank guarantee to Lloyd's which was lodged as part of the deceased's underwriting business. Initially, the Special Commissioners had held that the land itself was business property, albeit that its value was several times the value of the guarantee, but this decision was swiftly overturned by the High Court.

Remember that a guarantee that has not been called in may not be allowed by HMRC at its full value for the purposes of deduction. It may be necessary to negotiate a value to be deducted, to take account of the likelihood, at the date of death, that the guarantee would be called in. For this purpose an unsecured guarantee might carry a lower valuation for deduction purposes than a secured guarantee. Alternatively, it might even lapse with the guarantor and not be deductible at all.

TAX PLANNING FOR AGRICULTURAL PROPERTY: AGRICULTURAL COTTAGES AND THE FARMHOUSE

12.102

> **Focus**
>
> The APR qualification of the farmhouse remains one of the most contentious areas and HMRC challenge can and should be anticipated in any case where values are significant. The availability of the relief is very much driven by case law and thus dependent on the precise facts in each case. This is a fluid area subject to constant testing by both HMRC and the taxpayer and as a consequence it is vital to remain abreast of current developments in this area.

IHTA 1984, s 169 is a little-known provision which provides that, whether or not the ownership conditions for APR are satisfied, where cottages are occupied by persons employed in agriculture, their valuation will be on the basis that they are only suitable for that purpose. Accordingly, they command a lower transfer value for gifting purposes.

The difficult case of *Starke (Brown's Executors) v IRC* [1995] STC 689, CA suggests that reference in *IHTA 1984, s 115(2)* to 'agricultural land or pasture' should be given the narrow meaning of the bare land, not the wider meaning under the *Interpretation Act 1978* which automatically includes buildings on the land. As a consequence, HMRC argue that, for IHT purposes, a farmhouse or building will qualify for APR only if its occupation is ancillary to that of agricultural land.

On the facts in *Starke*, a six-bedroom farmhouse on 2.5 acres did not qualify for APR. *Starke* is a special case, decided on the basis of an undertaking given during the proceedings that limited the scope of the judgment. However, some weight should be given to the observations of Morritt LJ that some nexus, other than ownership of land, might link a house to the farmland.

12.103 In *Williams (personal representative of Williams, dec'd) v HMRC* [2005] STC (SCD) 782, it was held that broiler houses situated on land leased to a company and used for the intensive rearing of birds were not agricultural property within *IHTA 1984, s 115(2)*. The broiler houses were not 'ancillary' to the deceased's farm but instead dominated it. They were not a subsidiary part of the purpose of an overall agricultural activity carried out on the land.

Example 12.15 – APR on a retained interest

An estate owner gave 85% of his farm to his daughter and retained 15% together with the farmhouse.

If the estate owner continues to be involved in the farming business (ie through a partnership) the farmhouse may be eligible for 100% APR but it is a question of degree – it is possible to have a 100% interest in the farmhouse and a 15% interest in the partnership. It is also suggested that a service contract be entered into between the partnership and the 'farmhouse' owner setting out the specific administration and other farming duties he must satisfy.

The judgment in *Starke* (see above) contains *dicta* that admit the possibility that land may be agricultural property by virtue of some nexus other than direct unity of ownership. This was challenged in *Rosser* (see below), but here the taxpayer acted in person and in a review of the case report, the case was not fully argued. Interestingly, the point is still not formally decided and a further test case is anticipated.

12.104 In *Harrold v IRC* [1996] STC (SCD) 195, APR was in point in considering the clawback provisions. APR was claimed under the seven-year occupation test but as the house in question, though qualifying in other respects as a farmhouse, was unoccupied at the donor's death, APR was denied on the basis it was not occupied for the purposes of agriculture since it was not occupied at all.

In *Dixon v IRC* ([2002] STC (SCD) 53, a claim for APR failed through lack of substance – the agricultural use was derisory, comprising only an orchard of 0.6 acres.

The farmhouse must be of a 'character appropriate' to the agricultural property (*Lloyds TSB (personal representative of Antrobus, dec'd) v IRC* [2002] STC (SCD) 468. In that case, a six-bedroom country house situated in approximately 126 acres of agricultural land and pasture, which had been farmed by the Antrobus family since 1907 and had been a working farm, was held to be of a character appropriate to the agricultural land and pasture within *IHTA 1984, s 115(2)*.

12.105 By contrast, in *Higginson's Executors v IRC* [2002] STC (SCD) 483, the deceased lived in a lodge in a landed estate but that lodge was not a typical farmhouse. The Special Commissioner held that the lodge was not a farmhouse within *IHTA 1984, s 115(2)*. For that purpose, the land and house must be part of an agricultural unit, in which the land dominated. However, in this case the lodge dominated evidenced by the fact that when sold, it commanded a substantial price, far more than a 'real' farmer would pay for an agricultural investment. In essence this was a house with land and not land with a house.

In *Rosser v IRC* [2003] STC (SCD) 311 the estate owners/farmers made lifetime gifts of some 39 out of 41 acres of farmland, but retained the 'farmhouse' and a barn which were still held on the relevant death. The claim for APR on the home failed on grounds that it had clearly become merely a 'retirement home'. The moral emerging is to leave such gifting until death which also then benefits from the CGT death exemption and market value uplift (*TCGA 1992, s 62*).

12.106 The determination of whether a farmhouse is agricultural property is largely driven by the purpose of occupation, rather than the actual use put to it by the owner or occupier. In an article written for *Taxation*, published on 15 June 2000, the late Peter Twiddy (Assistant Director, HMRC Capital Taxes Office), described the test adopted by the then Capital Taxes Office (CTO) as follows:

> '... The CTO asks the District Valuer to consider the appropriate test through the eyes of the rural equivalent of the reasonable man on the Clapham omnibus ...'

The CTO in its previous guidance applied eight tests when determining whether a farmhouse is of a 'character appropriate' to the agricultural property. These were replaced in subsequent HMRC guidance by the following (IHTM24051):

- 'Is the farmhouse appropriate when judged by ordinary ideas of what is appropriate in size, layout, content, and style and quality of construction in relation to the associated land and buildings?
- Is the farmhouse proportionate in size and nature to the requirements of the agricultural activities conducted on the agricultural land? You should bear in mind that different types of agricultural operation require different amounts of land. This is an aspect on which the VOA will be able to give advice.

- Within the agricultural land does the land predominate so that the farmhouse is ancillary to that land?
- Would a reasonable and informed person regard the property simply as a house with land or as a farmhouse?
- Applying the "elephant" test, would you recognise this as a farmhouse if you saw it? Although this test involves some subjectivity it can be useful in ruling out extremes at either end of the scale.
- How long has the farmhouse and agricultural property been associated and is there a history of agricultural production? The matter has to be decided on the facts as at the date of death or transfer but evidence of the farmhouse having previously been occupied with a larger area of land may be relevant evidence.
- Considering the relationship between the value of the house and the profitability of the land, would the house attract demand from a commercial farmer who has to earn a living from the land, or is its value significantly out of proportion to the profitability of the land? If business accounts have been supplied, copies should be forwarded to the VOA. Business accounts can give a useful indication of the extent of the agricultural activity being carried on, although a loss-making enterprise is not on its own considered to be a determinative factor.
- Considering all other relevant factors, including whether land is let out and on what terms, is the scale of the agricultural operations in context?
- There must be some connection or nexus between "such cottages, farm buildings and farmhouses, together with the land occupied with them" and the property to which they must be of a character appropriate. The argument that the nexus must be derived from common ownership rather than common occupation was accepted by the Special Commissioner in *Rosser v Inland Revenue Commissioners* [2003] STC (SCD) 311.'

12.107 It is worth noting that in HMRC's revised guidance (see **12.62**) the original eight tests were extended to nine, the seventh and ninth bullet points above were added, and the following instruction (in IHTM24052) inserted:

> '… It is not a question of "how many factors have to be failed" in any given case before a house is judged not to be of a character appropriate to the property. It is necessary to consider all the various factors about the house and the land and come to a judgement …'

The notorious 'elephant test' relates to something which is difficult to describe, but is nonetheless recognised on sight. However, whereas there may be a consensus as to what an elephant is and what is not, an equivalent measure of certainty will not always be present when dealing with a question of fact and degree. A particular area of difficulty is in deciding to what extent any of the reported cases merely turn on their own unique facts.

Whilst the bullet points set out above are still part of the guidance, it is clear that a 'points test' as such does not apply: it must be stressed that each case must be considered on its own merits whilst accepting as a general premise that large houses on small estates and houses on estates that are largely let, will not easily qualify for relief.

12.108 The case of *Executors of D Golding Deceased v Revenue & Customs Commissioners* [2011] UKFTT 351 (TC) produced a very interesting outcome in favour of the taxpayer and introduced a bold view, namely that profitability and scaling back of active farming due to age or infirmity are not necessarily a determining factor when considering the 'character appropriate' test.

In that case, the deceased had for many years until his death at age 81, farmed a smallholding of just 16.29 acres – the diverse farming trade comprised some 600 chickens, seven to ten cattle, harvesting of fruit from trees and growing vegetables. The farm produced milk and crops of wheat and barley were produced for sale. It was accepted that old age and infirmity led to scaling back of activities confined to selling of eggs, fruit and vegetables which produced a net profit of approximately £1,500 pa on average over the last five years – equal to less than 25% of the deceased sustainable income. Even so in the early years the farm had been sufficient to sustain a family albeit not to any great state of luxury. The farmhouse was small in size, without electricity in parts and in a very poor state of repair. HMRC had implied acceptance that the house in which the deceased lived and from which he carried out his farming activities, was a farmhouse for agricultural purposes but disputed that the property was of 'character appropriate' – the argument rested to a great extent on the profitability of the farm.

In a refreshingly simple and clear analysis of the facts as presented, the tribunal in finding for the taxpayer stated '… we do not accept that the lack of substantial profit is detrimental to the decision that the farmhouse was of character appropriate …'.

12.109 HMRC did not like and have not warmed to the decision in *Golding* (although this is now referred to in HMRC's Inheritance Tax Manual at IHTM24053) and HMRC subsequently warned taxpayers seeking to rely on *Golding* that 'each case is judged on its own particular facts. It is unlikely that the facts will be the same as those of *Golding* in many cases and as the decision is not of binding precedent the decisions in the cases of *Rosser*, *Higginson*, *Dixon*, *Antrobus 1* and *2* and *McKenna* are still relevant'.

12.110 Case authority, as opposed to HMRC Guidance, on what constitutes a farmhouse is *McKenna v HMRC* [2006] SSCD 800 (SpC 00565), where an estate comprised Rosteague House, a lodge, a cottage and a stable flat and 188 acres. Some 52 acres were coastal slope and 100 acres were agreed to be agricultural land. HMRC denied APR on the house and the taxpayer's appeal from the decision failed.

The case is worth reading in full but as a broad summary, the title went back to the thirteenth century. The house was part Elizabethan, part eighteenth century, listed Grade II but at the relevant time, it had fallen into dilapidation and needed very considerable repair. There was evidence of farming from 1365 onwards but during the twentieth century farming was mainly done by others, the owner living in London until retirement to Rosteague in 1978. As long as his health allowed, the estate owner ran the farm from the house but eventually it was managed by an agent and over time the extent of agricultural activities declined. Mr McKenna relied on a pension and not on the farm for his living.

The estate was eventually sold, and importantly not as a farm but as residential property. The land was incidental, being mentioned only briefly in the sales literature and of the sale price of £3.05m as much as £2.03m might fairly be attributable to the house alone.

The Special Commissioner held that:

- the decision in *Antrobus (No 2)* as to what constitutes a farmhouse should be approached with some caution;
- it was necessary to decide on the basis of the words of *IHTA 1984, s 115(2)* rather than apply general principles, though the idea that a farmer is the person who farms the land on a day-to-day basis was a helpful one;
- a farmhouse is a dwelling from which the farm is managed;
- the farmer is the person who farms the land on a day-to-day basis, rather than the person who is in overall control;
- it is not occupation that matters so much as the purpose of that occupation;
- if the premises are 'extravagantly large for the purpose for which they are being used' then even though used for farming they may have become 'something much more grand';
- each case turns on its own facts, to be judged by ordinary ideas of what is appropriate in size, content and layout.

On the facts as presented and evidenced, the farming activity had been reduced and was no longer conducted from the house. The house was considered too grand for the level of farming activity carried out.

Critically, it was recognised that a farmer need not make a profit (and this lack of profitability has been reaffirmed in the *Golding* case – see above), but it certainly did not help the taxpayer on the facts in this case. It was held that it was not a farmhouse. However, even if it had been accepted as a farmhouse it was not of a character appropriate: it was 'at the very top end of the size of a farmhouse in Cornwall'. Applying the tests of *Antrobus (No 1)* in turn, it failed. It also failed the occupation test: neither Mr nor Mrs McKenna occupied for the purpose of farming: they were prevented by ill health from farming. This particular aspect, where the occupier of the house does little active farming, forms a central plank in the HMRC argument to deny relief.

Notwithstanding the judgment, there are still some issues unresolved, which the following example may illustrate:

Example 12.16 – Gift of farmhouse

On 30 June 2017, Mr and Mrs Gilliam, lifelong farmers, retire and, as in *Rosser*, give their farm to their daughter who takes over the farming. Mr and Mrs Gilliam continue to live in the farmhouse and the daughter lives elsewhere.

In those circumstances, the farmhouse ceases to be agricultural property because there is no common occupation by the same person who farms the land (the daughter runs the farm from other premises). The solution may be for the Gilliams to retain some partnership interest in the overall farm.

Example 12.17 – Life interest in farmhouse

Consider instead that Mr and Mrs Gilliam occupied a farmhouse as life tenants under a pre-*FA 2006* qualifying life interest trust. The land is separated from the trust interest and is now held by the daughter in her own right. The Gilliams give up occupation of the farmhouse to their daughter, retiring into a bungalow nearby. The daughter moves into the farmhouse and runs the farm from there.

The daughter is a farmer of the type favoured by *Antrobus (No 2)*: she actually farms the land from the farmhouse. It is arguable that there is such a close connection between the house and the land that, on the death of Mr Gilliam or of Mrs Gilliam, APR should be given on the house (this very point was discussed in the *Hanson* case below).

Consider then the more recent decision in *Joseph Nicholas Hanson as Trustee of the William Hanson 1957 Settlement v Revenue & Customs* [2012]

UKFTT 95 (TC). In this case, the First-tier Tribunal held that when determining whether a farmhouse qualifies for APR, both it and the land (to which the farmhouse is of 'character appropriate') must be in the same occupation but not necessarily in the same ownership.

The facts of the case were straightforward. Immediately before his death in December 2002, Joseph Charles Hanson was the life tenant of a trust created by his father in 1957. The trust held a property which HMRC agreed was a 'farmhouse' for APR purposes with an agreed market value in December 2002 of £450,000. Mr Hanson's son lived in the farmhouse which he had occupied since 1978 under a rent-free licence. From there the son farmed 215 acres of land of which 128 acres was owned by the son and 25 acres was part owned by Mr Hanson. The remainder of the 215 acres comprised 20 acres rented by the son from a third party and a further 42 acres whose ownership was unspecified. The only land in common ownership and common occupation with the farmhouse was the 25 acres part owned by Mr Hanson and farmed by the son.

Following Mr Hanson's death his executors claimed APR on the value of his interest in the farmhouse. HMRC denied the relief on the basis that there was insufficient agricultural land in both common ownership and common occupation with the farmhouse for the farmhouse to pass the 'character appropriate' test. The son appealed the decision in his capacity as sole trustee of the trust arguing that common occupation was the only connecting factor required between the farmhouse and the agricultural land to which it was of a character appropriate. The Tribunal agreed.

However, HMRC made it clear at the outset in the hearing before the First-tier Tribunal that this was, for them, an important point and thus it was inevitable that HMRC would look to the Upper Tribunal on appeal. The Upper Tribunal (*HMRC v Hanson* [2013] UKUT 0224 (TCC)) in finding for the taxpayer delivered a resounding judgment of strong common sense based on intricate academic examination of the statute, relevant case discussion and of analytical construction of all the arguments brought to the appeal. It was particularly encouraging that the Upper Tribunal did not lose sight of the fact that the Hanson land was very much a working farm, with livestock, and had little reliance on outside contractors. It was the exact sort of operation that 'ought' to qualify for APR. HMRC leave to appeal was denied.

This welcome decision is of significance in situations where a downsizing farmer has moved out of the farmhouse and gives away much of the agricultural land.

12.111 Following *IRC v Forsyth-Grant* [1943] 25 TC 369, if the grant of a farm business tenancy gives the owner a grant of herbage ('profit a prendre') but with responsibility for mowing, seeding and fertilising the land which is actually carried out, then 100% APR will apply to both the land and the farm buildings including the farmhouse (but of course subject to the 'character appropriate' tests set out above).

The potential availability of relief for short-term grazing lets or licences is referred to in the Inheritance Tax manual's APR guidance (see **12.62**). However, that guidance also includes the following note of caution in relation to farmhouses (IHTM24074):

> '… It is unlikely that a landowner who has allowed most or all of the agricultural land to be occupied on a grazing licence agreement where he does nothing but collect the rent and maintain boundaries, will be considered to be in agricultural occupation of that land. Consequently, as there is no farming activity actually being carried out, any associated house cannot be considered to be a farmhouse and therefore would not be eligible for APR ….'

The matter of whether pasture land was truly 'occupied for the purposes of agriculture' was considered by the Special Commissioner in *Re Executors of Walter Wheatley (dec'd)* [1998] STC (SCD) 60. It was held that grazing by horses such as draught animals could qualify because the horses would have a 'connection with agriculture' and by the same token grazing by horses used for leisure pursuits did not so qualify. Arguably, the issue is the exact basis of occupation. If there is a tenancy, the *dicta* in *Wheatley* should apply; but if there is a licence, the owner-occupier is producing an agricultural crop, grass, whatever eats it. However, in the light of the *McCall* case, this will seldom amount to a business, so only APR will be available.

To avoid the house being treated as an excepted asset within *IHTA 1984, s 112(2)*, by reason of its use wholly or mainly for the personal benefit of the transferor (*IHTA 1984, s 112(6)*), an arm's-length contract of employment should be considered. It is strongly recommended that the exact basis of occupation of the land is formally recorded. However, it is accepted that, in real life, land is often occupied by the neighbouring farmer or grazier who has known the landowner for many years such that there is no commercial reason to produce and sign a contract. In such a case the test is one of fact: what is the land used for? In completing IHT400 and its supporting schedules, the more precise the detail of occupation and use that can be given, the better – but be prepared for HMRC challenge.

The precise terms of conacre or agistment agreements were considered in detail in *McCall and Keenan (personal representatives of McLean, dec'd) v Revenue and Customs Commissioners* [2009] NICA 12, where it appeared that some of the agreements were negotiated orally and only later, if at all, recorded in writing.

In an interesting case, a special and technical rule was initially thought to have come to the aid of the taxpayer in *Atkinson and Smith (Executors of Atkinson*

Deceased) v HMRC [2010] UK FTT 108 (TC). It concerned occupation of a farm bungalow that had been the residence of a farmer for many years but in which he was not living at the time of his death, being then in a nursing home. This is a common problem and, in the past, HMRC had been successful in their argument that lack of occupation for the purpose of agriculture by its owner at the chargeable event date denied access to APR.

The distinguishing feature in *Atkinson* was that the land on which the bungalow stood was, with other land, let to a family partnership of which the deceased was still a partner at his death. It was established that he had originally occupied the bungalow and the partnership occupied all the land for the purpose of agriculture. Thus at the death, although he was not in residence, he was still taking an interest in the family business; his personal belonging and furnishings were still there; no-one else moved in and he wanted to go back there but as he aged that became less likely. The occupation was by the partnership as a whole but that was thought sufficient.

However, the success was short lived and the case was overturned on appeal by HMRC ([2011] UKUT B26 (TCC)), although it should be noted that the taxpayer was unrepresented due to lack of financial resources such that HMRC succeeded as much by default than by persuasive argument. Notwithstanding this, it does demonstrate the continued aggressive stance taken by HMRC as they continue to rebut any and all challenge to their interpretation of the qualifying farmhouse.

TAX PLANNING FOR AGRICULTURAL PROPERTY: FALLOW LAND AND OTHER FARMING ASSETS

12.112 Fallow land (ie under an EEC set-aside scheme) qualifies for APR provided that it is not used for another business purpose. Until recently much arable land was not actively farmed, because the return was far less attractive than doing nothing and relying on entitlement to Single Farm Payment (as to which see below). Accordingly, the question arose whether such land was truly occupied for the purpose of agriculture, or whether its nature had changed by reason of the passive purpose of drawing subsidy. As a consequence the farmer did well to take seriously his duties to keep the land in good order, even if he did not grow a crop.

Holiday lettings are not agricultural property and are unlikely in the main to qualify for BPR either (see below), unless the landlord contributes active management and services. In other words, it is necessary to show that the activity in question constitutes 'trading' and not 'a mere investment'. See the Special Commissioners' decisions in *Martin (Moore's Executors) v IRC* [1995] STC (SCD) 5 and *Burkinyoung (Burkinyoung's Executors) v IRC* [1995] STC (SCD) 29.

12.113 HMRC's original guidance on furnished holiday lettings indicated that BPR would normally be allowed if the lettings were short term (ie weekly or fortnightly) and there was substantial involvement with the holidaymakers both on and off the premises. This applied even if the lettings were for only part of the year. However, HMRC subsequently revised their guidance (IHTM25278), which now indicates that close attention will be given to the level and type of services, rather than who provided them.

The issue was highlighted following the initial unexpected First-tier Tribunal decision in the now much-publicised case of *Pawson (deceased) v Revenue & Customs* [2012] UKFTT 51 (TC). Its swift reversal in favour of HMRC on appeal (as discussed earlier (see **12.6**)) was perhaps to be expected, given the weakness of the case, but the summary analysis and judgment was so damning as severely to dampen optimism that BPR could ever be applied to furnished holiday lets. The position has been further damaged by the more recent case of *Green v Revenue & Customs* [2015] UKFTT 0236 (TC) (see **12.6**), which again made specific reference to the importance of and in this case the lack of 'extra services' so needed to support the reality of a trading business.

The case of *Farmer and another (executors of Farmer, dec'd) v IRC* is often quoted in support of claims to BPR where the landowner puts his land to mixed use. That case concerned an estate of over 400 acres, but there is little case law or HMRC direction which definitively confirms the smallest acreage that may qualify for BPR by applying the *Farmer* principles – perhaps that is not perceived as an issue, provided it constitutes a 'landed estate' and is managed as such.

12.114 Diversification within the same ownership to non-agricultural use (eg a golf course) will deny access to APR but may well attract BPR in its place such that all is not lost. As previously stated, in that circumstance there is no requirement to own such business property for two years in order to gain access to BPR, provided it was previously owned as qualifying agricultural property and the aggregate is at least two years.

In past times, it was common to create tenancies to achieve substantial tax savings by reason of the double discount namely the capital transfer tax agricultural property discount plus the reduction in value from open market vacant possession value. However, since 1 September 1995, there is little point as land let on new tenancies qualifies for APR at 100%. This situation is dependent on maintaining the current generous APR rate. Thus, if the 100% APR rate is reduced in the future, the double discount plan might revive.

12.115 In an era where vacant possession gives access to full 100% APR, the continuing grant of a tenancy is not generally advisable for IHT purposes. Instead of family-type tenancies, consider a partnership with vacant possession (or at least vacant possession within 12 or 24 months). Licensing arrangements that do not constitute leases or tenancies are also acceptable, for example for grazing, provided that vacant possession can be obtained within only 12 months. However, in this context it should be noted that ESC F17 (which extends the vacant possession period to 24 months) is restricted to 'tenanted' land and does not extend to land under licence.

The case of *Lubbock Fine & Co v Customs and Excise Commissioners* Case 6-63/92 [1994] STC 101 reinforces that surrenders of leases are exempt from VAT. However, it must be borne in mind that tenants who currently have security of tenure may be reluctant to agree to a surrender. Furthermore, the income tax and capital gains tax implications of retaining a tenancy should also be factored in as part of the overall review.

TENANT FARMERS

12.116

Focus

The more onerous seven-year landlord ownership rule can be replaced by the lesser two-year test where the underlying tenant later acquires the freehold. In such circumstances there is no requirement to restart the clock as the earlier tenancy period may count towards the two-year qualification.

A cash-rich tenant farmer perhaps should consider purchasing the freehold title in order to acquire exempt IHT assets thereby reducing his liquid estate not otherwise eligible for APR/BPR. This is because a tenant who has been in occupation as tenant for a minimum of two years prior to acquisition of the freehold will qualify for 100% APR immediately without a further waiting period.

Example 12.18 – Tenant purchase of freehold

Evan and Ifor are brothers who inherited farms from their father some years ago. Evan farmed until his health failed at which point he let his farm to Ifor, advising that he would be happy to sell any time it suited Ifor to buy. Ifor carried on farming.

Road widening in their Welsh Valley consumed part of Ifor's farm and provided a welcome cash payment of £300,000 into his bank account. This event, occurring shortly before his 75th birthday, provided some consolation not only for the loss of the land but also for the doctor's advice that for health reasons he should now cut back on his workload and perhaps give up the land he rented from his brother.

Ifor took advice from both his doctor and his lawyer. The former told him he had at most 18 months to live; the latter that he should buy the freehold of Evan's land nonetheless. He did, dying much sooner than predicted. No tax fell due on the value of Evan's land by reason of APR/BPR.

The arrangements for occupation of farmland are often informal, as was recognised when considering agistment in the Northern Ireland case of *McCall* (see **12.64**). Be aware that HMRC guidance urges Inspectors to call for evidence of the terms of occupation and, for example, to ask for substantive evidence that consideration has been given for occupation – such HMRC approach is now becoming increasingly routine in practice.

In real life, a landowner in later years may not be well enough to care for livestock or to manage crops and may enter into a quite genuine, but oral arrangement under which he retains occupation but another, whom he may have known all his life, carries out the necessary agricultural operations on their behalf. This practical and workable arrangement may cause problems through lack of formal evidence of that intention. What did the parties intend? Were they related? Was the consideration shown on the landowner's tax return? Informed practitioners should seek both to resolve and record the issues between the parties. Despite its failure on appeal the *Atkinson* case described at **12.111** might well have fallen at the first fence, but for the existence of a tenancy agreement.

FARMING COMPANIES

12.117 Farming companies (*IHTA 1984, s 122*) are at a clear disadvantage since 100% APR is only available if the transferor controls the company (but note the use of the related property rules in *IHTA 1984, s 161*, which may serve to preserve control in a spousal/civil partner scenario) – no relief is available to the minority shareholder.

Contrast this with BPR, where a 100% 'discount' is currently available whatever the size of the holding in an unquoted trading company. A holding in a farming company of 50% or less will be denied APR, but if it can be proved that the farm is a business, 100% BPR should be available to restore the status quo. Timing here is not critical, since control need exist only at the moment of transfer.

However, the company must fulfil the same requirements and minimum periods for APR as an individual. The shareholder transferor must (*IHTA 1984, s 123(1)*) have owned the shares for whichever of the two- or seven-year minimum periods is appropriate to that company.

Example 12.19 – Gift of farm or farming company shares?

On 10 October 2016, Angela, a widow whose late husband had fully utilised his nil rate band, gave her farm to her niece – that was a PET and thus was not tested for APR at that point. The farm consisted of a house worth £350,000 and 450 acres worth £5,000 per acre (ie £2,250,000) resulting in a total value of £2,600,000.

Assuming that 70% of the value of the farmhouse qualifies for APR, the part not so qualifying is £105,000 (£350,000 @ 30%). The agricultural value of the property given was therefore £2,495,000 ((£350,000 @ 70%) + £2,250,000). Angela had already used both her own nil rate band and her annual exemptions and prior to the gift she had occupied the farm and farmed it herself for 20 years.

The niece farmed the land until Angela's death on 10 February 2017, with the PET (which became a chargeable transfer with no tapering relief), of £105,000 attracting at 40% a tax charge of £42,000 payable over ten years by instalments. Interest (see *IHTA 1984, s 234(1)*) runs only from the due date of each instalment.

The wording of *FA 2009, Sch 53, para 7* is somewhat convoluted. It first appears to impose late interest charges from the due date for payment of an instalment on woodland (here meaning the timber, not the underlying land); or on business interests; but then excludes from the extra charge (see *FA 2009, Sch 53, para 7(4)* onwards) shares in a 'genuine' trading business, ie not one that fails the 'wholly or mainly' test. The legislation could have been more simply drafted to specify what does attract the charge rather than what does not. Farmland is excluded under *FA 2009, Sch 53, para 7(3)*.

If Angela had rolled over her farming business (including the land) into a company, A Ltd, a year before the transfer, that transfer of her shareholding to her niece, instead of the farm itself, would still qualify for relief if the niece kept the shares at least until Angela's death. The niece could add together the separate periods of occupation of both Angela and A Ltd. IHT would similarly be payable by instalments which, if paid on time, would carry no interest.

HABITAT SCHEMES

12.118 Land that is subject to habitat schemes, for the protection of the environment and preservation of the countryside, qualifies for APR even though the land is not 'occupied' for the purposes of agriculture (*IHTA 1984, s 124C*).

SPECIAL TYPES OF FARMING

Farm sharing

12.119 Farm sharing is very popular with those land investors who do not have the time or inclination to do any actual farming. The arrangement involves:

- a joint contractual venture between the owner of the farmland and the operator (who actually farms the land);
- provision by the owner of land, and sometimes fixed equipment and machinery;
- the supply by the operation of working machinery and labour;
- the purchase and supply by the owner of seed etc (but this is usually organised by the operator); and
- the sharing of gross outputs.

The outcome of that arrangement may be summarised as follows:

- there is no partnership established;
- the owner and operator have separate businesses;
- there is no landlord/tenant relationship;
- for IHT purposes 100% APR should be available on any farmland, though it is perhaps harder to secure a claim on the farmhouse.

Both parties should have vacant possession rights. In particular, the owner should be involved in policy-making decisions and exercise rights of inspection: this becomes particularly relevant in supporting the APR claim on the farmhouse, where it must be shown that the 'farmer' physically lives there.

HMRC appear to agree with some reluctance that farm-sharing arrangements qualify for capital gains tax reliefs such as rollover relief, and constitute trading as farmers for income tax purposes (*ITTOIA 2005, ss 9* and *859(1)* for income tax purposes, and *CTA 2009, s 36* for corporation tax).

Contract farming

12.120 It is also necessary to consider contract farming where the estate owner owns the farm but the actual farming activity is subcontracted out and usually to someone who is self-employed. In their guidance, HMRC state that contract farming may perhaps be better viewed as 'farming with contractors' (IHTM24082). Again, 100% APR should normally be available.

However, great care must be taken over the invoicing arrangements. Thus, for example, the purchase of seed and fertiliser should be done by the owner of the land. The same issue arises over the eligibility of the farmhouse, particularly in the light of *McKenna v HMRC*. HMRC's guidance states the following in relation to farmhouses:

> '... While the existence of a Share or Contract Farming agreement is unlikely to affect the availability of agricultural relief on the farmland, it may have an impact upon any the relief available on the farmhouse. This is a question of fact and degree to be decided in each case and may involve consideration of aspects such as:
>
> – The degree of financial risk for the deceased
> – The deceased's involvement in the day to day agricultural activity including the regularity and scope of any meetings with the share/ contract farmer
> – The deceased's involvement in decisions relating to the selection of crops, sowing, harvesting, sales, and so on ....'

The sale of grasskeep or agistment or (in Northern Ireland) conacre can give rise to special problems. Properly drafted, it was previously thought that such arrangements left the landowner in occupation of the land and thereby still engaged in the business of producing the agricultural crop (grass) to which the other party is entitled to take by means of grazing animals. However, this view has been challenged in light of case law – for a detailed review of the principles, see the decision of the Court of Appeal in *McCall and Keenan (personal representatives of McClean, dec'd) v Revenue and Customs Commissioners* [2009] NICA 12, considered in detail earlier in this chapter (see **12.4**).

SINGLE FARM PAYMENT SCHEME

12.121 The Basic Payment Scheme (formerly known as the Single Farm Payment Scheme) effectively separated farming subsidies from production. Entitlement potentially arises in the hands of farmers and non-farmers but is subject to various conditions and standards, such as keeping the land in good agricultural and environmental condition. A substantial payment of the entitlement in 2005 was expected to provide income support for the following eight years but, thereafter, anyone wishing to receive the subsidy could only do so through acquisition of an entitlement from someone entitled to receive it.

For IHT purposes, the entitlement is subject to the normal IHT rules concerning transfers of value and the death estate and thus the transfer of the entitlement may attract IHT as with any other asset. It is, though, a separate asset falling outside the definition of 'agricultural property' in *IHTA 1984, s 115(2)*, and cannot therefore qualify for APR, although BPR may be available. However, transfers of entitlement as an individual asset by non-traders (as opposed to a business or interest in a business) will not qualify for BPR.

'BUY AND SELL' AGREEMENTS/ARRANGEMENTS

12.122 APR and BPR (see **12.35**) are not available if the partners or company directors or shareholders have entered into a 'buy and sell' agreement under which, on the death of one of them before retirement, his personal representatives are obliged to sell and the others are obliged to buy his interest or his shares. Such an agreement, being more than a mere option, is regarded as a binding contract for sale within *IHTA 1984, s 124*.

However, in practice, an option arrangement can achieve the desired result without penalty. In theory cross-options (ie a put and call) are equivalent in substance to a binding contract for sale, on the grounds that the terms will be beneficial to one party or the other and thus a sale is inevitable, but the argument is seldom seen or tested in practice. If cross-options are used, they should be made successive in time and carry different exercise periods.

12.123 Automatic accrual arrangements between members of a partnership may seem similar to binding sale contracts, but IHTM25292 states:

> '… agreements under which the deceased's interest passes to the surviving partners, who are required to pay the personal representatives a particular price … do not constitute contracts for sale. So they do not prevent the interest from qualifying from business property relief by reason of *IHTA 1984, s 113*.'

WOODLANDS RELIEF

INTRODUCTION

12.124

> **Focus**
>
> Albeit descriptive, the use of the term 'relief' is misleading. Woodlands relief operates as a deferral mechanism and should not be confused with or regarded as full exemption akin to APR or BPR. Accordingly, it must be recognised that the deferred liability will spring back into charge at some later point.

Forestry used to be a very popular investment by reason of the favourable income tax treatment, but those advantages have been seriously eroded over time. Nevertheless, it is still seen as a good investment, especially for small 'amenity' parcels that might not qualify for APR or BPR.

The principal IHT relief provisions for woodlands are contained in *IHTA 1984, ss 125–130* and apply only to trees and underwood. Although the underlying land is excluded, its value will usually be relatively low and will be eligible for APR if occupied with, and ancillary to, agricultural land or pasture: see the detailed discussion of the need of cattle for shade in *Williams v HMRC* [2005] SSCD 782 (SpC 500).

The word 'woodland' is defined as a wood of sizeable area and to a significant extent covered by growing trees capable of being used as timber. Accordingly, a plantation of Christmas trees, which does not have the maturity, the height or the size to be useful as timber, and which resembles bushes rather than trees, does not constitute woodland (as discussed in *Jaggers v Ellis* [1997] STC 1417). The analysis in that case provides useful guidance on the meaning of woodland in the context of IHT legislation. Thus, a small remnant of ancient woodland (and known by that title), useful for walking a dog or for watching wildlife, whilst no doubt a delightful investment, is unlikely to qualify for relief because the timber is not felled but merely preserved. Furthermore, its value will be in the land rather than in the timber and, of course, it is only the latter which qualifies for the relief, as discussed below.

It should be noted that woodlands relief is potentially affected by changes introduced in *FA 2013*, where there is a liability attributable (directly or indirectly) to financing the acquisition of land, trees or underwood, or planting the trees or underwood, or maintaining or enhancing the value of the trees or underwood (*IHTA 1984, s 162B(5), (6)*).

The effect of the changes is that the liability must (as far as possible) reduce the value of the trees or underwood, so as to prevent the liability being secured against other assets on which no woodlands relief (or APR or BPR) is due.

NATURE OF RELIEF

12.125 IHT relief on death only is available if claimed by *notice in writing* within two years of death, or such longer period as HMRC will allow. It applies to woodlands other than agricultural property to which APR may attach. The value of the timber is left out of account at death but IHT may be payable on later disposal (*IHTA 1984, s 126*). In this way, it must be recognised that woodlands relief is a deferral mechanism and not a complete exemption.

The deferred IHT is eventually payable on a disposal in relation to the last death on which the timber passes and it is the person entitled to the sale proceeds, or who would be entitled if the disposal were a sale, who is liable for the tax (an inter-spouse/civil partner disposal is ignored). IHT is only charged on the first disposal of the trees or underwood following the death (*IHTA 1984, s 126(3)*).

IHT is calculated on the net sale proceeds or, if not a sale, on the net value at the date of disposal. Importantly, the tax rate scale is the one which would have applied if the chargeable value had been included in the estate in relation to the latest death on which it passes and represented the highest part of that estate (*IHTA 1984, s 128*). If the IHT charge crystallises after a reduction in the rates, the reduced rates apply (*IHTA 1984, Sch 2, para 4*).

12.126 Where the woodlands are being managed commercially (ie would have qualified for BPR), the amount on which IHT tax is charged under *IHTA 1984, s 126* is reduced by 100%. However, if there is a woodland postponement election under *IHTA 1984, ss 125–127* (see below), only 50% BPR will be available on a later sale.

Where woodland relief has been given on death, and the later disposal is also subject to IHT as a chargeable transfer, there will be two IHT computations – the first will relate to the earlier death and the second to the later chargeable transfer. However, the IHT relating to the first death may be deducted from the value of the chargeable transfer to arrive at the IHT liability on the latter (*IHTA 1984, s 129*). Since, by *IHTA 1984, s 3A(4)*, a PET made within seven years of death will fail and be treated as a chargeable transfer, it appears that the IHT on the earlier death may be deducted not only against lifetime chargeable transfers but also against those PETs that ultimately become chargeable.

CONDITIONS OF RELIEF

12.127 Relief is only available if the deceased held the land beneficially throughout the five years preceding his death, or acquired it otherwise than for money or money's worth. In tandem with APR, the restriction that the land must be situated in the UK was partly lifted with effect from 22 April 2009 (*FA 2009, s 122*). Under the post-*FA 2009* rules, land which is within the European Economic Area, Channel Islands and Isle of Man at the time of the transfer may qualify for the relief: see *IHTA 1984, s 115(5)(b)*.

Net values are after selling expenses and expenses of replanting within three years, or such longer period as the Board may allow (*IHTA 1984, s 130(2)*), except to the extent that these expenses are allowable for income tax (*IHTA 1984, s 130(1)(b)*).

Where the woodlands are being managed commercially and would qualify as relevant business property for BPR under *IHTA 1984, ss 103–114*, the amount on which IHT is charged is reduced by 100%, as was noted above. However, if there is an election under *IHTA 1984, ss 125–127* to leave the value of the woodlands out of account in determining the value of the estate on death, only 50% BPR will be available on an eventual sale (*IHTA 1984, s 127(2)*).

Obviously, if at all possible, it is sensible for the owners of woodland to endeavour to manage the woodlands in a commercial and active manner in order to preserve access to the more valuable 100% BPR. To assist this treatment, separate accounts should be kept in relation to the woodlands and these accounts should not be included in the overall farming accounts.

Example 12.20 – Woodlands relief claim

Hawker died on 30 September 1991 and left the following estate, there having been no lifetime transfers:

	£
Sundry assets	285,000
Value of timber	80,000
Total	365,000

Before claiming woodland relief, IHT on death would have been charged on £225,000, after deducting the then nil rate band of £140,000, ie £90,000 ((£365,000 – £140,000) @ 40%); but, on the basis that Hawker's executors made the claim, IHT on death would have been actually charged on £145,000 (£285,000 – £140,000), resulting in a reduced IHT liability of £58,000.

On 1 May 2017, the timber was sold for £200,000 (on which 50% BPR is due), after allowing for selling and replanting expenses, so that IHT is payable on:

	£	£
Value of timber (net of BPR @ 50%)	100,000	
Other assets at death	285,000	
	385,000	
IHT payable (at current rates)		
First £325,000 @ 0%		Nil
Next £60,000 @ 40%		24,000
Less: Payable (current rates) on estate of £285,000 on death		Nil
Payable on sale of timber		24,000

If no claim to woodland relief had been made but instead BPR had been claimed at 50% (ie the rate in force prior to 9 March 1992), on £80,000, then IHT on death prior to 9 March 1992 would have been on an estate of £325,000:

First	£140,000	Nil
Next	£185,000 @ 40%	£74,000
Total		£74,000

Time limits do apply to claims in connection with woodland relief. The time limit for claiming CGT holdover relief (which may in turn depend on the availability of IHT woodland relief) was reduced to four years in respect of claims made on or after 1 April 2010.

TRANSFERS OF WOODLANDS SUBJECT TO A DEFERRED ESTATE DUTY CHARGE

12.128 Under the estate duty regime, duty on a death on woodlands could be deferred until the heir felled or sold the timber. If the heir died before the timber was sold, estate duty on his death replaced the earlier deferred charge and could itself again be deferred. Under *FA 1986, Sch 19, para 46* any transfer which includes woodlands subject to a deferred estate duty charge is denied PET treatment so that there is an immediate lifetime chargeable transfer and the deferred estate duty is treated as discharged.

The problem with that, taken literally, would be that any single large transfer which included some small part of woodlands subject to deferred estate duty would be refused PET treatment. Extra-statutory Concession F15 restricts the denial of PET treatment only to such part of the transfer as consists of the woodlands subject to the deferred estate duty. Thus, there is an immediate IHT charge on the woodlands subject to the deferred estate duty, but the remaining part of the transfer constitutes a PET.

Chapter 13

Private residence relief

Jackie Anderson LLB, ACA, CTA, LHA Consulting Ltd

SIGNPOSTS

- **Introduction** – Private residence relief, available on the disposal of a taxpayer's main residence, is an extremely valuable relief which generates ongoing case law and legislative developments, and plenty of planning opportunities and pitfalls too (see **13.1–13.4**).
- **What constitutes a residence?** – 'Dwelling house' and 'residence' are not defined in the legislation, so guidance must be taken from the decided cases. The nature of the property, the 'curtilage', the quality of occupation, and the 'permitted area' are all factors which need to be considered in this context (see **13.5–13.9**).
- **Other uses of a residence** – The impact on private residence relief of other property uses – for business purposes, as a property let, for adult care and dependent relatives, and in relation to employer purchases – also need to be considered (see **13.10–13.17**).
- **Periods of occupation** – In determining periods of occupation for the purposes of private residence relief, there are provisions covering a delay in taking up occupation, deemed occupation (for the final few months), periods of absence due to work, and job-related occupation (see **13.18–13.22**).
- **Two or more residences** – There are provisions for the taxpayer to nominate (or 'elect' for) one of two or more properties to be regarded as their 'main residence', and to vary the notice (see **13.23–13.28**).
- **Trusts and estates** – Private residence relief may be claimed by trustees – of interest in possession and discretionary trusts – and by personal representatives (see **13.29–13.33**).
- **Marriage, separation and divorce** – Spouses and civil partners (living together) can only have one main residence for private residence relief purposes, with the facility to make an election where they own more than one residence between them. Transfers

of property, separation and divorce also need to be considered in this context (see **13.34–13.40**).

- **Administration** – Private residence relief is automatic and does not require a claim, with disclosure in the taxpayer's tax return only required in certain circumstances. Proper documentation, however, should always be kept where HMRC might contest the nature of the taxpayer's residence at a property (see **13.41–13.43**).
- **Planning opportunities and pitfalls** – The potentially significant value of private residence relief means that consideration needs to be given to the planning opportunities and pitfalls, particularly in relation to the main residence election, and the development and sale of land (see **13.44–13.49**).

INTRODUCTION

13.1 The relief from capital gains tax (CGT) on any profit arising on the disposal of the taxpayer's main private residence, commonly known as 'private residence relief', is an extremely valuable relief for homeowners in the UK (although many won't be aware of it as they will simply assume that they can profitably sell their family home without a tax charge arising!).

The corollary of CGT relief for a gain is, of course, that private residence relief prevents the taxpayer from claiming tax relief for any capital loss incurred on the disposal of their main private residence.

Key features of private residence relief

13.2 Private residence relief (*TCGA 1992, ss 222–226B*) is available where the taxpayer meets all of the following conditions:

- the 'dwelling house' has been their 'only or main residence' (see **13.5–13.8**) throughout their 'period of ownership';
- the 'garden or grounds' (including the buildings on them) are not greater than the 'permitted area' (see **13.9**);
- no part of the home has been used exclusively for 'business purposes' during their period of ownership (see **13.11**);
- they have not been absent, other than for an allowed period of absence or because they have been living in 'job-related accommodation', during their 'period of ownership' (see **13.18–13.22**).

Whilst let properties do not generally qualify for private residence relief – as a let property cannot also be the taxpayer's main residence at the same time – there is a form of relief where the taxpayer lets their main residence (see **13.14**).

Planning aspects of private residence relief

13.3 Private residence relief commonly provides planning opportunities and pitfalls in relation to the following areas:

- main residence elections (see **13.44**);
- development of land – in particular:
  - trading transactions (see **13.45**);
  - intention to reside (see **13.46**);
  - surplus land (see **13.47**);
  - residual building plot (see **13.48**); and
  - enhancing the value of the property (see **13.49**).

Recent developments

13.4 Some recent case law and legislation developments in relation to private residence relief include the following:

- A new charge of non-resident capital gains tax (NRCGT) applies from 6 April 2015 to gains made on the disposal of UK residential property owned by non-resident taxpayers. Non-resident individuals may be eligible to claim private residence relief for their UK property in certain circumstances (see **13.24**).
- The *Finance Act 2014* reduced the deemed period of occupation for taxpayers who have been resident in their dwelling house at some point in their period of ownership from 36 months to the last 18 months for properties disposed of after 5 April 2014 (see **13.20**).
- In *Hartland v Commissioners for Revenue and Customs* [2014] UKFTT 1099 (TC), the intention of the taxpayer to reside in the property was helpfully considered and was proved to be sufficient in relation to one property, but not in relation to a second property (see **13.8**).
- The case of *Wagstaff and another v HMRC* [2014] UKFTT 43 (TC) confirmed that a right to occupy the property under the inferred intention to create a trust could create an entitlement to private residence relief (see **13.31**).
- The First-tier Tribunal ruled that the quality of occupation had an insufficient degree of permanence, continuity or expectation of continuity

to justify describing that occupation as 'residence' in *Iles & Kaltsas v HMRC* [2014] UKFTT 436 (TC) (see **13.8**).

- In *John Arthur Day and Amanda Jane Dalgety v HMRC* [2015] UKFTT 139 (TC), the First-tier Tribunal similarly confirmed that private residence relief was not due where the taxpayer had no intention of occupying the property as his main residence (see **13.8**).
- The recent case of *Oates v Revenue & Customs* [2014] UKUT 409 (LC) considered the 'just and reasonable' apportionment of sales proceeds between a house and land for the purposes of private residence relief (see **13.13**).
- The case of *Fountain v HMRC* [2015] UKFTT 419 (TC) decided that, whilst it is possible for a garden detached from a residence to be covered by a private residence claim, in this case the taxpayer had not provided any evidence in support of this contention (see **13.9**).
- The nature and quality of the taxpayer's residence, for private residence relief purposes, was considered by the First-tier Tribunal in the recent cases of *Richard James Dutton-Forshaw v HMRC* [2015] UKFTT 478 (TC) and *Kothari v HMRC* [2016] UKFTT 127 (TC) (see **13.8**).
- A recent development which further enhances the value of private residence claims arises from the Autumn Statement 2015 proposal, from April 2019, for CGT due on the sale of residential property to be paid within 30 days of completion – except where there is no CGT liability due to private residence relief.
- The recent case of *Desmond Higgins v HMRC* [2017] UKFTT 236 (TC) demonstrated that the period of ownership for private residence relief purposes began and ended with the dates of the contracts to acquire and sell the property (see **13.19**).
- In *Paul Munford v Revenue and Customs Commissioners* [2017] UKFTT 19 (TC), the burden of proof as to whether the property had been occupied as his main residence fell on HMRC, which they could not discharge (see **13.8**).
- *Oliver v Revenue and Customs Commissioners* [2016] UKFTT 796 (TC) considered the quality of the taxpayer's 'residence', concluding that there was no indication of an intention to permanently reside (see **13.8**).

WHAT CONSTITUTES A RESIDENCE?

'Dwelling-house' and 'residence'

13.5 Private residence relief is provided by *TCGA 1992, s 223* which states that: 'No part of a gain to which section 222 applies shall be a chargeable gain if the dwelling-house or part of a dwelling-house has been the individual's only or main residence throughout the period of ownership …'.

> **Focus**
>
> The legislation does not define 'dwelling house', 'residence' nor 'only or main residence', so guidance must be taken from the decided cases. HMRC's views on what constitutes a 'dwelling house' (at CG64230–CG64328) and 'only or main residence' (at CG64420–CG64555) should also be considered.

There are three key issues to consider as to what constitutes a 'dwelling house', a 'residence' and the 'only or main residence' in this context:

- the nature of the property (see **13.6**);
- the 'curtilage' (see **13.7**) and 'permitted area' (see **13.9**);
- the quality of occupation (see **13.8**).

The nature of the property

13.6 A 'dwelling house' can include a house or a flat, and certain other structures not commonly regarded as dwelling houses – for example, rooms within a factory or hotel (CG64320).

There must be an element of permanence, hence a mobile caravan does not qualify for relief (*Moore v Thompson* 61 TC 15) – but may be exempt from CGT as a tangible moveable wasting asset anyway – but a static one connected to the mains services may qualify (*Makins v Elson* 51 TC 437). Similar principles would apply to yachts and houseboats, etc.

The 'curtilage'

13.7 Private residence relief can extend to other properties within the 'curtilage' of the house (CG64245). The 'curtilage' is a legal concept which helps to define the extent of the dwelling house, and whether it includes outbuildings, etc. The curtilage is the house, not the grounds, but can include any unconnected buildings that have a residential purpose and obviously 'go with' the house.

Case law has established two principal tests to determine whether a separate building qualifies with the main part of the dwelling, namely:

- The building must be used in conjunction with the enjoyment of the main dwelling to form part of one residence. Thus a cottage to house a caretaker and another for a gardener were held to be occupied for the benefit of the main house and so formed part of the main residence (*Batey (Inspector of Taxes) v Wakefield* [1981] STC 521).

- The building must be adjacent or at least quite close to the main house. For this reason, a cottage on the opposite side of a large estate to the main house (175 metres away) was considered not to be part of the main residence (*Lewis (Inspector of Taxes) v Rook* [1992] STC 171). Whereas in *Batey v Wakefield,* a cottage built for the caretaker which was separated from the main house by a narrow strip of land was eligible for relief.

The quality of occupation

13.8 Occupation of the dwelling house is a key factor which turns a house into a home, and thus a 'residence' for relief purposes. There are many cases which concern the redevelopment of a property, or the temporary occupation of a property.

Private residence relief was denied in *Goodwin v Curtis (Inspector of Taxes)* [1996] STC 1146 where a director purchased a newly developed farmhouse from his company for his own use. He took up occupation and had the services and telephone connected. The property was offered for sale within a matter of days, and soon after contracts were exchanged to sell the property at a very substantial profit. There was little evidence that he intended to make the property his permanent home – he lived in the property for only five weeks. It was held that it was necessary for the occupation to have 'some degree of permanence, some degree of continuity or some expectation of continuity'.

In this context, the following facts will be relevant to indicate where the taxpayer resides:

- where he is registered to vote;
- where the children of the family go to school;
- where the family spends most of its time;
- the correspondence address for bank accounts, credit cards, etc;
- where his main place of work is;
- where he is registered with a doctor or dentist;
- where the individual's car is registered and insured; and
- which property is the main address for council tax.

The quality of the occupation was examined in *Harte v HMRC* [2012] UKFTT 258 (TC). The Hartes inherited the property which was close to their own home. They elected for the property to be treated as their main residence for a short period before sale, but this claim was rejected on the basis that the taxpayers did not demonstrate any degree of permanence or expectation of continuance and, in particular, did not:

- take any personal possessions to the property;
- acquire a TV licence at the property;
- have a computer or internet connection at the property;
- entertain there or have anyone to stay; or
- change the name on the bills from 'occupier'.

In the cases of *Anthony Metcalf* [2010] TC753, *Malcolm Springthorpe* [2010] TC 832 and *Alison Clarke v HMRC* [2014] TC4062, the courts referred to the low level of power consumption in electricity bills in concluding that there was insufficient occupation to be eligible for the exemption.

In the recent case of *Hartland v Commissioners for Revenue and Customs* [2014] UKFTT 1099 (TC), the taxpayer contested HMRC's refusal to allow the appellant's claim for CGT private residence relief under *TCGA 1992, s 222* in relation to two properties. Private residence relief was allowed for *Primrose Cottage* – despite quite extensive works being undertaken – supported by the facts that the property was used as the appellant's correspondence address, he paid for energy supplies, the building and its contents were insured and the cottage contained furniture. However, relief was denied for *Grey Cottage*, where the First-tier Tribunal was satisfied that the acquisition, demolition, rebuilding and sale were undertaken in the course of a property development trade. The property was not fit for family occupation when the appellant purchased it, and there was no evidence he ever lived there. It was sold almost as soon as it had been rebuilt, and the appellant's mortgage application for the property described him as a self-employed builder with an income well over double that declared on his tax return for the relevant year. A different address was used on his mortgage application and no letter or other communication addressed to the appellant at *Grey Cottage* was produced.

And, in *Iles & Kaltsas v HMRC* [2014] UKFTT 436 (TC), the First-tier Tribunal examined the intention of the taxpayer to make the property a permanent or long-term home, as opposed to a temporary residence. The taxpayers occupied a small flat for 24 days after it had been let for some time and just prior to its sale. The Tribunal ruled that the quality of occupation had an insufficient degree of permanence, continuity or expectation of continuity to justify describing that occupation as 'residence'.

However, in *David Morgan v HMRC* [2013] UKFTT 181 (TC), the taxpayer bought a property to occupy with his fiancée, but she broke off the engagement.

Mr Morgan occupied the property for only 10 weeks before it was let. The Tribunal decided that he had intended the property to be his home, and accepted the private residence relief claim.

Whereas in *John Arthur Day and Amanda Jane Dalgety v HMRC* [2015] UKFTT 139 (TC), the First-tier Tribunal confirmed that private residence relief was not due where the tax payer had not occupied the property, and whilst he might have had a row with his partner, they had not split permanently and he had no intention of occupying the property as his main residence.

In *Richard James Dutton-Forshaw v HMRC* [2015] UKFTT 478 (TC), the property in question was only occupied by the taxpayer for two months out of a total ownership period of 44 months, but still judged to be the taxpayer's only residence as he had no other residence during that two-month period.

In the recent First-tier Tribunal case of *Kothari v HMRC* [2016] UKFTT 127 (TC), the decision went against the taxpayer on the basis that his six-month period of occupation did not have a sufficient degree of permanence or continuity, as he put the property on the market just one month after moving in.

In *Paul Munford v Revenue and Customs Commissioners* [2017] UKFTT 19 (TC), HMRC challenged a private residence relief claim, but because a discovery assessment was made outside the normal time limits, the burden of proof as to whether the property had been occupied as his main residence moved from the taxpayer to HMRC, and HMRC could not discharge that burden.

Oliver v Revenue and Customs Commissioners [2016] UKFTT 796 (TC) was another case in which the taxpayer's quality of 'residence' was considered. Here, although the taxpayer may have stayed at the property, there was no indication of an intention to permanently reside there – including no telephone or internet connection.

The 'permitted area'

13.9 The CGT relief for the gain on a taxpayer's main residence extends to 'land which he has for his own occupation and enjoyment with that residence as its garden or grounds up to the permitted area' (*TCGA 1992, s 222(1)(b)*) (CG64800 *et seq*).

The permitted area is defined as being an up to 0.5 of a hectare (including the house), and being the part of the grounds that is 'the most suitable for occupation and enjoyment with the residence'.

TCGA 1992, s 222(3) states that a larger area may be recognised where it is 'required for the reasonable enjoyment … having regard to the size and character of the dwelling-house'. This is a stricter test than for areas of less than 0.5 of a hectare where it is sufficient to show that the land was part of the garden or grounds of the house.

Land that is physically separated from the house by a road, fence or other houses, can qualify for exemption; HMRC recognise that cottage gardens may lie across the village street (CG64367).

It is not sufficient for this purpose that the property owner has his or her own special requirements. For instance, an individual may use extra grounds to keep horses or vintage cars. That does not mean that area is necessary for the reasonable enjoyment of the property, as other occupiers may not have this requirement (*Longson v Baker (Inspector of Taxes)* [2001] STC 6).

The case of *Fountain v HMRC* [2015] UKFTT 419 (TC) decided that, whilst it is possible for a garden detached from a residence to be covered by a private residence claim, in this case the taxpayer had not provided any evidence in support of this contention. He had built a new property which was then sold, with private residence relief being claimed on the sale of a separate plot which the taxpayer argued was the garden of the sold property.

OTHER USES OF A RESIDENCE

13.10 Full private residence relief will completely eliminate any chargeable gain arising on the sale of the taxpayer's 'dwelling house'. However, relief may be restricted, and the chargeable gain apportioned according to qualifying and non-qualifying elements of the gain, where there are 'other' uses.

Focus

The main 'other' uses of a residence to be considered in this context are:

- business purposes (**13.11**);
- property lets (**13.14**);
- adult care (**13.15**);
- dependent relatives (**13.16**); and
- employer purchases (**13.17**).

Note that, where an individual lets out a room under the 'rent-a-room' scheme (where a lodger shares the house), private residence relief is still available for the whole house (including the room let out).

Business purposes

13.11 Private residence relief is available in respect of the entirety of a dwelling house or of a part only. However, a separate apportionment is recognised by *TCGA 1992, s 224(1)* for dwelling houses or parts of dwelling houses which are exclusively used for a trade, business, profession or vocation (CG64660). This will be the case where a person works from home and either has an annex or outbuilding designated as an office, or has a room within his property which is exclusively used for office work.

Example 13.1 – Property partly used for business

Alice lives in a small house from which she runs a business. She also owns a small row of lock-up garages adjoining her home. Alice uses one garage for her domestic car, one for her delivery van, one for the stock of finished goods, and she lets the remainder. She uses the dining room to make curtains, but there is just enough room to have family meals in there as well.

On disposal of the house and the garages at a gain, Alice must apportion the gain between the different parts of the property. The garages that were let are a simple investment and taxable as such, with no relief under *TCGA 1992, s 222*. The garages used for the storage of stock and to house the delivery van have been used exclusively for the business and not for any domestic purpose, and are therefore also outside the scope of *TCGA 1992, s 222*.

The remainder of the property qualifies for private residence relief, even though Alice may have claimed a proportion of the costs of services etc against her business profits. There is only one dining room and the family spends considerable time in there; it is not used exclusively for the business. The garage for the family car is not used for business.

Alice would need to agree a reasonable apportionment of the gain with HMRC between the qualifying and non-qualifying elements.

'Just and reasonable' apportionments

13.12 As indicated at **13.11**, an apportionment is required for the purposes of establishing private residence relief if there is 'mixed' (ie residential and exclusively trade or business use) of the dwelling house. In certain circumstances (eg a change of use), the relief is adjusted on a 'just and reasonable' basis (*TCGA 1992, s 224(2)*).

A 'just and reasonable' approach may also be necessary (under *TCGA 1992, s 52(4)*) if, for example, an individual's only or main residence forms part of a larger disposal of land, some of which does not constitute the residence. In such cases, the sale proceeds may need to be apportioned to determine the amount attributable to the residence for private residence relief purposes.

13.13 In *Oates v Revenue & Customs* [2014] UKUT 409 (LC), the taxpayers sold a house with adjoining land for development. HMRC issued a determination to the taxpayers, apportioning the sale proceeds of £725,000 as to £170,000 for the house and £555,000 for the land. The taxpayers appealed, on the grounds that the correct apportionment should be £325,000 for the house and £400,000 for the land.

The Upper Tribunal (Lands Chamber) noted that the Valuation Office Agency's (VOA's) Capital Gains and Other Taxes Manual (at para 8.61; see http://app.voa.gov.uk/corporate/publications/Manuals/CapitalGainsTaxManual/sect8/b-cgt-man-s8.html#P75_1171) used a formulaic approach to find constituent values for apportionment purposes. Whilst finding the formula in the VOA manual to be 'less than satisfactory', the Tribunal decided to adopt it. The Tribunal concluded that a 'just and reasonable' apportionment of the sale proceeds was £325,000 for the house and £400,000 for the adjoining land. The taxpayers' appeals were therefore allowed.

Property lets

13.14 Let properties do not qualify for private residence relief as a let property cannot also be the taxpayer's main residence at the same time. However, there is a specific relief in *TGCA 1992, s 223(4)* which can apply where a person lets all or part of his own home, either while he also occupies the property (see **Example 13.2**), or during another period of the ownership when the property is fully let (see **Example 13.3**). (See CG64700 *et seq.*)

The tax relief is limited to the lowest of the following amounts:

- the part of the gain which is exempt because it was used as the taxpayer's main home;
- the gain attributed to the let period; and
- £40,000 per owner.

Example 13.2 – Letting part of the home

Henry bought an urban terraced property for £480,000 of which 25% is represented by the value of accommodation in the basement that could be occupied separately; the remainder relates to the ground floor and upper floor. He lives there, allowing a lodger to occupy the basement, and later sells the entire property for £660,000.

There is valuation evidence that the basement flat is still worth 25% of the whole.

The gain from the upper 75% of the property of £135,000 (75% × 180,000) is exempt under *TCGA 1992, s 222*. The gain on the basement is £45,000, of which £40,000 is exempt under *TCGA 1992, s 223(4)(b)* (being the lowest figure of £135,000, £45,000 and £40,000).

Example 13.3 – Letting the second home

Jane bought her cottage in Dorset on 1 June 2000 and owned it for exactly 14 years. She occupied it as her sole residence for the first three months, let it for eight years, and used it as a second home for the remainder of the period. The gain is £280,000 or £20,000 per year of ownership.

The taxable gain of £210,000 is calculated by reducing the capital gain of £280,000 before tax relief by £35,000 (being the main home exemption for 3 months, plus the last 18 months of ownership – £280,000 × 21/168 months – see **13.18**) and a further £35,000 (being the relief for letting restricted to lowest of (i) the gain exempt because it was used as the taxpayer's main home – £35,000, (ii) the gain attributed to the let period – £160,000 (8 months × £20,000), and (iii) £40,000).

Adult care

13.15 Under the adult placement scheme, a carer provides accommodation for the adult who needs care in the carer's home, and the carer is regarded as carrying on a caring business from that property. The adult who needs care will normally require exclusive use of part of the property. Where these circumstances apply, the exclusive use of the property for the caring business is disregarded for the purposes of the relief for disposals made on or after 9 December 2009 (*TCGA 1992, s 225D*) (CG64695).

Dependent relatives

13.16 Property owned by a taxpayer and occupied rent-free by a dependent relative on or before 5 April 1988 is treated as if it had been the only or main residence of the taxpayer (regardless of the fact that the taxpayer may have had another residence qualifying for relief) for as long as the dependent relative lived there (*TCGA 1992, s 226*) (CG65550).

Employer purchases

13.17 As part of an employment relocation, the employer may agree to buy the employee's home, thereby providing the employee with the capital to purchase a new home in the new area. In some cases, the employer (or a company acting on behalf of the employer) and employee enter a 'home purchase agreement', under which they agree to share any profit made on the disposal of the old home when it is eventually sold to a third party. In this situation, CGT relief is given to the employee on his share of the profit under that agreement (*TCGA 1992, s 225C*).

PERIODS OF OCCUPATION

13.18 To benefit from the relief in *TCGA 1992, s 222*, the dwelling house must be the taxpayer's only or main residence throughout the period of ownership. Otherwise, subject to the concessions and reliefs discussed below, some apportionment of the gain may be required between different periods of ownership.

Delay in taking up occupation

13.19 HMRC will, under concession ESC D49, ignore a short delay in taking up occupation, when considering whether *TCGA 1992, s 222* relief applies to the full gain on disposal of the property. For example, delays might arise where the taxpayer has acquired land and is having a house built on the land, or where the taxpayer has acquired a property but alterations and decorations are being carried out before the taxpayer occupies that property.

Provided that the delay is no more than one year, this period of non-residence is treated as if it were a period of residence (provided that the taxpayer moves in within that time). If a taxpayer needs more than one year, he may have a second year if there are good reasons for delay.

In *Henke v HMRC* [2006] SSCD 561, a married couple purchased land in 1982 with planning permission for the construction of a house, which commenced in December 1991. The couple took up residence in the house in June 1993. The Special Commissioner held (among other things) that the 'throughout the period of ownership' condition (in *TCGA 1992, s 223(1)*) was not met. An apportionment was therefore required (under *TCGA 1992, s 223(2)*), limiting private residence relief to the period of ownership from the first occupation of the house as the taxpayers' private residence in 1993.

The recent case of *Desmond Higgins v HMRC* [2017] UKFTT 236 (TC) considered the impact of a delay in taking up residence of a new flat which was being built. The First-Tier Tribunal decided that the period of ownership for private residence relief purposes began when the purchase had been physically and legally completed, and when the taxpayer had the right to occupy.

Deemed occupation

13.20 Homeowners may experience significant delays in finding purchasers, whilst personal circumstances compel them to move into a new residence before disposing of the old. *TCGA 1992, s 223(2)(a)* provides that if the taxpayer has been resident in the dwelling house at some point in his period of ownership, the last 18 months of ownership will qualify to be treated as a period of occupation as the main residence 'in any event'.

For properties disposed of before 6 April 2014, this deemed period of occupation was 36 months. This period was reduced to 18 months by *Finance Act 2014, s 58*.

Apart from that deemed period of occupation, the basic rule is that private residence relief is calculated on a time-apportionment basis and is allowed in respect of periods of occupation but not of periods of absence.

Since the last 18 months of ownership of a main residence will always qualify for exemption, even if it has not been occupied as such in that period, two properties may qualify at the same time.

Finance Act 2014, s 58 also introduces a new *TCGA 1992, s 225E*, to provide for a 36-month final exempt period where the disposer or their spouse is a disabled person or is a long-term (three months) resident in a care home. The additional period only applies where the disposer or their spouse have a single private residence relief, and does not extend the period for those with more than one home.

'Sandwich' reliefs

13.21 A person may be unable to continue to live at a property throughout his period of ownership but, if the dwelling house was the only or main residence of the taxpayer both before and after the period of absence, the following periods of absence can be deemed to be periods of occupation under *TCGA 1992, s 223(3)*:

- any length of time during all of which the taxpayer worked outside the UK;
- a period, up to four years, or periods together not exceeding four years, during which the taxpayer could not live at the residence because of

where he was working or as a result of any condition imposed by his employer that required him to live elsewhere;

- any other period of absence up to three years, or periods together not exceeding three years.

Example 13.4 – Periods of absence

Hosking buys a house in July 1999 for £180,000. After living there for three years, in July 2002 he and his family are sent abroad by his employer.

On his return in July 2016, it was valued at £600,000.

Hosking sold the house in August 2016, without resuming occupation. The CGT position in 2016/17 would be:

		£
Sale proceeds		600,000
Cost – July 1999		(180,000)
Total gain		420,000
Exempt		
Occupation as main residence	36 months	
Last 18 months	18 months	
	54 months	
Total ownership	204 months	
Exempt 54/204 × £420,000		(111,176)
Gain before annual exemption		308,824
Annual exemption – 2016/17		(11,100)
Chargeable gain		297,724
Tax at 28%		83,363

If Hosking had resumed ownership for a short period, the entire gain would have been exempt.

Job-related accommodation

13.22 If a property or part of it has been purchased with the intention that it should eventually be a residence, but the owner for the time being lives in job-related accommodation, the owner is deemed to occupy the property. It does not matter that the house is never, in fact, occupied, provided that the intention to occupy can be proved (CG64555).

Accommodation is job-related where a person or his spouse or civil partner has some kind of employment that meets the following conditions (*TCGA 1992, s 222(8A)(a)*):

- it is necessary for the proper performance of the work to live in specific accommodation;
- it is provided by the employer for the better performance by the employee of his duties and it is customary in that trade or employment to provide living accommodation for employees; or
- it is provided as part of special security arrangements, as there is a special threat to the security of the employee.

Where the taxpayer, his spouse or civil partner is self-employed, two conditions must be satisfied (*TCGA 1992, s 222(8A)(b)*):

- the worker is required as part of the contract to carry on the work on premises that are provided by another person (who may, but need not, be the other party to the contract); and
- it is a term of the contract that the contractor should live on those premises or on some other premises provided by the other party to the contract.

TWO OR MORE RESIDENCES

Nomination of a property as the main residence

13.23 Where the taxpayer has two or more residences, they may nominate, by notice (or 'election') to HMRC which of those residences is to be treated as his main residence for the purposes of private residence relief (*TCGA 1992, s 222(5)(a)*).

The election must be made within two years of the date on which the second or subsequent residence became available. (Note that it is not the date of acquisition of a second or subsequent property which triggers the need for this notice, but the date the second property is first used as a residence (CG64495).)

> **Focus**
>
> The taxpayer does not have to nominate the property which has the greatest use as a residence (being the one which is factually his main residence). The nomination can apply to any property which is actually a residence (CG64485).

If no action is taken by the taxpayer to nominate a residence as the main residence, the question of which property is the main residence is one of fact (CG64575).

Example 13.5 – Main residence elections

Renee has several houses outside the UK in which she spends five months of the year, with the rest of the time in the UK. On 1 September 2010 she acquires a London flat and makes a main residence election in respect of it. On 31 January 2011, she acquires a country house in Surrey and makes a main residence election in respect of that instead. On 1 September 2012 she decides to acquire a Scottish estate as many of her friends enjoy countryside pursuits. She makes a main residence election in respect of the Scottish property. She divides the seven months she spends in the UK between her various residences, spending the week in London and the weekend in her Surrey home and holidays in Scotland. Hence, all of them are occupied as a residence.

Dissatisfied with the London flat, she sells it in August 2013 and buys a larger house in Chelsea, again making a main residence election in respect of that property. Shortly afterwards, fed up with the British weather, she sells the Surrey home and purchases a property in the south of France instead. However, she does not make a main residence election in respect of the French property. By September 2015, she decides that she prefers France and sells all her properties in the UK.

All of Renee's UK properties have been nominated as her main home for some period, so the last 36 months of ownership of each property, or 18 months for properties sold after 5 April 2014, will qualify for the CGT exemption.

Non-resident capital gains tax

13.24 The *Finance Act 2015* introduced a new charge of non-resident capital gains tax (NRCGT) from 6 April 2015 which applies to gains made on the disposal of UK residential property owned by non-resident taxpayers. Where a loss arises on a disposal potentially subject to NRCGT, that loss can only be set against gains arising on disposals of other UK residential property.

For further commentary on the NRCGT provisions, see **9.73–9.78**.

13.25 Non-resident individuals may be eligible to claim private residence relief for their UK property, but only in relation to qualifying tax years in which:

- the taxpayer (or spouse or civil partner) satisfies a residence requirement for these purposes; or

- the taxpayer satisfies a 'day count' test (within *TCGA 1992, s 222C*), ie broadly by spending at least 90 days in the property in the tax year (or 90 days spread across all the properties the person owns in the country where the property is located). This day count test is adjusted in respect of 'partial tax years' (ie where only part of a tax year falls within the individual's period of ownership).

If neither of the above conditions is satisfied, the tax year broadly falls to be treated as a 'non-qualifying tax year'. The dwelling house is treated as not having been occupied as the individual's residence at any time within that tax year (or a 'non-qualifying partial tax year'). This rule does not apply for tax years before 2015/16, except in the case of NRCGT disposals (*TCGA 1992, s 222B*).

Note that UK residents who want to nominate a property located in another country (where they are not tax-resident) as their main home, will have to meet the 90-day requirement for that overseas property from 2015/16 onwards.

13.26 Where an individual disposes of a dwelling house that was occupied as a residence at any time during their period of ownership, and it is a NRCGT disposal (within *TCGA 1992, s 14B*), an election is available to nominate which of two or more residences (one of which was the dwelling house) was their main residence for any period within its ownership period.

The election must be given in the NRCGT return in respect of the relevant disposal, and cannot subsequently be varied (*TCGA 1992, s 222A*).

Varying the notice

13.27 The taxpayer may vary a notice given under *TCGA 1992, s 222(5)(a)* by giving further notice to HMRC. The statute does not require any minimum period during which a person must reside at a property in order to claim relief. However, the quality of occupation in the nominated property must be such as to constitute 'residence'. The nomination may be varied to apply to a second home for very short period, even a few days, which will give that second home a CGT exemption for gain arising in respect of the last 36 or 18 months of ownership (CG64510) (see **13.20**).

Focus

It is essential to file the notice under *TCGA 1992, s 222(5)* within the set two-year period and to submit any variation of that notice within the same time period.

Licence or tenancy

13.28 It was originally thought that any residence could trigger the need for an election under *TCGA 1992, s 222(5)* but, since October 1994, HMRC interpret *TCGA 1992, s 222(5)* purposively so that it is not appropriate to consider notice of election where the second residence is merely occupied under licence and the taxpayer has neither a legal nor an equitable interest in it (CG64536).

TRUSTS AND ESTATES

Trusts

13.29 Where a beneficiary occupies a trust property under the terms of the trust as their main residence, then on a disposal private residence relief should be available where the trustees make a claim in accordance with *TCGA 1992, s 225*.

13.30 Most trusts are created by a formal written trust deed (ie an 'express trust'). These are considered further below. However, HMRC acknowledge that trusts can sometimes be created by operation of the law (ie 'implied trusts') as opposed to creation by the express intention of the settlor. Furthermore, HMRC recognise that relief under *TCGA 1992, s 225* may be available in such cases to the legal owner of the property, as they hold the property as trustee.

HMRC sub-divides these implied trusts into resulting and constructive trusts. A 'resulting trust' can broadly arise where someone other than the legal owner has made a material contribution to the acquisition of a property. A 'constructive trust' can arise if a person has agreed with the legal owner that the property should be held in some particular way and the person has acted on that agreement.

In practice, a lack of evidence as to the existence of an implied trust is often an impediment to claims for private residence relief under *TCGA 1992, s 225* on the subsequent disposal of the property. However, successful claims can be possible depending on the particular circumstances and the documentary and/or other evidence available (see, for example, *Wagstaff and another v Revenue & Customs* [2014] UKFTT 43 (TC)).

Constructive and resulting trusts are beyond the scope of this chapter. Detailed commentary on HMRC's view and approach in relation to such trusts is included in its Capital Gains Manual (at CG65406 *et seq*).

Interest in possession trusts

13.31 Although a trust may have multiple life tenants, only one life tenant needs to occupy a property as their main residence in order for the trustees to obtain private residence relief. In other words, relief is not restricted to the extent that the occupying life tenant has an interest in the trust fund (so, for four equal life tenants, relief is not restricted to 25%). This can produce some helpful planning opportunities where a trust owns a property but not all the life tenants can occupy the property.

Where there is more than one residence held by the trustees for the use of the beneficiary, the trustees and the beneficiary can jointly elect under *TCGA 1992, s 222(5)(a)* as to which property is to be treated as the main residence for CGT purposes.

Similarly, where a beneficiary occupies a trust property as a residence but also occupies their own residence, private residence relief will only be available in respect of one property, but this can be decided by a joint election made by the trustees and the beneficiary.

The recent case of *Wagstaff and another v HMRC* [2014] UKFTT 43 (TC) confirms that, where property is held subject to certain legal obligations, the intention to create a trust may be inferred. In this case, the property was purchased by Mrs Wagstaff's son at an arm's length price, subject to an underlying written agreement that Mrs Wagstaff had a right to occupy the property at no cost for the remainder of her life or until she remarried. A private residence relief claim under *TCGA 1992, s 225* was allowed on the subsequent sale of the property.

Discretionary trusts

13.32 Where a trust instrument gives the trustees complete discretion over what benefit may be enjoyed by any of the objects of the trust, the effect is that, until the trustees take action, none of the beneficiaries actually has a right to any of the trust assets. Hence, no private residence relief would be available under *TCGA 1992, s 225*, because they do not have a right to occupy as required by that section.

In *Sansom v Peay* [1976] STC 494, the discretionary trust allowed the trustees 'to permit any beneficiary to reside in any dwelling house or occupy any property or building ... for the time being subject to the trust hereof upon such conditions ... as the trustees ... think fit'. Beneficiaries occupied a trust property and it was held that the occupations resulted from the exercise by the trustees of their powers under the deed. When the beneficiaries moved into the house, they were entitled to stay there unless and until permission was withdrawn by the trustees. As at the date of the disposal of the house, the beneficiaries were still entitled to occupy it and were occupying it under the terms of the trust deed. The gain was therefore sheltered by private residence relief.

Estates in administration

13.33 Sometimes there will be a substantial increase in the value of a dwelling house from the date of the death of its owner to the date on which the property can be sold. Delays can arise where there is a dispute about the terms of a will or where a claim is made under the *Inheritance (Provision for Family and Dependants) Act 1975* or where, quite simply, everything takes rather longer than it should.

Where an individual occupies a property and then the owner dies, but under their will the individual is entitled to at least 75% interest in the property either absolutely or as an interest in possession, then any gain made by the personal representatives will be eligible for private residence relief. This may occur where the deceased spouse owned the home but jointly occupied it with their spouse, and they then leave it to the surviving spouse absolutely or via an interest in possession trust. See *TCGA 1992, s 225A* for further details.

MARRIAGE, SEPARATION AND DIVORCE

Spouses and civil partners

13.34 An individual living with his spouse or civil partner can have only one main residence for both of them as long as they are living together (*TCGA 1992, s 222(6)*). A couple must nominate a residence jointly.

> **Focus**
>
> Where each party to a relationship has a residence, each may claim private residence relief unless and until they begin to be treated as living together within the context of marriage or a civil partnership.

Two or more residences

13.35 The taxpayer has an opportunity to make or vary a notice each time another property becomes a residence, or from the date of a marriage/civil partnership when the partner to the marriage already owns a residence (*Griffin v Craig-Harvey* [1994] STC 54).

> **Example 13.6 – Only one private residence relief for a married couple**
>
> Liz owns a flat in London whilst her fiancé Phil owns a house in the country. They both work in London during the week, so live in Liz's flat during the week, before they both return to Phil's cottage to enjoy weekends.

Prior to their marriage, both properties will qualify for private residence relief, but following their marriage, they have two years to jointly elect for one of their properties to be treated as their main residence, otherwise HMRC will base this on the facts of the case.

However, where one party to the marriage owns two or more residences, but the other does not own any property, then HMRC take the view that the marriage does not provide a new two-year opportunity to make an election, as a joint election is only required where it affects both parties.

Transfers of property

13.36 When a property or an interest in a property is transferred between spouses (or civil partners) who are living together, the transfer is treated as taking place on a no gain, no loss basis (*TCGA 1992, s 58*).

However, where an interest in the sole or main residence is transferred, the recipient spouse's period of ownership is deemed to commence at the date of the original acquisition by the transferor spouse, and not at the date of transfer of the interest between the spouses (*TCGA 1992, s 222(7)*). Similarly, on a death, the surviving spouse inherits the period of ownership of the deceased spouse.

Where one spouse is eligible for private residence relief under *TCGA 1992, s 223(3),* as a result of living in work-related accommodation elsewhere in the UK, the other spouse is also treated as satisfying the condition provided they are living together.

Year of separation

13.37 A common feature of the breakdown of marriage or of civil partnership is the disposal, by one party, of an interest in the residence that was formerly shared. Timing is everything, because a disposal between the parties that takes place within the tax year of separation is treated by *TCGA 1992, s 58* as if made on a no gain, no loss basis; whilst a disposal delayed into the following or even a later year may attract CGT.

Example 13.7 – Transfer within year of separation

Selena and Richard decide to divorce. They bought their flat for £500,000 on marriage, 75% with Selena's money, with Richard taking a mortgage for the balance. It is worth £900,000 on 31 December 2015.

Richard leaves the flat on 31 December 2015. Selena pays him £225,000 to go, completing the arrangement on 31 March 2016. This is treated as the disposal by Richard of his share to Selena for £125,000 (on a no gain no, loss basis) and his true gains of £100,000 are sheltered, not by private residence relief but by *TCGA 1992, s 58*.

Selena is treated as acquiring Richard's share at an undervalue, but that does not worry her: even if she later sells that share of the flat for more than the deemed acquisition value of £125,000, that gain will be sheltered by private residence relief.

Mesher orders

13.38 *TCGA 1992, s 225B* (formerly ESC D6) provides relief on disposals in connection with divorce (or dissolution of a civil partnership) etc. The relief seems to acknowledge that divorce may result in a court order that is often referred to as a *Mesher* order (so-called after a case of that name), under which the house is broadly occupied by one of the spouses for a limited period.

For example, a *Mesher* order may provide that upon the spouse ceasing to occupy the matrimonial home (the husband, in this example), his interest is held on trust until the couple's youngest child reaches the age of 18 or ceases full-time education, and that the other spouse shall continue to occupy the home during the trust period.

HMRC guidance (at CG65365) points out that the *Mesher* order results in a transfer into trust, which constitutes a disposal for CGT purposes (within *TCGA 1992, s 70*) by the husband in the above example. However, if the conditions in *TCGA 1992, s 225B* are satisfied, private residence relief is available.

When the trust period comes to an end (ie when the youngest child ceases full-time education in the above example) there is a deemed disposal of his property interest as a trustee (*TCGA 1992, s 71(1)*), but private residence relief under *TCGA 1992, s 225* ('Private residence occupied under the terms of settlement') should then apply. However, the husband in this example is still potentially liable to CGT on any increase in value between the trust ending and the property being sold.

13.39 It should be noted that relief under *TCGA 1992, s 225B* is subject to certain conditions being met, one of which is broadly that the individual potentially seeking to claim the relief has not made a main residence election under *TCGA 1992, s 222(5)* (see **13.44**). The individual will therefore need to consider whether or not relief under *TCGA 1992, s 225B* will be beneficial, compared to a possible loss of private residence relief on his or her new home. Interestingly, HMRC makes this planning point in its own guidance (see CG65375).

It should also be noted that private residence relief under *TCGA 1992, s 225B* requires a claim by the individual concerned (*TCGA 1992, s 225B(5)*).

13.40 For detailed commentary on separation and divorce, the matrimonial home and the CGT main residence exemption, together with *Mesher* orders (including the possible IHT implications of trust arrangements), see **16.39–16.61**.

ADMINISTRATION

How the relief takes effect

13.41

> **Focus**
>
> Private residence relief arises under *TCGA 1992, s 222* and is automatic (ie it does not have to be claimed by an individual).

Tax returns

13.42 Taxpayers do not need to complete the capital gains pages of their tax returns in relation to homes disposed of with private residence relief. However, if not all of the conditions are met, and a claim for partial relief is being made, then the relevant tax return pages do need to be completed.

Proper documentation

13.43 In any event, it is essential to ensure that an individual's 'residence' of a property is properly documented.

The case of *Paul Favell* [2010] TC00642 is an illustration of a decision being found in HMRC's favour, purely due to there being a 'complete absence of objective documentary evidence' to support the taxpayer's claim that he resided at the property in question.

PLANNING OPPORTUNITIES AND PITFALLS

Main residence elections

13.44 Where a taxpayer varies (see **13.27**) a notice given under *TCGA 1992, s 222(5)(a)* (see **13.23**) by giving further notice to HMRC, the variation may apply to a second home for very short period, even a few days, which will give that second home a CGT exemption for gain arising in respect of the last 36 or 18 months of ownership (see **13.20**).

This is the process known as 'flipping', and is considered to be 'acceptable' tax planning by the GAAR guidance, which states: 'Buying properties that are occupied as residences and then using the main residence election is using a relief afforded by statute and is not an abusive arrangement. The legislation places no limit on the number of times the election may be swapped'. The following example is based on GAAR guidance:

Example 13.8 – Varying the election for multiple residences

Renee has several houses outside the UK in which she spends five months of the year, with the rest of the time in the UK. On 1 September 2009 she acquires a London flat and makes a main residence election in respect of it. On 31 January 2010, she acquires a country house in Surrey and makes a main residence election in respect of that instead. On 1 September 2011 she decides to acquire a Scottish estate as many of her friends enjoy countryside pursuits. She makes a main residence election in respect of the Scottish property. She divides the seven months she spends in the UK between her various residences, spending the week in London and the weekend in her Surrey home and holidays in Scotland. Hence, all of them are occupied as a residence.

Dissatisfied with the London flat, she sells it in August 2012 and buys a larger house in Chelsea, again making a main residence election in respect of that property. Shortly afterwards, fed up with the British weather, she sells the Surrey home and purchases a property in the south of France instead. However, she does not make a main residence election in respect of the French property. By September 2014, she decides that she prefers France and sells all her properties in the UK.

All of Renee's UK properties have been nominated as her main home for some period, so the last 36 months of ownership of each property, or 18 months for properties sold after 5 April 2014, will qualify for the CGT exemption.

Development of land

Trading transactions

13.45 Private residence relief will be denied where the property was acquired wholly or partly for the purpose of making a gain from the disposal where there was no intention that the house would be occupied as a main residence (*TCGA 1992, s 224(3)*). This is in contrast to the position where an individual genuinely intends to occupy the property as their main residence but also naturally hopes it will appreciate in value over time.

Hence, cases where renovation of the property is followed by a quick sale may be vulnerable to HMRC challenge. In such cases, HMRC may not only deny the private residence relief, but they might also seek to treat the gain as arising from 'trading' transactions and so subject to income tax (and not CGT). This vulnerability could also extend to the conversion of a house into flats, the conversion of outbuildings into dwellings, or the acquisition by a leaseholder of a superior interest in the property.

In *Lynch v Edmondson (Inspector of Taxes)* [1998] STI 968, a bricklayer purchased two plots of land, developed them into two flats, and immediately let one of the flats at a premium for a term of 99 years. The Special Commissioner summarised the various tests that led to the final decision to deny private residence relief with the transaction instead considered to be consistent with a trading transaction:

- land is a commodity in which it was possible to trade;
- the taxpayer realised substantial money from one of the units by letting it as soon as it was built;
- much of the cost of the development was repaid from the premium that was taken on the grant of the lease of the first unit to be finished;
- the original purchase of the land was divided up into units for sale; and
- the taxpayer had told the bank that had lent him the money that he would sell one of the flats.

Where a clear pattern of dealing can be discerned, for example, where a person buys properties, renovates them and resells them on a regular basis, HMRC may well regard this as trading.

This can give rise to some cause for concern. A house purchaser often expects that the property value will increase over a period of time and there is an anticipation of gain on a future sale. Many individuals and couples acquire properties which they know they will be selling in, say, two or three years' time to buy larger properties.

The exclusion of the main residence exemption is clearly not aimed at normal home purchases and sales. The fact that the house has been purchased because it may have been a 'bargain' or was expected to appreciate in value does not itself prevent the exemption from applying.

Intention to reside

13.46 Where a residence is purchased and sold at a profit within a short period, it may be necessary to demonstrate the following facts to the Inspector:

- That the intention was to occupy the property as a main residence. This might be evidenced by reasons as to why the house and location, together with any local amenities, were particularly desirable. It may also be useful to give positive reasons for leaving the previous residence.
- That the property was actually occupied as a main residence. Whilst intention to occupy will help refute any contention that the property was bought with the objective of selling at a profit, no exemption will be available unless the property is actually occupied as a main residence (*Goodwin v Curtis* [1998] STC 475). Apart from the family's furniture being moved there, it should also be seen that the family slept in the house; cooked and entertained there; received mail there; the address was used for local amenity purposes (eg with libraries); and the occupants were registered there in the electoral register.
- The intention to sell should have arisen after the property was acquired. It may be necessary to demonstrate special reasons for a short-term sale such as financial problems, job requirements, problems with neighbours or any other reasons why the location or house may have become unsuitable.
- The timing of any advertising of the property for sale or its placement with estate agents should be consistent with the facts referred to in the points above.

Where the relief under *TCGA 1992, s 222* applies to any gain arising on the main residence, any loss made on the disposal of the same property is not an allowable loss for CGT purposes. The taxpayer in *Jones v Wilcox (Inspector of Taxes)* [1996] STI 1349 was unsuccessful in their attempt to use *TCGA 1992, s 224(3)* to create an allowable loss from disposal of his own home (to set against a separate and unconnected gain).

Surplus land

13.47 Private residence relief extends to 'up to the permitted area' (*TCGA 1992, s 222(1)(b)*), which is an area of up to half a hectare, or more where appropriate to the size and character of a dwelling house.

Where the grounds exceed half a hectare, HMRC must be satisfied that the extra area is required for the reasonable enjoyment of the property *(TCGA 1992, s 222(3))*. In that case, it may be crucial that the land is bought and sold with the house. If it is bought or sold separately, this would indicate that a previous or subsequent owner did not 'require' this land for the 'reasonable enjoyment' of the residence, so the gain would not be covered by private residence relief.

Example 13.9 – Selling part of the grounds

Belinda lives in the Old Coach House, built in 1850 as part of a much more extensive property. The Old Coach House has 1 hectare of garden which includes a former stable block and access to a side road. Belinda secures planning permission to convert the stable block into a mews residence, which she sells with 0.25 of a hectare of land.

It is difficult for Belinda to resist the HMRC argument that, if she is now selling the stable block and a parcel of land, that land is not 'required for the reasonable enjoyment of the (retained) dwelling house'. Clearly, if Belinda goes on living at the Old Coach House, the land is not now so required.

Residual building plot

13.48 At the time when land is sold, it must have been owned and used for enjoyment with the house. This condition cannot have been met where any portion of the land had been kept after the sale of the house – even if the original total area was less than half a hectare.

This common pitfall is illustrated by the case of *Varty v Lynes* [1976] STC 508. In that case, Mr Lynes sold his home and retained part of the garden which he sold at a later date. The High Court found that the relief in *TCGA 1992, s 222* could not apply to the later sale of the garden, as at the date of the sale it was no longer part of the residence occupied by Mr Lynes. The wording in *TCGA 1992, s 222(1)(b)* is precise in distinguishing the house from its grounds on this point (CG64377).

The above technically applies regardless of whether the gap between the sale of the house and the land was several years or one day. HMRC have confirmed this view in CG64377–64387.

Example 13.10 – Sale of land after sale of the home

Charles owned and occupied a large property with a 5-hectare plot. He obtained planning permission for a single dwelling on the plot. He then put both his home and the plot with planning permission on the market. In the end, the contracts for sale of his former house were exchanged before the sale of the adjoining plot. Any gain on the sale of the house itself, after apportionment, is covered by private residence relief.

Unfortunately for Charles, in general there can be no CGT relief on the eventual sale of the building plot. It would have been better for Charles to have sold the house and the plot together but with the benefit of the planning permission.

HMRC are prepared to relax the strict rule in CG64377 where all the land was formerly occupied as garden, and the land is disposed of between the date the contracts are exchanged on the house and the contracts are completed with conveyance of the house to the new owner. In that situation, the relief under *TCGA 1992, s 222* is given in respect of the land sold separately, but not if the land is sold after conveyance of the former home (CG64385).

Enhancing the value of the property

13.49 If any construction, refurbishment or improvement work is carried out on a main residence to enhance its value on sale, part or all of the gain arising may not be eligible for private residence relief.

Gains attributable to expenditure incurred wholly or partly for the purpose of realising a gain on the sale of the property are excluded from the main residence CGT exemption (*TCGA 1992, s 224(3)*). Therefore, any development and building profit arising from applying for planning permission and incurring construction costs could be fully assessable to CGT. The related provision is also sufficiently wide to catch any improvements that increase the value of the property on sale. This includes the acquisition of the freehold reversion by a leaseholder. Note that simply incurring expenditure on planning permission, or having a restricted covenant released, will not itself result in any loss of the exemption (CG65243).

Improvements may well be carried out with the expectation that the value of the house will be increased as a result. Any such expenditure could, technically, result in a restriction of the exemption. Accordingly, it may be necessary to demonstrate, where appropriate, that the whole or main objective of any work done was to improve the amenities of the property for the owner's benefit and not to realise a profit.

If the property is sold shortly after any work is carried out, this must add support to a possible argument that the expenditure was incurred with a profit motive. Where this inference is incorrect, the taxpayer may have to be prepared to present to the Inspector evidence that the intention to sell arose after the work commenced.

Where an opportunity arises to commercially develop a main residence, it might be appropriate to transfer the property to a company or partnership before any work is carried out. This could help ensure that the gain to the date of transfer will be exempt from tax. The further gain on the property in the hands of a company or partnership would almost certainly be taxable as income. This would most likely be as trading income (under *CTA 2009, s 201*).

Chapter 14

Tax planning with trusts

Robert Maas FCA, FTII, FIIT, TEP, Consultant, CBW Tax Ltd

SIGNPOSTS

- **Introduction** – Trusts have a long history. Despite a large number of attempts by successive governments to limit their use, they can still be an important tax-planning tool (see **14.1–14.7**).
- **Types of trust** – There are two basic types of trust: interest in possession and discretionary trusts. There are, however, a large number of variants on these basic models (see **14.8–14.20**).
- **Taxation of UK-resident settlements** – A UK-resident settlement is fully within the charge to UK tax. In some circumstances income (but not capital gains) can be treated as income of the settlor instead of that of the trust (see **14.21–14.41**).
- **Taxation of non-UK resident trustees** – A non-UK trust is outside the scope of UK tax except in relation to certain types of UK income and in some circumstances where there was a UK settlor. For 2015/16 onwards the trustees are liable to CGT on the disposal of UK residential property. However, income can be taxed on the settlor, and so can gains unless the settlor was non-UK domiciled. Both income and gains can alternatively be taxed on a beneficiary who receives a distribution or, in some cases, a benefit from the settlement (see **14.42–14.58**). A new type of protected settlement has been introduced from 6 April 2017 to cater for the situation where the settlor was non-UK domiciled when he created the trust but subsequently becomes deemed domiciled in the UK (see **14.59–14.60**).
- **Inheritance tax** – A special IHT regime applies to trusts. Under this an IHT charge can occur on the creation of the settlement, on each tenth anniversary and on property leaving the settlement. A different regime applies to some interest in possession trusts (see **14.61–14.88**).
- **Tax planning with trusts** – There is still a lot of scope for the use of trusts in IHT planning, however, there are a number of pitfalls that need to be considered (see **14.89–14.91**).

INTRODUCTION

14.1 Trusts have always been an important tool in tax planning. They can be very flexible vehicles. They effectively allow assets to be held in suspense and for the three main attributes of an asset, capital value, income and control, to be separated out.

Not surprisingly, tax authorities do not like trusts because these attributes facilitate tax planning. There are, accordingly, many anti-avoidance provisions in relation to trusts. One of the earliest UK anti-avoidance provisions was the *Statute of Uses 1535*. A use was an early form of trust. A landowner would transfer his land jointly into the name of two or three friends, for the benefit (or use) of either himself or his children. The feudal dues would then not be payable on the death of the original landowner (as he no longer owned the land) or on the death of one of the title holders, as on his death the land passed to the others (and a new title holder could be added to ensure that the ownership never reverted to a sole name).

The *Statute of Uses* deemed the land to belong to the person for whose use it was held. The statute was nominally introduced to protect the interests of the user as instances occurred where on the original landowner's death the title holders simply disinherited his children. It is generally accepted though that the real reason was to protect the royal revenues and other feudal dues that fell due to the king or a local lord on the death of a landowner.

14.2 A trust is a development of the medieval use. A settlor transfers assets to trustees to be held on the terms laid down by the settlor for the benefit of a beneficiary or a number of beneficiaries.

No formalities are needed to create a trust (other than whatever is needed to transfer legal title of the asset to the trustees, although even that is not strictly necessary as direct tax depends on beneficial ownership, and not legal title). A trust can be oral unless land is involved. However, it is obviously sensible to have a formal trust deed. This both evidences the creation of the trust and avoids misunderstandings as to both the terms of the trust and the identity of the beneficiaries.

14.3 A trust can have a single trustee. However, this creates a problem if the trustee dies, as someone will need to apply to the court to appoint a new trustee. Furthermore, a trust cannot dispose of land unless there are at least two trustees, which again would require the expense of an application to the court if there is a single trustee. It is accordingly normal to have a minimum of two trustees. There is no upper limit on the number of trustees but, as trustees must act unanimously unless the trust deed specifies otherwise (and even where it does all of the trustees are entitled to be involved in decision making), a large number of trustees can make operating the trust unwieldy.

14.4 Many people are suspicious of trusts. There are too many anecdotal horror stories in circulation of where things have gone wrong. Many of these date from times when trusts were far less flexible than a modern trust and it was common to have as the trustees one's solicitor and accountant – so a lot of such stories are actually instances of professional trustees declining to follow the wishes of a settlor because the trust deed did not give them the necessary power to do what the settlor was asking them to do.

14.5 There is actually no need to have any professional trustees (although that is obviously desirable for a charity or other public trust). There is no reason – either under trust law or tax law – why the settlor and his spouse should not be the sole trustees of a family trust. Indeed, as the settlor and his spouse might be expected to be uniquely placed to determine what is in the best interests of their own children, this would in many cases be the sensible thing to do.

One situation where some people think this may not be desirable is if the settlor and/or his spouse are amongst the beneficiaries of the trust, as there would be a potential conflict between their duty as a trustee to consider the needs of all of the beneficiaries and their interest as beneficiaries. There could then be a risk that a beneficiary could successfully challenge decisions of the trustees through the courts unless there is an independent trustee who was involved in the decision making. Many parents are happy to accept the risk of being sued by their children though, as they view such a possibility as remote.

14.6 Another deterrent from the use of trusts is that a trust deed looks complicated. The average trust deed runs to 20 or 30 pages. However, this is not because the trust is complicated (although obviously some are), but because a trust is a creature of statute. As such the trustees are entitled to do only what either trust law or the trust deed itself permits them to do. If the law or deed is silent on what they need to do – such as insure the trust assets – they need either to apply to the court to approve the proposed action or to go ahead and risk challenge by a beneficiary. Accordingly, only two or three pages of a typical trust deed actually set out the terms on which the trustees hold the trust property. The rest contains rules for administering the trust, such as the means for appointing and removing and remunerating trustees (a trustee is not entitled to be paid for his services unless the deed authorises it) and a long list of powers to enable the trustees to operate sensibly in relation to the trust assets and obviate the need to obtain court approval for a whole range of things that experience has taught the draftsman trustees frequently need or want to do.

14.7 Many trusts are created by a person's will to take effect on their death. Curiously, such trusts are normally expressed fairly briefly and most seem to operate effectively even though the will does not contain the numerous pages of powers that solicitors write into lifetime settlements. A trust created in a will is often called a will trust.

Trusts are of course not simply, or even primarily, tax-avoidance devices. What they actually do in many cases is remove an obstacle that stands in the way of arranging ownership of family assets in a sensible manner. This obstacle is normally either a reluctance by the settlor to give up control over an asset in circumstances where he does not believe that his children have the expertise to exercise such control properly, or a reluctance to give a child a large amount of either income or capital at the stage where his parents do not think he has the maturity to handle such funds sensibly.

The term 'trust' (ie the terms on which property is settled) and 'settlement' (the act of creating a trust) are generally used interchangeably to refer to a trust. 'Settlement' has a different specific meaning in land law in relation to certain trusts of land but is used in the tax legislation to mean a trust as commonly understood.

Types of trust

14.8

> **Focus**
>
> Trusts can be very flexible provided that the necessary powers are contained in the trust deed. When setting up a trust, understand what the client wants to achieve and discuss with them whether they might need greater flexibility in the future. However some clients are wary of too much flexibility if this requires giving to trustees who may be strangers to them a lot of discretion over the use and distribution of the funds. It is not necessarily sensible to give the trustees powers that they do not need to meet the client's objectives 'just in case' things change in the future.

There are two main types of trust; interest in possession (IIP) and discretionary. Under an IIP trust someone has an entitlement to the income. Under a discretionary trust no one is entitled to the income; it is at the discretion of the trustees (within the terms of the trust deed) how the income is dealt with.

There are a number of other types of trust that have been created as such by the inheritance tax legislation. These are either hybrids of IIP and discretionary trusts, or are IIP trusts which must also meet specific statutory conditions.

14.9 An 'accumulation and maintenance trust' is a discretionary trust for the benefit of an infant or infants which automatically converts to an IIP trust for the benefit of the infant when they reach 18 (25 in the case of some trusts created before 22 March 2006) or an earlier age specified in the trust deed.

14.10 A 'trust for bereaved minors' is a will trust for the benefit of an infant child or children of the deceased settlor under which the minor must become absolutely entitled to the assets at or before age 18 and until then it is either an IIP trust of which the minor is the principal beneficiary or a discretionary trust where the discretion of the trustees is limited to paying the income to or for the benefit of the minor or accumulating it.

14.11 An 'age 18-to-25 trust' is similar to a trust for bereaved minors and, like it, can be created only by will and only by a deceased parent for his own children, but the child need not become entitled to the assets (or attain an IIP) until age 25.

14.12 An 'employee benefit trust' is, as the name suggests, a discretionary trust for the benefit of the employees of a particular employer or persons engaged in a particular trade or profession (and their spouses or civil partners and dependants).

14.13 A 'newspaper trust' is a type of employee benefit trust which can also include UK newspaper publishing companies or newspaper holding companies amongst its beneficiaries and whose only or principal asset are shares in a newspaper publishing company or newspaper holding company.

14.14 A 'trust for a disabled person' is a discretionary trust which includes a disabled person (as defined in the legislation) as a beneficiary and provides that the settled property is applied during his lifetime for that person's benefit, subject to relatively small monetary limits.

14.15 Mention should also be made of a 'charitable trust' which is a trust whose income and assets can be used only for charitable purposes (although the special tax rules relating to charities are not dealt with in this chapter) and a protective trust. This is an IIP trust which automatically becomes a discretionary trust, the beneficiaries of which are the person with the interest in possession and his family, if the person with the interest in possession does or tries to do anything which divests him of his right to the income. For example, he becomes bankrupt or tries to sell his interest.

Although there is a basic distinction between an IIP and a discretionary trust it is possible for a person to have an interest in possession in only some of the income of a trust with the trustees having discretion over the remainder, or for sub-trusts to exist within a trust under which some of the assets are held on different trusts to the remainder. In addition, many IIP trusts give the beneficiary a right to income only, leaving the destination of the capital to the discretion of the trustees.

Residence of trustees

14.16

> **Focus**
>
> It is important to realise that having one UK trustee is sufficient to make the trust UK resident even if there are five non-UK trustees and all decisions are taken overseas. In particular, a UK resident settlor cannot be a trustee of his offshore trust.

Like an individual a trust can be UK resident or non-UK resident. The residence determines which tax rules apply to the trust – and which anti-avoidance provisions might apply to the settlor or beneficiaries.

For income tax and capital gains tax purposes a trust is resident in the UK (and prior to 6 April 2013, also ordinarily resident) if either:

- all of the trustees are UK resident; or
- at least one of the trustees is UK resident and at the time of creation of the settlement (or immediately before his death in the case of a will trust or other trust arising on death such as on an intestacy) the settlor was either resident, ordinarily resident or domiciled in the UK.

(*ITA 2007, ss 475, 476*; *TCGA 1992, s 69*)

14.17 In applying these tests a person who acts as trustee in the course of a business which he carries on in the UK through a branch, agency or permanent establishment in the UK must be treated as if he were UK resident if he is not (*ITA 2007, s 475(6)*; *TCGA 1992, s 69(2D)*).

If neither of these conditions is met the trust is neither resident nor ordinarily resident in the UK (*ITA 2007, s 475(3)*; *TCGA 1992, s 69(2E)*).

Different rules applied before 5 April 2007 but the above rules apply from that date irrespective of when the trust was created. Under the old rules, the test for CGT was where the majority of the trustees were resident. Accordingly, trusts with one UK trustee and the majority non-UK would have been non-UK resident but will automatically have become UK resident on 6 April 2007.

Extended meaning of settlement

14.18 A settlement is not defined as such for income tax and capital gains tax. The legislation states that (unless the context otherwise requires) 'settled property' means any property held in trust and that references to property comprised in a settlement are references to settled property (*ITA 2007, s 466(2), (4)*; *TCGA 1992, s 68*).

However, property held by a person as nominee for another person or as trustee for another person absolutely entitled as against the trustee, or for another person who would be so entitled but for being an infant or other person lacking legal capacity, is not settled property (*ITA 2007, s 466(3)*; *TCGA 1992, ss 60, 68*). Such a trust is called a bare trust.

For most tax purposes the assets and income are treated as that of the beneficiary, not the trustee. A person is absolutely entitled to property as against the trustee if he has the exclusive right to direct how the property is to be dealt with (subject to the trustees' right to use the property for the payment of duty, taxes, costs or other outgoings) (*ITA 2007, s 466(5)*; *TCGA 1992, s 60(2)*). Where a person becomes absolutely entitled to property as against the trustees, the trustees cease to be trustees and become nominees for the beneficiary if they do not transfer the assets to him.

14.19 For the purpose of *ITTOIA 2005, s 619* (amounts treated as income of settlor) a settlement is defined to include 'any disposition, trust, covenant, agreement, arrangement or transfer of assets' (*ITTOIA 2005, s 620*). However, the courts have cut down the very wide scope of this wording a little by requiring there to be an element of bounty. This was affirmed by the House of Lords in *IRC v Plummer* (1979) 54 TC 1, where Lord Wilberforce said:

> 'These sections, in other words, though drafted in wide, and increasingly wider language are nevertheless dealing with a limited field – one far narrower than the field of the totality of dispositions, or arrangements, or agreements which a man may make in the course of his life. Is there any common description which can be applied to this? The courts which, inevitably, have had to face this problem, have selected the element of "bounty" as a necessary common characteristic of all the "settlements" which parliament had in mind.'

The *Plummer* case was a tax-avoidance scheme which involved the sale of an annuity to a charity. This was held not to create a settlement.

14.20 Transactions which have been held to create a settlement include:

- The allotment of shares at a low price to children of the directors of a company coupled with the payment of a dividend on those shares (*Copeman v Coleman* (1939) 22 TC 594).
- An outright gift of shares by a father to his minor children (*Hood Barrs v IRC* (1946) 27 TC 385).
- Payments into a savings account in the name of minor children (*Thomas v Marshall (Inspector of Taxes)* (1953) 34 TC 178).

- The allotment of shares in a new company to children of a director, coupled with the payment of dividends and the parent providing the company with the opportunity to earn profits (*Butler (Inspector of Taxes) v Wildin* (1989) 61 TC 666).
- The surrender by a life tenant of his interest in a settlement so that the right to income passed to his children under the terms of the settlement (*IRC v Buchanan* (1957) 37 TC 365).
- The creation of a settlement by a grandparent for the benefit of a child coupled with its subscribing for shares in a company and the child's father generating income for the company by working for it at a very low salary (*Crossland v Hawkins* (1960) 39 TC 493).
- A loan by a settlement to the beneficiary's father carrying interest coupled with the father re-lending the money interest free to a company and the settlement distributing the interest to the beneficiary (*IRC v Leiner* (1964) 41 TC 589).
- A covenant to make annual payments to a company controlled by the covenanter until such time as the company was wound up with the payments being used by the company to pay dividends to a third party (*IRC v Payne* (1940) 23 TC 610). The transfer was similarly held to be a settlement in *IRC v Morton* (1941) 24 TC 259 and *Dalgety v IRC* (1941) 24 TC 280, where assets were transferred to the company instead of covenanting annual payments.
- The assignment of a life policy to trustees and covenanting with the trustees to continue paying the premium (*IRC v Tennant* (1942) 24 TC 215).
- A reorganisation of share capital so that trustees ended up with preference shares carrying high dividend rights for five years (*IRC v Prince-Smith* (1943) 25 TC 84).
- The issue of preference shares to the wives of the controlling shareholders combined with the declaration of substantial dividends on those shares (*Young (Inspector of Taxes) v Scrutton* (1996) 70 TC 331).
- A gift of shares to a charity with an option to repurchase, combined with the declaration of substantial dividends (*Vandervell v IRC* (1976) 43 TC 519).
- The guarantee of a bank overdraft secured by the deposit of cash, with the bank agreeing to pay no interest on the deposit and charge only 1% pa on the overdraft and dividends being paid by a company to enable the overdraft to be repaid and the deposit to be released (*IRC v Wachtel* (1970) 46 TC 543).
- An actress entering into an agreement with a company to render her services at a nominal salary combined with a settlement by her father for her benefit of the shares in the company (*Mills v IRC* (1972) 49 TC 367).

Although some of these transactions involved the creation of formal settlements, it was not that settlement that was discerned by the court but a separate deemed settlement resulting from the overall arrangement.

THE TAXATION OF UK-RESIDENT SETTLEMENTS

Income tax

14.21 The normal rule is that income of trustees is chargeable at the 20% basic rate, the savings rate or the dividend ordinary rate, as the case may be (*ITA 2007, ss 11, 12, 14*).

However, if accumulated or discretionary income arises to the trustees (and the trust is not a charitable trust) it is instead charged either at the trust rate, which is 45%, or the dividend trust rate, which is 38.1% (*ITA 2007, ss 9, 479*).

Income is accumulated or discretionary income if either it is required to be accumulated or it is payable at the discretion of the trustees or of any other person (*ITA 2007, s 480(1)*). In particular income is payable at a person's discretion if he has discretion over whether, or the extent to which, it is to be accumulated, the persons to whom the income is to be paid, or how much is to be paid to any person (*ITA 2007, s 480(2)*). Income is excluded from being accumulated or discretionary income if it is deemed to be the income of some person other than the trustees, it is held for the purpose of a superannuation fund relating to undertakings outside the UK (and not held as a member of a property investment LLP) or is income from residential property service charges (*ITA 2007, s 480(3)–(6)*).

The income of an IIP trust belongs to the person with the interest in possession and is taxable on him. Accordingly, in practice, the 20% rate applies only where the trustees are taxable as being the person in receipt of the income and the trust is an IIP trust. If it is not an IIP trust, the 45% trust rate applies.

14.22 Deemed income under the following provisions are also taxable at that rate (unless they are already so taxable) even if the trust is an interest in possession trust so that actual income is taxable on the beneficiaries. The reason is probably because under trust law these items are capital so would not be taxed as income at all unless they are taxed at trust level:

1 a payment by a company on the redemption or purchase of its own shares;

2 accrued income profits under *ITA 2007, s 628(5)* or *630(2)*;

3 offshore income gains under *Offshore Funds (Tax) Regulations 2009 (SI 2009/3001), reg 7*.

4 deemed income of employee share ownership trusts under *FA 1989, s 68(2)* or *71(4)*;

5 the income element of premiums on leases under *ITTOIA 2005, ss 276–307*;

6 profits from deeply discounted securities under *ITTOIA 2005, s 429*;

7 gains from life insurance contracts under *ITTOIA 2005, s 467*;

8 gains on transactions in deposits under *ITTOIA 2005, s 554*;

9 gains on disposals of options under *ITTOIA 2005, s 557*;

10 proceeds of sale of foreign dividend coupons under *ITTOIA 2005, s 573*;

11 deemed income from transactions in land under *ITA 2007, ss 752–772*.

Amounts within 1 above are taxed at the dividend trust rate, but that under the other heads (including, curiously, head 10) is taxed at the 45% trust rate (*ITA 2007, ss 481, 482*).

14.23 Where the trust rate or the dividend trust rate applies, a deduction is allowed for expenses of the trustees which are properly chargeable to income (ie legally chargeable ignoring the express terms of the settlement) (*ITA 2007, s 484*).

Broadly speaking, expenses are properly chargeable to income only if they solely benefit the income beneficiaries (although the appropriate part of an expense where some of the cost can meet this test is also allowable) (*HMRC v Peter Clay Discretionary Trust* [2009] STC 469).

Any unrelieved expenses can be carried forward to subsequent years (*ITA 2007, s 485*). Expenses are set first against dividend income from UK companies (and stock dividends or the release of a loan to a participator in a close company). Any excess is set against other dividend income, then against savings income and finally against other income. The relievable expenses must be grossed-up, so relief is not obtainable at the basic rate, dividend rate or savings rate (*ITA 2007, s 486*).

14.24 The trust rates and dividend trust rates do not apply to the first £1,000 pa of income. Where the settlor has created more than one settlement, the £1,000 figure is divided by the number of settlements but if there are more than five the first £200 in each settlement is taxable at the basic rate, savings rate or dividend rate as the case may be (*ITA 2007, ss 491, 492*).

Where the trustees make a discretionary payment to a beneficiary the payment is grossed-up at the trust rate and the beneficiary (or the settlor if the payment is made to a minor child of the settlor) is treated as having paid tax at that rate – and so can claim a refund if he is not taxable or is taxable at the basic rate only (*ITA 2007, s 494*).

14.25 The trustees must account to HMRC for the grossing-up amount to the extent that it exceeds the balance of their tax pool. This is the accumulated tax suffered by the trustees. However, notional tax, including tax credits in respect of dividends is not included in the tax pool.

It will be seen that an interest-in-possession trust is taxed more lightly than a discretionary trust. The income is treated as that of the beneficiaries, with the trustees being liable to tax at the basic rate only as the person in receipt of the income. Accordingly, where the beneficiaries of a trust are not higher rate taxpayers it is preferable from an income tax point of view to use an interest-in-possession trust. There are inheritance tax consequences in doing so where the trust was created before 22 March 2006, but for trusts created after that date this is no longer a problem in most cases.

A discretionary trust used to be particularly disadvantageous where the main assets of the settlement were UK shares, because the loss of the tax credit meant that the balance of the tax pool was often less than the tax payable on distributions to beneficiaries, but this problem has disappeared with the abolition of tax credits.

14.26 Using an interest-in-possession trust does mean having to fix the division of income amongst the beneficiaries in advance. However, a well-drawn trust is a very flexible entity. There is no reason why the trustees should not have power to revoke all or part of an interest in possession and instead grant an interest in possession in that part of the income to a different beneficiary. By this means it should be possible to divide the income broadly as the trustees would have done with a discretionary settlement, but using future rather than past income to adjust the share going to each beneficiary. However, it will not allow income to be accumulated instead of distributed, unless the power includes turning the trust into a discretionary one.

Charge on settlor

14.27 In some circumstances trust income is treated as income of the settlor (and not of the trust). This can happen in three circumstances (*ITTOIA 2005, s 624*):

- where the settlor retains an interest in the settlement;
- where income is paid to an unmarried minor child of the settlor;
- where the settlor receives a capital sum from the settlement or a body connected with the settlement.

14.28 A settlor has an interest in the settlement if there are any circumstances in which the settled property or any related property (which includes the income from the settled property) is payable to the settlor or to his spouse or civil partner, or is applicable for the benefit of any such person (or will or may become so payable or applicable) (*ITTOIA 2005, s 625(1)*).

There are a number of exceptions:

- If the only circumstance in which that can happen is:
  - the bankruptcy of a beneficiary (or a potential beneficiary);
  - the assignment or charging of the trust property by a beneficiary (or potential beneficiary);
  - in the case of a marriage (or civil partnership) settlement, the death of both parties to the marriage and of all or any of the children of one or both of them;
  - the death at or before age 25 of a child of the settlor who had become beneficially entitled to the property or any related property.
- If the only circumstance in which that can happen is the bankruptcy of a beneficiary or the assignment or charging of the beneficiary's interest in the trust, whilst that person is alive and under 25.
- The settlor does not have an interest in the trust property if his spouse or civil partner dies and they are separated under an order of the court or a separation agreement, or in circumstances that the separation is likely to be permanent.
- The settlor does not have an interest in the trust property merely because his widow or surviving civil partner may do so at a future time.
- The settlor does not have an interest in the settled property at a time when he is unmarried merely by virtue of the fact that he may subsequently marry (or become a civil partner of) a beneficiary.
- For income arising after 21 March 2012, the settlor does not have an interest in the settled property if the settlor is not an individual (*ITTOIA 2005, s 625*).

An outright gift of property from one spouse (or civil partner) to the other is not a settlement provided that:

- the gift carries a right to the whole of the income from the property gifted; and
- the property gifted is not wholly or substantially a right to income.

(*ITTOIA 2005, s 626(1)–(3)*)

A gift is not an outright gift for this purpose if it is subject to conditions or if there are any circumstances in which the property gifted (or any related property) is payable to the donor, or is (or will or may become) applicable for the benefit of the donor (*ITTOIA 2005, s 626(4)*).

14.29 It is important to realise that, as an arrangement can constitute a settlement, the property gifted by the donor is not necessarily the settled property; that may simply be part of the machinery making up the settlement. Thus, the fact that a gift of shares carries with it the right to dividends will not necessarily take the dividends out of the section if the arrangement is that the donor will work for the company for a nominal salary and the company will use the income generated by his work to pay dividends.

That was HMRC's contention in *Jones v Garnett (Inspector of Taxes)* [2007] STC 1536. The House of Lords rejected the argument in that case on the basis that ordinary shares carry a bundle of rights and are not substantially a right to income. However, the HMRC argument would be likely to prevail if the shares are preference shares or are a special class of shares with limited voting rights or rights to capital. It should also be borne in mind that the case concerned the exclusion for gifts which are not wholly or substantially a right to income and that this exclusion applies only to gifts to a spouse or civil partner; there is no corresponding exemption for gifts to infant children.

14.30 The settlor is not taxable under these provisions in relation to income which:

- arises under a settlement made by one party to a marriage (or civil partnership) by way of provision for the other after the dissolution or annulment of the marriage (or civil partnership) or while they are separated under an order of a court, under a separation agreement, or where the separation is likely to be permanent, where the income is payable to (or applicable for the benefit of) the other party;
- consists of annual payments made by an individual for commercial reasons in connection with the individual's trade, profession or vocation;
- consists of qualifying donations to charity (within *ITA 2007, s 416* (gift aid));
- consists of a benefit under a registered pension scheme (or other specified pension scheme) (*ITTOIA 2005, s 627*); or
- is donated by the trustees to a charity in the tax year in which it arises (and it is income to which a charity is entitled under the terms of the trust) (*ITTOIA 2005, s 628*).

14.31 Income is also treated as income of the settlor (and not of any other person) if it is paid to, or for the benefit of, a child of the settlor (including a stepchild) who is under 18 and unmarried (and not in a civil partnership) (*ITTOIA 2005, s 629(1), (7)*). This does not apply if the total amount of income paid to (or for the benefit of) the child during the tax year does not exceed £100 (*ITTOIA 2005, s 629(2)*). As with *ITTOIA 2005, s 624*, there is also an exception for income donated to charity by the trust (*ITTOIA 2005, s 630*).

If the trustees retain or accumulate income as an addition to capital and a payment is subsequently made in connection with the settlement to (or for the benefit of) a minor unmarried child of the settlor, that payment must be treated as a payment of income up to the amount of income retained or accumulated (*ITTOIA 2005, s 631*).

14.32 Any capital sum paid directly or indirectly in any tax year by a settlement to the settlor (or to his spouse or civil partner) is treated as income of the settlor for that year, up to the amount of 'income available' up to the end of that year. This is the income of the settlement from inception which has neither been distributed nor treated as income of the settlor under some other provision (and less tax at the trust rate on that undistributed income less any part taxed on the settlor under *ITTOIA 2005, s 624* or *629*) (*ITTOIA 2005, s 635*).

The capital sum is treated as a net amount from which tax has been deducted at the trust rate, so the taxable amount is the grossed-up figure (*ITTOIA 2005, s 640*).

If the capital sum exceeds the income available, the excess is carried forward and taxed as income of the settlor in future years (up to a maximum of ten future years) (*ITTOIA 2005, s 633(3), (4)*).

14.33 A capital sum for this purpose is:

- a loan;
- a loan repayment;
- any other payment which is made otherwise than as income and not for full consideration in money or money's worth; and
- any sum paid by the trustees to a third party either at the settlor's discretion, or as a result of the assignment by the settlor of his right to receive that sum, or which is otherwise paid or applied for the benefit of the settlor.

(*ITTOIA 2005, s 634*)

References to the settlor include his spouse and the settlor (or his spouse) jointly with some other person (*ITTOIA 2005, s 634(7)*).

Trust expenses which, in the absence of any express provision of the settlement, would be properly chargeable to income are deducted in calculating the available income (*ITTOIA 2005, s 636*).

14.34 If this charge is triggered by the making of a loan, and the loan is subsequently repaid, income arising after the date of repayment is not taxed on the settlor (*ITTOIA 2005, s 638(1)*).

If the settlement makes a loan to the settlor, and there have been previous loans to him that have been wholly repaid, the new loan attracts the tax charge only to the extent that it exceeds the amount previously taxed on the settlor by reference to the earlier loan (*ITTOIA 2005, s 638(2), (3)*).

If the capital sum is the repayment of a loan by the settlor and he subsequently makes a fresh loan which is at least equal to the capital sum, the income arising after the date of the fresh loan is not caught by the section (*ITTOIA 2005, s 638(4), (5)*).

If the capital sum is a loan and a tax charge has been triggered on the settlor on the release of that loan under *ITTOIA 2005, s 416* (release of loan to participator in close company) the amount taxed is not also taxable under *ITTOIA 2005, s 633* (*ITTOIA 2005, s 639*).

14.35 If a capital sum is paid to the settlor by a body corporate connected with the settlement and an associated payment has been, or is, made (directly or indirectly) to that body by the settlement, the capital sum is treated as having been paid to the settlor by the settlement (*ITTOIA 2005, s 641*).

There is an exception where the whole of the loan is repaid within 12 months and no loans to or by the settlor to the body corporate within the previous five years have been outstanding for more than 12 months (*ITTOIA 2005, s 642*). This will ensure that a director's loan account which is cleared regularly by voting remuneration or dividends will not trigger the charge.

A body corporate is connected with a settlement if it is a close company (or would be if it were UK resident) in which the trust is a participator or if it is controlled by such a company (*ITTOIA 2005, ss 637(8), 643(2)*). An associated payment is a capital sum paid to the body corporate by the trust and any other sum paid, or asset transferred by the trust other than for full consideration in money or money's worth in the five years preceding or the five years following the payment of the capital sum to the settlor (*ITTOIA 2005, s 643(3)*).

Although the provision refers only to the settlor, HMRC consider that it applies also to a payment to his spouse (Company Taxation Manual CT61060). It is not clear why. The extension of *ITTOIA 2005, s 633* to a spouse is contained in *ITTOIA 2005, s 634(7)*, but that provision is expressed to apply only for the purpose of *ITTOIA 2005, ss 633–638*. It may be because *ITTOIA 2005, s 643* provides that any question in *ITTOIA 2005, s 641* or *642* whether a capital sum has been paid to the settlor by a body corporate is determined in the same way as any question under *ITTOIA 2005, s 633* whether a capital sum has been paid to the settlor by the trustees, although it seems doubtful whether such wording is apt to import *ITTOIA 2005, s 634(7)* into *ITTOIA 2005, s 641*.

It should particularly be noted that these provisions cannot apply to an interest in possession settlement as the income of such a settlement belongs to the beneficiaries and so cannot be retained or accumulated by the settlement.

Capital gains tax

14.36 Capital gains of trusts are taxable at the full 20% or 28% rate depending on the type of asset (28% on disposals before 5 April 2016) irrespective of whether the trust is a discretionary one or there is an interest in possession (*TCGA 1992, s 4(1AA)*).

The CGT annual exemption for a trust is lower than that for an individual. For 2017/18, it is a maximum of £5,650. However, where a person is a settlor of more than one settlement (ignoring one created before 6 June 1978), the £5,650 figure is divided by the number of such settlements to determine the annual exemption of each, subject to a minimum exemption of £1,130 per settlement (which will apply where there are more than five) (*TCGA 1992, Sch 1, para 2*).

Accordingly, a settlement can be unattractive from a CGT point of view if the beneficiaries do not normally utilise their annual exemption in full or if their personal taxable income and capital gains are under £33,500 (for 2017/18) so that they would pay CGT at only 10% or18% if they were to realise the gain personally.

14.37 There are two exceptions. In arriving at the annual allowance of a settlement, no account is taken of any other settlement for a disabled person (see below), any settlement that is non-UK resident throughout the tax year or of any charitable settlement or sponsored superannuation scheme (*TCGA 1992, Sch 1, para 2(7)*).

A settlement for a disabled person attracts the full £11,300 annual exemption (for 2016/17). The settlement must secure that during the lifetime of the beneficiary all of the settled property which is applied (or all other than £3,000 or 10% of the value of the trust property if smaller) is applied for the benefit of that beneficiary.

The beneficiary must be either mentally disabled (within the *Mental Health Act 1983*) so as to be incapable of managing his own affairs, or in receipt of attendance allowance (under *Social Security Contributions and Benefits Act 1992, s 64*) or disability living allowance (within *SSCBA 1992, s 71*) by virtue of entitlement to the care component at the highest or middle rate or the mobility component at the higher rate). If a person creates more than one such settlement by the same settlor the annual exemption must again be divided by the number of settlements subject to a minimum of £1,130 per settlement – but disabled persons' settlements are not aggregated with other settlements for this purpose (*TCGA 1992, Sch 1, para 1*). A non-resident settlement does not attract any annual exemption but when its gains are taxed on a UK-resident beneficiary or settlor the individual can utilise his own annual allowance against the trust gains.

14.38 The transfer of property into a settlement is a disposal by the settlor and will trigger CGT on the settlor by reference to the market value of CGT assets put into the settlement (*TCGA 1992, s 70*). It will also trigger IHT, as a lifetime gift to a trust is not a potentially exempt transfer.

If the asset settled is a business asset (within *TCGA 1992, s 165*) the settlor can elect to treat the disposal as being at a no gain, no loss price in which case the settlement will be deemed to have acquired the asset at that price for CGT purposes (*TCGA 1992, s 165*). A similar election can be made by the settlor in relation to other assets if the settlement is within the IHT discretionary trust regime (*TCGA 1992, s 260*). Virtually all settlements created after 22 March 2006 (other than some will trusts) will come within this regime.

If the gift to the settlement is covered by an IHT exemption – as opposed to being within the nil rate band – hold-over relief will not apply (unless the exemption is that for transfers to political parties, to maintenance funds for historic buildings or of heritage property) (*TCGA 1992, s 260(2)(b)*).

14.39 There is a deemed disposal by the trust (and a reacquisition by the trustees as nominee for the beneficial owner) at market value where a beneficiary becomes absolutely entitled to any settled property as against the trustee, ie where he became entitled to the asset or would do so but for being an infant or other person under a disability (*TCGA 1992, s 71(1), (3)*). Again, the tax can sometimes be deferred by making an election under *TCGA 1992, s 165* or *260*. Such an election can also reduce the tax rate if the beneficiary is taxable at only 10% or 18% on the gains or is able to utilise entrepreneurs' relief against them.

It needs to be realised that a beneficiary can become entitled to assets as against the trustees automatically as a result of a provision of the trust deed. For example, if the deed provides that the assets shall be held in trust for A whilst he is under 30 and that when he reaches 30 A will become entitled to the assets, A will become beneficially entitled to the assets as against the trustee on his thirtieth birthday, so triggering a tax charge, without the need for any decision by the trustees.

14.40 If a loss accrues to the trust on a person becoming absolutely entitled to an asset as against the trustees and the trust cannot utilise that loss in relation to disposals of other assets before that time, the loss is treated as accruing to the beneficiary but can only be utilised by him against gains from the same asset (or, if the asset is an interest in land, from that interest or any other asset deriving from it) (*TCGA 1992, s 71(2)*).

If on the death of a life tenant IHT is payable in relation to the settled property (as will apply to a pre-22 March 2006 IIP settlement and many post-22 March

2006 will trusts) the assets in which the interest subsisted are deemed to be disposed of and reacquired at their market value at the date of death – but no chargeable gain is treated as accruing to the settlement, ie there is simply an uplift in the settlement's CGT base cost of the assets (*TCGA 1992, s 72*).

If a beneficiary disposes of his interest in a settlement that disposal is exempt from CGT provided that the interest was created by, or arose under, the terms of the settlement and the settlement has never been non-UK resident. The exemption extends to a disposal by any other person, other than one who acquired (or derived his title from someone else who acquired) his interest in it for a consideration in money or money's worth.

Trusts with a vulnerable beneficiary

14.41 Special rules apply to trusts with a 'vulnerable beneficiary'. This is a disabled person or a relevant minor. A disabled person is one who is incapable of administering his property or managing his affairs by reason of mental disorder (within the Mental Health Act 1983); a person in receipt of attendance allowance; a person in receipt of disability living allowance by virtue of entitlement to the care component at the highest or middle rate or the mobility component at the higher rate; a person in receipt of personal independence payment; a person in receipt of (armed forces) constant attendance allowance; or a person in receipt of armed forces independence payments (*FA 2005, s 38* and *Sch 1A* inserted by *FA 2013, Sch 44, paras 19, 18* and amended by *FA 2014, s 284*). The definition was slightly different prior to 6 April 2013 and, in some respects, prior to 5 April 2014 also.

A non-resident disabled person can qualify for the relief provided that he shows that he would have been entitled to the appropriate allowance had he met the requirements for that allowance but does not do so only because he does not meet the UK residence and UK presence requirements. A person who ceases to be entitled to attendance allowance, disability living allowance or personal independence payments because her or she is in receipt of alternative benefits is treated as continuing to qualify.

A relevant minor is a person who is aged under 18 and at least one of whose parents has died (*FA 2005, s 39*).

The trustees of such a trust can make a claim to reduce their income tax liability to what the liability on the income would have been had it arisen directly to the vulnerable person. Such an election can be made even if the trust is non-UK resident, but only in relation to UK income. The claim is an annual one.

If the trust is UK resident (and the vulnerable beneficiary does not die during the tax year) and the vulnerable beneficiary election is made for the tax year, the CGT payable by the trust is similarly reduced to the amount that would have been payable by the beneficiary had he realised the gain direct (*FA 2005, ss 30–32*).

The property of the trust (or of a sub-trust) must be applicable only for the benefit of the vulnerable beneficiary and no part of the income can be distributable to anyone else. From 6 April 2013, this latter requirement is relaxed to allow up to £3,000 of income and capital gains (or, if less, 3% of the maximum value of the trust assets during the tax year) to be applied to other beneficiaries (*FA 2005, ss 25, 28, 34, 35* as amended by *FA 2013, Sch 44, paras 14, 15*).

THE TAXATION OF NON-RESIDENT TRUSTEES

> **Focus**
>
> There are a large number of anti-avoidance provisions in relation to overseas trusts with UK resident beneficiaries. If the settlor is UK domiciled these are likely to apply even where the funds remain in the trust. If the settlor is non-UK domiciled they generally apply only where funds are distributed or a benefit is provided by the trust.
>
> It is important to consider the impact of these provisions before making a distribution from the trust. If there are both UK and non-UK beneficiaries the order in which distributions are made can alter the tax charges.

Income tax

14.42 The normal rule is that non-UK residents are chargeable to income tax only on UK earnings and property income and on other income only to the extent that tax is deducted at source (*ITA 2007, ss 811–814*).

However, this rule does not apply to a non-resident trust if it has a beneficiary who is either an individual who is resident in the UK (ordinary resident prior to 6 April 2013) or a UK-resident company (*ITA 2007, s 812*). A beneficiary for this purpose includes an actual or potential beneficiary who is (or will, or may, become) entitled under the trust to receive some or all of any income of the trust (or capital which represents amounts originally received as income) or to whom some or all of any income of the trust may be paid or for whose benefit such income might be used in the exercise of a discretion conferred by the trust (*ITA 2007, s 812(2)–(5)*).

It should be noted that the provision does not apply if all of the income beneficiaries are non-resident but trust capital can be paid to a UK resident.

Accordingly, a trust with a non-resident life tenant and a resident remainderman would not be caught. Where a trust falls within *ITA 2007, s 812*, it will of course be taxable on UK-source income only, as the territoriality principle will prevent the UK taxing a non-resident on non-UK source income.

14.43 The provisions in relation to UK settlements that attribute income of a settlement to the settlor in certain circumstances (*ITTOIA 2005, ss 624–629*) apply equally to non-resident settlements. So do the provisions that tax the income of a settlement (other than an interest-in-possession settlement) at the trust rate (*ITA 2007, ss 479–482*).

Where a non-resident settlement has both UK and non-UK source income the deduction for trustees' expenses is restricted in the proportion that non-UK (or other non-taxable) income bears to the total trust income (*ITA 2007, s 487*).

It also needs to be borne in mind that the anti-avoidance rules in relation to the transfer of assets to a non-resident as a result of which a person who is resident (or, prior to 6 April 2013, ordinarily resident) in the UK has power to enjoy the income of the non-resident or receives a benefit from the non-resident (*ITA 2007, ss 714–751*) apply to non-UK trusts and, where relevant, their underlying companies, in the same way as with other non-residents.

Capital gains tax

14.44 A non-UK settlement, like any other non-UK resident, is not liable to UK capital gains tax (except in relation to assets used for the purpose of a trade) (*TCGA 1992, s 2(1)*). For 2014/15 onwards, this does not apply to gains from UK residential property which are chargeable to NRCGT, a special version of CGT applying only to non-residents. The application of NRCGT is dealt with at **9.73–9.78**.

However, the gains of a non-UK settlement can be attributed to either the settlor or to beneficiaries.

Trust gains can be taxed on the settlor (as such) only if he is domiciled in the UK at some time during the tax year in which the gain accrues and he is resident here at some time during that year (*TCGA 1992, s 86(1)(c)*). In addition, the settlement must be a 'qualifying settlement' and the settlor must have an interest in the settlement at some time during the tax year concerned (*TCGA 1992, s 86(1)(a), (d)*).

14.45 A settlement is a qualifying settlement if it was created after 18 March 1991 or if it was created before that date and subsequent to 18 March 1991 one of the following applies (*TCGA 1992, Sch 5, para 9(1)–(6A)*):

- property or income is provided directly or indirectly for the purpose of the settlement otherwise than under a transaction entered into at arm's length (and otherwise in pursuance of a liability incurred before 19 March 1991) – but any additions solely to meet a deficit on the trust expenses can be ignored;

- the trust became non-UK resident (or fell to be regarded as non-resident under a double tax agreement);
- the terms of the settlement are varied so that either the settlor, a spouse or civil partner of the settlor, a child or grandchild of the settlor or the settlor's spouse, the spouse or civil partner of a child or grandchild, or a company controlled by any such person or persons (or associated with a company so controlled) becomes for the first time a person who will or might benefit under the settlement (and under the terms of the settlement as they stood at 18 March 1991 that person would not have been capable of enjoying a benefit from the settlement after that date); or
- the settlement ceases to be a 'protected settlement' at a time after 5 April 1999.

14.46 A settlement is a protected settlement if it was formed before 19 March 1991 and at 5 April 1999 (and at all times thereafter) the only beneficiaries of the settlement were:

- children of the settlor (or of a spouse or civil partner of the settlor) who are under 18 (at the end of the tax year immediately preceding that in which the gain arises);
- unborn children of the settlor (or of a spouse or civil partner of the settlor or of a future spouse or civil partner of the settlor);
- future spouses or civil partners of any children (or future children) of the settlor or a spouse or future spouse (or civil partner or future civil partner) of the settlor;
- a future spouse or civil partner of the settlor; or
- persons outside these defined categories (ie he is not a person whose relationship to the settlor (or any of the settlors if there is more than one) would give the settlor an interest in the settlement (*TCGA 1992, Sch 5, para 9(10A), (10B)*)).

In applying these tests a person is a beneficiary if there are any circumstances whatsoever in which any of the settled property (or income therefrom) is, or will or may become, applicable for his benefit or payable to him or he enjoys a benefit directly or indirectly from any of the settled property or the income therefrom (*TCGA 1992, Sch 5, para 9(10C), (10D)*).

14.47 The settlor has an interest in the settlement if any of the settled property, or income therefrom, is (or will or may become) applicable for the benefit of (or payable to) a defined person in any circumstances whatsoever, or any defined person enjoys a benefit directly or indirectly from any of the settled property or income therefrom (*TCGA 1992, Sch 5, para 2(1)*).

The defined persons are:

(a) the settlor;

(b) the spouse or civil partner of the settlor;

(c) a child of the settlor (or of the settlor's spouse or civil partner);

(d) the spouse or civil partner of any such child;

(e) any grandchild of the settlor (or of the settlor's spouse or civil partner);

(f) the spouse or civil partner of any such grandchild;

(g) a company controlled by one or more of the above; and

(h) a company associated with a company controlled by one or more of the above.

(*TCGA 1992, Sch 5, para 2(3)*)

14.48 There are the usual exceptions where the defined person can benefit only in the event of the bankruptcy or similar event of someone who is not a defined person (*TCGA 1992, Sch 5, para 2(4)(5)*).

Heads (e) and (f) do not apply to a settlement created before 17 March 1998 unless property is added to it after that date, it becomes non-resident after that date, its terms are varied after that date, or a grandchild (or spouse) receives a benefit after that date he could not have received under the terms of the settlement as they stood at 17 March 1998 (*TCGA 1992, Sch 5, para 2A*).

It will be seen that this provision is significantly wider than the corresponding income tax provision, which does not include either grandchildren or adult children of the settlor.

14.49 If the settlor does not have an interest in the settlement the trust gains are attributed to beneficiaries. The amount to be attributed in a tax year is of course the trust gains for the year plus any unattributed gains (after taper relief where appropriate) of earlier years (*TCGA 1992, s 87(1), (2)*). NRCGT gains or losses (ie on UK residential property – see **9.73**) are excluded from the calculation as they will already have been taxed on the trustees (*CTGA 1992, s 87(5A)*).

The amount so calculated is attributed to beneficiaries (including, curiously, non-resident beneficiaries) who receive capital payments from the settlement in the tax year or who received capital payments in earlier years which have not yet been matched with gains. The gains are then attributed to those beneficiaries in proportion to their capital payments up to the amount of such payments. Any unattributed part of the gains is carried forward to the next tax year (*TCGA 1992, s 87(4), (5)*).

Gains attributed to a beneficiary who is not domiciled in the UK are taxable here but subject to any application of the remittance basis. The domicile of the settlor does not affect the taxability of the beneficiary. Gains attributed to beneficiaries who are UK resident and domiciled are treated as gains realised by the beneficiary.

14.50 If the settlement migrates to the UK without all of the past gains having been attributed to beneficiaries the attribution continues so as to attribute those gains to beneficiaries who receive capital payments from the settlement in subsequent years (*TCGA 1992, s 89*).

To the extent that gains are not matched with capital payments in the same tax year or the year following that in which the gain arises, the beneficiary is also liable to a surcharge on the tax. The surcharge is 10% pa for the period from 1 December following the tax year in which the gain arose to 30 November in the tax year following that in which the capital payment is made. The surcharge cannot run for more than six years though, so it is effectively limited to 12% of the gain (60% of the 20% tax rate) (*TCGA 1992, s 91*). This gives an effective CGT rate of 32%.

14.51 If the settlement distributes assets to another settlement the unallocated trust gains of the first are treated as trust gains of the second settlement and allocated to beneficiaries who receive capital payments from the second settlement. If part only of the settled property is transferred then only a proportionate part of the unallocated gains of the first settlement is transferred to the second (*TCGA 1992, s 90*).

The normal exemption for a disposal by a beneficiary of his interest in a settlement does not apply to an interest in a non-resident settlement (*TCGA 1992, ss 76(1A), 85*). Such a disposal is accordingly chargeable to CGT.

In addition, where the interest is disposed of for consideration and the trustees were UK resident at any time in the tax year in which the disposal occurs, the settlor was UK resident or ordinarily resident in that year or in any of the five previous tax years, and the settlor has an interest in the settlement in that or in the previous two tax years, the trustees must be treated as having sold and immediately reacquired the relevant underlying assets of the settlement, ie the part of the assets in which the beneficiary's interest subsisted (*TCGA 1992, Sch 4A, paras 1–8*). *TCGA 1992, Sch 4A* displaces the charge on the beneficiary, unless that would be greater than the charge on the trustees (or there would be a lower loss on the disposal) under *TCGA 1992, Sch 4A* – in which case, *TCGA 1992, s 76(1A)* displaces the *TCGA 1992, Sch 4A* charge (*TCGA 1992, Sch 4A, para 10(2)*).

14.52 If a UK-resident settlement ceases to be UK resident at any time, the migration triggers a deemed disposal and reacquisition of all of the trust assets at the time of the migration so as to create a taxable gain while the settlement is UK resident (*TCGA 1992, s 80*). There is an exception where the migration occurs because of the death of a trustee provided that the settlement becomes UK resident again within the following six months (and the assets have not been disposed of during the period of non-residence) (*TCGA 1992, s 81*).

If the tax due on the migration of a settlement is not paid within six months of the due date, HMRC can recover it from anybody who was a trustee at any time in the 12 months prior to the migration. They cannot recover the tax from a person who ceased to be a trustee some time before the migration and can show that at the time that he ceased to be a trustee there was no proposal that the trust should emigrate (*TCGA 1992, s 82*).

14.53 If it is wished to migrate a settlement, it needs to be borne in mind that *Trustee Act 1925, s 37(1)(c)* provides that a trustee should not be discharged from his trust unless there will be either a trust corporation or at least two individuals to act as trustees to perform the trust. In most cases a trust corporation is a company incorporated in either the UK or another EU country.

In *Jasmine Trustees Ltd v Wells & Hind (a firm)* [2007] STC 660, UK trustees resigned and were replaced by an Isle of Man company. It was held that the resignation was ineffective, with the result that the previous UK trustees were still the trustees, so the trust remained UK resident and all of the acts of the new trustees must have been entered into as agent for the real trustees.

14.54 If the trustees of a non-resident settlement with a UK-resident beneficiary or a UK resident and domiciled settlor makes a transfer of value and that transfer is linked with trustee borrowing, the trustees are deemed to dispose of and immediately reacquire the whole (or a proportion of) the chargeable assets of the settlement (*TCGA 1992, Sch 4B, para 1*).

For this purpose trustees make a transfer of value if they:

- lend money or any other asset to any person;
- transfer an asset to any person either for no consideration or at an undervalue; or
- issue a security of any description to any person either for no consideration or at an undervalue.

14.55 The transfer of value is treated as made when the loan is made, the transfer is effectively completed (ie the transferee becomes for practical purposes unconditionally entitled to the asset) or the security is issued, as the case may be (*TCGA 1992, Sch 4B, para 2*).

A transfer of value is linked with trustee borrowing if at the time of the loan or transfer there is outstanding trustee borrowing, ie either:

- any loan obligation is outstanding; or
- there is trustee borrowing that has not been either applied for normal trust purposes or triggered a tax charge under *TCGA 1992, Sch 4B* in relation to an earlier transfer of value.

(*TCGA 1992, Sch 4B, para 5*)

14.56 A borrowing is applied for normal trust purposes if it is used to acquire a trust asset either at arm's length or at no more than an arm's-length price, is used to repay an earlier borrowing for such a purpose, or is used to meet bona fide current trust management expenses (*TCGA 1992, Sch 4B, para 6*).

The deemed disposal is of the whole of the trust assets unless the amount of value transferred is either:

- less than both the amount of outstanding trustee borrowing and the effective value of the remaining chargeable assets, in which case the deemed disposal and reacquisition is of the proportion of each of the remaining chargeable assets given by:

$$\frac{\text{amount of value transferred}}{\text{effective value of the remaining chargeable assets}}$$

- less than the effective value of the remaining chargeable assets (but not less than the outstanding trustee borrowing) in which case the deemed disposal and reacquisition is of the proportion of each of the remaining chargeable assets given by:

$$\frac{\text{amount of outstanding trustee borrowing}}{\text{effective value of the remaining chargeable assets}}$$

14.57 The effective value of the remaining chargeable assets is their aggregate market value less so much of that value as is attributable to trustee borrowing (*TCGA 1992, Sch 4B, para 11*). The value of an asset is attributable to trustee borrowing to the extent that the trustees applied the borrowing to acquire or enhance the value of the asset (or the asset represents directly or indirectly an asset whose value was attributable to the trustees having so applied the proceeds of trustee borrowing) (*TCGA 1992, Sch 4B, para 11*).

14.58 Where *TCGA 1992, Sch 4B* applies the gains are of course attributed to the settlor (if he has an interest in the settlement) or to beneficiaries who receive capital payments from the settlement (if he does not) (*TCGA 1992, Sch 4C*).

This provision prevents avoidance of the tax charge by the trustees borrowing against the trust assets and distributing the money borrowed instead of selling the assets and distributing the proceeds. It was aimed against what was known as the 'flip-flop' scheme under which trust 1 would borrow and distribute the amount borrowed to trust 2 and in the next tax year sell the assets and use the gain to repay the borrowing. As trust 1 made no capital payment to beneficiaries and trust 2, which did make capital payments, realised no gains this was thought to avoid the tax charge.

In fact, in the light of the subsequent decision in *West (Inspector of Taxes) v Trennery* (2003) 76 TC 713, the scheme probably did not work but the very complex legislation in *TCGA 1992, Schs 4B* and *4C* nevertheless remains.

Settlements with non-UK domiciled settlors

14.59 Broadly speaking, the non-UK income and gains of a settlement with a non-UK domiciled settlor and non-UK domiciled beneficiaries were outside the scope of the anti-avoidance rules on both income tax and capital gains tax up to 5 April 2017, provided that, if the income or gain was distributed to the beneficiary, it was not remitted to the UK. Following the changes to the domicile rules, such an overseas settlement, where the settlor is resident in the UK and was born in the UK with a UK domicile of origin, is brought fully within the anti-avoidance rules from 6 April 2017 (although prior income and gains of the settlement continue to be tax-free while they remain in the settlement, and any distribution of them to UK resident beneficiaries continues to be taxed in the UK on a remittance basis).

However, the *Finance (No 2) Bill 2017* creates a new form of protected settlement. The CGT settlor charge (see **14.44**) does not apply where the settlor was non-UK domiciled and remains non-UK domiciled (or deemed domiciled until he has lived in the UK for 15 out of 20 tax years). It also does not apply where the settlor has become deemed domiciled under the '15 out of 20 years' rule, provided that he does not (directly or indirectly) add any property to the settlement after 5 April 2017 (*TCGA 1992, Sch 5, para 5A*, inserted by *Finance (No 2) Bill 2017*). There are exemptions: for added property or income that is provided on arm's length terms (ie the settlor sells something to the settlement at market value); for a loan on arm's length terms (including a pre-5 April 2017 loan, if the terms are amended to provide for a market rate of interest), provided that the interest is actually paid annually; for a loan repayment by the trustees to the settlor; and for property or income provided to meet the trust's expenses of administration (or taxation), to the extent that such amounts exceed the trust's income for the year (*TCGA 1992, s 86(5B)*).

14.60 There is a similar exemption for protected foreign source income of a non-UK settlement. This is income that: would be relevant foreign source income (as defined in *ITTOIA 2015, s 830*) if it were income of a UK resident; is derived from property originating from a non-domiciled settlor (and non-deemed domiciled, if the settlement is created after 5 April 2017); arises in a year in which the settlor is a non-domiciled person (and is not deemed domiciled under the '15 out of 20 years' rule); and is not provided (directly or indirectly) to the settlement by the settlor (or by another settlement of which the settlor is settlor or a beneficiary) at a time when the settlor is UK domiciled or deemed domiciled under the '15 out of 20 years' rule (*ITTOIA 2005, s 628A*, inserted by *Finance (No 2) Bill 2017*). The same exceptions for added property or income as apply for CGT purposes also apply for this purpose (*ITTOIA 2005, s 628B*). The exemption is, of course, carried through to the tax charge on the settlor that applies where the trust distributes income to his minor child (*ITTOIA 2005, s 630A*) and to the charge on capital payments to the settlor (*ITTOIA 2005, s 635(3)*). *ITA 2007, ss 721* (undistributed income which the settlor has power to enjoy) and *729* (capital receipts) are similarly amended to exclude protected foreign source income from being taxed on the settlor under that provision (*ITA 2007, ss 721(3B), 721A, 721B*). The rules on capital receipts are also amended so that a capital payment to a non-domiciled settlor after 5 April 2017 cannot be matched with protected foreign source income (*ITA 2007, ss 728(1A), 729A*).

However, such a settlor is brought within *ITTOIA 2005, s 731* (receipts by persons other than the settlor), so that an actual distribution to the non-domiciled settlor will attract income tax in the same way as distributions to other beneficiaries (*Finance (No 2) Bill 2017*).

The effect of these changes is to keep income and gains of a qualifying settlement with a non-UK domiciled settlor out of the scope of both UK income tax and capital gains tax while it remains within the settlement. This applies to both pre- and post-6 April 2017 income and gains. However, a distribution from the settlement of the income or gains to the settlor will trigger both income tax and CGT in the same way that a distribution to a beneficiary previously did.

Inheritance tax

14.61 Trusts are within the scope of inheritance tax (IHT) but are taxed under a special IHT regime – or to be more precise a number of different IHT regimes. The residence or domicile of the settlor is irrelevant, except to the extent that non-UK assets of a settlement are excluded property (and therefore outside the scope of IHT) if the settlor was non-UK domiciled (and not deemed UK domiciled) at the time that the settlement was made (*IHTA 1984, s 48(3)*).

There are two main trust regimes, the interest-in-possession regime and the relevant property regime. Relevant property simply means property not falling into the IIP regime. The relevant property regime applies to all trusts created after 22 March 2006 including *inter vivos* interest-in-possession trusts (but excluding special forms of will trust). The interest-in-possession regime applies to interest-in-possession trusts created before 22 March 2006 and to some will trusts created after that date.

The relevant property regime

14.62 There are three possible occasions of charge to IHT:

- on the settlor on creation of the settlement (the 'entry charge');
- on the settlement on each tenth anniversary (the 'ten-yearly charge');
- on distributions from the settlement or the termination of the settlement (the 'exit charge').

The entry charge

14.63 Transferring assets into settlements constitutes a gift. A gift into settlement is generally not a potentially exempt transfer, so it attracts IHT but at 50% of normal rates, ie the tax charge is 20% of the value of the assets put into the settlement in excess of the £325,000 nil rate band (for 2016/17). As with other gifts, prior gifts within the seven years prior to the gift into settlement are aggregated with the gift into settlement to determine how much, if any, of the nil rate band is available to utilise against the gift.

The entry charge does not apply in the case of a will trust, as the death of the deceased will have triggered IHT and the creation of the trust is simply the disposition of part of the assets on that death.

The ten-yearly charge

14.64 The ten-yearly charge is imposed on each tenth anniversary of the creation of the settlement (*IHTA 1984, s 64*). If extra assets are added to the settlement the addition is not treated as a separate settlement; there is only one anniversary date for the entire settlement.

The charge is at a special rate of 30% of half the normal IHT rate. This gives a maximum rate of 6% of the value of the assets in the settlement at the anniversary date (30% of 50% of 40% = 6%) (*IHTA 1984, s 66(1)*). In most cases the charge is significantly less than 6% as the nil rate band applies in the normal way.

14.65 The tax rate is based on the tax that would be payable on a gift equal to the value of the trust assets at the anniversary date by a deemed donor who had made gifts in the prior seven years equal to the gifts made by the actual settlor in the seven years prior to the initial gift into settlement (*IHTA 1984, s 66(3)*).

Accordingly, if the actual settlor had made no gifts in the seven-year period the full £325,000 nil rate band would be available in calculating the tax payable under the ten-yearly charge. If assets have been added to the settlement in the ten-year period the gifts in the seven years prior to that addition are used as the starting point if they are greater than those in the seven years prior to the creation of the settlement (*IHTA 1984, s 67*).

The tax is calculated by computing the average rate and applying that to the value of the relevant property, ie the capital assets held by the settlement. However, if assets have been added to the settlement since the previous ten-year anniversary, the tax attributable to such assets is pro-rated by reference to the number of quarter years that the assets were in the settlement (*IHTA 1984, s 66(2)*). This reduction does not apply to uncapitalised interest which is deemed to be capital under *IHTA 1984, s 64(1A)* (*IHTA 1984, s 66(2A)*).

For transfers after 6 April 2014, income received is treated as relevant property, ie as capital, for the purpose of the 10-yearly charge if it arose more than five years before the anniversary date, arose (directly or indirectly) from property comprised in the settlement which at the time was relevant property, and at the time it arose no one had an IIP in the property from which the interest derives (*IHTA 1984, s 64(1A)* inserted by *Finance Act 2014, Sch 21, para 4*). This is intended to prevent trustees with a power to accumulate income from delaying a decision to capitalise the income until after the next 10-year anniversary. It is, however, a somewhat odd provision as it applies only to income generated by the trust capital (including income that has been actually accumulated). It will not affect income under, say, a deed of covenant or income from the investment of past income that has not been formally capitalised. The reason for this distinction is not readily apparent.

Where the settlor was not UK domiciled at the time the settlement was made, income which is situated outside the UK or which is represented by a holding in an authorised unit trust or a share in an OEIC is disregarded for this purpose. So is income represented by IHT on exempt gifts provided that all known persons for whose benefit the capital or income might be applied meet the terms of the exemption.

Example 14.1 – Ten-year anniversary charge

Joe created a settlement on 1 June 1976. On 1 June 2016, the value of the assets in the settlement was £2,025,000. £400,000 of those assets were added by Joe to the settlement on 31 December 2014. Joe had made no gifts in the seven years prior to the creation of the settlement or in the seven years prior to 31 December 2014.

The tax on £2.025m is	£325,000 @ nil%	£ nil
	£1,700,000 @ 40%	£680,000
		£680,000
The average rate is		33.56%
30% of 50% of 33.56% is		5.03%
The tax payable is		
5.03% of £1,625,000		£81,737.50
6/40 × 5.03% of £400,000 (as the property was in the settlement for only six quarters in the ten-year period)		£3,018.00
Tax payable		£84,755.50

The exit charge

14.66 If there is other property in the settlement which is not subject to the ten-yearly charge, such as property in which there is an interest in possession, the value of that property at the time that it was put into the settlement has to be added to the value subject to the charge in order to calculate the effective rate of tax. So does the value at the date of the settlement of property put into a related settlement (one made by the same settlor on the same day) (*IHTA 1984, s 66(4)*).

The reason is that these are in effect gifts made by the settlor in the seven years up to the creation of the settlement. If property has been distributed since the last ten-year anniversary the amount on which tax was charged on such distributions also has to be added in to calculate the rate of tax on the next ten-year anniversary (*IHTA 1984, s 66(5)*).

The exit charge is similar to the ten-yearly charge. It is payable when assets are distributed from the settlement. It is in effect the proportion of the ten-yearly charge attributable to the number of quarters (or part quarters) for which the property was in the settlement since that charge last arose (*IHTA 1984, s 69*).

14.67 The rate of tax used for the exit charge is however based on the average rate at the previous ten-year anniversary (*IHTA 1984, s 69(1)*). On a distribution before the first ten-year anniversary the rate is that payable by a notional transferor at the time of the creation of the settlement who had made transfers equal to the value of the property settled (at the time it was settled) plus the value of any gifts made by the settlor in the seven years prior to the creation of the settlement (*IHTA 1984, s 68*).

The effect of this is that if no tax was payable on the creation of the settlement nothing is payable on a distribution of the assets prior to the first ten-year anniversary, however high the value of those assets might be at the time of the distribution. That is not wholly correct. There is a tax trap if the assets settled qualified for business property or agricultural property relief. The notional transfer by the deemed transferor is not a transfer of such property. Accordingly, it is only if the value before business or agricultural property relief fell within the nil rate band that the tax payable on a distribution will be nil. Of course, this may not matter if the property that is distributed itself qualifies for 100% business property relief as, in such a case, the value to which the rate is applied is nil, so the rate does not matter.

No exit charge is payable if the distribution takes place within three months after a ten-year anniversary (*IHTA 1984, s 65(4)*).

The interest-in-possession regime

14.68 The interest-in-possession (IIP) regime applies to:

- interest-in-possession trusts created before 22 March 2006;
- some accumulation and maintenance trusts created before 22 March 2006;
- will trusts with an 'immediate post death' interest;
- trusts for disabled persons;
- protective trusts.

It should be borne in mind that where property is added to an existing settlement that addition is actually a separate settlement held on the trusts of the existing one (except for the purpose of the ten-yearly charge) (*IHTA 1984, s 43(2)*).

Accordingly, property added to a pre-22 March 2006 IIP trust after that date will be governed by the relevant property regime not the IIP one.

Pre-22 March 2006 IIP trusts

14.69 The settled property is treated for IHT purposes as belonging to the life tenant (or other person with the IIP) even if he has no right to capital (*IHTA 1984, s 49(1)*). There is no ten-yearly charge on such a settlement but IHT at the full rates is payable on the death of the life tenant, treating the settled property as the top slice of his estate. The trustees are liable for payment of the tax, but if they do not pay it the tax can be collected from the deceased's estate, any person who receives a benefit from the settlement after the death or, in the case of a non-resident settlement, the settlor (*IHTA 1984, s 201*).

If the interest in possession terminates during the life of the beneficiary with the IIP he is treated as making a gift of the settled property. The effect is that if the property remains in the settlement, eg it becomes a discretionary settlement or an IIP is created in relation to someone else, he is treated as creating a new discretionary settlement, thus triggering an entry charge liability, but if the property passes to an individual the deemed gift will be a potentially exempt transfer on which IHT will be payable only if the beneficiary dies within the next seven years.

14.70 Prior to 22 March 2006, if the property remained in the settlement but a different beneficiary became entitled to an IIP this was also treated as a PET. This treatment continued to apply if the IIP came to an end before 6 October 2008 (*IHTA 1984, s 49C*). This effectively gave a short window within which the identity of the person with the IIP could be altered. For example, an IIP in favour of a parent could be terminated by creating a new IIP in favour of his child (provided, of course, that the trust gave the power to do so).

It also continues to apply if the IIP comes to an end by the death of the beneficiary after 5 April 2008 and the spouse or civil partner of the beneficiary becomes entitled to an IIP on the death of the beneficiary (*IHTA 1984, s 49D*).

It also continues to apply where the settled property is an insurance contract, the person with the IIP dies after 6 April 2008 and a different person acquires an IIP on the death. This treatment will continue if a new beneficiary takes over the IIP on the second beneficiary's death and so on, provided that there is an unbroken sequence of IIPs from 22 March 2006 (*IHTA 1984, s 49E*).

14.71 Where a beneficiary has an IIP in only part of the trust assets the IIP treatment obviously applies only to that part (*IHTA 1984, s 50(1)*). If the interest is a right to a fixed annual sum (or to the trust income less a fixed annual sum) special rules apply to determine the amount in which the IIP is deemed to exist (*IHTA 1984, s 50*; *CTT (Settled Property Income Yield) Order 2000, SI 2000/174*).

If an IIP beneficiary disposed of his IIP (and the trust is within the IIP regime at the time) the disposal is not charged to CGT but the interest of the beneficiary is instead deemed to terminate so triggering the IHT charge that would arise on a termination of the IIP (*IHTA 1984, s 51*). No charge arises if the disposal is a gift for the maintenance of the life tenant's family (*IHTA 1984, s 51(4)*).

If the IIP beneficiary sells his interest (or otherwise disposes of it for money or money's worth) the consideration is deducted from the value of the settled property in calculating the IHT (presumably because the sale proceeds remain in the beneficiary's estate) (*IHTA 1984, s 52*). No tax is of course chargeable in relation to any of the trust assets which are excluded property (non-UK assets of a settlement created by a non-UK domiciled settlor) (*IHTA 1984, s 53(1)*).

14.72 There is also an exception if the trust property reverts to the settlor or his spouse or civil partner (or to his widow or surviving civil partner if he died within the previous two years) on the termination of the IIP and the settlor or spouse, etc is alive at that time and (except in the case of a revertor to the settlor) domiciled in the UK (*IHTA 1984, s 53(3), (4)*). The exemption does not apply if the settlor or spouse, etc acquired the reversionary interest for a consideration in money or money's worth (*IHTA 1984, s 53(5)*).

The revertor to settlor exemption also applies if the reversion is brought about by the death of the life tenant (*IHTA 1984, s 54*).

Accumulation and maintenance settlement

14.73 An accumulation and maintenance (A&M) settlement is a cross between a discretionary trust and an IIP trust. The settlement must have been created before 22 March 2006, and the settled property must be held for one or more persons who will become entitled to an interest in possession in it on or before age 18, and while no interest in possession subsists the income must be either accumulated or applied to, or for the benefit of, such beneficiaries (*IHTA 1984, s 71(1)*).

In addition either all of the beneficiaries must be grandchildren of a common grandparent (or surviving children of a deceased grandchild) or all of the beneficiaries must acquire their IIP within 25 years of the creation of the settlement (*IHTA 1984, s 71(2)*). No IHT charge arises on the death of a beneficiary before he obtains his IIP or on the attainment of the IIP, and after he does so the normal IHT rules apply (*IHTA 1984, s 71(4)*).

14.74 Prior to 6 April 2008, the IIP could be deferred until age 25. The *FA 2006* change gave a short window in which to amend existing A&M settlements to preserve the tax benefits. However, most people do not want children to acquire substantial assets at 18 for fear that the child may be financially immature at such a comparatively young age. Accordingly, it is unlikely that many people will have taken the opportunity to amend their A&M settlements in this way. An A&M settlement that does not meet the new rules came into the discretionary trust regime from 6 April 2008 (except of course to the extent that any beneficiary may have already become entitled to an IIP in part of the settled property). Where this happened there was, however, no IHT charge by reference to that event (*FA 2006, Sch 20, para 3(3)*)

14.75 If the settled property ceases to qualify as an A&M settlement in any other circumstances (other than by being used to meet trust expenses) IHT is chargeable at a special rate (*IHTA 1984, s 71(5)*). This is based on the period during which the property was held on A&M trusts (but ignoring any period before 13 March 1975). It is:

- 0.25% for each of the first 40 quarters;
- 0.20% for each of the next 40 quarters;
- 0.15% for each of the next 40 quarters;
- 0.10% for each of the next 40 quarters;
- 0.05% for each of the next 40 quarters.

(*IHTA 1984, s 70(6)*)

For example, if a property is held in A&M trusts for 22 years and the assets are then distributed to an adult beneficiary (other than the one with the IIP) the charge would be 4.8% of the value of the asset (0.25% for ten years plus 0.20% for ten years plus 0.15% for two years).

Immediate post-death interests

14.76 An immediate post-death interest is an interest in possession in settled property where the settlement was created by will or under the laws of intestacy, the beneficiary became entitled to the IIP on the death of the testator or intestate and he has remained entitled to it since that time (*IHTA 1984, s 49A*).

As with pre-22 March 2006 trusts, the beneficiary is treated as owning the assets for IHT purposes, so the discretionary trust regime will not apply even though the testator's death occurred after 22 March 2006 (*IHTA 1984, s 49*).

14.77 This provision was introduced to preserve the IHT exemption where an IIP in the testator's estate is left to his surviving spouse on his death. As the surviving spouse is deemed to beneficially own the assets, on the death the exemption for a gift to the spouse applies to the assets in which the IIP is created.

However, an immediate post-death interest is not limited to assets passing to the surviving spouse or civil partner; such an interest can be created in favour of anybody. If the beneficiary is someone other than the surviving spouse or civil partner, IHT will of course be payable on the death, but no further IHT charge will arise until the termination of the IIP.

Trusts for disabled persons

14.78 A trust for a disabled person is one under which during the life of the disabled person no interest in possession in the settled property exists but the trusts secure that during the disabled person's life any distribution is applied for the benefit of the disabled person.

For money put into the settlement prior to 8 April 2013 only, at least half of the settled property that is applied by the trustees during that person's life must be applied for his benefit (*IHTA 1984, s 89(1)* as amended by *FA 2013, Sch 44, para 6*).

In relation to property transferred to the settlement after 7 April 2013, the trust can still qualify as one for a disabled person if the trustees have power to pay up to £3,000 of income and capital gains (or 3% of the maximum value of the trust property during the tax year, if less) otherwise than for the benefit of the disabled person. They can also have the power of advancement under *Trustee Act 1925, s 32* (including with a less restrictive limitation than the Act allows) (*IHTA 1984, s 89(3), (3A), (3B)* as substituted by *FA 2013, Sch 44, para 6*).

A disabled person has the same meaning as in *FA 2005, Sch 1A* (see **14.41**). In relation to property transferred into the settlement before 8 April 2013, a disabled person is one who, when the property was settled, fell within one of the following categories:

(a) incapable by reason of mental disorder (within the meaning in the *Mental Health Act 1983*) of administering his property or managing his affairs;

(b) in receipt of attendance allowance under *SSCBA 1992, s 64*;

(c) in receipt of a disability living allowance under *SSCBA 1992, s 71*, by virtue of entitlement to the care component at the highest or middle rate or the mobility component at the higher rate;

(d) a person who would have met (b) or (c) but for the exceptions for persons in a hospital undergoing treatment for renal failure or for whom certain accommodation has been provided; or

(e) any other person who satisfies HMRC that he would have met (b) or (c) had he met the prescribed conditions of residence under *SSCBA 1992, s 64(1)* or *71(6)*, and had the provisions made by regulations under *SSCBA 1992, s 67(1), (2)* or *72(8)* been ignored (these conditions require the person to be resident in the UK, so this head will cover trusts for non-UK resident disabled persons).

(*IHTA 1984, s 89(4)–(6)*)

Where these conditions are met the disabled person is deemed to have an interest in possession in the settled property and the IIP regime accordingly applies to the settlement even if it is created after 22 March 2006 (*IHTA 1984, s 71(2)*). The qualifying conditions for trusts created before 10 March 1981 are slightly different (*IHTA 1984, s 74*).

Settlement by a person with a condition likely to lead to disability

14.79 If a person creates a settlement for his own benefit at a time (after 21 March 2006) when he can satisfy HMRC that he has a condition that is likely to lead to him becoming a disabled person within the meaning of *FA 2005, Sch 1A* (see **14.41**) (or would be one if he were resident in the UK), he is treated as being beneficially entitled to an interest in possession in the property (*IHTA 1984, s 89A*).

The property must be held on trusts under which the individual does not have an interest in possession in the settled property and which secure that, during his lifetime, the settled property (and the income from it) can only be used for his benefit and if the trust is terminated, either he will become absolutely entitled to the settled property or a disabled person's interest will subsist in the settled property. As with a trust for a disabled person, this applies the IIP regime to the trust. A disabled person's interest is an interest in possession to which a disabled person (or a person within *IHTA 1984, s 89A*) is treated as beneficially entitled; an interest in possession in settled property to which a disabled person becomes beneficially entitled after 21 March 2006; or an interest in possession in settled property to which the settlor is entitled and for which the settlor satisfies HMRC that the conditions of *IHTA 1984, s 89A* (other than the requirement for no interest in possession) exist (*IHTA 1984, s 89B*).

As with a disabled person's settlement, for assets settled after 7 April 2013 the trust can still qualify if the trustees have power to pay up to the £3,000 or 3% of assets limit to someone else (*IHTA 1984, s 89A(6A)–(6C)* inserted by *FA 2013, Sch 44, para 7*).

Where a person is or is likely to become disabled, it is clearly sensible to ensure that any trust meets the conditions to qualify for this special treatment.

Protective trusts

14.80 Property is held on protective trusts if it is held on trusts to the like effect as those specified in *Trustee Act 1925, s 33(1)* (*IHTA 1984, s 88(1)*). This is a trust in which a person ('the principal beneficiary') has an IIP but if the principal beneficiary does, or attempts to do or suffers, any event or thing whereby he would be deprived of the right to the trust income (eg he becomes bankrupt or tries to sell his interest in the trust) the income instead comes to be held on discretionary trusts for the maintenance or support (or otherwise for the benefit of) the principal beneficiary and his spouse, children or remoter issue (or for the principal beneficiary and the persons who would become entitled to the trust property on his death if he has no spouse or descendants).

The principal beneficiary is treated for IHT purposes as continuing to have an IIP in the settled property even if the trust has become discretionary. The IIP regime will accordingly continue to apply if the trust was created before 22 March 2006. It will not, however, apply if the trust was created after that date unless the beneficiary's interest is an immediate post-death interest, a disabled person's interest or a transitional serial interest (ie a post-21 March 2006 IIP arising in succession to a pre-22 March one) (*IHTA 1984, s 88*).

Special trusts

14.81 Special rules apply to:

- trusts for bereaved minors;
- age 18-to-25 trusts;
- charitable trusts;
- employee trusts and newspaper trusts;
- maintenance funds for historic buildings.

Trusts for bereaved minors

14.82 A trust for a bereaved minor is one established under the will of a deceased parent of the minor or under the Criminal Injuries Compensation Scheme and which provides that:

- the bereaved minor will become absolutely entitled to the settled property (and any accumulated income) at or before age 18;
- any income applied for the benefit of a beneficiary whilst the minor is under 18 is applied for the benefit of the bereaved minor; and
- any other benefit provided out of the settled property whilst the minor is under 18 is applied for the benefit of the bereaved minor.

(*IHTA 1984, s 71A(1)–(3)*)

The statutory trust created on the intestacy of a parent for the benefit of a bereaved minor also qualifies (*IHTA 1984, s 71A(1)*). A bereaved minor is a person who is under 18 and at least one of whose parents had died (*IHTA 1984, s 71C*).

No IHT charge arises on the bereaved minor obtaining his right to the settled property, or dying under 18, or on any capital distribution to the bereaved minor while he is under 18 (*IHTA 1984, s 71B(2)*). The special tax charge described above in relation to A&M settlements applies if the settled property ceases to be held for the benefit of the bereaved minor in any other circumstance (other than it being used to meet trust expenses) (*IHTA 1984, s 71B(3)*).

In relation to property transferred into a settlement after 7 April 2013, a trust can still qualify as one for a bereaved minor if it allows up to £3,000 of income and capital gains (or 3% of the maximum value of the settled property in the trust during the tax year, if less) to be applied otherwise than for the benefit of the bereaved minor (*IHTA 1984, s 71A(4), (4A)* inserted by *FA 2013, Sch 44, para* 2). There is also no tax charge on a distribution other than to the bereaved minor provided that it falls within the £3,000 or 3% of capital figure (*IHTA 1984, s 71B(2A), (2B)* inserted by *FA 2013, Sch 44, para 3*).

Age 18-to-25 trusts

14.83 An age 18-to-25 trust is similar to a trust for a bereaved minor, and like it can only be created by will or under the Criminal Injuries Compensation Scheme, but the beneficiary need not become entitled to the asset until age 25 (*IHTA 1984, s 71D*). Many people are unwilling to take the risk that a child may be financially immature at age 18 and thus are unlikely to be attracted to a trust for a bereaved minor. Some such people may be more willing to create such a trust if the beneficiary does not take the assets until age 25.

The trust must provide that the beneficiary will become absolutely entitled to the capital, any income arising from it and any accumulated income on or before age 25, that any distribution while he is under 25 is applied for his benefit and that any distributions are applied for his benefit (*IHTA 1984, s 71D(6)* as amended by *FA 2013, Sch 44, para* 2).

The income can be held on protective trusts but only for the beneficiary (*IHTA 1984, s 71D(6A)* inserted by *FA 2013, Sch 44, para 4*). As with trusts for deceased minors, in relation to property transferred into the settlement after 7 April 2013, a trust can still qualify if up to £3,000 or 3% of the capital value is applied for a different beneficiary (*IHTA 1984, s 71D(7)(za), (7A)* inserted by *FA 2013, Sch 44, para 4*).

As with a trust for a bereaved minor, IHT is not charged on the death of a beneficiary under the age of 18 (not 25), or on a distribution of capital to the beneficiary at or under the age of 18. Nor is it charged in respect of assets used to meet trust expenses, or to make distributions to other beneficiaries within the £3,000 or 3% of assets limit (*IHTA 1984, s 71E(2), (3), (4A)* as amended by *FA 2013, Sch 44, para 5*).

14.84 There is, however, a tax charge on the death of the beneficiary over the age of 18, on the distribution of assets to the beneficiary after that age, and on the beneficiary becoming entitled to the assets. The charge is calculated in the same way as the exit charge on a discretionary settlement but on the assumption that the settlement started on the beneficiary's eighteenth birthday (*IHTA 1984, s 71F*).

Accordingly, the maximum charge is 4.2% of the value of the assets, ie 7/10ths (or 28/40ths) (as the assets can be held for a maximum of seven years out of the ten-year period) of the value of the settled property multiplied by 30% of the rate payable on a chargeable lifetime gift (a maximum rate of 20%) by the notional transferor.

If the property ceases to be held for the benefit of the beneficiary in any other circumstances the special charge described earlier in relation to A&M settlements applies.

Charitable trusts

14.85 A charitable trust is outside the scope of IHT. The transfer of property to such a trust is exempt from IHT (*IHTA 1984, s 23*).

If settled property held in an A&M trust, a trust for a bereaved minor, an age 18-to-25 trust, an employee or newspaper trust, or old protective trusts or trusts for a disabled person, is transferred to a charity or comes to be held on charitable trusts without limit of time, the normal IHT charges that would otherwise have arisen do not apply (*IHTA 1984, s 76*).

If property is held in a temporary charitable trust, ie where the property is held for charitable purposes only until the end of a period (whether deferred by date or in some other way), a tax charge at a special rate applies when it ceases to be charitable. This is the special rate outlined earlier in relation to A&M settlements. This charge does not arise if the property is transferred to a permanent charity (or the limitation on the charitable period is removed) or to the extent that the funds are used to meet trust expenses (*IHTA 1984, ss 70, 76(1)*).

Employee trusts and newspaper trusts

14.86 An employee trust is one where the settled property is held on trusts which do not permit it to be applied otherwise than for the benefit of persons of a class defined by reference to employment in a particular trade or profession or employment by, or office with, a body carrying on a trade, profession or undertaking (or spouses, civil partners or dependants of such persons) or for such a purpose and charitable purposes. If the trust applies to employees of a particular body the class must comprise all or most of the persons who work for that body (or it must be for the purpose of an approved profit-sharing scheme or approved share-incentive plan) (*IHTA 1984, s 86*).

A newspaper trust is an employee trust whose class of beneficiaries also includes a newspaper publishing company or a newspaper holding company (*IHTA 1984, s 87*).

Such trusts are outside the scope of IHT. However, if any of the assets cease to be subject to the trusts the special tax charge described under A&M settlements applies (*IHTA 1984, s 72*).

Maintenance funds for historic buildings

14.87 Such funds are outside the scope of IHT. The relevant conditions are contained in *IHTA 1984, Sch 4*. If any part of the funds ceases to be held for the qualifying purposes, the special tax charge described under A&M settlements applies.

Other points

14.88 If property is transferred from one settlement to another it is treated for IHT purposes as remaining comprised in the first settlement (unless in the interim some person has become beneficially entitled to the property, eg it has been distributed to a beneficiary and remitted by him (*IHTA 1984, s 81*)).

Tax planning with trusts

14.89

> **Focus**
>
> Trusts are still very useful tax planning tools in the right circumstances. However they are hedged around with anti-avoidance rules and undistributed income and gains can be taxed at a higher rate than if the income or gain arose direct to the beneficiary. These higher rates can often be avoided, but only by structuring things right before they arise.

The changes made to the IHT trust regime by the *Finance Act 2006* mean that, in some cases, trusts will be used in different ways in future to those in the past. The following principles now apply to such IHT planning:

- It no longer makes any difference for IHT purposes if a new lifetime trust is a discretionary trust, an accumulation and maintenance trust or an interest-in-possession trust. This decision can now be based solely on family considerations. However, income tax considerations may affect the decision. The income of an IIP trust is taxed as income of the beneficiary so may attract tax at a lower rate than the 45% one which applies to a discretionary trust.

- It is still worth putting business assets into a trust if they attract 100% BPR and are likely to be sold at some stage. There is no IHT on the initial transfer and when the assets are sold and replaced by non-business assets the only IHT is the future ten-yearly charges and exit charge.
- Similarly, it is still worth putting into trust assets worth less than the £325,000 IHT nil rate band, which are likely to increase in value. Again this avoids the entry charge and gets the assets out of the settlor's estate subject only to the ten-yearly and exit charges.
- When the value exceeds £325,000 it may be worth selling the asset to a trust at a £325,000 undervalue leaving the sale proceeds outstanding. The outstanding amount remains in the donor's estate but the growth in value is in the trust and subject only to the ten-yearly and exit charges.
- The creation of a trust to hold non-UK assets is still virtually a must for those who are non-UK domiciled and not yet deemed domiciled here. And remember that if a person is deemed domiciled here his infant children may well not be, as they must themselves meet the '15 out of 20 years' test to be deemed domiciled. Of course, a very young child probably does not have the legal capacity to create a settlement but a teenager is likely to be competent to do so. Such trusts also give capital gains tax exemption while the gain remains in the trust, even for gains on UK assets (other than residential property), in most cases.
- Bare trusts can still be used where the beneficiary is under 18 and unmarried as the beneficiary is deemed to be beneficially entitled to the assets in the trust.
- If the main concern that prevents a gift direct to the beneficiary is a fear that the beneficiary might squander the money, a gift subject to a condition, eg that management of the money is carried out by a specified third party and that the beneficiary will not call on the fund until he is 25 or 30 or whatever, is worth considering. However, that would not protect the assets from creditors of the beneficiary.
- The strategy for wills is likely to be:
  - A trust for the surviving spouse (or civil partner) should be an interest-in-possession trust with power to advance capital to the spouse or to pay capital to a second class of beneficiary. There will then be no IHT on the death and any capital appointed to someone other than the spouse will constitute a potentially exempt transfer

by the surviving spouse (or civil partner) so there will be no IHT if the spouse survives for seven years after the appointment.

- Assets put into trust for an infant child should go into a trust for a bereaved minor or an age 18-to-25 trust provided that it is intended that the child should become entitled to the assets at or before age 25.
- If, as is likely to be the case, it is not wished to give an infant the assets at age 25 then a discretionary trust should probably be used. There is no charge on creating such a trust by will (as IHT already has to be paid on death where the assets go to someone other than the surviving spouse or civil partner and no trust creation charge arises in addition) so the only additional IHT will be the ten-yearly charge and exit charge, which could well be acceptable if the child is to take the assets at say, age 35.
- Trusts for adult children should be discretionary trusts. Again there is no trust creation charge. Depending on the age of the child, the total ten-yearly charges and exit charge may well be less than the 40% that would be payable on the child's death.
- Trusts for other people who would in the past have been given a life interest should probably now be discretionary trusts.

It can be sensible to put assets into trust even if this triggers the entry charge, as the £325,000 nil rate band can have a significant impact on the effective tax rate. For example:

			Tax on death		
Value of asset	*tax on settling*		*ten-yearly charge*		*under IIP regime*
£250,000	–	–	–	–	£100,000
£500,000	£35,000	7.00%	£10,500	2.1%	£200,000
1,000,000	£135,000	13.50%	£40,500	4.05%	£400,000
1,500,000	£235,000	15.67%	£70,500	4.70%	£600,000
2,000,000	£335,000	16.75%	£100,500	5.03%	£800,000

A 40% rate on death has been assumed as the individual normally has sufficient assets to use up his nil rate band. The tax under the ten-yearly charge assumes that the settlor had made no gifts in the seven years prior to the creation of the settlement.

If a person aged 60 creates a settlement of £1,000,000 now there is likely to be a maximum of four ten-yearly charges during his lifetime. Accordingly, the total IHT will be:

Entry charge	£135,000
Four annual charges	£162,000
	£297,000

This is a saving of over 25% of the tax that would be payable on death if he were to retain the asset. In reality of course the asset is likely to increase in value so the saving will be greater as the entry charge and the first couple of ten-yearly charges are likely to be payable on a significantly lower amount than the value of the assets at the time of the settlor's death.

14.90 For older settlors the saving is greater. If an 80-year-old creates a settlement of £2m and dies at age 91, the total charge will be £435,500 (plus an exit charge of around £10,000 if the assets are then distributed), compared with the £800,000 that would otherwise have been payable on death.

It should also be borne in mind that, if assets pregnant with CGT are put into a trust that is governed by the IHT relevant property regime, the CGT can be deferred until the trustees sell the asset concerned (and can be deferred again if they distribute it to a beneficiary).

Things to avoid

14.91

- It no longer normally makes sense to create a trust of which the settlor is a beneficiary. This triggers the initial IHT charge but the property remains in the settlor's estate under the reservation of benefit rules so it creates double taxation. There are no longer income tax or CGT benefits in creating such a trust, unless the settlor is non-UK resident or is taxable on the remittance basis and will not breach the '15 out of 20 years' rule for several years. Even in such cases, for a UK resident the IHT on creation of the settlement needs to be weighed against the anticipated income tax and CGT advantages.
- Similarly, it will normally no longer make sense to create a lifetime trust of which the settlor's spouse or civil partner is the main beneficiary, as a gift direct to the spouse avoids the trust creation charge of up to 20%.
- Careful thought needs to be given to the use of a trust for CGT planning where a person is non-UK domiciled but deemed domiciled; in such a case, it has been sensible in the past to set up an offshore IIP trust for the

settlor's own benefit to obtain the CGT and income tax advantages of such a trust. This may no longer make sense if it will trigger an immediate IHT charge – although it might still be worth selling the assets to the trust rather than gifting them.

- Where an individual is deemed domiciled under the '15 out of 20 years' rule, great care needs to be taken to avoid adding anything to pre-5 April 2017 trusts. Provided that such a trust remains untainted, it is a 'mini tax haven' for the UK resident family while the funds remain in the trust.
- A similar issue arises where a person wants to let his principal private residence but wants to stop time apportionment eroding the exemption already achieved. In such cases, putting the property into trust for oneself has achieved that objective in the past. Again, a sale to a trust rather than a gift may still be viable.
- There is no longer any benefit in holding a UK residential property through an overseas trust structure.

Chapter 15

Payments made on the termination of employment

Donald Pearce-Crump BA (Hons), LLB, CTA (Fellow), ATT

SIGNPOSTS

- **Scope** – A discussion of the main tax issues that arise when a lump-sum payment or benefit is made to an employee on the termination of his employment and how planning in this context is geared towards structuring a termination payment so that it falls within *ITEPA 2003, Pt 6, Ch 3* in order to access the many reliefs given in respect of such payments and to ensure that the payment thereby falls outside the scope of NIC.
- **Conditions** – The main condition that a payment has to meet in order that it falls within the above legislation is that it must not otherwise be charged to income tax. Avoiding the other four heads of charge that might apply to a termination payment (**15.3**) makes planning in this context a complex matter.
- **Practical issues** – Adopting the correct approach to analysing a termination package (**15.5**) is fundamental to identifying the correct tax treatment of its constituent payments and benefits. Navigating a payment away from the other four heads of charge requires a detailed consideration of the documents and other evidence that govern the relationship between an employer and an employee generally and which relate to the making of the termination payment in particular. In some cases it may be possible to get assurance from HMRC that a payment will be afforded the favourable treatment sought (**15.107**).
- **Employment law** – The common law and employment law treatment of termination payments may be determinative of their tax treatment and a sound understanding of these matters should not be overlooked.

- **Structure** – This chapter starts with the identification of the legislative provisions dealing with termination payments (**15.2**) and how termination packages are analysed (**15.5**). It then identifies the types of termination payment that benefit from the benign tax and NIC treatment intimated above (**15.8**) and discusses the many exceptions from tax afforded such payments (**15.23**). Termination payments within the other categories of employment income are then identified (**15.64**), concentrating on those payments that are charged to tax in full as earnings (**15.65**). The discussion concludes with a number of miscellaneous planning points (**15.104**).

INTRODUCTION

15.1 This chapter will examine the main tax issues that typically arise when a lump-sum payment or benefit ('termination payment') is made to an employee (or officer) on the termination of his employment (or the vacation of his office). However, there will be excluded from the discussion lump-sum payments made by any type of pension fund established for an employee as part of his service agreement or to which an employee may belong as part of his terms of service. The discussion applies for 2017/18 and earlier tax years. An added dimension to the discussion is the proposal for tax and national insurance changes to the tax treatment of termination payments which are expected to take effect in 2018/19 and subsequent tax years. These proposals are described as appropriate throughout this chapter and are summarised in **15.109**.

Tax planning in this context is, usually, planning to secure an advantage, namely that a termination payment should be structured so that it falls within *ITEPA 2003, Pt 6, Ch 3* (all statutory references in this chapter are to *ITEPA 2003*, unless otherwise stated). The reasons for this objective are twofold; first so that access can then be gained to the many reliefs available for such termination payments, and secondly because such termination payments are not charged to national insurance contributions.

However, as is the case for much tax planning, a taxpayer who is leaving his employment should primarily ensure that his legal and financial position is secured and only then seek to find a tax-efficient way of structuring a termination payment. It may not always be the case that the two objectives coincide, but to the extent that they can the best tax outcome is achieved if the payment falls within the scope of the above legislation. Indeed, seeking this tax-driven outcome may, in many cases, coincide with securing a sound financial outcome for an employee given the benefit of the reliefs available to such payments.

THE SCHEME OF LEGISLATIVE PROVISIONS DEALING WITH TERMINATION PAYMENTS

15.2 As intimated above, the optimum tax treatment of a termination payment is that found in *ITEPA 2003, Pt 6, Ch 3* which is entitled 'Payments and benefits on the termination of employment etc'. However, the title is misleading. The true nature and scope of that part of the legislation is dictated by *ITEPA 2003, s 401(3)* which reads as follows: 'This Chapter does not apply to any payment or other benefit chargeable to income tax apart from this Chapter'. This clearly indicates that *ITEPA 2003, Pt 6, Ch 3* is a residual category of employment income within *ITEPA 2003*. By implication, therefore, termination payments (whether made in cash or kind) may fall within other categories of employment income set out in *ITEPA 2003.*

15.3

> **Focus**
>
> It is essential to know the categories of employment income within which a termination payment may fall in order to appreciate how many hurdles, practically speaking, need to be considered before concluding that the payment falls within the favourable residual category.

The categories of employment income within which a termination payment might fall are the following:

(a) earnings from employment;

(b) the benefits-in-kind code;

(c) restrictive undertakings;

(d) employer-financed retirement benefits scheme (EFRBS),

(e) termination payments within *ITEPA 2003, Pt 6, Ch 3* ('residual termination payments').

Together these categories are, in this chapter, called the scheme of legislative provisions dealing with termination payments. The residual category of termination payments applies to payments and other benefits received directly or indirectly in consideration or in consequence of, or otherwise in connection with, the termination of a person's employment by the person, or the person's spouse or civil partner, blood relative, dependant or personal representatives (*ITEPA 2003, s 401(1)*).

15.4 It is important to note the order in which the categories of employment income are set out in the above list. If more than one of the categories prima facie applies in relation to a termination payment, priority sections in the legislation dictate that a category mentioned earlier in the list has priority over a category mentioned later in the list. So for example, if a lump sum payment made to an employee on the termination of employment is for his giving an undertaking not to divulge his former employer's industrial know-how after he leaves his employment, then the payment is charged to income tax as a payment for a restrictive undertaking (category (c)) and not as a residual termination payment (category (e)), even though the payment may satisfy the conditions for the application of the residual category as set out above. If the employee and employer are going to plan for the tax-efficient treatment of a termination payment, they are going to have to avoid its falling within categories (a) to (d). In some cases, however (as will be discussed later), the circumstances of their employment relationship or the nature of the payments made are such that they have no choice in the matter, in which case their planning opportunities in the sense described above will be limited. It should be appreciated that they may not always be able to pick and choose which category of employment income is applicable given the terms of their relationship which were agreed upon at the time their relationship commenced (see **15.6**).

ANALYSING TERMINATION PACKAGES

Focus

It is essential to have an informed understanding of the process to follow in analysing a termination package so that the correct tax treatment of its constituent payments and benefits may be identified. Particular attention has to be paid to locating and analysing the myriad documents and other pieces of evidence that govern the relationship between an employer and an employee as the content of that relationship is often determinative of the tax treatment of the elements of a termination package. Parties must guard against jumping to conclusions and determining the tax treatment of a payment merely by what it is called.

15.5 A contract of employment may end for a variety of reasons and when it does, an employee may receive a package comprising a variety of payments and benefits. In order to identify the tax treatment of the component elements of the package two steps have to be taken:

(a) First the nature of each component within the package has to be determined (but without having undue regard to the label attached to the component by the parties as their descriptions may not always be accurate).

(b) The next step is to match the scheme of legislative provisions dealing with termination payments to the component so analysed in order to ascertain the correct tax treatment of that component. Each category of employment income in the scheme charges income tax but each has its own set of exemptions and other relieving provisions associated with it. Only some of the categories of employment income in the scheme are subject to national insurance contributions. The application of the appropriate provision in the scheme on termination payments will depend on the occasion on which a payment or benefit is made and upon its nature.

15.6 If the parties are in the position where they are able to plan for the making of a tax-efficient termination payment, they should appreciate that each component of the package must be analysed separately: they must understand in substance and in truth the bargain that they are making in the context of their existing relationship and understand what each payment is for (*Henley v Murray (HM Inspector of Taxes)* 31 TC 351).

In achieving this level of understanding it is necessary for the parties to know the parameters in which they are able to work:

(a) They may be constrained by their existing relationship (*Henry v Foster* 16 TC 605). They will have to consider their conduct and all the documents and other evidence which govern their relationship generally and which relate to the making of the termination payment in particular.

(b) They must understand that the language used by them to describe a constituent element of a termination package (eg 'compensation for loss of office') is not the factor that determines its tax treatment. Rather they have to decide the nature of the payments made (*Henley v Murray (H M Inspector of Taxes)* 31 TC 351).

(c) They will be able to take comfort in the fact that HMRC must analyse any termination package as put together by the parties themselves (*Chappell & Co Ltd v Nestle Co Ltd* [1960] AC 87) and it is not open to HMRC to re-arrange a package genuinely agreed. Consequently, where the parties identify a number of components of a package and allocate a consideration to each or some of those components, generally speaking, HMRC will analyse the package in accordance with the agreed terms (EIM12805–EIM12810).

(d) In drawing up a termination package, the parties should consider carefully whether a single, lump sum payment should be agreed for all or a number of the elements comprised in the package. Depending upon the construction of the terms of the package (as contained, for example in a compromise agreement), it may be that a single sum that is payable for two or more separate and identifiable considerations is properly apportioned between to the two (*Wales (HM Inspector of Taxes) v Tilley* 25 TC 136; *A G Reid v RCC* [2016] UKFTT 79 (TC)). In such a case an apportionment may give rise to an outcome not expected by the parties (as was the case in *Carter v Wadman* 28 TC 41 – see **15.12**), although it may be that an apportionment can fall in the taxpayer's favour (see *Johnson v RCC* [2013] UKFTT 242 (TC) in **15.14**). In other cases an apportionment may not be possible and valuable tax reliefs may be lost as a result. For example, in *Owolabi v RCC* [2012] UKFTT 334 (TC), although the taxpayer argued that part of her payment for loss of office (as sub-postmaster) was a payment of capital and compensation for the expenditure she had originally incurred in buying and adapting her post office business (which was now ceasing), there was no evidence showing that the payment had a character of something other than compensation for loss of office and hence a residual termination payment, taxable as such.

Example 15.1 – Components of a termination payment

A payment of £66,000 is paid to an employee on the termination of his employment by reason of redundancy. This comprises the following elements:

- £5,000 as a contractual payment in lieu of notice
- £15,000 as a bonus owing at the time of termination
- £20,000 for an undertaking not to disclose confidential information after termination
- £26,000 on account of redundancy

On a proper analysis only the final amount falls to be treated as a residual termination payment. The first two amounts are earnings and the third amounts falls to be treated as a payment for a restrictive undertaking.

15.7 As already intimated in **15.1** above, a taxpayer who has secured his legal and financial position on the termination of employment, may be able to plan (in conjunction with his former employer) his termination package in such a way that most (if not all) of the components are treated as residual termination payments.

This chapter will develop along the following lines:

- It will discuss the types of payment within the residual category of termination payments so that it will be understood by the parties whether their circumstances are such that it is possible for them to take advantage of that category.
- It will then discuss the exceptions and reliefs associated with that category.
- It will then discuss the circumstances in which payments fall within the other categories of employment income comprising the scheme of legislative provisions dealing with termination payments so that the parties will understand when they cannot take advantage of the residual category; suitable planning opportunities will then be highlighted in these cases.
- Finally, it will discuss a number of miscellaneous planning and other points.

THE TYPES OF TERMINATION PAYMENT THAT FALL IN THE RESIDUAL CATEGORY

Introduction

15.8 The types of termination payment that fall in the residual category are set out in **Table 15.1**.

Table 15.1 – Residual termination payments

- Redundancy payments
- Payments made under compromise agreements
- Payments in lieu of notice (PILONs)
- Payments to compromise legal action generally
- Damages for breach of contract
- Payments made under employment protection legislation
- Payments made under anti-discrimination law
- Ex gratia payments

Redundancy payments

> **Focus**
>
> If a termination payment is paid by reason of an employee being made redundant, its favourable treatment as a residual termination payment is assured (even if it is paid under the contract of employment between the parties). It is essential to ensure though that the termination of employment occurs by reason of redundancy and that the payment is made to alleviate only the consequences of redundancy and is not made for some other work-related reason. UK legislation provides a specific definition of redundancy and, unless the reason for a dismissal satisfies it, the process is not a redundancy dismissal at all and payments made on the termination of employment will not be redundancy payments.

Statutory redundancy payments

15.9 A contract of employment will come to an end by reason of redundancy if the dismissal is attributable to:

(a) the fact that his employer has ceased, or intends to cease, to carry on the business for the purposes of which the employee was employed by him, or has ceased, or intends to cease, to carry on that business in the place where the employee was so employed; or

(b) the fact that the requirements of that business for employees to carry out work of a particular kind, or for employees to carry out work of a particular kind in the place where he was so employed, have ceased or diminished or are expected to cease or diminish.

It is clear from this definition that redundancy involves a reduction in an employer's need for employees because of, for example, the disposal of part of his business, its relocation or the introduction of new methods of work that reduces the number of employees needed. It includes the case of a 'bumped redundancy' where employee A's job disappears but it is employee B who is made redundant because the employer wants to retain employee A. Such redundancies may be common in large-scale redundancy programmes.

The *Employment Rights Act 1996 (ERA 1996), s 136* provides that, if a qualifying employee (basically one who has been employed for at least two years) is made redundant, then he is entitled to a redundancy payment (quantified in accordance with the Act) which is compensation for the loss of the particular job from which he is being dismissed. Such a payment is not taxed as the employee's earnings from his employment (*ITEPA 2003, s 309(1)*), but it does count as a residual termination payment and hence uses up part of the £30,000 threshold (*ITEPA 2003, s 309(3)*) (see **15.24**).

Non-statutory redundancy payments

15.10 It is not unusual for employers to make additional payments upon the termination of an employee's employment by reason of redundancy. Such payments can be determined and paid at the time of the redundancy in question or they may be made in accordance with the conditions under which an employee has given service during the subsistence of his contract (eg under a non-statutory redundancy scheme which may be provided for in the employee's contract of service or some other work-related document such as a staff handbook, a letter of appointment, a side letter to the main employment contract or an employer-trade union agreement).

Such non-statutory redundancy payments are charged to tax as residual termination payments (*Mairs (Inspector of Taxes) v Haughey* [1993] STC 569; *Colquhoun v RCC* [2010] UKUT 431, [2011] STC 394). This treatment is so even where the payment is made under the terms of an employee's contract (or other work-related document) and so is an important exception from the general treatment (as earnings) of termination payments made under a contract of employment (see **15.67**). Further, in *Colquhoun v RCC* [2010] UKFTT 34 (TC) it was held that a payment to buy out contractual redundancy rights was a residual termination payment even where the employment did not end until several years after the payment. However, it must be a non-statutory redundancy payment that is made in order for it to benefit from the above treatment; a contractual payment in lieu of notice made on an employee's redundancy is (correctly) treated as earnings despite it being paid on the occasion of an employee's redundancy (*Andrew v RCC* [2015] UKFTT 514 (TC)) (see **15.12** and **15.70**).

HMRC Statement of Practice 1/94 confirms this treatment and acknowledges that the scheme may be a standing one which forms part of the terms on which the employees give their services or it may be an ad hoc scheme to meet a specific situation such as the imminent closure of a particular factory (see SP 1/94, para 2). The statement is restricted to payments 'genuinely made solely on account of redundancy' and paragraph 4 of the Statement states that HMRC are:

> '... concerned to distinguish between payments under non-statutory schemes which are genuinely made to compensate for loss of employment through redundancy and payments which are rewards for services in employment or more generally for having acted as or having been an employee.'

In paragraph 3 of the Statement, HMRC say that where payments made under a non-statutory redundancy scheme do not compensate for the loss of employment through redundancy, then *ITEPA 2003, Pt 6, Ch 3* may not apply, and quote as an example a case where a terminal bonus is disguised as a non-statutory redundancy payment. The statement gives as examples payments made for meeting production targets or doing extra work in the period leading up to redundancy. Also included are payments which are conditional on continued service in the employment for a time if they are calculated by reference to any additional period served following the issue of a redundancy notice. In the case of *Allan v CIR* [1994] STC 943, payments were made to all employees in a company only some of whom were made redundant. The payments to those employees whose employments continued were held to be taxable in full as earnings from their employments.

Care must always be taken to ensure that a payment is actually made under a non-statutory redundancy scheme if it is to be treated as a residual termination payment. For example, a contractual term may provide that an employer must make a payment to an employee on the termination of his employment 'for any reason'. If a termination of employment occurs on account of the redundancy of the employee, then any payment made by the employer will not count as a non-statutory redundancy payment. At EIM13765, HMRC explain that redundancy may have triggered the payment, but any type of termination would have done so and the character of the payment (as earnings – see **15.67**) remains the same whatever the trigger.

HMRC go on to say, however, that if the contractual terms specify redundancy (eg the contract provides that a payment be made on the termination of employment 'for any reason (including redundancy)'), then it may be accepted that the intention of the employer is to pay compensation for loss of employment by reason of redundancy. In this case the payment made on redundancy will be treated as a residual termination payment.

If an employer who operates a non-statutory redundancy scheme wants to be certain that a payment made under the scheme is to be treated as a residual termination payment, then he may make an application in writing to HMRC for clearance (see **15.107**). Such an application must be accompanied by the scheme document together with the text of any intended letter to employees which explain its terms. The clearance procedure is available only in respect of a scheme in its final documented form, and is not available for schemes in the process of development and cannot be used to assist in that development (see EIM13190).

Other comments regarding redundancy payments

15.11 Provided that a redundancy is genuine, subsequent re-engagement by the same employer or an associated employer does not normally affect the treatment of a redundancy payment. This will also be the case where an employer outsources part of the business so that the employees working in that part are made redundant and those same persons become employees of the concern that takes on that business. Again the tax treatment of their redundancy payments should not be affected where the arrangement is genuine.

Payments made under compromise agreements

> **Focus**
>
> Always read (or draft) compromise agreements carefully, as any part of any termination payment made under the agreement in full and final settlement of an employee's unpaid remuneration is taxable otherwise than as a residual termination payment. It will not benefit from the benign treatment afforded such payments. Be particularly wary of compromise agreements that fructify the terms of an employee's contract of employment and avoid altering an employee's contract of employment by way of a compromise agreement.

Compromise of employees' contractual rights

15.12 A compromise agreement in this context is one made between an employer and employee whereby they agree to end their relationship under a subsisting contract of service. In consideration of entering into the agreement and giving up his employment, the employee receives a lump sum payment. In practice, this most commonly occurs where an employee is serving under a fixed-term contract (usually one that does not provide for notice) or where he is serving his contractual notice, be it indefinite or one for a fixed-term. It is agreed that the contract of service should be brought to an end before the expiry of the respective periods. This compares with a garden leave situation where a contract of employment is not ended but allowed to run its course; rather the employer waives his right to call on the employee to work during the period concerned (ie the period of garden leave). A payment made during a period of garden leave is the salary due to the employee for the period and is taxable as earnings (see **15.67**).

A payment made under a compromise agreement (which may be labelled a payment in lieu of notice) falls within the residual category of termination payments where it is attributable wholly to the loss of employment occasioned by the total abrogation of the employee's contract of employment (*Henley v Murray (H M Inspector of Taxes)* 31 TC 351; *Clayton v Lavender* 42 TC 607; *Essack v RCC* [2014] UKFTT 159 (TC); *Michael Phillips v RCC* [2016] UKFTT 174 (TC); *Tottenham Hotspur Ltd v HMRC* [2016] UKFTT 389 (TC)). It is not necessary that there has to be a breach of the employment contract in order for a payment made under a compromise agreement to be so categorised (*Tottenham Hotspur Ltd v HMRC* [2016] UKFTT 389 (TC)). Whether an employment contract has been terminated following a breach of contract or whether the contract has been terminated by mutual consent, a payment made under a compromise agreement which abrogates entirely the contract of employment falls within the residual category.

An element of care must be exercised here, however, as a payment made under a compromise agreement entered into in the above circumstances may satisfy some other right in an employee's contract (eg a right to a bonus not yet paid) in addition to being compensation for the loss of employment. Where this is the case, a part of the payment will be attributed to that right and be taxed accordingly (probably as earnings) (*Carter v Wadman* 28 TC 41). So care must be exercised where a compromise agreement is stated to be 'in full and final settlement of all claims' that an employee may have against his employer at the time of the termination of his employment. This issue is forcibly illustrated in *Andrew v RCC* [2015] UKFTT 514 (TC) where the taxpayer was made redundant. His employer exercised his power under the contract of employment to terminate the contract without notice and the taxpayer entered into a compromise agreement which was expressed to be in full and final settlement of all and any claims the employee had in respect of his contract of employment and its termination. The payment made under the compromise agreement was then expressed to a payment of the salary and benefits which would have been paid during the notice period to which the taxpayer was entitled and was being paid instead of giving notice. It was held, that despite his redundancy, the payment under the comprise agreement, described as it was, was a payment made in lieu of notice in accordance with the right given to the employer to do so by the employment contract itself. Consequently the payment was the taxpayer's earnings and did not fall within the residual category (see **15.70**). The exception for non-statutory redundancy payments (see **15.10**) did not apply in this case as no redundancy payment was in fact made under the compromise agreement.

Care must also be exercised where a compromise agreement fructifies (ie gives effect to) the terms of an employee's contract of employment, that is to say where the compromise agreement is the mechanism by which the terms of a contract of employment are effected (see **15.80**).

The case of *Hill v RCC* [2015] UKFTT 295 (TC) illustrates other circumstances where a payment made under a compromise agreement may not be treated as falling in the residual category. In that case the taxpayer was paid a sum as a result of a change in the terms of his contract of employment. The taxpayer's contract of employment had been transferred from one employer to another under the *Transfer of Undertakings (Protection of Employment) Regulations 2006, SI 2006/246* (the '*TUPE Regulations*'). Whereas his contract stipulated that he was not required to work more than 10 miles from an address in Luton, his new employer required him to work in London. The taxpayer complained and under a compromise agreement he was paid a sum for agreeing to the change to his contract of employment. He argued that he was being paid a sum on the termination of his employment with his former employer for agreeing not to pursue a claim for damages in respect of a breach of the terms of his contract (see rather than simply for agreeing to work for his new employer on varied terms). The judge refused to accept that distinction and held that the tax treatment of the payment would be the same in both cases. He stated that in both cases the effect of the compromise agreement was that the taxpayer was paid a sum of money in return for agreeing that he would work for his new employer at a place more than 10 miles from Luton. Consequently, in accordance with the principles laid down in *Hamblett v Godfrey (Inspector of Taxes)* [1987] STC 60 and *Kuehne & Nagel Drinks Logistics Ltd v RCC* [2012] EWCA Civ 34, it was held that the taxpayer received a payment from his employer as compensation for a change in the terms of his employment contract and the payment was properly characterised as earnings from employment.

The judge stated that he did not need to decide the case on the basis of the effect of the *TUPE Regulations* (see **15.108**); the case was decided simply on the point that, on the facts, the payment was made by the taxpayer's new employer for the taxpayer agreeing to a change in the terms of his employment following the transfer of his employment contract. He pointed out, interestingly, that the outcome may have been different if there had been no transfer under the *TUPE Regulations* and instead the taxpayer had, following the termination of his employment, been paid a sum by his former employer for a breach of its obligations during the time the employee was employed by it. In such a case, the payment made may have come within the residual category (although it should be pointed out that such a payment would have to be connected with the termination of the employment (see **15.105**).

Compromise of legal action

15.13 A compromise agreement in this context is also one whereby an employee, having been wrongfully dismissed, agrees to refrain from instituting or continuing legal proceedings against his former employer in consideration of receiving a payment (ie he gives up his cause of action to sue for wrongful dismissal). The agreement may be reached where there is a threat of court proceedings or court proceedings have started but not completed. 'Tomlin orders' (ie an order which records that an action is stayed by the agreement of the parties on terms set out in a schedule) are also included within this category of payment.

Compensation paid under such agreements is taxed as a residual termination payment (*Du Cros v Ryall (H M Inspector of Taxes)* 19 TC 444; *Wilson v Clayton* [2005] STC 157). However, in certain respects care must again be exercised. A principal feature of a compromise agreement is the employee's undertaking to give up his right to sue his employer. Indeed, although the consideration for the payment is most likely to be his giving up the pursuit of his cause of action, any amount specifically paid for this restriction in the employee's future behaviour may be charged to tax in full under the restrictive covenant category of employment income (*ITEPA 2003, s 225*) (see **15.93–15.95**).

Compromise agreements that vary an employment contract

15.14 In addition to the special case of a compromise agreement that gives effect to the terms of an employee's contract of employment (see **15.12**), care must be exercised where a compromise agreement is made before a termination of employment is in prospect. Such an agreement may amount to a variation of the terms of the employee's contract of employment so that any payment subsequently made will simply be a payment under the employment contract and taxable as earnings (see **15.67**).

Conversely, where compromise agreements are stated to supersede all previous agreements and understandings between the parties, this could have the effect of turning a non-taxable payment to the employee into a taxable one. In *Reid v RCC* [2012] UKFTT 182 (TC), an employer granted his employee an option for a sum of money and agreed to refund the amount should his contract of service be terminated. In the event the contract was brought to an end under a compromise agreement which included a term that declared the compromise agreement to 'constitute the entire agreement between the parties' and to 'supersede' all previous agreements between them. The compromise agreement therefore had the effect of negating the earlier promise to make the refund. As the compromise agreement failed also to mention that a refund was actually being made, it was held that no part of the payment made under the compromise agreement comprised the (tax free) refund; it was held that to the extent that the payment under the compromise agreement was in excess of £30,000, it was taxable as a residual termination payment. (Also see *Sjumarken v RCC* [2016] UKUT 568.)

However, it must be emphasised that each case depends on its own facts, as illustrated in *Johnson v RCC* [2013] UKFTT 242 (TC) where a compromise agreement providing for a payment made in full and final settlement of the employee's claims against his employer did include (even though it was not expressly stated) the (tax free) refund of £30,000 paid during his employment for the grant of an EMI option (which lapsed when his employment ended). The difference between the two decisions lies in the proper construction of the compromise agreements in each case. The case usefully sets out the principles laid down by the House of Lords in *Investors Compensation Scheme v West Bromwich Building Society* [1998] 1 WLR 896 by which contractual documents are construed, namely:

(a) Interpretation is the ascertainment of the meaning which the document would convey to a reasonable person having all the background knowledge which would reasonably have been available to the parties in the situation in which they were at the time of the contract.

(b) The background may be referred to as the 'matrix of fact'. Subject to the requirement that it should be reasonably available to the parties and to the exception to be mentioned next, the background includes absolutely anything which would affect the way in which the language of the document would be understood by a reasonable man.

(c) The law excludes from the admissible background the previous negotiations of the parties and their declarations of subjective intent. They are admissible only in an action for rectification. The law makes this distinction for reasons of practical policy and, in this respect only, legal interpretation differs from the way utterances in ordinary life are interpreted.

(d) The meaning which a document (or any other utterance) would convey to a reasonable man is not the same thing as the meaning of its words. The meaning of words is a matter of dictionaries and grammar; the meaning of the document is what the parties using those words against the relevant background would reasonably have been understood to mean. The background may not merely enable the reasonable man to choose between the possible meanings of words which are ambiguous but even (as occasionally happens in ordinary life) to conclude that the parties must, for whatever reason, have used the wrong words or syntax.

(e) The 'rule' that words should be given their 'natural and ordinary meaning' reflects the common sense proposition that it is not easily accepted that people have made linguistic mistakes, particularly in formal documents. On the other hand, if one would nevertheless conclude from the background that something must have gone wrong with the language, the law does not require judges to attribute to the parties an intention which they plainly could not have had. If detailed semantic and syntactical analysis of words in a commercial contract is going to lead to a conclusion that flouts business common-sense, it must be made to yield to business common-sense.

Payments in lieu of notice (PILONs)

Focus

Take care to ensure that the correct type of PILON has been identified before concluding that it falls to be taxed as a residual termination payment. Other types of PILON are discussed at **15.68** (contractual PILONs), **15.76** (so- called auto-PILONS) and **15.79** (garden leave payments).

15.15 In the present context a payment in lieu of notice is one which may be described as follows:

> 'Without the agreement of the employee, the employer summarily dismisses the employee and tenders a payment in lieu of proper notice … The employer is in breach of contract by dismissing the employee without proper notice.'

In this case the employer tenders the payment in lieu of notice to make good his breach of contract and such a payment is in the nature of damages. The tax treatment of such a PILON (ie as a residual termination payment) follows that for damages as discussed in **15.17**. It does not matter that the payment may be included in a compromise agreement. This position is confirmed in *Rubio v RCC* [2012] UKFTT 361 (TC).

Nothing turns on the label used to describe the payment as defined above. The PILON label is used to describe a range of payments made in a variety of legal situations (*Delaney v Staples (t/a De Montfort Recruitment)* [1992] 1 AC 687). It should be carefully noted that this category of PILON applies only where the contract of employment between the parties makes provision for notice only and not where it allows the employer a choice as to how to end the contract of employment – that is *either* by giving notice *or* by making a payment in lieu of notice (PILON). Such PILONs are taxed as earnings (see **15.68**). Nor does the present category of PILON apply to circumstances properly analysed as garden leave; a PILON made to an employee on garden leave is taxable on him as his earnings (see **15.78**). Neither does the present category apply to a PILON made at the end of an employment where the employer and the employee agree that the employment is to terminate forthwith on payment of a sum in lieu of notice. Such a payment is probably treated in the same way as a payment made under a compromise agreement (see **15.12**). In such a case, the employer is not in breach of contract in dismissing summarily and the payment in lieu is not remuneration for work done during the continuance of the employment.

However, care must be taken where an employer has established a practice of making termination awards which would create an expectation for all employees to receive PILONs on the termination of their employment; HMRC are of the opinion that a payment that is expected and received may be earnings (see **15.76**).

Payments to compromise legal action generally

15.16 This category of payment includes any payment made by an employer to compromise legal action. In *Clinton v RCC* [2009] UKFTT 337 (TC) the employee had been constructively dismissed and a payment made to her by her employer was motivated by the desire to obviate her taking proceedings for wrongful or unfair dismissal so that it did not have to admit that its actions had amounted to constructive dismissal. The payment so made was held to be a residual termination payment. Payments under agreements to compromise legal action (**15.13**) and PILONs within **15.15** are examples of payments within this broader category.

Damages for breach of contract

Unliquidated damages

15.17 A fundamental breach of a contract of service by an employer allows an employee to treat the contract as at an end. A cause of action to sue accrues to him under the common law and, if a tribunal or court gives judgment in his favour, the employer will be under an obligation to pay damages (called unliquidated damages) ordered by the court or tribunal. To constitute damages the lump sum must be awarded unconditionally by the court (including a consent order) as distinct from an amount which a party to a dispute agrees to pay out of court so as to settle the action or threatened action against him. (The tax treatment of compensation received for agreeing to compromise a cause of action is dealt with at **15.15** above.)

Damages compensate for loss suffered owing to breach of contract and seek to ensure that the injured party is put in the same position, so far as money can do it, as if he had not suffered the loss occasioned by the breach. Damages for wrongful termination of a contract of service are residual termination payments (*Du Cros v Ryall (H M Inspector of Taxes)* 19 TC 444; *Henley v Murray (H M Inspector of Taxes)* 31 TC 351).

Liquidated damages

15.18 Although the point has not been settled by the courts, there are *dicta* in *Henley v Murray (H M Inspector of Taxes)* 31 TC 351 and *Clayton v Lavender* 42 TC 607 to the effect that, even though liquidated damages are provided for in a contract of employment, unliquidated and liquidated damages are treated in the same way. Liquidated damages clauses in contracts of employment operate so as to provide a pre-arranged statement of the damages to be paid on termination of employment; provided the clause is properly structured and drafted so that it is enforceable as a matter of law and so that the amount provided for is a genuine pre-estimate of loss, such damages that compensate for that loss will not be treated as earnings but as a residual termination payment even though they are specified in the contract of employment itself. (See *Dale v de Soissons* 32 TC 118 (**15.67**) in which liquidated damages clauses are specifically distinguished from other payments made pursuant to the terms of an employee's service; see **15.67** and **15.72.**) A payment of liquidated damages is not given as a reward for services; it seeks to compensate the employee for the loss suffered as a result of the breach of the employment contract and so it has the same compensatory nature as a payment of unliquidated damages. Consequently, it should be treated no differently.

Comment

15.19 At EIM13922 HMRC sound a warning in relation to payments of damages. They say that damages for a breach of contract may not always be treated as a residual termination payment. They give as an example a failure to pay wages due when an employment ends. This is a breach of contract but the remedy given by the court may be to enforce the contractual terms so that the so-called damages are merely an unpaid debt. In this case the payment will be one of wages paid under the contract of employment and taxable as earnings (see **15.65**).

Payments made under employment protection legislation

15.20 Employment protection legislation in the UK gives an employee a wide variety of rights in relation to the termination of his employment, and regardless of how that legislation describes a payment to which an employee may be entitled under any aspect of that legislation, the tax treatment of such a payment must, as ever, be determined according to its substance (see **15.5**(a)).

The following payments have been treated as falling in the residual category of termination payments:

(a) Compensation paid for unfair dismissal (*Walker v Adams (Inspector of Taxes)* 2003 SpC 344). An employee who has been employed for at least one year has the statutory right not to be unfairly dismissed. Where he is unfairly dismissed, he may be awarded compensation consisting of a basic award, a compensatory award, an additional (or higher additional) award and a special award (*ERA 1996, s 112*). The same treatment applies to sums payable where the employee is re-instated or re-engaged by the employer. Such payments (although described by the ERA 1996 as remuneration) compensate for any benefits (including arrears of pay) that the employee would have had if he had continued as an employee for the period from the date of dismissal to the date of his re-instatement or re-engagement. However, it is HMRC's view that such a sum is compensation for unfair dismissal and so is taxable only as a residual termination payment (see EIM12960). (It should be noted however the *Social Security Contributions and Benefits Act 1992 (SSCBA 1992), s 112(3)(a)* deems sums payable in respect of arrears of pay in pursuance of an order for re-instatement or re-engagement to be earnings subject to Class 1 national insurance contributions.)

If a tribunal orders a payment of compensation for an employer's failure to comply with a re-instatement or re-engagement order under *ERA 1996, s 117*, that payment too is treated as a residual termination payment. However, HMRC state that where, exceptionally, there is as a matter of fact continuous employment between the two dates, any payment for the period is earnings. They say that this may happen where an employee is dismissed and immediately re-employed to allow a provision to be left out of his contract and the date of re-instatement or re-engagement is later than the re-employment date.

Finally, when making a claim for unfair dismissal an employee may also claim that his employer failed to provide a written statement for the reasons of dismissal. If this claim is upheld, the tribunal may award compensation (*ERA 1996, s 93(2)(b)*) and this too is taxable as a residual termination payment.

(b) Protective awards under the *Trade Union and Labour Relations (Consolidation) Act 1992, s 189* paid for failure by an employer to follow the consultation process on redundancy *(Mimtec Ltd v IRC* [2001] STC (SCD) 101; *K&N Drink Logistics Ltd v RCC* [2010] UKUT 457). (It should be noted however that *SSCBA 1992, s 112(3)(c)* deems protective awards to be earnings subject to Class 1 national insurance contributions.)

(c) Statutory redundancy payments (see **15.9** above).

Payments made under anti-discrimination law

Focus

Analyse payments made under anti-discrimination law carefully, as some may be outside the scope of income tax altogether (and hence not taxable).

15.21 Apart from the *Employment Rights Act 1996* and other labour-related Acts, the Equality Act 2010 (which was enacted to harmonise equality law and restate the greater part of earlier enactments relating to discrimination and harassment related to certain personal characteristics) provides rights to compensation for various forms of discrimination by employers (ie claims in respect of discrimination on the grounds of age, disability, gender reassignment, marriage and civil partnership, pregnancy and maternity, race, religion or belief, sex and sexual orientation). Compensation for such discrimination may be paid under different heads such as for loss of earnings, for injury to feelings, personal injury and so on.

The tax treatment of such compensation payments made at the time of termination of employment depends upon whether they have been paid 'in connection with' the termination. If, on the one hand, a payment is not so connected, it will not fall within the residual category of termination payments (*A v HMRC* [2015] UKFTT 189 (TC)). If, on the other hand, a payment is so connected, then it will fall within the residual category of termination payments (*Walker v Adams* [2003] STC (SCD) 269; *Mr A v HMRC* [2009] SpC 734; *Chidi Anthony Oti-Obihara v HMRC* [2010] UKFTT 568 (TC); *Krishna Moorthy v RCC* [2014] UKFTT 834 (TC); [2015] UKUT 13). In the last-mentioned case the First-tier Tribunal approached the question of taxability of such payments by reference to the correct statutory principles and provides a rigorous analysis of the law which was lacking in the earlier cases. The tribunal analysed the earlier cases and discussed the deficiencies in the reasoning in them. The Upper Tribunal in that case did not disagree with the reasoning of the First-tier Tribunal.

Any such payment that is attributable to discrimination occurring before the termination of employment and not connected with the termination is unlikely to be a residual termination payment (and indeed is likely to escape income tax altogether, being outside the scope of all the categories of employment income and hence entirely outside the charge to income tax levied by *ITEPA 2003* on employment income – see, in particular, **15.65**). This is illustrated in the case of *A v HMRC* [2015] UKFTT 189 (TC) where a payment was made at the time of an employee's redundancy but in respect of a claim for race discrimination which occurred sometime before the redundancy situation arose.

So if a payment relates only to the consequences of termination (eg loss of future earnings) or is made to compensate for discrimination that occurred at the time of and was connected with the termination of employment (eg compensation for sex discrimination due where an employee is dismissed because she is pregnant), then such a payment will most likely be treated as a residual termination payment. (There is nothing in the legislation that restricts the charge to tax on amounts paid in connection with the termination of employment only to the extent that they represent compensation for financial loss; there is no distinction in *section 401* between non-pecuniary aspects of a termination package, such as injury to feelings, and pecuniary aspects such as financial loss.) By contrast, compensation for sex discrimination occurring over a period leading up to termination and inherent in the termination itself may be reasonably apportioned and only the latter element taxable as a residual termination payment. This is a summary of the law as set out by HMRC in EIM12965. In the Upper Tribunal in *Krishna Moorthy* it was observed that there appears to be an anomalous distinction between payments of compensation for discrimination before termination (which are not taxable as earnings) and such compensation paid in connection with termination which is taxed as a residual termination payment. But that is a consequence of the provisions of *ITEPA 2003, s 401* which deem such payments to be taxable.

However, even where a payment pursuant to a claim for discrimination does fall within the residual category of termination payments, it may be that it benefits from one of the exceptions from the charge to tax thereby imposed (see **15.23**). However, and in particular, a payment for injury to feelings does not benefit from the exception afforded to payments made on account of injury to any employee (see **15.38**) (*Krishna Moorthy v RCC* [2015] UKUT 13). Although in *Wilton v Timothy James Consulting Ltd* [2015] UKEAT 82, the Employment Appeals Tribunal held that a payment for injury to feelings benefited from that exception (holding, following *Orthet Ltd v Vince-Cain* [2005] ICR 324, that the term 'injury, in *ITEPA 2003, s 406(b)* encompassed injury to feelings), these decisions have been expressed to have been wrongly decided by the Upper Tribunal in the *Krishna Moorthy* case. *Finance (No 2) Bill 2017* provides that, from 6 April 2018, in *ITEPA 2003, s 406(2)*, 'injury' does not include injured feelings unless they amount to a psychiatric injury or other recognised medical condition.

On a practical level, where a compromise agreement does not apportion an award of damages between taxable and non-taxable elements, it is for the employee (and not the employer) to sort out the position with HMRC. The employer should deduct tax from the entire award of damages (subject to the £30,000 exemption) when they are paid (*Norman v Yellow Pages Sales Ltd* [2010] EWCA Civ 1395). Where possible this situation should be avoided so that the employee does not suffer adverse cash-flow consequences and so that he does not have the extra burden of having subsequently to deal with HMRC to sort out the matter.

Ex gratia payments

15.22 Termination payments that are pure gifts which are not charged to tax as earnings from employment (see **15.84**) or as benefits from an EFRBS (see **15.96–15.103**) are taxed as residual termination payments. It is possible to make tax-efficient gifts when an employee leaves his employment, and the suggested wording for any letter or minute or memorandum conferring such a payment is simply as follows: 'That the payment is made as a mark of the employer's goodwill'. In EIM13914, HMRC give the following example of a payment falling under this head. An employee with nine months' service is made redundant. Because he has worked for less than two years, he has no right to a statutory redundancy payment. But, as a gesture of goodwill, the employer decides to pay £1,000 to the employee on account of redundancy; it is taxable as a residual termination payment.

An example of a case where an ex gratia payment was taxed as a termination payment (rather than as a reward for services) is *Resolute Management Services Ltd v RCC* [2008] STC (SCD) 1202. In that case a company involved in the Lloyd's insurance market was set up with the intention of dealing with a number of liabilities. This entailed it working itself out of business as it settled each problem and claim. The taxpayer was employed by the company as HR director. Once it achieved its objectives the company began to downsize and the taxpayer's job changed from managing high volume of staff recruitment and establishing HR policies for the company to managing a planned redundancy programme over a five-year period. When the taxpayer considered that her task had been accomplished, she resigned from the company and in so doing she forfeited her own redundancy benefit and other long-term incentive payments to which she was contractually entitled. She was motivated to do 'the right thing' by the company. In recognition of this, the company made an ex gratia payment of £150,000 to her. HMRC contended that the payment was the taxpayer's earnings. The company contended that it was a payment made in connection with the termination of the taxpayer's employment.

The Special Commissioner found that the payment was not earnings for the purposes of *ITEPA 2003, s 62*, as it was paid in recognition of the fact that the taxpayer had done the right thing in resigning her position. On the facts the payment was truly a gift. The taxpayer had no contractual entitlement to the payment and had done nothing to earn it. Whilst it is true that had she not resigned the payment would not have been made, yet it was not paid in return for the resignation and neither was it paid in respect of any service that the taxpayer had rendered or was obliged to render. The payment was a residual termination payment. Although it was made 'for doing the right thing', the right thing was resigning and accordingly the payment was in consequence of, or in connection with, the termination of her employment.

EXCEPTIONS FROM THE RESIDUAL CATEGORY OF TERMINATION PAYMENTS

Introduction

15.23 There are several exceptions from income tax in respect of residual termination payments. These exceptions apply only to residual termination payments and are therefore incentives to structuring a termination payment so that it falls in this category of employment income (see **15.1**).

The exceptions in **Table 15.2** are selected for discussion in this chapter (the list not being exhaustive).

Table 15.2 – Exceptions from the residual category of termination payments

- £30,000 threshold
- Payments made on death
- Payments made for injury or disability
- Contributions to registered pension schemes
- Foreign service exception
- Foreign service relief
- Payments of certain legal costs
- Counselling and other outplacement services
- Retraining courses
- Long-service awards

£30,000 threshold

Focus

The application of the £30,000 threshold can sometimes be quite complicated. Ensure that it is correctly applied where employers are associated or where a termination package comprises both cash payments and benefits, especially if they are made or provided over a number of years.

15.24 All residual termination payments that count as the employment income of an employee on the termination of his employment are aggregated and it is the total amount that is considered in relation to the £30,000 threshold. If the aggregate amount exceeds £30,000, the amount in excess of that threshold is counted as the employee's employment income (*ITEPA 2003, s 403(1)*). Where the aggregate amount does not exceed the threshold (or to the extent that it does not exceed it), then, as it is not charged to tax under any of the other categories of employment income, it is free of income tax. Neither is such an amount chargeable to capital gains tax.

Other rules

Termination packages made by associated employers

15.25 The £30,000 threshold is available to an individual only once in respect of each employment of his that has been brought to an end (*ITEPA 2003, s 404(1)(a)*).

The first implication of this rule is that where a termination package is received by an employee in instalments over a number of tax years, the £30,000 threshold is not available each year; one £30,000 amount applies to the package no matter when it is received.

Example 15.2 – The £30,000 threshold

Charles's payment of £46,000 from his company's non-statutory redundancy scheme is to be paid in two equal instalments on 1 March 2017 (ie in 2016/17) and 1 July 2017 (ie in 2017/18). Only one £30,000 threshold is available and the excess payment of £16,000 falls into charge to tax (in 2017/18).

15.26 The second implication of this rule is that where an employee suffers the termination of more than one employment (whether held by him concurrently or successively), then separate £30,000 thresholds are available in respect of each employment that has been brought to an end.

Example 15.3 – Separate £30,000 thresholds

Albert is made redundant on 7 April 2017 and receives a payment of £30,000. This is exempt (*ITEPA 2003, s 403(1)*). He finds a new job with a new employer (who is not associated with his former employer) in May 2017, but is made redundant from that job in February 2018 when he is again paid £30,000. This, too, will be exempt. Consequently, in 2017/18, Albert has, in his circumstances, had the benefit of two £30,000 thresholds.

15.27 It is an important fact that in the immediately preceding example, the two employers are independent of one another (ie they are not 'associated'). Where employers are 'associated' then only one £30,000 threshold is available to an individual. This is also the case where an individual has different employments with the same employer.

Example 15.4 – Same employer

James is made redundant on 7 April 2017 and receives a payment of £30,000. This will be exempt (*ITEPA 2003, s 403(1)*). He finds a new job with the same employer in May 2017, but is made redundant from that job in February 2018 when he is again paid £30,000. This will not be exempt and a charge to tax arises in relation to the whole of the second £30,000 payment. This is because James's employer, in both cases, is the same person and so only one £30,000 threshold is available to James. (This contrasts with the example of Albert above where his successive employers are different persons.)

Example 15.5 – Associated employers

Aragon Ltd owns all the shares of Seymour Ltd. Henry worked for Aragon Ltd from 1 January 2009 until 1 May 2016 when his employment was ended by compromise agreement. A payment of £27,000 was made to him on that date. This falls wholly within the £30,000 threshold and is not taxable. Henry then started work with Seymour Ltd but was, after he had worked his notice period, made redundant in June 2017 and received £5,000 as an ex gratia payment. This payment is exempt as to £3,000 only – ie the amount of the payment that is equal to the balance of the £30,000 threshold that is left after the payment made in respect of the May 2016 termination. This is because at the time of the termination of his employment with Seymour Ltd (ie June 2017), that company was associated with Aragon Ltd and so only one £30,000 threshold is available in respect of Henry's two employments.

15.28 In the light of the above treatment, it is important to know when two or more employers are associated. There are three alternative tests.

First test. Employers are associated if, on the date of the termination of the employment in question, one of them is under the control of the other (*ITEPA 2003, s 404(2)(a)*). For example, if A Ltd owns all the share capital of B Ltd and both companies are concurrent or successive employers of Mr X, then A Ltd and B Ltd are associated employers.

Second test. Employers are associated if, on the date of the termination of the employment in question:

(a) one of them is under the control of a third person, and

(b) that third person controls the other (first limb of *ITEPA 2003, s 404(2)(b)*).

For example, if Mr X owns all the shares in Y Ltd and Z Ltd and both companies are the concurrent or successive employers of Mr Q, then Y Ltd and Z Ltd are associated employers.

Third test. Employers are associated if, on the date of the termination of the employment in question:

(a) one of them is under the control of a third person, and

(b) that third person is under the control of the other (second limb of *ITEPA 2003, s 404(2)(b)*).

For example, if M Ltd owns all the share capital of N Ltd which owns all the share capital of P Ltd, and M Ltd and P Ltd are the concurrent or successive employers of Mr Z, then M Ltd and P Ltd are associated employers.

Composition and terms of payment of a termination package

15.29 The rules on the application of the £30,000 threshold also take on an element of complexity in relation to the possible composition of a termination package and the terms under which the components may be paid. A termination package may comprise both cash payments and non-cash benefits which are paid (or given or made available) by instalments either in a single tax year or in two or more tax years.

Instalment payments in a single tax year

15.30 If more than one cash benefit is received in a tax year in which the £30,000 threshold is exceeded, the exempt amount (or the balance of it) is set against the amounts of cash benefits as they are received (*ITEPA 2003, s 404(5)(a)*). Cash benefits are treated as received when payment is made of or on account of them, or when the recipient becomes entitled to require payment of or on account of them (*ITEPA 2003, s 403(3)(a)*).

Example 15.6 – Termination package: two instalments

Andrew's termination package of £40,000 (which is a package of residual termination payments) is to be paid in two equal instalments in July and December 2017. The application of the £30,000 threshold is as follows:

	£
July instalment	20,000
Threshold	(20,000)
	Nil
December instalment	20,000
Threshold (30,000 – 20,000)	(10,000)
	10,000

For 2017/18, therefore, £10,000 of the total package is counted as Andrew's employment income.

15.31 If a termination package comprises both cash and non-cash benefits, and if at the end of the tax year in question any amount of the £30,000 threshold (having first been used in relation to any cash benefits) remains unused, then the balance is set against the aggregate amount of non-cash benefits received in that year (*ITEPA 2003, s 404(5)(b)*). Non-cash benefits are treated as received when they are used or enjoyed (*ITEPA 2003, s 403(3)(b)*). This is a question of fact. In the case of corporeal property, mere physical possession constitutes its enjoyment even if the item is not used until a later date. In the case of incorporeal property, the ownership of a right constitutes its enjoyment.

Example 15.7 – Termination package: cash and benefits

Edward's termination package (which is a package of residual termination payments) comprises £24,000 cash to be paid in two equal instalments in July and December 2017 and the transfer of an asset in September 2017 worth £8,000. The application of the £30,000 threshold is as follows:

	£
July instalment	12,000
Threshold	(12,000)
Nil	
December instalment	12,000
Threshold	(12,000)
	Nil
Asset transfer	8,000
Threshold (30,000 – 24,000)	(6,000)
	2,000

For 2017/18 the amount treated as Edward's employment income is £2,000.

15.32 This second rule is of benefit to employees. Since cash payments are treated as exempt in priority to non-cash benefits, the PAYE regime has no application. The former employee thereby achieves a cash-flow advantage. Under the PAYE regime, income tax is deducted from the cash component of a termination package by the employer making the payment. The rate at which tax is deducted depends upon when a payment is made. If it is made before the end of the employment (usually the date on which the P45 is issued), tax must be deducted in accordance with the employee's notice of coding using the appropriate tax tables. By contrast, if the payment is made after the employment ends, then tax using the 0T code (on a week 1/month 1 non-cumulative basis) must be deducted from the payment and accounted for to HMRC (*Income Tax*

(Pay as You Earn) Regulations 2003, SI 2003/2682, reg 37) (see **15.104**). To the extent that cash payments are exempt, no deduction will occur. Non-cash benefits will be returned by the employee himself under the self-assessment regime and tax on them will be due only on the 31 January in the tax year following that in which the non-cash benefit is received.

Instalment payments in two or more tax years

15.33 If cash and non-cash benefits are received in different tax years, the £30,000 threshold is set against the amount of payments and other benefits received in earlier tax years before those received in later tax years (*ITEPA 2003, s 404(4)*). This rule does not displace the rules on instalment payments made in a single year (as described in **15.30** above) or the rule that allocates the threshold to cash payments in priority to non-cash benefits (as described in **15.31** above); it is applied in addition to them, so that in any one tax year, the £30,000 amount is first set against cash and then against any non-cash benefits.

Example 15.8 – Cash and benefits package: separate years

Elizabeth's termination package (which is a package of residual termination payments awarded under an agreement made on 1 January 2017) provides for:

(a) £39,000 to be paid in three equal annual instalments on 1 January 2017, 1 January 2018 and 1 January 2019;

(b) the use of a car, the cash equivalent of which is £2,000, £7,000 and £7,500 in 2016/17, 2017/18 and 2018/19 respectively.

The total value of the package is £55,500 in respect of which only one £30,000 threshold is available. It will be allocated as follows:

(a) *2016/17:* total taxable value is £13,000 cash plus £2,000 in respect of the car. This £15,000 is within the threshold, leaving a balance of £15,000 to be carried forward to 2017/18.

(b) *2017/18:* total taxable value is £13,000 cash plus £7,000 in respect of the car. This £20,000 is exempt as to £15,000, £13,000 of the threshold being set against the cash, then the balance of £2,000 being set against the cash equivalent of the car, leaving £5,000 taxable (in respect of the non-cash component of the package in this year).

(c) *2018/19:* total taxable value is £13,000 cash plus £7,500 in respect of the car. This £20,500 is taxable in full, no balance of the threshold being available.

The £30,000 threshold and foreign-service relief

15.34 Where an employee's service under his contract of employment includes foreign service which does not, on account of the inadequacy of the duration or timing of that service, qualify for the foreign-service exception (see **15.46**), he will be able to claim foreign-service relief. It must be noted, however, that the £30,000 threshold applies before a deduction is taken for foreign service relief (*ITEPA 2003, s 414(2)*).

Example 15.9 – Foreign-service relief

Alexandra is employed in an employment for five years. In respect of two of those years, she receives earnings in respect of foreign service. At the end of the fifth year she receives a payment of £100,000 which is a residual termination payment. The amount which is counted as her employment income is:

	£
Termination payment	100,000
Less: threshold	(30,000)
	70,000
Less: foreign service relief 70,000 × 2/5	(28,000)
Taxable amount	42,000

Payments made on death

Focus

Take care not to fall into the trap of thinking that termination payments made on death are necessarily not charged to income tax. Ensure that such payments which are ex gratia are not taxed as payments under an employer-financed retirement benefits scheme and so taxable in full (see **15.101**).

15.35 *ITEPA 2003, s 406(a)* provides that a payment or other benefit provided in connection with the termination of employment by the death of an employee does not fall to be taxed as a residual termination payment. All payments, whether ex gratia or made under some form of obligation (whether legal or not), are capable of coming within this exception. However, care must be exercised here to ensure that the payment is not chargeable to tax as a payment under an EFRBS (see **15.101**) as the payment will not then be a residual termination payment.

15.36 The rule is drafted very widely and is satisfied if the making of the payment merely has something to do with the termination of the employment which has been brought about by the death of the employee. This should cover all possible circumstances in which a death might arise – be it from natural causes, by accident or otherwise (eg as the result of a criminal act).

15.37 There are no conditions imposed by the exception as to the circumstances in which death occurs. It is not necessary that the employee be carrying out his employment duties at the time of the death. A payment following a fatal car crash, for example, whilst the employee is on holiday would also be within the exception.

Payments made for injury or disability

Focus

Take care not to fall into the trap of thinking that termination payments made on account of injury are necessarily not charged to income tax. There are a number of complex conditions that have to be satisfied for such a charge not to arise.

15.38 *ITEPA 2003, s 406(b)* provides that a payment or other benefit provided on account of injury to, or disability of, an employee does not fall to be taxed as a residual termination payment. Again, all payments, whether ex gratia or made under some form of obligation (whether legal or not), are capable of coming within this exception provided the other conditions for the exception are met.

15.39 In order to be within the exception, the payment must be provided 'on account of' the injury or disability. In contrast to the exception on death, the condition relating to the provision of the payment in this context is more stringent for it must be established as a subjective fact that the injury or disability is the motive for making the payment (*Horner v Hasted (Inspector of Taxes)* [1995] STC 766). If the employer decides to dismiss an employee on commercial grounds (eg the employee's work has deteriorated and is adversely affecting the performance of the employer's business), then any payment made upon dismissal is unlikely to come within the disability exception even if the reason for the deterioration in the employee's work is, in turn, due to a disability. In order to establish entitlement to the exception, the injury or disability must motivate or induce the making of the payment. In *Flutter v RCC* [2015] UKFTT 249 (TC) the taxpayer, who suffered from a hearing disability that impinged on his ability to carry out his employment duties (which involved the extensive use of the telephone), was made redundant and received a termination payment. Although the taxpayer's hearing loss was more likely than not a significant contributory factor to the timing of the termination of his employment, it was found that the payment made by the employer was not motivated by his disability and so the exception afforded by *section 406(b)* was not available in respect of it.

15.40 What type of injury comes within the exception? An injury is a physical injury (eg the loss of a limb or a sense (eg sight) that renders the victim incapable of carrying out the duties of his employment. In EIM13610, HMRC state that a psychological injury is also within the exception so that compensation for injury to feelings where the injury amounts to a recognised psychological illness may be exempt. In *Wilton v Timothy James Consulting Ltd* [2015] UKEAT 82, the Employment Appeal Tribunal, following *Orthet Ltd v Vince-Cain* [2005] ICR 324, held that the term 'injury, in *ITEPA 2003, s 406(b)* encompassed injury to feelings occasioned by acts of harassment by an employer related to the sex of one of its employees. However, these cases have been held by the Upper Tribunal in *Krishna Moorthy v RCC* [2015] UKUT 13 to have been wrongly decided. In *Krishna Moorthy*, after a rigorous review of the authorities, the Upper Tribunal held that 'injury' refers only to a medical condition and does not include injury to feelings. Nevertheless, HMRC's position may still be correct as it is not the injury to feelings per se that are regarded as the injury, but the psychological illness that results. *Finance (No 2) Bill 2017* provides that, from 6 April 2018, in *ITEPA 2003, s 406(2)*, 'injury' does not include injured feelings unless they amount to a psychiatric injury or other recognised medical condition.

However, the injury does not have to be sustained during working hours while the employee is carrying out the duties of his employment. Neither does it necessarily need to be suffered by accident. But the injury must occur to an individual while he is an employee, not after he has ceased to be an employee.

15.41 Understanding what comes within the scope of the term 'disability' is more problematic. In *Horner v Hasted (Inspector of Taxes)* [1995] STC 766 it was held that a disability is a condition that amounts to a total or partial impairment (which may arise from physical, mental or psychological causes) of the employee's ability to perform the functions or duties of his employment.

HMRC in SP 10/81 accept that 'disability' means the incapacity to fulfil the duties and responsibilities of the employment resulting from sudden affliction (eg coronary thrombosis), or arising out of the culmination of a process of deterioration of physical or mental health caused by chronic illness (eg bronchitis). Disability, therefore, encompasses ill health, but it is unclear why HMRC limit their practice to chronic illness only. Certainly, the legislation does not indicate that such a restriction be imposed, and this is in keeping with the definition of the term found in the Shorter Oxford English Dictionary which defines the word as a physical or mental condition (usually permanent) that limits a person's activities or senses, especially the ability to work. HMRC do not regard the normal process of ageing as a disability within the exception (EIM13620). In the *Horner* case, the taxpayer's distress and insomnia caused by his work were not considered to be a disability qualifying for exception even though they affected his work. In that case there was insufficient evidence to show that this caused a medical condition which disabled or prevented the taxpayer from carrying out the duties of his employment.

HMRC will give formal binding answers in relation to the meaning of disability under SP 10/81 and to enquiries on the application of this disability and injury compensation exception in any particular case (see **15.107**).

15.42 EIM13630 makes the following points (based on the *Horner* case) in relation to the disability exception.

First, there must be an identified medical condition that disables or prevents the employee from carrying out the duties of the employment. Any injury or disability must be established as an objective fact. Medical evidence confirming the precise nature of the disability must therefore be provided in all cases, and it must be clear that the nature of the disability prevents the employee carrying out the specific duties of the employment.

Secondly, the payment must be made on account of the disability and on account of nothing else. If, for example, the employer is unaware of the disability when the employee leaves, then the payment cannot be made 'on account of' disability. Similarly, if any part of the payment is a reward for specific services, or due on termination regardless of the cause, it cannot be 'on account of' disability. HMRC will frequently require seeing all documentation to establish why the employer made the payment.

Thirdly, it is important to ensure that the medical condition and its employment consequences are considered by reference to the situation at the point of termination of employment, and not at any other time. For example, evidence of a medical condition existing, say, two years before termination is not determinative.

Contributions to registered pension schemes

> **Focus**
>
> This exception is perhaps the most valuable tool in termination payment planning as it may often be combined with the £30,000 threshold to make larger payments entirely tax free. Take care though not to overfund a pension scheme or exceed an employee's annual allowance.

15.43 *ITEPA 2003, s 408(1)* provides that a contribution to a registered pension scheme (ie under *FA 2004, Pt 4, Ch 2*) or an employer-financed retirement benefit scheme (EFRBS) is not counted as a residual termination payment if the contribution is made:

(a) as part of an arrangement relating to the termination of the person's employment (*ITEPA 2003, s 408(1)(a)*), and

(b) in order to provide benefits for that person in accordance with the terms of the scheme or approved personal pension arrangements (*ITEPA 2003, s 408(1)(b)*).

15.44 It will be noted that the contribution must be made as part of an arrangement relating to the termination of the employee's employment (eg under a compromise agreement). It would appear that the exception will not apply where a payment is made to the former employee who then makes a contribution to the pension scheme. The amount of the contribution must be within the limits imposed by the scheme rules, which will have to be checked whenever such a contribution is made. Similarly, care should be taken to ensure that any contribution made to a registered pension scheme is within the employee's cumulated annual allowance to avoid an annual allowance charge arising on him (*FA 2004, s 227*) or that it does not negate any transitional protection regime that he may enjoy on account of the reduction of the pension lifetime allowance to £1m from 6 April 2016 (or any other protection regimes that are in place on account of earlier reductions in the lifetime allowance).

15.45 This exception is a most valuable one and should not be overlooked in planning. For example, where a termination package within the residual category provides that a payment of £50,000 be made to a former employee, it is possible to shelter the whole amount from income tax through a combination of the £30,000 threshold and a contribution to a registered pension scheme (assuming a £20,000 special contribution to the pension fund is within its funding limits and the individual's current annual allowance). Where a contribution is made to an EFRBS however, although the payment is not regarded as a residual termination payment, consideration must be given as to whether a charge to tax may arise in respect of the contribution in accordance with the rules on employment income provided through third parties (*ITEPA 2003, Pt 7A*).

Foreign service exception

> **Focus**
>
> This exception is another valuable tool in termination payment planning as payments to which it applies are entirely tax free regardless of their amount.

15.46 The normal rules on residence and domicile in so far as they relate to the taxation of general earnings (*ITEPA 2003, Pt 2, Chs 4, 5*) do not apply in relation to the imposition of a charge to UK income tax on residual termination payments and such payments are prima facie within the charge to UK income tax no matter where in the world they are made or to whom they are made (*Nichols v Gibson* [1996] STC 1008). However, this worldwide application of this category of employment income is limited by the foreign service exception.

Whether the exception for foreign service is to apply in respect of a residual termination payment, the employment in respect of which it is made must include 'foreign service' as defined in *ITEPA 2003, s 413(2)–(6)*. Service in or after the tax year 2013/14 is foreign service to the extent that it consists of duties performed outside the UK in respect of which earnings are not relevant earnings; so if the employee serves abroad for a period but his earnings for that period of service are relevant earnings, then that period will *not* count towards the exception. Relevant earnings are those for a tax year in which the employee is resident in the UK (including overseas earnings in respect of which a claim for the remittance basis has been made, including a claim under the overseas workday relief provisions). In short, therefore, an employee has a period of foreign service for the purposes of this exception only if his duties are performed outside the UK at a time when he is not resident in the UK (as determined using the statutory residence test). If the employee finds himself in any other position, his period of service does not count as foreign service. This will typically be the case where the employee is not resident in the UK and his duties are performed here. Similarly, the UK duties of a UK resident cannot qualify as foreign service even if they meet the overseas workday relief provisions (*ITEPA 2003, s 26A*).

Strictly speaking, the definition of 'foreign service' relates to service in a single employment, although HMRC will treat employments with different group companies as a single employment for the purpose of calculating periods of foreign service, provided that the termination payment relates to the service with those group companies as a whole (EIM13975).

HMRC will give formal binding answers in relation to the application of the foreign service exception in any particular case (see **15.107**).

15.47 A residual termination payment is exempt if paid in respect of an employment in which the employee's service has:

(a) included foreign service; and

(b) that foreign service falls within one of three qualifying classes (*ITEPA 2003, s 413(1)*).

An employee's foreign service must satisfy the requirements of any one of the three qualifying classes in order for the exception to apply. Each class requires that a proportion of the employee's period of service be comprised of foreign service. This requires one to ascertain the length of his foreign service and compare this to the length of his total period of service ending with the date of termination of his employment. Where the exception applies, it should be emphasised that the whole termination payment is exempt from tax, not only that part of it which is attributable to the period of foreign service.

15.48 Foreign service falls within the first qualifying class where:

(a) the employee's total period of service has exceeded 20 years (a period of 20 years exactly being insufficient); and

(b) the foreign service:

  (i) comprises one-half or more of that period; and

  (ii) includes any ten out of the last 20 years (*ITEPA 2003, s 413(1)(c)*).

It is not necessary that the period of foreign service be continuous, so long as in aggregate all such periods meet the conditions set out in paragraph (b) above.

Example 15.10 – Foreign service: first qualifying class

An individual is employed by Chancellor Ltd. His employment commenced on 6 October 1997 and was wrongly terminated on 5 April 2018 when he was paid £100,000 in damages. He was in foreign service for two periods, namely 6 October 1998 to 5 October 2001, and 1 January 2006 to 30 June 2013. His period of service comprises 20½ years, and so, prima facie, it is within the first qualifying class. His period of foreign service totals 10½ years which is more than one-half of the total period. The last 20 years of service comprise the period 6 April 1998 to 5 April 2018. The periods 6 October 1998 to 5 October 2001, and 1 January 2006 to 30 June 2013, together comprise a ten-year period falling in the last 20 years during which there was foreign service. This confirms that the first qualifying class applies and the damages are tax free.

15.49 Foreign service falls within the second qualifying class where:

(a) the employee's total service has exceeded ten years (a period of exactly ten years is insufficient); and

(b) the foreign service comprises the whole of the last ten years of that period (*ITEPA 2003, s 413(1)(b)*).

This class includes periods of total service of 20 years or more. Where the period exceeds 20 years, therefore, *prima facie*, the first and second qualifying classes are in point. The further conditions of each class will then determine which one is applicable (if at all). The conditions in paragraph (b) are met where at least the whole of the last ten years of service are made up of foreign service. In this case though, and by way of contrast to the provisions of the first qualifying class, there must be foreign service continuously throughout the final ten years of service.

15.50 Foreign service falls within the third qualifying class where:

(a) the employee's total period of service is of any length; and

(b) the foreign service comprises three-quarters of that period (*ITEPA 2003, s 413(1)(a)*).

The class is not limited to cases where the foreign service is exactly three-quarters of the whole period of service. It is sufficient if at least three-quarters of that period is made up of foreign service. It is also important to appreciate that this qualifying class applies to periods of service of any length, even those contemplated by the other two qualifying classes. Where the additional conditions of those classes are not satisfied it is still possible that the third qualifying class may apply.

Example 15.11 – Foreign service: third qualifying class

An individual is employed by Computer Services Ltd. His employment commenced on 1 January 2005 and was terminated on 31 December 2017 when he received £45,000. During this period he had ten years of continuous foreign service which began on 1 March 2005. Although his period of service was in excess of ten years (but less than 20 years), it does not fall within the second qualifying class as the whole of the last ten years does not comprise foreign service. However, it does fall within the third qualifying class as his period of foreign service represents 76.9% of his total service. The £45,000 is, therefore, not charged to income tax.

Foreign service relief

> **Focus**
>
> If a payment does not qualify for complete exception under the foreign service exception, do not overlook foreign service relief, but take care to apply it and the £30,000 threshold correctly (see **15.34**).

15.51 A residual termination payment made in respect of an employment in which the service of the employee includes foreign service may not, on account of the inadequacy of the duration or timing of that service, qualify for the foreign service exception. In such a case, however, a taxpayer will be able to claim foreign service relief (*ITEPA 2003, s 414(1)*). The relief operates by allowing a deduction to be made from the termination payment before it is charged to income tax (*ITEPA 2003, s 414(2)*).

15.52 The amount of any termination payment which is left in charge to tax (ie the 'taxable proportion' (Z)) after the application of the relief is calculated as follows (*ITEPA 2003, s 414(3)*):

	£
Termination payment	P
Less: P × F/T	(X)
Taxable proportion	£Z

where:

P is the amount of the termination payment which is 'chargeable to tax' before the relief is given

F is the length of the employee's period of foreign service

T is the length of the employee's total period of service before the date of termination.

The amount (P) of the termination payment which is 'chargeable to tax' before the relief is given is calculated after applying the £30,000 threshold (*ITEPA 2003, s 414(2)*) (see **15.34**). As this deduction is made before the relief for foreign service is given, the effect is that the benefit of the £30,000 threshold is restricted.

It is important to note that the reduction must be claimed within four years after the end of the tax year to which it relates; this must not be overlooked as the other exceptions tend to apply automatically. This is an important point for employers; because the relief has to be claimed by the employee, no account should be taken of it when operating PAYE. However, in practice HMRC may agree that the employer may operate PAYE taking into account foreign service relief where it has requested permission in advance of making a termination payment.

Finally, in the context of a payment qualifying for foreign service relief, it may be the case that a residual termination payment may have suffered tax in the country in which foreign service was rendered. In this case, any double tax agreement with the foreign country concerned should be consulted to see whether relief for that tax is available. The provisions in UK domestic law for unilateral double tax relief should also be considered.

Payments of certain legal costs

> **Focus**
>
> Take care to structure the discharge of an employee's legal fees in such a way that the stringent conditions applicable to this exception are satisfied. The same advice goes for payments for outplacement counselling (**15.54**) and retraining courses (**15.57**).

15.53 Legal costs paid by an employer on behalf of an employee in connection with the termination of his employment will be regarded as a residual termination benefit received by the employee. An exception is provided however for legal costs that meet two conditions (*ITEPA 2003, s 413A(1)*).

The first is that the payment must meet the whole or part of the legal costs incurred by the employee exclusively in connection with the termination of his employment (*ITEPA 2003, s 413A(2)*). Legal costs are the fees payable for the services and disbursements of a lawyer (as defined below) (*ITEPA 2003, s 413A(4)*).

The second condition is set out in *ITEPA 2003, s 413A(3)* and is in the alternative. It provides that:

(a) the payment must be made pursuant to an order of a court or tribunal, or

(b) the termination of the employee's employment results in a settlement agreement between the employer and the employee, the agreement provides for the payment to be made by the employer and the payment is made directly to the employee's lawyer (ie a qualified lawyer as defined in the *ERA 1996, s 203(4)* or the *Employment Rights (Northern Ireland) Order 1996, art 245(5)*).

It is essential that if the second alternative of the second condition is to be satisfied there must be a settlement agreement (ie compromise agreement) and it must contain two terms. First, it must provide that the payment is to be made by the employer; secondly it must make it clear that the payment be made directly to the employee's lawyer by the employer. The agreement should also state that the legal costs concerned relate exclusively to the termination of the employee's contract and not to any other matters. Care must therefore be taken in the drafting of such compromise agreements. The fees of accountants and other professionals must not be settled direct by the employer, otherwise the exception will not apply; such expenses should be billed as the lawyer's disbursements and settled by him out of the payment made to him by the employer. Also the employee should not first pay his solicitor and then seek reimbursement from his employer if the exception is to apply.

Counselling and other outplacement services

15.54 When an employee loses his employment, his employer may pay for him to receive professional advice and assistance designed to help him cope with his new situation and find a new job. Such professional advice is known as outplacement counselling and may consist of anything from a single advisory interview to ongoing assistance for a period of several months. It is a fairly common feature of redundancy packages offered by employers.

15.55 Payments for counselling services which meet certain conditions qualify for exemption from the charge to income tax levied on all categories of employment income comprising the scheme of legislative provisions dealing with termination payments (and so on residual termination payments in particular) (*ITEPA 2003, s 310*). No liability to income tax arises in respect of:

(a) the provision of services to a person in connection with the cessation of the person's employment; or

(b) the payment or reimbursement of:

  (i) fees for such provision, or

  (ii) travelling expenses incurred in connection with such provision,

if Conditions A to D and, in the case of travel expenses, Condition E are met.

15.56 Condition A is satisfied if the only or main purpose of the provision of the services is to enable the person either to adjust to the cessation of the employment or to find other gainful employment (including self-employment), or indeed both of these matters.

Condition B is met if the services consist wholly of any of the following:

(a) giving advice and guidance;

(b) imparting or improving skills;

(c) providing or making available the use of office equipment or similar facilities.

Condition C is met if the person provided with the services has been employed full time in the employment which is ceasing throughout the period of two years at the time when the services begin to be provided or, if earlier, at the time when the employment ceases.

Condition D is met if the opportunity to receive the services, on similar terms as to payment or reimbursement of any expenses incurred in connection with their provision, is available generally to employees or former employees of the person's employer in that employment or to a particular class or classes of them.

Condition E is met if the travel expenses are expenses in respect of which mileage allowance relief would be available if no mileage allowance payments had been made or which would be deductible as expenses of the employment under *ITEPA 2003, Pt 5*.

Condition E operates off the back of an assumption that receiving the services is one of the duties of the employee's employment, the employee incurs and pays the expenses and the employment continues even though it may, in fact, have ceased.

Retraining courses

15.57 *ITEPA 2003, s 311(1)* provides that no liability to income tax arises under any category of employment income comprising the scheme of legislative provisions dealing with termination payments (and so including the residual category of termination payments in particular) in respect of the payment or reimbursement of retraining course expenses (including certain travel expenses) by a person ('the employer') if a number of conditions are met. There are four categories of conditions that have to be satisfied in order for the exemption to be available:

(a) conditions relating to the employer;

(b) conditions relating to the expenses;

(c) the course conditions; and

(d) the employment conditions.

Conditions relating to the employer

15.58 The employer must incur expenditure in paying or reimbursing qualifying expenses (see **15.59**). Clearly, such expenditure will have been incurred by him where he has actually paid the expenses or reimbursed someone else. The condition is also satisfied where the employer has the obligation to pay or reimburse the expenses.

There is no bar on who pays the course provider. It could be the employer for he would then satisfy the condition that he pays the relevant expenses. However, if the employee or another person pays the expenses initially, his expenses must be reimbursed by the employer. The employee or other person is not allowed merely to take a deduction from his earnings for his expenditure; reimbursement is essential.

Conditions relating to the expenses

15.59 The expenses to which the exemption relates must be within the following list (*ITEPA 2003, s 311(2)*):

(a) fees for attendance of the employee at a training course;

(b) fees for any examination which is taken during or at the conclusion of the course;

(c) the cost of any books which are essential for a person attending the course; and

(d) travelling expenses incurred in connection with the course.

Any expenses incurred that do not fall within this list and which are paid or reimbursed by the employer are outside the scope of the exemption and will, in the absence of the application of any of the other categories of employment income comprising the scheme of legislative provisions dealing with termination payments, fall into charge to tax as residual termination benefits or payments.

As regards (d) above, the travel expenses must be expenses in respect of which mileage allowance relief (see *ITEPA 2003, Pt 4, Ch 2*) would be available if no mileage allowance payments had been made or which would be deductible as expenses of the employment under *ITEPA 2003, Pt 5* (*ITEPA 2003, s 311(5)*).

The conditions relating to qualifying expenses operate off the back of an assumption that attendance at the course is one of the duties of the employee's employment, that the employee incurs and pays the expenses, and that the employee continues to be employed by the employer even if his employment has, in fact, ceased (*ITEPA 2003, s 311(6)*).

The course conditions

15.60 *ITEPA 2003, s 311(3)* provides that the course must be a qualifying training course in that it must:

(a) provide training designed to impart or improve skills or knowledge relevant to, and intended to be used in the course of, gainful employment, including self-employment, of any description;

(b) be entirely devoted to the teaching or practical application of such skills or knowledge (or to both such teaching and practical applications); and

(c) not exceed two years in duration.

The employment conditions

15.61 In order to qualify for exemption all the following conditions in *ITEPA 2003, s 311(4)* relating to the employee must be satisfied.

The employee must:

(a) begin the course while he is employed by the employer or within one year of ceasing to be employed by the employer;

(b) either have left the employment before the course begins or have left the employment not later than the end of the period of two years beginning at the end of the course;

(c) not be re-employed by the employer within a period of two years of the employment ceasing;

(d) be employed by the employer throughout the period of two years up to the time he begins to undertake the course or, if it is earlier, at the time he ceases to be employed by the employer; and

(e) have been given the opportunity to attend the course and have the cost met or reimbursed by the employer on the same terms as offered to employees or former employees generally or to a particular class or classes of employee or former employee.

If an employee's liability to tax has been determined on the assumption that *ITEPA 2003, s 311* applies and subsequently condition (a) is not met because he fails to begin the course within one year after ceasing to be employed or conditions (b) and (c) of the above employment conditions are not met because of his continued employment or re-employment, then HMRC will withdraw the exemption and raise an assessment to collect any tax due

(*ITEPA 2003, s 312*). It is HMRC's view, however, that the *ITEPA 2003, s 311* exemption is not withdrawn or withheld if an employee does not find a job or start a business or if the employment or self-employment subsequently undertaken is in a field unconnected with the course, so long as all the other conditions are satisfied.

Example 15.12 – Retraining courses

An individual is employed by Traill Ltd. His employment commenced on 1 April 2015 and was terminated by reason of redundancy on 1 January 2017. As part of the individual's redundancy package, Traill Ltd pays the qualifying costs of a qualifying retraining course. The course began on 1 July 2017 and ended three months' later. The costs incurred by Traill Ltd will not be exempt under *ITEPA 2003, s 311*. Although the course began on 1 July 2017 which was within one year after the end of the employment which occurred on 1 January 2017 and the employee had ceased to be employed before the course began, he was in employment for the period 1 April 2015 to 1 January 2017 (the date of cessation of employment being taken as it is earlier than 1 July 2017 when the course started) and this was not a period of two years' continuous employment. Hence the employment conditions for the application of the exemption are not satisfied.

Long-service awards

15.62 *ITEPA 2003, s 323* provides that no liability to income tax arises under any category of employment income in respect of a long-service award which meets the following conditions:

(a) The award must be made to an employee to mark not less than 20 years' service with the same employer. Service is treated as being with the same employer if it is with two or more employers, each of whom is a successor or predecessor of the others, or one of whom is a company which belongs or has belonged to the same group as the others or a predecessor or successor of the others. A group comprises a body corporate and its 51% subsidiaries.

(b) The amount of employment income which would be charged to tax in respect of the award apart from the exemption does not exceed £50 for each year of service in respect of which the award is made. If the amount of the award exceeds this ceiling, then the excess only is outside the scope of the exemption and charged to income tax accordingly.

(c) The award must take one of the following forms – tangible moveable property, shares in a company which is, or belongs to the same group (as defined above) as, the employer; or the provision of any other benefit except a cash payment, a cash voucher, a credit token, securities, shares other than those just mentioned, or an interest in or rights over securities or shares.

This means that, for example, cash, cheques, premium bonds, National Savings Certificates and options over any shares may not be given as a long-service award; however, non-cash vouchers (eg travel tickets) are not excluded and may be so given, as may most other non-cash awards, including land, intellectual property or other intangible assets (eg the benefit of a contract such as the provision of a holiday). If a non-cash award fails to meet the conditions of the exemption or exceeds the monetary limit, then the employer may be prepared to pay the tax arising under a PAYE Settlement Agreement (treating the award as a minor benefit – see SP 5/96).

15.63 The exemption for long-service awards does not apply to a later award if an earlier award to mark a particular period of service with the same employer has been made to the employee in the period of ten years ending with the date on which the later award is made (*ITEPA 2003, s 323(4)*).

So the first time that a long-service award is made is after 20 years' service. On this occasion the maximum tax-free amount is £1,000. Thereafter, awards may only be made at ten-yearly intervals, but the calculation of the tax-free element of the award may take into account all years of service down to that later anniversary. So, an award made to an employee on the anniversary of 30 years' service may be tax free up to £1,500, even though an earlier award of £1,000 was made to him at the 20-year anniversary.

The time limits imposed by the section mean that it is likely that the exemption will be used only once or twice in a typical working life time. No exemption is due if an employee has received another long service award, for service with the same employer, within the previous 10 years. An employee who receives an award after 25 years and then again after 30 years, cannot benefit from the exemption for the award given on the 30-year anniversary because the 10-year rule is not satisfied. In the application of the 10-year rule it does not matter if the earlier award did or did not qualify for exemption. All earlier awards in respect of service with the same employer are taken into account for the purpose of the 10-year test, whether taxed or not.

Despite its restrictions, this exemption is quite valuable when used in connection with the termination of an employee's employment in the appropriate circumstances.

Example 15.13 – Long service awards (see EIM01510)

An employee receives long service awards from her employer as follows (all the awards being made on or after 13 June 2003):

- after 20 years' service, an article costing £1,000
- after 30 years' service, an article costing £500
- after 35 years' service, an article costing £625
- after 40 years' service, an article costing £1,000

The application of the exemption for long services awards is as follows:

The 20-year award is not taxed. This is the first award received, the 20 year condition is satisfied, and the cost does not exceed £50 for each year of service (20 × £50 = £1,000). If the article had cost £1,500, tax would have been charged on the excess over £1,000.

The 30-year award is not taxed. It satisfies the conditions for exemption and it does not matter that the employee has already received a tax-free award.

The 35-year award is taxed in full. It is within the monetary limit (35 × £50 = £1,750), but no exemption is due because the employee received a similar award within the previous 10 years.

The 40-year award is taxed in full. It is within the monetary limit (40 × £50 = £2,000), but no exemption is due because the employee received a similar award within the previous 10 years. The 35-year award is counted even though it was taxed in full.

TERMINATION PAYMENTS WITHIN THE OTHER CATEGORIES OF EMPLOYMENT INCOME

Introduction

15.64 The other categories of employment income into which termination payments may fall have been listed in **15.3**. Attention now focuses on dealing with each of those other categories in turn in the order in which they should be applied in ascertaining the treatment of a termination payment (see **15.3**) and discussing the types of payments that come within them. As intimated in **15.4**, it may be the case that the terms of the employment relationship between an employer and his employee (which were agreed upon at the time their relationship commenced) are such that the parties have little or no choice as to which category of employment income is applicable to a termination payment made by the employer to his employee. However, even if a payment falls to be treated otherwise than as a residual termination payment, it should not be forgotten to consider whether there are any exemptions available in respect of the category of employment income into which it falls.

Earnings from employment

15.65 Termination payments which are in the nature of rewards for services or which are attributable only to the employer-employee relationship are payments that fall to be taxed as earnings from employment (see *ITEPA 2003, s 9(6)*) notwithstanding the time of making the payment is deferred to the end of the employment or a time following that. The main types of payment within this category that will be discussed in this chapter are set out in **Table 15.3**.

Table 15.3 – Termination payments that are earnings

- Deferred remuneration
- Payments made pursuant to express terms of service
- Contractual PILONs
- Payments made pursuant to implied terms of service
- Payments that are expected on account of employer behaviour
- Payments for employment-related rights
- Payments for garden leave
- Payments under certain compromise agreements
- Termination payments that are inducement payments
- Ex gratia payments

Where, however, a payment is not in the nature of a reward for services or is not one which is attributable only to the employer-employee relationship, it will not be earnings. In *A v HMRC* [2015] UKFTT 189 (TC) a payment which was made to settle a claim for race discrimination was held not to be earnings from employment. Although HMRC had argued that the payment was designed to make good shortfalls in salary and bonus received by the taxpayer and was therefore earnings, the Tribunal found that the payment was made to settle his claim for race discrimination and so was not earnings, being as it was not a reward for services but a sum paid for some reason other than just the employment relationship. This was so even though the payment was calculated by reference to underpaid earnings. The Tribunal stated that while the discrimination may have manifested itself through the way in which the employee was remunerated, the compensation payment arose not because the employee was under-remunerated but because the underpayment was discriminatory.

Deferred remuneration

15.66 Where a contract of service provides expressly or impliedly that a payment is to be made upon the termination of the contract, and the payment is described as (or on a proper construction of the terms of the contract is in substance) a payment of deferred remuneration for services rendered, then such a sum is taxable as earnings 'from' the employment (*Allen and Another (as Murray's Executors) v Trehearne (HM Inspector of Taxes)* 22 TC 15; *Henry v Foster* 16 TC 605). Such a payment cannot therefore be a residual termination payment.

Payments made pursuant to express terms of service

15.67 The terms upon which an employee serves may expressly provide that a payment is to be made to him upon termination of his employment. The source of such terms is not limited to the contract of employment itself, but includes all sources which contain the terms of an employee's engagement, including a company's articles of association, staff handbooks, trade union agreements, oral arrangements and so on.

Payments made pursuant to such express terms are earnings from employment (*Dale (H M Inspector of Taxes) v de Soissons* 32 TC 118; *Williams (Inspector of Taxes) v Simmons* [1981] STC 715). The specific example of a payment falling within this head, namely a statutory PILON, is dealt with separately below.

Excepted from such treatment is a payment made under a genuine, non-statutory redundancy scheme whether the scheme is brought into existence and the payment is determined and paid at the time of redundancy or whether the payment is made at the time of redundancy but in accordance with a scheme that has been provided for in an employee's contract of employment and so part and parcel of the conditions under which he has given service during the subsistence of his contract (see **15.10**).

Contractual PILONs

> **Focus**
>
> It is often assumed that a contractual PILON clause in an employment contract is an absolute bar to the application of the residual category of employment income to a termination payment made under the clause. It is a fundamental misconception that once a contract of employment contains a provision for a PILON, it becomes impossible for there to be a wrongful dismissal and hence a payment that is a residual termination payment (see **15.70**). But care must be exercised here as there may be other adverse employment law consequences where an employer breaches a contract.

15.68 In the present context a payment in lieu of notice is one paid under a contract of service which expressly provides that an employment may be terminated either by notice or, on payment of a sum in lieu of notice, summarily. The following is an example of such a clause:

Pay in lieu of notice

'(1) One party has the duty to give three months' notice to the other of his intention to terminate the contract.

(2) However, the employer reserves the right to terminate the contract without giving notice upon the payment of three months' salary in lieu of notice.'

15.69 The clause bestows upon an employer the freedom to choose which of the two methods provided for in the contract he will use to end the contract. When the choice is made there will be no breach of contract, the employer having infringed none of the employee's rights (*Rex Stewart Jeffries Parker Ginsberg Ltd v Parker* [1988] IRLR 483; *Abrahams v Performing Rights Society Ltd*, *The Times*, 5 June 1995; *Delaney v Staples* [1992] 1 All ER 944). The freedom here is created by the parties themselves and the effect is that it absolves the employer from the duty which he would otherwise have had under clause (1). Once the employer has made his choice, only then does he fall under a contractual duty. Under choice (1), the employer is obliged to give notice (*Woolridge v Sumner* [1962] 2 All ER 978) and to allow the employment relationship to subsist for the agreed period. Under choice (2) the employer is under a duty to make a payment.

15.70 The payment of a sum in lieu of notice in this context is a payment of earnings from employment (*EMI Group Electronics Ltd v Coldicott (Inspector of Taxes)* [1999] STC 803). Such a payment is made in pursuance of a contractual provision, agreed at the outset of employment (or subsequently by variation of the employment contract), which enables the employer to terminate the employment on making that payment. The employee is entitled under the bargain struck at commencement of employment (or at the time of the subsequent variation of its terms) either to security or continuity of employment – or the security or continuity of salary – for a given period or to an additional payment on summary termination. In both cases the terms are agreed upon as terms under which service will be given by the employee and so the payment made under those terms falls squarely within the tests laid down by the House of Lords in *Hochstrasser v Mayes* 38 TC 673 as a payment made in return for acting as or being an employee and in *Shilton v Wilmshurst* 46 TC 78 as being an emolument from being or becoming an employee. This is the case whether that term was part of the contract of employment from the outset (as in the *EMI Group Electronics Ltd* case itself) or whether it was introduced by a subsequent amendment (for example, as in *SCA Packaging Ltd v RCC* [2007] STC 1640). Although such a clause reduces the scope for dispute where termination of employment occurs, the tax treatment of a payment that might be made under it needs to be understood when the contract is signed as the clause restricts the planning opportunities of the parties when the contract ends (see **15.6**).

The above principle does not apply where a contract contains an express provision permitting early termination of a fixed-term contract by mutual consent and the parties agree that, on the employer making a payment, the contract will be terminated. In such a case the employee is not receiving the security, or continuity, of salary which he required as an inducement to enter the employment. This is because the parties' right to terminate a contract arises as a result of general contract law; it does not come from the contract itself. Moreover, an employee entering into such a contract has no greater security or continuity of salary that he would obtain by entering into a fixed-term contract which did not expressly include a right to terminate by mutual agreement. Therefore, an employee employed under such a contract is in the same position as one employed under a fixed-term contract that is silent as to the circumstances in which it is terminated early (*Tottenham Hotspur Ltd v HMRC* [2016] UKFTT 389 (TC)). Payments made under compromise agreements that bring to end a contract of employment by mutual consent are payments that fall into the residual category (see **15.12**).

15.71 Even where a contract of employment contains a contractual PILON clause, on the authority of *Cerberus Software Ltd v Rowley* [2001] IRLR 160, it is still open to the employer to breach the term of an employment contract providing for a contractual PILON (although the employer will lose the benefit of any restrictive covenants in the contract). The employer may both dismiss the employee summarily and fail to make the PILON. The Court of Appeal has in these circumstances held that the employee has no automatic right to the payment in lieu of notice; his claim is for damages and he is under an obligation to mitigate his loss. In such a case, any subsequent payment by the employer to remedy such a breach or any payment of damages awarded by a tribunal or court to compensate for such a breach should be treated as a residual termination payment (see **15.16**, **15.18** and **15.19** respectively).

In *Tax Bulletin*, Issue 63 (February 2003), HMRC acknowledge this position but warn that it is crucial to establish and examine the facts in cases where it is claimed a contract with a contractual PILON clause has been breached and that damages have been paid instead of the payment promised in the contract. They list the following factors that need to be taken into account as guidelines in determining the matter.

(a) Although each case will depend upon its own facts, a settlement that is substantially the same in value as an exercise of the discretion would have produced is likely to be viewed as made by exercise of the discretion. They cite the case of *Richardson v Delaney* [2001] STC 1328 (see **15.80**) as an example of this – that in the absence of an identifiable breach of contract, the source of the payment lies in the employer's discretion to make a payment. They say that the case demonstrates that a payment made by the exercise of the employer's discretion need not be made precisely in either the sum or in the form provided for by the contract.

(b) A payment resulting from a decision not to exercise discretion could be expected to have characteristics normally associated with compensation or damages for breach of contract rather than those associated with a contract payment.

    (i) One such characteristic is apparent in *Cerberus* where the payment was reduced (or mitigated) to reflect the fact that the employee had secured alternative employment before the end of the notice period and by doing so had reduced the loss or damage caused by the employer's breach.

    (ii) Other adjustments are common when calculating such payments, for example, to reflect the difference in tax and NIC consequences between an emolument from employment (taxable and liable for Class 1 NICs) and a payment of damages (taxed only in excess of the £30,000 threshold and not subject to NICs).

    (iii) A damages payment will normally take into account all salary and benefits that would have been available in the notice period.

(c) A decision by an employer not to exercise its discretion might be evidenced in writing.

All factors need to be weighed in the balance in deciding whether the discretion has been exercised. Essentially the matter is a question of fact (see **15.80** for cases where the discretion has been treated as exercised). Problems in deciding the correct position are often caused by incomplete documentation of the events surrounding termination and the calculation of the payment made.

Payments made pursuant to implied terms of service

15.72 The above discussion of the tax treatment of payments made pursuant to express terms of service may, of course, apply equally to payments made pursuant to implied terms of service. In this context, an implied term is one properly implied as a matter of contract law.

As a matter of contract law, a term will be implied if a court can presume that it would have been the intention of the parties to include it in the agreement. In order to make such a presumption, the court must be satisfied that:

(a) the term is necessary to give the contract business efficacy; or

(b) it is the normal custom and practice to include such a term in the contract; or

(c) the term is implied by the conduct of the parties; or

(d) the term is so obvious because the parties must have intended it.

15.73 As a matter of contract law, terms may be implied into employment contracts if they are regularly (but not necessarily universally) adopted in a particular trade or industry, in a particular locality or by a particular employer. It will be assumed that the parties were aware of the custom and tacitly agreed that it should be part of their contract without any need to put it in writing (*Sagar v H Ridehalgh & Son Ltd* [1931] 1 Ch 310). So, the usual requirement for a term to be implied by custom and practice is that the custom must be reasonable, notorious and certain. This means it must be fair and not arbitrary, that it must be generally established and well known, and that it must be clear-cut. Where a practice is discretionary, the fact that it had been carried out for a number of years will not necessarily convert it into an implied term. In *Quinn v Calder Industrial Materials Ltd* [1996] IRLR 125 (EAT) it was held that redundant employees had no implied right to enhanced redundancy payments. The employers' policy of making such payments was not incorporated into any agreement and details of the policy had never been communicated to the employees. Although the policy had been followed in every case over a period of years, the payment remained discretionary. In *Pellowe v Pendragon plc* EAT 804/98, the employers had for 20 years given redundant employees a payment greater than their statutory redundancy pay. The chart for calculating the amount was contained in a management manual which was not publicised to staff. An employee who was paid only statutory redundancy pay sued for a larger amount but it was held that he had not acquired a contractual right, through custom and practice, to the enhanced payment. It had not been made known to staff that they would receive enhanced payments and so the term could not be said to be notorious.

Another way in which an implied term might come into being is to look at how the parties have operated the contract of employment in practice. This approach may demonstrate that the contract had been performed in such a way as to suggest that a particular term existed (*Mears v Safecar Security Ltd* [1982] ICR 626).

15.74 HMRC adopt a very robust practice in this regard and seek to treat as earnings any termination payment which an employee expects to receive, without much concern for the detailed application of the presumptions that bring about the existence of an implied term. However, what the above cases show is the high degree of certainty and knowledge required before a term becomes an implied term of a contract, and so practitioners should rely on this to test an allegation by HMRC that a payment is taxable as earnings from employment on the grounds that it is expected. This point was made in *Clinton v RCC* [2010] UKFTT 337 (TC) where HMRC argued that the taxpayer expected a termination payment pursuant to an implied term in her contract of employment and so was taxable in respect of it as her earnings. Judge Aleksander noted that the threshold for custom and practice to have the effect of implying terms into employment agreements is high. 'Expectation' in the context of employment law means more than a mere hope (akin to the expectation of a legacy under a will) – the expectation has to rise to the level of an enforceable contractual certainty. It is submitted therefore that HMRC would have to show that the expectation is held on the part of every employee in the employment of the employer in question because they knew of the practice and that they had a reasonable expectation of receiving the payment upon the termination of their employment. Alternatively, there must be a well-established custom.

15.75 Despite their practice regarding payments that are expected by an employee, it is useful to note that, as stated in *Tax Bulletin*, Issue 63 (February 2003), HMRC accept that it is unlikely that an implied term in relation to payment in lieu of notice can exist. It is stated that contract law suggests that if something conflicts with an express or written contractual term, then it cannot be implied. Since contracts generally include a right to receive notice of termination of employment (whether directly or through the application of the *ERA 1996*), then an implied right to receive a payment in lieu of notice would appear to conflict with the express term that the employee is entitled to receive notice of termination. So where an employer regularly dismisses employees summarily, it cannot be argued that payments in lieu of notice made to compromise actions for breach of contract are made under an implied term of their contracts.

Payments that are expected on account of employer behaviour (auto-PILONs)

> **Focus**
>
> HMRC are very quick to allege (even on the slightest pretext) that a termination payment made to an employee is expected by him and hence is to be taxed as earnings from employment. However, this is not a settled area of the law and careful consideration should be given to this and the preceding paragraphs on implied terms of service.

15.76 Despite acknowledging payments made under an implied term of a contract of employment and the difficulty of identifying such a term, HMRC contend that a termination payment made automatically, habitually or by practice may be chargeable as an employee's earnings otherwise than under an implied term of his employment contract.

At EIM12977 they cite as an example an employer that makes a payment for any notice period that is not worked where nothing is written down about the payment. They say that this may be described as a custom, habit, practice or expectation and that if the payment is made as an automatic response it is arguable that the payment is earnings (although it is acknowledged that damages paid in this way are not treated as earnings).

HMRC go on and say that if the payment is not one of damages then the fact that an individual employee does not know about the practice is not crucial; what is more important is whether it is part of the employment relationship where the individual works, namely whether it is perceived as a normal part of the employer–employee relationship rather than as a specific response to not receiving due notice at that time. It is less important, they say, how long the practice has been in place than whether it is an automatic part of the employment. So where it is clear that an employer intends to follow a particular path in the future, a practice can come into being very quickly.

However, it is not HMRC policy to argue for this treatment where there is a procedure for making a genuine critical assessment in the making of a payment, so that they are not made automatically. They give as an example the case where an employer makes PILONs instead of giving notice, but where each payment is looked at under an internal written procedure that assesses what payment is to be made. The result is that some employees may be forced to sue for compensation or some may receive less than the equivalent gross salary and benefits. HMRC observe that a critical assessment will essentially seek to identify adjustments typical of a damages payment. Such PILONs are dealt with as damages (which are residual termination payments – see **15.17–15.19**), because an individual employee cannot be certain that a payment equal to salary due in the notice period will automatically be made and so is not part of the working relationship between employer and employee. Such adjustments are not mandatory and an employer may have valid commercial reasons not to make them (eg in a large-scale programme where employees predominantly have short notice periods, the gain from making adjustments might be outweighed by the cost of doing so and the potential bad feeling generated in the workforce may also be a factor). Any such reasons must be taken into account when deciding whether the character of the payment is that of damages.

Payments for employment-related rights

15.77 An employee's termination package may contain an amount paid in lieu of holidays to which he was entitled but had not taken by the time he left employment. In some cases this is because the employee had a contractual right to such a payment. Such payments are earnings from employment and taxable as such (*ITEPA 2003, s 9(6)*) because they are payments made to compensate for the loss of a right directly connected with an employee's employment (ie if the employment did not exist there would have been no right to take holidays) (*Hamblett v Godfrey (Inspector of Taxes)* [1987] STC 60). Even where a right to such a payment does not exist, nevertheless, payments made voluntarily by the employer may also be charged as the employee's earnings because they arise from the employer–employee relationship and for no other reason (*Laidler v Perry (Inspector of Taxes)* 42 TC 351).

'Garden leave' payments

15.78 'Garden leave' is a colloquialism used to describe the case where an employer, in fulfilment of obligations under a contract of service, gives due notice of termination to an employee. The employee's right to receive notice will therefore have been observed. The contract remains in force and will come to an end only at the expiry of the notice period. However, at the start of, or during the course of, the notice period, the employee is asked to remain at home and is told that he will not be called upon to render any service until the termination date. This device of garden leave is useful where the employer wishes to keep the employee bound by the covenants of the contract (eg those relating to confidentiality and fidelity) and yet take the employee out of the marketplace for a short period so that he cannot work for competitors. The employer waives the right to call on the employee to render service, but it does not absolve him from the duty to pay the remuneration to which the employee is entitled. At the same time that the employer tells the employee no longer to report for duty, he gives the employee, as a lump sum, the remuneration attributable to the notice period (ie there is an advance payment of remuneration). This is sometimes referred to as a PILON.

15.79 Regardless of the terminology used, viewed from the perspective of the employee, there is no reason for the receipt of the payment other than the employer–employee relationship, and so the payment is earnings from employment and cannot be a residual termination payment (*Ibe v McNally* [2005] STC 1426).

Payments under certain compromise agreements

15.80 This category of earnings arises from the case of *Richardson (Inspector of Taxes) v Delaney* [2001] STC 1328. The taxpayer had been employed under a service agreement which included a contractual PILON clause (see **15.68**). The employer gave the employee notice. Whilst he was serving his notice, an agreement was made by the parties to end the contract of employment before the expiry of the notice period on the payment of an agreed sum. The court held that the payment was taxable as earnings and not taxable as a residual termination payment under a compromise agreement (see **15.12**). The effect of the compromise agreement in this case (and indeed in the later cases of *Goldman v RCC* [2012] UKFTT 313 (TC) and *Manley v RCC* [2013] UKFTT 99 (TC)) was to fructify the terms of the service agreement, in particular the PILON clause. In other words, the compromise agreement was the mechanism by which the PILON clause was effected, or putting it another way, there was effectively the specific performance of the contract of employment. It does not matter that the payment made under the compromise agreement does not equal the amount provided for in the contract of employment if the compromise agreement was aimed at enforcing, to the maximum amount attainable, the employee's contractual entitlement. The fact that an employee is unable as a practical matter to obtain full enforcement of his contractual entitlement and is obliged to settle for less is not a relevant factor in deciding whether the payment is earnings.

15.81 In order to avoid the decision in *Richardson* applying in any case, it is important that a replication of the precise facts of the case should be avoided where a compromise agreement is used to bring a contract of service to an end. In other words, where an employment contract gives an employer the liberty of choosing to end the contract either by the giving of notice or by the payment of a sum in lieu, a compromise agreement between the parties must be avoided once notice has been given. Unless this is done, then *Richardson* is likely to apply to a payment made under such an agreement, and accordingly it will not be taxable as a residual termination payment.

15.82 The case is, however, unlikely to apply to determine the taxation of payments made in the following circumstances which are distinguishable from the facts of *Richardson*:

(a) where a contract of service gives an employer the liberty of choosing to end the contract either by the giving of notice or by the payment of a sum in lieu, and a compromise agreement is entered into without the exercise of this liberty at all (see **15.12**) (now confirmed in *Brander v RCC* [2007] STC (SCD) 582, in which case the amounts actually paid under a compromise agreement exceeded the amounts payable under the contract of employment);

(b) where a contract of service provides only for the giving of notice to bring the contract to an end, and a compromise agreement is entered into whether before or after such notice has been given (see **15.15**);

(c) where a contract of service has been wrongfully or unfairly ended by an employer, legal proceedings have been initiated by the employee, and a compromise agreement is entered into between the parties to settle the dispute out of court (see **15.16**);

(d) where a contract of service which gives an employer the liberty of choosing to end the contract either by the giving of notice or by the payment of a sum in lieu, is amended to remove these clauses from the contract, and subsequently a compromise agreement is struck to terminate the employment (see **15.12**). However, the pitfalls associated with compromise agreements that vary an employment contract must be avoided (see **15.14**).

The effect of the case is also avoided if a contract of service is breached and a payment is made by an employer as damages or compensation for that breach (see **15.17** and **15.71**). There may be employment law reasons why, in any particular case, this may not be a viable way of proceeding in order to avoid the effects of *Richardson*, but it is nonetheless a possibility to be considered (but see **15.71** above).

Termination payments that are inducement payments

15.83 Care needs to be exercised where a payment made on the termination of employment is a form of inducement to an employee to take up service with another employer. In *Shilton v Wilmshurst* [1991] STC 88 the taxpayer was employed by a football club which negotiated his transfer to another club. In order to induce the taxpayer to agree to the move, the first club promised to make a payment to him when he left. The payment was held to be a reward for future services and taxable as earnings from his (future) employment. (Also see *Glantre Engineering Ltd v Goodhand (Inspector of Taxes)* [1983] STC 1.)

Particularly vulnerable to this treatment are payments made by a new employer to an employee to compensate him for the loss of rights connected with his former employment (eg loss of deferred remuneration rights contingent on his remaining in employment) (*Teward v IRC* [2001] STC (SCD) 36). By contrast, however, payments that are made to a new employee to compensate him for giving up benefits of a personal nature (unconnected with any service he may render) are not treated as earnings (*Jarrold (HM Inspector of Taxes) v Boustead* (1964) 41 TC 701; *Pritchard (HM Inspector of Taxes) v Arundale* (1971) 47 TC 680).

Ex gratia payments

15.84 It may be the case that an ex gratia payment (ie a gift) made to an employee on the termination of employment is taxable as earnings. In *McBride v Blackburn (Inspector of Taxes)* [2003] STC (SCD) 139, having reviewed the authorities, the Special Commissioner listed the following occasions when this might be the correct treatment of a gift:

(a) if it is received by an employee in respect of the discharge of his duties;

(b) if it accrues by virtue of the employment or if it is in return for acting in the employment;

A payment is not taxable however if it retains its characteristics as a gift (ie an exercise of bounty intended to benefit the donee for reasons personal to him), even though it is given in recognition of services rendered. Also a gift is not taxable if it is peculiarly due to the personal qualities of the recipient or if it is to mark his participation in an exceptional event. Relevant factors to be taken into account in determining the tax treatment of a gift are: whether the payment is made by the employer; whether the office is at an end; whether other remuneration is paid; whether the payment is exceptional; whether there is an element of recurrence; and whether the recipient is entitled to the payment (see *Moore v Griffiths (H M Inspector of Taxes)* 48 TC 338).

Category (b) above is the category that may be relevant to the discussion on auto-PILONs and holiday pay in **15.76** and **15.77** above.

The benefits code

General

15.85 Benefits given to an employee on the termination of employment will not be treated as residual termination payments where they are taxable under the benefits code. The benefits code in *ITEPA 2003, Pt 3, Chs 2–10* applies, generally speaking, only during the currency of an employment (ie benefits must be received or enjoyed whilst the employee is in employment). Consequently, as a general rule the code does not apply to benefits to be enjoyed after the termination of employment, even though their provision may be agreed upon whilst the employment is still in existence. So, for example, the code will apply where the employee enjoys benefits whilst on garden leave, but will not apply where the benefit in kind is given as part of a compromise agreement to be enjoyed after the termination of his employment.

At EIM12815, HMRC confirm that as a matter of practice benefits that straddle the termination of employment should be apportioned on a time basis, those falling after termination being taxed as a residual termination payment (where appropriate). For example, an employer pays a non-refundable lump-sum premium of £12,000 into a health scheme for his (higher paid) employee on 6 April 2017 to cover the provision of health care until 5 April 2018. That employee is dismissed on 5 January 2018. He will be charged to tax under the benefits code on only three-quarters of the premium.

15.86 The general rule just described is subject to an important exception in the case of the release or the write-off of an employment-related loan (*ITEPA 2003, s 188(2)*) (see **15.88–15.91**).

Benefits as residual termination payments

15.87 Benefits in kind given to employees as part of their termination package that do not fall under the benefits code are likely to be residual termination payments (unless they are given as consideration for the giving by the employee of a restrictive undertaking) (**15.93–15.95**). *ITEPA 2003, Pt 6, Ch 3* contains its own mini benefits code (*ITEPA 2003, s 402*) under which the quantification of benefits follows the benefits code itself. However, it should be appreciated that the mini code is wider than the main code and it is unlikely that something provided as part of a termination package falls outside its scope. For example, in tax years before 2016/17, whereas lower paid employees were outwith the benefits code, benefits provided to such persons on the termination of employment become taxable as residual termination payments. Also, if a benefit is exempt from the benefits code, do not assume that it is exempt from the charge on residual termination payments. It will only be so exempt if an employment-income exemption (as opposed to an earnings-only exemption) applies in respect of it. This will depend upon the wording of each exemption described in *ITEPA 2003, Pt 4*, but typically exemptions for counselling and other outplacement services (**15.54**), retraining courses (**15.57**) and long-service awards (**15.62**) are such exemptions. Additionally, the following benefits are exempt from the mini termination benefits code under *ITEPA 2003, s 402(2), (4)*:

(a) benefits connected with taxable cars and vans and exempt heavy goods vehicles;

(b) non-cash vouchers or credit tokens to obtain goods or services (or money to spend on goods or services) in connection with taxable cars or vans or exempt heavy goods vehicles;

(c) one mobile telephone;

(d) the right to receive a residual termination payment or benefit.

Employment-related loans

Focus

Where an employment-related loan is written off after an employee's contract has ended, take care to tax the amount written off in full and do not treat is as benefiting from the £30,000 threshold.

15.88 A director or employee may be given a loan at a beneficial rate of interest by reason of his employment. In such a case (ie of an employment-related loan that is a taxable cheap loan), a benefit in kind arises under *ITEPA 2003, ss 173–175* calculated by reference to the interest that would have been paid by the employee had the loan carried interest at the official rate.

A second, separate benefit arises when any employment-related loan (be it at a beneficial rate of interest or not) is released or written off in a tax year whether in whole or in part. *ITEPA 2003, s 188(1)* provides that, where, at the time of the release or write-off, the employee holds the employment in relation to which the employment is an employment-related loan, the amount released or written off is to be treated as earnings from the employment for that year.

15.89 An employee who leaves employment at a time when such a loan has not been repaid is regarded as in receipt of earnings when the loan is written off or released under the above provision by the operation of *ITEPA 2003, s 188(2)* which provides as follows:

> 'But if the employment has terminated ... and there was a time when –
>
> (a) the whole or part of the loan was outstanding, and
>
> (b) the employee held the employment, and
>
> (c) [before 2016-17] the employment was not an excluded employment [ie held by a lower-paid employee],
>
> subsection (1) applies as if the employment had not ended ... '

The effect of this section is to deem the individual's employment to continue. The result is that he will be treated as being in receipt of earnings chargeable to income tax when the employment-related loan is released or written off in an amount equivalent to the amount of the loan released or written off.

15.90 It will be noted that the operation of *ITEPA 2003, ss 173–175* (ie the benefit related to the beneficial rate of interest in respect of taxable cheap loans) is not so preserved on the termination of employment; only *ITEPA 2003, s 188* (ie the benefit related to the release or writing-off of the loan) continues to operate. Since a charge to tax arises otherwise than under the provisions dealing with residual termination payments, the release or writing off of a loan cannot benefit from the exceptions and reliefs that apply to such payments.

Example 15.14 – Benefits post-termination of employment

An employee enjoys a remuneration package which includes the provision of a £52,000 loan at a rate of interest of 2.75%. The employee is made redundant on 31 December 2017 and receives a cash payment of £25,000 and the use of a company car until the expiry of the lease in 2019. On 5 April 2018 it is subsequently agreed that the employee will be released from the obligation to repay the loan. The official rate of interest being 3%, the taxable amount arising in relation to the redundancy in 2017/18 is:

	£
ITEPA 2003, s 401	
Cash payment	25,000
Loan benefit (52,000 × (3 – 2.75)% × 3/12)	32
Car benefit (say)	1,675
	26,707
Less: threshold (restricted)	(26,707)
	Nil
ITEPA 2003, s 188	
Loan release	52,000
Taxable amount	52,000

The balance of the threshold of £3,293 will be carried forward to 2018/19 and used in relation to the cash equivalent of the car benefit arising as a residual termination payment in that year; it cannot be used against the charge on £52,000 arising on the release of the loan under *ITEPA 2003, s 188*.

15.91 In order to avoid the operation of *ITEPA 2003, s 188(2)* an employee may wish to pay off the loan using personal funds. Funds could be made available for this purpose by increasing the termination award through an ex gratia payment (which payment is likely to be regarded as a residual termination payment (see **15.22**)).

Also, it must be noted that *ITEPA 2003, s 188* does not apply where a release or writing off of an employment-related loan takes place on or after the death of an employee (*ITEPA 2003, s 190*). Thus, the section does not apply where an employment terminates on account of the death of the employee. In such a case the normal rules apply (see **15.85–15.86**).

Payments for restrictive undertakings

> **Focus**
>
> Take considerable care when drafting compromise agreements that contain restrictive undertakings. Do not inadvertently cause payments made under such agreements to become wholly or partly taxable by falling into the restrictive undertaking category of employment income (see **15.3**). In particular, follow carefully the advice contained in SP 3/96 wherever possible.

15.92 A payment made on termination of employment may be for the giving by the employee of a restrictive undertaking (ie an undertaking whereby the employee agrees to restrict his conduct once he has left employment). Prima facie such payments fall to be charged to income tax under *ITEPA 2003, s 225*. It has to be considered whether such payments can ever be residual termination payments.

Payments for conventional restrictive covenants

15.93 An employee may receive a payment in connection with the termination of his employment for agreeing to restrict his future conduct or activities after the employment comes to an end. Such covenants conventionally fall into the following categories:

(a) non-competition covenants under which the employee undertakes not to work for a competitor or within a specified area or within a specific time;

(b) non-solicitation covenants under which the employee undertakes not to contact former suppliers or customers or poach former colleagues;

(c) confidentiality covenants under which the employee agrees to keep secret privileged information.

These covenants may be contained in an employee's contract of employment or in a compromise agreement made at the time the employment ends. Very often a compromise agreement reaffirms the covenants given in a contract of employment.

15.94 Where an employee receives a specific payment on the termination of his employment for making such an undertaking, that sum will be treated as earnings and not as a residual termination payment (*RCI (Europe) Ltd v Woods* [2004] STC 315).

However, very often no payment is actually allocated for agreeing to the restrictions contained in the covenants. They are merely terms of the agreement in which they are contained. As no part of any termination payment will be attributable to the giving of the covenants, *ITEPA 2003, s* 255 cannot apply (see **15.95**). Also, in some compromise agreements the departing employee is asked to confirm that the restrictions set out in his contract of employment continue to apply. If the employee does so and is given no consideration for that confirmation, then again *ITEPA 2003, s 225* cannot apply (see **15.95** and EIM03605 and EIM03606 and *Vaughan-Neil v IRC* [1979] STC 644). However, HMRC do warn that, where it is not possible to account for all of any lump-sum termination payment under the categories contained in a compromise agreement, it may be possible that an oral agreement beyond the written agreement has been reached and that some of the consideration is given for that oral agreement. In the final analysis, however, the allocation of a consideration to the giving of a restrictive covenant is a question of fact and a matter of evidence.

SP 3/96

15.95 SP 3/96 applies to undertakings contained in a financial settlement relating to the termination of an employment whereby the employee:

(a) accepts the termination package in full and final settlement of all his outstanding claims relating to the employment; and/or

(b) undertakes not to commence or, if already commenced, to discontinue, any legal proceedings in respect of those claims; and/or

(c) reaffirms any covenants about his conduct or activity after termination which formed part of the terms on which the employment was taken up.

HMRC accept that where a sum is paid under a compromise agreement for the loss of employment, no portion of that amount will be attributed under *ITEPA 2003, s 225* to such undertakings.

However, care must still be exercised, as SP 3/96 does not cover the case where a severance agreement is framed in two distinct parts, the one an agreement for the payment of a sum of £X in consideration of the loss of employment, the other an agreement for the giving of a restrictive undertaking in consideration of a separate sum of £Y. The latter amount will still be taxed as earnings (*Appellant v Inspector of Taxes* [2001] STC (SCD) 21).

Compromise agreements often contain a 'repayment clause'. Such a clause provides that if the employee does later initiate proceedings before a tribunal or court – despite giving an undertaking not to do so – then the sum paid under the agreement must be repaid to the employer. HMRC will not argue that such a clause means that a sum is being attributed to the undertaking not to pursue claims. In virtually all cases, the sum paid under the agreement can be fully attributed to the settlement of the claims being dealt with. So there is no sum remaining to be attributed to that undertaking, even where there is a repayment clause. However, it should be noted that if the employee does repay such sums, there is no provision in the legislation that gives any deduction or relief for that payment.

Example 1 (see EIM03626)

An employee is made redundant by his employer. He is advised by a solicitor and enters into a 'compromise agreement' provided by *The Trade Union Reform and Employment Rights Act 1993*. The agreement contains a clause that states that the agreement is 'in full and final settlement of any and all claims that the employee may have against the former employer'. No consideration is attributed for agreeing to the clause. No other restrictive undertakings are contained in the agreement. Consideration of £40,000 is paid to the employee under the terms of the agreement.

The Inspector contends that all of the £40,000 is within *ITEPA 2003, s 225* as nothing would be paid if the employee did not agree to the restriction.

Comment

It is true that the settlement sum of £40,000 would not be paid unless the employee agreed to the conditions set out in the document. However, it is also clear that amounts within the lump sum are paid for other reasons:

- payment in lieu of notice;
- statutory redundancy pay;
- holiday pay.

The only restriction contained in the agreement is the 'in full and final settlement' clause and no consideration is attributed to that. In consequence, Statement of Practice 3/96 applies. Any part of the sum that is not earnings will fall to be treated as a residual termination payment and may attract the exemptions afforded to such payments.

Example 2 (based on EIM03620)

An employee's contract of employment contains a covenant to the effect that he shall not work within a 25-mile radius of the employer's premises or contact any customer or supplier of the employer for a period of 18 months after the termination of his employment. In a subsequent compromise agreement the employee merely confirms the conditions set out in his employment contract. *ITEPA 2003, s 225* does not apply in this case as no consideration has been paid for the giving of the undertaking and no new undertakings were made in the compromise agreement. If the compromise agreement identified a payment of say £25,000 for the re-affirmation of the covenant, then *ITEPA 2003, s 225* would have applied to the payment.

Payments from employer-financed retirement benefits schemes

Focus

The making of a gift on the termination of employment needs careful consideration. It could be taxable as a payment under an employer-financed retirement benefits scheme (especially where the recipient is retiring) or as his earnings (see **15.84**); such a payment is not automatically treated as a residual termination payment (see **15.22**). As to whether an employee is retiring is not an easy question to answer and special regard should be had to HMRC practice in this matter (see **15.103**). HMRC are quick to allege that payments are made under schemes (so as to bring them within this category of employment income) but this should be resisted in appropriate cases (see **15.97–15.99**).

15.96 The recipient of relevant benefits provided under an employer-financed retirement benefits scheme (EFRBS) is charged to income tax (*ITEPA 2003, s 393(1)*). This category of employment income is particularly relevant in the context of a termination payment where an employer makes an ex gratia payment (ie a gift) on the death or retirement of an employee (and the discussion here is limited to this case). In such a case, as the employer is making a payment direct to an employee *under* an EFRBS (and is not giving an undertaking to make a contribution *to* an EFRBS), the rules in *ITEPA 2003, Pt 7A* (Employment income provided through third parties) (the so-called 'disguised remuneration' rules) are not engaged, do not displace the application of the rules on EFRBS and do not have to be considered further.

It will be seen that three alternative arguments can be relied upon to avoid the application of this category of employment income applying to an ex gratia payment on the death or retirement of an employee – that there is no scheme under which it is made, that the payment is an excluded benefit or that the employee has not retired.

An 'employer-financed retirement benefits scheme' is a scheme for the provision of benefits consisting of or including relevant benefits to or in respect of employees or former employees of an employer (*ITEPA 2003, s 393A*). The term 'scheme' is defined as including any deed, agreement, series of agreements or other arrangements (*ITEPA 2003, s 393A(4)*). The scheme does not have to be formally constituted and it does not have to adopt any particular form.

15.97 At EIM15048, HRMC explain that a scheme includes:

(a) a decision taken at an employers' meeting (to make a payment);

(b) a decision taken by an employee (eg a personnel manager) with delegated authority or in accordance with a policy (to make a payment);

(c) the making of a payment under a plan, pattern, policy, practice, decision-making process or custom.

15.98 It is not entirely clear from doubt that a payment made in these circumstances is one paid under a scheme. In *Allum v Marsh* [2005] STC (SCD) 191, the taxpayer and his wife ('the taxpayers') were the directors and shareholders of an unquoted trading company. The company voted to purchase all the shares held by the taxpayers out of distributable profits. Later the same day, the taxpayers resigned as directors leaving their son as the only director. The next day, the board agreed to make voluntary payments of £30,000 each to the taxpayers 'following the resignation due to retirement, in appreciation of their services to the company over many years'. The board also approved the contract to purchase the taxpayers' shares and cheque payments were made accordingly.

HMRC sought to assess the payments contending that the voluntary payments made by the company to the taxpayers after they ceased to be directors were payments under (what is now) an EFRBS. It was held, however, that on the facts, the payments were not paid under a scheme. The Special Commissioner stated that there was no arrangement as there was no prior formal or informal understanding with the taxpayers that the payments would be made. The matter had not previously been discussed with them and they were both surprised and gratified when the company decided to make the payment. There was no expectation of reward. There was no system, plan, pattern or policy connected with the payments. Furthermore, the request by the board to the company's accountant to budget for the payment was not the establishment of a scheme or arrangement but merely a means of ensuring that the decision taken by the board to make the payment could be implemented. Consequently, it was held that the payments were not made under an EFRBS.

15.99 In *Barclays Bank plc v RCC* [2006] STC (SCD) 100, [2007] STC 747 by contrast, the bank made payments to pensioners who had retired from employment with the bank. The payments were made by way of compensation for the termination of an arrangement whereby a subsidiary of Barclays offered to those pensioners (and their widows or widowers) a free service for the preparation of their annual tax returns. The payments were made in order to avoid an adverse reaction from the pensioners similar to one that had occurred at an earlier time when it was mooted that the service be withdrawn. The amount of the compensation was calculated according to the age of the pensioner and the complexity of his affairs. HMRC contended that the payments were benefits provided under (what is now) an EFRBS.

The Special Commissioner commented (*obiter*) that there was an arrangement and hence a scheme under which the payments were made. He made the following observations in relation to the definition of a scheme:

(a) That arrangements need not be bilateral (as a deed can be a unilateral instrument).

(b) That since a benefit must be received under the arrangement, the arrangement is distinct from the benefit. The components of an arrangement must have a commercial life separate from the mechanics which merely implement the conferring of the benefit under the arrangements.

(c) The motivation that informs the conferring of a benefit is irrelevant as to whether there is a scheme. The meaning of scheme or arrangement calls attention to whether there is a construct comprised of one or more elements. The motivation behind the construct plays no part in informing the meaning of scheme or arrangement.

(d) Whether or not there is an arrangement or scheme is a question of fact. Thus an arrangement must have terms and it must seek to achieve a particular objective. There can be no arrangement in the abstract which cannot be fructified according to its terms. Equally there can be no arrangement which cannot be implemented on its terms because say there is a legal or factual impediment which prevents its implementation.

In this case there was an arrangement and therefore a scheme. The work done to calculate the compensation payments was not the arrangement. However, the letter informing the pensioners that the bank's subsidiary was to be sold, that the tax services would be withdrawn and that one-off payments would be made by the bank to the pensioners constituted the framework, distinct from the mechanics of calculating and implementing the mechanics of the payments, under which the payments were to be made. The letter raised an expectation of payment. It revealed a plan to enable the payments to be made. That plan was distinct from the mere mechanics of the payments. So when the payments arrived, the payments fructified the plan embodied in the letter.

That letter articulated and constituted an arrangement. Contrast the position in *Allum* where a voluntary payment out of the blue did not fructify any prior expectation that had been raised through the existence of an arrangement.

In *Moffat v HMRC* [2006] STC (SCD) 380, the taxpayer was a former employee of Scottish Bus Group which was privatised. He received an ex gratia payment from the government on the winding up of the group's pension schemes. A surplus amount had arisen in the pension scheme and it was agreed by the Scottish Executive and the Treasury that the surplus be paid to the United Kingdom Exchequer following the winding up of the schemes. However, when this was done it was understood that a large part of the surplus funds would be paid on an ex gratia basis, calculated by reference to the previous entitlement under the pension scheme and length of service, to members of the pension scheme. Although a legal entitlement to these payments did not exist, the decision was made to make the payments in order to mirror the payments made in relation to a settlement from a court action from the privatisation of the National Bus Company, which had operated in England and Wales. The terms of the payments were broadly similar to those of the payments made to the members of the National Bus Company.

HMRC argued that the payment received by the taxpayer was made under (what is now) an EFRBS and the Special Commissioner agreed. There was a scheme because there existed arrangements providing for relevant benefits. The arrangements stemmed from the agreement between the Scottish Executive and the Treasury that effect would be given in Scotland to the distribution broadly equivalent to what had happened in England and Wales. There was most certainly an expectation that such distribution would be made. The mechanics of payment were distinct from the arrangements enabling the payments.

So it would appear from the above two cases that there cannot be a scheme for the purposes of the rules on EFRBS, unless the employee is aware of the arrangements under which he may benefit.

15.100 In order for a scheme to be an EFRBS it must make provision for benefits consisting of or including relevant benefits. 'Relevant benefits' are defined in *ITEPA 2003, s 393B(1)* as meaning any lump sum, gratuity or other benefit (including a non-cash benefit) provided or to be provided (*inter alia*):

(a) on the retirement or in anticipation of the retirement of an employee or former employee;

(b) on the death of an employee or former employee; or

(c) after the retirement or death of an employee or former employee in connection with past service.

However, excluded benefits are not relevant benefits (*ITEPA 2003, s 393B(2)*). Excluded benefits include benefits in respect of ill health or disablement of an employee during service, benefits in respect of the death by accident of an employee during service, and benefits defined in regulations as excluded (*ITEPA 2003, s 393B(3)(d)*) (see **15.102**).

Benefits in respect of death or early retirement through ill health

15.101 Particular attention needs to be paid to the application of the EFRBS rules to ex gratia payments made on an employee's death or early retirement through ill health. In relation to a payment made on an employee's death, the first point to note is that a 'relevant benefit' does not include any lump sum paid in respect of the death by accident, of a person occurring during his service (*ITEPA 2003, s 393B(3)(b)*). If a payment is not a relevant benefit, the arrangement to pay it alone cannot, by definition, be an EFRBS.

In order to be within the exemption it is necessary to ask whether it was only the accidental death that motivates the making of the payment. HMRC interpret this requirement quite loosely. The condition is regarded as satisfied if the accident occurs during the subsistence of the employment contract. It does not necessarily have to occur during the time that the employee is on duty so that an accident does not have to be workplace-related. For example, an ex gratia lump sum payable following an employee's death while travelling to work would not be a relevant benefit. So the issue is whether the individual was in employment at the time of the death, not whether he was working. The death must, however, occur by accident. Death through natural causes does not fall within the exclusion and a payment made in such a case would be a relevant payment.

As regards lump-sum payments on early retirement through ill health, a payment which is afforded in respect of the employee's ill health or disablement occurring during his service is also, by definition, not a relevant benefit (*ITEPA 2003, s 393B(3)(a)*). It will be noted that the employee's ill health or disablement does not have to occur on account of an accident; disablement that occurs otherwise than by accident (eg the loss of sight through a progressive illness) is also within the scope of the provision. The EFRBS rules cannot, therefore, apply to such payments.

Benefits defined in regulations as excluded

15.102 The *Employer-Financed Retirement Benefits (Excluded Benefits for Tax Purposes) Regulations 2007, SI 2007/3537* provide for certain benefits to be excluded benefits for the purposes of *ITEPA 2003, s 393B(3)(d)*. These benefits fall under the following heads (and the regulations should be referred to for the detailed rules):

(a) welfare counselling;

(b) recreational benefits;

(c) annual parties;

(d) writing of wills etc;

(e) equipment for disabled former employees;

(f) living accommodation;

(g) removal expenses;

(h) repairs and alterations to living accommodation;

(i) council tax paid for living accommodation;

(j) annual health screening and medical check-ups;

(k) trivial benefits; and

(l) certain benefits given to armed forces personnel.

15.103 The term 'retirement' is not defined in the legislation, but in the case of *Venables v Hornby (Inspector of Taxes)* [2002] STC 1248 (which had to do with the construction of the terms of the trust deed under which a pension scheme was constituted) it was held in the Court of Appeal that whether a person had retired was a matter of fact and degree to be judged in a common sense and commercial way, and connoted withdrawing from active work. It did not, however, mean or include a mere reduction in workload or a change in the nature of service as an employee (eg by changing roles from managing director to non-executive director). On the other hand, as the case shows, a retirement can occur where the individual concerned continues to be interested to a small degree in the work of his former employer (perhaps by being an unpaid, non-executive director whose experience the employer could draw on from time to time).

In the later case of *Ballard v RCC* [2013] UKFTT 87 (TC) (which had to do directly with the construction of the EFRBS legislation in *ITEPA 2003*) it was again confirmed that the word 'retirement' has no special meaning. In particular, it is not linked with qualifying for a pension of any sort, nor is the individual's age of any relevance (although the older a person is when he leaves employment the more likely it is that he will not seek alternative employment and will effectively retire). Where a person makes a firm decision not to seek further employment he may be said to retire (as happened in the case). The occasion on which the individual concerned makes this decision is not a relevant factor (eg it could be taken during a redundancy consultation process) and making such a decision does not require the agreement of the former employer. The decision to terminate an individual's employment may be taken by an employer but the decision to retire is the employee's alone.

In the light of the *Venables* case, HMRC have (at EIM15300) set out how they regard this decision applying in specific cases (although they do point out that it is only a guide as each case depends on its own facts):

(a) A long-service employee leaves to take a senior executive position in another company at the age of 60. The person has retired from the first employment.

(b) A division of the company is sold and the 55-year-old manager responsible for running it leaves to take a job with the purchaser. Again the employee has retired from the first employment.

(c) A person in his 50s has a heart attack and is advised by his doctor to leave and seek a less stressful position. This is regarded as a retirement. (But if the ex-gratia payment made is purely consolation for loss of health that results in the premature termination of employment, it would not be regarded as made in connection with retirement.)

(d) An employee aged 50 leaves to take a job nearer home to be able to nurse her aged parents. The employee has retired.

However, in the light of the First-tier Tribunal's comments in *Ballard* it appears that these examples are open to doubt. The tribunal dismissed the idea that age was determinative of the question whether an individual had retired (although it did acknowledge that a person's' age affected the burden of proving that he had retired). It observed that a person whose employment comes to an end may make no decision about his future employment at all. He may actively look for further employment; he may wait and see what happens; or he may make a firm decision not to seek further employment – and there are probably other alternatives. In *Ballard* itself the individual had made a firm decision not to seek further employment and made that clear to his employer. It was held that he had retired. In the final analysis it will always be a question of fact whether a person has withdrawn from active work and hence retired.

MISCELLANEOUS PLANNING AND OTHER POINTS

Timing issues

> **Focus**
>
> When making a termination payment take into account the fact that if it is paid after the employee's contract of service has ended, it may (in part) have tax deducted from it under PAYE at the maximum rate of 45%.

15.104 When structuring a termination package, consideration should be given to when it should be paid to (ie received by) the employee. If it can be paid by instalments over two or more tax years, that may result in the employee not being a higher rate (or additional rate) taxpayer in either (see **15.33**).

Consideration should be given to making the payment just before the employment ends. If a payment is made after the end of the employment, the employer is obliged under the PAYE rules to deduct tax from the payment using a 0T code (see **15.32**). This means that a taxable payment of more than £12,500 in 2017/18 will have tax deducted from it at the rate of 45% to the extent that it exceeds that amount (although of course the employee will be able to claim a refund for any excess tax deducted).

Payments that have no connection with the termination of employment

15.105 In very limited circumstances a termination payment may be entirely tax free because it has no connection with the termination of the employee's employment (but this will not be the case merely because there is an extended period of time between the termination of employment and the making of the payment). A payment is made 'in connection with' the termination of an employment if it really and substantially has something to do with the termination (*Walker v Adams (Inspector of Taxes)* 2003 SpC 344). The test of connection is one of fact and degree (*Barclays Bank plc v RCC* [2006] STC (SCD) 100).

In *Crompton v RCC* [2009] STC (SCD) 504, the taxpayer, an ex-soldier, was enlisted in the Territorial Army and had taken up a post as workshop clerk. When it was decided that he was no longer eligible for that post, he applied for a number of other posts. Due to procedural failures of the selection boards, he was not appointed to any of these posts even though he was correctly qualified and had priority over other candidates. Shortly before he was made redundant from the workshop clerk post, he accepted the post as a store man. However, due to a misunderstanding about the conditions, the taxpayer took up the redundancy and left the army. He received a redundancy payment. He was, after he had complained, also offered compensation for financial losses suffered as a consequence of the selection boards' failings. HMRC alleged that this payment was a payment made in connection with the termination of his employment with the army and charged it to tax as a residual termination payment. The taxpayer argued that the payment was not in fact connected with the termination of his employment. The actual termination was his dismissal by redundancy from the store man position; there was no causative link between that and the selection boards' failures for which he was compensated. The Special Commissioner agreed with the taxpayer, with the result that the payment was not liable to income tax. It was held that a connection had to be some sort of link, joint or bond between two things. There was no such link between the compensation received and the termination of the taxpayer's employment with the army. The payment was for the selection boards' unfair treatment of the taxpayer but that did not lead to his leaving the army. He left the army at the time he left the store man post on account of redundancy and not because of his failure to be selected for the posts for which he had applied. Consequently, the compensation was not a payment made in connection with the termination of his employment.

At EIM13910 HMRC provide the following example of where there is a link between a payment and the termination of employment. An employee is dismissed. The company wants to make sure that there is a complete break and so insists that all the employee's shares in the company are sold. The employee protests about the costs and the possible loss of future gains on the shares. It is agreed that the shares will be sold, but the company will pay £10,500 as compensation. The sale price received by the employee for the shares is not a payment in connection with the termination of his employment. Although the sale was required by the termination agreement, the transfer of ownership of the shares, rather than the loss of employment itself, wholly explains the payment. So none of that receipt came to the employee even indirectly as a payment for the termination itself. The payment arose as a consequence of the sale; all that arose as a consequence of the termination was a requirement to sell the shares, and that requirement of itself yielded no payment. By contrast, the compensation of £10,500 is in connection with the termination. None of this payment represents the value of the shares. Its receipt is wholly explained by the company's decision to make a payment to settle claims arising from the termination agreement.

Recipient of payment

15.106 Generally speaking little planning can be achieved with regard to whom a termination payment is made to. A payment is taxable if it is received by the former employee, or is provided on his behalf or to his order (eg the employee directs his employer to make the payment direct to his bank to discharge his mortgage liability). It is also taxable if it is paid to his spouse or civil partner, blood relative, dependant or personal representatives. The only gap in this list is a cohabitant of the employee who is not also his dependant. But then the payment cannot be made to the order of the employee. So a payment is still taxable if the employee directs that the payment is made to his cohabitant; it is likely not to be taxable however if paid under the direction of a court to the cohabitant of an employee suffering severe psychological problems or to a former cohabitant after the employee's death but these are unlikely to be common occurrences.

Seeking HMRC guidance

> **Focus**
>
> HMRC are committed to giving clearances on many aspects of the tax treatment of termination payments. Follow the guidance below to see where that will be the case.

15.107 EIM12825 sets out HMRC's approach to handling enquiries in relation to termination payments. It states that formal binding answers will be given in relation to the meaning of disability under SP 10/81 (see **15.41**) and to clearances for redundancy schemes under SP 1/94 (see **15.10**). EIM12827 extends formal binding answers to be given to enquiries on the disability and injury compensation exception (see **15.38–15.42**), the foreign service exception (see **15.46–15.50**), how the £30,000 threshold applies to payments from third parties, and non-cash provisions. It may be useful to take advantage of these when structuring termination packages.

Termination of employment

15.108 It is axiomatic that a payment be made on the termination of employment before it can be argued that it falls within the residual category of termination payment as regards its tax treatment. This requires that a contract of employment be brought to an end as a matter of the Common Law. In this regard it is not settled as to how the *TUPE Regulations* operate. Those regulations specifically provide that a transfer of employment under the regulations 'shall not operate so as to terminate the contract of employment of any person employed by the transferor … but any such contract shall have effect after the transfer as if originally made between the person so employed and the transferee'. In other words, by virtue of the regulations the transferee stands in the shoes of the transferor following the transfer. In the absence of the regulations there would have been the termination of the employee's contract of employment with the transferor and the commencement of another employment with the transferee.

The view taken by the First-tier Tribunal in *Kuehne & Nagel Drinks Logistics Ltd v RCC* [2009] UKFTT 379 (TC) and *A G Reid v RCC* [2016] UKFTT 79 (TC) was that the deeming language of the *TUPE Regulations* were limited to its particular purpose and should not be taken into account in applying *ITEPA 2003*. In other words, the transfer of a contract of employment under the *TUPE Regulations* would nevertheless be treated as being brought to an end for tax purposes. In *Hill v RCC* [2015] UKFTT 205 (TC), however, the tribunal expressed the view that the tax legislation should be applied on the basis of the fiction contained in the regulations (ie that there is no termination of employment and that the employee has a single ongoing employment). However, it was not necessary for the tribunal to decide the case on the basis of the observation (see **15.12**).

CONCLUSION

15.109 The termination of an employee's employment affords an opportunity to the parties concerned to structure a payment in a tax-efficient way should the nature of their contractual relationship allow it. Yet this is an opportunity that arises in the context of an area of tax law where the relevant rules interact in a complex way. Careful consideration has to be given to all those rules and their interaction if satisfactory results are to be achieved. An added dimension to such complexity and planning is likely to come into play in respect of termination awards made on or after 6 April 2018. *Finance (No 2) Bill 2017* tightens and clarifies the treatment of payments that fall into the residual category. The changes that are to be made include classifying the first slice of a residual termination payment (but excluding a statutory redundancy payment) as earnings. The amount of the first slice of a termination package that will be treated as earnings equals the amount of the affected employee's basic pay (as defined) that he would have received if he had worked his notice period in full, even if he is not paid a contractual PILON. The deemed earnings amount will apply irrespective of the nature of the residual payments (other than statutory redundancy payments). Additionally, a new *National Insurance Bill* is expected to impose, with effect from 6 April 2018, a liability to employer's national insurance contributions (ie secondary Class 1 NICs) in respect of payments in the residual category that are not classified as earnings and that exceed £30,000.

Chapter 16

Separation and divorce

George Duncan Solicitor, CTA, TEP, Partner, Charles Russell Speechlys LLP

SIGNPOSTS

- Tax issues are often thrown up by the financial arrangements made in the context of divorce and relationship breakdown. There are few if any opportunities for achieving an artificial advantage through tax planning. However there are some sensible planning steps that can be taken and many pitfalls to avoid. The main role of the tax adviser will usually be to spot pitfalls in advance and either suggest a way around them or at least quantify them so that they can be taken into account in financial negotiations.
- The UK tax code is wildly inconsistent in the way in which it treats divorce and relationship breakdown. For some tax purposes the key date is the date of permanent separation of the couple, for other tax purposes the key date is the end of the marriage on decree absolute, and for yet others the key date is the end of the tax year of permanent separation.
- The chapter starts with an outline of the steps involved in a divorce where significant financial issues exist. It then looks at the taxes which are most likely to be an issue in the context of divorce and relationship breakdown and examines the main issues which are likely to arise. It then looks at the tax issues which arise in some specific scenarios including dealings with the matrimonial home, the issues raised where beneficial ownership of property differs from the legal ownership and the assignment of life policies. The chapter looks very briefly at pension sharing. At the end of the chapter there is a table summarising some tax consequences of the different stages of the process of separation and divorce.

INTRODUCTION

16.1 This chapter examines the main tax issues typically raised by separation and divorce. The breakdown of civil partnerships will raise the same tax issues.

Tax planning in this context is, usually, planning in the sense of planning to avoid disasters, rather than planning to secure an advantage.

AN OUTLINE OF THE STEPS INVOLVED IN A DIVORCE WHERE SIGNIFICANT FINANCIAL ISSUES EXIST

16.2 In broad outline the typical pattern will be as follows.

First, sadly, the relationship will break down leading to the permanent separation of the parties. The date of permanent separation is significant for certain tax purposes. It is a question of fact and will be referred to in various documents lodged with the court in the process of the matrimonial proceedings. It is not possible to specify a date of permanent separation for tax purposes different from that which has been acknowledged in documents submitted to the court.

16.3 The question whether a separation is permanent tends to be judged with the benefit of hindsight. However, the test is whether the separation is likely to be permanent, not whether it actually proves to be permanent. In *Bradley v Revenue & Customs Commissioners* – see **16.45** below – the tribunal accepted that a separation had been likely to be permanent even though a reconciliation had unexpectedly taken place. This is very much a question of fact and in *Benford v HMRC* [2011] UKFTT 457 (TC) the tribunal found that the taxpayer had not discharged the burden of proof required to demonstrate that his separation from his wife had been likely to be permanent.

Separation for these purposes is separation in the family law sense. It is possible, though rare, for a couple to be separated in the family law sense if they are living separate lives under the same roof, but also possible for a couple not to be separated if they are resident in different jurisdictions, for example where one of them has gone to live overseas for employment purposes and the other has stayed at home.

For the circumstances where husband and wife may be considered to have separated while still living under the same roof see *Holmes v Mitchell (Inspector of Taxes)* [1991] STC 25, where the General Commissioners found that a husband and wife were living as separate households under the same roof and Vinelott J as he then was accepted the conclusion that they were living apart with the consequence that the husband was not entitled to the higher personal allowance.

Permanent separation will, typically, be followed by the commencement of court proceedings for the dissolution of the marriage.

Example 16.1 – The difference between separation for tax purposes and in the geographical sense

Mr and Mrs A and Mr and Mrs B are all four resident in the UK. They live next door to each other.

Mr A receives an attractive offer of a job in one of the Gulf states. This is a permanent position and all the duties of his employment will be performed outside the UK. After discussion with Mrs A he decides that he will accept the offer, which he does.

However, Mrs A does not wish to accompany him. She does not like hot climates. Moreover, she has an equally good job in the UK. Therefore, Mr A departs for that Gulf state while Mrs A remains in the UK. Mr A easily satisfies the requirements in the statutory residence test introduced by *FA 2013, Sch 45* so that he ceases to be UK resident. However, Mr and Mrs A remain happily married. Modern technology allows them to keep in regular touch with each other and they spend as much time with each other as they can.

However, sadly, there is a falling out between Mr and Mrs B. Although they continue to live under the same roof, they come to lead quite separate lives and everything indicates that their separation will be permanent.

Therefore Mr and Mrs A are still living together as husband and wife, even though they are resident in different continents, while Mr and Mrs B are permanently separated even though they are living under the same roof.

16.4 The parties and their advisers will then try to agree 'minutes of order'. This is a document that will be submitted to the court by consent of both parties as being a form of order which both parties consider it would be appropriate for the court to make. The minutes of order are *not* a binding contract on which anyone can sue. They are an agreed recommendation to the court. However, it requires unusual circumstances for the parties not to be held to the substance of them: see *Xydhias v Xydhias* [1999] 2 All ER 386. The court said in *Xydhias* that the purpose of negotiation was not to finally determine the liability but to reduce the length and expense of the process by which the court carried out its function.

The judge will often make a consent order in the form of the minutes which have been supplied to him, but only if he considers it just to do so.

16.5 The court has wide powers when dealing with marriage breakdown. The court may order either party to the marriage to make periodical payments to the other party for that party's own benefit or for the benefit of children of the marriage. It can also order the payment of lump sums and the transfer of property between the parties, the settlement of property for the benefit of the other party to the marriage and of the children of the marriage, or either or any of them, and sharing or attachment of pensions. Attachment orders are merely a type of periodical payments or lump sum order. It also has power to vary the terms of pre-existing settlements but only if they are 'nuptial' or 'antenuptial' settlements.

Sometimes the court order will be made on the basis of undertakings given by one or both of the parties that they will do things which the court could not directly order itself.

The making of the court order dealing with financial matters will typically be preceded by the decree nisi and then, on the application of either party, followed by the decree absolute. The decree absolute ends the marriage for all legal purposes and it is then that the court order takes effect. Maintenance pending suit orders can take effect before decree nisi or absolute.

16.6 Property adjustment orders made before decree absolute take effect only on decree absolute.

It is possible under certain circumstances for financial matters to be left unresolved at decree absolute, in which case an order of the court dealing with financial matters may be made after decree absolute. Any order for payment of a lump sum or adjustment of property made after decree absolute will normally come into immediate effect.

There are of course many variations to this general pattern. If agreement cannot be reached on financial matters between the parties then there will be a contested court hearing and the court will make whatever order it thinks just. In some cases the parties will enter into a binding separation agreement which may or may not be followed by divorce proceedings. Couples who separate may make their own financial arrangements independently of the court but, in that case, the court might order different financial arrangements if it deemed it just to do so. Moreover, a reconciliation may take place leading to an abandonment of the court proceedings.

INCOME TAX

Focus

Income tax relief for maintenance payments is now no longer a major issue. Maintenance payments are not subject to income tax in the hands of the recipient. However there are points to watch out for. If one spouse provides for the other by making an outright transfer of capital then the income from that capital will be taxable in the normal way. Interest paid on overdue principal sums will also be taxable. The special rules for property jointly held by husband and wife cease to apply on a permanent separation and in some cases this may make a major change to the income tax position of the parties.

Maintenance payments

16.7 Tax relief for maintenance payments was at one time a key issue on marriage breakdown. However tax relief was greatly restricted by *FA 1988* and has subsequently become even more restricted so that it is currently seldom an issue. Relief for 'qualifying maintenance payments' survives in a very truncated form in the *Income Tax Act 2007* (*ITA 2007*), *Pt 8, Ch 5*, though only in a case where either of the parties to the marriage or civil partnership was born before 6 April 1935 or, in the case of certain child support maintenance payments, where either the person who made the payment or the person to whom it was made was born before that date. The amount of this truncated relief is a tax reduction of 10% of the lesser of the total amount of qualifying maintenance payments made by the individual in question which fall due in the tax year in question and the minimum specified in *ITA 2007, s 43* (£3,260 for 2017/18).

16.8 In other cases although maintenance payments are annual payments for tax purposes they attract no tax relief in the hands of the payer and they are tax free in the hands of the recipient. It is irrelevant whether the maintenance payments are secured or not. This treatment applies also to maintenance payments made by order of an overseas court (though they may attract tax relief overseas).

The statutory basis for this is contained in the Income Tax (Trading and Other Income) Act 2005 (*ITTOIA 2005*), *Pt 6, Ch 8*. *ITTOIA 2005, s 727* provides that no liability to income tax arises under *Pt 5* in respect of an annual payment if it:

(a) is made by an individual; and

(b) arises in the UK.

There are certain exceptions to this which are not relevant to maintenance payments.

ITTOIA 2005, s 730 (Foreign maintenance payments) provides that no liability to income tax arises under *Pt 5* in respect of an annual payment if:

1 it is a maintenance payment;

2 it arises outside the UK; and

3 had it arisen in the UK it would be exempt from income tax under *ITTOIA 2005, s 727* (certain annual payments by individuals).

The section goes on to explain that a 'maintenance payment' is a periodical payment which meets one of two conditions. Condition A is that the payment is made under a court order or a written or oral agreement. Condition B is that the payment is made by a person:

1 as one of the parties to a marriage or civil partnership to, or for the benefit of, and for the maintenance of, the other party;

2 to any person under 21 for that person's own benefit, maintenance or education; or

3 to any person for the benefit, maintenance or education of a person under 21.

The word 'marriage' is defined as including a marriage that has been dissolved or annulled.

Both *ITTOIA 2005, ss 727* and *730* are extended to certain payments made by an individual's personal representatives.

It should be noted that these exemptions for maintenance payments do not extend to income arising under an outright transfer of capital by one party to the marriage to the other. If there is such an outright transfer of capital then income arising from that capital will be taxed in the hands of the recipient in the normal way.

It should also be noted that these exemptions apply only to maintenance payments made by individuals. Sometimes the financial arrangements made in the context of divorce or relationship breakdown involve the provision of income to one party in the form of payments made by trustees, either of a pre-existing trust or of a new trust established by one of the parties for the purpose. Such trust income will not fall within these exemptions and will be taxable in the hands of the recipient in the normal way unless, exceptionally, it falls within the income tax settlement rule, on which see below, so as to be attributed to the settlor.

Interest payments

16.9 There is no tax exemption for interest received on a principal sum paid under an order of the court made in the context of divorce or marriage breakdown. Such interest will therefore be subject to tax in the hands of the recipient, being caught by the general income tax charge on interest imposed by *ITTOIA 2005, s 369* (see SAIM2070). This is notwithstanding that the payer will obtain no tax relief for the interest payment. If it is envisaged that there will be a delay in the making of a lump sum payment it may therefore be advantageous for periodical payments, which will be tax free in the hands of the recipient, to continue, or to continue at a higher rate, until the lump sum payment is received, rather than interest being paid.

Tax reductions for married couples and civil partners

16.10 The married couple's allowance now survives only in a truncated form (though it has been extended in a similar truncated form to civil partnerships). It is now represented by a tax deduction given under *ITA 2007, Pt 3, Ch 3* and applies where, for the whole or part of a tax year, the couple are living together (although it is reduced in the tax year of marriage or entry into civil partnership). It is therefore available in full for the tax year of permanent separation but not thereafter. It is available only where one of the spouses or civil partners in question was born before 6 April 1935.

The relief is lost if the payer claims the remittance basis of taxation (*ITA 2007, s 809G*). Rather curiously, the relief for maintenance payments does not however seem to be lost in these circumstances.

Transferable tax allowance for married couples and civil partners

16.11 The *FA 2014* introduced a very limited provision enabling the transfer of the personal allowance between spouses and civil partners (*FA 2014, s 11*, inserting *Ch 3A* of *Pt 3* in *ITA 2007*). The broad effect of the new provision is to enable the transfer of a proportion of one spouse or civil partner's personal allowance to the other in a case where neither is a higher rate taxpayer and part of the personal allowance of the one who makes the transfer would otherwise be wasted.

One of the requirements for a transfer to be made is that neither of the spouses or civil partners in question makes a claim for the married couple's allowance in respect of the tax year in question.

If the other conditions for the making of an election are satisfied then an individual may make the election for a transfer if he or she is married to, or in a civil partnership with, the same person for the whole or part of the tax year concerned and when the election is made. Thus the ending of a marriage or civil partnership ends the ability to make the election, even if the intention is to make a retrospective election in respect of a year during which the marriage or civil partnership was subsisting.

An individual is not entitled to more than one tax reduction under this new provision for the tax year, regardless of whether the individual is a party to more than one marriage or civil partnership in the tax year.

The new provision came into force in the tax year 2015/16 when the maximum transferable amount of the allowance was £1,060. For the tax year 2016/17 and subsequent tax years, the maximum transferable amount is 10% of the individual personal allowance. There is no requirement that the spouses or civil partners should be living together when the election is made, or during the tax year affected by the election. However, a decree of judicial separation is treated as ending a marriage.

Jointly held property

16.12 Where income-producing property is held in the joint names of a married couple or civil partners who live together, they are treated for income tax purposes as beneficially entitled to the income in equal shares (*ITA 2007, s 836*), unless they make a joint election of unequal beneficial interests in which case the income will be taxed in accordance with the actual beneficial ownership (*ITA 2007, s 837*). Certain types of income are excluded from these provisions. This presumption of equal entitlement ceases to apply on the date of permanent separation (see TSEM9836). In a case where significant income was involved and there was a marked disparity in beneficial entitlement permanent separation could thus have a significant effect on the income tax position of the parties.

Example 16.2 – Effect of permanent separation upon the tax treatment of income from assets held in joint names

Mr C has a substantial income and is an additional rate taxpayer. He has a substantial portfolio of shareholdings in UK companies and is therefore liable to tax on dividends from those holdings, beyond the first £5,000, at the dividend additional rate. Mrs C, however, has only a very small Stock Exchange portfolio and her income is well under the higher rate threshold.

In order to reduce the family's overall exposure to income tax, Mr C persuades Mrs C that they should combine their portfolios so that they are held in joint names. However, there are limits to Mr C's generosity. He persuades Mrs C to join in a Declaration of Trust recording that the joint portfolio belongs to them beneficially in the proportions in which they had contributed, Mrs C's beneficial interest thus being very small.

Mr and Mrs C deliberately have refrained from making an election of unequal beneficial interest. Consequently, the dividends from the joint portfolio are treated for income tax as belonging to them in equal shares. Mrs C's income is still not enough to bring her above the higher rate threshold so she will have no income tax liability on the first £5,000 of the dividends allocated to her and will pay tax at only 7.5% on the excess.

However, the relationship between Mr and Mrs C breaks down and they separate permanently. One consequence of this is that, from the date of their permanent separation, Mr C becomes liable to tax at the dividend additional rate on the proportion of the dividends from the joint portfolio which belongs to him beneficially. Thus his income tax liability significantly increases.

The settlement rules

16.13 The settlement rules are contained in *ITTOIA 2005, Pt 5, Ch 5*. Where these rules apply some or all of the income arising under the settlement will be treated as income of the settlor. For these purposes, 'settlement' is broadly defined (*ITTOIA 2005, s 620(1)*). It is, however, established by case law that the settlement rules can apply only where there is an element of bounty and, in most cases, it will be hard to argue that there is any element of bounty in a settlement made by one party to a marriage or civil partnership under the compulsion of a court order or as a result of arm's length negotiation (or both). There are three limbs of the settlement rules.

ITTOIA 2005, s 624 provides that income which arises under a settlement is treated for income tax purposes as the income of the settlor and of the settlor alone if it arises:

(a) during the life of the settlor, and

(b) from property in which the settlor has an interest.

ITTOIA 2005, s 625(1) explains that a settlor is treated for the purposes of *ITTOIA 2005, s 624* as having an interest in property if there are any circumstances in which the property or any related property:

(a) is payable to the settlor or the settlor's spouse or civil partner,

(b) is applicable to the benefit of the settlor or the settlor's spouse or civil partner, or

(c) will, or may, become so payable or applicable.

However, *ITTOIA 2005, s 625(4)* provides that, in sub-section (1), 'the settlor's spouse or civil partner' does not include:

(a) a spouse or civil partner from whom the settlor is separated under an order of the court or a separation agreement, or

(b) a spouse or civil partner from whom the settlor is separated where the separation is likely to be permanent.

Moreover, *ITTOIA 2005, s 627* (Exceptions for certain types of income) excepts certain types of income from this key rule. One of these exceptions is that the rule in *ITTOIA 2005, s 624* does not apply to income which:

- arises under a settlement made by one party to a marriage or civil partnership by way of provision for the other:
  - after the dissolution or annulment of the marriage or civil partnership; or
  - while they are separated under an order of the court, or under a separation agreement, or where the separation is likely to be permanent; and
- is payable to, or applicable for the benefit of, the other party.

The second limb is contained in *ITTOIA 2005, s 629* and provides that income which arises under a settlement is treated for income tax purposes as the income of the settlor and of the settlor alone for a tax year if, in that year and during the life of the settlor, it:

(a) is paid to, or for the benefit of, a relevant child of the settlor, or

(b) would otherwise be treated, apart from the section, as income of the relevant child of the settlor.

This provision does not apply to income which is treated as income of the settlor under *ITTOIA 2005, s 624*.

For these purposes, 'relevant child' mean a minor child who is unmarried or not in a civil partnership.

ITTOIA 2005, s 631 supplements this by providing that, if the trustees of a settlement retain or accumulate income arising under the settlement and a payment is subsequently made in connection with the settlement to, or for the benefit of, a child of the settlor who is unmarried or not in a civil partnership, the payment is treated for the purposes of *ITTOIA 2005, s 629(1)* as a payment of income, but only so far as there is retained or accumulated income available.

This second limb of the settlement rules could be an issue in a case where a capital settlement is made for the benefit of the children of the marriage as well as, or instead of, one of the spouses.

In *Harvey v Sivyer* [1986] Ch 119, Nourse J explained an earlier decision of the House of Lords on the basis that the natural relationship between parent and young child was one of such deep affection and concern that there must always be an element of bounty by the parent, even where the provision is, on the face of things, made under compulsion.

16.14 It follows, as one would expect, that no income tax advantage may be obtained by maintaining a minor child through the making of a capital settlement on the occasion of a divorce: distributions from such a settlement for the benefit of a minor child would be likely to be caught by *ITTOIA 2005, s 629*.

The third limb of the settlement rules is contained in *ITTOIA 2005, s 633* and applies where a capital sum is paid directly or indirectly in any tax year by the trustees of a settlement to the settlor. Such a capital sum is, broadly speaking, treated as income of the settlor up to the amount of income which has been accumulated within the settlement.

This is supplemented by *ITTOIA 2005, s 638* (capital sums paid by way of loan or repayment of loan) and *ITTOIA 2005, s 641* (capital sums paid to settlor by body connected with settlement).

This third limb will not usually be relevant in the context of the breakdown of marriage, although it could be relevant if one of the spouses sought to raise funds by persuading the trustees of a settlement which was otherwise outside the settlement rules to make a capital distribution to him or her.

The settlement rules will not often be an issue in a financial settlement made on the occasion of marriage breakdown, but the possibility of their application should always be considered where a capital settlement is made, especially where the children of the marriage may benefit. Since tax relief for maintenance payments has almost ceased, the rules could be an issue only in the context of a settlement of capital, rather than of income only.

The transfer of assets abroad rules in ITA 2007, Pt 13, Ch 2

> **Focus**
>
> This legislation betrays its age in that it treats a married couple as a unit and contains no concessions for permanent separation. In some cases this might leave one spouse being subject to income tax on income from which he had no prospect of benefiting.

16.15 A transfer of assets made in the context of divorce or relationship breakdown will not often itself be a transfer falling within these rules. However, problems may result from previous transfers, reflecting the fact that the legislation treats spouses, or civil partners, as a unit and there is no relieving provision that applies in the event of permanent separation. This is a feature of the legislation that goes back to its origins in the *FA 1936*. Consider the following example.

Example 16.3 – Permanent separation has surprisingly little effect on the transfer of assets abroad rules

Mr and Mrs D are resident in the UK. Mr D is in the fortunate position of having £1m to invest. He decides to invest it through an overseas company, so he purchases an off the shelf company incorporated in Jersey. (No particular significance attaches to the choice of this jurisdiction.)

Mr D invests his £1m by subscribing for shares in his Jersey company, in which he is the sole shareholder. The company invests the money and income arises to the company as a result. None of the exemptions contained in the legislation apply. The income arising to the company is thus squarely within the transfer of assets abroad rules. Income has arisen to a 'person abroad' as a result of a transfer of assets made by Mr D, Mr D has 'power to enjoy' that income within the meaning of the legislation, that income is then treated as arising to Mr D under *ITA 2007, s 721* and he is charged to tax on that income under *ITA 2007, s 720*. He does however have the consolation that, if the company distributes the income to him, the income received will be treated as not being his income for income tax purposes, under the relieving provision contained in *ITA 2007, s 743* (no duplication of charges) (as amended by *FA 2013*).

Mr D is a generous as well as a wealthy man. He proceeds to make an outright gift of the entire issued share capital in the Jersey company to Mrs D. However, from the point of view of income tax, not much changes as a result of this gift. The gift is not a settlement within *ITTOIA 2005, Pt 5, Ch 5* because it is an outright gift to his spouse and not a gift of property which is wholly or substantially a right to income (*ITTOIA 2005, s 626*). However *ITA 2007, s 714(4)* provides that in that chapter references to individuals include their spouses or civil partners. Thus, although Mr D no longer has power to enjoy the income in question, the fact that his spouse has power to enjoy that income is in itself enough to make him liable. He rather than his spouse is still the transferor. It is not even clear that *ITA 2007, s 743* will apply to any distribution of the income in question by the company to Mrs D, so as to prevent a second charge to tax on Mrs D in respect of the same income. (In practice, it could probably be assumed that HMRC would not seek to charge the same income twice, unless perhaps very aggressive tax avoidance was involved.)

Unfortunately, differences arise between Mr D and Mrs D. They separate permanently. However, neither wishes to divorce. Their separation has no effect upon Mr D's liability under these rules. Mrs D is still his spouse and she still has power to enjoy the income in question. He therefore remains liable to tax on that income. The legislation gives him no right of indemnity against Mrs D, nor even a right to obtain any information from her, or from the company. He would be well advised to negotiate such rights if he can.

Capital gains tax

Focus

This tax is often a major issue in the context of divorce and relationship breakdown. There is no general exemption for gains realised on disposals made in this context.

Disposals made between spouses before the end of the tax year of permanent separation fall within the 'no gain no loss' rule and it will sometimes be advantageous to accelerate the transfer of assets so that they fall within this rule.

Transfers between spouses made after the end of the tax year of permanent separation will usually be treated as made at open market value. However holdover relief may sometimes be available.

The timing of the CGT disposal is crucial. In some cases this will be the date of decree absolute and in some cases it will be the date of actual transfer of the asset. For detailed rules, see below.

16.16 The financial arrangements made in the context of divorce and relationship breakdown will often involve the transfer of assets between the parties. They may also involve the sale of assets to third parties to raise funds and the transfer of assets into or out of a settlement. With two exceptions explained below the legislation contains no specific exemptions and major liabilities often arise. CGT is now generally charged at a flat rate of either 10% or 20% but at 18% or 28% in the case of gains from residential property and carried interests. The rate is 10% where entrepreneurs' relief is available.

For both income tax and CGT, a married couple or civil partners are treated as living together unless:

- they are separated under an order of a court of competent jurisdiction;
- they are separated by deed of separation; or
- they are in fact separated in circumstances in which the separation is likely to be permanent.

See *TCGA 1992, s 288(3); ITA 2007, s 1011.*

Disposals between spouses before the end of the tax year of permanent separation

16.17 Disposals before the end of the tax year of permanent separation take place at 'no gain, no loss' in accordance with *TCGA 1992, s 58* (see CG22202).

Thus it will often be advantageous to accelerate the transfer of assets standing at a gain to a time before the end of the tax year of permanent separation. However, such transfers, while they will avoid any immediate CGT liability for the transferring spouse, may store up future problems for the recipient spouse who will thus take with a reduced CGT acquisition cost.

Example 16.4 – Advantages of prompt transfer of property following permanent separation

Mr and Mrs E separate permanently early in the 2017/18 tax year. Mr E is the sole owner of a valuable country property which the couple have used but which does not in any way qualify for the principal private residence relief. It shows a gain of £1m.

It is agreed in the course of negotiations that, as part of the financial settlement, Mr E will transfer this property into the outright ownership of Mrs E.

Mrs E intends to move to the country and to occupy this property as her main residence.

If the transfer takes place before 6 April 2018 then 'no gain, no loss' will apply. Mr E will have no CGT to pay. Mrs E will take a reduced CGT acquisition cost, but this is of no concern to her since she intends to occupy the property as her main residence.

If, however, the transfer takes place after 5 April 2018, Mr E will be exposed to CGT on his gain of £1m.

It should be noted that *TCGA 1992, s 58* applies even where the recipient spouse or civil partner is non-UK resident and thus outside the scope of CGT (see CG22300).

Thus, a transfer falling within *TCGA 1992, s 58* could have the effect of removing a gain permanently from the scope of CGT, for example where the recipient spouse goes to live permanently overseas as a result of the breakdown of the marriage.

Transfers between the end of the tax year of permanent separation and decree absolute

16.18 During this period transfers no longer qualify for 'no gain, no loss' treatment. However, the spouses will still be connected persons within *TCGA 1992, s 286* with the result that transfers will be deemed to take place at open market value in accordance with *TCGA 1992, s 18*.

Transfers between spouses after decree absolute

16.19 Following decree absolute the couple will no longer be connected persons for CGT purposes (unless they are connected for some other reason). However, it will be wise to assume that, one way or another, transfers of assets between them made under a court order or as part of the financial arrangements made between them in the context of the divorce will fall within *TCGA 1992, s 17* and thus be treated as taking place at open market value, unless they are, as a question of fact, the result of arm's-length bargains.

Hold-over relief

16.20 The view of HMRC is that where there is a disposal of an asset from one spouse to another after the end of the year of assessment in which they separate but prior to decree absolute this is, where there is no recourse to the courts, usually made in exchange for a surrender by the donee of rights which they would otherwise be able to exercise to obtain alternative financial provision. HMRC thus take the view that the value of the rights surrendered represents actual consideration of an amount which would reduce the gain potentially eligible for hold-over relief to nil. They accept that, exceptionally, there may be a substantial gratuitous element in the transfer so that hold-over relief will be available in the case of an appropriate asset.

16.21 HMRC formerly took this view in the case of transfers under a consent order. However, they now accept that, because a court order reflects the exercise by the court of its independent statutory jurisdiction and is not the consequence of any party to the proceedings agreeing to surrender alternative rights in return for assets, there is no actual consideration. Thus hold-over relief under *TCGA 1992, s 165* may be available for transfers of assets under a court order, even a consent order. This may be an extremely useful relief in the case of business assets, including shares in unlisted trading companies, and agricultural land. However hold-over relief reduces the acquiring spouse's acquisition cost and may thus store up problems for the future. The relief requires the consent of the acquiring spouse. This approach represents a change in the Revenue's prevailing practice following consideration of judicial observations made in the case of *G v G* [2002] EWHC 1339, [2002] 2 FLR 1143 (see CG67192).

There is some tension between *G v G* and the decision of the Court of Appeal in a non-tax case, *Haines v Hill and Another* [2007] All ER (D) 56 that a wife did give valuable consideration for the transfer of an asset to her by her husband under a court order made in matrimonial proceedings with the result that the court could not set that transfer aside as a transaction at an undervalue under the *Insolvency Act 1986, s 339* on the application of the trustee in bankruptcy of her former husband. However, that decision, which clearly reflects the desire of the Court to achieve a balance between the interests of creditors and those of estranged spouses, seems not to have affected the views of HMRC.

The time of the CGT disposal

16.22 It will be important to establish this. This is not only because disposals made before the end of the tax year of permanent separation will qualify for 'no gain, no loss' treatment but because the timing of the disposal will determine when any CGT has to be paid and the availability of exemptions and reliefs, including the annual exemption and loss relief. Moreover, the value of the asset may change as time goes on.

In the case of assets transferred outside the framework of a court order the normal rules apply. The date of disposal will thus be the date of actual transfer except in a case where the transfer was made in accordance with a binding contract, in which case the date of the contract will be the date of the disposal (unless it was a conditional contract, in which case the date of disposal will be the date when the condition is fulfilled). This is governed by *TCGA 1992, s 28* in the usual way.

16.23 The position is more difficult where the disposal is made in accordance with a court order. The view of HMRC, as set out in CG22423, is as follows:

- **Asset transferred under a court order before the date of decree absolute or before the dissolution of the civil partnership is made final.** Court orders of this type do not take effect until decree absolute has been granted or until dissolution has been made final. It is well established in case law that until the order takes effect, it is contractual in nature. Therefore, where an asset is transferred in pursuance of such an order before the date of decree absolute or the dissolution of the civil partnership is made final, the transfer is treated as a disposal under a contract. The parties are treated as entering into the contract on the date of the court order.

- **Asset transferred after the date of decree absolute or after the dissolution of the civil partnership is made final, in pursuance of a court order made before the date of decree absolute or before the dissolution of the civil partnership was made final.** A court order embodying the terms of the settlement made before the decree absolute or before the date of dissolution of the civil partnership remains contractual in nature until the date of the decree absolute or the date the dissolution is made final. After that date the court order ceases to be contractual and the terms derive their legal effect from the court order itself.

  So where an asset is transferred following the date of decree absolute, or following the date the dissolution is made final, in pursuance of an order made before decree absolute or before dissolution is made final, the date of disposal is the date of decree absolute or the date the dissolution is made final.

- **Asset transferred in pursuance of a court order made after the date of decree absolute or after the date the dissolution of the civil partnership is made final.** Where a court order is made after the date of decree absolute or after the date that the dissolution of the civil partnership is made final and an asset is transferred in pursuance of that order, the date of disposal is the date of the order.

The first part of this guidance is, presumably, contemplating a consent order. One would have thought that, if an asset is actually transferred before a court order comes into effect, the disposal will have taken place on any possible view, unless there was something suggesting otherwise in the particular terms on which the transfer was made.

HMRC expressly reject the view that, where the parties have approached the courts for an order to give effect to a prior agreement between them for the division of the assets of the marriage or civil partnership, and a consent order is obtained, the prior agreement is a binding contract so that the date of the agreement is the date of disposal for CGT purposes. See CG22420 which quotes the following extract from the judgment of Lord Diplock in *de Lasala v de Lasala* [1980] AC 546:

> 'Financial arrangements that are agreed upon between the parties for the purpose of receiving the approval and being made the subject of a consent order by the Court once they have been made the subject of the Court Order no longer depend upon the agreement of the parties as the source from which their legal effect is derived. Their legal effect is derived from the Court Order.'

It should be noted that this guidance attaches no importance to any delay between the coming into force of a court order requiring the transfer of an asset and its actual transfer. This is consistent with the decision of the Court of Appeal in the non-tax case *Mountney v Treharne* [2003] Ch 135 that it is the matrimonial court order, not the subsequent transfer of the asset which transfers the beneficial interest to the recipient spouse.

16.24 It will be seen that there is some scope for planning here. If desired and with goodwill the disposal of an asset could be accelerated by actually transferring the asset in advance of a court order (in which case any subsequent court order could leave its ownership unchanged). Alternatively, the disposal could be deferred by slowing the litigation.

The receipt of lump sums under court orders

16.25 There is no CGT on the receipt of a lump sum under a court order in itself. The authority for the payment of the lump sum comes from the court order, not from the disposal of any asset. HMRC accept that this principle extends to lump sums ordered by the court when discharging previous orders for periodical payments (see RI 227, April 2001).

See below for the special circumstances applying to disposals of the main residence.

Entrepreneurs' relief

16.26 Entrepreneurs' relief is now an extremely valuable relief from CGT, allowing gains of up to £10m to be charged at the rate of only 10%. The relief can be extremely useful when assets are to be transferred in the context of financial arrangements made on divorce or marriage breakdown. However, the relief may easily be lost. Note in particular the position where one spouse owns shares in a family trading company and is also an officer or employee of that company, owning at least 5% of the ordinary share capital and being entitled to exercise at least 5% of the voting rights by virtue of that holding. If the arrangements made on marriage breakdown involve that spouse both transferring his or her shareholding to another family member and resigning from the office or employment then the relief will be available (if its other conditions are satisfied) if the transfer takes place before resignation but will be lost if the order of events is reversed. See *TCGA 1992, ss 169I(6)* and *169S(3)*.

Inheritance tax

> **Focus**
>
> For various reasons an outright transfer of capital between spouses in the context of divorce or relationship breakdown will not usually be a chargeable transfer for IHT purposes. However the circumstances need to be carefully examined in each particular case. One of the protections, that given by *IHTA 1984, s 10*, is in fact relatively restricted.
>
> However the transfer of capital into settlement may well give rise to an immediate IHT charge and, even if it does not, in most cases the settlement will be exposed to the ten-yearly and exit charges following the changes made by *FA 2006*.
>
> Great care should be taken if assets to be transferred qualify, or may qualify, for reliefs or exemptions from IHT, such as business and agricultural property relief. A transfer may well lead to the loss of a relief or exemption. Transfers of assets which have been the subject of a potentially exempt transfer during the seven-year 'waiting period' within which the death of the transferor may trigger an IHT charge are especially hazardous.
>
> For IHT purposes the date of decree absolute is important rather than the date of permanent separation. In particular the spouse exemption will continue to apply to outright transfers of capital made before the date of decree absolute. The ability to transfer the nil rate band is not lost on permanent separation but only on decree absolute.

16.27 Until the enactment of *FA 2006*, IHT was rarely an issue in the context of divorce and relationship breakdown. This was for a number of reasons.

First, dispositions made on divorce for the benefit of a former spouse, whether under a court order or as a result of arm's-length negotiations, are normally accepted as being within *IHTA 1984, s 10* (dispositions not intended to confer gratuitous benefit) (see IHTM04165).

It must however be borne in mind that the protection given by *IHTA 1984, s 10* is all or nothing. If a disposition does not fall wholly within *IHTA 1984, s 10* then *IHTA 1984, s 10* gives no protection at all. A disposition cannot fall within *IHTA 1984, s 10* if it is made in a transaction or series of transactions which, with any associated operations, fails to meet the requirements of *IHTA 1984, s 10*. HMRC seem to have developed a more aggressive approach to *IHTA 1984, s 10* at least in the context of contributions to employee benefit trusts. See Revenue & Customs Brief 18/11 (Employee Benefit Trusts: Inheritance Tax and Income Tax Issues), which expresses the view that the slightest possibility of gratuitous intent will take a contribution to such a trust outside the protection of *IHTA 1984, s 10*.

In an interesting First-tier Tribunal decision *Parry (as personal representative of Staveley deceased) and Others v Revenue & Customers Commissioners* TC3548 [2014] UKFTT 419 (TC), HMRC failed in an attempt to argue that *IHTA 1984, s 10* did not apply to a transfer that formed part of a series of transactions (although they succeeded on another issue). In 2000, following her acrimonious divorce, Mrs Staveley transferred her pension fund from an occupational pension scheme linked to her ex-husband's company to a *Finance Act 1981, s 32* buy out policy. She was advised that on her death a substantial part of the funds could revert to the company for the benefit of her ex-husband. In order to prevent this, in November 2006 Mrs Staveley, who by then knew she was suffering from terminal cancer, requested that the policy be transferred to a personal pension plan and signed a Statement of Wishes that the death benefit should be paid equally to her two sons, who were beneficiaries under her will. Six weeks later she died, without having drawn any benefits from the plan. HMRC argued that the transfer into the personal pension plan had been a transfer of value for IHT purposes. However, the tribunal rejected that. Part of the tribunal's reasoning was that the transfer had not in itself been intended to confer a gratuitous benefit and, although it had affected the same property as the omission to draw benefits, it was not an associated operation with that omission because there was no connection of intent: operations had to be linked by the intention to confer gratuitous benefit if they were to be 'associated operations'.

The Upper Tribunal upheld the decision on this point and allowed the taxpayer's appeal on the point on which the First-tier Tribunal had found for HMRC ([2017] UKUT 4 (TCC)).

Such dispositions may also fall within *IHTA 1984, s 11* (dispositions for the maintenance of family). This applies to dispositions made by one party to a marriage in favour of the other party or of a child of either party which are either:

- for the maintenance of the other party; or
- for the maintenance, education or training of the child for a period ending not later than the year in which he attains the age of 18 or, after attaining that age, ceases to undergo full-time education or training.

Even in the absence of *IHTA 1984, ss 10* and *11* the straightforward transfer of an asset in pursuance of a matrimonial court order should not represent a transfer of value since the reduction in the value of the transferor's estate would already have occurred when the order came into effect. However, the position would be less straightforward if the transferor had given an undertaking as a basis for the court order or if the parties implemented a court order in such a way as to make greater provision for the children of the marriage than would have been required to satisfy the court.

HMRC will allow a deduction, in calculating the value of a person's estate chargeable to IHT on his death, for enforceable financial obligations to a former spouse or civil partner. See IHTM28090 following.

16.28 *IHTA 1984, s 11* expressly extends to dispositions made on the occasion of the dissolution of a marriage. However the provision is still somewhat limited in its effect, especially in the light of the decision of the Special Commissioner in the *Phizackerley case* (2007) SpC 591, [2007] STC (SCD) 328 that the provision of housing, in the context of a transfer from husband to wife, was not the provision of maintenance.

Unlike *IHTA 1984, s 10*, *IHTA 1984, s 11* can apply to part only of a disposition, as in *McKelvey v Revenue & Customs Commissioners* SpC 694 [2008] STC (SCD) 944 where a daughter had given two investment properties to her elderly and dependent mother and the Special Commissioner held that *IHTA 1984, s 11* applied to part only of the value of the gift.

Dispositions falling within either *IHTA 1984, s 10* or *11* are not transfers of value for IHT purposes.

16.29 In any case, since a married couple are still husband and wife until decree absolute, the spouse exemption will still apply to outright transfers made up to decree absolute, even after permanent separation, unless restricted by the domicile of the recipient spouse. Correspondingly, on decree absolute the related property rule (under which the property of husband and wife is aggregated for valuation purposes) ceases to apply (*IHTA 1984, s 161*).

Major difficulties have, however, been caused by the changes made by *FA 2006* to the IHT treatment of settled property. It often happens that, as part of the financial arrangements made on divorce or relationship breakdown, an interest-in-possession settlement will be established. Typically, this will take the form of a life interest for the spouse/former spouse with remainder to the children of the marriage. In this case the inclusion of the remainder interest for the children, rather than a reverter to the settlor, may well take the transfer into settlement outside *IHTA 1984, s 10*.

16.30 The difficulty is that, even though the transfer of capital into the settlement will often (though not necessarily) fall within *IHTA 1984, s 10* and thus not be a transfer of value the settled property will, under the post-2006 rules, be 'relevant property' exposed to the ten-yearly and exit charges, notwithstanding the former spouse's interest in possession.

This change discourages the establishment of such settlements and causes particular difficulties in the context of the former matrimonial home, on which see below.

Reliefs and exemptions from inheritance tax: some pitfalls

Business and agricultural property relief

16.31 If the ownership of assets is to change as a result of financial arrangements made in the context of divorce or relationship breakdown, then it is important to find out whether those assets qualify for any relief or exemption from IHT and, if so, whether that relief or exemption will be lost, permanently or temporarily, on the change of ownership.

One difficulty lies in the length of ownership requirement for business property relief (*IHTA 1984, s 106)* and the length of occupation or ownership requirement for agricultural property relief *(IHTA 1984, s 117)*. The provisions for replacement (*IHTA 1984, ss 107* and *118*) are unlikely to help in the case of a transfer of property made in the context of divorce or relationship breakdown. The provisions for successive transfers (*IHTA 1984, ss 109* and *121*) may help if assets otherwise qualifying for business property relief or agricultural property relief are transferred in the context of divorce or relationship breakdown and are subsequently the subject of a transfer of value made by the recipient on his death, but not in the event of a lifetime transfer by the recipient. Moreover the provisions for successive transfers only help if there has been an earlier transfer of value, so seem not to help if the only other transfers fell within *IHT 1984, s 10* or *11* in which case they will not have been transfers of value.

There may thus be an IHT exposure on the assets transferred until the transferee has satisfied the length of ownership or length of occupation or ownership requirements in his or her own right.

Another pitfall lies in wait where an asset which is transferred has previously been the subject of a potentially exempt transfer (*IHTA 1984, s 3A*) and the seven-year 'waiting period' following that previous transfer has not yet expired. In that case, should the original transferor die within that seven-year period and the potentially exempt transfer thus become chargeable, relief may be lost.

Even if the asset in question qualified for business property relief or agricultural property relief in the hands of the original donor at the date of the potentially exempt transfer these reliefs will not be available in calculating the tax payable as a result of the subsequent death of the original donor unless (*inter alia*) the asset in question is still owned by the original donee at the date of the original donor's death (or at the earlier death of the original donee) (*IHTA 1984, ss 113A* and *124A*). There are provisions for replacement property (*IHTA 1984, ss 113B* and *124B*), but these help only where the transferee has disposed of all or part of the property in question before the death of the transferor and the whole of the consideration received by him for the disposal has been applied by him in acquiring other property, so they will not help where no consideration has been received by the original transferee on making his disposal.

A further difficulty is that, should a potentially exempt transfer 'fail' because of the death of the transferor within seven years and should the property in question have been transferred in the meantime to the estranged spouse of the original donee for no consideration, then not only would business property relief or agricultural property relief be lost but the estranged spouse would then be one of the persons liable for the tax on the 'failed' potentially exempt transfer (*IHTA 1984, s 199*) because the estranged spouse would be a person in whom the property was vested at any time after the transfer. Even if the transfer to the estranged spouse took place on arm's-length terms the estranged spouse would not be a 'purchaser' and thus protected from liability under *IHTA 1984, s 199* unless he had acquired the property in good faith for a consideration in money or money's worth (*IHTA 1984, s 272*), which would seemingly not be the case if the transfer had been made by order of the court. However the practice of HMRC is to treat the transferee of a 'failed potentially exempt transfer' as primarily liable for tax (IHTM30042).

Example 16.5 – Hazards of transferring business property which has been the subject of a PET

Mr and Mrs F separate and divorce. Mr F transfers to Mrs F, in accordance with a court order, a block of shares in an unlisted trading company worth £1m which would qualify for business property relief at 100% in his hands.

Five years previously that same block of shares had been given outright to Mr F by his father, this transfer being a potentially exempt transfer. At the time of that gift the shares qualified for 100% business property relief in the hands of Mr F's father. The shares were also worth £1m at the date of the gift to Mr F by his father.

One year after the transfer by Mr F to Mrs F, Mr F's father dies and the potentially exempt transfer thus 'fails'.

Since Mr F no longer owns the shares at the date of his father's death and since he had not sold them and applied the proceeds in purchasing replacement business property no business property relief is allowed in calculating the tax payable on the 'failed' potentially exempt transfer. If HMRC encounter difficulties in recovering the tax from Mr F then they may seek to recover it from Mrs F.

Entitlement to business property relief in respect of certain shares and securities of a company depends upon the owner having control of the company in question (*IHTA 1984, s 105(1)(b)* and *(cc)*) with the result that eligibility for further relief may be lost if the result of a transfer is to separate ownership of a block of shares or securities from control of the company in question.

Entitlement to business property relief in respect of certain categories of land or building, machinery or plant depends upon the owner (or beneficial owner if the assets are settled property) having control of a company which uses those assets for the purposes of its business or being a member of a partnership which uses those assets for the purposes of its business in which case entitlement to relief in respect of those assets may be lost if they are transferred separately from control of the company in question or membership of the partnership in question (*IHTA 1984, s 105(1)(d)*).

Example 16.6 – Separation of assets from business ownership

Mr and Mrs G carry on business as retail newsagents in partnership with their son. The partnership business is carried on from a number of different premises, the freeholds of which are held outside the partnership by Mr and Mrs G as beneficial tenants in common in equal shares. Mr and Mrs G have owned the freeholds for many years and they have been used in the partnership business for many years. Thus, as matters stand, the freeholds will qualify for business property relief at the lower 50% rate in accordance with *IHTA 1984, ss 104(1)(b)* and *105(1)(d)*.

The partnership occupies the premises under leases granted by Mr and Mrs G.

Mr and Mrs G separate and divorce. As part of the associated financial arrangements Mrs G resigns from the partnership. However, in order to provide her with a continuing income, Mr G assigns to her his interest in the freeholds so that she becomes the outright owner of them and receives the whole of the rent payable by the partnership. Consequently, the freeholds will no longer qualify for business property relief. The link with the partnership will have been broken. Mrs G will also lose any possibility of obtaining entrepreneurs' relief under *TCGA 1992, Pt V, Ch 3* on a subsequent disposal of the freeholds.

Conditional exemption

16.32 The advantage of owning property which has attracted conditional exemption from IHT usually lies in pride of ownership rather than in any immediate financial returns, so such property is not a natural subject of a financial settlement made on the occasion of divorce or relationship breakdown. However it should be borne in mind that any disposal of such property, whether by sale or gift or otherwise, is prima facie a 'chargeable event' on which tax may be charged (*IHTA 1984, s 32(3)*). A disposal otherwise than by sale is not a 'chargeable event' with respect to any property if:

- the disposal is itself a conditionally exempt transfer of the property; or
- fresh undertakings are given by such persons as the Board thinks appropriate in the circumstances of the case presumably in most cases the transferee (see *IHTA 1984, s 32(5)* and *(5AA)*).

Thus, should conditionally exempt property be transferred otherwise than by sale, in order to avoid a 'chargeable event', either the exemption must be renewed (which, broadly speaking, would not be appropriate or possible unless the transfer would itself otherwise occasion an immediate charge to IHT) or the undertakings must be renewed. In either case the broad effect would be to pass liability for the tax that would be payable when and if the conditional exemption was lost to the transferee, who would be severely inhibited in his use of the property by the undertakings which he would probably have been required to give.

Growing timber

16.33 *Chapter III* of *Part V* of *IHTA 1984* provides that where part of the value of a person's estate immediately before his death is attributable to the value of land on which trees or underwood are growing but which is not agricultural property, the value of the trees or underwood may (subject to certain conditions) be left out of account in valuing that person's estate on death in which case tax is charged on the disposal of the trees or underwood. However there is no tax charge on a disposal made by any person to his spouse or civil partner (*IHTA 1984, s 126(2)*). Thus, in some cases it would be possible to avoid a tax charge on the transfer of trees or underwood by making the transfer before decree absolute.

The transferable nil rate band

16.34 It is a requirement of the provisions for the transfer of unused IHT nil rate bands introduced by the *FA 2008* and now contained in *IHTA 1984, ss 8A, 8B* and *8C* that (*inter alia*) a person has died who, immediately before his death, had a spouse or civil partner and who had unused nil rate band on his death. However it is not necessary that such spouses or civil partners were living together at the time of the first death, or that the second deceased spouse or civil partner benefited from the estate of the first deceased person. This may give rise to unexpected results. The same will apply to any transfer of the residential nil rate band introduced in relation to deaths on or after 6 April 2017 under *F(No 2)A 2015*. See *IHTA 1984, s 8G*.

Example 16.7 – Separation and transfer of nil rate band

Mr and Mrs H separate permanently after having been married for a number of years. One of the reasons for the breakdown of their relationship is that Mrs H does not share Mr H's great love for animals. Neither of them wishes to divorce. Mr H changes his will, wholly excluding Mrs H and leaving his entire estate to an animal welfare charity. He then dies and the provisions of this will are implemented. His nil rate band was intact at the time of his death and, since the only gift made by his will qualifies for the charity exemption from IHT, it is not used on his death.

When Mrs H dies (assuming no change in the law), her executors will be able to claim Mr H's unused nil rate band, notwithstanding that they had separated permanently during his lifetime and that she did not benefit from his estate. The beneficiaries of Mrs H's estate may thus be better off (at current tax rates) by £130,000 (£325,000 @ 40%).

Election to be treated as domiciled in the UK

16.35 *FA 2013, s 177* has made it possible, if certain conditions are satisfied, for a person to elect to be treated as domiciled in the UK for IHT purposes, thus securing the spouse exemption for transfers to that person. Such an election may also be made under certain circumstances by the personal representatives of a deceased person. It should be noted that, although the election is only possible if the person in question had a spouse or civil partner who was domiciled in the UK at the effective date of the election, a subsequent divorce or dissolution of the civil partnership would neither prevent an election nor invalidate one which had been made (*IHTA 1984, ss 267ZA* and *267ZB*).

Example 16.8 – Divorce and election for deemed domicile

At the start of the 2013/14 tax year, Mr and Mrs I have been married for a number of years. Both are resident in the UK. Mr I is domiciled in the UK but Mrs I is not, neither does she have a deemed domicile under *IHTA 1984, s 267*.

Mr I is a wealthy man. However, all is not well. Unknown to Mrs I, Mr I is conducting an affair with Miss X. Moved by guilt he decides to make Mrs I an immediate gift of £1m, which he makes on 6 April 2013.

This gift is intended to confer gratuitous benefit so it does not fall within *IHTA 1984, s 10*, nor is it a disposition for the maintenance of Mrs I so it does not fall within *IHTA 1984, s 11*. Mr I has two annual exemptions available so the first £6,000 of the gift is exempt. The spouse exemption is also available but, because of Mrs I's overseas domicile, even with the more generous provision introduced by the *FA 2013* applying to transfers made on or after 6 April 2013, the spouse exemption is still restricted to the amount of the nil rate band, thus £325,000. This is a lifetime limit but suppose that Mr I had not previously used any part of it. Suppose that Mr I has not previously used his nil rate band. Thus the first £331,000 of the gift is exempt but the balance of £669,000 is a potentially exempt transfer that will fall into charge to IHT should Mr I fail to survive for seven years, though the first £325,000 will be taxed at a nil rate.

Mrs I then discovers the relationship between Mr I and Miss X, which leads to a rapid disintegration of the relationship between Mr and Mrs I. This is followed by their permanent separation and divorce. The decree absolute is obtained later in the 2013/14 tax year and this is immediately followed by the marriage of Mr I to Miss X.

Under the financial settlement made on the divorce, Mrs I retains the £1m, this being taken into account in the divorce settlement.

Mr I then dies within the course of the 2017/18 tax year. This means that the potentially exempt transfer has 'failed' and there is an immediate liability to IHT which HMRC may recover from Mrs I.

It is, however, open to Mrs I to make an election under *IHTA 1984, s 267ZA* to be treated as domiciled in the UK from and including 6 April 2013. This is well within the period of retrospection permitted by the legislation. For the making of the election it is sufficient that she was married to Mr I at the effective date of the election: the facts that they were subsequently divorced and that he remarried are irrelevant. Mrs I cannot revoke the election but if she is not resident in the UK for income tax purposes for the period of four successive tax years (as the law currently stands) beginning at any time after the election was made, the election ceases to have effect at the end of that period (*IHTA 1984, s 267ZB(10)*). Mrs I should, however, consider carefully, before she makes the election, whether she has herself made any transfers of value that might become chargeable as a result of the election and whether she might in future make such transfers while the election is in force.

Mrs I would, clearly, have been well advised to obtain an indemnity in respect of the April 2013 gift as part of the financial settlement with Mr I, though even if she did she might reasonably have been expected to mitigate her loss by making the election.

One unintended consequence of the election is that Mr I's nil rate band is no longer set against the April 2013 gift so it will be available either to his executors or, if the spouse exemption is available because he leaves his entire estate to his new wife, to be transferred to the executors of the former Miss X.

Stamp duty land tax and stamp duty

16.36 In the past, SDLT has rarely been an issue in the context of separation and divorce. It has been more common for it to be an issue in the financial arrangements made on the breakdown of a relationship between cohabitees. However, the breakdown of a relationship may well lead to the purchase of a new home bringing with it an SDLT charge and in some circumstances the 3% surcharge introduced by the *FA 2016*.

There is a very wide exemption contained in *FA 2003, Sch 3, para 3*, which provides that a transaction between one party to a marriage and the other is exempt from charge to SDLT if it is effected:

- in pursuance of an order of a court made on granting in respect of the parties a decree of divorce, nullity of marriage or judicial separation;
- in pursuance of an order of a court made in connection with the dissolution or annulment of the marriage, or the parties' judicial separation, at any time after the granting of such a decree;
- in pursuance of:
  - an order of a court made at any time under *Matrimonial Causes Act 1973, s 24A;* or
  - an incidental order of a court made under *Family Law (Scotland) Act 1985, s 8(2)* or by virtue of *Family Law (Scotland) Act 1985, s 14(1)*;
- at any time in pursuance of an agreement of the parties made in contemplation or otherwise in connection with the dissolution or annulment of the marriage, their judicial separation or the making of a separation order in respect of them.

(This statement of the legislation omits some wording which is obsolete because of changes to matrimonial law.)

A similar wide exemption for transactions in connection with the dissolution of civil partnerships is contained in *FA 2003, Sch 3, para 3A*.

16.37 Even in the absence of this exemption, SDLT would not often be an issue because, in the context of separation or divorce, there would usually be no chargeable consideration for SDLT purposes given for the transfer of an interest in land. SDLT would, however, in the absence of this exemption, be an issue if, for example, land was transferred subject to a mortgage. Transfers of mortgaged properties between cohabitees, or changes in the beneficial ownership of mortgaged properties by cohabitees, or indeed exchanges of properties between cohabitees, may well give rise to SDLT issues.

It should be noted that this exemption does not extend to transfers made by or to third parties, for example to a child of the marriage, as part of financial arrangements made on the occasion of separation or divorce.

There is a similar wide exemption from stamp duty contained in *FA 1985, s 83*.

The higher rate SDLT charge for additional dwellings has been introduced by *FA 2016* inserting *Sch 4ZA* into *FA 2003*. In broad outline the effect of the new rules is that if a taxpayer purchases a dwelling and, at the end of the day of completion, owns another dwelling as well, then he will have to pay SDLT on the purchase at higher rates, those higher rates representing a surcharge of 3% on the rates that would otherwise have applied. Dwellings are excluded from this surcharge if they cost less than £40,000 or if they are subject to a lease with an unexpired term of more than 21 years. The surcharge does not apply if the purchased dwelling is intended to be the purchaser's only or main residence and replaces another dwelling which had previously been the purchaser's only or main residence. The precise conditions for this relief for replacements are somewhat technical and the relief does not apply in some circumstances where one might have expected it to.

In deciding whether the surcharge applies, spouses or civil partners are treated as a unit if they are living together for which the same tests apply as for the purposes of income tax. Thus, for example, if husband and wife are living together, the husband alone owns the matrimonial home and the wife purchases a holiday home (or vice versa) the purchase will normally attract the surcharge, even though the spouse who makes the purchase has no interest in the other property.

The surcharge may well apply to a property transaction entered into as a consequence of marriage breakdown.

Example 16.9 – Divorce and higher rate SDLT charge for additional dwellings

Mr and Mrs J occupy a house in London which is their matrimonial home and their main residence. This property is owned solely by Mr J. They also have a holiday home in Cornwall which is owned solely by Mrs J. Both properties are unencumbered freeholds worth considerably in excess of £40,000. They own no other properties at any relevant time.

They separate permanently and commence divorce proceedings. After the date of permanent separation, but before Decree Absolute, Mr J sells the London property. He uses part of the proceeds of sale to purchase a smaller property for his own occupation and transfers the other part to Mrs J, who herself buys a smaller property for her own future occupation.

Mr J is clearly not liable for the surcharge on his purchase since he owns only one dwelling at the end of the day of completion and because of the permanent separation he is no longer 'aggregated' with Mrs J for these purposes.

It is also seems that Mrs J escapes the surcharge. Although she will own two dwellings at the end of the day of completion, the new dwelling seems to qualify as a replacement for the previous matrimonial home for the purposes of *paragraph 3(6)* of the *Schedule*. This requires Mrs J to intend the purchased dwelling to be her only. or main. residence, which she does. It also requires that:

- in another land transaction the purchaser or the purchaser's spouse or civil partner at the time disposed of a major interest in another dwelling which itself had been the purchaser's only or main residence; and
- at no time during the period beginning with the effective date of the previous transaction and ending with the effective date of the transaction concerned, that is her purchase, had the purchaser or the purchaser's spouse or civil partner acquired a major interest in any other dwelling with the intention of it being the purchaser's only or main residence. (There are time limits specified in the legislation but assume for the purposes of the example that these are satisfied.)

There is no requirement that the purchaser had any beneficial interest in the previous dwelling nor that, if the sale is undertaken by the purchaser's spouse rather than by the purchaser himself or herself, the couple should have been living together at the time.

The position would, however, be different if Mr J had sold the matrimonial home after the Decree Absolute, when he was no longer a spouse of Mrs J. In that case, she could not benefit from the replacement relief and would have to pay the surcharge on her own purchase.

The position would also be different if, rather than selling the former matrimonial home, Mr J retained it for his own occupation and instead raised money from another source to pay to Mrs J to finance her purchase of a property for her own occupation.

Although this legislation is new, it is already clear that it will sometimes apply in an unexpected way and that its application is sensitive to the timing of transactions.

Pre-owned assets tax

16.38 This is seldom an issue.

The disposal of any property is an 'excluded transaction' in relation to any person if, *inter alia*:

- the property was transferred to his spouse or civil partner (or, where the transfer has been ordered by a court, to his former spouse or civil partner);
- it was a disposal by way of gift (or, where the transfer is for the benefit of his former spouse or civil partner, in accordance with a court order), by virtue of which the property became settled property in which his spouse or civil partner or former spouse or civil partner is beneficially entitled to an interest in possession (see *FA 2004, Sch 15, para 10(1)(b)* and *(c)*).

PARTICULAR ISSUES

The matrimonial home and the CGT main residence exemption

Focus

In a case where a couple own more than one home the application of the main residence exemption may not be straightforward and it is important to establish the facts before any transfer takes place.

The 'three-year rule' was often extremely helpful and its reduction to 18 months will greatly increase the problems in this area. In other cases the former *ESC D6* now *TCGA 1992, s 225B* may be helpful.

16.39 The breakdown of a relationship will almost invariably lead to one or both parties to the marriage leaving the matrimonial home. It will also often lead to the transfer of the former matrimonial home, or of an interest in it, from one spouse to the other, or from one spouse into a settlement for the benefit of the other. Relationship breakdown will also often be followed by the sale of the former matrimonial home to a third party. The situation is even more complicated if the couple have owned or occupied more than one property.

The first step will be to establish to which (if any) of the properties in question the main residence exemption applies. It should be borne in mind that, in the case of an individual living with his spouse or civil partner, there can only be one main residence for both, so long as they are living together, and where a notice as to which residence the exemption is to apply to affects both the individual and his spouse or civil partner, it must be given by both (see *TCGA 1992, s 222(6)*).

16.40 Moreover, in the case of an individual living with his spouse or civil partner, if there is a disposal of, or of an interest in, a dwelling-house which is their only or main residence from one to the other, then the recipient inherits the transferor's history of entitlement to the exemption (see *TCGA 1992, s 222(7)* and CG64950). If the exemption is restricted in the hands of the transferor, this problem thus passes on to the transferee.

There may be scope for planning if a property is to be transferred that has qualified for the exemption during part only of its ownership by the transferor but which will qualify without restriction in the hands of the transferee: if the transfer can be effected within the 'no gain, no loss' rule but outside *TCGA 1992, s 222(7)* the chargeable element of the gain falls away.

Example 16.10 – Transfers where the main residence exemption is restricted

Mr and Mrs K occupy a property which is owned outright by Mr K. Their main residence exemption currently attaches to it but there was a period earlier in Mr K's ownership during which the exemption did not attach to it.

The property shows a gain of £1m. Differences have, unfortunately, arisen between Mr and Mrs K. They are still living together in the property but are contemplating separation followed by divorce proceedings. They envisage that, if they separate, Mr K will transfer the property into the outright ownership of Mrs K who will thereafter occupy it as her only residence while Mr K will live elsewhere.

Mr and Mrs K decide to press ahead with the transfer while they are still living together. Mr K therefore transfers his interest in the property to

Mrs K. Soon afterwards they separate permanently. Mrs K continues to occupy the property in question as her only residence while Mr K goes to live elsewhere.

Mrs K will now have her own separate entitlement to the exemption, which will automatically attach to this property since this is her sole residence as a question of fact. However, *TCGA 1992, s 222(7)* applies. The result is that Mrs K's entitlement to the exemption is 'contaminated' by Mr K's history of non-entitlement. Mrs K will inherit Mr K's acquisition cost under the 'no gain, no loss' principle.

Consequently, when Mrs K comes to sell the property a proportionate part of the gain she realises will be taxable, subject to whatever other exemptions and reliefs are then available.

Contrast the position if the transfer of the property was postponed until after the date of permanent separation. In that case, so long as Mrs K occupied the property continuously as her only or main residence until a time within 18 months of her disposing of it, the exemption would apply in full to the gain she realised on its disposal, notwithstanding that there had been restricted entitlement to the exemption before the date of transfer.

In most cases, the main residence exemption will attach to the former matrimonial home, though if the couple have occupied more than one residence they may have made a joint election for the exemption to attach to a residence which is not, on the face of things, their main residence. The restriction upon the ability of non-UK residents to make elections as to which property the exemption attaches to, introduced by *FA 2015, s 37* and *Sch 9* inserting *TCGA 1992, ss 222A–222C*, will now need to be taken into account.

In this context the 'three-year rule' formerly contained in *TCGA 1992, s 223(1)* was extremely helpful and the reduction of the period, in most cases, to 18 months by *FA 2014, s 58* is unhelpful. If the main residence exemption attaches to the former matrimonial home then, if a spouse has ceased to occupy that former matrimonial home as a result of the breakdown of the relationship, he has 18 (formerly 36) months in which to transfer his interest in the property before losing entitlement to the exemption (though bearing in mind that it may be restricted in some other way, for example by a previous period of non-occupation).

Once a couple have separated permanently, each becomes separately entitled to the main residence exemption and may make a separate election for the exemption to attach to a separate property, if otherwise entitled to do so. Prompt action may be needed to make the best use of the exemption.

Example 16.11 – Advantages of prompt election for main residence exemption

Mr and Mrs L own two properties, a house in the country and a flat in London, in each case as beneficial tenants in common in equal shares. Both have appreciated greatly in value. They divide their time between the two but have made a joint election for the London flat to qualify for the exemption, on the basis that it is increasing in value more quickly and that it is likely to be sold first.

The relationship breaks down and as a result Mr L ceases to occupy the London flat. He acquires rented accommodation in London for his own use. However, he continues to make regular use of the country house at weekends (when Mrs L is not there).

It is less than two years since these changes happened. It is anticipated that, when a settlement is negotiated between the parties, Mr L will assign to Mrs L his interest in both the country house and the London flat. Mr L also intends, at a later stage, to purchase a further London property for his future occupation, in which case he will give up his rented accommodation.

Mr L will probably be well advised to make an immediate election in favour of the country house. This will prevent his exemption from attaching to his rented accommodation where it would be wasted. It will give him at least 18 months' worth of the exemption in respect of the country house, where it will be more useful. This will not prejudice his entitlement to the exemption in respect of the London flat which will continue to apply for up to 18 months after his departure from it. When he acquires his new property in London, he should consider whether to make a fresh election in favour of that property, to make sure that it attaches to that property, if he thinks it will be more useful there.

TCGA 1992, s 225B (formerly Extra-statutory Concession D6)

16.41 In cases where the transfer of a property, or of an interest in it, will not in any case be exempt under the 18-month rule, it may be advantageous to claim the benefit of *TCGA 1992, s 225B* which has replaced ESC D6 for disposals made on or after 6 April 2009. This provides as follows:

'(1) Where an individual –

(a) ceases to live with his spouse or civil partner in a dwelling-house or part of a dwelling-house which is their only or main residence, and

(b) subsequently disposes of, or of an interest in, the dwelling-house or part to the spouse or civil partner,

then, if conditions A to C are met, *ss 222* to *224* shall apply as if the dwelling-house or part continued to be the individual's only or main residence until the disposal.

(2) Condition A is that the disposal mentioned in *subs (1)(b)* is pursuant to –

(a) an agreement between the individual and his spouse or civil partner made in contemplation of or otherwise in connection with the dissolution or annulment of the marriage or civil partnership, their judicial separation or the making of a separation order in respect of them, or their separation in other circumstances such that the separation is likely to be permanent, or

(b) an order of a court –

(i) made on granting an order or a decree of divorce or nullity of marriage, for the dissolution or annulment of the civil partnership, or for judicial separation,

(ii) made in connection with the dissolution or annulment of the marriage or civil partnership or the parties' judicial separation and which is made at any time after the granting of such an order or decree,

(iii) made at any time under *s 22A*, *23*, *23A*, *24* or *24A* of the *Matrimonial Causes Act 1973*,

(iv) made at any time under *art 25* or *26* of the *Matrimonial Causes (Northern Ireland) Order 1978*,

(v) made under *s 8* of the *Family Law (Scotland) Act 1985*, including incidental orders made by virtue of *s 14* of that Act, or

(vi) made at any time under any provision of *Sch 5* to the *Civil Partnership Act 2004* that corresponds to any of the provisions mentioned in paragraphs (iii) and (iv).

(3) Condition B is that in the period between the individual ceasing to reside in the dwelling-house or part of the dwelling-house and the disposal to the spouse or civil partner, the dwelling-house or part continues to be the only or main residence of the spouse or civil partner.

(4) Condition C is that the individual has not given notice under *s 222(5)* that another dwelling-house or part of a dwelling-house is to be treated as the individual's main residence for any part of that period.

(5) *Section 223* (as applied by this section) shall apply only on the making of a claim by the individual.'

16.42 The limitations of this relief should be noted. In particular, it applies only in relation to transfers between spouses or civil partners, thus not to a sale on the open market, and it requires the spouse or civil partner who claims the benefit of the relief to give up the main residence exemption in respect of any other property for the period in question, thereby potentially storing up CGT problems for himself in the future. It is therefore much less beneficial than the 18-month rule, in cases where that rule applies.

16.43 A series of decisions of the courts and tax tribunals have addressed the question of what quality of occupation of a dwelling is needed to turn that occupation from mere occupation into residence so that the dwelling in question becomes the taxpayer's residence, rather than merely a dwelling which he is occupying on a temporary basis, so that he will be entitled to main residence relief on disposing of it if the other conditions of the relief are satisfied. This is a sensitive issue in the context of relationship breakdown which is very likely to lead to upheaval in the lives of those concerned.

In *Goodwin v Curtis* [1998] STC 475, a case where the taxpayer, who was separated from his wife, had occupied the dwelling in question, a farmhouse, for just over one month and it had already been put on the market when he moved in, the Court of Appeal held that the relief was not available. Millett LJ accepted the substance of the Commissioners' finding that the nature, quality, length and circumstances of the taxpayer's occupation of the farmhouse did not make his occupation qualify as residence. Schiemann LJ accepted the Revenue's contention that in order to qualify for the relief the taxpayer must provide some evidence that his residence in the property showed some degree of permanence, some degree of continuity or some expectation of continuity.

The difficulty is that, in the nature of things, the breakdown of a relationship is likely to lead to a lack of continuity and permanence in the lives of those concerned.

16.44 The issues are illustrated by four decisions of the First-tier Tribunal Tax Chamber reported in 2013, *Bradley v Revenue & Customs Commissioners* [2013] UKFTT 131(TC); *Moore v Revenue & Customs Commissioners* [2013] UKFTT 433 (TC); *Wade Llewellyn v HMRC* [2013] UKFTT 323 (TC) and *Morgan v HMRC* [2013] UKFTT 181 (TC). It is worth looking closely at these decisions.

16.45 In *Bradley v Revenue & Customs Commissioners*, Mrs Bradley had at all relevant times been married to Mr Bradley. Until August 2007 they lived together at 118 Ashley Road, which was owned by them jointly. In addition Mrs Bradley owned 124 Exning Road and 68 Weston Way, both of which were normally let to tenants.

In the year or so leading up to August 2007 differences arose between Mr and Mrs Bradley and in August 2007 Mrs Bradley left Ashley Road. As the flat at

Weston Way was vacant she moved there. When the tenancy at Exning Road ended she moved from Weston Way to Exning Road.

At that stage her intentions were to separate permanently from her husband with a view to obtaining a divorce following a two-year separation.

Mrs Bradley moved into Exning Road in April 2008. She made certain improvements to make it more a 'home'. However, she had already, in March 2008, placed Exning Road on the market for sale. Although no offers were forthcoming the property was never taken off the market.

During the autumn of 2008 Mr and Mrs Bradley became reconciled and Mrs Bradley moved back to Ashley Road in November 2008. She then sold Exning Road in January 2009. The point at issue was whether the main residence relief applied to Exning Road because of Mrs Bradley's occupation between April and November 2008.

The tribunal decided that Mrs Bradley had not occupied Exning Road in such a way as to qualify for the relief. At the time she moved into Exning Road she had already placed it on the market and she never withdrew her instructions to the estate agents. She never intended to live permanently at Exning Road; it was always only ever going to be a temporary home, and therefore it was never her residence for the purposes of the relief.

It is noteworthy that the tribunal considered the fact that Mrs Bradley had been occupying Exning Road and no other dwelling during the period in question was not in itself sufficient to secure the relief.

Another interesting feature of the decision is that the tribunal accepted the separation of Mrs Bradley from her husband was likely at the time to have been permanent, so that she and her husband were separately entitled to the relief, on the basis of her intentions at the time, even though in the event the separation proved not to be permanent.

16.46 *In Moore v Revenue & Customs Commissioners*, Mr Moore purchased 110 Headlands, a two-bedroom house, on 5 November 2002. This and all the properties concerned were in Huntingdon. He let the property out from November 2002 until November 2006. When the last tenant left, Mr Moore's first marriage was in difficulties. Mr Moore moved out of the matrimonial home, 9 Church Street and into 110 Headlands, his first wife remaining at 9 Church Street.

Mr Moore took some furniture with him from 9 Church Street and bought further furniture for his own use. He also took all his clothes with him as he knew he would not return to 9 Church Street to live there.

Mr Moore had a lady friend, subsequently his second wife on their marriage in January 2011, who lived at 64 Orthwaite. Mr Moore said in evidence that it was around March or April 2007 that his relationship with this lady developed to the point that they decided they would live together.

After Mr Moore had moved to 110 Headlands, some correspondence continued to be sent to him at 9 Church Street and some correspondence to 64 Orthwaite. His evidence was that during the period in which he lived at 110 Headlands, he spent pretty much every night there. His financial circumstances were unsettled because of impending divorce proceedings and his evidence was that he lived at 110 Headlands until his financial circumstances became clearer. However, fairly soon after moving into 110 Headlands, he began to look for another property. At this point, the position is complicated by the fact that Mr Moore produced further evidence to the tribunal after an adjournment: he produced documentary evidence that his estate agents commenced marketing 110 Headlands in April 2007. Contracts were exchanged on the purchase and completion took place in August 2007.

The property of the lady who became Mr Moore's second wife was put on the market by her in May 2007 and sold with completion also taking place in August 2007. Mr Moore and his second wife jointly purchased a further property, 10 Church Close, the purchase being completed in July 2007. This was a four-bedroomed house and, unlike 110 Headlands, had the space needed to accommodate Mr Moore, his second wife and her two sons.

There were produced to the tribunal letters written by Mr Moore to HMRC in 2010 suggesting that during the relevant period he had been living in 110 Headlands only temporarily.

Mr Moore moved money between different building society accounts in February 2007 and the judge concluded that this was preparatory to a move which Mr Moore knew at that time he would be making.

Mr Moore showed that he had been charged council tax on 110 Headlands for the period from November 2006 to July 2007 with a discount appropriate to single occupancy.

The judge accepted that Mr Moore had been living in 110 Headlands between November 2006 and July 2007. The question was whether his occupation had had the necessary degree of permanence, continuity or expectation of continuity.

The judge rejected Mr Moore's argument that when he moved into 110 Headlands he simply did not know how he was placed financially and that he was expecting to live there until his financial affairs were sorted out, which could have taken a long time. He decided that the most important factor which determined Mr Moore's expectation at any time of what the continuity or permanence of his occupation of 110 Headlands would be was the state of his relationship with the lady who subsequently became Mrs Moore. Mr Moore conceded that it was around March or April 2007 that his relationship with Mrs J Moore developed to the point that they decided they would live together. However, the judge had difficulty in accepting he had no serious hope or expectation that he would be able to buy a house with Mrs J Moore before March 2007. In that case, matters had moved on with almost unbelievable speed after that. The judge accepted that in matters of the heart things can move with such rapidity but had to consider that on the balance of probabilities Mr Moore had had such a serious hope or expectation before March 2007. He concluded that Mr Moore had failed to discharge the burden of proof which was on him to satisfy the judge that for any significant period after he moved to 110 Headlands he did not have an expectation of being able to move from there and set up a home jointly with Mrs J Moore. The judge emphasised the fact that post had been delivered during the relevant period to other addresses and the fact that Mr Moore had been unable to show any bills other than council tax documentation recognising his address as 110 Headlands in the relevant period. He concluded that Mr Moore had never envisaged 110 Headlands as a long-term home and that his occupation lacked the necessary degree of permanence, continuity or expectation of continuity.

16.47 In *Wade Llewellyn v HMRC*, Mr Wade Llewellyn had lived with his partner at 10 Netley Terrace, Southsea for a number of years. However, Mr Llewellyn began to experience personal difficulties with his partner. He purchased another property, 10 Henderson Road, which was in a very poor state. He moved into the property with a chair, sleeping bag and kettle. There was no evidence that he had established his base at 10 Henderson Road and he returned to 10 Netley Terrace to pick up his post. The relationship later healed and after about ten months he moved back permanently to Netley Terrace, letting out Henderson Road. The tribunal decided that there was no evidence to show that his occupation of Henderson Road had amounted to residence there with some degree of permanence, some degree of continuity or some expectation of continuity so as to qualify for the relief.

16.48 In *Morgan v HMRC*, Mr Morgan purchased a property intending to live there with his fiancé. Unfortunately for Mr Morgan, shortly before he moved in, his fiancé broke off the engagement and the property could no longer fulfil his intended purpose of being the matrimonial home. Mr Morgan nevertheless moved into the property hoping for a reconciliation. It became clear that this was not going to happen and, in the event, he only lived in the property for some two and half months. The tribunal found the case to be extremely finely-balanced but decided that Mr Morgan had intended when he moved in to make the property his permanent residence and that his occupation of the property did qualify it as a residence for the purposes of the relief.

16.49 Another interesting decision of the First-tier Tax Tribunal came in 2015 in *Dutton-Forshaw v HMRC* [2015] UK FTT 0478. One interesting feature of this decision is that the taxpayer had again occupied the property concerned for quite a short time, about seven weeks, but the tribunal still found that he had been occupying it as a residence and that the exemption applied.

The facts of this case were rather complicated. During the period of 12 years considered by the tribunal, the taxpayer had occupied nine different properties and also sometimes stayed on his boat moored in Lymington Harbour. He had divided his time in rather a complicated way between Lymington and London. During the period in which he occupied the property in question, 32 Cornwall Gardens, SW7 in August to September 2006, he had had strong ties to London where his business was, but his ex-wife and infant daughter were living in Lymington. After this short period of occupation of 32 Cornwall Gardens he moved back to Lymington, where he had lived previously and where he owned another property. This was because of a concern that his former wife, whose new husband was living in Spain, might herself go to live in Spain and take with her the taxpayer's daughter. The taxpayer was very much against this idea partly because he did not want to be separated from his daughter and partly because of concerns about his former wife's health. He was faced with the possibility that the only way of preventing his daughter's move to Spain would be for him to move back to Lymington to look after her. Cornwall Gardens was then rented out.

The tribunal considered that the question of permanence or continuity should not be over-stated. It was simply one of the factors to be taken into account in weighing up whether the property in question was a 'residence'. The tribunal found that, when the taxpayer moved into Cornwall Gardens, he had hoped to live there on a continuous basis but was aware that circumstances might arise which would require him to move to live full-time in Lymington. In that sense he was in a similar position to that of Mr Morgan (see **16.48** above). Although the taxpayer's bank statements and other formal correspondence continued to be sent to an address in Lymington, it was not essential to change this as the taxpayer could continue to pick up his post from his property in Lymington when he visited Lymington to see his daughter. The tribunal attached more importance to the fact that he registered his car at Cornwall Gardens and obtained a parking permit from Kensington & Chelsea, in the knowledge that the parking permit system in Kensington & Chelsea was policed very carefully. The tribunal found that 'the nature, quality, length and circumstances' of the taxpayer's occupation of Cornwall Gardens did make that occupation qualify as residence for the purposes of the exemption and, since he had had no other residence during the relevant period, Cornwall Gardens had been his only residence during that seven-week period, so the private residence relief and lettings relief were both available.

This decision contains a careful analysis of the earlier case law and the tribunal must be right in its conclusion that the question of whether a person's occupation of a dwelling is mere occupation or residence is a more subtle question than the question whether there is an element of permanence or continuity in his occupation.

16.50 All the above decisions were heavily fact-dependent and some of them were complicated by some dispute over the facts. However, the following lessons may be drawn for the taxpayer who moves to a new home as a result of a relationship breakdown and wishes to demonstrate that his new home is a residence rather than merely somewhere he is occupying on a temporary basis:

- so far as possible, arrange for correspondence to be addressed to that property;
- notify that address as the taxpayer's permanent address for official purposes such as council tax and the electoral roll, notifying HMRC would be a good start;
- move furniture and possessions to the property and try to demonstrate that the taxpayer is not just 'camping out' there; do not just take your chair, sleeping bag and kettle;
- spend as much time in that home as possible, especially nights (to demonstrate that it is a residence);
- formulate no plans for moving elsewhere and, above all, do not place the property on the market – or remove it from the market if it has already been put on the market. It seems to have been this point above anything else which undermined the position of Mrs Bradley and, indeed, Mr Goodwin.

Although some of these cases concerned relatively short periods of time, no doubt they were considered worth fighting because of the extension of the main residence exemption to the last 18 months (formerly 36 months) of ownership and in some cases to periods of letting.

Position where the former matrimonial home is to be retained following separation of the couple for occupation by one spouse only and where the non-occupying spouse wishes to keep a stake in the property

Focus

This area has become extremely difficult following the changes to the IHT treatment of settled property made by the *FA 2006*.

An arrangement under which one spouse has the sole right to occupy the former matrimonial home during his life or until the happening of a specified event without being entitled outright to the sale proceeds is likely to constitute a settlement for both CGT and IHT purposes. The CGT position is likely to be favourable but such an arrangement may well lead to IHT charges.

One alternative is to transfer a property into the outright ownership of the occupying spouse but subject to a charge granted to the non-occupying spouse linked to the value of the house. However the tax treatment of a gain realised on the redemption of such a charge is unclear. The intuitive answer is that the gain will be subject to CGT because the gain will be capital in economic terms. However, there are arguments that the gain will be subject to income tax. On the other hand, if tax was paid only when the charge was redeemed there would be funds available to pay the tax.

16.51 Here one enters difficult territory.

One traditional approach is to seek a *Mesher* order. Under this type of order, one spouse will have the sole right to occupy the property (perhaps with the children of the marriage) during his life or until the happening of a specified event, such as all the children of the marriage attaining a specified age or completing their tertiary education, but on the death of the occupying spouse or on the happening of that event, the property is to be sold and the proceeds divided between the two spouses (or their estates).

In such a case, the view of HMRC is that the making of such an order results in the property becoming settled property for CGT (see CG65365).

16.52 There will thus be disposals by both spouses of their entire interests in the property. However, this will usually be of no consequence for CGT purposes. Almost invariably, the occupying spouse will qualify for the main residence exemption and, usually the non-occupying spouse will be protected by the 18-month rule.

Once the property has become settled property then, since usually the occupying spouse will occupy as his main residence, the main residence exemption will apply, subject to the making of a claim as required by *TCGA 1992, s 225*.

16.53 A *Mesher*-type order is thus attractive from the point of view of CGT, except in a case where there has been a long interval since the departure of the non-occupying spouse from the former matrimonial home with the result that he is exposed to CGT on the disposal he is deemed to make on the making of the order.

Once the house is settled property, the interests of the former spouses in the property will be interests in settled property and thus, in a normal situation, exempt from CGT under *TCGA 1992, s 76*.

A similar result follows if the property is expressly settled upon the occupying spouse for life or some lesser period.

16.54 In an interesting First-tier Tax Tribunal decision, *Wagstaff and Another v Revenue & Customs Commissioners* [2014] UKFTT 43 (TC), the tribunal took a broad view of what constitutes settled property for CGT purposes. In that case, a husband and wife had purchased a flat from the wife's mother. The sale was subject to a brief agreement which allowed the mother/mother-in-law to continue to occupy the flat for the remainder of her life or until remarriage, in return for a lump-sum payment. The tribunal concluded that, in acquiring the flat on terms that included the agreement, the husband and wife were assuming the role of trustees and did not become at that time absolutely entitled to the flat with the exclusive right to direct how it should be dealt with. Thus the flat had become settled property and the principal private residence exemption was available.

In other words, if a property becomes subject to a legally binding arrangement which has the characteristics of a trust, then it will become settled property for CGT (and, indeed, for other legal purposes) even if the arrangement is not formally labelled as a trust.

16.55 However, since *FA 2006*, such an arrangement has become unattractive from the point of view of IHT. Although the definition of settled property for CGT purposes is quite distinct from the definition of a settlement for IHT purposes (these definitions being contained in *TCGA 1992, s 68* and *IHTA 1984, s 43* respectively), if property is settled property for the purposes of CGT, it will usually be hard to deny that it is comprised in a settlement for the purposes of IHT. The occupying spouse will normally insist, for his own protection, upon an exclusive right to occupy the property. Any arrangement under which one person has the exclusive right to occupy a property rent free but without being the exclusive beneficial owner seems likely to constitute a settlement for IHT purposes, unless the occupation is under the terms of a lease other than for life.

For a broad view of what can constitute a settlement for IHT purposes see *Smith and Others v Revenue & Customs Commissioners* [2009] SpC 742, [2009] STC (SCD) 386 (building society account in joint names, arrangement that one joint holder would be solely entitled to interest during her life and the other joint holder to the capital on her death).

If the property has become comprised in a settlement for IHT purposes then it will be 'relevant property' and thus exposed to the ten-yearly and exit charges. These charges will, as the law currently stands, be at a maximum rate of 6%. They may, however, be irksome depending upon the value involved, particularly because, by definition, there will normally be no liquid funds comprised in the settlement from which the charges could be paid.

Planning strategies based upon securing multiple nil rate bands would be difficult to deploy in this scenario as they would involve fragmenting the ownership of the property between different settlements when the essence of the arrangement must be that one spouse is entitled to occupy the property as whole.

16.56 Furthermore, although the former matrimonial home will thus be relevant property, the capital interests of the former spouses in it will also be within their estates for IHT purposes as reversionary interests in settled property to which the settlors are entitled (*IHTA 1984, s 48(1)(b)*) (assuming both spouses previously had interests in the property).

One alternative approach would involve the transfer of the property into the outright beneficial ownership of the occupying spouse, the non-occupying spouse being given a deferred charge over the property redeemable only on the happening of the events under which a sale of the property would have been triggered under a *Mesher*-type order. The amount needed to redeem the charge would be linked to the value of the property at that time.

In the author's view, it is important to look at the arrangements, whether or not comprised in a court order, as a whole. The details of the arrangement might well be such as to make the property settled property for CGT, as in the *Wagstaff* case. If, for example, the property is supposed to be in the outright beneficial ownership of the occupying spouse but cannot be sold without the consent of the other spouse, it seems likely that it would be treated as settled property for both CGT and IHT purposes.

If the property is not settled property for CGT, then one enters especially different territory in the tax treatment of the deferred charge. It is reasonably clear, in the author's view, that the 'profit' realised by the non-occupying spouse on the redemption of the charge would be subject, one way or another, either to income tax or to CGT, subject to whatever of the usual reliefs and exemptions were available.

It is, however, harder to see precisely how the gain would be charged to tax, or how any tax would be calculated. The general view seems to be that the gain would be subject to CGT, which seems intuitively the right answer, but the position is far from clear.

One disquieting possibility is that the gain might be subject to income tax as interest. This is counter-intuitive: a gain linked to the growth in value of a capital asset would not normally be characterised as interest. However, the view of HMRC is that, where the trustees of the estate of a deceased person make loans linked to the retail prices index, or a similar index, to the surviving spouse, the uplift in value above the principal sum lent constitutes interest and is taxable as such (HMRC Trusts and Estates Newsletter April 2017). This is not a directly analogous situation (and, in any case, HMRC may well be wrong) but there are points of similarity and the views of HMRC should be borne in mind. In *Pike v Revenue & Customs Commissioners* [2014] All ER (D) 172 (Jun) the Court of Appeal upheld decisions of the First-tier Tribunal and the Upper Tribunal that an additional sum payable on redemption of loan stock was interest, even though it was not payable periodically and was not labelled as interest by the parties.

16.57 Depending upon the drafting of the charge, it might qualify as a 'deeply discounted security' within *ITTOIA 2005, Pt 4, Ch 8*. In that case there would be a charge to income tax on the difference between the redemption proceeds and the amount paid to acquire the security (*ITTOIA 2005, s 439*). However it might, depending upon the drafting, qualify as an 'excluded indexed security' under *ITTOIA 2005, s 433*, on the basis that its value was linked to the value of an asset within the scope of CGT and thus not be a 'deeply discounted security'. This presupposes that a financial instrument issued in a family as opposed to a commercial context can be a security for tax purposes, but this did not seem to trouble the tax tribunal in *Audley v Revenue & Customs Commissioners* [2011] UKFTT 219 (TC).

Another possibility is that *ITA 2007, Pt 9A* might apply on the basis that the charge was land and was acquired with the sole or main object of realising a gain from disposing of the land. *ITA 2007, s 517S* provides that, in that Part, the word 'land' includes *inter alia* any estate, interest or right in or over land.

It is known from *Page v Lowther* [1983] STC 799 that what is now *ITA 2007, Pt 9A* can apply to transactions not specifically designed to avoid tax.

(It would seem very hard to apply *ITA 2007, Pt 9A* to a beneficial interest in the former matrimonial home under a *Mesher*-type order, since this would normally be, in substance, retention of a pre-existing beneficial interest in the property.)

16.58 If the profit realised on redemption of the charge was not subject to income tax then it would, in the writer's view, be subject to CGT.

One of the difficulties would lie in establishing the acquisition cost of the charge since its market value on creation would clearly reflect the delay before it was due to be redeemed and the uncertainty as to when this would happen, as well as the possibility of an increase in value.

Thus, the choice seems to lie between incurring small but recurrent charges to IHT or what might be a more substantial income tax or CGT charge at a future date, but when there would be funds to pay the tax.

Legal and beneficial ownership

Focus

The beneficial ownership of an asset held in the joint names of spouses or in the sole name of a husband or wife may differ from the legal ownership. In most cases it is the beneficial rather than the legal ownership which is important for tax purposes.

The question of beneficial ownership will not usually be litigated in matrimonial proceedings because of the very wide powers the court has to adjust ownership. However it is important to establish the beneficial ownership of an asset for tax purposes.

The beneficial ownership may be difficult to establish except in a case where the parties have clearly recorded this when the asset was acquired. There is a great deal of case law arising from disputes between cohabitees over property held in joint names and an important decision of the Supreme Court seems to give the court more latitude in determining beneficial ownership of jointly held property than was previously the case.

The practice of HMRC in most circumstances is to accept an agreement between the parties as to beneficial ownership of a home held in the sole name of one of the spouses, or a recognition of an equitable interest by the court.

If both spouses have a beneficial interest in a property it is vital to establish whether they hold as beneficial joint tenants or tenants in common. In the former case the joint tenancy can be severed leading to ownership as tenants in common.

16.59 It is important to bear in mind that, for most tax purposes, it is the beneficial rather than the legal ownership of a property that counts. If a property is held in the sole name of one spouse, then the other spouse may well have a beneficial interest. It is also possible that, where a property is held in joint names, the interests of the spouses are not equal.

This is a complex area and only the barest outline of the issues can be given here.

In general the beneficial ownership of a property will not be an issue in matrimonial litigation because the court has such wide powers to order changes to the beneficial ownership. This, however, does not alter the importance of beneficial ownership in the tax context.

In some cases the intended beneficial ownership of a property will have been recorded at the time of its acquisition, for example by a declaration of trust. In such a case it may be unnecessary to look further.

In the absence of such a written record of the intended beneficial ownership it may be necessary to look at contributions to the purchase price and to consider the application of the equitable presumptions. If a husband funds the acquisition of a property in the name of his wife then there is a presumption of advancement: the husband is presumed to have intended a gift to his wife. If, however, a wife funds the acquisition of a property in the name of her husband then the husband is presumed to hold on resulting trust for her. These, however, are only presumptions which can be readily rebutted by a contrary intention. If a dispute about beneficial ownership comes to court then the court may be expected to look at whatever evidence is available of the express or implied intention of the parties.

The presumption of advancement will be abolished, prospectively, by *Equality Act 2010, s 199* when *Pt 15* of that Act comes into force.

The beneficial ownership of a property is more likely to be litigated when a relationship between unmarried cohabitees breaks down, in which case the court lacks the wide powers it has in the case of the breakdown of a marriage or civil partnership. In *Stack v Dowden* [2007] 2 AC 432 the House of Lords decided, in a case involving the breakdown of a relationship between an unmarried couple, that a conveyance into joint names, in the domestic consumer context, established a prima facie case of joint and equal beneficial interests unless and until the contrary was proved. The contrary could be proved by looking at all the relevant circumstances in order to discern the common intention of the parties. In the particular case, the House of Lords upheld the decision of the Court of Appeal that the beneficial ownership was unequal, while emphasising that this was an unusual conclusion based upon the particular facts.

16.60 The Supreme Court addressed the difficulties raised in ascertaining the beneficial ownership of a property following the breakdown of a relationship between cohabitees, where there was no express declaration of trust, in the case of *Jones v Kernott* [2012] 1 AC 776.

In that case the parties met in 1980 and formed a relationship. They did not marry. They had two children. In 1985 the parties bought a property in their joint names. In 1993 the parties separated. Thereafter, the claimant assumed sole responsibility for the outgoings on the property they had purchased in 1985. In 1995 the parties cashed in a joint life insurance policy and the proceeds were divided between them to enable the defendant to put down a deposit on a home of his own. The claimant had conceded that in 1993 when the couple separated there had been insufficient evidence to displace the presumption that their beneficial interests in the property they had bought in 1985 followed the legal title, so that they were then joint tenants at law and in equity. However, she contended that the purchase of the second property, along with other events since the separation, was evidence that their intentions with regard to the beneficial interest in the first property had changed. Thus, the point at issue was whether, although the couple had originally had equal beneficial interests in the first property, those beneficial interests had subsequently changed, without any express agreement or documentation.

The court held that the following principles were to be applied in cases where the family home was bought in the joint names of a cohabiting couple who were both responsible for a mortgage but without any express declaration of their beneficial interests. The starting point was that equity followed the law and that they were joint tenants both at law and in equity. However, that presumption could be displaced by showing (a) that the parties had had a different common intention at the time when they acquired the home, or (b) that they had later formed a common intention that their respective shares would change. Their common intention was to be deduced objectively from their conduct. In those cases where it was clear either (a) that the parties had not intended joint tenancy at the outset, or (b) that they had changed their original intention, but it was not possible to ascertain by direct evidence or inference what their actual intention had been as to the shares in which they would own the property, the answer was that each was entitled to that share which the court considered fair having regard to the whole course of dealing between them in relation to the property. The 'whole course of dealing' had to be given a broad meaning, enabling a similar range of factors to be taken into account as might be relevant to ascertaining the parties' actual intentions. Each case would turn on its own facts and, whilst financial contributions were relevant, there were many other factors which might enable the court to decide what shares were intended, in a case where it was possible to ascertain their intentions, or fair, in a case where it was not possible to infer what their actual intention had been.

This decision seems to give the courts more latitude in determining what the beneficial ownership of a property held in joint names is than had previously been the case, especially in circumstances where there is a reason to believe that the intentions of the parties as to beneficial ownership have changed since the original acquisition of the property. In such circumstances, there will be more scope for the court to decide what is fair. However, the court still cannot make a finding as to the beneficial ownership of a property contrary to whatever evidence exists showing what the parties actually intended. Thus, the discretion of the court when dealing with disputes as to the beneficial ownership of a property between cohabitees is still very much more limited than in the case of the breakdown of a marriage or civil partnership.

16.61 The practice of HMRC in the situation where it is claimed that a spouse or civil partner has an equitable interest in a home held in the sole name of the other spouse or civil partner is recorded in CG65310. This (sensible) practice is that if there is an agreement between the parties or recognition by the court of such an equitable interest, it should be accepted that the wife or civil partner had an equitable interest in the home from the outset. Moreover, their equitable interest of up to one half should be accepted without investigation, unless exceptionally there is obvious evidence to contradict it. Presumably, the same practice would apply in reverse in the case of a house held in the sole name of the wife where it is claimed that the husband has an equitable interest.

It should also be borne in mind that, under the *Law of Property Act 1925, s 53(1)(c)*, a disposition of an equitable interest subsisting at the time of the disposition must be in writing signed by the person disposing of the same, or by his agent thereunto lawfully authorised in writing or by will. However, this section does not affect the creation or operation of resulting, implied or constructive trusts. Thus, in general, once an equitable interest exists, it can only be disposed of in writing.

Where a property is owned by husband and wife beneficially then they will be either equitable joint tenants or equitable tenants in common. If they are equitable joint tenants then their interests will be co-extensive: neither can have a greater beneficial interest than the other. If, however, they are equitable tenants in common then they will hold separate shares in the equity which may be equal or may be of different sizes.

An equitable joint tenancy can always be 'severed' thus converting it into an equitable tenancy in common. If there is initially a declaration of a beneficial joint tenancy which is later severed then the parties will become tenants in common in equal shares, even if the initial contributions to the purchase price were unequal (see *Goodman v Gallant* [1986] 1 All ER 311).

Conventionally, an undivided share in a property is valued for tax purposes at a 10% discount to the corresponding percentage share of the overall value of the property, except where the inheritance tax related property rule applies. However, the extent of the discount and the allocation of value between spouses are now a matter for negotiation if one of the co-owners has occupation rights under the *Trusts of Land and Appointment of Trustees Act 1996*. See *IRC v Arkwright* [2004] STC 1323 and IHTM09737.

PARTICULAR SITUATIONS

Extracting funds from companies and settlements

Focus

Funds often need to be extracted from companies or trusts in the context of divorce and relationship breakdown but there are no special exemptions that apply in such a situation and extraction may well trigger tax liabilities.

16.62 Financial arrangements made in the context of relationship breakdown and divorce will often involve the extraction of funds from companies and trusts. There are no special exemptions which apply in this situation and all of the usual tax difficulties in extracting funds from companies and trusts will need to be considered.

If one spouse has much of his capital tied up in a trust or company structure, and if the other spouse is seeking to obtain a lump sum that can only be paid if funds are extracted from that structure, then the spouse seeking the lump sum can be expected to press for funds to be distributed to the other spouse first. In that case, any adverse tax consequences will fall upon that other spouse and the funds will reach the recipient spouse in a 'clean' form.

In *Ebsworth v Revenue & Customs Commissioners* [2009] UKFTT 199 (TC); [2009] SFT 602, the First-tier Tribunal (Tax Chamber) in allowing an appeal against a notice issued under *TA 1988, s 703* accepted that certain transactions in securities had been undertaken for the purpose of separating the personal and commercial interests of the taxpayer and his estranged wife and none of the main objects of the transactions had been the avoidance of tax.

If funds seem likely to reach the recipient spouse with tax liabilities attached to them then, clearly, those tax liabilities must be quantified in order to ascertain the adequacy of the capital payment.

This will be especially significant if funds are to be extracted from an offshore trust. A capital payment to a beneficiary out of an offshore trust may attract an income tax liability under *ITA 2007, s 731* or a CGT liability under *TCGA 1992, s 87*.

16.63 Permanent separation and decree absolute may have a beneficial effect upon the liability to income tax or CGT of a spouse who is a settlor in relation to a settlement.

Following permanent separation, the fact that the permanently separated non-settlor spouse (or civil partner) may benefit under the settlement will not in itself be sufficient to bring that settlement within the settlement rule (*ITTOIA 2005, s 625(4)(a)* and *(b)*).

The fact that a former spouse or civil partner of a settlor is a beneficiary or potential beneficiary of an overseas settlement will not, in itself, be sufficient to give that settlor an interest so as to bring the settlement within *TCGA, s 86* leading to the attribution of its gains to the settlor. Moreover, the fact that any other person related to the settlor only by a marriage or civil partnership which has ended may benefit will not in itself be sufficient to give the settlor such an interest (even if it would have done before the marriage or civil partnership ended). This applies to the whole of the tax year during which the marriage or civil partnership ends, ie during which decree absolute is obtained or the civil partnership is dissolved (*TCGA 1992, Sch 5, para 4(4)*)).

Close companies

> **Focus**
>
> On decree absolute a husband and wife cease to be 'associates' of each other for the purposes of the close company legislation and this may give rise to a range of consequences which should always be considered in such a situation.

16.64 On decree absolute, a husband and wife cease to be 'relatives' and thus 'associates' of each other for the purposes of the close company legislation (*CTA 2010, s 448*). This could, under certain circumstances mean that a company ceased to be close, because the rights and powers of one spouse could no longer be attributed to the other in determining whether that other spouse had control of the company for the purposes of the close company provisions now contained in *CTA 2010, Pt 10* (see *CTA 2010, ss 450* and *451*). An expense incurred by a close company in providing a benefit to a former spouse could not be treated as a distribution under *CTA 2010, s 1064* as a benefit provided to an associate of a participator (see *CTA 2010, s 1069*). However, a benefit provided to a former spouse of a participator in a close company could still, presumably, be treated as a benefit to that participator if it discharged a financial obligation imposed on that participator under the terms of a court order or agreement reached in the context of the breakdown of the marriage, thus limiting planning possibilities.

One consequence of divorce or the dissolution of a civil partnership is that relief under *ITA 2007, s 383* for interest on a loan taken out to buy an interest in a close company might be lost, either because the company ceased to be close or because the former spouses or civil partners no longer had a 'material interest' in the company as defined in *ITA 2007, s 394* since their interests would no longer be aggregated for the purposes of that definition.

Spouses with non-UK domicile

> **Focus**
>
> Great care must be taken if one or both spouses are remittance basis users, especially in view of the *FA 2008* changes. A spouse is still a 'relevant person' for the purpose of the remittance rules even if permanently separated.
>
> When either spouse has overseas connections it is important to consider the possibility of a charge to tax in another jurisdiction.

16.65 If one or both spouses have non-UK domiciles and are taxable on the remittance basis, then the greatest care should be taken that the financial arrangements made in the context of relationship breakdown and divorce do not involve any remittance of funds to the UK such as to give rise to a UK tax liability unless this is unavoidable.

This area has become more difficult following the changes to the remittance rules made by the *FA 2008*. Under the new rules, which are contained in *ITA 2007, Pt 14, Ch A1*, the overseas income or chargeable gains of an individual taxable on the remittance basis will be treated as remitted to the UK, *inter alia*, if the income or chargeable gains are brought to, or received or used in, the UK by or for the benefit of a 'relevant person'. A husband or wife or civil partner is a 'relevant person' for these purposes even if permanently separated (*ITA 2007, s 809M(2)(b)* and *(c)*). Where spouses are estranged and a spouse who is a remittance basis user makes payments to the other spouse out of funds potentially taxable on the remittance basis, the payer may be in a difficult position as he may become liable to tax as the result of a remittance wholly outside his control and of which he may have no knowledge. If circumstances allow, indemnities should be obtained in such a situation combined with undertakings to notify the paying spouse of any remittance.

Note that even after decree absolute a minor child of the dissolved marriage will still be a 'relevant person' in relation to both former spouses. A former spouse who is a remittance basis user may therefore be liable to tax on funds used in the UK by his or her former spouse for the benefit of a minor child even after decree absolute (*ITA 2007, s 809M (2)(d)*).

Where either spouse has overseas connections, the possibility of financial arrangements or asset transfers triggering overseas tax liabilities should always be borne in mind.

Although overseas taxes are outside the scope of this chapter, it is worth sounding a warning about the special difficulties that may arise if one spouse is a US taxpayer, especially where a spouse who is a US taxpayer is to transfer assets to a spouse who is not.

Liabilities to US tax may arise when there is no liability to UK tax. Since the USA imposes tax upon the basis of citizenship as well as a territorial basis, even a long-term UK resident may remain within the scope of US tax.

The assignment of life policies

Focus

It is common for life policies to be assigned in the context of divorce and relationship breakdown and tax liabilities may arise. There may be advantages in transferring the ownership of policies under the court order rather than by a separate agreement between the spouses.

16.66 The financial arrangements made in the context of relationship breakdown or divorce will often involve the assignment of life policies, or interests in life policies, between spouses.

If a non-qualifying life policy or, in certain limited circumstances, a qualifying life policy is assigned for money or money's worth then there may be a charge to higher rate tax in accordance with *ITTOIA 2005, Pt 4, Ch 9.*

For the purposes of that chapter, however, an assignment of rights under a policy or of a share in such rights is ignored if it is made between spouses or civil partners living together (*ITTOIA 2005, s 487*).

16.67 The Revenue previously took the view that the transfer by one spouse to the other of all or some of the rights under a policy as part of a divorce settlement was invariably for money or money's worth, thus potentially leading to a higher rate income tax charge. However, HMRC now accept that transferring ownership of the rights conferred by a life insurance policy under a court order is not for money or money's worth and no gain can arise because of it (see RI 267 (December 2003)). This change of policy followed the change of policy in relation to CGT hold-over relief.

It follows that, if it is desired to avoid the higher rate income tax charge that may arise on the assignment of a life policy or of an interest in a life policy for money or money's worth, and if such an assignment is intended to take place in the context of a divorce, it would be as well to make sure that the assignment took place in pursuance of a court order.

This HMRC change of practice may enable an immediate tax charge to be avoided but it is not all good news since the recipient spouse is, sooner or later, likely to be faced with an income tax charge when a 'chargeable event' arises in relation to the policy in question, if the policy is of a type subject to this charge.

CGT is seldom an issue on the assignment of a life policy, or of an interest in a life policy, made in the context of relationship breakdown or divorce. *TCGA*

1992, s 210 has the effect of taking life policies out of the scope of CGT unless they are 'secondhand policies'. The section provides that a gain accruing on a disposal of, or of an interest in, the rights conferred by any policy of insurance or contract for a deferred annuity is not a chargeable gain unless:

(a) (in the case of a disposal of the rights) the rights, or any interest in the rights; or

(b) (in the case of a disposal of an interest in the rights) the rights, the interest or any interest from which the interest directly or indirectly derives (in whole or in part)'

have or has at any time been acquired by any person for actual consideration. However actual consideration for a disposal which is made by one spouse or civil partner to the other or is an 'approved post-marriage disposal or an approved post-civil partnership disposal' is to be treated as not constituting actual consideration.

For these purposes a disposal is an approved post-marriage disposal or an approved post-civil partnership disposal if:

(a) it is made in consequence of the dissolution or annulment of a marriage or civil partnership by one person who was a party to the marriage or civil partnership to the other;

(b) it is made with the approval, agreement or authority of a court (or other person or body) having jurisdiction under the law of any country or territory or pursuant to an order of such a court (or other person or body); and

(c) the rights disposed of were, or the interests disposed of was, held by the person by whom the disposal is made immediately before the marriage or civil partnership was dissolved or annulled.

See *TCGA 1992, s 210(6)*.

The broad effect of this is that the transfer of a life policy between spouses in the context of divorce will not bring that policy within the scope of CGT, as a second-hand policy acquired for value, even if the assignment was for actual consideration.

FA 2013 imposed a general limit of £3,600 per annum upon the premiums that may be paid under a qualifying policy. All policies under which an individual is a beneficiary are aggregated for this purpose. This limit does not generally affect policies taken out before 6 April 2013. However, the assignment of a pre-6 April 2013 policy in the context of divorce or the dissolution of a civil partnership may bring such a policy within the new rules, either making it non-qualifying or making it a 'restricted relief qualifying policy'. Such a policy is subject to tax charges on the happening of a chargeable event to the extent that, broadly, premiums in excess of £3,600 per annum are paid after it becomes a restricted relief qualifying policy. If a qualifying policy issued on or after 21 March 2012 is assigned in this context and the assignment causes the assignee to breach the annual premium limit, taking his other qualifying policies into account, it will become non-qualifying. See *ICTA 1988, Sch 15, Pt A1, paras A1* and *A2, ITTOIA 2005, ss 463A–463D* and IPTM2081.

Transfers of assets in respect of which tax reliefs have previously been obtained

16.68 Great care needs to be taken if assets which are to be transferred in the context of divorce or relationship breakdown have previously attracted tax reliefs. See above for the issues where assets have been the subject of a potentially exempt transfer or are conditionally exempt from IHT. Another example is EIS relief, which may be clawed back if shares which have attracted the relief are transferred between spouses or civil partners no longer living together, in which case the relief for transfers between spouses or civil partners no longer applies (*ITA 2007, s 209(4)*). There is a similar rule for SEIS relief (*ITA 2007, s 257FA(4)*) and for social investment relief (*ITA 2007, s 257R(1)(d)*). However, holdover relief for gains reinvested in social enterprises is not clawed back on a disposal within marriage or civil partnership (*TCGA 1992, Sch 8B, para 6(1)(a)*).

If an individual subscribes for shares and then transfers them to another individual, at a time when transferor and transferee are living together as spouses or civil partners, the transferee is treated for the purposes of investors' relief as having subscribed for the shares (*TCGA 1992, s 169VU(3)*, inserted by *FA 2016, Sch 14*).

Note that share loss relief may be available if a person subscribes for shares in certain types of trading company and transfers those shares to his spouse or civil partner who subsequently realises a loss on their disposal (*ITA 2007, s 135(3)*). Thus an effect of postponing a transfer of shares between spouses until after decree absolute, in circumstances where the relief is not available to the transferor in relation to the transfer itself, may be to lose the share loss relief that might otherwise have been available on a subsequent disposal to a third party by way of a bargain at arm's length. The spouses or civil partners need not be living together at the date of the transfer.

Statutory residence test

16.69 For the purposes of the statutory residence tax, a person has a family tie for a tax year if he has a relevant relationship at any time in that tax year with another person who is resident in the UK for that year and a relevant relationship exists between two people at any time, inter alia, if they are husband and wife or civil partners and not separated, applying the usual income tax test of separation. Under certain circumstances a person would therefore lose a 'family tie' at the end of the tax year of permanent separation which, if he was on the cusp of satisfying the statutory residence test, might result in his ceasing to be UK resident for tax purposes. See *FA 2013, Sch 45, para 32.*

Example 16.12 – Effect of permanent separation on the statutory residence test

Mr M is an international businessman. He has homes and business interests in a number of different countries. He is married to Mrs M.

Mr M regularly spends more than 45 but not more than 90 days in the UK in the course of a tax year. He does not meet any of the automatic UK tests or any of the automatic overseas tests. Therefore his residence status depends upon the number of his ties.

Mrs M has many ties to the UK and is undoubtedly UK resident. Therefore, so long as Mr M is married to Mrs M and they are not permanently separated, he has a family UK tie. He owns a house in the UK which is available for him to live in, so he has an accommodation tie. He regularly spends at least 40 days in the course of a tax year working in the UK, so he has a work tie. However, he has no other UK ties. There are no children of the marriage, so he has no other family ties.

Since Mr M spends more than 45 but not more than 90 days in the UK in the course of a tax year, and since he has three UK ties and (suppose) he has been resident in the UK for a number of years, he is resident in the UK under the statutory residence test.

However, Mr and Mrs M separate permanently early in the 2017/18 tax year. Mrs M ceases to use the UK house which belongs to Mr M, but Mr M retains it and continues to use it. This means that Mr M will continue to be UK resident until the end of the 2017/18 tax year but (assuming nothing else changes) he will cease to be UK resident at the end of that tax year as he will have only two UK ties.

Pension sharing

> **Focus**
>
> A number of issues need to be considered if the court makes a pension sharing order. One of these is the ability of the spouse whose pension rights have been reduced to rebuild his entitlement by making additional contributions. This is a complex area in which care must be taken. The flexibility for members of defined contribution pension schemes aged 55 and over to withdraw funds introduced by the *Taxation of Pensions Act 2014* may provide an alternative to pension sharing, although such withdrawals may give rise to immediate and substantial income tax charges.

16.70 This is a complex subject and only the barest outline will be given here.

The *Welfare Reform and Pensions Act 1999, Pt III* gives the court power to make pension-sharing orders in connection with proceedings in England and Wales for divorce or nullity of marriage.

This power applies to most though not all forms of pension scheme. It applies not only to registered pension schemes, but also to unapproved schemes and to the earnings-related element of the state scheme. It does not apply to overseas schemes.

Where the court makes an order under this power the entitlement of one spouse under the scheme in question is reduced (a 'pension debit') and the other spouse is given rights of corresponding value (a 'pension credit').

The pension debits and credits must be expressed as a percentage of the cash-equivalent transfer value of the spouse whose rights are reduced.

A pension-sharing order can be made in respect of pensions that are in payment as well as in respect of rights to pension benefits which have not yet been drawn.

Where a pension-sharing order is made in respect of a funded scheme, the rights created for the spouse who acquires a pension credit may be given effect to either by creating rights for that spouse within the scheme or by making a transfer into a separate scheme.

Pension debits and credits will, respectively, reduce and increase the value of the pension rights of the spouses to be set against their lifetime allowances under *FA 2004*. It should, however, be borne in mind that the calculation of the value of pension rights for the purpose of this test is quite distinct from the calculation of the cash-equivalent transfer value.

It may therefore be possible for the spouse whose rights have suffered from the pension debit to make additional contributions, beyond those which would otherwise have been permissible under the *FA 2004*, to rebuild his entitlement. However, the greatest care must be taken in the event of a taxpayer with transitional rights under *FA 2004* wishing to make further contributions. Note in particular the warning set out at PTM029000. If the member has enhanced protection, fixed protection or fixed protection 2014, paying extra contributions may cause the member to lose their protection. See *FA 2004, Sch 36, para 13.*

If the rights of a scheme member with primary protection under *FA 2004* are reduced by a pension debit on or after 6 April 2006, then the value of that member's pension rights under primary pension protection will be recalculated and the member will be given a new personal lifetime allowance.

The reduced personal lifetime allowance applies to all benefit crystallisation events that take place after the member's rights have been reduced by the pension debit. The reduction occurs on the effective date of the pension-sharing order, not when the order is implemented.

Where the pension debit reduces a member's protected pension rights value below £1.5m, the member will lose primary protection and reverts to the standard lifetime allowance. See *FA 2004, Sch 36, para 11* and PTM092300.

If an individual has (at any time after 5 April 2006 but before the benefit crystallisation event) acquired rights under a registered pension scheme by reason of having become entitled to a pension credit, the pension credit derived from the same or another registered pension scheme, and the rights under that registered pension scheme which became subject to the corresponding pension debit consisted of or included rights to a post-commencement pension in payment, then that individual becomes entitled to a lifetime allowance enhancement factor with respect to that benefit crystallisation event. This reflects the fact that the pension credit will already have been tested against the lifetime allowance so it would be unreasonable to test it twice (see *FA 2004, s 220*). This section applies only if notice of intention to rely on it is given to HMRC in accordance with regulations made by HMRC. See PTM095200.

Finance Act 2011, Pt 4 made major changes to the taxation of pensions, including reductions to the annual allowance and lifetime allowance. Further restrictions have been introduced by the *FA 2013, FA 2014* and *FA 2016*. In each case there are transitional provisions.

Overview

16.71 In a rational world the breakdown of a relationship would not lead to any windfall tax-planning opportunities; nor would it lead to any windfall receipts for the Exchequer. The existing legislation does, broadly speaking, achieve the former objective, but not the latter! It is especially difficult to see why, as a matter of policy, transfers of assets ordered by the court on the occasion of marriage breakdown should lead to windfall CGT receipts for the Exchequer or why a settlement established for purely asset-protection reasons on the occasion of marriage breakdown should be exposed to the IHT ten yearly and exit charges.

Moreover, in a rational world, tax law would take a coherent and consistent approach to relationship breakdown, avoiding the many anomalies which exist at present. To single out one particular anomaly, it is extremely difficult to see why, under the *FA 2008* changes to the remittance basis of taxation, if a taxpayer who is a remittance-basis user separates from his spouse and cohabits with someone else then both his estranged spouse and the person with whom the taxpayer is cohabiting are 'relevant persons' in relation to the taxpayer. This seems to be having it both ways! Consequently, a remittance to the UK by either the estranged spouse or the cohabitee might impose a tax liability upon the taxpayer, even though a remittance by the estranged spouse might well be completely beyond the control or even the knowledge of the taxpayer.

Table 16.1 – Summary of some tax consequences of the different stages of the process of separation and divorce

Event	*Tax consequences*
Permanent separation of the couple	The transferor spouse's history of entitlement to the CGT main residence exemption will no longer pass to the transferee spouse on a disposal of, or of an interest in, the dwelling-house which is occupied as their only or main residence between the spouses. If one spouse is a settlor in relation to a settlement, then the fact that the other spouse may benefit under that settlement will no longer in itself be sufficient to bring that settlement within the settlement rule (*ITTOIA 2005, s 625(4)*). An assignment of rights under a policy of life insurance, a contract for a life annuity or a capital redemption policy between the spouses is no longer ignored for the purposes of *ITTOIA 2005, Pt 4, Ch 9* (which charges to tax certain gains arising on such assignments if made for money or money's worth).

	The presumption of equal beneficial entitlement to the income of jointly held property ceases to apply: *ITA 2007, s 836*. EIS relief and SEIS relief previously given may be clawed back on a subsequent transfer of company shares between the couple. Social investment relief will be lost on a subsequent transfer of the investment between the spouses. Shares subsequently transferred between the spouses cannot entitle the transferee spouse to investors' relief on their disposal by virtue of their having been subscribed for by the transferor spouse. If one spouse subsequently purchases a dwelling, any dwellings owned by the other are not taken into account in deciding whether the higher rates of SDLT for additional dwellings apply.
End of tax year of permanent separation	Transfers of assets between the spouses cease to qualify for 'no gain, no loss' treatment for CGT purposes. Entitlement to the married couple's allowance for income tax ceases, even if it was previously available. The spouses can no longer have family ties to the UK by virtue of their relationship.
Decree absolute	If one spouse is a settlor in relation to an overseas settlement the fact that the other spouse is a beneficiary or potential beneficiary of that settlement will no longer, in itself, be sufficient to bring that settlement within *TCGA 1992, s 86*. The couple cease to be 'connected persons' for tax purposes, unless they are so treated for some other reason. The inheritance tax spouse exemption ceases to apply to transfers of value between the couple and the inheritance tax related property rule ceases to apply to the valuation of their property. Unused IHT nil rate band can no longer be transferred between them.

The couple will no longer be 'relatives' and so 'associates' for the purposes of applying the close company legislation: *CTA 2010, s 448*.

The couple cease to be 'relevant persons' in relation to each other for the purposes of the extended remittance rules introduced by *FA 2008*. Any other persons who were previously 'relevant persons' in relation to one spouse solely through a connection with the other also cease to be 'relevant persons' in relation to that first spouse.

The possibility of share loss relief will no longer be preserved on transfers of certain shareholdings between the couple.

Chapter 17

Research and development relief

Anne Fairpo Barrister, CTA (Fellow), ATT

SIGNPOSTS

- **Qualifying R&D** – the project must seek an *advance* in overall knowledge in an area of science or technology by resolving an *uncertainty* that is not readily resolved by a competent professional in the field (see **17.1–17.7**).
- **Reliefs** – There are three forms of relief:
  - the small companies' relief – a super-deduction of 230% on qualifying R&D revenue expenditure (see **17.19**);
  - the repayable tax credit – available where the small companies' relief creates or increases a loss, which provides a repayment equivalent to up to 33.35% of qualifying expenditure in exchange for the surrender of the loss (see **17.54–17.58**); and
  - the R&D expenditure credit for large companies (see **17.21** *et seq*);

  The large companies' relief, which was a super-deduction of 130%, has been phased out and replaced with the R&D expenditure credit.
- **Qualifying expenditure** – relief is available on specific revenue expenditure relating to the R&D activities, including staff costs, costs of consumables (including power and fuel) and subcontracted work for SME relief (see **17.29–17.46**). Receipts of grants or subsidies may affect the amount of expenditure qualifying for relief (see **17.47**).
- **Points to note** – the definition of SME is double the usual thresholds, and there is no geographical restriction on where the expenditure is incurred (see **17.22–17.28**). Similarly, there is no geographical restriction on ownership: provided that the SME criteria are met, the R&D company can be a subsidiary Or permanent establishment of an overseas company. Where an SME does not meet the criteria for SME relief (except on a going concern basis), it can claim a deduction that is equivalent to the large company R&D relief instead of the SME relief.

- **Capital expenditure** – this does not qualify for the R&D reliefs, but there is an R&D capital allowance which provides 100% relief for capital expenditure on qualifying R&D, including expenditure on providing buildings and facilities for such R&D.

WHAT IS 'RESEARCH AND DEVELOPMENT'?

17.1

Focus

R&D (for tax purposes) is not the broad phrase often used in business – covering market research, commercial product development and other such activities that do not qualify as relevant R&D for tax purposes.

In the first instance, R&D for tax purposes has the same meaning that it does in generally accepted accounting practice (*CTA 2009, s 1138(2)*), excluding oil and gas exploration and appraisal. That definition is somewhat too wide for the government's purposes when giving the enhanced reliefs, and so the definition for the purposes of these reliefs is further constrained by the R&D Guidelines (see below).

HMRC now offer an advance clearance process to allow 'smaller' companies making their first R&D claim to apply to HMRC for assurance that their project involves qualifying R&D.

Accounting definition

17.2 The corporate intangibles tax rules outsource the definition of research and development by ensuring that an activity will broadly qualify as research and development for tax purposes if it would be treated as research and development under generally accepted accounting practice (GAAP) for companies in the UK under FRS 102.

Under UK accounting practice, R&D is defined in FRS 102 as:

- 'research', which is 'original and planned investigation undertaken with the prospect of gaining new scientific or technical knowledge and understanding'; and
- 'development', which is 'the application of research findings or other knowledge to a plan or design for the production of new or substantially improved materials, devices, products, processes, systems or services before the start of commercial production or use'.

The international accounting standards' definition of research and development (IAS 38) is the same as the UK GAAP definition:

- 'research' is original and planned investigation undertaken with the prospect of gaining new scientific or technical knowledge and understanding, and
- 'development' is the application of research findings or other knowledge to a plan or design for the production of new or substantially improved materials, devices, products, processes, systems or services prior to the commencement of commercial production or use.

R&D Guidelines

17.3 For tax purposes, the accounting practice definitions are modified by Guidelines (the 'Guidelines on the Meaning of Research and Development for Tax Purposes') which cover in some detail the meaning of 'research and development' with examples indicating what can and cannot qualify as R&D. HMRC have published their commentary and interpretation of the Guidelines in the Corporate and Intangibles Research and Development (CIRD) Manual, starting at CIRD81900.

The Guidelines take precedence over accounting definitions for tax purposes; activities that are R&D for accounting purposes may not, therefore, be regarded as R&D for tax purposes.

The principal distinctions between the tax definition and the UK accounting definition of R&D are in the area of development: research (as defined for accounting purposes) should qualify as R&D for tax purposes. However, development will only qualify as R&D for tax purposes where it concerns *appreciable* (rather than substantial) improvements to products, materials, and devices, etc. Development related to installation of new processes and systems will generally not be R&D for tax purposes, under the Guidelines, unless there is also a technological uncertainty that needs to be resolved, advancing technology, in the process.

The tax definition of R&D is also considerably narrower than the accounting definition – that has no requirement either that any technological uncertainties be resolved, or that any advance in science or technology is sought.

The focus of the Guidelines is on activity, rather than attempting to formulate a definition of 'research and development'. Instead, R&D is described as activities that take place within a qualifying project.

In the Autumn Statement 2015, the Government announced that it planned to update the Guidelines but, to date, no revision has been published.

Project

17.4 A project is defined by the Guidelines as a collection of '*activities* conducted to a method or plan in order to achieve an *advance* in *science or technology*' (para 19; italicised words defined below). The beginning and end of a project are not always straightforward to determine, as projects may arise out of other projects and activities.

For the project to qualify as R&D for tax purposes the Guidelines state that it must seek to achieve an advance in science or technology (para 3). For example, periodic updating or modification of a product will not be research and development unless that updating or modification involves an appreciable element of innovation.

The project must seek to achieve the advance through resolution of scientific or technological uncertainty (para 4). This point was emphasised in the case of *BE Studios v Smith & Williamson* [2006] STC 358, where the company claiming the relief could not show the necessary advance in scientific or technological knowledge. Merely being 'cutting edge' and 'innovative' was not sufficient; the R&D had to resolve some scientific or technological uncertainty.

Identifying when a project starts is important to ensure that R&D tax relief is maximised: the project begins when the work to resolve an uncertainty begins, once the uncertainty has been identified, and there is no qualifying R&D until that uncertainty has been identified.

The project will end either when the uncertainty has been resolved or the project is abandoned. Uncertainty will, generally, be considered to be resolved when the knowledge obtained from the project can be expressed in a tangible form – perhaps as a prototype, or as a published document.

A project does not need to succeed in order for its activities to qualify as R&D (para 10) – it is the intention of the project that is important, not the outcome. Arguably, a failure of the project can still be considered to be an advance in science or technology – by failing, the project has expanded the knowledge of what does not work.

Activities

17.5 R&D activities are those which directly contribute to attempting to resolve the underlying *uncertainty* (see below) which would lead to an advance in either science or technology (paras 4, 26). These include:

- scientific or technological design, testing and analysis undertaken to resolve the scientific or technological uncertainty;

- scientific or technological planning activities; and
- activities to create or adapt software, materials or equipment needed to resolve the scientific or technological uncertainty, provided that the software, material or equipment is created or adapted solely for use in R&D (para 27).

The Guidelines also include a list of activities which do not directly contribute to the resolution of scientific or technological uncertainty:

- commercial and financial activities;
- non-scientific or non-technological aspects of a new or appreciably improved process, material, device, product or service;
- production and distribution of goods and services;
- administration and other supporting services;
- general support services; and
- qualifying indirect activities (para 28).

Qualifying indirect activities

17.6 In addition to the activities which directly contribute to resolving the uncertainty, certain indirect activities are also regarded as R&D activities (para 5). The status of qualifying indirect activities has been in doubt from time to time, but HMRC have confirmed that qualifying indirect activities do constitute R&D for relief purposes (see, eg CIRD81300).

The Guidelines provide an exhaustive list (para 31) – if an activity is not on this list, it cannot be a qualifying indirect activity (para 32):

- indirect supporting activities: maintenance, security, administration and clerical activities, and finance and personnel activities, insofar as undertaken for R&D;
- ancillary activities essential to the undertaking of R&D (eg taking on and paying staff, leasing laboratories and maintaining research and development equipment including computers used for R&D purposes);
- training required to directly support an R&D project;
- research by students and researchers carried out at universities;
- research (including related data collection) to devise new scientific or technological testing, survey, or sampling methods, where this research is not R&D in its own right;

- feasibility studies to determine the strategic direction of a specific R&D activity; and
- scientific and technical information services for the purpose of R&D support (eg the preparation of the original report of R&D findings).

It should be noted that the range of qualifying expenditure (see **17.29** onwards) is not altered by the inclusion of qualifying indirect activities: for example, leasing laboratories is a qualifying indirect activity, but rental costs are not qualifying expenditure. In practice, it is likely that only staff time spent on dealing with a laboratory lease would qualify.

Science or technology

17.7 Science is defined in the Guidelines as 'the systematic study of the nature and behaviour of the physical and material universe' (para 15), and specifically excludes any study of the arts, humanities and social sciences. Included within science is work in physics, chemistry, engineering (civil, mechanical, etc).

Technology is defined as 'the practical application of scientific principles and knowledge' (para 17).

It is the particular project that is important; the overall business need not be specifically focused on science or technology.

Example 17.1 – Qualifying R&D project

A logistics trucking company develops a new low-cost refrigeration unit for its trucks, subcontracting much of the work. The project requires the resolution of an area of technological uncertainty with regard to the refrigeration material and the refrigeration material developed represents an advance in scientific knowledge.

The project will be qualifying R&D, although the principal business of the company – logistics, trucking goods around the country – does not initially appear likely to involve R&D.

Advance

17.8 Activities may be research and development if the project of which they form part is concerned with achieving an advance through (paras 6–12):

- the use of new scientific or technological principles in an existing area of investigation; or

- the adaptation of existing scientific or technological principles to a new area of investigation.

Advances in science or technology sought by a project must be advances in *overall* knowledge in that field, not simply in the company's knowledge. Overall knowledge is that which is publicly available or readily deducible by a competent professional in that field; companies are not expected to know their competitors' trade secrets, for example (paras 20–22).

Uncertainty

17.9 The Guidelines do not specifically state what is or is not uncertainty; instead, it is considered to be present when certain factors exist (paras 13–14):

- where the ability to achieve the scientific or technological objective is unknown;
- where the method of achieving that objective is not readily ascertainable;
- where a particular type of method of achieving an objective is not readily ascertainable – for example, producing a low-cost version, or improving reliability.

Uncertainty is more than simply a lack of knowledge; if the competent professional in the field could readily resolve the problem, then that problem is not considered to be uncertainty under the Guidelines.

Commercial development

17.10 Commercial development is excluded under the Guidelines; it may be difficult in some areas to decide whether development is commercial or not and the guidelines suggest that what is important is the motive behind the development; if it is being carried on to test the viability of the R&D then it may be classed as R&D itself.

For example, drug development may involve testing to ensure that the delivery mechanism (the tablet casing or bindings in which the active ingredients are bound to enable a patient to take the drug) does not interfere with the drug itself. The dyes used in a casing could potentially interfere with the drug, for example, so expenditure on establishing the colour of the final product may be qualifying R&D. Expenditure on establishing the best colour for a new type of mobile phone, however, is very unlikely to be qualifying R&D, even where the phone itself contains technology developed through qualifying R&D.

If the scientific or technology uncertainty which the R&D sought to overcome is no longer in question, the continued development is likely to be considered to be commercial; expenditure on commercial development will be dealt with under the general rules.

In some cases, R&D activities may overlap with non-R&D development – for example, where work continues on resolving the scientific or technological uncertainties underlying a project to develop a particular product whilst, at the same time, carrying out market research to support work on the aesthetic development of the product.

Careful analysis of the various activities involved in a project is necessary to be able to support a claim for R&D tax relief; there is no single methodology that can be applied to distinguish qualifying activities from non-qualifying activities, so each project must be considered on its facts.

Particular cases

Prototypes

17.11 The boundary between experimental development (which is R&D for tax purposes) and pre-production activity (which is not) can be extremely grey in respect of prototypes in engineering work. The design, construction and testing of a prototype will generally involve qualifying R&D expenditure.

There can be more than one prototype before the R&D activities of a project are completed; either the initial prototype continues to be modified, or the project generates a series of prototypes. A series of prototypes will be produced where testing renders the previous prototype unusable, or where multiple models are required for field-testing. For example, electronic equipment used in racing cars is likely to need to be tested in races as part of the R&D process – the R&D will not be complete until it has been established that the electronics can perform in the harsh environment of a race; where the cars complete in a race series open to a variety of cars, the equipment will need to be tested in all the cars to ensure that it can operate not only in the conditions but also in each of the types of cars. Each of the prototypes will, at this stage, still be within qualifying R&D if the resolution of uncertainties is being tested (eg to check whether a new type of anti-vibration system functions). It is generally not cost-effective to attempt to reproduce this type of race environment simply for testing purposes!

Once testing is satisfactorily completed and the uncertainty has been resolved, further work will be classed as pre-production and subsequent prototypes will be commercial development, which will not qualify for the enhanced relief.

17.12 This has, historically, been an area of contention between taxpayers and HMRC. Paragraph 28(c) of the Guidelines explicitly excludes production activity from the definition of R&D.

The area of contention is around 'first in class' products and other one-off items that may be produced as prototypes but, if they work, would then be sold to a customer. It is not necessarily economically appropriate to scrap the prototype and rebuild it for sale, particularly where it is a bespoke item and there is no intention to produce any further quantities for sale. HMRC accepted that if the sole aim of producing the prototype was for use in R&D but it was later sold to a customer, this would not change the nature of the activity in constructing the prototype. The particular problem was with projects where the intention was, on creation of a successful version, to sell that version to the customer – ie where the intention to sell arose later, after the R&D.

This did not entirely accord with other areas of the Guidelines, as para 34 states that '... an R&D project ends ... when a prototype or pilot plant with all the functional characteristics of the final process, material, device, product or service is produced.' That is, the R&D ends after the prototype/pilot has been produced and not before.

17.13 After much discussion, HMRC have produced a revision to their Manual section CIRD81350 which acknowledges that, if the main aim of creating a prototype is experimentation to resolve an uncertainty, part the costs of producing the prototype can still be part of R&D, even where it is successful and is intended to be sold to a customer in the event of success.

The guidance indicates that HMRC do now accept that 'where production trials are necessary to test whether the scientific or technical advance has been made, the whole or part of the expenditure on such a trial may be on R&D, depending on the degree of uncertainty existing within the process at a particular time'.

As a result, HMRC will be looking for information as to when in the production trial the uncertainty was resolved, for example, so some consideration of the point will need to be made and recorded. This does extend to bespoke products (or 'first in class' products, as HMRC refer to them), where part of the 'costs ... would qualify for R&D relief, even though the total build costs would not'. Again, the company will need to determine where in the process the uncertainty was resolved.

In *FA 2015*, the qualifying expenditure which can be included in an R&D relief claim in respect of such prototypes was amended so that consumables costs relating to a prototype which is sold cannot be included in the claim (*FA 2015, s 28* inserting *CTA 2009, ss 1126A* and *1126B*).

Computer software

17.14 Software development can be either the object of R&D or to produce a tool for use in a research and development project – a modelling system, for example, or data-handling software (CIRD81960).

Qualifying software research and development includes theoretical computer science, the development of new operating systems and new languages, significant technical advances in algorithms, and artificial intelligence investigation.

However, routine software activities are not research and development. These include:

- supporting existing systems;
- converting or translating programming languages;
- de-bugging systems;
- adapting existing software; and
- producing user documentation.

Where software is used to achieve research and development, expenditure on the software element of the project may still qualify for enhanced R&D relief even though there is no technical advance to the software itself involved. The types of project that are likely to qualify would include:

- drug design; and
- aerospace innovation

as both of these fields make extensive use of computer modelling. This will require expenditure on creating computer software to do the modelling and will be part of the qualifying R&D expenditure on the pharmaceutical or aerospace project, even where creating the software alone would not be qualifying R&D.

Using software simply to simulate aerodynamics or fluid dynamics, though, will probably not qualify as R&D expenditure. However, developing new software to provide such 'in silico' simulation might qualify (provided that the necessary advance in scientific or technological knowledge could be shown).

Capitalised software

17.15 Where internally developed software is classed as a tangible asset in the accounts – because it is software included within hardware costs as being 'directly attributable to bringing a computer system or other computer-operated machinery into working condition for its intended use within the business' – then the included software would not be within the intangibles regime and so the expenditure would not be able to be excluded from the regime to fall within the R&D reliefs. The overall capital expenditure on the system as a whole, including the software, would generally be eligible for plant and machinery capital allowances.

Other internal software development (not so linked to hardware) should be within UK GAAP as the result should be an intangible fixed asset.

Expenditure on an intangible fixed asset that is qualifying R&D expenditure is excluded from the intangible fixed asset rules, even where the expenditure has been capitalised (*CTA 2009, s 814*), so that it can come within other tax rules on R&D, including the R&D reliefs.

Capitalisation of R&D under UK GAAP is an option even where the specific conditions are met, rather than a requirement, so it should be possible to ensure that the expenditure is not capitalised in the first place.

Pharmaceuticals

17.16 HMRC have issued additional guidance on the availability of R&D relief for activities in pharmaceutical R&D (CIRD81920).

In practice, HMRC will generally accept that research activities of discovery, pre-clinical development and Phase I to III clinical trials (required for licensing of medicines by a regulator) will usually be concerned with the resolution of scientific and technological uncertainty.

Phase IV clinical trials are carried out post-licensing and are focused on longer term safety and efficacy; the scientific advance has generally been established by the time the licence for the medicine is granted and so HMRC will not expect companies to claim R&D relief for these trials. That said, they accept that in unusual circumstances qualifying R&D may be done in Phase IV trials.

This does not override the general principles of what activities qualify as R&D – brand name research and development work, for example, will not qualify.

Generics

17.17 Once a patent on a pharmaceutical drug has expired, other companies can produce generic versions of that drug. To get a licence for a generic drug, the company generally only needs to demonstrate that their product is bio-equivalent and has equal clinical safety to the previously patented product. Neither of these demonstrations is likely to involve the resolution of any scientific or technological uncertainty and so a generic drug manufacturer is unlikely to have qualifying R&D activities.

RESEARCH AND DEVELOPMENT TAX RELIEF

17.18 There are, in effect, two reliefs – the small- and medium-sized companies' relief and the R&D expenditure credit – and a repayment credit. Revenue expenditure of a small and medium-sized enterprise (SME) that does not qualify for the SME relief may, in some circumstances, be eligible for the R&D expenditure credit.

The R&D reliefs are only available for companies, not partnerships, individuals or other non-corporate entities.

SME relief

17.19 The SME R&D relief provides an enhanced deduction for tax purposes of an additional 130% (125% for the period 1 April 2012–31 March 2015, 100% for the period 1 April 2011–31 March 2012, 75% for the period 1 August 2008 to 31 March 2011, and 50% prior to 1 August 2008) of qualifying revenue expenditure on qualifying R&D, in addition to the 100% deduction already available for revenue expenditure under the normal tax rules (*CTA 2009, s 1004(8)*, as amended by *FA 2012*).

Example 17.2 – R&D tax deduction – SME

SMECo carries out qualifying R&D, and its qualifying costs for the accounting period starting on 1 April 2017 are £150,000. It will be able to claim a total deduction in respect of R&D of £345,000:

Expenditure	£150,000
R&D tax relief @ 130%	£195,000
Total deduction	£345,000

Large company relief

17.20 The large company R&D relief provided an enhanced deduction of 30% in addition to the standard 100% deduction for revenue expenditure. This relief has been abolished and replaced by the R&D expenditure credit for expenditure incurred on or after 1 April 2016.

R&D expenditure credit

17.21 The R&D expenditure credit was introduced in *FA 2013* as a replacement for the large company relief. It is the only relief available for large companies for expenditure incurred on or after 1 April 2016; between 2013 and 2016, a company could elect to use the R&D expenditure credit instead of the large company relief. The R&D expenditure credit is also available for SMEs in respect of certain expenditure for which the SME relief is not available.

The R&D expenditure credit is calculated in a very different way to the SME relief and large company relief; instead of increasing deductible expenditure, a direct credit of 11% (10% prior to 1 April 2015) of qualifying expenditure is brought into account and then deducted from tax (repayable for loss-making companies).

SMALL- AND MEDIUM-SIZED COMPANIES' RELIEF

What is 'small and medium-sized' (CTA 2009, ss 1119–1120)

17.22

> **Focus**
>
> Before 1 August 2008 the standard EU definition of an SME applied to establish the companies entitled to the SME. From that date, the standard EU thresholds were doubled (for R&D relief purposes only) so that the small- and medium-sized companies' relief is now available to 'larger SMEs' that have:
>
> - fewer than 500 employees in a year and either, or both, of:
> - an annual turnover not exceeding €100m; and
> - a period-end balance sheet total not exceeding €86m.
>
> The company must also be independent, and must be a going concern: these points are considered below.

Independence

17.23 In all cases, to be an SME or larger SME, the company must be independent: that is, less than 25% of its capital or voting rights can be owned by one or more companies that are not SMEs (unless such companies are venture capital companies or institutional investors and public investment corporations, provided that they do not have actual control of the SME – CIRD91700).

The calculation of these limits may include the employees, turnover and balance sheet total of other enterprises, including linked enterprises and partner enterprises, if the company in question is not a stand-alone company. Note that, although only *companies* may claim R&D tax relief, the tests take into account *enterprises*, which may not be corporate entities – an enterprise is any entity carrying on an economic activity, regardless of its legal form, and so can include even an individual.

Linked enterprises

17.24 Linked enterprises are those in which one enterprise can exercise control, directly or indirectly, over the affairs of the other(s) (CIRD91600) by:

- having more than 50% of the shareholders' or members' voting rights in another enterprise, either directly or as a result of provisions in a shareholder agreement;
- having the right to appoint or remove a majority of the members of the administrative, management or supervisory body of that other enterprise;
- having the right to exercise a dominant influence over another enterprise as a result of the terms of a contract entered into with that enterprise or as a result of a provision in its memorandum or articles of association.

Enterprises can also be linked if a relationship of the sort listed above exists through an individual or group of individuals acting together, but only if the enterprises are engaged (wholly or partly) in the same markets or adjacent markets in a vertical supply chain.

The limits are applied to the aggregate of the figures for *all* the enterprises with which the company under consideration is linked, together with those of the company itself.

Partner enterprises

17.25 Partner enterprises are those in which one enterprise does not control another but where, either alone or in connection with linked enterprises, one enterprise owns 25% or more of the share capital or voting rights of the enterprise under consideration. In this case, the limits are applied to the aggregate of the figures of the enterprise under consideration together with the appropriate percentage of the figures of the partner enterprises. However, note that venture capital companies, business angels, universities and institutional investors (see CIRD91700 for full list) may own more than 25% (but not more than 50%) of the company without being considered to be a partner enterprise of the company.

Subsidiaries

17.26 The independence requirement does not mean that the SME cannot be part of a group; provided that the group as a whole meets the SME criteria, a subsidiary (including a subsidiary of an overseas company) can be within the scope of R&D relief.

Change in size

17.27 The EU definition of an SME provides a 'year of grace' for companies which exceed the SME thresholds. Such a company will not change status from SME to large unless it exceeds the thresholds for two years in a row, in which case it will become large with effect from the second year (CIRD92000).

This 'year of grace' only applies in respect of the staff, turnover and assets thresholds: if a company ceases to be an SME because it has been taken over by another enterprise, the year of grace will not apply and the company will be treated as large from the beginning of the accounting period in which it was taken over.

Going concern

17.28 The accounts of an SME claiming the SME relief or the repayment credit must be prepared on a going concern basis (*CTA 2009, ss 1046* and *1057*), but this must not be only because it is expected that R&D relief will be received. There must be other reasons for enabling the accounts to be prepared on a going concern basis (*CTA 2009, s 1106*).

A company will not be a going concern at any time if it is in administration or liquidation (*CTA 2009, s 1046*; after amendment by *FA 2012, Sch 3, para 10*). This amendment was introduced because a company's going concern status is determined by the most recent set of accounts; these may have been prepared several months ago, and the company's financial position could have changed substantially in the meantime.

Note that where a company fails to qualify for the SME relief on a going concern basis, it will not be able to claim *any* R&D relief, either under the SME relief or the R&D expenditure credit. Where a company fails to qualify for the SME relief for other reasons, it can usually claim the RDEC instead (see **17.46** below). This option is not available to companies that fail on a going concern basis.

Qualifying expenditure

17.29

> **Focus**
>
> The expenditure that qualifies for relief (*CTA 2009, ss 1052–1053*) must be:
>
> - revenue expenditure;
> - relevant to the trade of the SME;
> - relating to:
>   - the cost of qualifying staff involved;
>   - software and consumable items used;
>   - qualifying subcontractor costs;
>   - costs of externally provided workers (for expenditure incurred after 26 September 2003); and
>   - payments to the subjects of clinical trials (for expenditure incurred after 1 August 2008).
>
> All these are considered in more detail below.
>
> Note that the expenditure does not need to be incurred in the UK; this is one of the more generous aspects of the UK R&D tax relief – many other countries restrict relief to expenditure incurred in that country alone.

Minimum expenditure (historic)

17.30 For accounting periods beginning before 1 April 2012, there was a requirement that the company spend a minimum of £10,000 on R&D before being able to claim the relief (*CTA 2009, s 1050* before amendment by *FA 2012, Sch 3, para 3*).

Maximum relief

17.31 There is an overall cap on the amount of relief that can be obtained by an SME under the SME relief (and, prior to 1 April 2012, vaccine research relief) in aggregate on any one project, of €7.5m (*CTA 2009, s 1113*). This cap was introduced in *FA 2008*, following agreement with the EU in order to get approval for the changes in rates and the size of qualifying SMEs for the SME relief, which is an EU State Aid.

A formula is used to test whether the cap has been exceeded in an accounting period. Where an SME exceeds the cap, it can claim the R&D expenditure credit on qualifying expenditure in excess of the cap amount.

Revenue expenditure

17.32 For the expenditure to be eligible for R&D relief, it must be allowable as a deduction in calculating in the profits of the trade (*CTA 2009, s 1044*).

UK GAAP – accounting treatment of research costs

17.33 FRS102 generally requires that pure and applied research costs should generally be deducted immediately in the profit and loss account as they are incurred.

Where the outcome of a project can be identified and technical and commercial feasibility established, then it may be possible to capitalise the expenditure on creating the intellectual property rather than writing the expenditure off immediately through the profit and loss account – in practice this will not happen often during the research phase of a project, given the inherent uncertainties over intellectual property research.

UK GAAP – accounting treatment of development costs

17.34 Development activities are considered to be easier to identify for accounting purposes, and easier to match to actual or potential future revenues. However, even at a development stage there can often still be areas of uncertainty over features of a project and so, given the accounting concept of prudence, development costs will still be deducted in the profit and loss account if the future economic benefit is not sufficiently certain.

Note, however, that only development which still relates to scientific or technical uncertainties will be qualifying R&D for tax purposes (see above).

International accounting standards

17.35 The basic principle in IAS 38 is that all research costs should be expensed (IAS 38.54), and that development costs can be capitalised only once the technical and commercial feasibility of the asset for sale or use has been confirmed (IAS 38.57).

Where it is not clear whether the research phase has completed and the development phase has begun, IAS 38 requires expenditure to be expensed and not attributed to an asset; HMRC will not be so forgiving when it comes to

R&D tax relief and so the fact that R&D expenditure is expensed under IAS 38 will not automatically mean that the expenditure (assuming it is a qualifying project) will qualify for relief.

An R&D project acquired in a business combination is treated as an asset under IAS, even where part of the cost of the project is research. Any subsequent expenditure on that project is accounted for as any other research and development cost, so subsequent research expenditure will usually be expensed (IAS 38.34).

Capitalised expenditure

17.36 Where development expenditure has been capitalised in the accounts, then it may still be possible to obtain R&D relief for that expenditure. This will usually be where the company has adopted international accounting standards, as IAS38 requires the capitalisation of development costs, but there is still scientific or technological uncertainty so that the activities remain within the scope of qualifying expenditure for R&D relief purposes. This will be unusual; as noted above, IAS 38 requires capitalisation where the technical feasibility of the asset has been confirmed, which would usually be after the point at which scientific or technological uncertainties had been resolved.

In this case, R&D tax reliefs and vaccine research tax relief (for large companies only from 1 April 2012 to 1 April 2017) are available for qualifying revenue expenditure on research which is added to the capitalised costs of an intangible asset in the accounts in accordance with UK GAAP or IAS (*FA 2004, s 53*; CIRD98500).

Relevant to the trade (*CTA 2009, s 1042*)

17.37 Research and development expenditure is 'relevant' expenditure in respect of a company if it relates to a trade carried on by the company, including R&D that could lead to an extension of that trade. Broadly, most R&D expenditure incurred by a company is likely to be relevant expenditure as it is unusual for a company to spend money on pure 'blue sky' R&D with no thought as to how that R&D might benefit the trade. An extension of the trade can be the possibility of licensing out any resulting intellectual property – it does not have to be used by the company in producing goods and services directly.

Where the trade of the company is the carrying out of R&D (eg where a single group company provides all R&D functions for the group, creating new intellectual property for the group to exploit), then the R&D carried out is still considered to be relevant to that trade.

Finally, relevant R&D expenditure will also include expenditure on medical research that is particularly relevant to the welfare of workers employed in the trade of the company. This will generally only apply to trades where there are specific risks to workers (eg in the mining sector).

Qualifying staff

17.38 Qualifying staff are employees (generally, someone with whom the company claiming the relief has an employment contract – CIRD83000) and directors who are directly and actively involved in the R&D – researchers, managers, etc, who organise and carry out or support the R&D activity (*CTA 2009, s 1124*).

Any support function must still be directly and actively involved to qualify – for example, directing technical activity will qualify for the relief, but long-term strategic planning and contract administration will not qualify, and neither will equipment maintenance. It is the actual activity that is important and not the title of the individual. The staff costs must be apportioned for staff members who are not involved full time with the R&D activity.

Example 17.3 – Qualifying staff costs

RD Co has three employees, including the managing director. Total staff costs are £110,000 per annum. One employee, a researcher, is paid £30,000 per annum and spends all his time on R&D activities. The managing director is paid £60,000 per annum and spends 50% of her time on R&D activities, 35% of her time maintaining investor relationships and seeking new funding, and 15% of her time on other general administration activities. The third employee, paid £20,000 per annum, supports both of the others and spends around 75% of his time on R&D activities.

The qualifying staff costs are therefore:

Researcher: 100% of £30,000	£30,000
MD: 50% of £60,000	£30,000
Assistant: 75% of £20,000	£15,000
Total qualifying staff costs	£75,000

The allowable staff costs (*CTA 2009, s 1123*) include:

- emoluments paid by the company, including all salaries, wages, bonuses and other perquisites, but not benefits in kind;

- secondary Class 1 NICs paid by the company; and
- pension fund contributions paid by the company.

The exclusion of benefits in kind can be an issue for small technology companies that reward staff with share options, to participate in the growth in the company, and can only afford to pay small salaries – only the salaries will count as R&D expenditure. The share options are benefits in kind and so are not qualifying staff costs.

Note that *CTA 2009, s 1123* also includes expenses paid to staff as qualifying costs; HMRC has stated that, to qualify for R&D relief, such expenses must be attributable to relevant R&D and that the expense must be incurred for the employee to perform the requirements of their job. This interpretation appears to be rather more restrictive than the wording of the legislation, and HMRC's interpretation remains potentially subject to challenge.

Where staff are seconded, intra-group and salary costs incurred by another group company are recharged to the R&D company. These are not qualifying staff costs for the purposes of R&D relief, although they may qualify as costs of externally provided workers (see below).

Software and consumable or transformable material

17.39 Consumable items include supplies directly used up in the R&D activity – essentially materials and equipment, but only where the equipment has a short useful life. Consumable items also include utilities such as power, water and fuel (*CTA 2009, ss 1125–1126*).

Spending on consumables that are only indirectly used for the R&D activity – generally, administration consumables, such as paper – will not qualify for the relief.

HMRC will accept claims for relief on expenditure on materials (such as chemicals) that are recycled provided that the materials are actually used in the first place and (in practice, although not stated in guidance) will generally accept expenditure on catalyst materials which, by their nature, are not transformed or used up (CIRD82400).

If the software, materials or utilities are only partly used for R&D, an apportionment needs to be made – any practical apportionment can be made, such as by floor area or staff headcount, between R&D activity utilisation and non-R&D activity utilisation. Where an R&D function makes heavy use of utilities, it may be cost-effective to have separate metering for the R&D areas to evidence that utilisation.

Example 17.4 – Allowable costs

TechCo has electricity bills of £250,000 per annum for the building in which its offices and labs are based. The labs make up 80% of the area of the building and so TechCo makes an R&D claim for 80% of £250,000 = £200,000 in respect of the power costs.

As noted above, TechCo should consider whether it would be better to have separate meters for the labs are and the administration area if the R&D activity is an intensive user of power, as apportionment by area may not adequately reflect the R&D element of the power costs.

TechCo has also spent £100,000 on a software licence – the software is used by one administration employee and 12 R&D researchers. In this case, one-thirteenth of the licence cost will not qualify, but the balance of £92,308 will qualify for R&D relief.

Capital equipment – R&D allowances only

17.40 Equipment that is expected to have an enduring benefit to the company is capital expenditure and does not qualify for the R&D tax relief – but it should qualify for the 100% R&D allowance.

Subcontracted R&D

17.41 Expenditure on subcontracted qualifying R&D will qualify for R&D relief for an SME, and the subcontractor to an SME cannot claim R&D relief on its costs (*CTA 2009, ss 1065–1068*).

The subcontractor does not have to be a small or medium-sized company for the relief to be available to the claimant and it need not be in the UK. The work done by a subcontractor need not, on its own, qualify for R&D relief provided that it is part of a larger project of the SME that will qualify.

For example, some testing procedures are better outsourced than done in house by a claimant because it would not be cost-effective for the claimant company to purchase the equipment needed for testing. The testing procedure alone would not be considered to be R&D because it does not involve any innovation. However, where it is a part of an activity that does meet the definition of R&D, the costs of the subcontract will be part of the qualifying R&D costs for relief.

Where the company and the subcontractor are connected persons (as defined in *CTA 2010, s 1122*), the company can claim relief on the lower of:

- the costs which the subcontractor includes in his year-end accounts in respect of staff and consumables costs relating to the work done;
- the amount of the company's payment to the subcontractor (*CTA 2009, s 1134*).

If the company and the subcontractor are not connected, they may still elect to use the connected persons treatment (*CTA 2009, s 1135*). The election needs to be made within two years of the end of the accounting period of the company in which the subcontract is entered into. As the election needs to be joint, the company should ensure that any contract relating to the subcontract work requires the subcontractor to sign such an election when requested to do so.

This election also, in effect, requires the subcontractor to disclose to the R&D company information that would indicate the profit being made on the contract: the subcontractor may be reluctant to provide this information and so may not agree to enter into the election.

If the joint election is not made, the company can claim relief on 65% of the payment made to the subcontractor (*CTA 2009, s 1136*).

Example 17.5 – Subcontracted R&D

RD Co subcontracts a specialist testing routine to Sub Co for a payment of £100,000. The two companies are not connected.

Sub Co's accounts show qualifying costs in respect of that subcontracted test of £75,000; the rest of the charge to RD Co reflects the use of equipment, which is not a qualifying cost, and a profit margin.

If no election is made, RD Co can claim 65% of the payment made, ie £65,000.

If RD Co and Sub Co make the election, RD Co can claim the lower of its actual payment (£100,000) and Sub Co's costs (£75,000). RD Co would be better making the election, if it can persuade SubCo to do so, as this will enable it to claim £75,000 rather than being restricted to the 65% (£65,000) otherwise available.

Externally provided workers

17.42 Relief is available for workers who are not employed by the company carrying out the SME but, instead, are employed by an intermediary company to provide services to the SME (*CTA 2009, s 1127*). A staff provider may also include another company within the same group as the company carrying out R&D.

There are strict requirements that must be met for the expenditure to be eligible (*CTA 2009, s 1128*), requiring that the worker:

- must be an individual;
- cannot be a director or employee of the R&D company (confirmed in *Gripple* [2010] STC 2283);
- must provide services through a staff provider;
- must be subject to the control of the R&D company; and
- must personally provide services to the R&D company through a contract between the worker and *someone other than the R&D company* (amendment introduced in *FA 2012, Sch 3, paras 33–37*. Prior to 1 April 2012, the contract had to be directly with the staff provider. This change allows for other intermediaries to be included in the chain, such as a personal service company).

The requirement to provide services personally to the R&D company under the contract means that general temporary staff costs will not usually be eligible, as they are not usually contracted to provide services to a specific company. This can also be an area where group employment companies can fail to qualify, if employee contracts simply require them to work for the group as a whole and not for the specific R&D company.

Relief is available on the expenditure paid by the company to the intermediary in respect of the services supplied by the external workers; it does not include payments in respect of ancillary costs, such as any recruitment costs incurred by the intermediary.

The external workers must be directly and actively engaged in relevant R&D. Where only a proportion of the external workers' time is spent on relevant R&D activities, relief is available for only that proportion of the costs.

Self-employed consultants

17.43 As a result of these requirements, R&D relief is *not* available for the costs of self-employed consultants (although, of course, the normal revenue deduction will still be available), as the staff provider must be a company – this can be resolved if the consultant operates through a personal service company, as the relief should then be available, provided that the contracts are properly structured.

IR35

17.44 Similarly, where the external worker is self-employed through a personal service company, it is unlikely that the requirements will be met where the arrangements are such that IR35 does not apply.

IR35 is a set of rules that are intended to ensure that employment is not disguised by the use of a worker's personal service company; where the rules apply, the worker's personal service company is required to account for PAYE and NICs on 95% of the income from the engagement. The tests as to whether IR35 applies are broadly the same as the normal employment status tests; the detail of these is outside the scope of this chapter but, in brief, where the engaging company (the R&D company in this case) has control over the worker, it is likely that the IR35 rules will apply.

Deduction

17.45 The deduction which can be made for the R&D tax relief in respect of expenditure on externally provided workers is calculated in a similar way to expenditure on subcontractors.

Where the R&D company and the staff provider are not connected, the SME can claim R&D relief on 65% of the qualifying payments to the staff provider (*CTA 2009, s 1131*).

Where the company and the intermediary are connected, the qualifying expenditure is the lower of:

- the costs which the intermediary includes in his year-end accounts in respect of remuneration incurred in providing the company with the staff; and
- the amount of the company's payment to the intermediary (*CTA 2009, s 1129*).

If the company and the intermediary are not connected, they may still elect to use the connected persons treatment (*CTA 2009, s 1130*). The election needs to be made within two years of the end of the accounting period of the company in which the contract is entered into. As the election needs to be joint, the company should ensure that the contract relating to the externally provided workers requires the intermediary to sign such an election when requested to do so.

If the joint election is not made and the parties are not connected, the company can claim relief on 65% of the payment made to the intermediary.

Relief for expenditure on work subcontracted to an SME

17.46 An SME can claim the R&D expenditure credit (RDEC) from 1 April 2016 (or could claim it earlier by election) where the company incurs qualifying expenditure on R&D that has been subcontracted to it by either:

- a large company; or
- any person otherwise than in the course of a UK taxable trade, profession or vocation (broadly, such persons are likely to be foreign companies).

The reason for this exception is that, otherwise, all R&D relief would be lost in respect of such subcontracted R&D because a large company cannot claim R&D relief on work that it subcontracts to others. A foreign company could, in theory, set up a UK subsidiary to carry out R&D; that subsidiary would be able to claim R&D relief on qualifying expenditure. In each case, an SME to which the work is subcontracted can claim the RDEC on its expenditure so that some relief is therefore granted. Large companies, in particular, should take note of this and endeavour to negotiate the costs of the contract accordingly, taking into account the enhanced relief that the SME will receive as a result of the subcontract.

Grants and subsidies

State Aid

17.47

> **Focus**
>
> Where a notified State Aid is received in connection with an R&D project *none* of the expenditure on that project will qualify for the SME R&D tax relief (*CTA 2009, s 1138*; CIRD81670), even if the State Aid grant is intended to cover capital expenditure. This is because the SME R&D relief is a State Aid, and EU rules do not permit the accumulation of State Aid – most government/EU funding is also a State Aid.
>
> Where the receipt of a State Aid grant means that the company cannot claim the SME R&D relief, then the R&D Expenditure Credit can be claimed by the SME (from 1 April 2016, or earlier by election) for the R&D expenditure on the project instead.

'Project' is not defined and HMRC state that each case depends on its own merits; in practice, good documentation prepared to establish the scope of a project and supporting the independence of that project from others carried on by the company will assist in any queries that HMRC may raise over the allocation of expenditure between grant-supported and non-supported projects.

An SME carrying out qualifying R&D should, therefore, take care to establish the effect of the receipt of a grant as it may be considerably less advantageous to accept the grant. The RDEC is given at a lower rate and does not cover subcontracted expenditure.

Example 17.6 – R&D relief vs government grant

R&D Co has two projects underway. It is considering making an application to the local RDA for a grant for research and development in respect of one of those projects.

The budget for the project in question is £1.5m; the maximum grant for which the company qualifies is £200,000.

If the company does not make the application, it will be able to claim SME R&D relief on the expenditure; assuming that all the expenditure qualifies, the additional R&D relief deduction available during the life of the project will be:

130% of £1.5m = £1,950,000

Assuming that the company is loss-making, this can be surrendered in exchange for a repayable tax credit (see below). The overall repayment available over the life of the project will be:

14.5% of (£1,500,000 + £1,950,000) = £500,250

Net effect if no grant received: £500,250 repayment available, no loss carried forward.

In comparison, if the company decides to apply for – and receives – the grant, it will only be able to claim the R&D expenditure credit in respect of that project (note: any R&D relief claim in respect of the other project, for which no grant is claimed, is *not* affected by the grant received for this project, provided they are independent projects).

The R&D expenditure credit is worth (overall) 8.8% of qualifying expenditure, so that the value of the credit to R&D Co would be £132,000.

This assumes that all of the expenditure is incurred in-house: if, for example, £500,000 of the £1.5m project expenditure is subcontracted costs, the R&D expenditure credit value will only be £88,000.

The R&D expenditure credit can be repaid to loss-making companies, although 20% notional tax will be deducted from the repayment and carried forward as a credit against future tax.

Net effect of receipt of grant: £200,000 immediately available (from grant) and a potential repayment of £105,600, compared with the potential repayment of £500,250 if no grant is claimed.

Not State Aid

17.48 Other grants and subsidies will reduce qualifying expenditure for the purposes of the SME R&D relief but will not disqualify all expenditure on the project (*CTA 2009, s 1052*; CIRD81650).

For that part of the project expenditure that is covered by a grant or subsidy, the R&D expenditure credit will be available; SME relief continues to be available for expenditure on the project that is not covered by the non-State Aid grant or subsidy.

In practice, non-State Aid and subsidies are often given for capital expenditure which is not covered by the R&D relief and, where this is the case, they will have no effect on the R&D relief.

Pre-trading expenditure

17.49

Focus

Where a company is undertaking R&D in order to be able to trade, but is not yet doing so as part of a taxable trade, there are specific rules to allow the company to claim the SME R&D tax relief immediately in respect of qualifying expenditure (*CTA 2009, s 1045*). Without such rules, the company could not claim relief until it began trading, when such expenditure would be treated as having been incurred on the first day of trading.

The company can elect to be treated as having incurred a trading loss for the accounting period equal to 230% (from 1 April 2015; 225% for the period 1 April 2012–31 March 2015, 200% for the period 1 April 2011 to 31 March 2012, 175% for the period 1 August 2008 to 31 March 2011, and 150% before 1 August 2008) of the amount of its qualifying expenditure in that period.

The company can therefore surrender the deemed loss and claim the payable R&D tax credit immediately (see below), to assist with cash flow through the pre-trading period. The usual pre-trading rules are disapplied in respect of that expenditure so that it is not brought into account again on the first day of trading.

The deemed trading loss cannot be carried back against any profits that may have been made by the company in an earlier period, although it can be used for group relief or carried forward if not surrendered for repayment.

If an election is made, it must be made in respect of *all* of the qualifying R&D expenditure for that accounting period. An election cannot be made in respect of part only of that expenditure.

The election must be made in writing to HMRC within two years of the end of the relevant accounting period. The election must specify the accounting period for which it is made, as a separate election is required for each accounting period in which pre-trading R&D expenditure is to be treated as a trading loss.

Where the company does not yet have an accounting period, it is treated for these purposes as though an accounting period began when the relevant R&D activity began.

Form of the SME R&D relief

17.50 Provided that the SME is carrying on a trade, the relief is taken as an expense, a deduction for tax purposes (*CTA 2009, s 1044(7)*) reducing a profit or increasing a loss (to reduce future profits) then, if the business is loss-making, the additional loss arising from the relief can be surrendered in exchange for an immediate repayment from HMRC (see below, repayable tax credit).

Deduction from profits

17.51 The relief is given by allowing a business to deduct 130% (for expenditure from 1 April 2015; see above for rates before that date) of its qualifying expenditure when calculating profits/losses for tax purposes, in addition to the 100% deduction already available under the general rules.

For a tax-paying company, this will reduce the tax liability. For a loss-making company it will increase the loss available to carry forwards or backwards, use against other income of the period, surrender as group relief, or surrender for the repayable tax credit.

Example 17.7 – R&D deduction

Net Co spends £40,000 of qualifying expenditure on relevant R&D activity in a year. The company can deduct £92,000

(£40,000 + (£40,000 × 130%))

from turnover when calculating its profits/losses for that year.

Claiming the relief

17.52 The relief must be claimed within two years of the end of the accounting period to which the claim relates (*FA 1998, Sch 18, para 83B* (as amended)). The relief should be claimed on the company's self-assessment return or by an amended return.

Maximum relief

17.53 An SME can only claim R&D relief to the extent the total combined R&D relief and vaccine research relief claimed for expenditure on a particular project does not exceed €7.5m in total. This is a lifetime limit on relief for each project (*CTA 2009, s 1113*).

There is a formula to calculate the total R&D relief received to date, to identify whether the cap has been reached, and a recalculation is required each year (*CTA 2009, s 1114*).

Where the cap is reached for a particular project by an SME any qualifying R&D expenditure in excess of the threshold may qualify for the R&D expenditure credit on that excess.

PAYABLE RESEARCH AND DEVELOPMENT TAX CREDIT

17.54 If the SME is loss-making once the R&D relief has been deducted, the option of surrendering the loss relating to the SME R&D tax relief and qualifying expenditure and taking the credit as immediate cash is available – but the payment from HMRC is less than the tax ultimately saved if the relief is carried forward as a loss. The repayment option may be preferential for a company that has cash-flow issues, where the longer term financial disadvantage is less important than the short-term need for cash.

In exchange for surrendering the loss relating to the SME R&D tax relief and qualifying expenditure, the company can claim a repayment that is effectively up to 33.35% of the qualifying costs, calculated according to the loss surrendered by the company.

Any trading loss carried forward arising in the relevant accounting period is reduced by the loss surrendered to obtain the tax credit repayment.

Surrenderable loss

17.55 The company can surrender a loss equal to the lower of (*CTA 2009, s 1056*):

- the R&D reduction – 230% (from 1 April 2015) of the qualifying R&D expenditure;
- the total loss of the trade, less;
  - any claim made, or which could be made, to set the loss against other profits or gains of the same accounting period; and
  - any other relief claimed in respect of the losses, including losses carried back to an earlier accounting period or surrendered by group or consortium relief.

Example 17.8 – Loss surrender calculation

LossCo, an SME, spends £250,000 of qualifying expenditure on R&D activity in a year, incurs other losses of £500,000 and has taxable income of £100,000 in that same year from subletting part of its office space.

LossCo's total deduction for R&D is:

£250,000 + (£250,000 × 130%) = £575,000

LossCo can surrender the lower of:

R&D deduction: £575,000

Total losses: £(500,000 + 575,000 – 100,000) = £975,000 (the total loss of the company after setting losses against income)

As the R&D deduction is less than the total losses, LossCo can surrender the whole of the R&D deduction (£575,000) to obtain a repayment.

Once the surrenderable loss has been determined, the company can claim a maximum repayment of (*CTA 2009, s 1058*, as amended by *FA 2014, s 31*) 14.5% of the surrendered loss in respect of expenditure incurred on or after 1 April 2014 (11% for expenditure between 1 April 2012 and 31 March 2014; 12.5% from 1 April 2011 to 31 March 2012; 14% from 1 August 2008 to 31 March 2011; 16% prior to 1 August 2008).

At the 20% corporate tax rate, this equates to 33.35% of the qualifying R&D expenditure (32.625% from 1 April 2014 to 31 March 2014, 24.75% from 1 April 2012 to 31 March 2014; 25% from 1 April 2011 to 31 March 2012; 24.5% from 1 August 2008 to 31 March 2011; 24% prior to 1 August 2008).

The company is not required to surrender the maximum amount possible; part of the loss arising from the SME R&D tax relief can be retained to carry forwards and, where the full R&D relief cannot be surrendered, must be retained to carry forward to set against future profits.

PAYE/NIC limitation (historical)

17.56 For expenditure prior to 1 April 2012, the repayment was limited to the total amount of relevant PAYE and Class 1 NICs paid by the company for PAYE periods ending in the relevant accounting period (*CTA 2009, s 1059*; repealed by *FA 2012, Sch 3, para 15*).

PAYE periods end on the fifth day of the month, and the relevant PAYE and NICs were those *paid* in the accounting period, not liabilities accrued to the end of the accounting period. Where a company had, for example, an accounting period ending on 31 December, the relevant PAYE and NICs were those actually paid in the PAYE periods ending on 5 December.

Claiming the repayment

17.57 The repayment credit must be claimed within two years of the end of the accounting period to which the claim relates, and must be made in the company's corporation tax return or by amended return (*FA 1998, Sch 18, para 10(2)* (as amended)). The claim must be quantified when it is made.

Although HMRC generally pay the repayment credit to the company soon after receipt of the claim, that payment can be withheld if the corporation tax return for that period is subject to enquiry before the R&D repayment has been made.

No payment will be made until the company has paid all the PAYE and Class 1 NICs for the accounting period of claim. In addition, HMRC can use the repayment credit to discharge any corporation tax liabilities of the company (*CTA 2009, s 1060*).

Deduction or repayment – which is more useful?

17.58 To make the decision between taking a repayment (potentially equivalent to 33.35% of expenditure) and keeping a deduction (potentially equivalent to 43.7% of expenditure, at the current 19% corporate tax rate), the company will need to consider the cost of the capital employed in the business (ie the interest cost, any returns due on preference shares, etc), and balance that cost against the benefit of a loss going forwards. If a deduction is taken, no benefit as such is received until the business moves into profit, when it will defer the point at which the business exhausts its losses and begins to pay tax on profits.

The company therefore needs to be funded until it moves into profit and becomes self-sustaining; if the deduction is taken more funds (either raised by borrowing or from the sale of equity) will be needed than if a repayment is taken. If the cost of that additional borrowing or equity sale, less the future tax saving, is more than the difference between the repayment and the future tax saving then it is likely to be better to take the repayment and have the cash immediately, reducing the funding requirement.

Group relief

17.59 Alternatively, an SME which is a member of a group may be able to surrender the loss to another, profitable, UK group company by way of group relief (*CTA 2010, Pt 5*).

A surrender of losses through group relief will reduce the profits of the other company so that the group as a whole benefits more than it would have done if the R&D company had surrendered the loss for a repayment. Where there are cash-flow issues for the R&D company, the profitable company to which the loss is surrendered can pay the R&D company for the surrendered loss; such a payment is ignored for corporation tax purposes provided that it does not exceed the corporation tax saved (*CTA 2010, s 183*).

No consortium relief

17.60 An SME may be owned by a consortium rather than a group; a company will be owned by a consortium where at least 75% of its ordinary share capital is owned by two or more companies, each of which owns at least 5% of the share capital (*CTA 2010, s 153*). Provided that such companies were also SMEs, a company could be owned by a consortium and still qualify as an SME itself (see the independence test above).

A company can surrender trading losses to consortium members (*CTA 2010, s 143*) but, where an SME is owned by a consortium, it cannot surrender any R&D relief losses to the consortium members (*CTA 2009, s 1049*).

LARGE COMPANIES' RELIEF

17.61 The large companies' relief was abolished from 1 April 2016; large companies may now only claim the R&D expenditure credit on expenditure incurred on or after that date.

A large company is any company that does not meet the definition of a small- or medium-sized company (*CTA 2009, s 1122*).

Qualifying expenditure

17.62 Expenditure that qualified for the large companies' R&D tax relief is the same as the qualifying expenditure for the R&D expenditure credit (see **17.67**).

Large company relief-equivalent claims by SMEs

17.63 Where an SME could not claim the SME R&D relief because the qualifying R&D expenditure:

- had been subsidised (see **17.47–17.48**); or
- was over the €7.5m project cap (see **17.31**); or
- had been sub-contracted to the SME by a non-SME (see **17.64**),

the SME could claim an additional deduction equivalent to the large company relief for that qualifying R&D expenditure (*CTA 2009, s 1068*).

Subcontracted work

17.64 An SME could claim an additional deduction equivalent to the large company relief for qualifying R&D expenditure where the R&D was subcontracted to the SME by a larger company or a person not carrying on a trade that is subject to UK tax (*CTA 2009, s 1063*). However, the activities subcontracted to the SME still had to be qualifying R&D for the SME on a stand-alone basis.

No repayment credit was available for an SME in respect of the large company relief.

Form of the large company R&D relief

17.65 The research and development tax relief for large companies was given by allowing the company to deduct 30% (25% for expenditure incurred prior to 1 April 2008; *FA 2008, Sch 8, para 2*) of its qualifying expenditure on R&D (in addition to the 100% deduction given under the normal rules) when calculating its profits for tax purposes; this either reduced the tax payable by the company or, if it was loss-making, increased the loss available to the company.

Example 17.9 – Large company R&D tax relief

If a company spent £100,000 on qualifying R&D, it could deduct £130,000 – £100,000 was deducted under the normal rules and £30,000 was deducted under the R&D tax relief:

- if the company was tax paying, this would reduce tax by up to £6,000 (at the 20% rate of corporation tax, on the £30,000 R&D tax relief); or
- if the company was loss-making, the additional loss could be used as a trading loss of the period and either carried forward or, if appropriate, set against other income of the period, carried back to earlier periods or surrendered as group relief.

The large company relief did not provide an equivalent to the SME repayable credit.

Claim for relief

17.66 As with the SME R&D tax relief, a claim had to be made within two years of the end of the accounting period in which the qualifying expenditure was incurred. The claim was made either in the company's corporation tax return or by way of amended return.

R&D EXPENDITURE CREDIT

17.67 The R&D expenditure credit can be claimed by large companies (defined as a company that is not an SME, as above) in respect of their qualifying expenditure (*CTA 2009, Chapter 6A, Pt 3*). For expenditure incurred on or after 1 April 2016, this is the only R&D relief available to large companies. The R&D expenditure credit may also be claimed by SMEs in certain circumstances.

Early election

17.68 For expenditure incurred on or after 1 April 2013 but before 1 April 2016, a large company could elect to claim the R&D expenditure credit rather than the large companies' relief. Such an election was irrevocable; the company had to continue to use the R&D expenditure credit in subsequent accounting periods, even if these were before 1 April 2016.

SME claims

17.69 The R&D expenditure credit can be claimed by an SME company in respect of certain expenditure that does not qualify for the SME relief, specifically (*CTA 2009, s 104A(3)*):

- qualifying expenditure that exceeds the €7.5m cap on total relief for a project (see **17.31**);
- subsidised qualifying expenditures (see **17.47**); and
- R&D subcontracted to the SME by a large company or an entity outside the scope of corporation tax (see **17.64**).

An SME could, similarly to a large company, elect to use the R&D expenditure credit in preference to the large company-equivalent relief for this sort of expenditure incurred on or after 1 April 2013 but before 1 April 2016. For relevant expenditure incurred on or after 1 April 2016, the R&D expenditure credit is the only R&D relief available for such expenditure.

Qualifying expenditure for large companies

17.70 Expenditure that qualifies for the R&D expenditure credit for large companies is similar to that for SME relief, wth some modifications. A company can claim the R&D expenditure credit on (*CTA 2009, s 104A(4)*):

- in-house direct R&D;
- sub-contracted R&D (in very limited circumstances); and
- contributions to independent research.

Subcontracted work

Work subcontracted by a large company

> **Focus**
>
> Expenditure by large companies on R&D that is subcontracted to another party will not be eligible for the R&D expenditure credit, unless the work is subcontracted to one of the following:
>
> - a qualifying body (universities and other higher education institutions; charities; scientific research organisations; NHS bodies); or
> - an individual; or
> - a partnership of individuals.

17.71 A qualifying body does not have to be based in the UK, but must be approved by HMRC before payments will qualify. A list of already-approved non-UK qualifying bodies is maintained by HMRC (CIRD82250). If the body in question is not on the list then approval should be sought from HMRC for the body to be designated as qualifying; the enquiry can be made to the R&D specialist office, who will refer it to the CT International and Anti-Avoidance (Technical) department.

In each of these cases, if work is subcontracted by a large company, no R&D relief would be available to anyone as the entities carrying out the subcontracted work cannot claim R&D relief.

Where work is subcontracted to an SME, that SME can (if it is qualifying R&D for the SME) claim the R&D expenditure credit on the expenditure it incurs in performing the subcontracted work (see above) and so no R&D relief can be claimed by the large company commissioning the work.

Where the R&D expenditure credit (or, formerly, the large company relief) can be claimed on the costs of subcontracting, the full costs can be eligible for relief: there is no requirement to take only 65%, or use connected parties relief, as there is for the SME relief (*CTA 2009, s 1078*).

Work subcontracted to a large company

17.72 Where a large company has work subcontracted to it, expenditure by the company on the R&D can qualify for R&D relief where the work has been subcontracted by either:

- another large company; or

- any person otherwise than in the course of a UK taxable trade, profession, vocation (principally where the work is sub-contracted to the company from overseas).

The activities subcontracted to the large company must still be qualifying R&D (see above) for the company on a stand-alone basis.

This requirement is modified where the work is subcontracted to the company by another group company which pays for the work, the activities of the two group companies are considered together to determine whether the activities are qualifying R&D. Where the aggregate activities are qualifying R&D, the company carrying out the work will be able to claim the R&D expenditure credit (or, formerly, the large company relief), even if the specific activities would not qualify as R&D expenditure on a stand-alone basis (*CTA 2009, s 1082*).

Where work is subcontracted by an SME to a large company, the large company will not be able to claim any relief, to prevent double relief being claimed, as the SME can usually claim the SME R&D relief on some or all of the expenditure it incurs in commissioning that subcontracted work (see above).

Contributions to independent research

17.73 Payments to qualifying bodies in respect of their research will also qualify for relief where the work is not actually subcontracted (ie where the company does not receive the benefit of the work done by the organisation (*CTA 2009, s 1079*)). However, for the expenditure to qualify, the R&D carried out by the organisation must be relevant to the trade of the company. Where the contribution is made to an individual or a partnership, the company must not be connected to the individual or to any member of a partnership.

Going concern

17.74 Note that a large company must be a going concern in order to claim the R&D expenditure credit, as must an SME. The company will be a going concern if its latest accounts are prepared on a going concern basis and the company has not since gone into administration or liquidation. The accounts must not have been prepared on a going concern basis solely because the R&D expenditure credit was expected to be received (*CTA 2009, s 104T*).

Form of the R&D expenditure credit

17.75 The R&D expenditure credit is given in a very different way to the SME relief or the former large company relief.

The R&D expenditure credit amount (11% of qualifying R&D expenditure; 10% from 1 April 2013–31 March 2015) is first brought into account as a receipt of the trade of the claimant company, increasing the profits of the company (or decreasing a loss). This may affect the quarterly instalment payments of the company. The same amount is then given as a credit against corporation tax. If the amount is more than the corporation tax due (or where the company is loss-making), a repayment may be available to the company.

Note that, as this is a credit, it is not taken into account in calculating quarterly instalment payments so that, overall, the expenditure credit may lead to a slight increase in quarterly instalment payments for a company. The credit may, however, be used to discharge future quarterly instalment payments once a return has been submitted and a claim made for credit (CIRD89870).

Example 17.10 – R&D expenditure credit

A company has taxable profits of £750,000 and spends £100,000 on qualifying R&D and claims the R&D expenditure credit, it must first bring into account £11,000 as a receipt of the trade for corporation tax purposes, so that its taxable profits are increased to £761,000.

Assuming a corporation tax rate of 19%, the corporation tax due on profits of £761,000 would be £144,590. However, a credit of £11,000 is now given against this as a result of the R&D expenditure credit, so that the actual corporation tax due is £133,590.

If the profits of the company had been, instead, £25,000 (with the same qualifying R&D expenditure) then the R&D expenditure credit would have the effect of increasing taxable profits to £36,000. The corporation tax due on £36,000 would be £6,840. After the R&D expenditure credit of £11,000 is given against corporation tax, the company would be potentially entitled to a repayment of £3,370, with a carried-forward tax credit of £790.

Payment of the R&D expenditure credit

17.76 Where a company claims the R&D expenditure credit, the credit against tax is given in accordance with a specific sequence of steps (*CTA 2009, s 104N*):

1 deducted from any corporation tax liability (as above);

2 any remaining credit is reduced by the main rate of corporation tax (eg if the main rate of corporation tax is 20%, the remaining credit is reduced by 20%);

3 the remaining net credit is compared to the company's total PAYE and NIC liabilities for the accounting period. If the remaining net credit is more than the PAYE and NIC liabilities, then the excess over the amount of those liabilities must be carried forward to use as a credit in a future accounting period;

4 the element of the net credit which is equal to or less than the PAYE and NIC liabilities is then used against any other outstanding corporation tax liability of the company – any excess is carried forwards to get set against tax liabilities in future years;

5 any remaining net credit can now be (but is not required to be) surrendered to another group company;

6 the net remaining net credit is used to reduce any other outstanding tax liability of the company (eg VAT, PAYE etc); and

7 finally, any net remaining credit is repayable to the company.

Notional tax availability

17.77 The notional tax deducted at step 2 can be carried forward and will be available to reduce the corporation tax liability of the company in a future accounting period. It can also be surrendered to another group company to reduce its corporation tax bill for the current accounting period.

Example 17.11 – Payment of R&D expenditure credit

Taking the example above, and looking at each of the steps:

1 The R&D expenditure credit of £11,000 has been deducted from the company's corporation tax liability of £6,840, leaving remaining credit of £4,160.

2 The remaining credit is reduced by the main rate of corporation tax. If this is 19%, then the net remaining credit available is £3,370. The £790 'notional tax' deducted will be carried forward or can be surrendered to a group company.

3 Assuming that the company has PAYE and NIC liabilities for the accounting period of £2,500, then £870 is carried forward to use as a credit in a later accounting period.

4 Assuming that the company has no outstanding corporation tax liabilities, the remaining £2,500 continues to be available.

5 If the company chooses not to surrender the remaining credit to a group company, then £2,500 continues to be available.

6 Assuming that the company has no outstanding tax liabilities, the net remaining credit of £2,500 continues to be available.

7 The net remaining credit of £2,500 will be repayable to the company.

PAYE and NIC liabilities

17.78 The PAYE and NIC liabilities which are taken into account in comparing the repayable credit are the PAYE and NIC liabilities which relate to staff involved directly in R&D activities (*CTA 2009, s 104P*).

In addition, the company can bring into account the PAYE and NIC liabilities (if any) incurred by a group company in providing externally provided workers to the R&D company. This is limited to the percentage of such liabilities which corresponds to the percentage of staff costs for which R&D expenditure is actually claimed; claims for group externally provided workers are generally limited to a proportion of the actual costs (see above).

Claim for the R&D expenditure credit

17.79 As with the other R&D tax reliefs, a claim must be made within two years of the end of the accounting period in which the qualifying expenditure was incurred. The claim is made either in the company's corporation tax return or by way of amended return.

REFUNDS OF EXPENDITURE

17.80 Where R&D relief has been claimed on:

- contributions to independent research;
- subcontractor payments;
- subsided expenditure; or
- capped R&D expenditure

and these payments are subsequently refunded to the company, that refund is treated as taxable trading income of the company. This applies to both large companies and SMEs.

An additional 30% of the refund is also treated as taxable trading income of the company (*CTA 2009, s 1083*), regardless of the size of the company, and regardless of whether the claim was for the SME relief or the large company relief.

ANTI-AVOIDANCE

17.81 There are anti-avoidance provisions attached to the R&D tax relief (*CTA 2009, s 1084*) and the R&D expenditure credit (*CTA 2009, s 104X*).

If the transaction leading to the relief is connected with arrangements undertaken wholly or mainly for a disqualifying purpose, that transaction is not taken into account when determining the amount of R&D relief (including pre-trading relief).

A disqualifying purpose is one in which the main object, or objects, of the arrangements is to enable the company to obtain an amount (or an increased amount) of R&D relief than that which it would otherwise be entitled to; in other words, the R&D is entered into purely to obtain the tax relief and not for the purposes of the trade.

Chapter 18

The patent box

Anne Fairpo Barrister, CTA (Fellow), ATT

SIGNPOSTS

- **Qualifying patents** – these include UK patents, patents granted by the European Patent Office, and national patents of some EEA countries (see **18.3**).
- **Qualifying companies** – a claimant company must have carried out, or have a group company that carried out, relevant development in respect of the patent or products derived from it. An intellectual property (IP) holding company will usually need to actively manage its patents to qualify for the patent box (see **18.4–18.15**).
- **Points to note** – the patent box calculation can result in a patent box loss as well as a patent box profit; the loss does not affect the corporation tax charge for the accounting period, but it must be set against any patent box profits of the group or the company in that year, or carried forwards (see **18.16–18.43**).
- **Losses** – the relief is being phased in: only 60% of the relief could be claimed in 2013–14, the year of introduction. The amount that can be claimed will be increased by 10% each until the full relief becomes available in 2017–18 (see **18.48** and **18.49**).
- **New rules from 1 July 2016** – in order to comply with the framework for patent box regimes introduced by the OECD's BEPS project, the patent box rules changed for new IP, and new entrants to the regime, from 1 July 2016. The principal difference is to the calculation, introducing a restriction on the patent box benefit where R&D has been substantially outsourced to group companies, or where the claim substantially dependent upon acquired IP. Claimants within the new regime will need to calculate profits at the level of an IP asset, and will need to track R&D expenditure on qualifying IP more closely; the range of claimants and qualifying IP will not change.

WHO CAN CLAIM?

18.1

> **Focus**
>
> The patent box deduction is available to companies within the scope of UK corporation tax which have patent income, regardless of size. It is also available to partnerships in respect of the profits of one or more of the corporate partners of the partnership – it does not provide relief for non-corporate partners.
>
> Where an individual owns the patent used by a company, take care in planning to use the patent box in the company: a sale of patent rights by an individual to a company will give rise an income tax charge on the profit/gain on sale (*ITTOIA 2005, s 587*), and if the patent is a post-1 April 2002 asset for the company, the sale will be deemed to take place at market value (*CTA 2009, s 845*). Where the sale of patents is subject to income tax, the individual will not be able to use capital gains tax reliefs to reduce the tax charge.

Election

18.2 An election is required for a company to use the patent box (*CTA 2010, s 357A*). The election is made by giving notice to an officer of HMRC in writing, specifying the first accounting period to which it applies, and must be given within two years of the end of that accounting period (*CTA 2010, s 357G*). In practice, this means that the election should be sent with the tax return (or amended return) on which the patent box relief is first claimed.

Note that elections can be made within this two year period to elect into the regime in respect of pre-1 July 2016 IP and profits, provided that the company meets the conditions for the patent box regime at 30 June 2016; there is no requirement to have made the election before 1 July 2016.

An election by one group company does not affect any other group company – each must make its own election. Similarly, each corporate partner in a trading partnership with relevant income must make a separate election.

An election will apply to subsequent accounting periods unless, and until, it is revoked by notice in writing to an officer of HMRC (*CTA 2010, s 357G(5)*). The notice must specify the first accounting period from which the revocation will have effect, and must be given within two years of the end of that accounting period.

Once a company has revoked an election in respect of the patent box regime, it cannot re-elect into the regime for any accounting period that begins within five years of the day after the last day of the accounting period from which the revocation has effect (ie the company must be out of the regime for at least six years before it can elect back in) (*CTA 2010, s 357GA(5)*).

Under the pre-July 2016 rules, the election applies to all of the trades of the company (*CTA 2010, s 357G(4)*), and the patent box is calculated on a trade-by-trade basis for the company.

Under the new rules, applying from 1 July 2016 to new IP and new entrants, the patent box calculation is still operated on a trade-by-trade basis but also requires that the calculation of the patent box profits for each trade be calculated on an asset-by-asset basis for the company (an IP asset will be a patent, a product or a product category, or a process, whichever is most appropriate to the business).

Nevertheless, under the new rules, a small company (see **18.39**) can make a global streaming election (*CTA 2010, s357BNC*) to opt to calculate the patent box using a single IP stream.

A company which qualifies for the old rules may, nevertheless, elect to calculate the patent box on the basis of the new rules from 1 July 2016 (*CTA 2010, s357A(11)(b)*).

QUALIFYING INTELLECTUAL PROPERTY

Focus

Only income from qualifying intellectual property rights will be eligible for the patent box relief. The intellectual property rights which are eligible are (*CTA 2010, s 357BB*):

- UK patents, granted under the *Patents Act 1977*;
- patents granted under the European Patent Convention (ie granted through the European Patent Office, *not* patents of the individual European countries, although some of these may be eligible separately – see below);
- inventions which are not granted a patent solely because the application contains information prejudicial to national security or safety (ie where the inventor is notified under *s 18(4)* of the *Patents Act 1977*);
- plant breeders' rights, granted under the *Plant Varieties Act 1997* or EC Regulation 2100/94;

- Supplementary protection certificates (issued under Regulation (EC) No 469/2009 – medicines – or Regulation (EC) No160/96 – plants);
- EU marketing authorisations (data exclusivity for medicinal products for human use, orphan medicinal products and veterinary products).

Note that there is no change to the range of qualifying intellectual property under the new rules from 1 July 2016, although the range of qualifying intellectual property in the OECD BEPS framework is wider than that in the UK regime.

Foreign intellectual property

18.3 The range of qualifying intellectual property can be extended by Treasury Order and, so far, patents granted by the patent offices of a number of European countries have been included (the *Profits from Patents (EEA Rights) Order 2013, SI 2013/420*):

- Austria;
- Bulgaria;
- The Czech Republic;
- Denmark;
- Estonia;
- Finland;
- Germany;
- Hungary;
- Poland;
- Portugal;
- Romania;
- Slovakia;
- Sweden.

QUALIFYING COMPANIES

Focus

A company must meet the relevant ownership conditions (*CTA 2010, s 357B*) *and* the development condition (*CTA 2010, s 357BC*) in respect of the qualifying intellectual property. These requirements are not changed for the new regime.

Ownership condition

18.4 The company must meet either the current or the prior ownership conditions and a company that is part of a group must *also* meet the active ownership condition.

Current ownership

18.5 A company will meet the current ownership condition for a particular accounting period where, during that accounting period, it either:

- owns qualifying intellectual property rights; or
- has an exclusive licence in respect of qualifying intellectual property rights.

Note that intellectual property acquired by a company on or after 2 January 2016 from certain foreign connected parties, where the main purpose, or one of the main purposes, of the transfer was the avoidance of tax, cannot benefit from the grandfathered rules; any patent box profits for such IP must be calculated using the new rules, even if the company has elected into the patent box for a period prior to 1 July 2016.

Prior ownership

18.6 A company will meet the prior ownership condition for an accounting period where it has income during the accounting period which is derived from a qualifying intellectual property right which the company previously owned, or to which it previously had an exclusive licence.

However, the income must be derived from an event which occurred when the company:

- owned or had an exclusive licence to the intellectual property; *and*
- had elected into the patent box regime.

As a result, the patent box relief will not be available for income from patents which were sold or expired before the patent box rules come into force on 1 April 2013: no election can be made before that date.

Active ownership (group companies only)

18.7 This condition must be met in addition to either the current ownership condition or the prior ownership condition, but applies to group companies only: it is intended to ensure that the company owning the intellectual property is not simply a passive holding company within the group.

In order to fulfil the condition for an accounting period, all, or almost all, of the qualifying intellectual property held by the company must be intellectual property for which the company either (*CTA 2010, s 357BE*):

- carries out a significant amount of management activity; *or*
- carries out the development itself (ie the development condition is not met by attribution of another group company's activity).

'Management activity' means 'formulating plans and making decisions in relation to the development or exploitation of the rights'. 'Significant' is not defined; whether the level of activity is 'significant' will depend on all the relevant circumstances, including the resources and responsibilities of the company within the group. 'Almost all' is also not defined, and there is no information in the HMRC guidance (CIRD210210) as to its meaning. In practice, it likely that this will mean at least 90% of the qualifying intellectual property will need to be actively managed or have been developed by the group company owning it.

Note that, under the post 1 July 2016 regime rules, if a group company meets the active ownership requirement through management activity rather than development activity, it may find that the benefit of the patent box is restricted (see below).

Exclusive licence

18.8 An exclusive licence is a licence which (*CTA 2010, s 357BA*):

- is granted by the person who holds either the qualifying intellectual property rights, or holds an exclusive licence to those rights; *and*
- gives the licensee (alone or with others authorised by the licensee) specific rights over the qualifying intellectual property rights.

These specific rights are:

- rights over the qualifying intellectual property to the commercial exclusion of all others, including the grantor, in a commercially distinct area of business in at least one country; and either

- the right to bring proceedings for infringement of the rights without consent of the grantor or any other person; or
- the right to receive the whole (or greater part) of any damages awarded in respect of any infringement.

Groups

18.9 The requirement to include specific rights is relaxed for licences between group companies (CIRD210120). In particular, where the licence is granted by one group company to another, it will still be regarded as exclusive where the group as a whole has all the necessary rights. This allows the group intellectual holding company, for example, to retain the rights to enforce, assign or licence the intellectual property so that it can continue to manage the intellectual property portfolio of the group as a whole. Note, there must be some evidence as to the intra-group licencing: this can be in the form of a group policy document, but the licence terms must be clear and demonstrate that the requirements of the legislation as to the terms of the exclusive licence are met.

Development condition

18.10 The company must have either (*CTA 2010, s 357BD*):

- created, or significantly contributed to the creation of, the intellectual property; or
- performed a significant amount of activity for the purposes of developing the intellectual property or any item or process incorporating the intellectual property.

'Significant' is, again, not defined but – as for the active ownership condition – all relevant circumstances need to be taken into account. Merely applying for a patent in respect of acquired rights, or acquiring the rights to and marketing a fully developed patent or invention, or product incorporating the invention, will not be 'significant' activity.

Meeting the development condition

18.11 A company can meet the development condition through meeting *one* of four conditions:

- **Condition A:** The company has carried out the qualifying development activity at any time and has not since joined or left a group.

- **Condition B:** The company previously carried out qualifying development activity, has since left or joined a group, but has continued to carry out development activity of the same description for at least 12 months after leaving or joining the group.
- **Condition C:** The qualifying development activity was carried out by another company which was a member of the same group at the time it carried out the development.
- **Condition D:** The qualifying development activity was carried out by another company which at some point in time was a member of the same group and that other company continued to carry out development activities for at least 12 months after joining the group and did not leave the group during that time.

In effect, if a company enters or leaves a group, it must undertake development activity for 12 months after doing so in order to continue to, or start to, claim the patent box – this is a point which should be noted for corporate acquisitions or buyouts from groups, in particular.

Note that meeting the development condition through either Condition C or Condition D is likely to result in a restriction on the benefit of the patent box under the new rules (see below).

Partnerships

18.12 A partnership will meet the development condition in respect of qualifying intellectual property if it has itself carried out qualifying development in relation to the right, or if a relevant corporate partner (one that is entitled to at least a 40% share of profits or losses of the partnership) has done so.

The active ownership condition will be met by the partnership if the development condition is satisfied by the partnership, but not if it is satisfied by a relevant corporate partner only (*CTA 2010, s 357GB*).

GROUP COMPANIES

Focus

The definition of a group for the purposes of the patent box regime is substantially wider than most tax definitions of group: 'a company ("company A") is a member of a group at any time if any other company is at that time associated with company A' (*CTA 2010, s 357GD(1)*). This definition is broad, and has no geographical restriction.

Associated

18.13 A company (A) will be associated with another company (B) at a particular time (the 'relevant time') if *any* of the following applies:

- in the accounting period in which the relevant time occurs, the financial results of the two companies are, or are required to be, consolidated in group accounts (under UK or foreign law) or would be required to be consolidated if an exemption did not apply; or
- for company A's accounting period which includes the relevant time, the companies are connected; or
- at the relevant time, one of the companies has a major interest in the other; or
- in the accounting period which includes the relevant time, the financial results of company A are consolidated in group accounts with the results of a third company, and at the relevant time that third company has a major interest in B; or
- for an accounting period which includes the relevant time, there is a connection between A and a third company, and at the relevant time that third company has a major interest in B.

Connected

18.14 Two companies are connected if they meet the connection tests in *CTA 2009, ss 466–471*.

Major interest

18.15 A company has a 'major interest' in another company if it meets the tests in *CTA 2009, ss 473–474*.

CALCULATING THE PATENT BOX RELIEF

18.16 Under the grandfathered rules, there are two routes through the calculation:

- the standard calculation, using an apportionment method (*CTA 2010, s 357C*); and
- the alternative streaming calculation (*CTA 2010, s 357D*) which may be chosen by a company or required by HMRC in certain circumstances.

A separate calculation is required for each trade of the company.

Under the new rules, the calculation must be done on the streaming basis, and a separate calculation is required for each patent or, where it is not reasonably practicable to stream by patent, then for each product using patents or each product category using patents (each stream then being a IP stream) (*CTA 2010, s 357BF(2)*, inserted by *s 60* of the *Finance Act 2016*).

GRANDFATHERED RULES: THE STANDARD (APPORTIONMENT METHOD) CALCULATION

> **Focus**
>
> There are a number of steps to the calculation, depending on the company's position:
>
> - Steps 1–3 calculate the pro-rata profits of the trade that relate to qualifying intellectual property;
> - Step 4 deducts a 'routine return' – if the result at this step is a patent box loss, Steps 5–6 are ignored;
> - Steps 5 or 6 (these are alternatives) are intended to eliminate any element of the patent box profit that relates to brand intellectual property (trademarks etc);
> - An optional last step, applying only in the year of grant of a patent, allows a company to get some relief for pre-grant qualifying IP profits in the year of grant
>
> Any patent box losses must be taken into account once a patent box profit is calculated, and the final calculated profit is then subject to a formula to determine the deduction from total taxable profits before calculating corporation tax (see **18.48**).

Steps to the standard (apportionment method) calculation

Step 1 – calculate 'TI', the gross trade income for the accounting period

18.17 'Gross trade income' of the trade includes:

- all income which is brought into account in calculating the trading profits for tax purposes; and
- damages, insurance proceeds and other compensation relating to the intellectual property which is not included above; and

- receipts that are brought into account as receipts under *CTA 2009, s181* (ie where there has been a change of accounting policy and an amount falls out of GAAP recognition); and
- amounts brought into account as a credit on the sale of intangible assets under the corporate intangibles tax rules, if not already included; and
- profits from the sale of patent rights held for the purposes of the trade which are not within the corporate intangibles tax rules (ie, pre-1 April 2002 patent rights which have not been acquired since that date from a third party).

'Gross trade income' specifically excludes financial and similar income.

Step 2 – calculate X%, being RIPI/TI × 100

18.18 Having established TI in Step 1, it is now necessary to calculate the trade's relevant intellectual property income (RIPI) and then calculate X% – the percentage of total income that relates to relevant intellectual property income.

Relevant IP income is income falling within any of five specific 'heads':

- Head 1: income from the worldwide sale of:
  - items wholly or partly protected by a qualifying IP right;
  - items which incorporate a qualifying item, or designed to incorporate a qualifying item which is sold with that item at a single price; and
  - items which are wholly or mainly designed to be incorporated in items included above (ie spare parts).

  Where one such item is sold as part of a package with other non-patented items under a single agreement, the income from that sale must be apportioned between the qualifying and non-qualifying items on a just and reasonable basis.
- Head 2: income from licensing qualifying intellectual property for granting rights over:
  - qualifying IP rights (including rights out of an exclusive licence);
  - a qualifying item or process (eg where the non-UK/EPO patents over that item or process are licensed to third parties); and
  - other associated IP rights under an agreement granting one or more of the rights above.

- Head 3: proceeds of sale etc, of qualifying intellectual property

  This covers income from the sale, realisation or other disposal of qualifying intellectual property rights, or from the sale etc of a qualifying exclusive licence.

- Head 4: infringement income

  This covers amounts received by the company as compensation for infringement (awarded by a court) or alleged infringement (under a settlement agreement) of qualifying intellectual property rights.

- Head 5: damages, insurance, etc

  This covers income which is not directly related to infringement of the qualifying intellectual property and so does not fall within Head 4.

Notional royalty: on election

18.19 The notional royalty provisions are available to companies who use patents in their processes, so that such companies can calculate income that can be treated as RIPI for patent box relief purposes. A company that has elected to bring in a notional royalty can include in RIPI an 'appropriate percentage' of the income derived from the use of the qualifying intellectual property.

The 'appropriate percentage' is the proportion of any IP derived income which the company would pay a third party on an arm's length basis for the use of the IP, if it did not already have the right to use the IP. Once established, the appropriate percentage will continue to apply for each following accounting period for which the company holds the rights.

Step 3 – calculate X% of the profits of the trade for the accounting period

18.20 The taxable profits of the trade must be adjusted under the patent box rules, to account for excluded income and to allow R&D relief to be available at the company's normal corporate tax rate.

The following must be added back to to the taxable profits of the trade:

- debits relating to loan relationships and derivative contracts (as these are excluded);
- the *additional deduction* from R&D relief given by superdeduction (ie 130% for SMEs, 30% for large companies or SMEs claiming the 30% relief; see **Chapter 17**);
- any *additional deduction* claimed as relief for production of television programmes, video games or theatrical productions; and

- any R&D shortfall (in first four years – see **18.21**).

The following must be *deducted* in calculating the taxable profits of the trade:

- the amount of any R&D expenditure credit brought into account (see **17.67**); and
- any finance income brought into account.

Note that these adjustments are *only* for the purposes of calculating the patent box relief: the actual profits of the trade for tax purposes are not adjusted by these amounts.

R&D shortfall adjustment

18.21 This adjustment relates to actual accounts R&D expenditure of the company, *not* the amounts deducted for tax purposes under the R&D relief rules (CIRD220410).

This adjustment is intended to bring into the patent box expenses relating to earlier R&D costs, where the expenses of the company in the current accounting period do not properly reflect the development costs of the items etc, from which patent box income is derived. This is meant to ensure that the company does not receive disproportionately more patent box relief by electing into the regime only once all R&D has been completed.

The shortfall deduction must be considered in the first accounting period in which the company elects into the patent box regime, and then in each accounting period that begins within the four years that begin with that accounting period.

Shortfall

18.22 There will be a shortfall where the actual R&D expenditure (ie *not* the amount of the R&D relief) in the accounting period in which the patent box relief is claimed is less than 75% of the average annual R&D expenditure over the four years before the company elects into the patent box regime.

Adjustment to deduction

18.23 In calculating the deduction, the actual R&D expenditure during the first four years *after* the company elects into the patent box regime must be considered: any expenditure in those years above the average must be carried forward and used to add to future accounting periods in which expenditure below 75% of average before any adjustment is made.

Deduction

18.24 Where the company's actual R&D expenditure, after adding in any brought-forward above-average expenditure from the first four years within the patent box regime is less than 75% of the average R&D expenditure during the four years before election into the regime, then the amount added back in adjusting the profits to which X% is applied in this step is the difference between:

(a) the total of actual and any brought-forward; and

(b) 75% of the pre-patent box average.

Where the brought-forward above-average expenditure is more than required to bring up the actual expenditure to 75% of the pre-patent box average, the excess over that requirement is carried forward again.

Where the actual R&D expenditure together with any brought-forward amounts is still less than 75% of the average pre-patent box expenditure, the amount added back is deemed to be 75% of the average R&D expenditure.

Step 4 – deduct the routine return

18.25 The routine return is calculated as X% of 10% of the following expenses:

- capital allowances deducted in calculating taxable profits;
- premises costs (rent, rates, repair, water, fuel, power, etc);
- staff costs (costs of employing directors and employees, and costs of externally provided workers);
- plant and machinery costs (other than capital allowances: includes leasing costs, construction and modification costs, maintenance, services, operations, etc);
- professional services (consultancy, professional fees, administration and management);
- other services (software, telecoms, post, transport, waste, legal, accountancy, etc).

Where some or all of these expenses are incurred by another group company on behalf of the company claiming the patent box, the expenses are included in the calculation as if they had been incurred by the patent box claimant.

R&D expenses excluded

18.26 Any expenditure in these categories which qualifies for R&D tax relief is not included in the calculation of routine expenses, and neither is the R&D tax relief given on that expenditure. R&D capital allowances and patent allowances are also excluded (but *not* know-how allowances).

Deduction

18.27 Once the routine expenses have been established, the routine return is calculated as being 10% of the routine expenses, and then X% of this figure is calculated to arrive at the amount to be deducted from the profits attributed to relevant intellectual property income (calculated at Step 3).

If the result is a profit then this is termed the qualifying residual profit (QRP) of the company, and further adjustments are required to establish the amount of the patent box relief.

Where the result is negative (or nil) then there is a patent box loss (relevant IP loss, or RIPL) and no further adjustment is needed – the next step in the calculation for a patent box loss is Step 7, if relevant.

Steps 5 or 6 – exclude profits relating to trademarks etc

18.28 As the patent box relief is intended to give relief on income from a limited range of intellectual property only, these Steps 5 or 6 (they are alternatives) will deduct an amount intended to adjust for the profits attributable to trademarks and other marketing intangibles included in QRP.

Step 5 is a formula calculation that takes no account of the actual contribution of brand and marketing intangibles. It can be used by election, provided that a company meets specific conditions. Where the company does not meet the conditions, or chooses not to elect to use Step 5, then the more detailed calculation at Step 6 must be used instead. In practice, Step 5 can substantially reduce the benefit of the patent box claim.

Step 5: small claims election

18.29 A company can elect to use the small claims treatment for a trade where it meets *one* of two conditions:

(a) the RIPP for all the trades of the company in aggregate does not exceed £1,000,000 (patent box losses are ignored in the aggregate); or

(b) the aggregate RIPP of the trades of the company does not exceed the relevant maximum *and* the company has not used the Step 6 calculation method for excluding non-qualifying intellectual property in the previous four years.

The 'relevant maximum' is calculated as:

$$\frac{£3,000,000}{(1 + N)}$$

where N is the number of associated companies of the company in the relevant period. The maximum is reduced pro-rata where the accounting period is less than twelve months. 'Associated' means that the companies are grouped for patent box purposes and have elected into the patent box regime.

As a result, for a solo company with a single trade, the options are:

- QRP < £1m: can always elect to use Step 5;
- QRP > £3m: can never elect to use Step 5;
- QRP ≥ £1m and ≤ £3m: will be able to elect if it has not used the Step 6 calculation method in the previous four years.

Calculation

18.30 Where the company meets one of the conditions and elects to use the small claims treatment then the patent box profits amount on which the patent box relief is based is the *lower* of:

(a) 75% of QRP for the trade (as calculated in Step 4); and

(b) the small claims threshold for the company divided by the number of trades of the company.

The small claims threshold is:

$$\frac{£1,000,000}{(1 + N)}$$

where N is, again, the number of companies associated with the company in the relevant period which have elected into the patent box regime. Where the accounting period is less than twelve months, the small claims threshold is reduced pro rata.

In practice, this formula will usually substantially reduce the value of the patent box to a company; it will usually be more appropriate to consider using the provisions of Step 6 instead.

Step 6: marketing assets return

18.31 Where a company does not qualify for Step 5, or does not elect to use Step 5 where it qualifies, the company must calculate a 'marketing assets return' amount to deduct from QRP to establish the relevant IP profits (RIPP) of the trade.

Marketing assets return amount

18.32 The marketing assets return is the difference between:

- the notional marketing royalty of the company; and
- any actual marketing royalty paid by the company.

However, the marketing assets return is deemed to be nil where the difference is:

- negative (ie the actual marketing royalty exceeds the notional marketing royalty); or
- less than 10% of the QRP for the accounting period.

This is supposed to assist companies, so that they are not required to undertake an expensive valuation exercise where the contribution from the marketing royalties is small and HMRC have said that they will take a pragmatic approach (not requiring calculation of the notional marketing royalty; CIRD220490) where the circumstances are such that it is reasonably clear that the trademark and marketing intangibles contribution is less than 10% of QRP (usually in business-to-business situations where the products are sold on the basis of cost or technical specification).

Notional marketing royalty

18.33 This is the percentage of relevant intellectual property income for the accounting period (as calculated at Step 2 of the standard calculation, or Step 1 of the streaming calculation) that the company would pay to a third party on an arm's length basis in order to be able to use the brand/marketing intangibles if the company did not already own those intangibles.

The brand/marketing intangibles which need to be considered are:

- trademarks and design rights (registered or unregistered; UK or foreign);
- signs or indications of geographic origin of goods or services; or
- customer information used for marketing purposes.

The notional marketing royalty should be assessed in each accounting period, although it is likely to stay the same in respect of a stable product. In contrast, where a company is actively promoting a new product which has an associated trademark (for example), the notional marketing royalty in respect of that product is likely to increase year-on-year as the trademark becomes more valuable with the success of the product.

Actual marketing royalty

18.34 In comparison, the actual marketing royalty is reasonably straightforward to calculate: this is a proportion of the royalties actually paid by the company to use brand/marketing intangibles (as defined above).

The proportion is X%, and the amount paid is: the aggregate royalties and other sums paid to acquire or exploit the relevant marketing assets, provided that they have been brought into account in calculating taxable profits. This will include amortisation deductions where the marketing asset was acquired outright and is being amortised over its useful economic life.

Where the streaming calculation has been used, with the alternative Steps 1–4, then there is no need to take X%. Instead, the amount of the actual marketing royalty is that which has been allocated to the RIPI stream on a just and reasonable basis.

Optional, year of grant only – additional relief for pre-grant profits

18.35 This step is another elective step, rather than a compulsory element of the calculation. It is intended to provide a measure of patent box relief for profits which a company makes from a product etc, before a patent over that product is actually granted.

The company can look back up to six years before the grant, but can only take into consideration accounting periods in which it had elected into the patent box regime. The company must also elect to claim the pre-grant relief, and such election should be made with effect from the year of application to ensure maximum pre-grant relief (the election must be made within two years of the end of the accounting period from which pre-grant relief is to be first claimed).

The amount which can be added to patent box profits for relief purposes is the difference between:

- the actual aggregate patent box profits for each accounting period whilst the patent application was pending (to a maximum of six years before grant); and

- the aggregate patent box profits which would been calculated for those accounting periods if the patent had been granted at the date of application.

The effect of this additional amount is (in effect, through the calculation mechanism) a corresponding decrease in the taxable profit of the company, so that less is taxed at the mainstream corporation tax rate – in effect, recovering a proportion of the tax which was paid on the relevant income when it actually arose.

Deduction from tax

18.36 At the end of the calculation, the calculated patent box profit of the trade is adjusted to take into account any patent box losses. If there is still a profit following that adjustment, the patent box relief is given as an additional deduction in calculating the profits of the trade for corporation tax purposes.

This deduction is:

$$\frac{RP \times (MR - IPR)}{MR}$$

where:

- RP is the RIPP of the trade after adjusting for patent box losses;
- MR is the main rate of corporation tax; and
- IPR is the patent box tax rate (10%).

Note that the main rate of corporation tax is used in the formula, even if the company was subject to tax at the small profits rate prior to the abolition of that rate from 1 April 2015.

Where the company has more than one trade, the patent relief must be calculated separately for each trade so there may be a series of deductions (one for each trade).

The relief is given by way of deduction from profits to get around problems that might otherwise arise with losses and other reliefs if, instead, a rate of 10% were to be applied directly.

Phasing in

18.37 The relief was phased in over four years by applying a percentage to the patent box profits (after adjustment for patent box losses) to reduce these before the patent box relief is calculated. The percentages were:

2013–14:	60%
2014–15:	70%
2015–16:	80%
2016–17:	90%

The full relief is available from 1 April 2017. Where the accounting period straddles a tax year, the relief must be pro-rated and the relevant percentage applied.

STEPS TO THE STREAMING CALCULATION (PRE JULY 2016 AND UNDER THE NEW RULES)

Focus

In some cases, a company's income and profits are such that a straightforward apportionment of profits between IP income and non-IP income does not give a reasonable approximation of the actual profits that arise from exploitation of qualifying IP rights, so that the profits attributed to qualifying intellectual property in the standard calculation (at Step 3) are much lower than actually is the case.

In this case a company can elect to use streaming to allocate profits, to allocate expenses and profits to income streams on a just and reasonable basis. Once an election is made, it will continue to apply until the company elects otherwise, and the company will use the following Steps 1–4 in place of those in the standard calculation.

Under the new rules, this method of calculation is the only method available.

Grandfathered rules: mandatory streaming

18.38 The streaming calculation *must* be used where any one of three conditions are met:

- **Condition A:** the gross income of the trade includes a substantial amount of credits brought into account in calculating taxable trade profits, but not fully recognised as revenue under GAAP (eg transfer pricing adjustments); or
- **Condition B:** the gross income of the trade include a substantial amount of licensing income that is not relevant intellectual property income (eg trademark licensing etc); or

- **Condition C:** the trade generates income that is not relevant intellectual property income and the company also receives a substantial amount of relevant intellectual property income from licences granted, where those licenses are granted out of exclusive licences held by the company (eg conduit arrangements).

In this case, 'substantial' has been defined – licensing income from non-qualifying IP rights will be substantial if it is more than:

(a) £2m; or

(b) (if lower) 20% of the gross income of the trade for that accounting period.

There is a de minimis level so that, if the licensing income from non-qualifying IP rights is no more than £50,000, it will not be regarded as substantial even where it is more than 20% of gross income.

New rules: small claims elections

18.39 Under the new rules, three elections are available to companies with lower levels of patent box profits to simplify the calculation of the patent box for such companies. These are the global streaming election (see **18.40**), the notional royalty election (see **18.19**), and the small claims figure election to calculate the marketing assets return (see **18.44**).

In order to make these elections, a company must calculate its patent box profits using the new rules and must meet the following conditions:

- the company must have only one trade; and
- the company must have qualifying residual profits for the accounting period (see below) of less than:

  (a) £1,000,000; or

  (b) the relevant maximum (see below) for the accounting period, if higher.

However, even if a company meets these conditions, it cannot make any of these elections if (*CTA 2010, s 375BN(3)*):

(a) the company's qualifying residual profits exceed £1,000,000 for the accounting period; and

(b) the company has calculated patent box profits on the basis of the new rules in any of the previous four years; and

(c) the company did not make the relevant election in each of the years in that prior four year period in which it used the new rules to calculate patent box profits.

'Qualifying residual profit' for the purposes of establishing eligibility to make these elections, is effectively the aggregate result of the patent box calculation under the new rules, up to and including Step 4, ignoring any sub-stream with a negative result.

The 'relevant maximum' is £3,000,000 where the claimant company has no related 51% group companies. Where it has got related 51% group companies, then the 'relevant maximum' is (£3,000,000)/(1+N), where N is the number of related 51% group companies that are elected into the patent box (whether under the old rules or the new rules).

Step 1 – identify the streams of income

18.40 Grandfathered rules: the taxable income of the trade (ie all amounts brought in as taxable credits), after deduction of finance income, must be apportioned into two streams of income:

(a) relevant intellectual property (RIPI) income (this is the same as the RIPI established at Step 2 of the standard calculation; and

(b) all other income.

New rules: the taxable income of the trade (as above) is apportioned between IP and non-income streams. The IP stream is then divided into "relevant IP income sub-streams" so that each sub-stream consists of income attributable to a particular qualifying IP right or to a particular kind of IP item (a product or product category), where it is not practicable to stream on the basis of qualifying IP rights, such as where the claimant company produces products covered by multiple qualifying IP rights.

A company with small patent box profits (see **18.39**) can make a global streaming election (*CTA 2010, s 357BNC*) in order to calculation the patent box on the basis of a single IP stream, as under the grandfathered rules – although note that the R&D fraction is still applied to this stream.

In addition, a company with small patent box profits with IP-derived income which is not in Heads 1–5 of the definition of RIPI (see **18.18** above) can elect to use a notional royalty (as in **18.19**) and further may elect to use a fixed percentage of 75% of the IP-derived income instead of calculating the 'appropriate percentage'.

Step 2 – allocate expenses between the income streams

18.41 **Grandfathered rules:** the expenses of the trade (ie all debits deducted in calculating taxable profits except finance debits, the additional deductions for R&D relief or television programme relief, video games relief, or theatrical production relief) plus any R&D shortfall amount, are allocated to the income stream to which they relate on a just and reasonable basis. This should result in the RIPI stream having intellectual property-related expenses allocated to it and all other expenses allocated to the non-RIPI stream. All debits must be allocated to one of the two streams.

New rules: the expenses of the trade are allocated on a just and reasonable basis between the "all other income" (non-IP) stream and each of the relevant IP income sub-streams (or to the global IP stream where a company with small patent box profits has elected to use global streaming). Finance debits, the additional deductions for R&D relief or television programme relief, video games relief, and theatrical production relief continue to be excluded, but the R&D shortfall adjustment is not included in the new rules.

What is 'just and reasonable' will depend on the company's particular circumstances and, once established, the same method of allocation must be used in each accounting period unless there is a change of circumstances relating to the trade of the company which makes the method inappropriate.

Under the grandfathered rules, where the allocation method is no longer appropriate, the company can either chose a different method or elect out of the streaming calculation where it is not mandatory. There is no restriction on a company later electing back into the streaming calculation in a later accounting period, if it becomes appropriate again.

Under the new rules (or where HMRC required the use of streaming under the grandfathered rules) the company must amend the methodology if it ceases to be appropriate.

Step 3 – calculate the net relevant intellectual property income amount

18.42 This is straightforward: deduct the amount calculated in Step 2 from the amount calculated at Step 1 in respect of each sub-stream (or from the global IP stream where a company with small patent box profits has elected to use global streaming).

Step 4 – deduct the routine return

18.43 **Grandfathered rules:** the routine return is 10% of the routine expenses which are included in the RIPI stream.

New rules: the routine return is 10% of the routine expenses which are included in the relevant IP income sub-stream (or in the global IP stream where a company with small patent box profits has elected to use global streaming).

'Routine expenses' are the same as those for the standard calculation (see **18.25–18.27**).

Step 5/6 - deduct marketing assets return

18.44 If the result of the calculation at the end of Step 4 is a figure greater than nil, a marketing return is then calculated and deducted.

The marketing return is calculated as in the apportionment method, using either the small claims figure (calculated as set out in **18.30**, and available by election for company with small patent box profits, for which see **18.39**) or by using the notional marketing royalty as for the apportionment method (see **18.28** onwards), for each trade (pre-July 2016 rules) or relevant IP income sub-stream (or to the global IP stream where a company with small patent box profits has elected to use global streaming) (new rules).

Note that the small claims figure election is not available to a company for qualifying residual profit of more than £1,000,000 which was elected into the patent box under the old rules in any of the previous four years, but did not elect to use the small claims treatment available under the old rules in each such year.

As with the apportionment method, if the marketing assets return is less than 10% of the amount of the relevant IP income stream (grandfathered rules) or sub-stream (or to the global IP stream where a company with small patent box profits has elected to use global streaming) (new rules), or the actual marketing royalty exceeds the notional marketing royalty, the marketing assets return is taken to be nil.

New rules – new Step seven – apply R&D fraction

18.45 The BEPS framework requires that patent boxes be limited by the amount of economic substance/activity in the jurisdiction where the patent box is offered. As there are many ways that economic substance could be measured, the proposals opt for research and development activity as a proxy. Accordingly, patent boxes are required to limit the tax benefit in accordance with the proportion of R&D undertaken by the claimant in respect of the specific patent or product for which the patent box is claimed.

The UK follows the framework closely, setting out an 'R&D fraction' which must be applied to each IP asset's patent box profits (or to the global IP stream where a company with small patent box profits has elected to use global streaming) to establish the deduction that will be available.

This is set out as the lower of:

$$\frac{(D + S) \times 1.3}{(D + S + A + R)} \text{ and}$$

where:

D = direct (in-house) R&D costs

S = costs of R&D subcontracted to third parties

A = IP acquisition/licensing costs

R = costs of R&D subcontracted to related parties

D, S, A and R are calculated on a cumulative basis, over the life of the relevant IP asset; it will be necessary to identify R&D expenditure, and acquisition costs, relating to an IP asset and maintain records of that expenditure for up to 20 years.

In effect, patent box claims will effectively be limited where the company outsources a substantial amount of R&D to related parties – even if those related parties are in the UK. Groups could well need to rethink their R&D arrangements accordingly. The limitation relating to acquired/licensed IP costs may, in practice, be less of an issue – if the company is spending that much, comparatively, on the relevant acquired/licensed IP, it may well not meet the development condition.

The *Finance (No 2) Bill 2017* includes provisions regarding cost-sharing arrangements, to ensure that companies are neither advantaged nor disadvantaged by such arrangements in calculating the nexus fraction. These provisions take effect from 1 April 2017.

In exceptional circumstances, where the R&D fraction is not an accurate reflection of the position, the company can increase the R&D fraction (although it can never increase above 1). This may, for example, arise where a company has acquired intellectual property which later turns out to contribute very little value to the eventual product.

Following the application of the R&D fraction, all the IP sub-streams of the trade are added together (unless the company has elected to use global streaming).

Pre-grant relief and deduction calculation

18.46 The calculation of pre-grant relief and the deduction (and phasing in, to April 2017) is the same for the streaming method as for the apportionment method (see **18.35–18.37** above).

Note that the pre-grant relief adjustment is made after the R&D fraction under the new rules; the calculation of the amount of the relief for earlier years will have included the R&D fraction and so it does not need to be applied again when the relief is actually given.

TRANSITION FROM GRANDFATHERED RULES TO NEW RULES

18.47 As noted above, the grandfathered rules continue to apply until 30 June 2021 to existing IP (ie that applied for before 1 July 2016) of companies who have elected into the patent box with effect from a period before 1 July 2016.

For companies that continue to develop intellectual property, it is likely that over that five-year period, new qualifying IP will start to apply to existing products as they continue to be developed. Such products will, therefore, be covered by both new and grandfathered IP. Provided that the core IP of the product is grandfathered (pre-1 July 2016) IP, then the income from that product will continue to be within the grandfathered rules.

Where the core IP underlying the product becomes new IP, but the product remains covered by some grandfathered IP, it will be necessary to apportion the profit from the product between the grandfathered rules and the new rules, following the proportion of grandfathered IP to total qualifying IP.

From 1 July 2021, the new rules will apply to all companies elected into the patent box, in respect of all qualifying IP.

PATENT BOX LOSSES

Focus

18.48 Patent box losses (relevant intellectual property losses, or RIPL) are a product of the patent box calculation, whether standard or streaming, and can arise in otherwise profitable companies – broadly, a patent box loss will arise where the expenses relating to relevant intellectual property income exceed that income.

Where a trade generates a patent box loss, that loss *must* be set against patent box profits of (in order):

(a) other trades of the company;

(b) other group companies; and

(c) future accounting periods of the company or other group companies.

Any patent box loss set off against patent box profits will reduce the amount of the patent box deduction in calculating the taxable profits of the company. Essentially, a company cannot have the benefit of the patent box relief until all patent box losses of that company or any of its group companies have been utilised.

Losing the losses

18.49 The patent box losses of a company are not necessarily extinguished by the company:

- ceasing to trade; or
- revoking its election into the patent box regime; or
- ceasing to be within the corporation tax charge.

If there are any patent box losses in a company when one of these events occurs, those losses must be transferred to any other group company that is a qualifying company at that time. Only if there are no other group companies elected into the patent box are the patent box losses extinguished if the company ceases to trade etc.

ANTI-AVOIDANCE

Principal anti-avoidance rule

18.50 The main anti-avoidance rules applies where a company which has elected into the patent box regime is party to a scheme, one of the main purposes of which is to obtain a relevant tax advantage (*CTA 2010, s 357FB*).

A 'relevant tax advantage' is obtained where patent box profits are increased as a result of the scheme and the scheme is:

- designed to avoid the application of any part of the patent box rules; or

- designed to create a mismatch between expenses and income relating to a qualifying IP right (eg where a company enters a group);
- designed to recognise non-IP income as something other than revenue (to increase the proportion of IP income).

Anti-avoidance – exclusivity

18.51 Where a licence is made exclusive and the main purpose (or one of the main purposes) of the exclusivity is to get the benefit of the patent box, the patent box relief will not be available. That is, exclusivity in a licence should be commercially justifiable for income derived from that licence to qualify for the patent box relief.

Anti-avoidance – incorporation of patented items

18.52 An anti-avoidance rule also applies where a patented item is incorporated into a product simply to bring the sale of the product within the patent box regime – there must be some commercial reason for the inclusion of the patented item within the overall product.

Example calculations

18.53 The examples below illustrate the pre-1 July 2016 rules and the new rules.

Example calculation – post 1 July 2017 rules

Assume that this relates to a company's accounting period for the calendar year 2018, and that the company has only one (old) patent and no associated companies, and the following financial information:

Trade turnover (from the accounts)	£10,000,000
Of which, IP income is:	
Income from sales of patent product	£6,000,000
Settlement award relating to patent	£1,000,000
Interest income	£1,000,000
Interest expense	£250,000
Routine expenses	£1,250,000
R&D expenses within routine expenses	£300,000

Total R&D tax relief claimed	£450,000 (tax relief only, not including costs)
Taxable profits (before patent box)	£4,000,000

Step one: calculate TI: 'trade income'

Gross trade turnover	£10,000,000
Less finance-related income	(£1,000,000)
TI	£9,000,000

Step two: establish RIPI: 'relevant IP income' and X%

Income from sale of patented items	£6,000,000
Infringement income	£1,000,000
RIPI	£7,000,000

$$X\% = \frac{\text{RIPI}}{\text{TI}} \times 100$$

$$\frac{£7,000,000}{£9,000,000} \times 100 \qquad 77.78\%$$

(Note: if the company had elected to use the streaming calculation, this would be Step 1 of the calculation. Step 2 would be an analysis of all expenditure, allocating it between IP and non-IP streams, on a just and reasonable basis. For reasons of space, no example of the streaming calculation differences has been given.)

Step three: establish X% of adjusted profits

Taxable profits	£4,000,000	
Add back R&D tax relief claimed	£450,000	
Add back loan relationship debits	£250,000	
Less R&D adjustment	(£200,000)	– see below
Less finance-related income	(£1,000,000)	
Adjusted profits	£3,500,000	
X% of adjusted profits		
77.78% × £3,500,000	£2,722,300	

(Note: if the company had elected for the streaming calculation, this step would be simply to deduct the figure in Step 2 from the figure in Step 1.)

Early years R&D average spend adjustment

Assume that in the four years prior to electing into the patent box, the company's average R&D expenditure in the accounts was £1m. Accounts R&D expenditure in each of the accounting periods in the four years following entry into the patent box is (assume 12-month accounting periods):

AP1 (2013):	£1,050,000	>100%, no adjustment and £50,000 c/f
AP2 (2014):	£800,000	>75%, no adjustment but <100% so no additional c/f
AP3 (2015):	£500,000	<75%, use £50,000 b/f to increase, but adjustment of £200,000 still required to match pre-patent box average

The company will need to check R&D expenditure again in AP4, but not thereafter.

Step four: establish QRP: 'qualifying residual profit'

Routine costs (from tax computation)	£1,250,000
Less routine costs on which R&D relief claimed	(£300,000)
Routine expenses	£950,000
10% of routine expenses	£95,000
X% of routine expenses	
77.78% (from step three) × £95,000	£73,891
QRP (X% of adjusted profits less X% of routine expenses)	
£2,722,300 – £73,891	£2,648,409

(Note: if following the streaming calculation, only those routine costs in the IP expenses stream calculated at Step 2 would be taken into account, and QRP would be 10% of those routine costs.)

Step five: establish RIPP by formula deduction of marketing royalty (by election, if qualifying)

Company will qualify as QRP < £3,000,000 and QRP also < £3,000,000/associates/trades

Adjusted QRP = **lower** of 75% × QRP/associates/trades **or** £1,000,000

75% × QRP/associates/trades   75% × £2,648,409/1/1 = £1,986,307

As this is more than £1,000,000, QRP would be reduced to £1,000,000 if an election to use this step was made.

Step six: establish RIPP by marketing royalty deduction (where step five not used)

Assuming the company does not pay any marketing royalties

Notional marketing royalty (from valuation)	£250,000
Actual marketing royalty	£0
Net marketing royalty	£250,000
This is less than 10% of the QRP calculated above, so no adjustment required	
RIPP	£2,648,409

In this case, it would not benefit the company to elect to use the formula in Step 5, as that will more than halve the amount of patent box relief available. Even with the costs of a valuation exercise taken into account, Step 6 would seem more likely to be beneficial.

Step seven: pre-grant relief (by election)

In 2015 the company is granted a patent it applied for in 2010. The company had elected into the patent box when first able to do so, in 2013. The additional RIPP that would have been included in the patent box calculation if the patent had been granted in earlier years is:

2013:	£300,000
2014:	£500,000
Total	£800,000 added to 2015 RIPP if elect to do so
RIPP for 2015, on election	
£2,648,409 + £800,000	£3,448,409

Phasing-in adjustment

As the accounting period (calendar year 2018) is not within the phasing-in period, no adjustment to RIPP is required.

Patent box deduction

The deduction from taxable profits is given by the formula:

$$\frac{\text{RIPP} \times (\text{main rate of corporation tax-patent box rate})}{\text{main rate of corporation tax}}$$

Deduction (as 2018 corporation tax rate is 19% and patent box rate is 10%)

$$\frac{£3{,}448{,}409 \times (19-10)}{19} = £\ 1{,}633{,}457$$

Corporation tax

The company's taxable profits before the patent box deduction were £4,000,000 (as at Step 3) so, following deduction of the patent box, total taxable profits are:

£4,000,000 – £1,633,457	£ 2,366,543
and corporation tax payable is reduced from	
£4,000,000 @ 19%	£760,000
to	
£2,663,741 @ 19%	**£449,643**

Example calculation – new rules

Assume that this relates to a company's accounting period for the calendar year 2018, and that the company has only one (new) IP asset and no associated companies, and the following financial information:

Income from sales of patented product	£6,000,000
Settlement award relating to patent	£1,000,000
Routine expenses	£1,250,000
R&D expenses within routine expenses	£300,000
Taxable profits (before patent box)	£4,000,000

Step one: IP income

Allocate any income taken into account in calculating the profits of the trade (ignoring any finance income) between a non-IP income stream and an IP income stream.

Income from sale of patented items	£6,000,000
Infringement income	£1,000,000
IP stream	£7,000,000

Step two: sub-divide IP streams

For companies with multiple IP assets, the IP income stream will need to be divided into IP sub-streams, one for each IP asset. The non-IP income stream is disregarded for the rest of the calculation. In this example, the company has only one IP asset and so the IP sub-stream is the same as the IP stream above.

Step three: allocate expenditure

Allocate expenditure brought into account in calculating the profits of the trade (ignoring loan relationship debits and additional deductions for R&D relief, television production relief, video game relief or theatrical production relief) relating solely to non-IP income to the non-IP stream. Allocate expenditure relating solely to each IP asset to the IP sub-stream for that IP asset. Establish one or more methodologies for allocating overhead expenses between the IP sub-streams and the non-IP expense stream.

As methodologies will vary substantially between companies, this example does not set out any methodologies

IP income stream	£7,000,000
Allocated expenses (ignoring R&D relief)	(£3,500,000)

Step four: deduct expenses allocated and routine return

For each IP sub-stream, identify the routine expenses allocated to that sub-stream, less any non-routine deductions (such as R&D expenses) and calculate 10% of such expenses to establish the routine return for that sub-stream.

Routine expenses in sub-stream	£1,250,000
Less routine costs on which R&D relief claimed	(£300,000)
Routine expenses	£950,000
Routine return: 10% of routine expenses	£95,000

IP stream income	£7,000,000
Less: IP stream expenses	(£3,500,000)
Less: routine return	(£95,000)
IP stream	£3,405,000

Step five: deduct marketing royalty by formula deduction (by election, if qualifying)

Company will not qualify as QRP > £3,000,000, so no election can be made.

Step six: deduct marketing royalty (where Step five not used)

Assuming the company does not pay any marketing royalties:

Notional marketing royalty (from valuation)	£250,000
Actual marketing royalty	£0
Net marketing royalty	£250,000
This is less than 10% of the QRP calculated above, so no adjustment required	
IP stream	£3,405,000

Step seven: apply the R&D fraction

Assume that:

- cumulative direct R&D costs on the IP asset ('D') are £1,500,000
- cumulative third party sub-contracted R&D costs ('S') are £0
- cumulative acquisition costs ('A') are £500,000
- cumulative group R&D costs ('R') are £0

The R&D fraction is the lower of ((D+S) × 1.3)/(D+S+A+R) and 1

Applying the formula gives: ((1,500,000+0) × 1.3)(1,500,000+0+500,000+0) = 0.975

As this is lower than 1, this is the fraction used.

Applying this to the IP stream gives: £3,405,000 × 0.975 = £3,319,875.

Step eight: add together IP streams

Having repeated Steps two to seven to establish the IP sub-stream for each IP asset, add together the IP sub-streams to establish the total patent box profits.

In this example, there is only one IP asset, so the total patent box profit is £3,319,875.

Step nine: pre-grant relief (by election)

Assume that the patent for which patent box profits are being calculated was granted in 2018, having been applied for in August 2016. The company had elected into the patent box when first able to do so, in 2016. The additional patent box profit that would have been included in the patent box calculation if the patent had been granted in earlier years is:

2016:	£300,000
2017:	£500,000
Total	£800,000 added to 2018 patent box profits if elect to do so
Additional patent box profits for 2018, on election	
£3,319,875 + £800,000	£4,119,875

Patent box deduction

The deduction from taxable profits is given by the formula:

$$\frac{\text{IP stream} \times (\text{main rate of corporation tax-patent box rate})}{\text{main rate of corporation tax}}$$

Deduction (assuming 19% corporation tax rate and patent box rate is 10%)

$$\frac{£4,119,875 \times (19 - 10)}{19} = £1,951,520$$

Corporation tax

The company's taxable profits before the patent box deduction were £4,000,000 so, following deduction of the patent box, total taxable profits are:

£4,000,000 – £1,951,520	£2,048,480
and corporation tax payable is reduced from	
£4,000,000 @ 19%	£760,000
to	
£2,048,480 @ 19%	**£389,211**

Chapter 19

Investors' relief

Chris Williams LLB

This chapter includes material originally adapted from the book *Capital Gains Tax Reliefs for SMEs and Entrepreneurs* (Bloomsbury Professional) by Satwaki Chanda and Chris Williams.

SIGNPOSTS

- **Operation of the relief** – Which disposals qualify, shareholding requirements, interests in shares (see **19.3–19.12**).
- **Comparison with other reliefs** – The differences from entrepreneurs' relief and EIS are handily summarised (see **19.3–19.4**).
- **What companies and shares qualify** – No listing at time of issue, what is an ordinary share, trading requirements (see **19.13–19.21**).
- **Who can claim the relief** – Which individuals, what sort of trusts and what connections they can have with the company, when relief is denied (**19.22–19.26**).
- **Order of disposal** – Qualifying, potentially qualifying and excluded shares, special share identification rules for IR, lifetime limit for IR (see **19.27–19.37**).
- **Share reorganisations** – Reconstructions and share exchanges (see **19.38–19.42**).
- **Overseas matters** – Remittance basis, temporary non-residents (see **19.43–19.45**).
- **Trustees** – Need for a qualifying beneficiary, what are the trust business assets, how much relief can be claimed, how to make that claim, offshore trusts (see **19.46–19.57**).

INTRODUCTION

19.1 *Finance Act 2016, Sch 14* introduced *TCGA 1992, ss 169VA–169VY* and *Sch 7ZB* which add investors' relief (IR) to the range of CGT reliefs. Announced in the 2016 Budget as an extended form of entrepreneurs' relief (ER), investors' relief (IR) shares both the 10% rate of CGT and £10 million lifetime relief limit but little else. In particular, IR only applies to company shares and the provisions are deliberately drafted to ensure that there is minimal overlap between IR and ER; it would be virtually unheard of for a person to be eligible for both IR and ER on shares in the same company.

The discrete nature of the two reliefs is something of a double-edged sword in that they do not overlap and an individual's shareholding that qualifies for IR will not also be eligible for ER and vice versa, so it is essential that the right relief be identified. But this is not all bad news, in fact the separation provides a great advantage because each is subject to a lifetime limit of £10 million, both of which may be used. Thus an individual may be able to take advantage of 10% rates on gains of up to £20 million.

IR can apply to shares:

- subscribed for by the claimant;
- issued on or after 17 March 2016; and
- disposed of on or after 6 April 2019,

subject to the qualifying conditions being met.

Every individual has a lifetime IR allowance (currently £10 million), of gains against which relief may be claimed. Trusts do not have a separate limit but may use a beneficiary's allowance. The IR allowance is separate from and additional to the individual's IR limit.

IR does not apply automatically but must be claimed (see **19.57**). This enables the taxpayer to choose whether claiming the relief is in his best interests, perhaps not to claim in order to use another roll-over or deferral relief, or to preserve the lifetime limit so it can be used for another disposal. Sometimes, a protective IR claim may be advisable, such as where the taxpayer is non-resident or non-domiciled, but there is a possibility that he may resume UK residence within five years, after the time limit for claiming IR has passed (see **19.45**).

Legislation

19.2 The IR legislation is *TCGA 1992, ss 169VA–169VY* and *Sch 7ZB*.

TCGA 1992, s 169VA acts as a contents section for the main IR provisions thus:

- *TCGA 1992, s 169VB* defines 'qualifying shares', 'potentially qualifying shares' and 'excluded shares';
- *TCGA 1992, s 169VC* creates the relief, to be known as 'investors' relief';
- *TCGA 1992, s 169VD* deals with disposals from holdings consisting partly of qualifying shares;
- *TCGA 1992, ss 169VE* to *169VG* contain rules to determine which shares remain in the holding out of which previous disposals have been made;
- *TCGA 1992, ss 169VH* and *169VI* make provision about disposals by trusts;
- *TCGA 1992, s 169VJ* makes provision about disposals of interests in shares;
- *TCGA 1992, ss 169VK* and *169VL* cap the amount of IR that can be claimed;
- *TCGA 1992, s 169VM* makes provision about claims for investors' relief;
- *TCGA 1992, ss 169VN* to *169VT* make provision for IR following a company's reorganisation of its share capital, an exchange of shares or securities or a scheme of reconstruction;
- *TCGA 1992, ss 169VU* to *169VY* contain definitions; and
- *TCGA 1992, Sch 7ZB* contains provisions about disqualification of shares where the investor receives value within the 'period of restriction'.

As at the end of June 2017, no HMRC guidance had been published beyond the Budget announcement (tinyurl.com/j9ef9pg).

COMPARISON WITH ENTREPRENEURS' RELIEF AND EIS/SEIS

Entrepreneurs' relief

19.3 Although the reliefs are superficially similar it cannot be stressed enough that they are designed to operate as separate, mutually exclusive reliefs: hence the duplication of the lifetime limits on gains qualifying for relief. There are numerous differences between the reliefs, reflecting the fact that ER is intended to reward owner-participators whilst IR is specifically intended to act as an inducement to attract investment from participators who will not be involved in the business at all when they invest and are not expected to become involved at the time when they invest.

The table below summarises key differences

	Investors' relief	**Entrepreneurs' relief**
Type of business	Company only	Company or partnership
Qualifying activity	Any trade, must be carried on for a qualifying period of at least one year, ending on disposal or ceasing to be a trading company within three years before disposal	Any trade, must be carried on throughout a period of 12 months ending on either the date of disposal or, if the company has ceased to be a trading company, within the three years preceding disposal
Share acquisition	Subscription only: shares may not be acquired by gift except inter-spouse transfers	Any method of acquisition
Ownership period	Minimum ownership period three years Only the original subscriber (or spouse) may claim IR: the shares must be held throughout the period from issue to disposal without any break	One year
Minimum interest	No minimum shareholding requirement	Minimum shareholding 5% of voting and assets except where shares acquired through EMI
Assets used in the business	No relief for any asset other than the IR shares	Associated disposals relief available if the individual is entitled to ER
Trusts	Trustees may hold shares for benefit of any beneficiary	Trustees may hold shares for benefit of any beneficiary who holds the required minimum interest for the company to be his personal company

Activity in the business	Investor may not be an employee or director other than an unremunerated director at the time when the shares are issued. Subject to conditions, an investor may subsequently become an employee or remunerated director without invalidating IR	Shareholder must be an officer or employee of the company

In most cases the would-be investor will not have a choice between IR and ER at the time when the investment is made because of the restrictions relating to employment status:

- an existing employee or office-holder other than an unremunerated director cannot qualify for IR;
- a non-employee cannot qualify for ER at the time of the investment but may find that he can claim ER when he comes to sell his shares if he has become an employee in the meantime and acquired the requisite shareholding interest; and
- an investor who has become eligible for ER may not have shed his entitlement to claim IR when disposing of his shares.

EIS and SEIS

19.4 Unlike entrepreneurs' relief (ER) which is specifically targeted at participators in the business, IR is a relief that competes with the Enterprise Investment Scheme (EIS) and Seed EIS (SEIS) as a means of attracting investment from investors who are not involved in running the business.

The table below summarises key differences

	Investors' relief	**EIS/SEIS**
Activity	Any trade but the investee company must be a trading company throughout the period of ownership	Restricted to qualifying trades through the three year qualifying period from issue/ starting to trade
Nature of relief	Reduced rate of CGT on disposal	Income tax relief as a percentage of investment • Shares exempt from CGT • Hold-over relief for gains reinvested in shares

Share acquisition	Subscription only: shares may not be acquired by gift except inter-spouse transfers	Subscription only: shares may not be acquired by gift except inter-spouse transfers
Ownership period	Minimum ownership period three years Only the original subscriber (or spouse) may claim IR: the shares must be held throughout the period from issue to disposal without any break	Minimum ownership period three years from later of issue and commencement to trade Only the original subscriber (or spouse) may claim IR: the shares must be held throughout the period from issue to disposal without any break
Minimum interest	No minimum shareholding requirement	No minimum shareholding requirement
Trusts	Trustees may hold shares for benefit of any beneficiary	Trustees may hold shares for benefit of any beneficiary who holds the required minimum interest
Activity in the business	Investor may not be an employee or director other than an unremunerated director at the time when the shares are issued. Subject to conditions, an investor may subsequently become an employee or remunerated director without invalidating IR	Shareholder must be an officer or employee of the company

Investors in companies eligible for SEIS or EIS will generally find that EIS/SEIS is the preferred option because of SEIS and EIS offer much greater advantages than the reduction in CGT rate that is the sole tax advantage of IR.

Planning tip

Shares in an EIS/SEIS company may lose their status, so that the EIS/SEIS relief is withdrawn. This is most likely to happen because the investor receives value from the company or the company's trade ceases to meet the strict qualifying trade rules for EIS/SEIS. But there is no provision in *TCGA 1992* that excludes IR where EIS or SEIS relief has been claimed, whether or not the relief has been withdrawn. There is also no need to claim IR at the time of investment, only following disposal. Therefore an EIS/SEIS investor would still be able to claim IR if the IR relief conditions were met in relation to shares on which EIS/SEIS relief had been claimed but on which the relief had been withdrawn.

OPERATION OF THE RELIEF

What disposals qualify?

19.5 IR is available on gains made by an individual who disposes of qualifying:

- ordinary shares;
- in a trading company or holding company of a trading group;
- issued to the claimant when none of the company's shares or securities is listed on a recognised stock exchange, on or after17 March 2016;
- held for a minimum period of three years; and
- disposed of on or after 6 April 2019.

Although no claims will be possible until 6 April 2019, it is essential that would-be claimants ensure that the conditions for a claim are observed and maintained throughout the period from issue of the shares until their disposal.

A disposal for IR can be:

- a sale;
- a gift or transfer at undervalue;
- where a capital distribution is received in respect of shares held in a company, for example on the liquidation of that company; or
- a capital sum derived from an asset.

No minimum shareholding required

19.6 In contrast with ER, IR carries no minimum or maximum limit on the size of the qualifying shareholding. This simplifies matters considerably in the sense that investors do not need to be wary of their shareholdings falling below any threshold.

Qualifying shares

19.7 *TCGA 1992, s 169VB* applies the qualifying share (QS) test at the point immediately preceding disposal. However, all but one of the criteria must be satisfied throughout the investor's 'share-holding period'.

The shares must be subscribed for by the investor. The subscription conditions are that:

- the investor subscribes for the shares personally, in his own right;
- the shares are issued to the investor, ie not to a nominee or trustee;
- the only consideration for subscription is cash;
- the shares are fully paid up at the time of issue;
- the shares are subscribed for and issued for genuine commercial reasons and not as part of arrangements the main purpose, or one of the main purposes of which, is to secure a tax advantage to any person; and
- the subscription is an arm's length bargain (*TCGA 1992, s 169VU(1)*).

Married couples and civil partners

19.8 The investor can transfer qualifying shares to their spouse or civil partner, at a time when they are living together as a married couple/civil partnership, without losing the benefit if IR. In this case the transferee is treated as if he had subscribed for the shares on the date on which they were issued to the transferor. Because a transferee spouse is treated as having been the subscriber they too can transfer the shares back to the original subscriber or to a new spouse (*TCGA 1992, s 169VU(3), (4)*).

Planning point

The freedom to transfer qualifying shares between spouses offers more than just flexibility: if one spouse held shares on which the gains would exceed their lifetime allowance, he/she could transfer those shares to their spouse or civil partner at any time up until immediately before disposal so as to take advantage of the transferee spouse's lifetime limit.

Jointly held shares

19.9 IR is available on shares issued to the individual or trustee holder and to interests in shares that they subscribed for within the meaning given by *TCGA 1992, s 169VU*:

> '(1) For the purposes of this Chapter (other than this subsection) a person "subscribes for" a share in a company if –
>
> (a) that person subscribes for the share,
>
> (b) the share is issued to that person by the company for consideration consisting wholly of cash,

(c) the share is fully paid up at the time it is issued,

(d) the share is subscribed for, and issued, for genuine commercial reasons and not as part of arrangements the main purpose, or one of the main purposes, of which is to secure a tax advantage to any person, and

(e) the share is subscribed for, and issued, by way of a bargain at arm's length.'

However, *TCGA 1992, s 169VJ* explicitly provides for disposals of joint holdings and interests in shares. This creates a mess of confusion because, whilst more than one individual may subscribe jointly for shares (though only the first-named holder may be recorded on the company's statutory register) it is not possible to subscribe for an interest in shares.

Joint ownership

19.10 Unless it is accepted that a joint owner can be treated as a subscriber, even though the shares were not actually issued to them, the provisions allowing for joint ownership appear to be restricted to married couples and civil partnerships. *TCGA 1992, s 169VU* provides specifically for a transferee spouse to be treated as if they were the original subscriber for the shares and so obtain IR. Therefore, the only certainty in relation to joint ownership and interests in shares is that IR will be available to spouses and civil partners who receive their interests from their spouse who was the original subscriber. This will cover shares transferred into joint names and cases where the subscriber spouse does not transfer legal ownership but creates an interest for their spouse in any other way, such as by a declaration that they hold shares on bare trust for themselves and their spouse as joint owners.

If the subscriber creates an interest for a non-spouse that will be a disposal, on which IR may be claimable, but the transferee will not be able to claim IR on their subsequent disposal of the shares.

Interests in shares

19.11 It would appear that the references to disposal of an interest can only apply to a subscriber who makes a part disposal by creating an interest over the shares that they continue to legally own. The one case where an interest in shares will clearly be eligible for IR concerns married couples: if the husband subscribes for shares and subsequently makes a declaration of trust, sharing beneficial ownership with his wife, they will both be able to claim IR.

Continuous ownership from subscription until disposal

19.12 Any shares acquired as qualifying shares will cease to be qualifying shares if they are disposed of, other than to a spouse or civil partner. Therefore, the investor cannot sell and reacquire the shares and hope to obtain IR on their eventual disposal (*TCGA 1992, s 169VB(2)(b)*).

WHICH COMPANIES AND SHARES QUALIFY?

No stock exchange listing at time of issue

19.13 The company may not have any of its shares listed on a recognised stock exchange at the time when the IR shares are issued. A recognised stock exchange does not include AIM and the application of this requirement only at the time of issue means that early investors in companies that later become listed will still be able to benefit from IR when they eventually dispose of their shares (*TCGA 1992, s 169VB(2)(d)*).

This continuity of treatment may be affected if there is a reorganisation, reconstruction or disposal of the company in exchange for shares, because special rules apply in such cases and continuity cannot always be guaranteed (see **19.38–19.42**).

Shares must be ordinary shares

19.14 This requirement does not apply throughout the share-holding period, only at the times:

- when the share is issued; and
- immediately before disposal.

The definition of an ordinary share has been the subject of a number of legal cases in relation to EIS and ER and there may be problems with shares carrying fixed dividend rights, a specified 'zero-dividend' right or no dividend rights at all (see **19.15**).

Ordinary shares

19.15 Ordinary share capital is defined in *ITA 2007, s 989* as all of a company's issued share capital (however described), other than capital the holders of which have a right to a dividend at a fixed rate but have no other right to share in the company's profits. The interpretation of this apparently simple definition has caused a number of problems and led to tribunal decisions that have not entirely clarified matters.

The latest case to consider this issue is *McQuillan v HMRC* [2016] UKFTT 305 (TC) in which the First-tier Tribunal (FTT) had to consider whether redeemable non-voting shares which were not entitled to any dividend should be regarded as ordinary shares. HMRC argued that entitlement to no dividend was not the same as being entitled to a fixed dividend of 0% which would have brought the shares within the scope of *ITA 2007, s 989*. In this instance the NV shares had been created for a specific non-tax purpose and were not intended to unbalance the rights and entitlements attaching to the other shares which all the shareholders regarded as the true ordinary share capital. The FTT decided that in this respect *ITA 2007, s 989* was ambiguous and it was just that it should be interpreted in a way that did not create an absurd result.

This contrasts with another ER case, decided only two months earlier than *McQuillan*: in *Castledine v HMRC* ([2016] UKFTT 145 (TC)) the FTT decided that non-voting deferred shares which carried no dividend rights and entitlement to a small share of assets in a winding up were ordinary share capital. The FTT found that although the chance of those shares participating in the company's profits was vanishingly small, that chance nonetheless existed and so the deferred shares did form part of the company's ordinary share capital. The FTT's view on this occasion was that *ITA 2007, s 989* was unambiguous and had to be followed to the letter.

The uncertainty over the definition of ordinary share capital is unlikely to cause as many problems under IR as it can for ER because investors will normally want shares that participate fully in dividends and capital; care is nevertheless needed to ensure that shares subscribed for in the hope of obtaining IR do meet this criterion.

Fixed rate preference shares do not count as ordinary share capital, but it is not always clear whether the preference shares are fixed rate. The coupon on a preference share can be fixed at the outset, but the actual amount may vary. Where the share has a stepped coupon, such that the actual percentage changes from year to year, HMRC do not regard those shares as being fixed rate. Where shares carry no dividend rights, HMRC consider those shares to be ordinary shares, not shares with a fixed-rate dividend of 0% (see Employee Share Schemes User Guide at ESSUM23230).

Appendix 11 to the HMRC Capital Gains Manual provides a discussion of what HMRC consider to be ordinary share capital, which may be particularly helpful when dealing with non-UK companies. Note that there is no requirement for the company to be resident in the UK, or trading in the UK, for the shares to qualify for IR.

Trading company or holding company of a trading group

19.16 This requirement will apply throughout the share-holding period, ie from issue until immediately before disposal which could be a long time. The government is clearly conscious of its need to prevent companies being used at any time as investment-holding vehicles; this requirement is significantly different from the ER requirement that the company should have been a trading company or holding company of a trading group only for a final 12-month period. This is examined further in **19.17**.

Trading activities

19.17 Trading activities are those carried on by the company or group in the course of, or for the purposes of, a trade that it is carrying on, or it is preparing to carry on (*TCGA 1992, s 165A(4)*). HMRC regard trading activities as including those activities that a company or group has to carry out before it can start trading. In such cases, trading activities may include developing a business plan, acquiring premises, hiring staff, ordering materials and incurring pre-trading expenditure (CG64065).

HMRC highlight the distinction between trading and investment activities. HMRC give the example of land bought either as trading stock or as a fixed asset to be used to support the trading business, in which case the buying of the land would be a trading activity. Conversely, the land may be held as an investment to generate rental income, which is not a trading activity (CG64060). In some circumstances, the making and holding of investments may be part of the company's or group's trading activities; whether those activities are trading activities can only be decided on the facts (see **19.19** regarding the letting of surplus business property).

HMRC acknowledge that companies and groups may acquire shares other than for investment reasons. They may be paid in shares in place of cash, or be required to hold shares in a trade organisation. The holding of such shares will be considered to be a trading activity if HMRC can be convinced of the trading reason to hold the shares (CG64080).

It is quite common for a company, which is reaching the end of its useful life for the owners, to hold a significant cash balance that has been generated from trading activities, but has not been paid out as dividends or otherwise invested in business assets. It may not be clear whether such a company has become an investment company, due to the ratio of investment activities (cash balances) to trading activities. The HMRC guidance is that short-term lodgement of surplus funds in a deposit account could count as a trading activity rather than an investment activity. Also, funds retained to distribute as dividends would not be an investment activity. However, the long-term retention of surplus earnings would be considered an investment activity unless those funds had been preserved for a particular trading purpose (CG64060).

Trading activities can include activities undertaken with a view to the company acquiring or starting to carry on a trade, or with a view to its acquiring a 'significant interest' in the share capital of another company that is a trading company or the holding company (see **19.20**) of a trading group (so long as, where the acquiring company is a member of a group of companies, it is not a member of the target company's group). These activities qualify as trading activities only if the acquisition is made, or (as the case may be) the company starts to carry on the trade, as soon as is reasonably practicable in the circumstances (*TCGA 1992, s 165A(5)*). HMRC accept that a company that has disposed of its trade and invested the proceeds and is 'actively seeking' to acquire a new trade or trading subsidiary might still be a trading company if it does not have substantial non-trading activities. What is 'reasonably practicable in the circumstances' will depend on the particular facts of the case (CG64075).

Trade

19.18 Trade means anything which:

- is a trade, profession or vocation within the meaning of the *Income Tax Acts*; and
- is conducted on a commercial basis with a view to the realisation of profits (*ITA 2007, s 989*).

The commercial letting of furnished holiday accommodation (FHL) is deemed to be a trade for the purposes of IR and certain other CGT reliefs (*TCGA 1992, s 241(3A)*). The conditions that must be met for a deemed FHL trade are discussed in more detail in Chapter 2 of Chanda and Williams, *Capital Gains Tax Reliefs for SMEs and Entrepreneurs* (Bloomsbury Professional).

Activities that a company carries on as a member of a partnership may be included in the company's trading activities. There is no exclusion of such activities for IR equivalent to that which applies for ER.

Substantial extent

19.19 Where a company carries on activities other than trading activities, the existence of those non-trading activities will not disturb the trading status of the company if they are not carried on to a substantial extent (*TCGA 1992, s 165A(3)*). This measure of trading activities is the same as used in the substantial shareholding exemption, and is identical to the test previously used for taper relief.

HMRC regard 'substantial extent' as meaning more than 20% (CG64090). However, the legislation only refers to the word 'substantial' and, in the first instance, the normal everyday meaning should be used, being an equivalent word to 'considerable', 'solid' or 'big'. The words of Viscount Simon in *Palser v Ginling* [1948] AC 291 should be heeded:

> 'If the judgement of the Court of Appeal in *Palser*'s case were to be understood as fixing percentage as a legal measure, that would be going beyond the powers of the judiciary. To say that everything over 20% of the whole rent should be regarded as substantial portion of that rent would be to play the part of the legislator.'

Even if the 20% boundary is taken as being reasonable, it is not clear from the legislation which attributes of the business should be categorised into trading and non-trading, to prove that the trading activities of the whole business do exceed 80% of the whole. HMRC indicate the following attributes of the business will be indicators of the trading or non-trading activities:

- income from non-trading activities, such as investment property;
- the company's trading and non-trading asset base, taking account of intangible assets such as goodwill or trademarks;
- expenses incurred, or time spent, by officers and employees of the company in undertaking its trading and non-trading activities; and
- the company's history over several years or seasons.

These measures should not be regarded as individual tests which all need to be passed; they are just factors which may point one way or the other. The HMRC officer is instructed to weigh up the relevance of each measure in the context of the individual case and judge the matter 'in the round', as demonstrated by the approach of the Special Commissioner in *Farmer (Farmer's Executors) v IRC* [1999] STC 321.

Where a company lets property that is surplus to its current requirements, HMRC do not consider that the following activities necessarily indicate non-trading activities (CG64085):

- letting part of the trading premises;
- letting properties that are no longer required for the purpose of the trade, where the company's or group's objective is to sell them;
- sub-letting property where it would be impractical or uneconomic in terms of the trade to assign or surrender the lease; or
- the acquisition of property (whether vacant or already let) where it can be shown that the intention is that it will be brought into use for trading activities.

If the company is uncertain as to whether it does qualify as 'trading', it may ask HMRC for an opinion in accordance with the non-statutory business clearance procedure, as described in the HMRC Non-Statutory Business Clearance Guidance (see checklist at tinyurl.com/NSBCAnnex). HMRC have confirmed that an opinion will be given to the company in these circumstances, but they will not enter into correspondence with the individual shareholders on this matter (CG64100).

Holding company

19.20 A holding company is a company that has one or more 51% subsidiaries (*TCGA 1992, s 165A(2)*).

A 51% subsidiary is defined in *CTA 2010, s 1154* as a company where more than 50% of its ordinary share capital is owned directly or indirectly by another body corporate. Thus, a company where 50.1% of its ordinary shares were held by another company would count as a 51% subsidiary.

Where the group has a number of intermediate holding companies owning trading subsidiaries, and an ultimate holding company at the top of the group, it is not clear whether a shareholding in the intermediate holding company would qualify. In such a situation, a ruling or clearance may be sought from HMRC (see **19.19**).

Trading group

19.21 A group of companies means a company that has one or more 51% subsidiaries.

When looking at whether the group is trading, the activities of all the members of the group are taken together as one business (*TCGA 1992, s 165A(8)*). This allows the group to contain one or more companies that are not trading and still qualify as a trading group. The intra-group transactions are ignored.

However, where a minority individual shareholder disposes of shares in a subsidiary company, that particular subsidiary company must be a trading company in order to qualify for IR.

WHO CAN CLAIM THE RELIEF?

Employees and office holders

19.22 The general rule in *TCGA 1992, s 169VW* is that IR on shares is not available to 'relevant employees'. A relevant employee is a person who is an employee or office-holder of the company or any connected company at any time in the relevant period (ie from issue of the shares until immediately before disposal).

Specific exceptions to this rule apply to people who become employees (see **19.23**) and unremunerated directors (see **19.24**).

Employees

19.23 A person who is already an employee or office-holder, but not a director, cannot subscribe for IR shares but a person who has subscribed for shares may still obtain IR on disposal if:

- he becomes an employee more than 180 days after the shares are issued; and
- at the time when he subscribed for the shares there was not a reasonable prospect of him becoming an employee (*TCGA 1992, s 169VW(5)*).

Unremunerated directors

19.24 Unremunerated directors can qualify for IR if they have never previously been either:

(a) connected with the issuing company; or

(b) involved in carrying on (whether on the person's own account or as a partner, director or employee) the whole or any part of the trade, business or profession carried on by the issuing company or a company connected with that company (*TCGA 1992, s 169VW(4)*).

TCGA 1992, s 169VX defines an unremunerated director as a director who neither receives nor is entitled to receive a 'disqualifying payment' from the company.

A disqualifying payment is defined by *TCGA 1992, s 169VX(2)* as any payment other than:

> '(a) a payment or reimbursement of travelling or other expenses wholly, exclusively and necessarily incurred by the person concerned in the performance of his or her duties as a director,
>
> (b) any interest which represents no more than a reasonable commercial return on money lent to the issuing company or a related person,

(c) any dividend or other distribution which does not exceed a normal return on the investment to which the dividend or distribution relates,

(d) any payment for the supply of goods which does not exceed their market value,

(e) any payment of rent for any property occupied by the issuing company or a related person which does not exceed a reasonable and commercial rent for the property, or

(f) any necessary and reasonable remuneration which is–

  (i) paid for qualifying services that are provided to the issuing company or a related person in the course of a trade or profession carried on wholly or partly in the United Kingdom, and

  (ii) taken into account in calculating for tax purposes the profits of that trade or profession.'

This exclusion applies throughout the relevant period, ie from the date of issue of the shares until immediately before disposal. It includes payments received by the director and any relative or person connected with them.

Receipt of value by investors

19.25 The investor is denied relief if he receives value from the company.

This restriction applies to all investors: any investor who receives a payment in the 'period of restriction' which begins one year before the shares are issued and ends immediately before the third anniversary of their issue has their shares disqualified from IR (*TCGA 1992, s 169VB(5)* and *Sch 7ZB*).

The restrictions take the wide-ranging form that is customary in such cases, extending to any form of uncommercial bargain including loans left unpaid.

Receipt of value

19.26 Receipt of value is defined in *TCGA 1992, Sch 7ZB, para 2(1)* thus:

'(1) For the purposes of this Schedule the investor receives value from the company if the company –

(a) repays, redeems or repurchases any of its share capital or securities which belong to the investor or makes any payment to the investor for giving up a right to any of the company's share capital or any security on its cancellation or extinguishment,

(b) repays, in pursuance of any arrangements for or in connection with the acquisition of the shares, any debt owed to the investor other than a debt which was incurred by the company –

(i) on or after the date of issue of the shares, and

(ii) otherwise than in consideration of the extinguishment of a debt incurred before that date,

(c) makes to the investor any payment for giving up the investor's right to any debt on its extinguishment,

(d) releases or waives any liability of the investor to the company or discharges, or undertakes to discharge, any liability of the investor to a third person,

(e) makes a loan or advance to the investor which has not been repaid in full before the issue of the shares,

(f) provides a benefit or facility for the investor,

(g) disposes of an asset to the investor for no consideration or for a consideration which is or the value of which is less than the market value of the asset,

(h) acquires an asset from the investor for a consideration which is or the value of which is more than the market value of the asset, or

(i) makes any payment to the investor other than a qualifying payment.'

Qualifying payments

19.27 Qualifying payments to the investor, ie payments that do not create a receipt of value are defined in *TCGA 1992, Sch 7ZB, para 2(4)* thus:

'(4) In this paragraph "qualifying payment" means –

(a) the payment by any company of such remuneration for service as an officer or employee of that company as may be reasonable in relation to the duties of that office or employment,

(b) any payment or reimbursement by any company of travelling or other expenses wholly, exclusively and necessarily incurred by the investor to whom the payment is made in the performance of duties as an officer or employee of that company,

(c) the payment by any company of any interest which represents no more than a reasonable commercial return on money lent to that company,

(d) the payment by any company of any dividend or other distribution which does not exceed a normal return on any investment in shares in or other securities of that company,

(e) any payment for the supply of goods which does not exceed their market value,

(f) any payment for the acquisition of an asset which does not exceed its market value,

(g) the payment by any company, as rent for any property occupied by the company, of an amount not exceeding a reasonable and commercial rent for the property,

(h) any reasonable and necessary remuneration which –

  (i) is paid by any company for services rendered to that company in the course of a trade or profession carried on wholly or partly in the United Kingdom; and

  (ii) is taken into account in calculating for tax purposes the profits of that trade or profession, or

  (iii) a payment in discharge of an ordinary trade debt.'

The £10 million lifetime limit

19.28 The lifetime IR limit is completely separate from the ER limit of the same amount and may be used in addition to the ER limit, allowing for gains of up to £20 million on qualifying investments to enjoy the reduced CGT rate.

As is detailed below, each individual's limit applies to their own IR claims and claims by trustees on shares in which they are interested as an eligible beneficiary (*TCGA 1992, s 169VK*).

ORDER OF DISPOSAL

Excluded shares

19.29 Any share that meets all of the criteria, except for the share-holding period, is a potentially qualifying share (PQS).

Any share that meets all of the criteria including the share-holding period is a qualifying share (QS).

Any share that is neither qualifying nor potentially qualifying is an excluded share (E) and cannot ever become a QS or PQS again, so the opportunity to claim IR on that share is lost.

This distinction will need to be considered whenever a disposal is in prospect, although it will usually be impossible to rectify any defects other than the shares not being ordinary shares immediately before disposal.

Share identification rules for IR

19.30 There are special identification rules that determine which shares are disposed of first for the purposes of IR but not for any other purposes. These rules are benignly drafted, ie they operate in a way that generally gives the best chance of retaining IR on mixed holdings.

Some of the holding qualifies for IR

19.31 When the investor disposes of shares and claims IR it may be necessary to distinguish between shares that do and do not qualify for IR. *TCGA 1992, s169VD* rules that where IR is claimed and the shareholding out of which the disposal is made consists only partly of qualifying shares, it is the qualifying shares that are deemed to be disposed of first: *TCGA 1992, s 169VD* expresses this simple concept through a clumsy fraction but that is what it means. The fraction of the shares disposed of that qualifies for IR is Q/T where:

- if the number of qualifying shares in the entire holding is less shares than the number disposed of, Q = the number disposed of;
- if the number disposed of is no greater than the number of qualifying shares in the holding, Q = the number of qualifying shares in the holding; and
- T is the total number of shares disposed of.

Therefore, where IR is claimed it is used up to the maximum possible by the current disposal. There are specific rules for subsequent disposals which determine which shares are deemed to be disposed of according to whether IR was claimed on the previous disposal(s).

No claim – no waste of IR

19.32 *TCGA 1992, ss 169VC–169VE* must be read carefully, otherwise the false impression could be gained that qualifying shares are always deemed to be disposed of first. These ordering rules only apply to cases where IR is being claimed because *TCGA 1992, ss 169VD–169VE* refer to cases where 'a disposal' ('the disposal concerned') is made as mentioned in *TCGA 1992, s 169VC(1)*; this refers specifically to a disposal where IR is claimed.

Therefore, if there is a disposal on which IR is not claimed there is no requirement at that time to identify which shares are deemed to be disposed of and in what order: that only becomes relevant when IR is actually claimed on a later disposal.

If IR is never claimed, there is clearly never any need to work out the order of disposal but it is likely to be the case that IR will be claimed at some time, so keeping a record of the 'IR pool' will usually be worthwhile.

IR claimed on previous disposal

19.33

- When IR has been claimed on an earlier disposal, *TCGA 1992, s 169VF* must be applied to the last disposal to work out which, if any, of the shares disposed of in that earlier disposal were excluded shares or potentially qualifying shares. The starting point is the shares on which IR was claimed, ascertained under *TCGA 1992, s 169VD* as above (see **19.31**).
- The next tranche of shares deemed to have been disposed of in the earlier transaction comes out of any excluded shares held at the time of that earlier disposal.
- If those excluded shares do not account for all the remaining shares, the next tranche to be reduced are the shares that were potentially qualifying shares, again, at the time immediately before the last disposal.

This order of set off is the most advantageous to investors in that it means that the potential for an IR claim is not lost.

19.34

Example 19.1 – Some shares are excluded from IR claim

Barney subscribes for 10,000 shares in Pugh Pews Ltd in three tranches:

- 5,000 on 31 March 2016;
- 2,500 on 31 July 2017; and
- 2,500 on 31 January 2018.

On 31 March 2018 he becomes an employee of Pugh Pews which makes shares acquired in the preceding six months (ie those acquired on 31 January 2018) excluded shares (see **19.29**).

He then disposes of 7,000 shares on 31 July 2019 and the remaining 3,000 on 1 August 2020, claiming IR on both occasions.

Disposal 1

At the time of this disposal the only qualifying shares are the initial investment of 5,000 shares which are the only ones that have been held for more than three years: they are deemed to have been disposed of first, so Pugh can claim IR on 5,000/7,000 and the remaining shares (against which he sets his annual exemption) are taxable at the full CGT rate (20% unless rates change).

The question of share identification does not make a difference to Barney's 2019/20 liability but it does become relevant when we come to consider the second disposal.

Disposal 2

When Barney sells his remaining 3,000 shares it is more than three years since he acquired his second tranche, so they are no longer PQS: they are now qualifying shares but the question is how those 3,000 shares are divided between excluded and qualifying shares. This is where *TCGA 1992, s 169VF* applies.

TCGA 1992, s 169VF says that the first shares to be considered after qualifying shares disposed of on 31 July 2019 are the excluded shares. So the 2,000 non-IR shares in that disposal, on which Barney has paid full-rate CGT anyway, are deemed to come out of the 2,500 shares acquired on 31 July 2017 which became excluded shares when Barney became an employee. This benefits Barney because it means that all 2,500 of the shares acquired on 31 January 2017 qualify for IR as qualifying shares and only 500 shares are taxed at the full CGT rate as excluded shares.

IR not claimed on previous disposal

19.35 The rule, in *TCGA 1992, s 169VG*, is simpler than that applying where IR has previously been claimed in respect of holdings in the same company (*TCGA 1992, s 169VF*).

TCGA 1992, s 169VG simply states that the first shares deemed to have been disposed of in the previous disposal are those that were excluded shares at the time of the disposal.

19.36

Example 19.2 – No previous IR claim

Cuthbert subscribes for 10,000 shares in AIM company Dibble & Grubb plc (D&G) in three tranches:

- 5,000 on 31 March 2018;
- 2,500 on 31 July 2021; and
- 2,500 on 31 January 2022.

He sells 7,000 shares on 31 August 2021 but does not claim IR because he has losses in the same year which are automatically set off against the gains, meaning he has no net chargeable gains for 2019/20.

On 30 September 2021, Cuthbert becomes an employee of D&G which means that the shares acquired in the preceding six months (ie those acquired on 31 July 2019) are excluded shares (see **19.29**).

He then sells the remaining 3,000 on 1 August 2025, claiming IR.

Cuthbert can only claim IR on 500 of the 3,000 shares sold now: the identification rules still help him but in a different way.

He cannot claim that the shares that became excluded when he became an employee should be matched with the earlier disposal as *excluded* shares because they had not become excluded at that point.

Out of the 7,000 shares disposed of on 31 August 2021, 2,000 were part of the 2,500 he acquired on 31 July 2021, meaning they were *potentially qualifying* shares at the time of the earlier disposal; as such they must be matched with the earlier disposal. Those shares subsequently became excluded shares when Cuthbert became an employee.

This means that, as 2,000 of those shares have been treated as part of the earlier disposal, covered by losses, only 500 excluded shares remain in the 'pool', so Cuthbert can still claim IR on 2,500 of the shares sold on 1 August 2025.

19.37 It would be impossible to give examples of all possible permutations but the examples given here show the need to keep a careful check on all shareholdings that may qualify for IR.

REORGANISATIONS, RECONSTRUCTIONS AND SHARE EXCHANGES

19.38 The normal rules whereby, on a reorganisation, reconstruction or takeover the new shares received stand in the shoes of the old, are amended in the case of IR. These rules are applied at the time of disposal but must be considered at the time of the reorganisation to ensure that the investor is not denied IR on ultimate disposal.

Share reorganisation where no new consideration given

19.39 Where the company's share capital has been reorganised within the meaning of *TCGA 1992, s 126* and the investor provided no new consideration for the new shares, those new shares are treated as having the same proportions of qualifying (Q), potentially qualifying (P) and excluded shares (E) as were comprised in the original share-holding before the reorganisation. Shares in the new company are deemed to have been subscribed for at the same date and held continuously for the same period as the corresponding shares in the original company. Therefore, there should be no automatic disqualification from investors' relief, as long as no consideration is given for the new shares.

Share reorganisation where new consideration was given

19.40 Where the investor provided consideration as part of the reorganisation, the position is different. For the purposes of investors' relief, any shares received in exchange for consideration are treated as having been issued when they were actually issued. The holding would therefore need to be split, notionally, between the replacement shares which stand in the shoes of the original shares, and the new shares which may be either excluded or at best potentially qualifying shares which must wait for three years to become qualifying shares.

Take-over or reconstruction

19.41 Following a share exchange within the meaning of *TCGA 1992, s 135* or a scheme of reconstruction in line with *TCGA 1992, s 136*, there are new rules in *TCGA 1992, ss 169VL–169VN* that explain the treatment after those exchanges or reconstructions. These rules include a requirement that the conditions that the conditions in *TCGA 1992, s 169VB(2)(f)* – trading company or holding company of a trading group – and *TCGA 1992, s 169VB(2)(g)* – investor not to be connected with the company – must be met:

- in relation to the original share, from its issue date until the reorganisation or reconstruction; and

- in relation to the new share, from the reorganisation or reconstruction to the disposal.

Whilst this emphasises that great care is needed ensure that access to investors' relief is preserved, it also means that those tests do not need to be applied at times when they are not really relevant.

Investor may elect for *TCGA 1992, s 127* not to apply

19.42 An election can be made to disapply the treatment outlined above. This ensures that investors' relief is not lost if the original share-holding would have qualified at the time of the reorganisation but the new one does not (or might not).

If this election is made, a gain arises on the point the old shares are surrendered for new ones and investors' relief can be claimed. The disadvantage of making this election is that no consideration will have been received with which to pay the tax due.

OVERSEAS MATTERS

19.43 There are three categories of taxpayer who may pay CGT on gains in a current tax period, when the underlying gain actually accrued in an earlier tax period. This can cause problems for the calculation of, and elections relating to, IR. The categories of taxpayer are:

- remittance basis users (see **19.44**);
- temporary non-UK residents (see **19.45**); and
- settlors and beneficiaries of offshore trusts (see **19.57**).

The HMRC Capital Gains Manual guidance does not currently consider the position of any of the above taxpayers for either IR or ER. However, ICAEW TaxGuide 1/12 does address some of these issues. Where an unusual situation arises, guidance may be sought from HMRC through the non-statutory clearance service (see **19.19**).

Remittance basis

19.44 IR can apply to gains made on assets situated outside the UK and on shares or securities held in overseas companies.

For a more detailed discussion of the remittance basis, refer to Booth & Schwarz, *Residence, Domicile and UK Taxation* (Bloomsbury Professional).

In brief, CGT is not charged on gains accruing on the disposal of assets situated outside the UK to individuals who claim the remittance basis for the particular tax year in question, and those overseas gains are not treated as being received in the UK.

The general rule is that an amount is treated as received in the UK in respect of a gain if it is:

- an amount paid, used or enjoyed in the UK; or
- an amount transmitted or brought in any manner or form to the UK.

Where a gain is not remitted directly but is invested in other assets, the gain is traced through those assets in order to establish whether the gain has been remitted to the UK. HMRC take the view that such tracing can take place through 'any number of investments, deposits to bank accounts, transfers between accounts etc' (CG25350). Thus, gains may be remitted to the UK many years after they arose.

HMRC may accept that IR can be claimed by remittance basis users and that the delay between the time when the gain arises and when the remittance is made is no bar on the claiming of IR, provided a valid claim is made within the required time limit. This would be consistent with HMRC's view that an ER claim must be made by the first anniversary of 31 January following the tax year in which the gain was realised, not the year in which the gain was remitted (see ICAEW TaxGuide 1/12).

It is understood that HMRC's settled view with regard to ER is that the lifetime limit to apply with respect to remittance basis gains is that limit which was in force when the gains arose, and not the limit that applies when the gains are remitted to the UK. This issue will need to be clarified before the first disposals eligible for IR take place on or after 6 April 2019.

Temporary non-residents

19.45 The definition of temporary non-residence that applies for departures from the UK before and after 6 April 2013 is discussed in detail in Booth & Schwarz, *Residence Domicile and UK Taxation* (Bloomsbury Professional).

In brief, an individual is treated as a temporary non-resident (*TCGA 1992, s 10A*) if his residence status would otherwise mean that he escaped CGT having left the UK, and the following applies:

- the individual was UK resident for at least four of the seven tax years prior to departure; and

- the period of non-residence is less than five years (before 6 April 2013 this period is measured in 'tax years').

In this case, gains arising in the year of departure are chargeable in that tax year, and gains arising during the period of non-residence are chargeable in the year in which UK residence for tax purposes is resumed (*TCGA 1992, s 2*). Gains on assets that are both acquired and disposed of during the period of non-residence, are outside the charge, subject to certain anti-avoidance provisions.

Trustees

19.46 Under *TCGA 1992, s 169VH* trustees are eligible to claim IR in a way that is similar to but not identical with ER. As with ER the trustees do not have an entitlement to IR for the trust itself but only in respect of an 'eligible beneficiary'.

The share acquisition and holding rules apply to trustees in the same way as to individual investors (*TCGA 1992, s 169VH(5)* applies *TCGA 1992, s 169VB(2)(g)*). This means that for trustees to claim IR it is the trustees who must have made the initial investment: IR cannot apply to shares acquired by an individual and then settled on trust.

Qualifying beneficiary

19.47 An eligible beneficiary is a beneficiary who, as against the trust:

- has a life interest in possession in the shares concerned immediately before the disposal;
- held that interest throughout the three years immediately preceding the disposal;
- has not been a 'relevant employee' (see below) of the company at any time in those three years; and
- has elected to be treated as an eligible beneficiary in relation to the disposal.

Eligible interests in possession

19.48 An interest in possession (IIP) cannot be for a fixed time only (*TCGA 1992, s 169VH(4)*). The legislation does not elaborate on how interests subject to reappointment at the trustees' discretion are to be treated. Similarly, where a beneficiary has an interest in shares that have been sold and IR claimed the IIP may be extinguished by the trustees appointing the net sale proceeds to the beneficiary.

Beneficiary needs not own any shares personally

19.49 Unlike ER where the 'personal company' requirement means that a beneficiary must personally own shares, there is no such requirement under IR. This is logical, given that IR carries no minimum interest requirements for individual investors.

Election for treatment as an eligible beneficiary

19.50 The beneficiary may elect to be treated as an eligible beneficiary at any time before the trustees make the IR claim. The claim does not need to be made to HMRC, it is sufficient for the beneficiary to inform the trustees of the election, in writing or orally and the election may be withdrawn and/or reinstated at any time until the trustees make the claim.

Trustees' claims

19.51 Trust claims must be made jointly by the trustees and the beneficiary. The time limit is the first anniversary of 31 January following the end of the year in which the disposal takes place.

Period of share ownership

19.52 Whilst the requirements of *TCGA 1992, s 169VB* must be satisfied by the trustees, where applicable, throughout the trusts period of ownership, ie from issue on subscription until disposal, the beneficiary only needs to satisfy the Eligible beneficiary requirements throughout the three years leading to the disposal. Before then the trustees may hold the shares on any other interest for any other beneficiary.

19.53

Example 19.3 – Trust and beneficiary holdings

Mr Onion died on 1 June 2017 leaving his entire estate on a discretionary trust for the benefit of his grandchildren, Clive and Charlotte.

On 18 March 2018 the trustees subscribed for 100,000 £1 ordinary shares in Scallion plc, an AIM listed trading company.

On 6 April 20219 Garlic plc makes a cash offer for all the shares in Scallion. Considering this to be a good offer the trustees vote in favour of acceptance and on 1 May 2021, before the offer is accepted unconditionally, appoint unlimited interests in possession in the shares; half each to Clive and Charlotte.

This scenario satisfies the conditions for the trustees to claim IR jointly with either or both of Clive and Charlotte, subject to their not having used their lifetime allowances.

Restriction on trustees' relief

19.54 Whilst *TCGA 1992, s 169VH* refers to the beneficiary having a settled interest in possession in the shares, implying that it is not possible to give one beneficiary the IIP in the income but not the asset itself, ie the capital, *TCGA 1992, s 169VI* puts a different slant on things by requiring gains of joint beneficiaries to be allocated to them in proportion to their shares in the *income*, not interests in the capital of the trust. This is not really a restriction on the relief, merely a requirement that joint beneficiaries be treated in the same way as joint owners of shares.

Trustees may claim IR on the aggregate of all eligible beneficiaries' shares in the gain.

Trustees share the beneficiary's lifetime limit

19.55 The amount of IR that can be claimed by the trustees will be restricted by the amount of the unused lifetime limit which is available to the qualifying beneficiary, and this will be reduced by claims for IR already submitted by:

- the qualifying beneficiary for gains made in his own name;
- the trustees in conjunction with the same qualifying beneficiary; or
- the trustees of any other trust in conjunction with the same beneficiary.

The amount of the beneficiary's lifetime limit that is assigned to the trust is controlled by the qualifying beneficiary, not by the trustees and not by the date on which gains are made. The beneficiary may choose to retain all of his lifetime limit to use against personal gains made in the same tax year, or to be made in a later year.

The amount of the trust gains that can be relieved using the qualifying beneficiary's lifetime limit is also limited to that beneficiary's relevant proportion of the gain. If the beneficiary is only entitled to 50% of the income from the trust assets which were disposed of, only up to 50% of the gain can be relieved using that beneficiary's lifetime limit.

Planning point

Trust ownership offers investors flexibility with regard to transferring shares that is not available if shares are held personally

19.56

Example 19.4 – Flexibility of trust holdings

Anna is interested in investing in Morels and More Ltd, but regards this as a long-term investment which may take a long time to bear fruit. She believes the investment will grow rapidly and wants it to benefit her children, Jordan and Nicole. However, Jordan and Nicole are still young and Anna would be reluctant to give them shares outright. She is also concerned that she may need to access the shares, or their sale proceeds, for her own benefit.

Therefore Anna creates a trust which subscribes for the shares using money that she has provided and retains to herself the power to appoint interests to beneficiaries. This enables Anna to take an interest in possession herself for as long as she needs to, but appoint a life interest in possession to Jordan and Nicole once she no longer requires to retain the interest. Provided Jordan and Nicole meet the requirements to be qualifying beneficiaries (see **19.47**) and the shares are not disposed of within three years of the appointment, the trustees will be able to make a joint IR claim with the beneficiaries. This option may be particularly beneficial if the shares' value has mushroomed because the IR available to cover the trustees' gains will not be a single £10m, nor will it depend on Anna's lifetime limit. Instead the shares representing each beneficiary's interest will benefit from that beneficiary's lifetime limit. Therefore, if the trust's shares produce gains totalling £20m, divided equally between Jordan and Nicole, and they have not claimed any IR already, they may join with the trustees and claim IR on the entire £20m gain.

This arrangement depends on the trustees being the subscribers for the shares and Anna being able to settle cash on trust without incurring a lifetime inheritance tax charge when she creates the trust: settlements that are within her IHT nil-rate band (NRB) or which consist of assets on which IHT is not chargeable (eg business or agricultural assets) may be suitable for this purpose.

Claims

19.57 A claim for IR will need to be made jointly by the trustees and the individual within the same period as a claim made by an individual, ie by the first anniversary of 31 January following the end of the tax year in which the disposal occurred (*TCGA 1992, s 169VM*)).

A problem may arise on the death of the relevant beneficiary who is the sole life tenant of the trust. This death will mean the trust has ceased to exist. Where this life tenant became entitled to the interest in possession on or after 22 March 2006, his death will trigger a deemed disposal of the trust assets (*TCGA 1992, s 71(1)*), which is not exempt from CGT (*TCGA 1992, s 73(2A)*). If the beneficiary met the qualifying conditions for the relief up to the date of death, IR should apply to the trust assets. This would be the same treatment as HMRC have confirmed applies under ER (see ICAEW Tax Guide 1/12). However, a valid claim needs to be signed both by the trustees (who are technically no longer trustees, as there is no trust) and on behalf of the deceased beneficiary. In this situation HMRC will accept a claim signed by the personal representatives of the deceased beneficiary, and the trustees.

Offshore trusts

19.58 The capital gains tax rules that apply to offshore trusts are very complex; for an excellent summary, refer to Chapter 27A of *Revenue Law: Principles and Practice* (Bloomsbury Professional, 32nd edition).

Capital gains realised by an offshore trust may be attributed to the settlor under *TCGA 1992, s 86*, and in some cases to the beneficiaries of the trust under *TCGA 1992, s 87*. In that case no claim for IR would appear to be possible because the taxpayer who is deemed to realise the gain is not the person to whom the shares were issued and so the condition in *TCGA 1992, s 169VB(2)(a)* is not met.

Chapter 20

Extracting funds from the company

Peter Rayney FCA, CTA (Fellow), TEP, Peter Rayney Tax Consulting Ltd

This chapter includes material originally adapted from *Tax Planning for Family and Owner-Managed Companies 2017/18* (Bloomsbury Professional) by Peter Rayney.

SIGNPOSTS

- **Surplus profits: retain or extract?** – There are various potential issues to consider in the decision whether to retain or extract surplus profits from the family or owner-managed company. For example, retaining profits in the company may be attractive to some individual shareholders if entrepreneurs' relief would be available on a disposal of their shares. It is possible to extract funds or value from the company in a number of ways. The overall tax cost of the various extraction methods will vary, and it is important to determine the tax implications and efficiency of each one in advance (see **20.1–20.6**).
- **Capital receipts versus income receipts** – A purchase of the company's own shares, liquidation or sale of a company tend to be the most common 'exit routes' for shareholders of family or owner-managed companies. The tax liabilities under the income and capital routes should be compared well in advance of these transactions, in order to determine the most tax-efficient route (see **20.7–20.8**).
- **Bonus versus dividends** – Factors to consider in the decision whether to extract company profits as bonuses or dividends include the NIC impact on bonuses, the national minimum wage and national living wage rules (where applicable), the level of the company's distributable reserves in relation to dividends, the 'dividend allowance', and whether the company has tax losses (see **20.9–20.20**).
- **Implications of paying a bonus** – These include corporation tax relief (if the bonus is commercial and not excessive), the timing of relief for accrued remuneration, PAYE/NIC and cash flow, and reporting requirements under real-time information (see **20.21–20.25**).

- **Payment of dividends** – Any such payments must comply with company law requirements. The 'bonus versus dividends' decision will often also be influenced by factors including pension provision, protecting the state pension and social security benefits, the effect on share valuations, the spread of shareholdings, and personal borrowing. There is no substitute for doing the relative computations to compare the combined effective tax rates (for the company and its owner-manager(s)) for each extraction method (see **20.26–20.28**).

- **Remuneration paid to other family members** – Tax savings are often possible if income can be paid to other members of the owner-manager's family in order to use their annual personal allowances and benefit from their lower marginal tax rates. However, remuneration payments must be commercial and not excessive in relation to the duties performed, and care is needed to ensure that dividends to spouses (or civil partners) or other family members are not 'caught' by anti-avoidance provisions (see **20.29–20.38**).

- **Charging rent for personally owned assets** – The company's owner-managers will sometimes own the trading property (and/or other assets used in the company's trade) personally. In such cases, the owner-manager can extract funds from the company by charging it a market rent for the use of the property. In addition to the tax effects of extracting profits via rent, issues to consider potentially include SDLT, the implications for entrepreneurs' relief purposes on any subsequent 'associated disposal' of the property, and VAT (see **20.39–20.43**).

- **Selling an asset to the company** – Owner-managers might consider extracting a capital sum from their company by selling personally owned assets (eg trading premises) to the company. Issues to consider potentially include SDLT for the company, CGT for the vendor on a capital gain, and VAT (see **20.44–20.46**).

- **Charging interest on loans to the company** – Owner-managers who make loans to the company, or have credit balances on their current account, could consider charging the company interest on the loan or credit balance, up to a commercial rate. Corporation tax relief would generally be available to the company under the 'loan relationship' provisions (see **20.47–20.49**).

- **Loans from the company** – Such loans (including overdrawn director's loan accounts) will generally have implications for closely controlled companies under the 'loans to participator' rules, and benefit-in-kind implications for owner-managers under the 'beneficial loan' provisions. Anti-avoidance provisions aimed at circumventing tax charges under the loans to participator (and also benefits to participators and return payments to the company) rules may also need to be considered. If loans to shareholders are waived, further tax (and NIC) implications potentially arise (see **20.50–20.72**).

- **Benefits-in-kind to non-working shareholders** – Expenses or benefits provided to a close company shareholder (or an associate of a shareholder) may be taxable as distributions, unless the expense or benefit is already taxed under the employment income rules in *ITEPA 2003* (see **20.73**).
- **Appendix** – A planning checklist of strategies for extracting funds from the company is included at **20.74**.

SHOULD SURPLUS PROFITS BE RETAINED OR EXTRACTED?

Main issues

20.1

Focus

Family and owner-managed companies can freely decide how much of their profits should be returned to the shareholders or retained within the business. The 'working' shareholders will need to extract a basic level of income from the company to satisfy their personal requirements.

Hitherto, the comparatively lower income tax rates tended to encourage companies to extract surplus profits. Companies that relied on bank borrowings or institutional finance may, however, have been prescribed financial limits on the amount of dividends and other payments which can be made to the owner-manager shareholders.

From a commercial perspective, the company's cash flow and working capital requirements must be considered when determining the timing and amount of funds to be taken out. Given that the extraction of funds (see **20.5**) gives rise to a tax charge, which will be particularly expensive where large sums are involved, there is little point in taking them out by bonus, dividend, etc unless they are required by the owner-manager for their personal/family's needs. With the current high levels of income tax rates many owner-managers are likely to retain more profits within their companies. Within these constraints, some owner-managers may still wish to regularly remove 'surplus' cash from the business so as to remove it from any further business risk (subject to the requirements of the *Insolvency Act 1986*, for example, the 'two year' look-back period for 'preferential' or 'under-value' transactions under *IA 1986, ss 238* and *239*).

A further factor to consider is the potential double charge to tax, which arises where profits retained in the company are invested in appreciating assets. The appreciation in asset values could potentially be taxed both in the company and when the value is realised by the shareholders, perhaps on a sale or liquidation of the company. However, if the company is eventually sold for a price based on a multiple of earnings, the value of the shares may bear little relationship to the level of retained profits. Furthermore, the 'double charge' effect would not be a problem where the company's shares are to be passed down as a family heirloom on death. Owners of personal service companies are effectively forced to extract 'tainted' income and additional factors will come into play.

Entrepreneurs' relief (ER) and investors' relief (IR)

20.2 Owner-managers of trading companies enjoy particularly favourable CGT treatment, with a current 'exit' ER CGT rate of 10% (up to a cumulative lifetime gains, limit of £10 million). However, since 6 April 2016, all other 'non-ER' significant gains are taxable at 20% (except those arising on the sale of residential property).

Finance Act 2016 introduced Investors Relief (IR), which provides a 10% CGT-rate of the disposal of qualifying shares after three years. Like ER, the IR 10% CGT rate is subject to a separate £10 million lifetime gains limit. As a general rule, 'business angels' should normally be eligible for IR but employees and 'paid' directors cannot qualify.

Retention of profits

20.3 With a current ER limit of £10 million, the overall tax costs of realising retained profits as a capital gain (for example, by liquidation or sale – see **20.4**) have remained identical to the pre-6 April 2008 business taper regime (assuming the (cumulative) gains are below £10 million).

Retained profits only suffer corporation tax at the company's marginal tax rate and may ultimately be realised at low CGT rates.

The ability to reinvest profits within company structures at relatively low tax rates has encouraged many sole traders and partnerships to incorporate their businesses. For 2017/18, unincorporated businesses earning substantial profits will generally suffer a marginal 47% combined income tax/Class 4 NIC rate on their profits, regardless of whether the profits are 'ploughed-back' within the business or extracted.

All companies pay corporation tax at 19% from 1 April 2017 (previously 20% since 1 April 2015). Thus, the total effective rate of taking profits as a capital sum is 27.1% (ignoring the impact of any base cost, etc) calculated as follows:

	£
Profit	100
Corporation tax at 19%	(19)
Retained profit = chargeable gain	81
CGT @ 10% (assuming ER)	(8.1)
Net realisation	72.9
Total effective tax rate	28%

If ER is not available at the time the retained profits are taken as a 'capital distribution', the overall effective rate increases to 35.2% (assuming a 20% CGT rate). The rates on retained profits compare very favourably with the current top income tax rates.

Taking profits as capital gains

20.4

> **Focus**
>
> Unless the owner-manager is making a complete, or almost complete, 'exit' from the company, it may be difficult to find an effective method of converting profits into a capital sum. Taking the profits as a capital distribution on a subsequent winding-up is not a realistic option if the business is continuing.This means that the individual will have to sell their shares either back to the company or by way of an external sale.

Given the relatively wide gap between CGT and dividend tax rates, HMRC are likely to use the Transaction in Securities rules where shares in close companies are sold to a commonly controlled company, Employee Benefit Trust, pension fund, etc but not normally on commercially driven sales to third parties. However, unless there is *complete certainty* that transaction will satisfy the post-sale 'no-connection' test, it is recommended that the advance clearance procedure in *ITA 2007, s 701* is used to obtain assurance that HMRC are satisfied that the transaction is not driven by the avoidance of income tax.

If the company is likely to be sold, the level of its *retained* profits will not normally influence its sale price, which is normally based on a multiple of its post-tax earnings. With the relatively low rates of CGT, however, it is tempting to 'gross up' the price for the retained earnings rather than strip them out as a pre-sale dividend.

Taking all the above factors into account, a balanced approach between retention and extraction of profits will generally be required in practice. Ultimately, the decision must depend on whether the shareholders need the money for their personal requirements and whether they are able to obtain a better 'return' on the funds than the company.

Extracting funds or value from the company

20.5

> **Focus**
>
> It is possible to extract funds or value from the company in a number of ways, although (a) to (c) below are usually available only for those shareholders who work in the company as a director or employee.

The most important methods of extracting value are listed below:

(a) directors' remuneration or bonuses and paying salaries to other family members (see **20.9–20.37**);

(b) provision of benefits in kind and company shares;

(c) pension contributions;

(d) dividends (see **20.12–20.18**, **20.26–20.28**);

(e) charging rent on personally owned property which is used in the company's trade (see **20.39–20.43**);

(f) selling assets to the company for value (see **20.44–20.46**);

(g) charging interest on loans to the company (see **20.47–20.49**);

(h) loans or advances from the company (see **20.50–20.66**);

(i) purchase of own shares;

(j) repayment/reduction of share capital; and

(k) liquidation of the company.

The overall tax cost of the various methods of extraction will vary and it is important to determine the tax efficiency for each method of extracting funds/value.

20.6 On an on-going basis, the working shareholders may well, in addition to drawing a normal salary, decide whether to extract surplus profits by means of a bonus or dividend. This aspect is considered in further detail at **20.9–20.37**. In addition, owner-managers will often ensure that adequate provision is made for their future pension and that tax efficacious benefits in kind are provided. Owner-managers may also consider extracting funds through a loan account, but this too involves a tax cost.

CAPITAL RECEIPTS VERSUS INCOME RECEIPTS

Basic planning techniques

20.7 A purchase of the company's own shares, liquidation or sale of a company tend to be the most common 'exit-routes' for shareholders when they wish to leave the company, retire or realise capital value.

In the context of a purchase by the company of its own shares, it is usually possible to structure the transaction either as a capital gains receipt within *CTA 2010, s 1033*, or as a distribution.

Similarly, if the company is about to be wound up, value can be extracted by means of an income dividend if the amount is paid prior to liquidation. Amounts distributed during the winding up should be a capital distribution (liable to CGT) for the shareholder. However, where the liquidation is mainly driven by 'unacceptable' phoenixing to extract the company's retained profits at beneficial CGT rates, the *FA 2016* 'anti-phoenix' Targeted Anti-Avoidance Rule ('TAAR') is likely to apply. If the liquidation falls within the TAAR, the liquidation distributions would be taxed at dividend *income tax* rates (as opposed to CGT).

Comparing income and capital gain positions

20.8

> **Focus**
>
> It is particularly important to compare the tax liabilities under the income and capital route *well in advance* of these transactions in order to determine the most tax-efficient route.

For individual shareholders, an income distribution in 2017/18 will generally carry a tax charge of 32.5% or (where the taxpayer's income exceeds the £150,000 top tax rate bracket), 38.1%.

The tax efficiency of taking a capital gain will therefore depend on the shareholder's potential effective CGT rate (maximum of 20% with reduction to 10% if ER or IR is available).

Any planning steps which are then necessary, for example, to characterise the transaction as income, can then be implemented with minimal risk of an HMRC attack under the *Furniss v Dawson* doctrine (*Furniss v Dawson* [1984] STC 153). The potential application of the GAAR may also be a consideration, where HMRC consider the relevant planning to be abusive or egregious.

BONUS VERSUS DIVIDENDS

Impact of national insurance contributions (NIC)

20.9 Although the working shareholders can reward themselves in a number of ways, the main choice often lies between whether to pay a bonus or a dividend. The high levels of NIC rates have meant that more owner-managers tend to draw a substantial part of their profits in the form of dividends. Profits extracted as 'earnings' (ie salary or bonus) are now subject to significant NIC charges. For 2017/18, the first £157 per week (or, if earnings are calculated on an annual basis, £8,164 per year) does not suffer employers' NIC. Above this 'secondary threshold', the company pays NIC on all earnings at 13.8%. Most P11D benefits in kind are subject to a NIC Class 1A charge of 13.8% (without any threshold).

For 2017/18, directors and employees suffer NIC at the rate of 12% on their earnings and benefits between £157 and £866 per week (or, if earnings are calculated on an annual basis, £8,164 and £45,000. An additional employee NIC charge of 2% is levied where the individual's total earnings/benefits exceed the 2017/18 upper earnings limit of £45,000. This means that a 2% employees' NIC charge arises on all earnings, etc above the £45,000 threshold with no restrictions.

For 2017/18, companies will still be able to deduct (up to) £3,000 from their first remittance of employer's NIC's providing the director is *not* the sole employee.

For those owner-managers with the 'work till you drop' ethos, it is perhaps worth noting that employees' NIC ceases to be payable on their earnings after they have reached 'pensionable age'. This is currently 65 years old for men, 60 years old for women born before 6 April 1950, and 65 for women born after 5 April 1955 (with a sliding scale operating between those dates). From December 2018, the state pension age will start to increase for both men and women.

However, employers' (ie secondary) NICs continue to be paid on an individual's earnings beyond their pensionable age.

An employer's NIC charge under Class 1A applies to the majority of benefits in kind, including company cars and private fuel. The Class 1A NIC charge is based on the total benefits taxed as 'employment income' under the *ITEPA 2003* rules.

National minimum/living wage

20.10 Owner-managers will need to adhere to the national living wage (NLW) and national minimum wage (NMW) legislation. The NLW effectively replaced the NMW on 1 April 2016 for employees aged 25 and over. The NMW continues to apply for those employees who have not reached their 25th birthday. HMRC are responsible for policing the minimum wage legislation on behalf of the Department for Business, Innovation and Skills (BIS).

The NLW and NMW legislation only applies where an individual has a contract of employment. In law, the directors' rights and duties are defined by that office. They can be removed from office by a simple majority of the votes cast at a general meeting of the company. Clearly, if the director *actively* works in the business, receives a salary, and enjoys other rights accorded to employees, an employer/employee relationship will be established.

In contrast, an employee's rights and duties are expressed in a contract of employment, which need not be in writing and can be an implied or oral contract. Due to the informal nature of the arrangements in many small companies, there may be some uncertainty as to whether an employment contract exists between the company and its controlling director. The question of whether an office holder is employed will clearly depend on the facts of each case. Where there is no explicit contract, the NMW and NLW rules are unlikely to apply, even where the director carries out a wide range of activities, which might include 'working in the company's shop'. In such cases, the work would be regarded as done in the director's capacity as an office holder.

Indeed, BIS confirms that if there is no written employment contract or other evidence of an intention to create an employer/worker relationship, it will not seek to contend that there is an unwritten or implied employment relationship between a director and his company.

However, a prudent course of action would be for 'owner-manager' directors to pay themselves (and of course their staff) sufficient remuneration to satisfy the requirements of the NLW and NMW legislation.

The current NLW/NMW rates are as follows:

Age	From 1 April 2017 Hourly rate
Employees aged 25 and over (NLW)	£7.50
Employees aged 21–24	£7.05
Development rate (employees aged 18–20)	£5.60
Young workers rate (aged 16–17)	£4.05
Apprentices under 19, or over 19 and in first year	£3.50

Dividends cannot be treated as remuneration for this purpose, nor can benefits in kind, other than the provision of living accommodation.

Employers that do not comply with the NLW/NMW will have to pay the 'underpaid' amount to its workers at current minimum wage rates. HMRC will issue a Notice of Underpayment (NoU) to start this process.

Breaking the NLW/NMW law can be an expensive business, since non-compliance is subject to penalties of up to 200% of the underpaid amount (with a 50% reduction if paid within 14 days). The overall maximum penalty is 'capped' at £20,000 for each worker.

The Government will 'name and shame' most exploitative employers, which may cause reputational damage to their businesses. For example, nearly 350 of the worst offending employers' were published on the government's website in February 2017. Compliance with the NLW/NMW should therefore be taken very seriously!

Determining appropriate amount to extract from company

20.11 Most discussions about profit extraction usually start by focusing on the amount available to be paid out to the owner-manager(s). This is generally influenced by one or more of the following factors:

- the amount required for future retention in the business (to satisfy future working capital or capital investment purposes);
- the level of the company's distributable reserves and 'free' cash flow;
- any provisions or restrictions laid down in Shareholder Agreements or a company's Articles, particularly where venture capital finance has been used;
- the desire to 'de-risk' part of the 'surplus cash' generated by the business by taking it out of the company;

- the shareholders' personal 'income' requirements and tax position (and the impact of the 45% income tax rate!);
- 'one-man-band' type service companies may be affected by IR35 and 'spousal' settlement considerations in fixing the level of 'remuneration' to be paid out, although the House of Lords decision in the *Arctic Systems* case gives potentially vulnerable taxpayers greater comfort in this area.

Having broadly determined the appropriate level of profits that can be 'extracted' by the owner-manager(s), attention then usually shifts to deciding whether the amount should be paid out as a bonus and/or dividend.

Comparison between bonus and dividends

20.12

> **Focus**
>
> If the company pays tax at the small profits' rate it is nearly always beneficial to extract surplus funds by means of a dividend as the now relatively high cost of NICs is avoided. The substitution of dividends for remuneration is not regarded as an abnormal pay practice for NIC purposes (*Social Security and Benefits Act 1992, Sch 1, para 4(c)*).

It is possible, however, that the National Insurance Contributions Office (NICO) may seek to challenge dividends which have not been declared in accordance with the relevant *Companies Act* formalities. If the correct legal procedures are not followed, it can be asserted that a payment is not a 'valid' dividend and hence must be 'NIC-able' earnings.

The recent Court of Appeal ruling in *HMRC v PA Holdings Ltd* [2011] EWCA Civ 1414 demonstrates that the judiciary may seek to treat purported dividend payments as employment income where aggressive tax avoidance schemes have been used.

20.13 The dividend regime radically changed on 6 April 2016. For 2017/18 the key aspects for owner-managers are summarised as follows:

- Dividends do not carry any form of tax credit.
- Owner-managers have a £5,000 dividend tax allowance (decreasing to £2,000 from 6 April 2018), which essentially represents a 'nil rate' band for their dividend income.
- Dividend income represents the highest slice of income and is allocated to the tax bands *before* the £5,000 dividend 'nil rate' band.

- Subject to personal allowances and the £5,000 dividend 'nil rate' band, dividends are taxed at the following rates:

Total taxable income	**Tax rate applied**
Below basic rate income threshold – £33,500	7.5%
Between basic rate threshold and £150,000	32.5%
Above £150,000	38.1%

20.14 Some owner-managers may be tempted to extract their income entirely in the form of dividends, but it is often sensible to extract a reasonable level of salary. In any event, if the owner-manager has no other taxable income, it is often beneficial to pay at least a sufficient salary to maintain NIC records such that each year is a qualifying year for state pension 'accrual' purposes.

Various tax comparisons between extracting surplus profits as a bonus or a dividend for 2017/18 are shown in the worked examples below. The various factors listed at **20.27** may also influence the decision, depending on the relevant circumstances of each case.

Bonus versus dividend comparison – 2017/18

20.15 **Example 20.1** (assuming a marginal income tax rate of 40%) and **Example 20.2** (assuming a marginal income tax rate of 45%) below illustrate that it will often be beneficial to extract surplus profits as a dividend for 2017/18 (despite the recent increase in dividend tax). However, this is subject to the other factors cited at **20.27**.

It should be noted that, where a company pays a bonus, there is an additional NIC cost – but corporate tax relief is given on the total cost of the bonus and related NIC, ie the company does not pay corporation tax on this part of its profits. On the other hand, a dividend is not tax deductible and hence profits earmarked for a dividend suffer corporation tax.

Example 20.1 – 2017/18: Bonus versus dividend comparison (owner-manager's marginal tax rate of 40%)

Greaves Limited is likely to have surplus profits available of £100,000 for the year ended 31 March 2018, which could be paid to its sole shareholder, Mr Jimmy, as a bonus or dividend. Mr Jimmy already draws a monthly salary of £4,000 (ie in excess of the basic rate threshold upper earnings limit), and therefore his marginal tax rate is 40%.

The relevant tax and NIC effects are compared below.

			Bonus		*Dividend*
	£		£	£	£
Available profits			100,000		100,000
Less: Employer's NIC –					
£87,873 @ 13.8%			(12.127)		
Corporation tax @ 19%					(19,000)
			87,873		81,000
Income tax thereon					
Bonus	87,873	@ 40%	(35,149)		
Employees' NIC @	87,873	@ 2%	(1,758)		
2% (rate on earnings					
above upper limit)					
Dividend:					
Tax	76,000*	@ 32.5%			(24,700)
Net cash available			50,966		56,300
Tax and NIC liabilities					
Employer's NIC			12,127		
Corporation tax					19,000
PAYE and NIC					
(£35,149 + £1,758)			36,907		
Dividend tax liability			000,000		24,700
			49,034		43,700
Effective overall tax rate			49.0%		43.7%

Tax saved by paying a dividend = £5,334 (£49,034 less £43,700).

* Dividend of £81,000 less £5,000 dividend 'nil rate' band

Example 20.2 – 2017/18: Bonus versus dividend comparison (owner-manager's marginal tax rate of 45%)

Bonds Limited is likely to have surplus profits available of £100,000 for the year ended 31 March 2018, which could be paid to its sole shareholder, Mr Billy, as a bonus or dividend. Mr Billy already draws a monthly salary of £15,000 and therefore his marginal income tax rate is 45%.

The relevant tax and NIC effects are compared below.

			Bonus		*Dividend*
	£		£	£	£
Available profits			100,000		100,000
Less: Employer's NIC –					
£87,873 @ 13.8%			(12,127)		
Corporation tax @ 19%			(000,000)		(19,000)
			87,873		81,000
Income tax thereon					
Bonus	87,873	@ 45%	(39,543)		
Employees' NIC @ 2% (rate on earnings above upper limit)	87,873	@ 2%	(1,758)		
Dividend					
Tax	76,000*	@ 38.1%			(28,956)
Net cash available			46,572		52,044
Tax and NIC liabilities Employer's NIC			12,127		
Corporation tax					19,000
PAYE and NIC					
(£39,543 + £1,758)			41,301		
Dividend tax liability			000,000		28,956
			53,428		47,956
Effective overall tax rate			53.4%		48.0%

Tax saved by paying a dividend = £5,472 (£53,428 less £47,956).

* Dividend of £81,000 less £5,000 dividend 'nil rate' band

Shareholders paying tax at the basic rate

20.16 For 2017/18, where the shareholder only pays tax at the basic rate, their dividend income would simply be subject to income tax at 7.5%. This should still give a reasonable tax 'extraction' rate (especially where the £5,000 dividend nil rate band is available)

Example 20.3 – 2017/18: Dividend tax and £5,000 nil rate band (basic rate tax payer)

Terry's expected taxable income during the year ended 5 April 2018 is as follows:

- Employment income – £11,500
- Dividend from Blues Ltd – £15,000

Terry's income tax liability is £750, calculated as follows:

	Total	*Personal Allowance*		*Basic rate band*
	£	*£*	*£*	*£*
Employment income	11,500	11,500		
Less: Personal allowance		(11,500)		
Dividend	15,000			15,000
Dividend nil rate band	(5,000)			(5,000)
Taxable	10,000	nil		10,000
Taxed at 7.5%				750

20.17 The above examples have been simplified to show the relevant tax that would be payable at relevant marginal rates. There will, of course, be many cases where tax/NIC is payable over two or more rate bands and detailed calculations will be required. With the post-5 April 2016 changes, dividends should still be preferred but will offer less tax savings than before.

As a result of the large 'gap' between individual and corporate tax rates, companies will become increasingly attractive as a vehicle to earn and retain income. Many highly profitable sole traders, partnerships and LLPs have either recently incorporated or are considering incorporation in the near future. However, the sale of goodwill of an unincorporated business to a company no longer qualifies for entrepreneurs' relief (ER) (for post-2 December 2014 disposals). Thus, the transfer of goodwill would normally be taxed at 20% (rather than the 10% ER CGT rate).

COMPANIES WITH TAX LOSSES

20.18 If the company has tax losses, the payment of a bonus will increase the tax-adjusted trading loss. If there is scope to carry back the loss against the previous year, corporation tax relief is effectively obtained. The rate of relief would depend on the level of the prior year's profits. If there is no scope to relieve the bonus by loss carry-back (or group relief), then it will be included as part of the company's carried forward trading losses and the tax relief is effectively deferred until the losses are offset against future trading profits.

Carried forward trading losses arising after 1 April 2017 are subject to more generous offset rules. In such cases, companies can offset their unused losses against profits from different types of income (and profits of other group companies). However, 'very large' companies may be subject to certain restrictions in the amount of losses they can offset.

Repayment interest would accrue on tax repaid for the previous year, from nine months after the end of that period.

In contrast, a dividend would not create an additional loss.

The 'bonus versus dividend' equation therefore depends, amongst other things, on the effective rate of company tax relief and the amount of any repayment interest.

WHEN SHOULD THE 'BONUS VERSUS DIVIDEND' COMPARISON BE MADE?

20.19 It is generally preferable for the computational 'bonus versus dividend' profit extraction comparison to be made *before* the year end. From the owner-manager's viewpoint, there may of course be a timing point regarding the particular tax year into which the bonus/dividend should fall (particularly if there is a need to avoid the top tax rate).

20.20

> **Focus**
>
> The position with bonuses is more flexible since it is also possible to make a provision in the year end statutory accounts and obtain tax relief in that

period, provided the bonus is paid within nine months of the year end (see **20.22**). In the vast majority of cases, such a provision must comply with FRS 102/FRS 105, which requires a legal or constructive obligation to pay the bonus to exist at the balance sheet date.

In practical terms, this means that the anticipated results should be considered before the year end and an agreement should be in place for any required bonuses. It may also be preferable to look at the anticipated results of the company for other reasons. For example, this would enable the directors to consider the amount of any pension contributions which must be paid before the year end to ensure that tax relief is obtained in the current period. This means that reliable management accounting figures should be available.

DETAILED IMPLICATIONS OF PAYING A BONUS

Corporation tax relief

20.21 In the case of a trading company, the remuneration or bonus should be deductible against profits. It is very rare for an Inspector to challenge the level of remuneration paid to working director shareholders. The amounts paid to owner-managers will generally stand up to scrutiny as being a commercial rate, given their role in the company and the responsibility involved. In contrast, HMRC often seek to limit the tax deduction for directors' fees paid by investment companies to a very modest amount. In such cases, extracting funds via a dividend is likely to be more tax efficient.

If the Inspector challenges the corporation tax deduction for the remuneration and denies relief for the amount considered to be excessive, this amount will still be subject to PAYE tax and NICs. However, by concession, HMRC are prepared to refund the PAYE tax paid on this amount, provided the excess amount is formally waived by the director and the amount is actually reimbursed to the company (see ICAEW Tax Faculty Technical Release TAX 11/93). However, any NIC liability will still stand as the NICO does not apply this concession.

Relief for accrued remuneration

20.22 A special rule applies to remuneration which is accrued or unpaid at the end of a company's accounting period, such as a provision for a bonus. Such remuneration can only be deducted against the company's taxable profits for that period if it is paid within nine months after the period end (*CTA 2009,* *ss 1288* and *1289*). The date when remuneration is deemed to be paid is defined in *ITEPA 2003, s 18* (this rule also applies for PAYE purposes.

In the case of directors, the date of payment will often be the time when payment is actually made, or when the director becomes legally entitled to the amount (although the statutory definition also includes other events). In practice, HMRC will accept that a bonus is 'paid' when it is credited to a director's current account.

Unless a director has a service agreement, his remuneration can only be determined when it is approved by the shareholders at the company's AGM, which will normally be the date on which the company's annual accounts are signed. However, where appropriate, reliance can be placed on the decision in *Re Duomatic* [1969] 1 All ER 161 (applied more recently in *Cane v Jones* [1981] 1 All ER 533). This case decided that, where the directors agree in their capacity as shareholders the amount to be paid to them as directors' remuneration, this agreement will have the same effect as a resolution passed at the AGM. Consequently, where the AGM is likely to occur after the end of the nine-month period, it should still be possible to trigger a 'payment' of the bonus within the nine-month period by agreement of the director shareholders, which should be formally minuted. It will be appreciated that bonuses provide a convenient way of reducing a company's taxable profits after the year end.

20.23 If the shareholder director is fortunate enough to have a healthy credit balance on their loan/current account, they can draw amounts from the account during the accounting period without attracting any PAYE or NIC charges. The loan/current account can then be 'topped up' by a bonus following the year end and the exercise repeated next year.

The tax deduction rules for accrued bonus/remuneration may be used to obtain earlier corporation tax relief for amounts to be paid within the nine months following the year end. Provided the statutory accounts have not been signed-off, a provision can be made for bonuses paid (or to be paid) within nine months of the year end. Care must be taken that any such provision is FRS 102/FRS 105 complaint. This would require there to be a 'present obligation' at the balance sheet date to pay a bonus. This could be evidenced by minutes of a board meeting held prior to the year end, or even by the fact that such bonuses are regularly made. A provision written into the accounts after the year end (which does not satisfy current UK GAAP) would be open to challenge from HMRC, since they could seek to disallow the deduction in the year. HMRC are increasingly looking at accounting and accounting standards as part of their enquiries.

When providing for accrued directors' remuneration in the accounts, it is normal practice to provide also for the PAYE and NIC (including employer's

NIC) liabilities in the accounts to which the remuneration relates. If this practice is not adopted the amount would be provided gross and when the directors' final remuneration is approved (at the AGM, if not earlier), the net remuneration would then be credited to the relevant director's accounts. At that date, the PAYE and NICs must then be accounted for (ICAEW Tax Faculty Guidance Note TAX 11/93).

PAYE and cash flow

20.24 The payment of the bonus will, of course, attract a PAYE/NIC liability. PAYE at the basic rate (and higher rate, if applicable) and Class 1 NICs are normally payable 14 days after the end of the month in which the bonus is 'paid' or 'made available' (*SI 2003/2682, reg 69*). If the director receives a relatively low monthly salary and a high bonus payment once a year, further NICs are likely to become due on the annual re-calculation (this is because the NICs accounted for will have been subject to the monthly 'upper earnings limit').

If the tax due on the bonus was incorrect (for example, if the PAYE code was wrong), there may be additional tax to pay when the individual submits their tax return (at the latest by 31 January following the relevant tax year). However, provided the unpaid amount is less than £3,000 and the tax return is submitted early (say) by 31 October after the tax year for a paper return and 31 December after the tax year (if filed online), HMRC will adjust the PAYE code for the following tax year, enabling that tax to be collected on a gradual basis over the next tax year.

With a bonus, the owner-manager only receives the net amount after deducting PAYE and NIC. By contrast, where a dividend is paid, the owner-manager receives the full cash amount and does not have to pay the higher rate tax until a later date. Payments of tax on the dividend are made in accordance with the normal self-assessment rules. This requires interim tax payments to be made on 31 January in the tax year and on 31 July following the tax year (based on the previous year's tax liability), with a final payment being due on the following 31 January. Where a regular payment of dividends is established, the tax may become factored into the interim payments. Some owner-managers alternate between bonuses and dividends to prevent tax on dividends being factored into their payments on account.

In some cases, it may be beneficial to defer the payment of a dividend from say March to 6 April or later, as this may defer the higher rate liability (particularly if the director/shareholder's interim tax payments are based on a low prior year tax liability).

The tax cash flow implications therefore need to be considered, which will vary according to the individual circumstances of each case. When interest costs have been taken into account, this may affect the 'bonus versus dividend' comparisons considered above.

REAL TIME INFORMATION (RTI)

20.25 Under RTI, details of payments of earnings to directors must now be sent to HMRC every time a payment is made. The report must be made in the form of a Full Payment Submission (FPS).

With the introduction of the RTI system for reporting PAYE it is even more important for owner-managers to be clear about the status of all payments made to them at the time they are made. Furthermore, evidence must be retained to support the relevant treatment.

For example, if amounts drawn by a director (and debited to their loan account) are later considered to be a salary/bonus, they will not have been reported 'on or before the payment is made' in accordance with the RTI rules, which may lead to penalties being imposed by HMRC.

Care must be taken to ensure that amounts drawn by a director and debited to their loan account are *not* regarded as a payment on account of earnings, which would be reportable under RTI. HMRC will not consider such amounts to be earnings in the absence of evidence as to their exact true nature (EIM42280). It should also be noted that HMRC appear to be making increased use of the rule in *ITEPA 2003, Ch 3* which provides that any personal expenses paid by the company should be treated as (advance) payments of earnings. If *ITEPA 2003, Ch 3* catches these payments, they would be subject to PAYE and NICs. For owner-managers it is therefore important to place on record that overdrawn loan accounts are to be cleared by dividends or personally by the director and are not paid as expenses.

Under the RTI regime, many owner-managed companies have had to develop greater financial discipline. As part of this process, companies should produce proper *contemporaneous* evidence to support dividends, salaries and bonuses.

One sensible approach is for owner-managers to develop an agreed payment plan at the start of the tax year. Assuming the company has sufficient reserves, it would be sensible to bring the loan account in credit by paying an appropriate dividend at the start of the year. The owner-manager can then draw down regular amounts during the year (whilst keeping their loan account in credit). A one-off salary payment can be made in the last month of the tax year, which would avoid regular monthly RTI reporting. Consideration might also be given to applying for annual RTI reporting.

ICAEW RTI Helpsheet 3 published in April 2013 contains further guidance relating to the impact of RTI on directors' remuneration.

PAYMENT OF DIVIDENDS

20.26 In the context of a family or owner-managed company, the company's directors decide on the maximum level of the annual dividend that should be paid, based on the company's annual accounts and general financial position. Their proposed dividend is then put forward to the shareholders (in many cases, the same or largely the same individuals as the directors), who vote (by ordinary resolution) whether to pay the suggested figure or a *lower* amount.

Dividends are paid proportionately to the number of shares held (of the same class), although it is possible for shareholders to waive all or some of their dividend entitlement. Some companies have different classes of shares enabling them to alter the level of dividend paid on each separate class. It is only possible to pay dissimilar levels of dividend on different classes of shares. Once the vote has been passed, the dividend becomes 'declared' when it is then strictly regarded as having been made for tax purposes.

Directors usually have the power to make interim dividends before the final dividend is made. It is, therefore possible to pay dividends on a regular basis. However, many owner-managers find it easier just to pay one 'large' dividend, which is then credited to their current account with the company, upon which they can draw through the year. In practice, HMRC treat the 'crediting' of a dividend to a loan/current account as having been paid for tax purposes.

BONUS VERSUS DIVIDEND – OTHER FACTORS

20.27

> **Focus**
>
> The 'bonus versus dividend' decision will often be influenced by a number of other factors. The main ones are set out below.

(a) ***Pension provision*** – In the past, owner-managers often enjoyed considerable flexibility regarding the level of contributions they were able to make. However, they can currently only enjoy tax relief on pension contributions of up to £40,000 in the relevant tax year (plus any unused 'allowance' brought forward from the three previous years).

The 'annual allowance' limit applies to both personal and *company* contributions. It cannot therefore be side-stepped by routing pension contributions through the company.

Personal contributions only rank for income tax relief if the payer has sufficient 'relevant earnings' since relief is available on up to 100% of their relevant earnings for the tax year. However, if they have little or no earnings, relief is always given on gross contributions of up to a maximum of £3,600. Thus, where the owner-manager decides to draw little or no salary, they will still be able to fund a personal pension scheme at a rate of up to £3,600 (gross) per year. It should be noted that dividend income does not count as relevant earnings.

Owner-managers will need to have a reasonable level of salary/bonuses/ benefits to make worthwhile (tax relievable) pension contributions. Thus, where additional pension provision is required, it will often be necessary to pay appropriate bonuses. The bonus would not attract any income tax if it can be sheltered by a matching pension contribution (made within the relevant limit). However, a personal pension payment would *not* shelter the employers' and employees' NIC liability on the bonus. These NIC costs can be avoided where the company undertakes to pay the individual's pension contributions (instead of the bonus). Although the company is discharging a pecuniary benefit of the individual, this does not give rise to a taxable benefit.

(b) ***Protecting social security and basic state retirement benefits*** – Dividends do not attract NICs and therefore a certain level of remuneration is required to secure certain earnings-related social security benefits and the National Insurance Retirement Pension ('NIRP'). It is only necessary for an individual's earnings to be above the lower earnings limit (£113 per week for 2017/18) to qualify and, therefore, a small salary should always be paid (also possibly to satisfy the national living wage requirements – see **20.10**). In fact, provided the earnings exceed the lower earnings limit but are below the primary earnings threshold (£157 per week for 2017/18), basic state retirement benefits can be protected without incurring any NIC liability.

(c) ***Share valuations*** – A history of dividend payments might increase the value of minority shareholdings for tax purposes. This is because the valuation of a minority shareholding may be determined by the expectation of dividend income. Share valuations for controlling shareholders are unlikely to be affected.

(d) ***Spread of shareholdings*** – as shareholders receive dividends in proportion to their holdings, the amount of dividends received by each shareholder may not provide a fair reward for the working shareholders and may prove too generous for the non-working or 'passive' shareholders. On the other hand a bonus can be a problem where the company's shareholdings have become widely spread over time. A 'dividend waiver' may be the answer here, provided it does not create any 'settlement' problems. Use of a separate class of shares for the non-working shareholders might be a more elegant solution on a long term basis.

(e) ***Personal borrowing and other issues*** – some lenders may not understand the methodology of profit extraction used by owner-managed companies and only focus on 'remuneration/salary' (as opposed to bonuses and dividends) when providing mortgages, loans, etc. Remuneration is also used to calculate redundancy pay and remains important for income protection plans. PHI cover can be provided to take salary/bonus as well as dividends into account.

EXTRACTING SURPLUS PROFITS – SOME CONCLUSIONS

20.28 The various worked examples in this chapter largely concentrate on the extraction of 'surplus' profits where a reasonable level of salary has already been paid. It is often considered beneficial to pay a modest level of salary. However, where tax-efficiency is paramount, there is no substitute for doing the relative computations to compare the combined effective tax rates (for the company and its owner-manager(s)).

Since 1 April 2015, all companies pay tax at the same rate of tax, which is 19% from 1 April 2017 (20% between 1 April 2015 to 31 March 2017). This is subject to limited exceptions. On the basis of effective tax rates, the payment of dividends should be marginally preferable. Dividends also offer the added potential of a longer deferment in the payment of income tax.

Where shareholders only pay tax at the lower or basic rates, dividends will invariably be more tax efficient.

However, the above broad generalisations may be overturned by various other factors. Thus, a relatively high bonus payment might be required to enable the owner-manager to augment their personal pension fund with tax allowable contributions (subject to the annual allowance limits). In certain situations, the payment of a bonus may provide a useful way of keeping a company outside the quarterly instalment regime for corporation tax.

In summary, family and owner-managed companies should consider a sensible combination of bonuses and dividends and, in appropriate cases, pension contributions. The precise mix would depend on the particular circumstances of each company and its shareholders.

REMUNERATION PAID TO OTHER MEMBERS OF THE FAMILY

20.29

Focus

As a general rule, tax will be saved if income can be paid to other members of the owner-manager's family in order to use their annual personal allowances and benefit from their lower marginal tax rates. Inspectors are likely to scrutinise salaries paid to members of the family to see whether they are paid at or above the market rate for the duties performed.

Where the amount clearly exceeds the commercial rate, the Inspector will seek to disallow the 'excess' element on the grounds that it has *not* been incurred wholly and exclusively for the purposes of the company's trade. In practice, the agreement of an 'allowable' amount is likely to be negotiated.

TRANSFERRING INCOME TO THE SPOUSE

Income tax for spouse or civil partner

20.30 For the sake of brevity, but at the risk of appearing sexist(!), the following commentary (in particular) is couched exclusively in terms of the husband being the one who owns and runs the company and puts income into his wife's hands. However, the comments below apply equally to those situations where the wife owns the company and the roles are reversed. (The same considerations also apply to same-sex couples, either married or registered as civil partners.)

Under independent taxation, each spouse has their own personal allowance and personal basic rate bands. It is generally beneficial to bring the spouse in as a director or employee and pay them a salary, provided the following conditions are met:

(a) the salary is taxable at a lower rate of tax (than that suffered by the owner-manager on his income);

(b) this income tax saving is not exceeded by the additional NIC liability (see **20.40**); and

(c) the company is able to obtain a tax deduction for the salary (see **20.42**).

In all such cases, it is recommended that the remuneration (or dividend – see **20.44**) should not be paid into a joint bank account, but one in the spouse's sole name. The same benefits may also apply to bringing in a civil partner as an employee/director.

20.31 Many spouses only work on a 'part-time' basis. However, part-time workers also fall within the national living wage (NLW) legislation. Hence, the amount paid to the spouse (providing they are over 25 years old) must not be lower than the current rate of £7.50 per hour requirement (see **20.10** for further details). However, if the spouse works for the company without any remuneration at all, she may well not be an employee, and hence the NLW legislation will not apply as the relationship may be explained by a desire to assist the company voluntarily (ICAEW Tax Guide 7/00).

Universal credit

20.32 The 'Universal Credit' system replaces almost all social security benefits and tax credits system.

Details of the Universal Credit are set out in the *Welfare Reform Act 2012*. Universal credit for working people is administered and 'underpinned' by the RTI system (see **20.25**).

Universal credit replaces the following:

- Income-based Jobseeker's Allowance
- Income-related Employment and Support Allowance
- Income Support
- Child Tax Credits
- Working Tax Credits
- Housing Benefit

Universal Credit is firmly targeted at jobseekers and low paid workers and so it offers few benefits to most owner-managers. It will supply a standard allowance plus additional amounts for disability, housing, children and other caring responsibilities. Claimants under the current benefits system are guaranteed to be no worse off under the Universal Credit system.

The amount payable will be restricted by reference to income thresholds for earned and unearned income at rates of 65% to 100% for unearned income. Most owner-managers would have a withdrawal rate of 100% where they extract profits by way of dividends and thus are unlikely to receive any benefits under the Universal Credit system.

Spouse's NIC liabilities

20.33 The income tax benefits of giving a salary to a spouse are often reduced by the NIC cost. In 2017/18, if the spouse earns £157 or more per week (or more than £8,164 on an annual basis), *employees'* NICs are payable at 12% on earnings between £157 and £866 per week (£8,164–£45,000 per year). The first £157 per week is free of NICs. Contracting out is no longer possible from 6 April 2016.

When the spouse's total annual earnings reach the upper earnings limit of £45,000, a 2% NIC 'surcharge' is levied on any amount exceeding the limit.

For 2017/18, *employer's* NICs are levied at the standard rate of 13.8% for earnings exceeding £157 per week with no maximum limit. (The first £157 per week (£8,164 per year) is NIC free.)

An annual salary of up to £8,164 can therefore be paid in 2017/18 without any income tax or NIC liability.

TAX DEDUCTION FOR REMUNERATION PAID TO SPOUSE

20.34

> **Focus**
>
> The optimum amount to be paid to the spouse must therefore be carefully considered. Unless the spouse works for the company on a full-time basis, HMRC will require the amount to be substantiated in relation to the duties performed. Inspectors often critically assess the amount of remuneration paid to a wife in relation to the work she performs. It may be helpful to draw up a job specification listing all the wife's duties (for example, secretarial, certain administrative duties, etc) together with some indication of the time commitment.

There must also be some evidence of payment to the spouse. Unsurprisingly, in *Moschi v Kelly* (1952) 33 TC 442, tax relief for the wife's wages was denied since they were charged to the owner's own drawings account!

If the wife is appointed as a director, then the legal obligations and responsibilities assumed in that position alone should justify a reasonable level of remuneration. Provided the amount paid to the wife reflects the work she *actually* carries out, the company should have no difficulty in obtaining a tax deduction. (Similar considerations apply to remuneration paid to a civil partner, etc.)

A further advantage of paying remuneration to the wife is that it can be used to support company pension contributions to provide her with a pension in her own right, subject to the spouse's overall package meeting the 'wholly and exclusively' requirement (and the pension payment being within the annual allowance).

A spouse could also pay tax-deductible personal pension contributions up to 100% of her salary.

The Copeman v William Flood & Sons Ltd case

20.35 Where HMRC consider the level of remuneration to be excessive, they will challenge it using the decision in *Copeman v William Flood & Sons Ltd* (1940) 24 TC 53. (Similar issues apply to the tax deductibility of company pension contributions.) This case enables them to disallow the 'excess' part of the remuneration charged in the accounts on the grounds that this element was not paid wholly and exclusively for the purposes of the company's trade (*CTA 2009, s 54*).

In the *Copeman* case, the Revenue contested the deduction for remuneration of £2,600 paid in 1938 to a pig dealer's daughter, for dealing with telephone queries. This would be equivalent to remuneration of well over £75,000 in current day values! The case was remitted to the Commissioners to determine the amount which should be disallowed.

Waiving 'disallowed' remuneration

20.36 If HMRC succeed in substituting a lower figure for the tax deductible remuneration, the wife would strictly be taxable on the *full amount* of the remuneration. However, provided the 'excess' element is formally waived and paid back to the company, HMRC will generally restrict the income tax charge to the *deductible* element of the remuneration (EIM42730).

If the spouse is also a shareholder, the Inspector may treat any non-waived 'disallowed' amount as a distribution, which should not increase the tax liability. However, HMRC will still retain any NIC liability.

Paying dividends to a spouse

20.37 If the wife does little or no work for the company, no relief can really be justified. In these cases, it is generally better to structure the shareholdings so that the spouse receives dividend income instead. Provided fully-fledged ordinary shares are provided to the spouse, HMRC are unlikely to challenge it now, following their defeat in *Garnett v Jones* [2007] STC 1536 – the so-called *Arctic Systems* case. On the other hand, if the shares issued only contain dividend rights (such as non-voting preference shares), HMRC will probably be able to counter the relevant arrangements, as they successfully did in *Young v Pearce* [1996] STC 743.

Dividend-splitting may also be considered by those owner-managers affected by the 'top' (2017/18) dividend tax rate of 38.1%. In many cases, owner-managers will seek to pay their spouses part of 'their' dividend entitlement to avoid paying this tax rate on their dividends.

HMRC were very keen to introduce legislation to negate these types of income-shifting/income splitting arrangements as soon as the *Arctic Systems* ruling went against it. However, the Treasury seems to have lost the appetite to introduce appropriate new legislation to counter income splitting between married couples. It is recommended that any spousal dividend should be paid into their own bank account (rather than an account in joint names).

Focus

Following the changes to the dividend tax regime in 2016/17, spousal dividend planning still remains. For example, a 'non-tax paying' spouse could take a *tax-free* dividend of £16,000 (ie an amount equal to their personal allowance and dividend nil rate band).

Most owner-managers prefer taking advantage of the 7.5% 'basic-rate' band. Thus, assuming spouses have no other taxable income, they could receive a dividend in 2017/18 of £45,000 at a tax cost of only £2,137, as calculated below:

	£
Cash dividend	45,000
Personal allowance	(11,500)
Taxable dividend	33,500
Basic rate band is £33,500 but	
First £5,000 – nil rate	–
Next £28,500 @ 7.5%	2,137
Tax Liability	2,137

Where spouses take dividends, they would have little or no relevant earnings for pension purposes. However, it is still possible for them to make annual tax-deductible gross pension contributions of up to £3,600 gross (£2,880 net of basic rate tax relief relieved at source), provided this can be justified in terms of their 'commercial' pay package.

Example 20.4 – Salary or dividend for spouse

Mr Astle is the controlling shareholder of Astle Ltd, which is based in the West Midlands. His wife holds 20% of the ordinary shares in Astle Ltd.

Mr Astle is deciding whether to pay £20,000 to his wife as a salary (before NICs) or dividend for the year to 31 March 2018. She has no other income.

Mrs Astle performs secretarial and administrative duties for the company which should be sufficient to justify corporation tax relief for the salary.

		Salary	*Dividend*
	£	£	£
Available Profits		20,000	20,000
Less Employer's NIC (13.8% on £18,565 – £8,164)		(1,435)	
Gross pay		18,565	
Less Employees' NIC 12% × (£18,565 – £8,164)		(1,248)	
Corporation tax at 19%			(3,800)
		17,317	16,200
Less Income tax thereon			
On Salary			
Salary	18,565		
Less PA	(11,500)		
Taxable	7,065		
Income tax (£7,065 at 20%)		(1,413)	
On Dividend			
Cash	16,200		
Less PA	(11,500)		
Taxable dividend	4,700		
Within dividend nil rate band of £5,000		–	–
Post-tax receipt		15,904	16,200

EMPLOYING THE CHILDREN

20.38 The owner-manager's children may also work for the company at weekends, or in their school/college/university holidays. The company will need to comply with the appropriate legislation and by-laws for employing children aged under 16. Children cannot be employed in a factory and those under 13 cannot be employed except for light duties in limited circumstances.

The national living wage (NLW) rules must be adhered to for children aged 25 or over and the national minimum wage (NMW) rules for children aged between 16 and 24 (see **20.10** for current applicable rates).

If the children have taken out student loans, then the company may be liable to make appropriate deductions from their salary towards repayment of their loan. No student loan deductions are currently required where the salary is less than £17,775 per year in 2017/18.

The wages received by the children can be paid tax free up to their personal allowance, with any excess being liable at the basic rate or higher rate, as appropriate. Once again, HMRC will seek to establish the commercial justification for the payment in relation to the work done by the children. Payments made to the owner-manager's children which constitute 'disguised pocket money' will be disallowed (see *Dollar v Lyon* [1981] STC 333). There will, of course, be cases where a fairly reasonable amount can be substantiated as a genuine trading expense of the company. For example, the author is aware of a case where a teenage son of an owner-manager was paid a justifiable commercial wage for trial testing computer games that had been developed by the business. In such cases, such amounts will clearly be allowable as a trading expense.

Under the current pension regime, pension contributions of up to £3,600 gross (£2,880 net of the basic rate tax relief contributed at source by HMRC) can be made for each child, even in the absence of any relevant earnings.

CHARGING RENT ON PERSONALLY OWNED ASSETS USED BY THE COMPANY

Rationale for holding property personally and tax treatment of rent

20.39

> **Focus**
>
> A number of owner-managers leave the trading property outside the company to mitigate the effect of the potential 'double-tax' charge and to create wealth outside the company (free from the claims of its creditors (subject to personal guarantees), etc). In such cases, the owner-manager can extract funds from the company by charging the company a market rent for the use of the property.

The rent may be paid under a formal lease agreement between the owner-manager and the company. If the property is jointly-owned, for example, by the owner-manager and their spouse, then the rent would be paid to both in the appropriate shares.

SDLT is payable where (and to the extent that) the chargeable consideration for the lease exceeds £150,000 (for commercial property). A 2% charge applies for chargeable consideration falling within the '£150,001 to £250,000' band, with any excess over £250,000 being charged at 5%.

In broad terms, the chargeable consideration represents the net present value of the future rental income, with special rules applying to variable and/or contingent rents. It is not possible to mitigate the SDLT charge by charging a low rent, since a deemed market rental value applies where the property is let to a 'connected company' (as will generally be the case). If the SDLT charge is prohibitive, it may be worth considering granting a simple 'licence to occupy' the property since this is an *exempt* interest in land for SDLT purposes. In broad terms, a licence to occupy represents a non-exclusive right of occupation so it is important that any documentation does not grant the company the sole exclusive right to occupy the property (*FA 2003, s 48(2)(b)*).

The rent paid by the company would be deductible against its profits (provided it represents a market rent) and the rent received would be taxable in the owner-manager's hands as property income (but no NIC liability would arise). The owner-manager can deduct, as property business expenses, the normal expenses of running the let property, including repairs (not capital improvements), service expenses, insurance, security costs and relevant professional fees. Interest paid on personal loans taken out to purchase or improve the property will also be tax-deductible (subject to the income tax relief restriction for interest costs which is being phased in from 2017/18).

Where the owner-manager has borrowed money to purchase the property, he would normally charge rent to secure immediate tax relief for the interest (*ITTOIA 2005, s 272*). Clearly, if only part of the building is let, then only a corresponding part of the costs can be deducted as property business expenses.

Where personally held property is subsequently sold alongside a disposal of the owner-manager's shares, it may be possible to claim Entrepreneurs' Relief (ER) on the property gain under the associated disposal rules. Provided the owner-manager has 'ER capacity' after relief has been claimed against the share sale, a 10% ER CGT rate can be applied to the property gain. Since 18 March 2015, shareholders' must sell at least a 5% stake in the company to qualify for 'associated disposal' relief.

In such cases, the gain qualifying for ER would be denied or restricted where the owner-manager has previously charged a rent for the use of the property.

Interest on borrowings and capital allowances

20.40 In some cases, the owner-manager may not charge a rent, but will arrange for the company to pay the interest on their personal borrowings that were taken out to purchase or improve the property. Such 'interest' would be deductible in computing the company's trading profits as it represents consideration for occupying the property for trading purposes. Following normal accountancy principles, the company's interest payment on the owner-manager's behalf is counted as a property business receipt in the owner-manager's hands, but this would be offset by the owner-manager's actual obligation to pay the interest (subject to the proposed phasing out of full income tax relief (see **20.39**)). (If the company does not pay rent or interest, the owner-manager cannot secure any income tax relief for the interest.)

Other allowable deductions include capital allowances on integral features and plant attached to the building.

VAT issues

20.41 Provided the property is used for normal commercial (non-residential) purposes, the owner-manager can elect to opt to tax it. Where the owner-manager is personally VAT registered, VAT would be added to the rent charged to the company (as well as on any service charges). An option to tax would almost certainly be required where VAT was charged on the purchase price paid for the property (or on any substantial improvements). Provided the election is in place, this will enable the owner-manager to recover VAT on any expenses incurred in relation to the property in their capacity as a landlord. However, it also means that if the property is sold, VAT would have to be charged on the sale proceeds (unless it was possible to use the 'transfer of going concern' exemption.

Provided the company is fully taxable (for VAT purposes), VAT charged on the rents would be fully recovered. Thus, overall, charging VAT on the rent is likely to be cash neutral whilst enabling VAT to be reclaimed on property improvements and running expenses.

Where the owner-manager is only likely to suffer minimal VAT costs, it may not be worthwhile to opt to tax (unless of course VAT was charged on the original purchase cost which needs to be recovered).

Extraction of profits via rent

20.42 The tax effect of extracting profits via a rent is similar to the payment of remuneration, except that no PAYE or NIC is payable.

Example 20.5 – Rent charged to company for use of owner-manager's property

Mr Downing owns the entire share capital of The Downing Cross Company Ltd. The factory used by the company was, however, purchased by Mr and Mrs Downing in equal shares many years ago.

For the year ended 31 March 2018 the company was charged a rent of £30,000. Mr and Mrs Downing's claim for allowable property expenses were £3,000 each. They had no finance costs.

Assuming that, for the year ended 31 March 2018, the company's taxable profits before charging the rent were £260,000, the tax consequences are as follows:

	Company	*Mr Downing*	*Mrs Downing*
	£	£	£
Taxable profits before rent	260,000		
Less: Rent charged	(30,000)	15,000	15,000
Taxable profit (after rent charge)	230,000		
Less: Corporation tax @ 19%	(43,700)		
Post-tax profit	186,300		
Less: Allowable property expenses		(3,000)	(3,000)
Taxable rent		12,000	12,000
Company tax saving on rent			
£30,000 @ 19%	5,700		
Income tax payable:			
Marginal tax rate @ 40%		6,000	
Marginal tax rate @ 20%			3,000

Subsequent sale of property

20.43 If the owner-manager subsequently sells the property, any capital gain will generally be taxed at the main current CGT rate of 20%.

Where the property is being sold along with an ER-eligible disposal of shares in the company, the owner-manager *may* be able to obtain a 10% rate on any unused ER entitlement against the property gain under the 'associated disposal' rules (subject to any restriction for rent charges) (see also **20.39**).

SELLING AN ASSET TO THE COMPANY FOR VALUE

Background

20.44 The controlling shareholder may personally own the company's trading premises. This means that the property should not be exposed to the company's creditors on a winding up, although in many cases, banks or other lenders will secure a charge on the property. Consequently, as far as the commercial risk is concerned, there may be little difference whether the property is owned by the company or shareholder.

> **Focus**
>
> Owner-managers might consider extracting a capital sum from their company by selling the (personally-owned) property to the company. The disposal would generate a capital gain in their hands, which will now generally be taxed at 20%. (Note that 'associated disposal' ER relief is not available for 'separate property sales'.)

SDLT may be payable on the purchase by the company. In such cases, SDLT would normally be levied on the market value of the property irrespective of the actual sale price paid by the company (see **20.46**). The transfer of the property to the company may also improve the owner-manager's business property relief position for IHT purposes.

Care is necessary to ensure that the property is not sold at an over-value, since the excess amount could be taxed as employment income (or as a shareholder distribution) (*CTA 2010, s 1000*).

CGT treatment

20.45 An immediate chargeable gain can be avoided by selling the property to the company at its original base cost (which will be the March 1982 value where the property was held by the owner-manager at that date). Although the disposal computed by reference to market value, the 'unrealised element' of the gain can be held over under the business asset gift relief provisions in *TCGA 1992, s 165* (which must be claimed on form IR295). This relief is not affected by any previous rent charges. By concession, it is not necessary to agree the market value of the gifted asset with HMRC. The 'transferor' owner-manager and the company must request this treatment in writing (SP8/92).

Where the owner-manager sells the asset at its original base cost/March 1982 value, the company will effectively acquire it at that amount.

Where the asset is sold to the company at its original base cost or a lower amount, this will be the acquisition cost on the company's balance sheet. However, it is possible to bolster the company's balance sheet by subsequently revaluing the asset. The uplift in valuation would be credited to a revaluation surplus account within shareholders' funds.

VAT and SDLT

20.46 The owner-manager will normally be connected with the company within *CTA 2010, s 1122*, since they either control it in their own right or together with their family members. Consequently, the 'deemed market value' rule in *FA 2003, s 53* will apply for SDLT purposes, irrespective of the actual consideration paid by the company. The amount of SDLT payable on the acquisition of the property by the company will therefore depend on its market value (which is treated as the 'chargeable consideration'). However, if the property was previously owned by a 'connected' family partnership, the special partnership SDLT provisions take precedence over the deemed 'market value' rule, which may result in a reduction or elimination of the SDLT charge.

The SDLT chargeable consideration normally includes any VAT chargeable on the sale and it appears that HMRC require any potential VAT to be added to the 'deemed' market value consideration for these purposes.

Where the property is subject to a VAT option to tax (see **20.41**), the owner-manager will need to charge VAT on the purchase price (which is normally recoverable by the company). Some care is required over the timing of the transaction to ensure that the company is able to recover the input VAT before it is paid over by the owner-manager. Although the property may have been previously let to the company at a commercial rent, the sale cannot be treated as a transfer of a going concern since the same letting business would not be carried on by the company (the property would then become 'owner-occupied').

CHARGING INTEREST ON LOANS TO THE COMPANY

Commercial implications

20.47

> **Focus**
>
> Where owner-managers make a loan to the company or have a credit balance on their current account, there is nothing to stop them charging the

company with interest on the loan. The interest rate charged should be at a commercial rate, which (depending on the company's financial position and creditworthiness) could be several base points above the bank base lending rate. This would recognise the 'risk' element of non-recovery if the company gets into financial difficulty, although it may be possible to secure the lending (for example) against the company's property.

If the interest charged by a shareholder-director materially exceeds a commercial rate, HMRC may seek to treat the 'excess' amount as a salary (seeking PAYE and NIC) or dividend distribution.

ACCOUNTING FOR OWNER-MANAGER'S LOAN TO COMPANY

20.48 FRS 102 requires all financing transactions to be accounted for on a consistent basis. Consequently, where owner-managers make an interest-free or below market interest loan to 'their' companies, this is seen as giving additional financial benefits to the company as compared with arm's length borrowing transactions.

Loans with a fixed repayment term (of longer than 12 months) are shown as a non-current liability on the balance sheet. Where the loan is interest-free (or below commercial interest rates), it must be valued at amortised cost, ie the present value of the future payments discounted at a market rate of interest for a similar debt instrument. Consequently, the loan is discounted to its present value. In subsequent periods, the interest is unwound by debiting the profit and loss account.

This treatment produces an intial gain and notional finance charges for accounting purposes, which are dealt with through the profit and loss account. There is an exception if the loan is provided by an owner-manager, when the initial gain is recognised as a capital contribution from the owner-manager. This reflects the economic substance of the transaction and would be recorded with shareholders' 'capital'.

For loans made in accounting periods starting *after 31 December 2015*, the initial gain and the subsequent notional interest adjustments are completely ignored for tax (*CTA 2009, s 446A*).

These accounting complications do not arise where the loan is repayable on demand *or* where interest is charged at a commercial rate. Furthermore, if the company is small and accounts under FRS 105, these rules do not apply.

Company's tax deduction for interest

20.49 Under the 'loan relationship' rules, the company normally obtains relief for interest charged in its accounts on an accruals basis, ie on the amount charged against its profits. However, any loan to a close company from an individual shareholder (or an associate of a shareholder) is subject to the 'late interest' rule. (Although the *Finance Act 2015* repealed much of the late interest rules, they still apply for loans from owner-managers and other individual shareholders.)

Under these rules, the corporate tax deduction for any interest that remains unpaid more than 12 months after the accounting period end, is deferred until the interest is actually paid (*CTA 2009, ss 373* and *375*).

A close company therefore only gets relief for the interest on a loan from its owner-manager on an accruals basis provided it is paid in, or within 12 months after the end of, the relevant accounting period.

If the period of the loan exceeds (or can be extended beyond) one year, the interest would be treated as 'annual interest'. Since the interest is paid to an individual, the company must deduct lower rate tax (of 20%) at source when the interest is paid. (Only interest on bank and building society loans can be paid 'gross' from 6 April 2016.) This interest is reported and paid over to HMRC on Form CT 61. The recipient shareholder-director is taxed on the ('grossed up') interest *received* (with credit being given for any tax deducted at source). The interest does not constitute earnings and therefore no NICs are payable.

Focus

In some cases, it may be possible to secure a timing advantage by exploiting the late interest rule within the constraints of the rules.

For example, a company could accrue interest on an owner-manager's loan account in its accounting period ended 31 March 2018 with the interest being paid in (say) June 2018. Thus, the interest would still be deductible against the company's profits for the year ended 31 March 2018 (with the benefit of the tax reduction being obtained on 1 January 2019). On the other hand, the recipient would be taxed on a 'received' basis in 2018/19, with the income tax liability being payable on 31 January 2020.

Example 20.6 – Charging interest on a director's loan account

Mr Cresswell is a 75% shareholder of Aaron 3 Ltd. Over the years, he has ploughed back most of his dividend income to provide additional working capital for the company.

During the year ended 31 March 2018, the balance outstanding on his loan account with the company was £300,000 on which he charged interest at 8% per year.

The company's taxable profits (*before* charging interest on Mr Cresswell's shareholder loan account) for the year ended 31 March 2018 were £780,000.

The tax position for the company and Mr Cresswell is as follows:

Year ended 31 March 2018	
Company	£
Taxable profits before interest	780,000
Less: Interest charge	
£300,000 × 8% =	(24,000)
Taxable profit after interest charge	756,000
Corporation tax @ 19%	(143,640)
Profit after tax	612,360
Company tax saving on interest	
£24,000 @ 19%	£4,560

The company will only obtain tax relief in the year ended 31 March 2018 provided the interest is actually paid to Mr Cresswell by 31 March 2019. Relief will not be given if the interest is simply 'rolled-up' as a credit to his loan account and remains outstanding at 31 March 2019.

Mr Cresswell	
Interest received net of tax deducted by company	
£24,000 less £4,800 (ie 20% × £24,000)	19,200
Less: Income tax payable	
£24,000 @ (say) 40% = £9,600 less £4,800 (tax deducted at source by company)	(4,800)
Net amount received	14,400

LOANS FROM THE COMPANY

Companies Act restriction

20.50 Since 1 October 2007 private companies have been able to make loans to directors (provided they have been approved by shareholders) (*CA 2006, s 197*).

Loans to those connected with the director are also subject to the same 'shareholder approval' rules. (Connected persons under the *CA 2006* include spouses, minor and adult children, parents, and so on.)

The *CA 2006* does not require any approval for small loans/quasi-loans (£10,000) and minor credit transactions (£15,000).

If the company fails to obtain the required resolution of its shareholders, the loan is voidable under *CA 2006, s 213*. This means that the company could rescind the loan and recoup its money.

Scope of CTA 2010, s 455 charge

20.51 Strictly, the *CTA 2010, s 455* charge only arises on loans made to 'participators' (invariably shareholders) of a close company, and the vast majority of owner-managed companies will be 'close' for these purposes.

Consequently, owner-managers will normally be subject to a *CTA 2010, s 455* charge of 32.5% (25% for pre-6 April 2016 loans) where the company makes a loan or advance to them which is not repaid within nine months of the company's year-end (see **20.61**).

The charge can also apply where a loan is made to an 'associate' of the shareholder, such as a spouse, parent, grandparent, child, grandchild, brother or sister, as well as a business partner (*CTA 2010, s 448(2)*).

For FRS 102-related accounting issues for (overdrawn) directors' loan accounts, see **20.58** and **20.59**).

Changes introduced in *FA 2013* have widened the scope of *CTA 2010, s 455* in relation to loans made to 'related' partnerships and trusts after 19 March 2013 (see **20.52**).

Furthermore, *FA 2013* also introduced:

- special rules to deal with 'bed and breakfasting arrangements (see **20.61**); and
- an anti-avoidance charge on 'benefits' enjoyed by shareholders (under arrangements that would not otherwise be caught by *CTA 2010, s 455*) – see **20.70**.

There is a separate rule which deems a *CTA 2010, s 455* liability to arise where a participator (or associate) incurs a debt to the company – for example, where the shareholder buys a 'personal' asset on credit in the company's name (*CTA 2010, s 455(4)*). This particular trap can also occur with management charges that remain due to a 'parallel' partnership service company (for longer than six months (see exemption (b) below)). Any debt incurred by the partnership would fall within *CTA 2010, s 455(4)* (see *Grant v Watton; Andrew Grant Services Ltd v Watton* [1999] STC 330).

There are various exemptions from the *CTA 2010, s 455* tax liability, but they are of little assistance to most family and owner-managed companies:

(a) loans up to £15,000 in total are exempt where the borrower works full time for the company and does not own more than 5% of the ordinary share capital (*CTA 2010, s 456(4)*);

(b) indirect loans involving the supply of goods on credit by the close company are exempt provided this is made in the normal course of trade (except where the credit given exceeds six months) (*CTA 2010, s 456(2)*);

(c) the tax charge does not apply where the company is a lending institution which makes the loan or advance in the ordinary course of its business (*CTA 2010, s 456(1)*). HMRC only regard this exemption as being available where the company is carrying on the business of money lending and this is part of its general business activities.

Although *CTA 2010, s 455* is generally regarded as a 'deposit' tax (since it is repayable when the loan/advance is repaid), it is still treated as 'an amount of corporation tax' and thus is liable to interest and penalties in the normal way. It is therefore important that all *CTA 2010, s 455* loans are disclosed on the CT 600 return, even if the relevant tax liability is discharged by repayment of the loan within nine months of the company's year-end (see **20.54**).

Loans to 'related' trusts and partnerships/LLPs

20.52 A *CTA 2010, s 455* charge will now firmly catch loans made to the trustees of a settlement in which at least one of the trustees or beneficiaries (actual or potential) is a participator (or an associate of an individual of a participator).

FA 2013 ensures that loans made to a trust are caught by *CTA 2010, s 455*, irrespective of whether the trust holds shares in the company. All that is required is that either:

- (at least) one trustee; or
- a beneficiary of the trust

is a shareholder of the 'lending' company.

For loans made after 19 March 2013, the *FA 2013* confirms that a loan or advance to a partnership/LLP in which *at least one* participator (or their associate) is a partner/member is caught by *CTA 2010, s 455*. Furthermore, the new *CTA 2010, s 455(1)(c)* also catches loans made to a partnership/LLP that includes at least one corporate partner/member. A *CTA 2010, s 455* charge can therefore easily apply where there is no significant overlap between the company's shareholders and the partners/members.

Unfortunately, the *FA 2013* provisions do not include any 'commercial purpose' exemption, which had been widely called for. *CTA 2010, s 455* will therefore apply to commercially based loan arrangements, such as where a 'related' close company makes a loan to a property development LLP to fund a new development.

Partners or members often inject funding into the partnership/LLP through their capital accounts, which reflects the nature of their investment or proprietorial interest in the relevant firm. Since partners do not have a right to demand repayment of their capital account, many would strongly argue that this cannot be viewed as a 'loan or advance' within the meaning of *CTA 2010, 455(1)(c)*. Consequently, where a corporate partner/member makes a capital contribution to a partnership/LLP, it should *not* be subject to a *CTA 2010, s 455* charge.

Example 20.7 – Application of *CTA 2010, s 455* to loans made to partnerships/LLPs

Mr Allen is a 40% shareholder in Gills Ltd and a 50% member of Allen LLP, as shown below:

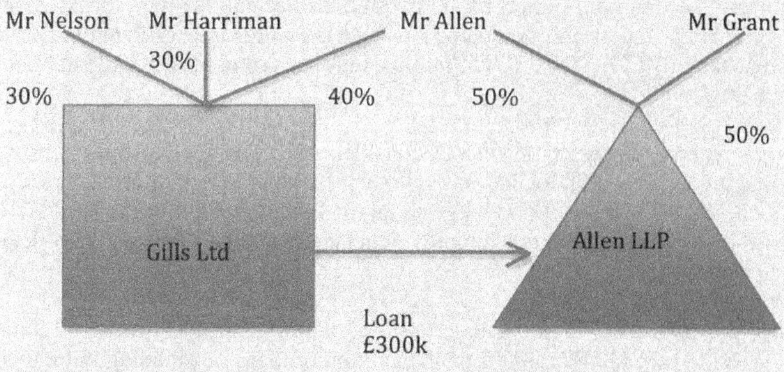

In June 2017 Gills Ltd made a loan of £300,000 to Allen LLP to provide additional working capital.

The loan of £300,000 to Allen LLP would be caught by *CTA 2010, s 455*. This is because Mr Allen is both a partner (member) of the LLP and a participator in the 'lending' company (Gills Ltd).

Beneficial loan charge

20.53 Since owner-managers will also be within the scope of the directors'/ employment/benefit, any loan made to them by the company will also fall within the scope of the beneficial loan provisions. Thus, if the company does not charge any interest on the loan (or the interest charge is less than the official rate), a taxable benefit will arise on the 'interest' benefit (*ITEPA 2003, s 175*).

Mechanics of CTA 2010, s 455 charge

20.54 The aim of this legislation is to levy tax on what would otherwise be an easy method of extracting cash from the close company on a tax-free basis. *CTA 2010, s 455* requires the company to account for tax at the rate of 32.5% on the loan/advance. For loans/advances made before 6 April 2016, *CTA 2010, s 455* tax is charged at 25%.

The *CTA 2010, s 455* tax therefore represents a stand-alone charge which is deposited with HMRC. If the loan or overdrawn account is repaid in whole or in part (or is released (see **20.70**)), the appropriate portion of the *CTA 2010, s 455* tax is discharged or refunded (*CTA 2010, s 458(2)*). Any repayment from HMRC must be claimed within four years from the end of the *financial year* in which the loan is repaid/released.

For companies that are not subject to the Quarterly Instalment Payment (QIP) regime, the *CTA 2010, s 455* liability falls due nine months after the end of their company's accounting period (in line with their normal due date for payment of tax). However, if the company pays its tax under the QIP regime, any (undischarged) *CTA 2010, s 455* liability must be factored into its instalment payments.

Some owner-managers may wish to consider extracting funds from company by making a substantial loan to mitigate their income tax liabilities. There will be a one-off *CTA 2010, s 455* charge equal to 32.5% (25% for pre-6 April 2016 loans/advances) and an annual employment benefit charge based on the official rate of interest.

Thus, the *CTA 2010, s 455* charge on a £100,000 loan advanced on 1 June 2017 would be £32,500 (assuming the amount remains outstanding more than nine months after the company's year-end) and the tax on the 'interest' benefit would be just £1,200 for a 40% taxpayer (ie £100,000 × 3% × 40%).

If the loan is repaid before the *CTA 2010, s 455* tax is due for payment, the liability is discharged and the tax does not have to be paid over. However, if the loan remains outstanding after the nine month due date, HMRC will seek the *CTA 2010, s 455* tax and charge interest from the due date until the tax is paid.

When the loan is subsequently repaid, the repayment of the *CTA 2010, s 455* tax is deferred until nine months after the *end of the CTAP in which the loan is repaid or reduced,* with repayment interest arising on any delayed repayment. Given this lead time for repayment of the *CTA 2010, s 455* tax, owner-managers should always try to avoid triggering a *CTA 2010, s 455* liability by repaying their loans within nine months of the balance sheet date.

Directors' overdrawn loan accounts

20.55 HMRC insist that the company's record keeping should ensure that balances of directors' loan accounts are accurate and kept up to date. HMRC are concerned that poorly kept records 'may result in non-business expenditure incurred by the directors being incorrectly recorded or mis-posted in the business records and claimed in error as an allowable expense'. Particular risk areas include the payment of personal bills, such as credit cards, personal expenses paid by company, and personal entertaining.

20.56 In practice, there is usually a potential *CTA 2010, s 455* exposure on overdrawn director-shareholder's current or loan accounts.

Focus

In many cases, an overdrawn loan account may not be established until sometime after the balance sheet date, eg when the accounts are completed or following certain audit adjustments. It is therefore important to establish the proper balance before the 'nine-month' due date for the *CTA 2010, s 455* tax. This will enable the owner-manager to decide whether to clear the balance by voting an additional bonus or declaring an appropriate dividend.

Dividends must be properly declared and documented to demonstrate that the debt due to the company has been repaid. Repayment via cheque to the company is the most robust way of demonstrating repayment.

20.57 If an overdrawn balance remains after the 'nine month' due date, the *CTA 2010, s 455* tax falls due and interest will begin to accrue. Where regular advances/loans are made to a company's shareholder director, HMRC will often contend that these have the character of 'earnings' and seek to apply PAYE and NIC on the relevant amounts. Proper loan documentation will help to rebut such challenges. To avoid HMRC seeking (unexpected) PAYE and NIC liabilities on regular withdrawals, where the owner-manager wishes to extract regular amounts from the company, it may be better for them to pay regular 'quarterly' dividends instead (see also **20.25**).

In cases where frequent advances have been accepted as loans under an HMRC enquiry, there may be insufficient evidence as to the amounts that have been cleared by subsequent repayment(s). Inspectors normally seek to apply the rule in *Clayton's* case (1816 MR Ch Vol 1, 572), which provides that repayments are set against the oldest debts first. Given that loans or advances may have been subject to different *CTA 2010, s 455* tax rates, it may be preferable to allocate the repayments against the loans/advances liable to the 32.5% rate in priority to those subject to the 25% charge.

Inspectors will not accept that separate 'director's' accounts can be aggregated or netted off each other since the *CTA 2010, s 455* charge arises where a close company 'makes any loan or advances any money' to a shareholder. HMRC seem to accept that genuine book entries (with supporting documentation) can be made where a credit balance is used to repay a debit balance. However, the ICAEW Tax Faculty Guidance Note TAX 11/93 recommends that a company should draw a cheque to pay off the whole or part of the credit balance with another cheque being paid into the company to clear the debit balance. This will therefore provide firm evidence of the date the loan is repaid.

Interaction of FRS 102 and directors' loan accounts

20.58 Many owner-managed companies are now required to adopt FRS 102. (Micro-entities can adopt the simplified FRS 105 (for accounting periods starting after 31 December 2015.)

The application of FRS 102 could have implications for the way in which directors' loan accounts are accounted for going forward.

There is an argument that the build-up of entries in the directors loan account over an accounting period is not a financing transaction, provided the loans are intended to be settled within a year. In practice, transactions between the directors and 'their' companies are often entered into on an informal basis. Therefore, to avoid the potential complexities of FRS 102 accounting treatment, owner-managers should specifically record that their loan accounts are repayable on demand. The loan accounts can then be recorded at 'cost' under FRS 102 (as was historically the case).

On the other hand, if the transactions on a directors' loan account are considered to be 'financing transactions', FRS 102 requires the balances to be accounted for under the amortised cost basis using the effective interest method. However, this can normally be avoided if a commercial rate of interest is charged. In such cases, there should be no (material) difference between the initial recognition amount and the amount received/settled on maturity. Furthermore, if the rate of interest charged is at least equal to HMRC's official rate, no tax charge arises under the 'beneficial loan' legislation (see **20.53**).

20.59 If no interest is charged (or is charged at less than a commercial rate) the loan account balance must be recorded at present value. This is likely to give rise to a 'shortfall' between the face value of the loan and its present value. In this case, the resultant debit would be treated in the company's books as a 'distribution' (para 11.13 of FRS 102). This reflects the benefit of the interest-free/cheap interest being provided to the shareholder.

Example 20.8 – Treatment of 'long-term' interest-free loan to a director-shareholder

Andre is a 100% shareholder of Ayew Ltd, which draws up accounts to 31 March each year. On 1 April 2017, the company provides a £20,000 interest-free loan to him repayable on 31 March 2020. A comparable market interest rate is 6%.

The accounting entries would be:

	Dr	Cr
Director's loan account	16,792*	
Discount (= distribution)	3,207	
Cash		20,000

* This is the present value of £20,000 received in three years' time at a discount rate of 6%

Under normal corporation tax 'loan relationship' rules, the discount would normally be regarded as a (deductible) non-trading debit. However, for loans arising after 31 December 2015, the 'discount' would not be deductible for corporation tax purposes.

20.60 The 'individual' directors/shareholders tax treatment is *not* based on the FRS 102 accounting treatment. Consequently, any taxable benefit is calculated using the beneficial loan rules (see **20.53**). Also the *CTA 2010, s 455* charge is still based on the actual amount of the loan or advance (see **20.51**).

'Bed and breakfasting' of loan accounts

20.61 HMRC introduced specific legislation to counter the use of 'bed and breakfasting' arrangements in *FA 2013*.

> **Focus**
>
> Under the *FA 2013* changes, which apply for loans repaid after 19 March 2013, *CTA 2010, s 458* repayment relief can be denied in two different situations, as indicated below.

The 30-day repayment restriction

20.62 The new *CTA 2010, s 464C(1)* will apply where within a 30-day period:

- a shareholder has made repayments of 'their' *CTA 2010, s 455* loan (exceeding £5,000) ('relevant repayments'); and
- In a *subsequent accounting period*, new loans/advances (exceeding £5,000) are made to the same person or their associate (relevant chargeable payments).

This therefore catches the clearest form of bed and breakfasting arrangement. In such cases, *CTA 2010, s 458* repayment relief is only given *if and to the extent* that the *relevant repayments exceed the relevant chargeable payments.* In effect, the legislation only recognises the 'real' repayment (since repayments are matched with the amounts that have been re-lent shortly after the end of the relevant accounting period are).

An illustrative diagram showing the operation of the '30-day' rule is given below:

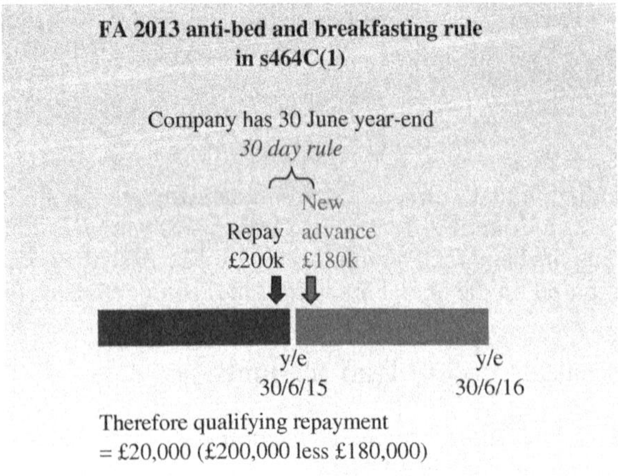

However, importantly, this restriction does *not* apply if the amount repaid gives rise to an income tax liability in the individual shareholder's hands (*CTA 2010, s 464C(6)*). This would typically arise where a bonus is voted for or dividend is paid to 'clear' the shareholder-director's loan account, as is often the case in practice.

In practice, HMRC accept that the crediting of an interim dividend to a loan account represents 'payment' at the time the relevant book entry is made, since the amount is then 'placed unreservedly at the disposal of the directors/shareholders as part of their current accounts with the company'. Some company law purists would argue with that approach, contending that a payment requires a transfer of cash.

On a strict analysis of *CTA 2010, s 464C(6)*, the 'repayment' itself *must* give rise to the income tax charge. The Chartered Institute of Taxation (CIOT) (see *TAX Adviser, May 2014*) pointed out to HMRC that it is the entitlement to the bonus or dividend itself that gives rise to the income tax charge. Worryingly, recent correspondence between the CIOT and HMRC suggests that HMRC are taking a strict interpretation of this 'exemption'. It appears that HMRC consider that the exemption would only apply if the loan account were cleared by a book entry 'crediting' the relevant bonus or dividend from the (lending) company.

Many would argue that an appellate tribunal would adopt a purposive approach so that the 'income tax payment' requirement would be met where, for example, a company actually pays a *cash* dividend to a director, who then uses these monies to repay a loan account.

Focus

HMRC have confirmed that the exemption would not apply where the loan account is cleared by, for example, rent or interest payments received from the company (although it is difficult to see how this view is supported by the legislation).

Example 20.9 – Operation of *CTA 2010, s 464C(1)* restriction

Thierry is a (UK resident) executive director of, and also a 75% shareholder in Henry Ltd, which makes up accounts to 31 March each year.

The company has incurred some large personal expenses on Thierry's behalf during the year ended 31 March 2017, with the result that Thierry owes the company £25,000 before the week leading up to its 31 March 2017 year-end.

Thierry arranges to repay the £25,000 from his personal funds, with his cheque clearing the company's bank account on 28 March 2017. However, on 2 April 2017, he arranges for the company to advance a new loan of £20,000 to him.

Since the £25,000 repayment on 28 March 2017 was made within 30 days of a new loan of £20,000 (falling in the subsequent accounting period), it is matched with the new £20,000 loan first, so that only the excess amount is eligible for *CTA 2010, s 458* repayment relief, as follows:

	£
Repayment	25,000
Matched with new loan	(20,000)
Qualifying repayment	5,000
Therefore repayment of *CTA 2010, s 455* tax = £5,000 × 32.5%	£1,625

There is no restriction in the repayment claim if the amount repaid gives rise to an income tax charge on the relevant shareholder or their associate. Thus, if Thierry had credited a dividend of £25,000 from Henry Ltd to his loan account, it would be treated as a full repayment of the loan, and the company would obtain the full *CTA 2010, s 455* tax repayment of £6,250. This is logical since HMRC will collect income tax from Thierry on the dividend payment.

The arrangements rule

20.63 The 'complementary' provision in *CTA 2010, s 464C(3)* potentially applies where the total amount of a shareholder's *CTA 2010, s 455* loan exceeds £15,000 before any repayment. If it does, the provisions in *CTA 2010, s 464C(4)* are triggered when a repayment is made, provided:

- arrangements had been made for one or more chargeable payments to be made to replace some, or all, of the amount repaid…' and
- the amount of those chargeable payments exceeds £5,000.

In other words, this provision broadly requires that arrangements (which is a wide-ranging term) be in place (typically by the company and/or the relevant shareholder) to 'replace' some or all of the repayment. In such cases, the amount qualifying for repayment relief under *CTA 2010, s 458* is computed as:

Loan repayment(s)	X
Less: New loans/advances for which arrangements are in place	(X)
Qualifying repayment	X

It should be a little easier to prove whether there are arrangements actually in place for the company to grant fresh loans/advances. However, (as the CIOT Technical Team put it) 'any arrangement for a re-borrowing is likely to have involved a negotiation between the participator and the company that took place inside the head of the shareholder-director'. It is to be hoped that HMRC will adopt a sensible approach when applying this provision.

As with the '30 day' rule (see above), *CTA 2010, s 464C(3)* does *not* apply if the 'repayment' transaction gives rise to a taxable bonus or dividend (or waiver). Thus, if the loan is credited with a bonus (which is subjected to PAYE/NIC), this 'credit' will give rise to a valid repayment claim under *CTA 2010, s 458*.

Example 20.10 – Operation of *CTA 2010, s 464C(3), (4)* restriction

Winston holds 100% of the issued share capital of Reid Ltd, which makes up accounts to 30 September each year.

The management accounts show that Winston owed the company some £50,000 at 31 August 2017, which had been built up over the last 11 months.

Winston wishes to clear the loan account to avoid the *CTA 2010, s 455* liability. However, he cannot personally afford to repay it at present. Winston therefore asks his friend's company, Vaz Tê Ltd, for a short-term loan on the understanding that he would repay it within two months by taking a new loan from his company.

There is a significant risk that HMRC would contend that the 'arrangement' with Vaz Tê Ltd would be caught by *CTA 2010, s 464C(3)* and thus deny any claim for repayment relief.

On the other hand, Winston could clear his loan account with a dividend payment of (say) £70,000 on (say) 27 November 2017. Since his loan account was cleared by a taxable dividend, the repayment will qualify for *CTA 2010, s 458* relief (*CTA 2010, s 464C(6)*). As the loan would be 'cleared' by a taxable amount within nine months of the 30 September 2017 year-end, the *CTA 2010, s 455* tax would be discharged under *CTA 2010, s 458*.

Winston would not be liable to pay the income tax on his dividend (in 2017/18) until 31 January 2019.

CTA 2010, s 464A anti-avoidance charge on 'benefits' provided to shareholders

20.64 *FA 2013* introduced a completely new weapon for dealing with 'indirect benefits' (as opposed to loans) enjoyed by close company shareholders. *CTA 2010, s 464A* imposes a 32.5% deemed 'corporation tax' charge on the relevant close company where:

- it is a party to tax avoidance arrangements (which are widely defined); and
- as a result of those arrangements, a 'benefit' is directly or indirectly conferred on a shareholder of the company (or their associate).

Where the shareholder receives the benefit before 6 April 2016, it is charged at the 25% tax rate.

The *CTA 2010, s 464A* charge will *not* apply where the benefit conferred on the participator would be subject to the 'normal' *CTA 2010, s 455* tax charge or an income tax charge.

HMRC consider that the *CTA 2010, s 464A* charge would be invoked in certain 'hybrid' partnerships where:

- an individual partner's capital account becomes overdrawn (after 19 March 2013); and
- that overdrawn account has effectively been financed by the undrawn profits (or capital introduced) of a corporate partner.

HMRC's explanatory notes indicate that the main target of this provision is to levy a tax charge where *individual* partners benefit as a result of the retention of profits in the partnership/LLP by a corporate partner. This 'benefit', which would otherwise be tax-free, would typically arise where individual partners reduce their own capital account or take sufficient drawings to overdraw their current/capital accounts.

In such cases, the (close) corporate partner could be liable to an *CTA 2010, s 464A* charge on the individual partner's overdrawn capital/current account (or, if lower, the amount funded by the corporate member).

Given that *CTA 2010, s 464A* can only be triggered where there are tax avoidance arrangements, we would expect the 32.5%/25% tax charge to be restricted to those cases where there is *deliberate* 'transfer of value' to 'related' individual partners via the partnership/LLP arrangements.

CTA 2010, s 464B contains a mechanism for repayment of the *CTA 2010, s 464A* tax charge if payments are returned to the company. However, such cases are likely to be rare since (in contrast to a loan), the 'benefit' conferred on the shareholder does not give rise to any repayment obligation.

It is hoped that HMRC would not use these widely drawn provisions as a carte blanche to attack normal commercial arrangements where individual partners/members simply draw profits earned in accordance with their profit share entitlements – it should be possible to show there is no tax avoidance motive here. Similarly, *CTA 2010, s 464A* should not apply where an individual partner's/member's drawings are 'financed' entirely from their own capital account (ie without relying on the capital account of a fellow corporate partner/member).

Example 20.11 – Scope of *CTA 2010, s 464A* charge

Gareth is a 75% shareholder in Bale Ltd (a close trading company).

Both Gareth and Bale Ltd became equal partners in 'The Bale Partnership' on 1 April 2011, which draws up accounts to 30 September each year.

Under the terms of the partnership agreement, Bale Ltd and Gareth share profits in the ratio of 75%:25% respectively.

During the year ended 30 September 2017, the partnership generated profits of £1,500,000, which were shared as follows:

	£
Bale Ltd (75%)	1,125,000
Gareth (25%)	375,000
Total	1,500,000

Bale Ltd's profits are credited to its capital account and are left retained in the partnership business. On the other hand, Gareth has drawn over £800,000 from the business and, by the end of September 2017, his partnership capital account is overdrawn by some £400,000.

HMRC are likely to contend that *CTA 2010, s 464A* should apply to Gareth's overdrawn capital account.

The assertion would be that:

- the 'overdrawn' element represents a benefit conferred on Gareth; and
- this has been funded by Bale Ltd's undrawn profits.

The CTA 2010, s 459 charge – deemed close company loans for certain arrangements

20.65 The normal *CTA 2010, s 455* charging rules are supplemented by a special *CTA 2010, s 459* charge, which may apply where a *CTA 2010, s 455* charge does not normally bite.

In broad terms, a 32.5% (25% pre-6 April 2016) tax charge may be triggered under *CTA 2010, s 459*, where:

- under arrangements made by someone,
- a close company makes a loan that is *not* within the normal *CTA 2010, s 455* charge; and
- a person (other than the close company) makes a payment to a participator (or their associate), which is *not* subject to an income tax charge (*CTA 2010, s 459(3)*).

In such cases, the loan is treated as having been made to the 'participator' under *CTA 2010, s 455*.

CTA 2010, s 459 primarily aims to catch certain 'back-to-back arrangements' – such as where a close company deposits cash with (say) a bank on the understanding that the bank will make an advance or loan to a participator of that close company. These arrangements would firmly fall within this legislation.

However, the wording of *CTA 2010, s 459* is sufficiently wide to catch ('financial assistance' type) loans made in connection with certain type of company takeover (especially management buy-out deals), as illustrated below:

3. Newco makes a payment to the sellers of Target which is not subject to income tax in their hands (they are participators of Target since they would be on the share register of Target when the deal is completed).

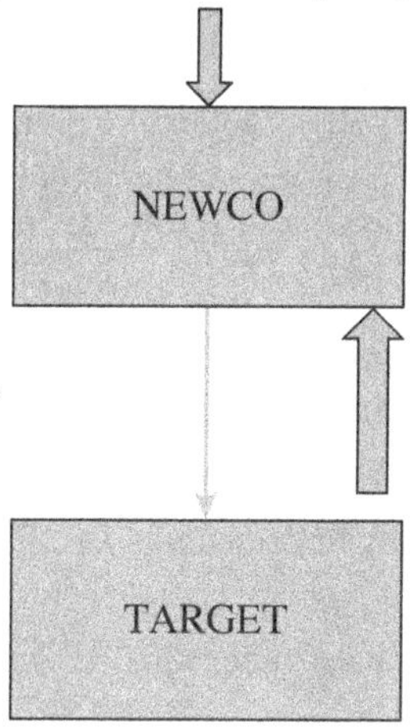

1. Newco acquires 100% of Target

2. To finance all or part of Newco's purchase consideration for its acquisition of Target, Newco procures a loan from Target – this is not within CTA 2010, s455 (*as the loan is not to an individual shareholder*)

In practice, it is often possible to 'plan out' of the potential *CTA 2010, s 459* charge by arranging for Target to make an appropriate dividend to Newco (rather than a loan). The 'tax-free' dividend monies received by Newco are then used to discharge the purchase consideration payable to the sellers of Target. Since there is *no* loan to Newco, *CTA 2010, s 459* cannot apply.

HMRC continue to confirm that, where the relevant conditions (as summarised above) are satisfied, they will seek to apply the *CTA 2010, s 459* provisions.

CTSA reporting obligations for CTA 2010, ss 455 and 464A tax

20.66 Under corporation tax self-assessment, the *CTA 2010, s 455* tax must be reported on the corporation tax return form CT600 and various details of loans made to participators, etc must be given on the supplementary page CT600A (even if the *CTA 2010, s 455* liability has been discharged by repayment or waiver). Companies that are liable to pay their corporation tax in instalments must include any anticipated or actual *CTA 2010, s 455* tax in their instalment liabilities. The same obligations also apply to any *CTA 2010, s 464A* tax (see **20.64**).

The CT600 return form must normally be submitted within 12 months from the end of the company's accounting period. Late returns attract a flat rate penalty of £100 increasing to £200 if the return is more than three months late.

(These penalties become £500 and £1,000 respectively, if the company was subject to a flat penalty charge in each of its two preceding accounting periods.)

Companies must take care to ensure they report all *CTA 2010, s 455* loans correctly since they are potentially exposed to HMRC penalties. Penalties are now charged according to the underlying taxpayer behaviour that gave rise to the error. Thus, HMRC will charge a greater penalty where they can show that the understatement of the tax liability was deliberate (as opposed to an innocent error).

Penalties are based on the relevant amount of tax that has been understated, the nature of the taxpayer's behaviour and the extent of disclosure. For example, a penalty of:

- *up to 30%* will arise on any understated *CTA 2010, s 455* tax due to lack of reasonable care: or
- *up to 70%* on any deliberately understated *CTA 2010, s 455* tax.

For these purposes, in arriving at the understated *CTA 2010, s 455* tax, no reduction is made for any offset under *CTA 2010, s 458(2)* (where the loan has been subsequently repaid (see **20.54**)).

The relevant penalty would be substantially reduced where the taxpayer makes full disclosure or takes active steps to correct the mistake. No penalty should arise where the taxpayer makes a genuine mistake.

Example 20.12 – *CTA 2010, s 455* tax and interest on overdrawn director's loan

Mr Noble, a shareholder in Claret & Blue Captain Ltd (a close company), overdrew his director's loan account by £20,000 in November 2017. This amount was still outstanding at the end of the company's accounting period on 31 December 2017, although it was entirely cleared by the payment of a bonus on 30 June 2018.

The company's accounts, corporation tax computations and return form CT600 for the year ended 31 December 2017 were submitted to HMRC in September 2018.

The company must complete the supplementary page CT600A and submit it with the return. In Part 1, the company must show the loan of £20,000 made to Mr Noble during the period, but would also claim relief from the *CTA 2010, s 455* liability (in Part 2) as the loan was repaid by 30 September 2018 – ie within nine months of the end of the accounting period.

Mr Noble would also be subject to an employment income charge on the benefit of the interest-free loan. The company would also be subject to a Class 1A NIC charge on the same amount.

WAIVER OF LOANS TO SHAREHOLDERS

Income tax charge on shareholder

20.67 An income tax charge arises if the company releases or simply writes off a loan to a shareholder (or an associate of a shareholder) (*ITTOIA 2005, s 415*). The loan must be formally waived (which must be documented by a formal legal deed), as opposed to merely not being collected by the company.

Focus

Since 6 April 2016, loans formally waived or released no longer get the benefit of the 10% tax credit. Instead, the amount of the loan waived/released is taxed at the post-5 April 2016 'distribution' tax rates. The amount waived is treated as dividend income under *ITA 2007, s 19(1)(d)*. Thus, loan waivers can also benefit from the £5,000 'dividend' nil rate band.

Thus, depending on the level of the shareholder's other income, the deemed 'dividend income' is taxed as the top slice of their total income in 2017/18 as shown below (ignoring the £5,000 dividend nil rate band):

Amount of loan waived/released	*Tax rate applied*
Up to £33,500	7.5%
£33,501 to £150,000	32.5%
More than £150,000	38.1%

Where the shareholder is a director (or an employee), the *ITTOIA 2005, s 415* charge also takes priority over any employment income tax charge on the waiver under *ITEPA 2003, s 188* (due to the statutory priority rule in *ITEPA 2003, s 188*). However, HMRC have recently been trying to assert that the waived amount should be regarded as earnings under general principles (see **20.68**).

It is fairly clear that, if a waiver or release was in contemplation at the time the original 'loan' was made, then it is unlikely to be treated as a loan in the first place – there would be strong arguments for treating the payment as 'income' which would be characterised according to the underlying facts!

Provided any HMRC challenge to treat the loan waiver as 'earnings' can be successfully rebutted (see **20.68**), the loan waiver, release, or write-off should be taxed as dividend income under *ITA 2007, s 19*.

HMRC contention that amount waived is earnings

20.68 In recent times, HMRC have been trying to challenge loan waivers on the grounds that the amount waived was earnings based on basic principles within *ITEPA 2003, s 62* (as opposed to the deemed *ITEPA 2003, s 188* employment charge – see **20.67** above).

Many advisers remain unconvinced by HMRC's view on this. However, in the case of *Stewart Fraser Ltd v HMRC* [2011] UKFTT 46 (TC), the company had written off a loan to a shareholder-director. The taxpayer contended that the write-off was made in his capacity as a shareholder rather than a director, and therefore not considered to be earnings. Nevertheless HMRC successfully contended that the write-off was 'earnings' which gave rise to an NIC liability.

In giving their evidence, HMRC said that they considered that:

> 'Had they (the loans) been waived for him in his capacity as a shareholder then HMRC would have expected to see this discussed and approved at a shareholders' meeting involving all the shareholders.'

Following this useful statement, it would therefore be advisable for waivers/write-offs of loans to participators to be approved at a general meeting of the shareholders or by an elected written resolution under *Companies Act 2006, ss 292* and *293*.

NIC treatment of loan waivers

20.69 Although the *ITTOIA 2005, s 415* charge takes precedence over the *ITEPA 2003, s 188* 'employment income' charge for income tax purposes, any such release is likely to be treated as 'earnings' for NIC purposes. 'Earnings' is widely defined for NIC purposes to include 'any remuneration or profit derived from the employment' (*SSCBA 1992, s 39(1)(a)*). HMRC's view is that, given this wide coverage, the release of a director's loan would be seen as rewarding the director for services rendered and would thus be liable to Class 1 NICs.

However, following the ruling in the *Stewart Fraser* case (see **20.68** above), it may be possible to side step an NIC charge by following appropriate corporate procedures. In the *Stewart Fraser* case, the company lost its appeal that the loan write-off was made in Mr Fraser's capacity as a shareholder. The Tribunal could find no evidence for this since the *directors* had approved the write-off, not the shareholders. To demonstrate that Mr Fraser's loan had been waived in his capacity as a shareholder, HMRC would have expected to see this discussed and approved at a meeting of all the shareholders. Thus, applying this reasoning, provided a loan waiver is approved at a general meeting of the shareholders (or by a written shareholders resolution (see **20.68**)), it should be possible to avoid an NIC charge.

Clearly, if the shareholder is neither a director nor an employee, there can be no question of an NIC charge being levied on the release.

Novation of loans

20.70 The case of *Collins v Addies* [1992] STC 746 held that the novation of a shareholder loan gives rise to a release. The company had advanced a loan to its two director shareholders and the company was subsequently sold. As part of the sale, the purchaser of the company agreed to take over these debts. Thus, the shareholder loans were novated so that the target company released the shareholders from their debts and the purchaser agreed to take them over. The court held that novation of the £68,000 debt constituted a taxable release under what is now *ITTOIA 2005, s 415*.

As illustrated by this case, the debtor (borrower) cannot assign the debt. A novation takes place under which the existing debtor is released from the debt and a new 'lender' (assignee) takes on a new debt (with the debtor). *ITTOIA 2005, s 415* will therefore catch situations where the creditor assigns the loans to someone else.

Recovery of CTA 2010, s 455 tax

20.71 Where a loan is released or waived, the company can recover from HMRC any tax paid under *CTA 2010, s 455*. The amount is due for repayment nine months after the accounting period in which the loan is waived (see **20.64**).

Note that a loan waiver (upon which an *ITTOIA 2003, s 415* liability would arise) would enable the *CTA 2010, s 455* tax to be repaid in a 'bed and breakfasting' arrangement and the special rules in **20.61** would not apply.

Corporation tax treatment of loan waiver

20.72 A properly executed release of a loan (provided it is properly accounted for under GAAP) would reduce the amount of loan that is due to be paid which would be written-off against the company's profits.

However, the *FA 2010* introduced legislation preventing almost all owner-managed companies from claiming a loan relationship (non-trading) tax deduction for the release or write-off of a loan made to a shareholder (or associate thereof) (*CTA 2009, s 321A*). This rule (which applies to close companies) affects amounts that are written-off after 23 March 2010. Nevertheless, despite these changes, it remains possible for companies to deduct amounts written-off in respect of other loans (where the borrower is not a shareholder or one of their 'associates').

Before 24 March 2010, the loan relationship legislation (*CTA 2009, s 324(1)*) contained an apparent loophole, since it permitted relief to be claimed on the write-off of shareholder loans as well as other 'third party' loans. However, in practice, HMRC have been known to resist claims for 'non-trading' debit relief under the loan relationship rules, contending that they are (already) blocked by various anti-avoidance provisions, such as *CTA 2009, s 444* (transactions not conducted on an arm's length basis).

Example 20.13 – *ITTOIA 2003, s 415* tax liability on release of shareholder loan

In June 2016, Hotspur Ltd (which is a close company) advanced an interest-free loan of £90,000 to Mr Alli, who is a 30% shareholder of the company. He does *not* work for Hotspur Ltd.

The loan remained outstanding nine months after the 31 December 2016 year end and therefore *CTA 2010, s 455* tax of £29,250 (32.5% × £90,000) was paid to HMRC on 1 October 2017.

In November 2017, the company decided to waive the £90,000 loan due from Mr Alli. Mr Alli and Hotspur Ltd entered into a formal deed to release the debt.

Hotspur Ltd

Since the company is 'close' and Mr Alli is a shareholder ('participator'), the *CTA 2009, s 321A* restriction applies to the amount written-off. Thus, the consequent loan relationship debit of £90,000 is not deductible for corporation tax purposes.

The *CTA 2010, s 455* tax of £29,250 also becomes repayable (which must be claimed), being due for repayment on 1 October 2018, ie nine months after the end of the accounting period in which the loan is waived – the year ended 31 December 2017.

Mr Alli

Assuming Mr Alli's total income (including the waiver) exceeds £150,000, his *ITTOIA 2005, s 415* charge in 2017/18 will be as follows:

	£
Amount waived less dividend 'nil rate' band (£90,000 – £5,000)	85,000
Tax at 38.1%	32,385

It is important to note that if Mr Alli were a *director or employee* of Hotspur Ltd, the *ITTOIA 2005, s 415* charge would still prevail, but HMRC would also seek to impose a Class 1 NIC charge. Recently, HMRC have contended that amounts of loans waived should be treated as earnings under *ITEPA 2003, s 62* – see **20.68** above.

BENEFITS IN KIND TO NON-WORKING SHAREHOLDERS

20.73

Focus

Certain expenses or benefits provided to a close company shareholder (or an associate of a shareholder) are treated as a distribution under *CTA 2010, s 1064*. Without these special provisions it would be possible to provide benefits to a non-working shareholder on a tax-free basis.

This 'deemed distribution' treatment does not apply where the expense or benefit is already taxed under the employment income rules in *ITEPA 2003*. Consequently, in practice, these rules would effectively apply to non-working shareholders being provided with living accommodation and other benefits or services (to the extent that they are not made good by the shareholder or their associate). These rules do not include pensions or lump sums payable on death or retirement.

The value of the distribution is taken to be the same amount that would have applied if the amount had been treated as an employment-related benefit. The recipient shareholder would be taxed on this amount in accordance with the relevant 'dividend taxation' rules.

The amount of the 'distribution' cannot be deducted against profits for corporation tax purposes

If a non-working shareholder was provided with a car, the distribution would be based on the scale benefit charge. This would not be the same figure as the depreciation and running costs that would have to be disallowed in calculating the company's taxable profits (since being incurred for a non-working shareholder, they would not generally be for the purposes of the trade).

APPENDIX – PLANNING CHECKLIST

20.74

PLANNING CHECKLIST – STRATEGIES FOR EXTRACTING FUNDS FROM THE COMPANY

Company

- The extraction of funds is often influenced by the company's cash flow and working capital position.
- Where appropriate, shareholders can loan funds back to the company to restore liquidity and provide working capital.
- Dividend payments can easily be timed for optimum income tax efficiency in the hands of the shareholder(s).
- Corporate tax relief for bonuses can be effectively back-dated by making provision in the statutory accounts under the nine-month rule. However, care must be taken to ensure such provisions also comply with current UK GAAP, such as FRS 102/FRS 105.

Working shareholders

- Generally require a sensible mix of remuneration/bonuses and dividends. Adopting a profit extraction model of 'low salary/high dividends will often be tax-efficient.
- Some owner-managers wish to extract surplus cash funds from the company to remove them from any further business risk.
- To avoid high income tax rates on substantial salaries and bonuses, owner-managers could consider providing 'cheap' loans from the company. Such loans would only suffer employment tax at

1.2%/1.35% (ie official rate 3% × 40%/45%) for a complete tax year. The loans can be repaid when appropriate, although a *CTA 2010, s 455* charge will also arise if the loans are not repaid within nine months of the company year-end in which they were made.

- A *CTA 2010, s 455* liability is now likely to be triggered where an owner-managed company makes a loan to a 'related' partnership or LLP (even where it is being made for genuine trading purposes). Similarly, a *CTA 2010, s 455* charge may also arise on loans to the trustees of a 'connected' trust.
- To avoid having to discount the value of directors' loan accounts under FRS 102, it is recommended to make the loans repayable on demand.
- Following *FA 2013*, the 'bed and breakfasting' of *CTA 2010, s 455* loans is no longer effective as a means of avoiding the *CTA 2010, s 455* tax or securing its repayment. However, these rules do enable the *CTA 2010, s 455* tax to be avoided/repaid where the loan account is cleared by means of a taxable bonus, dividend (or waiver of the loan).
- Owner-managers should consider bringing their loan accounts into credit by paying a dividend or 'large' bonus early in the tax year, thus enabling amounts to be drawn at a later date with no tax repercussions or RTI issues.
- It may be possible to avoid incurring Class 1 NICs on the waiver of directors overdrawn loan accounts by ensuring that this is approved at a general meeting of all the shareholders (or by a shareholders' written resolution)
- Dividends still remain attractive for shareholders who are only liable to lower or basic rate income tax. A small salary is usually worthwhile to provide a 'credit' for state pension purposes.
- Owner-managers can mitigate income tax on their earnings to the extent that they are paid out as pension contributions. Income tax relief for pension contributions is subject to the annual £40,000 'annual allowance' restriction. Also take into account any potential unused relief from the previous three years.
- Where the company's trading premises are personally owned by the controlling shareholder, it may be desirable to sell them to the company to obtain a tax-efficient extraction of cash.

Other employees

- Employees generally look for good remuneration packages with tax-efficient benefits (although there is now an increasing preference for cash).
- In appropriate cases, an incentive-based bonus scheme should be considered.

Non-working shareholders

- Dividends are much more tax-efficient as the company cannot claim tax relief for 'remuneration', particularly for non-working spouses. However, some care must be exercised to avoid the dividend being taxed on the owner-manager(s) under the settlement legislation.
- Consider paying pension contributions of up to £2,808 net (tax relief of up to £792 is added at source by HMRC) for non-working shareholders.

Index

[*all references are to paragraph number*]